Twentieth-Century
Literary Criticism

Guide to Gale Literary Criticism Series

For criticism on	Consult these Gale series
Authors now living or who died after December 31, 1959	*CONTEMPORARY LITERARY CRITICISM (CLC)*
Authors who died between 1900 and 1959	*TWENTIETH-CENTURY LITERARY CRITICISM (TCLC)*
Authors who died between 1800 and 1899	*NINETEENTH-CENTURY LITERATURE CRITICISM (NCLC)*
Authors who died between 1400 and 1799	*LITERATURE CRITICISM FROM 1400 TO 1800 (LC)* *SHAKESPEAREAN CRITICISM (SC)*
Authors who died before 1400	*CLASSICAL AND MEDIEVAL LITERATURE CRITICISM (CMLC)*
Black writers of the past two hundred years	*BLACK LITERATURE CRITICISM (BLC)*
Authors of books for children and young adults	*CHILDREN'S LITERATURE REVIEW (CLR)*
Dramatists	*DRAMA CRITICISM (DC)*
Hispanic writers of the late nineteenth and twentieth centuries	*HISPANIC LITERATURE CRITICISM (HLC)*
Native North American writers and orators of the eighteenth, nineteenth, and twentieth centuries	*NATIVE NORTH AMERICAN LITERATURE (NNAL)*
Poets	*POETRY CRITICISM (PC)*
Short story writers	*SHORT STORY CRITICISM (SSC)*
Major authors from the Renaissance to the present	*WORLD LITERATURE CRITICISM, 1500 TO THE PRESENT (WLC)*

ISSN 0276-8178

Volume 72

Twentieth-Century Literary Criticism

**Excerpts from Criticism of the
Works of Novelists, Poets, Playwrights,
Short Story Writers, and Other Creative Writers
Who Lived between 1900 and 1960,
from the First Published Critical
Appraisals to Current Evaluations**

Jennifer Gariepy
Editor

Thomas Ligotti
Associate Editor

GALE

DETROIT • NEW YORK • TORONTO • LONDON

STAFF

Jennifer Gariepy, *Editor*

Thomas Ligotti, *Associate Editor*

Susan Trosky, *Permissions Manager*
Kimberly F. Smilay, *Permissions Specialist*
Sarah R. Chesney, *Permissions Associate*
Steve Cusack, Kelly A. Quin, *Permissions Assistants*

Victoria B. Cariappa, *Research Manager*
Michele P. LaMeau, Andrew Guy Malonis, Barbara McNeil, Gary J. Oudersluys, Maureen Richards, *Research Specialists*
Julia C. Daniel, Tamara C. Nott, Tracie A. Richardson, Norma Sawaya, Cheryl L. Warnock, *Research Associates*

Mary Beth Trimper, *Production Director*
Deborah L. Milliken, *Production Assistant*

Christi Fuson, *Macintosh Artist*
Randy Bassett, *Image Database Supervisor*
Robert Duncan, Michael Logusz, *Imaging Specialists*
Pamela Reed, *Photography Coordinator*

Library of Congress Catalog Card Number 76-46132
ISBN 0-7876-1174-3
ISSN 0276-8178

Printed in the United States of America
10 9 8 7 6 5 4 3 2 1

Contents

Preface vii

Acknowledgments xi

Preface

Since its inception more than fifteen years ago, *Twentieth-Century Literary Criticism* has been purchased and used by nearly 10,000 school, public, and college or university libraries. *TCLC* has covered more than 500 authors, representing 58 nationalities, and over 25,000 titles. No other reference source has surveyed the critical response to twentieth-century authors and literature as thoroughly as *TCLC*. In the words of one reviewer, "there is nothing comparable available." *TCLC* "is a gold mine of information—dates, pseudonyms, biographical information, and criticism from books and periodicals—which many libraries would have difficulty assembling on their own."

Scope of the Series

TCLC is designed to serve as an introduction to authors who died between 1900 and 1960 and to the most significant interpretations of these author's works. The great poets, novelists, short story writers, playwrights, and philosophers of this period are frequently studied in high school and college literature courses. In organizing and excerpting the vast amount of critical material written on these authors, *TCLC* helps students develop valuable insight into literary history, promotes a better understanding of the texts, and sparks ideas for papers and assignments. Each entry in *TCLC* presents a comprehensive survey of an author's career or an individual work of literature and provides the user with a multiplicity of interpretations and assessments. Such variety allows students to pursue their own interests; furthermore, it fosters an awareness that literature is dynamic and responsive to many different opinions.

Every fourth volume of *TCLC* is devoted to literary topics. These topic entries widen the focus of the series from individual authors to such broader subjects as literary movements, prominent themes in twentieth-century literature, literary reaction to political and historical events, significant eras in literary history, prominent literary anniversaries, and the literatures of cultures that are often overlooked by English-speaking readers.

TCLC is designed as a companion series to Gale's *Contemporary Literary Criticism,* which reprints commentary on authors now living or who have died since 1960. Because of the different periods under consideration, there is no duplication of material between *CLC* and *TCLC*. For additional information about *CLC* and Gale's other criticism titles, users should consult the Guide to Gale Literary Criticism Series preceding the title page in this volume.

Coverage

Each volume of *TCLC* is carefully compiled to present:

- criticism of authors, or literary topics, representing a variety of genres and nationalities

- both major and lesser-known writers and literary works of the period

- 6-12 authors or 3-6 topics per volume

- individual entries that survey critical response to each author's work or each topic in literary history, including early criticism to reflect initial reactions; later criticism to represent any rise or decline in reputation; and current retrospective analyses.

Organization of This Book

An author entry consists of the following elements: author heading, biographical and critical introduction, list of principal works, excerpts of criticism (each preceded by an annotation and a bibliographic citation), and a bibliography of further reading.

- The **Author Heading** consists of the name under which the author most commonly wrote, followed by birth and death dates. If an author wrote consistently under a pseudonym, the pseudonym will be listed in the author heading and the real name given in parentheses on the first line of the biographical and critical introduction. Also located at the beginning of the introduction to the author entry are any name variations under which an author wrote, including transliterated forms for authors whose languages use nonroman alphabets.

- The **Biographical and Critical Introduction** outlines the author's life and career, as well as the critical issues surrounding his or her work. References to past volumes of *TCLC* are provided at the beginning of the introduction. Additional sources of information in other biographical and critical reference series published by Gale, including *Short Story Criticism, Children's Literature Review, Contemporary Authors, Dictionary of Literary Biography,* and *Something about the Author,* are listed in a box at the end of the entry.

- Some *TCLC* entries include **Portraits** of the author. Entries also may contain reproductions of materials pertinent to an author's career, including manuscript pages, title pages, dust jackets, letters, and drawings, as well as photographs of important people, places, and events in an author's life.

- The **List of Principal Works** is chronological by date of first book publication and identifies the genre of each work. In the case of foreign authors with both foreign-language publications and English translations, the title and date of the first English-language edition are given in brackets. Unless otherwise indicated, dramas are dated by first performance, not first publication.

- Critical excerpts are prefaced by **Annotations** providing the reader with information about both the critic and the criticism that follows. Included are the critic's reputation, individual approach to literary criticism, and particular expertise in an author's works. Also noted are the relative importance of a work of criticism, the scope of the excerpt, and the growth of critical controversy or changes in critical trends regarding an author. In some cases, these annotations cross-reference excerpts by critics who discuss each other's commentary.

- A complete **Bibliographic Citation** designed to facilitate location of the original essay or book precedes each piece of criticism.

- **Criticism** is arranged chronologically in each author entry to provide a perspective on changes in critical evaluation over the years. All titles of works by the author featured in the entry are printed in boldface type to enable the user to easily locate discussion of particular works. Also for purposes of easier identification, the critic's name and the publication date of the essay are given at the beginning of each piece of criticism. Unsigned criticism is preceded by the title of the journal in which it appeared. Some of the excerpts in *TCLC* also contain translated material. Unless otherwise noted, translations in brackets are by the editors; translations in parentheses or continuous with the text are by the critic. Publication information (such as footnotes or page and line references to specific editions of works) have been deleted at the editor's discretion to provide smoother reading of the text.

- An annotated list of **Further Reading** appearing at the end of each author entry suggests secondary sources on the author. In some cases it includes essays for which the editors could not obtain reprint rights.

Cumulative Indexes

- Each volume of *TCLC* contains a cumulative **Author Index** listing all authors who have appeared in Gale's Literary Criticism Series, along with cross references to such biographical series as *Contemporary Authors* and *Dictionary of Literary Biography*. For readers' convenience, a complete list of Gale titles included appears on the first page of the author index. Useful for locating authors within the various series, this index is particularly valuable for those authors who are identified by a certain period but who, because of their death dates, are placed in another, or for those authors whose careers span two periods. For example, F. Scott Fitzgerald is found in *TCLC*, yet a writer often associated with him, Ernest Hemingway, is found in *CLC*.

- Each *TCLC* volume includes a cumulative **Nationality Index** which lists all authors who have appeared in *TCLC* volumes, arranged alphabetically under their respective nationalities, as well as Topics volume entries devoted to particular national literatures.

- Each new volume in Gale's Literary Criticism Series includes a cumulative **Topic Index**, which lists all literary topics treated in *NCLC, TCLC, LC 1400-1800,* and the *CLC* yearbook.

- Each new volume of *TCLC*, with the exception of the Topics volumes, includes a **Title Index** listing the titles of all literary works discussed in the volume. In response to numerous suggestions from librarians, Gale has also produced a **Special Paperbound Edition** of the *TCLC* title index. This annual cumulation lists all titles discussed in the series since its inception and is issued with the first volume of *TCLC* published each year. Additional copies of the index are available on request. Librarians and patrons will welcome this separate index; it saves shelf space, is easy to use, and is recyclable upon receipt of the following year's cumulation. Titles discussed in the Topics volume entries are not included *TCLC* cumulative index.

Citing *Twentieth-Century Literary Criticism*

When writing papers, students who quote directly from any volume in Gale's literary Criticism Series may use the following general forms to footnote reprinted criticism. The first example pertains to materials drawn from periodicals, the second to material reprinted from books.

[1]William H. Slavick, "Going to School to DuBose Heyward," *The Harlem Renaissance Re-examined,* (AMS Press, 1987); excerpted and reprinted in *Twentieth-Century Literary Criticism,* Vol. 59, ed. Jennifer Gariepy (Detroit: Gale Research, 1995), pp. 94-105.

[2]George Orwell, "Reflections on Gandhi," *Partisan Review,* 6 (Winter 1949), pp. 85-92; excerpted and reprinted in *Twentieth-Century Literary Criticism,* Vol. 59, ed. Jennifer Gariepy (Detroit: Gale Research, 1995), pp. 40-3.

Suggestions Are Welcome

In response to suggestions, several features have been added to *TCLC* since the series began, including annotations to excerpted criticism, a cumulative index to authors in all Gale literary criticism series, entries devoted to criticism on a single work by a major author, more extensive illustrations, and a title index listing all literary works discussed in the series since its inception.

Readers who wish to suggest authors or topics to appear in future volumes, or who have other suggestions, are cordially invited to write the editors.

Acknowledgments

The editors wish to thank the copyright holders of the excerpted criticism included in this volume and the permissions managers of many book and magazine publishing companies for assisting us in securing reproduction rights. We are also grateful to the staffs of the Detroit Public Library, the Library of Congress, the University of Detroit Mercy Library, Wayne State University Purdy/Kresge Library Complex, and the University of Michigan Libraries for making their resources available to us. Following is a list of the copyright holders who have granted us permission to reproduce material in this volume of **TCLC.** Every effort has been made to trace copyright, but if omissions have been made, please let us know.

COPYRIGHTED EXCERPTS IN *TCLC,* **VOLUME 72, WERE REPRODUCED FROM THE FOLLOWING PERIODICALS:**

American Heritage, v. 22, June, 1971. Copyright © 1971 Forbes Inc. Reprinted by permission of American Heritage Magazine, a division of Forbes Inc.—*Clues: A Journal of Detection*, v. 2, Fall-Winter, 1981. Reproduced by permission of the Bowling Green State University Popular Press.—*ELH*, v. 50, 1983, for "Jude the Obscure: Reading and the Spirt of the Law" by Ramon Saldivar. Copyright © 1983 Johns Hopkins University Press. Reproduced by permission of The Johns Hopkins University Press.—*English Literature in Transition: 1880-1920*, v. 24, 1981; v. 37, 1994. Copyright © 1981, 1994 *English Literature in Transition: 1880-1920*. Both reproduced by permission.—*English*, v. XXXVIII, Autumn, 1989 for "Sexual Ideology and the Narrative Form in Jude the Obscure" by Phillip Mallett. Copyright © 1989 by The English Association. Reproduced by permission of the publisher and the author./ v. 22, Summer, 1972. Copyright © 1972 by The English Association. Reproduced by permission of the publisher.—*Essays and Studies*, v. 5, 1952. Copyright 1952 by The English Association. Reproduced by permission of the publisher.— *Essays in Criticism*, v. XXV, July, 1975, for "Sue the Obscure" by Mary Jacobus. Reproduced by permission of the Editors of *Essays in Criticism* and the author.—*International History Review*, v. 11, August, 1989. Copyright © 1989 International History Review. Reproduced by permission.—*International Journal*, v. 30, Winter, 1974-75. Copyright © 1975 Canadian Institute of International Affairs. Reproduced by permission.—*Journal of American History*, v. 71, September, 1984. Copyright © 1984 Organization of American Historians. Reproduced by permission.—*Journal of Presbyterian History*, v. 49, Summer, 1971. Reproduced by permission.—*London Magazine*, v. 19, February, 1980. Copyright © 1980 *London Magazine*. Reproduced by permission.—*Monumenta Nipponica*, v. XXXII, Autumn 1977. Copyright © 1977 by *Monumenta Nipponica*. Reproduced by permission.—*Nineteenth Century Fiction*, v. 20, 1966, for "Hardy's Sue Bridehead" by Robert B Heilman. Copyright © 1966 by The Regents of the University of California. Reproduced by permission of The Regents of the University of California and the author./ v. 38, 1983. Copyright © 1983 by The Regents of the University of California. Reprinted by permission of the publisher.—*Novel: A Forum on Fiction*, v. 25, Spring, 1992. Copyright © 1992 by Novel Corp. Reproduced by permission.—*PMLA*, v. 87, May, 1972. Copyright © 1972 by the Modern Language Association of America. Reproduced by permission of the Modern Language Association of America.—*Political Science Quarterly*, v. 65, 1950. Copyright 1950. Renewed 1978 by *Political Science Quarterly* Editors. Reproduced by permission.—*Sight and Sound*, v. 47, Spring, 1978. Copyright © 1978 by The British Film Institute. Reproduced by permission.—*Studies in English Literature: 1500-1900*, v. XVIII, Autumn, 1978. Copyright © 1978 William Marsh Rice University. Reproduced by permission of *SEL: Studies in English Literatrure 1500-1900.— Studies in the Novel*, v. 11, 1970; v. XII, Spring, 1980; v. XIII, 1981. Copyright © 1970, 1980, 1981 by North Texas State University. All reprinted by permission of the publisher.—*The New York Herald Tribune Books*, v. 13, January 24, 1937. Copyright 1937 by The New York Times Company. Reproduced by permission.—*The South Atlantic Quarterly*, v. 50, January , 1951. Copyright 1951, renewed 1978 by Duke University Press, Durham, NC. Reproduced by permission.—*The Southern Review*, Louisana State University, v. 6, 1940-41, for "Jude the Obscure As a Tragedy" by Arthur Mizener. Copyright, 1940 by Arthur Mizener. Reproduced by permission of the author.—*The Victorian Newsletter*, No. 82, Fall, 1992, for "Individuation and Consummation in Hardy's 'Jude the Obscure': The Lure of the Void" by Mary Ann Kelly.

COPYRIGHTED EXCERPTS IN *TCLC*, VOLUME 72, WERE REPRODUCED FROM THE FOLLOWING BOOKS:

Abdoo, Sherlyn. From *The Existential Coordinates of the Human Condition: Poetic-Epic-Tragic*. Edited by Anna-Teresa Tymieniecka. D. Reidel Publishing Company, 1984. Copyright © 1984 by D. Reidel Publishing Company. All rights reserved. Reproduced by permission.—Alvarez, A. From *Jude the Obscure*. New American Library, 1961. Reproduced by permission of New American Library, a division of Penguin USA.— Andrew, Dudley. From *Film in the Aura of Art*. Princeton University Press, 1984. Copyright © 1984 by Princeton University Press. All rights reserved. Reprinted with permission of Princeton University Press.—Barzun, Jacques, and Wendell H. Taylor. From *A Book of Prefaces to Fifty Classics of Crime Fiction, 1900-1950*. Garland Publishing, 1976. Copyright © 1976 by Jacques Barzun and Wendell H. Taylor. All rights reserved. Reproduced by permission.—Berman, Jeffrey. From *Narcissism and the Novel*. New York University Press, 1990. Copyright © 1990 by New York University Press. All rights reserved. Reproduced by permission.—Blyth, R. H. From *A History of Haiku, Vol. II*. The Hokuseido Press, 1964. Copyright © 1964 by R. H. Blyth. All rights reserved. Reproduced by permission.—Bock, Audie E. From *Japanese Film Directors*. Kodansha International Ltd., 1978. Copyright © 1978 by Audie E. Bock. All rights reserved. Reproduced by permission of the author.—Brome, Vincent. From *Four Realist Novelists*. Longmans, Green & Co., 1965. Copyright © 1965 by Vincent Brome. Reproduced by permission of the author.—Cannaday, Marilyn. From *Bigger than Life: The Creator of Doc Savage*. Bowling Green State University Popular Press, 1990. Copyright © 1990 by the Bowling Green State University Popular Press. Reproduced by permission.—Cohen, Robert N. From "Why Does Oharu Faint? Mizoguchi's 'The Life of Oharu' and Patriarchal Discourse" in *Reframing Japanese Cinema: Authorship, Genre, History*. Edited by Arthur Nolletti, Jr., and David Desser. Indiana University Press, 1992. © 1992 by Indiana University Press. All rights reserved. Reproduced by permission.—Craig, Gordon A. From *War, Politics, and Diplomacy: Selected Essays*. Frederick A. Praeger, Publishers, 1966. © 1966 by Frederick A. Praeger, Inc. All rights reserved. Reproduced by permission.—Goode, John. From *Women Writing About Women*. Edited by Mary Jacobus. Croom Helm, 1979. Reproduced by permission.—Goulart, Ron. From *Cheap Thrills: An Informal History of Pulp Magazines*. Arlington House, 1972. Copyright © 1972 by Ron Goulart. All rights reserved. Reproduced by permission of Random House, Inc.—Langland, Elizabeth. From *The Sense of Sex: Feminist Perspectives on Hardy*. Edited by Margaret R. Higonnet. University of Illinois Press, 1993. Copyright © 1993 by the Board of Trustees of the University of Illinois. Reproduced by permission.—McDonald, Keiko I. From *Cinema East: A Critical Study of Major Japanese Films*. Fairleigh Dickinson University Press, 1983. Copyright © 1983 by Associated University Presses, Inc. Reproduced by permission.—Mellen, Joan. From *The Waves at Genji's Door: Japan Through Its Cinema*. Pantheon Books, 1976. Copyright © 1976 by Joan Mellen. All rights reserved. Reproduced by permission of the author.—Morgenthau, Hans J. For "John Foster Dulles" in *An Uncertain Tradition: American Secretaries of State in the Twentieth Century*. Edited by Norman A. Graebner. Copyright © 1961 by the McGraw-Hill Book Company, Inc. All rights reserved. Reproduced by permission of the editor.—Murray, Will. From *Doc Savage Omnibus: Number 13*. Bantam Books, 1990. Copyright © 1997 by Will Murray. Reproduced by permission of the author.—Murray, Will. From *The Man Behind Doc Savage*. Robert Weinberg, 1974. Copyright © 1974 by Will Murray. Reproduced by permission of the author.— Pritchett, V. S. From *The Living Novel & Later Appreciations*. Random House, 1964. Copyright © 1964, 1975 by V. S. Pritchett. Reprinted by permission of Peters, Fraser & Dunlop Group Ltd. on behalf of The Literary Estate of V. S. Pritchett.—Pruessen, Ronald W. From *John Foster Dulles and the Diplomacy of the Cold War*. Edited by Richard H. Immerman. Princeton University Press, 1990. Copyright © 1990 by Princeton University Press. All rights reserved. Reproduced by permission.—Rimer, J. Thomas. From *A Reader's Guide to Japanese Literature*. Kodansha International, 1988. Copyright © 1988 by Kodansha International Ltd. All rights reserved. Reproduced by permission.—Sarris, Andrew. From "Ugetsu: A Meditation on Mizoguchi" in *Favorite Movies: Critics' Choice*. Edited by Philip Nobile. Macmillan Publishing Co., Inc., 1973. Copyright © 1973 by Philip Nobile. All rights reserved. Reproduced by permission of the editor.—Stevens, John. From an introduction to *Mountain Tasting: Zen Haiku* by Santoka Taneda. Translated by

John Stevens. Weatherhill, 1980. All rights reserved. Reproduced by permission.—Wood, Robin. From *Personal Views: Explorations in Film*. Gordon Fraser Gallery Ltd., 1976. Copyright © 1976 by Robin Wood. Reproduced by permission of the author.

PHOTOGRAPHS AND ILLUSTRATIONS APPEARING IN *TCLC*, VOLUME 72, WERE RECEIVED FROM THE FOLLOWING SOURCES:

Dent, Lester, photograph. UPI/Corbis-Bettmann. Reproduced by permission.—Dulles, John Foster, photograph.—Glyn, Elinor, wearing hat and pearls, photograph. Archive Photos, Inc. Reproduced by permission.—Hardy, Thomas (checked tie), photograph. Corbis-Bettmann. Reproduced by permission.—Mizoguchi, Kenji (wearing white kimono), photograph. The Kobal Collection. Reproduced by permission.

Ernest Bramah

1868-1942

(Full name Ernest Bramah Smith) English short story writer and novelist.

INTRODUCTION

Primarily a short story writer in the genre of detective fiction, Bramah is best remembered for his creation of the blind sleuth Max Carrados and for his mannered tales of the Far East recited by the fictional Chinese storyteller Kai Lung. The shrewd, erudite, and superhumanly observant Carrados presides over Bramah's inventive, atmospheric, and at times humorous tales in the tradition of Sir Arthur Conan Doyle's Sherlock Holmes stories. With Kai Lung, Bramah ranges into satire by evoking a stylized version of the Far East peopled by rogues, hoods, and evil mandarins. Using Kai Lung's affected, aphoristic style—ostensibly intended for the moral edification of his listeners—Bramah combines humor and what Norman Donaldson called the "meticulous touch of a rare literary craftsman," to create lively and engaging tales that won him a small but ardently devoted readership in the first half of the twentieth century.

Biographical Information

Bramah was born near Manchester, England in 1868 to Charles Clement Smith and Susannah Brammah Smith (in his pen name he later dropped the second "m" as well as the surname Smith). He attended Manchester Grammar School and upon graduation began a three-year period of his life as a farmer—later recounted in his humorous *English Farming and Why I Turned It Up* (1894). Beginning in 1890 Bramah began submitting a weekly column to the *Birmingham News*, his success with writing and the financial assistance of his father allowing him to travel to London two years later in order to pursue a full-time career in journalism. He served as secretary to Jerome K. Jerome, editor of the London magazine *To-day*, and later as an editorial assistant for the publication. In 1895 Bramah left *To-day* to become editor of another magazine, the *Minister*. He remained with this journal until late 1897, at which time he married Lucie Maisie Barker and embarked upon a career as what he termed an "outside writer." His first work of fiction, *The Wallet of Kai Lung* appeared in 1900 and featured the engaging figure of Kai Lung, a Chinese tale spinner who also narrates Bramah's later collections *Kai Lung's Golden Hours* (1922), *Kai Lung Unrolls His Mat* (1928), and the novel *The Moon of Much Gladness, Related by Kai Lung* (1932; also published as *The Return of Kai Lung*). The Kai Lung stories afforded Bramah a certain measure of notoriety, which was expanded considerably with the 1914 introduction of his blind detective Max Carrados in

his collection of short stories under the same title. The popularity of *Max Carrados* led to Bramah's publication of three more volumes of tales, *The Eyes of Max Carrados* (1923), *The Specimen Case* (1924), and *Max Carrados Mysteries* (1927), and a novel, *The Bravo of London* (1934), featuring Carrados as its protagonist. Bramah published his last collection of fiction, a return to his early tales of the Far East in *Kai Lung Beneath the Mulberry-Tree*, two years before his death in 1942.

Major Works

Bramah's primary contribution to English literature lies in his creation of two characters, Kai Lung and Max Carrados, both of whom appear most convincingly in several collections of short stories. More of a storyteller than an active protagonist, Kai Lung has been described by William White as a kind of "Chinese Chaucer" whose function is akin to that of Scheherazade in *The Thousand and One Nights*. Seized by the evil mandarin Shan Tien, Kai Lung endeavors to forestall his torture and death by diverting his captor with a variety of wondrous tales. In his at once didactic and ironic stories, Kai Lung reveals a highly-mannered society based upon Bramah's imagined conception of the Far East (an area of the world he never visited). The tales are filled with Kai Lung's stylized language and aphoristic wit, and engage in satire as much as fantasy. In *Max Carrados*, Bramah created one of the most enduring figures in detective fiction. Although blind, Carrados possesses a keen intelligence, uncanny powers of observation, and highly trained senses that allow him to, for example, read newspaper headlines with his fingertips. The beneficiary of a large inheritance from an American relative, Carrados is foremost a gentleman who undertakes sleuthing only as an avocation. Among his most memorable exploits is that related in "The Tragedy of Brookbend Cottage" (1914), in which Carrados attempts to prevent a jealous husband from making his wife's murder appear to be an accident. This story, considered among Bramah's best, demonstrates his skill with dialogue and characteristic blending of tragedy and lighthearted humor.

Critical Reception

Between the publication of *The Wallet of Kai Lung* and *Max Carrados* Bramah produced his first novel, a work of science fiction entitled *What Might Have Been: The Story of a Social War* (1907). The book's near total neglect by critics illustrates the common opinion that Bramah's greatest successes have been in short fiction. Since their publication in 1900 the earliest Kai Lung stories have maintained a modest but devoted readership.

Bramah's Max Carrados tales were also much praised by contemporary reviewers and have likewise earned him a noteworthy position in the history of the British detective story, making him one of the most admired practitioners of the genre from the prewar era through the 1920s. In the latter half of the twentieth century, however, Bramah's writings have elicited very little scholarly interest, though the original Kai Lung and Max Carrados stories are still considered highly readable examples of genre-writing, and many have since been reissued.

PRINCIPAL WORKS

English Farming and Why I Turned It Up (prose) 1894
The Wallet of Kai Lung (short stories) 1900
The Mirror of Kong Ho (short stories) 1905
What Might Have Been: The Story of a Social War [also
    published as *The Secret of the League*] (novel) 1907
Max Carrados (short stories) 1914
Kai Lung's Golden Hours (short stories) 1922
The Eyes of Max Carrados (short stories) 1923
The Specimen Case (short stories) 1924
Max Carrados Mysteries (short stories) 1927
*The Story of Wan and the Remarkable Shrub and The
    Story of Ching-Kwei and the Destinies* (short stories)
    1927
Kai Lung Unrolls His Mat (short stories) 1928
*A Guide to the Varieties and Rarity of English Regal
    Copper Coins: Charles II-Victoria, 1671-1860* (non-
    fiction) 1929
Short Stories of To-day and Yesterday (short stories)
    1929
A Little Flutter (short stories) 1930
The Moon of Much Gladness, Related by Kai Lung [also
    published as *The Return of Kai Lung*] (novel) 1932
The Bravo of London (novel) 1934
The Kai Lung Omnibus (short stories) 1936
Kai Lung Beneath the Mulberry Tree (short stories) 1940

CRITICISM

J.C. Squire (essay date 1921)

SOURCE: "The Wallet of Kai-Lung," in *Life and Letters*, George H. Doran Company, 1921, pp. 44-51.

[*In the following essay, Squire favorably assesses the Chinese stories of* The Wallet of Kai Lung.]

Everybody knows about Mr. Thomas Hardy, Shakespeare, Lord Byron and Lord Tennyson. This does not detract from one's enjoyment of their works; but there is

a peculiar and intense delight in good books which are not commonly known. English literature is sprinkled with them, and one's own favourites of the kind one talks about with a peculiar enthusiasm. For myself I continually urge people to read Trelawney's *Adventures of a Younger Son* and *Coryat's Crudities,* which, famous enough in the auction room, is seldom enough talked about outside it. The present age, like other ages, produces these books that are less celebrated than they ought to be, and one of them is Mr. Ernest Bramah's *The Wallet of Kai-Lung*. This work was first published by Mr. Grant Richards in the year 1900. For all I know to the contrary, it fell quite flat; at any rate since that date Mr. Belloc has frequently informed an inattentive public that it is one of the best of modern books, but one has never heard it mentioned by any other critic. Largely, I take it, on account of Mr. Belloc's recommendation, Methuens have now issued it in their 1s. 3d Library. It is a volume of Chinese stories.

One does not need to have read many translations from the Chinese to understand that there is a distinctive, a unique, Chinese way of looking at things. The late Count Hayashi, in his memoirs, observed that his own countrymen, whatever their material successes, could not help feeling inferior in the presence of the civilisation, the rounded philosophy and perfect manners, of the Chinese gentleman. A man who reads Chinese poetry is in contact with a mastery of the Art of Life. Religion does not come in much except for rather decorative gods and good spirits and demons; once admit religion in our sense and the Chinese conception of life will not hold water. But granted their rationalistic epicureanism they certainly carry it out to perfection. They keep so superbly their balance. Moved by the passions, they stand outside themselves and watch themselves with sympathetic humour. They would have grief but not its abandonment, joy but not its paroxysms; they are conscious of the sweet in the bitter and the bitter in the sweet. They bear pain, and the spectacle of pain, with equanimity; yet their calm does not degenerate into callousness, and their comments on the spectacle of life fall through the air like particoloured petals, which flutter noiselessly in the wind and show in constant alternation the grey side of irony and the golden side of tenderness. They enjoy beautiful things with an exquisite sensibility, but a careful moderation: wine, flowers, and the sky, snow upon the mountains, reflections in the water, song and the laughter of girls. They yield a little to everything, but surrender to nothing, save to death; and there they submit courteously, with dignity, and throwing back a glance of no more than whimsical regret. The old Chinese literature is steeped in this philosophy. They have, it is alleged, no literature now on a higher level than that which comes out on the tea-boxes. But the manners and the restraint remain. When the fall of the Pekin Legations was in doubt the then Chinese Minister here, a most enlightened and charming man, was asked what would happen to the diplomatists if the rebels got in. "They will be decahpitated," he said, with a slight inclination. "But what will happen to the women and children?" continued the lady. "They will be decahpitated," he said. "But you, who are so pro-English, what would happen to you if you were there?" "I should be decahpitated." He thought that adequate: it was only decorous to leave any anxieties or strong emotions he had to be guessed.

Mr. Bramah, in his book, has got the Chinese equanimity wonderfully; the most moving and the most horrible things are told with mild deprecation; the most grotesquely farcical situations are analysed and developed with a full sense of their rich ludicrousness but with the very slightest loss of gravity on the part of the narrator. All the characters behave consistently, veiling their actions and their intentions behind the most transparent lies and subterfuges and saying the most offensive things in the politest possible way. For it is to the comic side of the Chinese genius that Mr. Bramah chiefly inclines. Now and then he uses China as an illustration of Europe. By transplanting customs and phrases he at once suggests the unity and the absurdity of mankind. In **"The Confession of Kai-Lung"** he is frankly preposterous. He describes Kai-Lung's early career as an author in terms precisely applicable to a European literary failure. He began by falling in love with Tiao T'sun, the most beautiful maiden in Pekin, whom he frequently met

> at flower-feasts, melon-seed assemblies, and those gatherings where persons of both sexes exhibit themselves in revolving attitudes, and are permitted to embrace openly without reproach

(which reminds one of the old lady's comment on the Tango, in one of the late "Saki's" books: "I suppose it doesn't matter if they *really* love one another"). Kai-Lung was successful in his suit. Then, "on a certain evening," he says:

> this person stood alone with Tiao upon an eminence overlooking the city and watched the great sky-lantern rise from behind the hills. Under these delicate and ennobling influences he gave speech to many very ornamental and refined thoughts which arose within his mind concerning the graceful brilliance of the light which was cast all around, yet notwithstanding which a still more exceptional light was shining in his own internal organs by reason of the nearness of an even purer and more engaging orb. There was no need, this person felt, to hide even his most inside thoughts from the dignified and sympathetic being at his side, so without hesitation he spoke—in what he believes even now must have been a very decorative manner—of the many thousand persons who were then wrapped in sleep, of the constantly changing lights which appeared in the city beneath, and of the vastness which everywhere lay around.

> 'O Kai-Lung,' exclaimed the lovely Tiao, when this person had made an end of speaking, 'how expertly and in what a proficient manner do you express yourself, uttering even the sentiments which this person has felt inwardly, but for which she has no words. Why, indeed, do you not inscribe them in a book?'

He does. But while he is absorbed in his labour Tiao accepts "the wedding gifts of an objectionable and excessively round-bodied individual, who had amassed an inconceivable number of tales by inducing persons to take part in what at first sight appeared to be an ingenious but very easy competition connected with the order in which certain horses should arrive at a given and clearly defined spot." He completes his work, publishes it at great expense and great loss, and makes a last desperate bid with an effort to prove that the works of the great national poet were not sheer imitations. Here, in adaptations from Shakespeare, we lapse into burlesque. There are several quotations like: "O nobly intentioned but nevertheless exceedingly morose Tungshin, the object before you is your distinguished and evilly-disposed-of father's honourably-inspired demon"—though after all a Boer dramatic adapter *did* render the same passage as "I am thy papa's spook." This excursion, however, does show Mr. Bramah's style. That style is almost impeccable.

He keeps it up from start to finish; ceremonial to the point of absurdity, embellished with an unending flow of maxim and euphemism. It is not possible here to detail the complicated plots of his extremely ingenious stories. The best of all is **"The Transmutation of Ling."** Ling is a studious youth who passes the public examination and, to his horror, is awarded, not a cosy nook in the Whitehall of Pekin, but the command of a very white-livered band of bowmen who have to resist the continual onslaughts of exceedingly ferocious bandits. His adventurers are numerous and diverse. As I say, I will not tell the story, which Kai-Lung recounts, standing with a rope around his neck and his toes touching the ground, to a brigand chief with a formidable snickersnee. But one may perhaps quote some of the incidental proverbs, which add much to the grace of the tales.

> Before hastening to secure a possible reward of five tales by dragging an unobservant person away from a falling building, examine well his features lest you find, when too late, that it is one to whom you are indebted for double that amount.

> The road to eminence lies through the cheap and exceedingly uninviting eating-houses.

> Although there exist many thousand subjects for elegant conversation, there are persons who cannot meet a cripple without talking about feet.

Whether Mr. Ernest Bramah has been to the East or has merely caught the atmosphere of its literature I do not know. I have only recently learnt who he is. But it is not surprising that one who likes good satire, good humour, good romance and good English should find the book worthy of being an inseparable companion.

Hilaire Belloc (essay date 1922)

SOURCE: Preface to *Kai Lung's Golden Hours,* Jonathan Cape, 1922, pp. vii-xii.

[In the following essay, Belloc offers praise for the artistry of The Wallet of Kai Lung *and* Kai Lung's Golden Hours.*]*

Homo faber. Man is born to make. His business is to construct: to plan: to carry out the plan: to fit together, and to produce a finished thing.

That human art in which it is most difficult to achieve this end (and in which it is far easier to neglect it than in any other) is the art of writing. Yet this much is certain, that unconstructed writing is at once worthless and ephemeral: and nearly the whole of our modern English writing is unconstructed.

The matter of survival is perhaps not the most important, though it is a test of a kind, and it is a test which every serious writer feels most intimately. The essential is the matter of excellence: that a piece of work should achieve its end. But in either character, the character of survival or the character of intrinsic excellence, construction deliberate and successful is the fundamental condition.

It may be objected that the mass of writing must in any age neglect construction. We write to establish a record for a few days: or to send a thousand unimportant messages: or to express for others or for ourselves something very vague and perhaps very weak in the way of emotion, which does not demand construction and at any rate cannot command it. No writer can be judged by the entirety of his writings, for these would include every note he ever sent round the corner; every memorandum he ever made upon his shirt cuff. But when a man sets out to write as a serious business, proclaiming by the nature of his publication and presentment that he is doing something he thinks worthy of the time and place in which he lives and of the people to whom he belongs, then if he does not construct he is negligible.

Yet, I say, the great mass of men to-day do not attempt it in the English tongue, and the proof is that you can discover in their slipshod pages nothing of a seal or stamp. You do not, opening a book at random, say at once: "This is the voice of such and such an one." It is no one's manner or voice. It is part of a common babel.

Therefore in such a time as that of our decline, to come across work which is planned, executed and achieved has something of the effect produced by the finding of a wrought human thing in a wild. It is like finding, as I once found, deep hidden in the tangled rank grass of autumn in Burgundy, on the edge of a wood not far from Dijon, a neglected statue of the eighteenth century. It is like coming round the corner of some wholly desolate upper valley in the mountains and seeing before one a well-cultivated close and a strong house in the midst.

It is now many years—I forget how many; it may be twenty or more, or it may be a little less—since *The Wallet of Kai Lung* was sent me by a friend. The effect produced upon my mind at the first opening of its pages

was in the same category as the effect produced by the discovery of that hidden statue in Burgundy, or the coming upon an unexpected house in the turn of a high Pyrenean gorge. Here was something worth doing and done. It was not a plan attempted and only part achieved (though even that would be rare enough to-day, and a memorable exception); it was a thing intended, wrought out, completed and established. Therefore it was destined to endure and, what is more important, it was a success.

The time in which we live affords very few of such moments of relief: here and there a good piece of verse, in *The New Age* or in the now defunct *Westminster:* here and there a lapidary phrase such as a score or more of Blatchford's which remain fixed in my memory. Here and there a letter written to the newspapers in a moment of indignation when the writer, not trained to the craft, strikes out the metal justly at white heat. But, I say, the thing is extremely rare, and in the shape of a complete book rarest of all.

The Wallet of Kai Lung was a thing made deliberately, in hard material and completely successful. It was meant to produce a particular effect of humour by the use of a foreign convention, the Chinese convention, in the English tongue. It was meant to produce a certain effect of philosophy and at the same time it was meant to produce a certain completed interest of fiction, of relation, of a short epic. It did all these things.

It is one of the tests of excellent work that such work is economic, that is, that there is nothing redundant in order or in vocabulary, and at the same time nothing elliptic— in the full sense of that word: that is, no sentence in which so much is omitted that the reader is left puzzled. That is the quality you get in really good statuary—in Houdon, for instance, or in that triumph the archaic *Archer* in the Louvre. *The Wallet of Kai Lung* satisfied all these conditions.

I do not know how often I have read it since I first possessed it. I know how many copies there are in my house—just over a dozen. I know with what care I have bound it constantly for presentation to friends. I have been asked for an introduction to this its successor, *Kai Lung's Golden Hours*. It is worthy of its forerunner. There is the same plan, exactitude, working-out and achievement; and therefore the same complete satisfaction in the reading, or to be more accurate, in the incorporation of the work with oneself.

All this is not extravagant praise, nor even praise at all in the conversational sense of that term. It is merely a judgment: a putting into as carefully exact words as I can find the appreciation I make of this style and its triumph.

The reviewer in his art must quote passages. It is hardly the part of a Preface writer to do that. But to show what I mean I can at least quote the following:—

> "Your insight is clear and unbiased," said the

gracious Sovereign. "But however entrancing it is to wander unchecked through a garden of bright images, are we not enticing your mind from another subject of almost equal importance?"

Or again:

"It has been said," he began at length, withdrawing his eyes reluctantly from an unusually large insect upon the ceiling and addressing himself to the maiden, "that there are few situations in life that cannot be honourably settled, and without loss of time, either by suicide, a bag of gold, or by thrusting a despised antagonist over the edge of a precipice on a dark night."

Or again:

"After secretly observing the unstudied grace of her movements, the most celebrated picture-maker of the province burned the implements of his craft, and began life anew as a trainer of performing elephants."

You cannot read those sentences, I think, without agreeing with what has been said above. If you doubt it, take the old test and try to write that kind of thing yourself.

In connection with such achievements it is customary to-day to deplore the lack of public appreciation. Either to blame the hurried millions of chance readers because they have only bought a few thousands of a masterpiece; or, what is worse still, to pretend that good work is for the few and that the mass will never appreciate it—in reply to which it is sufficient to say that the critic himself is one of the mass and could not be distinguished from others of the mass by his very own self were he a looker-on.

In the best of times (the most stable, the least hurried) the date at which general appreciation comes is a matter of chance, and to-day the presentation of any achieved work is like the reading of Keats to a football crowd. It is of no significance whatsoever to English Letters whether one of its glories be appreciated at the moment it issues from the press or ten years later, or twenty, or fifty. Further, after a very small margin is passed, a margin of a few hundreds at the most it matters little whether strong permanent work finds a thousand or fifty thousand or a million of readers. Rock stands and mud washes away.

What is indeed to be deplored is the lack of communication between those who desire to find good stuff and those who can produce it: it is in the attempt to build a bridge between the one and the other that men who have the privilege of hearing a good thing betimes write such words as I am writing here.

Louise Mansell Field (essay date 1924)

SOURCE: "Ernest Bramah and His Blind Detective," in *The Literary Digest International Book Review*, Vol. II, No. 6, May, 1924, pp. 464-65.

[*In the following review, Field highlights the extraordinary skills of Bramah's blind detective Max Carrados and calls the stories in* The Eyes of Max Carrados *"perplexing, entertaining, ingenious, and very well written."*]

The immense contribution which failure has made to Anglo-Saxon letters is at once a curious and an entertaining subject for speculation. The failure, that is, which persons who have since accomplished worthwhile literary work made in the professions first chosen by them. Cold shivers run down one's spine at the thought of the loss which we might have suffered had Algernon Blackwood's dairy-farm, for instance, been a success; and now it appears that Ernest Bramah, whose Kai-Lung stories have won so much well-deserved praise, and whose new book, *The Eyes of Max Carrados,* is just off the press, also intended to become a farmer, tho his experiment was conducted, not in Canada, but in Warwickshire. Fortunately, the venture lost money continuously and consistently; meanwhile, a paragraph casually sent to a newspaper resulted in a commission which ensured the author the magnificent income of ten shillings a week! This remuneration, declares Mr. Bramah, "inculcated in me a fondness for the lucrative fruits of literature that has pursued me ever since."

A gain of shillings being preferable to a steady loss of pounds—a loss which the Manchester business man, who was certainly a most "agreeable" father, endured without reproach—young Mr. Bramah presently went up to London, to see, as he himself remarks, "if there was any newspaper work that required doing there." Protected by a comfortable allowance from home against the starvation-in-an-attic phase, through which all artists are popularly supposed to pass, he found employment with Mr. Jerome K. Jerome. At first the work was secretarial, but soon it became closely connected with the magazine-journal, *To-Day,* which Mr. Jerome was then editing. From that time, Ernest Bramah was immersed in the congenial atmosphere of printer's ink, first with *To-Day,* among whose contributors were such writers as Thomas Hardy, Stanley Weyman, Rudyard Kipling, George Moore and many others, including our own Bret Harte, "the only writer," he says, "whom I ever went to see personally" when a letter could have been made to serve instead of a visit. Later he joined a new firm with "enterprising ideas"—which presently came to grief—and then, with some others of its staff, started another publishing business. Two years of this sufficed, and since 1897 Mr. Bramah has been what he calls an "outside" writer.

Altho only a comparatively few years have passed since *The Wallet of Kai-Lung* became a popular book, it was originally published nearly a quarter of a century ago—in 1900. Another Chinese-named book followed, *The Mirror of Kong Ho,* a volume "frequently found amusing by those who can not stand Kai-Lung," so Mr. Bramah tells us. Then came a romance, *What Might Have Been* in England under a Socialist Government, and in 1914 *Max Carrados,* the book to which this new one is a companion rather than a sequel, since both volumes consist of collections of short stories centering about the wealthy blind man, Max Carrados, one of whose hobbies was criminal investigation.

His other hobby was the collecting of antique Greek coins, and in this connection it is interesting to note that his creator has himself compiled a manuscript on the English regal copper coinage "of such proportions and detail that at the sight of it no English publisher can repress a shudder." But Max Carrados could "see" his treasures only through the medium of his extraordinarily sensitive finger-tips, finger-tips with which he could read the headlines and even some of the smaller print in an ordinary newspaper. For when a twig flicked across his eyes one day when he was out on horseback, and the apparently trivial accident deprived him of his sight, Max Carrados, with that wonderful courage so often displayed by the blind, went to work so to educate his other senses that they might, in great measure, take the place of the one he had lost. And presently he found that even blindness was not entirely without its compensations: "A new world to explore, new experiences, new powers awakening; strange new perceptions; life in the fourth dimension."

Some of the achievements of Max Carrados would seem almost incredible did not Mr. Bramah preface this new account of his hero's exploits with extracts from the biographies of other blind men, notably one John Metcalf, *Blind Jack of Knaresborough,* to whom, oddly enough, he has since discovered that he is himself related. Max Carrados played cards and golf, bowls and cricket; he could punt and fish, and within two miles of his own house, The Turrets, he was "quite independent of any guidance," while the peculiar alertness of his other senses, especially those of touch and hearing, enabled him to perceive much that others ignored. So whenever his friend Carlyle, the private inquiry agent, came across a particularly puzzling case, he enlisted the services of Max Carrados, and whether the mystery concerned the very peculiar behavior of **"The Ghost at Massingham Mansions"** or **"The Mystery of the Poisoned Dish of Mushrooms,"** or the very singular **"Disappearance of Marie Severe,"** the blind man never failed to discover the truth, a truth which not infrequently amazed all those concerned.

Readers of the Kai-Lung books will not need to be told of Mr. Bramah's gift for phrasing, nor of the fine craftsmanship of his highly polished style. He has applied them to these mystery tales, and with them no small amount of ingenuity of invention and cleverness of characterization. Altho a trifle marred by the introduction of an American woman who talks as American women never do outside of English fiction ("He's a piece too mean-spirited to have the nerve," she remarks at one important moment), **"The Disappearance of Marie Severe"** is not only an excellent puzzle, but its motivation, besides being plausible, seems distinctly novel.

The achievement of a certain "painstakingly conscientious young man" in connection with **"The Virginiola Fraud,"** the story of which opens the book, is well contrasted with the gruesome **"Secret of Dunstan's Tower,"** into which strange affair of Druid stones and ancient legend Max Carrados was brought by his friend Dr. Tulloch, the same Dr. Tulloch who figures in **"The Eastern Mystery,"** the last and weakest story in the book.

It is not only that these tales are perplexing, entertaining, ingenious and very well written; they have an attention to detail, an air of verisimilitude, which makes the reader believe in the reality of the events they record. The book is full of flesh-and-blood characters and dextrously turned phrases, phrases which will give abundant delight to the lover of fine craftsmanship in the art of writing.

William White (essay date 1959)

SOURCE: "Kai Lung in America: The Critical Reception of Ernest Bramah," in *The American Book Collector,* Vol. 9, No. 10, June, 1959, pp. 15-19.

[*In the following essay, White surveys Bramah's writings and laments the general lack of criticism on the author's works.*]

Almost sixty years ago Ernest Bramah wrote *The Wallet of Kai Lung,* in which Chinese ways of thinking and speaking were adapted to the English language: the most horrifying events told blandly, the most farcical situations described with a straight face, and the most evil characters tell the most transparent lies in the politest possible way, with aphorisms on every other page. For example: "It has been said . . . that there are few situations in life that cannot be honorably settled, and without loss of time, either by suicide, a bag of gold, or by thrusting a despised antagonist over the edge of a precipice on a dark night." But the translation of this mannered Far Eastern society and speech into Western idiom under Bramah's hand became something more than farce. Character and situation are often fined to a sharp edge of satire, which cuts no less deep for the humaneness and benevolence that constitute one of Bramah's most appealing qualities. It is not every inmate of a pitch-black dungeon who would protest against personal injury and indignity in such tones as these: "If it is not altogether necessary for your refined convenience that you stand on this one's face, he for his part would willingly forego the esteemed honor."

However, the first eight publishers who read the manuscript of *The Wallet of Kai Lung* turned it down; after British publication it had to wait 23 years before an American house printed it in 1923. In both England and America it created a small coterie of Bramah lovers, so that Clifton Fadiman asked in June 6, 1928 *Nation* on the publication of the third Kai Lung volume: "Is it possible, as rumor runs, that there are those who have no relish for these sly Oriental suavities, these delicate evasions of language, this restrained Gongorism carried to a point of fine art?" The answer to the 30-year-old question must be yes, many must have no such relish. For today 16 years after Bramah's death, you cannot even buy a Bramah book in a bookstore in America—he is long out of print. You must either order one of the three or four Kai Lung books still available from the British Book Centre in New York or buy them directly from England. No critic (apart from book reviewers) in this country and no literary historian has paid the slightest attention to Ernest Bramah. He has had no critical reception.

Of course, one is first tempted to ask: should we pay any attention to him? Before this can be answered, certain other questions must be taken care of: who is Ernest Bramah? what has he written? what popular or serious consideration has he received in England? and why has he been, to a large extent, ignored by readers and students of the novel in America? It is these problems with which I should like to deal in in this paper.

Very little is known about the life of Ernest Bramah—born Ernest Bramah Smith—and even less has been written: a page or two here and there is everything a diligent search turns up. Not even the date of his birth is known, but from his first book, the semi-autobiographical *English Farming and Why I Turned It Up* (London, 1894), we may infer that it was about 1869. (His obituaries give both this date and 1868.) He told the editors of *Twentieth Century Authors* (New York, 1942, p. 1304), Stanley J. Kunitz and Howard Haycraft, "I am not fond of writing about myself and only in a less degree about my work. My published books are about all I care to pass on to the reader." We do know that he was born in Manchester, England; that at 17 he chose farming as a profession, giving it up after three years of losing money, and turned to journalism. Penguin Books, which still publishes some of his tales, says: "He started as a correspondent on a typical provincial paper, then went to London as secretary to Jerome K. Jerome, and worked himself into the editorial side of Jerome's magazine, *To-day,* where he got the opportunity of meeting the most important literary figures of the day. But he soon left *To-day* to join a new publishing firm, as editor of a publication called *The Minister;* finally, after two years of this, he turned to writing as his full-time occupation."

There is reason to believe that Bramah spent some time in the Far East, the *New York Times* obituary stating flatly that he "lived for many years in China," the locale of his Kai Lung volumes. If this is true, it is most likely that he was there before 1899, for in July of that year he sent to Grant Richards, the English publisher, the manuscript of *The Wallet of Kai Lung*. Richards said that Smith, Elder, Chatto, Cassell, Heinemann, Constable, Lawrence and Bullen, Macmillan, and Fisher Unwin all turned down the *Wallet*; Richards writes (*Author Hunting,* London and New York, 1934, p. 272) "that it was a careful typescript, sewn bookwise into a brown paper wrapper, and that every manuscript of Ernest Bramah's that I have seen since has looked exactly like it." Richards's edition of 1,000 copies, plus 500 for a special

Colonial Edition and 750 for a Boston firm did not sell out for seven years: one could hardly call it a publishing success. Richards describes Bramah as "one of the kindest and the most amiable of men . . . , small and—may I say—he does not look ferocious; I believe him to be uncarnivorous, and indeed I think that he eschews the pleasures of the table—whether from compulsion or inclination I cannot say." Richards wrote Bramah twice a year for a successor to the *Wallet* (reprinted by Methuen & Co. in a cheap edition in 1917) until *Kai Lung's Golden Hours* was published in 1922; and in the next year both the *Wallet* and the *Golden Hours* were first issued in America as companion volumes under the George H. Doran imprint. While Richards says Doran "had a considerable success with" the set, I think "considerable" is an overstatement.

Meanwhile, however, Bramah had written three other books: *The Mirror of Kong Ho* (London, 1905), *What Might Have Been: The Story of a Social War* (London, 1907), and *Max Carrados* (London, 1914). The last two have never been published in America, and the first did not get an American imprint until 1930, when Doubleday, Doran & Company (George H. Doran's successor) brought it out. By then Bramah's literary career was in full swing: he was appearing in British fiction magazines and (later) in anthologies on both sides of the Atlantic, especially with his Carrados stories about the blind detective. Two collections of these short pieces were published, *The Eyes of Max Carrados* (London, 1923) and *Max Carrados Mysteries* (London, 1927), but only the former was issued in this country—by George H. Doran in 1924. Another collection, *The Specimen Case* (London, 1924; New York, 1925), came out between these two: it contains 21 stories by Bramah, each one a single example of what he calls a "literary exercise." His ninth book was *Kai Lung Unrolls His Mat* (London and New York, 1928), which with *The Wallet of Kai Lung* and *Kai Lung's Golden Hours* make up *The Kai Lung Omnibus* (London, 1936). His writing career, which is about all one can mention in recounting his life, was not yet over. The next volume was a piece of nonfiction in an area which had long interested him and which even crops up in his Max Carrados stories, *A Guide to the Varieties and Rarity of English Regal Copper Coins, Charles II-Victoria, 1671-1860* (London, 1929). It has never been published in this country, nor was his next book, *A Little Flutter* (London, 1930), a light-hearted novel. Two years later he turned back to Kai Lung, this time a full-length narrative in which the Chinaman does not himself appear but his name appears in the title: *The Moon of Much Gladness, Related by Kai Lung* (London, 1932), published in America after a delay of five years and by a small firm, Sheridan House, as *The Return of Kai Lung* (New York, 1937). His last two books, *The Bravo of London* (London, 1934), the only novel in which Max Carrados appears, and *Kai Lung Beneath the Mulberry-Tree* (London, 1940) were not printed in America, perhaps because the earlier ones did not sell well, for it was a time of financial depression.

Ernest Bramah's total output was fifteen books, only seven of which were issued with American imprints. He also wrote two one-act plays which, according to Penguin Books, "are often performed at London variety theatres, and many stories and articles in leading (British) periodicals." Grant Richards tells us, again in *Author Hunting* (p. 274): "There is one thing that I think few Bramah admirers know. On 21 February 1931 at 2:30 the Men Students of the Old Vic Shakespeare Company presented *Kai Lung's Golden Hours,* 'a Chinese Comedy, adapted for the stage by Allan D. Mainds, A.R.S.A.'" To which Richards adds, "But I prefer my Kai Lung within the pages of a book." Bramah died in Somerset, England on June 27, 1942; the *New York Times* reported the next day: "The life of the writer of detective fiction was somewhat of a mystery, as he lived in great seclusion, his widow even asking suppression of the place of death." From Bramah's own preface to *The Specimen Case,* however, one gets the impression that the notion of being a "mystery" amused him. For he reports a controversy in London periodicals, with his publisher Grant Richards writing, "I am asked all sorts of questions about (*The Wallet of Kai Lung*) and its author. Is there really such a person as Ernest Bramah? and so on. . . . Finally, I do assure his readers that such a person as Ernest Bramah does really and truly exist. I have seen and touched him." Bramah's American publisher told him in a letter, "I have always had a feeling that you were a mythical person," to which Bramah replied, "There is something not unattractive in the idea of being a mythical person . . . though from the heroic point of view one might have wished that it could have been 'a mythological personage.'"

So much for the life of the creator of Kai Lung and Max Carrados. What about his writings? It is these, after all, which are the reasons he is being discussed in the present paper. Of the fifteen books, several of them can be dismissed in a few words. For example, his first work, the autobiographical *English Farming and Why I Turned It Up:* the copy I read (and it is a rare book) came from the Library Company of Philadelphia. A notation indicates that it was bought August 22, 1894, the year of its publication. It was first taken out on December 7, 1894, and once more after that, on April 22, 1913, before I got it on Interlibrary Loan in December 1957. There was hardly a mad rush in Philadelphia reading circles for the book; but then it was catalogued under "Agriculture," which might account for its burial. And an early reader has made a marginal annotation on the first page of the text: "This book was written by an English 'Smarty.' Don't waste time on it." (Incidentally, the Library Company saw so little future demand for *English Farming* that it was sold to me for $3.00.)

Bramah's book on numismatics, *A Guide to the Varieties and Rarity of English Regal Copper Coins,* has been called an authoritative work on the subject; but it is not literature in the sense I am using the term in this paper. He did, however, draw on his expert knowledge in this area for several of his stories. One more book that is different from anything else Bramah wrote, except as another expression of his humor, is *A Little Flutter*. It is a novel about the last surviving specimen of the Patagonian Groo-Groo, which has been sent to the aviary of a man left a legacy on the condition that he spend his life studying birds. Complications become outlandish when an escaped convict is disguised in the skin of the deceased bird. Which is enough said about this book. This leaves us with the detective stories and the Chinese ones, and *The Specimen Case,* in which both Kai Lung and Carrados appear.

There are four books which have the blind detective as a central character: *Max Carrados,* the first one; *The Eyes of Max Carrados,* which came second and contains a long and interesting introduction on blindness and detection; *Max Carrados Mysteries,* the final collection of short stories of a police nature; and *The Bravo of London,* the one novel and not a very good one in which Carrados is a character. (*Twentieth Century Authors* is wrong saying, "There is no full-length Carrados novel.") These stories bring up a provocative question: is the detective novel worthy of serious discussion as a literary type? George Sampson's *Concise Cambridge History of English Literature* (Cambridge and New York, 1941) devotes a few pages (p. 978, for instance) to the subject, not without some sneers. Professor William York Tindall's *Forces in Modern British Literature, 1885-1946* (New York, 1947, pp. 143-144) is far more generous. But an affirmative answer to the question may be suggested by Howard Haycraft's *Murder for Pleasure: The Life and Times of the Detective Story* (New York, 1941), a full-length account of police fiction as literature. Mr. Haycraft mentions Bramah more than once and gives two pages of information (pp. 77-79), some of which—including the no Carrados novel mistake—he repeats in *Twentieth Century Authors.* Max Carrados is also discussed briefly a few times in Mr. Haycraft's *Art of the Mystery Story* (New York, 1946). He calls Bramah skillful, able, conscientious; however: "Occasionally the tales lean a little too far in the direction of intuition, and at other times they partake of the monotony of the arm-chair method; but for the most part they have a basis of sound investigation and deduction, imaginatively set forth." Mr. Haycraft concludes: "Wise, witty, gentle Max Carrados is one of the most attractive figures in detective literature—and a worthy protagonist to bring the (Sherlock Holmes, 1890-1914) epoch to an end."

My own opinion on rereading these stories is that from a literary view they do not hold up; they are far below in quality, to cite one other writer in the same field, Dorothy Sayers. But Bramah surely belongs in a historical survey of detective fiction, and in most of his obits in 1942 he was referred to as a writer of mystery stories and police fiction. In the eyes of many, the Max Carrados tales gave him some popular fame in America at least.

Coming in 1924, *The Specimen Case* is an important book for anyone who is studying Ernest Bramah as a literary figure. At the time he had written two Max Carrados books and two concerning Kai Lung; the new collection, he says in his preface, consists "of a suitable example taken at convenient intervals over the whole time that I have been engaged in writing stories—a span of thirty years." Not only is the preface of more than passing interest on Bramah and what he has to say about writing, but the collection traces, counter-clockwise (from the first tale, dated 1923, to the last, dated 1894) Bramah's development as an author. The 1894 piece, **"From a London Balcony,"** is a "shocker," a little item of journalism; the 1923 piece, **"Ming Tseuen and the Emergency,"** is a brilliant gem of a Kai Lung story. Comparing this with the Carrados story which *The Specimen Case* contains, **"A Bunch of Violets,"** one can easily see the Kai Lung material as far superior. While the stories as a whole show technical proficiency and writing skill of a high order, nothing a professional author need be ashamed of, the Kai Lung stories in this book and elsewhere approach much closer to genuine literature. One can also see in *The Specimen Case* that satire was Bramah's metier. If Bramah is to have any claim to fame it is to be in his satirizing of social conventions, especially in England during his period, and in the unique style of Kai Lung's tales.

In addition to the first story in *The Specimen Case,* there are five Kai Lung books (if I may repeat titles already mentioned) published in this order from 1900 to 1940: *The Wallet of Kai Lung, Kai Lung's Golden Hours, Kai Lung Unrolls His Mat, Return of Kai Lung* (called *Moon of Much Gladness, Related by Kai Lung* in England), and *Kai Lung Beneath the Mulberry-Tree.* (There are two other books, *The Transmutation of Ling* and *The Story of Wan and the Remarkable Shrub, and The Story of Ching-Kwei and the Destinies,* but they are merely taken from Kai Lung volumes and issued separately.) Finally, there is *The Mirror of Kong Ho,* which some (including Penguin Books) have called a Kai Lung book: it is in a similar genre, but Kai Lung does not appear in it, nor has he anything to do with it. It has what I might call Kai Lung "qualities"; hence its discussion here. Kai Lung himself does not appear in *The Return of Kai Lung*—as he does in the other four books as both a character and a storyteller—but Bramah regards him as the teller of this full-length novel; thus he has his name in the title.

The basic pattern of the Kai Lung books is relatively simple. He is a kind of Chinese Chaucer, as Clifton Fadiman calls him, an ingenious and ingenuous professional storyteller among thieves, rogues, and mandarins. Accused of many crimes, he tells his wonderful tales to postpone the verdict (*á la Arabian Nights*) or get himself out of difficulties by charming his captors from day to day. There are of course other complications, such as in *Kai Lung Unrolls His Mat,* when he must rescue his beautiful Golden Mouse from the vicious mandarin Ming Shu, who also desires her. These adventures themselves are of small importance: it is the satirical element, the style, and the aphorisms that are everything. In *Kong Ho,* with the locale shifted from China to London and the characters changed from these thieves, rogues and man-

darins to Englishmen, the effect is exactly the same, as Kong Ho—in the Chinese spy tradition—writes letters from England to his father in the Orient about British customs and the situations he gets himself into. In addition to the satire, which so many reviewers have not given its due, there is a delightfully elaborate and circuitous way of expressing the most obvious and simple notions. This polished, exaggeratedly refined verbiage slows each tale down to a less-than-tortoise pace just as the tale itself has completely stopped Kai Lung's own adventure. But a reader never minds: for the framework on which to hang all this is a minor matter.

It is impossible to describe the style of Ernest Bramah in these books, for there is nothing else quite like it. One can only give examples: "After secretly observing the unstudied grace of her movements, the most celebrated picture-maker of the province burned the implements of his craft, and began life anew as a trainer of performing elephants." And though all of the characters are invariably polite, rigidly ceremonial, and totally insincere, there is sometimes a loss of temper, as in this ordinary slang phrase turned into a high-flown Chinese idiom: "Thou concave-eyed and mentally bedridden offspring of a bald-seated she-dog." And again from *The Return of Kai Lung:* "To regard all men as corrupt is wise, but to attempt to discriminate among the various degrees of iniquity is both foolish and discourteous." A final quote from the same book: "It is possible to escape from an enemy carrying a two-edged sword but not from the interference of a well-meaning woman." When Bramah is talking of the Hereditary Confederacy of Superfluity Removers and Abandoned Oddment Gatherers, he is referring to garbage collectors; and when he speaks of the Kochow Throng of Hechild Track-Followers, Kai Lung has in mind the Boy Scouts of the neighborhood.

In spite of the high-level performance of Ernest Bramah in these Kai Lung stories over a period of years, and in spite of the very high praise he got in England from Hilaire Belloc, Sir Arthur Quiller-Couch, Sir John C. Squire and S. P. B. Mais, critical attention in Britain has been negligible. A chapter in Squire's *Life and Letters: Essays* (London, 1920; New York, 1921, pp. 44-51); another in Mais's *Some Modern Authors* (London and New York, 1923, pp. 45-51; Grant Richards's introduction to *The Wallet of Kai Lung* (London, 1923) and his pages on Bramah in *Author Hunting* (London and New York, 1934, pp. 272-275); and Belloc's Preface to *Kai Lung's Golden Hours* (London, 1922), which is included in every edition of the book in both England and America—these and the book reviews as the various volumes were published just about sum up all the writings about Bramah. In America, as in Great Britain, he is mentioned in no histories of English literature that I am aware of, and I've searched hundred, no studies of the novel, no critiques of contemporary fiction, not in the *Cambridge History* or the *Oxford Companion to English Literature,* though William Rose Benét does give Bramah (under his real name, Ernest Bramah Smith) six lines in *The Reader's Encyclopedia* (New York, 1948, p. 1042).

Other than book reviews of seven of the books published in this country, the obituary notices, and the three Haycraft books cited above (*Twentieth Century Authors* and the histories of detective and mystery stories), Bramah has been ignored. Not one single article that could be called criticism.

Some of the reviews, on the other hand, are worth citing, though not all are fulsome in their praise. *The Nation* of January 9, 1924 had this to say about the **Wallet:** "The measure of one's delight in such a narrative as this is on the basis of one's fondness for humor which is deliberate, satire which is philosophical, and action which is aloof. There is a great deal of color in this story—and an equal apportionment of Oriental calm. If these elements coincide with one's temperament, Ernest Bramah will be quite to the taste; otherwise he is inclined to be insidiously soporific." *The Outlook* of May 16, 1928 wrote that *Kai Lung Unrolls His Mat* was "subtle, suave, and intricately satirical," and concluded: "We only refrain from saying these books are the best of their kind because we know of no others that are at all like them. They are really unique." Mary McCarthy's notice of **The Return of Kai Lung** in *The Nation* for October 23, 1937 ought to be quoted in full:

> This little book, set in the never-never land of dynastic China, has for its ostensible subject the loss of a mandarin's pigtail. In the rigidly ceremonial Chinese world which Mr. Bramah predicates, this deprivation is synonymous with the loss of dignity, sexual and bureaucratic; and the quest of the missing pigtail becomes a national problem. The agent of its recovery is a Chinese girl, disguised in boys' clothes, who has an anachronistic acquaintance with English detective stories. The book is a satire of detective-story writers, who are habitually referred to as "the barbarian sages"; it is also a gentle, ironic commentary of the eternal, international venality and mutability of human nature and the absurdity of accepted social forms. It is, of course, a little démodé, both in its kindly, eclectic cynicism and its comic method. Most of its effects are gained through what H. W. Fowler classifies as polysyllabic or pedantic humor. It assumes that if a Western custom is described in ornate, Oriental verbiage, the reader will find both the incongruity and the custom funny. As a matter of fact, the reader frequently does. Mr. Bramah has an enormous vocabulary and a droll, supple hand. With this equipment, and with considerable effort, he does manage to squeeze a number of laughs out of the old topsy-turvy joke.

Many reviewers have said, with truth, that Bramah writes for a special audience. *The Bookman* (October 1930): "The pages of Bramah have the bouquet of the rarest tea, of a kind not imported, and drunk only by mandarins of the highest button, and in this amber atmosphere live his amiable personages, displaying, even under the most excruciating trials, that affable demeanor which is the conscious art of the countrymen of the polite Confucius." And *Time* (September 6, 1937): "(Bramah's) **Kai Lung**

stories . . . have long delighted patient readers on both sides of the Atlantic. Their low-keyed humor, chess-game pace and subacid satire gave them an effect somewhat less than sidesplitting, but for readers who like slyness slow and stately, Ernest Bramah is a lordly dish. . . . Their chief delight, however, is an apt aphorisms: 'Two resolute men acting in concord may transform an Empire, but an ordinarily resourceful duck can escape from a dissentient rabble.'" Finally, one of the longest reviews of **Kong Ho,** by John Carter in the *New York Times Book Review* of December 14, 1930, which speaks of the Kai Lung tales being "to China what 'Hajji Baba of Ispahan' is to Persia. Here is satire of a sort which stands on its own feet and needs neither apology nor explanation." Mr. Carter continues, "Mr. Bramah is an English savant and philosopher and Kong Ho is a purely ficticious character. This is a device which recommended itself to the greater satirists, to Voltaire as to Goldsmith. . . . East and West, Mr. Bramah reminds us, are not opposite; they are sideways from each other. . . . 'The Mirror of Kong Ho' is something more than an ordinary production. It is part of the carefully distilled and rarefied humor and wisdom of one of the few modern writers of whom it can be truthfully said that they should write far more than they do, but that it would be a pity if they did. Kong Ho takes his place beside, or a little beneath, Mr. Bramah's immortal Kai Lung." Mr. Carter concludes: "This is one of the few books which no intelligent man ought to neglect, as it is one of the few which every intelligent man will enjoy rereading."

Such was the reception from American book reviewers. The reception from book buyers in America was considerably less than in England. All fifteen of his books were published in London, and of the seven published in this country, all are out of print. The Kai Lung books are still in print on the other side of the Atlantic, in both paperback editions and in hard covers; many more editions were issued there than here. Only the **Wallet** and **Kai Lung's Golden Hours** were reprinted in hard covers—there were no paperbacks here—by Doubleday, Doran; and the printings were never large. Today, to repeat what I said at the outset, the books can only be obtained in America through direct import from Britain—or through the antiquarian bookseller.

More than thirty-five years ago Hilaire Belloc wrote in a preface to **Kai Lung's Golden Hours** an apt conclusion to what I have been trying to say:

> In connection with such achievements (of Ernest Bramah's) it is customary to deplore the lack of public appreciation. Either to blame the hurried millions of chance readers because they have only bought a few thousands of a masterpiece; or, what is worse still, to pretend that a good work is for the few and that the mass will never appreciate it—in reply to which it is sufficient to say that the critic himself is one of the mass and could not be distinguished from the others of the mass by his very own self were he a looker-on.

In the best of times (the most stable, the least hurried) the date at which general appreciation comes is a matter of chance, and to-day the presentation of any achieved work is like the reading of Keats to a football crowd. It is of no significance whatsoever to English Letters whether one of its glories be appreciated at the moment it issues from the press or ten years later, or twenty, or fifty. Further, after a very small margin is passed, a margin of a few hundreds at the most, it matters little whether strong permanent work finds a thousand or fifty thousand or a million of readers. Rock stands and mud washes away.

What is indeed to be deplored is the lack of communication between those who desire to find good stuff and those who can produce it: it is in the attempt to build a bridge between the one and the other that men who have the privilege of hearing a good thing betimes write such words as I am writing here.

William White (essay date 1972)

SOURCE: "Ernest Bramah on China: An Important Letter," in *PMLA*, Vol. 87, No. 3, May, 1972, pp. 511-13.

[*In the following essay, White presents a letter from Bramah to his publisher, Grant Richards, that proves the author of* The Wallet of Kai Lung *and several other books set in China never visited the Far East.*]

If Ernest Bramah, born Ernest Bramah Smith (1868-1942), is to find a place in English literary history, it will be for his Kai Lung tales, centered on this Chinese storyteller and "philosopher" in *The Wallet of Kai Lung* (1900), *Kai Lung's Golden Hours* (1922), *Kai Lung Unrolls His Mat* (1928), *The Moon of Much Gladness, Related by Kai Lung* (1932, called, in America, *The Return of Kai Lung*), and *Kai Lung Beneath the Mulberry-Tree* (1940). The pattern in all of them is pretty much the same: Kai Lung, finding himself among thieves, rogues, and mandarins, is accused of many crimes but postpones the torture or verdict by charming his captors from day to day with marvelous tales. This is an ancient device, but it is not so much the matter of stories as the manner, the style, the satire, and his endless and ingenious aphorisms.

The China that Bramah created—its people, its manners, its landscape—is so real and comprehensively Chinese, obviously of an earlier period, that many readers and reviewers of the Kai Lung stories have tended to ask about their source. For example, Grant Richards, Bramah's publisher, wrote in the Introduction to a reissue of *The Wallet of Kai Lung* (London: Grant Richards, 1923), "I thought it would be great fun to explore the deeper recesses of Mr. Bramah's mind and memory for some remains of the mental and physical experiences that led to the creation of Kai Lung himself and to the evolution of the style, so seemingly inevitable and so lucidly involved, in which Kai Lung's words and actions are set down."

And Richards probed into matters that troubled all of Kai Lung's admirers:

> How long, I asked in effect, were you in China? And when? Has Chinese literature always had a fascination for you? I know you have not visited the East in recent years—in that time have you kept your Oriental knowledge and sympathetic understanding alive by frequenting the society of Chinese diplomats and students? To each of these questions our author made a bland, evasive and, as I now suspect, characteristic reply. (pp. v-vi)

A few years later, Sir J. C. Squire, one of Bramah's champions, wrote in a Preface to *The Mirror of Kong Ho* (London: Grant Richards and H. Toulmin [Cayne Press], 1929), "How far Mr Bramah faithfully reflects the attitude of the practical masses of Chinamen in this or any other age I do not know. I do not even know if he has ever been to China, though he had all the literary and superstitious jargon at his fingers' ends" (p. xii). The *New York Times* obituary of Bramah, 28 June 1942, said he "lived for some time in China"; Stanley J. Kunitz and Howard Haycroft's entry for Bramah in *Twentieth Century Authors* (New York: Wilson, 1942, p. 1304) says that Kai Lung's China "is a deliberately 'fantastic conventional bogus China,' but is yet sufficiently verisimilar to suggest the author's sometime residence in the Far East." *Chamber's Biographical Dictionary*, edited by J. O. Thorne (New York: St. Martin's Press, 1962), simply states that Bramah "lived for a while in China"; and a columnist in the London book publishers' periodical, *Smith's Trade News,* upon the publication of a collection of Kai Lung stories in 1963, said just as explicitly that Bramah "spent some part of his life in China and never got over it." W. P. Watt, Bramah's literary agent, who was left the copyright to his novels and stories, told a member of his staff, Miss Patricia Butler, "something about Bramah going to China," which she reported to me in 1965 but was not able to verify her information.

There have been some who doubted that Bramah was in China. Another of his stoutest and most generous admirers, Hilaire Belloc, once wrote to the editors of a Hong Kong magazine to ask what was known in China of Kai Lung; he received no reply. Thus, according to John Connell's Introduction to the latest collection of Kai Lung stories, *The Celestial Omnibus* (London: John Baker, 1963, pp. 8-9) and "The Recluse Who Created Kai Lung," *The Listener,* 29 May 1947, "I am afraid there is not one scrap of evidence that Bramah ever went out of Europe in his life. I think we must accept it, therefore, that his knowledge and love of China and of things Chinese were products entirely of his own mind and temper" (p. 841).

If by any chance Bramah visited the Orient, it must have been before 1896, for his earliest Chinese tale, **"The Story of Yung Chang,"** as **"Narrated by Kai Lung, in the Open Space Before the Tea-Shop of Celestial Principles, at Wu-Whei,"** was published in *Chapman's Magazine of Fiction* (London, 5 Oct. 1896, 142-53. It was included in *The Wallet of Kai Lung* in 1900). Further, it was written earlier, for in a letter (in the University of Texas Humanities Research Center), dated 12 November 1895, from Quiller-Couch to Bramah, reference is made to these Chinese stories, which Cassell & Co. declined to publish. However, Bramah could not have gone to the Far East by then, as his whereabouts can be well accounted for from his birth in Manchester in 1868, his schooling in the Manchester Grammar School and others from 1874 to 1885, farming from 1885 to 1892 (including his work as correspondent for the *South Birmingham News,* 1890-92), and his studying and editing and writing in London from 1892 to 1895. Of course he made a "bland, evasive reply" to Grant Richards: he was never in China.

We now know this for certain, for a typed letter, signed by Bramah, has come to light, and permission to publish has been granted by Kathleen M. Watt, of Cambridgeshire, holder of the copyright:

> 210 Hamlet Gardens.
> Ravenscourt Park. W. 6.
>
> 27th. April. 1923.
>
> Dear Richards,
>
> I am hastening to reply to yours because I rather gather that you wish to have any material I can give you soon. I have an ever-growing note of things that I have to write to you about but the only one that gives me any concern is the first enquiry of your letter and on that subject I feel apologetic, because on it I can find so little to say.
>
> Specifically, I have never been in China, but I do not know that (to others) it is diplomatic to be specific on this point. It has seemed to me that an attitude might be: (a) if I have lived in China then the stories are probably merely translations or at all events not entirely original [;] (b) if I have not been in China and have no special knowledge, then the whole fabric is imaginary and unreliable as a picture of Chinese life; so that I have in general rather evaded the direct question, desiring personally only that the books should be taken as they stand. However, that blameless secret is now in your keeping and I shall not reproach you whatever use you make of it.
>
> Beyond that, I suppose that by now I have assimilated a considerable amount of miscellaneous Chinese literature—at all events all that has come my way, and the only book in which I could find nothing of interest or novelty was one written by a Chinaman who had long resided in America. He seemed to have completely lost every Celestial touch and to have forgotten what China was (or, perhaps, ought to be) like. Also I have casually known some of the people but I do not take much account of that. If I am genuinely Chinese (and I have frequently been told by those who ought to know me best that my everyday way of looking at ordinary things is more than half Chinese) it must be ascribed to

> my having lived there in a previous existence. Sometimes the extent of intimate inside knowledge credited to me by the well-meaning is more than a little embarrassing. A few years ago I contributed a harmless Anglo-Chinese story to a leading magazine, to find myself described in a serious footnote to the tale when it appeared as "perhaps the greatest living English authority on China"— or words very much to that effect. "Perhaps", as the Editor wisely put it, but it sent me hot and cold for weeks afterwards. And only a few weeks ago an earnest student of Chinese custom wrote to me—apropos of one of the stories in the *Golden Hours*—to enquire if I had not been guilty of a slight technical oversight in connection with the behaviour of a "senior concubine."
>
> As regards the mere process of writing I do not know that there is anything beyond the very obvious to say. I suppose that if you or I sat long enough opposite a Chinese screen or an ivory carving we should write a tale about it. In my case, unfortunately, the sitting period is rather long (averaging at least that of the ordinary hen) but when a satisfactory central idea does evolve its elaboration is more or less automatic, though still (this is partly owing to my unfortunate habit of altering each day every word that I have written on the previous one) painfully slow. A spontaneous and extraneous germ idea is a godsend. For instance, at the Whitechapel Chinese Art Exhibition some years ago there was an item: 'Poor Chinese student, reading by the light of glow-worms held in a gauze bag' and there you have The Story of Lao Ting and the Luminous Insect practically complete. Frazer (*Golden Bough*) mentions that the essential idea of the burial robe is the vital principle emanating from the maker, which seems to me to cover everything contained in The Story of Wang-ho and the Burial Robe. If only I could come upon a ready supply of these great ideas of someone's providing, I daresay that it would not take me more than two or three months to write a story regularly.
>
> Now as regards other things. [The remaining two pages of the letter concern business matters, payment for stories, the price of his books, and other comments not pertinent to this discussion.]
>
> Possibly there are other things but this is all I remember at the moment.
>
> Yours sincerely,
> Ernest B. Smith [signed]
>
> Grant Richards, Esq.

From the date of this letter, 27 April 1923, and the date of Richards' introduction to *The Wallet of Kai Lung,* May 1923, we know that the publisher had sent Bramah the "questionnaire" (as Richards calls it) about China; but the novelist's reply was not revealed here or in Richards' *Author Hunting, by an Old Literary Sportsman: Memories of Years Spent Mainly in Publishing 1897-1925* (London: Hamish Hamilton, 1934). This four-page letter, signed the way he usually signed letters and everything except his stories and books, is the most important one by Bramah yet published. It definitely settles the did-he-go-to-China question, and, in addition, makes some lively comments on the creative process. Even here, in a private letter, Ernest Bramah Smith writes in a way that leaves small doubt why his Kai Lung books have gone through numerous editions in America (issued by George H. Doran, later Doubleday & Company) and in England. There they were published by several houses, including Penguin Books, and they are still in print.

Jacques Barzun and Wendell H. Taylor (essay date 1976)

SOURCE: "Ernest Bramah: Max Carrados," in *A Book of Prefaces to Fifty Classics of Crime Fiction, 1900-1950,* Garland Publishing, 1976, pp. 23-4.

[*In the following essay, Barzun and Taylor briefly introduce* Max Carrados, *Bramah's first book of tales featuring his famous blind detective.*]

Just as the classic novelist wants to make his hero or heroine differ in character or circumstance from all previous ones, so the writer of detective tales feels obliged to make his investigator in some way singular. The demand leads to some dreadful temptations, one of which is to make the detective a blind man. Ernest Bramah was so tempted, but unlike others, who have variously gone in for bumblers, drunkards, paraplegics, and certifiable idiots, he achieved an unquestioned triumph in Max Carrados. This able and amiable man of otherwise independent means is but little dependent on help for the remarkable things he does, and these are not more than can be done without eyesight—let doubters read the authoritative work by T. D. Cutsforth on *The Blind in School and Society.*

The present volume [*Max Carrados*] inaugurated in 1914 the series of twenty-six cases in which Carrados and his friend, the inquiry agent Louis Carlyle, prevent or help avenge crime. The situations range from the serious to the comic without disturbing either the poise of the blind man or the slightly raffish tone of his associate. Throughout their adventures the reader will also enjoy the note of quiet derision which is typical of the writer who, besides Carrados, created Kai Lung and his pseudo-Chinese predicaments. It is perhaps this satirical attitude that makes the Carrados stories sound so fresh, though they were written more than half a century ago and are concerned with matters of daily life one tends to think vastly changed.

The test of this classic quality is best seen in **"The Tragedy at Brookbend Cottage"**, where the mood is still felt as tragic—and the pebbles rattling on the window pane as a master touch. The broader effects, at once alarming and farcical, in **"The Comedy at Fountain Cottage"** and **"Harry the Actor"** are equally memorable and credible, as is the very modern motive for the railway disaster.

Ernest Bramah tried only once to use his blind man in a full-length book, ***The Bravo of London*** (1934). It turned out an unconvincing thriller. For a writer who had so much humor and so wide a choice of interests—he once wrote a book on English farming and another on rare coins—he seems to have made few acquaintances among his contemporaries and left no perceptible mark as a person. The chief first-hand account of him is a brief passage in Grant Richards' *Author Hunting,* where in successive editions may be found two different photos of the elusive man who in real life was, appropriately enough, E. B. Smith.

FURTHER READING

Haycraft, Howard. "England: 1890-1914 (The Romantic Era)." In *Murder for Pleasure: The Life and Times of the Detective Story*, pp. 62-82. New York: D. Appleton-Century Company, 1941.
   Briefly mentions *Max Carrados* as among the last and most successful detective novels in the premodern period of the genre.

The following sources published by Gale Research contain additional coverage of Bramah's life and career: *Contemporary Authors,* Vol. 156; *Dictionary of Literary Biography,* Vol. 70.

Lester Dent

1904-1959

(Also wrote under the pseudonyms Kenneth Robeson and Tim Ryan) American novelist and short story writer.

INTRODUCTION

A tremendously prolific writer specializing in the genres of mystery-detective and science fiction, Dent is largely remembered for the nearly two hundred Doc Savage novels he produced in the 1930s and 1940s. Writing under the pseudonym of Kenneth Robeson, which was imposed by his publishers in New York, Dent churned out scores of novels featuring the hero-adventurer Dr. Clark Savage, beginning with 1935's *The Man of Bronze*. In addition to his many pulp fiction works, Dent also wrote several mystery novels, including the notable Chance Malloy tale *Dead at the Take-off*. Two of Dent's short stories, "Sail" and "Angelfish," are moreover thought to typify the gritty, laconic style of the *Black Mask* magazine, a detective-mystery publication that enjoyed considerable popularity in the 1930s under the editorship of Joseph T. Shaw.

Biographical Information

Lester Dent was born in La Plata, Missouri in 1904. He spent most of his early formative years in relative isolation on his father's ranch outside Pumpkin Buttes, Wyoming, but his family's return to Missouri allowed Dent to receive his early education in La Plata. While still in school Dent envisioned himself becoming a banker and began attending Chillicothe Business College in Chillicothe, Missouri. In 1924 he took a job as a telegraph operator instead, believing that he could make more money by doing so. The following year he moved to Oklahoma, gaining employment with the Associated Press as a telegrapher. In 1926 a coworker of Dent's in Tulsa informed him that he had sold a short story for a significant sum of money to a pulp magazine publisher. Soon after Dent began writing his own stories for the pulps while working the night shift for Associated Press. His success in the field attracted the attention of Dell Publishing in New York City. A representative of Dell contacted Dent in 1929 and offered him a substantial salary to become a house writer. He accepted, relocating to New York with his wife, Norma Gerling, in 1931. At Dell Dent began writing his popular Doc Savage novels under a house pseudonym. Meanwhile, he attempted to expand the scope of his writing, and contributed two well-received detective stories, "Sail" and "Angelfish," to the acclaimed *Black Mask* magazine in 1936. While earning considerable wealth for his writing, Dent pursued a broad range of avocational activities, including mountain-climbing, boating, treasure-hunting, piloting, and

aerial photography, as he continued to write an extraordinary amount of salable fiction for Dell and similar publishers. In 1940 he and his wife retired to La Plata to settle on a dairy farm, a move that signaled a significant decrease in Dent's literary output, though he continued to write Doc Savage titles and produced several other detective novels. In February of 1959, after completing by some estimates more than two hundred and seventy-five novels as well as numerous short stories, Dent was hospitalized following a heart attack; he died less than one month later on 11 March 1959.

Major Works

Preeminent among Dent's fictional output are the scores of pulp novels he wrote featuring the superhuman hero Doc Savage. Raised by experts to possess incredible physical and mental capabilities, Savage relies primarily on his host of technological gadgets to fight evil across the globe. His opponents are typically criminal masterminds who pervert technology and exploit the innocent in order to acquire power and satisfy their sinister desires.

The adventures themselves present a blend of science fiction and fantasy adventure. Some of the novels, including *The Majii* and *The Squeaking Goblin*, for example, rely on myth and folklore while others, such as *The Land of Terror* and *The Land of Always-Night*, carry Savage and his team to exotic locales and lost worlds. During the World War II era, Dent injected a great deal of realism into his previously fantastic plots, notably accentuating the potential fallibility of Savage by revealing his capacity for self-doubt. By the end of the 1940s, however, Dent had returned to the earlier, more imaginative pulp-style formula for the Savage novels, apparent in the final Savage adventure *Up from Earth's Center*. In contrast, Dent's more complex mystery novels, written in the 1940s and 1950s, depart considerably from the style of the Savage stories. Of these Dent's 1946 novel *Dead at the Take-off*, featuring the character Chance Malloy, is representative. A tale of adventure and intrigue, the story follows Malloy's efforts to respond to the underhanded scheming of several corrupt individuals as they attempt to destroy his small airline company. Among Dent's most highly esteemed works are the short stories "Sail" and "Angelfish." In both tales the unusually tall private detective Oscar Sail employs violence and deception to achieve his professional goals.

Critical Reception

Critics have attributed Dent's literary success to his use and refinement of the popular pulp fiction formulas that were already established by the early 1930s in his almost two hundred Doc Savage novels. Some have acknowledged, in addition, that Dent's humor in these works, unlike that of most of his contemporaries, was largely intentional and that his action-filled Savage stories reflect certain developments of plot and character as well as a clever use of imagery and metaphor that transcends their otherwise formulaic nature. Overall, however, commentators have observed that these novels were intended solely for mass consumption and quick sales rather than for literary quality—Dent himself once opined that his writing and that of his colleagues might have improved if they were allowed to put their own names on the novels, but his publishers flatly refused to do so. While several of Dent's Doc Savage novels do stand out as exemplary among the rest, and although the series exhibits an almost timeless appeal, the works have been considered simply as adequate examples of genre writing, marred by the flaws of conventionality, especially noticeable in the dozen or so Savage stories that were undertaken by Dent's ghost writers. In contrast, Dent's mysteries, such as *Dead at the Take-off* and *Cry at Dusk* have been more highly esteemed, as have his *Black Mask* stories, which have been said to epitomize the magazine's hard-boiled style at its best.

*PRINCIPAL WORKS

The Land of Terror (novel) 1935

The Man of Bronze (novel) 1935
The Fiery Menace (novel) 1942
The Derelict of Skull Shoal (novel) 1944
The Three Devils (novel) 1944
King Joe's Cay (novel) 1945
The Thing That Pursued (novel) 1945
Dead at the Take-Off [also published as *High Stakes*] (novel) 1946
The Devil Is Jones (novel) 1946
Five Fathoms Dead (novel) 1946
Lady to Kill (novel) 1946
Measures for a Coffin (novel) 1946
Terror and the Lonely Widow (novel) 1946
Danger Lies East (novel) 1947
Let's Kill Ames (novel) 1947
No Light to Die By (novel) 1947
The Angry Canary (novel) 1948
I Died Yesterday (novel) 1948
Lady Afraid (novel) 1948
The Pure Evil (novel) 1948
Terror Wears No Shoes (novel) 1948
Return from Cormoral (novel) 1949
Up from Earth's Center (novel) 1949
Lady So Silent (novel) 1951
Cry at Dusk (novel) 1952
The Lost Oasis (novel) 1965
The Fantastic Island (novel) 1966
The Land of Always-Night (novel) 1966
The Phantom City (novel) 1966
Death in Silver (novel) 1968
The Dagger in the Sky (novel) 1969
Dust of Death (novel) 1969
The Red Snow (novel) 1969
The Squeaking Goblin (novel) 1969
The Golden Peril (novel) 1970
The Mental Wizard (novel) 1970
The Green Death (novel) 1971
The Majii (novel) 1971
Poison Island (novel) 1971
Mad Mesa (novel) 1972
Land of Fear (novel) 1973
The Crimson Serpent (novel) 1974
The South Pole Terror (novel) 1974
The Mountain Monster (novel) 1976
The Red Terrors (novel) 1976
Mystery on Happy Bones (novel) 1979
The Whiskers of Hercules. The Man Who Was Scared (novels) 1981
One-Eyed Mystic. The Man Who Fell Up (novels) 1982
The Shape of Terror. Death Has Yellow Eyes (novels) 1982
The Talking Devil. The Ten Ton Snake (novels) 1982
The Golden Man. Peril in the North (novels) 1984
The Laugh of Death. The King of Terror (novels) 1984
Three Times a Corpse (novel) 1990

*Years of publication later than 1959 reflect dates of reprinted editions rather than of original publication.

CRITICISM

Ron Goulart (essay date 1972)

SOURCE: "Doc Savage and His Circle" in *Cheap Thrills: An Informal History of Pulp Magazines*, Arlington House, 1972, pp.75-84.

[*In the following essay, Goulart explores the origins and style of Dent's* Doc Savage *novels.*]

> Recently it had occurred to Doc Savage he might be turning into too much of a machine—becoming, in fact, as superhuman as many persons thought he was. He did not like that idea. He had always been apprehensive lest something of the kind occur. The scientists who had trained him during his childhood had been afraid of his losing human qualities; they had guarded him against this as much as possible. When a man's entire life is fantastic, he must guard against his own personality becoming strange.

> —Kenneth Robeson,
> ***The Dagger In The Sky***

You never know what sort of monument you'll get or what you'll be remembered for. Lester Dent had hoped to have a chance to write what he felt were first rate books and stories, the kind of thing that shows up on slick paper and best seller lists. Instead he got hired to write the Doc Savage series and he spent nearly two decades hidden behind the penname Kenneth Robeson. The current Bantam paperback revivals of the old Doc Savage novels have now sold over twelve million copies and so Dent has become, some ten years after his death, one of the best selling authors of the century.

The official version of the inception of Doc Savage is that the entire concept was originated by Henry W. Ralston of Street & Smith. More probably, the character developed out of the numerous conferences on new titles which followed the unexpected success of *The Shadow*. "*The Shadow* was going so good, it fooled hell out of everybody," recalls Walter Gibson. "Ralston wanted to start another adventure magazine, but for a long time he didn't even have a title." John Nanovic, who edited both *The Shadow* and the new *Doc Savage* magazines, was also in on the planning of the new series. Basically the Doc Savage format—that of a strong and brilliant hero and his coterie of gifted and whimsical sidekicks—is Frank Merriwell and his chums updated. And there were numerous other successful gangs of fictional do-gooders around in the 1920's and '30's that might have served as inspiration, especially Edgar Wallace's *Four Just Men*. Street & Smith might even have noticed a series one of their own authors was doing over at Fiction House. A year before the debut of Doc, Theodore Tinsley was writing novelets about a manhunter named Major Lacy, who had his headquarters in "the towering pinnacle of the Cloud building" and was aided by a variously gifted quartet of his ex-Marine buddies. Clark Gable influenced the development of Doc, too. When artist Walter Baumhofer was called in to paint the cover for the first issue of *Doc Savage Magazine* he was handed this description of the character: "A Man of Bronze—known as *Doc*, who looks very much like Clark Gable. He is so well built that the impression is not of size, but of power." Baumhofer ignored this and made Doc look like the model he was using at the moment. In the stories, of course, Doc's full name is Clark Savage.

When he took on the Doc Savage job in 1933, Lester Dent was in his early thirties and already a prolific writer of pulp stories. A contemporary describes him as being then "a huge, red-headed man, six feet three and weighing around two hundred pounds." Dent grew up on his family's farm in La Plata, Missouri and despite his later wanderings he continued to refer to himself as "just a Missouri hillbilly." In the mid 1930's, writing about himself in the third person for a publicity release, Dent depicted his early years this way:

> As a small boy, Lester Dent was taken across Wyoming in a covered wagon. Six weeks were required for a trip which can be made by automobile today in three hours.

> Dent lived as a youth on a Wyoming cow ranch. Also lived on a farm near La Plata, Mo.

> Dent was nineteen years old before his hair was ever cut by a barber.

> Dent has only a High School education, but he attended Chillicothe Business College, learned to telegraph, and went to work for $45.00 a month.

> Dent studied law nights.

> While working a night telegraph job—from midnight until eight in the morning—Dent turned his hand to writing adventure stories. His first thirteen stories, nobody would buy. The fourteenth story sold for $250.00.

> A few months later, a large New York publishing house, after reading the first story Dent sent them, telegraphed him to the effect that, "If you make less than a hundred dollars a week on your present job, advise you to quit; come to New York and be taken under our wing, with a five-hundred-dollar-a-month drawing account."

> After telegraphing friends in New York to inquire around about the publisher's sanity, Dent went to New York. That was in 1931.

The publisher who called Dent away from his Associated Press job in Tulsa was Dell. He wrote stories for their *War Aces, War Birds, All Western, Western Romances* and *All Detective*. He eventually wrote for many of the other pulp outfits and had sold to Street & Smith's *Popular* and *Top Notch* before taking up the Savage assignment. Though much of the pulp writing Dent did sounds like the work of a man who is enjoying himself, he often privately referred to it as "crud." Asked to explain Doc Savage to a reporter, Dent said, "He has the clue-following ability of Sherlock Holmes, the muscular tree-swinging ability of Tarzan, the scientific sleuthing of Craig Kennedy and the morals of Jesus Christ."

The first issue of *Doc Savage Magazine* was dated March, 1933, and sold for ten cents. The Baumhofer cover showed a slightly tattered Doc standing in front of a piece of Mayan ruin that had several sinister natives lurking behind it. Baumhofer, who did every cover of the magazine for the next several years, has yet to read a Doc Savage novel. He usually based his cover paintings on a short synopsis provided by one of the art editors. He got seventy-five dollars per oil painting. The interior illustrations were drawn by Paul Orban. Orban followed directions and so inside the new magazine Doc did indeed look like Clark Gable for awhile. "I actually read all the stories," Orban told me. "The editors never interfered or suggested what to draw. The artists were on their own. . . . The going price was fifteen dollars a drawing and thirty dollars for a double page spread." Unlike Baumhofer, who never encountered Lester Dent, Orban did meet him once, though briefly.

The maiden Doc Savage adventure was titled **The Man Of Bronze**. This inaugural novel about Clark Savage, Jr. and his group is written in a breathless turgid prose that is not characteristic of Dent and probably indicates some editorial committee work. It begins, "There was death afoot in the darkness," and ends, "The giant bronze man and his five friends would confront undreamed perils as the very depths of hell itself crashed upon their heads. And through all that, the work of Savage would go on!" In between the reader is introduced to Doc, who possesses "an unusually high forehead, a mobile and muscular, but not too-full mouth, lean cheeks." He looks like a statue sculptured in bronze, is what he looks like, and "most marvelous of all were his eyes. They glistened like pools of flake gold." He also has nice teeth. "This man was Clark Savage, Jr. Doc Savage! The man whose name was becoming a byword in the odd corners of the world!" This exclamatory novel also introduces Doc's crew of five. Here they are, walking into Doc's headquarters atop one of the tallest buildings in New York:

> The first of the five men was a giant who towered four inches over six feet. He weighed fully two fifty. His face was severe, his mouth thin and grim. . . . This was "Renny" or Colonel John Renwick. . . . He was known throughout the world for his engineering accomplishments.

> Behind Renny came William Harper Littlejohn, very tall, very gaunt. . . . He was probably one of the greatest living experts on geology and archaeology.

> Next was Major Thomas J. Roberts, dubbed "Long Tom." Long Tom was the physical weakling of the crowd. . . . He was a wizard with electricity.

> "Ham" trailed Long Tom. "Brigadier General Theodore Marley Brooks," Ham was designated on formal occasions. Slender, waspy, quick-moving . . . and possibly the most astute lawyer Harvard ever turned out.

> Last came the most remarkable character of all. Only a few inches over five feet tall, he weighed better than two hundred and sixty pounds. He had the build of a gorilla . . . "Monk!" No other name could fit him!

Besides looking like an ape, Monk is a chemical wizard.

The rest of the first novel details Doc's avenging the recent death of his father, exploring Mayan ruins in the Central American republic of Hidalgo, unmasking a villain known as the Feathered Serpent and finding enough gold to finance the remaining years of his pulp career.

In the issue after this came a lost world novel, **The Land Of Terror,** and next a Southern swamp adventure, **Quest Of The Spider**. As the series progressed a distinct Dent type of book developed. The dime novel aura which was present in the first stories faded and both the plots and the prose dropped much of their melodrama. Dent's sense of humor moved closer to the surface and by the mid 1930's the Doc Savage adventures had some resemblance to the screwball movies of the period. He was more and more mixing adventure and detective elements with wackiness and producing a sort of pulpwood equivalent of films like *The Thin Man, Gunga Din* and *China Seas*. These movies, despite different locales and themes, shared a fooling-around quality that was current then in a good many Hollywood pictures. In his Doc Savage novels Dent pushed the usual pulp adventure and science fiction plots often quite close to parody, whether he was dealing with infernal machines, plagues, master thieves, pixies or ogres. While quite a few of his competitors can now be read for their unconscious humor, all of the laughs in Dent are intentional. He excelled in devising villains who were both bizarre and baggy-pantsed. For instance:

> Off to one side was a child's crib. It was an elaborate thing, with carvings and gilt inlays, and here and there rows of pearl studding. . . . The crib was about four feet long. The man who occupied it had plenty of room. . . . He was a little gem of a man.

> His face had that utter handsomeness which pen-and-ink artists give their heroes in the love story magazines. He wore little bathing trunks and a little bathrobe, smoked a little cigar in a little holder, and a toy glass on a rack at the side held a toy drink in which leaned a toy swizzle stick.

Dent was also partial to slender, salty tomboy heroines and they appear in most of the novels.

> The big eyes were blue, a nice shade. There was more about her that was nice, too. Her nose, the shape of her mouth. Long Tom had a weakness for

slender girls, and this one was certainly slender. She wore stout leather boots, shorts, a khaki blouse and a khaki pith helmet.

"Don't stand there staring!" she snapped. "I want a witness! Somebody to prove I saw it."

She was a redhead. In height, she would have topped Doc's shoulder a bit. . . . Altogether her features could hardly have been improved upon. She wore an amazing costume—a loose, brocaded Russian blouse, drawn in at the waist with a belt fashioned of parallel lines of gold coins. From this dangled a slender, jewelled sword which Doc was certain dated back at least four centuries. There was also an efficent, spike-nosed, very modern automatic pistol.

Dent's action was often presented in choppy, quick-cut movie style. As in this assault from the novel, **Red Snow**:

Doc Savage put on speed. He came in sight of the basement window just in time to see the golf-hosed legs of his quarry disappearing inside. Then, in the basement, a man saw Doc and bellowed profanely. What might have been a thick-walled steel pipe of small diameter jutted out of the window. Its tip acquired a flickering red spear-point of flame. The weapon was an automatic rifle of military calibre and its roar volleyed through the compound.

Doc Savage had rolled behind a palm, which, after the fashion of palms when stunted, was extremely wide at the base. The tree shuddered, and dead leaves loosened and fluttered in the wind. A cupro-nickel-jacketed slug came entirely through the bole. More followed. The bole began to split. The racket was terrific.

He also worked out a distinctive and personal way of starting a story. These were often abrupt and unlike the usual slow and moody Street & Smith openings so much favored by writers like Walter Gibson. For example:

When Ethel's Mama blew up, she shook the earth in more ways than one.

When the plane landed on a farmer's oat-stubble field in the Mississippi bottoms near St. Louis, the time was around ten in the morning.

The farmer had turned his cattle on to the stubble field to graze, and among the animals was a rogue bull which was a horned devil with strangers.

The bull charged the aviator.

The flier killed the bull with a spear.

The street should be very clean. The long-faced man had been sweeping it since daylight.

Never completely reverent of Doc, Dent extemporized abilities for him that went beyond the wildest talents of your average everyday super-hero. In one novel, for in-

stance, Doc Savage displays not only a remarkable knack for fashion designing but an exceptional skill for leading a dance band.

Doc Savage Magazine proved to be another best-selling title for Street & Smith and it stayed on the stands for sixteen years all told. The periodical remained monthly until after the war and then declined down through bi-monthly and finally quarterly publication. There were 181 separate novels devoted to Doc Savage, all credited to Kenneth Robeson. Of these Dent seems to have written all but about two dozen. The official Street & Smith records, now looked after by Conde Nast Publications, show nine Doc Savage novels are the work of the ubiquitous Norman Daniels, four are by Alan Hathway and three by William Bogart. All three men were S&S hacks in the '30's and '40's. Laurence Donovan, another undistinguished workhorse, is also sometimes mentioned as having contributed to the corpus. The major period of ghosting was in 1936 and 1937. According to Frank Gruber, "along about 1936 Lester Dent began to tire of Doc Savage. He thought the stories too juvenile and he thought that he should be trying to write more adult fiction." During these same years Dent acquired the forty-foot Albatross, which he referred to as his "treasure hunt schooner," and he was spending a good deal of time aboard it. Besides the ghost writers who made the official list at Street & Smith, Dent hired a few others on the side. Ryerson Johnson, an affable little pulp writer, remembers doing at least three Doc Savages in 1935. "I did **Land Of Always-Night,**" he told me. "Another one, and something about the Galapagos Islands and giant turtles." Dent made $750 per novel and he paid Johnson $500 out of that. Johnson remembers being handed $500 in cash on a street corner in Manhattan after doing the giant turtles book.

As a merchandising property Doc Savage didn't equal The Shadow. There were no movies, no serials. There was a radio show, but it ran only in the East during one wartime summer. The Doc Savage comic book never did well either. A number of cartoonists drew the feature, including William A. Smith, later a *Saturday Evening Post* illustrator and currently a gallery painter. As with many of their later characters, Street & Smith's timing was off. They didn't think of using him as a comic book hero until 1940 and by then there was Superman. It's obvious Jerry Siegel and Joe Shuster had recognized Doc Savage's potential much earlier. Dedicated pulp readers, the two young Cleveland boys borrowed considerably from Dent's character for their own super-hero. It isn't because of coincidence that Superman's name is Clark Kent and that he was initially billed as the Man of Steel. In the pulp magazines themselves there were a number of imitation Docs. None of them, such as Captain Hazard, survived beyond the '30's. Street & Smith tried, too, most notably with a sea-faring adventurer named Cap Fury. The captain and his crew had their own magazine for awhile. It was called *The Skipper* and the busy Norman Daniels ghosted the novels.

Lester Dent died just ten years after his character had folded. That was in 1959 while he was, once more, on a treasure hunting cruise. A year prior to that Dent, who never substantially realized his ambition to progress to slicks and bestsellers, was asked to reminisce about his pulp days. He had by then written hundreds of short stories and nearly two hundred novels, earning as much as $4,000 a month. All he spoke well of out of all that material were the two short stories he'd done for *Black Mask* in the 1930's. He sold the stories, both of which dealt with a lean Florida detective named Sail, to editor Joseph Shaw. He admired Shaw for being "gentle with his writers. You went into *Black Mask* and talked with him, you felt you were doing fiction that was powerful, you had feelings of stature." In 1936 Shaw was fired from the magazine. This, Lester Dent felt, "is what kept me from becoming a fine writer. Had I been exposed to the man's cunning hand for another year or two, I couldn't have missed. . . . Instead I wrote reams of saleable crap which became my pattern, and gradually there slipped away the bit of power Shaw had started awakening in me."

Will Murray (essay date 1974)

SOURCE: "The Bronze Genius", in *The Man Behind Doc Savage,* Robert Weinberg, 1974, pp. 9-14.

[*In the following essay, Murray discusses Doc Savage's many fantastic gadgets, inventions, and vehicles.*]

Bronze was Doc Savage's symbol. Bronze because his skin had been kilned to a metallic hue by tropic suns and arctic winds; but also it denoted his forte, science. For bronze was the first alloy, its creation the first dabbling into science attempted by early man, heralding the Bronze Age and the end of the Stone Age. Just as Doc Savage alloyed science and human courage to end the Age of Menace.

Out of The Wizard's Den of his 86th floor headquarters or the secret Fortress of Solitude laboratory came literally hundreds of inventions, devices, gadgets and scientific discoveries applicable to every phase of human existence—medicine, aviation, warfare, agriculture and most notably, crime-fighting.

For most of his adventurous career, Doc Savage employed a fantastic diversity of gadgets whose purposes were to locate and nullify his evil opponents while at the same time protecting Doc and his men from harm.

One of the earliest inventions used by Doc and company were the supermachine pistols, also called superfirers, rapidfirers, or mercy pistols. When first introduced, (in *The Man of Bronze*), they are described as being automatic pistols with machine gun capabilities. Rams' horn shaped magazines fitted into the grips, which contained sixty ordinary bullets. By the time of *The Man Who Shook the Earth,* they would be equipped with drum magazines as well, fitting just in front of the trigger. The drums contained mercy bullets, hollow shells filled with an anaesthetic which barely broke the skin, but reduced victims to unconciousness. The weapons were most often described as being slightly larger than an automatic, intricate looking, and capable of firing single shot as well as so fast that it produced the familiar bull fiddle moan. In fact, they fire over 600 shots a minute. Other drums contain smoke, gas, and demolition bullets laced with tracers. Special compensators absorb recoil and two secret safeties prevent unauthorized use. The mercy pistols are used constantly throughout the series, except for a period in the late forties. One time that they do appear, in *Terror and the Lonely Widow,* they are described as being smaller than a Thompson or Reising gun, weighing as much as a Colt automatic, and using .22 Hornet cartridges. Instead of mercy bullets, they fire a mushrooming bullet capable of tearing a man to pieces. In the same story, Doc uses a .220 Swift rifle, which is described as being his favorite rifle. Other times, he uses an ordinary revolver. Near the end, they again use the mercy pistols.

Doc also carries a pocket knife that fires a single mercy bullet from the hilt in *The Mountain Monster*. A rapid firing elephant gun with special recoil check is another Savage invention.

To protect themselves from the inevitable return fire such weapons might generate, the Doc Savage organization all wear bullet-proof suits under their clothes. Described as being either an alloy mesh or chain mail construction, they resemble long underwear. A hood-like attachment fits over the head.

Between the armor and his street clothes, Doc wears his equipment vest. On the outside, ordinary looking; the underside is lined with numerous pockets that contain a vast assortment of small devices used exclusively by Doc. The vest, like the machine pistol shoulder holsters, is padded so not to be conspicuous under a suit coat. The assortment of gadgets changes from time to time, but some of the more familiar follow:

A small flashlight powered by a spring generator that is wound by hand. As long as it is wound up, it will not fail, being waterproof as well as containing spare bulbs within. It can be adjusted to throw a thin beam as well as a wide ray. It had an ultraviolet attachment and the generator could power a radio transmitter or an electrical detonator. It could also shock a man badly.

A small folding grappling hook with a knotted silk line. The hook is encased in rubber tubing to silence its action.

Pills, which when swallowed, provide the body with oxygen and make it unnecessary to breathe for a half hour. These are a relic of the adventure *Mystery Under the Sea* and, though not Doc's invention, they are quite often used.

A diving lung consisting of goggles, a spring nose clip and a mouthpiece that feeds from a small oxygen tank usually strapped to the chest. The lung can be used either as a gas mask or for underwater travel. A mouth filter can be used instead of the oxygen apparatus during gas attacks.

Another, simpler gas mask, is a transparent hood which slips over the head. An elastic seals it around the neck and it is effective for only a short time, having no oxygen supply other than what the hood would ordinarily contain. Used with the oxygen pills, it is good for longer periods of time. The hood has a cape-like attachment which protects the body from gases capable of affecting a person through the pores. This can be worn over street clothes and weighs next to nothing.

A listening device consisting of headphones, amplifier, and velocity microphone. A similar device has a coil antenna instead of mike, which when held near phone wires, will pick up conversations.

A short wave transmitter and receiver, slightly larger than a cigarette pack.

Glass marbles containing an odorless, colorless anaesthetic that neutralizes itself in less than a minute so that the initiated can escape its effects by holding one's breath. These are unleashed simply by throwing or stepping on them, being very breakable. Doc often carries them in flat cases and sometimes secreted so that they will break when he flexes his muscles. They come in two sizes, as small as marbles and about egg size. The effect of the gas varies, depending upon the potency of the mixture and can be counteracted by an injection of chemical.

Various types of grenade, the size and shape of eggs actuated either by a firing pin or timed lever. These are color-coded in Navy fashion. Checkers denoting smoke bombs; red for gas, yellow for explosion and white for shrapnel.

Special goggles with dark lenses the size of condensed milk cans that are used with an ultraviolet light projectors for night fighting. Doc and his aides often leave messages for each other with a chemical chalk. The chalk will write on any surface and leaves no visible mark. But, under the black light, messages glow an electric blue. Certain buttons from their clothes are also of this material.

A small medical kit containing various pills, hypodermics and simple surgical instruments.

Burglar tools such as glass cutter, lock picks and suction cups.

Vials containing chemicals such as acids, fluorescent powders and chemicals, including a concoction of every scent known to cause fear reactions in animals. It is effective as shark repellent, and it discourages watchdogs.

For a while in the late thirties (most notable in *The Living Fire Menace* and *Merchants of Disaster*), Doc abandons his vest in favor of an equipment belt, but returns to the vest. Probably because it would hold more gadgets. The belt resembles an army cartridge belt, being a string of pockets sewn over a wide belt.

Not all of Doc's gadgets repose in his vest. Besides a metal skull cap that simulates his bronze hair, Doc's clothing is chemically treated.

His undershirt is impregnated with tear gas, his coat and shirt contain a potassium compound which bursts into flame when moistened, shoe heels often contain compounds or devices. Doc's buttons are a thermite compound. When crushed into powder and rolled up in his tie, it will burn through anything. The lining of his trouser watch pocket, when removed, will flame when scraped like a match and ignite the thermite.

Doc has two false wisdom teeth in his upper jaw. Chemicals within these, when combined, form an explosive. Another false tooth contains a coil saw.

False skin over his calves and a false scar on his back conceal explosives and other chemicals. In addition, Doc carries a multi-purpose device invented for him by an optical expert who fled Europe because of the Nazis. This is a tubular, telescopic arrangement with interchangeable lenses capable of converting into a periscope, microscope, or telescope. Filters and a mechanical attachment enable it to amplify minute quantities of light, making for an effective night sight scanner. Stripped of its lenses, it also makes a good snorkel.

On occasion, he also wears a light parachute beneath, or within, his suitcoat. The material is called fabrikoid, (developed by Monk) stronger and lighter than silk. A button on his vest, when pulled, acts as a rip cord.

With all these gadgets secreted about his person, it's no wonder Doc's foes consider him a terror in bronze. Whenever captured, Doc is usually stripped down to the bathing suit trunks he habitually wears, but invariably something (false teeth, toenails, chemicals in his hair or somesuch) is overlooked. In *The Submarine Mystery,* his captors go so far as to strip him completely; scrub his clothes and hair with soap and brush to remove chemicals and sound out his teeth with hammer and chisel, all while he is drugged, naturally. Even then, he is not out of tricks, for he had previously treated Monk and Ham's pets' fur with knockout powder. (Left to his natural resources, Doc is still a massive headache. Besides being so strong that his captors often have to bind him with heavy chain or steel bands, he is capable of hypnotizing the unwary with his flake-gold eyes or rendering them either unconscious, paralyzed, or in such a state that they can't help but tell the truth, with just some pressure on a nerve in their neck. Before he perfected the nerve trick, he wore bronze finger caps equipped with a tiny anaesthetic-charged hypo; a brief contact and his foe is out cold.)

Naturally, not all his equipment can be carried on his person. Larger devices are carried in numbered equipment cases. These cases might contain spare ammunition; a compact chemical laboratory, an experimental, portable television set, a black box which can be clamped beneath a car and which sends a radio signal that can be traced with a loop-antenna compass, wire recorders, light bulb transmitters, or an assortment of emergency suits which Doc has developed.

These suits are largely experimental. They are invariably designed to provide protection in hostile environments. Some of the more interesting follow—

For laboratory work, such as working with dangerous gases or germs, Doc wears a rubberized, coverall suit equipped with a glass hood.

For underwater exploration, Doc has a number of different suits. In *Death in Silver,* he uses flexible, mailed suits replete with twin tanks in back to supply oxygen and regulate ballast, transparent helmets, transmitters, depth gauge, and knives. A similar suit has been used (and depicted on the cover) in *Repel.* A light, waterproof fabric now covers the chain mail, and pistol-like cutting torches are part of the equipment. These have two foot long barrels with bulbs attached to the grips. They burn a chemical gas which ignites under water. In *Devils of the Deep,* he uses a flexible, completely transparent suit together with a supply of oxygen tablets.

For arctic travel, he wears a parka and hood with bearskin trousers and moosehide moccasins. This is essentially the type of covering used by eskimos and is quite efficient by itself. But to this Doc has added an electrically-warmed mask, spectacle-like binoculars, and a zippered, electrically-warmed coverall.

In *The Land of Fear,* Doc, Monk and Ham are trapped in a burning building. They escape through the expedience of Doc's new fireproof suits. These are thin, transparent coveralls composed of a new form of asbestos. Used with hoods and the convenient oxygen pills, they can resist almost any temperature due to the insulating air pocket within the suit. Later, in *The Mountain Monster,* these suits are used again in conjuction with another device. When Doc and company are trapped in their crashed plane, they don these suits and two jets on a metal ball are opened. Gas forms a great bubble around them which becomes a fire-quenching foam. In some fashion, the bubble rolls out of the destroyed plane with them in it.

Yet another kind of fire suit is used in *Merchants of Disaster.* This time, it's Doc and Long Tom who are trapped in a blazing building. When the fire dies out, what appears to be two snowmen step out of the smoldering building. These prove to be Doc and Long Tom encased in a double layered suit of the same clear asbestos as used in the other suit. In this one, however, an ammonia-like solution and tiny condensers lie between the lay-

ers. When subjected to intense heat, the suits act like refrigerators, producing cold and the snow deposit on the material's outer layer.

Other types of protective apparel are not so successful, such as the artificial skin used in *The Laugh of Death.* This is a type of plastic (possibly similar to the transparent asbestos) which is applied to the skin to form an overskin. It's a perfect insulator against heat and cold; unfortunately, perspiration causes it to split and crack.

Other suits are used to combat a particular menace and are never used again. In *Red Snow,* Doc escapes destruction as the weird scarlet stuff descends upon him by jumping into a sack-like affair of metallic, yellow-red cloth. Although not a suit proper, it serves the same purpose. In *The Headless Men,* a death ray similar to the X-ray is the prime menace. Doc's suit is a two-layer affair composed of platinum and lead, the only metals which can halt the ray. The suit is silvery, but when subjected to the ray, it glows cherry-red.

These suits are improvisations, but, when the time and materials are not available, other substitutes are used. In *Dust of Death,* he coats his body with an anaesthetic in order to ward off the microscopic parasites which kill on contact. And in *The Land of Fear,* a paste applied to his skin prevents the moisture from being drawn from his body and thus reducing him to a skeleton due to the villain's death device.

Another of Doc's infrequently used devices was his atomic gun. When he uses it in *The Golden Peril,* it resembles a cannon with a solid steel barrel and is hooked up to a dynamo for power. It shoots bolts of electricity which release the atomic energy of whatever it hits with explosive force. An improved form of this weapon appears later in *The Motion Menace.* By that time, it resembles a camera with a black lens and is small enough to be carried on the bronze man's person. It is fired in the same way that one would take a picture. The effects of this version seem no different than the earlier one.

Doc used a couple of different wrist devices during his career. In the early Thirties, he wore a wrist-sized television receiver. For a time in 1939-40, he and his men communicated using a wrist watch apparatus. This emitted heat flashes which the wearer could feel on his skin. The impulses were sent in code form and were a silent means of communication. Interestingly enough, these were not Doc's own invention, but rather devices that they captured from a spy ring in *Merchants of Disaster.*

Doc's avowed purpose in life, that of righting wrongs and punishing evil-doers, by necessity, was to take him to the four corners of the Earth. But in this connection, the inventions that he would use would run into the most difficulties. His planes, autogyros, and, especially his dirigibles would all encounter the most horrendous obstacles in trying to reach one point on the globe from another.

Doc's fleet of cars and trucks, which he kept in the basement garage of his headquarters, were on the surface as innocuous a set of conveyances as could grace any depression-era used car lot. Mostly they were drab coupes or roadsters and an occasional beat-up delivery van. But, within they were rolling juggernauts. They came equipped with super-charged engines, armour plate, bulletproof glass, sponge-rubber tires and very wide wheelbases. They were also sealed so as to be gas-proof (they had to be; tanks under the chassis spewed a smoke and anaesthetic combination as well as a gas that affected foes through their pores). Short wave transmitters, infra-red lights, and windshields treated to prevent snow from sticking are also attributes of Doc's fleet. The delivery truck is especially formidable. Besides the aforementioned, it is equipped with racks containing superfirer pistols, body armour, gas masks, grenades and even a small field gun which fires a two-inch shell.

Doc's air and sea craft are kept in a warehouse-hanger that fronts upon the Hudson River. These were an amazing assortment of ships of all varieties. A bullet-shaped, padded pneumatic car runs between the skyscraper and the hanger.

These craft, being mostly for the dual purpose of transporting and exploring, are generally not armed; although they do carry weapons within, usually spare pistols and similar small arms.

Doc's planes, of which there are about a dozen or so, are mostly amphibious craft. This is a necessity as Doc's journeys often have unknown destinations and his landing place might be a lake just as it might be a more conventional airfield. They can also be equipped with skis for snow landings. The planes are armored. The exhausts can be silenced although this does cut down on the performance of their supercharged motors. They can be guided by remote control using a robot-pilot.

The plane most often used by Doc is his tri-motored speed plane, based on the streamlined Stinson. First used in *The Man of Bronze,* it and its successors, for the craft was repeatedly destroyed, were described as being the very latest in streamlined, all-metal ships. It boasted retractable landing gear and a cruising speed of two hundred miles per hour. Sometimes, it was painted bronze, but most often it was silver or gray. It carried within it another of Doc's inventions. One side of the craft hinged down to form a ramp. Out of it could be rolled a gyro-plane. This resembled a small, wingless plane. It had four caster wheels, the windmill vanes of a helicopter, and was equipped with aero bombs that contained sleep gas and were fired torpedo-fashion. Unlike an autogyro, (which Doc also possessed) this was not a fast craft, but it had the advantage of being able to rise and land vertically. Doc's autogyros were fast craft having wings as well as the rotor-like windmill vanes. They could hover, but they did require a landing strip; though a smaller stretch than a plane was needed.

After the tri-motor era, Doc flew a variety of aircraft, ranging from twin-engine speed planes to giant ocean-spanning flying boats similar to the four-motored Pacific Clippers that came into use in the late Thirties. During the war, he designed several pursuit-type planes and once experimented with an aircraft built of transparent materials so as to be virtually invisible at high altitudes.

After the second World War, Doc experimented with jet aircraft. In *The Pure Evil,* he first uses such craft and in *Return from Cormoral,* the jet is used again. Although these jets are very advanced, Doc had first used the principle about ten years earlier, in *The Mountain Monster.* In this story, one of Doc's transport planes is equipped with rocket tubes in the tail section. These are used to supply emergency thrust so that the plane can get out of range of a ray which has disabled its ordinary motors.

Doc did a lot of experimenting with lighter-than-air craft. He held the curious belief that such craft were not as outmoded as most people thought. (His theory is coming true today; there is renewed talk of bringing back dirigibles for commercial use as they use little fuel compared to jet craft). Unfortunately for his theory, most of Doc's dirigibles came to grief in varied corners of the globe.

His first encounter with such airships was in *The Lost Oasis,* where he ends in possession of the lost dirigible, *Aeromunde.* Although Doc later returns it to its rightful owners, in *Land of Always-Night,* he has one of his own. This ship is of Doc's own construction; streamlined with alloy motors enabling it to fly at nearly two hundred miles per hour. A synthetic, noninflammable gas made it fireproof. This ship enjoys the distinction of being one of the few to survive an adventure intact.

In *Dust of Death,* Doc's stratosphere dirigible is unveiled. This craft boasts of rocket tube propulsion, infra-eye scanners, self-sealing gas cells, and an auxiliary plane. It escapes one sabotage attempt only to fall into another.

In *Murder Mirage,* an airship that seems to be the one used in *The Land of Always-Night,* manages to get to Arabia before being dissolved by a terrible weapon.

The stratosphere dirigible again sees action in *The South Pole Terror,* but is blown to smithereens amid Antarctic snows.

In *Land of Long Juju,* the Wing is revealed. This experimental ship is a wing-shaped dirigible propelled by heated gases and capable of over five hundred miles per hour. Although an incredibly advanced craft, the Wing is destroyed during its maiden voyage to Africa.

Another experimental craft, the *Zephyr,* debuted in *Terror of the Navy.* Built for the Navy by Doc, this ship was an attempt to prove that such craft were still practical. She was a floating destroyer, designed as the ultimate war machine and every precaution was incorporated into her design so that she would be unimpregnable. The *Zephyr* is all-metal, with honeycomb gas cells so bullets could not down her, equipped with a radar-type device, auxiliary planes and in an emergency, her motor nacelles converted to life boats. She was so strong that a mile-long fall would not damage her greatly. On her initial run, she is forced down on the high seas and annihilated by thermite bombs. After this setback, Doc's experiments with dirigibles would be limited. His next such craft, a small all-metal job with enclosed cabin is stolen during the weird adventure of *Ost.* The smallness of the ship indicates that Doc has given up on larger dirigibles; also the *Hindenburg* disaster had taken place only a few months earlier. Doc recovers this ship intact; which must have been heartening.

A full-sized airship carries Doc to South America in *The Green Death,* but it meets its end, also. Yet another is destroyed in *The Crimson Serpent.*

Doc's last such ship just manages to clear the warehouse hanger in *The Headless Men,* before going the way of all the others. He completes his journey by plane and never-more flies by airship.

He had better luck with his submarine, the *Helldiver,* fortunately. First used in *The Polar Treasure,* this submersible is one he acquired from another explorer. Designed for under-ice travel, she came equipped with steel runners along her hull and had no conning tower to speak of. After Doc purchased the sub, he made numerous improvements in her. These included: a sounding device, collapsible seaplane, chemicals to melt ice or turn sea water black, a collapsible shield that doubles as a navigating bridge, spring-steel bowsprit ram, infrared television scanners, a listening device that identifies passing ships by the beat of their propellers and others. The *Helldiver* saw action again in *The Phantom City,* (where she was almost lost) *Death in Silver,* and lastly in *Devils of the Deep.*

In *Haunted Ocean,* Doc makes use of a small glass sub. This is a cylinder consisting of a double hull of glass. It's an emergency craft, possessing only an oxygen and chemical light supply. Chemicals introduced into the envelope between hulls, give it lifting power.

Doc's yacht, *Seven Seas,* first sails in *Fantastic Island,* where she piles up on some rocks. Doc must have salvaged her, for she again appears in *The Land of Fear.* She is a rakish, diesel-powered craft faster than any in her class. In *The Red Terrors,* she is used to transport Doc's sub-sea tank on its first trial run. The tank is built like an army tank, with caterpillar treads, but instead of a cannon, it sports numerous collapsible arms that can pick things off the ocean floor. It functions not unlike a diving bell and is lowered from the yacht by a cable.

Probably the most unusual of Doc's gadgets and inventions is his Arctic Fortress of Solitude. A great blue dome of a substance having properties of both metal and glass,

this retreat houses Doc's great laboratory as well as some of the most terrible inventions developed by man. Guarded by a tribe of Eskimos, it is Doc's greatest secret. In *The Devil's Playground,* criminals locate the Fortress and send bombers to destroy it, though they fail. The possibility of discovery makes Doc model it differently so that by *The Laugh of Death,* it resembles a great chunk of ice.

After the war, Doc abandons most of his gadgets and inventions (curiously, he still carries his tiny grapple), and many of them end up in a little museum set up by Pat Savage. His reasons for this are the same as his reasons for not carrying a gun; simply, that a man who depends too much on devices grows dependent upon them, and is doubly ineffective when stripped of them. Doc now prefers to rely upon a quick wit and a sharp mind. Pat seems to think that Doc is simply trying to live down the former phase of his career. As Doc's postwar adventures are much less fantastic than his earlier ones, the gadgets are really not essential.

In his last few adventures, however, many of the gadgets return without explanation. This is not surprising, as these stories are more along the line of his early depression escapades.

In the final analysis, Doc Savage's supple bronze intellect is one of the most amazing ever to probe and apply itself to the twin fields of science and crime-fighting. From the smallest gadget designed to render a criminal helpless, to the advanced surgical technique that permanently reforms the evil forever, Doc Savage's grasp of every possible contingency and inroad makes him the most thorough and effective of all fictional crime-fighters, a true genius of science.

Will Murray (essay date 1974)

SOURCE: "The Sunset of the Superman," in *The Man Behind Doc Savage,* Robert Weinberg, 1974 pp. 56-62.

[*In the following essay, Murray recounts Doc Savage's exploits in Dent's World War II era novels, and the changes Savage's character underwent during this period.*]

Doc Savage was a superman. His men were near-supermen. Originally, they got together during the first World War where the excitement got into their blood. They decided to band together as a small army after it was all over for the avowed purpose of fighting evil. The war must have had a great effect on Doc and his men. It was there that they saw their first action and much of their equipment was patterned after military hardware.

It was only natural, then, that when the second World War broke out they would do their best to scramble back into uniform. Indeed, that is precisely what they did try to do; but there was a stumbling block. Doc and Company were now national figures; men whose scientific prowess overrode their fighting ability.

Many times, Doc flew specially down to Washington, D.C. to meet with government leaders, trying to convince them that he and his men belonged back in uniform and in the front lines. They wanted action; they got a run-around.

In **The Fiery Menace** (Sept. 1942) Doc meets with the President, the Secretary of the Navy, and other officials in a vain effort to see action. He is politely rebuffed and promised that he will be summoned should any difficulty arise requiring his special talents. Doc does not like it, but he accepts the situation at first; continuing his crime fighting activities on the home front. In the course of his adventures, he comes into contact with various enemy subversives, whether Nazi or Japanese. This whets his appetite for real war action.

As the war goes on, Doc's men are often called to Europe to work on defense projects; dams, pipelines, and similar matters. His men, in effect, become government trouble-shooters and are away so often that he is sometimes forced to press Pat Savage into service as an aid, something he would never do under ordinary circumstances.

Although Doc Savage never does see action on the front, he certainly manages to become involved behind enemy lines. The action that he encounters in enemy territory, in fact, proves to be among the most hair-raising of his career.

The first such episode, **The Black, Black Witch** (March 1943) begins with Doc and Monk parachuting into occupied France, responding to a message from an American diplomat being held by the Nazis. They immediately fall into the hands of some very polite and respectful Nazis, who are very glad to meet the illustrious Doc Savage. Besides being very polite, they are very excited, from Hitler on down, about something called the secret of the black, black witch. They even get more excited when the diplomat, along with the secret, escape to America. Doc and Monk get loose also, and follow the dignitary home. Back in New York, they unravel the story of Peterpence, a man who lived in the time of Nostradamus. This Peterpence—the black, black witchs—seems to have been developed a gas that bestows the power of foretelling the future upon one. By the time Doc discovers all this, it becomes apparent that the Nazis had accidentally destroyed the secret back in France.

Doc's next important brush with the Axis is an interesting one. It (**Hell Below,** Sept. 1943) begins with Doc again in Washington, trying to get into uniform. He, Monk and Ham get into a violent argument with a war official over their current status. Doc, especially, gets hot under the collar and walks out in a huff. They walk into a mess and end up captives aboard a Nazi subskippered by a German commander, who is on the trail of two escaped Nazi leaders. On a ranch in Mexico, they catch up with the two, Der Hase (Hare) and Das Seehund (Seal) who are obviously Himmler and Goering. They, along with much Axis gold, are on the run, convinced that Germany will lose the war. There is an interesting scheme wherein Der Hase attempts to seduce Doc into becoming part of his new plan for a master race. Of course, Doc refuses; what is interesting about Doc's attitude is that he, himself, is proof that the superman concept is a viable one.

Doc was reared to become a scientific superman by his father. He accepted this at first, without any feeling that there might be unfortunate achievement in the condition. But, with the rise of Nazi supermanism, some qualms must have crept in. The concept became subverted in the light of what the superman could mean to mankind. His conclusions are pretty well summed up in the novels **Hell Below** and **The Time Terror**. In **Hell Below** he considers the whole idea barbaric, and in **The Time Terror** (Jan. 1943), when he wrests a superman-evolving chemical from the Japanese, Doc decides to suppress the stuff because it would destroy the principle that all men are created equal and thus destroy the fabric of human civilization. This realization, that the superman is an entity unfair to mankind and inimical to democracy and world freedom, would seem to have had an impact upon Doc, for in succeeding adventures, he gradually becomes less and less a superman.

The climax of **Hell Below** comes when Doc stages a ruse which leads to a falling out between the two Nazis, in which Das Seehund kills Der Hase, then flees back to Germany. Doc lets the comical sub-commander escape so he can tell the Fuehrer the true story of Das Seehund's defection.

For the next few months, Doc continues to stumble upon Axis activities and has yet to be called upon by the government to get involved in anything really big.

According to Plan of a One-Eyed Mystic (Jan. 1944) starts off with Renny waking up in the body of another man because he had insulted a little brown man with one eye. Shifting events lead to a Nazi sub off Labrador where the selling of a plane-destroying missile is effectively stopped.

Death Has Yellow Eyes (Feb. 1944) concerns a pair of detectives named Nat and Jay, a girl named Doris Day, an Axis financier and pairs of floating eyes. Doc and Company are framed for murder-robbery and then flown to Roumania by Nazi plane. There they are framed for murder-robbery and then flown to Roumania. They find war loot and suits of translucent cloth that enable the wearer to become invisible.

The Three Devils (May 1944) is the name of a Canadian lumber town that appears to be haunted by a ghost bear, called Black Tuesday. Numerous spooky occurences are laid at his doorstep, causing the inhabitants of Three Devils to evacuate the place and its pulp mills. The whole thing turns out to be a Nazi plot, first hatched 20 years previous, that slowly built up the Black Tuesday legend so that it could be used to close down Canada's pulp industry in wartime.

The Shape of Terror (Aug. 1944) is the first of a handful of tense, red-hot assignments that the Allies saddle Doc with. It begins with Doc being led aboard a RAF plane which crashes on an English flying field. Monk and Ham investigate, only to be blocked by officials. Then, they too are declared dead when their car crashes. All this is to convince the enemy that Doc and Company are dead. The trio then are taken to a meeting where the combined heads of Allied Intelligence give them their assignment: free Czech scientist Johann Kovic from Dabelsky Dum, a concentration camp in Prague. The Germans, it seems, have invented a terrible secret weapon that threatens civilization. Kovic has a defense for it, and he is the only man alive who knows the secret. Doc must free Kovic or the war is lost.

After escaping being poisoned in London, Doc and Kovic's daughter are flown to Czechoslovakia by a Nazi turncoat who nearly turns them over to Germany. In Prague, they rendezvous with Monk and Ham, who flew in separately and are caught up in a running series of incidents involving the Gestapo and a bogus British agent. Monk and Ham are captured, and land in Dabelsky Dum. Finally, Doc with the help of the Czech Underground, breach the castle-like camp and break out again with Monk, Ham, and Kovic in tow. An American plane returns them to London, where Kovic spills the defense that renders Germany's last chance for victory useless.

Jiu San (Oct. 1944) is an enormously important novel. A disguised Doc Savage shows up in an Alaskan POW camp, where Japanese soldiers are being held. Just prior to this, he has been demoted from Brigadier General (detached service during the present war), to Sergeant for alleged pro-Japanese leanings.

Here, Doc engineers a mass breakout of prisoners and leads them to a waiting plane piloted by Monk, who knows nothing about the whole business, except that Doc is officially a traitor. Confronted by the horde of escapees, Monk, in a very distraught frame of mind, demands of Doc that he return the Japs to the camp. Doc floors him. Monk winds up in Yokohama, where he has become a prisoner.

In prison, he meets an English actor who is disguised as Savage. Monk is whisked away, leaving the Englishman in his place. At a private home, Doc and Monk are reunited amid an assortment of characters, including a group of high Japanese officials. The situation is made clear.

The end of the war is now in sight with the fall of Japan just a matter of time. In order to shorten the mopping up after the final collapse, the Allies have contacted this group of respectable leaders with the notion of setting them up as heads of the post-war government. But there's a toad in the soup; one of them, calling himself Jiu San (Mr. Thirteen) has threatened to expose the plot to the Emperor if he is not made Emperor of the new administration. Doc's job—unmask Jiu San.

What follows is considerable violence and running around with the end result of no progress and Doc and Company ending up in the hands of Jiu San's men. Now captives, things look bleak. But a disguised Ham Brooks turns out to be one of their captors (he had parachuted into Japan some time previous).

In the final scenes, Doc, unable to unmask his foe, resorts to a bluff. His sudden announcement that he's uncovered Jiu San causes same to bolt, where one of the Japanese working with Doc butchers him. A quick escape to a waiting plane, and they're home.

Doc Savage is a very tense and frightened man in *The Lost Giant* (Dec. 1944) when the State Department hands him another terrible mission. So affected is he, that he turns to a Hollywood makeup man for his disguise, upon which hinges the success of his assignment and, ultimately, the course of the war.

A train ride to a ski lodge in Lake Placid is Doc's first move. The lodge is swarming with unsavory characters all with a single purpose: find a flier named Chester Wilson. Wilson has been kidnapped by persons unknown. For some reason, he is the key to some great thing. Doc joins up with a pair of very vicious types who also seek Wilson. The two penetrate Doc's disguise, but don't let on to the fact. Unknown to them, Doc knows they know who he is, which makes for a very hairy situation.

Monk and Ham show up; stumble upon two foreign agents who are to meet with Wilson's captors. They take the agents' places and make the contact successfully. They are flown to Wilson's location and then on to Devon Island in the Arctic, while Doc, still playing cat-and-mouse with his two unsavory types, trails behind.

In the Arctic, the whole affair explodes into violent clarity. In an unarmed plane, Doc gets into a dog fight with a pair of German Heinkels, succeeding by luck more than anything else. The wild battle that follows occurs in and around a wrecked army transport where Winston Churchill (not mentioned by name) is stranded. Churchill's plane went down some time ago in a cold front, after eluding some Nazi fighters. Wilson, in his own plane, got away from the wreck. He's the only one who knows Churchill's location. Thus, he was kidnapped. And thus the resulting affray. Doc digs in with Churchill, while Monk and Ham grab a downed Heinkel and raise hell with the encroaching Axis. When all is set to rights, Doc learns that one of the two unknowns he's been running around with, is actually a State Department agent, sent to back him up. Doc is hardly overjoyed to learn this; the double agent having contributed mightily to his emotional strain.

Violent Night (Jan. 1945) is as hellish an assignment for Doc Savage as *The Lost Giant,* which immediately preceded it. Doc's emotional state is very similar; unending tension, a feeling of being made responsible for things too big for one man to handle himself—even a superman.

Lisbon is where it begins. Doc rendezvous with Monk and Ham and discovers to his horror, that Pat Savage was following them from London, where her war correspondent's clearance was revoked for raising hell over the fact that she was not allowed to go to Europe and see action. (Just like Doc.)

Doc's situation and emotions are so precarious that, for once, he allows Pat to horn in without an argument. This has the effect of scaring her somewhat, as well. Doc is in Lisbon at the request of the White House, where he will receive full instructions though he has a good idea what he's been saddled with. From the beginning, they are shadowed by a red-haired man. The four manage to collar this worthy, who gets the drop on them with Pat's old six-shooter. The red-head gets away, though Doc reclaims Pat's pistol.

At a secret meeting, Doc gets his assignment in a nice neat package from the head of combined Allied Intelligence and other officials. Germany nears collapse. Hitler (again, not mentioned by name) has fled Germany leaving a double in his place who is to be assassinated. The assassination will make Hitler a martyr, thus prolonging the war and possibly leading to the reemergence of Nazism twenty years hence. Doc has two days to locate Hitler and expose the plot to the German people. He has no clue to the Fuerher's whereabouts; only that he is in disguise and the Allies have a set of fingerprints that will definitely establish his identity.

While Doc is mapping his strategy, Monk, Ham, and Pat get mixed up with a man named Carter and his toughs who are after, of all things, Pat's shooting iron. Monk and Ham, in typical fashion are held captive, while Pat gets away. She meets a girl, Barni Cuadrado, who is working with her cousin, Hans Berkshire (the red-haired man) in trying to foil Hitler's plan.

Unbeknownst to Pat, Carter is working for Doc, trying to scare Pat into going home. The ploy succeeds, with Pat going home by clipper plane. But, unbeknownst to Doc, Carter is actually a Nazi agent who overtakes Pat and again demands the six shooter, which Doc secretly holds.

Meanwhile, Doc and Barni meet with Hans Berkshire, who decides to let Doc do the actual catching of Hitler for the purpose of authentication, rather than having his underground do it. Berkshire seems to know where Hitler might be; accordingly, they all fly to Switzerland.

There, in a great mansion, all the principals involved in the affair gather. In a tense and terrible standoff, Carter and some Nazis hold Barni, Pat, Monk, and Ham at gun-point and demand that Doc turn over the six-shooter. At the time, Doc is standing holding the pistol on Adolph Hitler—Hans Berkshire in disguise!

It's a hellish moment, with strung-out Doc Savage screaming that he'll kill Hitler at the slightest provocation. As the tension mounts, it comes out that Hitler only passed himself off on Barni as her cousin. The scramble for the pistol stemmed from the time Hitler (as Berkshire) grabbed the weapon in Lisbon, leaving fingerprints on its handle.

Then, the Nazis throw down their guns and rush Doc and friends. The ensuing fracas sees Doc victorious and Hitler in Allied hands.
In this very difficult assignment, there is an interesting scene where Doc falls under the spell of Hitler briefly, as the disguised dictator attempts to sway Doc into working with him.

Although *Strange Fish* (Feb. 1945) takes place in America and is something that Doc happens to stumble across, it is similar to some respects of *Jiu San.* In New York, WAC Paris Stevens runs into trouble over something called a belonesox. The trouble leads to a ranch in Oklahoma crawling with Nazi agents. The belonesox, when uncovered, turns out to be an unusual fish, in whose tank is a roll of film. The film reveals the Allied-picked head of Germany's post-war government as an ex-Gestapo officer responsible for the execution of countless Nazi prisoners.

Cargo Unknown (April 1945) is another tense tale peripherally related to the war as Renny, Monk, and Ham are assigned to ride the *Pilotfish,* a sub from London to New York. The sub has a secret cargo in a sealed compartment, which triggers sabotage that sinks the sub. Renny escapes leaving Monk, Ham and crew trapped. Renny reaches Doc and together they wade through violence, frustrating setbacks, and terror as time runs out for the trapped men. Step by step, they are blocked by those who are after the U-boat spirited out of Germany so that it wouldn't fall into the wrong hands.

The Screaming Man (Dec. 1945) takes place after the war's end. Doc and Company are in Manila, looking for Johnny Littlejohn who has been missing for the past six months. Doc does some poking around POW camps and becomes involved with a lady Economic Planning Representative, assorted heavies and a Dutchman, Van Zandt Basset with his friend, Jack Thomas.

The Thing That Pursued (Oct. 1945) takes place in America at the close of the war. It concerns a dangerous little man named Pansy Orchid Heather and glowing balls of light which dog aircraft for mysterious reasons. The tale attempted to explain the phenomenon popularly called Foo Fights, which bedeviled Allied pilots during the war. The bad guys are after the device which creates the fireball effect, unaware that the Nazi invention has little practical use.

When the lady, Annie Flinders, gets into difficulties and is spirited aboard a ship, *Empress Margaret,* because of her prying into Doc's presence in Manila, Doc boards the ship. The ship is ferrying Nazi and Japanese POWs to the States. For some reason, the prisoners begin to act strangely during the voyage; exhibiting signs of extreme fear without just cause.

As the journey wears on, and strange things continue to pop up, we learn that Johnny has been on the trail of a near-legendary genius called Jonas Sown, a man at whose doorstep is laid the blame for World War Two. The reason for this lies in a device which is supposed to control the minds of great masses of people. This device, it seems, is aboard and affecting the POWs. Further, Sown may be aboard, as might Johnny—a prisoner and the only man who might identify Sown. Johnny, for some reason, is being referred to as the Screaming Man.

As things get hotter, the prisoners become increasingly unstable. Doc finds Johnny a prisoner and together they move toward the final confrontation, where Basset—a Dutch againt—learns the secret of Jonas Sown and shoots the unmasked supervillain very dead. The mind-control device that supposedly created the psychological atmosphere that led to war in Europe is lost when Sown's henchmen cast it into the ocean.

With *The Screaming Man,* Doc's activities directly related to the war close. A few later stories have their roots in the war, however. *Terror and the Lonely Widow* is the inevitable lost atom bomb story. *Death Is a Round Black Spot,* concerns illegal Axis securities. *Fire and Ice* is about a gang that smuggles war criminals, for a price. Finally, *The Exploding Lake* deals with a fugitive Nazi scientist who's perfecting a device that turns lead into gold.

Doc emerges from the war no longer the superman that he was; nor is he quite the free agent of the thirties. He is now strongly identified with Washington and the State Department. As stated in *Rock Sinister* (May 1945) Doc has become an international figure, thrust into prominence as a result of his involvement in the affairs of the collapsing Axis nations. In fact, in this novel, Doc is framed by a South American dictator in order to put America's good neighbor policy in a bad light. As time passes though, this tie fades as Doc's activities center on detective work, and his industrial holdings, though he would still become involved with international intrigue (*Danger Lies East* and *Terror Wears No Shoes,* most notably). Curiously, while he's held in such esteem by the government, Doc is currently under suspicion from the police—a problem that always plagued him—but one which apparently reached a critical point in *The Three Wild Men* (Aug. 1942) because the difficulties he encountered therein were referred to in succeeding novels as the authorities only slowly and grudgingly reaccept him.

His critical missions all occur during the last stages of the war, by which time he has worked himself into a state of nervous expectation, very, very, anxious to participate in a significant way to the war effort. His aides are anxious too and are pressed into service on government projects and their loss is greatly felt, especially on the critical missions. During this compressed and hectic period, the bronze man is saddled with missions upon which depend the future of many governments.

Doc's feelings of being involved with overpowering events which threaten to swamp him into failure greatly undermine his effectiveness. Most of his handicaps during this period are psychological; his evident doubts and disgust with the superman concept as well as the fact that each mission is only one battle in a war that he cannot stop. In addition, Doc is no longer a free agent, as he was during the Thirties. He is acting with the ever-present threat of being shot as a spy hanging over him. Further, to his disgust, he is always being called in at the penultimate moment and asked to straighten out what everyone called has either botched up or cannot handle.

The war years gradually stripped away Doc's self-control and effectiveness, making him a very tense and brittle man; at the war's end, he emerges a different person.

His state is best described in *The Screaming Man,* where Doc reflects that the war gives people all kinds of complexes (meaning himself) and, though the Army's iron-fisted methods rather jolted him, he remained very sensitive to it because they made him go through the war out of uniform. This is understandable at a time where it was both suspect and un-American for a healthy male not to be in the service. Later, seeing the bombed-out ruins of Manila, Doc gets an empty feeling again because he was kept out of the war.

Though Doc may have felt that he was left out of the action, his bronze hand managed to affect the end of the war drastically, as well as touch the fates of most of the governments, both Allied and Axis. Not to mention the fact that he became involved with most of the leaders of the period. (In the pre-war adventure, *Peril in the North,* (Dec. 1941) he becomes embroiled in a chase after a fugitive European dictator, Mungen, who seems to be Mussolini, adding yet another such figure to the list. Interestingly enough, this Mungen was supposed to have been killed and fed to a zoo alligator alive, by his subjects, echoing eerily Mussolini's true fate. Doc discovers Mungen alive still and pursues him and the dictator dies a second time.)

In the final analysis, Doc Savage, superman that he may well have been, was just another citizen caught up in the rush of events that was World War Two; a war that not only chewed up governments, ordinary people and boundaries, but also sounded the death knell of the superman concept. The racial superman symbolized by the Nazis and the scientific superman represented by Doc Savage both died in that holocaust that was Ragnarok,

Gotterdammerung, the Twilight of the Gods and the Sunset of the Superman.

Will Murray (essay date 1981)

SOURCE: " Lester Dent: The Last of Joe Shaw's *Black Mask* Boys", in *Clues: A Journal of Detection,* Vol. 2, Fall-Winter, 1981, pp. 128-134.

[*In the following essay, Murray investigates the publishing history of Dent's two acclaimed short stories, originally published in the* Black Mask *magazine, "Sail" and "Angelfish."*]

Lester Dent (1904-1959) enjoys an unusual dual reputation in the mystery field. Under the house name Kenneth Robeson he ground out between 1933 and 1949 over 150 pulp adventure novels featuring his superhuman hero Doc Savage. Under his own name, he was responsible for unnumbered pulp and slick magazine stories, in addition to five well-received, but long out of print, crime novels. Of this group, only two stories, each written a few weeks apart back in 1936, would be reprinted as often as his Doc Savage novels.

These stories were **"Sail"** and **"Angelfish,"** both of which appeared in *Black Mask* during its hard-boiled period, in the closing weeks of Joseph T. Shaw's magnificent decade as editor. *Black Mask* produced quite a body of "tough guy" literature in its day and had an enormous influence upon not only the mystery field but also on American literature. Yet for all of its influence, comparatively little *Black Mask* fiction remains in print today. In fact, only the contributions of three writers have been consistently reprinted since then.

Two of these writers are of course Dashiell Hammett and Raymond Chandler. The third is Lester Dent.

It is not only because Dent wrote only two *Black Mask* stories that they have seen frequent reprintings; it is because these two stories are so undeniably excellent, so quintessentially, *Black Mask* that anthologizers have seen fit to include them in virtually all significant hard-boiled collections. Consider the three major anthologies in this area: Joseph Shaw's *Hard-boiled Omnibus* (1946) reprinted **"Sail,"** while Ron Goulart's *Hardboiled Dicks* (1965) and Herbert Ruhm's *Hard-boiled Detective* (1977) both reprinted **"Angelfish."** The stories have also appeared in various Ellery Queen anthologies. Further, Dent is almost invariably cited as one of the major exponents of the *Black Mask* school by scholars and researchers who seem unaware that his total contribution was so slim—at least as measured in pulp pages.

It was an interesting, if inevitable, chain of circumstances which led Dent to *Black Mask.* He began writing pulp adventure stories in 1929 in his spare time (he worked as a teletype mechanic for the Associated Press in Tulsa, Oklahoma) and had been a part-time writer only a year when he received a telegram from Dell's Richard E. Martinsen offering him a job as a contract writer. Martinsen needed fresh blood to fill the pages of his growing list of pulp magazines. Dent accepted with alacrity. In meeting Martinsen for the first time, he recalled that Martinsen "tossed a copy of Dashiell Hammett's latest book at me and said, 'This is the sort of thing we want you to do. For what impresses us about your writing is the fast movement, the brittle violence of emotion and action'."

At Dell, Dent began, for the first time, to write in the detective genre. First it was a series of novels about a tough, hulking agency detective named Curt Flagg in Dell's *Scotland Yard.* When that magazine folded—along with most of the magazines for which Dent was contracted to fill—he went over to the Magazine Publishers Group. He did Lynn Lash for *Detective-Dragnet.* Lash was a scientific detective of the old school, along the lines of Craig Kennedy, but the stories were told in the unmistakable *Black Mask* style. That was in 1932. In 1933 he created Lee Nace, another tough, gadget-happy private detective, for *Ten Detective Aces.*

By 1933, Dent was also under contract to produce the monthly 60,000 word novel for Street & Smith's new *Doc Savage Magazine.* At first he kept up a fair share of outside writing (including another wild detective, Foster Fade, in *All Detective*) but the grind soon caused him to curtail much of this, to his regret. He itched to crack the better pulp markets and then go on to the slicks like *Colliers* and *The Saturday Evening Post.* The better markets included *Detective Fiction Weekly, Argosy* and *Black Mask,* all of which he read consistently. He was especially fond of *Mask*'s Frederick Nebel whose tough style Dent absorbed to the betterment of his Doc Savage novels. Early on, Dent had tried repeatedly to break into *Detective Fiction Weekly* without success; after a number of his manuscripts met with rejection, feeling his name meant an automatic turn-down, he tried submitting under a pseudonym. When that didn't work, he gave up and concentrated on *Doc Savage.*

This novel-a-month routine continued until 1935, when Dent's publishers decided to issue *Doc Savage* every two weeks. The prospect of writing two of those every month produced absolutely no enthusiasm on Dent's part. Street & Smith hired another writer, Laurance Donovan, to write the alternate novels. After Donovan had generated nine Docs, the firm changed its mind. *Doc Savage* would remain a monthly. However, the push to go twice-a-month resulted in a two-year inventory of Doc novels by year's end. Happily, Lester Dent now had the freedom to concentrate on other writing.

Coincidentally he had recently acquired a forty-foot schooner, a Chesapeake bugeye, and a yen for treasure-hunting. He spent the early months of 1935 and 1936 prowling the waters off Florida in search of pirate gold and story ideas. It was an interesting hobby but not conducive to serious writing. Several times while treasuring nasty hurricanes pounced on his boat, the *Albatross,* and one time she was thrown up on a reef. These experiences, in time, cooled Dent's treasure-hunting fever.

When not at sea, Dent and his wife lived on the boat anchored at the City Yacht Basin in Miami. There, inspired by the locale and his recent adventures, he wrote a short story he called simply **"Sail."** The story was aimed at *Black Mask* for which he was, by then, eminently qualified to write.

Returning to New York City sometime in July, 1936, Dent paid Shaw the first of several visits at *Black Mask*'s Madison Avenue office, probably with **"Sail"** in hand. He was tremendously impressed by Cap (as he was affectionately known), who had a reputation for being rather paternalistic toward his writers—even the would-be ones. Dent found Shaw "a man who could breathe this pride of his into a writer. Cap didn't think I was a pulp hack. Joe felt I was a writer in step with the future. He thought that of all his writers. He had a way, with this device or some other device, of breathing power into his writers." At that first meeting, Shaw shared with Dent a particularly sensitive letter from Raymond Chandler. Dent was also given a paragraph of prose from one of the better *Mask* writers and asked to cut it a little. Dent couldn't—but that was the point: if you wished to write for Joe Shaw's magazine, you had to write lean.

Shortly after this meeting, Shaw rejected **"Sail."** His rejection letter is a fascinating glimpse of the inner-workings of *Black Mask*'s editorial mind and deserves to be quoted in full:

Dear Lester Dent:

We're simple folk; really—we've kidded ourselves so long in trying to gauge average intelligence receptibility that for all practical purposes we're it.

Style—we were unwary enough to state that we weren't concerned with style, method or technique so long as entertainment should be provided. Perhaps we are still right about that, since understanding must introduce entertainment and stand by throughout.

You've done things with this darned good story **"Sail"**—particularly with the first half. You've given a series of pictures that are designed to provide movement, plot and its development. Some of these pictures are gorgeous in their plentitude of descriptive material of a rare authenticity and almost as rare recognizability. Mr. Average Reader would have to go through the dictionary a score of times to a page. In the first place, he hasn't the dictionary, and in the second, if he had, it is extremely doubtful if he would bestir himself to do so even once. He doesn't appreciate the value of such pearls, and he'd say "Nuts" or "Rats"—or some equally absurd and irrefutable New Deal argument.

So what?

Your method of presenting the story by the disjointed picture system, plus the remarkably full amplification of each, ties up Mr. Average Reader in a confused maelstrom of noodle aches more severe than Sail's cramps. You are altogether too nimble for him in their swift sequence and in the still remaining too abrupt scene and angle changes.

There are approximately seventeen pages of this— and it's a darned good story. And would it lose any of its effectiveness if these seventeen pages were told in the straight-running, non-switching, simple narrative language of Mr. Average Reader?

Confidentially—many of those pictures fascinate me; but that was when I relapsed from my role. And in it once more, I an convinced that this method doesn't beget clarity and constant under-standability, and without these we are gutted and sunk.

Man, can you write.

Incidentally, this is not the *Black Mask* method. It is not Hammett's. Curiously, it chances to be exactly Jim Moynahan's conception of Hammett's style or method. Jim is not so far wrong that his machinery creaks and moans. Yours does not; you have oiled it so darn well. But it is there—in places in the first seventeen odd pages, and it confuses and obfuscates, when the narrative should ring as clear as the winding of the silver horn on a winter morning.

How's your patience?
I'd tackle the do-over of this part myself—for sake of the work you've given it—but I couldn't do it justice. I'm not that much of a sailorman, and there are some pearls that must be saved.

Sincerely,
Editor

Plainly Dent had gone overboard in his desire to achieve a strikingly different effect. He also had a habit, in *Doc Savage,* of using exotic words gotten from a Thesaurus. Dent hated rewriting. If an editor suggested revision, Dent would simply send that editor a new story and sell the other to another magazine, when he could. But *Black Mask* was different, and Dent applied himself, revising and honing **"Sail"** through several drafts.

The result was excellent, and **"Sail"** was accepted and published in the October 1936 issue.

The story is set mostly around the familiar City Yacht Basin in Miami. Its protagonist, an unusually tall and laconic individual, is Oscar Sail who runs the one-man Marine Investigations agency out of his jet-black schooner, a Chesapeake Bay bugeye named *Sail*—evidently after himself. (Dent's boat was white and it didn't have the traditional five-log hull described in the story.) The tale is a treasure hunt. Virtually every Doc Savage novel Dent ever wrote is a treasure hunt. This one is about an oil man's yacht which is sunk during a hurricane, along with his wife's diamonds. Sail and a number of very violent characters are all after the location of the wreck. Sail has been hired by an insurance company to recover the jewels. Almost everyone is double-crossing everyone else in the course of the quest. The characters are well-drawn, from Sail to a father and son cop team, and nicely hard-boiled. They were just the sort of characters one expected of *Black Mask,* although Oscar Sail, the too-tall detective, is as much an extrapolation of earlier characters Dent created as he was anything else.

Shaw thought so much of **"Sail"** that he called the story to the attention of Chandler, who read it with interest and remarked, "It can't happen again." Presumably, he meant the story was a fluke, inasmuch as it came from an obvious hack who had nothing better to do than to write *Doc Savage.* Shaw's reply consisted of two words: "Read **'Angelfish'.**"

"Angelfish" was the sequel to **"Sail"** Dent turned in weeks later. It featured Oscar Sail once again and appeared in the December 1936 *Black Mask,* this time rating the cover illustration.

The story is, predictably, another Miami treasure hunt. There are some more vivid characters, including a peg-legged cab driver and two slightly comical gunmen, and this time Sail is sketched a bit more in the traditional private eye manner: when he's fired by the woman who hired him, he sets out to help her out of some obvious trouble even though he isn't especially fond of her. This time, the hunt is for some aerial photos of a possible oil field location in New Mexico. (The oil-wealth motif in both stories is no coincidence—Dent soaked up considerable oil lore during his Tulsa days.)

But in **"Angelfish,"** the violence of man against man is sublimated, and the violence of an approaching hurricane acts as both a spur to the plot and a counterpoint to the action. *Mask* stories seldom if ever involved the man-against-nature theme; that was more of an adventure story device. But Dent used it and used it with extraordinary skill. **"Angelfish"** has been correctly termed a tour de force.

Both Dent and Shaw were excited about Oscar Sail and planned more stories. Dent discussed with Shaw a third yarn—Dent always called his fiction "yarns"—which would have a foreign locale, but circumstances intervened. Before Dent could turn his attention to it, he received a letter from Shaw dated 8 October 1936, saying he had been fired and was about to try his hand at agenting. He requested the third Sail story for that purpose. Not long after, Fanny Ellsworth, who had taken over the editorship and under whom **"Angelfish"** had been published (she copyedited it), also asked about a third Sail adventure. Dent's reply to either query is unknown, but in later years he explained, rather paradoxically, that he didn't write for *Black Mask* again because Shaw was no longer there and didn't do the story for Shaw because Shaw couldn't guarantee him the "money-apple" of a *Black Mask* sale.

The fact of the matter is that Shaw's firing (reportedly due to a financial squeeze requiring a less expensive editor) was as cruel a blow to Dent as it was to Shaw and to the magazine. He never again submitted to it, although in December he once more tried to crack *Detective Fiction Weekly* with a story which may have used the title and some of the ideas of the aborted third Sail story. **"Windjam"** was about Cyrus Peace of the Admiralty Investigations in Miami. He was a somewhat rustic character who carried an unusual arsenal of booby-trapped corncobs. It was a good story, with international complications, but it wasn't up to the standards of Dent's recent work. It met with a polite rejection, causing Dent to finally give up on *DFW.* A year later, he reworked **"Windjam"** as an entry in his Gadget Man series for *Crime Busters,* cheapening the story a good deal.

Shaw eventually did become Dent's agent (after Dent unsuccessfully tried to arrange for him a job at Street & Smith's) and sold several pieces, including a serial to *Argosy,* **"Genius Jones,"** in 1937. Dent had previously cracked that market about the time of the Sail stories. But his outside writing quickly once again fell victim to the renewed demands of *Doc Savage.* (He also sold the *Albatross* early in 1937; it was later reported sunk off Haiti.) As for Shaw, now with the firm of Wilson, Powell & Hayward, he soon began promoting a Boston-based writer named Mark Harper to the detriment of his agenting. Harper never caught on, and it later came out that "Harper" was Shaw himself. Dent subsequently found a new agent and concentrated on his long-held dream of selling to the slicks but without success.

Over the years, Dent and Shaw lost track of each other until 1946 when Shaw contacted Dent—then busily writing mystery novels for Doubleday—about reprinting **"Sail"** in his forthcoming *Hard-boiled Omnibus.* Dent was flattered and gave permission. About the same time *Ellery Queen's Mystery Magazine* inquired after Dent's *Black Mask* stories and was concerned to learn Shaw had already scooped up one of them but relieved when told **"Angelfish,"** which the editor considered the superior of the two, was still available. *EQMM* reprinted it in 1947 as **"Tropical Disturbance"** and **"Sail"** in 1952 as **"V Marks the Spot."**

Since then, both stories have been often collected, as they well deserve to be. They can still be read as exquisitely crafted examples of the *Black Mask* school. This craft, which Dent called "word savagery," was his chief accomplishment. Even though Dent was simply recycling his pulp formulas in the Sail stories, those formulas were honed and told in a drumhead-tight voice, and they were told with the telling authenticity of experience.

If there is anything that raises these stories above the pulp level, which makes **"Sail"** so taut and **"Angelfish"** a true tour de force, it is not just the *Black Mask* prose, but the infusion of Dent's sailing experiences. This is especially true of **"Angelfish."** It was inspired by a fierce hurricane which ravaged Miami in November 1935. Dent was absent at the time, but when he drove down to check his boat (which was intact), he was awestruck by the devastation and the freakish display of the gale's power. When he speaks of "the railroad rails tied in knots half a mile back in the mangroves" on Matacumbe Key and "the tug that was put three quarters of a mile inshore on Knight's Key" in **"Angelfish,"** Dent is describing what he saw with his own eyes, photographs of which exist among his papers.

After Shaw was fired, a number of writers felt strongly that *Black Mask* couldn't be the same without him and, out of loyalty, stopped submitting there. Among these were Raymond Chandler, who went on to greater accomplishments in hardcover, and Frederick Nebel, who went over to the slicks and undeserved obscurity. But perhaps the greatest casualty of all was Dent himself, who arrived on the scene barely in time to be the last of Shaw's "discoveries." Had Shaw remained, Dent would have unquestionably produced more Sail stories of high quality and who knows what else. But this was not to be.

In 1958, a year before his death and six years after Shaw's passing, Dent ventured a frank and possibly unfair self-assessment when he said that Shaw's dismissal was "what kept me from becoming a fine writer. Had I been exposed to the man's cunning hand for another year or two, I couldn't have missed. . . . Instead I wrote reams of salable crap which became my pattern, and gradually there slipped away the bit of power Shaw had started awakening in me."

That Lester Dent's work is still read and discussed over twenty years after his death belies this judgment.

Marilyn Cannaday (essay date 1990)

SOURCE: "Lester Dent and Doc Savage: Heroes and Adventurers", in *Bigger Than Life: The Creator of Doc Savage,* Bowling Green State University Popular Press, 1990, pp. 85-94.

[*In the following essay, Cannaday examines affinities between Lester Dent and his fictional hero Doc Savage.*]

> To 'live dangerously' is for them an act of self-indulgence, not loyalty.
>
> Paul Zweig, *The Adventurer*

Lester Dent and Doc Savage were seekers of adventure, risk-takers whose lives were interwoven. Dent invented imaginative, far-flung adventures for Doc Savage and experienced them vicariously through the writing process; meanwhile, his own travels and exploits enriched the Doc Savage stories. Not one to sit at his desk at home creating fantasies, Dent was an inquisitive explorer, a man of great energy and action who carried his writing with him whether traveling in Europe or sailing his schooner.

Paul Zweig in his book *The Adventurer* (Princeton University Press, Princeton, N.J., 1974) talks about his perception of the adventurer in literature—an idea that seems particularly relevant to Dent's stories. In fact, Zweig cites Doc Savage in one of his examples:

"The popular craving for adventure reached an extraordinary peak during the 1920s and 1930s, in pulp magazines like the Doc Savage series, in westerns, in the soaring cult of movie stars, in the creation of instant legends around figures like Rupert Brooke and Lawrence in England [Lawrence of Arabia], and Lindbergh in the United States."

Zweig makes an interesting distinction between the hero and the adventurer in literature. He says the hero has qualities of courage, loyalty and selflessness which he uses for moral purposes; however, the adventurer, while he may do moral actions, does them for enjoyment—the exhilaration of the adventure itself. He may, in fact, have a fascination for evil. For example, Beowulf, a character from early English literature, is fascinated with the demonic world. "He longs to plunge into it for nothing but the exaltation of adventure itself," Zweig says.

An idea that is often repeated in the Doc Savage sagas is:

> Carelessness would not go together with his [Doc's] strange career . . . of righting wrongs and punishing evildoers in the far corners of the earth. Or pursuing adventure. The pursuit of venture was doubtless a better description of it.
>
> Not as romantic, of course, the plain designation of adventurer. But it might amount to that. There was no denying that pure love of adventure was at the bottom of much of his career. And surely it was this thing that held his five aides to him so inseparably. They were also held together by friendship and mutual admiration, but those things were not the real glue. Those things were ingredients of peace and quiet, whereas the thing that made this organization was more dynamic, volatile, explosive, breathless. It was a liking for adventure that was never fully satisfied. (**"Mystery on Happy Bones"**)

To suggest that Doc Savage and his pals were fascinated by evil and "longed to plunge into it" may be stretching a point; still I think a case can be made for their being drawn to fighting crime for kicks or thrills—as well as for some of their more noble motives.

The seminal document, "Doc Savage, Supreme Adventurer," by Henry Ralston and John Nanovic, that set the tone for all future Doc Savage stories, expressed a love for adventure:

> From this time on, this tiny group of adventurers had their task set before them. The thought of gold was already out of their minds. The thoughts they now had were only of the road ahead—the battles that they had to face, the experience they would undergo in doing what the elder Savage wanted them to do—going out to whatever part of the world needed them, answering whatever call was

urgent, giving their help and support to causes which needed them. People, tribes and nations would gain their help when sore pressed. Industry would be served by them. Art and science would profit by their daring.

But, most of all, the yearning for adventure, the longing for a life of thrill and excitement, which burned within the heart of each of them, would get its fill in their future experiences together.

Doc's five aides, like the adventurer Zweig defines, are hungry for action, a phenomenon of sheer energy; they always seem ready for a fight.

The character Doc Savage is described on the covers of paperback editions of the stories as "America's supreme superhero" and "the greatest hero who ever lived." (Blurb writers of course hardly ever are interested in fine literary distinctions such as those between "hero" and "adventurer.") Interestingly enough, Nanovic, who wrote the first description of Doc Savage, called him a "supreme *adventurer*" [italics mine]. I am not suggesting that Doc Savage did not have a moral purpose; to do so would be ridiculous, as the fight of good against evil is the main theme for every episode. But according to Dent—from the mouth of Doc Savage himself at times—Doc is in the business of fighting evil *partly* for the adventure, the thrill of it all. To be sure, he has admirable heroic qualities, and the moral purpose is always there, but those aspects seem to be almost secondary at times. The character of Doc Savage seems to fall somewhere between that of hero and adventurer.

I found Paul Zweig's book relevant not only for the hero/adventurer concept but also because it helped me understand the wide appeal of adventure stories in general and where those stories—as popular literature—fit into literary history. Adventure is the oldest subject matter in the world—going all the way back to mythology—with a good example of adventure for its own sake being Homer's *Odyssey*. Doc Savage is a little like the character Odysseus in that he is more attuned to action than to feelings.

It's easy to see that most modern readers are saturated with adventure stories from childhood on—fairy tales (which are usually adventurous quests), books like *Alice's Adventures in Wonderland, The Adventures of Huckleberry Finn* and *Treasure Island,* and in general, westerns, mysteries, romances, and science fiction. In addition, visual stories such as soap operas and B-grade movies further cultivate our taste for adventure.

In the twentieth century the adventure story has fallen from favor; we are accustomed to hearing it called "second rate" and "trashy." Yet pulp fiction has enjoyed tremendous popularity, and there are several possible explanations.

The story of adventure contains moments of heightened intensity, such as we have all experienced, if only briefly. For example, we may have started out on a long trip in the middle of a blizzard, or had a brush with the law;

maybe that intense experience was a new relationship when something sparked magically or seemed dangerous. At such moments adrenalin pumped through our veins; our nerves and muscles were taut; we were up for the experience, excited, and intensely alive. The adventure story magnifies these moments of essential experience that seem to be universally recognized, and the reader is seduced by them.

When you combine the need for emotional excitement with the tendency to fantasize—to escape the mundane world through another reality that is only in the mind—you have a key to the appeal of the Doc Savage stories, and perhaps a key to understanding Lester Dent's life as well. Dent said as much himself:

> I didn't realize how many people wanted to be superman. It's more clear to me now. A man comes in from driving a taxicab all day to find his wife threatening to throw him out on his ear for not bringing home more tips to turn over to her. Naturally he wants to be a superman. Or a barber who has to vegetate in his shop all day, don't you reckon he yearns for a chance to get out and reorder the life of whole continents? Doc is sort of the what-I-would-like-to-be dream of everybody, including me. (Murray, "Doc Savage: The Genesis of a Popular Fiction Hero")

An adventure story is an escape from the world of the ordinary—the domestic world of house and garden and a regular job; escape from the world of the farm and the small town where nothing much happens. Thoreau said men live out their lives "in quiet desperation." Not so for Dent and Doc; they were two of a kind in their quest for change and excitement.

Looking at Doc Savage as a hero in the traditional sense, it is not difficult to understand his appeal. The hero has had a universal appeal down through the ages in legend, history and literature. Joseph Campbell, in *The Hero with a Thousand Faces,* identifies archetypal patterns common to heroes in mythology and religion. He describes an exalted hero that existed in the mystical traditions of the past; the modern hero by comparison is more self-determined, more individualistic, but also is endowed with extraordinary abilities—a description that places Doc Savage in the modern era.

Dent may have been unconscious of the power of the hero image he created. While he was no doubt aware that his stories reflected the accepted values of his time, some of the effects he achieved were probably accidental in that he was simply following a formula used by other writers at that time. On a conscious level, he may have described in Doc his own ideal of what it was to be a man.

Dent gave readers what they wanted—escape into a world of danger and adventure in which a man was defined by action—and the Doc Savage stories found their place in popular literature of the thirties and forties.

A further connection can be seen between adventure and the art of storytelling itself. The adventurer travels physically to another country while the storyteller travels in his fantasy. The narrative art may have begun as the need to tell an experience—a need we still have today. I have heard my father say, "A funny thing happened to me when I went to town." (Maybe it was funny, or strange, or unusual.) What happened then for a brief moment held our interest, no matter how trivial the incident. Maybe he would describe how a deer had run across the road, or a clerk had tried to shortchange him. A narrative as simple as this has long been considered what is worth talking about.

Raised to the level of the written story, that narrative creates a kind of time warp which transports the listener beyond the familiar world, one that may bring him into a controlled encounter with what Zweig calls the "raw power surging over and around that world . . ." one that exposes him to "a further reach of darkness [in man's experience] which is exposed to the clarity of words." The story is the thing. The story *becomes* the adventure, and the writer fuses and confuses storytelling with life/adventure. I believe this is a clue to understanding Lester Dent and the interrelatedness of his life and writing. The restless heart of Lester Dent became Doc Savage; Doc fed Dent's need for excitement and adventure and became his rationale for going out to look for it.

Sometimes Dent hardly knew where truth left off and fiction began. The story goes that Dent booked passage for himself, his wife and secretary on the Hindenburg for their return from Germany in 1937. At boarding time they were not allowed on the dirigible, because Dent was carrying too much cash. Frantically he rushed out to spend the excess money on fancy camera equipment. But it was too late, for when he returned the dirigible had taken off without them. As we know, the dirigible exploded when it reached its mooring place in New Jersey. It was said that after the accident, Doc Savage never again travelled by dirigible.

I asked Norma to authenticate the story. "It isn't true," she told me. I also noted the date of the disaster did not coincide with the date of their only trip to Europe. But who could have invented the story, which was published with precise details (albeit with some skepticism)? Surely Dent himself was toying with the idea of what might have been a dramatic story, and he may have tried it out on someone!

Dent wrote glowing accounts of his own exploits, especially when asked to send a biographical sketch. He knew how to make himself sound good on a flier advertising his lectures. When he sent news releases to newspapers, his yacht grew magically from forty to fifty feet in length. Maybe it was advertising license necessitated by trying to be his own sometimes-press agent. Perhaps he had done and written so many fantastic things the edges became blurred in his mind.

There were many parallels between Dent and his brainchild Doc Savage. In the first place they both were big and strong and brown. Dent was described by a reporter as "big and brown as some of his swashbuckling heroes"; another said, even in middle age with a paunch, Dent was "dashing." A friend, Ryerson Johnson, told the story of how they worked in Johnson's yard to dislodge a boulder. They had dug all around it, but still couldn't get it out even by using pry bars. Finally, Dent just grabbed hold of it and heaved it out by himself. "Like Doc Savage," Johnson said.

Doc Savage is described as being six-feet-eight and weighing 270, although, according to Dent's notebook, he seems to have started out at six feet, 200 pounds in the first story, *The Man of Bronze,* closer to Dent's size of six-feet-two, 215 pounds at age thirty-two. Doc grew bigger than life in later stories, while Dent remained about the same except for the shifting of his cargo in middle age. Doc is handsome; his forehead is unusually high, his nose straight, his lips mobile and not too full, his cheeks lean, his chin square, and his jaw strong but not massive. His hair is a beautiful bronze, straight and close to his scalp. His bronze skin is "deeply tanned by many tropical suns and arctic winds" and his eyes are "light tawny with gold flecks." The written description evokes a picture of the young Lester Dent. Only Dent's brown wavy hair and blue eyes were different from Doc's. (However, there were vast differences in early and late *artists'* interpretation of the description of Doc Savage.) Regardless, both Dent and Doc would have stood out in a crowd.

Dent and Doc also were both highly intelligent. Dent's formal education was sketchy but he became largely self-educated on a wide variety of subjects from plumbing to chemistry. He read voraciously; his taste encompassed the classics, poetry, *Popular Mechanics,* how-to books, and books about the mind. Among his books were *Maltese Falcon,* Dashiell Hammett, *The Case of the Counterfeit Eye,* Erle Stanley Gardner, and *Tarzan of the Apes,* Edgar Rice Burroughs. Dent also owned a series of books on language—the Marlborough Self-Taught Series, which he used as references for details of dialogue and setting when he wrote a story set in a foreign country. They included: Japanese, Norwegian, Polish, Roumanian, Russian, Spanish and several others. Doc Savage's knowledge of languages and dialects was an important aspect of his character, and, as a world traveler, he spoke many languages fluently. He had been highly educated, but he continued to learn, just as Lester Dent did. He and his aides had a secret language they spoke only to each other, the Malayan language.

Dent was particularly interested in the Mayan culture in South America—an interest that manifested itself in Doc's ties to the same country. Doc's father had connections there and had left his son a legacy of a small tract of practically inaccessible mountain land in the Central American nation of Hidalgo. It was inhabited by a lost clan of Mayan Indians. Doc proved to the Mayans his worthiness to carry on his father's work and received title to a secret cache of gold.

Both Dent and Doc were essentially loners. Zweig says, of adventurers, "the very energy which defines their greatness—creates for them a kind of exile, a solitude vanishing only in the fullness of action. . . . At their moments of splendor they belong only to themselves."

Doc Savage, a man of silence and mystery, often retreated to his Fortress of Solitude to "brush up on the newest developments in science, psychology, medicine and engineering, and to conduct experiments in his laboratory." The fortress presumably had been suggested by Doc's father when he presented him with this Gibbons quote: "Conversation enriches understanding, but solitude is the school of genius." Dent had his own retreats; he may have enjoyed climbing aboard the schooner and setting out to sea for the solitude it gave him.

> I was never able to visualize Eternity till now. I am not sure that I believe in such a state, but after these weeks at sea I have had a foretaste of what it might be like. One's spirit expands in the strong sunlight and salt air. The fog closes in with the soft chill of infinity. Stars loom large with importance when one knows that one's course is being set by them, and it is strange how differently people move and talk in the middle of the Atlantic. Their voices grow less sharp and hurried. They speak simply and gravely of life and death, even of God sometimes to a comparative stranger. (Unpublished manuscript)

Though Dent had friends, he was essentially an individualist—a loner whose plan for life did not include a lot of socializing. As a writer, he worked primarily alone, sometimes into the wee hours of the morning.

Dent and his alter ego both showed benevolence toward the needy. Dent gave the proceeds from his lectures to the area school to buy lunches, eyeglasses and other necessities for children. To enable an Ohio paralytic, who was a ham radio operator, to get the surgery he needed, Dent spearheaded a drive among other operators, raising $1,200 to cover hospital costs. Then he and another pilot personally flew the young man to Kansas City for surgery.

Doc Savage also helped people. He would stop on the street and help an old woman, give $50 to a man who was unemployed and then help him find a job. He gave free medical care and operations to those in need.

But when it came to things mechanical and to technical knowledge, Dent and Doc were two of a kind. Dent seemed to enjoy giving this aspect of his imagination free rein in all of Doc's gadgets. His technical knowledge was mentioned as being one of the reasons Street and Smith sought him out to write the Doc Savage series. But he no doubt went far beyond their expectations.

Dent incorporated electronic devices into his stories long before they were in common use: gadgets using sophisticated adaptations of radio and television for surveillance and sending messages, electronic door openers, paging devices. He anticipated the Polaroid camera by ten years or more and he described the use of radar as early as 1934. The character Long Tom even had an electrical device in his car that killed bugs! Doc wore a vest full of gadgets in the early episodes: compasses, smoke bomb, trail markers, periscopes, marbles full of chemicals that broke like birds eggs when he tossed them. Even his jewelry—rings and watches—turned into useful tools and weapons. Philip José Farmer (in *Doc Savage: His Apocalyptic Life*) counted 350 gadgets in all!

Dent incorporated his love for technology into another series of stories about Gadget Man that were published from 1937 to 1940. He also played with gadgets in his own life. The house he planned and built was nicknamed the House of Gadgets because it had conveniences and gimcracks that were not commonly used until about ten years later. He built and operated his own powerful ham radio station. He invented the "treasure-finder," a magnetic device for sounding out metals on the bottom of the ocean.

And of course both Dent and Doc could pilot a plane, sail a ship or drive anything on wheels.

Dent didn't believe in killing; he did some limited hunting for game, but he really didn't take to it as a sport. The Doc Savage series, in its maturity, followed the policy of never depicting the killing of anyone unless absolutely necessary. Bad guys were shot with mercy bullets, which merely stunned them; they were drugged or gassed, hit over the head or captured alive and taken away to the "college" where Doc performed a delicate operation on them to remove all memory of their criminal past; they were rehabilitated, given jobs and returned as productive members of society.

Truly Dent and Doc were both good guys—Boy Scouts at heart. Dent actually helped with the scouts in his hometown, and a Doc Savage code that had echoes of the scout pledge was both printed in the *Doc Savage* magazine for the fan club and read at the conclusion of the radio program. The code is:

> Let me strive, every moment of my life, to make myself better and better, to the best of my ability, that all may profit by it. Let me think of the right, and lend all my assistance to those who need it, with no regard for anything but justice. Let me take what comes with a smile, without loss of courage. Let me be considerate of my country, of my fellow citizens and my associates in everything I say and do. Let me do right to all, and wrong no man.

Drawing parallels between Doc and Dent's attitudes toward women is difficult—but there are similarities. Dent had complained about never having known any little girls as a child. He was taught and nurtured more by his mother than by his father, and he had a stable and loving relationship with his wife Norma. A quotation from a character who sounded very much like Dent (from his novel, **Smith Is Dead**) said he put all women on a pedestal.

In keeping with the general beliefs of the era, Dent accepted the idea that women had their place and that was in the background. Doc, of course, reflected the same view. The adventure story in the thirties was a man's domain. Any serious reference to girls was "sissy stuff." Women were thought to represent a threat to heroes and adventurers alike—they would either seduce men and bind them with domestic ties, or worse. As in Grimm's fairy tales, women were seen as demonic witches, bad fairies and cruel stepmothers. Any self-respecting adventurer would naturally try to avoid them in the bedroom as well as in the forest—to sidestep their seduction and sorcery.

A statement in one of Dent's plot outlines (for a story other than a Doc Savage tale) certainly expressed the fear an unknown character had of being domesticated: "He hasn't married. He knows why. It is because he hasn't found a kindredness in any woman. They want to quell his restlessness, want to strip him of it, so he will be a controlled animal. He couldn't stand that. So he hasn't married." We can't assume this is Dent's philosophy since he was apparently happily married, but we can only note that this thought crossed his mind.

Women appear in the Doc Savage sagas as "dames," "babes," and "chicks." Monk and Ham are always chasing "skirts." All five of Doc's aides prefer bachelorhood, and Doc himself is not married. His stated reason for avoiding all romantic liaisons is that his life is so dangerous, if he did have a "girl" he liked, some of the bad guys would try to get to him by hurting her, a chance he cannot take. So he eschews all female entanglements—which is not to say he is immune to temptation!

Of course, certain conventions were observed in writing for the pulp magazines, one being, no girls allowed. Doc Savage admits he is afraid of women, and Dent conveniently depicts them as shallow, two dimensional characters. Only one female character appears more than three times in the series. Pat Savage, Doc's beautiful cousin, plays a part in thirty-seven of the novels. According to Philip Farmer, "Doc doesn't like girls cluttering up the landscape and hampering him." But in a way, his cousin was like one of the guys. She has a compulsive love for adventure, excitement and danger, and she carries an old six-shooter which she can use when necessary. She takes her share of punishment like a man, having been knocked unconscious many times, usually with the butt of a gun. Stubborn and independent, she certainly doesn't fit the stereotype of the helpless or evil woman.

Lester Dent and Doc Savage shared many experiences and similarities, but the experience of writing the Doc Savage stories became for Dent the biggest adventure of them all.

Will Murray (essay date 1997)

Source: "Six Decades of Doc Savage," in *Doc Savage Omnibus* #13, Bantam Books, 1990, pp. 419-30.

[*In the following essay, which is a slightly revised and expanded version of the afterword to the* Doc Savage Omnibus #13, *Murray discusses the origins and development of Doc Savage.*]

No one writer or editor conceived Doc Savage, the Man of Bronze, whose adventures originally appeared in *Doc Savage Magazine,* which ran 181 issues from March 1933 to the Summer 1949 issue. Doc was the product of the greatest hero-making factory ever—he Street & Smith Publishing Company, which had been responsible for such still-famous icons as Nick Carter, Buffalo Bill, and Frank Merriwell during its dime-novel days and, after they switched over to publishing pulp magazines, new heroes like The Shadow, The Avenger, Bill Barnes, and many others.

Doc Savage came into being by accident. The accident was the mania caused by a popular radio show *The Detective Story Hour,* which in 1931 sponsored by Street & Smith's announcer known only as The Shadow.

The Shadow's creepy voice electrified Depression-era America. It also electrified Street & Smith business manager Henry W. Ralston when he realized that such fame was sure to create imitators and knockoffs. He commissioned a one-shot magazine to trademark The Shadow's name.

Perhaps Ralston was surprised when the first issue of *The Shadow* sold out. Perhaps not. For Ralston had been a fan of Street & Smith's dime-novel heroes during his youth, and had particularly doted on Nick Carter. During the summer of 1898 he first went to work in the Street & Smith mail room, and liked it so much he quit Aldelphi College to make the firm his career.

By 1931 he was a business manager in charge of the growing Street & Smith pulp-magazine line. Impressed by the time reading public's appetite for *The Shadow,* Ralston guessed the time was ripe to revive the kind of virtuous, two-fisted heroes he loved in his dime novel-devouring youth. He began laying plans for a revival of Nick Carter and for a new adventure character. Not another wisecracking roughneck such as ran through the pages of countless rival pulps, but one who would tower over them all. "The supreme adventurer," Ralston dubbed his nameless hero, envisioning him as "the poor man's Monte Cristo."

Ralston's thoughts drifted back to a colorful man he had once known, a tall, steely-eyed soldier, diplomat, engineer, lawyer, and author of over forty books, including *A Monte Cristo in Khaki,* whom Street & Smith had published.

A man named Savage.

Colonel Richard Henry Savage (1846-1903) is a forgotten man today. A West Point graduate, Savage enjoyed a distinguished military career, beginning with the U.S. Corps of Engineers and a stint in the Egyptian Army. He went on to become U.S. vice-consul in Rome and Marseilles, joint commissioner on the Texas-Mexico frontier, and chief engineer of the Corpus Cristi and Rio Grande Railroad. He passed the bar in 1890, and the next year published his first book, *My Official Wife,* later made into a silent film. It proved so successful Savage stopped practicing law. When the Spanish-American War broke out he reenlisted, seeing combat in Cuba. It is said Savage personally hoisted the first U.S. flag over conquered Havana.

And although his death was ignominious—on October 3, 1903, Colonel Savage was run over by a horse-drawn delivery wagon while crossing Sixth Avenue in Manhattan—Ralston thought Savage the perfect model for the hero he had in mind.

Since Ralston had plans to update old Nick Carter as a hard-boiled detective, he looted the original Nick of elements he liked. Nick had been raised by his father to be the perfect specimen of humanity, physically powerful and intellectually keen. So, too, would the new character be. But rather than possessing just the required skills of a master detective, Ralston's hero would be a true superman—superhumanly strong as well as the ultimate expert in *every* field. And like Nick Carter, he would live by the Carter family's old code: "Keep your mind, your body, and your conscience clean." Updated, of course.

Ralston had a premise and a last name. But not a first name. It was traditional for dime-novel heroes to be christened to reflect their dominant qualities. Thus, Frank Merriwell—an athlete who was truthful, good-humored, and healthy. Since Ralston already had a surname that signified his supreme adventurer's physical prowess, he gave him a thinking man's first name. Clark, after the most popular actor of that day, Clark Gable. His nickname would be indicative of his great scientific knowledge: Doc.

Thus, Doc Savage—a genius in the body of a Hercules.

Ralston bounced the developing Doc Savage off a new Street & Smith editor he'd hired for *The Shadow.* John L. Nanovic was fresh out of Notre Dame and bursting with ideas. They decided Doc would have a group of assistants, as Frank Merriwell had. Under Ralston's guidance Nanovic prepared a lengthy blueprint for the first Doc Savage novel and sketched out the characters of Doc and his four aides, each of whom were inspired by historical figures and colorful people Ralston had known. A Ralston acquaintance named Ham Peck became Ham Brooks, for instance, and Thomas Jefferson, whose nickname had been "Long Tom," served as Long Tom Robert's namesake.

By the fall of 1932, after months of planning, Ralston and Nanovic had everything they needed to launch *Doc Savage Magazine.* Except a writer.

Enter Lester Dent, a six-foot-two former telegraph operator and Missouri farmboy. Dent had sold his first pulp story to Street & Smith's *Top-Notch Magazine* in 1929. Ralston noticed one of Dent's stories, *The Sinister Ray,* in a rival pulp magazine. It featured a scientific detective obviously patterned after Arthur B. Reeve's then-popular scientific detective, Craig Kennedy, battling a superscientific menace with inventive gadgets. This was exactly the modern approach Ralston wanted for Doc Savage.

Dent was offered the opportunity to write a Shadow novel, and produced *The Golden Vulture.* This proved to Ralston and Nanovic that he could deliver an exciting novel, and Dent was let in on their plans. The original Doc Savage blueprint, called *Doc Savage: Supreme Adventurer,* was only twenty-eight pages long. There was a lot of room for further development.

An imaginative man, Dent had ideas of his own. He wanted to change Doc Savage's name. Ralston balked; he saw Doc Savage as his brainchild. Dent also objected to Doc's trilling sound, later calling it "a patent steal from The Shadow." To the original group of four Doc Savage aides, Dent added a fifth—Renny Ren-wick—and remodeled the others after earlier pulp characters he had written.

Although Ralston originated Doc, Lester Dent fleshed out the character, putting an entirely different spin on the Man of Bronze than Ralston ever dreamed. As Dent once explained it:

> I looked at what people had gone for already. So I took Sherlock Holmes with his deductive ability, Tarzan of the Apes with his towering physique and muscular ability, Craig Kennedy with his scientific knowledge, and Abraham Lincoln with his Christliness. Then I rolled 'em all into one to get— Doc Savage.

Years later Ralston recalled Doc this way:

> We grabbed him right out of thin air. We made him a surgeon and scientist, because we wanted him to know chemistry, philosophy, and all that stuff. We also made him immensely wealthy—he'd inherited a huge fortune from his father. He crusaded against crime of all kinds—plots against the United States, against industry, against society at large. He was very strong physically, a giant of a man of bronze, with eyes whose pupils resembled pools of flake gold, always in gentle motion.

No one remembers who envisioned Doc's metal motif. Bronzed, metallic-haired characters had appeared in Dent pulp stories before Doc Savage. He was also a fan of an *Argosy* magazine hero called Peter the Raven, sometimes called the Man of Bronze, so Dent likely dreamed up those elements.

The source for Doc's flake-gold eyes is noteworthy. During the summer of 1932, while waiting for Ralston and Nanovic to give him the go-ahead on Doc Savage, Dent went to Death Valley to prospect for gold. He was fascinated by the stories surrounding Death Valley Scotty, a hermit who lived in a magnificent desert castle maintained, it was said, by a secret source of gold. Although Dent never found Scotty's gold mine, he did return with a vial of golden flakes he'd panned from a river.

Those shifting gold flakes inspired Doc's unique eyes.

And the experience gave him the idea for Doc Savage's secret source of gold in the Valley of the Vanished in Central America. Scotty's castle may have given Dent the idea for Doc's mysterious Fortress of Solitude—later appropriated by Superman—although its design apparently came from a favorite childhood book containing instructions for building an eskimo igloo. Impressed by the brand-new Empire State Building, Dent selected it as Doc Savage's headquarters.

After expanding the basic Doc Savage elements in a black notebook used as a writing reference, Lester Dent sat down to writer the premier Doc Savage novel, **The Man of Bronze,** in December 1932. It was based on *Doc Savage: Supreme Adventurer,* which contained the same device used to launch Nick Carter's career—the death of the hero's father. He finished the novel three week's later and immediately started on the second, **The Land of Terror.** By the time the first issue of *Doc Savage Magazine* appeared on the third Friday of February 1933, Dent had already written four Doc novels.

The timing seemed to be perfect. It was the worst year of the Depression. President Franklin Roosevelt had just declared his famous bank holiday. *King Kong* was about to premiere nationwide. America craved escape and an untarnished hero.

Lester Dent gave it something more. He produced the world's first superhero, one who inspired later heroes as diverse as Superman and *Star Trek's* Mr. Spock.

Like *The Shadow, Doc Savage Magazine* became an overnight success. Soon it was selling as well as *The Shadow*—a reported two-hundred thousand copies each month—and this without a radio show to promote it. That soon changed. In 1934 a Doc Savage radio show was syndicated nationally, written by no less than Lester Dent himself.

Sometime in 1934 the pressure of all this frenetic writing finally caught up with Dent. While hunched over his typewriter, he looked up to see two of his characters standing there. They started a conversation and Dent answered. When it sank in that he was conversing with figments of his own imagination, Lester Dent took off for a sudden and very necessary Florida vacation. There he was bitten again by the treasure-hunting bug and bought an ungainly boat, the *Albatross,* on which he and his wife, Norma, lived. He wrote Doc Savage, hunted treasure with a magnetic metal detector right out of *Doc Savage,* and calmed his frazzled nerves.

In 1935 Street & Smith made a decision calculated to give Dent a permanent nervous breakdown. It laid plans to publish *Doc Savage* every two weeks, as they were doing with *The Shadow.* Dent, who had his sights on one day escaping the low-paying pulp magazine market, refused to take on such a crushing burden. Street & Smith quickly hired a pinch-hitter Kenneth Robeson named Laurence Donovan, who ultimately contributed nine *Doc Savages,* ranging from the excellent *Cold Death* to the terrible *Land of Long Juju.* (Donovan's Docs have sometimes been miscredited to another pulp writer, Norman A. Daniels, who never contributed to the series.)

Ultimately, Street & Smith reconsidered, and *Doc Savage* continued as a monthly.

Luckily for Lester Dent, Harold Davis ultimately learned to write Doc novels well enough that Dent no longer needed to rewrite him so heavily—or at all. He was responsible for Docs such as **Merchants of Disaster, The Living-Fire Menace, The Munitions Master,** and others. Dent was so confident in his friend that in 1937 he allowed Davis to write **The Golden Peril**—the long awaited sequel to **The Man of Bronze.**

But Davis alone wasn't enough. So in 1938 Dent hired a former *Doc Savage* associate editor, William G. Bogart, to back up Davis. Although not as imaginative as Davis, Bogart proved a fast and competent Kenneth Robeson, beginning with his first Doc, *World's Fair Goblin.* Bogart would go on to write fourteen Docs, among them *Hex* and *The Angry Ghost,* making him the most prolific Doc ghost writer.

Dent, who had aspirations of following fellow pulp writers Dashiell Hammett and Raymond Chandler to greater writing fame, probably would have eventually turned *Doc Savage* over to his growing battery of ghosts, but for circumstances that conspired against his plans.

Early in 1940 Harold Davis was hired as *Newsday*'s first managing editor. That left Dent with just Bogart. Street & Smith brought in a crony of Davis, newspaperman Alan Hathway, to pick up the slack, but Hathway was transferred to another Street & Smith magazine hero, *The Whisperer,* after writing **The Headless Men** and three other Docs. Later he would also replace Davis as *Newsday*'s managing editor.

Then, on Christmas Eve 1940, Dent was informed that his *Doc Savage* rate had been reduced due to a company-wide austerity move. It was a sad Christmas that year. Effectively, this ended Dent's ability to afford ghost writers and quashed his plans to move on. He had just hired the writing team of pulp editors Jack Schiff and Mort Weisinger to write **Birds of Death.** Unable to afford their services, he wrote the novel himself.

By this time, Dent had sold his boat and left New York for his hometown, La Plata, Missouri, where he built a house which boasted more gadgets than Doc Savage's headquarters. He took up flying light planes, and continued grinding out a Doc Savage novel every month without fail.

Punishing competition from radio and comic books began to eat away at the pulp audience, and with World War II raging in Europe and Asia, Street & Smith found itself losing not only readers, but writers, artists, and editors as the draft swept up many men of fighting age. Paper shortages shrank its pulp line, and in 1943 John L. Nanovic moved on after a brilliant decade guiding *Doc Savage*'s editorial destiny. He was replaced by Charles Moran, who decided Doc Savage needed to be updated. He instructed a reluctant Lester Dent to retool his writing style and make Doc Savage less of a superman, made him scrap his original plot to *Death Had Yellow Eyes* and *The Derelict of Skull Shoal* and write them as suspense novels. The latter story was run under Dent's name at his request—a decision soon reversed by Henry Ralston.

Although Moran was replaced by William DeGrouchy after six months, his editorial dictates forever changed the tone of the Doc Savage stories. This was the era of tense, realistic war-era Doc novels such as *Violent Night* and *The Shape of Terror.* As Moran told Dent:

> Doc should always be the plausible man, ready to come to grips with wrongdoers, eager for combat, though not a superman who bowls over mountains if they get in his way.

The novels were much shorter in this phase, since *Doc Savage* had become digest sized. Dent didn't find the shorter length any easier to write. He struggled with the new restrictions and an edict that Doc could no longer rely on his familiar gadgets.

By 1945, with the war over, Dent again looked toward the day he would bolt from the pulps to the next plateau of writing. His old rate had been restored by Moran, so he rehired both Harold Davis and William Bogart. But Davis's new story, *The Exploding Lake,* proved so much a throwback to the pre-Moran Doc Savage that Dent was forced to completely rewrite it. Street & Smith's efforts to find a writer on its own were dropped when first choice, John D. MacDonanld, declined to pen a Doc novel. To Dent's relief, William Bogart slid comfortably back into the Kenneth Robeson groove—so comfortably, in fact, that Dent temporarily turned the series over to him. It was Dent's hope that he could at last give up being Kenneth Robeson.

Events once more conspired to thwart his plans. *Doc Savage* was rechristened *Doc Savage, Scientist Detective* and scaled back to bimonthly frequency. His Doc income reduced by half, Dent released Bogart and hunkered down to the new mystery-oriented Doc Savage. Although it was an unhappy event for Dent, he took advantage of the new editorial guidelines under his latest editor, Babette Rosmond, and experimented with fresh approaches to what was by now a very old chore. It was in this period

that Dent produced the quintet of Docs told in the first person. He also recycled several unsold mystery novels into Docs, which explains why some later stories such as *The Devil Is Jones* and *Death Is a Round Black Spot,* read strangely. Originally, they were not Doc novels!

By 1948 the Street & Smith pulp line was on its last legs. *Doc Savage, Scientist Detective* still sold reasonably well, but the pulp industry in general had fallen on hard times, the victim of increasing competition from the burgeoning paperback book and the new home entertainment phenomenon, television—which Doc had been experimenting with as far back as 1933. In a last-ditch effort to restore sales, the firm restored its digests to magazine size and put them under the editorial control of the improbably named Daisy Bacon. Bacon found Dent churning out polished Cold War stories such as *Terror Wears No Shoes,* and put a quick stop to this latest new direction. One Doc novel, *The Red Spider,* fell through the cracks during the transition, and finally saw print in 1979 under the Bantam Books colophon.

Dent found it hard working with Daisy Bacon, even though she wanted him to return to the original high-adventure slant. Bacon complained about Dent's work, often criticizing or rejecting his plots. She had Dent revise the first of the retro-thirties Docs, *The Green Master,* and forced him to replot the next, *Return from Cormoral,* several times before she was satisfied.

In frustration Dent wrote Bacon a long letter outlining various Doc Savage plot ideas, hoping to hit upon one that she would like. One of these plots concerned a man who, while exploring a cavern, uncovers the entrance to hell and is pursued by an imp.

Bacon liked the idea, but thought Dent's suggested ending—that it was all hoax—too much of a cheat and suggested he give the story a fantasy twist. Dent's opinion of the suggestion is not known. He had always avoided the supernatural in his fiction. But Bacon was his editor and he duly gave her what she wanted.

Thus, the classic *Up from Earth's Center* actually came about by accident! Dent had no inkling it would mark the end of the series. In fact, he was preparing another Doc plot when Bacon asked him to hold off. Street & Smith had instituted a buying freeze on their entire pulp line, which had been rolled back to quarterly publication.

While awaiting further word, Lester Dent suffered a heart attack. He was recuperating when he received the news. *Doc Savage* had been cancelled. Not due to sales, but because Street & Smith had decided to fold its entire pulp-magazine and comic-book line to concentrate on their growing string of women's magazines such as *Mademoiselle.*

Doc continued in Great Britain and elsewhere in reprint and translation, while Lester Dent settled down to farming and occasional writing. Unhappy over Street & Smith's abandonment of its heroes, Henry Ralston retired in 1950. And Street & Smith became absorbed by Condé Nast Publications in 1961 after nearly a century in business. Today, the company name survives only on the mastheads of sports annuals.

It would be fifteen years before Doc Savage would return in Bantam Books editions. Lester Dent, who once scoffed at the idea of reprinting his Doc novels, saying "they would be so outdated today they would undoubtedly be funny," never lived to see that day. He died on March 11, 1959, while convalescing at the Grim Smith Hospital in Kirksville, Missouri. He had suffered another, fatal heart attack.

The man who wrote the best of the Doc Savage series would never write again.

But this was not the end of Doc.

In October 1964, with the simultaneous release of Kenneth Robeson's **The Man of Bronze, The Thousand-Headed Man,** and **Meteor Menace,** Bantam Books began its ambitious Doc Savage reprint program. No one then could have imagined more than a dozen or so of these Depression-vintage pulp adventure novels would ever see paperback editions.

For in 1964 the concept of packaging a paperback series in consecutively numbered editions was untried. Adventure heroes of Doc Savage's era were considered passe. This was the time of James Bond, Mike Hammer, and other cynical types. What chance had a Galahadian relic known as the Man of Bronze

Surprisingly, Doc Savage caught on. Soon the books were being released on an unheard-of monthly schedule and selling millions of copies. All through the 1960s and 1970s a new Doc Savage reprint was a familiar sight on bookstore and newsstand racks. They were translated into French, German, and Spanish. *Time* and *Newsweek* took notice of the phenomenon, quoting from the innumerable Doc Savage fanzines being cranked out by diligent fans. There were Marvel comic-book adaptations. A "biography" of his life was written by the noted author Philip José Farmer. Doc reached the silver screen in 1975 with the release of George Pal's *Doc Savage—The Man of Bronze.*

But competition from modern adventure series like The Executioner, The Destroyer, and countless others—all of which borrowed the Doc Savage numbered-package format—pushed Doc into the background during the late seventies. Bantam, looking for new ways to keep the series going, published a lost Doc Savage novel, **The Red Spider,** in 1979 amid much fanfare.

It took Bantam Books until October, 1990 with the publication of *Doc Savage Omnibus* #13 to finally reprint every installment. A year later, the publisher inaugurated a series of new adventures, beginning with Philip José Farmer's *Escape from Loki.* There followed seven period Docs, written by Will Murray from Lester Dent's unused outlines and uncompleted manuscripts. These were *Python Isle, White Eyes, The Frightened Fish, The Jade Ogre, Flight into Fear, The Whistling Wraith,* and *The Forgotten Realm.*

The venerable series ended in 1993, sixty years after it was launched, with its 190th entry. A further revival is not out of the question.

FURTHER READING

Blosser, Fred. "The Man from Miami—Lester Dent's Oscar Sail." *Armchair Detective* 5 (1971-72): 93.
> Examines Dent's short stories "Sail" and "Angelfish" as "splendid examples of the *Black Mask* school at its best."

Farmer, Philip José. *Doc Savage: His Apocalyptic Life.* Garden City, N. Y.: Doubleday & Company, 1973, 226 p.
> Biography of Dent's fictional hero Doc Savage.

Lachman, Marvin. "Original Sins." *Armchair Detective* 22 (Summer 1989): 274.
> Includes a light-hearted but laudatory review of Dent's first Doc Savage novel *The Man of Bronze* occasioned by its re-release in 1989.

Murray, Will. *Secrets of Doc Savage.* Greenwood, Mass.: Odyssey Publications, 1981, 36 p.
> Includes four essays on various topics relating to Doc Savage and Dent's writing of the Savage novels. The first and longest of the four recounts many of Dent's story ideas and fragments that never appeared in print.

The following source published by Gale Research contains additional coverage of Dent's life and career: *Contemporary Authors,* Vol. 112.

John Foster Dulles

1888-1959

American statesman.

INTRODUCTION

The United States Secretary of State between the years 1953 and 1959, John Foster Dulles is remembered as a preeminent shaper of American foreign policy in the postwar era. Taking an incontrovertible stance against international communism, calling it a "moral evil," the Republican Dulles is considered one of the early architects of America's decades-long Cold War policy, which envisioned the United States as the protector of freedom and moral bulwark against the spread of Soviet-style communism in the second half of the twentieth century. As Secretary of State Dulles implemented President Dwight D. Eisenhower's "New Look" defense policy, a course of action that called for a shift away from conventional military parity and emphasized technological superiority and the stockpiling of nuclear arms in an effort to deter nuclear war. As a statesman Dulles is also typically associated with the terms "massive retaliation" and "brinkmanship," the former alluding to the U.S. threat of nuclear reprisal against its political and military opponents, the latter referring to Dulles's controversial willingness to steer the nation to the brink of war in order to achieve his diplomatic goals and ultimately ensure peace.

Biographical Information

Dulles was born in Washington, D.C., in 1888, the son of a Presbyterian minister. Both his maternal grandfather, John W. Foster, and his uncle, Robert Lansing, had been Secretaries of State. Dulles spent his childhood in Watertown, New York, and attended public schools until enrolling at Princeton University in 1904. In 1907 he traveled with his grandfather to the Second Hague Peace Conference, an experience that shifted his intentions of becoming a minister toward an interest in international politics. He graduated from Princeton in 1908, then studied for a time at the Sorbonne in Paris. He attended law school at Georgetown University, and upon obtaining his degree in 1911 began working for a New York law firm. Already known as a distinguished international lawyer, Dulles joined President Woodrow Wilson's staff in 1917 to negotiate the Versailles peace treaty at the close of World War I. In the ensuing years Dulles became actively involved in the pursuit of a lasting international peace and outlined his evolving political philosophy in his 1939 monograph *War, Peace, and Change*. In the 1940s Dulles became Republican presidential candidate Thomas E. Dewey's foreign policy adviser. Additionally, Dulles, although a Republican, acted as adviser to the Democratic Truman administration. At the close of

World War II in 1945, Dulles was appointed a U.S. delegate to the United Nations Conference in San Francisco and continued to serve as a delegate to the newly formed organization between 1946 and 1948, and again in 1950 following a brief appointment to the United States Senate. Dulles published his second book on international affairs *War or Peace* in 1950 and the next year assisted in negotiating the formal peace treaty with Japan. In 1953, shortly after Republican Eisenhower's landslide victory in the 1952 presidential election, Dulles was appointed U.S. Secretary of State.

As Secretary of State Dulles implemented his anticommunist foreign policies wherever possible. He responded to tensions between the Soviet Union and the governments of Warsaw Pact nations in Eastern Europe, including Poland, East Germany, and Hungary. In 1954, after the siege of the French fortress at Dien Bien Phu by communist Vietnamese forces, Dulles initiated the creation of the Southeast Asia Treaty Organization (SEATO) designed to contain the expansion of communism in that part of the world. In 1954 and 1955 Dulles negotiated with communist China over its bombing of the Nationalist-controlled islands of Quemoy and Matsu near Formosa (now Taiwan). Using the threat of nuclear retaliation, Dulles ordered communist China to cease its shelling of the islands—an interruption in hostilities that prevailed for several years until Soviet premier Nikita Krushchev countered Dulles's tactic with a promise to respond with his nation's own nuclear weapons. In 1956 Dulles supported a United Nations cease-fire in Egypt, thwarting a combined British, French, and Israeli attack on the government of Egyptian nationalist leader Gamal Abdel Nasser over contested international rights to the Suez Canal. Attempting to check European colonialism and prevent a large-scale war between the West and the radical nationalist Nasser, Dulles emerged on the side of successful negotiators who sought to place the canal under the control of the United Nations. Diagnosed with terminal cancer in 1958, Dulles was compelled to resign his post as Secretary of State in April of 1959 due to severe illness. He died on 24 May 1959.

Major Works

Dulles's literary corpus consists primarily of two political monographs and several essays which explore the subject of international relations and the state of foreign policy from the early World War II era to the time of his death in 1959. In his first book, *War, Peace, and Change*, Dulles enumerated his political philosophy—based in large part upon a Wilsonian belief in the necessity of a worldwide community of nations to mediate foreign policy and promote international peace and understanding. Such later essays as "A Righteous Faith for a Just and Durable Peace" (1942) and *The Six Pillars of Peace* (1943) emphasize Dulles's belief in the moral foundations of foreign policy, whereas "Thoughts on Soviet Foreign Policy and What to Do About It" (1946) makes explicit his strongly anticommunist views and his goals to counter Soviet expansion throughout the world. In his second book, *War or Peace*, Dulles evaluated the early stages of Cold War foreign policy and specifically attacked President Harry S Truman's policy of "containment" toward the Soviet Union, arguing that such a strategy is insufficient to combat the growing menace of communism.

Critical Reception

Both during and after his tenure as U.S. Secretary of State Dulles was regarded as a controversial figure in international politics. His reputation among European leaders suffered in large part from his unbending anticommunism and unwillingness to negotiate with the Soviet Union, a policy that historians observe fueled the Cold War in the 1950s. After Dulles's death, scholars have noted, U.S. policies shifted somewhat away from the Secretary's often dogmatic and moralistic pronouncements, emphasizing both military disarmament and improved relations with the Soviet Union, communist China, and the Third World. In more recent years, historians have also attempted to re-evaluate the simplified

and to a degree stereotypical portrayal of Dulles as single-minded in his Christianity, Republicanism, and hatred of communism. Commentators have since offered more balanced appraisals of the private and public Dulles. Likewise, many critics have examined Dulles's relationship with President Eisenhower in an attempt to uncover the true extent to which Dulles may be said to have dominated U. S. foreign policy during the Eisenhower administration.

PRINCIPAL WORKS

The Panama Canal Controversy between Great Britain and the United States (essay) 1913
"As Seen by a Layman" [published in periodical *Religion in Life*] (essay) 1938
War, Peace, and Change (political treatise) 1939
"Churches' Contribution toward a Warless World" [published in periodical *Religion in Life*] (essay) 1940
"A Righteous Faith for a Just and Durable Peace" [published in periodical *Life*] (essay) 1942
The Six Pillars of Peace (essay) 1943
"Thoughts on Soviet Foreign Policy and What to Do About It" [published in periodical *Life*] (essay) 1946
"Moral Force in World Affairs" [published in periodical *Presbyterian Life*] (essay) 1948
War or Peace (political treatise) 1950
"A Diplomat and His Faith" [published in periodical *Christian Century*] (essay) 1952
"A Policy of Boldness" [published in periodical *Life*] (essay) 1952
"Policy for Security and Peace" [published in periodical *Foreign Affairs*] (essay) 1954

CRITICISM

William T. R. Fox (essay date 1950)

SOURCE: Review of *War or Peace*, in *American Political Science Review*, Vol. XLIV, No. 3, September, 1950, pp. 751-53.

[*In the following review, Fox summarizes the argument of Dulles's* War or Peace, *calling it "a sensible book which ought to be widely read."*]

There is still a group which believes that peace is inevitable and security assured if we do the one right thing; that otherwise all is lost. What this one right thing is—create a world federation or an Atlantic Union, support the United Nations more fervently, or swear off power politics—the dwindling group is not agreed upon. Mr. Dulles makes short shrift of it (p. 204).

Against another and growing group which finds equally uncongenial the limitless series of painful choices involved in attempting to preserve an acceptable peace with the Russians, a group which believes that war is inevitable with the only question one of the time and the place, Mr. Dulles strikes harder. His whole book is devoted to supporting the thesis that as free men we do not have to accept submissively the dictate of a stern fate, that we do not have to leave to the future and to the Russians the question of whether there shall or shall not be a third World War, that we can in some measure be masters of our own destiny. It is unfortunate that in his discussion of civilian-military relations he almost implies (p. 241) that the military tend to believe in inevitable war and that civilians do not.

With the author's conception of peace not "as isolation, or as world domination by the United States, or as stagnation" but rather as "condition of community, of diversity and of change" we must agree. In this context he discusses realistically the role of the United Nations in American policy. His important share in developing that policy gives special interest to this part of the analysis. It should go far to counteract the cynicism of the disillusioned who can never forgive the United Nations for not turning out to be a vehicle of automatic salvation. His analysis suggests that even at San Francisco official American policy placed more emphasis on the UN's forum function than on its enforcement function. Of course, neither Mr. Dulles nor the government could have foreseen that one of the Soviet Union's periodic boycotts of UN activities, this time over the presence at Lake Success of a delegation from Nationalist China, would permit the Security Council to order enforcement action in the Korean crisis.

Mr. Dulles probably also did not foresee that by the time *War or Peace* appeared in print he would have returned to the Department of State. The bitterness of the Lehman-Dulles senatorial contest apparently had destroyed his further usefulness in developing a bipartisan foreign policy. Yet the savage attack on the Department of State led by Senator McCarthy changed all this; and, paradoxically, the extreme partisanship of the New York senatorial campaign gave added value to the demonstration of bipartisan unity involved in his return. Foreknowledge that he would again be serving under a Democratic president might well have caused him to modify his chapter on "Bipartisanship in Foreign Policy." Throughout the book there is the suggestion that the *Democrats* at critical moments played party politics, while counting on Mr. Dulles and the Republicans to forego partisan advantage in the national interest.

War or Peace is a sensible book which ought to be widely read, even if in its autobiographical aspects it does suggest that John Foster Dulles has batted 1,000 and that his Democratic collaborators do not have quite such a spectacular batting average.

Basil Rauch (essay date 1950)

SOURCE: Review of *War or Peace,* in *Political Science Quarterly,* Vol. 65, No. 4, 1950, pp. 592-54.

[*In the following review, Rauch calls* War or Peace *a "primer for Everyman" that asserts "the primacy of moral issues in international affairs," but nevertheless observes that the work occasionally fails to surmount Republican partisanism.*]

This book suggests comparisons with Wendell Willkie's famous *One World*. In both, Republican leaders better than any Democrats stated for the whole public the form and content of evolving United States foreign policy. But Willkie's book was a rapt vision of utopia; John Foster Dulles' book is a sober redemption of hope after five years of discouragement. The two books are signposts marking the distance we have traversed from the dream of One World right away to an awakening with attendant determination to prevent sad experience from reconciling us permanently to two worlds.

Wendell Willkie reported on his trip, which was little more than an inspirational junket, to the allied nations during the war. Mr. Dulles reports on his experience in the actual making of administration policy. Thus the two books are also signs of the rapid development of bipartisanship in the conduct of our foreign relations. *War or Peace* is furthermore a primer of recent and current events and a preachment of the necessity to strengthen internationalist doctrine and practice as the best means to prevent a third world war.

It is the best primer available to spell out for citizens the essentials of what has been happening in the main arenas. Specialists will be appalled by Mr. Dulles' distortions-by-omission, which are sometimes severe even for a primer. But specialists rarely speak to the average citizen to any purpose, and Mr. Dulles has a purpose which must be achieved if we are to construct a viable peace or at least win if we are forced to fight. His purpose is to convince Americans that our policy since 1945 has been sound and that no other policy than collective security—neither appeasement in hope of an easy peace nor isolation in hope of security nor aggression in hope of victory over communism—is practicable.

The author is aware that the crux of the struggle between the United States and Russia is their competition for the moral leadership of humanity. He does not stress the religious ambience of his own morality; but his association with a major effort to find a common denominator among religious groups has evidently convinced him that all human beings share the essentials of morality. Honesty, he believes, is really our best policy. He gives us evidence that keen moral sense and respect for it in mankind have guided crucial decisions of our government in recent years. He concludes that the view of the small free nations after the war that they might remain neutral in the struggle between the United States and

Russia, that it was merely another old-fashioned, a-moral sruggle for power, was demolished by the actual conduct of the United States.

Specialists will want to know more than Mr. Dulles tells them of recent international relations before they accept his conclusion that good and evil are entirely polarized between the United States and Russia. Busy with data on Arabian oil, West German cartels, dollar shortages abroad, and so forth, political scientists may delude themselves that the value judgments in which Mr. Dulles deals are naïve. A primer for Everyman is just the place to assert the primacy of moral issues in international affairs. Unless everything changes, the American people will in the long run see to it that their government's policy is plainly moral.

As an account of the author's experience in recent international negotiations, *War or Peace* is a disappointment. The text gives the impression that it was dictated from memory unaided by notes, and Mr. Dulles claims a great deal of credit for himself. He implies that his advice to Secretary Byrnes during the September 1945 London Council of Foreign Ministers (p. 30) ended "the epoch of Teheran, Yalta, Potsdam," and inaugurated the policy of "no appeasement". It is not true that in the Atlantic Charter "no mention was made of an international organization" (p. 33). Section Eight declares Roosevelt's and Churchill's belief that, after disarmament of the aggressor nations, a "permanent system of general security" should be established. Mr. Dulles states that private effort, including that of a committee which he headed for the Federal Council of Churches, "transformed the attitude" of the government (p. 34). He claims that postwar bipartisanship in foreign policy had its "birth" in August 1944, when Governor Dewey asked him to confer with Secretary Hull on the projected United Nations (p. 123). Bipartisanship was actually "born" on September 20, 1939, when President Roosevelt conferred with Alfred M. Landon and Frank Knox on the repeal of the arms embargo, and Wendell Willkie certainly helped bipartisanship to grow.

Mr. Dulles rises above partisan history in the passages of *War or Peace* which plead for strengthened internationalism among our people and in our policy. Besides exhortations, he offers in chapter vi, "The United Nations in Operation", a solid analysis designed to show that its successes were notable even prior to Korea. Other chapters also contain penetrating expositions and arguments in support of collective security.

The book does a great deal to make the meanings of recent world affairs and of our policy available to the public. Its wide popularity encourages hope that public understanding may keep pace with at least the broad outlines of the world situation and that popular American support of the United Nations will survive the failure to realize immediately Willkie's dream of One World.

Theodore Rapp (essay date 1951)

SOURCE: Review of *War or Peace,* in *The South Atlantic Quarterly,* Vol. 50, No. 1, January, 1951, pp. 124-26.

[*In the following review, Rapp argues that Dulles's general thoughts on sustaining world peace and containing communist expansion as outlined in* War or Peace *are "more important than his specific recommendations."*]

Mr. John Foster Dulles believes that a Third World War, though probable, is not inevitable and that an intelligent American foreign policy still has at least a good chance of keeping the peace. As in Britain, our foreign policy is bipartisan, not because of any love lost among the politicians, but because of what Stalin would call the "logic of facts," the desperateness left by the two most destructive wars in modern history. "There is no simple formula for peace, and no single act that will assure peace," while those who believe in violent methods of political change can often catch us off guard, as they have done in South Korea. But those are the hazards of a policeman's life. The real world, as Mr. Dulles sees it, is no place for "realistic" simple solutions, a fact which makes his book much harder reading than the optimistic accounts of those converted Middle-Westerners, Mr. Willkie and Mr. Wallace. Mr. Dulles writes clearly about some very muddled situations, but he is too clear-headed to see any immediate solution for our difficulties. Except in Moscow, the brave new world is not just around the corner, and the general sense of relief at our decision to use force in Korea should not be allowed to conceal the fact that merely taking that stand does not automatically solve our problems. This is the sort of book which the harried Mr. Acheson might have written if Mr. Dewey had won the election and an equally harassed Mr. Dulles had been given the job of explaining the facts of life to certain United States Senators. There are some mild headlines in Mr. Dulles's work, but his account of what we are trying to do and why we are trying to do it is more important than his specific recommendations.

Like Mr. Truman and Mr. Acheson, Mr. Dulles does not like the type of "peace" proposed by the Russians. Their idea of "peace . . . is a condition where everyone agrees with everyone else, where there is no disharmony, and where the productive machine is running smoothly under the direction of the political leaders acting as master mechanics. Any who do not conform are like grit in the wheels of the machine and have to be cleaned out." Our idea of "peace" is different. Some of us still "think of peace as a condition in which our nation is isolated from all external forces and lives its own solitary life. To accept this idea is to invite war and defeat." Others "rather naively . . . assume that a world at peace will conform to *our* ideals and *our* wishes." But "that kind of peace can be won only by war; and under modern conditions there can never be a successful 'war to end war.' A third misconception is that in a world at peace everything stands still and remains as it is. That is the idea of those who are satisfied. . . . One great weakness of the League of Nations was its attempt to preserve the *status quo.* Peace must be a condition where international changes can be made peacefully . . . , of community, of diversity, of change." If this formula is difficult and unromantic, that is the fault of the world and not of our foreign policy.

Such is the core of Mr. Dulles's good advice. These matters are not going to be explained or worked out in ten or a hundred easy lessons. We are holding Western Europe and have won a sort of victory in Yugoslavia, but the Russians have consolidated their zone in the east of Europe, and the Communists have won an even greater victory in China. We made some major errors in China, but hindsight is always better than foresight, and treason in the State Department certainly had little to do with Red victory. In any event, we must get on with the job and not spend our time in mutual recrimination. In so short a tour of the world Mr. Dulles cannot go into detail, but what he has to say will be a good starting point for every citizen who wishes to get the general background of the policies we were trying to follow in the spring of 1950. Here is his advice on South Korea, written some months before that area erupted. There is as much good sense in his discussion of almost all the rest of the specific areas he examines.

> In South Korea we have responsibilities due to the fact that we were in occupation of that area and primarily sponsored its transition to independence. We were remiss in the early years in not encouraging the local authorities to develop a loyal and disciplined security force. That omission is now being made good. But there is continuing need of economic support and of some military aid, if this young nation which we helped bring into the world is to survive.

If this is aggressive, war-mongering talk, then most of us stand convicted, but it is hard to see how we can act otherwise when so large a "part of the man power and the natural resources of the world is despotically controlled by a group who have no scruples against war as a means of getting what they want, who act in secrecy, and who could strike without warning."

John Foster Dulles (essay date 1953)

SOURCE: "Morals and Power," in *The Puritan Ethic in United States Foreign Policy*, edited by David L. Larson, D. Van Nostrand Company, Inc., 1966, pp. 139-44.

[*In the following essay, originally delivered as an address before the National War College at Washington in 1953, Dulles outlines the mechanisms of Soviet power and ideology, which, he contends, may be defeated by the "supremacy of moral law."*]

Since I have been secretary of state, I have been to Europe, the Near East, and South Asia. Before that, in connection with negotiating the Japanese peace treaty, I had an excellent chance to get a firsthand look at our foreign representatives in Japan, Korea, and other parts of the Far East.

One of the things that most impressed me in these areas was the down-to-earth cooperation which existed between our civilian and military officials. The North Atlantic Treaty Organization is an outstanding example of large-scale military-civilian cooperative effort.

The current negotiations in embattled Korea are being carried on by General Harrison. And, to my way of thinking, he is doing an excellent job under very exacting conditions.

But behind General Harrison stands a team of Defense and State Department officials which, once again, testifies to the effectiveness of military and civilian cooperation.

I might mention that one of my first acts as Secretary of State was to invite the Joint Chiefs of Staff and their chairman to lunch with me at the State Department. They kindly responded and the five of us had an intimate exchange of views about the world situation and U.S. security. Ever since, we have cooperated with no single trace of friction. That, I am glad to say, is typical. Of course, there are often initial differences of opinion. But, by and large, our military and civilian officers both here in the United States and on duty overseas rise above differences when the chips are down. In today's world, the chips are down almost everywhere.

It is teamwork between the military and civilian which has given us the necessary strength whenever and wherever we have needed it.

I should like to talk for a few minutes about power in a material sense, such as is represented by our splendid military establishment. What is the purpose of this power? Admiral Mahan is credited with one of the best answers to this question. It is that the role of power is to give moral ideas the time to take root. Where moral ideas already are well-rooted, there is little occasion for much military or police force. We see that illustrated in our own communities. Where the people accept the moral law and its great commandments, where they exercise self-control and self-discipline, then there is very little need for police power. Under these circumstances, it is sufficient to have a very modest force to take care of the small minority always found in every community which disregards the precepts of the moral law.

Where, however, there are many who do not accept moral principles, then that creates the need of force to protect those who do. That, unfortunately, is the case in the world community of today.

At the present time, there is no moral code which has worldwide acceptance. The principles upon which our society is based—the principles which we believe to be both humanitarian and just—are not accepted by governments which dominate more than one-third of mankind.

The result is that we have a world which is, for the most part, split between two huge combinations. On the one hand, there is the United States and its free-world associates. This is a voluntary alliance of free peoples working together in the recognition that without unity there could be catastrophe.

On the other hand, there is the totalitarian bloc led by the Soviet Union—an artificial, imposed unity which cannot be called an alliance in the sense that we use the word.

These huge concentrations are in conflict because each reflects differing aims, aspirations, and social, political, and economic philosophies. We must assume that they will continue to remain in basic conflict, in one way or another, until such time as the Communists so change their nature as to admit that those who wish to live by the moral law are free to do so without coercion by those who believe in enforced conformity to a materialistic standard.

This is one of the hard facts of international existence which we must accept. We cannot close our eyes to it. It will not go away simply because we hope that it will do so.

We must plan accordingly.

"KNOW YOUR ENEMY"

There is a sound military principle which we must take into consideration in our planning. It is "know your enemy."

What makes the Soviet Union—the fountainhead of world communism—act as it does? Why do the Soviets seek power and more power?

These complex questions are not simply answered. There are many forces which motivate the Soviet drive for power. Among these forces are these which I should like to mention: ideology, the historic imperialist urge, and the chronic insecurity complex which besets those who rule by force.

Take first the question of Communist ideology. Soviet theorists, as you know, refer to their ideology as Marxian-Leninist-Stalinism. Whose name will next be added remains to be seen.

Through the years, Communist ideology has taken a number of twists, turns, and shifts in emphasis. Upon occasion, it has almost seemed as if the ideology has been stood on its head to justify a policy which Soviet leaders have had to adopt to meet a given international or domestic crisis. Thus, in October 1939, the Soviet leaders proclaimed that Hitler was the peace lover and the British and French the aggressors.

There can be no question but that Soviet leaders use shifty tactics.

But the Soviet leaders have never departed from a certain basic thesis laid down by Marx. It is called "dialectical materialism."

It is important for us to remember that this Marxist principle continues to be basic to the Soviet credo despite any changes that have been made by Lenin and Stalin. Stalin's last published article, written shortly before his death, was based upon original Marxist assumptions when he predicted that the United States and its allies inevitably would split because of inner, economic contradictions.

The entire creed of Soviet communism is based upon this "dialectical materialism," the theory that there is no such thing as a moral law or spiritual truth; that all things are predetermined by the contradictory movements of matter; that so-called capitalism is historically fated to collapse; and that communism is the movement predestined to effect that collapse.

Now, let us look briefly at another of the springs of Soviet action, that of historical imperialism. This urge to expand is not something patented by the Communists of Soviet Russia. This urge has long been found with the "Great Russians" in the Eurasian heartland. It is a national urge, though it is clear that today communism has greatly intensified it.

The present Soviet Communist exertions in the Near East, Far East, and East Europe are a duplication of many past performances. Early in the 19th century Tsar Alexander, the most powerful ruler of his time, organized the so-called "Holy Alliance" in an effort to dominate the world.

Has the historic imperialist urge played a role in the Soviet drive for power? I think it is clear that it has.

The third and last influence which I will mention is that chronic sense of insecurity which pervades police-state rulers. Those who rule by force inevitably fear force. In a police state the rulers have a monopoly or near monopoly of weapons. But it is never possible to arm enough policemen to rule an unruly mass without in the process arming some who themselves may prove unruly. Also, the rulers of a police state greatly fear any weapons which they do not control, and they seek to extend their power to bring these weapons under control. They cannot imagine that armaments in the hands of others may be designed purely for internal security and self-defense. That is why the Soviet leaders have so consistently and so violently expressed their opposition to the North Atlantic Treaty Organization and fought the creation of a European Defense Community. To us their fears seem mere pretense. But perhaps they do have fear, because they do not understand that if force is in the hands of those who are governed by moral law, it will not be used as a means of aggression or to violate the principles of the moral law.

This picture which I have given of the international situation is not a pleasing one. It does not hold out the prospect of any quick change for the better or any early elimination of our need for power in order to permit moral principles to take root rather than be uprooted.

However, if we do maintain power, and if we do subject it to moral law and use it truly to enable moral principles to survive, and thrive, and spread in the world, we can have hope in the future. For we know that in the long run the fruits of a spiritual faith prevail over the fruits of materialism.

The great weakness of Soviet Communist doctrine is that it denies morality. That is its Achilles heel, of which we must take advantage. We can take advantage of it if—but only if—we ourselves accept the supremacy of moral law.

"RECAPTURING THE MOOD OF OUR FOREBEARS"

Our nation was founded by the men who believed that there was a Divine Creator who endowed men with unalienable rights. They believed, as George Washington put it in his farewell address, that religion and morality are the great pillars of human happiness and that morality cannot prevail in exclusion of religious principles.

Our Federal and State Constitutions, our laws and practices, reflect the belief that there is a Being superior to ourselves who has established His own laws which can be comprehended by all human beings and that human practices should seek conformity with those laws.

Seeking first the Kingdom of God and His righteousness, many material things were added to us. We developed here an area of spiritual, intellectual, and material richness, the like of which the world has never seen. What we did caught the imagination of men everywhere and became known everywhere as "the Great American experiment." Our free society became a menace to every despot because we showed how to meet the hunger of the people for greater opportunity and for greater dignity. The tide of despotism, which at that time ran high, was rolled back and we ourselves enjoyed security.

We need to recapture that mood.

Today some seem to feel that Americanism means being tough and "hard-boiled," doing nothing unless we are quite sure that it is to our immediate short-term advantage; boasting of our own merit and seeing in others only demerit.

That is a caricature of America. Our people have always been generous to help, out of their abundance, those who are the victims of misfortune. Our forebears have traditionally had what the Declaration of Independence refers to as a decent respect for the opinion of mankind. They sought to practice the Golden Rule by doing to others as they would have others do unto them. Their conduct and example made our nation one that was respected and admired throughout the world.

So, in conclusion, I say to you who graduate from the National War College: Be proud of your association with U.S. power, which is indispensable in the world today; but remember that that power is worthy only as it is the shield behind which moral values are invigorated and spread their influence; and accept, as citizens, the obligation to preserve and enhance those moral values. They are the rich heritage that has been bequeathed us. It must be our ambition that future generations shall look back upon us, as we look back upon those who preceded us, with gratitude for the gift to our Republic of the qualities that make it noble, so that men call it blessed.

Richard M. Nixon (essay date 1959)

SOURCE: "An Appreciation of John Foster Dulles," in *Great Readings from "Life,"* Harper & Brothers Publishers, 1960, pp. 433-36.

[*In the following essay, originally published in 1959, Nixon honors Dulles for his firmness, integrity, and skill in negotiating foreign policy as United States Secretary of State.*]

I have had the privilege of knowing and working with John Foster Dulles since the time I first met him in 1948. And it was my great fortune that since the fall of 1955 the association between us was particularly close.

In a city where a political leader learns that the number of his friends goes up and down with his standing in the public opinion polls, I found Mr. Dulles' loyalty to his friends was no more affected by the latest poll than was his adherence to his own policies.

He was not unaware of his unique abilities. But he was one of those rare individuals who could accept—and even demand—from his friends constant critical examination of both his policies and his leadership. He was never guilty of that most deadly sin—unreasoned pride and conceit.

I recall at least four occasions when he was under attack when he asked for my advice. His question was not as to his policies, which he believed to be right (a view I shared), but whether he, himself, might have become too controversial to be the best spokesman for those policies.

"I never want to be a burden on the President," he often used to say to me. "As a friend, I want you to tell me whenever you believe that I have become a burden, either politically or otherwise."

He recognized the fundamental truth that a public man must never forget—that he loses his usefulness when he as an individual, rather than his policy, becomes the issue.

This trait was most in evidence on his last arduous journey to Europe when he had to call into play all his superb diplomatic talents in order to help unify the Western position on Berlin. There was seldom a moment on this trip when he was without pain. He was unable to keep down a single meal.

I asked him how he was able to carry on.

He answered, "I told my associates that they were to watch me carefully and that they were to inform me immediately whenever it appeared that my physical condition in any way impaired my ability to carry on the negotiations in which we were participating." But he was never better at the negotiating table than at this most difficult period of his life.

He afterward told me, "I never felt any pain while the negotiating was taking place. Then at the end of the day it would come down on me like a crushing weight."

So much for the quality of the man. His policies will be judged not by his dedication or his skill at the conference table but by what happens in the years ahead, when men like [Secretary of State] Christian Herter build on the foundations Mr. Dulles erected.

But whatever happens there are certain great principles which he advocated which will forever stand as a monument to his memory.

He believed that those who are called to positions of leadership in a democracy have the responsibility to lead, not just to follow public opinion. During the crisis over Quemoy and Matsu the mail, the polls and the opinion makers seemed to be overwhelmingly against the position he advocated. He told me that we had to try to change public opinion by informing the people of facts of which they might not be aware. If, after they learned the facts, the people held the same opinion, theirs of course should be the final judgment. But in this instance, his leadership helped to convince the people and thereby averted a Communist victory that could have destroyed the free world position in Asia.

History will also record that the "inflexibility" and "brinkmanship" for which he was criticized in truth represented basic principles of the highest order.

At a time when the political and intellectual climate in the West appeared to be moving slowly but steadily toward advocacy of short-sighted, opportunistic arrangements with the Soviets, Mr. Dulles' stubborn constancy sometimes appeared like an anachronism. Yet he made an unchallengeable argument for firmness where fundamentals were involved. Speaking before the National Council of Churches of Christ last November, Mr. Dulles said: "Communism is stubborn for the wrong; let us be steadfast for the right. A capacity to change is indispensable. Equally indispensable is the capacity to hold fast to that which is good. So it is that while we seek to adapt our policies to the inevitability of change, we resist aspects of change which counter the enduring principles of moral law."

When he was attacked for "brinkmanship" Mr. Dulles stood on an ancient and honorable principle—that by looking a great danger in the face we may avert it and lesser perils. He was simply taking the same position which Winston Churchill saw so well in 1939: "If you will not fight for the right when you can easily win without bloodshed; if you will not fight when your victory will be sure and not too costly; you may come to the moment when you will have to fight with all odds against you and only a precarious chance of survival."

But it is in a third area in which Mr. Dulles leaves to the free world perhaps his most lasting and valuable legacy. Some of his critics have scoffed at his advocacy of peaceful liberation of the Communist-dominated peoples and at his often reiterated faith in the eventual collapse of Communism.

Yet, what other tenable position can self-respecting free peoples take? The Communists have no hesitancy in proclaiming their faith in the eventual domination of the world by dictators. Can we be less determined in our dedication to the cause of freedom from tyranny for all people?

If we want a foreign policy and a national attitude that bends before every Communist breeze, if we have come to the point where liberty is not worth our lives, if we are becoming convinced that the future is in the hands of dictators rather than in those of free men, then we no longer need the Dulleses or their legacy. But while American greatness and American hope endure, John Foster Dulles will be remembered as one of their most effective and eloquent champions.

Hans J. Morgenthau (essay date 1961)

SOURCE: "John Foster Dulles," in *An Uncertain Tradition: American Secretaries of State in the Twentieth Century,* edited by Norman A. Graebner, McGraw-Hill Book Company, Inc., 1961, pp. 189-308.

[*In the following essay, Morgenthau examines Dulles's role as Secretary of State in relation to several factors, including Congress, the President, and general public opinion. Overall, Morgenthau argues that Dulles's work was essentially a continuation of his predecessors' foreign policies, and was aimed at maintaining the status quo while appearing to be innovative.*]

A contemporary American Secretary of State must perform two basic and difficult tasks: he must defend and promote the interests of the United States abroad, and he must establish and defend his position at home. Whereas the former task is inherent in the office, the latter is a result of five interconnected constitutional and political factors inherent in the American system of government. The position of the Secretary of State must be secured, first of all, against competition from four quarters: the President, Congress, other agencies of the executive branch, and other members of the Department of State. The fifth factor is public opinion, and it, of course, affects the Secretary's relation to the other four.

The President bears, according to the constitutional scheme, the chief responsibility for the conduct of foreign policy. This he is supposed to discharge with the help of the Secretary of State as his principal adviser and administrative officer. Yet, in actuality, the distribution of responsibility between the President and the Secretary of State has run the gamut from Presidential predominance—the President determining foreign policy without the advice and administrative support of the Secretary of State—to the predominance of the Secretary of State— the latter determining and administering foreign policy and the President merely ratifying his decisions.

The competition between the executive branch and Congress for control of American foreign policy began in Washington's administration and is the result of a constitutional distribution of functions which, in the words of Professor Corwin, "is an invitation to struggle for the privilege of directing American foreign policy." It is also the result of the dynamics of the American political system, which deprives the Secretary of State of most of the political weapons of rewards and reprisals with which the President and other members of the Cabinet can stave off congressional opposition and secure congressional support.

The need for the Secretary of State to maintain the prerogatives of his office against competition from other executive departments arises from the dispersal of responsibility for the conduct of American foreign policy among a multitude of executive departments. In 1949, the Hoover Commission, which investigated the organization of the executive branch, found that about forty-five executive agencies, aside from the Department of State, were dealing with one or another phase of foreign policy. The Secretary of State must maintain, against the parochial interests of all these agencies, the over-all direction of foreign policy.

The Secretary of State must also establish and maintain his authority within his own Department. He must keep in check the members of his staff who owe their position to political influence or who otherwise enjoy political support for independent policies.

Finally, the accomplishment of these four competitive tasks depends in great measure upon the ability of the Secretary of State to marshal public opinion at large to the support of his person and his policies. Without the support of public opinion, the Secretary of State is bound to be utterly vulnerable to competition from any of the quarters mentioned, especially, however, from Congress, which in most circumstances is likely to enjoy the public support that the Secretary of State is lacking. On the other hand, with that support secured, the Secretary of State is in a strong position vis-à-vis his competitors, especially those who, like himself, draw much of their strength from public opinion.

Thus the American Secretary of State must perform a domestic political task of great complexity and delicacy as a precondition for the performance of his primary task in the field of foreign policy. Nor are these two tasks separate in execution. Quite to the contrary, each impinges upon the other. The kind of foreign policy the Secretary of State pursues exerts an influence, favorable or unfavorable, upon his domestic position. The kind of domestic position he is able to make for himself predetermines in good measure the limits within which he is able to move on the international stage. The attempt to reconcile the demands of foreign policy and those of domestic politics, without sacrificing the indispensable substance of either, involves more complications and calls for greater finesse than any of the tasks previously mentioned. It is here that the Secretary of State faces the supreme test of his ability to do justice to the requirements of his office.

II

How has John Foster Dulles performed those tasks which impose themselves with existential force upon whoever occupies the office? What conception of the office did he bring to these tasks, and in what concrete terms did he execute them? The answers to these questions must be sought in three factors that exerted a fundamental influence on Dulles: his sense of mission, the state of mind of the Republican party, and the example of his predecessor, Dean Acheson.

Dulles's appointment to the position of Secretary of State must appear to the observer as the natural culmination of a development foreshadowed by his family background and prepared for step by step by his diplomatic career. Both his maternal grandfather, John W. Foster, after whom he had been named, and his uncle, Robert Lansing, had been Secretaries of State. Dulles had started his diplomatic career virtually at the earliest possible moment: in 1907, when he was nineteen and a junior in college, he acted as his grandfather's secretary at the Second Peace Conference at The Hague. He served in 1917 as a member of the Second Pan-American Scientific Congress and as a special agent of the Department of State in Central America. In 1918-1919 he was counsel to the American Commission to Negotiate Peace, and in 1919 he became a member of the Reparation Commission and of the Supreme Economic Council. He was a member of the American delegation to the San Francisco Conference of 1945 and to the United Nations General Assembly in 1946, 1947, 1948, and 1950. He served as adviser to the Secretary of State at meetings of the Council of Foreign Ministers in 1945, 1947, and 1949 and as consultant to the Secretary of State in 1950. In 1950-1951, as special representative of the President with the rank of ambassador, he negotiated the peace treaty with Japan and the security treaties with Australia, New Zealand, the Philippines, and Japan. When Thomas E. Dewey ran for the Presidency in 1944 and 1948, Dulles was generally regarded as his choice for Secretary of State.

To Dulles himself, this record seemed to reveal a providential design which had singled him out to be Secretary of State, which had endowed him with the qualities required for that position, and which would not let him fail. In a speech to the staff of the Department of State on the assumption of his office, Dulles pointed to the fact that his grandfather had been Secretary of State, that his uncle had been Secretary of State, and that he was now Secretary of State. His conviction that there was something virtually inevitable and foreordained in his holding this exalted position accounts at least in part for Dulles's confidence in his ability to shoulder alone the momentous responsibilities of his office and to face alone the dreadful uncertainties of foreign policy. The self-confidence which all statesmen need, faced as they are with these responsibilities and uncertainties, and which others have found in superstitions, such as astrology or other forms of soothsaying, exhaustive information and advice, or a simple faith in divine guidance, Dulles found in his sense of predestination, derived from his family background and his career and supported by a strong, self-reliant personality.

Dulles was destined to become Secretary of State as a member of a party whose support for an active but restrained foreign policy—moving somewhere between isolationism and imperialism—was still precarious at the beginning of the fifties. The Republican party had entered World War II committed to isolationism and had emerged from it with a split personality. Senator Vandenberg, strongly influenced and supported by Dulles and a minority of his party, initiated bipartisanship in foreign policy. Thus one wing of the Republican party came to approve the fundamental changes by which American foreign policy was transformed in the forties, whereas another wing, more vociferous and more influential with public opinion at large and represented by men like Senators William E. Jenner and Joseph McCarthy, remained in uncompromising opposition. Between these two groups stood a vacillating center which hankered back to isolationism but would almost, though not quite, admit that isolationism was beyond the reach of a rational foreign policy. Senator Taft was the most eminent spokesman of this group.

Dulles had to come to terms with the problem of gaining the support of his own party for his person and policies. Two roads were open to him. He could attempt to impress the internationalist wing and the wavering center with the rationality and even the inevitability of the foreign policy to which he was committed, letting the intransigent right wing wither on the vine, or else he could try to gain the support of the right wing by giving the appearance of being really one of them and of actually pursuing their policies. Dulles chose the latter course, primarily under the impact of what had happened to his predecessor.

The third fundamental experience which molded Dulles's conception of his office, and the policies realizing it, was the opportunity of witnessing, and contributing to, the fate that befell Dean Acheson. Here was a Secretary of State who was intellectually at least as well equipped for

the office as any of his predecessors since John Quincy Adams, whose dedication to the common good was exemplary, and whose achievements in fashioning a new foreign policy for the United States commensurate with its interests were outstanding. In short, in terms of the requirements of foreign policy, here was one of the best Secretaries of State the United States had ever had. Yet here was also, in terms of the requirements of domestic politics, one of the least successful Secretaries of State. For large sectors of American public opinion Acheson's State Department became synonymous with softness toward communism—if not toleration of, or even connivance in, treason. When Acheson's loyalty was attacked and his resignation asked for in Congress, not a member dared to come to his defense. Only the President's support kept him in office.

Witnessing the terrifying spectacle of a good and able man—as great a Secretary of State in terms of foreign policy as Dulles could ever hope to be—being haunted as a threat to the Republic and shunned as an outcast, Dulles resolved that what happened to Acheson would not happen to him. In consequence, to secure his domestic position became his overriding concern. To that end, he set out to achieve three objectives: to create for the American public the image of himself as a stanch and dynamic fighter against communism and thus as a Secretary of State without any of the faults attributed to his predecessor; to prevent at all costs the development of an opposition in Congress to his person and policies; and to establish and maintain a relationship with the President which would assure his control of foreign policy.

III

The creation of the image of a foreign policy radically different from that for which the preceding administration had been responsible proceeded essentially through six spectacular pronouncements: "liberation," the unleashing of Chiang Kai-shek, "agonizing reappraisal," the "new look," intervention in Indochina, and "brinkmanship."

During the election campaign of 1952 and during the first months of his tenure of office, Dulles and other spokesmen for the new administration announced that the old policy of containment, which Dulles had called in the Republican platform of 1952 "negative, futile and immoral," was to be replaced by a policy of liberation. Yet, as the London *Economist* put it as early as August 30, 1952, "Unhappily 'liberation' applied to Eastern Europe—and Asia—means either the risk of war or it means nothing. . . . 'Liberation' entails no risk of war only when it means nothing." The Eisenhower administration, however, shied away from the risk of war at least as much as had its predecessor. And when the East German revolt of June, 1953. and the Hungarian revolution of October, 1956, put the policy of liberation to the test of actual performance, it became obvious that liberation was indistinguishable from containment.

In his State of the Union message of February 2, 1953, following Dulles's public and private advice, President Eisenhower declared: "In June, 1950, following the aggressive attack on the Republic of Korea, the United States Seventh Fleet was instructed both to prevent attack upon Formosa and also to insure that Formosa should not be used as a base of operations against the Chinese Communist mainland." In view of the Chinese intervention in the Korean conflict, the President declared that he was "issuing instructions that the Seventh Fleet no longer be employed to shield Communist China." This announcement implied a fundamental change in the Far Eastern policies of the United States from the preservation of the *status quo* to the active attempt to restore Chiang Kai-shek's rule on the Asiatic mainland. In actuality, no such change occurred. Quite to the contrary, the Eisenhower administration seems to have been at least as anxious as its predecessor to limit the military activities of Chiang Kai-shek to strictly defensive measures. By making this limitation part of the agreements negotiated with Chiang Kai-shek at the end of 1954, the Eisenhower administration went even beyond the unilateral declaration of policy contained in President Truman's instruction to the Seventh Fleet of June, 1950.

On December 14, 1953, Dulles declared at the meeting of the North Atlantic Council: "If, however, the European Defense Community should not become effective, if France and Germany remain apart, so that they would again be potential enemies, then indeed there would be grave doubt whether Continental Europe could be made a place of safety. That would compel an agonizing reappraisal of the basic United States policy." This statement implied that in certain contingencies the United States might lose its interest in the military defense of Europe and leave it to its fate. This threat called forth much comment but little anxiety in Europe and elsewhere. As an incentive for France to ratify the European Defense Community, it was ineffective. For in order to take this threat seriously, one would have had to assume that the United States had committed itself to the defense of Western Europe, not because it deemed its own security dependent upon it, but because it happened to approve of the policies of certain European nations. Few observers, and no responsible statesmen, were willing to make such an assumption.

The most far-reaching and most widely commented-upon announcement of this kind, however, was Dulles's speech of January 12, 1954, proclaiming a "new look" in American foreign policy as the result of "some basic policy decisions" which the President and the National Security Council had taken. This new policy was anchored to the concept of "massive retaliation." Lester Pearson, then Canadian Secretary of State for External Affairs, thought as late as March 15, 1954, that this speech "may turn out to be one of the most important of our times." The present writer, on March 29, 1954, published an article in the *New Republic* interpreting and evaluating this speech as if it meant what it said. Yet Walter Lippmann could say on March 18 that "the official explanations of the new look have become so voluminous that it is almost a career in itself to keep up with them." Characterizing Dulles's speech as "a case of excessive salesmanship," Lippmann concluded: "There is no doubt that the words of the text convey the impression that something momentous and novel has been decided. But everything that has been said since then by the Chiefs of Staff, notably by Admiral Carney, and no less so by Mr. Dulles himself, make it plain that there has been no radical change in our strategic policy."

On the same day, the *Manchester Guardian* summed it all up by saying: "The 'new look' in American military strategy is mainly old merchandise in a new package. There is really nothing new in relying on 'massive mobile retaliatory power' as the principal safeguard of peace—nothing new, that is, except the sales campaign by which the Administration is trying to persuade the American people that some small changes make the strategy of 1954 fundamentally sounder than the strategy of 1953." On March 19, the Senate Committee on Foreign Relations was the scene of the following dialogue between Senator Mike Mansfield and Dulles, who for all practical purposes buried the "new look" under the cover of military secrecy:

> Senator Mansfield: Do you consider this new policy a new policy?
>
> Secretary Dulles: It certainly has new aspects.
>
> Senator Mansfield: What are they?
>
> Secretary Dulles: Well, I am sorry I cannot go into that here. All I can say to you, and you will have to take it on faith, is that a series of new decisions have been taken by the National Security Council and many have been involved, close, and difficult decisions, but there is today on the record a series of decisions which are largely derived from this basic philosophy which were not there a year and a half ago.

Although the "new look" was the most sweeping of these announcements, the official declarations concerning the Indochina War were politically and militarily the most serious; for they dealt, not with general principles of United States policy, but with a concrete situation which required action here and now. On March 25, 1954, the President declared at his news conference that the defense of Indochina was of "transcendent importance." On March 29, the Secretary of State announced: "Under the conditions of today, the imposition on Southeast Asia of the political system of Communist Russia and its Chinese Communist ally, by whatever means, would be a grave threat to the whole free community. The United States feels that that possibility should not be passively accepted, but should be met by united action. This might have serious risks, but these risks are far less than would face us a few years from now if we dare not be resolute today." The President and the Secretary of State referred to Indochina as the cork in the bottle of Southeast Asia and as the first in a row of dominoes whose fall would necessarily cause the downfall of the others. Yet no action of any kind reflected even faintly the conception of policy which these words seemed to convey. It was, in the words of the *Economist* of August 21, 1954, this "spectacle of vociferous in-action" which led to the "worst diplomatic disaster in recent American history."

The most sensational and also the most patently implausible of these pronouncements concerned "brinkmanship." In an article in *Life* magazine of January 16, 1956, Dulles was reported as having declared, in the course of an interview, that his policy of firmness and daring, fully supported by the President, saved the peace and protected the interests of the United States on three occasions: in Korea, Indochina, and the Formosa Straits. "Of course," Dulles was quoted as having said, "we were brought to the verge of war. The ability to get to the verge without getting into the war is the necessary art. If you cannot master it, you inevitably get into war. . . . We walked to the brink and we looked it in the face. We took strong action." The article praises this technique as "the greatest display of personal diplomacy since the great days of the Franklin-Adams-Jefferson triumvirate in the Europe of the 1780's."

Although this is obviously not the place to test these claims in detail against the available historic evidence, it must be pointed out that, in regard to Indochina, Dulles was prevented from going to war by the unwillingness of the President and of Great Britain to do so. Whether the government of the United States had really resolved to use atomic weapons against Manchuria in June, 1953, if the Communists renewed the war in Korea and whether the Communists were deterred by that knowledge are at present matters of speculation. It is also a moot question whether the congressional resolution of January, 1955, authorizing the President to defend the offshore islands in the Formosa Straits under certain conditions was interpreted by both the administration and the Chinese government as a threat implying the certainty of atomic war. Yet what in actuality was either speculative or simply untrue was presented, in the *Life* article, as a set of historic facts supporting a most favorable evaluation of Dulles's policies.

Dulles's six major pronouncements served the purpose of creating the image of a new, forceful, aggressive foreign policy in order to gain the support of public opinion for both the person of the Secretary of State and the foreign policies he pursued, policies which were not essentially different from those of his predecessor and were certainly not different in the respects in which they were claimed to be. These endeavors culminated in the first Cabinet meeting ever televised, in which Dulles reported on the London Conference which met from September 28 to October 3, 1954. Arthur Krock recalled in the *New York Times* of May 6, 1960, that "the television show . . . was billed as a 'Cabinet meeting' . . . and turned out to be more of a sham performance than any rigged quiz program." In the *Manchester Guardian Weekly* of October 23, 1954, Alistair Cooke gave a striking account of that performance:

The whole show had a relaxed, closed-door air, almost like a Cabinet meeting. In the lead part . . . Mr. Dulles gave a naturalistic performance of great ease and articulateness. Mr. Henry Cabot Lodge made the most of a single-sentence tribute to the President for his peaceful atomic energy proposals. Cast as the unsleeping watchdog of the people's purse, Mr. Secretary of the Treasury Humphrey expressed with moving verisimilitude his concern that the Paris Agreement should not cost the American taxpayer one extra nickel. Mrs. Hobby conveyed an intelligent anxiety over the Saar.

Only Secretary of Agriculture Ezra Benson, an artless man from the West, had to be prodded into his line by Mr. Dulles, who suggested after an anxious pause that some of them might now be wondering "how the Soviet Union is taking this." Mr. Benson was indeed wondering just that, and made an alert retrieve. It was the only missed cue in an otherwise flawless performance, surely an enviable record for any amateur dramatic company.

IV

The position of the Secretary of State vis-á-vis Congress was secured by two basic tactics. Dulles disarmed the potential congressional opposition, consisting of the right wing of the Republican party, by pursuing its policies and by allowing it to exert a governing influence, at least temporarily, over certain personal and substantive matters which remained but nominally under the control of the Secretary of State.

Dulles's execution of the personnel policies of the congressional right wing was predicated on the assumption, with which the Republican party had attacked the preceding administration, that the Department of State at the very least was not a reliable guardian of the interests of the United States vis-á-vis other nations and, more particularly, Communist ones. In carrying out these policies, Dulles proceeded in two stages: the first was a purge and the second the application of stringent security regulations. By the end of 1953, most members of the Foreign Service who had held high positions in the Department of State had been dismissed, had voluntarily resigned, or had been transferred to politically nonsensitive positions.

Executive Order No. 10450 of April 27, 1953, as applied to the Department of State, in effect institutionalized the purge by establishing extremely stringent security regulations for employment, promotion, and surveillance. The case of John Paton Davies, Jr., a prominent member of the Foreign Service, who underwent nine security investigations before he was dismissed, is but an extreme example of what was then a fairly typical situation. His case is typical also in that it reveals clearly the political purpose of the purges which, in so far as the Secretary of State was concerned, were undertaken primarily in order to satisfy the potential opposition in Congress. Davies, who had been stationed in China after World War II and who afterward joined the Policy Planning Staff, was a favorite target of that opposition. There can be no doubt, even though the documentary evidence to prove it is not yet available, that Davies was deliberately sacrificed, regardless of the merits of his case, and was subjected to as many security investigations as were necessary to prove him a security risk. It is revealing in this connection that, after the last investigating board had rendered the desired unfavorable verdict and Davies had been dismissed, he received a telephone call from the Secretary of State congratulating him upon his attitude before the board and authorizing him to use Dulles's name as a reference in his search for a new position.

Executive Order No. 10450, which provided the legal basis for these proceedings, was a general order, issued under the authority of the President for all executive departments. Yet since this order left wide discretion to the heads of the departments, the Secretary of State was responsible for the way it was implemented in his own Department. Not only did he establish, and suffer to be established, a rigid system of security regulations, but he also added to this system measures of his own. Department Circular No. 95 of April 15, 1954, for instance, imposed upon all officials of the Department of State the duty to be informers:

> I am aware that no agency of the government can improve, or even maintain its level of effectiveness unless it is receiving a stream of new ideas and constructive criticisms. I hope that the inspection operation will be the focal reception point of that stream. I have told Mr. McLeod that in his capacity as administrator of the inspection operation he should be available at any time to receive personally from any of our people the benefit of their thinking on improving operations and procedures or on other problems, official and personal.
>
> In brief, I regard the internal inspection operation of the Department as one of its most important concerns. Its success will depend upon the cooperation and aid received generally from employees of the Department.

Dulles's efforts to disarm the potential opposition by pursuing its policies were assured success by the ability of that opposition to place its representatives in key positions within the Department of State. The right-wing bloc thus came to dominate the Bureau of Security, whose leading officials controlled, directly or indirectly, security, consular affairs, personnel, and inspection of United States missions abroad. The bureau adopted the political philosophy and the policies of the congressmen to whom its principal members owed both their positions and their primary loyalties. It reported to them and executed their orders. To an extent which changed with the ebbs and tides of political fortune, it was these congressmen, and not the President or the Secretary of State, who determined the operations of the Department of State and its affiliated agencies.

The most spectacular instance of this extraconstitutional influence that has come to light is provided by the Inter-national Information Administration. The report published by Martin Merson, the chief consultant to the Director of that agency, leaves no doubt that, at least from February through July, 1953, Senator McCarthy and his friends in Congress had taken over the functions which, according to the Constitution, the President and the Secretary of State are supposed to perform. These members of Congress determined, in large measure, both the substantive and the personnel policies of the International Information Administration. It was to them that the top officials of the agency reported, it was their approval which they had to seek, and it was their orders which they were supposed to execute. And when they finally incurred the displeasure of their congressional masters, they had to resign.

In the *New York Times* of January 17, 1954, five of the most distinguished older diplomats of the United States, four of whom have been Ambassadors and an equal number Under or Assistant Secretaries of State, summarized the "sinister results" of these policies:

> The conclusion has become inescapable, for instance, that a Foreign Service officer who reports on persons and events to the very best of his ability and who makes recommendations which at the time he conscientiously believes to be in the interest of the United States may subsequently find his loyalty and integrity challenged and may even be forced out of the service and discredited forever as a private citizen. A premium therefore has been put upon reporting and upon recommendations which are ambiguously stated or so cautiously set forth as to be deceiving.
>
> When any such tendency begins its insidious work it is not long before accuracy and initiative have been sacrificed to acceptability and conformity. The ultimate result is a threat to national security. In this connection the history of the Nazi and Fascist foreign services before the Second World War is pertinent.
>
> The forces which are working for conformity from the outside are being reinforced by the present administrative set-up within the Department of State which subordinates normal personnel administration to considerations of security.
>
> It is obvious, of course, that candidates for the Foreign Service should be carefully investigated before appointment and that their work should at all times be under the exacting scrutiny of their professional superiors. But when initial investigation attaches undue importance to such factors as even a temporary departure from conservative political and economic views, casual association with persons holding views not currently in fashion or subscription to a periodical labeled as "liberal"; when subsequent investigation is carried to the point of delaying a promotion list for a year and routine transfers from one post to another; when investigations of individual officers must be kept up-to-date to within ninety days; when an easy path has been opened to even the anonymous

informer; and when the results of these investigations are evaluated not by persons experienced in the Foreign Service or even acquainted at firsthand with conditions abroad, but by persons of quite different experience, it is relevant to inquire whether we are not laying the foundations of a Foreign Service competent to serve a totalitarian government rather than the government of the United States as we have heretofore known it.

Fear is playing an important part in American life at the present time. As a result the self-confidence, the confidence in others, the sense of fair play and the instinct to protect the rights of the non-conformist are—temporarily, it is to be hoped—in abeyance. But it would be tragic if this fear, expressing itself in an exaggerated emphasis on security, should lead us to cripple the Foreign Service, our first line of national defense, at the very time when its effectiveness is essential to our filling the place which history has assigned to us.

As far as personnel policy in the State Department and Foreign Service was concerned, the potential opposition was conciliated simply by the dual device of pursuing its policies and handing over to it in good measure the control of those policies. With regard to substantive policies, three different devices were used to propitiate the opposition. First, the great pronouncements, which, as we have seen, were intended to impress public opinion at large with the novelty, dynamism, and aggressiveness of Dulles's foreign policy, served the same purpose for congressional opinion. Although the foreign policies which had been established by the preceding administration and which had proved their worth by their success were essentially continued, the Secretary's pronouncements created the impression of a succession of drastic innovations. Second, the Department shunned actual initiative and innovation where they were called for by new conditions, for a new departure in foreign policy might antagonize the potential opposition and was bound to create the domestic political complications that Dulles was resolved to forestall. Thus the twofold need of giving the appearance of innovation and avoiding it in practice resulted in a consistent contrast between what American foreign policy was declared to be and what it actually was.

In regard to the Far East, however, Dulles did permit a certain degree of innovation. His third major conciliatory tactic was to adjust the substance of foreign policy to the preferences of the potential opposition for the cause of Chiang Kai-shek, both by identifying himself, at least to some extent, with those preferences and by handing over the control of foreign policy in that area to men committed to pursue those preferences vigorously. There can be no doubt that the majority of the leading officials who advised Eisenhower on foreign affairs during his first years in office were opposed to his policies in the Far East. That majority was composed of two groups: by far the larger of these groups wanted to advance toward a more aggressive position, even at the risk of a limited war with Communist China; the smaller group would have liked to retreat into less exposed positions. The

actual policy of the United States was to maintain an intermediate position between those two extremes, which followed the line of least resistance by trying neither to advance nor to retreat but to maintain the *status quo.*

Yet a rational examination of the forces opposing each other in the Far East and their probable dynamics could only lead to the conclusion that a commitment to the *status quo* was not likely to be tenable in the long run. Both the United States and Communist China would have to go forward or backward; they were not likely to remain indefinitely where they were. Why, then, was the policy of the United States based upon an assumption that could not be supported by rational argument? The answer is to be found in the surrender to the concepts, if not the policies, of an opposition whose reasoning, contradictory in itself, could not provide the basis for a rational policy but whose voice, by default of the executive branch, was powerful enough to mold public opinion.

Public opinion with regard to Communist China was dominated by two strong contradictory desires: to make good somehow the defeat which the United States had suffered through the defection of China to the Communist camp and to do so without getting involved in a major war on the continent of Asia. The opposition presented a program designed to meet these two emotional demands. It promised the overthrow of the Communist regime of China and the restoration of Chiang Kai-shek's rule through aerial bombardment and a naval blockade, using Formosa as a springboard. Yet a careful reading of the minutes of the joint congressional committee investigating, in 1951, the dismissal of General MacArthur can leave no doubt in the mind of the unbiased reader about the military and political emptiness of this program. For the opposition could not devise any policy, short of all-out war, that would assure the destruction of the Communist regime of China. In short, the program of the opposition served as an effective instrument to achieve an illusory reconciliation of policy with popular demands, but since the two could not be reconciled in practice, it offered no basis for a rational policy.

Nevertheless, the Eisenhower administration, frightened like its predecessor by the specter of public opinion, at least appeared to have accepted the objectives and expectations of the opposition and thus allowed its own policies to be judged by the standards of the opposition. By these standards, its policies could not help being found wanting. For, on the one hand, the administration was responsible enough not to embark upon military adventures; on the other, it committed itself at least to the defense of Formosa, whose indispensability for the defense of the United States was accepted as a dogma by government and opposition alike. In consequence, the executive branch found itself continuously on the defensive, apologizing, as it were, for not living up to its own standards and feeling compelled from time to time to substitute for policy a momentous announcement or a grandiose gesture suggesting the imminence of forceful action. The executive branch had thus become the prisoner of the opposition. Too responsible to do what the opposition wanted it to do but prevented by its fear of public opinion from devising and executing a positive policy of its own, the President and Secretary were reduced to having no policy at all, while trying to make it appear as though they were following, however cautiously, in the footsteps of the opposition.

V

Dulles's task of making his position and policies secure with public opinion and Congress was greatly complicated by his uncertainty about the extent to which public opinion and Congress were willing to endorse him as Secretary of State and to support his policies. It was this uncertainty, amounting in Dulles's mind to extreme doubt, which resulted not only in his opening the gates of the State Department to the potential opposition and allowing it to influence substantive policies but also in his making pronouncements on foreign policy that contrasted with the policies he actually pursued.

Dulles's task of making his position and policies secure with the President encountered no such complications and hence necessitated no such complex measures for its achievement. President Eisenhower very soon trusted Dulles so completely and admired his ability as Secretary of State so unreservedly that he gave him, for all practical purposes, a free hand to conduct the foreign policy of the United States as he saw fit. Although Dulles was continuously and deeply concerned with the support he could expect from Congress and public opinion, he did not need to worry about the President's support.

Echoing Thomas E. Dewey's statement that Dulles was "no ordinary mortal" in his ability to understand and conduct foreign policy, President Eisenhower paid frequent tribute to Dulles as the greatest Secretary of State he had known. On the occasion of Dulles's fiftieth anniversary as a diplomat, on June 15, 1957, President Eisenhower wrote him a personal letter, saying: "Your accomplishments will establish you as one of the greatest of our Secretaries of State." And when Dulles's tenure as Secretary of State was at an end, President Eisenhower said in his press conference of April 18, 1959: "I personally believe he has filled his office with greater distinction than any other man our country has known—a man of tremendous character and courage, intelligence and wisdom." The President acted in accordance with his estimate of Dulles's ability, for he almost always followed his Secretary's advice in things great and small. The only important instance on record of Dulles's having been overruled by Eisenhower occurred in 1954 when the President refused to accept Dulles's advice to intervene with military means in the Indochina War.

Although Dulles did not need to exert much effort to create his extraordinary relationship with the President, he was from the very outset careful lest it be disturbed by third parties. And, as in his relations with public opinion and Congress, it was his knowledge of what had happened to other Secretaries of State in this respect that determined his attitude. According to a report by James Reston in the *New York Times* of February 2, 1958, Dulles remarked privately at the beginning of his tenure of office "that he would oppose any system of divided authority between the White House staff and the State Department for the conduct of foreign policy." He called attention to the examples of his own uncle, Robert Lansing, who had been hampered by the influence Colonel House had exerted upon Woodrow Wilson, and of Edward R. Stettinius, Jr., many of whose Secretarial functions had been performed by Franklin D. Roosevelt's assistant, Harry Hopkins. Dulles concluded, therefore, that "he could not take lightly any attempt to establish in the White House a competing center of foreign policy information and negotiation."

Thus Dulles opposed successfully a plan, devised by the White House staff, to reorganize the office of the President by creating three Vice Presidents, one of whom would have been in charge of foreign policy. He did not oppose, in 1956, the appointment of General Bedell Smith, who had served as his Under Secretary, as special adviser to the President in the field of foreign policy; this appointment fell afoul of the opposition of Herbert Hoover, Jr., then Under Secretary of State. But the men who were actually appointed to similar positions, however limited in scope—C. D. Jackson, Nelson A. Rockefeller, William Jackson, and Harold Stassen—met with Dulles's opposition and sooner or later had to yield to it by resigning. Of these conflicts, the most dramatic was the controversy with Stassen, the President's adviser for disarmament. Stassen, who had strong ideas of his own on the conduct of disarmament negotiations, challenged openly the authority of the Secretary of State, and the latter did not hesitate to take up the challenge. To this conflict over policy was added a clash of personalities. The result was a complete triumph for Dulles. In February, 1958, Stassen was forced to resign, the possibility of his further employment by the Eisenhower administration having come to an abrupt end.

VI

The position of Dulles vis-à-vis other executive departments and the Department of State itself was made secure both by his unique relationship to the President and by his extraordinary forensic ability and force of personality. When Dulles spoke in the councils of the government, he spoke not only as the President's principal adviser on foreign affairs, as would any Secretary of State, but also and patently as the President's alter ego. When Dulles spoke, it was for all practical purposes the President of the United States who spoke. The voice of so trusted and admired a servant was not challenged lightly. This relationship between the President and his Secretary of State made it impossible from the outset for any executive department to bypass the Secretary of State by gaining the ear of the President and to pursue a foreign policy of its own in competition with that of the Secretary of State. Yet that same relationship allowed the Secretary of State to bypass other executive departments, either singly or assembled in the National Security Council, and to obtain without bureaucratic complications the President's approval for what he had decided.

The voice of the Secretary of State, however, carried an authority derived not only from his identification with the President but also from the qualities of Dulles's personality and mind. In force of personality, only the Secretary of the Treasury, George Humphrey, was his equal in the councils of government; in knowledge of foreign affairs and skill of argumentation, Dulles was clearly superior to all the President's other advisers. Thus, in the National Security Council, the Cabinet, and the informal discussions on foreign policy, Dulles generally carried the day. He was in uncontested control of American foreign policy. In its conduct he had no rival above him, that is, in the President; beside him, that is, in other executive departments; or below him, that is, in the Department of State itself.

Rivalry from within the Department was precluded by two facets of Dulles's *modus operandi*. It has been frequently asserted that Dulles carried American foreign policy under his hat. Although this is an exaggeration, it contains an element of truth. It is true that Dulles used to confer with a small number of aides and that these conferences, especially during President Eisenhower's first term, were frequently characterized by a vigorous give-and-take. But they apparently served less to provide the Secretary with information and advice than to give him an opportunity of trying his ideas out in informal debate. The Department of State at large was not affected by these debates in its day-by-day operations and was hardly aware of them. Nor was the Secretary of State, in either his thinking or his decisions, much affected by what the Department of State knew and did. Dulles devised the foreign policies of the United States by drawing upon his own knowledge, experience, and insight, and the Department of State merely implemented these policies.

Dulles assumed personal responsibility, not only for formulating American foreign policy, but also, in good measure, for carrying it out, at least on the higher levels of execution. The public image of Dulles as a constant traveler comes indeed close to reality. During his tenure of office, he traveled 559,988 miles, of which 479,286 were outside the United States. He visited 47 nations— France, 19 times; Great Britain, 11 times; Italy, 4 times; and West Germany, 6 times. By personally performing many of the major political functions which had traditionally been performed by high-ranking diplomats, Dulles greatly reduced opportunities for the latter to take political initiative of any kind. By divorcing his operations to a considerable degree from those of the Department of State and at the same time taking over the higher political functions of the Foreign Service, Dulles for all practical purposes disarmed the Department of State as a rival in the management of foreign affairs. It must also be kept in

mind that the purge of 1953 and the regime of surveillance accompanying and following it had made it inadvisable for a member of the Department of State to develop a foreign policy of his own.

Thus the *Life* article quoted above had a point when it commented:

> Dulles . . . altered drastically the basic concept of the job of Secretary of State. . . .
>
> President Truman's Secretaries of State worked essentially in the pattern of the administrative executive. They counted time away from Washington as serious neglect of the Department. Dulles took the opposite view. He regarded too much time spent in Washington as neglect of the U.S. task of free world leadership.
>
> Reverting to an older tradition, he undertook personal direction of the country's foreign affairs, assigning himself the role of No. 1 diplomat of the U.S. The day-to-day routine of departmental administration he has delegated to his undersecretaries. . . .

However, operational efficiency was bound to suffer from Dulles's methods of securing his position from the rivalry of subordinates and of other executive departments. The price of his success was lack of political coordination for all concerned. In some cases the Secretary made decisions without regard to political and military information available in the Department of State and other executive agencies; in other cases he neglected to prepare the Department of State and the related agencies for the policies to be adopted. For instance, the concept of massive retaliation, taken at its face value, was obsolete from the military point of view when Dulles presented it as the "new look" of American foreign policy in 1954. On the other hand, the decision to intervene in Lebanon in 1958 took many high officials of the State Department by the same surprise that it did the general public.

VII

Comparing Dulles's conception of the office of Secretary of State with the results of his administration of the office, one cannot doubt that he was eminently successful. Everywhere he seemed to achieve his purposes. When he took office, he resolved that what had happened to Dean Acheson would not happen to him; that he would make himself master of American foreign policy, without competition from any of the quarters from which such competition had traditionally come; that he would give the appearance of being the initiator of new, dynamic, and successful foreign policies. Dulles accomplished what he had set out to do. Yet it is characteristic of the dilemma which of necessity faces a modern Secretary of State that Dulles had to pay a price for his triumph in making his position and policies secure on the domestic political scene, just as Acheson had to pay a price for shielding his foreign policies from the intrusion of domestic politics. Although what happened to Acheson did not happen to Dulles, something else did. The price Dulles had to pay for his domestic success consisted in the stagnation of American foreign policy and the diminution in prestige that both his person and his office suffered abroad.

Although Dulles consistently strove to make it appear that his foreign policies were different from, and superior to, the foreign policies of his predecessors, it is a historic fact that he essentially continued those very policies. Refusal to recognize the legitimacy of the *status quo* in Europe and defense of the *status quo* in Europe and elsewhere through containment, as well as foreign aid, were the cornerstones both of his and his predecessors' foreign policies. Dulles introduced only two major variations: he endeavored to extend the policy of military containment, originally applied to Europe, systematically to the Middle East and Asia through a network of alliances, and he postulated the inadmissibility of violence as an instrument of national policy, putting that principle into effect by opposing the 1956 invasion of Egypt by France, Great Britain, and Israel.

Regardless of the intrinsic merits of these policies, it is hardly open to doubt that they were not sufficient to meet the new issues arising from the growing military, economic, and political power of the Soviet Union, the emergence of Africa from colonial rule, the unrest in Latin America, and the endemic crisis of the Atlantic alliance. A case can of course be made in support of the thesis that Dulles, acting essentially as the resourceful advocate of his client, the United States, was contitutionally incapable of transcending his responsibility to defend the position in which he found his client, that is, the *status quo,* and of creating new situations by virtue of new policies more in tune with the interests of the United States in a new environment. However, even if Dulles had had the attributes of the creative statesman, he would have been greatly handicapped in his creative task by his overriding concern with his domestic position. To stand as still as possible while appearing to move was the safest course to take in view of this concern, and so was the limitation of any actual movement to the military sphere. A fresh political initiative, a really creative political effort, would in all likelihood have raised a domestic political issue, dividing Congress and public opinion at large into supporters and opponents, and it was such a division which Dulles was resolved to forestall.

The support which Dulles enjoyed at home was not matched by a similar response from abroad. Neither his person nor his policies were popular with foreign statesmen and foreign peoples. To a degree, unpopularity is the price that powerful nations and forceful personalities pay for their power and force, and to that extent it cannot be helped. In Dulles's case, however, the negative foreign reaction was in good measure the direct result of the preoccupation with domestic support that dictated both the conception and the administration of his office. For-

eign public opinion and foreign statesmen were more sharply aware than American public opinion could be of the contrast between what American foreign policy was declared to be and what it actually was. Once this contrast had developed into a consistent pattern, Dulles's public and private pronouncements were bound to be carefully scrutinized abroad for their real meaning. Since foreign statesmen could not be sure that Dulles's policies would conform to his pronouncements, they lost confidence in his person and his policies.

Dulles's *modus operandi* also contributed to the distrust he ultimately encountered abroad. By concentrating not only the direction but, to a large extent, also the implementation of foreign policy in his own hands, he escaped the handicap of involvement with the bureaucracy of the State Department, but he thus created another hazard. By taking over the functions ambassadors have traditionally performed, Dulles deprived himself of that protection with which ambassadors are intended to shield their chiefs from too frequent contacts with their opposite numbers. Such contacts breed not only familiarity but also distrust; for it is in the nature of diplomacy to try, sometimes by devious means, to use other statesmen for its own purposes. The statesman who has been so used for some length of time is likely to get tired of, and lose confidence in, the man who has so used him, and then it is time to replace that man. For that reason ambassadors frequently become expendable after a few years of service in a particular capital and are transferred elsewhere. The foreign minister who assumes the task of his ambassadors simultaneously in many capitals cannot easily be replaced when, for the same reason, his usefulness has been impaired. Thus he carries on with his prestige damaged and his trustworthiness compromised.

Dulles compounded the liability inherent in his *modus operandi* by his use of the advocate's technique. The advocate, trying to advance his client's case as far as possible, can afford to disregard the interests and reactions of other parties who have advocates of their own, both relying upon the judge to sift the truth from ex parte statements, hyperbole, and deception. What the advocate can afford, the foreign minister cannot. For the foreign minister is not only the advocate of his nation, but, in a manner of speaking, also the advocate of the other side and the judge who recognizes and respects the interests of the other side and at least tentatively decides how the two interests ought to be reconciled. The foreign minister who limits himself to being the advocate of his nation will be acclaimed at home as the stanch defender of the national interest, but he will be handicapped in his conduct of foreign policy because he will be distrusted personally and will be incapable of performing the supreme task of diplomacy: to create out of disparate and contradictory national interests a higher harmony. [A close associate of Dulles has graphically described in private conversation one facet of Dulles's technique and its results. He compared Dulles dealing with two foreign ministers with a man who had to explain the same landscape to two associates. Knowing that foreign minister A was interested in mountains, he would tell him only about the mountains. Knowing that foreign minister B was interested in valleys, he would tell him only about the valleys. When the two foreign ministers later compared notes, they both felt that they had been deceived.]

Such was the price in terms of substantive foreign policy that Dulles had to pay for his domestic triumph. Did it have to be paid? The answer to that question depends upon one's judgment of the strength of the potential domestic opposition and of the need for different foreign policies. This writer is convinced that the price was unnecessarily high by far; for Dulles, fully supported by President Eisenhower's unprecedented prestige, could have pursued whatever foreign policies he chose without fear of a domestic opposition. But, then, would different foreign policies have been desirable, and would Dulles have wanted to pursue them had he not feared that opposition? Future historians will debate these questions, and perhaps history will one day answer them.

Gordon A. Craig (essay date 1964)

SOURCE: "John Foster Dulles and American Statecraft," in *War, Politics, and Diplomacy: Selected Essays,* Frederick A. Praeger, Publishers, 1966, pp. 262-80.

[*In the following essay, originally delivered as a lecture in 1964, Craig surveys Dulles's qualifications and tenure as secretary of state. While acknowledging Dulles's faults, such as occasional lapses of precision or tact, Craig emphasizes his successes and particularly grants him "credit for the recovery of western unity and will."*]

It may be that some of what follows will arouse disagreement, for my subject makes this almost inevitable. Let me begin, therefore, with a statement that would be hard to contest: namely, that John Foster Dulles was not a popular man. Indeed, it would be difficult to think of an American Secretary of State who was less beloved during his term of office than Dulles. In his own country he was detested by liberals in general and the Democratic Party in particular. Even in his own party he was the object of bitter criticism, which came not only from the extreme right wing but also from Republicans who occupied leading positions in the Department of State and the missions abroad. Finally, large sections of the populations of foreign lands regarded him with aversion, and these included the subjects of some of his country's closest allies. A lot of water will have to flow down the Spree before a John-Foster-Dulles-Allee[1] graces London or Paris, and I know of no such boulevard in Washington.[2] A movement to repair this omission is hardly to be expected as long as the Democrats remain in power or even—if I interpret Senator Goldwater's interview with *Der Spiegel* correctly[3]—in the event that that statesman should be elected in November.

Dislike of Dulles as a person has also characterized a good part of the literature about him and the events with which he dealt. Thus, his critics are generally not content to list what they consider to be his faulty judgments and his errors of commission or omission but seem to feel compelled to ascribe these to moral obliquity and weakness of character, the more violent of them charging that he was not only wrong but hypocritical, disingenuous, treacherous, and, under pressure, cowardly. Typical of this kind of writing is Herman Finer's book on the Suez crisis of 1956, in which the author scoffs at Dulles' religious faith (with ponderous asides about his pharisaism, his "Calvinistically zealous" behavior, his "religiosity," "sanctimoniousness," and "self-righteousness," and with low-burlesque passages like: "October 25 was a particularly glorious day in Dulles' office. . . . The Soviet Empire was on the decline. Faith had been justified. The sinners were being whipped at last. God was not mocked!") and accuses him of "open and disguised panic before Russian power," of being "intimidated by what Moscow *might* do," of "quailing" before the Russian specter, and of much else.[4] Finer is a liberal, but his kind of criticism is not restricted to the left; during Dulles' lifetime, similar charges, couched in ideological rather than biblical terminology, were made about him by people whose political position was close to that of the John Birch Society.

It is not my purpose here to defend John Foster Dulles, but rather to try to explain why his policy as Secretary of State made such extreme (and, all things considered, unjustified) criticisms credible to so many people; to show how his diplomatic style was determined not only by his own personality and character, but also by the domestic political situation in which he found himself; and, finally, to hazard a tentative appraisal of his accomplishment and his stature. I use the word tentative deliberately, for it is obviously impossible at this time to say anything that would be final. Not until the Dulles Papers, currently being assembled at Princeton University, are made available to scholars will a definitive judgment of the career of this extraordinarily difficult man be feasible; and it is unlikely that those files will be opened for at least another decade.[5]

I

One of the crimes most frequently laid at Dulles' door by his critics is the fact that he had the temerity to want to be Secretary of State. Exactly why this should be considered reprehensible in a country in which every red-blooded American boy is, or was, supposed to want to grow up to be President is not at all clear. Part of the reason is doubtless that many Americans have always had a deep suspicion of the Department of State, because it deals with foreign affairs and, indeed, with foreigners, a dangerous and obviously un-American occupation.[6] But there is also a tendency among some writers to regard Dulles' ambition as both vain and presumptuous.

Yet it is easy to find a more generous explanation. If Dulles persisted in defying the parochialism of many of his countrymen, it was partly because the career of diplomacy was a kind of tradition in his family; and if he had confidence in his own abilities in the field of foreign affairs, he had good reason to do so, for he had a long and systematic apprenticeship in this calling before becoming Secretary. Both his grandfather on his mother's side, John Watson Foster, and one of his uncles by marriage, Robert Lansing, served as Secretaries of State, the first under President Benjamin Harrison and the second under Woodrow Wilson; and it would have been unnatural if this had had no effect upon the young Dulles in the formative stages of his career. He once said that, after the Bible and Shakespeare, his grandfather's memoirs was the work to which he most frequently returned;[7] and after he became Secretary himself his desk at the Department was flanked by portraits of Foster and Lansing.[8]

His own practical experience in diplomacy had begun long years before those pictures were hung and, indeed, some years before his uncle had moved into the gray pile on Pennsylvania Avenue which used to be the heart of American statecraft. In 1907, while still an under-graduate at Princeton University, he accompanied John Watson Foster to the Second Hague Peace Conference, where his grandfather served as counsel to the Chinese delegation and he himself as its secretary. It was an unusual assignment for an American college student (although he apparently did not think so, writing of it quite matter-of-factly in the fifth reunion yearbook of his class[9]), but it was not an inappropriate one, for it began the preoccupation with the tangled problem of devising means for preserving international peace which he possessed for the rest of his life.

After graduating from Princeton in June 1908 as class valedictorian, Dulles studied for a time at the Sorbonne and then buckled down to the task of qualifying himself for the practice of the law. But the war in Europe soon drew him back into the world of diplomacy. In March 1917 he was selected by President Wilson and Robert Lansing for the job of special envoy of the Department of State to Panama, Costa Rica, and Nicaragua, apparently to make soundings concerning the possibilities of alliance in the event of American involvement in the European conflict, but also, by his own admission, to investigate rumors of German subversion in those countries.[10] After the United States became a belligerent, he was commissioned in the army and made head of the Economic Section of the Positive Military Intelligence Division of the General Staff. Six months later, he was seconded to the War Trade Board, where he not only served as liaison officer with the War Industries Board and the General Staff and coordinator of the joint planning of the three bodies but also carried on extensive negotiations with Dutch shipping firms and with trade delegations from Denmark, Switzerland, and Spain, with a view to limiting neutral exports to Germany by means of preemptive buying.

When the war ended, Dulles resigned his commission and was immediately appointed to the United States delegation to the Paris Peace Conference as counsel on reparations matters. In this capacity he helped formulate the American position, defended it in discussions with other governments, and, once the principles had been agreed upon, helped to draft the reparations sections of the treaty itself.[11] Nor did the signature of the Treaty of Versailles terminate his part in the European settlement. At the President's request, he remained in Paris to work out the reparations and financial aspects of the treaties with Austria-Hungary and Bulgaria; he participated in the first negotiations with the Germans concerning deliveries of shipping and coal and was the American member of the Inter-Allied Commission that established political authority in the areas of occupation; and, in the first months of 1920, after a brief period in the United States, he was back in Europe, studying the effects of the economic clauses of the treaty in Germany, Austria-Hungary and Czechoslovakia. In March 1920 he witnessed the first of the ominous convulsions that were in the end to destroy the Weimar Republic—the Kapp *Putsch* in Berlin and the subsequent Communist disorders in the Rhineland.[12]

The years that followed were devoted for the most part to the law, and in 1921, at the age of 32, Dulles became partner in the prominent New York firm of Sullivan and Cromwell. But this position too broadened his acquaintance of foreign affairs, for Sullivan and Cromwell had many European interests, and Dulles traveled continually to the continent and took part in a series of important cases that involved dealings with international or foreign firms and banks. At the same time, he gave legal advice to the underwriters of the Dawes loans, cooperated in the formulation of the Young Plan, and collaborated with Jean Monnet in working out the Polish Stabilization Plan.[13] In this way, he came to know Europe well, particularly France and Germany. During these years he also visited China and Japan and methodically informed himself about those countries.

In the years before the outbreak of the Second World War, Dulles became concerned about the fragility of the world order and increasingly interested in the part that organized religion might play in building a better basis for security and international justice. It was logical, therefore, that in 1939 he should have taken a leading part in the foundation of the Commission for a Just and Durable Peace, whose parent body was the Federal Council of Churches, representing some 25 million Christians. The Commission was designed to work for an international comity of peaceful nations that would revise the international treaty structure once peace was restored, adjust the public law to changed world conditions, promote the liberation of colonial dependencies, and secure recognition of the right of all peoples to intellectual and religious liberty.

Dulles became so well known through his work for the Commission that, in 1944, when Thomas E. Dewey became Republican candidate for the Presidency, he asked him to serve as the party's chief spokesman on foreign policy. In the years that followed, he won equal recognition from the Democrats. In 1946, 1947, 1948, and 1950 he was invited to join the United States delegation to the U.N. General Assembly; and, as special adviser to Secretaries of State Byrnes, Marshall, and Acheson, he took part in the meetings of the Council of Foreign Ministers in London in 1945, in London and Moscow in 1947, and in Paris in 1949. In the course of these meetings, he acquired a first-hand knowledge of Soviet techniques of negotiation, which he later described in his book *War or Peace*[14] and which he put to good use in 1950, when he served as special adviser to the State Department and negotiator of the Peace Treaty in Japan. The manner in which Dulles carried out this difficult assignment, and particularly the adroitness with which he defeated Gromyko's attempt to vitiate the negotiations with Japan by means of the wrecking tactics that had frustrated the conclusion of a German treaty, won grudging admiration from some of his sharpest critics.[15]

In view of all this, Dulles was justified in believing that he was qualified to serve in the highest diplomatic post in the government of his country when the Republican Party came to power in 1952. He certainly possessed more experience in foreign affairs than any other member of his party, and it may indeed be true that he was better qualified in this respect than any previous Secretary of State. That he had the strongest claim to the office was recognized in both parties, and no one was surprised when President Eisenhower asked him to fill it. Whether this was a wise request, however, and whether Dulles' achievement in office measured up to his qualifications, is another question, and one that is not easy to answer.

II

If dedication to his country, knowledge of foreign parts, mastery of the mechanics of international discourse, and experience in negotiation were all that were needed to make a man a great statesman, Dulles' place in history would be unquestioned. But there are other talents that are required of the diplomat. Anyone who looks into the handbooks and treatises left to us by such past practitioners as Hotman, Wicquefort, Callières, Martens, and Satow[16] will not fail to note that they all emphasize the importance of such qualities as precision, due respect for the legitimate interests of other countries, patience, restraint, and tact. It is fair to say that Dulles was not richly endowed with these gifts.

It is possible that a legal education is not the best preparation for diplomacy, not only because lawyers are less willing to admit the possible intrusion of *imponderabilia* into matters of business than professional diplomats should be, but also because they use language differently than diplomats. Finley Peter Dunne once wrote that what seemed to the eye of the ordinary citizen to be a brick wall looked like a triumphal arch to the eye of a constitutional lawyer. These were words that might easily have dropped from the lips of Dulles' allies in 1956, who repeatedly grumbled that what had seemed to them to be clear promises of support were transformed out of all

recognition once Dulles had interpreted them; all of his notes seemed to have hidden escape-hatches through which the Secretary of State disappeared when they called upon him for assistance.

"My difficulty in working with Mr. Dulles," Anthony Eden wrote sadly in his memoirs, "was to determine what he really meant and in consequence the significance to be attached to his words and actions."[17] Part of the trouble was that Dulles sometimes used strong words for their own sake, with little reference to their precise meaning. Robert Murphy has noted in this regard:

> One never could be quite sure of the thoughts in the innermost recesses of the Dulles mind. He was entirely capable of suddenly ejaculating in the midst of a critical situation, "It's about time we started throwing bombs in the market place!" But that type of statement was a relief from the pressures and was to be taken with a warehouse full of salt.[18]

People close to Dulles might be aware of this tendency, but how were foreign statesmen to know when the words used were meant seriously and when not? In August 1956, when the Secretary of State told the British and French Foreign Secretaries that "a way must be found to make Nasser disgorge what he is attempting to swallow,"[19] it is understandable that Eden should have been impressed by the determination of this forthright utterance, and he can be forgiven for being aggrieved later on when he discovered that he had read too much into Dulles' words.

On those occasions when his allies were misled in this way, Dulles always found it possible to demonstrate that his language had not said what they thought it said—that, in fact, *he* was precise and *they* were muddled. He could never be convinced that there is a difference between the precision that one finds in a legal contract and the precision of expression which, in diplomatic discourse, conveys an intention. Paul Nitze once explained this distinction by telling a story of Henry L. Stimson when he was Secretary of War. Stimson objected to the lack of clarity of a statement drawn up by his staff and was told that "all of the points he had in mind were covered somewhere in the language they had prepared." His reply was that in the world of politics one should never forget that any public statement is to be judged as though it were a poster, not a photograph. The over-all impression, not just the detailed words, must correspond with the thought that is intended."[20]

Dulles' failure to appreciate this, and his proneness to the kind of indulgence Murphy has described, frequently confused and angered his allies, and, in one unhappy hour, it persuaded some of them to react violently and tragically against what they considered to be lack of honesty on his part.

It is possible that the Secretary might have corrected this failing if he had been able to see things from another vantage point than his own, but this always appeared to be difficult for him. It seemed, for instance, to puzzle him when his ambassadors resented being left in the dark concerning matters that affected their missions and about which the governments to which they were accredited were likely to ask questions; and, in dealing with his allies, he was rarely capable of that sympathetic penetration of the minds of others which makes for mutual confidence. Because of this, he was capable even of startling and dismaying the Germans, his most intimate associates within the NATO alliance. At the end of 1958, his sister had to explain patiently to him that certain of his statements concerning the feasibility of dealing with East German guards on the *Autobahn* to Berlin as agents of the Soviet Union and of achieving German reunification without free elections were doubtless legally sound, but that they could not but make informed Germans fear that the United States was considering a basic change in its German policy.[21] To the very end of his term of office, Dulles remained unaware of the effect of his words on others and incapable of putting himself, even momentarily, in their shoes.[22]

This insensitivity to the feelings of others—and Dulles' failure to live up to Satow's definition of diplomacy as the application of intelligence and tact to the regulation of relations among states—was apparent not only in his private communications to other statesmen and his remarks in press conferences concerning specific issues, like the ones just mentioned, but also in his more comprehensive public declarations of policy. In these he had a preference for the kind of idealistic rhetoric that had characterized the speeches of Woodrow Wilson, Dulles' teacher and first chief in foreign policy and a man whom he greatly admired. But, whereas Wilson's speeches had lifted the hearts and aspirations of his domestic and foreign auditors, Dulles often left his fellow Americans in embarrassment, while infuriating people abroad. Walter Lippmann once wrote that his public statements always seemed to say that the United States was not only the richest, most highly developed, and strongest country in the world, but the best as well. He was "too noble about our ideals and never humble at all about our human, our very human, failures and faults. This alienates, indeed enrages, those who are by national interest our friends and allies. . . . For with great power, which is always suspect, there should go a decent humility." Mr. Dulles made all this worse, Mr. Lippmann continued, by threatening other countries with dreadful consequences whenever they failed to follow our advice, a habit doubly harmful since the implied threat never materialized.[23] The criticism was sound, but it was unfortunately lost on the Secretary, and his speeches continued to be arrogant, moralistic, and, not infrequently, threatening, to friends as well as to foes.

In justice to Dulles, however, it has to be said that he was in a sense compelled to adopt the kind of attitude and language which Mr. Lippmann and others found objectionable by the context in which he had to work and the state of American public opinion when he took office.

III

In a sense that is true to the same degree in no other great nation, American foreign policy has always been determined by the people. Dexter Perkins has written:

> There were debates on foreign policy in the first days of our national history. There have been such debates ever since. Uninstructed though the average citizen may be in the facts of international life, he still has an opinion with regard to them. If he does not know, he thinks he knows. And this conviction on his part is one that cannot be disregarded.[24]

No one was more keenly aware of this than John Foster Dulles, for he had seen how the foreign policy of his idol Woodrow Wilson had been destroyed by a sudden swing in public opinion and by his loss of control over Congress. And no one knew better than Dulles how strong a possibility there was in 1952 that the pressures of public opinion would make a coherent and effective foreign policy impossible. For the public mood was both frustrated and inflamed. The long-drawn-out war in Korea, with its heavy casualties, had caused wide dissatisfaction with America's allies—because their contributions in manpower were small and they opposed expanding the war as General MacArthur and his followers desired—and with the Democratic administration that had tolerated this behavior. A morbid suspicion arose that the government—to say nothing of the governments of its allies—had been undermined by Communists. A vocal desire was heard for a through housecleaning in Washington and "a victory over international Communism," whatever that might mean. At the same time, it was demanded that our allies should pay more of the costs and, simultaneously, be more obedient to our orders.

It is no exaggeration to say that the national mood imposed upon Dulles a diplomatic style that could not but annoy and frighten our friends abroad, and one which, in the strictest sense of the word, was dishonest. When he became Secretary of State, he knew what he wanted to accomplish in foreign policy, and he knew that it did not differ essentially from what the Truman administration had been seeking to do. To one of his ambassadors, he said, "I believe in the policy of the previous administration, but more firmly than they did." On the other hand, he dared not admit this publicly. From his favorite sport he had learned to trim sail to prevailing winds, and he did that now. With respect to the Department of State, he bowed to the public demand for a shakeup that became so extensive that it came close to making a shambles of morale in the Department itself and in the foreign service.[25] He did so in the apparent belief that an attempt to combat McCarthyism openly would merely paralyze the administration of foreign policy and that concessions to it were, therefore, necessary. In the field of international politics in general, he yielded to the popular desire for a "new foreign policy" more positive than the containment policy of the Truman administration. In his first television appearance after his assumption of office, therefore, he announced that the Eisenhower government would follow a policy of "liberation of the captive peoples" and of "rolling back the Communist world empire." In subsequent speeches, he threatened to respond to new Communist attacks with "massive retaliation" and to meet any failure by his allies to show the same united will and determination as the United States with "an agonizing reapprasial" of the country's position.

The new aggressive tone of Dulles' foreign policy, which was supported by sudden and not always welcome lightning trips to capitals in the spotlight[26]—(a bad American pun spoke of his "infinite capacity for taking planes")—aroused dismay and concern in friendly nations. Later, as it became apparent that "liberation of the captive peoples" did not exactly mean what the words implied (the American reaction, or lack of reaction, to the East German rising of 17 June 1953 made this clear, and it was underlined during the Hungarian revolution of 1956), as "massive retaliation" was defined and redefined to the point of meaninglessness, and as the "agonizing reappraisal" did not take place, even when the French Assembly failed to ratify the agreement for a European Defense Community, publicists had a field day writing pieces about Dulles' hypocrisy and dishonesty—and they are still doing so.

And yet it can be seen that, however devious and lacking in candor his tactics may have been, they had succeeded in bringing American foreign policy out of the paralysis into which it had fallen during Truman's last days. Even if it was only by means of verbal attitudinizing (and Americans are a people, but surely not the only people, who take big words seriously), a reasonably solid public support had been created for the same policy that had been threatened with repudiation before November 1952; and, even if it was only by means of spreading irritation and insecurity in allied capitals, the western governments had by his urgency been galvanized into renewed activity in the field of rearmament and European federation. The result was that, even when the long negotiations for EDC ended in the defeat in Paris, another solution was quickly found in the form of the West European Union and the admission of Federal Republic of Germany to NATO. The commonly accepted version of this story is that, when the French Assembly issued EDC's death certificate, Dulles succumbed to a fit of the sulks and Anthony Eden saved the day by promising a permanent British contribution to European defense, thus making possible both the creation of the WEU and the expansion of NATO's membership. When one remembers the British coolness toward EDC, however, it is difficult to account for this sudden generosity, and we should perhaps not assume that Dulles' role was wholly negative in the crisis. When the records are opened, it is not unlikely that they will show that American pressure in London played some part in its resolution.

While these matters were being straightened out, the stabilization of the situation in the Far East had also been proceeding. The Korean War had come to an end, not least of all because of Dulles' intimation in New Delhi that further delays by North Korea in the negotiations would mean that the war would have to be carried north of the Yalu into Manchuria.[27] In the same way, the Communist thrust toward Indochina was stopped by a warning to the Chinese that, however many successes they might win in Vietnam, the United States would not tolerate a complete victory or anything like the absorption of Southeast Asia. It was this policy which—after an even stronger Dulles line had failed to win British support at the time of the Dienbienphu crisis—paved the way for the Geneva Conference of 1954. The British writer Richard Goold-Adams has written: "Without the American stand, the Conference could never have taken place on the basis that it did. And. . . . neither Eden nor Bidault could have kept the Conference going without Dulles' shadow in the background."[28] His firmness had stopped the possibility of Chinese expansion and made possible treaty arrangements that were not seriously challenged until the re-opening of Communist pressure in Laos at the end of 1960.

These were undeniable achievements, and the momentary easing of tension in 1955 was so apparent that the view prevailed in liberal circles at home and abroad that it should be exploited by means of new conversations with the Russians aimed at resolving other outstanding questions. This was the mood that led to the Geneva Summit Conference, which awakened so many vain hopes. It is worth noting that Dulles was opposed to this meeting on the grounds that nothing good could come out of unstructured talks between heads of state unless there was some concrete proof ahead of time of a desire on the part of the Soviets to negotiate earnestly; he agreed to American participation only because refusal would have had unfortunate repercussions in countries to which the United States was allied. His worst presentiments were confirmed. The Summit Meeting of 1955 and the subsequent meeting of the Foreign Ministers contributed nothing to a solution of Europe's problems. On the other hand, they led to a relaxation of the rearmament efforts of NATO's members and to new differences of opinion concerning the attitude that should be adopted toward the Soviet Union. There followed agitated exchanges of notes among the United States and its allies with respect to force levels, and new public concern in America over European foot-dragging and unreliability.

In this atmosphere of less than complete harmony, the Suez crisis threatened to destroy allied collaboration, and the NATO alliance that embodied it, completely. It would be idle to deny that the faults of Dulles' diplomatic style, which have been touched on above, played a significant role in this western débâcle. If it is unsound to blame the crisis on his abrupt withdrawal of his offer to finance the Aswan dam, it must be admitted that it was sharpened by it. In the subsequent period, the Secretary of State was determined that the differences between Britain and France on the one hand and the Egyptian leader Nasser on the other should not be allowed to lead to hostilities. It is unfortunate that he never succeeded in making this entirely clear to his allies, who thought that he had broken promises to them and gradually came to the conclusion that he was being dishonest in his communications to them.[29] In this lack of mutual understanding, an important part was played by personal differences between Dulles and Eden, which had their origins in the days of the negotiation of the Japanese Peace Settlement[30] and had been complicated by Eden's refusal to supply troops for the defense of Dienbienphu in 1954. In 1956 the two statesmen were not speaking the same language, and out of this incompatibility, and the French intrigue with Israel into which Eden allowed himself to be drawn, much evil came. The Israeli aggression, and the Anglo-French support given it, enraged Dulles, because hostilities were begun before he had exhausted his efforts to find a peaceful solution and, above all, because the events in the Near East destroyed the moral advantage the western alliance possessed when Hungary revolted against Soviet domination, an advantage Dulles doubtless hoped to exploit in a general and a specific sense. As far as the Near East was concerned, that was now impossible. The west had been brought down to the same level as the Soviet Union.

Even if he had been able to overcome his own indignation, it is doubtful whether Dulles could have controlled public opinion, which was shocked by the allied action, to say nothing of the feelings of the President. It has become fashionable to regard President Eisenhower as a political Trilby under the influence of a Svengali-like Dulles, but the President had a will of his own, and it was he, in the last analysis, who made American policy. In November 1956 he regarded the Anglo-French action as a personal affront and a blow against that policy of preserving the peace to which he had dedicated himself. Robert Murphy has indicated that it was Eisenhower rather than Dulles who determined the American course after the attack took place and that it was he also who insisted that his allies should be censured in the General Assembly of the U.N.[31]

It is clear today that blame cannot be attributed exclusively to any of the participants in the Suez muddle, and it is ludicrous to write as if Dulles were the villain of the piece, motivated by a desire "to indulge his own conceit as a potent maestro of world political *savoir-faire* and to secure leverage over the American public and Congress and President Eisenhower."[32] His motive was not personal aggrandizement. He was seeking to balance conflicting claims in a tense and developing situation, to retain the support of public opinion, to maintain alliance solidarity, to avoid alienating the uncommitted nations, and to preserve the peace. Thanks in part to faults of method and language, he failed; and his failure will probably be enough to deny him the right to be regarded as one of the United States' greatest Secretaries of State. For it was a big failure. In his first years of office, Dulles had demonstrated his ability to appease aroused public opinion; he had brought the Korean War to an end; and his hard line had contributed to the ceasefire in Southeast Asia. But in the area that the United States Government had for twenty years regarded as of fundamental strategi-

cal importance, that is, in Europe, his style and actions had weakened the alliance that the Truman administration had forged for Europe's protection, and the violence of Eisenhower's reaction to the attack on Suez had come close to destroying NATO.

IV

And yet Dulles learned from these mistakes, and, in the wake of the crisis, he sought, with not inconsiderable success, to repair the damage done. He was doubtless aided in this by accidental factors. The implied Soviet threat to rocket-bomb London and Paris reawakened fear of the ultimate intentions of the Soviet Union, while at the same time the merciless repression of the Hungarian rising reminded people of the brutality of which the Soviet Government, despite Khrushchev's smiles, was capable. In addition, the successful launching of the *Sputniki* helped (once the initial panicky reaction was overcome) to inspire new efforts to close what now seemed to be a frightening gulf between Soviet military capabilities and those of the west.

Even so, Dulles himself deserves credit for the recovery of western unity and will. With a tact that was in sharp contrast to his behavior on previous occasions, he set about the difficult task of effecting a reconciliation with allies whom he had, not long before, arraigned before the bar of justice. By the end of 1957, he had won such a measure of success that, in a moment of anger, Khrushchev himself gave public testimony to it. The Soviet Premier called upon the United States Senate to investigate the activities and policy of the Secretary of State, an outburst that strengthened Dulles' position in his own country and simultaneously caused his stock to rise in European capitals.[33] Indeed, in 1957, when the danger of Soviet imperialism seemed greater than at any time since Stalin's death, it was reluctantly admitted that, in contrast to many wishful thinkers, Dulles had never wavered in his determined insistence that vigilance must not be relaxed, that Soviet intentions were what they had always been, and that, as he had written in 1950, there was "no greater and more dangerous illusion than that Soviet objectives can be changed by persuasion. . . . Power is the key to success in dealing with the Soviet leadership."[34]

The restoration of European confidence in the United States, badly shaken by the Suez crisis and to some extent also by the launching of the Soviet satellites, was advanced also by the sureness with which Dulles went about his work in 1958, a year that has been rightly called his greatest as Secretary of State. He found himself facing three crises in this year, and he met them all with confidence and tactical skill. In July there occurred the *coup d'état* in Iraq, and the pro-western government of Lebanon was placed in serious jeopardy. Dulles met this danger promptly and effectively, responding to President Chamoun's request for assistance by sending U.S. Marines to the imperilled country. This action dispelled the prospect of Communist domination of the Near East and made idle Khrushchev's hope that he might be able to exploit the Near Eastern troubles so as to force a summit conference on his own terms.[35]

As this situation eased, a new crisis broke out in the Far East where the Chinese Communists began their bombardment of Matsu and Quemoy in August. Despite cries of anguish raised by his liberal critics at home and in Europe, Dulles had too keen an appreciation of the potential effects of any retreat under Communist pressure to give way in this matter. Instead, he brought the U.S. Seventh Fleet into the picture in such a way as to make it clear that any Communist attempt to invade the islands would lead to American intervention. After several tense days, the bombardment stopped.

Finally, in November 1958, came Khrushchev's Berlin note, with its six-month ultimatum. Dulles' first reaction to this struck many Germans as being inadequate, for it was on this occasion that he spoke to the press of the possibility of dealing with the East Germans as "agents" of the Soviet Union and said that there were possibly other routes to reunification besides free elections. These statements, which can be seen today as tactical responses to the legalism of the Soviet note, were perhaps designed to persuade critics in London and the United States that he was not wholly inflexible in his German policy and that he was capable of responding to a reasonable and positive approach from the east. But he had no intention of yielding to threats, and, essentially, his views on the possibility of reaching a viable agreement with the Soviet Union on Germany were the same as they had been when he took office. At the Berlin conference of 1954, he had asked one of his aides whether he would be satisfied if Molotov suddenly gave up all his objections and accepted free elections. "Why, yes," was the answer. "Well, that's where you and I part company," Dulles said, "because I wouldn't. There'd be a catch in it."[36] He was firmly opposed to accepting any form of agreement that did not place the essentials of the Western position under an effective guarantee, and he had no intention of giving way to military pressure before that had been realized. Despite his statements to the press, therefore, he took advantage of Anastas Mikoyan's visit to the United States in January 1959 to have a ninety-minute talk with the Soviet official, in the course of which he apparently made it clear that the United States would not yield in Berlin; and from that moment on the Soviet drive on the city began to run out of gas, although that was not immediately evident.

That was really Dulles' last significant political action. In February he made one more trip to Europe, principally to see his friend Konrad Adenauer and to explain his recent statements about Germany. At the end of the same month, he went into the hospital, and three months later he was dead.

v

What can be said, even tentatively, about his place in the history of American statecraft? Perhaps more on the negative than on the positive side. As director of the machinery of American foreign policy, he showed no great ability to coordinate the varied resources at his command or to use them effectively. He lived apart from the Department of State psychologically and, thanks to his penchant for travel, physically,[37] and he was never, in a real sense, its leader. Many of its officers never fully forgave him for condoning the purge effected in his first days by Scott McLeod, just as many of his ambassadors came to resent what appeared to be his willingness to disregard their reports and to supplant them in their proper functions. As the man who, with the approval of the President, was charged with the task of giving form and expression to American foreign policy, he will not be remembered for striking new conceptions, like the Marshall Plan, or for new doctrines. (It is easy to remember the Truman Doctrine, which marked a turning point in American foreign policy, but who can recall with any clarity the purpose of the Eisenhower Doctrine?) As spokesman for American goals in the world, he cannot be placed on the same level as Woodrow Wilson or Franklin Roosevelt or John Kennedy, who were able to use the wordy idealism so beloved of Americans in such a way as to mobilize energies for realistic and constructive goals. Dulles' attempts to strike the same note always sounded moralistic or boastful. Finally, as his country's chief negotiator, he was, at least until the last years, more successful in dealing with enemies than with friends, who often failed to understand his objectives and sometimes came to the point of distrusting his motives.

And yet there is a positive side which may, with the passing of time, place these negative qualities in the shadow. In a time of great danger, Dulles was a tough and determined fighter for peace and the public law, and one who recognized that these things could be maintained only by sacrifice and risk. "You have to take chances for peace, just as you must take chances in war," he was quoted as saying, in a famous *Life* magazine article in January 1956. "The ability to get to the verge without getting into war is the necessary art. If you cannot master it, you inevitably get into war. If you try to run away from it, if you are scared to go to the brink, you are lost."[38] This article brought a storm of criticism down on Dulles' head, but the London *Economist* said a little later:

> His central thought . . . is of the need for certainty. He believes that the only risk of total war is as a result of miscalculation by an aggressor, owing to his not knowing how far he can safely go. . . . There cannot be any certainty unless the alliance of free nations will draw the line clearly and give the aggressor no reason to doubt their determination to defend it. . . . Surely it is the lesson of the years from 1933 to 1939, which should not be forgotten so quickly that a statesman who tries to re-emphasize it, however clumsily, should be held up to obloquy.[39]

John Foster Dulles had some of the same aversion to sentimentality in politics that Bismarck possessed, and this must also be credited to the positive side of his account. He regarded with scorn those people who desired peace so avidly that they responded hungrily and uncritically to every Soviet blandishment, and he successfully resisted pressure to make concessions to the Soviet Union in the hope of getting something in return. For his steadfastness in this regard, he has been accused of pursuing a wholly negative policy,[40] a complaint that assumes greater credibility now that we have achieved something in the nature of a *détente* with the Russians than it possessed during his lifetime, when the Soviet threat was palpable and the opportunities for useful negotiation few. The historian will not be able to achieve anything like a balanced assessment of Dulles unless he can recapture the atmosphere of the 1950's and remember the sense of foreboding and even panic that sometimes affected men in responsible positions. In those circumstances, Dulles stood like a rock; and perhaps the best answer to those who now criticize him for rigidity is the evidence that the Russians had enormous respect for him,[41] doubtless because they acknowledged his sound judgment with respect to their own designs. It may even be true, although admittedly hard to prove, that his toughness and steady nerves helped to blunt the arrogant self-confidence that was so marked in their behavior in that dangerous decade and to start them on the road to what became in the 1960's a tentative accommodation with the west.

"John Foster Dulles und die amerikanische Staatskunst" was first delivered as a Public Lecture at the Otto Suhr Institute of the Free University of Berlin, 23 July 1964.

[1] The John-Foster-Dulles-Allee starts at Schloss Bellevue, the official Berlin residence of the Bundespräsident, runs in an easterly direction along the southern bank of the Spree, and then, turning southeast, goes past the Kongress-Halle, slips between the Platz der Republik and the Soviet War Memorial, and finally joins the Friedens-Allee and the Strasse des 17. Juni at the Platz vor der Brandenburger Tor.

[2] Washington does, however, have a Dulles Airport, which, in view of the Secretary's extensive travels while in office, is an entirely appropriate memorial.

[3] *Der Spiegel,* No. 28/1964 (8 July 1964). Without mentioning him by name, Senator Goldwater made remarks that could be considered critical of Dulles' policy, at least in 1956. He expressed the opinion that the United States should have sent troops into Hungary in that year and added: "If the United States had fulfilled its duty to Hungary in this way, Hungary would be a free country today."

[4] Herman Finer, *Dulles over Suez: The Theory and Practice of His Diplomacy* (Chicago, 1964), pp. 7, 16, 17, 21, 31, 60, 72, 76, 78, 172, 173, 258, 322, 347, 371.

[5] In turning over his papers to Princeton University, Dulles expressed the wish that access to them be granted as widely as possible, and become unlimited after the expiration of twenty-five years from the date of his death.

[6] "Somewhere along the line, perhaps deeply rooted in our history and character, there must have been implanted an attitude of mind toward diplomacy—which is to say the conduct of foreign affairs—that creates a combination of distrust and depreciation. The long history of isolationism has something to do with it. So has a sense of inferiority that made us believe the British and the French and other foreigners were more astute, more clever, more subtle, more experienced than our diplomats." "The Foreign Service," Editorial, *The New York Times,* 30 August 1957.

[7] Richard H. Rovere, *Affairs of State: The Eisenhower Years* (New York, 1956), p. 53. John W. Foster's term as Secretary lasted only eight months, but he had entered the diplomatic service in 1872 and had a long and rich experience in it. See John W. Foster, *Diplomatic Memoirs* (2 vols.; Boston, 1909).

[8] Finer, *op. cit.,* p. 1.

[9] Class of 1908 Fifth Reunion Yearbook (Princeton, 1913).

[10] *Approaching the Fifteenth.* Class of 1908 Reunion Yearbook (Princeton, 1922), p. 87. He had some previous knowledge of Central America and had written a book, *The Panama Canal Controversy between Great Britain and the United States,* which the Princeton University Press published in 1913.

[11] He was partly responsible for that preamble to section 231 which came to be called "the war guilt clause" because it appeared to justify the exaction of reparations by attributing sole responsibility for the war to Germany and its allies. He was later to admit that it was the revulsion of the German people from this article of the treaty which, as much as any other factor and more than most, paved the way for Adolf Hitler's conquest of Germany.

[12] *Approaching the Fifteenth,* p. 88.

[13] J. F. Dulles, ed., *Poland, Plan of Financial Stabilization, 1927: Documents* (New York, 1928). Printed for private distribution by Messrs. Sullivan and Cromwell.

[14] John Foster Dulles, *War or Peace* (New York, 1950), especially pp. 27 ff.

[15] On the negotiation of the treaty, see especially Bernard C. Cohen, *The Political Process and Foreign Policy: The Making of the Japanese Peace Settlement* (Princeton, 1957), especially chapters 2 and 7.

[16] See, *inter alia,* Jean Hotman de Villiers, *L'Ambassadeur* (Paris, 1604); Abraham de Wicquefort, *The Ambassador and His Functions* (trans. John Digby) (London, 1716); *The Practice of Diplomacy,* being an English rendering

of François de Callières, *De la manière de négocier avec les souverains,* presented with an introduction by A. F. Whyte (London, 1919); Sir Ernest Satow, *A Guide to Diplomatic Practice* (3rd ed.; London, 1932); and Heinrich Wildner, *Die Technik der Diplomatie: L'art de négocier* (Vienna, 1959).

[17] *Full Circle: The Memoirs of Anthony Eden* (Boston, 1960), p. 71.

[18] Robert Murphy, *Diplomat among Warriors* (New York, 1964), p. 386.

[19] *Full Circle,* p. 487.

[20] Paul Nitze, "The Impossible Job of Secretary of State," *The New York Times Magazine,* 24 February 1957, pp. 9 ff.

[21] Eleanor Lansing Dulles, *John Foster Dulles: The Last Year* (New York, 1963), pp. 221, 224.

[22] Sympathy, it may be noted, is less highly thought of in the practice of law, where identification with the thoughts and interests of others can have unfortunate results.

[23] Walter Lippmann, "The Grace of Humility," *The New York Herald Tribune,* 24 September 1957.

[24] Dexter Perkins, "The Department of State and American Public Opinion," in Gordon A. Craig and Felix Gilbert, eds., *The Diplomats, 1919-1939* (Princeton, 1953), p. 282.

[25] This is admitted even in such a friendly biography as John Robinson Beal, *John Foster Dulles: A Biography* (New York, 1957), pp. 138 ff.

[26] "Mr. Dulles flies in for a few days, delivers a couple of dour Calvinist forecasts of doom and retribution, and then heads back out to Bangkok or Rio or wherever." Rovere, *op. cit.,* p. 267.

[27] Beal, *op. cit.,* p. 182.

[28] Richard Goold-Adams, *John Foster Dulles: A Reappraisal* (New York, 1962), pp. 129-30.

[29] See *Full Circle,* pp. 540-41, 557, 634.

[30] *Ibid.,* pp. 21-22.

[31] Murphy, *op. cit.,* pp. 392-93.

[32] Finer, *op. cit.,* pp. 492-93.

[33] Goold-Adams, *op. cit.,* p. 255.

[34] Dulles, *War or Peace,* p. 16.

[35] Eleanor Dulles, *op. cit.,* pp. 139 ff.

[36] Goold-Adams, *op. cit.,* p. 293.

[37] On 12 July 1956, under the heading "Stop Over in Washington Some Time, Mr. Secretary," R. H. Shackford reported in the *Washington Daily News* that Dulles had traveled a distance equal to eleven times around the earth in the last three and a half years, and he quoted Dr. Henry Wriston's opinion that less travel on the part of the Secretary of State would improve the efficiency of the Department and the morale of the chiefs of mission abroad.

[38] *Life,* 16 January 1956, p. 70.

[39] *The Economist* (London), 21 January 1956, quoted in Beal, *op. cit.,* pp. 217-18.

[40] Henry A. Kissinger, *The Necessity for Choice* (New York, 1960), p. 193.

[41] So Louis Joxe, one of de Gaulle's aides, to Eleanor Dulles. *The Last Year,* p. 223.

R. D. Challener and John Fenton (essay date 1971)

SOURCE: "Which Way America?: Dulles Always Knew," in *American Heritage,* Vol. 22, June, 1971, pp. 13, 84-93.

[*In the following essay, Challener and Fenton use Dulles's correspondence and the taped recollections of his friends and colleagues to present a more complicated view of Dulles than the common stereotype of him as a one-dimensional, Christian anti-communist.*]

About a dozen years ago Carol Burnett's nightclub repertoire included a number, "I Made a Fool of Myself over John Foster Dulles." In 1971, in an era of massive discontent with American foreign policy, Miss Burnett would be unwise to restore it to her program. For even though the song is pure camp, some youthful member of her audience would certainly jump to his feet with a denunciation of Dulles as the archetypal villain of the foreign-policy establishment he repudiates. To the new generation Foster Dulles stands condemned as the very model of the Modern Cold Warrior. To them he is the moralist whose platitudes reduced the world situation to a struggle between Western "good" and Communist "evil" and the brinkman who stood poised on the edge of Armageddon and revelled in the confrontation. His veto of United States assistance in the building of Egypt's Aswan Dam, the indictment further runs, alienated Gamal Abdel Nasser and began the fatal series of steps that led to a massive Soviet influence in the Middle East, against which we are now contending. At the real brink, some of his other critics assert, he frustrated the Anglo-French-Israeli armed intervention at Suez, without providing any countermeasure to preserve the Western position in that area. Finally, it is charged, his efforts to maintain staunch anti-Communist leadership in power in Saigon after 1954 make the Vietnam war in good part his legacy.

John Foster Dulles dominated American foreign policy during the more than six years that he was Secretary of State, and was always a controversial figure. In his speeches, especially those that were televised, he presented the image of a one-dimensional man, the stern Presbyterian whose stock in trade was an unbending stance against "atheistic communism" (and, as anyone who heard his speeches will recall, the adjective was as important as the noun). One Washington correspondent privately referred to the Secretary as "a card-carrying Christian." Even before his untimely death in 1959 there were more than a few critics who argued that his militant anticommunism blinded him to changes in the Soviet world and condemned American diplomacy to a global rigidity. Yet to his many dedicated admirers, and especially to President Eisenhower, he was a man of principle and conscience, a Secretary of State who would never settle for a policy of expediency. Those who worked with him in the Cabinet or National Security Council were impressed with his almost total knowledge of all the facts in a given situation, his ability to present the relevant evidence, and his talent, as a lawyer, to write a brief resting upon seemingly irrefutable logic.

John Foster Dulles was, paradoxically, everything that both his critics and his admirers claimed. But he was, most emphatically, not simply one-dimensional; his personality had many and varied facets. A wide variety of experiences shaped the outlook and perspectives of this complex man. His involvement in American foreign policy was, in many respects, the working out of a family drama. His grandfather (to whom he was particularly close) was John W. Foster, Secretary of State to Benjamin Harrison; his uncle, Robert Lansing, served Woodrow Wilson in the same capacity. Thus through family associations he gained an early exposure to the world of diplomacy and the workings of American foreign policy. He was also deeply affected by certain personal, firsthand experiences with the conduct of United States foreign policy from 1919 onward. Yet, despite his unique qualities and background, Dulles was a "typical" American in his response to the international issues that faced his country. The movement of his ideas was not far removed from the main currents of public opinion, except perhaps in the 1920's when he was more of an "internationalist" than all but a few of the surviving Wilsonians. Certainly in 1919 he was caught up in the general enthusiasm for the Wilsonian program, and, on the eve of World War II, he had no desire to see America involved. But once we were in it, he was again caught by the enthusiasm for internationalism and, like F.D.R., was hopeful that there could be postwar cooperation with the Soviet Union. Like most Americans, his suspicions of the Russians came largely after Yalta; they were founded on the disillusionment that arose when the wartime hopes were destroyed. Indeed, in the immediate postwar period, more than a few militant anti-Communists charged Dulles with not recognizing sufficiently the menace of the Soviets.

The purpose of the piece that follows is to illuminate some of the many facets of John Foster Dulles that have

been noted in this brief introduction—above all, to suggest that he was far more complicated than the popular stereotype. It is based entirely upon two sources: first, his correspondence for the years 1919-1952, now on deposit in the Firestone Library of Princeton University; and second, transcripts of the Dulles Oral History Project, in the same library. The Oral History Project, directed by Philip Crowl, then of the Department of State and now chairman of the History Department at the University of Nebraska, taped the recollections of over three hundred persons who had known and worked with Dulles—Cabinet members, churchmen, colleagues in Wall Street and in the State Department, officers of the military services. They reveal aspects of the man not to be found in any letters or published sources. One cautionary note is in order. "Oral history" is not documented history; it rests on the fragile memories of men who, long after the fact, were asked to put their recollections on tape. The men cited in this article told it as they remembered it, not necessarily as it actually was.

John Foster Dulles was reared in Watertown, New York, where his father was pastor of the local Presbyterian church. Many years later his sister, Mrs. Margaret Edwards, recalled what it was like to grow up in a small town parsonage on the shores of Lake Ontario and what kind of boy her older brother had been:

> He was an adventurous little boy. He wasn't foolhardy—never was—all his life. But he loved to climb the highest apple tree out in the back yard, and I would climb up after him as fast as I could. And when we shot off firecrackers on the Fourth of July, I just hated the noise, but I never let him know.

> Our Sundays were quite strict, but they were happy days. In fact, I think we looked forward to Sundays. And every Sunday morning, as our family grew up, we five children, led by my mother, walked sedately up the church aisle and took our places next to the front pew. And each of us was equipped—this was my father's idea—with pencil and notebook. We were to take notes on the sermon. Of course, for the younger ones, my two little brothers, this didn't amount to very much. But for my brother Foster, and myself, and my brother Allen, it was a very serious undertaking. We felt that we were reporters on our father's sermon. And then at Sunday dinner our notes were brought forth, and we discussed the sermon. . . . My father would always say that if our notes were not clear, then he must have preached a very poor sermon. He always took the blame himself. So that made us very eager—because we loved our father—to make our notes as accurate as possible.

The family's intellectual horizons, however, were never limited to the view from the parsonage. Their father was, by the standards of nineteenth-century theology, a liberal; and he set broad educational goals for all the children—"being a world citizen, learning foreign languages, getting to know people face to face." To Mrs. Edwards, "all of those things that came out when Foster was Secretary of State . . . were all started by my father." Then, too, every year the Dulles children spent time in Washington visiting their grandfather, John W. Foster, no longer Secretary of State but still quite active in international affairs:

> The Washington houses . . . were always centers of international personages, so that we kind of took that for granted. The Mexican ambassador lived next door, and the Chinese ambassador lived not far away . . . and they came and went from our house. My grandparents "received" every Monday, and, of course, social life and protocol was very detailed, and one made no mistakes . . . [Foster and I] would glue our faces to the windowpane to see these equipages roll up with their coachmen and their footmen, and then somebody would get out all dressed in regalia . . . so that I suppose it was in our blood when we were quite young.

It was a close-knit family, the children always in competition with one another but ever united against any outsider. Throughout their lives both Foster and Allen Dulles were resolute defenders of the family reputation. In the 1930's, for example, they edited the memoirs of their uncle, Robert Lansing and, in the opinion of the publisher, eliminated interesting but possibly unflattering material about Lansing's work with Woodrow Wilson. In a letter to his brother, Allen conceded having cut a section that "rather tended to indicate that Robert Lansing had been on the sidelines in connection with the preparation of the 14 Points message."

From Watertown High School, Foster Dulles went to Princeton, where he graduated in 1908. (The Princeton record is obscure. Young Dulles was apparently a brilliant but shy and unsocial person; in later years few of his classmates could recollect much more than the fact that he had been with them at Princeton.) After college there was a year at the Sorbonne, with language study and philosophy courses under Henri Bergson, and then law school at George Washington University—so that he could be close to his grandfather. In 1913 Dulles joined the prestigious Wall Street law firm of Sullivan & Cromwell. There is more than a suspicion that it took the assistance of Grandfather Foster to land him his first job. As an old friend of the family later remembered:

> Well, when he graduated, his grandfather, of course, wanted him to get a job so he brought him up to New York to Sullivan & Cromwell. And his grandfather knew Mr. Cromwell, and they had a meeting in Mr. Cromwell's office. And General Foster said, "Now, here is my grandson, just graduated from law school, so perhaps you could find a place for him." And Mlle. Reynard [Cromwell's secretary] said that Mr. Cromwell was so interested in the way Mr. Dulles behaved. This young man never raised his eyes from the floor. He was very shy, you know, at having his grandfather ask for a job rather than . . . getting it for himself.

Even in these years there were signs of an interest in international affairs. When his grandfather was named as one of the American delegates to the Second Hague

Peace Conference in 1907, young Dulles accompanied him as his secretary. In 1913, when he was just beginning at Sullivan & Cromwell, Uncle Lansing tempted him with a chance to do some legal work for the State Department in Washington. In 1917-18, after America had gone to war and Dulles had temporarily left Wall Street for an Army commission, there were a few Lansing-inspired minor diplomatic missions to Central America. But Foster Dulles' first significant involvement with American foreign policy came in 1919 when he was a member of the American delegation in Paris to help Wilson write the Versailles Treaty.

Dulles worked on the issue of German reparations—how much Germany was to pay the victors for war damages—and, to his sorrow, lost many of the battles to keep the figures from being so high as to impede Germany's recovery. He was not alienated by the completed treaty. Throughout the twenties he continued to regard himself as a Wilsonian and moderate internationalist. But he was increasingly disturbed by the way in which the reparations question was handled.

Eustace Seligman, his law partner at Sullivan & Cromwell since prewar days, described the evolution of Dulles' attitude:

> Dulles felt that the Versailles reparation burden on Germany was an impossible burden and would dislocate the economies of all the European countries. . . . Then, in 1939, he published a book in which he pointed out, without ever justifying any of their aggressions, that Germany, Italy, and Japan had been restricted in their economic and political development by French and British policies . . . and he advocated a recognition of the legitimacy of the demands of these countries—for which he was somewhat criticized.

All of this created a certain ambivalence in Dulles' attitude toward the rise of Adolf Hitler, as a letter he wrote to the editor of the *Forum* in 1937 indicates:

> I am in receipt of your letter of September 20, with reference to Professor [Emil] Ludwig's article on Hitler.
>
> One may disagree, as I do, with many of Hitler's policies and methods. But such disagreement should not lead one into the error, as I conceive it, of disparaging his abilities. One who from humble beginnings, and despite the handicap of alien nationality, has attained the unquestioned leadership of a great nation cannot (as Ludwig maintains) have been "utterly lacking in talent, energy, and ideas." Professor Ludwig asserts that because Hitler's policies are blindly stupid, they are more apt than those of Mussolini to lead to war. This is a highly speculative prediction. . . . Admittedly Hitler's methods involve primarily an appeal to the emotions and the use of the arts of propaganda. Emotionalism is dangerous, whether in a people, a dictator, or an historian. But the user of emotional methods is not necessarily himself a mental incompetent.

As he became more involved in the arena of international finance, Dulles was a frequent speaker at business gatherings and at such organizations as the newly established Council on Foreign Relations. He was an internationalist by the standards of the 1920's; that is, he shared the view of many members of the Wall Street community with transatlantic financial interests, who felt that the United States, as the world's leading creditor nation, had a role to play in the world scene.

But in the late 1930's, as war shadows lengthened, Dulles became increasingly disillusioned about the state of international affairs. Believing, like a good Wilsonian, in the need for peaceful change, he insisted that another European conflict was threatening because no nation was prepared to live up to the implications of Article 19 of the Versailles Treaty, which had called for the revision of treaties that had become outmoded. He was wary of American involvement in such a struggle. When Charles A. Lindbergh began to emerge as the outspoken champion of isolationism, Dulles wrote him in guarded but sympathetic terms:

> I am very glad you spoke as you did. I do not agree with everything that you said, but I do agree with the result, and I feel that there is grave danger that, under the influence of emotion, we will decide upon a national policy which is quite the reverse of what we had more or less agreed upon when we were thinking clearly.

The emotional reaction that Dulles feared was a commitment to defend democracy that might be impossible to fulfill. In the spring of 1940, he wrote to a friend advocating American assistance to Britain and France:

> So far as Europe is concerned, I do not think there is anything we can do, or that any one can do, that will prevent the present war from impoverishing the nations of Europe and creating social and economic conditions such that a regime of personal and individual liberty, such as we aspire to, will be impracticable. This will, I fear, be true no matter who "wins."

And his concluding paragraph scarcely suggests the later Secretary of State who would be accused of being an "immobilist" frozen into fixed positions:

> If the defeat of England and France can only be prevented by the United States assuming the role of the guarantor of the *status quo* in Europe and Asia, then, indeed, we would have assumed a heavy responsibility. For, as I have said elsewhere, change is the one thing that cannot be permanently prevented, and the effort to perpetuate that which has become artificial will inevitably break the person or the nation committed thereto.

Yet in these same years, Foster Dulles, the son of a minister, began to find answers to pessimism in the peace efforts of American Protestantism. The year 1937 was crucial in his intellectual development. First, he attended an international conference on problems of war and peace that was held in Paris and sponsored by the League of Nations; then he crossed the Channel and attended a similar church-sponsored conference at Oxford. His son Avery recalled the contrast between the way his father responded to the two conferences:

> In the summer of 1937, when he was in Paris . . . he had this great conference with many of the leading thinkers on financial and political matters in various countries. . . . But [he] . . . was rather dissatisfied with the results, because he felt that the people attending were not able to rise above their immediate national self-interest and prejudices. And then, right after it, he attended a conference of the Life and Work Group—which was one of these groups that later joined in the World Council of Churches—at Oxford on "Church, Community, and State." And he said that the atmosphere was so completely different when all these men were gathered together under Christian principles to discuss many of the same problems. He found that people of different nationalities were able to reach agreements transcending their short-term national self-interest and prejudices and see things in a much larger perspective. I think the contrast of these two conferences on world affairs in the summer of 1937 convinced him that Christianity was of tremendous importance for the solution of world problems of peace and international justice.

After 1937 Dulles plunged heavily into the work of the churches in world affairs, soon becoming a regular speaker at church-sponsored conferences and meetings on the problems of war and peace. His papers at Princeton contain an admiring note from his mother written about this time:

> . . . just a few lines to tell you how much I appreciate what you are doing in the cause of Peace and Religion. I remember that after graduation [from college] when you told me that you were going into the law and not into the ministry, that you said that you thought you could do as much good in that field, and you are proving it, for your reputation gives weight to all you say.

Early in 1940, after the war had started in Europe, Dulles accepted the chairmanship of a major church-sponsored study group—the Commission on a Just and Durable Peace—established by the Federal Council of Churches. As head of that group Dulles became the lay spokesman for American Protestantism on the subject of war aims. Dulles and the commission insisted on the need to create a new international organization to replace the old League of Nations and, above all, hoped to establish a new international system that would create the possibility of peaceful change.

The churches, still smarting under charges that their outlook in the 1930's had been dominated by pacifism, found in Dulles a lay leader of conservative instincts and a Republican lawyer with impeccable credentials. He worked closely with some of the most liberal leaders of

American Protestantism—men such as Reinhold Niebuhr and John Coleman Bennett—and, according to all accounts, was successful in the role. Bennett, later the president of Union Theological Seminary, recalled:

> I should want to emphasize the fact that he was really the creative leader . . . the leader, indeed, of this effort for about a decade. He was, in dealing with these people, open, and he listened. . . . He always did his homework, he always had drafts, he always knew the line he wanted to take—a line having to do with the period after the war. . . . He was certainly opposed to a peace based primarily on a vindictive attitude—very open to the German people. And also, I thought, he was open toward the revolutionary part of the world to a considerable extent.

In the 1950's, when Dulles had become the alleged brinkman and advocate of massive retaliation, many church leaders looked back in some confusion. Was this the same Dulles with whom they had worked so closely during the war years? Former associates became critics, and there was strain in old relationships. In 1958 Dulles was asked to give a major speech at the annual meeting of the National Council of Churches in Cleveland. In it he insisted that the United States could not and should not give diplomatic recognition to Red China. He had scarcely returned to Washington when the five hundred delegates, by a wide margin, endorsed a resolution that called for U.N. recognition of the Red Chinese. Ernest Gross, a friend of the Secretary and a church delegate at Cleveland, recalled:

> It [the vote] was strong and bitter medicine to Mr. Dulles, because word came back almost at once to us that he really felt it a personal blow and a repudiation.

But these discords were still in the future in the immediate postwar period, when Dulles clearly emerged into national prominence as an authority on American foreign policy. In both the 1944 and 1948 election campaigns he was Thomas E. Dewey's principal consultant on foreign affairs. Indeed, in 1948, on that historic occasion when Dewey (the Republican candidate) "snatched defeat from the jaws of victory," it was widely assumed that Dulles would be the next Secretary of State. All of this caused no little embarrassment. At the time of the election Dulles was in Paris attending a meeting of the U.N. General Assembly, and as the Israeli foreign minister, Abba Eban, recalled the circumstances:

> At that time, in the early part of November and late October, everybody in Paris who talked to Dulles assumed that he was talking to the prospective Secretary of State, and all sorts of dinner parties and meetings were held on this assumption, which nobody questioned at the time. Dulles himself was inviting delegates and groups of delegates to have dinner, during which he would lay down future lines of policy. It fell to me to be invited on November 4, the day after the election, and the occasion had all the melancholy of a funeral . . .

Dulles' stature was enhanced by his position as delegate at several U.N. General Assembly meetings. He became both an official and unofficial Republican adviser to the Department of State. He was asked to negotiate and carry through the Japanese Peace Treaty. The important aspect of the years from 1948 to 1952, however, was the change in his views toward the Soviet Union and his emergence as one of the architects of the postwar bipartisan foreign policy of containment and resistance. Dulles was relatively slow to emerge as a militant anti-Communist; throughout the late 1940's he continued to express fears about the global spread of American commitments, worried about the fragmentation of the United Nations, and on occasion doubted whether the East-West split was irrevocable. On the very eve of Truman's enunciation of the Truman Doctrine, Dulles wrote Joseph Barnes of the New York *Herald Tribune:*

> I read with great interest your piece in today's "Tribune." I am in general agreement with it except that I do not feel that the Soviet ideological challenge "would prove embarrassing and costly to us even if it never produced a war." My personal feeling is that, if the Soviet challenge does not produce a war, and I think it will not, it may prove to be a useful and invigorating thing. I do not know whether you are familiar with Toynbee's story of History and his study of the rise and fall of civilizations in terms of "challenge and response." Without periodic challenge it seems that civilizations decline and pass away.

In 1952 Dulles emerged as Eisenhower's choice for Secretary of State. The two men, however, scarcely knew each other until the spring of that year, when a carefully planned meeting was arranged in Paris so that they could sound each other out and determine if they could work together. It had always been assumed by those who knew Dulles that, consciously or unconsciously, he had always sought the position of Secretary of State. Yet when the first overtures came from Dwight Eisenhower's camp, Dulles had hesitations. His long-time partner, Eustace Seligman, remembered what happened when Lucius Clay, who handled the arrangements, first called:

> I remember I went up to Foster's room and asked if he could go over to Paris the next week and told him what it was about. Foster got another of our partners, Arthur Dean, and the three of us discussed it. And this is something that people I've told it to don't believe. Foster said, "I don't think I really want to become Secretary of State." And the reason was, he didn't want the administrative detail. He didn't want the political business of having to go up to the Hill to persuade people. He said, "The job I would like to have would be head of the planning group—to plan foreign policy and not to have to worry about these other unimportant things."

Dulles, quite obviously, resolved his doubts, realizing that he would not have the necessary authority or control without the actual position as Secretary of State. To be sure, he never really "ran" the State Department in any full managerial sense; he administered, as Robert Murphy, a career diplomat who had worked with Eisenhower since the North African invasion in 1942, put it, "sporadically." Moreover, though he and the President eventually established a close and personal relationship, at the outset of the new administration there were those who thought the two men were incompatible and who wondered if Dulles would survive as Secretary for even a year. Emmet John Hughes, journalist and speechwriter for the administration, insisted that in the early days of the Eisenhower-Dulles association the President was "just plain bored" by his new appointee:

> It was so emphatic and obvious a boredom that I found it embarrassing, even though I was not terribly sympathetic to Foster Dulles . . . I recall, too, that after some of these rather long conferences broke up, during which the President-elect would just stare up at the ceiling as if in a trance every time Foster Dulles talked, C. D. Jackson and I would remark on this, and we both had identical reactions to the phenomenon. We both reached the conclusion, that would seem to be inescapable, that this was a human relationship that could not endure.

In later years the Eisenhower temper flashed when he was questioned about the accuracy of Hughes's observations: "That's a complete distortion of fact. Matter of fact, the man [Hughes] knew nothing about it. How did he know what my reactions were? Matter of fact, I admired Dulles from the very beginning . . ." But others also noted the roughness in the early relationship of President and Secretary. Robert Murphy was forcibly struck by the difference between the way Dulles and Walter B. Smith, the new Undersecretary of State, approached the President (General Smith had been Eisenhower's Chief of Staff at SHAEF during the war):

> He'd [Smith] call up on the phone . . . or the President would call him, and he'd say, "Ike, I think you ought to do this" or "I think that's a hell of a thing. Don't do that." . . . Then I'd go from Smith's office, maybe, to Dulles' office, and Dulles would be on the phone to the President, and he'd be all deference and politeness, and "Mr. President," and there was no informality there.

Like many of the newcomers Dulles apparently feared that many officials of the State Department had been corrupted and brainwashed by twenty years of service to Democratic administrations. In his first talk to members of the department he called for a new regime of "positive loyalty," and, as Douglas MacArthur II recalled the incident, thereby alienated many with whom he would have to work:

> He addressed the Foreign Service and the State Department shortly after he took over, and he presented his remarks in a way which was interpreted by many . . . to have cast some doubt on their loyalty to the government. It was one of those things where the Secretary did not have a text, and I think he could have said what he had to say and put it in a different way . . .

A strained atmosphere was also created by the feeling of many in the State Department that Dulles was willing to tolerate right-wing attacks on alleged "subversives" in their ranks and to appease the congressional followers of Communist-hunting Senator Joseph R. McCarthy. "There was quite a bit of feeling in the Foreign Service," Theodore Achilles noted, "that he was not standing up strongly in the defense of some people, including Chip Bohlen, who was the most prominent case at that time and who was under attack by McCarthy." The recollections of Edward Corsi, New York State commissioner of labor, were bitter. Corsi, a liberal Republican, was invited to take on a State Department assignment handling refugee problems, but he had scarcely arrived in Washington before he came under intense attack from the House Un-American Activities Committee for alleged Communist sympathies. As the furor mounted, suggestions were made to Corsi that the best way out was for him to resign his post in Washington and, in its place, accept "a roving ambassadorship in Latin America." Corsi flatly rejected this "solution" and sought a personal meeting with Dulles:

> Finally, I couldn't take it. I had to have a showdown with John Foster Dulles himself. . . . My house was filled with reporters and people trying to create this into a huge national scandal of some kind. . . . I had to get a clearance from the Secretary one way or the other.
>
> I went there at four o'clock. Of course downstairs was just packed up with dozens of photographers. . . . I ducked them and got into the Secretary's office. . . . He sat there. He looked like a beaten man. It seemed that the tragedy was more his than mine. And he said, "You know, Ed, we have to depend on Congress for our appropriations."
>
> "Very true, Mr. Secretary," I said. "What is the meaning of this? Do you want me to leave?"
>
> "No," he said, "no, Ed, why don't you accept [the ambassadorship]?" I said, "Because I'm not interested in that offer."
>
> Then he went off into a spiel about what these same elements had done to him on the Hiss case. And he said, "Don't you know that I went through this kind of thing with all these people? You can't pacify these people; there's no reasoning with [them]. They've got the cards in their hands. They can stop our appropriations. They can do a great many things." And so on.
>
> I realized, the more I talked, the more I was dealing with a man who was determined to put an end to this thing, and the way to put an end to it was to run away from it.

These incidents, to be sure, occurred early in the new administration, at a time when things often go wrong for Washington newcomers. With the passage of time many of these problems were solved, sorted out, or simply shelved. With the fall of Senator McCarthy the attack on the State Department waned, and departmental morale improved. Dulles himself gained increased respect for the Foreign Service. His relationship with the President firmed; indeed, it became exceptionally close. Emmet Hughes, returning to the White House in 1956, found a harmony he had never expected. President Eisenhower later recalled that "there were so many telephone calls with Dulles, that you just didn't attempt to keep track of the number. I'd just reach for the phone myself and call, and he'd do the same thing. . . . We'd be in close touch all the time. I suppose some days eight or ten times . . . I'd call him, or he'd drop in, or send somebody over, just for a few moments about something. . . . But always— I suppose there was no one I kept in as close touch with as I did with Foster."

All of this was to the occasional annoyance of Sherman Adams, the granite Cerberus from New Hampshire, whose task it was to guard access to Dwight Eisenhower. Adams was devoted to keeping the President's schedule "orderly," a chore made all the more difficult because, in his words, Eisenhower was "a friendly man who would have welcomed all":

> Dulles was the only member of the Cabinet who took literally Ike's invitation to come in any time and, when not occupied, simply to walk in. Dulles would walk in here, ask Shanley, Stevens, etc. if the President was busy, and, if not, Dulles just opened the door and walked in.

Once, Adams barred Gerard Smith, Dulles' adviser on nuclear matters and disarmament, from a White House meeting despite Smith's insistence that Dulles had sent him over as his personal representative. Said Smith:

> . . . I went back and reported the thing . . . to Foster. And then he said, "You know, Gerry, Adams talks to me that way sometimes." And then he added, "But not very often."

Dulles soon established himself, in both the Cabinet and National Security Council, as one of the most influential and respected members of the administration. His reputation was based upon his mastery of facts and detail, his total command of every aspect of a problem under discussion, his ability to marshal evidence and mount his case. The laconic Sherman Adams was eloquent on the point:

> There were occasions, when, at the Cabinet table, Mr. Dulles really took his hair down. . . . Although he would not show impatience toward some remark which Mr. [Ezra] Benson or some other member of the Cabinet would make, he nevertheless occasionally gave the Cabinet a—well, I thought they were grand lectures. He would start with the various elements that made up a situation with which we were faced, to look at the alternatives, and so unmistakenly bring the Cabinet to a conclusion that he really took Mr. Humphrey and some of the others into camp.

What impressed General Matthew Ridgway, himself no stranger to professional briefings, about Dulles' presentations in the National Security Council was his "ability to take the whole complex international situation and, in the course of fifteen or twenty minutes . . . brief the NSC without a note before him, in a most lucid manner, with beautiful continuity. It was a really marvelous display of intellect and memory and grasp of the whole situation."

It was quite simple to Dwight Eisenhower:

> I admired the man from the very beginning for two reasons. One, his obvious sincerity and dedication to the problems that were put before him, and secondly, the orderliness of his mind. He had a little habit before he started to speak—probably in his youth, he may have had a little bit of stammering—he waited, sometimes it would be three or four seconds, before he'd start to talk. But when he did, it was almost like a printed page.

There was also a certain ineffable quality about Dulles that made him both the spokesman for and symbol of the foreign policies of the Eisenhower administration. It was his successor, Christian Herter, the gentle man from Massachusetts, who most clearly sensed this quality:

> The major differences between ourselves was my own feeling that the President was the constitutional officer responsible for foreign affairs. Whether he made the policy, or didn't make the policy, he still ought to be out in front in connection with it. I didn't want it to be known as a Herter policy; I'd much rather have it an Eisenhower policy . . . [pause] . . . I think Foster rather liked it being a Dulles policy.

Whether it was a strength or a weakness, the "lawyer's mind" of Dulles can readily be detected in many of his policies. SEATO, for example, was deliberately designed to meet a series of constitutional, political, and legal problems far more than it was intended to be simply a military alliance on the NATO model. Richard Bissell, deputy director of the CIA, insisted that it was a lawyer's and not a soldier's concept. Recalling the occasion when Dulles first discussed the idea for SEATO, Bissell emphasized that the Secretary had placed great stress upon the factors that had prevented American intervention in Indochina when the French position collapsed in 1954 and also had made it clear that he did not expect the nations of Southeast Asia to provide any appreciable military power or political stability to the proposed treaty:

> Dulles made a great deal of the fact that the circumstances which had tied our hands at the time of Dien Bien Phu and [prevented] a possible direct military intervention, were in part the lack of a position in international law which would justify an intervention and in part a domestic constitutional problem. . . . Dulles argued at the meeting . . . that an appropriate regional treaty in Southeast Asia would have, in effect, made possible the

overcoming of these legal obstacles to military intervention in the area should we ever be faced with a situation in which that might be necessary. In the first place, as a treaty it would have been debated in the Congress and ratified by the Senate. Therefore, in its domestic aspect, this would be a legislative action with a legislative history that would clearly augment Presidential powers to react quickly. . . .

Internationally the point was more obvious that if a government in the area required our assistance, the treaty would provide a recognized . . . legal basis for rendering such assistance.

But if colleagues saw the lawyer dominant, many also saw the Presbyterian moralist rampant. He was, to them, the churchman in politics whose religious rejection of "atheistic communism" made him identify the Soviets and their allies with the forces of evil. Roscoe Drummond, the New York *Herald Tribune*'s man in Washington, noted the prevailing view among the press corps that "Dulles wrapped his temporal views in theological clothes in a way that made him seem smug and moralistic." Even his friends noted the same quality. To James Hagerty, the President's press secretary:

> Dulles was a tough old boy. . . . He was a Roundhead, a Puritan, and I'm quite sure that in the Cromwell era his ancestors were chopping down the Cavaliers in the name of their religious beliefs.

Christian Herter made the same point, but in different language:

> I think that you have to give some allowance to the fact that Foster was essentially a very religious person, and I think that the very thought of communism, and the ungodliness of communism . . . was something he felt very deeply inside.

A senior American diplomat, the late George V. Allen, long remembered an evening when he was a guest in the Dulles home. During the after-dinner conversation, Allen made a few unflattering comments about the democratic leadership provided by Syngman Rhee and Chiang Kaishek. Dulles leaned forward in his chair, and, as Allen recalled it, his eyes were blinking:

> Well, I'll tell you this. No matter what you say about them, these two gentlemen are modern-day equivalents of the founders of the church. They are Christian gentlemen who have suffered for their faith. They have been steadfast and have upheld the faith . . .

At a meeting in the State Department, someone once made a Biblical reference. The Secretary waved his finger and, as Robert Murphy recalled, said, "I want it understood that I know more about the Bible than anybody else in this Department." Gerard Smith had a first-hand experience with that knowledge. He was on a transatlantic flight with Dulles and working on a speech that the Secretary was to deliver concerning the state of NATO.

Unwisely, as it turned out, Smith decided to include a Biblical quotation, "When a strong man is armed, his castle is in peace":

> I handed Dulles the manuscript, and he called me to the back of the plane and said, "Where did you get this quote?" And I told him, and he said, "Well, is there a Bible aboard?" And I dug into the reference books and found a Bible, and pointed out the passage. He looked and looked at it.

> Finally, the next day he called me in and said—he knew that I was a Roman Catholic—"What do your theologians say is the meaning of that passage? . . . My sense of it is that this is a reference to Satan."

> So I called up someone learned in the New Testament and recited it to him—"When a strong man is armed, his castle is in peace." I said, "Who does this refer to?" He replied, "Why, Satan, of course. . . . Look at the next line, for it says, 'But when a stronger man comes, he overcomes him'— and that's the reference to Christ."

> Well, I went shamefacedly to Dulles. He got a great kick out of it. "Just think what my Presbyterian friends would have said, if they heard me saying that to the country at large."

Yet those who saw only the stern face of the Secretary on TV or who knew him only for his incantations about the evils of communism were unaware that the Secretary was also a man with a sense of humor and kindness. Behind the preaching of the brinkman there was warmth of personality.

Thomas Gates, Undersecretary of the Navy, remembered the first time he and his wife attended an official Washington dinner party at which the Secretary of State was present. Mrs. Gates, apprehensive that she would be seated next to the austere Dulles, found that he was indeed her dinner partner:

> And she sat down, and Dulles started to pull the candle grease off the candles and eat it. . . . And my wife said, "Now, Mr. Dulles." He said, "I know it's awful, it's a terrible habit, but I just love to chew candle grease. I've done it all my life." My wife said, "Well, you shouldn't do it. I've scolded my children all their lives, and it messes up the tablecloth." And he laughed, and they got along swimmingly.

> Well, my wife went out and bought two boxes of those bee's honey candles that are made out in San Diego in some missionary place and sent them up to his camp in the Thousand Islands. And she got back a letter which she thinks is the greatest letter she's ever had. It said, "Dear Mrs. Gates: The candles arrived. They look good, they light good, and they chew good."

One Saturday the Secretary was about to depart on one of his frequent trips abroad. He and Douglas MacArthur II spent most of the day working on papers they would have to take with them. Around midafternoon Dulles announced that he was going home and would meet MacArthur at the airport at nine in the evening. "And I want you to go home, too," he told MacArthur, "and see something of your family before we're off tonight. And that's an order." MacArthur promised to quit in a few more minutes, though, knowing how much work still remained to be done, he had no intention of leaving. He kept on sorting papers. About 6:30 the phone rang:

> I was feeling tired, and when the phone rang, I said, "Yeah, who's this?"
>
> And this voice replied, "This is Dulles. You better go home, boy. Your home front is crumbling . . . I mean it. You go home right away."
>
> So, I immediately hung up the phone and called my wife. I said, "I'll be home in about an hour to pick up my clothes. But I just got this strange phone call from the Secretary. Do you know what it's all about?" And I repeated what he said to me.
>
> My wife said, "Yes, I do know what it's all about. About fifteen minutes ago, the telephone rang, and a voice said, 'I want to speak to Mr. MacArthur.'"
>
> And she said, "Who's calling please?" And this voice replied, "Secretary Dulles."
>
> My wife, thinking it was one of the Secretary's minions, said in a rather hard voice, "Well, you go back and tell the Secretary that Douglas MacArthur is where he is every Saturday, every Sunday, every night. He's down in that damned State Department."
>
> The voice replied with a chuckle, "I will give that message to the Secretary." Of course it was the Secretary himself.

Two phrases—"brinkmanship" and "massive retaliation"—will long be irrevocably associated with John Foster Dulles. Both were controversial and, as shorthand, capsule statements of complex policies, helped to create the image of Dulles as the dogmatist who revelled in the confrontation between East and West. Ernest Gross was present when the "massive retaliation" speech was given before the Council on Foreign Relations on January 12, 1954, and remembered the negative impact it made on him and many other council members:

> A group of council members went to the hotel bar afterwards. And really we all expressed a sense of shock and consternation at that speech. A group of really knowledgeable people gathered afterwards, and we all shook our heads and were really worried.

In this speech, as in many others, Dulles was his own worst enemy. He sincerely desired to communicate his ideas to the American public and thereby secure broad acceptance of administration policies. But to command attention he often used dramatic, abbreviated phrases—

and failed to realize that these could be counterproductive. Robert Bowie, twice member of the Policy Planning Staff, noted the ironies emerging from the massive-retaliation speech:

> I am quite certain that Dulles' concepts . . . assumed the capacity for more limited force. In private discussion he would always express the view that there must be an opportunity for a flexible use of force, and not simply one choice. . . . But in speaking he was so anxious to get things clear and simple and forceful and to have them get attention, that he gave the picture of a mind that had all . . . the qualities of simplification in black and white.

Much the same thing happened with respect to the equally famous "brinkmanship" article that appeared in *Life* magazine in January of 1956 and that rounded out the impression of Dulles as a man who was sufficiently bellicose to atomize large portions of the globe on less-than-massive provocation. The article, "Three Times to the Brink," was based on a tape recording that Dulles made with three journalists who worked for various Luce publications. On the actual tape Dulles had been trying to explain why, in his opinion, a nation confronted with a grave crisis and dealing with a remorseless enemy could not, in advance, afford to indicate that it would yield to pressure. To do so, Dulles argued, might tempt the enemy to press too far, to assume that the nation lacked will, and therefore, to miscalculate—thereby actually increasing the prospect of war. But in taping his remarks the Secretary had used such phrases as "the ability to get to the verge of war without getting into war as the necessary art," had talked about not being "scared to go to the brink," and had described President Eisenhower as "coming up taut" on several crucial decisions. No journalist could resist the potential in such copy, and *Life* further compounded the problem by tightening the piece, inserting provocative subheads, and adding the title "Three Times to the Brink" on the cover. James Shepley, who wrote the article on the basis of the Dulles tape, admitted:

> We had committed the sin of oversensationalizing what he had said at that point. . . . Because of the way we headlined and covered the thing, it was readily subject to the misinterpretation that . . . he appeared to be bragging about taking the country to the brink of war.

Henry Luce, publisher of *Life* and long an admirer of Dulles, said:

> Shepley's mistake was putting something in quotation marks which should not have been put in quotation marks. . . . He should have . . . given the sense of the thing—and the sense of the thing was that in very tense world affairs, there are times when you have to be willing to go to the brink of war. You can't carry out your policy without any risk of war whatever. . . . But Dulles had put this a little dramatically in saying, "going to the brink."

Two men—Richard Nixon and Dwight Eisenhower—admired Dulles almost beyond all others. To Nixon the great strength of the Secretary was his firmness and, above all, his willingness to pursue a policy that he felt was correct even though unpopular:

> So, let me put it this way: some political leaders in the decision-making process would put their finger in the air and say, What do people want? Dulles never believed in decision-making by Gallup Poll. . . . He said, "After all, you don't take a Gallup Poll to find out what you ought to do in Nepal. Most people don't know where Nepal is, let alone most Congressmen and Senators. But what you do is to determine what policy should be, and then if there's a controversy and if there's need for public understanding, you educate the public."

Richard Nixon also felt a personal debt to Dulles for the assistance that the Secretary gave him in 1955, when President Eisenhower suffered his heart attack and the young Vice President was thrust into a position of both national leadership and vulnerability. On this occasion the wheel came full circle. Dulles, the nephew of Robert Lansing, could draw on family experience in the matter of Presidential disability and had strong views about what had gone wrong when Woodrow Wilson was struck down in 1919. In Nixon's words:

> Basically, there had to be, at that time, some one on whom I could rely . . . Dulles was one—he was the first. Dulles was the one who, because of the accident that he had been through it before with his uncle, advised me and guided me. [He] was my major adviser as to what I should do and the role that I should play. And he was also the one that urged Sherman Adams to go out to Denver so that we would not have the Wilson experience of just Mrs. Eisenhower and a press secretary out there. . . . He also urged that Cabinet meetings be held, and that the National Security Council meetings be held, and that the President write me a note—in fact, I would say that Dulles was really the general above all at that point. Others contributed to what we ought to do, but we never did anything in that period without checking it with Dulles.

The man whom Dwight Eisenhower remembered was the man of moral principle:

> Not only were our relations very close and cordial, but on top of that I always regarded him as an assistant and an associate with whom I could talk things out very easily, digging in all their various facets and tangents—and then, when a final decision was made, I could count on him to execute them. . . . On top of that, the man was possessed of a very strong faith in moral law. And, because of that, he was constantly seeking what was right, and what conformed to the principles of human behavior as we'd like to believe them and see them. . . .
>
> And it was a tremendously serious blow to me when that second operation showed that Foster was filled up with cancer. I not only liked the man—

and I just hated to think of going on without his brain—but it's one of those things fate brings along and you have to learn to live with it.

Wiley Buchanan, chief of protocol in the State Department, handled the funeral arrangements when John Foster Dulles died in the spring of 1959:

> The first time I was in the President's office after the funeral, I started out the door, and he said, "Wiley, come back here for a minute." I went over by the window, looking out at the lawn of the White House—out of his oval office. And he said, "I just wanted to thank you and your people for arranging the funeral. It couldn't have been better, and I was well pleased with it." Then he lowered his eyes, and, actually, tears filled them, and he said, "It's a great loss."

John M. Mulder (essay date 1971)

SOURCE: "The Moral World of John Foster Dulles: A Presbyterian Layman and International Affairs," in *Journal of Presbyterian History*, Vol. 49, No. 2, Summer, 1971, pp. 157-82.

[*In the following essay, Mulder investigates the religious and moral sources of Dulles's approach to international affairs.*]

In his three roles as lawyer, churchman, and Secretary of State, John Foster Dulles revealed himself as a complex personality. To many there seemed to be a private Dulles—warm, cordial, flexible, knowledgeable, and articulate, as well as a public Dulles—austere, aloof, rigid, moralistic, and self-righteous. This paper is an attempt to probe something of the enigma which still surrounds the man in death, and in particular it will focus on the nature of Dulles' religious faith and activity in order to illuminate better his appearance to many as the pious Presbyterian in politics.

Such an analysis is admittedly deficient and incomplete, for while the importance of Dulles' religious background and work in the churches is considerable, John Foster Dulles was also a skilled international lawyer and an astute student of international affairs. His Christian faith inevitably interacted with his professional life, and the difficult job of his biographers is to determine the way in which these factors were related in his personality. This analysis of Dulles' religious faith and activity is further complicated by the ambiguity inherent in any man's profession of religious convictions; that is, religion can be both a source of strength and motivation as well as a facile means of rationalization and justification. In addition, religious ideas can be used for a multiplicity of purposes depending on historical situations. Thus, the onerous task of the historian is both to respect the integrity of Dulles' Christian faith and yet to remain suspect of the possibility of self-justification.

John Foster Dulles was born on February 25, 1888, in Washington, D.C., but was raised in the parsonage of the First Presbyterian Church of Watertown, New York. His father, Allen Macy Dulles, was the minister of the Presbyterian church in Watertown from 1887-1904, and was then named to the post of professor of apologetics at Auburn Theological Seminary where he taught until 1930. The Dulles home was consequently a religious one, and family life included a measure of religious discipline and training which had a profound effect upon the eldest child, John Foster. In 1949, Dulles returned to his father's pulpit in Watertown and told the congregation, "This is the pulpit from which my father preached for many years, and from which he radiated an influence which is still felt here and elsewhere." In that address he recalled the rigors of being a minister's son—attendance at three services on Sunday, as well as Sunday school, memorizing Bible verses and hymns every Sunday, reading of religious periodicals or literature such as *Pilgrim's Progress* on Sunday afternoons, and church activities during the week. "Sunday then was a holy day," Dulles said, "but hardly one of rest." Eleanor Lansing Dulles later recollected that even in play the Dulles children were not unaware of their religious environment. The landscape around their northern New York home became dotted with landmarks named after Pilgrim's ordeal: a bluff became the Hill of Difficulty and a low place was labeled the Slough of Despond.

Although his father had received the Calvinist theological education then offered at Princeton Theological Seminary, he had been exposed to the liberal German theology of the nineteenth century during his tenure as a student at the University of Leipzig and the University of Berlin. His theology was thus considerably more liberal than that of many of his colleagues. At one point he created a sensation by arguing that the Virgin Birth was not essential for the Christian faith, and his nomination to the professorial chair at the liberal Auburn Seminary was a recognition of his humanized Calvinism. John Foster said later that his home life was "rigorous," but "it was not distasteful."

John Foster's sister, Margaret Dulles Edwards, recollects that because of their father's international study, he "was a great believer in travel" and that this gave all of the children an interest in foreign affairs. As children they accompanied their parents to Europe, and when John Foster received a fellowship upon graduation from Princeton University in 1908, the whole family went to Europe. There he studied at the Sorbonne under Henri Bergson and in the spring travelled to Spain to learn Spanish.

By this time Dulles had decided not to follow his father's lead and enter the ministry but to become a lawyer. He explained to his parents that his desire was to be "a Christian lawyer" and an active layman because he felt that he could accomplish more in that way. Margaret says that his parents took the news well. "I don't recall any sense of 'This is too bad,' or 'We're disappointed in you,' or 'You've let us down,' or anything like that at all," she says. However, Henry P. Van Dusen, former president of Union Theological Seminary in New York and one of Dulles' close clerical friends during his work with the churches, remembers that a minister once suggested to Dulles: "Foster, your mother must have been terribly disappointed when you didn't become a minister." "Nearly broke her heart," was his gruff reply.

His decision to enter law was also influenced by his maternal grandfather, John Watson Foster, who served as Secretary of State under Harrison and after whom Dulles was named. He often regaled his young grandson with tales of his diplomatic experiences during visits to the Dulles family. Even before his graduation from Princeton, John Foster received his first taste of international diplomacy, accompanying his grandfather to the Hague Peace Conference in 1907. After studying in Europe, Dulles entered George Washington Law School and finished the three-year course in two years, passing his bar examination in 1911. However, the young lawyer found it difficult to find a job because he had graduated from the less prestigious George Washington Law School. His grandfather finally interceded in his behalf, and he became a member of Sullivan and Cromwell, a leading Wall Street firm.

At the close of World War I, Dulles once again received experience in international affairs by joining the American peace delegation at Paris. Wilson's Secretary of State, Robert Lansing, was Dulles' uncle, and in Paris Dulles was assigned the responsibility of working on the issue of war reparations. His personal experience at Versailles and the failure of the Wilsonian settlement served as a touchstone throughout his later years against which he measured his own approach to international affairs.

European travel with his parents, the influence of his grandfather and uncle, and his early experience in diplomacy gave Dulles a lifelong interest in international affairs, and to some observers it imbued him with ambition to maintain the family tradition by becoming Secretary of State. Dulles himself admitted the force of family tradition in his initial statement to State Department employees. Recalling his great-great uncle's service as an early minister to the Court of St. James, his maternal grandfather's as Secretary of State under Harrison, his uncle's as Secretary of State under Wilson, his brother's and sister's as officers in the foreign service, and his own "at least sporadic association," he concluded: "So you can see, from the standpoint of background and tradition, it is to me an exciting and thrilling thing to be with you here today as Secretary of State." One of Dulles' partners at Sullivan and Cromwell, David R. Hawkins, states that "he prepared himself, undoubtedly, all his life to be Secretary of State." A personal friend, Clarence Dillon, thinks that Dulles "always had in the back of his head, . . . the hope that someday he might be Secretary of State. . . . It may not always have been his conscious wish to be Secretary of State, but I wouldn't be surprised if it was."

Conscious or unconscious, Dulles' desire to become Secretary of State was confined during the 1920s to the practice of international law and the avocation of studying international affairs. He rose quickly in the ranks of Sullivan and Cromwell, and by 1927 he was head of the firm. According to one of his partners, Dulles as head of the firm was primarily engaged in general practice in New York City, with only the smaller part of his professional time available for international affairs. Yet he soon became known as a lawyer to consult on international matters.

During the 1920s Dulles and his wife were members of the Park Avenue Presbyterian Church in New York, and he served as an elder on the church's session. Dulles' thinking about the Church's responsibility in international affairs was stimulated by an Armistice Sunday sermon by Roswell P. Barnes, associate pastor at the Park Avenue Church from 1928-1932. He was particularly interested in Barnes' favorable portrayal of Woodrow Wilson's policies, and after the sermon Dulles stopped to compliment him on his ideas and invited him to his home to discuss the subject at greater length. This was the beginning of a growing friendship between Dulles and Barnes, and it is one of the earliest indications that Dulles was beginning to appreciate the role which the churches might play in foreign affairs.

Because of Dulles' reputation in the problems of foreign policy and his interest in the contribution which the Church might make in this area, he was one of the American churchmen selected to attend the Oxford Conference on Church, Community, and State in 1937. This conference, by Dulles' own admission and in the opinion of the churchmen who knew him well, represented a "turning point" in his life. Van Dusen says, "It was a milestone in Mr. Dulles' own intellectual development that any biographer ought to take serious account of." Dulles acknowledged that it was "one international event that, to me, stands out above all others," and in 1940 he described the impression which the conference had made on him. "I have seen conference after conference break down. . . . In contrast I have attended church conferences such as those at Oxford and Geneva where I have seen Christians from different lands come readily to accord on matters which would have baffled any conference not permeated with a Christian spirit."

One reason for the sizeable impression which the Oxford Conference made on Dulles was that it followed his trip to Paris to a conference on "Peaceful Change" convened by the League of Nations. There he was discouraged by the disagreement and strife between the different delegations, a characteristic which he claimed was conspicuously absent from the Oxford meeting. In an article in 1938 describing the conference, Dulles candidly admitted that "despite the fact that my beliefs are somewhat diluted," his hope that the Christian churches could provide the leadership to bring peace to the world was reinvigorated.

At Oxford Dulles worked on the committee dealing with "The Universal Church and the World of Nations" which concluded:

> All law, international as well as national, must be based on a common ethos, that is, a common foundation of moral convictions. To the creation of such a common foundation in moral conviction the church, as a supra-national society with a profound sense of the historical realities and of the worth of human personality, has a great contribution to make.

These ideas—a universal moral law, the contribution of the church to international affairs, the supreme worth of the individual—later provided the core of Dulles' approach to international affairs and foreign policy. Furthermore, the basic methodology adopted by the conference groups was one which was congenial with Dulles' legal training and one which would also shape and define his foreign policy as Secretary of State. As John A. Mackay, former president of Princeton Theological Seminary and the chairman of Dulles' committee at Oxford, later explained, the participants recognized that there were two basic approaches to the solution of international problems. One was to move from the multiplicity of nations with their own vital interests toward agreement and international peace. The other was to move from a central or unifying principle—Jesus Christ and the moral law—toward the resolution of international conflict.

Dulles was seized by this latter approach to world problems. Samuel M. Cavert, General Secretary of the Federal Council of Churches and one of Dulles' associates at Oxford, thought that he saw "great possibilities for creating an international ethos [through the church] which would be essential as any foundation for any lasting international political structure."

The 1937 Oxford Conference was therefore significant in Dulles' life for a number of reasons. First, it marked the beginning of his active involvement in the Church on a broader scale and his realization of the contribution which the churches might make in the amelioration of international conflict. Second, the discussions provided much of the philosophical or theological foundation which Dulles used in formulating his own approach to foreign affairs. This foundation included at least three essential elements: there is a God; there is a moral law which is created by God and which man can know and must uphold; and individuals are created by God and given "a spiritual dignity and worth which all others should respect." Third, it marked a renewal of Dulles' interest in the church and its role in the world.

At approximately the same time as the Oxford Conference, Dulles fell under the influence of Lionel Curtis, an Englishman who published a massive study, *Civitas Dei,* in 1934, which surveyed the entire course of human history and attempted to apply a Christian solution to the world crisis. Curtis' *Civitas Dei* is faintly reminiscent of the eighteenth century American Thomas Prince who started a "Chronological History of New-England" with creation but died before he reached 1631. Curtis' effort, however, met with a more felicitous personal result, for he survived the book's completion. In its account of human history since the beginning of man, it is no less ambitious, and Curtis concluded that history is a gradual development and evolution toward the Kingdom of God. He defined the Kingdom as the ethical ideal which was viewed and expounded by Jesus and summarized in the two great commandments—love God and love one's neighbor as oneself.

This largely moral principle as the dynamic force in history and the goal toward which history is moving found a receptive audience in Dulles. Furthermore, Curtis contended that "the churches alone can create the necessary public opinion" for the establishment of the commonwealth of God. "When political thinkers provide the necessary guidance," wrote Curtis, "the churches can then begin to change public opinion and so enable the statesmen to act." These ideas apparently influenced Dulles' decision to become active in the church, for Dulles' son maintains that Curtis had a sizeable impact on his father's thinking. "I think," says Avery Dulles, "Mr. Curtis' thoughts had considerable influence on his own. . . . He'd have meetings with him and sort of sit at his feet and listen to him as a prophet."

Later, it seems that Curtis and Dulles did not continue their relationship through the war years when their thinking about a postwar international organization began to diverge. It is significant, however, that Dulles was stimulated in the late 1930s by Curtis' ideas of civilization evolving toward the Kingdom of God and the gradual development of an international organization to secure peace. Much of Dulles' writing during the war years and later reflects a similar conception of world order, and while a major influence undoubtedly came from the theologians with whom Dulles was working, the effect of Curtis' somewhat bizarre religious-political philosophy can hardly be ignored.

Dulles' first book, *War, Peace, and Change,* published in 1939, reflects the influence of his contact with the churches, and his thinking shows some parallels with that of Curtis. While Dulles is vague on the structure of an international organization and even on the necessity for it, he does argue for the principle of peaceful change through international agreement. Some changes are necessary in the status quo, and change must be encouraged and controlled in order to prevent war, the rise of totalitarian governments, and the destruction of essential human values. In addition, one of the prerequisites for change is an alteration of public attitudes toward the need for cooperation between nations. This he describes as "the ethical solution" which is the core of any "political solution." *War, Peace, and Change* appears to be Dulles' philosophical statement of the foundation of international affairs, and although it is characterized primarily by abstractions and ambiguities, it is a striking indication of Dulles' flexibility, his belief in peaceful change, and his conviction that the solution to any international problem must have an ethical as well as a political basis.

In 1939 Dulles also attended another church conference on international affairs. Convened in Geneva, it was one of the meetings which helped to establish the World Council of Churches. Dulles' obvious interest in working with the churches on international problems attracted the attention of church leaders, and in February 1940 the Federal Council of Churches met in Atlantic City to create the Commission to Study the Bases for a Just and Durable Peace. Dulles was named chairman, and his first contribution was the phrase, "just and durable peace," which would have wide circulation during the war years.

Dulles' motivations for accepting the position as chairman of the commission are somewhat unclear, but all the evidence indicates that he did not actively seek the position. His former minister, Roswell Barnes, who was serving at that time as Associate General Secretary of the Federal Council of Churches, maintains that he was reluctant at first to assume the new responsibility. Barnes remembers visiting Dulles at his office at Sullivan and Cromwell in New York and that Dulles immediately questioned him about the purpose of the commission to determine whether it was really intended to accomplish something. Barnes believes that Dulles had no intention of using his position with the churches to further his political career, and he cites Dulles' offers to resign from the commission in possible conflicts with his political activity as indications that he did not want to make political capital out of his post with the commission.

Samuel Cavert, General Secretary of the Federal Council, asserts that Dulles was chosen chairman because during the late 1930s he had distinguished himself as "the person who had the contribution of both competence and experience and also of real orientation to the Christian approach." His willingness to sacrifice time to attend conferences impressed the churchmen. As Cavert recalls, "He was one of the people willing to be very generous with his time. . . . It sounds a little overly pious maybe, but I think he really had a sense of Christian vocation about this."

It is also apparent that despite Dulles' obvious contributions of time, energy, and knowledge, the churchmen were flattered that a man of Dulles' stature would be willing to take on the leadership of the churches' Commission. Henry Smith Leiper, a commission member and Foreign Secretary of the FCC, reflects something of this impression in his recollection that "the thing that I have always thought was highly significant in a case of a man who was so engrossed in legal and financial matters was his sensitivity for the really key people in the religious world."

Dulles' "sensitivity," of course, was interpreted by some as his desire to be projected into national political prominence through publicity of his activity in the church. Journalist Marquis Childs describes Dulles involvement in the commission's work as "shrewd," but most of the church leaders who worked closely with Dulles deny any ulterior motive in his participation and leadership of the church's work. An exception is Richard M. Fagley, who served as a commission staff member and who argues that Dulles' motivation for accepting the position of chairman were more complex than simple religious vocation. "Mr. Dulles—as all big men—was complex," he says, "There were many levels of motivation. . . . I think one could argue that his political future—he may have felt unconsciously, at least—was being advanced by his work in connection with the largest body of Protestant and Orthodox opinion in the country." Fagley insists that the leaders of the church were not conscious of this factor in Dulles' activity, but they never felt that he was using the commission solely for his own purposes. "We knew that obviously he had political ambitions," Fagley continues,

> and he wanted to have a responsible role in the making of peace and this group [was] in favor of conscientious laymen making their contribution in the secular sphere. But I would say that we had no particular feeling that he was trying to use the Commission to put forward points of view that were political in character vis-a-vis his political future.

John A. Mackay, who served as a commission member for a period, also feels that Dulles saw in the commission not only an opportunity for him to make a contribution to the churches but to the country as well. His participation, Mackay says, "showed his very, very basic concern, at that time at least, not merely to win a war, but to see that the country would be worthy of its tradition and also worthy of the role which it would have to play in international affairs." Thus, whatever Dulles' motivations might have been, it is apparent that the church leaders sought and appreciated his contribution and that Dulles himself felt that his work might have an immediate constructive result.

After assuming the chairmanship of the Commission for a Just and Durable Peace, Dulles exerted the predominant leadership in the formulation of the commission's positions. Frederick Nolde, then a professor at Lutheran Theological Seminary and one of Dulles' closest associates on the commission, argues that "there's no question that he exercised the top leadership." Another commission member, Van Dusen, suggests that due to Dulles' strong personality, the commission was "really a one man show" and "a rubber stamp for John Foster Dulles' ideas." "The sad thing," says Van Dusen, "is that when Mr. Dulles disappeared from its chairmanship, . . . the keystone dropped out of the structure very largely." However, other commission members, including John C. Bennett and Henry Smith Leiper, maintain that Dulles was not rigid or domineering in his attempt to persuade commission members and that the final documents represented a meeting of minds. Leiper recalls, "I don't think . . . that there was any preponderant influence, let's say, coming from Mr. Dulles, which pushed the other views aside and persuaded people against their will to accept his views."

Bennett asserts that if Dulles did exert a major influence, it was due to his great interest in the commission's work and the knowledge and preparation he brought to it. "He was the leader of this effort for about a decade," Bennett says. "He was, in dealing with church groups, open, and he listened. He was not dominating in an objectionable sense. He always did his homework, he always had drafts, he always knew the line he wanted to take."

Thus, Dulles' acquaintance with international problems, his obvious commitment to the purpose of the commission, his preparation, and his flexibility made him an excellent chairman. Fagley says that one of Dulles' great abilities was in editing drafts and reconciling various positions in wording acceptable to the commission and in terms which would communicate to the American public. "One thing that Mr. Dulles always stressed was that getting a good statement was only half the battle," Fagley states. "To have it prepared in a form which could be communicated and which was supported by an active program of communication and education—this was just as important as having good principles." To this end, Fagley recalls, a public relations man was always present at commission meetings in order that the public statements or actions would be effectively communicated.

However, the relatively united front which the churchmen portray should not obscure the fact that Dulles was often opposed by others on the commission. Some observers have wondered how the moralistic Dulles could have worked effectively with men such as Bennett and Reinhold Niebuhr, who were regarded as consummate political realists. Fagley recalls that Niebuhr thought that Dulles was "too much concerned with the formal constitutional aspects of international affairs, the lawyer's approach, as over against the underlying realities." Bennett explains the success of their working relationship as due to Dulles' flexibility as chairman. "Dulles, himself," he says, "didn't polarize things as much in regard to the war as he did later with regard to communism."

In addition, the relative unanimity which characterized the commission's work is in part explained by the attitude of Niebuhr, Bennett, and others during the war. Niebuhr felt very strongly that the United States must effectively stop the rise of fascism in Europe, and to shape public opinion he founded the periodical *Christianity and Crisis* in 1941. While he had been an articulate critic of Roosevelt during the 1930s, he underwrote most of Roosevelt's foreign policy during World War II and became one of the State Department's most influential defenders. Thus, while many of the commission's statements were considered "quite revolutionary" measured against Dulles' later policies, it is also apparent that the threat of Nazi Germany brought Dulles and the more liberal commission members closer together.

The work of the Commission on a Just and Durable Peace was divided into making policy statements and circulating them through a comprehensive educational program in the churches. Dulles' primary task, of course, was the formulation of the statements, although he did make a number of speeches and imparted considerable prestige and influence to the commission because of his reputation in international affairs. The commission's first important statement was issued in April 1941, under the title "A Just and Durable Peace." Appearing before the attack on Pearl Harbor, the pamphlet urged Christians to become aware of the growing international crisis and to bring Christian principles to their judgment of the government policy. The predominant note of restraint reflects Dulles' own reluctance to encourage American involvement in the war at that time. Van Dusen remembers that " . . . after the fall of France, between then and Pearl Harbor, [Dulles] and I were . . . on opposite sides of a very sharp dividing line. . . . Foster Dulles was certainly not a pacifist and he was not an extreme isolationist but at this time he felt very strongly that the United States should remain aloof."

On September 18, 1941, the commission issued Dulles' critique of the Atlantic Charter, and the principles contained in that document proved to be highly influential in the church's campaign for a liberal peace and the establishment of a postwar international organization. Asserting the necessity for Christians to speak out on the international situation, Dulles assailed the Atlantic Charter and pointed to three failures: it did not commit America to a world organization which would guarantee the peace; it did not fulfill the Wilsonian dream and did not build upon the failures of the Versailles settlement; and it fell short of the ideals expressed by ecumenical councils. The striking characteristic of the document is Dulles' flexible approach to the problem of structuring the peace in the postwar world and his pointed, informed criticisms.

Dulles' next significant statement as chairman appeared in a pamphlet of essays, **"A Righteous Faith for a Just and Durable Peace,"** published in October 1942. The threat to America and the declaration of war had imparted a new note of urgency to Dulles' writing, and in his essay he emphasized the need for Christians to obtain a "righteous faith" which would guide the country. "We, too, need a faith," he wrote,

> a faith that will make us strong, a faith so profound that we, too, will feel that we have a mission to spread it through the world. Today we have it not. The American people believe in nothing with conviction. We are cynical and disillusioned. Even our war effort we look upon primarily as one of resistance, not of accomplishment, and victory as being that which will assure our being left alone. Such a spiritual state is conducive neither to a military victory nor, when victory is won, to subsequent peace. For again new faiths will arise to attack us, and in the long run we will succumb.

America's chosen mission, the note of impending doom, the erosion of religious faith by cynicism, and the threat of nationalism are combined by Dulles with a strong identification of Christian principles or the moral law with U.S. policy. In 1937 he had warned that "too often spiritual and secular motives become unconsciously

mixed, and it requires unusual practical experience to detect the pitfalls which the worldly constantly prepare to secure for themselves the appearance of church benediction." In contrast, in 1942 he assured Americans that "we can, therefore, be confident that in following Christ we are not jeopardizing the welfare of our nation."

Whatever the influence of Dulles' exhortations to faith and assurances of the righteousness of the American cause in the war, his most important wartime policy statement was the *Statement of Political Principles,* issued in March 1943, and reissued in May under the name which made it famous—*The Six Pillars of Peace.* The position paper was accompanied by a statement of guiding principles which were largely formulated by the theologians on the commission. *The Six Pillars,* however, was openly acknowledged as Dulles' work, and it basically called for a postwar international organization to guarantee peace, control of economic developments which have international implications, a flexible treaty to permit peaceful change, autonomy for subject people, control of military establishments, and religious and intellectual liberty.

Because religious language was largely absent, *The Six Pillars* illustrates clearly Dulles' desire to communicate the commission's position in secular terms that all Americans could understand. It is also significant as an indication of Dulles' liberal peace aims, "a creative and curative peace," as he often called it. His introduction to the document, however, reflects the way in which his religious ideas provided the foundation for his political principles. He prefaced his remarks with his favorite section from *The Federalist,* which one of the commission members described as "really his bible":

> It seems to have been reserved to the people of this country, by their conduct and example, to decide whether societies of men are really capable or not of establishing good government from reflection and choice, or whether they are forever destined to depend for their political constitutions on accident and force. The crisis at which we are arrived may be regarded as the era in which that decision is to be made, and a wrong election of the part we shall act may deserve to be considered as the general misfortune of mankind.

Dulles indicated that another crucial period was present in American history, and that the country must not make a wrong decision. The crisis was produced, he said, by "nonconformity with a moral order, the laws of which are as imperative and as inexorable as are those that order our physical world." The solution to the crisis is for Americans to submit to the moral law and to apply it to the international crisis. *The Six Pillars,* he wrote, is the result of the commission's attempt to relate the moral law to the chaos of a world immersed in war.

Dulles' prevailing conception of a world controlled by a moral law, the necessity for international political affairs to be organized according to the moral law, and the special role assigned to America to assure the establishment of a just peace are explicitly stated in this document and reveal the way in which his own ideas interacted with those of the theologians on the commission. While his ideas are not expressed in the moralistic language which often characterized his later statements as Secretary of State, he recognized and stated lucidly the new power of the United States "to influence decisively the shaping of world events" in the postwar world.

In July 1943 Dulles participated in the International Round Table of Christian Leaders. The conference was convened by the commission in Princeton, New Jersey, and involved more than seventy lay and clerical leaders from several countries. As chairman of the editorial committee, Dulles played an important role in the composition of the "Christian Message on World Order," issued by the conference. The report reiterated the principles of *The Six Pillars,* and it called for cooperation between nations after the war for the establishment of an international organization to preserve peace. The report stated that while the Russian revolution was "antireligious and materialistic," it also recognized that many communist objectives "are those which Christians have long accepted in principle but have largely failed to achieve in practice." The report further acknowledged the Russian need for security and anticipated a peaceful resolution of potential conflict with Russia after the war.

The year 1944 produced no commission document of major significance, but it did mark the beginning of Dulles' reentry into politics. The prestige which he had acquired as chairman of the commission and his experience in international affairs made him a valuable adviser for Thomas Dewey in his rise to Republican leadership. Although Dulles was sensitive to the possible conflict which this relationship implied, he retained the chairmanship of the commission. Many of its members deny that the involvement with Dewey damaged his effectiveness, but at least one member felt that it "unquestionably" affected "his influence with some elements in the churches." When Secretary of State Cordell Hull attempted to remove the issue of the United Nations from the campaign of 1944, Dewey sent Dulles to confer with Hull. Their agreement linked Dulles' name with "non-partisanship," and *Life* magazine immediately suggested that Dulles would be Dewey's Secretary of State. Although Dulles and Dewey had known each other as legal colleagues in New York, Dulles' position as Dewey's chief policy adviser was undoubtedly due in part to his leadership of the church's involvement in the formulation of American peace aims during the war.

Dewey's unsuccessful presidential bid in 1944 temporarily checked Dulles' desire to be in public life, and 1945 and 1946 marked two important years for the Commission on a Just and Durable Peace and its chairman. In August 1945, Dulles and Bishop G. Bromley Oxnam of the Methodist Church issued a statement on the explosion of the atom bomb, and given Dulles' later pronouncements on "massive retaliation," his reaction in 1945 is

illustrative of his perception of the world at the end of the war. Fagley recalls that Dulles' reaction to the explosion at Hiroshima and Nagasaki was "one of shock." He was concerned, according to Fagley who assisted in drafting the statement, with the atom bomb's excessive violence and its implications for reconstruction and reconciliation after the war. In September the Federal Council of Churches, in consultation with Dulles, issued a major statement on the atom bomb, and its significance consists in its call for international control of the bomb. The FCC thus became the first organization with a substantial membership to advocate such action.

In 1946 Dulles joined other churchmen in the founding of the Commission of the Churches on International Affairs at a conference in Cambridge, England. This commission represented an important achievement of the churches' ecumenical effort to work together for a common approach to world problems. The organization became the specialized agency of the World Council of Churches and the International Missionary Council for studying the church's relationship to international affairs.

In October 1946, Dulles and the commission issued a major policy statement on "Soviet-American Relations." Coming in the wake of the disintegration of the Allied alliance and the initial stages of the Cold War, the document is highly significant. It reveals Dulles' hope and willingness to deal with the Soviets while maintaining the sizeable ideological differences which divided the two powers. One commission staff officer who worked with Dulles on the statement says that Dulles regarded it "as important as any single statement issued by the Commission. At least it took more time in drafting. . . ." In the conclusion, the statement makes four recommendations—the acceptance of international toleration; the elimination of "certain prejudices and practices" from U.S. policy which create tension; scientific, economic, cultural and religious cooperation between the Soviet Union and the United States; and the pursuit of policies by the democratic powers that will "reflect the Christian doctrine of the sacredness of the individual personality" in order to make democratic institutions desirable.

The pamphlet is worth noting for its open attitude toward and hope for American-Soviet cooperation, and it certainly is far removed from the Dulles' rhetoric of the 1950's on atheistic communism and the evils of neutrality. Fagley says that the document was a compromise between Dulles and Niebuhr and others, who wanted to eliminate any note of self-righteousness from the document. It was, he states, a "working out of the interplay of these minds and points of view."

At this time, Dulles seemed to be convinced that world developments favored democracy, and he tended to share the general unconcern with the Russian threat that prevailed at the end of the war. He further believed that the United States was closer to realizing many of the goals for which the Soviets were also working but were pursuing them democratically. In September 1946, before a church group in Philadelphia, he even admitted that "it is understandable that some phases of our nation's armament and strategic defense policies may, to Soviet leaders, seem threatening." But, he assured them, they had reason to hope because of the United Nations, the moral law, and because "none of the competitors wants war."

The events of 1946-1948 apparently hardened Dulles' attitude toward communism and the Soviet Union. In a celebrated incident at the General Assembly of the World Council of Churches in Amsterdam in 1948, Dulles delivered a speech on "The Christian Citizen in a Changing World." In it he advanced his familiar argument that there was a supreme moral law which was ordained by God and which transcended national boundaries. This moral law implied the sanctity of each individual, said Dulles. However, he raised a furor when he suggested that because communism did not accept this religious view of man, conflict between the United States and Russia was inevitable. Theologian Joseph Hromadka, who had spent most of the war in the United States and returned to his native Czechoslovakia after the war, replied strongly to Dulles' address and said that the West itself was guilty of failing to live up to the principles which Dulles had enunciated. Hromadka appealed to the churchmen for a greater cooperation between the two victorious powers because "the problem of Germany cannot possibly be solved without a genuine cooperation of the West and the East, a cooperation on the basis of what is best in them." He reminded the delegates that "what has frequently been interpreted as Soviet expansion, or as a revived Russian nationalistic imperialism may be rather a manifestation of self-protection and self-defence."

Graphically spelling out the chaos of post-war Europe, Hromadka asked vehemently,

> How can we under these conditions expect a normally functioning democratic process? In such a situation, what matters is to help the people, to disarm wrongdoers, to assist, to save, to establish dams, to extinguish fires, to organize reconstruction, not to thrive on individual freedom or on freedom of reporting. In certain circumstances discipline, service, responsibility, self-control, self-dedication are superior to freedom and human rights.

One commission member, who witnessed the interchange, described the argument as "quite a hot one," and it represented a turning point in Dulles' relationship with church leaders. Most of them were unwilling to accept Dulles' rather superficial and facile portrayal of the evil of communism and the righteousness of democracy. In 1949 Dulles resigned as chairman of the commission and maintained only sporadic contact with the church leaders until he became Secretary of State.

Dulles' hardened attitude toward the Soviet Union is illustrated in his widely circulated book, *War or Peace,* which he published in 1950 during his campaign for the U. S. Senate from New York. In it he analyzed the teach-

ings of communism in a chapter entitled "Know Your Enemy," and he again pointed to the United Nations as a means of arbitrating international disputes. In addition, *War or Peace* also reveals the influence of his participation in the Church on his approach to world problems. "What we lack is a righteous and dynamic faith," he wrote. "Without it, all else avails us little. The lack cannot be compensated for by politicians, however able; or by diplomats, however astute; or by scientists, however inventive; or by bombs, however powerful." Dulles called upon religious leaders to provide spiritual leadership for the nation, and concluded, "Our greatest need is to regain confidence in our spiritual heritage. Religious belief in the moral nature and possibilities of man is, and must be, relevant to every kind of society, throughout the ages past and those to come."

If the period from 1946 to 1948 marked a decisive shift in Dulles' perception of the Soviet Union, it did not change his fundamentally optimistic view of the United Nations. Dulles resigned temporarily as chairman of the commission to become Senator Arthur Vandenberg's chief adviser at the San Francisco conference which established the U.N. in 1945. In that capacity he fought for the broadening of the U.N. which the commission had long advocated, and some observers feel that he was instrumental in bringing Vandenberg to a more internationalist stance. The commission lobbied at San Francisco, and church leaders with Dulles sought what he later called "a moral reorientation of the Charter," particularly in the sections dealing with justice, law, human rights, and self-government for colonial peoples.

This effort as well as the more important endeavor to mold American public opinion to accept membership in the United Nations was successful, and Dulles took great pride in his contribution to the creation of the U.N. In 1949, he told a church conference, "If our nation has abandoned political isolation, it is largely because our Christian people took the lead in developing the public opinion that not only permitted but that compelled our Government to work to establish a world organization and to work with it." Dulles' evaluation of the commission's work is echoed by Ernest Gross, a lay leader in the National Council of Churches and a delegate to the U.N. General Assembly several times. Dulles, he says, "was extremely influential and instrumental in bringing the church leadership into full support of the U.N. Charter." Fagley maintains that while the historical lesson of the failure of the League of Nations was "the major teacher," the commission through the churches "had a part in helping to awaken the American people to their need for a more responsible role in the post-war world."

Similarly, Dulles' knowledge of the complexity of international affairs helped the Church to articulate and support a realistic conception of an international organization with effective but limited powers. "I've always said," Bennett asserts,

> that I thought it's very interesting that the American

churches never went in heavily for world government, because of the influence of Reinhold Niebuhr and John Foster Dulles—Niebuhr providing, perhaps, the broader rationale, but Dulles also having this intuitive sense of the way things developed, that they didn't develop by fiat.

A recent monographic study similarly concludes that the work of Dulles and the commission was instrumental in winning the support of the Protestant churches and in securing public support for the ratification of the U.N. Charter.

As indicated above, Dulles' tenure as chairman of the commission also precipitated his political involvement, first as an adviser to Dewey in 1944, then as a consultant to Senator Vandenberg in 1945, and by 1948 it was assumed that he would be Secretary of State if Dewey defeated Truman. These connections in high Republican circles were partially a result of the public attention Dulles attracted as commission chairman as well as his firmly established reputation as an international lawyer.

After Dulles assumed his post as Eisenhower's Secretary of State, his former colleagues in the Church cooled considerably toward him. Samuel Cavert reflects some of the disillusionment which many felt. They "were disappointed in his conduct of this office," he said, "and wondered if he had changed his position or whether they had really understood him before." Similarly, Mackay notes that "looking at the matter objectively, there were two Dulleses—the Dulles that I knew in those contacts in church gatherings and the Dulles that emerged as Secretary of State." Leiper detected "a let-down at certain points," particularly when Dulles enunciated the principle of "massive retaliation."

Reinhold Niebuhr also became dissatisfied with the Secretary of State, especially his tendency to oversimply and moralize. In a 1958 article in the *New Republic,* Niebuhr complained about Dulles' "fanatic oversimplification of the Communists," and said, "Mr. Dulles' moral universe makes everything clear, too clear. . . . Self-righteousness is the inevitable fruit of simple moral judgments, placed in the service of moral complacency."

The growing gap between Dulles and his ecclesiastical friends was dramatically confirmed by an incident at a NCC Study Conference in Cleveland in November 1958. He had been invited to speak to the meeting, and in his address he warned of the dangers of admitting Red China into the United Nations. Within a few hours after his speech, the conference received a resolution urging that steps be taken to incorporate Red China in the U.N. Eleanor Lansing Dulles said that the action was "a real and deeply felt hurt," and Gross described it as "strong and bitter medicine to Mr. Dulles," "a personal blow," and "a most unfortunate, if not a deplorable aftermath coming on the heels of his visit and presentation."

The critical attitude which many liberals in the Church had taken toward Dulles as Secretary of State is reflected in the restrained tone of an editorial in *The Christian Century,* which appeared just after Dulles' death. "Debate over the wisdom of John Foster Dulles' policies of state will continue for a long time," the journal stated, "but there will be no argument over the strength of his loyalty to the church, nor over the depth of his devotion to the Lord of history."

Dulles' moralizing which irritated churchmen also provoked many members of the Washington press corps who described him as a "card-carrying Christian" and who felt with Richard Rovere that it was just "good politics" for him to phrase his policies in terms of moral absolutes. "I think that piety of his was awful junk," says Rovere, "and I've never known how much of it was in earnest, but I think this spirituality was for the birds." Marquis Childs thinks that Dulles reflected "the kind of piety that didn't seem to be very genuine with the inevitable ruthlessness that a corporation lawyer would have to have," and Roscoe Drummond contends that this impression of Dulles as smug and moralistic was prevalent among diplomats as well as the press.

Drummond, however, defends Dulles' moralizing because "he was a deeply, honestly, sincerely religious man, who didn't hesitate to express his own convictions that there was a great moral content to the policies that he was advocating." Cavert also believes that Dulles' lectures on ethics and foreign policy were genuine and not "an affectation or just a political gimmick. He had very deep moral conviction. I think he was essentially a puritan of the twentieth century."

Whether or not Dulles' attempt to portray his policies as righteous was sincere, it succeeded in both alienating many people and marshalling support behind some administration policies. In addition, it must be remembered that a moralistic tone pervaded the entire Eisenhower administration, as evidenced in part by the reputed prayers which began each Cabinet meeting. In Dulles' case, moral categories often led him to oversimplify and overstate his position, a habit which was often irritating to Eisenhower. Roscoe Drummond says that Eisenhower "felt that there were two minor weaknesses in Foster's conduct of foreign policy, . . . weaknesses of exposition, not of substance. And they were a tendency either to oversimplify or, on occasion, to overdramatize by a particular phrase." It does appear now that the oft-maligned Dulles phrases of "brinkmanship" and "massive retaliation" were, in effect, manifestations of his tendency to over-argue his case, to state his position too forcefully, to exaggerate what most considered a sound approach to the international conflict of the time.

A more serious implication of his moralizing is that it may have needlessly escalated the Cold War. Rovere argues that "the worst thing" Dulles did "was to transform the Cold War into a hot ideological dispute. . . . This was Dulles' doing. . . . The Cold War until 1952 had very little ideological content. Its aims were finite." Fagley also remembers that even before becoming Secretary of State Dulles saw the ideological conflict between communism and democracy "as something fundamental and hardly reconcilable." This failure to discern the difference between communist rhetoric and practice and Dulles' combative instinct to respond in kind probably did add a new dimension to the Cold War. In the wake of the McCarthy investigations, it calcified public opinion toward the Russians and severely limited the flexibility of American foreign policy.

Granted the limitations and the liabilities which were imposed on the conduct of American foreign policy by John Foster Dulles' moralizing, one is still confronted with the question of explaining why the Secretary of State chose to portray the international situation as an apocalyptic struggle between evil communism and righteous democracy. Rovere's suggestion that it was a good political ploy is a possible explanation, and with a somewhat cynical eye one could argue that Dulles' self-righteous defense of American interests was merely an attempt to win support. Or, Dulles may have felt that the American people would only support foreign policies which were based on clearly defined moral values. The fact that his moralizing was largely absent in his private conversations lends substantiation to both positions.

However, unless one is willing to write off the influence of Dulles' religious training as a youth and his involvement in the church for more than a decade, it seems a better explanation lies in Dulles' own religious background and faith. Former President Eisenhower described Dulles as a man who possessed "a very strong faith in moral law. And because of this he was constantly seeking what was right, and what conformed to the principles of human behavior. . . ." This conviction that all men were bound by a common ethical standard which was created by God and which man could know and obey formed the core of Dulles' approach to foreign affairs.

It was, of course, partially a product of his legal training, a philosophy of law in which positive or human law is a reflection of natural law, but through his activity on the Commission for a Just and Durable Peace, the moral law became both a religious and political principle which was thoroughly integrated into his view of the world. From the Oxford Conference to his resignation as chairman of the commission, Dulles' style of thinking was both influenced by and a reflection of theological modes of thought. While working with churchmen, he adopted the practice, congenial with his legal training, of moving from theological principles to specific situations, and since his theology consisted almost solely of a faith in moral law, it is not surprising that in his enunciation of policy he relied on moral categories.

Dulles' theology really was "secularized Calvinism," in which the ideas of grace and reconciliation had been watered down and practically eliminated. His speeches to church groups and his statements as chairman of the commission rarely contained references to sin, man's inability to create order in a chaotic world, or man's reli-

ance upon God for anything more than strength. Always present were the emphasis upon the existence of a moral law which man can know and obey, the deploring of man's refusal to obey that law, and the conviction of the supreme worth of the individual. In all his work with Reinhold Niebuhr, Dulles never seemed to comprehend Niebuhr's insistence upon the ambiguity involved in all ethical decisions, the dimension of finitude and fallibility in all human institutions, and the degree of self-interest, self-preservation, and self-righteousness implicit in every exercise of power.

Dulles' faith in the moral law, which he inherited from his home and his work in the church, illumines another characteristic of his foreign policy. He tended to make constitutional problems, that is, the structure of international order to permit peaceful change, the primary focus of his attention. In the process, he ignored some of the dynamic, revolutionary movements which arose in the turmoil of the postwar world and which defied the very structures Dulles sought to establish.

Furthermore, Dulles often linked the ideal of moral law to the special mission or role which the United States was destined or predestined to play in international affairs. This may explain in part his conversion of the Cold War into an ideological battle with the United States carrying the banner of righteousness for the free world. It also suggests an explanation of his abhorrence of neutrality and his desire to conclude security treaties which would check the spread of communism and guarantee the perpetuation of democratic political institutions.

Dulles' work with the churches and his attendance at church conferences coincided with the development of the ecumenical movement. The Oxford meeting, in fact, not only established the philosophy for the church's ecumenical approach to political and social problems for a generation but inaugurated one of the first concrete attempts of the churches to work together within one organization. The ecumenical movement was basically an attempt to reach common agreement on the essential components of the Christian faith and to work together for the communication and application of the faith to the rest of the world. In this light, Dulles' international security treaties, his organization of the free world into an allied organization, and his support for the U.N. as an organization committed to common moral principles represent a kind of secularized ecumenical movement. In Dulles' thought and policy, this movement's purpose was primarily negative—to check the spread of communism.

Many of the relationships between Dulles' faith and political activity suggested above are tentative and are probably incapable of being demonstrated conclusively. They do, however, offer a partial explanation of the "very complicated man" about whom journalists puzzled and whose policies determined the context and conduct of international affairs during the Eisenhower years. The influence of his religious faith and experience in the churches on his performance as Secretary of State was considerable, if not decisive, and the deficiencies in his record as Secretary of State are not totally unrelated to the superficiality and shallowness of his religious ideas. These enabled him to slip into moralizing; they had little sense of a transcending judgment of human affairs; they ignored the dimension of self-interest in all human activity; they had little awareness of a grace imparted to all men; and they produced a reliance upon force or the threat of force for obedience to a moral law. However, Dulles' policies were also based on what was considered then a realistic assessment of power in the world.

One of his favorite biblical texts was "by their fruits ye shall know them," and it is not a bad measure to hold to him. Despite all of his self-righteous moralizing and ideological combat, in the short run Dulles' efforts as Secretary of State did succeed in keeping the U.S. out of war. His policies and their fruits must also be judged in the longer run, and the tragic U.S. attempt to stem communism from the Bay of Pigs to the Dominican Republic to Vietnam and Laos are in part fruits of the moralistic Dulles legacy. At its best, Dulles' foreign policy was an attempt to secure world peace based on Christian principles. At its worst, it veered toward arrogance, chauvinism, and a self-righteous refusal to accept diversity and pluralism in the world.

Ole R. Holsti (essay date 1974)

SOURCE: "Will the Real Dulles Please Stand Up," in *International Journal,* Vol. 30, No. 1, Winter, 1974-75, pp. 34-44.

[*In the following essay, Holsti evaluates the largely negative assessment of Dulles presented in Townsend Hoopes's* The Devil and John Foster Dulles, *as well as other contemporary accounts, by comparing Dulles's record as secretary of state to that of Henry Kissinger.*]

Townsend Hoopes' *The Devil and John Foster Dulles* is the latest addition to a growing literature on the late secretary of state. From this bibliography the interested reader can select a wide variety of interpretations. At the most favourable end of the scale we find a biography by David and Deane Heller,[1] who portray Dulles as an heroic figure manning the ramparts of freedom. The book is unburdened by serious analysis or critical assessment of Dulles' diplomacy. Except for its publication after Dulles' death it might be mistaken for a campaign biography. John Robinson Beal's study appeared in two editions, one of which appeared while Dulles was still in office.[2] Although a substantially weightier effort than that of the Hellers, it depicted Dullesian diplomacy in generally favourable terms, finding little to criticize in either the conception or the execution of his foreign policies. Michael Guhin's recent biography is both scholarly and highly sympathetic.[3] Originally a doctoral dissertation, it is heavily documented but written in a lucid style that belies its origins. Guhin's thesis is that Dulles was a shrewd diplomat whose well-developed appreciation for

the art of the possible was unimpaired by excessive ideological or moral concerns. His rhetoric is dismissed as a realistic and necessary way of paying his dues to the realities of the American political scene during a period in which Senators Joseph McCarthy, William Knowland, and others were still a force to be reckoned with. But the attempt to portray Dulles as 'realist,' a Republican George F. Kennan, is ultimately unconvincing because Guhin is required to expend too much effort attempting to explain away evidence that appears to support the contrary thesis.

Other serious efforts to analyse Dulles include books by Eleanor Lansing Dulles (sister of the late secretary and herself a former official in the State Department), Richard Goold-Adams, Roscoe Drummond and Gaston Coblentz, and Louis Gerson.[4] Gerson's biography, part of a multi-volume series on American Secretaries of State and Their Diplomacy, challenges the conventional thesis that Dulles rather than President Eisenhower was the architect of American diplomacy during the period from 1953 to 1959.

Herman Finer's detailed analysis of the Suez crisis is exceedingly critical.[5] Finer concludes that, at the crucial point Dulles lost his nerve, thereby preventing the overthrow of Nasser by the combined French, British, and Israeli forces. Although Dulles' clumsy and at times dishonest diplomacy during this episode was indefensible, it is far from evident that military success by the invading Anglo-French-Israeli forces would have been in America's interest—or that of the world. Within hours of his speech at the United Nations, putting the United States on record as opposing its erstwhile allies, Dulles was felled by the first attack of cancer that would claim his life thirty months later. Whether his illness caused the 'loss of nerve' is neither clear nor especially relevant, for by that time the damage had been done.

Unflattering as Finer's portrait of Dulles may be, however, it is no more so than that which emerges from *The Devil and John Foster Dulles.* Hoopes, who had previously given us an excellent insider's account of American policy-making toward Vietnam,[6] undertook the study of Dulles largely as a way of tracing the roots of American involvement in that catastrophic venture. But this is a full-scale biography, not simply an account of American policy toward Indochina during the Eisenhower years.

The Dulles that emerges from these pages is attractive neither as a man nor as a diplomat. He is depicted as excessively ambitious, opportunistic, and almost wholly lacking in sensitivity to others, including his own children. But Hoopes has not written a psycho-biography (such as, for example, the Georges' classic study of Woodrow Wilson or Arnold Rogow's book on James Forrestal[7]). He does not make any systematic effort to relate Dulles' psychological needs and defences to the development of his thought about international politics, or to his performance as adviser to Thomas Dewey during two unsuccessful presidential campaigns, as an appointed Republican senator from New York and unsuccessful candidate for a full elected term, as an official during the Truman administration, or as secretary of state. Thus, some of the more interesting questions about Dulles' life, including his 'conversion' from a quasi-economic determinist to something of a spiritual determinist during the late 1930s and the early 1940s, remain largely unanswered.

Hoopes focuses his attention on Dulles as secretary of state.[8] His diplomatic style is characterized in the following terms.

1) Dulles' thought and diplomacy were guided by moral absolutes. As a consequence he repeatedly transformed conflicts with the Soviet Union into moral issues. (The 'Devil' in the title refers to communism.) His rigid and sometimes petulant behaviour—for example, his refusal to shake hands with Chou En-lai at the 1954 Geneva conference on Vietnam—served America poorly in the post-Korea, post-Stalin international environment. As Hoopes puts it, Stalin did Dulles a disservice by dying and Dulles responded by ignoring his death.

2) Despite his bitter denunciation of the Democrats during the 1952 election, Dulles failed to offer a single original idea on foreign policy during his six years in office. He had joined the chorus of right-wing senators who denounced 'containment' as 'immoral,' and he dismissed the architect of that policy—George F. Kennan—as a dangerous man. Nevertheless, the keystone of Dullesian diplomacy was the erection of new alliances (SEATO, CENTO, etc) that carried the concept of containment far beyond its successful application in Western Europe into essentially barren geopolitical terrain.

3) Except for his close relations with Konrad Adenauer, Dulles was often insensitive to the political needs of others, be they allies or non-aligned nations.

4) Dulles was essentially a tactician, a barrister throwing his immense energies into the case of the moment, rather than a strategist. As a consequence short-term considerations were often allowed to dominate American foreign policy.

5) Dulles' inability to deal effectively with multiple audiences was a source of considerable difficulty. When an American secretary of state makes a major policy pronouncement at a news conference, in a television speech, or in testimony before Congress, foreign ministries all over the world will be listening in and analysing his words. This was especially true in Dulles' case because it was known that he often wrote his own speeches, that he attached a good deal of importance to his own words, and that he expected his colleagues and subordinates to do likewise. Terms and phrases such as 'liberation,' 'agonizing reappraisal,' 'neutralism is immoral,' 'unleashing Chiang,' 'brinkmanship,' 'massive retaliation,' and others, however useful they may have been for domestic political consumption, were less well received abroad, especially among America's oldest friends. That the implied threats in many of these ringing pronouncements were not in fact carried out did little to enhance the credibility of American policy. By 1954 it had become clear that the much-heralded new direction in foreign policy consisted largely of hollow threats. In response to the East German uprising in June 1953 the United States offered free food packages for the victims of Soviet repression, and if French rejection of the European Defence Community resulted in any reappraisal of American policy, it would be engaging in hyperbole to describe it as agonizing.

Hoopes closes his devastating portrait of Dulles by suggesting that the 'fervent anti-communist absolutes' that epitomized Dulles were picked up by John F. Kennedy in his inaugural address: 'Let every nation know, whether it wishes us well or ill, that we shall pay any price, bear any burden, meet any hardship, support any friend, oppose any foe to assure the survival and success of liberty.'

Although Hoopes finds little to admire in Dulles' performance, he is not indiscriminately hostile. He criticizes the Secretary of State for permitting the offshore islands to become a major point of conflict between the United States and mainland China, but he recognizes that Dulles was instrumental in defusing the issue in the autumn of 1958. And he effectively rebuts the charge by I. F. Stone that the Korean War was plotted by Dulles and General Douglas MacArthur.

Is the Hoopes biography then a fair portrayal? His analysis is generally convincing, although one has the feeling that at times he leans over backward to pin the tail on Dulles. For example, Hoopes quotes a highly moralistic section of an address Dulles delivered in Dallas on 26 October 1956, just as the first rumblings of revolution were making themselves felt in Hungary. Yet he fails to quote key parts of the speech which were a clear signal to the Soviet Union that the United States would *not* intervene in Hungary, an action that might well have started a general war in Europe. Perhaps the problem arises from Hoopes' use of a secondary source (Finer) rather than the original, perhaps it is that Hoopes sometimes seems to work a bit too hard to find fault with Dulles. As a consequence he may also be forced to lean too far in giving credit to President Eisenhower for the most favourable aspects of American foreign policy during the period. Nevertheless, this is a well researched and well written book that has captured much of the essence of a complex and controversial figure.

With two relatively inconsequential exceptions (Christian Herter and William Rogers, neither of whom was a powerful force in foreign affairs), Dulles and Henry Kissinger have been the only Republican secretaries of state since Franklin D. Roosevelt entered the White House over forty years ago. Aside from the office that both held, there are a number of parallels in their careers and diplomatic styles. Both were highly ambitious, self-confident, solo operators. Being acutely sensitive to the realities of power in Washington, they were successful in repelling potential challengers to their primacy in the area of foreign affairs, effectively structuring the decision-making process so as to maintain a near monopoly on access to the president. Dulles and Kissinger achieved high office only after seeing their original patrons suffer political defeat. Dulles had served as foreign policy adviser to Thomas Dewey when the latter was defeated by Roosevelt in the 1944 election. Harry Truman's surprising victory over Dewey in 1948 appeared to end Dulles' ambition to achieve the office once held by his grandfather and uncle. Nelson Rockefeller's unsuccessful effort to gain the Republican presidential nomination in 1968 was a bitter blow to Kissinger, all the more so because the victor was a man for whom he had limited admiration—Richard M. Nixon.

Although both Dulles and Kissinger came to office in the midst of highly unpopular wars with ambitions to reshape the fundamental conceptions, goals, and direction of American diplomacy, they soon became enmeshed in the operational side of policy. The dominant public image of both men is that of global crisis managers who have spent much of their working time in jets en route to one or another meeting with foreign leaders. By-passing the normal diplomatic channels in favour of personal diplomacy was in part a response to the urgency of crises, but it also reflected a shared distrust of bureaucracies. Dulles' rather shabby demand for 'positive loyalty' from his State Department colleagues epitomized his doubts that holdovers from twenty years of Democratic administrations would serve him faithfully. Kissinger's characterization of bureaucracy as a major barrier to rational foreign policy was well developed long before his departure from Cambridge for Washington.[9] Suspicion that the bureaucracy would not be responsive to executive direction led him to bypass it in important aspects of his Vietnam policies. The failure of bureaucracy to 'tilt' toward Pakistan during the Indo-Pakistani war in 1971 led, according to the 'Anderson Papers,' to a severe tongue lashing from Kissinger. Even after moving to the State Department there is little evidence that this aspect of Kissinger's thinking or policy-making has materially changed.

Interesting as these parallels may be, they should not be pursued too far, for in a number of important respects Dulles and Kissinger differ significantly. Indeed, it was as a critic of the Eisenhower-Dulles defence policies that Kissinger first achieved public recognition. As a young assistant professor who had been denied tenure at Harvard, he accepted a position with the Council on Foreign Relations not long after Dulles announced a 'new look' in American defence policy. Publication of *Nuclear Weapons and Foreign Policy,* a critical analysis of the 'massive retaliation' doctrine, established Kissinger as a leading student of strategy in the nuclear age.

One notable difference between Dulles and Kissinger concerns the role of ideology in foreign policy. For the former the ideological differences between the free world and the communist bloc were critical and defined relations between them, whereas Kissinger's writing is re-

plete with assertions that ideology is a major barrier to effective foreign policy. He has at times suggested that his critics compare his position to that of John F. Kennedy's inaugural address—and, by implication, to that of Dulles. Admittedly the world has changed during the sixteen years between Dulles and Kissinger, but it is hard to imagine the circumstances under which the latter would be inclined to diagnose the sources of Soviet foreign policy in these terms: 'Soviet Communism starts with an atheistic, Godless premise. Everything else flows from that premise.'[10]

A second fundamental difference between Dulles and Kissinger is in their conception of the international system and America's place in it. The former accepted the premises of a bipolar world, and he sought to thwart communist advances by means of a series of bilateral and multilateral alliances. His distaste for summitry and direct dealing with the adversary arose in part from the fear that even limited steps toward détente would lull the American public and allies abroad into reduced vigilance, thereby endangering the vital structure of free world defences. Kissinger, on the other hand, has largely discarded the assumptions of bipolarity, and his image of a multipolar world would appear to incorporate a declining role for alliances of the type that marked the Dulles years.

Except in a pure conflict situation there are always some tensions between the requisites of alliance management and those of crisis management. The manner in which Dulles and Kissinger have attempted to cope with these tensions is also revealing. One strategy is to give top priority to alliance maintenance, even if doing so may entail some potential lost opportunities for reducing or resolving inter-alliance conflicts. Dulles adopted this approach during much of his tenure as secretary of state. Deviations from this policy—for example, agreeing to attend the Geneva summit conference of 1955—were grudgingly accepted only in response to intense pressures from allies, most notably Great Britain.

The Kissinger strategy has been almost diametrically opposite to that pursued by Dulles. Maintaining harmonious relations with allies has apparently become a secondary or tertiary priority, taking a back seat to the search for détente with China and the Soviet Union. The pursuit of the 'China opening' was undertaken without any prior consultations with Japan. Revelation of the Kissinger and Nixon trips to China (and the New Economic Policy of August 1971) caused considerable embarrassment to Prime Minister Sato, the ruling Liberal party, and the nation. Nor have relations with major NATO allies fared much better. Kissinger's harshest words have been reserved not for the Soviet or Chinese governments, but for those of the Western European allies; indeed, he has raised questions not only about the wisdom of their foreign policies, but also about the very legitimacy of their governments.

While their conceptions of alliances differed, neither Dulles nor Kissinger gets very high marks for alliance management. Dulles did not inspire great confidence in the foreign offices of America's partners. Although acutely aware of the need to build a base of political support in Washington, he often seemed almost studiously insensitive to the political position of allied leaders, with the exception of Konrad Adenauer. Others were used and manipulated when it suited Dulles' purposes. His handling of the Suez crisis is a classic in the art of alienating allies.

Kissinger's lack of success in this respect is more puzzling because much of his academic writing had criticized the policies of his predecessors for being insufficiently sensitive to Western European fears and aspirations. Yet today American relations with its natural allies—Japan and the NATO nations—are in a shambles, and it is far from clear that this was a necessary (or even acceptable) price to pay for the benefits that have thus far accrued from détente. There is an element of truth in a recent comment by Peter Jenkins of the *Manchester Guardian* that Kissinger 'regards Europe as he regards the State Department—as an adjunct to his personal diplomacy, to be seen and not heard.'

How will history ultimately judge Dulles and Kissinger? In the latter case it is obviously too early to make much more than a studied guess. Much will probably depend on: (1) the durability of détente; (2) Kissinger's ability to use the freedom from the constraints of superpower confrontations to cope creatively with critical post-cold war issues, many of which will require more than agility in great power manoeuvres; and (3) the extent to which a solo operator such as Kissinger is able to institutionalize policies that have thus far been largely the result of the most personal type of diplomacy.[11]

In assessing Dulles we should avoid doing so too much in the light of subsequent developments. Whatever the wisdom or foolishness of his Indochina policies, they should be judged in their own terms, not by the actions subsequently taken by Presidents Kennedy, Johnson, and Nixon in that unhappy part of the world. To do otherwise is to fall prey to a type of historical determinism, implying wrongly that those who followed Dulles had no freedom of choice with respect to Vietnam. Critics sometimes also accuse Dulles of having failed to take advantage of opportunities to seek a meaningful détente with the USSR, and perhaps China as well. Kissinger's successes are sometimes cited as proof of what might have been achieved a decade and a half earlier. But one need not be counted among Dulles' admirers to question whether he was the sole or even main obstacle to détente or to a stable settlement in Europe. In this respect perhaps the fairest judgment is that unique Scottish verdict: Not proven.

But even if we resist the temptation to assess Dulles in light of subsequent actions by others, the balance sheet on his diplomacy would seem to remain largely negative.[12] Consider just a few examples. The Aswan-Suez fiasco could scarcely have been handled more ineptly.

The long-term decline in State Department morale began when he caved in to right-wing pressures for a purge, especially among China experts who had reported unpalatable truths about the Kuomintang régime. And the education of the American people about the realities of international life was set back for six years while Dulles painted for them a picture of the world in bold strokes of black and white. Repeated assertions that only 'atheistic communism' stood in the way of perpetual peace were punctuated by periodic claims of diplomatic triumphs that were hastening the demise of the Soviet system. Whether his sermons did or did not reflect Dulles' 'true' beliefs—the evidence strongly suggests that they did—is quite irrelevant on this point. By merely having indulged in such rhetorical excesses Dulles was guilty of having served poorly the needs of the American people for realistic guidance from their leaders.

NOTES

[1] David and Deane Heller, *John Foster Dulles* (New York 1960).

[2] John Robinson Beal, *John Foster Dulles 1888-1959* (New York 1959).

[3] Michael Guhin, *John Foster Dulles: A Statesman and His Times* (New York 1972).

[4] Eleanor Lansing Dulles, *John Foster Dulles: The Last Year* (New York 1963); Richard Goold-Adams, *The Time of Power: A Reappraisal of John Foster Dulles* (London 1962); Roscoe Drummond and Gaston Coblentz, *Duel at the Brink* (New York 1960); and Louis Gerson, *John Foster Dulles* (New York 1967).

[5] Herman Finer, *Dulles over Suez* (Chicago 1964).

[6] Townsend Hoopes, *The Limits of Intervention* (New York 1969).

[7] Alexander L. George and Juliette L. George, *Woodrow Wilson and Colonel House* (New York 1956); Arnold Rogow, *James Forrestal: A Study of Personality, Politics, and Policy* (New York 1963).

[8] Hoopes has no doubt about the relative impact of Dulles and Eisenhower on American foreign policy. 'While Eisenhower knew his own mind in foreign policy and demonstrated at several critical junctures a humane, practical wisdom and a firm restraint, Dulles was indisputably the conceptual fount as well as the prime mover of United States foreign policy during those years. His was the informing mind, indeed almost the sole keeper of the keys to the ramified web of understanding and relationships that constituted America's posture of categorical anti-Communism and limitless strategic concern.' (p xiv)

[9] See, for example, Henry A. Kissinger, 'Domestic Structure and Foreign Policy,' *Daedalus,* xcv (spring 1966), 503-29.

[10] John Foster Dulles, *War or Peace* (New York 1950), p 8.

[11] As this is being written, Kissinger is for the first time coming under sustained attack in Congress. Previously critics tended to be confined to those who felt that Kissinger had not bargained as hard as he might have with the Soviet Union. His rather maladroit performance during the Cyprus crisis, and revelations about his possible role in covert CIA activities in Chile, have brought forth a number of public suggestions that Kissinger is no longer indispensable to the conduct of American foreign policy.

[12] In writing *The Devil and John Foster Dulles* Hoopes had access to materials unavailable to previous biographers, notably the *Pentagon Papers*. He also supplemented the Dulles Oral History data by interviewing many of Dulles' former associates. Useful as these sources are for filling in details, the character that emerges from this study does not really depend on them. Put somewhat differently, even had he been forced to rely only on materials that were public as early as a decade ago, I suspect that Hoopes' book would have been very similar. Whether his characterization of Dulles will remain valid as new archival materials become available remains to be seen. I would guess that it will.

Richard H. Immerman (essay date 1979)

SOURCE: "Eisenhower and Dulles: Who Made the Decisions?," in *Political Psychology,* Vol. 1, No. 2, Autumn, 1979, pp. 21-37.

[*In the following essay, Immerman puts forth evidence which questions the conventional view that Dulles dominated the president in his foreign policy decision-making during the Eisenhower administration.*]

Studies of American foreign policy during the Eisenhower administration have produced several continuing controversies. Probably the most heated debate revolves around the influence of Eisenhower's secretary of state, John Foster Dulles. As the title of Ole R. Holsti's article, "Will the Real Dulles Please Stand Up," succinctly reminds us, assessments of Dulles' character and performance differ radically.

Many analysts have concentrated on Dulles' theological inclinations. They depict him as a relentless crusader, whose fervent belief in his own moral rectitude and "strong, self-reliant personality" gave him the necessary confidence "to shoulder alone the momentous responsibilities of his office and to face alone the dreadful uncertainties of foreign policy." While most students of Dulles agree that his moral instincts drove him to initiate forceful policies, they vehemently disagree in their assessments of those policies. Sympathizers emphasize that his crusading spirit was harnessed to a realistic perception of the world. They argue that the firmness of his convictions combined with his knowledge of diplomatic subtleties enabled him courageously to defend the interests of the United States in the face of a dangerous communist threat. Detractors criticize him as a virtual fanatic who exaggerated the threat of communism and led the United States to the brink of war. In both of these theological interpretations, the strength of Dulles' personality is a constant.

A smaller school portrays Dulles in more secular terms. These writers present him as a man of great ambition, a man who above all wanted to be secretary of state. Rather than acting out of conviction, he acted out of expediency. He was an opportunist whose desire to be America's international leader caused him to echo the dominant cold war ethos. Accordingly, these authors argue that Dulles' hard-line anticommunism was more the result of the legacy of Dean Acheson's China policy and the rampages of Joseph McCarthy than it was of any fear of international atheism. His primary concern was with his career and Eisenhower's remaining in office, thereby permitting him to continue to live his lifelong dream of international leadership.

Somewhat surprisingly, these divergent opinions as to Dulles' character have had little effect on assessments of another fundamental issue concerning Eisenhower's foreign policy—"Who made it?" Some authors paint a portrait of Dulles as dominating his relations with Eisenhower, while others describe him as almost obsequious. Yet virtually all agree that Eisenhower's diplomacy from 1953-1959 was in fact designed by Dulles. This consensus is based to a large extent on the traditional image of Eisenhower. How could the conventional Dwight D. Eisenhower, a naive farm boy whose only experience in world affairs was thought to have been narrowly military, have been anything but a figurehead in his dealings with a man who had been Wall Street's highest-paid lawyer, and had been garnering diplomatic experience since the age of 19? The answer seemed so obvious it hardly required careful examination.

But if Dulles were indeed so influenced by domestic pressures as some have postulated, is it not possible that he was also influenced by his president? And was Eisenhower so naive and so easily dominated? Since the late 1960s, journalists such as Murray Kempton and Garry Wills have asserted that his personality was much more complex than generally assumed, and recent scholarly treatments have supported their assertions. Questions such as these require students of the Eisenhower-Dulles relationship to look carefully at both men's personalities, and to analyze closely their relationship on the basis of a systematic examination of the primary source record, rather than continuing to assume Dulles' dominance based on the imputed personal characteristics of the two men.

This study is the beginning of such an examination. Using illustrative evidence gathered from recently released archives and older sources that have been available but largely overlooked, it will set forth the case for the necessity of reexamining the conventional wisdom. I argue that the personalities of neither Eisenhower nor Dulles have been adequately understood, nor has the manner in which they viewed their respective roles within the constellation of the executive office. Citing representative examples from archival material, I will show that Eisenhower and Dulles interacted on various levels, calling into question the traditional assumptions concerning the nature of their relationship.

This study is interesting because it raises both a general issue and a concrete case for historical analysis. In general terms, it sheds light on the complex relationship between a president and a chief adviser. There have been altogether too few assessments of these types of interactions. Too little is known about the precise nature of the flow of influence in such relationships. Under what circumstances is the president the primary influence? Under what circumstances is it the adviser? When there is genuine collaboration, how does it occur? There are many such questions to consider, and these one-to-one relations have become so common that it is time they be meticulously examined, and eventually some comparisons drawn.

Specifically, reexamination of the Eisenhower-Dulles relationship will add another dimension to the growing revisionist literature on the Eisenhower administration, and on the president himself. Perhaps in no aspect of the conventional literature on Eisenhower is the Barber image of a passive/negative president so prevalent as it is in the standard interpretation of his relationship with Dulles. Traditional assumptions as to their respective personalities could not help but to have reinforced the model of a president who placed full control of foreign policy in the hands of his secretary of state.

A noteworthy illustration of this standard treatment is Lloyd S. Etheredge's new work, *A World of Men: The Private Sources of American Foreign Policy.* Etheredge, in attempting to rate quantitatively the personalities of various statesmen as to their general dominance over subordinates, cites the Eisenhower-Dulles relationship as an example. Using a 10-point scale derived from purported policy differences, he determined that Dulles' rating was 9.33 dominant, second only to Lyndon Johnson. Eisenhower, at 2.33, fell very near the bottom of the list. Hence Etheredge could conlude: "The traditional historian's judgments that . . . Eisenhower often took a back seat [to Dulles] is supported by . . . ratings as being of lower dominance." Etheredge's study thus quantifies the conventional wisdom. But as in all cases of quantification, the numbers are only as valid as the data they enumerate. And Etheredge uses secondary sources and published memoirs which are themselves based on inferences of the sort previously summarized, not close analysis of the actors' behavior to whom he assigns scores.

SOURCES ON EISENHOWER AND DULLES

A major reason why interpretations of the Eisenhower-Dulles relationship have remained so static over the years

is the unchanging nature of their sources. Etheredge, writing in 1978, documents as his primary evidence Sherman Adams' *Firsthand Report* and Emmet Hughes' *The Ordeal of Power,* which appeared in 1961 and 1963, respectively. These are both works by White House insiders, but neither of the authors was able to observe consistently Eisenhower's dealings with or attitudes toward Dulles. Adams was almost exclusively involved with domestic concerns, and Hughes' position was that of a part-time speechwriter. Furthermore, coming so close to the end of the Eisenhower administration, they suffer from a lack of historical detachment.

Others who have analyzed the Eisenhower-Dulles diplomatic record have relied heavily on two other kinds of sources. Journalists like Kempton and Wills used the public record to support inferentially their conclusions. The public record, of course, tells little about the decision-making process. Scholarly researchers have sought more primary material, and have therefore concentrated on the Dulles Papers and Oral History Project at Princeton. Unfortunately, Dulles' papers reveal very little of his relationship with Eisenhower, and few doubt that indiscriminate use of oral histories can lead to faulty generalizations. As I will explain, none of those who used the Dulles oral histories have subjected them to a close contextual analysis.

The acquisition by the Eisenhower Library in Abilene, Kansas, of the massive Whitman file permits the current researcher to go beyond this "first-cut" evidence. Named after the president's personal secretary Ann Whitman, the file is a bonanza, revealing more clearly what transpired behind the scenes of the Eisenhower presidency. Included are daily calendars and often detailed minutes of appointments and discussions, both formal and informal, and meetings, such as those of the cabinet, National Security Council, and legislative leaders. Perhaps even more enlightening are the numerous transcriptions of the many telephone conversations Eisenhower held each day, the huge volume of memoranda which he sent and received, and the prolific correspondence which he conducted with individuals within and outside of the administration. The communication between Eisenhower and Dulles, both written and verbal, is greater than that between the president and anyone else.

The Whitman File also contains an extensive array of the numerous drafts of Eisenhower's speeches. Prepared by official and unofficial speechwriters, normally with the significant input of department and agency chiefs, these drafts show that Eisenhower was intensely involved in and knowledgeable about virtually all aspects of the affairs of state, and in particular foreign policy. He never gave a major speech without his personal editions and additions. Nor, when time permitted, did one of his subordinates make a major address without his having had the opportunity to review it. Dulles showed virtually all his draft speeches to Eisenhower, and it is not uncommon to find the president's suggestions incorporated verbatim into the final text.

A final component of the Whitman File which requires special attention is Eisenhower's personal diary. The president actually began to keep a diary in the 1930s while serving as Douglas MacArthur's aide in the Philippines, and although he kept it only sporadically, it contains many insights into his personal thinking and actions. He comments on his philosophy, his analysis of specific episodes, and most beneficially from the standpoint of this study, his views on leadership and relationships with individual subordinates. The diary is essential to any study of Eisenhower's personality.

The new assessment of Eisenhower's role in American foreign policy and his relationship with Dulles, which emerges from the Whitman File, encourages the researcher to reexamine previously available sources. The logical place to begin this review is the Dulles Oral History Project. Containing close to 300 interviews, this collection has been the basic instrument for those interested in understanding Dulles, both as a person and a secretary of state. Careful scholars and popular historians alike have used this project to support the thesis that Dulles dominated Eisenhower's diplomacy.

A careful analysis of the Dulles Oral History Project reveals that virtually all interviewees who depict the Dulles-Eisenhower relationship traditionally were *outside* the inner circle of both the White House and the State Department. Those who *were within* one or both of these circles, who witnessed intimately how Eisenhower's foreign policy apparatus operated, almost unanimously support the hypothesis of an activist president who was the central figure in diplomatic decisions. These were the individuals closest to both Eisenhower and Dulles, who knew their personal habits, idiosyncracies, and modes of operation.

These views are substantiated by looking at the "other side of the coin." There are a large number of interviews on the Eisenhower administration in the Columbia Oral History Collection. These interviews have not been used by Dulles scholars when assessing his relationship with the president. Yet when Elmo Richardson used the Columbia Collection in conjunction with the Whitman File to study Eisenhower, he also concluded that the Eisenhower-Dulles relationship needs reexamination.

One final note on the sources. A striking feature of any record on the Eisenhower presidency, whether it be from the Whitman File or the Oral Histories, is the constant reference to Eisenhower the General. There is no doubt that Eisenhower brought with him to the White House the legacies of his long military service. Consequently, in order to understand fully Ike's personality and the nature of his relationships, it is essential to review his career as supreme allied commander and chief of NATO.

Two often overlooked studies of the military Eisenhower are by Kenneth Davis and Stephen Ambrose. They both present an individual brimming with self-confidence and blessed with an almost uncanny ability to understand and take advantage of the personal characteristics of his subordinates. They also show a general very much involved with the political as well as the military aspects of international relations. These traits can also be found in Ike's wartime memoirs, *Crusade in Europe.* Although this work creates the suspicions of any autobiographical account, his personal papers reinforce the view presented in the narrative. Once secluded in Abilene, and in other subdivisions of the National Archives, these papers are now being made readily available through the magnificently edited collection, *The Papers of Dwight David Eisenhower.*

SOME WHITMAN FILE EVIDENCE

Three representative selections from the Whitman material suggest the need to reexamine the nature of the relationship between Eisenhower and Dulles. Each illustrates a different manner by which the two men interacted. To show the type of give and take which indicates a mutual respect and confidence, I have chosen one of the numerous telephone conversations that took place between the two men practically every day. The incident under discussion was a relatively minor episode in the omnipresent cold war. In June 1954, a British airplane was shot down off Hainan, China. In attempting to locate survivors, two American search planes had themselves been shot down. Upon hearing the news, Dulles immediately informed Press Secretary James Hagerty, who told Eisenhower. The president called Dulles.

Eisenhower opened the conversation by asking Dulles how he suggested the matter be handled. Dulles replied that *if* the president approved, he would make "a protest against further barbarities in attempting to shoot down rescue-type planes." Eisenhower told Dulles that he had *already* spoken to the congressional leaders about lodging a protest, and they seemed to think it a good idea. But he had advised the leaders to keep the information secret until an official policy was decided upon. In addition, Eisenhower instructed Dulles that he should also send a message to British Foreign Secretary Anthony Eden urging that England take as equally a hard line as the United States in condemning the Chinese action. Eisenhower was concerned that if the British position differed from the American one, friction might be created between the two countries. Dulles agreed. They concluded their exchange with the understanding that Dulles would immediately make a public statement, while the president would delay any comments.

Clearly this was not a Dulles-dominated conversation. Eisenhower requested Dulles' advice, but in this case he had already arrived at the same judgments. Furthermore, it was Eisenhower who suggested the note to Eden, a note that was very much in keeping with his traditional concerns with Allied unity. Eisenhower was concerned with the overall strategy, and with the political ramifications. He would then have Dulles execute the decisions. The public would hear and see the secretary of state, not the president. The parallels to his former role as supreme allied commander are evident.

This telephone conversation is representative of the transcripts found in the Whitman File, and suggests the need for a new assessment of Eisenhower's interaction with Dulles. A more complete assessment will now be possible. Several days before the substance of this article was delivered as a paper, the staff of the Eisenhower Library completed the review of the Eisenhower-Dulles telephone conversations located in the Dulles Papers at Abilene. This series of documents contains over a thousand pages of detailed transcripts of the many conversations between the president and the secretary of state, whether or not Eisenhower was in the Oval Office when the conversations took place. They concern literally every aspect of United States foreign policy and related matters, and will unquestionably enable scholars to reach more definitive conclusions.

The second example shows Eisenhower soliciting Dulles' advice, but also using the secretary as a "sounding board" for his own ideas. Eisenhower would soon give a speech before the newspaper editors, and wanted Dulles' suggestions. His "personal and confidential" letter requesting the suggestions is revealing for two reasons. First, it indicates the respect the president had for Dulles' knowledge and judgments. Second, it calls into question the conventional assumption that since Eisenhower advocated conciliation and Dulles brinkmanship, the administration's hard-line anticommunism resulted from the secretary's dominating influence. This is one of many illustration's of Eisenhower's personal hard-line thinking.

Eisenhower began the letter by outlining his overall objective, which was to reach "some reliable agreements with the Soviets that will make it possible, with confidence, to reduce armaments." But he continued by discussing the difficulties in reaching such agreements. His emphasis was not on conciliation but firmness. I will quote from the letter at length, advising the reader to keep in mind that these are Eisenhower's words, not Dulles':

> It is, of course, quite comforting to recite all of the international difficulties that have, over the five years, been either surmounted or ameliorated. I've personally recited these in a number of speeches.
>
> But these specific successes cannot blind us to the most potentially dangerous of all the situations now developing. This is the credence, even respect, that the world is beginning to give to the spurious Soviet protestations and pronouncements. As their propaganda promotes this world confusion, the tone of Soviet notes and statements grows more strident. The more the men in the Kremlin come to believe that their domestic propaganda is swallowed by their own people and by the populations of other countries, including some we have counted upon as allies, the greater the risk of American isolation. One great step we can take to counter-act this trend is to make sure our own people are not deceived. . . .
>
> *I personally believe that one of the main objectives*

> *of our own efforts should be to encourage our entire people to see, with clear eyes, the changing character of our difficulties, and to convince them that we must be vigilant, energetic, imaginative and incapable of surrender through fatigue or lack of courage.* (emphasis added)

The final selection illustrates Eisenhower *instructing* Dulles. I have chosen a document from the 1956 Suez crisis because it has been an episode frequently cited by historians as an example of *Dulles'* foreign policy. Not only was the Suez crisis a dramatic confrontation, but for many scholars it indicated the force of Dulles' personality and the short-sightedness of *his* diplomacy.

This tendency is especially true of his critics, like Herman Finer, who in his *Dulles Over Suez* traces the secretary of state's every move. For our purposes Finer's work, in spite of its bias against Dulles, provides a fascinating study. He begins by proffering the standard view that Eisenhower had chosen Dulles "so that he could leave in his hands almost all of the direct and daily responsibilities for guiding this nation in its multitudinous and complex dealings with other nations. Dulles alone was in the driver's seat." He then goes on to recount Dulles' diplomacy, but his narrative continually illustrated Eisenhower's participation. Caught in a quandary, Finer eventually writes, "It must be added at this point, for unmistakable emphasis, that the President took a more active part in the Suez affair than in other diplomatic conflicts."

The Whitman material illustrates that Finer is incorrect in asserting that Eisenhower played more of a role in Suez than in other similar events. Furthermore, he was unaware of the extent of Eisenhower's activity in this particular crisis. For example, Finer spends several pages criticizing Dulles for failing to present Nasser with the Eighteen Nations' Proposals which developed from the London Conference. Predictably he places the blame for this failure squarely on Dulles. What he did not know is that on August 20, the very day Dulles, according to Finer, independently decided against presenting the proposals, the secretary of state received a message from Eisenhower. I quote:

> By no means should you become involved in a long wearisome negotiation, especially with an anticipated probability of negative results in the end. . . . Our government has expressed the opinion that in this problem, the peaceful processes of negotiation should prove equal to the development of a satisfactory solution. We cannot afford to do less than our best to assure success, and yet I repeat that it would be worse than embarrassing if you should get tied into drawn out conversations which would in the long run prove unsuccessful.

A NEW LOOK AT EISENHOWER

This small sampling of Whitman material certainly does not prove conclusively that the conventional wisdom on the Dulles-Eisenhower relationship is inaccurate. It does, however, indicate that a careful examination is necessary. Any such examination must proceed in three stages. The first is a reappraisal of the president's personality and role.

As mentioned, the Barber image of a passive/negative Eisenhower, with a relatively bland and unassuming personality, has dominated the extant literature. Only a few mavericks have attempted to challenge this portrayal, but none of their analyses has gained wide acceptance within academic circles. When Kempton opened his 1967 article with Richard Nixon's famous comment, "He [Eisenhower] was a far more complex and devious man than most people realized, and in the best sense of those words," many perhaps intuitively questioned the validity of Kempton's approach.

President Eisenhower was thought to be the same as General Eisenhower, allegedly an excellent "chairman of the board" but severely limited as an innovator or strategist. For this reason his purported role as a leader was constantly described as one of keeping the peace among more dynamic personalities who were really responsible for the specific courses of action. During World War II there were Omar Bradley, Bernard Montgomery, and George Patton. Once president, there were George Humphrey, Sherman Adams, and of course John Foster Dulles. According to this standard view, Ike did not assume responsibility, he delegated it. "Congenial Ike" was well prepared to act as a moderator, but incapable of conceiving or directing policies of his own. Writers consistently intoned that any man who employed a Walter Bedell Smith or Sherman Adams supposedly to shield himself from irritating controversies could not possibly hold his own in the numerous confrontations characteristic of the cold war. Ike left the controversies to Dulles while he practiced putting on the White House lawn.

In revising this assessment, let us begin with the image of a passive, bland, and unassuming Eisenhower, the type of personality who would be a pushover for a dynamic and forceful chief subordinate. From his earliest childhood he had never exhibited these characteristics. As a boy in Abilene, although most diligent in performing his responsibilities, he much preferred the adventure of climbing to the precarious pinnacle of the barn roof, or testing his ability against others on the athletic field. His prowess and determination earned him the respect of the entire neighborhood, including that of the boys from the "right" side of the tracks. Dwight Eisenhower would never give up, and he would never back down from anyone. The most illustrative instance of his indomitable will was his legendary, by Abilene standards, bout with Wesley Merrifield. Merrifield, the acknowledged champion of the more wealthy North Side of Abilene, was much stronger and quicker than young Ike. But challenged to defend his honor and that of his friends, Ike lunged to the attack. In spite of an initial beating that should have summarily ended the contest, he would not yield. Almost inconceiv-

ably the fight continued for more than two hours, with both boys suffering immeasurably. Finally Merrifield gasped, "Ike, I can't lick you," and wearily they decided on a draw. It took three days for Ike to return to school, but he had proven he could hold his own.

Ike never lost this indomitable spirit. While at West Point he could not totally resign himself to the strict regimentation. This is not to say that he was inherently insubordinate, but rather that he had individual drives that needed to be expressed. He expressed this personality wherever he went. For West Point this personality was a little too activist. Over the four years he received 307 demerits, and out of a graduating class of 164 members, his rank in conduct was 125.

Nor was Eisenhower passive in his later years, when he was supreme allied commander or president of the United States. There are numerous instances of his asserting himself in opposition to more cautious advice by deciding on an aggressive course of action. He was not reckless but he was firm. His decision to launch the D-Day invasion in spite of the problematic weather predictions and deeply divided advisers is well documented. A not so monumental but similar decision came in 1954 when, in spite of the objections of the assistant secretary of state and an estimated chance of success of only 20 percent, Eisenhower ordered that several planes be sent to Castillo Armas to help in the overthrow of Arbenz's government in Guatemala. The president's 1956 letter to his long-time friend and confidante "Swede" Hazlett illustrates Eisenhower's activist nature. Referring to the frequent occasions when he awakened "annoyingly" early, he confided:

> Ever since the hectic days of the North African campaign, I find that when I have weighty matters on my mind I wake up extremely early, apparently because a rested mind *is anxious* to begin *grappling* with knotty questions. Incidentally, I never worry about what I did the day before. Likewise, I spend no time fretting about what enemies or critics have said about me. I have never indulged in useless regrets. Always I find, when I have come awake sufficiently to figure out what may be then engaging my attention, that I am pondering some question that is still unanswered.
>
> So I think it is fair to say that it is not worry about the past, but a *desire to attack* the future, that gets me into this annoying habit. [emphasis added]

There is one other manifestation of Eisenhower's personality that I should mention in this connection, for it relates directly to his relationship with Secretary Dulles. All of his associates were aware of his great temper. Although he constantly fought to keep it under control, when it erupted he resembled, in the words of Special Assistant Bryce Harlow, "a human Bessemer furnace." It seems impossible that the conventional Eisenhower could have possessed such dynamism. Former head speech writer Arthur Larson recalls one incident in which an outburst of the Eisenhower anger clearly contradicts the interpretation of a president somewhat in awe of his secretary of state, perfectly happy to delegate all responsibility to him. Dulles was in doubt over the Girard case, which concerned a jurisdictional dispute between the United States and Japan. An American serviceman was accused of shooting a Japanese citizen. According to Larson, once Eisenhower had finished discussing the matter with Dulles over the phone, he violently slammed down the receiver and exploded, "Goddammit, nobody can ever do anything around here without me doing it for them." In this case it appears that Eisenhower wanted to delegate some responsibility, but found it impossible to do so.

But even if one accepts the notion that there were several dimensions to Eisenhower's personality, there remains the question as to his involvement in foreign policy. Did he *want* to shoulder the inherent responsibilities? The conventional characterization of Eisenhower is that he did not enjoy being president, and welcomed the opportunity to shift the burdens of his office to more capable subordinates. Supposedly, the secretary of state, full of self-confidence, willingly accepted the president's mandate. Did Eisenhower delegate all the responsibility for foreign policy to Dulles, responsibility that should properly have remained within the Oval Office? To answer this question we must look at Eisenhower the leader.

Long before entering the White House, Eisenhower had developed comprehensive theories of executive leadership. As might be expected, these theories were firmly rooted in his military experience. They were comprised of two essential components. The first has to do with the need for a systematically staffed administration. This applies to the general organizational structure of Eisenhower's presidency. The second, less well-recognized component was his view that any effective leader had to evaluate and make conscious use of the personalities of his chief subordinates. This latter aspect of his theory is central for understanding how Eisenhower related to John Foster Dulles.

Of these two components of executive leadership, Ike's use of a well-organized staff is the most discernible. Indeed, his reliance on his staff has often been used to evidence his excessive delegation of responsibility. What such critics have failed to consider is that Eisenhower's entire career *proved* to him the value of operating as a team. Many have remarked that much of Eisenhower's reputation prior to World War II resulted from his successes as a football coach. But as hackneyed as it may sound, his contact with football prepared him well for his more important assignments. His emphasis was always on coordinated effort as opposed to individual performances, and he preached that victory was the collective responsibility of all the participants. The analogy between football and life has certainly been overstated, but in this case the parallels are often appropriate.

Of course a successful football coach will not necessarily be a successful chief of staff, supreme allied commander, or president of the United States. A coach's role is not nearly as complex, nor is his responsibility nearly as great. It was really Eisenhower's World War II experience, and in particular the influence of General George C. Marshall, that crystallized his thinking. According to Eisenhower, Marshall thought highly of him precisely because, as the chief of staff's subordinate, he was willing to assume responsibility. Marshall wanted Eisenhower, he *needed* Eisenhower, to make certain decisions himself and not constantly check for approval. As Eisenhower wrote in *Crusade for Europe:*

> Another thing that annoyed him [Marshall] was any effort to "pass the buck," especially to him. Often he remarked that he could get a thousand men to do detailed work but too many were useless in responsible posts because they left to him the necessity of making every decision. He insisted that his principal assistants act on their own conclusions in their own spheres of responsibility. . . . By the same token he had nothing but scorn for any man who attempted to "do everything himself."

Eisenhower incorporated this reliance on staff administration into his overall team concept. Delegation of responsibility was not the same as encouraging independent action. The subordinate who is making a decision must make that decision through the eyes of his commander. He must, in fact, almost cease to be his own man. He certainly may discuss various alternatives with his chief, and argue contrary positions, but once in the field his opinions are no longer his own. He is a member of a team, and a team can have only one captain. Again Eisenhower's words are precise:

> The teams and staffs through which the modern commander absorbs information and exercises his authority must be a beautifully interlocked, smooth-working mechanisms. Ideally, the whole should be practically *a single mind.* [Eisenhower's emphasis]

The complexities of running a nation are certainly as great as those of running an army, and therefore President Eisenhower felt it important to develop a similarly well-organized staff network. Early in his first term he wrote his friend Amon Carter:

> . . . because of the way this government *must* be run, . . . I have to be guided largely by the opinions of those that I trust day in and day out . . . and who normally reach specific conclusions before they report to me.

In writing that he would be "guided," Eisenhower assumed that his staff's opinions would be based on informed judgments in keeping with *his* overall policies. And every one of his close advisers who was charged with carrying out delegated responsibilities was aware of Eisenhower's theories and approved of them. *Both* the Dulles and Columbia Oral Histories support this contention. Eisenhower's presidential subordinates knew what he expected of them. All important matters were to be brought directly to the president's attention. Less consequential matters, however, were to be handled at the staff level, but always within the context of the president's general directives. The number of Eisenhower's assistants who have expressed this theme is too large to list here. For this reason I will only cite the words of one—General Andrew Goodpaster. Goodpaster, as a special staff assistant at SHAPE, and then staff secretary in the White House, had a long and intimate connection with Eisenhower. His appraisal is directly to the point:

> If you know the President, if you know General Eisenhower at all, you know that he's a man who (a) knows how to delegate, and (b) when he delegates, he expects the people to carry the responsibility he has delegated to them, while keeping the whole thing in a context of overall policy and direction.

An understanding of Eisenhower's views on staff administration leads directly to the second component of his theory of executive leadership—an emphasis on personalities. Not all types of individuals are well-suited to such an administrative structure. Consequently, Eisenhower believed strongly that "the personalities of senior commanders and staff officers are of special importance." Chief subordinates must have the confidence and ability to carry out responsibility, to make decisions on their own. If they cannot, they should be dismissed. Furthermore, if the entire operation suffers because a subordinate fails to live up to these standards, the failure is with the commander who has selected him in the first place.

As is well-known, Eisenhower was plagued in this regard by Secretary of Defense Charles Wilson. Wilson insisted on bringing virtually all problems to Eisenhower, and often ignored the expert advice of his staff. In another one of his revealing letters to Swede Hazlett, the president explained his position. His use of the military analogy is instructive:

> Personally, I think there is nothing complicated about the line of authority and responsibility. The President is Commander in Chief. He delegates to a Service Secretary a certain amount of his constitutional authority and that Secretary becomes the President's representative.... The Secretary's orders are presumed to be the orders of the Commander in Chief. *If the Secretary is the type* who does not take the advice of his own military choices, or who is domineering and arbitrary in his decisions, then *it is the fault of the Commander in Chief for having selected such a person,* if things go wrong—as surely they would. [emphasis added]

Clearly, therefore, Eisenhower's assessments of individual personalities played a prominent role in his selection of subordinates. But he looked for more than just whether someone could assume responsibility, or could accept the advice of others. He sought to understand the strengths and weaknesses of all his associates, so that he could assure that they be used most effectively. Eisenhower was not callous, but his theory of executive leadership *called* for the use of subordinates.

To use World War II again as an example, Eisenhower constantly analyzed the personalities of his various associates in order to get the most out of their performances. One of his greatest challenges was George Patton. After the infamous incident when Patton struck a hospitalized soldier, Eisenhower admitted to Marshall, "George Patton continues to exhibit some of those unfortunate personal traits of which you and I have always known." Highest among these, according to Eisenhower's assessment, was "his habit of impulsive bawling out of subordinates." Nevertheless, Eisenhower continued, "he has qualities that we cannot afford to lose unless he ruins himself." These were, as he later wrote, "his emotional tenseness and his impulsiveness . . . that made him, in open situations, such a remarkable leader of an army. In pursuit and exploitation there is need for a commander who sees nothing but the necessity for getting ahead." Taking all this into consideration, General Eisenhower felt that he had to devise a means to minimize Patton's weaknesses and utilize his strengths. Patton's exploits at the end of the war attest to Eisenhower's success.

Bernard Montgomery also caused Eisenhower great difficulty. A tremendous egotist, he bitterly opposed playing a subordinate role to Eisenhower, or even an equal one to Bradley. As a result he threatened Ike's objective of promoting allied unity. But he had, in Eisenhower's opinion, "no superior in two most important characteristics." Specifically, Eisenhower mentioned Montgomery's ability to develop among his men "an intense devotion and admiration," and his "tactical ability in what might be called the 'prepared' battles." Ike's strategy toward Montgomery was to be firm, yet flattering and conciliatory. In a long letter to the field marshal in 1944, Eisenhower repeatedly complimented Montgomery, and highlighted their points of agreement. But, at the same time, he consistently maintained, "for any one major task on the battlefield there must be a *single battlefield* commander." Eisenhower left no doubt that this was to be himself. He was not cowed by Montgomery because, as he concluded to Marshall, he had "no lack of confidence in my ability to handle him."

To say that Eisenhower "handled" Dulles is perhaps to overstate the case. Yet, as with Patton and Montgomery, the president sought to understand the personality of his secretary of state. This understanding was a crucial aspect of his relationship with Dulles, and exemplifies the mode by which he executed presidential leadership, and made Dulles function as an efficient member of the Eisenhower administration.

A NEW LOOK AT DULLES

This study is concerned with those aspects of Dulles' personality that affected his conduct as secretary of state, and more specifically, those that affected his relationship with President Eisenhower. For the present purposes it is not necessary to attempt a detailed analysis of his religious and philosophical beliefs. Ole Holsti has already written an insightful article demonstrating the influence of Dulles' theological and intellectual perceptions on his postures and attitudes [in *Canadian Journal of Political Science* III, No. 1 (March 1970): 123-57]. Although, as mentioned earlier, there are opposing views on the nature of his strident anticommunism and often uncompromising diplomacy, there can be little doubt that they rested on a firm theoretical foundation. A serious student of international relations, Soviet communism, and the Bible, John Foster Dulles was in many respects the consummate cold warrior.

The evidence I have gathered does not contradict this impression. But it does indicate that there were more secular facets of Dulles' personality as well. He was not the one-dimensional, one-directional secretary of state so prevalent in the conventional literature. He was much more "human" than that. He had feelings, ambitions, and fears. He had strengths and weaknesses. By looking at some of these other sides to his character, we can better understand his relationship with the president.

I will begin with the common image of Dulles the intellectual loner, a man so firm in his convictions that he "carried the state department around in his hat," seeing no need to seek advice." Dulles was quite confident in his abilities. Perhaps no modern secretary of state has entered office with a better background or preparation. He was the grandson of John Watson Foster, who had served as Benjamin Harrison's secretary of state, and the nephew of Robert Lansing, who had held the same post under Woodrow Wilson. Although he gave his class's valedictory address at Princeton, he had taken time off to attend the World Peace Conference at the Hague, and when only 30 he had advised President Wilson at Versailles. Through his position as senior partner of the Wall Street law firm of Sullivan and Cromwell, and his chairmanship of the internationalist Federal Council of the Churches' Commission to Study the Bases of a Just and Durable Peace, Dulles had met many leading world figures. Later, his role as Thomas Dewey's chief foreign policy adviser in the 1944 and 1948 campaigns, his short stint as a senator, and the various activities which he performed for Dean Acheson, such as helping to organize the United Nations and negotiate the treaty with Japan, brought him recognition as an expert on international affairs. He even wrote two books on the subject. Small wonder that he expected to be Eisenhower's selection as secretary of state, and was confident of his ability to do well.

But Dulles was not so confident, nor so stubborn, that he did not seek advice. As a matter of fact, his operation of the State Department was not unlike that of President Eisenhower's White House. The primary difference is that Dulles tended to consult a group of his favorites, a sort of "kitchen cabinet." This group included both general advisers and experts in specific fields, such as Robert Bowie, John Hanes, Douglas MacArthur II, William Macomber, Livingston Merchant, Robert Murphy, Roderic O'Connor, and Herman Phleger. He held staff meetings each morning, during which time he would listen to the reports and the analyses of his subordinates. But he always reserved the final decision for himself.

It is true that Dulles normally approached his advisers with certain preconceived notions. But he did not want them merely to agree and complacently execute his policies. William Macomber states that he never saw Dulles make a decision without "talking it over with the elements in the Department that would have real experience and responsibility in that field." Herman Phleger concurs by adding, "I never met a person who was so interested in getting other people's views and . . . picking their brains for anything he could get out of them." The secretary's relationship with the Department's Planning Board chief Robert Bowie is a case in point. Bowie and Dulles disagreed on many fundamental issues. But Dulles invited, he demanded, that Bowie give his opinions on all major decisions. In this way, the secretary could guard against his overlooking alternative options, while at the same time forcing himself to think through his own position. As Bowie remarks, "He wanted somebody who would be forceful and direct in discussion. He didn't fear that." Bowie's comments reveal a side to Dulles which has been deemphasized. He was not so confident that he felt he did not need advice and criticism, and he was confident enough to accept it.

Although not very large, the group of people who worked closely with Dulles, along with others who knew him intimately, belie another generalization regarding his personality. Dulles was not the unapproachable, dour statesman who always seemed to have one foot on an airplane. Clearly he was less personable and less sensitive than Eisenhower, and enjoyed the spartan life of his Duck Island retreat. But both the Dulles and Eisenhower Oral History collections show that his associates and acquaintances saw him as warm, possessing a good sense of humor, and a pleasant companion. He not only inspired respect, but he inspired genuine affection.

Many have referred to his devotion to his wife Janet, how he took her everywhere with him, and how he appeared almost lost without her. His devotion to those outside his immediate family is less known. He was far from an extrovert, but once he became familiar with an associate, they frequently developed an intimate relationship. He teased and joked with his secretarial staff, and displayed an almost fatherly concern for his junior subordinates. Douglas MacArthur II remembers that after Dulles learned that MacArthur's wife resented the amount of time he was spending at work away from her, the secretary literally ordered him home, explaining that the young man's "home front was crumbling." On another occasion, Dulles took time off from his incredibly hectic schedule in order to make arrangements that the tropical fish which were kept in his cold State Department office found a warm home while he was away. Like Eisenhower, there was a public and a private Dulles. The words of MacArthur represent this general consensus:

> He was a fellow of great human warmth. He thought about people. He thought about family relationships. He didn't hesitate to work one very hard indeed, but at the same time he was somebody that one could joke with. And this aspect of him really didn't come out publicly. . . . I think Livy Merchant, Bob Bowie, and others of us that were privileged to work with him—all of us—we've had hilarious times with Dulles, traveling to and from conferences, when the work was over. He was a warm human being for whom I have a deep affection.

The preceding discussion is not meant to debunk completely the conventional image of a bellicose, seemingly belligerent secretary of state. Dulles' gruff exterior is a matter of public record, and numerous observers have commented on such incidents as his refusal to shake the hand of Chou En-lai at the 1954 Geneva Conference. As will be shown, Eisenhower was well aware of this aspect of Dulles' personality. What is also important to note is that Dulles himself was aware of it. This was one of the major reasons why he maintained Carl McCardle as his press secretary for such a long time in spite of advice to the contrary from so many others. (The other major reason is that he *liked* McCardle.)

A great intellect and forceful advocate, Dulles loved to coin a phrase. He always wrote his own speeches and statements. Unfortunately, he was often incapable of predicting how his words would affect the press, the public, or his opponents. He knew that McCardle, although obviously not infallible, had an uncanny ability to make such predictions. He was not a very knowledgeable journalist, and was extremely inarticulate, but he would force Dulles to listen to his opinions. I say "force" because McCardle could rarely explain why he felt as he did, which would frustrate and even anger a man who had spent much of his life as an attorney. Dulles realized, however, that McCardle possessed an ability which he did not, and by heeding McCardle's advice, Dulles was able to minimize his propensity to say the wrong thing to the wrong people at the wrong time.

Dulles' conduct during the McCarthy period raises another point about his character. Few studies of the secretary of state have not mentioned his early speech demanding "positive loyalty" from his desk officers and foreign servicemen, his hiring of Scott McLeod to conduct security investigations, and his general failure to protect the State Department from demoralizing witch hunts. There is debate as to Dulles' motives. Some analysts feel that he was forced into this passive position by Eisenhower's reluctance to confront McCarthy. Dulles, they theorize, was not sufficiently strong politically to take on McCarthy independently from the president. Others imply that to some extent Dulles sympathized with McCarthy, or at least agreed that security in the State Department had been lax and there was the possibility of communist infiltration. Another viewpoint, shared by, among others, Dulles' sister Eleanor, is that Dulles was too concerned with the political climates of the period, and felt it necessary to go along with McCarthy in order to assuage the right wing of the Republican party.

Dulles was probably influenced, in varying degrees, by all these considerations. However, another factor was also involved. Dulles was not so sure of himself, was not so contemptuously intractable, as many believe. Few have thought it possible that a man with the theological and intellectual convictions of John Foster Dulles could have been frightened by a man as crassly opportunistic as Joseph McCarthy. But he was, for Dulles, too, had his Achilles heel—Alger Hiss.

Dulles, of course, had worked with Hiss in organizing the UN, and had recommended him for the presidency of the Carnegie Foundation. His deep concern that his past connection would make him vulnerable to McCarthyite charges is illustrated by an interview with Edward Corsi. Corsi was the State Department's specialist in migration and refugee problems, and was attacked by McCarthy's staunch ally, Congressman Francis Walter, chairman of the House Immigration and Naturalization Subcommittee. At first, Corsi could not understand his isolation. The only help he was getting from the Department was an open-ended offer to become an ambassador to an unspecified Latin American country. Finally, he went directly to Dulles. Corsi's account of this encounter shows a side of Dulles very different from that of the indomitable titan:

> Finally I couldn't take this. I had to have a showdown with John Foster Dulles himself. And I called Mr. Dulles. I made an appointment. . . . He sat there. He looked like a beaten man. It seemed that the tragedy was more his than mine. . . . And then he went off into a spiel about what these same elements had done to him on the Hiss case. And he said, "Don't you know that I went through this kind of thing with all these people? You can't pacify these people. There's no reasoning with these people." . . . and he kept pleading with me. I never saw a man plead . . . I never saw a man so scared of this situation as he was.

This story is not intended to portray Dulles as a cowering weakling. It is meant rather to illustrate that there was more to him than vitriolic rhetoric, seemingly inexhaustible energy, and stoical self-denial. He had a multifaceted personality. Similarly, he had a multifaceted relationship with President Eisenhower.

THE EISENHOWER-DULLES RELATIONSHIP

It is too simplistic to assert that the respective personalities of two individuals wholly determine the manner in which they relate to each other. Environmental and situational factors all play a part. However, concentrating on the personality factor, I have argued thus far that neither Eisenhower nor Dulles conform to the conventional historical image. While these new assessments of their personalities do not necessitate a new interpretation of their relationship, they do necessitate that their relationship be reexamined.

Perhaps the most crucial component in any relationship is how the involved personalities perceive one another. Eisenhower, most have believed, felt innately inferior to Dulles. He deferred to his secretary of state's knowledge, intelligence, and power of advocacy. One Dulles biographer wrote, Ike "admired Foster and was a little frightened of him, sometimes referring to him as an Old Testament prophet." In relation to the other members of the cabinet, Eisenhower viewed Dulles, according to the journalist Roscoe Drummond, as "a peer among peers," and gave him his unwavering and unequivocal support.

According to this traditional interpretation, Dulles perceived Eisenhower as his client. In almost every Dulles biography or study there is the analogy to a lawyer and his client. Theoretically in such a relationship the lawyer advises and counsels, and the client listens. But the lawyer should not overstep his mandate. For this reason Dulles, many think, kept Eisenhower informed as to his every action. He never forgot how his uncle, Robert Lansing, had lost Wilson's confidence by pursuing too independent a course at Versailles. Dulles therefore nourished his relationship with extreme care, giving Eisenhower "advance notice of upcoming problems in need of decision, laying out his own analysis, and listening carefully to the President's comments." In fact, one gets the impression that the secretary was so attentive and held such a monopoly with Eisenhower concerning international affairs that there was little if any other input. As a result, in the words of another Dulles biographer, "Eisenhower came to see the world through Dulles' own spectacles."

On one score these generalizations concerning the manner in which Eisenhower and Dulles perceived each other are right on the mark. The president did greatly admire his secretary of state. As he wrote in 1954 to Edgar, his older brother and often critic, in his estimation Dulles was "the best informed man on international affairs that I believe lives in the world today." In addition, Eisenhower respected Dulles for being a "dedicated and tireless individual," as a patriot who "passionately believes in the United States, in the dignity of man, and in moral values." What responsible leader would not seek out and often accept the advice of an adviser whom he regarded so highly?

But to admire someone, to respect his outstanding abilities, is not the same as to be awed. Eisenhower had spent most of his life dealing with many of the most able and forceful individuals in the twentieth century. Being secure in himself he was not reluctant to bestow praise on others. Yet he was also not reluctant to find fault with them. We have seen how during World War II he analyzed both the strengths and weaknesses of chief subordinates like Patton and Montgomery so as to use their potential to the utmost. He did the same in the White House. A 1953 entry in his personal diary bears a remarkable resemblance to his previously cited letter to Marshall a decade earlier. Similar to his assessment of the chief officers under his command during World War II, Eisenhower as president reviewed his cabinet secretaries and White House staff.

He opened his discussion of Dulles by extolling the secretary of state's virtues. His second paragraph, however, illustrates the type of critical analysis necessary for his theories on effective leadership. Eisenhower understood that Dulles had faults as well as virtues, and as the leader he would have to be conscious of both. Consequently, he concluded his appraisal by writing:

> He is not particularly persuasive in presentation and, at times, seems to have a curious lack of understanding as to how his words and manner may affect another personality. Personally, I like and admire him; my only doubts concerning him lie in the general field of *personality,* not in his capacity as a student of foreign affairs. [Eisenhower's emphasis]

Perhaps some day the availability of additional documents will permit the researcher to uncover the spectrum of Eisenhower's views on Dulles. For the time being, however, it is enough to note that he was not so overwhelmed by Dulles that he was oblivious to his shortcomings. He perceived Dulles in the same ways he perceived Patton or Montgomery, based on all his feelings and his judgments. Eisenhower's mode of leadership required multifaceted approaches, and it required cooperation. When there is a mutuality of purpose, there must be a mutuality of understanding.

Interestingly, Eisenhower's reservations regarding Dulles' manner of presenting the United States position stemmed in part from the secretary's legalistic inclinations. Although most observers, including many within the administration, perceived the Eisenhower-Dulles relationship as that of a client to his lawyer, the president at times disapproved of the attorney-like approach. For example, in 1958, after dictating an insert to Dulles' draft note to the Soviet Union, Eisenhower commented to Andrew Goodpaster, "I sense a difference with Foster Dulles [in the approach to the Soviets]. His is a lawyer's mind." The difference, he explained, was that whereas Dulles methodically prosecuted the Soviets for their actions, he neglected to emphasize sufficiently the constructive aspects of United States policy. Eisenhower appreciated Dulles' power of advocacy, but preferred that the American position be presented more positively. As he told Goodpaster, "Of course we have got to have a concern and respect for fact and reiteration of official position, but we are likewise trying to 'seek friends and influence people.'"

By the same token, Dulles' perception of his role as Eisenhower's secretary of state was not merely that of a lawyer to client. He did believe that his background in international relations, and his assignment as chief of the State Department, dictated that he be the administration's key foreign policy advisor. He jealously guarded this position. This is the reason he felt he was selected in the first place. He knew that Eisenhower wanted his advice and counsel, that Eisenhower expected him, as he expected any subordinate, to carry out his responsibilities as fully and as aggressively as he could. He was confident in himself. But he was also confident in Eisenhower.

Perhaps no aspect of the Eisenhower-Dulles relationship has been less appreciated than this confidence which Dulles had in his president. Dulles did not confer so frequently with Eisenhower simply because he wanted to avoid the fate of his uncle, Robert Lansing. He conferred with him because he respected Eisenhower's opinions. He knew that the president's experience in the international arena and familiarity with many of the world leaders gave him a valuable perspective on the conduct of foreign policy. He also knew that Eisenhower possessed the type of political sensitivity and awareness that he himself was lacking.

Dulles acquired this respect for Eisenhower at the beginning of their association. Illustrative is an incident recounted by Dulles' long-time assistant Roderic O'Connor. During the Hotel Commodore period, while Eisenhower was organizing his administration prior to taking office, he received a long telegram from Premier Mohammed Mossadegh in Iran, asking for the administration's support. The president-elect understandably sent the wire to Dulles for a draft reply. As time passed and Eisenhower did not hear anything from the secretary of state-designate, he dictated a two-page reply to Ann Whitman, who brought it personally to Dulles for his comments. Dulles changed two words and then said to O'Connor, "You know, I don't know why General Eisenhower needs a Secretary of State."

The purpose of this study was not to prove that Eisenhower did not need a secretary of state, or even that he dominated foreign policy. The purpose was to show that there is reason to scrutinize the conventional wisdom on the relationship of Eisenhower and Dulles. Evidence indicates that the standard views of both men's personalities are problematic, as are the views of their interaction within the decision-making process. Any further conclusions will require more extensive research and analysis of the recently released archival material.

George C. Herring and Richard H. Immerman (essay date 1984)

SOURCE: "Eisenhower, Dulles, and Dienbienphu: 'The Day We Didn't Go to War' Revisited," in *Journal of American History,* Vol. 71, No. 2, September, 1984, pp. 343-63.

[*In the following essay, Herring and Immerman suggest that Dulles and Eisenhower had offered "a massive air strike to relieve the Vietminh siege of the French fortress at Dienbienphu" in 1954, thus bringing the United States close to war in Southeast Asia a decade before large-scale U.S. military involvement in Vietnam began.*]

America's role in the Dienbienphu crisis of 1954 has been a source of persisting confusion and controversy. In a *Washington Post* story of June 7, 1954, subsequently expanded into a *Reporter* article provocatively entitled "The Day We Didn't Go to War," journalist Chalmers M.

Roberts divulged that the Dwight D. Eisenhower administration had committed itself to a massive air strike to relieve the Vietminh siege of the French fortress at Dienbienphu. The United States would have intervened in the Indochina War, Roberts went on, had not the congressional leadership, after a secret meeting on April 3, made intervention conditional on British participation and had not the British refused. In their memoirs British and American officials confirmed some of Roberts's account. French memoirists went further, charging that Secretary of State John Foster Dulles and Admiral Arthur W. Radford, chairman of the Joint Chiefs of Staff (JCS), had proposed an air strike to save Dienbienphu, had even proposed the loan of atomic weapons, and then had callously reneged, sealing France's defeat in the war. On the other hand, administration officials at the time and Eisenhower later insisted that they had never seriously contemplated military intervention in Indochina. Eisenhower conceded only that he had attempted to put together an allied coalition to resist Communist encroachments in Southeast Asia but had been thwarted by the British.

Despite lingering uncertainty about what actually happened, scholars have advanced numerous interpretations of the administration's handling of the crisis. Early writers typically used it to show how a reckless Dulles nearly pushed the passive Eisenhower into war. In the aftermath of Lyndon B. Johnson's massive intervention in Vietnam, however, scholars increasingly praised Eisenhower for his caution and for his involvement of Congress in policy formation. Some writers speculated that he had cleverly used Congress to restrain his more impulsive advisers. Others argued that the open process established by Eisenhower promoted a high level of "multiple advocacy," thereby producing sound policy. Whatever the perspective, scholars viewed Eisenhower's decision not to intervene as exceptional in the long history of United States escalation in Vietnam.

Recent declassification of an abundance of United States documents permits a new look at one of the most significant episodes of the Eisenhower years. Those documents make clear that the memoirs of the participants are often inaccurate and misleading and that Roberts's standard account, on which most scholars have relied, contains important errors and suffers from the bias of its own sources. The documents compel modification at a number of important points of recent favorable interpretations of Eisenhower's diplomacy.

The Dienbienphu crisis stemmed at least indirectly from Franco-American adoption of the Navarre Plan in September 1953. To prevent the fall of Indochina to the Communist-ied Vietminh insurgents, the United States since 1950 had supported France with steadily growing volumes of military and economic assistance. United States officials deplored the cautious, defensive military strategy pursued by France, however, and they feared that as long as France was fighting for essentially colonial goals, it could not win the war. Certain that the Harry S. Truman administration had not effectively applied the leverage available to it, Dulles and Eisenhower conditioned further aid on French agreement to fight the war more aggressively and to make firm promises of independence for the states of Indochina.

Uneager to expand the war but unwilling to abandon it, the French bent to American pressure. The government of Joseph Laniel vaguely promised to "perfect" Vietnamese independence. The newly appointed commander of French forces in Indochina, General Henri Navarre, drew up a military strategy tailored to United States specifications, proposing to combine his scattered forces and to launch a major offensive in the Red River delta. Although Navarre himself was skeptical that the plan could produce victory, the French government adopted it to gain additional United States aid. Dubious of French intentions and capabilities, the Eisenhower administration nonetheless felt compelled to go along, fearing that otherwise Laniel's government might be replaced by one committed to negotiations.

Navarre abandoned his ill-fated plan before he had even begun to implement it. To parry a Vietminh invasion of Laos, he had to scatter the forces he had just started to combine. As part of a hastily improvised alternative strategy, he established in late 1953 a position at the remote village of Dienbienphu in northwestern Vietnam, where he hoped to lure the Vietminh into a set-piece battle. In a broad valley surrounded by hills as high as one thousand feet, he constructed a garrison ringed with barbed wire and bunkers and dispatched twelve battalions of regulars supported by aircraft and artillery. Vietminh commander Vo Nguyen Giap soon laid siege to the French fortress. By early 1954 twelve thousand of Navarre's elite forces were isolated in a far corner of Vietnam. Although uncertain that his troops could defend themselves against superior Vietminh numbers, Navarre decided to remain.

Shortly after, the contingency Americans had so feared became reality. Facing growing political opposition at home, an uncertain military situation in Vietnam, and a depleted treasury, the Laniel government decided that it must negotiate a settlement. Over Dulles's vigorous protests, it agreed to place the Indochina question on the agenda of an East-West conference scheduled to meet in Geneva, Switzerland, in late April 1954.

These developments generated great concern in Washington. An American military observer reported from Dienbienphu as late as February that the French fortress could "withstand any kind of attack the Vietminh are capable of launching," but United States officials could not ignore the possibility that the garrison might fall, causing a total French collapse. Reports of increased Chinese aid to the Vietminh raised additional fears that, as in Korea, China might intervene directly in the war. In any event, Americans suspected that French war-weariness might lead to a sellout in Geneva. "If the French were completely honest they would get out of Indochina," Dulles remarked, "and we certainly didn't want that."

Accordingly, the administration searched desperately for means to deter Chinese intervention and to bolster French resistance. Eisenhower sent the French forty bombers and two hundred United States Air Force mechanics to service them. Conceding the risk of expanded involvement, he insisted, "My god, we must not lose Asia—we've got to look the thing right in the face."

The administration concurrently began to face the prospect that United States forces might have to be used. Notwithstanding his determination to "keep our men out of these jungles," Eisenhower reminded the National Security Council (NSC) that "we could nevertheless not forget our vital interests in Indochina." He appointed a special committee to examine the circumstances under which direct United States involvement might be required and the means by which it could be made most effective. The study had not been completed by mid-March 1954, but the siege of Dienbienphu and the danger of a French cave-in at Geneva added a sense of urgency. The committee, headed by Under Secretary of State Walter Bedell Smith, had gone so far as to ask the JCS to develop a "concept of operations" for Indochina.

In mid-March the siege tightened. French and American military experts had predicted that the Vietminh would not be able to transport artillery up the hills surrounding the fortress, but by sheer human exertion they did. In a series of attacks beginning on March 13, the Vietminh seized two major hill outposts established by the French to protect the fortress and the airfield below. Heavy Vietminh guns quickly knocked out the airfield, making resupply possible only by parachute drop. The Central Intelligence Agency (CIA) estimated no better than an even chance that the vulnerable French garrison could hold out. It seemed increasingly clear that the United States might have to take drastic steps to save France or, in the event of a French collapse, to continue the struggle for Indochina on its own.

The visit of General Paul Ely to Washington in late March brought these pressing issues to the forefront. The Smith committee had invited the French chief of staff to discuss additional military assistance. It suspected, nevertheless, that he might request intervention. During his initial meetings with Radford and Dulles, Ely estimated a fifty-fifty chance that Dienbienphu might still hold and asked for the loan of twenty-five additional B-26 bombers and American volunteers to fly them. At that point he seems to have been concerned primarily with the threat of Chinese air intervention, and he inquired in writing what the United States would do if China sent aircraft into the war.

Ely's visit took the form of a game of international cat and mouse, graphically revealing the accumulated frustrations of four years of Franco-American collaboration in Indochina. The United States approved Ely's request for the additional bombers (without the pilots), although Radford expressed grave doubts about France's ability to maintain them and use them in combat. When Radford pressed for a larger United States role in training indigenous forces and in determining strategy, Ely complained of the "invading nature" of the Americans and their apparent determination "to control . . . everything of importance."

Dulles and Radford responded noncomittally to Ely's query about Chinese intervention. They agreed that they would make no commitments until they "got a lot of answers" from the French on issues that divided the two nations. Dulles informed Ely point-blank that the United States would not invest its prestige except under conditions where military success was likely, which would require France to extend to the United States a "greater degree of partnership" than had prevailed in the past. The result was a tightly qualified "agreed minute" that directed "military authorities [to] push their planning work as far as possible so that there would be no time wasted when and if our governments decided to oppose enemy air intervention over Indochina if it took place."

At Radford's request Ely remained in Washington for one more day, at which time the two men discussed the possibility of an air strike to relieve the siege of Dienbienphu. The idea apparently originated from American and French officers in Saigon. Code-named VULTURE, the plan called for massive night bombing attacks on Vietminh positions by as many as 300 United States aircraft launched from carriers in the region and perhaps from air bases in the Philippines. Who first raised the issue and what commitments resulted are impossible to determine. Ely later declared that Radford had enthusiastically endorsed the plan and had intimated that he had Eisenhower's support. Radford admits telling Ely that within two days of a formal French request as many as 350 United States aircraft could be deployed, but he insists that he made clear that intervention would require a decision at the highest level of government and congressional approval. It is possible, of course, that the two men misunderstood each other. They spoke without an interpreter, Ely's English was not good, and he may have missed or minimized the qualifications Radford says he included. Or the French general may have understood the qualifications quite well and only later professed to have been misled. More likely, Radford was less circumspect than he allows. An Asia-firster in the mold of Douglas MacArthur and a firm believer in air power, he often advocated intervention in Indochina and at times even urged the use of atomic weapons against China. Before his last meeting with Ely, he warned Eisenhower that the United States "must be prepared to act promptly and in force possibly to a frantic and belated request by the French for U.S. intervention." Even if he had included the qualifications, as he later maintained, his obvious zeal for intervention might have left the impression that formal authority could be readily obtained, an impression, given certain of Eisenhower's comments, Radford probably believed.

In the week after Ely left Washington, however, Radford was unable to generate support for VULTURE even among the JCS. Acting on his own initiative, he called a special meeting of the JCS on March 31 to consider the "necessity or desirability" of recommending to the president that the United States offer France naval and air units for use in Indochina. Army Chief of Staff Matthew B. Ridgway objected, arguing that the formulation of policy was "outside the proper scope of authority of the JCS." Undaunted, Radford came back two days later with a formal request from the secretary of defense for the JCS view on what the United States should do if the French asked for naval and air intervention. Only Air Force Chief of Staff Nathan F. Twining responded positively, and he insisted on conditions the French were unlikely to accept, including agreement to American training of indigenous forces and a grant of "true sovereignty" to the Indochinese states. With varying degrees of intensity, reflecting to some extent the interests of their respective services, the other chiefs warned that air intervention at Dienbienphu would not decisively affect the outcome of the war and questioned whether the limited tactical gains would be worth the risks of direct involvement.

Among top civilian leaders there was no enthusiasm for air intervention at Dienbienphu. Vice-President Richard M. Nixon has been frequently cited as an advocate of intervention—and he was—but he did not play a consequential role in shaping policy. Dulles, often portrayed as a "hawk" in this crisis as in others, was in fact quite cautious. Deeply concerned that the Chinese might intervene or that France might hand Indochina over to the Communists at Geneva, the secretary was prepared to take risks in Indochina. He seems not to have been persuaded that VULTURE was either feasible or necessary, however. He stated that if the Chinese intervened he would prefer such things as "harrassing tactics from Formosa and along the Chinese seacoast," measures, he added, that "would be more readily within our natural facilities than actually fighting in Indochina."

Eisenhower's position is equally interesting, if characteristically elusive. He is typically depicted as at least a closet dove in this crisis, and he later dismissed VULTURE as military folly. Indeed, as early as 1951 he had entered in his diary, "I am convinced that no military victory is possible in that kind of theater [Indochina]." On March 24, nevertheless, he told Dulles that he would not "wholly exclude the possibility of a single strike, if it were almost certain this would produce decisive results." A week later he alluded to the idea again, adding that such an operation would have to be covert and that "we would have to deny it forever." The president was probably thinking out loud. Like Dulles, he seems never to have been persuaded that the plan would work, and he was equally opposed to intervention in any form in the absence of satisfactory military and political agreements with France. In the week after Ely's departure, VULTURE was not discussed seriously at the top levels, and the administration never made a commitment to it.

Still, Eisenhower and Dulles recognized that something must be done, and between March 24 and April 1 they began to formulate an appropriate response. They proceeded with extreme caution, keeping numerous options open and covering their tracks so well that they baffled contemporaries and future scholars. Dulles labeled their plan "United Action." Based on a regional security program he had proposed under Truman when negotiating the peace treaty (Treaty of San Francisco, 1951) with Japan, United Action was designed to meet the many uncertainties and dilemmas of the Indochina crisis. It reflected the perceived lessons of the Korean War as well as the administration's concept of strategic deterrence and its New Look defense policy. The keystone of the plan was the creation of a coalition composed of the United States, Great Britain, France, Australia, New Zealand, Thailand, the Philippines, and the Associated States of Indochina and committed to the defense of Indochina and of the rest of Southeast Asia against the Communist menace. The mere establishment of such a coalition accompanied by stern warnings to the Communists might be sufficient to bolster the French will to resist and to deter Chinese intervention, thus making outside intervention unnecessary. It is even plausible, as one of Dulles's top aides later suggested, that United Action was merely a grand charade of deterrence and that Eisenhower and Dulles never seriously considered United States military involvement.

It is more plausible that United Action was designed to ensure that if the United States intervened it would do so under favorable circumstances. The evidence indicates that although the administration never committed itself to intervention during the Dienbienphu crisis, that option was left open to meet the contingencies of Chinese intervention, a French military collapse, or, preferably, a breakdown of the Geneva negotiations and a continuation of the war. Eisenhower and Dulles agreed that the United States should go in only as part of a genuinely collective effort and that United States ground forces must not become bogged down in Asia. United Action would provide a legal basis for collective action. A multilateral effort would remove the taint of a war for colonialism and would provide additional leverage to force the French to share political and military decision making. If, on the other hand, France pulled out, United Action would ensure that the United States did not have to fight alone. In keeping with the New Look doctrine, local and regional forces would bear the brunt of the ground fighting while the Americans did those things Dulles proclaimed "we can do better," providing air and naval support, furnishing money and supplies, and training indigenous troops.

The major problem was time. The Geneva conference was only a month away. Ely's query about a United States response to Chinese intervention needed to be answered promptly if it was to have the proper political effect in France. And on March 30 the Vietminh initiated the second stage of the battle for Dienbienphu, launching withering artillery barrages and a series of human-wave assaults against the hill outposts that constituted the outer defenses of the fortress. The French held the lines and even managed successful counterattacks at some points,

but the decisive battle seemed to be underway. The fate of the fortress and the outcome of the war might be settled in a matter of weeks.

Eisenhower and Dulles hence moved rapidly to lay the groundwork for United Action. In a March 29 speech designed to "puncture the sentiment for appeasement before Geneva," Dulles publicly unveiled the concept in deliberately vague terms. He warned that the Chinese now supported the Vietminh "by all means short of open invasion" and that Communist success in Indochina would lead to further aggression in Southeast Asia, the loss of which could have disastrous consequences for the entire free world. Using words that his aide Robert Bowie described as "deliberately picked" to sound" menacing without committing anybody to anything," the secretary declared that the possibility of a Communist conquest of Southeast Asia "should not be passively accepted but should be met by united action."

Having raised the possibility of intervention, Eisenhower and Dulles next consulted with the congressional leadership. The president has been rightly praised for involving Congress at that stage, but his move was based as much on political exigency as on abstract respect for the Constitution. The administration carefully monitored public opinion, which overwhelmingly opposed United States military involvement. Further, Eisenhower had only the barest majorities in both houses (48-47-1 in the Senate; 221-212-1 in the House). The Republican right wing had been notoriously unreliable, and the Army-McCarthy hearings were soon to begin. Although the Democrats had supported the president faithfully on foreign policy through much of 1953, bipartisanship had begun to erode. Some Democrats were in a vengeful mood. Recalling the vicious attacks on Truman and Dean Acheson, Hubert H. Humphrey warned Dulles, "As ye [sow], so shall ye reap, and, believe me, you have so sown and so you reap." By the time of the Dienbienphu crisis, even moderate Democrats had begun to challenge the administration's Indochina policy. Congressional restlessness had been made abundantly clear in February when Democrats and Republicans attacked the administration for failing to consult before sending United States Air Force mechanics to Vietnam. To calm the legislators, the president had publicly pledged that the United States would not become involved in war "unless it is a result of the constitutional process . . . placed upon Congress to declare it."

Eisenhower and Dulles perceived that whichever way they went they faced problems with Congress. Should they do nothing and Indochina fall, right-wing Republicans might join Democrats in condemning them for losing additional territory to Communism. If United States intervention were required, however, there would be little time for consultation and deliberation, and the experience of Korea left no doubt that intervention without some kind of congressional authorization would leave the administration politically vulnerable. Eisenhower thus had to implicate Congress at an early stage. "It might be necessary to move into the battle of Dien Bien Phu in order to keep it from going against us," he said in late March, "and in that case I will be calling in the Democrats as well as our Republican leaders to inform them." Remaining cautiously in the background, the president had Dulles and Radford arrange an unusual Saturday morning meeting with the legislative leadership on April 3.

Recently declassified documents make clear that notwithstanding Eisenhower's remark he did not seek authority for an immediate air strike to relieve the siege of Dienbienphu, as Roberts and others have long argued. At a top-level White House meeting on April 2, an obviously isolated Radford conceded that the outcome at Dienbienphu would be "determined within a matter of hours, and the situation was not one which called for any U.S. participation." The administration sought, rather, congressional endorsement of a broad, blank-check resolution, not unlike the Formosa Resolution of 1955, that would give the chief executive discretionary authority to use United States air and sea power to prevent the "extension and expansion" of Communist aggression in Southeast Asia. The draft resolution that Dulles brought to the White House and that Eisenhower approved stipulated that the authority would terminate on June 30, 1955, and would in no way "derogate from the authority of Congress to declare war."

Eisenhower and Dulles sought the resolution primarily to meet the immediate needs of United Action. Dulles indicated that he wanted the resolution mainly as a "deterrent" and to strengthen his hand in upcoming discussions with representatives of allied nations. The administration was also notably discreet in handling its presentation. Eisenhower insisted that the "tactical procedure should be to develop first the thinking of Congressional leaders without actually submitting in the first instance a resolution drafted by ourselves."

Dulles followed the script, but the drama took a direction the administration had not intended. Radford briefed the legislators on Dienbienphu, perhaps mistakenly convincing them that the White House wanted to intervene immediately. Dulles then portrayed the threat to Indochina in the gravest terms and urged that the president be given "Congressional backing so that he could use air and sea power in the area if he felt it necessary in the interest of national security." No one challenged the assessment of the crisis, but the legislators, particularly Democratic senators Richard B. Russell and Johnson, insisted that there must be "no more Koreas with the United States furnishing 90 percent of the manpower" and that there must be firm commitments of support from allies, specifically Great Britain. Dulles persisted, affirming that he had no intention of sending ground forces to Indochina and indicating that he could more easily gain commitments from other nations if he could specify what the United States would do. The congressmen were not swayed. "Once the flag is committed," they warned, "the use of land forces would surely follow." Sharing fully the administration's distrust of France, they also insisted that

the United States must not go to war for colonialism. They would only agree that if "satisfactory commitments" could be obtained from Britain and other allies to intervene collectively and form France to "internationalize" the war and to grant the Indochinese independence, a resolution authorizing the president to employ United States forces "could be obtained."

Although less dramatic than often assumed, the outcome of the meeting was significant. Neither Eisenhower nor Dulles differed fundamentally with the congressmen on the form intervention ought to take, but the conditions did tie their hands by virtually eliminating any possibility of unilateral intervention, an option that they had not entirely ruled out. The conditions weakened Dulles's position with allied leaders by requiring the allies' commitment prior to action by Congress, an order the administration would have preferred to reverse. Most important, they made collective intervention dependent on British support and French concessions, each of which would be difficult to obtain. Eisenhower and Dulles admitted that the meeting raised some "serious problems."

Ironically, at the very time the congressmen were setting guidelines for United States intervention, the French were concluding that Dienbienphu could be saved only by a United States air strike. Navarre had originally opposed United States involvement, fearing that it might provoke direct Chinese intervention. In the aftermath of the Vietminh offensive of early April, however, he revised his estimate, cabling the French government on April 4 that an air strike might spare the garrison if executed within the following week. After an emergency meeting that night, Foreign Minister Georges Bidault requested VULTURE, emphasizing that the extensive presence of Chinese matériel and advisers met the conditions under which United States involvement had been discussed by Radford and Ely.

It seems unlikely that Eisenhower and Dulles would have approved the request under any circumstances, but the conditions imposed by the congressmen clinched the decision and probably provided a convenient excuse. Manifesting no sense of disappointment, they agreed that approving the request without "some kind of arrangement getting support of Congress, would be completely unconstitutional and indefensible." Expressing some annoyance with Radford for leading the French to believe that the United States would respond positively, Eisenhower instructed Dulles to see "if anything else can be done" to help the French. But, he concluded firmly, "we cannot become engaged in war."

While the president and the secretary of state were setting policy, the NSC machinery was finally wrapping up the studies launched months earlier. The Smith committee report, dated April 5, recommended that the United States oppose any political settlement at Geneva and seek nothing less than a "military victory" in Indochina, using its own forces if necessary. An NSC planning board study, although hastily revised to incorporate the requirements of April 3, recommended that formal decisions about intervention ought to be reached at once and included a detailed annex itemizing the number and types of forces that might be employed in Indochina should intervention be required.

Not surprisingly, the NSC refused to go as far as either study recommended. Ridgway vigorously objected to the planning board proposals, arguing that, if naval and air forces were used, ground troops would inevitably be required and insisting that the number of troops specified in the annex would represent only the beginning of what might become a huge commitment. Although Ridgway later claimed a decisive influence on policy making, his opposition only reinforced prior decisions. At a meeting on April 6, the NSC postponed a recommendation on military intervention. "There was no possibility whatever of U.S. unilateral intervention in Indochina," Eisenhower declared "with great emphasis" at the outset, "and we had best face that fact." The NSC thus agreed that every effort ought to be made to create a "regional grouping" to defend Southeast Asia and that France ought to be pressed to grant full independence to the Associated States of Indochina. If those conditions could be met, the White House would seek congressional authorization for intervention. In the meantime, "military and mobilization planning" for possible later intervention "should be promptly initiated."

During the following week the administration prepared the way for United Action. Dulles conferred with the British and the French ambassadors, and Eisenhower wrote a personal letter to Prime Minister Winston Churchill urging British support for a coalition that would be "willing to fight" to defend Southeast Asia. At a news conference on April 7, the president outlined what came to be known as the "domino theory," explaining that if Indochina fell the rest of Southeast Asia would "go over very quickly," with "incalculable" losses to the free world. A carrier strike force already on station in the South China Sea was moved to within one hundred miles of Hainan Island and began air reconnaissance of Chinese airfields and staging areas.

On April 10 Dulles traveled to Europe for the first round of three weeks of frantic shuttle diplomacy. Stopping first in London, he encountered immediate opposition. The British did not share the American view that the loss of Indochina would threaten all of Southest Asia. Convinced that France retained sufficient influence to salvage a reasonable settlement at Geneva, they feared that outside intervention would destroy any hope of a negotiated settlement and perhaps would even provoke war with China. Most important, they had no inclination to entangle Britain in a war that could not be won. The persistent Dulles could get nothing more than Foreign Secretary Anthony Eden's grudging assent to participate in immediate multilateral talks to establish a common bargaining position at Geneva, with a coalition to be included on the agenda.

Dulles met further obstacles in Paris. He held out the prospect of United States intervention but only on condition that France resist a negotiated settlement at Geneva, agree to fight in Indochina indefinitely, concede to the United States a greater role in planning strategy and in training indigenous troops, and accept Vietnamese demands for complete independence. Like Eden, French Foreign Minister Bidault insisted that nothing should be done to jeopardize the success of the Geneva negotiations. He also indicated that French public opinion would not support continuation of the war if the ties between the Associated States of Indochina and France were severed, and he made plain French opposition to internationalizing the war. As from the British, Dulles could obtain from the French an agreement only to join preliminary talks to be held in Washington on April 20.

By the time Dulles returned to the United States, the administration's delicate strategy faced rising opposition at home. The possibility of some kind of intervention in Indochina elicited from members of Congress increasing protest about the danger of joining a war for French colonialism. In an April 6 speech that won praise from both sides of the aisle, Democratic Senator John F. Kennedy warned that victory could not be won so long as the French remained. Echoing Kennedy's sentiments, Senators Estes Kefauver, Wayne Morse, and Michael J. ("Mike") Mansfield demanded that France clarify its intentions regarding independence for Indochina. On April 7 Senator Henry Jackson hit closer to the point bothering many in Congress when he demanded that the administration reveal its own intentions in Indochina.

The day after Dulles's return, a high administration source, subsequently identified as Vice-President Nixon, set the pot boiling again. Speaking before the American Society of Newspaper Editors, Nixon, answering a "hypothetical" question about how the United States would respond to a French collapse in Indochina, affirmed that "we must take the risk by putting our boys in." Regarded at the time and since as a trial balloon, Nixon's remarks had not been authorized, and press secretary James Hagerty deemed them "foolish." Some administration officials rationalized that at least they might keep the Communists guessing, but the State Department, acting on instructions from Eisenhower, hurriedly put out an ambiguous statement to "clarify" United States policy without "cutting the ground from under Nixon."

Nixon's indiscretion immensely complicated Dulles's task. Receiving extensive publicity in Europe, Nixon's remarks conveyed an impression of American belligerency at the very time Dulles was trying to curry British and French support. Congress reacted so adversely that the secretary feared that on the eve of the Geneva conference Congress might attempt to foreclose his options, weakening his hand in dealing with allies and adversaries.

Worse, two days before the scheduled meeting with representatives of the proposed coalition, the British indicated that they would not attend. Dulles speculated that

Eden had been swayed by India's neutralist prime minister, Jawaharlal Nehru; but the British may also have been alarmed by the implications of the Nixon statement, and they may have recognized belatedly that attendance at the meeting would trap them into endorsing Dulles's policy. Whatever the cause, the decision struck a body blow at United Action. An outraged Dulles reluctantly agreed to a hastily drawn compromise by which the British would attend the meeting provided that it dealt only with Korea. The meeting had been designed at least in part to signal the Communists of the threat of allied intervention in Indochina, however, and the change deprived it of its significance.

The administration's strategy threatened from several directions, Dulles hastened back to Europe for a North Atlantic Treaty Organization (NATO) council session. The issue of United States air intervention at Dienbienphu immediately emerged. The situation of the French fortress had become perilous. Efforts to retake the inner hill positions had failed, costing France all its reserves. The beleaguered garrison had been reduced to about three thousand able-bodied fighting men, and resupply was virtually impossible. On April 22 Bidault, whom Dulles described as "totally exhausted mentally," hinted at French willingness to internationalize the war and warned that nothing short of "massive air intervention by the U.S." could save Dienbienphu. The following day the foreign minister showed Dulles an "urgent" cable from Navarre indicating that in the absence of an air strike Navarre would have no choice but to order a cease-fire.

Bidault's later claim that at that point Dulles offered him the loan of two atomic weapons seems highly implausible. No other evidence of the alleged offer exists in available French or American sources. Dulles did not have the authority to take such a step, and for him to have so exceeded his prerogatives would have been inconsistent with his usual conduct and with the caution he displayed throughout the Dienbienphu crisis. Dulles had shown little interest in JCS contingency plans that called for atomic bombs should the United States intervene. Eisenhower did discuss the possibility of lending France "new weapons" but not until April 30, while Dulles was in Europe. Shocked when he learned of the charges, the secretary could only surmise that as a result of Bidault's highly agitated state of mind or of problems of translation, Bidault had interpreted as an offer a random statement that United States policy now treated nuclear weapons as conventional. Dulles may have been correct. Bidault attempted to blame the Dienbienphu debacle on his American counterpart, and he may have used the alleged offer to damage the reputation of a man he came to despise thoroughly.

Whatever the case, Bidault's second request for United States air intervention sparked a week of the most intense and nimble diplomatic maneuvering in recent history. Hoping to save Dienbienphu and to strengthen their bargaining position at Geneva, the French sought an American air strike without incurring commitments that would restrict their freedom of action. Dulles could not, of course, commit the United States without first extracting agreements from both Britain and France. In any event, he was less concerned with the immediate situation at Dienbienphu than with the long-term defense of Southeast Asia, and he sought to keep France in the war and to use the opening provided by Bidault's overture to revive the flagging prospects of United Action. Unwilling to enter the war under any circumstances, Britain attempted to restrain the United States and to keep France committed to a negotiated settlement without provoking an irreparable split in the alliance.

From Dulles's standpoint, Britain was the key, and on April 23 and April 24 he relentlessly pressured Eden. He warned that the French would not continue the war without assurance of British and American support and insisted that the mere knowledge that a "common defense system was in prospect" would deter the Communists and would strengthen the allied hand at the Geneva conference. If Britain agreed, he added, the president would seek immediate congressional authorization for United States intervention. When Eden expressed doubt that an air strike would accomplish anything, Radford, who had joined Dulles in Paris, declared that at least it would "stabilize the situation." If the United States intervened, he went on, Navarre might be relieved of his command, and Americans from "behind the scenes" could exercise a "considerable voice" in the conduct of the war. To calm Eden's expressed fears of World War III, Radford minimized the risks of Soviet or Chinese intervention. The Americans also played down the anticipated cost of British participation, indicating that nothing more would be asked than the use of several air squadrons from Malaya and Hong Kong. Making clear his continued personal opposition, Eden agreed to return to London to consult with Churchill.

Even with the fate of Dienbienphu in the balance, the United States and France could not bridge the vast gap that had long separated them. France had finally agreed to Vietnamese independence, but the question of internationalization of the war remained unsettled. Moreover, the two nations differed sharply in their approaches to the short-term issues. Bidault warned Dulles that making intervention conditional on British participation would merely cause delays when speed was of the essence and added that the British contribution would not "amount to much of anything." To secure an immediate air strike, he cleverly played on established American fears. If Dienbienphu fell, he warned, the French people would insist on getting out of the war and would have no use for a coalition, which they would view as a sinister means of keeping them fighting indefinitely.

Not ruling out intervention while scrupulously avoiding anything that could be interpreted as a commitment, Eisenhower and Dulles urged Bidault to stand firm. In a carefully worded letter of April 24, Dulles informed the French foreign minister that an air strike would constitute "active United States belligerency" and would therefore require congressional authorization. That could not be obtained within a matter of hours, he added, and probably not at all except within the framework of United Action. He went on to insist that the fall of Dienbienphu need not cause a total French collapse—indeed, the Vietminh had incurred such heavy losses during the siege that the overall military balance would favor France. Dulles held out the prospect of future support through "collective action." Concurrently Eisenhower wrote Laniel, reminding him that France had "suffered temporary defeats" in the past and had still prevailed.

Anticipating a negative British response, the French pressed for unilateral United States action. Bidault informed Dulles that French military experts had concluded that a massive air strike could deliver a "decisive blow" because the Vietminh had so many men and so much matériel concentrated around Dienbienphu. The French pleaded for "armed intervention" through "executive action" or some other "constitutional way to help," warning of ominous consequences to the war in Indochina and to Franco-American relations if nothing were done.

Eisenhower and Dulles peremptorily rejected the French proposal. Dulles advised the administration that because the security of the United States was not directly threatened, the political risk could in no way be justified. Air intervention might not save Dienbienphu, he continued, and the United States could not be certain that France would continue the fight. Intervention without Britain would "gravely strain" relations with Australia and New Zealand as well as with Britain. There would not be time to "arrange proper political understandings" with the French, and "once our prestige is committed in battle, our negotiating position in these matters would be almost negligible." If necessary, it would be better to let Dienbienphu fall than to intervene "under the present circumstances." Eisenhower agreed. Years later, he contemptuously recalled Bidault's last-minute proposals to "solve . . . our 'constitutional problems' and launch a unilateral air strike—on their terms."

Eden settled the issue on April 25, when he delivered the unwelcome, but not unexpected, news. Not even the "diplomatic" language of a memorandum of conversation can conceal the tension that followed. Eden insisted that an air strike might not be decisive and added that it would be a "great mistake" in terms of world opinion. He assured Dulles that Britain would give France "all possible diplomatic support" toward reaching a satisfactory political settlement at the Geneva conference. If such a settlement could be obtained, he would join the United States in guaranteeing it and would agree to immediate discussions about a collective effort to defend the rest of Southeast Asia. If not, Britain would cooperate with the United States in exploring the possibilities of United Action. Dulles protested vigorously that the British position might lead to total French capitulation. To write off Indochina and to believe the rest of Southeast Asia could be held would be foolish, he argued. Eden retorted that

"none of us in London believe that intervention in Indochina can do anything."

Nor did direct appeals sway Churchill. The prime minister told Radford on April 26 that since the British people had let India go they could not be expected to give their lives to hold Indochina for France. At a formal dinner that evening, the old warrior went into a long and emotional discourse, asserting that the Indochina War could be won only by using "that horrible thing"—the atomic bomb—and noting Britain's vulnerability in the event of a nuclear war. "I have known many reverses myself," he concluded. "I have not given in. I have suffered Singapore, Hong-Kong, Tobruk; the French will have Dien Bien Phu." The British would not be drawn into what they feared would be "Radford's war against China."

The British and French responses to the crisis infuriated American leaders. Privately, Eisenhower vented his rage with his allies. The British had shown a "woeful unawareness" of the risks "we run in that region," he confided to his diary. The French had used "weasel words" in promising independence to the Vietnamese, he wrote an old friend, and "through this one reason as much as anything else have suffered reverses that have been really inexcusable." They wanted the Americans "to come in as junior partners and provide materials, etc., while they themselves retain authority in that region," and he would not go along with them "on any such notion."

For several days French and American officials toyed with various expedients. Dulles studied the possibility of proceeding without Britain and working for United Action with France, the ANZUS (Australia, New Zealand, United States) Pact, and the Associated States of Indochina. He also pondered the feasibility of having French forces withdrawn to defensible enclaves, where they could be supported by United States air and sea power, with the United States assuming responsibility for training indigenous forces. The French government warned Dulles that something must be done to compensate for the anticipated blow to French morale, imploring Dulles to create ad hoc machinery for allied consultation on measures to defend Southeast Asia or, as a last resort, to sponsor a public announcement that nations with vital interests in the area were consulting. French and American military officials explored the possibility of using United States C-119s, with American crews, to fly supplies and ammunition into the war zones to support a last-ditch effort to relieve Dienbienphu.

None of those options produced anything of substance, however, and after Eisenhower told the American public that the United States must steer a course between the "unattainable" and the "unacceptable," the decision against immediate intervention was formalized at a long and heated NSC meeting on April 29. The possibility of an air strike was reconsidered, and several of the conferees, led by Harold Stassen, administrator of the Foreign Operations Administration, proposed that the United

States intervene unilaterally and with ground troops if necessary to retrieve the situation. Vice-President Nixon suggested the establishment of a "Pacific Coalition" without Britain and the dispatch of a United States Air Force contingent to make plain American determination to resist further encroachments. The Communists must be put on notice that "this is as far as you go, and no further."

As with the April 6 meeting, the result was both inconclusive and anticlimactic. Eisenhower firmly reiterated that unilateral military intervention would be impossible. "Without allies . . . the leader is just an adventurer like Genghis Khan," he asserted. Moreover, "if our allies were going to fall away in any case, it might be better for the United States to leap over the smaller obstacles and hit the biggest one [the Soviet Union] with all the power we had." After extended discussion the NSC decided to "hold up for the time being any military action on Indo-China" pending developments at Geneva. In the meantime, the United States ought to explore the possibilities of establishing a coalition without Britain while urging France to hold on in the hope that "some formula may be found which would permit additional aid of some sort." In brief, there would be "no intervention based on executive action."

The American decision sealed Dienbienphu's doom. The hopelessly outnumbered defenders finally surrendered on May 7 after fifty-five days of heroic, but futile, resistance. The attention of the belligerents and of interested outside parties immediately shifted to Geneva, where the following day the Indochina phase of the conference was to begin.

The fall of Dienbienphu did not end discussion of United States intervention in Indochina. Throughout the first weeks of the Geneva conference, Dulles continued to promote United Action, hoping that Communist recalcitrance would force the French to accept American support on American terms. This time the plan was contingent merely on British acquiescence. The State Department drafted another joint congressional resolution authorizing the president to employ air and naval forces in Asia to assist friendly governments "to maintain their authority . . . against subversive and revolutionary efforts fomented by Communist regimes." Administration officials even drew up a detailed working paper outlining the day-by-day measures that would be taken and calling for a presidential request on June 2 for congressional backing. French and American military officials discussed possible military collaboration, and the JCS developed detailed plans of operation.

The United States and France still could not agree on the terms of United States intervention. The Eisenhower administration insisted on an unqualified French commitment to internationalize the war. Although Eisenhower privately conceded a willingness to use marines under certain contingencies, he would formally agree only to use naval and air forces in Indochina. Consenting merely to "discuss" the conditions proposed by the United States, France added unacceptable conditions of its own, including an advance commitment from the United States to use ground forces and a promise of full-fledged intervention if China entered the war. The talks ended in mid-June when the Laniel government fell and was replaced by a government headed by Pierre Mendès-France and committed to a negotiated settlement. From that point, the Eisenhower administration devoted its efforts to attaining the best possible settlement at Geneva and to salvaging what it could in Southeast Asia.

The evidence presented here permits firm conclusions about the role of the United States in the Dienbienphu crisis. Contrary to Roberts's view, the Eisenhower administration clearly was at no point committed to an air strike at Dienbienphu. Even when faced with a total French collapse in the frantic days of late April, the administration did not deviate from the position it had staked out before Dulles and Radford met with congressional leaders. At the same time, Eisenhower and Dulles seem to have been much more willing to intervene militarily than the president later indicated in his memoirs. United Action was certainly part bluff, but it also involved a willingness to commit United States military power if conditions warranted it and if the proper arrangements could be made.

The praise accorded Eisenhower for consulting with Congress seems overstated. The political situation left him little choice but to consult, and in any event his intent was to manipulate Congress into giving him a broad grant of authority not unlike that which President Johnson secured in 1964. Implicating Congress in the Dienbienphu decisions protected the administration's domestic flank, but it represented at best a hollow victory. Instead of a blank check, the administration got a tightly drawn contract, and Dulles later conceded that Congress had "hamstrung" his policy.

Because of congressional restrictions, British rejection was decisive in the defeat of United Action, but Franco-American differences played a larger role than scholars have recognized. Long divided on Indochina, the two nations never came close to agreeing on the form United States intervention ought to take, on their respective roles in the proposed coalition, or even on the purposes of the war. It seems likely, therefore, that had other conditions been met, Franco-American divisions might still have prevented United States intervention.

Recent praise for the decision-making process may also be misplaced. The NSC structure encouraged a full review of policy and a high level of multiple advocacy and team building, but what is striking about the Dienbienphu crisis is the extent to which the formal machinery was peripheral to the actual decision making. The NSC role was restricted to planning, but even in that realm it consistently lagged behind the unfolding of events in Indochina.

Regarding the quality of the decision, there seems little reason to quarrel with the view that the administration acted wisely in staying out of war in 1954. It may deserve credit only for making a virtue of necessity, however, and after the Geneva conference it made political commitments to South Vietnam fraught with fateful long-range consequences. The "day we didn't go to war" merely postponed for a decade large-scale United States military involvement in Vietnam, and the decision not to intervene militarily may well loom as less important than the political commitments made after the fall of Dienbienphu.

Roger Dingman (essay date 1989)

SOURCE: "John Foster Dulles and the Creation of the South-East Asia Treaty Organization in 1954," in *International History Review,* Vol. 11, No. 3, August, 1989, pp. 457-77.

[*In the following essay, Dingman discusses the successes and limitations of Dulles's involvement in the creation of SEATO, an organization that Dulles largely envisioned as designed to check possible communist aggression in Southeast Asia.*]

When John Foster Dulles resigned as secretary of state in 1959, newspapers provided readers with the statistics of his statesmanship. The record was impressive: he had travelled nearly half a million miles on more than a hundred visits to forty-six countries on every continent except Antarctica. Among Dulles's accomplishments during his tenure as secretary of state was the conclusion of three collective security pacts. These, when added to the three similar treaties he had negotiated for the Truman administration, linked the United States with ten Asia/Pacific states. Of all these treaties, perhaps none was more controversial than the pact signed at Manila in September 1954, which came to be known as the South-East Asia Treaty Organization (SEATO).

For thirty years and more, the treaty and its principal progenitor have drawn the critical fire of biographers and international historians. Their verdicts have varied wildly. Some have portrayed Dulles as a ruthless, bullying 'pactomaniac', who tilted at windmills of communist subversion rather than responding creatively to the emergence of a new South-East Asian *status quo*. Others have portrayed a man hoisted on his own petard—forced by Washington's inability to agree on intervention in the closing moments of the first Indochina War to conclude a sham pact in the wake of the Geneva accords. Two decades ago SEATO was called 'the alliance that never was', implying that it had little significance. More recently it has been called an important step on the road to US military intervention in Vienam.

Discord of this sort and a wealth of newly opened archival sources in Washington, London, Canberra, Wellington, and Manila oblige the historian to reconsider the creation of the South-East Asia treaty. What were the perceptions and intentions of its US progenitors in the summer of 1954? To what extent did their desires, the demands of

domestic politics, and the needs of their prospective allies coincide? How and why did they manage to reconcile frequently contradictory understandings of the situation in South-East Asia? What significance did they attribute to the pact they produced at Manila? Careful reconstruction of the circumstances attending the birth of SEATO may provide not only answers to these particular questions but also insight into the nature of US Asian diplomacy at mid-century.

An attempt to understand the creation of SEATO must begin by recognizing the deep divisions within and between its prospective members. The idea of a regional organization for South-East Asia had surfaced repeatedly during the five years prior to the alliance. It had foundered, however, on sharp disagreements among its prospective South-East Asian and Australasian members and on doubts of the State Department as to its necessity and efficacy. But with the election of Dwight Eisenhower to the presidency, the idea took on new life. The president-elect raised the possibility in talks with officials of the State Department prior to his inauguration. The prospect of a truce in Korea which might free Chinese communist forces for action elsewhere troubled Dulles and his subordinates. One of the most astute observers of South-East Asia among them, Charleton Ogburn, Jr., thought the emergence of an association of Asian and Western nations with interests in the region unlikely. But in March 1953, he proposed that Washington should proclaim its commitment to self-determination for Asian peoples, and also the determination of the United States and other Western powers to check any aggressor.

In the troubled spring of 1954, however, that determination appeared open to doubt. Faced with the prospect of the collapse of French resistance to what Dulles perceived as communist aggression in Vietnam, he revived the notion of a collective security arrangement for South-East Asia. What he said and did grew in part out of intellectual conviction. Two years earlier he had written in abstract terms about the value of nuclear weapons and collective security arrangements as deterrents; now he faced the challenge of translating his ideas into effective policy. Dulles's words and deeds also mirrored the desires of Americans. Fear of communism and belief in the strength of the threat it posed to US interests were real. Eisenhower reflected and amplified such fears when he spoke of the danger of South-East Asian states falling under communist control like 'a row of dominoes'. On Capitol Hill, Republicans as different as Senator William F. Knowland of California and New York Representative Jacob Javits championed collective security arrangements in the Asia/Pacific region. Polls taken during the first seven months of 1954 showed that nearly six out of every ten Americans thought the United States should sign a treaty for the collective defence of South-East Asia.

Dulles's understanding of the purpose of such a pact changed dramatically between March and August 1954. Facing the prospect of a French defeat at Dien Bien Phu late in March, he called for 'united action' to meet 'the

Red threat in Asia'. But a quick trip to London and Paris in mid-April revealed sharp differences with the Western allies over what should be done. Before the French garrison at Dien Bien Phu surrendered, Dulles hoped that efforts to create an alliance would stiffen the will of France to resist; after the surrender, he hoped his efforts would restrain the communists in the negotiations to end the war to be held at Geneva. When the negotiations led, however, to an agreement which left Ho Chi Minh in control of northern Vietnam and a chaotic political situation in the south, Dulles feared that communist pressure might topple all of the Indochinese dominoes. In the wake of his failure to achieve agreement on 'united action', Dulles came to regard a regional security pact for South-East Asia as a means of restoring the Eisenhower administration's badly tarnished image as 'leader of the free world'. Thus, by early summer, Dulles looked upon the pact not as a mechanism to facilitate military intervention in Indochina, but rather as a symbol of anti-communist unity which would make such action unnecessary.

Two obstacles stood in the way of that kind of collective security pact. One was Great Britain. Precisely as experts at the State Department had predicted, differences between Washington and London over East- and South-East Asian policy had grown apace since the end of the Korean War. Fearing a confrontation with China and thinking it foolish to act so long as the Geneva talks held any prospect of success, London spurned Washington's overtures for collective diplomatic action in South-East Asia. British hesitancy fuelled caution in Wellington and Canberra. Not until mid-June, when officials on both sides of the Atlantic grew worried about the health of the Anglo-American relationship, did London agree to begin talks on a possible South-East Asian pact. Even then, the British foreign secretary, Sir Anthony Eden, put forward a radically different view of its purpose. By suggesting that such an agreement might be part of a wider Locarno-like mutual guarantee of the post-Geneva *status quo,* he created a political and diplomatic uproar. The ensuing summit conversation between Eisenhower and the British prime minister, Sir Winston Churchill, barely glossed over that difference but did give officials the green light to draft a treaty.

In the negotiations that followed, the British sought to modify the purpose of the pact and soften its anti-Chinese overtones by broadening its membership to include Indonesia and the South Asian members of the British Commonwealth. Adding the so-called Colombo Powers might make economic aid rather than military deterrence the principal purpose of the pact. Dulles consented to talks with the states involved, but in the end, just as his subordinates predicted, the two most important among them— India and Indonesia—declined to join any collective security pact. To Washington's surprise and dismay, however, Pakistan, always in search of support in its struggle against India, accepted the invitation to take part.

The other major obstacle Dulles faced was the Pentagon. Always leery of a commitment to defend the mainland of South-East Asia, after Dien Bien Phu and Geneva the joint chiefs of staff wanted no part of a pledge to military action there. Instead, they preferred to attack the problem of possible Chinese aggression at its source. As their chairman, Admiral Arthur Radford, saw it, the threat of nuclear devastation made meaningful by the deployment of forces capable of carrying out such a threat, was the best way to deter a Chinese communist advance into South-East Asia.

Dulles found it difficult to overcome the Pentagon's lack of enthusiasm for meaningful collective security arrangements covering South-East Asia for two reasons. First, the public agreed with the Pentagon about how best to deal with threats to peace in the region. Polls showed that nearly fifty per cent of Americans thought nothing would be gained by fighting a war in Indochina and barely twenty per cent favoured sending troops there. Between January and July of 1954, moreover, support for striking China directly if Beijing attacked a third power jumped from less than thirty to nearly fifty per cent. Second, Eisenhower did not protect his secretary of state from Pentagon interference as much as Dulles would have liked. Eisenhower restrained but did not completely silence Radford. In May, he sent the secretary of defence, Charles E. Wilson, to East Asia, and in Manila, despite the misgivings of the State Department, Wilson agreed to the establishment of a United States-Philippine Defence Council.

By the third week of August 1954, public opinion and the differences within the Eisenhower administration had profoundly altered the draft treaty Washington had placed before its prospective allies. That text, completed and circulated a month earlier, had proclaimed Washington's desire to promote stability and well-being in South-East Asia; its support for people seeking and capable of sustaining their independence; its devotion to democratic principles; and, most important, its 'sense of unity' in the face of 'any potential aggressor'.

The heart of the proposed agreement was its fourth article, which identified two threats and posited different responses to them. In the unlikely event of overt armed attack upon the allies or on 'any states or territory in the area' which they had unanimously agreed to protect, each would act to meet the common danger 'in accordance with its constitutional processes'. In the more probable case of indirect aggression or subversion, the allies would immediately consult to determine the actions they should take to maintain 'the common defense . . . and peace and security in the area'. Other articles established a council to implement the terms of the treaty; provided for the accession of other states; and defined procedures for the ratification, implementation, and denunciation of a treaty of indefinite duration.

When the National Security Council (NSC) met in mid-August to consider the draft treaty in conjunction with a ponderous East Asian policy position paper, Dulles realized that the July text would have to be modified. The

Pentagon remained extremely critical of any commitment to action on the South-East Asian mainland. Dulles himself questioned the wisdom of committing US prestige in an area over which the United States had 'little control' and in which 'the situation was by no means promising'. But he thought the alternative—appearing 'to abandon the entire area without a struggle'—far worse. Thus, while dissenting from too rigid a definition of hostility towards China, Dulles accepted a limited and not entirely consistent definition of the pact's purpose. The treaty should provide a legal basis for retaliatory attacks on China in the event of armed aggression in South-East Asia and oblige allies to support US action there. But the treaty should neither limit Washington's freedom to use nuclear weapons nor promise the commitment of US forces to the region for local defence purposes. In other words, the treaty must preclude the ultimately fruitless manoeuvring for 'united action' of the preceding spring, yet leave the Pentagon free to fight only on its own terms.

Dulles's subordinates redrafted the treaty to meet these rather contradictory demands. The revised text made clearer the threat against which the parties were to unite. The preamble and article four specified that they stood together against 'communist aggression'. Ostensibly designed to preclude entanglement in extraneous disputes such as the quarrel between Pakistan and India, this language left no doubt that China was *the* threat to peace in South-East Asia. Two other changes defined the area to be defended with greater precision. The first excluded the Pacific north of 21°30'—ruling out any pledge to defend Hong Kong. The second strengthened the commitment to preserve the new *status quo* in the region by guaranteeing the territory of Laos, Cambodia, and 'the free Vietnamese Government'.

The revised draft gave Washington's would-be allies the opportunity to press for changes which suited their particular interests. The most significant objections came from Manila, Canberra, and London. The president of the Philippines, Ramon Magsaysay, must have been furious when he learned what Washington proposed late in August. Initially cool to the idea of such a pact (it had been proposed by his predecessor), he had with considerable difficulty persuaded militantly pro-Asian senators in his own party to agree to join by calling for the reaffirmation of the principle of national self-determination. At the request of London and Canberra, however, the new draft had eliminated earlier pledges of support for peoples striving to attain or sustain their independence. Magsaysay had to insist that the allies must promise to take 'effective practical measures' to aid the progress of the peoples of South-East Asia towards 'self-rule and independence'.

To defend himself against charges of toadying to Washington—claims whose credence was enhanced by persistent rumours that US funds had purchased his election the preceding year—and to hedge against the possibility that Washington might reject his call for explicit support of Asian nationalism, Magsaysay insisted upon two additional changes. First, Washington must promise to do more. The language of commitment to collective security should echo what his rival, Senator Claro Recto, perceived to be the stronger language of NATO, rather than the weaker language of the United States-Philippine and ANZUS treaties of 1951. In a gesture designed to please the armed forces whose support he needed, Magsaysay also let it be known that Philippine membership would be 'pointless' without an assurance of 'a substantial increment' in US military aid. Second, the prospective allies should do less on the South-East Asian mainland. Rejecting the advice of his friend, Colonel Edward Lansdale, and accepting the cautious counsel of roving ambassador and former foreign secretary, Carlos Romulo, Magsaysay cavilled at guaranteeing the security of Laos, Cambodia, and southern Vietnam. To avoid being dragged into a war on the mainland on Washington's coat-tails, Philippine officials argued that decisions in the proposed council should require a three-quarters majority vote.

The Australians shared that concern. Caught between a desire for greater US involvement in South-East Asian affairs and a reluctance to become militarily involved in the Franco-Vietnamese war, Canberra had chosen to avoid 'united action' by letting others raise objections to it. In April, the prime minister, Robert Menzies, followed the British lead in declining to rush into negotiations for a South-East Asian alliance. During the Geneva conference, his minister for external affairs, Richard Casey, had sought out Zhou Enlai and avoided any words and actions that the Chinese might regard as provocative. In July, Canberra had suggested that the commitment to act against subversion, as opposed to armed attack, should be softened in the US draft treaty.

But Egyptian nationalism and the turbulence of Australian domestic politics soon pushed Menzies in quite the opposite direction. In July 1954, Great Britain agreed to withdraw British Commonwealth forces from Egypt and in so doing destroyed the principal rationale for the maintenance of Australian armed forces capable of action at a distance from their homeland. At the same time, the uncertain state of affairs in post-Geneva South-East Asia caused alarm in Australia. Menzies's coalition had won a narrow election victory with Red-baiting tactics, but in its wake, Opposition spokesman Arthur Calwell challenged Menzies's claim to militant anti-communist leadership by pointing to the 'red lava' boiling southwards in Indochina. Editorials in the *Sydney Morning Herald* also repeatedly attacked Menzies's defence policies as inadequate.

Pressed by its critics and constrained by lack of money, the Menzies government found it difficult to follow a consistent policy: it opted for both membership of SEATO and an increase in Australia's armed forces. But what was to be the relationship between the two? A clear answer eluded Menzies and his colleagues. External affairs and defence officials thought that as long as the United States provided 'teeth' sufficient to deter Chinese expansion in South-East Asia, Washington need not be asked for clarification of its intentions. They were echoed by Casey, who probably saw a defence buildup more as a means of enhancing Australia's credibility as an ally than as a realistic response to South-East Asian unrest. Menzies, however, who regarded appeals from Australia's old protector in London and her new ally in Washington as the best way to obtain parliamentary votes for more defence spending, favoured pressing both for immediate discussions on military planning.

The outcome was a protest to Washington about the latest draft of the treaty, which threatened Australia with the worst of both worlds. Asians generally and the Chinese in particular might regard a South-East Asian alliance as provocative, yet Canberra had no assurance of additional protection. If the proposed pact were nothing more than 'a commitment to act . . . without any effective understandings among . . . Allies as to what that action should be', it would weaken Australia's value as an ally. The Menzies government would certainly be attacked at home for signing a treaty 'which seemed valueless'. Thus it was essential that the proposed pact establish 'effective military machinery' for planning the defence of South-East Asia.

That discreet if strongly worded appeal paled in comparison with British objections to the draft. The Churchill government was itself divided on China policy. Churchill was willing to follow Washington's lead if necessary, but Eden insisted upon a more independent, and decidedly less provocative, East Asian policy. While Dulles, whom Eden distrusted, was drafting the treaty, the former prime minister, Clement Attlee, captured the public's imagination by travelling to China for talks with Mao Zedong. Mindful of the tensions at home and between allies that had arisen during the Korean War, and resigned to the failure of his attempt to restrain the Americans by including India, Eden now pressed for significant modifications to the draft.

He let it be known that he was 'unalterably opposed' to the use of the word 'communist' in the preamble or anywhere in the text of the treaty. Moreover, article four should be rewritten so as to make it clear that force would be used in response to overt attack only in accordance with the terms of the United Nations Charter and seek only 'to restore and maintain the security of the treaty area'. The language of NATO rather than ANZUS should be copied, which, in London's interpretation, was preferable because it gave signatories 'considerable discretion' in deciding how to respond if an armed attack was 'not one which it is the real purpose of the proposed Treaty to guard against'. Behind these words lay London's very real fears, based on experience during the Korean War and the Indochina crisis in the spring, that Washington, acting rashly without meaningful consultation with its allies, would blunder into war against China. As if to cap his objections to Dulles's policy, Eden announced that he would not take part in the negotiations at Manila himself because the rejection of the European Defence Community by the French would oblige him to stay in London.

That was the last straw for Dulles, who angrily determined to resist British, Australian, and Philippine-proposed changes to the text of the treaty. He instructed the officials who would precede him to Manila to insist upon the phrase 'communist aggressor' in its preamble and in article four, and to oppose the creation of a permanent organization at a particular site. His hands were tied on both points by the administration's desire to make it virtually impossible for allies not to follow the US lead in the event of overt attacks. He recognized Eden's challenge to US leadership in his call for NATO language in article four, but rather than meet the challenge directly, hid behind supposed congressional sensibilities in rejecting that wording. He also rejected recommendations from his staff to cut the word 'communist' from the text so as to avoid a six-to-one lineup against the United States at Manila, claiming that his inability to consult with Senators Mike Mansfield and H. Alexander Smith, who were members of the US delegation, now about to depart, precluded a compromise. That may have been true. For Dulles personally, and for the Eisenhower administration generally, however, the conclusion of a South-East Asian treaty had become a test of political and diplomatic leadership.

For a moment, Dulles was inclined to flinch before the challenge. Already deeply annoyed at British and French opposition to 'united action' and their independent negotiation of the Geneva accords, he expressed 'great reservations' about the utility of a treaty. He wondered aloud whether the United States might not be better off acting alone. The prospective allies 'running away from the word "Communist"'; their unwillingness to allow unofficial Vietnamese, Laotian, and Cambodian observers to attend the conference; and his feeling that London and Paris were 'blocking everything we want to do'—all suggested that he should not go to Manila to negotiate a treaty. Only the argument that not going would doom the treaty and hand the communists 'complete victory . . . on a silver platter' in both Europe and Asia convinced Dulles that he must go. So stifling his doubts about the wisdom of an agreement with such 'weak and feeble' partners, he went.

During his long flight from Washington to the Philippines, Dulles had ample time to recover his temper and consider how best to reconcile his differences with the allies. When his plane landed at Manila in the evening of 3 September, he immediately plunged into conference with his deputy Douglas MacArthur II, who happily reported that after three days' preliminary talks among officials, only four problems remained to be solved.

The first and most serious question was how to define the threat against which the allies were uniting. Precisely as predicted, everyone but the Thais had objected to specifying 'communist aggression' as the threat, as being unduly provocative towards China. New Zealand had expressed the 'gravest doubts' about the phrase. Ostensibly worried that it would deter other Asian states from joining, in fact Wellington preferred vaguer language which might leave SEATO free to respond to new and different threats in the future just as similarly general words in the ANZUS agreement had done. Australia, in a phrase which echoed Great Britain's wishes, proposed to narrow the definition of threat to 'any renewal of . . . aggression in violation' of the Geneva accords. Such action was to constitute 'a matter of grave international concern' and trigger a collective response.

The second question was the nature and extent of the allied commitment. The Philippines had pressed for the use of NATO (rather than ANZUS or US-Philippine Security Treaty) language in defining the collective commitment. She had also tabled a Pacific Charter which would require its signatories to recognize Asian self-determination and independence. The State Department's European and South-East Asian experts had differed sharply on the merits of such a declaration when it had first been suggested. Now MacArthur criticized both proposals. The first was a 'booby trap'—the Magsaysay administration's public relations ploy to gain prestige abroad and popular favour at home—and it would never be accepted. He reportedly told the British delegation that he would have quashed the second proposal if he could have, for its strident anti-colonialism was 'clearly unacceptable' to Great Britain and France.

Australia had raised the third question with a proposal to establish, by unanimous consent, 'such subsidiary machinery as may be necessary' to reach the treaty's 'military and other objectives'. This demand for planning rather than a mere declaration of determination to resist was received coolly by the British and the French, while it positively alarmed Washington. The chairman of the joint chiefs of staff, Admiral Radford, thought it a covert British ploy to suck the United States into an unwise military commitment which she had not sought and ought not to make.

Radford's reaction served to remind Dulles of one of the limits to his freedom of action at Manila. But undaunted by it, he used the opportunity presented by a weekend of informal talks to strengthen his negotiating position. On the morning of the 4th, at a meeting of the United States-Philippine Defence Council, his hosts presented him with the draft of an executive agreement which promised massive US aid to all three Filipino armed services. Having broken off the meeting to study the text, Dulles instead found himself forced by news of Communist Chinese attacks on the Nationalist-held island of Quemoy, to spend the next hour and a half drafting a strongly worded message urging Washington to defend the island even if it was not militarily essential to the defence of Taiwan and even if doing so risked 'constantly expanding' operations against the Chinese mainland. With some hyperbole, he told an aide that he had had 'to determine within five minutes whether there will be war with China'. In fact, Dulles was advocating the same measured response in the Taiwan Strait that he felt should underlay any South-East Asian collective security treaty.

Dulles rejoined Magsaysay for lunch and used the Chinese attack on Quemoy to deflect the Philippine demands for more military aid, on the ground that the heavy demands on US forces would preclude giving the Philippines all the help asked for. Having thus evaded compliance with Magsaysay's request, Dulles left it to subordinates to hammer out the details of a military aid agreement that gave the Philippines much less than had been requested. The success of Dulles's manoeuvre, however, would make it all the more important for Magsaysay to succeed in his demand for a more explicit pledge of support for the independence of Asian peoples.

The Chinese attack sharply reminded Dulles of the divisions within his own camp. The British once again took alarm lest an incident in the Taiwan Strait should trigger a nuclear war. Top policy-makers in the Eisenhower administration, scattered as Dulles had feared from Washington to Denver to Manila, failed to agree quickly on what to do, and the joint chiefs split over whether or not the defence of Quemoy was strategically necessary. To make matters worse, Senator Mansfield, the Democratic talisman of bipartisanship on the US delegation at Manila, favoured a dovish response. Such discord in Dulles's own camp boded ill for success in the negotiations ahead.

Hoping to reduce the discord and to build a consensus on how far to compromise in the formal negotiations that lay ahead, Dulles met on the morning of the 5th with the US delegation at the residence of the US ambassador at Manila, Admiral Raymond Spruance. Dulles then said that he was ready to make changes to the preamble to the draft treaty. He could agree to the Australian-sponsored reference to the Geneva accords and was 'probably . . . willing' to drop the phrase 'communist aggression'. But Smith and Mansfield objected, saying that the senate would then almost certainly attach a reservation to the treaty stating that it was 'specifically designed' to deter communist aggression.

Dulles next made two proposals that reflected his lingering doubts about the viability of a non-communist regime in southern Vietnam and his continuing sensitivity to Pentagon objections to a greater military commitment in South-East Asia. In the presence of Vice-Admiral Arthur C. Davis, the joint chiefs' representative, he suggested that the situation in southern Vietnam was 'so precarious'—given the challenges to the Ngo Dinh Diem government from personal rivals, armed Buddhist sects, and the presence of French troops—that it might not be wise to guarantee all three non-communist Indochinese successor states against both external and internal aggression. Mansfield, however, at once pointed to the 'real disadvantages' of making any public distinction in the commitment to Cambodia, Laos, and southern Vietnam. Overriding Pentagon objections, Dulles then proposed agreeing to consultations on military planning in lieu of creating the 'subsidiary machinery' for strategic co-ordination proposed by Australia. That compromise troubled Smith, who doubted the efficacy of simply talking about strategic planning, but he accepted it as the most the United States could concede, given commitments elsewhere.

Fortified by agreement with his American colleagues, Dulles then renewed his efforts to gain the support of his prospective allies. At a meeting with Casey, he listened patiently while Australia's case was explained to him. The Menzies government had to be able to tell parliament that specific forces would be 'required to meet Australia's commitment under SEATO'. The planning machinery should co-ordinate ANZUS, the Five Power Military Staff Agency, and the defence plans of individual Asian nations. Dulles replied that Washington had 'no intention' of earmarking specific forces for SEATO, for US strategy was based on the concept of 'mobile reserve striking power'. The Australian nodded in understanding, then sent up an Anglo-Australian balloon: perhaps the treaty should apply solely to attack from outside a specified area. Dulles immediately rejected that assault on the notion of uniting against subversion as well as armed attack, though he did offer to drop the word 'communist' from the preamble, on the understanding that the United States would enter a reservation specifying that her commitment applied only to communist threats to peace. Casey replied that 'insofar as he was concerned' such a procedure would be 'entirely acceptable' and probably the best way to reach an agreement. Pleased with the outcome of the conversation, Dulles next sent MacArthur to talk with the Thais. His purpose was probably to soften the blow of excising the word 'communist' from the text of the treaty by promising to support a modified version of the Philippines' proposed Pacific Charter.

Dulles had shrewdly set the stage for the formal negotiations that followed during the next seventy-two hours, beginning with speeches by the heads of the various delegations. Smarting from press criticism of recent remarks in which he had stammered that Philippine foreign policy was US foreign policy, the vice president and secretary for foreign affairs of the Philippines, Carlos Garcia, called for an organization which would 'captivate [*sic*] the faith and imagination of the Asian peoples'. Casey stressed that 'defense is our keynote'; Prince Wan of Thailand the need to include Cambodia, Laos, and South Vietnam in an agreement substantially the same as NATO; and Great Britain's Lord Reading that the rumour that London preferred a 'toothless treaty' was false. Dulles closed this portion of the conference by stressing that the treaty should make it clear that an attack would produce 'a reaction so united, so strong and so well placed that the aggressor would lose more than it could hope to gain'. He admitted that there was no 'simple . . . single formula' for dealing with subversion but condemned it none the less. Signalling his support for Philippine demands and in an attempt to deflate communist charges of American racism, he emphasized the need to 'invigorate the independence' of new nations and to speed up the process by which others would become capable of 'winning and sustaining' their freedom.

That afternoon a closed working session disposed of the question of implementing machinery for a South-East Asian collective security organization. Casey opened the session by calling for 'a treaty with teeth in it', but the discussions ended with virtual agreement on Dulles's proposal simply to establish a council which would consult on 'military and other planning' as the situation demanded. Leaks to the press transformed that Australian defeat into what the *Sydney Morning Herald* trumpeted as a 'personal triumph' for Casey. The hyperbole, which may have been of American origin, undoubtedly pleased the minister for external affairs and may have strengthened his conviction that Australia need not enter a reservation similar to Dulles's intended stipulation that the object of the treaty was the prevention of communist attack.

On the 6th, the negotiators refined the definition of the threat and clarified the extent of their commitment to respond to it. Dulles formally offered to drop the phrase 'communist aggression' from the treaty so long as Washington could make a reservation limiting its commitment exclusively to response to such attacks. That compromise earned British Commonwealth support in exchange for US rejection of Thai and Philippine attempts to use NATO—rather than ANZUS—phraseology in spelling out the shared commitment to action. In the afternoon the negotiators accepted a French-sponsored protocol that extended the protection of the treaty to the three non-communist successor states in Indochina. To assuage lingering British fears of unilateral US military intervention, Dulles agreed to language which specified that the signatories would not intervene in any state without its permission. Completing the debate over the extent of territory covered by the treaty, the negotiators agreed to an Anglo-American statement that met the British desire to specify the area and the US determination to exclude Hong Kong from it.

These developments set the stage for what was to have been a final compromise on the nature of the commitment in the treaty. The many Philippine-sponsored references in its text to the right of national self-determination were to be excised in return for British Commonwealth acceptance of a Pacific Charter containing less stridently anti-colonial language. That bargain probably would have been struck on the last morning of the conference if New Zealand's minister for external affairs, T. Clifton Webb, had not spoken up. He raised the sensitive issue of small power-great power inequality. If Dulles's proposed reservation to the treaty were accepted, seven of its eight parties would bear a much heavier and broader burden than the United States.

Webb's remark momentarily disrupted the proceedings. The Philippine delegate, perhaps hoping to increase pressure for the final acceptance of the Pacific Charter and certainly chary of the domestic political dangers of approving anything that perpetuated inequality with Washington, said that his government, too, wanted to limit its commitment in the US fashion. That prompted the Thai and Pakistani delegates to say that if Manila did so, their governments would not approve the draft treaty. For a moment it appeared as if 'a chain reaction was about to destroy the Treaty', and the proceedings had to be recessed.

During the recess Dulles 'apparently spoke bluntly' to the Philippine secretary for foreign affairs, who withdrew his proposed reservation. Dulles had no such luck when he met Allen D. McKnight, one of Robert Menzies's private secretaries who was also a member of the Australian delegation. Dulles tried to persuade Canberra to drop a similar reservation. Unhappy at the inequality of commitment, worried that Pakistan might somehow take advantage of the treaty to demand support in her quarrel with India, and upset by the strong anti-colonial language of the proposed Pacific Charter, Menzies had put the issue of what to do before his cabinet colleagues. They decided to order Casey to sign the treaty only with a reservation similar to Washington's and only after Canberra had approved the final text.

Despite Casey's views of the acceptability of the US reservation and his objection to orders to sign the treaty only on identical terms with Washington's, the Australian cabinet responded by directing Menzies to telephone him and place its views 'firmly' before him. Behind the decision lay a sharp split within the governing coalition on defence policy generally and compulsory military service in particular. Country Party members were less hawkish on both subjects than Menzies's Liberals. But when Menzies telephoned Casey, a decision was postponed after Casey explained the morning's 'great developments'. It was essential to achieve 'the greatest possible area of unanimity', and parliament could be told that the US reservation was 'an inevitable concession to . . . domestic opinion'. Convinced by Casey that there was 'a new and very important element in the situation', Menzies agreed to reconvene the cabinet and ring again in an hour.

The most Menzies could persuade his colleagues to agree to was conditional permission for Casey to sign the treaty, provided he first explained Canberra's 'firm view' to the American and British delegates. If, in Casey's judgement, insistence upon an Australian reservation would produce 'an inevitable breakdown', and not merely a delay in concluding the treaty, then he could sign without formal reservation, but he must explain that the 'real purpose' of the treaty and the 'dominant purpose' of Australian defence policy was 'to present a concerted front against aggressive Communism'. The acting minister for external affairs then telephoned Casey, who in turn met Dulles and Webb to explain Canberra's position. Already sensitive to what he perceived as British and French faint-heartedness, Dulles was more determined than ever to achieve the symbolic, deterrent unity which in his view was the essence of any South-East Asian pact. Overreacting to Menzies's qualms, he made it clear that an Australian reservation to the treaty would pose 'serious danger' to American relations with Canberra

and Wellington. That implicit threat to the ANZUS relationship which both valued gave Casey an excuse to follow the less restrictive of Canberra's instructions, as he preferred. When the negotiations resumed, he voiced but did not formally register a reservation to the final treaty text.

Casey's manoeuvre permitted the Manila conference to close almost as Dulles had intended. The delegates signed the South-East Asian treaty on schedule. Four of them signed, and four initialled, the Pacific Charter. A kind of unity had been achieved, but it fell short of complete agreement. In their closing remarks, the Philippine, Thai, and Pakistani delegates stressed the importance of progress towards complete independence for Asian peoples, while the British Commonwealth representatives voiced reservations about what had been written. Casey repeated what he had written above his signature on the treaty: that Canberra reserved the right to review its text. Webb hinted that his government took the same position. Lord Reading emphasized Great Britain's desire for an early meeting of the council established by the treaty to lay more definite defence plans. Dulles glossed over these differences of emphasis by stressing two points on which he claimed everyone agreed: the necessity of deterring 'the evil of aggression' and the importance of assuring the independence of new states and the orderly progress of other peoples capable of sustaining it to that goal.

The delegates shared a sense of relief that the conference was over and pride in its accomplishments. But what had they achieved? And what was its significance?

Dulles and the men with whom he negotiated at Manila shied away from giving too expansive answers to such questions. In his report to Eisenhower and the National Security Council, Dulles stressed the beginnings of accommodation between newly independent Asian states on the one hand, and the former imperial powers plus Australia and New Zealand on the other. His televised speech to the nation emphasized deterrence of Chinese aggression but avoided any mention of commitment to military action. When he explained the treaty to the Senate Foreign Relations Committee, he praised the Pacific Charter as 'a notable achievement' but repeatedly denied that the SEATO pact committed the United States to armed intervention in Vietnam to quash subversion or revolution.

Magsaysay praised the pact as a step towards greater cooperation among Asian nations. While one cynical Australian diplomat condemned the Manila proceedings as 'a complete circus', Casey modestly claimed that the pact was 'just what I hoped it would be'. His subordinates elaborated on that point, describing SEATO as a reinsurance policy. It constituted a pledge of US assistance in the event of Chinese aggression that paralleled the guarantee against a threat from Japan already given in the ANZUS treaty. New Zealand diplomats shrewdly recognized that although the treaty was a product of contemporary South-East Asian circumstances and US political exigencies, its vague language made it valuable for dealing with a variety of possible future threats.

The caution and realism implicit in these evaluations and in worldwide commentary on the Manila conference point to four important conclusions about the birth of the South-East Asia Treaty Organization. First, the treaty had more than one parent. While its creation may have reflected Washington's determination to keep the Pacific an American lake, neither the United States nor Dulles was as successful in the pursuit of that goal as earlier writers have suggested. American strength was limited by the complexity of the problems that South-East Asia presented in 1954, of which Eisenhower and Dulles were fully aware. Washington's power was also reduced by divisions within the Eisenhower administration over how best to deal with the problems; the Pentagon was cautious and public opinion uneasy. The record also leaves no doubt of the restraining influence of the men with whom Dulles negotiated. They, no less than Dulles, were caught between conflicting perceptions of danger in South-East Asia and the political situation at home. Each fought for, and obtained, something of particular value at Manila: Magsaysay's endorsement of Asian nationalism, Menzies's mechanism for military planning, and Eden's restraint of US interventionism all found their way into the final text.

Second, Dulles himself played a different role from that caricatured by later admirers and critics. He was not the architect of a new Cold War Asian/Pacific international order but simply a diplomatic cobbler who pieced together parts inherited from his Democratic predecessors. The Manila agreements did not create a US commitment in South-East Asia but simply amplified and reified commitments that already existed. Dulles's manner of dealing with the twin problems of aggression and subversion in the region lacked the subtlety and logical elegance of proposals advanced by the British at the time and later by his critics. But his actions did mirror the uncertainties that East and South-East Asia presented after the truces in Korea and Indochina; the strident anti-communist mood of the American people at the time; and his own sense of the interconnection of communist provocations around the globe. Dulles recognized that SEATO was merely an imperfect and impermanent stopgap measure.

Third, Dulles's actions in this instance also suggest that he was a skilled practitioner of the politics and diplomacy of the possible. He was not a bully, nor was the what Winston Churchill dubbed him—a bull 'who carries his own China closet with him'. Dulles behaved angrily and pettily towards those whom he felt were betraying the anti-communist cause: never once during his sojourn in Manila did he meet alone with a British or French diplomat. But he recognized that British and French participation in a South-East Asian collective security arrangement, however limited, was essential. Making every effort to meet Manila's, Canberra's, and even Wellington's needs, Dulles was gracious and magnanimous in explaining how far he could go. At Manila, he proved himself a shrewd and subtle diplomatic tactician, preparing com-

promises, consulting privately with those who would have to make them, and allowing time for bargains to become acceptable. One might even go so far as to say that he was far-sighted. By overruling the objections of his subordinates and his British Commonwealth allies to the Pacific Charter, he did help to lay the groundwork for better understanding between the races in the Asia/Pacific region.

The limits to the Pacific Charter and the imperfect unity achieved at Manila point to a fourth and final conclusion. Like the architects of the Anglo-Japanese alliance at the beginning of the century, or the US, British, and Japanese practitioners of deterrent diplomacy in 1940-1, the fathers of SEATO resorted to diplomacy to conceal the inadequacy of their defences. They wanted to do with words what they could not do with arms. Like parents, they produced a child whose life and character would be shaped as much by developments yet unseen as by the events of the past. To see them as men who knowingly grasped at an imperfect solution to seemingly intractable problems rather than as gods or tragic figures whose actions determined the future is to begin to understand the significance of the agreements they signed at Manila in 1954.

Ronald W. Pruessen (essay date 1990)

SOURCE: "John Foster Dulles and the Predicaments of Power," in *John Foster Dulles and the Diplomacy of the Cold War,* edited by Richard H. Immerman, Princeton University Press, 1990, pp. 23-45.

[*In the following essay, Pruessen undertakes a survey of Dulles's actions and policymaking as U. S. Secretary of State. Pruessen maintains that Dulles's intellectual achievements far outnumbered his practical ones, and that his diplomatic endeavors in Europe proved much more successful than those in Asia, the Middle East, or Latin America.*]

Exiled for twenty years from the White House, Republicans were straining at the bit in 1952. John Foster Dulles was certainly among them: he turned down an offer to become the ambassador to Japan, explaining that he preferred the "power house" in Washington to "the end of the transmission line" in Tokyo. The exhilaration that came with control of the "power house" was quickly tempered, however, by the realities of being "in" rather than "out" of office. Though circumstances produced cynical overstatement, there was a kernel of broadly relevant truth in Harry Truman's late 1952 chuckle over the likely fate of his successor: "He'll sit here, and he'll say, 'Do this! Do that!' *And nothing will happen.* Poor Ike—it won't be a bit like the Army. He'll find it very frustrating."

There would be frustration for John Foster Dulles too—and it would spring from encounters with what might be called the predicaments of power: those things that complicate its exercise, that interfere with the ability of the wielder to do what he may want, and that may ultimately limit success or even bring defeat. Dulles found that power is never pure because it is never exercised in a vacuum. Moving in an environment in which other people and other states also move means that strength is always relative. Just as light or sound waves are affected by the nature of the medium through which they pass, moving faster or slower or not at all under different conditions, so the most influential of policymakers in the most influential of states would be inhibited by the circumstances of the real world in which he operates.

Like all modern secretaries of state Dulles had to struggle with several layers of predicaments, each layer inseparably related to the others while maintaining certain distinct characteristics of its own. Initially, he had to deal with the problems inherent in maintaining a personal power base in the Eisenhower administration. This meant developing and protecting a relationship with the president: an obvious enough priority for any cabinet officer, but Dulles was acutely sensitive to it because of memories of his uncle Robert Lansing's difficulties with Woodrow Wilson. There was also the need to vie for influence over policymaking with other members of the advisory and administrative structure that supported the president.

Secondly, Dulles had to cope with the complexities of the American political system that surrounded his bureaucratic base. Well before the 1950s, of course, democratic practices had given public opinion, especially as revealed in election results, a place in determining the international posture of the United States. The specific structure of U.S. government also gave Congress power over the shaping of foreign policies. Dealing both with voters and their elected legislators were thus inescapable concerns at any time; the particular atmosphere of the 1950s, however, made these tasks that much more complicated. McCarthyite hysteria, "China Lobby" vigilance, Sputnik, and "missile gap" paranoia, among other influences, generated an extraordinarily charged domestic political atmosphere.

Thirdly, and most important, there was confrontation with the predicaments of power in the international arena—with what Raymond Aron and the subtleties of the French language identify as *puissance* as opposed to *pouvoir*. Dulles attended to a cluster of closely related concerns that might all be placed under the heading "the political economy of power." Though universally recognized as the most powerful single state in the world of the 1950s, the United States, Dulles knew very well, was nevertheless but one nation in a global system. There were external forces and circumstances against which or through which it had to move as it sought to protect and advance its interests. There were, as well, significant limitations on the resources it could devote to dealing with those forces and circumstances. The most basic predicament with which Dulles ever had to deal was the process of balancing—or trying to balance—those interests and those resources.

In this respect Dulles's labors have ongoing relevance. The current controversy sparked by Paul Kennedy's *The Rise and Fall of the Great Powers,* among other writings, would have had a familiar ring to the secretary of state of three decades past. Sensitivity to the perceived interplay of resources and interests in the 1950s might well provide greater historical depth and intellectual heft to today's debates.

Some of the resource problems of that earlier decade are well known. Dulles and most other 1950s policymakers never lost sight of the fact that they had finite military power available to them. For example, military planners had to consider manpower constraints, and they recognized that not all weapons systems were appropriate to all situations. In addition, Dulles and the Republicans were highly sensitive to the severe economic strains that an active foreign policy imposed on the United States. Compounding these abstract military and economic limitations were some of the obvious political factors already mentioned: just how many soldiers would the American public be willing to send overseas, especially if those soldiers actually had to fight? Just how large a defense budget would Congress support, especially if it meant an increase in taxes or deficits?

Some of the resource problems of the 1950s—and today—are less traditionally emphasized. Dulles had a fascinating entanglement with the predicaments of *time,* for example. He saw it as a consistently complicating factor in the exercise of power. On an abstract, indeed philosophical level, he had had an almost lifelong respect for what he saw as the potency of time. As early as his graduate student days in Paris, he had been impressed with Henri Bergson's theories of "flux," of the irresistible force of "change" in human affairs. His own writings in the 1930s, especially *War, Peace, and Change,* had made the unending conflict of "static" and "dynamic" forces a key tool for analyzing international affairs.

The vicissitudes of time were not only an ongoing concern in the 1950s; they seemed to have grown more complex. On the one hand, Dulles saw the pace of change quickening to a dizzying speed, perhaps as a result of technological revolutions and the impact of war: "[I]t was a most uncertain world," he told Syngman Rhee in August 1953, "and impossible to anticipate as much as six months ahead." On the other hand, curiously, problems and struggles had taken on a semipermanent character, with a potential for exhaustion as one result. "One of the most dangerous characteristics of the Soviet Communist movement is that it regards itself as timeless," Dulles wrote Eisenhower. "It emphasizes that to achieve its results will require 'an entire historical era.'" On a more mundane, but equally complicated level, Dulles also found himself consistently *short* of time. Endless issues required attention and crises seemed to hound him at every turn: where was the time, where was the opportunity to learn enough about the issues in order to shape appropriate policies?

A final predicament for Dulles represents something of a category of its own because it grew out of efforts to deal with the other facets of "the political economy of power." Involved here is the issue of "allies" and the process of finding them, working with them, and keeping them. Dulles had not the slightest doubt of America's need for allies, or that this dependency was a function of the limitations on American resources. He was to learn, though, that this need was not easily fulfilled. There were unending problems connected with getting allies to do what Washington wanted them to do—or getting them to at least endorse or maintain some sort of "benevolent neutrality" toward what Washington itself wanted to do. Sometimes it was the stronger partners who caused difficulties: British and French attachment to colonial attitudes, for example, created what Dulles called a "very, very fundamental problem" for the United States. What Churchill once dubbed the "tyrannies of the weak" could complicate Dulles's life too: a Syngman Rhee or a Chiang Kai-shek "are not people, under normal circumstances, that we would want to support," Dulles told the Senate Foreign Relations Committee in 1953, and he could quickly have drawn up a list of frustrating maneuvers emanating from Seoul or Taipei. The national interest, the secretary nevertheless believed, gave the United States no choice but to gather allies both strong and weak. As he said of Rhee and Chiang, they were the "lesser of two evils."

The sources of the predicaments confronting John Foster Dulles were certainly varied. Some of them can almost be said to be inherent in the human condition. Others were more precisely located in place and time. Problems involving Congress or elections were in part a product of specifically American institutions and traditions, for example, though they were also a function of the uniquely charged atmosphere of the 1950s.

Whatever the sources, Dulles accumulated only a mixed record in his encounters with the predicaments of power, with the balance tipping more toward failure than success. His greatest strengths tended to be *intellectual:* Dulles was frequently sensitive to the problems inhibiting his role as secretary of state and sometimes thoughtful and articulate in discussing them. Awareness did not always translate into *achievement* or *practice,* however. In some situations predicaments were so great as to defy attempts to tame them. In others the policies adopted were not sufficiently aligned with the insights that preceded them. And at still other times—the most ironic or tragic of all—the very efforts that Dulles put forth spawned other, even more troubling problems.

Dulles may have enjoyed his purest success in the realm of bureaucratic politics. He faced the formidable twin tasks of safeguarding a relationship with a president who was not a longtime associate and navigating the complex shoals of a large executive branch. He worked hard at these tasks, and one might argue that if he had not, he would have had a much shorter tenure as secretary of state than he did.

Problems with Eisenhower might have become important, for example, if Dulles had not acted with considerable shrewdness and sensitivity. There were numerous potential pitfalls. Almost from the beginning of their association, the president had qualms about Dulles's "personality." "Foster's a bit sticky at first," he told Harold Macmillan, "but he has a heart of gold." Disagreement about important issues were present too. In the drawn-out battle over the Bricker Amendment, Dulles regularly pressed Eisenhower to be tougher than he seemed inclined to be. As late as May 1956 the secretary of state was complaining to Sherman Adams about the "awkward" and "embarrassing" situation created by the president's apparent refusal to "take the lead" on this matter. Dulles and Eisenhower never completely resolved differences concerning the use of nuclear weapons either, though a curious seesaw pattern emerged in which each tried to rein in the other on different occasions. In December 1953, for instance, the secretary of state argued with both the president and Pentagon officials about what he saw as their too-hasty readiness to turn to full-fledged war with China in the event of a violation of the Korean armistice. In September 1958, however, it was Eisenhower who questioned Dulles's proposals regarding a resort to tactical nuclear weapons during the second Quemoy-Matsu crisis.

In spite of the pitfalls, a very strong Eisenhower-Dulles relationship evolved. Dulles kept in constant touch with the president, explicitly saying time and again that he wanted to confirm mutual conceptions of policies and clear major speeches or releases. He could also be openly deferential, as when asking what his "place" would be in the follow-up to Eisenhower's "atoms for peace" proposal. Extensive consultation under such conditions allowed both men to recognize how many ideas and judgments they shared. The president certainly came to see it this way: he resisted a number of suggestions to replace his secretary of state, arguing that he was "as nearly indispensable as a human ever becomes." Ann Whitman commented on how "hard hit" Eisenhower was during the last stages of Dulles's cancer, and the president himself referred to his "unique relationship" with Dulles during one of his last visits to Walter Reed Hospital.

Dulles's solid relationship with Eisenhower, which is all the more impressive because of the fragile elements within it, served as both ballast and compass for navigating the executive branch's bureaucratic rapids. And rapids there were. The secretary was rarely able to forget that some of the most important policies he was involved in shaping were subject to input from potent colleagues; he was forced to participate in ongoing discussions, even struggles, with the Treasury Department and the Bureau of the Budget concerning foreign aid and Mutual Security expenditures. There were likewise constant maneuverings and tussles with the Defense Department and the JCS over issues as crucial as preparations for war with China, the future of NATO, and a nuclear test ban. Within the State Department itself there were disagreements on policy matters. These might have proved to be a two-edged sword for Dulles. On the one hand, conflicting advice on Asian issues from men like Walter Robertson and Philip Bonsal or on European developments from Douglas Dillon as opposed to David Bruce surely increased his sensitivity to options. On the other hand, evaluating those options—and stacking them up against those emerging from other segments of the executive branch—increased the complexity of decision-making.

Dulles worked hard at maintaining his influence in the bureaucracy surrounding Eisenhower. On one level, he seems to have calmly taken as a given the need to thrash out policies: where Eisenhower could get angry at Pentagon pressure for money, for example, Dulles could tell him that "it was not entirely surprising" that the military would make "maximum demands for the deliberate purpose of shifting the decision to the political branch." On another level, it was equally natural for him to be a tough advocate himself. He regularly argued budget issues, using what he once called his "day in court" to impress the president and others. Periodically he took swipes at military spokesmen. In May 1954, while coping with the crisis in Vietnam, Dulles pointedly criticized what he saw as too much JCS emphasis on atomic war with China and the Soviet Union and too little attention to "political" and "defensive" options. This, it might be added, was one of the many situations in which Eisenhower's essential agreement with him gave Dulles a successful handle on a policy deliberation. The secretary of state knew that this was a crucial ingredient in his bureaucratic clout, and he was determined to protect his access to the president so that opportunities for persuasion or opportunities for mutual discovery of shared views could continue unimpeded. About this he was blunt even with Eisenhower on the few occasions when the president toyed with reorganization ideas. In late 1956, for example, when the president was considering making the chairman of the Operations Coordinating Board (OCB) a sort of interdepartmental "inspector general," Dulles expressed worries about the possibility of an "undesirable conflict of jurisdiction." He insisted that "the Secretary of State should always have direct access to the President . . . and that if he lost that position, it would seriously impair the constitutional functioning of government." It is not clear whether Eisenhower deferred to Dulles or not; he did not carry through with the plan.

Dulles also worked tirelessly and experienced considerable success when confronting predicaments in the domestic arena outside the executive branch. He knew that his ability to achieve almost any foreign policy goal could be dramatically affected by the winning or losing of elections and the maintenance or loss of broad domestic support. As a result he turned his attention to a cluster of interrelated foci: public opinion, relations with the press, and, especially, relations with Congress.

Dulles's sensitivity to the relevance of public opinion was lifelong. Grandfather John Watson Foster drew him into electoral politics as early as the Taft presidency and involvement, usually with the Republican party, was

regular thereafter. More than thirty years before his association with Eisenhower, more than twenty years before his work with Thomas Dewey, Dulles was deliberating campaign strategy on foreign policy issues with men like Herbert Hoover and John W. Davis. By 1952 Dulles's sensitivity to public opinion could only have grown. The surprise results of the 1948 election had demonstrated the fundamental importance of attending to first things first. The intervening travails of Dean Acheson had similarly underlined in unmistakable fashion how a secretary of state could be grievously hurt by failing to tend enough of the fences that surrounded the electorate.

Dulles's interest in voter opinion never dwindled once a Republican finally gained the White House, and he at last assumed command at the State Department. Regarding the never-ending battle over foreign aid appropriations, for example, correspondence and minutes of meetings are liberally sprinkled with estimates of public support. And deliberations on several other specific issues were regularly punctuated by reference to confounding public relations problems. Walking with Anthony Eden on a beach in Bermuda in December 1953, Dulles pleaded for British cooperation on dicey questions concerning China: the new administration wanted to devise more "reasonable" policies, but was all too sensitive to the "political dynamite" still in its hands. In 1956 Dulles bemoaned the way "the White House staff was subject to strong political influences" on the subject of arms aid to Israel.

Thus prodded, Dulles devoted a portion of his prodigious energies to domestic political tasks. He was active in both the 1952 and 1956 election campaigns, of course, but also put a great deal of time into general public information efforts before and after the successful reelection drives. Such efforts produced mixed results. In 1949, when Dulles was campaigning for a Senate seat, Arthur Vandenberg had praised him for "the facility with which you have shed the language of a million dollar lawyer and dropped into the lingo of Joe Doakes." Throughout the 1950s, however, the "lingo" of a heavy flow of statements, speeches, interviews, and press conferences regularly sparked problems and criticisms. To this day, in fact, the mention of Dulles's name conjures up redolent phrases like "massive retaliation," "agonizing reappraisal," and "brinkmanship."

Media attention often served as the catalyst for criticism of public statements, and Dulles had problems with the press throughout his years at the State Department. When barely in office he had to tangle with the *New York Times* on a story about an informal dinner discussion with reporters that was supposed to have been "off-the-record"; there were testy telephone exchanges between the new secretary and Arthur Krock, complete with threats on never granting another interview. Rough as the press might be, however, Dulles assumed the costs of *not* working with it would be much higher.

Something of the same stoic determination characterized Dulles's approach to Congress. Congressional controls over budgetary allocations and military affairs would alone have compelled his attention; in addition to an uncomfortably large number of Democrats who required courting, the Republican bloc was a regular source of worry. There were prickly, even eccentric leaders, especially in the Senate, and there were prickly issues (like "China") on which it was impossible to devise a universally acceptable position. Yet the legislators' continuing efforts to reassert their power following the Roosevelt years made him that much more mindful of their sensitivities and prerogatives. Dulles saw a solid relationship with Capitol Hill as a factor in the international credibility of the Eisenhower administration. During debate on the Formosa Resolution in January 1955, for example, he admitted to the Senate Foreign Relations Committee that "[a]s a practical matter, of course, the authority of the President in this field cannot in fact survive effectively any indication on the part of Congress that it is not behind the President." In the context of the 1950s, keeping Congress "behind" desired policies proved to be a task dense with its own particular predicaments.

Dulles worked strenuously to tame them. Consultation with legislators was a constant necessity, with what he once called "Congressional education" taking place in many hours of committee hearings and White House meetings. Dulles also utilized the tried and true mechanism of roping Capitol Hill representatives into conference delegations and other official responsibilities. (It did sometimes prove difficult to carry off, as when he was unable to persuade a single Democrat or Republican to attend the various London conferences designed to deal with the Suez crisis.) Not surprisingly, Dulles singled out key leaders for special attention: Robert Taft was a major concern early on, and close private contacts with him helped cope with the awkward Bohlen confirmation problem; Democrat Walter George, who became chairman of the Senate Foreign Relations Committee, was probably Dulles's most intensively courted senator, though Mike Mansfield and Lyndon Johnson were important counterparts in the process of maintaining a "bipartisan" foreign policy.

All in all, Dulles's efforts to deal with electoral politics, public opinion, and congressional necessities paid some solid dividends. The major reelection success of 1956 was hardly his, of course, but his four years of work as secretary of state were not irrelevant either. Shortly after the election, Dulles pointed with pride to surveys showing a two-thirds public approval of his performance, in contrast to two-thirds disapproval of Dean Acheson some five years earlier. (It should be added that Dulles was honest enough to comment on the full range of the statistics, which also showed that 17 percent of those surveyed had never heard of him!) On the legislative front there were regular successes as well: though one can point to shortfalls involving matters like foreign aid or thorny tangles like the "missile gap" debate, it is likewise essential to cite the long record of congressional cooperation on many budgetary recommendations—the Bricker Amendment, the Formosa Resolution, the "Eisenhower Doctrine," and so on.

In retrospect, however, one must recognize that the costs of such successes were sometimes high—and that such costs are prominent reminders of the way predicaments surrounded Dulles's power. There was, for example, a drain on his time and energy: as early as 1953 he confessed that one set of hearings had been "exhausting" and his grumblings about the number of hours spent on Capitol Hill were heard regularly in later years. When public or congressional pressures resulted in modifying administration policies, other costs resulted. Perhaps the most obvious is the toll taken on allied relationships. What Dulles once referred to as a "delicate Senate problem" on China policy, for instance, greatly compounded already tricky Anglo-American coordination.

European allies in general—and some of Eisenhower's and Dulles's friends at home—also grew frustrated with the bending that took place toward Joseph McCarthy. There were angry indictments of the president's timidity on so dramatic an issue, and the secretary of state's readiness to cave in to the likes of Scott McLeod. What made the administration's posture regarding McCarthyism so distressing, it must be added, was the fact that both Eisenhower and Dulles were quite prepared to use shrewdness, toughness, or both to get around congressional or public recalcitrance when they saw the issue as important enough. Among the virtues of the Formosa and "Eisenhower Doctrine" resolutions overwhelmingly approved by Congress, for example, was the greater latitude allowed the executive to deal with Asian or Middle Eastern problems. In hearings on the former, Dulles admitted that "its purpose" was to allow even so extreme an action as a strike at China without further consultations with Congress.

Though Dulles had to struggle with the costs of policymaking at home, his most serious predicaments came within the international arena. There, grappling with military, economic, and political limitations on American control capabilities absorbed even more of his time and energy without necessarily producing commensurate achievements.

Dulles tried to deal creatively with the major problems he saw confronting the United States on almost every front. He came closest to success when working on the definition of a new "grand strategy" and closely related policies toward Europe.

The Eisenhower administration is well known for its early pronouncement of a "New Look," and there is no question that Dulles was one of its enthusiastic architects. Even before the 1952 election he had begun to speculate on what would soon be called the "Great Equation": finding a way to maintain adequate defense and an active foreign policy without going bankrupt. Dulles is most identified with the emphasis on nuclear weapons, traditionally seen as the key tool chosen for accomplishing this objective, particularly the concept of "massive retaliation." In the slang of the day, "more bang for the buck" could be secured by relying on atomic bombs rather than conventional ground forces, especially since the Soviet Union was seen as being "glutted with manpower."

The New Look, however, has often been analyzed too simplistically, the tendency being to overstate Dulles's attachment to nuclear weapons and to understate his and other policymakers' interest in "flexible" responses to problems and goals. The Eisenhower administration's European policies, for instance, suggest the fuller range of options that Dulles typically considered. There was, to be sure, a 1953-1954 push to bring NATO into line regarding reliance on atomic weaponry, a policy driven by financial as well as strategic considerations. Other policies were pursued, however, each designed to ease limitations or increase opportunities. Perhaps the best known was the struggle for the notorious European Defense Community, belatedly and successfully transformed into the Western European Union. Though Dulles inherited plans for EDC and had Anthony Eden to thank for the WEU alternative, he was a willing and important worker on behalf of both programs. Relatedly, Dulles steadily encouraged European economic integration via development of institutions like the European Coal and Steel Community and Common Market.

Dulles helped shape important achievements in the New Look and European policies. Simple accounting suggests one: the actual cutting of billions of dollars from defense budgets. The budgets in excess of $50 billion during the Korean War years were reduced to $40 billion by fiscal 1955; even congressional agitation over Sputnik and the "missile gap" produced increases to only $46.6 billion in fiscal 1959 and $45.9 billion in 1960. Other achievements are not so easily measured but are nonetheless impressive. Take Dulles's patience in dealing with old European allies, at least in the period before the Suez crisis. This may seem an odd claim on behalf of the author of the infamous "agonizing reappraisal" speech of December 1953; yet the long battle over EDC as a whole substantiates it quite well. Countless prods to anger and frustration were part of the EDC campaign, many (though by no means all) of them emanating from the byzantine intricacies of French politics and the interminable delays in securing ratification in Paris. Dulles, like many at the time, had his lapses from equanimity: the harsh "agonizing reappraisal" statement was one; a tendency to testiness in dealings with Pierre Mendès-France, another.

Usually, however, Dulles recognized the seriousness and legitimacy of French concerns, ably communicated to him by men like Georges Bidault and American representatives like David Bruce and Douglas Dillon. In any event Dulles decided that patience was the best way to get maximum results. Facing congressional criticism of his reluctance to use threats to achieve West German rearmament, Dulles shrewdly demurred: "When you have a machine that is running in a certain direction you can try to stop it abruptly, in which case you generally get an accident, or you can swing it through a curve, in which case you can conserve a good bit of what you have got." This was the typical Dulles approach until the much-de-

layed French ratification of WEU in December 1954. In his congratulatory telegram to Mendès-France, he specifically commented that "if we here said little [during the final ratification debate] it was because we felt that silence was the best contribution we could make."

Dulles's handling of the EDC-WEU tangle can be seen as the tip of an iceberg of strength as far as European policies are concerned. EDC was always explicitly connected with the problems of limitations on American resources; the WEU variation sensibly allowed allies to help deal with those problems while simultaneously proceeding with their own programs. The whole issue is therefore closely related to the "predicaments" of power.

At least some of Dulles's achievements in this area were the result of his being able enough—or lucky enough—to prevail over the shortage of time. Because of the nature of his previous life and work, Dulles came to European issues with more solid intellectual preparation than he could claim concerning any other foreign policy problems. For more than forty years he had traveled back and forth across the Atlantic, involved in government work at the Paris Peace Conference of 1918-1919 and meetings of the Council of Foreign Ministers in the 1940s, and involved in a highly successful law practice specializing in international business and finance. He had watched and thought and written; he had devoted the kind of time and accumulated the kind of experience required for a grasp of complexities. The evidence of this is abundant and underappreciated, though it can only be suggested here. One example certainly is Dulles's intense concern for what he described as the "suicidal strife" between France and Germany: an "old cycle" of war and revenge; a "firetrap" that had engulfed too many, he believed, and that had to be replaced by the weaving of "a European fabric of mutual understanding and common endeavor." Nor was military unification the only or even most important mechanism. "The supranational aspect of EDC [is] far, far more important than twelve German divisions," Dulles told Mendès-France. His own emphasis on economic integration, going back to the 1930s and shaped in cooperation with friends like Jean Monnet, suggested the specific direction in which he was most anxious to move.

Sensitivities like these also allowed Dulles to develop his approach to the thorny problem of dealing with the Soviet Union. Conscious of the indigenous nature of European problems, and congruent with his own concern for them as early as the 1920s, he placed Moscow's behavior into a more balanced, less distorted context than many other contemporary analysts. For example, he refused to oversell the anti-communist case for EDC: "Even if there were a genuine detente with the Soviet Union," he told Britain's Lord Salisbury in July 1953, "it would still be virtually necessary to press on with the integration of Europe"; "Even if the Soviet threat were totally to disappear," he told the North Atlantic Council six months later, "would we be blind to the danger that the West may destroy itself? Surely there is an urgent, positive duty on all of us to seek to end that danger which comes from within?" By 1955 Dulles was explicitly acknowledging the relaxation of the cold war in Europe. With West Germany safely nestled into NATO, with economic integration proceeding, and with the Austrian State Treaty concluded, Dulles described the Soviet Union as moving to a "less menacing" position in Europe. In a report on the Geneva summit to the Senate Foreign Relations Committee, he said further: "I think we are getting closer to a relationship [where] we can deal with [the Soviet Union] on a basis comparable to that where we deal with differences between friendly nations. We have differences, and they are hard differences, but we know they will not lead to war."

It would be reasonable to recall that Dulles's—and Eisenhower's—public rhetoric often failed to communicate this sense of historical complexity and/or incipient détente concerning European issues. Does this suggest a weak link in an often impressive chain of analysis and policymaking? Yes. Nor is it the only weak link. Though it is important to identify basic achievements in New Look and European policies, it is equally necessary to recognize that the achievements were compromised in important ways by problems emanating from those very policies. Attempts to cope with or tame predicaments could generate yet others.

Most striking perhaps are the weaknesses inherent in the "massive retaliation" component of the revised grand strategy. Melodramatic appraisals can be put aside, to be sure: neither Dulles nor Eisenhower were itching to charge over the brink to blast adversaries back to the Stone Age. Both of them, on the contrary, generally subscribed to "deterrence" theory in shaping their nuclear policies. And both, to their credit, came to appreciate the almost paralyzing character of nuclear weapons as numbers and destructive capacities increased. Nonetheless, nuclear weapons did remain the ultimate component of the American arsenal, and there were too many ways in which the brink might have been jumped in spite of intentions to the contrary. The president and secretary of state were each too enamored of "tactical" nuclear weapons, for example, and failed to appreciate the full potency of these presumably "bullet"-like tools. This is symptomatic of a certain cockiness about control capabilities as well, a sometimes frighteningly naive assumption that the decision to unsheath weapons of mass destruction would always be one's own and would only be taken after mature deliberation. It is in the very nature of nuclear technology, however, that it can take on a demanding life of its own. (David Lilienthal once remarked that trying to stop development of the hydrogen bomb in 1950 was like trying to say no to a steamroller.) The meshing of ever-developing technology with complex political realities further undercut pretensions to firm control. To illustrate, agitation over the Gaither Report and the "missile gap" forced Eisenhower and Dulles to accept budget increases they had no desire to endorse.

Abroad, something similar was possible. For instance, adversaries would influence the way conflict evolved:

who could be sure that some initial use of even "tactical" atomic bombs would not trigger an irresistible escalation to Armageddon? Foreign "friends" could be equally complicating. Dulles worried about Chiang Kai-shek's ability to drag the United States into a war with China that was bound to involve nuclear weapons. And within Dulles and Eisenhower themselves, the capacity for *self*-control was not as absolute as either imagined. Though it can certainly be demonstrated that both men kept cool heads about atomic bombs during the May 1954 crisis in Vietnam, for example, the same cannot be said about their handling of the Quemoy-Matsu tensions of 1954-1955 and 1958. In these cases the speed and psychological pressures of a crisis situation brought both men dangerously close to shooting from the nuclear hip over stakes they knew were nowhere near commensurate.

Nor were flaws lacking in some of the other tools Dulles turned to in his encounter with the predicaments of power. Psychological warfare and covert operations, for example, may have seemed appropriate for political and financial reasons, but they could bring serious problems in their train. In Europe, certainly, the reasons to doubt their value are plentiful and apply to programs involving balloon surveillance and propaganda campaigns in Italy, East Germany, and Hungary, among others. On an abstract level, "psywar" efforts and dirty tricks compromised American integrity in many quarters. They also compromised the intellectual consistency of Dulles's usually shrewder analysis of the European scene and how to deal with the Soviet Union there. More concretely, any number of covert operations threatened to explode in the face of the United States—or the faces of those directly involved, as the bloodshed in Hungary in 1956 amply illustrates.

Dulles's personal role in psychological warfare and covert operations is still unclear. At best, these may have been activities that he did not adequately control, activities that may offer one more demonstration of the perils of bureaucratic politics—even when they involve a brother. At worst, Dulles may have been able to control them but chose not to. Perhaps he indulged them as a sharper and potentially useful supplement to calmer, more traditional approaches to European problems? In the end, however, whether the story involves inability to control or indulgence, Dulles's record in this area was as dubious as that of any of his successors.

One additional example of possible limits on the strength of Dulles's European policies deserves mention. It does not involve blatant failure but suggests the irony that often plagues the policymaker: even apparently tamed predicaments have a way of evolving into other problems. Dulles took pride in the evolution of European integration in the 1950s. Politically, militarily, and especially economically, he interpreted his own efforts as contributing to those of many others to solve deep historical problems that had long concerned him. There was a trapdoor in such an achievement, however: it was built on a divided Germany. Dulles feared the destabilizing potential of a two-Germany Europe, feared the ability of the Germans to play off those around them against one another, and the ability of the Soviets to play to German desires for reunification. To repeat, there is irony here, not failure. It is easy to debate but not resolve the question of whether any better German-European arrangements could have been secured in the 1950s, and thirty years of relative stability are not irrelevant to the debate in any event.

The shaping of basic strategy and European policies were major components of Dulles's work as secretary of state, but they obviously do not comprise the whole story. Because he found it necessary to deal with other issues and other quarters of the globe, so must anyone interested in evaluating his performance. As Dulles turned in other directions, however, his efforts were consistently weaker.

Regarding Europe especially, Dulles invested the time and commitment required to understand highly complex problems, thereby allowing himself to shape policies that related to those problems. As well, these policies were in reasonable proportion to what the United States could do without severely straining its resources. In more instances than not these layers of mature policymaking were lacking when Dulles turned to Asia, the Middle East, and Latin America. Something like an inverse pattern actually became the norm in these areas, in fact, and the poorer results that were common seem all too logical because of the change.

This is not to say that elements of strength were absent from Dulles's approach to non-European issues. Even in the 1950s some impressive achievements were obvious, and the passage of time has allowed appreciation of others. Regarding Asia, for example, he shares in the credit for terminating the draining Korean conflict in 1953 and for avoiding a plunge into war in Indochina during the volatile days of 1954. Dulles could also be shrewd in his analytical grasp of the basic dynamics of Asian affairs. For example, he fully recognized the significance of Japan and the value of a close relationship with that former enemy. Though it produced opposite results, he also understood that China was a crucial factor in any regional equation. More to the point, because it contrasts with still common assumptions of U.S. obtuseness regarding Asia in the 1950s, Dulles was not inclined to treat the People's Republic of China (PRC) as a mere puppet of the Soviet Union. As early as December 1953, at the Bermuda conference, he talked at great length to Eisenhower, Churchill, Eden, and Bidault about the "strain" in the Sino-Soviet relationship and Mao Tsetung's status as an "outstanding Communist leader in his own right."

The same kind of sensitivity surfaced in his overall view of Middle Eastern developments. He knew full well that Arab nationalism had become the dynamic ingredient in that region and that the United States was being plagued by its allies' tendency to "commit suicide" in dealing with it: even the major crisis of 1956, Dulles said at one point, was "not a question of Suez, but . . . really a question of Algeria for the French and position in the Persian Gulf for the British."

In Europe such analytical sophistication was compromised by Dulles's confrontation with the predicaments of power; in Asia, the Middle East, and Latin America, the strengths were overpowered. This happened because the layers of successful policymaking present in the one area were absent in the others. A shortage of time and experience made the foundation for understanding complex problems too shallow, thus helping to produce responses or programs that were either unrelated to the fundamental nature of those problems or beyond the essential capabilities of the United States.

A shortage of time was one of the truly fundamental predicaments in these cases, as in others. "Today's trouble spot is the Gaza strip," was the first line of a 1955 Dulles memo to the president: it was an opening symptomatic of the "crisis" atmosphere that permeated the Eisenhower presidency. At many points the exigencies did not even wait their turn to hold the stage alone. It was bad enough to have to juggle the problems of the Geneva conference after the fall of Dien Bien Phu and then have to cope with Quemoy and Matsu after Geneva, for example; it was obviously even worse to have to simultaneously deal with the climacteric of the EDC imbroglio.

A crisis orientation, almost by definition, makes it more difficult adequately to collect thoughts, analyze complexities, and evaluate alternatives. Even when some of the raw materials for more capable policymaking are present, they may get shunted aside or inadequately utilized because of the confusing pressures of the moment. In the months before May 1954, for example, Dulles fully shared in the often perceptive Washington assessments of problems in Southeast Asia. He was emphatic that the French must thoroughly pull down colonial sails, for instance, and about the importance of maintaining an American sense of proportion: "[N]ot knowing what the French are going to do . . . I am determined not to make Indochina a symbol for all of Southeast Asia so if Indochina is lost we assume that the whole game is up." Such acumen did not survive in the pressure cooker of mid-1954, however, as Dulles helped shape policies that greatly expanded the U.S. role in the region. And hurried resort to mediums like SEATO and the Diem regime meant that the major new efforts would be unrelated to the fundamental problems involved in Vietnam as well.

Approaches to the Middle East in 1958 offer another example of the debilitating impact of a crisis orientation. In spite of earlier discernment about this region's complex politics and dynamics, Dulles and others responded to emergencies in Jordan and Lebanon with almost knee-jerk reactions. "Even though every alternative is 'wrong,'" Dulles admitted, the United States would have to intervene. Marines would be sent, the flag of resistance to communist aggression would be raised, and references to the lessons of the 1930s would be made before the largely irrelevant operation petered out. Though he was hardly one to talk, Anthony Eden caught something of the nature of the episode at the time: "These sudden gusts of improvization, which with Dulles pass for policy," he wrote, "are disastrous for the West. If this is one more of them there will not be much left in the Middle East."

To compound the complications of shaping policies under pressured conditions, it is worth remembering that the very perception of a "crisis" was not always germane to fundamental problems. President Camille Chamoun's maneuvers in Lebanon, for example, suggest the way in which a "crisis" could be created or manipulated. American policymakers were not averse to this themselves, as the Guatemalan episode of 1954 demonstrates. And whether fabricated and exaggerated or not, emerging policies could be equally damaged by being forged in such an atmosphere. In Guatemala Carlos Castillo Armas hardly offered genuine solutions to the problems requiring attention.

One more point about the predicaments of pressured policymaking deserves brief mention here. Policies conceived under duress may not only be inappropriate for the situations involved, but may actually make them worse. There are a number of examples of this, but the most dangerous probably came during the Quemoy-Matsu crises of 1954-1955 and 1958. Dulles knew that the overall Asian problem confronting the United States was, as he put it, a "ruptured balance of power" in that region; he also knew that Chiang Kai-shek was a wild-card ally and that the United States had become "over-committed" to "two exposed pieces of real estate." In spite of all this, he helped devise policies that coupled the most dangerous of his options: the United States would brandish and seriously discuss use of its nuclear weapons while simultaneously tending a relationship with Chiang that gave him ongoing opportunities to jeopardize a stable balance. That some of the misguided risks of this combination resulted from the domestic political context in which Dulles and Eisenhower were operating is true enough, but to recognize this is only to recall that this is another kind of pressure that can have deleterious effects on policymaking.

Explicit recognition of U.S. "over-commitment" regarding Quemoy and Matsu is a useful signpost to a last point about Dulles's predicaments in Asia, the Middle East, and Latin America: that in calculations of "the political economy of power" in these regions, he—and Eisenhower—tended to incur obligations that would severely, even tragically, strain the resources of the United States over time. Given articulate sensitivity to the pressures of the "long haul" and the New Look's emphasis on conserving strength, the 1950s witnessed an odd but real drift toward the kind of declining American power recently highlighted by Paul Kennedy and others.

Dulles and Eisenhower did successfully avoid the kind of vast vortexes that plagued other American policymakers. Though there were uncomfortably close calls in the Formosa Strait and the Middle East, for example, it is now often recalled that no Korean War and no grand-scale involvement in Vietnam began between 1953 and 1961. This is important and a distinct achievement, but it does not mean that a sense of proportion was always solidly in place. One sign of fragility in this regard was too great a tendency to put a foot in the door of Asian and Middle Eastern affairs or to inch further through already opened doors. Getting started and/or inching along has a way of seeming safe enough or limited enough while it is being done, but the experiences of the 1950s suggest that apparently minor steps have an insidious way of leading to more and more. What could be the harm in playing something of a friendly mediator's role in Anglo-Egyptian negotiations in 1953-1954? And was it not a finely calibrated move to provide assistance to France for its struggle in Indochina? But first steps in Cairo led to the explosive complications of the Aswan negotiations and to thoughts of replacing the British and French through most of the Middle East. And an arms-length role in Vietnam gave way to the elaborate process of organizing "United Action" to salvage something in Geneva and to the actual replacement of the French in Saigon. There was nothing inevitable about this step-by-step process of moving toward grave problems and disasters; decisions to stop or even turn back, however, require a strong, fully mature sense of proportion, and experience suggests that neither Dulles nor Eisenhower nor their successors had this in good enough measure. There is irony in this matter as far as Dulles is concerned. He could be perceptive about exactly this problem. In one early meeting at the 1954 Geneva conference, for example, he dismissed the likelihood of French withdrawal from Indochina by saying "it is one thing to talk about quitting, but another thing actually to quit." In 1957 too, while debating possible support for Turkish intervention in Syria, he told the president "there would be great difficulty in winding up the affair, as we had anticipated in the case of Britain and France in Suez."

In the real world of the 1950s, John Foster Dulles found complex circumstances that constantly hedged his ability to achieve what he would have seen as ideal results with ideal policies. In the end his struggle with those predicaments produced genuine success and serious failure.

Dulles started out with an impressive intellectual foundation, not the least element of which was his recognition that power was finite and that it required energy and creativity to make it as productive as possible. He also had the ability to mobilize his own energy and creativity over an extended period of time. In most aspects of his dealings with European issues, his intellect and his stamina worked well: he was able to understand many of the complexities of the European situation and to shape manageable policies that related to them. In his work on Asian, Middle Eastern, or Latin American issues, he performed less well. Here the predicaments of circumstances and resources often overpowered his efforts to tame them and tended to produce costly policies that were inappropriate and dangerous.

Why was Dulles less successful at grappling with the predicaments of power in some areas than in others? It is tempting to opt for a curt answer: like other human beings, he simply could not understand everything equally well. This is too bald an explanation, however, primarily because Dulles came intriguingly close to an *intellectual* grasp of many more things than is evident in the *policies* he helped shape. Even in Asia and the Middle East, for example, he often had more sophisticated *perceptions* than his *behavior* would suggest. The real question, then, is what interfered with the progression from sometimes shrewd analysis to less shrewd policymaking? Why did Dulles practice what might be called "intellectual brinkmanship" and fail to follow through his insights to their logical conclusions?

Part of the answer is surely tied up with the predicament of time, which complicated Dulles's work in several ways. His own life had given him extensive experience in European affairs but very limited contact with Asia or the Middle East. In the pressured, crisis-oriented years he served as secretary of state, would this not have made a difference? Is it surprising that deeper familiarity with one area gave views there a solidity that could survive the pressure—or that shallower, even if perceptive familiarity with other areas would prove more fragile?

In a sense the predicament of time can be said to have imposed itself in the path of Dulles's power, making it easier to detour away from directions his intellect might have suggested. The other obstacle that encouraged detour was self-imposed, though probably unconsciously. It involved the identification of goals or interests that were simply beyond the capacities of the United States, no matter how much time was available to tend them. For all his sensitivity to the limitations on American power, Dulles could allow ambitions and appetites to predominate his more abstract calculations of the political economy of power. Though he genuinely understood the scale of problems in Asia, for example, the thought of accepting the inevitability of a less prominent role there was just too unpalatable. On one hand he could tell Chiang Kai-shek's ambassador, Wellington Koo, that "even the Japanese had got themselves completely bogged down" in dealing with China—it "was a big country, with a lot of people." On the other hand, he could struggle for years to force the PRC to accept what the United States had decided were severe but necessary limitations on its regional role in spite of contrary advice from Japanese and Indian leaders, in spite of difficulties with allies, in spite of the blood of Korea and Indochina, and in spite of great numbers of problems elsewhere. John McCloy may have had just such an approach in mind when he once asked Eisenhower whether his administration's foreign policies had "too much of an 'Atlas' complex" about them.

Of course, Dulles was hardly unique in allowing appetite to sometimes triumph over logic. Like many of his Washington associates, like many American policymakers in other years, and like many leaders elsewhere throughout history, he experienced a tug of war often basic to human nature. Ironically, the attempt to make power do more than it is capable of doing seems to come most dramatically at those times when power is already great. In this respect, Dulles and other Americans of the cold war era had something in common with the Persians described by Herodotus or the "exorbitant court" of Louis XIV described by Ranke. Perhaps it has something to do with Henry Kissinger's notion that "power is the great aphrodisiac."

Nor was Dulles unique in *struggling* with his ambitions and the predicaments they brought, though here his company is more exclusive. One thinks of Napoléon, for example, who could advise Metternich that "he who wills a thing must also will the means to bring it about," but could also complain to one of his generals that "you write to me that it's impossible; the word is not French." Or one thinks of Bismarck, deeply troubled by German compulsions after 1890, but so responsible for having set them in motion. Dulles's similar confrontation with contradictory impulses makes him a figure equally worthy of careful study. Such similarity may offer no comfort, of course. The experiences of Napoléon's France and Bismarck's Germany—and Dulles's America—suggest all too clearly how high a price is paid for failing to carry the confrontation to a wise conclusion.

FURTHER READING

Biography

Beal, John Robinson. *John Foster Dulles: A Biography*. New York: Harper & Brothers, 1957, 331p.
　　Biography of Dulles focusing on his life and efforts to maintain world peace while serving as Secretary of State.

Pruessen, Ronald W. *John Foster Dulles: The Road to Power*. New York: The Free Press, 1982, 575 p.
　　Offers a "careful examination" of Dulles's entire life in order to trace his personal development and discern the experiences that later shaped his foreign policy decision making.

Stang, Alan. *The Actor: The True Story of John Foster Dulles Secretary of State, 1953-1959*. Boston: Western Islands, 1968, 346 p.
　　Explores Dulles's tenure as U.S. Secretary of State and his public activities prior to attaining this position.

Criticism

Arend, Anthony Clark. *Pursuing a Just and Durable Peace: John Foster Dulles and International Organization*. New York: Greenwood Press, 1988, 243 p.
　　Study of Dulles that highlights his career prior to becoming U.S. Secretary of State.

Berding, Andrew H. *Dulles on Diplomacy*. Princeton, N.J.: D. Van Nostrand Company, 1965, 184 p.
> Attempts "to show Dulles's thinking on the major issues of his day"—disarmament, Soviet expansion, problems in Southeast Asia, the possibility of German reunification, and others.

Chang, Gordon H. "To the Nuclear Brink: Eisenhower, Dulles, and the Quemoy-Matsu Crisis." *International Security* 12, No. 4 (Spring 1988): 96-123.
> Analyzes the 1954-55 confrontation between the United States and China, arguing that Eisenhower and Dulles brought the two nations closer to war than most historians have generally suspected.

Dulles, Eleanor Lansing. *John Foster Dulles: The Last Year*. New York: Harcourt, Brace & World, 1963, 244 p.
> Close study of Dulles's activities in 1958, his last year as Secretary of State.

Finer, Herman. *Dulles over Suez: The Theory and Practice of His Diplomacy*. Chicago: Quadrangle Books, 1964, 538 p.
> Examines Dulles's diplomacy and its "decisive effect" on the Suez Crisis of 1956.

Gerson, Louis L. *John Foster Dulles*. New York: Cooper Square Publishers, 1967, 372 p.
> Discussion of Dulles's varied diplomatic activities as Secretary of State preceded by an evaluation of the effect of his religious beliefs on his overall foreign policy.

Goold-Adams, Richard. *John Foster Dulles: A Reappraisal*. New York: Appleton-Century-Crofts, 1962, 310 p.
> Assesses Dulles's career, concluding that "his actual policies and the concepts that lay behind them deserve a higher place in the judgment of history than the methods by which he carried them out."

Guhin, Michael A. *John Foster Dulles: A Statesman and His Times*. New York: Columbia University Press, 1972, 404 p.
> Study of Dulles's diplomacy that endeavors to understand the reasons behind his decisions and to clarify several misconceptions about his motivations and personality.

Heller, Deane, and David Heller. *John Foster Dulles: Soldier for Peace*. New York: Holt, Rinehart and Winston, 1960, 328 p.
> Essentially laudatory study that seeks "to let Dulles' words speak for themselves—to let his philosophy of freedom and his strong religious beliefs shine through and illumine the man himself."

Marks, Frederick W., III. *Power and Peace: The Diplomacy of John Foster Dulles*. Westport, Conn.: Praeger, 1993, 266 p.
> Evaluates Dulles's statesmanship, treating his activities "on a comparative basis in terms of what his predecessors and successors achieved, or failed to achieve."

Toulouse, Mark G. *The Transformation of John Foster Dulles: From Prophet of Realism to Priest of Nationalism*. Macon, Ga.: Mercer University Press, 1985, 277 p.
> Investigates the religious underpinnings of Dulles's thought and the gradual transformation of his moral ideas over the course of his career.

The following sources published by Gale Research contain additional coverage of Dulles's life and career: *Contemporary Authors*, Vols. 115, 149.

Elinor Glyn

1864-1943

(Born Elinor Sutherland) English novelist, scriptwriter, and nonfiction writer.

INTRODUCTION

Glyn earned worldwide fame as a popular novelist specializing in stories with glamorous high society settings. Her most celebrated novel, *Three Weeks,* challenged conventional morality with its scandalous depiction of an adulterous love affair. Trading on the notoriety she gained with *Three Weeks,* Glyn also became an influential Hollywood screenwriter and commentator on the subject of romantic love, popularizing the word "it" as a slang term for sexual magnetism.

Biographical Information

While growing up on Jersey, one of the English Channel Islands, Glyn read extensively but had relatively little formal education. When she reached marriageable age, her family, which was economically middle-class with aristocratic pretensions, took her and her sister Lucy (who later earned fame as the fashion designer Lucile, Lady Duff Gordon) to London and Paris in order to introduce them to upper-class social circles. In 1892 she married the English country gentleman Clayton Glyn. Although the marriage provided her with the prestigious social connections she desired, she was not happy with her husband, who did not provide her with either the emotional satisfaction or the economic support she needed, and so she turned to a career in writing. Her first novel, *The Visits of Elizabeth,* was well-received and she established a popular following with subsequent light romantic stories set in upper class English society. With the publication of *Three Weeks,* however, she became an international celebrity. During the 1920s she established a successful second career as a screenwriter in Hollywood, collaborating on the photoplay for Metro-Goldwyn-Mayer's 1924 production of *Three Weeks* and other adaptations of her works, including the 1927 box-office hit *It,* which made actress Clara Bow famous as "the It Girl." She also wrote and directed two films in England, *Knowing Men* and *The Price of Things.*

Major Works

In novels such as *The Visits of Elizabeth, The Vicissitudes of Evangeline,* and *Elizabeth Visits America,* Glyn offered detailed, unconventionally frank observations about the manners and morals of the English aristocracy, featuring veiled descriptions of her own experiences and acquaintances. In contrast to these relatively decorous works, *Three Weeks* is a passionate

erotic fantasy that depends less on plot or character than on sensuous evocation of an exotic, romantic atmosphere. Focusing on a short-lived but intense affair between a young Englishman and an Eastern European queen traveling incognito in Switzerland and Venice, this novel, although not sexually explicit, stimulated tremendous controversy and remained an international bestseller for over two decades. Capitalizing on the lasting fame afforded her by *Three Weeks,* Glyn concentrated thereafter on writing mainly as a means of making money to support her lavish lifestyle, producing novels, screenplays, magazine articles, and nonfiction writings such as *The Philosophy of Love.*

Critical Reception

Because of her incomplete education, Glyn never mastered basic rules of grammar and style, and so even her most well-received works were noted for their popular appeal rather than their literary quality. In the decades following the publication of *Three Weeks,* her reputation declined as she wrote more quickly and carelessly, although her status as a popular culture icon solidified as a result of her talent for publicizing herself. Glyn's works are no longer widely read, but critics observe that *Three Weeks* remains noteworthy for having played a significant role in breaking down sexual censorship barriers in post-Victorian English literature.

PRINCIPAL WORKS

The Visits of Elizabeth (novel) 1900
The Reflections of Ambrosine (novel) 1902; also published as *The Seventh Commandment*
The Vicissitudes of Evangeline (novel) 1905; also published as *Red Hair*
Beyond the Rocks (novel) 1906
Three Weeks (novel) 1907
*Three Weeks (play) 1908
Elizabeth Visits America (novel) 1909
His Hour (novel) 1910; also published as *When His Hour Came*
The Reason Why (novel) 1911
Halcyone (novel) 1912; also published as *Love Itself*
The Sequence (novel) 1913; also published as *Guinevere's Lover*
The Man and the Moment (novel) 1915
The Career of Katherine Bush (novel) 1917
The Price of Things (novel) 1919
The Great Moment (screenplay) 1920
The Philosophy of Love (nonfiction) 1920
Man and Maid (novel) 1922
*Three Weeks (screenplay) 1923
It, and Other Stories (short stories) 1927
Knowing Men (screenplay) 1930
†The Price of Things (screenplay) 1930
Glorious Flames (novel) 1932
Love's Hour (novel) 1932
Did She? (novel) 1933
Saint or Satyr? and Other Stories (short stories) 1933
Sooner or Later (novel) 1933
Romantic Adventure (autobiography) 1936
The Third Eye (novel) 1940

*These works are adaptations of the novel *Three Weeks*.
†This work is an adaptation of the novel *The Price of Things*.

CRITICISM

The New York Times Book Review (essay date 1906)

SOURCE: "Smart Society," in *The New York Times Book Review*, November, 1906, 771 p.

[*In the following review, the critic reacts negatively to Glyn's* Beyond the Rocks, *citing the novel's "moral atmosphere" as "decidely unwholesome."*]

Elinor Glyn's new story, **Beyond the Rocks,** (Harper,) furnishes another of those saddening pictures of smart society for which she is already responsible to the number of two or three, though it has always been British smart society whose unseemliness she exposed. "Exposed" is perhaps not the best word, either, because one does not gather from the author's method of telling her story that she has the slightest idea of criticising the morals or manners of the set of people of whom she writes or of impressing her readers with their urgent need of missionaries. They are not labeled as bohemians, or free-thinkers, or eccentrics of any kind, but just exhibited as the ordinary run of nice (?) English men and women, pursuing their ordinary tactics in the game of life, but it strikes one looking at them from the provincial, and perhaps narrow-minded, Western shore of the Atlantic that they are hardly fit to associate with. One wonders if English people like the decidedly shady version of themselves which will get abroad through the medium of Mrs. Glyn's book, entirely without intention on her part, apparently.

But that is not the worst thing about **Beyond the Rocks**. The whole moral atmosphere of the book is of a decidedly unwholesome and vitiated character, since it not only condones the weaknesses and worse of its several characters, but actually expects us to accept them at their own valuation and rejoice in the combination of circumstances that landed the hero and heroine safely "beyond the rocks." though barely in time to save their reputations. At the opening of the story Theodora Fitzgerald has married a dreadful grocer, Josiah Brown, in order to provide her "exquisite" father with the means to go on his happy-go-lucky way without having to worry about the wherewithal to supply himself and his daughters with food and clothes.

Theodora is presented as beautiful as the dawn, as innocent as a baby, as pure as the stars, so good as to make all other women seem wicked beside her, yet she sells herself without a qualm to Josiah Brown, and when Lord Bracondale arrives on the scene a year later she receives his amazingly open attentions as eagerly as if the "too, too solid" Mr. Brown were an airy myth. Mr. Brown is blind to everything but his own ill-health, but one wonders if English husbands are really such negligible quantities as Theodora's was to that lady and her whole circle of friends. To be sure, the line seemed to be drawn against her really consigning Mr. Brown to limbo and attaching herself to Lord Bracondale, but all the preliminaries of such an event were gone through with as gayly as if there were no impediment—and then Theodora "for the first time realized whither she was speeding." As for Lord Bracondale, he never had any doubts, took everybody into his confidence, and implored everybody's help in securing for himself "happy hours" with his "white rose." His mother and sister were delighted to aid him, since it was far safer and nicer in their eyes to have an affair with a married woman than with the questionable Parisian ladies whom he had previously threatened to introduce into the family. Everybody adored Theodora and Bracondale and wondered what would happen to poor, luckless Josiah, whose plebeianism seemed to deprive him of all rights.

However, after months of blindness to her own special kind of villainy—though the author assures the reader at this point that Theodora "had no sentimental feeling of personal wickedness"—she decided to write her lover a letter of eternal farewell and her husband another concerning the train she would take up to London. A certain Morella Winmarleigh, with the worst intentions in the world, exchanged the two letters in their envelopes and Josiah immediately began to pine away with a mysterious illness, while Bracondale went off to hunt lions in Africa in order not to be an indelicate witness of his demise. The author does consent also to conceal the reason for the husband's death from Theodora, though it would take more than her word for it to convince that Theodora didn't know what a good turn Morella Winmarleigh had done her—and so, with all the rocks safely behind them, these two admirable lovers are left in the garden at Versailles, "looking out upon the realization of that fair dream of life," with not one visible twinge of conscience or regret, and murmuring, as they walk off into the sunset, that "there lived no greater gentleman" than the extraordinarily obliging Josiah Brown.

The New York Times Saturday Review of Books (essay date 1909)

SOURCE: "Mrs. Glyn's Ideas of America", in *The New York Times Saturday Review of Books,* May 22, 1909, 321 p.

[*In the following review, the critic praises Glyn's novel* Elizabeth Visits America, *but accuses Glyn of pandering to the American public with her portrayals of Americans.*]

Mrs. Elinor Glyn has made a book about her recent visit to the United States of America following upon the splutter and splash among the talkative and unsophisticated which was caused by the spectacular plunge of her lady of the famous tiger skin into public notice. To be sure, readers trained in the French school of scandal found it a dull *Three Weeks,* for all the black and gold glamour of the tiger skin and the regal splendor of the lady from Eastern Europe, with her taking ways. But *Three Weeks* obtained a certain vogue, and it gained for Mrs. Glyn, among other things, acquaintance with a large number of a hard-working and deserving class of artisans—the New York newspaper reporters.

It is of them she remarks in the present volume (*Elizabeth Visits America,* Duffield & Co.) that they "were perfectly polite, but asked direct questions," adding that they were, "all but two, of the same type—very prominent foreheads, deep-set eyes, white faces, origin south of France or Corsican mixed with Jew to look at, with the astounding American acuteness added, and all had the expression of a good terrier after a rat, the most intense concentration." It is clear that Mrs. Glyn enjoyed her meetings with these reporters—though she is rather spiteful toward what she calls "the female ones."

In the book itself Mrs. Glyn goes back to her earlier and more entertaining manner—the mixture of assumed simplicity and demure audacity which furnished the charm of *The Visits of Elizabeth, The Reflections of Ambrosine, The Vicissitudes of Evangeline,* and the rest. Resuming her Elizabethan disguise, (Elizabeth has had a little tiff with her Marquess: he has gone off to Africa to shoot lions and recover his temper, while she has left her "sweet angels of children, Hurstbridge and Ermyntrude," in the care of her mamma,) our lively author goes out to seek new adventures and to see America. Americans in general she finds—in one word—dears, though they speak a foreign language and are rather in the cub stage, while the smart set in New York and the pork-prosperous in Chicago are distinctly unprepossessing. The men, to be sure, are "of quite another sex to English or French—I mean you feel more as if you were out with kind Aunts or Grandmothers or benevolent Uncles than just men. They don't try to make the least love to you or say things with two meanings, and they are perfectly brotherly and serious, unless they are telling you anecdotes with American humor—and that is not subtle. It is something that makes you laugh the moment you hear it, you have not to think a scrap."

The men in Philadelphia, however, are different—quite human enough to flirt with, in fact—and Elizabeth meets one bronzed young Westerner who falls head over heels in love with her before he finds out that she is married and a Marchioness, and afterward behaves in the most thrillingly chivalrous manner. He is not only all of a man, but the finest of nature's noblemen. For a time you are not sure whether the Marquess may not return from his lions to find his Marchioness provided with an American divorce—but this is an Elizabeth-Ambrosine-Evangeline book. Of course, nothing really the least out of the way happens—it is only talked about.

Elizabeth not only sees New York, Newport, Long Island, Philadelphia—she goes West to Chicago and then quite across the continent to San Francisco and up into the most lovely Bret Harte mining camp—travels in a private car and meets a perfect darling of an enormously rich Senator. There is not much of a story but the episodes and the observations are highly interesting, both for the truth that is in them—there is a good deal—and the lack of it—there is much of that also. In short, Mrs. Glyn not only used her eyes and her imagination to her own great entertainment during her grand tour of the United States of America, but she has used her pen and her wits very cleverly in telling the Americans what she thinks it will amuse them most to have her say about them. Even when she is cruel she takes care to flatter the pet foibles of all but the grossly pork-prosperous and the smart set already mentioned.

For instance, she finds that the women—whatever else may be said about them—dress beautifully, and as to the men—though, to be sure, she compares them insultingly with grandmothers, and even aunts, "because they are so safe you could go off to Australia alone with one of them"—yet the worst of the sting is drawn even here. For she begins at once to bubble about "chivalry." The American men are harmless, indeed, but it is because they are splendid, high-souled creatures, not because they are, in the eloquent phrase of our childhood, "'fraid cats."

Mrs. Glyn takes pains to find all that is really American simply delightful—even a hold-up in a miners' hotel, where a gang of desperadoes stick the women of the party up against the wall in their nightclothes while they rob their rooms, is presented rather as a pleasant diversion than otherwise. If one of the ruffians just misses shooting the vivacious Elizabeth, Marchioness of Valmond, it is quite worth while, since it gives Elizabeth a chance to be saved by a bullet of her nature's nobleman, ending the ruffian's evil career on the spot.

It is only New York and Chicago—which are not American, as everybody knows—that come in for genuinely hearty condemnation. For the feverish New York money hunter and the "thick" Chicagoan, as social beings, she has very harsh and cutting words. But the most of these even are put in the mouth of some nice American, who, while he possesses all the virtues of his nation, makes no attempt to ape the fine perfections of the European.

Arnold Bennett (essay date 1917)

SOURCE: "Mrs. Elinor Glyn", in *Books and Persons: Being Comments on a Past Epoch*, George H. Doran and Company, 1911, pp. 271-277.

[*In the following essay, Bennett praises Glyn's novel* His Hour, *describing it as "magnificently sexual."*]

After all, the world does move. I never thought to be able to congratulate the Circulating Libraries on their attitude towards a work of art; and here in common fairness I, who have so often animadverted upon their cowardice, am obliged to laud their courage. The instant cause of this is Mrs. Elinor Glyn's new novel, **His Hour**. Everybody who cares for literature knows, or should know, Mrs. Glyn's fine carelessness of popular opinion (either here or in the States), and the singleness of her regard for the art which she practices and which she honours. Troubling herself about naught but splendour of subject and elevation of style, she goes on her career indifferent alike to the praise and to the blame of the mob. (I use the word "mob" in Fielding's sense—as meaning persons, in no matter what rank of life, capable of "low" feelings.) Perhaps Mrs. Glyn's latest book is the supreme example of her genius and of her conscientiousness. In essence it is a short story, handled with a fullness and a completeness which justify her in calling it a novel. There are two

principal characters, a young half-Cossack Russian prince and an English widow of good family. The pet name of the former is "Gritzko." The latter is generally called Tamara. Gritzko is one of those heroic heroes who can spend their nights in the company of prostitutes, and their days in the solution of deep military problems. He is very wealthy; he has every attribute of a hero, including audacity. During their very first dance together Gritzko kissed Tamara. "They were up in a corner; everyone's back was turned to them happily, for in one second he had bent and kissed her neck. It was done with such incredible swiftness. . . . " etc. "But the kiss burnt into Tamara's flesh" . . ."'How dare you? How dare you?' she hissed."

Later " . . . 'I hate you!' almost hissed poor Tamara." (Note the realistic exactitude of that "almost.") "Then his eyes blazed. . . . He moved nearer to her, and spoke in a low concentrated voice: 'It is a challenge; good. Now listen to what I say: In a little short time you shall love me. That haughty little head shall be here on my breast without a struggle, and I shall kiss your lips until you cannot breathe.' For the second time in her life Tamara went dead white. . . . " Then follow scenes of revelry, in which Mrs. Glyn, with a courage as astonishing as her power, exposes all that is fatuous and vicious in the loftiest regions of Russian fashionable society. Later, Gritzko did kiss Tamara on the lips, but she objected. Still later he got the English widow in a lonely hut in a snowstorm, and this was "his hour." But she had a revolver. "'Touch me and I will shoot,' she gasped. . . . He made a step forward, but she lifted the pistol again to her head . . . and thus they glared at one another, the hunter and the hunted. . . . He flung himself on the couch and lit a cigarette, and all that was savage and cruel in him flamed from his eyes. 'My God! . . . and still I loved you—madly loved you . . . and last night when you defied me, then I determined you should belong to me by force. No power in heaven or earth can save you! Ah! If you had been different, how happy we might have been! But it is too late; the devil has won, and soon I will do what I please.' . . . For a long time there was silence. . . . Then the daylight faded quite, and the Prince got up and lit a small oil lamp. There was a deadly silence. . . . Ah! She must fight against this horrible lethargy. . . . Her arm had grown numb. . . . Strange lights seemed to flash before her eyes—yes—surely—that was Gritzko coming towards her! She gave a gasping cry and tried to pull the trigger, but it was stiff. . . . The pistol dropped from her nerveless grasp. . . . She gave one moan. . . . With a bound Gritzko leaped up. . . ."

"The light was gray when Tamara awoke. Where was she? What had happened? Something ghastly, but where? Then she perceived her torn blouse, and with a terrible pang remembrance came back to her. She started up, and as she did so realized that she was in her stockinged feet. The awful certainty. . . . Gritzko had won—she was utterly disgraced. . . . She hurriedly drew off the blouse, then she saw her torn underthings. . . . She knew that however she might make even the blouse look to the casual eyes of her godmother, she could never deceive her maid." . . . "She was an outcast. She was no better than Mary Gibson, whom Aunt Clara had with harshness turned out of the house. She—a lady!—a grand English lady! . . . She crouched down in a corner like a cowed dog. . . ." Then he wrote to her formally demanding her hand. And she replied: "To Prince Milaslavski. Monsieur,—I have no choice; I consent.—Yours truly, Tamara Loraine." Thus they were married. Her mood changed. "Oh! What did anything else matter in the world since after all he loved her! This beautiful fierce lover! Visions of enchantment presented themselves. . . . She buried her face in his scarlet coat. . . . " I must add that Gritzko had not really violated Tamara. He had only ripped open her corsage to facilitate respiration, and kissed her "little feet." She honestly thought herself the victim of a satyr; but, though she was a widow, with several years of marriage behind her, she had been quite mistaken on this point. You see, she was English.

His Hour is a sexual novel. It is magnificently sexual. My quotations, of course, do less than justice to it, but I think I have made clear the simple and highly courageous plot. Gritzko desired Tamara with the extreme of amorous passion, and in order to win her entirely he allowed her to believe that he had raped her. She, being an English widow, moving in the most refined circles, naturally regarded the outrage as an imperious reason for accepting his hand. That is a summary of Mrs. Glyn's novel, of which, by the way, I must quote the dedication: "With grateful homage and devotion I dedicate this book to Her Imperial Highness The Grand Duchess Vladimir of Russia. In memory of the happy evenings spent in her gracious presence when reading to her these pages, which her sympathetic aid in facilitating my opportunities for studying the Russian character enabled me to write. Her kind appreciation of the finished work is a source of the deepest gratification to me."

The source of the deepest gratification to me is the fact that the Censorship Committee of the United Circulating Libraries should have allowed this noble, daring, and masterly work to pass freely over their counters. What a change from January of this year, when Mary Gaunt's *The Uncounted Cost,* which didn't show the ghost of a rape, could not even be advertised in the organ of The *Times* Book Club! After this, who can complain against a Library Censorship? It is true that while passing *His Hour,* the same censorship puts its ban absolute upon Mr. John Trevena's new novel *Bracken.* It is true that quite a number of people had considered Mr. Trevena to be a serious and dignified artist of rather considerable talent. It is true that *Bracken* probably contains nothing that for sheer brave sexuality can be compared with a score of passages in *His Hour.* What then? The Censorship Committee must justify its existence somehow. Mr. Trevena ought to have dedicated his wretched provincial novel to the Queen of Montenegro. He painfully lacks "savoir-vivre." In the early part of this year certain mysterious meetings took place apropos of the Censorship, between a sub-committee of the Society of Authors

and a sub-committee of the Publishers' Association. But nothing was done. I am told that the Authors' Society is now about to take the matter up again. But why?

Raymond Mortimer (essay date 1923)

SOURCE: "A Review", in *The New Statesman: A Weekly Review of Politics and Literature,* Vol. XXI, May, 1923, pp. 144-146.

[*In the following essay, Mortimer praises Glyn's ability to treat scandalous material, and calls her novel* The Great Moment *"a sociological phenomenon."*]

David Garnett and Elinor Glyn! Some like one, and some like the other, but is it not ridiculous to say that Mrs. Glyn's work is inferior to Mr. Garnett's? As well protest that the Hammam Turkish Baths are not so good as the operas of Mozart! *Lady into Fox* is a work of art (I take Mr. Garnett as an example because he has gained his reputation, not by splitting psychological hairs, but by his superb accomplishment in narrative). **The Great Moment** is a sociological phenomenon. The two books attain their different objects with equal certainty and completeness: they cannot be otherwise compared. But they are both prose fiction, and the wretched reviewer of novels has to discuss them both. Really the sociologist might come to the rescue!

Once dismiss the notion that art has anything more to do with popular novels than it has with the pictures at Burlington House, and it is possible to be just to them and even laudatory. But one must decide what their purpose is. They can, I think, be roughly divided into two main divisions, which, for lack of a better terminology, I call the *curiosity-type* and the *dream-type.* The novel of the former type is dramatic and depends upon situation. It may be subdivided into two classes, the novel of adventure and the problem-novel. The former appeals to man's love of vicarious excitement, the latter to his natural casuistry, of which the continual discussion of so-called Silly Season Topics in popular newspapers gives evidence. The curiosity-novel, in both its forms, arouses the detached or objective interest of its readers. It has always flourished.

The dream-novel, in its most decided form has only made its appearance rather recently, and the psychological processes on which it depends have only been defined by the modern pioneers of psychological theory. Art itself had its origin in sympathetic magic. The Palæolithic Cave-Man's priest painted on the wall an effigy of the coveted prey, and, when the cave-man went out to hunt, drew an arrow on top of it. The popular novelist describes an eminently desirable young person, and then puts a wedding-ring upon her finger. The dream-type of novel is an instrument of compensation and escape. It is an artificial dream, which gives to the mind of the reader the same satisfaction as real dreams or reveries to the mind of the dreamer. Even the opponents of Freud seem mostly to accept his theory that our dreams express our desires, and particularly those subconscious desires which we are prevented from realising; and that in expressing them they give a necessary, if insufficient, outlet to repressed energy. These desires, springing from the secret depths of our being, would many of them be intensely repellent to our conscious minds, and in order to reach the surface even in dreams, they have to assume symbolic or disguised forms. For even in sleep our consciousness exerts a censoring influence. But if there is any truth in the theory I am trying to suggest, the dream-novel fulfils its function as an artificial dream with the advantage that the so-called Censor is tricked from the beginning; for the novel is not the product of the reader's mind, though it does for the unconscious part of it what it has difficulty in doing for itself. The hero or heroine is not the reader, but is quickly identified with him or her. If people demand that a book should end happily, it is not out of altruism; and if that happy ending is usually a romantic, passionate and prosperous marriage, it is because that is the most usual of hopes and ideals, and one that is often never outgrown, even by the married. The dream-novel deals principally with sex, because that is both the strongest and the most suppressed instinct.

Writers of this type of novel provide what is wanted with wonderful exactness. They place their characters either in extravagant luxury or in idealised simplicity, for both of which most of us have corners in our hearts: love in a cottage and love in Grosvenor Square are delirious alternatives. And it is remarkable that the most successful of them often appeal to those forms of instinct which are considered anti-social and consequently are more likely to be repressed—the rudimentary sadism of men, for instance, and masochism of women. Of course, the writers usually do this unconsciously. I doubt if best-sellers are ever written with the tongue in the cheek, and I am confident that Miss Ethel Dell, for instance, does not owe her enormous popularity to any study of the unpleasant treatises of Havelock Ellis or Freud. But if her books are read with such avidity, it is because they, and not their less successful competitors, manage most closely to express the half-unconscious desires of the mass of half-educated humanity. Regarded in this light, this particular type of popular novel betrays the nature of its admirers as closely almost as a dream when analysed does that of its dreamer, and the results are what one would expect; the most popular dream-novels are those that paint the most primitive sorts of passion. And their value has no more to do with art than a Turkish bath has. The work of art exerts its cathartic influence by rousing objective pity and disinterested terror, thus reducing the importance of our personal wants to their proper proportion; the work of the dream-type, on the other hand, satisfies our self-pity, gives expression (perhaps hygienically) to our lower impulses, and invests our meannesses with magnificent robes.

The divisions I put forward are naturally not water-tight. The curiosity-novel will probably be partly a dream-novel, and *vice versa*; and the work of art will very frequently perform to some extent the functions of both of these as well as its own. But a rough classification can usually be effected according to which function appears in each case to be the most important.

Mrs. Glyn has a well-deserved reputation. Years ago, when external repression was severer than it is now, she was more audacious, and more perspicacious, than most of her contemporaries. *Three Weeks* may have been a *succès de scandale:* it was certainly a first-rate dream. In fantasy most men have fallen in love with Royal ladies—think of the deathless fascination of Mary of Scotland and Marie Antoinette, and most women have played with the idea of the Man as consort, at once their superior and subject. The most popular royal weddings are those to which one party is a commoner, and the one thing more exciting than a royal wedding is a royal indiscretion.

In her new book Mrs. Glyn has done her best to satisfy the subconscious requirements of any reasonable woman. The heroine's father is the haughtiest of English aristocrats, and her mother the most passionate of Russian gypsies. The mother having died, the girl is brought up in lonely magnificence by her proud old father, a situation with considerable attractions to any girl who has not tried it. She meets a young American who is Bayard by name as well as nature, and who has "killed his man." (What more could any woman want?) Our heroine throws over all else for "love in a shack," only to find herself in a noble house replete with tea-gowns, French maids, and every modern convenience: her Bayard rolls in riches after all! "What a woman wants," says Mrs. Glyn, "is a master—and lots of love." Her heroine gets both, and brings both in imagination to everyone who agrees with Mrs. Glyn. The girl is always dreaming about snakes: this is prophetic, for in the "big scene" she is bitten by a rattlesnake. Bayard holds her down by force, and she screams and struggles while he cuts the place out of her flesh! Mrs. Glyn knows the stuff to give us, and no mistake.

But apart from its conformity to the dream type, the most remarkable feature of the book is its portentously close connection with the cinema. In the past, novels have been turned on to films; it looks as if in the future it will be the films that will be made into novels. In form *The Great Moment* seems just a scenario written up, and some of the scenes would only make their proper effect upon the screen. At the happy end, for instance, the heroine converts an indoor costume into a travelling dress by cutting off its train and making a hat and a wrap of it. In the book that does not tell at all, but what an exquisite stunt for Nazimova! As for the style, well, every sensible woman who reads about Bayard will no doubt agree with the heroine, "Oh, what do I care about phrasing or grammar or anything. He's a *Man*."

Norman Douglas (essay date 1925)

SOURCE: "Fiction", in *Experiments,* Robert M. McBride and Company, 1925, pp. 23-32.

[In the following essay, Douglas provides a plot summary of Glyn's novel The Sequence *and praises Glyn's ability to write of events considered shocking—particularly sexuality—without being crude.]*

The Sequence is a simple tale. Guinevere, at the age of seventeen, is forced into a loveless marriage with a stern soldier twice, or possibly thrice, her own age. She is an old-fashioned, refined, and misunderstood female with "a demure air and a rebellious gleam in her eyes"—she lives in a state of trembling sensibility and in abject terror of her grumpy old male. So far good. But he, the husband, is a less probable creature; his harshness is rather overdone; he calls her a "hateful iceberg" and "the coldest bit of womankind I've come across." Ladies do not like being called icebergs. Such remarks are always rude, and sometimes incorrect. Guinevere, pondering sadly over them, comes to the conclusion that she has been caught by the wrong man. She has her son, of course—a bewilderingly beautiful lad who might have given her some interest in life; but what's the use of a son if he resembles the wrong man, his father? So she goes on pondering.

She is always pondering and dissecting her feelings; she belongs to that analyzing type of female who drives one nearly crazy. Such being the case, it stands to reason that she keeps a diary—a diary wherein she records minutely all the incidents of her adultery with the right man, Sir Hugh Dremont. He was bound to turn up sooner or later; and here he is. All the women are after Sir Hugh. He is "so utterly unapproachable, cynical, and attractive," so *soigné;* above all, so devilish rich. But he likes Guinevere best. It is consoling to learn that in this adventure both lovers are equipped with efficient aides-de-camp; the heroine has her sister Letitia, a worldly-wise go-between (to put it decently), and as to Sir Hugh—is there not a discreetly-silent butler, William, who always keeps his weather-eye open and supervises their amorous encounters in Richmond Park and elsewhere? For the rest, Sir Hugh is an old hand at captivating the sex; he has the true sporting instinct in such matters; he is in no hurry to land his fish—not he! and if the attractive picture facing p. 128 be a likeness of his lady-love Guinevere, we can only congratulate the gentleman on his masterly self-restraint. But do what we may, things will come to a head. On p. 46 the pair are beginning to be naughty; on p. 60 Guinevere learns from her sensible sister the proper definition of what stupid people call sin; on p. 99 she discovers that "one is not always master of oneself in supreme moments" (a great step forward); on p. 127 Sir Hugh's voice gets suspiciously hoarse; on p. 143 "I must," says he, "I will hold you in my arms"; on p. 152 he kisses her lips. Thank God, he has got as far as the lips at last; up to this point it was only her hand, gloved or *au naturel.* And soon enough he gets a good deal further.

This is the climax, and so far there has been no great hitch; the narrative has slipped along with an Elinor-glibness all its own. But here we are now, at the end of the romance, and in the middle of the book. Rather awkward,

this. The publisher, naturally enough, is shrieking for another 170 pages of *Sequence;* what's to be done? Well, since you cannot have a husband knocking about when another fellow is in the house, the old General is conveniently despatched to some queer foreign country; and to fill up the gap, certain other things happen which do not interest us profoundly. It is the grossest of padding, but this much is certain: readers who cannot extract their money's worth of illicit love out of this story must be hard to please. It simply reeks of sex. Amazing, how this writer can pack her pages with suggested improprieties and yet say nothing that is not more or less presentable. She is truly an adept at "Dublin tenders." But we like the aristocratic ladies best. This is how they talk:

> I do think you should have shown up, Ermyntrude," Lady Majoribanks announced. "We must play the game now, with the Radicals coming in, or we shall lose our influence. I am all for making these creatures pay for their footing among us, but you should have given them some return. . . .

And the way they swop lovers is enough to make their social inferiors burst with envy. Even the happily-married Letitia has her friend, Lord Alfred—but only for a season. As to Guinevere, the effects of her love-intrigue are these: firstly, everybody, even the family physician, notices how enormously her looks and health are improved under the hygienic influence of her adultery with Sir Hugh; and, secondly, from being an idealistic simpleton, she is transformed into a prudent lady. How love for a man not her husband will sharpen a woman's wits!

Then the old brute returns home and the game is up. The lovers, driven to desperation by his odious presence, begin praying to God to help them. Funny! Whenever people make fools of themselves, they always try to get God to pull them out of their scrapes. And, by Jove! sometimes they succeed. This is exactly what happens to Hugh and Guinevere. By a combination of unexpected happenings, by a veritable Russian salad of drownings, murders and other catastrophes all tending providentially to one end, the lovers are at last legally united. For our part, we confess that we are grateful to Providence for this consummation; thunderingly grateful. Let it not be forgotten that we have been on the sexual rack from 1905 to 1912. Whether the lovers remained truly grateful—that is quite another question. Legitimate wedlock, after so many moonlight amours, may well have seemed a trifle dull. One likes to think otherwise, of course; but perhaps—perhaps they got slightly bored with each other after all. One fears that they may have relapsed into the habits of all their friends and relatives; they may have discovered, as other people have done, that when you have a "recrudescence of worldly desires" there is something to be said for Letitia's swopping system.

Isabel Paterson (essay date 1937)

SOURCE: "A Review", in *The New York Herald Tribune Books,* v. 13, January 24, 1937, 13 p.

[*In the following essay, Paterson praises Glyn's autobiography* Romantic Adventure.]

The tiger skin was real. Readers who like to know whether or not a novel is "true" will be glad to check up on this historic item by turning to page 127 of Mrs. Glyn's autobiography [*Romantic Adventure*], in which she Tells All. They may, however, be a trifle disappointed by the innocent comedy of the facts. During the summer of 1902 Mr. and Mrs. Clayton Glyn made a brief sojourn in Lucerne. "The setting was ideally romantic," but Mr. Glyn apparently took scenery for granted, and laughed at his charming young wife's enthusiasm. One day it rained, and the atmospheric pressure caused a slight domestic disharmony—nothing serious. There was a fur shop adjoining the hotel, with a magnificent tiger skin on display. Mrs. Glyn explains: "I had always longed to have one, but Clayton would never give me this present, as he said I was too like the creature, anyway." But at the moment she had extra money in her pocket, royalties from her first novel, *The Visits of Elizabeth*. She went down to the shop unbeknownst to her husband, paid "a fabulous sum" for the trophy, and had it sent up to her sitting room. When it arrived she "stretched it out on the floor and lay on it and caressed its fur, looking, I imagine, much as my caricaturists have portrayed me ever since."

Here one would prefer to insert a few asterisks: but they might be misunderstood. For Mr. Glyn only laughed so heartily that the romantic lady never again reclined on that or any other tiger skin, though she has since had seven more presented to her by respectful admirers.

And when the Glyns continued their journey, "Clayton was really furious" because the tiger skin necessitated a special trunk. "He said it was bad enough to have to travel with a woman who had thirty-seven new dresses, a train of antique admirers, and a maid who fell out of bed, but to have a huge tiger-skin as well was more than an Englishman could stand."

Perhaps it would be well to explain further that the antique admirers and the gravitational maid were as innocent as the tiger skin. None of Mrs. Glyn's romantic adventures contravened the proprieties. A most disarming naivete is the dominant trait of her character, and of her book. It would be easy to pick out a string of harmless absurdities from her candid narrative, but not quite fair. Sometimes the author herself is aware of the humor of her memories, as in the case of the tiger skin: sometimes she is almost incredibly serious, as when she takes pride in her contribution to international good will through the medium of the films. Because while in Hollywood she succeeded in revolutionizing the movies by banishing aspidistras from the "sets" intended to represent ducal English country house interiors. Dukes do not have aspidistras in their drawing rooms. Any one who thinks so has been misinformed.

But Mrs. Glyn's memoirs are not wholly concerned with such high matters. And when she is simply recalling the aspect of the vanished social order in which she held an authentic position, she is agreeably informative, even in her point of view, which remains essentially unchanged and is therefore representative of the pleasant, ornamental, ephemeral privileged class of the pre-war world. It was a society whose members had nothing to do but amuse themselves, and plenty of money to supply the accessories. Discretion was the rule of conduct: birth, beauty, fame and of course wealth were the passports.

Mrs. Glyn saw it with the advantage of an alien background, and the right of inheritance. Her mother, Canadian born but of aristocratic connections, married a young Scottish engineer of the Sutherland family, apparently a man of unusual ability and charm. His profession took him all over the world, so that his daughters were born in Jersey. He died in South America: his beautiful young widow returned to her parents in Canada for a time. Later, to give her two girls the environment which she felt to be their due, she married again. The second husband was elderly, eccentric, selfish and domineering, but he had a comfortable income—he lost it later—and the right background. He took his wife and step-daughters back to Europe. Mrs. Glyn therefore spent the latter part of her childhood in Scotland, England, France and Jersey, and made her debut in the most exclusive social circles, at the time when Lily Langtry was the reigning beauty.

As a girl, Mrs. Glyn's red hair and green eyes were thought to be a disadvantage; but she got along just the same. She was determined to marry for love, and rejected even a duke, though "in those days to become a duchess meant a great deal." One would hardly consider it negligible now. But the duke "was absorbingly interested in the details of ecclesiastical apparel," a theme from which the lady was unable to extract a thrill. Perhaps he picked the wrong sister—Mrs. Glyn's sister Lucy is better known as "Lucille," Lady Duff Gordon. Anyhow, Miss Elinor Sutherland remained heart-free until she was twenty-seven, when Mr. Clayton Glyn, a jolly and highly eligible gentleman of a sporting temper—"a splendid shot, a great traveler and bon viveur"—heard an amusing story of how four of her suitors, after a hunt ball, had jumped into the lake at Hillersden in evening clothes at her behest. Mr. Glyn decided that a girl who could induce four solid, responsible Englishmen to jump into a lake at 3 o'clock of a winter morning "must be worth looking at." And after taking a good look, he married her out of hand.

Mrs. Glyn as a bride was presented at court: a photograph shows her in stately plumes and velvet. She had a country house, and the entree to the smartest and most amusing set in England. She traveled extensively, and in luxury, with her husband, who was good natured and lavishly generous. He was much diverted by the artless attitudes of his better half, and too sensible to be jealous when there was no real cause.

His romantic wife didn't know that he was spending the principal of his estate; but when it was all gone, she had no reproaches for him. They had had a good time, and a happy marriage; and she could earn money herself. She did so, took care of her mother, her husband in his last years, when he was ill, and her two pretty daughters. She made and lost a fortune on her own account as a novelist and scenario writer; she has been all over the world, met everybody of note, enjoyed everything, and has no regrets nor fears. Her novels, one gleans, are the imaginative excursions of an intrinsically good woman. She takes them quite seriously as literature, and cannot understand the slighting tone of the critical fraternity, since she has never done them any harm. She forgives them—and extraordinarily, one can believe that she really does forgive them, an example of magnanimity unparalleled in literature. And toward the conclusion of her memoirs she remarks that "the news from Pekin sounds rather interesting. Yes, I think it must be Pekin next."

The final chapter, "a vision of things to come," reveals a kindly, optimistic nature and a tendency to the non-sequitur, as, for instance, in the belief that "aviation which will soon enable the people of all countries to visit each other," will "develop the spirit of mutual understanding which will eventually bring about the universal reign of peace." This, perhaps, is why shipments of planes have to be rushed.

Anthony Glyn (essay date 1955)

SOURCE: *Elinor Glyn: A Biography,* Hutchinson, 1955, 356 p.

[*In the following excerpt, Glyn provides a biographical survey of Glyn's film screenplays.*]

It is difficult now, more than thirty years later, to re-create the extraordinary topsy-turvy atmosphere of Hollywood in 1920. The lusty young film industry, only a few years old, was finding its feet and was full of boisterous self-confidence. Everyone connected with the studios was firmly convinced that he or she knew all about everything, even ways of life far removed from his own, confirmed in this belief by the large box-office returns brought in even by the primitive silent films then being made.

They all believed they knew exactly what the public wanted and were perfectly capable of supplying it without any outside advice. Their efforts, however, were met with uncompromising hostility from almost all dramatic critics and a great number of distinguished people in the world of letters and art. The heads of the studios were pained by this criticism, to which they seem to have been particularly sensitive, and it was to combat this distrust and contempt for moving pictures in general that Lasky had invited his eminent authors to Hollywood.

It did not take the authors long to discover that their presence in Hollywood was only window-dressing. It was their names and not their literary abilities which were required by the studios. Elinor [Glyn] wrote in her memoirs:

The blatantly crude or utterly false psychology of the stories as finally shown upon the screen was on a par with the absurdity of the sets and clothes, but we were powerless to prevent this. All authors, living or dead, famous or obscure, shared the same fate. Their stories were rewritten and completely altered either by the stenographers and continuity girls of the scenario department, or by the Assistant Director and his lady-love, or by the leading lady, or by anyone else who happened to pass through the studio; and even when at last, after infinite struggle, a scene was shot which bore some resemblance to the original story it was certain to be left out in the cutting-room, or pared away to such an extent that all meaning which it might once have had was lost.

One by one, all the imported authors departed in varying conditions of rage, disappointment or sorrow. [W. Somerset] Maugham did not even stay to watch the shooting of his script but moved on quickly to his more familiar stamping-grounds across the Pacific. Elinor alone stayed on to fight it out.

There was, of course, another side to the story. Some of the authors whom Lasky had invited to Hollywood were no longer able or willing to learn their trade all over again. Their skill and their reputations were founded upon their mastery of words and they found it difficult now to adapt themselves to a wordless medium. Maeterlinck's first scenario was "a charming little tale about a small boy who discovered some fairies. I'm afraid," wrote Mr. Samuel Goldwyn, "my reactions to it were hardly fairy-like." Maeterlinck's second effort was a love story so daring that no censor could have passed it, and he returned to Europe in high dudgeon.

> A versatile woman, Elinor Glyn [wrote Mr. Goldwyn], and one whose name will always figure in any history of the film colony—though she didn't think much of Hollywood.

It may well be thought that Elinor's success there, under the given conditions, was the most remarkable achievement of her whole career.

. . . . .

Her first script, *The Great Moment,* was carefully devised for the silent screen and depended on plot, strong situations, vivid scenes and clear-cut characters, rather than the subtleties of human relationships. *The Kine Weekly* said of it:

> It is a highly-coloured, semi-sensational society drama but it has many good points to recommend it, including an original plot, definite characterisation, dramatic situations, a strong love interest and plenty of interest particularly suited to picturisation.

Sir Edward Pelham, a reserved, conventional English diplomat, has, in a moment of ecstatic passion, married a Russian gipsy girl, and in terror in case their daughter Nadine should grow up as wild as her mother, now dead, he keeps her virtually imprisoned in his English country house during her childhood. He also arranges for her to marry his distant cousin and heir, Eustace Pelham, a dull pompous young man. Nadine, in her loneliness and yearning to escape, dreams continually of a Knight Bayard who will come and set her free. She sees from her bedroom window a handsome young man whom she imagines to be Eustace coming to propose, but it is in fact the manager of her father's American gold-mine, Bayard Delaval.

Nadine is deeply disappointed by the real Eustace who arrives later, but accepts him. She falls ill and, on the doctor's recommendation, she, her fiancé and her father go to Nevada to inspect the mine and to have a holiday. There, of course, she meets Bayard again and falls in love with him. Riding back with him from the mine across the desert, she is bitten by a rattlesnake and Bayard in anguish saves her life by carrying her to a shack of his nearby and pouring a bottle of whisky down her throat. Nadine becomes very drunk and, her gipsy blood coming out, she makes passionate love to him. At this strong and compromising situation, her father and fiancé arrive on the scene.

Sir Edward is outraged and tells Nadine he never wishes to see her again; he leaves her with the man whom he imagines to be her seducer. Nadine falls unconscious, and when she wakes she does not recognise Bayard. He, suddenly realising that her passion the night before was only due to gipsy blood and the whisky, and not to love for him, sends her quickly away after her father, who forgives her a little bleakly. Poor Nadine, not understanding at all why her beloved Bayard should send her away so brusquely, is very unhappy. She goes to Washington to stay with friends and gets into the worst set. A millionaire called Hopper wishes to marry her and gives vast parties for her which turn into orgies and at which Nadine makes an exhibition of herself in her general misery and frustration.

However, through the influence of friends who understand the true story, Bayard arrives to claim her just before her marriage to Hopper. Nadine is radiantly happy, even at the thought of spending the rest of her life in a shack in the Nevada desert; and Bayard keeps as a surprise for her the knowledge that he is now retiring, a rich man, from gold-mining and is taking Nadine to live at his ancestral home in Virginia.

As was later conceded, *The Great Moment* was admirable material for a Hollywood silent film of 1920. It was, however, at first treated with contempt and the continuity writer proceeded to cut the story to ribbons. The director, Sam Wood, "in order to increase the suspense", decided to treat part of the film as a knockabout farce and there were moments when Elinor was herself on the verge of packing her bags and returning to England.

One day, at a conference on the set, the director remarked: "Say, boys, I guess you all think you know just what ought to be done, but I certainly can't think how to end this story myself." In the moment of silence that followed Elinor offered tentatively that perhaps, as the author, she could suggest an ending. Cecil B. de Mille, one of the most powerful of Lasky's producers, was walking through the studio at that moment and he caught Elinor's eye and laughed out loud. That one laugh, Elinor later realised, did her film career more good than anything else. With de Mille's support and influence behind her she was in a far stronger position to battle on for the ideals and objectives which had brought her to California.

The Great Moment was a considerable success at the box-office even in its mutilated, farcical form. This was due partly to the story itself, the hard core of which was still apparent; and partly to a vivid performance by Gloria Swanson as Nadine, wilful, passionate, bewildered, half child, half woman. Lasky was pleased and Elinor was signed on for a further picture on an improved contract.

. . . . .

She had by now seen enough of Hollywood studios to know that, even with de Mille behind her, she was powerless to prevent her stories being altered almost beyond recognition. But at least she could do something to make the sets a little more realistic. Indeed, this aspect of film-making seemed to her even more important than the story itself.

Few of the art directors, the scene designers, the costumiers or the hairdressers of Hollywood had been outside the States, but they would accept no advice or suggestions from Elinor. She was appalled to think that millions of Americans and Britons were going to see such travesties and presumably believe them to be accurate. In vain she protested that English Duchesses did not wear their hair like frizzy golliwogs; that the drawing-rooms of English country houses did not contain bamboo tables, aspidistras or the various knick-knacks usually associated with seaside lodging-houses; that ducal castles did not have a line of spittoons, even gold ones, down the middle of the drawing-room.

Elinor had always a passionate love of truth and she could not bear now to see the scenes she knew and loved so well misrepresented and held up to derision, even unintentionally. She was the sole representative of European high society in Hollywood and she felt her responsibility keenly.

It has often been said that Hollywood is a difficult place in which to retain a sense of proportion; Elinor found it as difficult as anyone else. One can sympathise with her indignation at seeing such travesties of English high life enacted on the sets, but at the same time one must feel that she often could not see the wood for the trees, and that it would have been better had she conserved her combative efforts for broad principles and general atmosphere rather than for details of scenery or clothes. However, one has only to recall many of the Hollywood films of the 'thirties, with their greater desire for accuracy not only of sets and clothes but also of speech, atmosphere and characters, to realise how far the cinema progressed in those ten years, at any rate in authenticity. And for that progress Elinor must be given a good deal of the credit.

. . . . .

> Elinor Glyn's name [wrote Mr. Goldwyn] is synonymous with the discovery of sex appeal for the cinema.

Elinor herself disliked the term "sex appeal", much preferring her own "it". But "it" was a quality which one either had or had not and which could never be taught. Romance, that spiritual disguise so necessary to human happiness, was the teachable quality. In 1907 she had been shocked by the lack of romance in America, by the indifferent mercenary attitude of American men and women to love, and, although the pendulum was now swinging the other way, she felt that a great deal still could and should be done to bring romance into the lives of ordinary people and to teach all gold-digging girls that true love meant giving unconditionally and not receiving or bargaining.

But she was soon made to realise that American girls were not wholly to blame for this attitude.

> I had not been long in Hollywood before I discovered that what I had always suspected was true; American men of those days simply could not make love! Not even the leading screen actors had any idea how to do it then. One after another screen tests of handsome young American film stars were shown me for approval, but in every case I considered that the performance was lamentable! I christened them all woolly lambs and besought the studio managers to find me someone who could treat differently, in front of the camera, the actress who was supposed to be his sweetheart from those who were supposed to be his aunts and sisters.

The best of them was Rudolph Valentino, not yet at his full fame, but even he had a lot to learn from Elinor in the art of making love convincingly before a camera. "Do you know," she would murmur in later years, "he had never even thought of kissing the palm, rather than the back, of a woman's hand until I made him do it!"

. . . . .

It is not quite clear who suggested *Beyond the Rocks* for Elinor's second film. Lasky himself had considerable misgivings about it and, indeed, the book with its very slight plot would not seem to be good silent film material. However, the story was approved and production started early in 1922.

Unlike *The Great Moment*, the whole action of *Beyond the Rocks* takes place in France and England and this gave almost unlimited opportunities for those anachro-

nisms and solecisms which Elinor so much abhorred. She and Sam Wood had disagreed many times in the first film; they were completely at loggerheads now and appalling rows went on between them on the set, each giving as good as received. Miss Ruby Miller, the Gaiety Girl, who was in Hollywood at the time, recalls that she went down to lunch with Elinor on the set, to find her in full battle over a shooting party which was assembled in hunting pink before a cottage on which rambler roses were in full bloom. By the time Elinor had sorted this out to her satisfaction, the day was almost over and neither she, Miss Miller nor anyone else had had any lunch.

> Like a lot of other women I know [wrote Mr. Goldwyn] she liked her own way, though it didn't always follow that she got it with me. She not only wrote the scenarios, but insisted on designing the dresses and arranging the drawing-room as a replica of her own room in London. When someone remonstrated with her about this, she retorted: "Do you think they would know how to arrange a gentlewoman's room but for me?"

The principal shortcomings in the completed picture of *Beyond the Rocks* were not in the settings, but in the acting and direction. The charm of the book, it will be remembered, lay in the effect of Theodora's innocence and purity upon Lord Bracondale's jaded man-of-the-world attitude. Both the principal actors seemed to misread their parts: Gloria Swanson played Theodora as a sophisticated minx and Rudolph Valentino, for all his charm and passion, portrayed Lord Bracondale as a young boy going through his first love affair. The continuity writers had taken every possible liberty with the story to introduce sensational effects. The scene at Versailles, in which Lord Bracondale tells Theodora the fairy story, was played in eighteenth-century clothes in and out of a sedan chair. Josiah, instead of dying quietly of a broken heart, was sent off big-game shooting in Africa to be brutally murdered by natives. There were also some rather surprising shots of Lord Bracondale galloping about a desert in a burnous, the studio having decided to put in some unused sequences from Valentino's previous film, *The Sheik*.

Altogether *Beyond the Rocks* was not, artistically, a great success. But with those stars and that author it could not fail at the box-office. Exhibitors were advised to "Boom the Author!"

> Conjure with the name of Elinor Glyn! The fact that the author has supervised this film may be mentioned but if it allows patrons to think that the book has been faithfully followed, they may be disappointed.

. . . . .

During 1922 Elinor was approached by another film company, Metro-Goldwyn-Mayer, who proposed that, when *Beyond the Rocks* and her contract with Famous Players-Lasky were completed, she should join Metro-

Goldwyn-Mayer to supervise the filming of *Three Weeks*. For years Elinor had been hoping that she would one day be given an opportunity to film her best-seller and she accepted the tempting new offer with alacrity— too great alacrity for the contract she might have won from them by harder bargaining.

The production was scheduled to begin in March 1923 and meanwhile Elinor decided to return to Europe to revisit her family and friends and familiar scenes. Her absence in America had prevented her, to her distress, from being present at either of her daughters' weddings, Margot's to Sir Edward Davson, and Juliet's to Sir Rhys Rhys-Williams, both of which had taken place in 1921. Now she was able to be present at a great family reunion and to meet her first two grandchildren (one of them myself), for whose schooling, with her newly acquired wealth and her instinctive generosity, she immediately started insurance policies. She installed her mother in a comfortable flat in Embankment Gardens and reopened her house in the Avenue Victor Hugo, Paris. She also went with Margot to Cannes and paid . . . visits to Spain and Scandinavia . . . and was back again in Hollywood at the end of February 1923, living now in a suite on the sixth floor of the Ambassador Hotel, Los Angeles.

During her visit to Europe she had been working on the film version of *Three Weeks* and we may with some justice regard the finished scenario as a considerable achievement, a yardstick of the degree to which in her first two years in Hollywood she had mastered the art of the silent film. Horniman had discovered how difficult it was to cast *Three Weeks* into a dramatic version. The greater part of the book, it will be remembered, is virtually one long love scene, and to get this across without any dialogue and without lapsing into either offensiveness or ribaldry made a considerable demand on Elinor's skill. To break up the love scene and in the interests of clarity, she was obliged to insert some sequences of the Balkan background, to show briefly the King's depravity, his unpopularity and the love and respect in which the Queen was held. She also put in, to increase the suspense, a fight on the edge of a Venetian canal between Vasili and one of the King's spies, but otherwise she stuck closely to the book, except that, at the demands of the studio, she was obliged to put in a brief reunion between Paul and the Queen in the villa before the final tragedy. The English part she left unaltered.

Her scenario, however, tested to the utmost the resources even of Metro-Goldwyn-Mayer's experienced continuity writer. For the scene in the Queen's boudoir in Lucerne where she lies on the tiger-skin, quivering with emotion and passion, he wrote, a little helplessly:

> scene 137 closeup
> INTERIOR THE LADY'S SUITE
>
> Better than describe this scene, I will simply mention that Mrs. Glyn will enact it for Mr. Crossland on the set. The Lady makes her decision

to accept Paul as her lover. She hears Paul outside and indicates for him to come in.

Elinor enjoyed working for Metro-Goldwyn-Mayer more than she had for the Lasky studios, finding the Art Department, under the direction of Cedric Gibbons, more amenable to her insistence on accuracy and beauty of setting. She cared terribly that *Three Weeks* should be worthily produced and several times she had scenes, which still dissatisfied her, reshot at her own expense.

There was also the shadow of the censor falling across this particular film. Elinor had cherished a faint hope that, in the interests of verisimilitude, Paul might be allowed to play the final love scene, on the night of the full moon, in pyjamas; but she was soon made to realise that this would never be permitted, and in the approved version the Queen tiptoed away, racked with sobs, leaving Paul asleep on the couch of rose-petals, still in full evening dress, his hair smooth and his white waistcoat uncrumpled. As a consolation for this, Metro-Goldwyn-Mayer allowed Elinor real rose-petals for the couch.

The part of the Queen was played by Aileen Pringle, looking astonishingly like Elinor, who had coached her assiduously. She gave a beautiful performance, dignified, regal yet passionate. Conrad Nagel's Paul was adequate, if a little weak, but the actor who played the King unfortunately burlesqued his part. As one critic remarked, the story as a whole could do with a little humour, but not in that particular character.

Three Weeks, however, fully deserved its enormous success at the box-office. In England the censor made a large number of cuts, including, rather strangely, the title, which was not allowed to appear even on a by-line. But despite this handicap *The Romance of a Queen* did very well and provided a strong resurge of interest in the original novel.

Three Weeks has never been filmed as a talking picture, though a proposal from Metro-Goldwyn-Mayer to do so in 1933, with Gloria Swanson as the Queen and Irving Thalberg as director, reached an advanced stage before it was abandoned in deference to a 'cleaner films' campaign then sweeping America.

It had occurred to several people that *Three Weeks* was well suited to musical treatment. In 1908 the book had been suggested to Puccini as a possible libretto and we may well think that the intensity, the drama and the passion of the story might have fired Puccini to write some of his most appealing music. He himself gave the book serious consideration but rejected it in the belief, erroneous as it turned out, that *The Girl of the Golden West* would have greater attraction in America. In any event, however, the projected operatic version must have encountered serious difficulties over the vexed question of the ownership of the American dramatic rights of *Three Weeks*.

In 1924 the Shubert brothers proposed to present the work as an operetta in New York. A musical score was commissioned and completed before the venture foundered on the unseen rocks that bar the way for so many Broadway productions.

. . . . .

The novel of *The Great Moment* was brought out by Duckworth in April 1923. In writing it Elinor adhered to her original scenario and the book makes no attempt to provide more than light entertainment. One may, indeed, regard it as her 'Western'. She herself proposed to Duckworth that the book should be brought out from the beginning in a cheap edition, without review copies, to demonstrate that she did not consider it in the same class as her more serious psychological studies such as *Three Weeks, Halcyone* and *The Career of Katherine Bush,* Duckworth, however, preferred to adhere to his normal practice—fortunately, as it turned out, for the book received good notices from everyone.

Elinor had clearly enjoyed herself in writing it and the enjoyment comes through to the reader. She had plenty of opportunity to bring landscapes and scenes to life—the English country house, the luxurious American trains, the desolate Nevada desert and its mining camp, 'Poppa Hopper's orgie' (*sic*) in Washington—the last two in vivid and deliberate contrast to each other.

The central weakness of the plot is still there, that of a father abandoning at a moment's notice his only daughter, for ever, in the middle of Nevada, to a man he thinks of as a cheap seducer, knowing the girl to be seriously ill from snake-bite; but such is Elinor's skill and technique that the point does not strike us until after we lay the book down.

The Great Moment is the first of Elinor's American novels, if we exclude *Elizabeth Visits America* which is hardly a novel, and we may discern clearly the change in her style of romance. Her American novels were usually based on silent film scenarios and they have far greater pace and plot than her English books, even *His Hour* or *The Reason Why*. There is no room in the film stories for elaborate studies of characters and human relationships, still less for discussions on philosophy. *The Great Moment* and its successors depend upon scene, dramatic and clearly apprehended situations, sharply defined and contrasting characters and, above all, suspense. Whether this was or was not an improvement is a matter of opinion; Elinor, as shown by her own view of *The Great Moment,* did not think so.

The philosophical basis behind the American novels is also different. In the English novels, as has been explained earlier, it is the woman who plays the part of Pallas Athene, inspiring the hero to great causes and great deeds. This conception would not have been acceptable or feasible in America, where the hero was already fully active and almost over-preoccupied with his career. In the American novels the woman is not the inspiration; she is the end in herself, without whom all the triumphs of the hero's career are as dust and ashes.

The heroines, from whose point of view the stories are always told, are usually distressed and unhappy, but their characters are so drawn that they exist, not so much to be comforted or pandered to, but to be fenced with, dominated and finally tamed. It is this relationship between the sexes which forms the basis for the most successful of Elinor's American stories, *"It"*.

We may again detect the strong influence of the cinema in her second American novel, *Six Days,* which was published in January 1924 and filmed later the same year. Here, once more, Elinor had devised a strong situation: David Lamont, an American special agent, and Laline Lester, a spoilt heiress, travel together to Europe, sparring with each other on the boat and in Paris. David is given six days' leave before he is sent on his secret assignment and the whole party, including Laline, David's best friend Jack, and a number of relatives set out on a tour of the battlefields.

David takes Laline into a deep derelict dug-out, where he had had an exciting experience in the war, and Laline steps on an unexploded bomb, seriously wounding the old *curé* who is showing them round and irretrievably blocking their escape. With his expiring breath the *curé* marries them and they are then left alone for the six days, buried alive in the dug-out, trying to dig their way out with their hands and making love to each other at intervals. They are finally rescued by Jack; Laline collapses, and when she recovers consciousness David has disappeared without trace, the letter he has written to her having gone astray.

She cannot imagine why she is so cruelly forsaken and wonders if David intends to repudiate the marriage to which there is now no witness. She realises that, if so, she has got to marry someone else very quickly, and in despair she accepts Jack, who has loved her for years, and to whom she tells the whole story. David returns from his secret assignment to learn what has happened. He dashes off at once to the church where the wedding is scheduled to take place that day, first by aeroplane, then by car and finally, all else failing, bareback on a thoroughbred horse which was grazing in a field beside the road; he jumps the ha-ha and arrives at the church in the nick of time to show cause and just impediment why Laline should not marry Jack. All ends happily for everyone except Jack.

The scenes in the dug-out are some of the best that Elinor ever wrote: the claustrophobia, the dank darkness, the hunger and thirst, the horror of the slow death awaiting the pair, their feverish efforts to dig their way out, their passionate desire to re-create themselves in those last hopeless hours, are vividly described. Elinor's loathing of enclosed places stimulated her imagination. We suck our last sliver of chocolate with Laline, we grope down old shafts, dropping stones into dug-outs half filled with water, we climb up and down fragile ropes made of our own clothes. It is the final section of the book which is the disappointment. The pattern of will-he-get-there-in-time has been worked on the films almost to death and we cannot accept it now, even in what must have been one of its earliest versions.

. . . . .

Elinor's views about American women, and perhaps the women themselves, had changed considerably since 1908. They were no longer the "fluffy little gold-diggers"; on the contrary they were as capable of love as European women. Now they wrote to her in their hundreds, following the publication of her newspaper articles, asking for help and advice: How were they to win the man they loved? How were they to hold his love? How could they rekindle his earlier love, now seemingly dead?

The popularity of Elinor's own novels, of Rudolph Valentino's films, showed only too clearly how desperately hungry the women of America were for love and romance; and Elinor thought it pitiful that they could only find it in print and in celluloid. Real life, she was convinced, was as full of potential romance as any book or film; but it was so easily smothered by dull, matter-of-fact routine, by sordidness or by excessive familiarity. She had been puzzled, even in the days of *Three Weeks,* as has already been shown, by the way the marriage ties so often proved fatal to love itself; her own marriage had been a case in point. Her cynical disillusioned spirit had, in *The Damsel and the Sage,* accepted this seemingly inevitable consequence of marriage with a shrug and a pout. It had always been so and would probably always remain so.

But her romantic heart rebelled. It should be possible, she argued—and the whole of her creed of life was based upon this premise—for men or women of any nationality to find all the romance they wanted in their own lives, not only before but even after marriage, without having to resort to novels and films—provided that they had the necessary skill and wisdom. And it was to provide this skill that she wrote for her American readers *The Philosophy of Love*.

The book contained many of the thoughts and conclusions of her own life and much of it was taken from articles she had already written on the subject. It dealt with many aspects of love and marriage, and especially with the problem of how to make love last. She coined a new word, to 'revulsh': less strong than to disgust, stronger than to put off, it covered all those little points of habit, speech and hygiene, those minute pinpricks, all of them almost negligible, which cumulatively killed love far more completely than the greater matrimonial crimes of cruelty or infidelity. This point has since been made by many others in books and newspaper articles.

She also campaigned against the touching and 'petting' which had become so prevalent since her first visit and which was partly a reaction from the chaperoned austerity of those days and partly, no doubt, the social consequence of the wider ownership of small, closed cars.

> Don't cheapen all agreeable emotions by being so physically friendly with every girl—that is, touching her at every moment, taking arms and so on, when you are not the least interested in her, or she in you. Touching ought to be reserved entirely for the loved one—that is, if you want to feel any thrills; and this advice applies to girls also. This continuous and promiscuous familiarity of pawing each other, is the first step towards destroying the capacity to love.

Quite apart from the practical results of disillusionment, such pawing was, in Elinor's view, "servants' behaviour", and she fought against it unwearyingly for the rest of her life. We can imagine that she must have regretted the passages in *Elizabeth Visits America,* in which she urged American girls to be less grudging and miserly with their kisses.

The Philosophy of Love also includes an extended analysis of the male and female characters and contains her division of the female sex into three parts: lover-women, mother-women and neuter-women; the characteristics of one or other group should, Elinor contended, be discernible even in early childhood.

The book is, on the whole, sensible and constructive, and is free of those wilder and more controversial theories about life which both enrich and mar Elinor's other works. It is full of earnest practical advice, some of it dull and a little obvious, other parts strong and outspoken. It was written in a sincere attempt to bring romance into lives of young Americans, particularly young American women, and for that reason it deserved the astonishing reception that America gave it.

When it was published in England, under the title *Love—What I Think of It,* it caused no great stir. But the American nation has an almost inexhaustible thirst for books of practical advice upon human relationships, as Dale Carnegie has found to his profit. *The Philosophy of Love* did not achieve his astronomical figures, but it sold a quarter of a million copies in its first six months of publication and its ultimate American sale was second only to that of *Three Weeks*.

The consequences of the book's widespread popularity were two-fold. One was an enormous increase in Elinor's own mail—letters from girls, young husbands, young wives, asking her further advice upon some particular point, and to each of which Elinor replied fully and conscientiously, despite the demand which they made upon her severely limited time. She found herself, in effect, running single-handed a marriage advice bureau and she continued this up to her departure from America in 1929. She liked the insight which it gave her into people's lives and problems, the feeling that she was bringing her romantic ideals into widespread practice, and especially the thought that she was repaying to the American people something for the kindness and hospitality they had always shown to her.

The other consequence of the success of *The Philosophy of Love* was more spectacular: an engagement to appear in vaudeville in New York, giving ten minute talks on love at a salary of five hundred pounds a week. This engagement she carried out during the winter of 1923; and one may wonder if, while she was waiting in the wings for her cue, she ever recalled the days when she would not have allowed anyone connected with the stage inside her house.

. . . . .

Elinor's second film for Metro-Goldwyn-Mayer, *His Hour,* was produced in 1924 and the making of this film was one of the happiest experiences Elinor had during her stay in Hollywood. She found her new director, King Vidor, a congenial person and for once there was no difficulty about the authenticity of the sets. Hollywood swarmed with emigré Russians, earning their living as film extras, and Elinor was both pained and amused to find several of them playing in her film very nearly the same part they had played in St. Petersburg in real life.

The story was only altered very slightly, the duel between Gritzko and Boris in the darkened room playing a rather more important part, and the climax in the hunting lodge being made a little less *risqué*. Aileen Pringle acted Tamara on rather a subdued note, as if she were determined to emphasise the difference between Tamara and the Queen in *Three Weeks*. John Gilbert as Gritzko showed very nearly as much "it" as the original Gritzko himself—a vivid, passionate performance in the Valentino manner which raised him at once to the heights of stardom. . . .

. . . . .

In 1925 Elinor produced a film version of *Man and Maid* for Metro-Goldwyn-Mayer. This followed the story of her novel, but a silent film could not carry all the subtle overtones of character and relationships which had distinguished the book and the film showed simply and rather sentimentally a poor typist marrying a rich hero. The settings included some glittering French interiors and the film was adequately acted by Lew Cody as Nicholas and Harriet Hammond as Alathea. There was also an excellent little performance by Renée Adorée as Suzette.

For her next film, *Love's Blindness,* which was made at the end of the same year, Elinor reverted to her English settings. Hubert, Earl of St. Austell, is involved in a spectacular money crash and to save himself and, even more, his friends, he agrees to Benjamin Levy's conditional offer of help. Levy has social ambitions and his condition is that Hubert should marry his daughter Vanessa. Hubert, trapped and humiliated, loathes the thought of Vanessa; he does not notice her beauty which is derived from her aristocratic Italian mother, and treats her with icy contempt. Vanessa, however, knows nothing of her father's machinations; she has adored Hubert from afar for some time and imagines that he is now marrying her for love. Hubert's treatment of her, the unconscious partner and witness of his degradation, breaks her heart and gives her a miscarriage. The final happy ending comes as something of a jolt.

The film's settings were costly and elaborate and evocative of an English country house, but it was acted by Pauline Stark and Tony Moreno with almost excessive restraint, and it aroused little enthusiasm among either the critics or the public. The book version of the story was published by Duckworth in February 1926 and was called by *The Times Literary Supplement* a "capable romance".

For her next film, *The Only Thing,* which was the last that she made for Metro-Goldwyn-Mayer, Elinor turned again to a Balkan kingdom. She put in popular and well-tried ingredients: the heroine, the beautiful queen; the old unattractive king; the handsome English diplomat in love with the queen; the queen's charming American girl friend, Sally; a handsome upright Balkan politician in love with Sally; a sinister blind beggar, the embodiment of evil, who stirs up the mob to revolution, killing the king and throwing the queen and the diplomat into prison. Elinor had in the past five years learned a great deal about negotiating with Hollywood film companies and at this point her draft synopsis breaks off abruptly with the words:

> The rescue from the prison and the final great situation which is very dangerous and exciting I do not propose to tell anyone, until the contract is made, as it is a unique and great situation.

Mr. Mayer accepted the bait thus held out to him, the contract was signed and Elinor revealed the missing scene, a new version of the *mariages de Nantes* in which the queen finds herself tied in the sinking barge to the diplomat who is disguised, to her unspeakable horror, as the blind beggar himself. This scene was to be shot partly under water by a method devised by Elinor herself. The closing sequences of the story were to show the queen and the diplomat married, living quietly in his English country home, while the people of the Balkan state acclaim their new republic and their new President and his wife Sally—a startling *dénouement* for such a royalist author.

The film was made in the summer of 1926, with the *mariages de Nantes* just as Elinor conceived them. But the American continuity writers took out Sally and the republic, and turned the diplomat, whom Elinor had made a commoner, into a duke.

. . . . .

One of Elinor's principal literary activities at this time was a series of articles called *The Truth,* which she wrote for the Hearst press. There were more than two hundred and fifty of them, and they dealt not only with love and marriage, but with almost every other subject under the sun.

She adopted in these articles an uncompromising forthright style, a ruthless didacticism, deliberately intended to strip away all self-deception and prevarication. She herself was both hurt and enfeebled when her own self-deceptions were stripped from her, but of these, her own self-deceptions, she was for the most part unaware. She had no compunction, when truth and honesty demanded it, in letting others see themselves and their actions in the cold light of realism.

The following quotation is taken from her article on unpunctuality and illustrates this point:

> What is the truth about unpunctuality? It comes from two roots, so to speak—inertia and selfishness. Take the inertia root first. The necessary force to start things going in the day is not as strong as it ought to be in millions of human beings. Their wills are weak and they allow the impulse of the moment to interfere with what they ought to do. They start the morning by being late and find it hard to catch up during the day. . . . Unpunctuality coming from the selfish root is more powerful. These people are late because they are really indifferent to others' feelings and convenience. They are only concerned with what they personally desire to do. . . . They are not worried at the rest of the company's having had to wait for them, or the annoyance for the hostess. It was their pleasure—and that's that! But if you are an unpunctual person—just stop and think that it means you are either a weakling or an egotist, and if you don't like being either—Change!

Coming from an unpunctual person, such a homily would be intolerable. But Elinor was never late for anything in her life. Her own weaknesses, as already shown, lay in other directions.

She also wrote at this time, at the commission of an American publisher, *The Elinor Glyn System of Writing*, a book of detailed practical advice for budding authors on how to write short stories and film scenarios. Much of the book is completely uncharacteristic both in its matter and its style and one feels that the work must have been considerably sub-edited in the publisher's office. It does, however, contain Elinor's own analysis of her short story *Fragments* and of her screen-play for *The Great Moment,* which are of some interest. The book also contains a list of the nineteen plots to be avoided. . . .

The most important and the most consequential piece of literary work which Elinor produced at this time was her famous *conte "It"*. In length *"It"* is more a short novel than a short story. It was serialised in *Cosmopolitan* and was published the following year by itself in America and by Duckworth in a volume containing four other short stories. *"It"* was deservedly a great success and one must

regard it not only as the cream of her American literary output, but as one of the most striking pieces she ever wrote.

"It", as the title suggests, is a study in personal magnetism. Since *The Man and the Moment* there had been in her novels and articles, letters, diaries and even, it is understood, in her conversation, several mentions of "it". And now in her new story she defined it once again.

> To have "It", the fortunate possessor must have that strange magnetism which attracts both sexes. He or she must be entirely unself-conscious and full of self-confidence, indifferent to the effect he or she is producing, and uninfluenced by others. There must be physical attraction, but beauty is unnecessary. Conceit or self-consciousness destroys "It" immediately. In the animal world "It" demonstrates in tigers and cats—both animals being fascinating and mysterious, and quite unbiddable.

Both the hero and the heroine of the story possess "it" to a marked degree. The hero, John Gaunt, has raised himself by his own exertions from the depths of the Bowery to the head of a prosperous New York business, but despite this and despite his attraction for women, he realises that there is something missing in his life. The girl, Ava Cleveland, is well-born, proud, impoverished, "a little sister of the rich", in continuous difficulties mainly through the financial irresponsibility of her scapegrace but charming brother, Larry.

Gaunt, deeply attracted to her, has mentioned that he will give her a job if ever she needs it, and finally in desperation she takes it. She finds herself sitting at a desk immediately outside his door, sorting press-cuttings at a large salary, resented by the other girls in the office and the supervisor, and acutely aware of her humiliating and invidious position. She is as strongly attracted to Gaunt as he to her, but she holds him firmly at arm's length.

Larry, also an employee of Gaunt's, continually runs up debts, even to the point of embezzlement, and Ava knows that her fate and Larry's is now completely in Gaunt's hands.

Gaunt names the price that he will require for forgiving Larry. Ava puts on her loveliest evening dress and goes to dine with Gaunt alone in his house, ready to pay the price. The scene that follows is perhaps the strongest that Elinor ever wrote. All through the dinner, behind their fencing and sparring, lies their acute awareness of each other's "it" and this gives a sharp tang to their words. After dinner Gaunt suddenly offers Ava her brother's freedom and pardon without demanding any price. Ava, almost overcome with longing for Gaunt, replies that her class does not accept favours from his, and that she prefers to pay.

> He took her forward into the apricot-rose bedroom. It had evidently been prepared for someone to stay there for the night; for filmy, gossamer raiment lay ready on the bed.

Intoxication filled Ava's brain—a divine madness permeated her being—Her ears but dimly heard, but her heart registered that John Gaunt's deep voice was saying sternly—"Tell me the truth—Is it for your brother—or for a cat-like desire for the conquest of a man?—Is it for the pride of taking me from another woman, that you are here?—Or is it just for the love of me—Ava?"

Her eyes, wet with dewy tears, looked up at him, while her willowy body grew limp in his embrace. His passionate regard devoured her—His head drooped closer and closer to her—Then his lips met hers in utter abandon of desire, which filled them both.

"Ah, God!"—at last, she said divinely—"What do I care for a price—or tomorrow—or the afterwards—I came because I love you—John Gaunt!"

All the dreams of heaven which he had dreamed of as a child when once he had strayed from the Bowery, all dirty and ragged into St. Patrick's Cathedral and heard High Mass sung, now seemed to return to him—Here was his heart's desire, won and in his arms—His to have and to hold from now for henceforth till death them do part—Given of herself without reservations, without bargainings, without vows.

Then he gave her a number of presents, her creditors' bills, paid and receipted, her treasures redeemed from the pawnbroker, and last of all, a glorious necklace of virgin pearls.

"These"—he said as he fastened the diamond clasp—"are for the lady I have *always* intended to marry"—Then when he saw that all the soul of love was gazing at him through Ava's tender eyes, suddenly he released her from his arms, and kneeling down he kissed her ivory hands.

The Times Literary Supplement reviewer, in the course of his notice, wrote:

The first story gives us a situation much favoured by Mrs. Glyn in which a powerful and wealthy lover subdues the persistent coldness and reluctance of the girl he means to win. Ava, with her coolness and restraint, reminds one a little of the heroine of Mrs. Glyn's novel *The Career of Katherine Bush*. Despite the author's slipshod English and a curious feeling one sometimes has that she is burlesquing her own style, these stories certainly let themselves be read.

From this view there can be few dissenting opinions.

· · · · ·

Elinor's last three films in Hollywood were made for her old company, Famous Players-Lasky, which was by now renamed Paramount. The films were all light comedies, a new genre in films for her. The first, *Ritzy,* was easily the worst of the three. It was founded very remotely upon a short story of Elinor's of the same name, about a bumptious American girl who tried to teach Paris society a lesson and got severely snubbed. In the film only the heroine's nickname and her dislikeable character remain. Ritzy Brown longs to marry a duke, but to her annoyance falls in love with a commoner. The duke and the commoner, however, turn out to have exchanged roles, to teach her a lesson, and so Ritzy gets it both ways. It says a good deal for the ingenuity and skill of all concerned that any laughs were got out of such a wretched little plot.

The second film was *"It"*. Once again there was no obvious resemblance between the film and the original story except the title. But this time Elinor wrote the screen-play herself. In the book the dominating character had been John Gaunt, but the Paramount studios wanted the chief part, the character who had "it", to be the girl. Further, it was to be a light comedy, and not, like the book, a tense study in human relationship.

For a while Elinor felt puzzled, but after she met Clara Bow, who was to play the heroine, she saw her way clear before her; and under the considerable stimulus and inspiration of Clara Bow's own personality, Elinor produced the scenario of her most famous and successful film.

In synopsis form the story seems very slight. A New York store proprietor, Cyrus Waltham (played by Tony Moreno) is strongly attracted by one of his shop-girls, the "pert and unabashed" Betty Lou Spence (Clara Bow). Going to call on her in her modest home, he finds her minding a friend's baby. He jumps to the conclusion that Betty Lou is an unmarried mother and offers her his protection. She is indignant at this supposed insult, but after some gay misunderstandings the story finally reaches a happy conclusion on Cyrus's yacht. The film was sparklingly directed by Clarence Badger and was, in the words of one critic, "as entertaining as it is disarming".

The screen's most piquant star [wrote *The Kine Weekly*] in an Elinor Glyn story, demonstrating the presence of an indefinable attraction. The comedy situations are excellently handled and the treatment is light, bright and vivacious.

"It" grossed more than a million dollars at the box office, at that time a prodigious figure for a film. It also boosted the reputations of all those concerned with the film, principally Elinor herself, who also reaped large financial rewards. *The Bioscope* wrote in a rather sardonic paragraph:

Few authors have boomed themselves so successfully as Elinor Glyn. Her latest effort is as astute as it is likely to be effective. Having written a book called *"It"*, she proceeds to get a picture produced explaining what "It" is, and incidentally appears in the picture and tells the hero what "It" is. Then for the past year she has been lecturing on "It", and the new cult has spread across the continent to the east coast.

Elinor's fan mail had been large ever since the publication of *The Philosophy of Love*. Now it swelled to proportions reminiscent of the days of *Three Weeks*. All over the world girls wrote asking exactly what "it" was and how they could acquire it. To this last question, of course, there was only one answer—that "it" could never be acquired. Elinor also wrote numerous articles on the subject, listing some of the well-known figures who had "it", and trying to show the difference between those who had it and those who had not. The press could not leave the subject alone and were for ever interviewing her about "it"; and Elinor was deeply gratified, finding herself back on the peak of fame and fortune, as high if not higher than she had reached twenty years before.

The film also made the reputation of Clara Bow. She was later to play many other parts of very different character, but for the rest of her career she was always thought of primarily as 'The "It" Girl'. She herself was keenly conscious of the debt she owed to Elinor. When she came on her honeymoon to see Elinor in England, she wrote on a photograph of herself, "To Elinor Glyn whom I respect and admire more than any other woman in the world."

Elinor's last Hollywood film, *Red Hair,* was made by the same team, author-producer, director and actress. The film, which was in colour, was designed as a vehicle for showing Clara Bow's versatility and for illustrating the passion inherent in red-heads. The heroine was a little manicurist, who received presents from three male admirers, of whom one saw her as a demure young miss, one as a 'vamp' and one as a temperamental young woman. She herself reformed when she met the right man, who was the nephew of two of her admirers and the ward of the third. They attempted to interfere with her new romance, but the handicap of their own pasts and the heroine's fiery temper frustrated them. The final and rather daring scene took place on a boat in which she undressed and returned them their presents of clothes in each other's presence, to their great consternation, before going off with the right man.

Once again the story provided a series of nicely contrived comic scenes, expertly directed by Clarence Badger, and once again Clara Bow was in excellent form. *Red Hair* was almost as successful as *"It",* grossing nine hundred thousand dollars at the box-office, and Elinor decided wisely to relinquish her Hollywood career on this note of triumph.

She had successfully achieved her triple objective for which she had first come to Hollywood seven years before. She had spread her romantic ideals, not only through her films but through her books and articles far wider through America than she had ever dared to hope. She had made her fortune. She had acquired a large number of new friends and a considerable insight into the American way of life. And she had re-established her fame in a way she had never even dreamt. Now, at last, she could afford to retire and lead a more leisured existence.

. . . . .

Elinor had never pulled her punches about America, either in the early days of *Elizabeth Visits America,* or more recently. She had never been one to indulge the shortcomings of others, except, perhaps, her husband. Though she was not so ungracious as to stint her admiration for the good aspects of the American scene, she never hesitated to pass severe and sometimes scathing comment on the parts which pleased her less.

She had during her seven years in America consciously resisted all efforts to Americanise her. In her books, especially *The Flirt and the Flapper,* we may note that she had a considerable command of American slang, but she never used a single Americanism in her own conversation. There was no trace of an American accent in her voice.

We cannot be surprised at this. It would, indeed, have been surprising if she, her habits, manners and speech trained in the style and tradition of the English and French aristocracy, should have moved so far from her rigid and proudly held standards, as to adopt, even for protective colouring, a form of outward behaviour, habit and speech which she had once thought uncouth. But underneath the purely outward, formal standards there had been a considerable change. In mind and in spirit she was now far closer to the American way of life, more nearly attuned to American ideals and geared to American tempo. She had also, not unnaturally, become very fond of a country and a people which had given her such splendid opportunities and which had rewarded her efforts so lavishly.

And so we find that when the moment came in 1927 when she was free to leave America and return to England, she found suddenly that she could not bear to go. She wanted, however, to leave California, even though she had so many friends there, and she went to live in New York, taking a flat on the top floor of the Ritz Tower, at that time the tallest inhabited building in the world.

Elinor loved the view from her flat, which had windows on all sides, the strange lights and shadows, the lightning and thunder and high winds around her, and, especially on calm nights, the city lights twinkling far below her as if they were stars reflected in a lake. She lived there for nearly a year, writing articles for Hearst and magazine stories.

One of these stories, **"Such Men Are Dangerous,"** she sold to Twentieth-Century Fox for six thousand pounds and it was the first of her stories to be produced as a talking-picture. The story dealt with an immensely rich and rather unattractive man, married to a dull wife, and longing for romance. In the middle of a flight across the Channel, he jumped out of the aircraft and disappeared for ever. In fact, he parachuted down and was picked up by a midget two-man submarine which he had arranged to be at a certain spot. He then went to Vienna and placed himself in the hands of a plastic surgeon, who lifted his face, remoulded his nose, altered the shape of his hands, stretched him on a rack, carried out a difficult operation on his shoulder muscles to alter the set of his shoulders, and gave his vocal cords and hair drastic treatment. The millionaire was now unrecognisable in every way and he set out to find romance. His wife, in the meantime, had brightened herself up and in due course the millionaire met her, fell in love with her and married her all over again, without ever telling her the true story.

The film followed the story in outline, if not in detail, and Warner Baxter gave a good performance as the millionaire. Elinor took no part in the production, but she was pleased by the finished picture, especially by the meticulous accuracy of the sets.

In the summer of 1928 Elinor returned to Hollywood, staying with Marion Davies at her Beach House. She thoroughly enjoyed luxuriating in her new-found idleness in the warm Californian climate and seeing her friends again, and, at Marion Davies's stern insistence, she stayed there for six weeks before leaving for Washington.

Washington had always appealed greatly to Elinor, with its old houses, its cosmopolitan atmosphere and its diplomatic society. She had many friends in the city and she now decided to make her home there. She bought a pleasant house of the 1790 period in Georgetown and spent the whole of the autumn and winter of 1928 redecorating it.

Her ideas of house decoration, never austere, had been encouraged in Hollywood by the sumptuous sets she had designed for her films. It was many years since she had last decorated a home of her own and in Washington now, secure in her newly acquired wealth, she gave her ruling passion and her lavish ideas full rein, denying herself nothing, however extravagant. The house in Georgetown was the most costly that she ever decorated for herself, and, ironically, it was the only one that she never lived in.

Shortly before she moved in, in the spring of 1929, she paid a visit to England, intending to spend a few weeks with her family and friends. In fact, she remained there for the rest of her life.

FURTHER READING

Biography

Etherington-Smith, Meredith, and Jeremy Pilcher. *The "It" Girls: Lucy, Lady Duff Gordon, the Couturière "Lucile," and Elinor Glyn, Romantic Novelist*. San Diego: Harcourt Brace Jovanovich, 1986, 274 p.
    Dual biography of Glyn and her sister.

Leslie, Anita. *Edwardians in Love*. London: Arrow Books, 1974, 352 p.
    Historical study of Edwardian society; includes references to Glyn.

Robinson, David. *Hollywood in the Twenties*. New York: Paperback Library, 1970, 176 p.
    Discusses Glyn's career as a screenwriter.

Criticism

"The Insoluble Problem." *The Bookman* 45, No. 267 (December 1913): 172-73.
    Guardedly affirmative review of *The Sequence*.

Payne, William Morton. "Recent Fiction." *The Dial* 30, No. 356 (April 16, 1901): 268-70.
    Short, positive review of *The Visits of Elizabeth*.

A review of *Beyond the Rocks*. *The Nation* 83, No. 2158 (November 8, 1906): 396.
    Brief, positive review of Glyn's novel.

A review of *Romantic Adventure*. *American Literature* 9, No. 1 (March 1937): 110.
    Short, mostly descriptive assessment of Glyn's autobiography.

Scott, C. A. Dawson. "All Sorts of Novels." *The Bookman* 64, No. 382 (July 1923): 203-4.
    Very brief, negative assessment of *The Great Moment*.

The following sources published by Gale Research contain additional coverage of Glyn's life and career: *Dictionary of Literary Biography*, **Vol. 158.**

Enrique González Martínez

1871-1952

Mexican poet, autobiographer, journalist, editor, and short story writer.

INTRODUCTION

While maintaining a career as a physician, then as a high-level public servant, González Martínez also became a significant force in Mexican literature. Challenging the conventions of literary Modernism, he played a key role in defining how that movement would affect modern Hispanic writing.

Biographical Information

González Martínez wrote his first poems as a teenager growing up in Guadalajara, winning an award in 1885 for his translation of a sonnet by John Milton. He regarded writing as a hobby, however, and while he continued to contribute poems to various Mexican journals, he attended medical school, eventually setting up a practice in Sinaloa. When in 1900 a false obituary of González Martínez appeared in a newspaper, the resulting outpourings of praise for the supposedly dead young poet caused him to revise his opinion of his writings and publish his first poetry collection, *Preludios* (1903). Thereafter he maintained an active career as a poet. He also served in various capacities in the national government following the 1911 revolution, including diplomatic posts in Argentina, Chile, Spain, and Portugal.

Major Works

Critics have noted the influence of the French Symbolist and Parnassian movements on González Martínez's poetry, with its emphasis on simplicity and formal beauty. His characteristic themes, expressed in the verse collections *Lirismos* (1907), *Silénter* (1909), and *Los senderos ocultos* (1915), include nature, solitude, and the contemplation of life and death. Although he is identified as a Modernist, his relationship to certain aspects of Modernism was antagonistic. In one of his most famous poems, the sonnet "La muerte de cisne" ("Death of the Swan,") he derided the art-for-art's-sake attitude espoused by Nicaraguan Modernist poet Rubén Darío and his followers, declaring that the poet's task is to express his or her true perceptions of life.

Critical Reception

Critics note that González Martínez's simple, intuitive approach to verse did not have any direct stylistic influence on other writers, and his works are not well known to contemporary readers. However, his reputation endures as one of Mexico's most distinguished poets.

PRINCIPAL WORKS

Preludios (poetry) 1903
Lirismos (poetry) 1907
Silénter (poetry) 1909
Los senderos ocultos (poetry) 1915
*Jardines de Francia [translator] (poetry) 1915
 Parábolas, y otros poemas (poetry) 1918
 La palabra del viento (poetry) 1921
Algunos aspectos de la lírica mexicana (prose) 1932
Poemas truncos (poetry) 1935
Poesía, 1898-1938. 3 vols. (poetry) 1939
Bajo el signo mortal (poetry) 1942
El hombre del buho: misterio de una vocación (autobiography) 1944
Segundo despertar, y otros poemas (poetry) 1945
Vilano al viento (poetry) 1948
Babel (poetry) 1949
La apacible locura, segunda parte de "El hombre del buho: misterio de una vocación" (autobiography) 1951
El nuevo Narciso, y otros poemas (poetry) 1952
Cuentos, y otras páginas (prose) 1955
Enrique González Martínez: Antología de su obra poética (poetry) 1971
Obras completas (poetry and prose) 1971

*Includes translations of works by Charles Baudelaire, Maurice Maeterlinck, Paul Verlaine, and other French poets.

CRITICISM

Isaac Goldberg (essay date 1920)

SOURCE: *Studies in Spanish-American Literature*, Brentano's Publishers, 1920, pp. 81-92.

[*In the following essay, Goldberg contends that González Martínez introduced a "new orientation of Modernism" with his emphasis on reason and contemplation of ethereal beauty.*]

[González Martínez] comes at a time when Mexico's need is for stern self-discipline, solid culture and widespread education, rather than for effete æstheticism and ultra refinement. The verses that he wrote as a child were probably of the same character as is produced by most gifted children; his training as a physician, however, with the necessary scientific application to concrete phenomena, must have had not a little to do with his substitution of the owl for the swan. Social need and a scientific discipline aptly merged with a poetic pantheism furnished the background for the physician-poet's new orientation of modernism. . . .

A host of contradictory influences have played upon the idol of young Mexico's poetry lovers. Lamartine, Poe, Baudelaire, Verlaine (the ubiquitous Verlaine!), Heredia, Francis Jammes, Samain. Yet here we find no morbidity, no dandyism, no ultra-refinement. Where other poets feel the passing nature of joy and cry out, admonishing mortals to "seize the day" ere it fly, González Martínez ("a melancholy optimist" de Icaza has termed him, in a paradoxical phrase that seems to sum up modern optimism) feels rather the transitory character of grief. He is what I may call an intellectual pantheist,—his absorption of nature is not the ingenuous immersion of the primitive soul into the sea of sights and sounds about him; it is the pantheism of a modern intellect that gazes at feeling through the glasses of reason, and having looked, throws the glasses away. . . . In all things, as he tells us in the beautiful poem **"Busca En Todas Las Cosas,"** from his collection *Los Senderos Ocultos,* he seeks a soul and a hidden meaning. The modernist poets are prodigal with poems upon their artistic creeds and practises. In this series of melodious quatrains González Martínez enlightens us upon his poetic outlook:

> Busca en todas las cosas un alma y un sentido
> Oculto; no te ciñes a la aparencia vana;
> Husmes, sigue el rastro de la verdad arcana
> Escudriñante el ojo y aguzado el oído.
>
> Ama todo lo grácil de la vida, la calma
> De la flor que se mece, el color, el paisaje;
> Ya sabrás poco á poco descifrar su lenguaje. . . .
> Oh, divino coloquio de las cosas y el alma!
>
> hay en todo los seres una blanda sonrisa,
> Un dolor inefable ó un misterio sombrío
> ¿Sabes tu si son lágrimas las gotas de rocío?
> Sabes tu que secretos va cantando la brisa?

That is the secret of the poet's charm. His pantheism is as much wonder as worship; as much inquiry as implicit belief. As he has told us in **"La Plegaría de la Noche en la Selva"**: "Now I know it, now I have seen it with my restless eyes, oh infinite mystery of the nocturnal shadows! To my engrossed spirit you have shown the urn in which with jealous care you hoard your deepest secrets." If poets must have heraldic birds, if Poe must have his raven, Darío his swan, Verlaine his hieratic cat, González Martínez has his owl and night is his ambient,—not the *Tristissima Nox* of a Gutiérrez Nájera, but that night which unto night showeth knowledge.

To Miss Blackwell I am indebted for versions of some characteristic poems by González Martínez. These reveal the poet's mood of communion as well as his peculiarly contemporary pantheism. The first selection is one of the most popular of modern Mexican poems and almost at once found its way into the anthologies:

"Like Brother and Sister"

Like brother with dear sister, hand in hand,
We walk abroad and wander through the land.

The meadow's peace is flooded full tonight
Of white and radiant moonlight, shining bright.
So fair night's landscape 'neath the moon's clear
　beam,
Though it is real, it seems to be a dream.
Suddenly, from a corner of the way,
We hear a song. It seems a strange bird's lay,
Ne'er heard before, with mystic meaning rife,
Song of another world, another life.
"Oh, do you hear?" you ask, and fix on me
Eyes full of questions, dark with mystery.
So deep is night's sweet quiet that enrings them,
We hear our two hearts beating, quick and free.
"Fear not!" I answer. "Songs by night there be
That we may hear, but never know who sings
　them."

Like brother with dear sister, hand in hand,
We walk abroad and roam across the land.

Kissed by the breeze of night that wanders wide,
The waters of the neighboring pool delight,
And bathed within the waves a star has birth,
A swan its neck outstretches, calm and slow,
Like a white serpent 'neath the moon's pale glow,
That from an alabaster egg comes forth.
While gazing on the water silently,
You feel as 'twere a flitting butterfly
Grazing your neck—the thrill of some desire
That passes like a wave—the sudden fire
And shiver, the contraction light and fine
Of a warm kiss, as if it might be mine.
Lifting to me a face of timid fear
You murmur, trembling, "Did you kiss me, dear?"
Your small hand presses mine. Then, murmuring
　low,
"Ah, know you not?" I whisper in your ear,
"Who gives those kisses you will never know,
Nor even if they be real kisses, dear!"

Like brother with dear sister, hand in hand,
We walk abroad and wander through the land.

In giddy faintness, 'mid the mystic night,
Your face you lean upon my breast, and feel
A burning teardrop, falling from above,
In silence o'er your languid forehead steal.
Your dreamy eyes you fasten on me, sighing,
And ask me very gently, "Are you crying?"
"Mine eyes are dry. Look in their depths and see!
But in the fields when darkness overspreads them,
Remember there are tears that fall by night,"
I say, "of which we ne'er shall know who sheds
　them!"

The two poems that follow are a delicate variation of a similar mood; note the attitude of wonder in the first, as well as the sense of repose in both.

"A Hidden Spring"

Within the shadowy bowl of mossy valleys,
Afar from noise, you come forth timidly,
Singing a strange and secret melody,
With silvery dropping, where your clear stream
     sallies.

No wanton fauns in brutal hunting bold
Have muddied you, or heard your voice that sings;
You know not even of what far-off springs
The unseen veins created you of old.

May rural gods preserve your lonely peace!
Still may the sighing leaves, the sobbing breeze,
Down the low murmurs of your scanty flow!
Forgive me that my momentary glance
Of your unknown existence learned by chance;
And hence, with noiseless footsteps, let me go!

"To a Stone by the Wayside"

O mossy stone, thou pillow small and hard
Where my brow rested, 'neath the starlight's
     gleam,
Where, as my weak flesh slept, my life soared up!
I give thee thanks for giving me a dream.

The gray grass gleamed like silver fair, bedewed
By a fresh-fallen shower with many a tear.
A bird upon the bough his music sighed
Beneath the twilight, hueless, thin and clear.

Yearning, I followed evening's concert sweet.
The shining ladder by a star-beam given
I climbed, with eyes fast closed but heart awake,
And ascended to the heights of heaven.

Like Jacob, there the marvel I beheld.
That in a dream prophetic glowed and burned.
In the brief space for which my sleep endured,
I sailed a sea, and to the shore returned.

O mossy stone, thou pillow small and hard!
Thou didst receive, beneath the starlight's gleam,
My aimless longing, my sad weariness;
I give thee thanks for giving me a dream.

His soul is quiveringly responsive to nature's every mood, which is his own.

Sometimes a leaf that flutters in the air,
Torn from the treetops by the breezes' strife,
A weeping of clear waters flowing by,
A nightingale's rich song, disturb my life.

And soft, sweet languors, ecstasies supreme,
Timid and far away, come back to me.
That star and I, we know each other well;
Brothers to me are yonder flower and tree.

My spirit, entering into grief's abyss,
Dives to the farthest bottom, without fear.
To me 'tis like a deep, mysterious book;
Letter by letter I can read it clear.

A subtle atmosphere, a mournful breeze,
Make my tears flow in silence, running free,
And I am like a note of that sad song
Chanted by all things, whatsoe'er they be.

Delirious fancies in a throng press near—
Hallucination, or insanity?—
The lilies' souls to me their kisses give,
The passing clouds all greet me, floating by.

Divine Communion! for a fleeting space
My senses waken to a sharpness rare.
I know what you are murmuring, shining fount!
I know what you are saying, wandering air!

I loose myself from all things, free myself
To live a new life—and I should not say
If I through all things am diffused abroad,
Or all come into me, and with me stay.

But all things flee me, and my soul takes flight
On heavy wings, 'mid faint and chilly breezes,
In an aloofness inconsolable,
Through solitude which terrifies and freezes.

Therefore, amid my pangs of loneliness,
The while my senses sleep, I bend mine ear,
O Nature, to receive thy lightest words—
I tremble at each murmur that I hear.

And that is why a falling, fluttering leaf,
Torn from the tree tops by the breezes' strife,
A tear of limpid water flowing by,
A nightingale's rich song, disturb my life.

González Martínez, indeed, is a strange union of the social spirit and the lonely contemplator of the universe. His loneliness is not, however, the seclusion of the hermit fleeing mankind, as of the spirit in advance of his fellows. "Genius," said Martí, "is simply anticipation; it foresees in detail what others do not behold even in outline, and as the rest do not see what the genius sees, it regards him with amazement, wearies of his splendor and persistency and leaves him to feed upon himself, to suffer." Something of this sense of isolation is in González Martínez's **"Sower of Stars"**:

Thou shalt pass by, and men will say, "What
     pathway does he follow,
Lo, the somnambulist?" But thou, unheeding
     murmurs vain,
Wilt go thy way, thy linen robe upon the air out-
     floating,
Thy robe of linen whitened with pride and with
     disdain.

Few, few will bear thee company—souls made of
     dreams and visions;
And when the forest's end is reached, and steeper
     grows the track,
They will behold the wall of rock that rises huge

before them,
And they will say with terror, "Let us wait till he
    comes back."

And all alone thou wilt ascend the high and
    crannied pathways,
And soon the strange procession of the landscapes
    will file by,
And all alone it shall be thine to part the cloudy
    curtains,
There where the lofty summits kiss the splendors
    of the sky.

Upon some night of moonlight faint, and sad,
    mysterious shadows,
Thou wilt come downward slowly, descending
    from the height,
Holding thine hands up, laden full, and, with a
    giver's gesture,
Sprinkling around thee, one by one, bright roses
    made of light.

And men, absorbed, will gaze upon the brightness
    of thy foot-prints,
And, many-voiced, that multitude will raise a
    joyful cry:
"He is a thief of stars!" And then thy generous
    hand forever
Will keep on scattering through life the stars from
    out the sky.

Is it strange, then, that he should have his moments of
temptation to climb up his ivory tower and renounce the
world? This is the spirit of **"The Castle."**

I built my castle on a summit high,
One of those peaks where eagles love to nest.
One window I left wide toward life's unrest;
The sounds, as of the far sea, rise and die.

There I shut up my dreams, beneath the sky—
Poor wandering caravan that haunts my breast.
Cloud girt, like some old mountain's hoary crest,
That far, strange stronghold greets the gazer's eye.

My dreams wait there till I shall close the door.
They will behold me from my home of yore
Cross the still halls, to be their guest for aye.

Latching the doors, the bolts I shall let fall,
And in the moat that girds the castle wall
Some night shall proudly cast the keys away.

"The thing which hath been, it is that which shall be; and
that which is done is that which shall be done; and there
is no new thing under the sun." Thus spake the Preacher.
But then, was it not Paul in his second epistle to the
Corinthians who said that "old things are passed away;
behold, all things are become new"? Between the two
statements might be placed all the battles that are forever
being waged around the newest of the new standards in
art. "Newness," after all, is a matter of spirit rather than
of chronology. The unimaginative poetaster of today who
shrieks his little theories and seeks to exemplify them in
chopped lines that are neither literary fish nor flesh, is
ancient even as he writes, while the great authors of all

time are freshly new because true to something more
durable than a love of novelty for novelty's sake. Nothing
ages so quickly as novelty. This, however, is no reason
for condemning an entire movement, for the new *spirit* is
always right, unless progress is to resolve into classic
stagnation. A Rémy de Gourmont may say that "the new
is always good because it is new," and a Villergas that
"the good is not new and the new is not good"; both, in
their excessive adherence to a school rather than to an
idea, over-emphasize the point; above all the rivalries of
school and precept (often merely verbal) there is a kinship among all true poets and creators. That modern view
which tends to break away from schools, that inherent
unity between the "new" and the "old," is deeply felt and
effectively expressed by González Martínez in his sonnet
"The Poets, Tomorrow . . .", wherein he sings the same
eternal questioning under different forms.

Tomorrow the poets will sing a divine verse that
we of today cannot achieve; new constellations will
reveal, with a new trembling, a different destiny to
their restless souls. Tomorrow the poets will follow
their road, absorbed in a new and strange blossoming,
and on hearing our song, will cast to the winds
our outworn illusion. And all will be useless, and
all will be vain; the task will remain forever—the
same secret and the same darkness within the heart.
And before the eternal shadow that rises and falls
they will pick up from the dust the abandoned lyre
and sing with it our selfsame song.

Extremes meet. In such a beautiful sonnet as this is in the
original, it seems that the new and the old join in a
golden circle. Great art is neither old nor new; it is ageless.

Robert Avrett (essay date 1931)

SOURCE: "Enrique Gonzáles Martínez: Philosopher and
Mystic," in *Hispania*, Vol. XIV, No. 3, May, 1931, pp.
183-192.

[*In the following essay, Avrett discusses the philosophy
underlying González Martínez's poetry.*]

Enrique González Martínez, physician, poet, journalist,
and diplomat, was born on April 13, 1871, in the city of
Guadalajara, capital of the state of Jalisco, Mexico. In
1893 he received his degree in medicine from the
Facultad of Jalisco. The young doctor soon moved to the
state of Sinaloa, where he settled down to the serious
practice of his profession. His first slender volume of
poems came out in 1903, under the very appropriate title
of *Preludios;* and it was followed in 1907 by *Lirismos,*
by *Silénter* in 1909, and by *Los senderos ocultos* in
1911. In the latter year he took up his residence in
Mexico City, where he was at once admitted into the
inner circles of the foremost men of letters of the capital.
González Martínez, however, did not permit himself the
luxury of idleness. In 1912 he founded the literary review
Argos, but it was short-lived. Within the same year he

became editorial writer for *El Imparcial,* and president of the Ateneo, whose membership included the most distinguished literary men of the capital. In 1913 he served for a brief period as undersecretary of public instruction and fine arts. Later, he was chosen secretary of state for Puebla; he became professor of French literature in the Escuela de Altos Estudios; and he was made director of the department of literature and grammar, and professor of Mexican literature in the Escuela Preparatoria. For a period, during the Carranza administration, González Martínez ceased to be prominently identified with public life. In 1920, however, he was sent as minister to Chile, where he remained for over a year before going to the Argentine Republic as minister plenipotentiary; and in 1924 he was sent as minister to Spain, in which capacity he has since served.

In spite of his busy public life, González Martínez has steadily built up his literary reputation; and he early acquired a very considerable following among the younger poets of his own country. His verses have been collected from time to time and published, each new volume adding to his popularity among literary circles, if not among the masses. In 1915 appeared *La muerte del cisne* and *Jardines de Francia,* the latter consisting of translations from modern French poets, with a prologue by Pedro Henríquez Ureña. In 1916 three volumes were published: a second edition of *Los senderos ocultos,* with a prologue by Alfonso Reyes; a second edition of *Silénter,* containing a prologue by Sixto Osuna and a portrait sketch of González Martínez by Saturnino Herrán; and *La hora inútil,* a reprint of poems selected from *Preludios* and *Lirismos.* Two more volumes were added in 1917: *El libro de la fuerza, de la bondad y del ensueño* and *Pensamiento de los jardines,* the latter a prose translation from the French of Francis Jammes. In 1918 appeared *Parábolas y otros poemas,* with a prologue by the distinguished Mexican poet Amado Nervo, and *Tres grandes poetas belgas, Rodenbach—Maeterlinck—Verhaeren,* a collection of translations into Spanish made by various poets, with a *conferencia* by González Martínez as an introduction. For the next several years the poet contributed occasional articles and poems to various periodicals, but it was not until 1921 that a new volume of verse appeared under the symbolic title of *La palabra del viento*. The year 1923 saw the publication of *El romero alucinado;* and in 1925 two more volumes were brought out: a second edition of *El romero alucinado,* with a prologue by E. Díez-Canedo, and *Las señales furtivas,* a new book of poems to which Luis G. Urbina contributed the prologue.

At first glance there might seem a bit of incongruity between the vocation of medicine and the avocation of poetry; but a moment's consideration will reveal that such a lack of harmony may be more apparent than real. To a man endowed with a sensitive, artistic temperament intimate daily contact with suffering humanity must, of necessity, bring about one of two reactions: he will become hardened spiritually and more or less indifferent to the misery of his surroundings, or he will become, as it

were, subtly attuned to mankind, seeking to fathom something of that impenetrable mystery of human existence and its significance, an enigma that is never quite solved to the seeker's satisfaction. Fortunately, González Martínez followed the second course. His poetry is intensely subjective, and his themes are frequently tinged with that mystical philosophy which comes only from profound introspection. Beginning with *Preludios,* his first published volume of verse. the poet made evident his interest in those things that lie within the human soul, rather than in the bare rehearsal of such things and events as may be perceived readily by the casual observer. As Pedro Henríquez Ureña points out:

> La autobiografía lírica de Enrique González Martínez es la historia de una ascensión perpetua. Hacia mayor serenidad; pero, a la vez, hacia mayor sinceridad; hacia más severo y hondo concepto de la vida.

In the poem **"Lucha eterna"** the poet indulges in a bit of faintly ironical philosophy, a tendency which has steadily developed in his subsequent works, although in a broader, more tolerant vein. The last two stanzas follow:

> Mujer, es fuerza batallar, prosigue
> Y sírvate de aliento la esperanza
> Para que al débil corazón fustigue,
>
> Que es ley ineludible y sin mudanza
> Huir de la ventura que nos sigue,
> Seguir el ideal que no se alcanza.

Yielding, apparently, to a temporary state of spiritual depression, the poet declares in **"Como sutil neblina . . .":**

> Mi vida es selva donde no hay el germen
> De una Ilusión y mis ensueños duermen
> Oculta bajo el ala la cabeza;
>
> Aves que esperan en su pobre nido
> El abrazo de nieve del olvido
> Y el ósculo glacial de la tristeza.

The indomitable spirit of González Martínez soon reasserts itself, however, and there is something heroic in the calm philosophy expressed in **"Resurgam"**:

> No importa que las iras de la suerte
> A mi ansia de ideal hieran de muerte
> Y hagan caer con ímpetu violento;
>
> Para cada tropiezo de la vida
> Yo tengo un claro sol que en la caída
> Trueca en iris triunfal mi pensamiento.

Lirismos, the poet's next volume, shows an added sureness of touch gained through a greater confidence in the value of his ideals and in his ability to express himself simply and harmoniously. There is a perceptible deepening of his tendencies toward mystic symbolism; both the ideals and the philosophy of Enrique González Martínez have expanded. There are times when he seems possessed of what, for want of a better term, may be called a certain mystic melancholy; he seeks to unravel the riddle of man's life and ultimate destination by a searching study of the world of nature, but he never quite discovers the key that will unlock the door of the future. In **"Creciente"** he watches the torrent of the river as it sweeps relentlessly onward, but he derives no answer to his problem. The great *why?* and *whither?* remain unknown. The last two stanzas sum up the spirit of the entire poem.

> Alamo enorme que tronchó la ira
> De sañudo huracán, cruzar se mira
> Como una barca gigantesca y rota,
>
> Llevando en la prisión de su ramaje
> Un ave implume que en extraño viaje
> No sabe cómo va ni adónde flota.

Much the same idea of the uncertainty of man's destination is conveyed in the seventh stanza of **"País de ensueño,"** wherein the poet exclaims:

> Tú misma no sabías á dónde los antojos
> Del céfiro empujaban tu barco de oro y gules,
> Y en pájaros de armiño y en vértices azules
> Ibas posando el ávido anhelo de tus ojos.

Silénter, published in 1909, marks a distinct step forward in the artistic development of the poet. Eduardo Colín, in a somewhat brief but discerning essay entitled "Enrique González Martínez," offers the following comment:

> Uno de los nuevos espectáculos que ha aparecido en la poesía hispanoamericana es Enrique González Martínez. Nuevo por razón de los años en que ha escrito y por la originalidad de su manera. Es el poeta esencialmente filosófico. Hay poetas como Olegario Andrade, Acuña y el propio Darío que son tenidos por bardos pensantes, pero en realidad no lo son como González Martínez; cantan asuntos concretos y de ellos derivan ideas. Los temas del autor de *Silénter,* son por sí mismos estados, impulsos abstractos del alma, motivos ideales. Y su singularidad también consiste en el modo de exhalar su pensamiento; no es en odas docentes como tantas escritas en América **"A la Ciencia,"** **"A Natura,"** **"A Dios,"** pura ideología versificada, sino que su filosofía es de temperamento, verdadera filosofía de poeta.

Philosophy is not to be attained without meditation; and nothing so induces meditation as solitude. It is solitude and freedom from the rude disturbances of the busy world of men that González Martínez is seeking. From silent and solitary communion with Nature the poet derives his greatest enjoyment, a calm, philosophical contentment that embraces the soul as much as the senses. The last stanza of **"Soledad"** is quite characteristic of this phase of the poet.

> Ante el cielo sin brumas y sin celajes
> Sueño con mis memorias y mis paisajes,
> Mis sombras familiares, mis pobres muertos
> Que han pisado la arena de otros desiertos . . .
> Y la tarde se muere, la tarde quieta,

> De las tardes amadas por el poeta,
> En que todo reposa, todo convida
> A meditar muy hondo sobre la vida.

With the publication of *Los senderos ocultos,* in 1911, it became evident that the poet's period of early uncertainty, of continuous groping toward the light which only his own soul could reveal to him, had ended. The man, as well as the artist, had found himself; there was revealed the calm purpose of the poet who, after frequent wanderings, had come to realize his mission and to formulate more clearly his philosophy of life. Henceforth, González Martínez might stray occasionally into the delightful realms of pure fancy, but he inevitably must return again to continue his explorations into the fascinating territory of the human soul. Philosophers throughout the ages have realized that joy must be tinged with grief—happiness and sorrow are more closely akin than the average mortal supposes. In **"Una vieja tristeza . . ."** this age-old truth is clothed in a mystic symbolism that renders the poem unusually appealing.

> Una vieja tristeza desanduvo el camino . . .
> Yo podaba mi huerto y libaba mi vino . . .
>
> Una constante charla de pájaros decía
> Las divinas canciones de la franca alegría;
>
> Los ajados rosales, los musgos del jardín,
> Y las fresas regadas, hablaban del festín
>
> Interrumpido; el aire fingía llevar esos
> Apagados murmullos de los furtivos besos,
>
> Y un viejo Pan de mármol en la rústica fuente
> De piedra, parecía reir paternalmente. . . .
>
> Y la vieja tristeza se detuvo á mi lado
> Y la oí levemente decir: ¿has olvidado?. . . .
>
> De mis ojos aun turbios del placer y la fiesta,
> Una lágrima muda fué la sola respuesta. . . .
>
> Mientras tanto, la charla de pájaros seguía
> Las divinas canciones de la franca alegría.
>
> Y la vieja tristeza se fué por donde vino
> Perdiéndose y perdiéndose por el mismo camino. . . .
>
> Yo podaba mi huerto y libaba mi vino. . . .

The last six lines of the sonnet **"Intus"** give in condensed form an entire philosophy of life, a philosophy with which we have every reason to believe that the poet himself is in accord.

> Hay que labrar tu campo, hay que vivir tu vida,
> Tener con mano firme la lámpara encendida
> Sobre la eterna sombra, sobre el eterno abismo. . . .
>
> Y callar. . . . mas tan hondo, con tan profunda
>   calma,
> Que absorto en la infinita soledad de tí mismo
> No escuches sino el vasto silencio de tu alma.

La muerte del cisne and *El libro de la fuerza, de la bondad y del ensueño,* published in 1915 and 1917, respectively, show a gradual deepening of the poet's regard for Nature and an increasing use of mystic symbolism. The philosophical tendency to probe to the soul of the material which he treats is generally more strongly pronounced than in his earlier works. It is not greatly surprising, therefore, that with *Parábolas y otros poemas,* which appeared in 1918, González Martinez should plunge frankly into the realm of the mystic. Luisa Luisi has analyzed with rare discernment this mysticism of the poet.

> Ama en las cosas el alma, y no la apariencia; y mucho menos el goce pasajero que prestan a nuestros sentidos. Esa honda espiritualidad de su poesía, que es al mismo tiempo su mayor nobleza, recuerda a la del catalán Fernando Maristany, aunque este último, como Amado Nervo. se sienta arrastrado al fin, por la corriente del neocristianismo. La dificultad estriba en mantenerse místico, sin caer ni en la religión, ni en el sensualismo. En **"La puerta,"** magnífico poema, en **"Un fantasma,"** esta actitud de sinceridad y de nobleza, adquiere toda su serena amplitud. El problema de la muerte lo atrae con fuerza invencible. Quisiera creer en la vida de ultratumba, pero la educación combate el anhelo del alma. Y este combate, que analizó magistralmente Unamuno en uno de sus mejores libros, está contenido todo él en **"La puerta"**:

> Los dos llamamos a la misma puerta
> para saber un día lo que esconde
> la lóbrega mansión. . . . En la desierta
> inmensidad, el eco nos responde.
>
> Largo llamar. . . . Los maltratados nudos
> de las manos ya sangran. Han corrido
> con el tiempo las lágrimas. . . . ¡ Oh, mudos
> huéspedes sin piedad y sin oído!
>
> A veces, un rumor de la lejana
> extensión nos anima; el ansia crece. . . .
> ¡ Oh, triste golpear!. . . . En la mañana,
> la ilusión de la noche desparece.
>
> Mas llegará la hora en que la herida
> mano rompa el orín de los cerrojos,
> y al último rincón de la guarida
> penetre la codicia de los ojos.
>
> Y cuando ceda al fin el oxidado
> gonce que afianza la cerrada puerta,
> sabrá nuestro dolor que hemos llamado
> ante el umbral de una mansión desierta.

The publication of *La palabra del viento,* in 1921, marked another forward step in the poetic development of Enrique González Martínez. The mysticism and the philosophical melancholy which had been so apparent in *Parábolas y otros poemas* finds in the later volume a fitting continuation; and there is sounded, moreover, in the versification a distinctly new and varied note that connects the author with the more progressive younger school of Mexican poets. This evidence of progressiveness is not surprising, coming as it does from a poet who had much earlier allied himself with the so-called *modernista* movement. Indeed, as Coester points out:

> González Martínez's poems mark the trend that modernistic poetry had already taken. Introspection and sensitiveness to the world, *"el alma colosal del paisaje,"* were rudimentary in modernistic poetry from the first. Sensations and the joy of experiencing them demand the attention of youth; reflection comes later. . . . There is something quite Mexican in the mystical attitude toward Nature. It appears continuously in Mexican poetry.

The appearance of *El romero alucinado,* which came out in 1923, was received with almost universal praise by the critics. Suárez Calimano has analyzed the characteristics of this volume very concisely.

> Toda una filosofía de la vida se desprende de la primera parte de este libro, en la que campea una gracia helénica y moderna al mismo tiempo, suave y elegante, bien ajena al vetusto y gris ropaje que a menudo le prestan ciertos poetas cuando la traen a sus jardines.

El romero alucinado is, in truth, a pilgrimage into that mystical region whose territory is entered through the single gateway of the human soul. The poet is still fascinated by the mysteries of life and death, but there is little bitterness when he fails to solve these phenomena. Instead, there is a patient continuation of the endless search for the hidden truth that is almost stoic in its resignation. The man of science recognizes that inevitable change which must come to every man—the beginnings of the physical dissolution that the years bring on, accompanied by torturing doubts as to the spiritual stability. The body is decaying—must the soul likewise decay? And yet, in spite of the unmistakable evidences of change which he recognizes in himself from day to day, the poet feels that there is within his own soul something that endures. This conception is expressed simply in the poem "¿. . . . ?," whose delicate beauty merits quotation in full.

> Cada día me cambia en otro hombre;
> ahora mismo soy otro ya.
> El hombre de ayer está muerto. . . .
> ¡ Descanse en paz!
>
> Son inútiles los propósitos.
> Arrepentirse. . . . ¿ Para qué?. . . .
> El hombre nuevo de mañana
> dictará su ley.
>
> Cada instante, con un olvido
> o con una nueva emoción,
> va cavando el abismo insondable
> de ayer a hoy.
>
> Y en la sucesión vertiginosa
> de este incesante *devenir,*
> la vida es un río que corre y que corre
> sin rumbo y sin fin. . . .
>
> Bajo la embriaguez de lo efímero,

mientras todo viene y se va,
"hoy es el hombre y mañana no parece"....
¡ Descanse en paz!

(Y, no obstante, cuando allá a solas
dialogamos tú y yo,
sentimos que hay algo que dura,
¡ oh, corazón!....

In *Las señales furtivas,* published in 1925, González Martínez sums up, as it were, the various characteristics of his earlier volumes. His varied verse forms, and especially his numerous short poems, proclaim the new spirit in poetry; yet there may be discerned something of the delicate mysticism and the poetic sensitiveness which were responsible for much of the charm of his earlier works, notably in portions of *Los senderos ocultos* and in *Parábolas y otros poemas*. His philosophy is frequently tinged with a slightly ironical humor that is wholly delightful. *Las señales furtivas* is indisputable proof that Enrique González Martínez is not yet ready to relinquish his leadership to younger contemporaries. He is not only the poet of the past, but he is the poet of the present as well. His own definition of his poetic ideal, given in an interview for a Costa Rican periodical, is perhaps the best possible explanation for the poet's continued popularity throughout Spanish America.

> Al tanto de la actual discusión relativa a la poesía pura . . . le pregunto al vate mexicano, ¿ cuál es su ideal poético? Casi sin pensarlo (maravilloso improvisador), me responde: *traducirme a mí mismo y expresar mi inquietud ante la contemplación de la vida.*

Because he has achieved this ideal, because he has "interpreted himself to himself and expressed his inquietude before the contemplation of life," González Martínez is able to share with others something of his own innermost feeling. He has interpreted himself, not to himself alone, but to his readers likewise; and thus he has depicted something of the perpetual struggle, something of the inquietude before the unfathomable mysteries of life and death, and something of the eternal quest that is as old as mankind, but which is ever new.

John Eugene Englekirk (essay date 1934)

SOURCE: *Edgar Allan Poe in Hispanic Literature,* Instituto De Las Espanas, 1934, 504p.

[*In the following essay, Englekirk explains the influence of the works of Edgar Allan Poe on González Martínez.*]

Francisco A. de Icaza testifies to the contradictory influences that have shaped the personal art of Enrique González Martínez:

> "Con gran agilidad rítmica y mental, pasa del sentimentalismo ordenado y pulcro de Lamartine a las alucinaciones y sacudimientos patológicos de Poe; refleja el 'clair de lune' de Verlaine, la idea

> hosca, encajada en el pulido verso de Baudelaire; la plasticidad objectiva del alejandrino de Heredia; el encanto primitivo, en forma y en idea, de Francis Jammes; el clasicismo vivido de Samain, y llega así a lograr esa técnica que caracteriza hoy su poesía original del todo, pues dió vida a las extrañas sin reclamar nada de ellas;—"

Goldberg corroborates the above-mentioned sources of the influences that have played upon Mexico's outstanding poet.

In the poems that proclaim González Martínez a spiritual brother of Nervo and a lineal descendant of their common ancestor, Gutiérrez Nájera, one finds the very acme of those characteristics that were emphasized in the studies on his fellow-countrymen as evidence of their spiritual affinity to Poe. The poet's exhortations to whet the senses for the appreciation of the deeper meaning of life, his questioning attitude in the face of the Eternal Query, and his passionate desire to sound the mysteries of that "ultimate dim Thule," are the obvious points of contact between the Mexican poet and Poe.

However, there is a very essential difference in the fundamental attitude of these two poets. Díez-Canedo aptly commented on the poet's lines:

> Mas como ya cayeron las sombras del ocaso
> como en la torre antigua ya resonó la hora,
> a mi redil del alma se vuelven paso a paso
> con la esperanza inútil de una imposible aurora.

when he wrote, "Una esperanza *inútil,* y además una aurora *imposible*. Mas la desolación de los adjetivos no llega a deshacer el encanto de los nombres: inútil, pero esperanza; imposible pero aurora." González Martínez has never succumbed entirely to the utter despair of Poe. This difference is brought out admirably by comparing **"Las tres cosas del romero"** of the former with "Eldorado" of the latter. "Esperanza inútil," yes, in this seeking of the "impossible dawn" by "el romero alucinado":

> En la noche y en el día,
> por el llano y el otero,
> aquel caminante no se detenía,
> como el primer día . . .

but hope still in those closing lines,

> Porque tres cosas tenía
> para su viaje el Romero:
> los ojos abiertos a la lejanía,
> atento el oído y el paso ligero.

But how despairingly void of all hope is the quest of Poe's knight:

> And as his strength
> Failed him at length,
> He met a pilgrim shadow—
> "Shadow," said he,

"Where can it be—
This land of Eldorado?"

"Over the Mountains
Of the Moon
Down the Valley of the Shadow,
Ride boldly ride,"
The shade replied,—
"If you seek for Eldorado!"

Save for this difference in the underlying tones of the poems, the resemblances are suggestive enough to imply that the Mexican bard was inspired by Poe's lines.

Reminiscences of Poe are particularly acute in the volume that stresses the melancholy strain of the Mexican's muse—*Parábolas y otros poemas*. There is an amazing similarity to one of Poe's favorite themes, the tragic horror of man's fate, in the poem "**Parábola de los viajeros.**" The following stanzas are very suggestive of such works as "The Masque of the Red Death" and "The Conqueror Worm":

> Y así fueron cayendo uno tras otro—
> El infante, del seno que agotó
> el frío de la muerte pende inmóvil
> como el fruto marchito de un dolor.
> Aquel que alzó los brazos codiciosos
> al mágico verdor
> de un laurel en la orilla de la ruta,
> en las manos guardó la crispación
> de su codicia, y en la abierta boca,
> su última imprecación.
> Y la serpiente de osamentas blancas
> iba creciendo. El grito que movió
> aquella multitud, sobre las rocas,
> de la montaña enhiesta se prendió;
> mas ya nadie escuchaba; ya los últimos
> quedaban allá abajo, en la feroz
> y cruel ansiedad de la fatiga;
> ni un grito, ni un adiós;
> y murió el postrer hombre y la postura
> ilusión.

Of a similar vein, and equally suggestive, is the poem "**Dolor.**" The reference is very obvious in the stanza that follows:

> Mientras vomitan lumbre las forjas de Vulcano,
> mientras la Muerte Roja tiende su calosfrío
> la tierra delincuente, bajo el pavor humano,
> es cual gota de sangre que rueda en el vacío . . .

Other compositions of the same volume that offer marked resemblances to Poe are "**Parábola del sol, del viento y de la luna,**" "**Tardes de aquellos años,**" and "**Parábola del huésped sin nombre.**" Similarly Poesque are such poems as "**Retorno,**" "**Un fantasma,**" "**Alguien se ha ido,**" "**La Pesadilla,**" and "**Las almas muertas.**" Certain elements in the poems "**La ciudad absorta,**" and "**La campana mística**" are very suggestive of the respective influences of Poe's "The City in the Sea" and "The Bells."

Helen P. Houck (essay date 1940)

SOURCE: "Personal Impressions of Enrique Gonzáles Martínez," in *Hispania,* Vol. XXIII, No. 4, December, 1940, pp. 331-335.

[*In the following essay, Houck discusses González Martínez's life and personality.*]

The title, Mexico's best-loved poet, which once belonged to Amado Nervo—and still does in a sense—may fittingly be applied to Enrique González Martínez. Certainly, as among living poets, the epithet would be given him by acclaim. Of Mexico's brilliant modern galaxy of poets, beginning with Manuel Gutiérrez Nájera, there remains only one of the major luminaries, González Martínez, conceded generally to be the greatest of them all. Hence the intellectuals prize him as the glory of modern Mexican letters and all who know him, of whatever class, esteem and love him as a man.

After many years of intense work as physician, politician, journalist, diplomat, teacher, and poet, González Martínez now lives a quiet life, occupying a modest government position as *consejero* of the Banco Nacional Agrícola, enjoying his family and his friends, his books and his creative work. In his beautiful home in Colonia del Valle, he lives with his son Hector and his family and with his grandson Enriquito, the son of Enrique González Rojo, who died May 9, 1939. Enriquito, at his grandfather's request, bears the name Enrique González Martínez. In the capital live also the poet's sister and his daughter with their families. The death of the poet's wife, doña Luisa Rojo de González Martínez, on April 8, 1935, and that of his elder son, the only one of the children to follow in his father's footsteps as a poet, were crushing blows, to which González Martínez has given noble expression in verse. Since these blows, the poet's friends have drawn even closer to him to give him the consolation of their warm affection.

In his study, opening upon the *sala* with its hand-carved furniture, reminiscent of his seven years in Spain, the poet spends much of his time. The four walls are lined with low bookcases that house a magnificent library, culled from the world's choicest literature. On the walls hang photographs and sketches of his literary friends and compeers, some of them no longer living: Gutiérrez Nájera, Rubén Darío, Luis G. Urbina, Amado Nervo, Enrique Diez-Canedo, Asaña, Eugenio d'Ors, and many others.

The predominant impression made by González Martínez' personality is that of serenity. He seems a man who has met and conquered all of life's difficulties, obstacles, sorrows, doubts, and restlessness. He appears to live in an atmosphere of tranquillity, of *"triste alegría,"* as someone has said. One is reminded of his own words: *"Yo voy alegremente por donde va la vida"* and of those other lovely verses:

> Dolor, si por acaso a llamar a mi puerta

llegas, sé bienvenido; de par en par abierta
la dejé para que entres . . .

. . . . .

No turbar el silencio de la vida,
ésa es la ley . . . Y sosegadamente
llorar, si hay que llorar, como la fuente
escondida.

Yet González Martínez is genial, at times jovial. His
conversation is interspersed with sparkling jests and with
choice anecdotes from his rich experience. His speech is
rapid—*atropellado,* he says that Amado Nervo called
it—and his hands are seldom at rest. The three gestures
which Moreno Villa classifies as typically Mexican are
frequently used by him. The "overtones" of which Luisa
Luisi speaks as characteristic of his poetry are felt in all
his words. Even a simple greeting has harmonics of genuine interest and kindness, enveloping the whole personality of the one addressed. This poet so in love with *"mi
amigo el silencio,"* so fond of contemplation, turns from
his intense inner life to give himself completely and utterly to the external world, to the pleasures of the senses,
and to the intimate joys of friendship. May this warm,
human quality be due in part to his seventeen years of
medical practice? Certainly something of the kind physician still remains in his solicitous attention to the individual. His friends refer to him affectionately as *"el doctor."* He says that he loved the profession of medicine.
During all those years he was writing poetry surreptitiously, publishing it in newspapers and journals distant
from Guadalajara and Sinaloa, for fear his patients would
lose faith in him as a doctor. He tells with enjoyment how
one of them mentioned having read a good poem "by a
man of the same name as yours." Even then he did not
confess to his *pecadillo.* Though poetry, years ago, over-
shadowed and crowded out medicine, there is still in
Enrique González Martínez something of the sympathetic
family doctor—*"el doctor," par excellence.*

Youthfulness is part and parcel of Dr. González Martínez'
personality. An Argentine critic has said of him as a poet:
"Ni se cansa ni se envejece: se transforma." Perhaps the
same could be said of him as a man. He himself has said,
though not with the same intent: *"Cada día me cambia en
otro hombre."* It is not only that the poet does not look
his sixty-nine years: he does not impress one as an elderly man by his conversation, his interests, or his outlook
on life. He is still looking forward. He seems specially at
home with and responsive to young people. The university students who have recently launched *Tierra Nueva*
have found in him a kind and interested adviser; his study
door is always open to them.

Another quality that endears the poet to his friends and
makes him a charming companion is his delightful humor. On one occasion when a friend, knowing his dislike
for adulation, was repeating the extravagant praise of a
rather frothy person, González Martínez exclaimed with
a jovial laugh: "You know sweets are not good for dia-
betics!" In the home of Valle Arizpe—one of the show-

places of Mexico, with its antiques worth millions of
pesos—he asked the host jocularly: "What day was it,
Artemio, that you invited me to bring my grandchildren
to play in your house?"

The warmth of the poet's personality is evident in the
smallest details of life. Recently the family of one of his
friends lost by death their faithful old *nana* who had
cared for two generations of children. The burial was
scarcely over before *"el doctor"* came to offer his
pésame. This humble, ignorant Indian woman was hon-
ored in death by the greatest living poet of Spanish
America, and that with simple naturalness. It would never
have occurred to González Martínez to do otherwise.

Though no longer in the teaching profession, González
Martínez is still a teacher. For the past five years he has
been giving weekly lectures on Wednesday evenings to a
group of his friends and admirers. The nucleus is made
up of old friends from Guadalajara, who like to be assured of seeing *"el doctor"* at least once a week. Some
of the Spanish colony attend, often students from one
institution or another or American teachers and scholars
visiting in Mexico. For a time the meetings were held in
the home of Sr. Salvador Martín del Campo; at present
they are in the home of Sr. Ignacio Helguera. The length
of time that these lectures have continued speaks for their
charming quality. In leisurely fashion the lecturer has
carried his listeners through Spanish and Mexican literature, being now occupied with seventeenth-century
French literature. With a few brief notes before him, to
which he seldom refers, González Martínez evokes the
life, character, and spirit of the authors, relating them one
to another and to other periods and countries. His kindly
humor and his deep human understanding enable him to
present each author as a living person. Indeed one would
say that he is speaking of intimate, well-loved friends,
whose weaknesses and foibles do not dim his affection
for them.

On the poet's latest saint's day, April 13, 1940, the group
gave him a surprise party after the "class," to which a
large number of friends were invited. Prominent musicians provided a program, some laudatory verses in Latin
were read by a youthful poet, the guest of honor was
presented with a handsome briefcase, and supper was
served in the dining room. *El día del maestro,* May 15,
gave the group another opportunity to entertain the poet-
teacher. This time the program was of popular character.
Professor Vaqueiro Foster of the Conservatorio Nacional,
who is making a study of the folk music of Mexico,
brought his *huapango* to provide hilarity. The rustic
musicians were in their best form, as they were on the
eve of leaving for New York to take part in the concerts
of Mexican music given in connection with the exhibition, "Twenty Centuries of Mexican Art." That morning
Sr. Vaqueiro Foster had explained to the "orchestra" the
occasion of their playing and had read them some poems
of González Martínez. One of them, the youngest and
most spirited, had composed some verses in his rude
style, interweaving the titles of the poems he had heard.

The reading of the jingles by Sr. Vaqueiro Foster won for the rude jongleur hearty applause and a cordial congratulatory handshake from the poet.

The affection and esteem in which González Martínez is held by the public was illustrated by a small incident on the occasion of the *homenaje* offered him by the Universidad Autónoma de México, on April 16, 1940. After the ceremony was over and the poet had gone with his family and a few friends to a Spanish *churrería* to partake of the traditional *chocolate y churros,* González Martínez drew from his pocket an object, which he passed around the table, telling the following story. As he was coming out of the University building after the program, a young man, probably a university student, stepped from the shadows, saying: "Doctor, I want to give you a token of my esteem and affection. I am giving you the thing dearest to me among all my possessions." It was a small Mickey Mouse. What story lay behind the pathetic, almost ludicrous incident? One of the men present recalled that his own most treasured possession was a toy of his little daughter who had died. Perhaps the Mickey Mouse held some tender association. Possibly the poet appreciated this little gift for its unusualness, even more than he did the warm, sincere expressions of scholars and students who had spoken at the *homenaje.*

Whoever wishes to know González Martínez the man, needs only to study his works, for he is his poetry and his poetry is he. This trite saying, applicable to most poets, is true in a special sense of González Martínez and finds explicit corroboration in his own words. Luisa Luisi, in an address on González Martínez delivered before the Argentine Women's Club, July 23, 1923—an address which the poet considers an excellent analysis of his work up to that point—closed with a similar idea, supporting it by the following poem of González Martínez, **"Para un libro":**

> Quiero con mano firme y aliento puro,
> escribir estos versos para un libro futuro:
>
> Este libro es mi vida . . . No teme la mirada
> aviesa de los hombres; no hay en sus hojas nada
> que no sea la frágil urdimbre de otras vidas:
> ímpetus y fervores, flaquezas y caídas.
> La frase salta a veces palpitante y desnuda;
> otras, con el ropaje del símbolo se escuda
> de viles suspicacias. Aquél a quien extrañe
> este pudor del símbolo, que no lo desentrañe.
> Este libro no enseña, no conforta, ni guía,
> y la inquietud que esconde es solamente mía;
> mas en mis versos flota, diafanidad o arcano,
> la vida que es de todos. Quien lea no se asombre
> de hallar en mis poemas la integridad de un hombre
> sin nada que no sea profundamente humano.

Jefferson Rea Spell (essay date 1946)

SOURCE: "A Review," in *Hispania,* Vol. XXIX, No. 1, February, 1946, pp. 155-156.

[*In the following essay, Spell reviews the first volume of González Martínez's autobiography,* El hombre del buho. Misterio de una vocación, *praising the work's "contribution to the cultural history of Mexico since 1880."*]

In this first volume of his autobiography **El hombre del buho. Misterio de una vocación,** Enrique González Martínez (b. 1871), one of Mexico's leading poets, re-creates the atmosphere of the Guadalajara of his childhood and youth; draws subtle pen-pictures of the members of his family, his teachers and friends; details his studies in medicine and the circumstances that led him to become a physician in Sinaloa in 1895; relives a happy married life, marred only by his gambling; pictures literary circles in the capital, to which he was drawn by men prominent in the Díaz regime; and describes his disillusionment and return to Mocorito, where a political post, too carelessly accepted, embroiled him in the Revolution of 1910.

A hard-working physician, he handled thousands of cases, many of them surgical, although it was later said that his skill in that line was confined to "twisting the swan's neck"—a reference to his indictment of Modernism in his celebrated poem **"Tuércele el cuello al cisne."** During the years in Sinaloa, he could call on few for either professional counsel or assistance, but he cared faithfully for rich and poor alike, and won confidence and respect, even while he squandered strength, time and money at the card table. Before 1905 poetry was merely an avocation; only **Preludios** had been published.

But this simple story of his early life is told some thirty years later with an artistry which places it on a level with poetry. Not only are people and places seen through the eyes of a poet, but the reader is transported, as on a magic carpet, along the way the poet had earlier traveled; and colorful details and incidents, both humorous and tragic, are pointed out with a flavor and zest for life which compel admiration for the narrator.

Not the least interesting bits are those that trace his literary interests and achievements—among them, the obituary and his reply published on the occasion of his supposed death in 1900, and his impressions of some of Mexico's leading writers that he came to know, five years later, in the capital. At that time Amado Nervo was there, embittered over his treatment by the literary clique; Joaquín Casasús was wealthy and influential, very generous with encouraging words but not with the material aid the young physician needed; Luis Urbina, generally recognized for his poetic ability, stood guard at the portal to Justo Sierra, distributor of governmental grants and positions to promising young artists and writers; and in the suburbs lived Jesús Valenzuela—editor of the *Revista Moderna,* best of Mexico's literary periodicals—sick, in reduced circumstances, and neglected by many of the friends of more prosperous days, but always kind. Stirred by these contacts but unable to find a means of livelihood, the physician returned to Mocorito to resume his practice and to try his hand at various literary forms, but not in the current *modernista* style. These efforts are to be found in *Lirismos* and a monthly literary journal, *Arte* (1907-1909). Sorrow over the death of his mother and son found outlet in *Silenter* (1909); at last, in these poems, he had found both himself and his field.

This re-creation of the atmosphere and the personalities that contributed to the development of a poet is a valuable contribution to the cultural history of Mexico since 1880, yet the charm of the work lies less in the facts presented than in the art of the story-teller in transforming the commonplace into the distinctive. Readers of this volume will surely await the appearance of the next with eager anticipation.

FURTHER READING

Bibliography

Anderson, Robert Roland. "Enrique González Martínez (1871-1952)." In *Spanish American Modernism: A Selected Bibliography*, pp. 71-6. Tucson: University of Arizona Press, 1970.
　　Cites critical sources, mostly in Spanish.

Criticism

Brushwood, John S. *Enrique González Martínez.* New York: Twayne Publishers, 1969, 166 p.
　　Survey of González Martínez's poetry.

Craig, G. Dundas. "Enrique González Martínez." In *The Modernist Trend in Spanish-American Poetry: A Collection of Representative Poems of the Modernist Movement and the Reaction: Translated into English Verse with a Commentary*, pp. 310-12. Berkeley: University of California Press, 1934.
　　Short overview of González Martínez's themes and techniques.

Schulman, Ivan A. "Antonio Machado and Enrique González Martínez: A Study in Internal and External Dynamics." *Journal of Spanish Studies* 4, No. 1 (Spring 1976): 29-46.
　　Identifies thematic and stylistic similarities between the two poets.

The following sources published by Gale Research contain additional coverage of González Martínez's life and career: *Hispanic Writers*

Jude the Obscure

Thomas Hardy

The following entry presents criticism of Hardy's novel *Jude the Obscure* (1895). For information on Hardy's complete career, see *TCLC*, Volumes 4 and 10; for discussion of his novel *Tess of the D'Urbervilles* see *TCLC*, Volume 18; for discussion of his novel *The Mayor of Casterbridge* see *TCLC*, Volume 32; for discussion of his novel *The Return of the Native*, see *TCLC*, Volume 48; for discussion of Hardy's poetry, see *TCLC*, Volume 53.

INTRODUCTION

Hardy's last and by most accounts bleakest novel, *Jude the Obscure* details the failed life and ignoble death of Jude Fawley, a bright and ambitious, but ultimately inconsequential, man. The central theme of the work is the inability of individuals to surmount the social and psychological forces that determine their lives. This theme also appears Hardy's earlier novels, notably *Tess of the D'Urbervilles* and *The Return of the Native*, which likewise dramatize his belief that individuals are powerless to affect their own lives in an attempt to achieve happiness. In *Jude the Obscure* Hardy further explores this theme in relation to the constricting forces he observed around him in Victorian society: class, religion, and sexuality. Thus, the novel recounts Jude's unrealized dream to enter the university at Christminster (Hardy's fictionalized version of Oxford University), and his powerlessness to remain happily with the woman he loves, Sue Bridehead, outside of the socially accepted institution of marriage.

Plot and Major Characters

Jude the Obscure opens as a young Jude Fawley watches his school teacher, Mr. Richard Phillotson, depart the small town of Marygreen and travel to the university at Christminster. Sharing Phillotson's goal of earning a degree, Jude hopes to one day follow the same path and so studies intently. Meanwhile, he lives with his great-aunt, Drusilla Fawley, and learns the trade of stonemasonry in order to earn money for his future. Several years pass and Jude, now nineteen years old, meets Arabella Donn, the daughter of a local pig farmer. Sensuous and physically attractive, Arabella pursues Jude, and the two become lovers. Eventually Arabella convinces Jude that she has become pregnant by him, and they marry. Quickly growing tired of her new husband, however, she leaves him and emigrates to Australia. Jude than resumes his original plan and journeys to Christminster. There he meets his distant cousin Sue Bridehead, an intelligent, unconventional woman with whom he immediately falls in love. He later learns that Sue has also attracted the

attention of Phillotson. Disheartened by this news and his inability to gain acceptance to the university, Jude departs Christminster for Melchester, where he hopes to pursue theological studies instead. Now also in Melchester at a training college, Sue spends time with Jude, but grows cold when he professes his love to her. After a fearful Jude reveals to her that he is married, she responds by proclaiming her own marriage, to Phillotson. However, the marriage is not to Sue's liking, and the return of Arabella, who has since married an Australian man, prompts Sue to change her mind about Jude.

At the funeral for Jude's recently deceased aunt, Sue kisses Jude passionately. Thinking himself no longer suitable for a career in the Church, Jude forsakes his theological studies. Sue, meanwhile, asks Phillotson for his permission to leave. Sue and Jude move in together in the nearby town of Aldbrickham, while Phillotson eventually grants Sue a divorce. After a year Sue still refuses to make love to Jude, until Arabella appears once again, and Sue and Jude, though unmarried, consummate their relationship for the first time. Arabella notifies Jude that they have a son together, a gloomy boy who is called Little Father Time. The boy arrives shortly from Australia to live with Jude and Sue. Meanwhile, public dislike for the couple's unwed lifestyle costs Jude his job, and the two leave Aldbrickham for Kennetbridge. More than two years pass, and Jude and Sue now have two children of their own, while Sue carries another unborn. When Little Father Time hears his adopted mother's unhappy reaction to the pregnancy he mistakenly believes that he and the other children are the source of the family's woes. He responds by hanging his siblings and then himself. He leaves a note nearby that reads "Done because we are to menny." Soon after, Sue delivers her child stillborn. Jude, meanwhile, falls ill and works only irregularly. Arabella then reappears—her Australian husband has since died—with a revived interest in Jude. She contacts Phillotson, who writes to Sue, urging her to return to him. Sue, feeling that she has been wrong to live with Jude unmarried, agrees. Arabella then contrives to get Jude back, and the two remarry. Jude, who has grown more and more ill over time, professes his enduring love for Sue, but both remain, unhappily, with their former spouses. When Jude dies one year later, having never realized his ambitions, he is attended only by Arabella and Mrs. Edlin, a family friend.

Major Themes

Hardy called his final novel "a tragedy of unfulfilled aims," and critics have since interpreted *Jude the Obscure* as his most thoroughly pessimistic statement on the inability of human beings to escape the deterministic forces of nature, society, and internal compulsion. For Jude such an escape lay in his dream of attaining a degree from the university at Christminster, yet the reality of Christminster proves wholly unlike Jude's fantasy. Because Jude is unable to enter the university, it becomes a source of bitterness and a symbol of defeat. Likewise, Jude's relationship with Sue Bridehead ultimately yields only futility and leads to another of the crucial conflicts critics perceive in the novel, that between the flesh and the spirit. Unable to give herself physically to Jude, Sue is trapped both by Victorian conventions of marriage and by her deeply held fear of sexuality and desire. Ironically, critics observe, Jude's love for Sue forces him to forsake the spiritual path he had set out for himself at Melchester, as he thinks himself unfit for the Church because of his physical longings for her—longings that she avoids for most of the novel. The result is to reinforce Hardy's overall theme of human inconsequentiality in the face of an insurmountable fate.

Critical Reception

The first complete appearance of *Jude the Obscure* in 1895 provoked a considerable uproar among Hardy's contemporaries. Most negative assessments objected to its frank portrayal of a man and woman living together out of wedlock, taking this to be a critique of the institution of marriage and the religious foundations upon which it is based. Hardy objected, contending that his novel was moral, but soon capitulated. He wrote in his postscript to the 1912 edition of *Jude the Obscure* that these reactions had the effect of "completely curing me of further interest in novel-writing," causing him to devote his literary attentions from that point forward solely to poetic and dramatic works. Still, many during Hardy's lifetime disagreed with this narrow interpretation and hailed the novel as a masterful work of art. Later criticism has generally shared this conclusion. With certain reservations, such as Hardy's occasional lapses into melodrama, critics have acknowledged *Jude the Obscure* as one of the masterpieces of late Victorian literature and a story that offers a glimpse of the ensuing modern era, an age forced to reckon with the crumbling certainties of the past.

CRITICISM

W. D. Howells (essay date 1895)

SOURCE: A review of *Jude the Obscure,* in *Thomas Hardy and His Readers: A Selection of Contemporary Reviews,* edited with a commentary by Laurence Lerner and John Holmstrom, Barnes and Noble Publishers, 1968, pp. 115-17.

[*In the following review, which was originally published in* Harper's Weekly *in December 1895, Howells praises the "artistic excellence" of* Jude the Obscure *and defends it to his contemporaries, many of whom found certain images and events in the narrative displeasing.*]

It has never been quite decided yet, I believe, just what is the kind and what is the quality of pleasure we get from tragedy. A great many people have said what it is, but they seem not to have said this even to their own satisfaction. It is certain that we do get pleasure from tragedy, and it is commonly allowed that the pleasure we get from tragedy is nobler than the pleasure we get from comedy. An alloy of any such pleasure as we get from comedy is held to debase this finer emotion, but this seems true only as to the whole effect of tragedy. The Greek tragedy kept itself purely tragic; the English tragedy assimilated all elements of comedy and made them tragic; so that in the end Hamlet and Macbeth are as high sorrowful as Orestes and Oedipus.

I.

I should be rather ashamed of lugging the classic and the romantic in here, if it were not for the sense I have of the return of an English writer to the Greek motive of tragedy in a book which seems to me one of the most tragical I have read. I have always felt in Mr. Thomas Hardy a charm which I have supposed to be that of the elder pagan world, but this I have found in his lighter moods, for the most part, and chiefly in his study of the eternal-womanly, surviving in certain unconscienced types and characters from a time before Christianity was, and more distinctly before Puritanism was. Now, however, in his latest work he has made me feel our unity with that world in the very essence of his art. He has given me the same pity and despair in view of the blind struggles of his modern English lower-middle-class people that I experience from the destinies of the august figures of Greek fable. I do not know how instinctively or how voluntarily he has appealed to our inherent superstition of Fate, which used to be a religion; but I am sure that in the world where his hapless people have their being, there is not only no Providence, but there is Fate alone; and the environment is such that character itself cannot avail against it. We have back the old conception of an absolutely subject humanity unguided and unfriended. The gods, careless of mankind, are again over all; only, now, they call themselves conditions.

The story is a tragedy, and tragedy almost unrelieved by the humorous touch which the poet is master of. The grotesque is there abundantly, but not the comic; and at times this ugliness heightens the pathos to almost intolerable effect. But I must say that the figure of Jude himself is, in spite of all his weakness and debasement, one of inviolable dignity. He is the sport of fate, but he is never otherwise than sublime; he suffers more for others than for himself. The wretched Sue who spoils his life and her own, helplessly, inevitably, is the kind of fool who finds the fool in the poet and prophet so often, and brings him to naught. She is not less a fool than Arabella herself; though of such exaltation in her folly that we cannot refuse her a throe of compassion, even when she is most perverse. All the characters, indeed, have the appealing quality of human creatures really doing what they must while seeming to do what they will. It is not a question of blaming them or praising them; they are in the necessity of what they do and what they suffer. One may indeed blame the author for presenting such a conception of life; one may say that it is demoralizing if not immoral; but as to his dealing with his creations in the circumstance which he has imagined, one can only praise him for his truth.

The story has to do with some things not hitherto touched in fiction, or Anglo-Saxon fiction at least; and there cannot be any doubt of the duty of criticism to warn the reader that it is not for all readers. But not to affirm the entire purity of the book in these matters would be to fail of another duty of which there can be as little doubt. I do not believe any one can get the slightest harm from any passage of it; only one would rather that innocence were not acquainted with all that virtue may know. Vice can feel nothing but self-abhorrence in the presence of its facts.

II.

The old conventional personifications seem drolly factitious in their reference to the vital reality of this strange book. I suppose it can be called morbid, and I do not deny that it is. But I have not been able to find it untrue, while I know that the world is full of truth that contradicts it. The common experience, or perhaps I had better say the common knowledge of life contradicts it. Commonly, the boy of Jude's strong aspiration and steadfast ambition succeeds and becomes in some measure the sort of man he dreamed of being. Commonly, a girl like Sue flutters through the anguish of her harassed and doubting youth and settles into acquiescence with the ordinary life of women, if not acceptance of it. Commonly, a boy like the son of Jude, oppressed from birth with the sense of being neither loved nor wanted, hardens himself against his misery, fights for the standing denied him, and achieves it. The average Arabella has no reversion to her first love when she has freed herself from it. The average Phillotson does not give up his wife to the man she says she loves, and he does not take her back knowing her loathing for himself. I grant all these things; and yet the author makes me believe that all he says to the contrary inevitably happened.

I allow that there are many displeasing things in the book, and few pleasing. Arabella's dimple-making, the pig-killing, the boy suicide and homicide; Jude's drunken second marriage; Sue's wilful self-surrender to Phillotson; these and other incidents are revolting. They make us shiver with horror and grovel with shame, but we know that they are deeply founded in the condition, if not in the nature of humanity. There are besides these abhorrent facts certain accusations against some accepted formalities of civilization, which I suppose most readers will find hardly less shocking. But I think it is very well for us to ask from time to time the reasons of things, and to satisfy ourselves, if we can, what the reasons are. If the experience of Jude with Arabella seems to arraign marriage, and it is made to appear not only ridiculous but impious that two young, ignorant, impassioned creatures should promise lifelong fealty and constancy when they can have no real sense of what they are doing, and that then they should be held to their rash vow by all the forces of society, it is surely not the lesson of the story that any other relation than marriage is tolerable for the man and woman who live together. Rather it enforces the conviction that marriage is the sole solution of the question of sex, while it shows how atrocious and heinous marriage may sometimes be.

III.

I find myself defending the book on the ethical side when I meant chiefly to praise it for what seems to me its artistic excellence. It has not only the solemn and lofty effect of a great tragedy; a work far faultier might impart this; but it has unity very uncommon in the novel, and especially the English novel. So far as I can recall its incidents there are none but such as seem necessary from the circumstances and the characters. Certain little tricks which the author sometimes uses to help himself out, and which give the sense of insincerity or debility, are absent here. He does not invoke the playful humor which he employs elsewhere. Such humor as there is tastes bitter, and is grim if not sardonic. This tragedy of fate suggests the classic singleness of means as well as the classic singleness of motive.

Edmund Gosse (essay date 1896)

SOURCE: A review of *Jude the Obscure,* in *Thomas Hardy and His Readers: A Selection of Contemporary Reviews,* edited with a commentary by Laurence Lerner and John Holmstrom, Barnes and Noble Publishers, 1968, pp. 117-22.

[*In the following excerpt from a review that originally appeared in* Cosmopolis *in January 1896, Gosse remarks favorably on characterization and plot in* Jude the Obscure, *calling the novel "irresistible." Gosse also notes that the* Jude *wanders into some improprieties, but observes that censure "is the duty of the moralist and not the critic."*]

[*Jude the Obscure*] is a study of four lives, a rectangular problem in failures, drawn with almost mathematical rigidity. The tragedy of these four persons is constructed in a mode almost as geometrical as that in which Dr. Samuel Clarke was wont to prove the existence of the Deity. It is difficult not to believe that the author set up his four ninepins in the wilds of Wessex, and built up his theorem round them. Here is an initial difficulty. Not quite thus is theology or poetry conveniently composed; we like to conceive that the relation of the parts was more spontaneous, we like to feel that the persons of a story have been thrown up in a jet of enthusiasm, not put into a cave of theory to be slowly covered with stalactite.

Jude the Obscure is acted in North Wessex (Berkshire) and just across the frontier, at Christminster (Oxford), which is not in Wessex at all. We want our novelist back among the rich orchards of the Hintocks, and where the water-lilies impede the lingering river at Shottsford Ash. Berkshire is an unpoetical county, 'meanly utilitarian,' as Mr. Hardy confesses; the imagination hates its concave, loamy cornfields and dreary, hedgeless highways. The local history has been singularly tampered with in Berkshire; it is useless to speak to us of ancient records where the past is all obliterated, and the thatched and dormered houses replaced by modern cottages. In choosing North Wessex as the scene of a novel Mr. Hardy wilfully deprives himself of a great element of his strength. Where there are no prehistoric monuments, no ancient buildings, no mossed and immemorial woodlands, he is Samson shorn. In Berkshire, the change which is coming over England so rapidly, the resignation of the old dreamy elements of beauty, has proceeded further than anywhere else in Wessex. Pastoral loveliness is to be discovered only here and there, while in Dorsetshire it still remains the master-element. All this combines to lessen the physical charm of *Jude the Obscure* to those who turn from it in memory to *Far from the Madding Crowd* and *The Return of the Native.*

But, this fortuitous absence of beauty being acknowledged, the novelist's hand shows no falling off in the vigour and reality of his description. It may be held, in fact, to be a lesser feat to raise before us an enchanting vision of the valley of the Froom, than successfully to rivet our attention on the prosaic arable land encircling the dull hamlet of Marygreen.

To pass from the landscape to the persons, two threads of action seem to be intertwined in *Jude the Obscure*. We have, first of all, the contrast between the ideal life the young peasant of scholarly instincts wished to lead, and the squalid real life into which he was fated to sink. We have, secondly, the almost rectilinear puzzle of the sexual relations of the four principal characters. Mr. Hardy has wished to show how cruel destiny can be to the eternal dream of youth, and he has undertaken to trace the lamentable results of unions in a family exhausted by intermarriage and poverty. Some collision is apparent between these aims; the first seems to demand a poet, the second a physician. The Fawleys are a decayed and wasted race, in the last of whom, Jude, there appears, with a kind of flicker in the socket, a certain intellectual and artistic brightness. In favourable surroundings, we feel that this young man might have become fairly distinguished as a scholar, or as a sculptor. But at the supreme moment, or at each supreme moment, the conditions hurl him back into insignificance. When we examine clearly what these conditions are, we find them to be instinctive. He is just going to develop into a lad of education, when Arabella throws her hideous missile at him, and he sinks with her into a resigned inferiority.

So far, the critical court is with Mr. Hardy; these scenes and their results give a perfect impression of truth. Later on, it is not quite evident whether the claim on Jude's passions, or the inherent weakness of his inherited character, is the source of his failure. Perhaps both. But it is difficult to see what part Oxford has in his destruction, or how Mr. Hardy can excuse the rhetorical diatribes against the university which appear towards the close of the book. Does the novelist really think that it was the duty of the heads of houses to whom Jude wrote his crudely pathetic letters to offer him immediately a fellowship? We may admit to the full the pathos of Jude's position—nothing is more heart-rending than the obscurity of the half-educated—but surely, the fault did not lie with Oxford.

The scene at Commemoration (Part VI.) is of a marvellous truth and vividness of presentment, but it would be stronger, and even more tragic, if Mr. Hardy did not appear in it as an advocate taking sides with his unhappy hero. In this portion of his work, it seems to me, Mr. Hardy had but to paint—as clearly and as truthfully as he could—the hopes, the struggles, the disappointments of Jude, and of these he has woven a tissue of sombre colouring, indeed, and even of harsh threads, but a tapestry worthy of a great imaginative writer. It was straightforward poet's work in invention and observation, and he has executed it well.

. . . It does not appear to me that we have any business to call in question the right of a novelist of Mr. Hardy's extreme distinction to treat what themes he will. We may wish—and I for my part cordially wish—that more pleasing, more charming plots than this could take his fancy. But I do not feel at liberty to challenge his discretion. One thing, however, the critic of comparative literature must note. We have, in such a book as *Jude the Obscure,* traced the full circle of propriety. A hundred and fifty years ago, Fielding and Smollett brought up before us pictures, used expressions, described conduct, which appeared to their immediate successors a little more crude than general reading warranted. In Miss Burney's hands and in Miss Austen's, the morals were still further hedged about. Scott was even more daintily reserved. We came at last to Dickens, where the clamorous passions of mankind, the coarser accidents of life, were absolutely ignored, and the whole question of population seemed reduced to the theory of the gooseberry bush. This was the *ne plus ultra* of decency; Thackeray and George Eliot relaxed this intensity of prudishness; once on the turn, the tide flowed rapidly, and here is Mr. Hardy ready to say any mortal thing that Fielding said, and a good deal more too.

So much we note, but to censure it, if it calls for censure, is the duty of the moralist and not the critic. Criticism asks how the thing is done, whether the execution is fine and convincing. To tell so squalid and so abnormal a story in an interesting way is in itself a feat, and this, it must be universally admitted, Mr. Hardy has achieved. *Jude the Obscure* is an irresistible book; it is one of those novels into which we descend and are carried on by a steady impetus to the close, when we return, dazzled, to the light of common day. The two women, in particular, are surely created by a master. Every impulse, every speech, which reveals to us the coarse and animal, but not hateful Arabella, adds to the solidity of her portrait. We may dislike her, we may hold her intrusion into our consciousness a disagreeable one, but of her reality there can be no question: Arabella lives.

It is conceivable that not so generally will it be admitted that Sue Bridehead is convincing. Arabella is the excess of vulgar normality; every public bar and village fair knows Arabella, but Sue is a strange and unwelcome product of exhaustion. The *vita sexualis* of Sue is the central interest of the book, and enough is told about it to fill the specimen tables of a German specialist. Fewer testimonies will be given to her reality than to Arabella's because hers is much the rarer case. But her picture is not less admirably drawn; Mr. Hardy has, perhaps, never devoted so much care to the portrait of a woman. She is a poor, maimed 'degenerate,' ignorant of herself and of the perversion of her instincts, full of febrile, amiable illusions, ready to dramatise her empty life, and play at loving though she cannot love. Her adventure with the undergraduate has not taught her what she is; she quits Phillotson still ignorant of the source of her repulsion; she lives with Jude, after a long, agonising struggle, in a relation that she accepts with distaste, and when the trag-

edy comes, and her children are killed, her poor extravagant brain slips one grade further down, and she sees in this calamity the chastisement of God. What has she done to be chastised? She does not know, but supposes it must be her abandonment of Philottson, to whom, in a spasm of self-abasement, and shuddering with repulsion, she returns without a thought for the misery of Jude. It is a terrible study in pathology, but of the splendid success of it, of the sustained intellectual force implied in the evolution of it, there cannot, I think, be two opinions.

One word must be added about the speech of the author and of the characters in *Jude the Obscure.* Is it too late to urge Mr. Hardy to struggle against the jarring note of rebellion which seems growing upon him? It sounded in *Tess,* and here it is, more roughly expressed, further acerbated. What has Providence done to Mr. Hardy that he should rise up in the arable land of Wessex and shake his fist at his Creator? He should not force his talent, should not give way to these chimerical outbursts of philosophy falsely so called. His early romances were full of calm and lovely pantheism; he seemed in them to feel the deep-hued country landscapes full of rural gods, all homely and benign. We wish he would go back to Egdon Heath and listen to the singing in the heather. . . .

A fact about the infancy of Mr. Hardy has escaped the interviewers and may be recorded here. On the day of his birth, during a brief absence of his nurse, there slipped into the room an ethereal creature, known as the Spirit of Plastic Beauty. Bending over the cradle she scattered roses on it, and as she strewed them she blessed the babe. 'He shall have an eye to see moral and material loveliness, he shall speak of richly-coloured pastoral places in the accent of Theocritus, he shall write in such a way as to cajole busy men into a sympathy with old, unhappy, far-off things.' She turned and went, but while the nurse still delayed, a withered termagant glided into the room. From her apron she dropped toads among the rose-leaves, and she whispered: 'I am the genius of False Rhetoric, and led by me he shall say things ugly and coarse, not recognising them to be so, and shall get into a rage about matters that call for philosophic calm, and shall spoil some of his best passages with pedantry and incoherency. He shall not know what things belong to his peace, and he shall plague his most loyal admirers with the barbaric contortions of his dialogue.' So saying, she put out her snaky tongue at the unoffending babe, and ever since, his imagination, noble as it is, and attuned to the great harmonies of nature, is liable at a moment's notice to give a shriek of discord. The worst, however, which any honest critic can say of *Jude the Obscure* is that the fairy godmother seems, for the moment, to have relaxed her guardianship a little unduly.

Margaret Oliphant (essay date 1896)

SOURCE: A review of *Jude the Obscure,* in *Thomas Hardy and His Readers: A Selection of Contemporary Reviews,* edited with a commentary by Laurence Lerner and John Holmstrom, Barnes and Noble Publishers, 1968, pp. 126-30.

[*In the following excerpt from a review originally published in* Blackwood's Magazine *in January 1896, Oliphant describes* Jude the Obscure *"as an assault on the stronghold of marriage."*]

THE ANTI-MARRIAGE LEAGUE

[The] inclination towards the treatment of subjects hitherto considered immoral or contrary to good manners, in the widest sense of the words—and the disposition to place what is called the Sex-question above all others as the theme of fiction—has gradually acquired the importance of a *parti pris*. It may be said that this question has always been the leading subject of romance; but this never in the sense of the words as now used. Love has been the subject of romance, and all the obstacles that have always come in its way, and the devotion and faithfulness of Lovers, the chosen Two, the perennial hero and heroine in whom the simpler ideals of life have been concentrated. What is now freely discussed as the physical part of the question, and treated as the most important, has hitherto been banished from the lips of decent people, and as much as possible from their thoughts; but is now freely given forth as the favourite subject for the chatter of girls, who no doubt in a great number of cases know nothing about what they are talking of, and therefore are more or less to be pardoned for following a hideous fashion which has the never-exhausted charm of shocking and startling everybody around. Indeed one of the things most conspicuous in this new method is the curious development of shameless Innocence, more dangerous than folly, more appalling almost than vice, because one does not know at any moment into what miserable quagmire its bold and ignorant feet may stumble. . . .

. . . Nothing, I think, but a theory could explain the wonderful want of perception which induces a man full of perceptions to make a mistake so fundamental; but it is done—and thus unconsciously affords us the strangest illustration of what Art can come to when given over to the exposition of the unclean. The present writer does not pretend to a knowledge of the works of Zola, which perhaps she ought to have before presuming to say that nothing so coarsely indecent as the whole history of Jude in his relations with his wife Arabella has ever been put in English print—that is to say, from the hands of a Master. There may be books more disgusting, more impious as regards human nature, more foul in detail, in those dark corners where the amateurs of filth find garbage to their taste; but not, we repeat, from any Master's hand. . . .

We can with difficulty guess what is Mr Hardy's motive in portraying such a struggle. It can scarcely be said to be one of those attacks upon the institution of Marriage, which is the undisguised inspiration of some of the other books before us. It is marriage indeed which in the begin-

ning works Jude's woe; and it is by marriage, or rather the marrying of himself and others, that his end is brought about. We rather think the author's object must be, having glorified women by the creation of Tess, to show after all what destructive and ruinous creatures they are, in general circumstances and in every development, whether brutal or refined. Arabella, the first—the pig-dealer's daughter, whose native qualities have been ripened by the experiences of a barmaid—is the Flesh, unmitigated by any touch of human feeling except that of merciless calculation as to what will be profitable for herself. She is the native product of the fields, the rustic woman, exuberant and overflowing with health, vanity, and appetite. The colloquy between her and her fellows in their disgusting work, after her first almost equally disgusting interview with Jude, is one of the most unutterable foulness—a shame to the language in which it is recorded and suggested; and the picture altogether of the country lasses at their outdoor work is more brutal in depravity than anything which the darkest slums could bring forth, as are the scenes in which their good advice is carried out. Is it possible that there are readers in England to whom this infamy can be palatable, and who, either in inadvertence or in wantonness, can *make it pay?* Mr Hardy informs us he has taken elaborate precautions to secure the double profit of the serial writer, by subduing his colours and diminishing his effects, in the presence of the less corrupt, so as to keep the perfection of filthiness for those who love it. It would be curious to compare in this unsavoury traffic how much of the sickening essence of his story Mr Hardy has thought his first public could stomach, and how many edifying details he has put in for the enlightenment of those who have no squeamish scruples to get over. The transaction is insulting to the public, with whom he trades the viler wares under another name, with all the suppressed passages restored, as old-book dealers say in their catalogues, recommending their ancient scandal to the amateurs of the unclean. It is not the first time Mr Hardy has adopted this expedient. If the English public supports him in it, it will be to the shame of every individual who thus confesses himself to like and accept what the author himself acknowledges to be unfit for the eyes—not of girls and young persons only, but of the ordinary reader,—the men and women who read the Magazines, the public whom we address in these pages. That the prophets should prophesy falsely is not the most important fact in national degradation: it is only when the people love to have it so that the climax is attained.

The other woman—who makes virtue vicious by keeping the physical facts of one relationship in life in constant prominence by denying, as Arabella does by satisfying them, and even more skilfully and insistently than Arabella—the fantastic *raisonneuse,* Susan, completes the circle of the unclean. . . . This woman we are required to accept as the type of high-toned purity. It is the women who are the active agents in all this unsavoury imbroglio: the story is carried on, and life is represented as carried on, entirely by their means. The men are passive, suffering, rather good than otherwise, victims of these and of fate. Not only do they never dominate, but they are quite incapable of holding their own against these remorseless ministers of destiny, these determined operators, managing all the machinery of life so as to secure their own way. This is one of the most curious developments of recent fiction. It is perhaps natural that it should be more or less the case in books written by women, to whom the mere facility of representing their their own sex acts as a primary reason for giving them the chief place in the scene. But it has now still more markedly, though much less naturally, become the method with men, in the hands of many of whom women have returned to the *rôle* of the temptress given to them by the old monkish sufferers of ancient times, who fled to the desert, like Anthony, to get free of them, but even there barely escaped with their lives from the seductions of the sirens, who were so audacious as to follow them to the very scene of the macerations and miseries into which the unhappy men plunged to escape from their toils. In the books of the younger men, it is now the woman who seduces—it is no longer the man.

This, however, is a consideration by the way. I have said that it is not clear what Mr Hardy's motive is in the history of Jude: but, on reconsideration, it becomes more clear that it is intended as an assault on the stronghold of marriage, which is now beleaguered on every side. The motto is, 'The letter killeth'; and I presume this must refer to the fact of Jude's early and unwilling union to Arabella, and that the lesson the novelist would have us learn is, that if marriage were not exacted, and people were free to form connections as the spirit moves them, none of these complications would have occurred, and all would have been well. 'There seemed to him, vaguely and dimly, something wrong in a social ritual which made necessary the cancelling of well-formed schemes involving years of thought and labour, of foregoing a man's one opportunity of showing himself superior to the lower animals, and of contributing his units of work to the general progress of his generation, because of a momentary surprise by a new and transitory instinct which had nothing in it of the nature of vice, and could be only at the most called weakness.' This is the hero's own view of the circumstances which, in obedience to the code of honour prevalent in the country-side, compelled his marriage. Suppose, however, that instead of upsetting the whole framework of society, Jude had shown himself superior to the lower animals by not yielding to that new and transitory influence, the same result could have been easily attained: and he might then have met and married Susan and lived happy ever after, without demanding a total overthrow of all existing laws and customs to prevent him from being unhappy. Had it been made possible for him to have visited Arabella as long as the new and transitory influence lasted, and then to have lived with Susan as long as she pleased to permit him to do so, which was the best that could happen were marriage abolished, how would that have altered the circumstances? When Susan changed her mind would he have been less

unhappy? when Arabella claimed him again would he have been less weak? . . .

Havelock Ellis (essay date 1896)

SOURCE: A review of *Jude the Obscure*, in *Thomas Hardy and His Readers: A Selection of Contemporary Reviews*, edited with a commentary by Laurence Lerner and John Holmstrom, Barnes and Noble Publishers, 1968, pp. 138-44.

[*In the following excerpted review, originally published in* The Savoy *in October 1896, Ellis calls* Jude the Obscure *"a singularly fine piece of art," adding "this book, it is said, is immoral, and indecent as well. So are most of our great novels."*]

. . . Your wholesome-minded novelist knows that the life of a pure-natured Englishwoman after marriage is, as Taine said, mainly that of a very broody hen, a series of merely physiological processes with which he, as a novelist, has no further concern.

But in novels, as in life, one comes at length to realize that marriage is not necessarily either a grave, or a convent gate, or a hen's nest, that though the conditions are changed the forces at work remain largely the same. It is still quite possible to watch the passions at play, though there may now be more tragedy or more pathos in the outcome of that play. This Mr. Hardy proceeded to do, first on a small scale in short stories, and then on a larger scale. . . .

I was not without suspicion in approaching ***Jude the Obscure***. Had Mr. Hardy discovered the pernicious truth that whereas children can only take their powders in jam, the strenuous British public cannot be induced to devour their jam unless convinced that it contains some strange and nauseous powder? Was ***Jude the Obscure*** a sermon on marriage from the text on the title-page: 'The letter killeth'? Putting-aside the small failures always liable to occur in Mr. Hardy's work, I found little to justify the suspicion. The sermon may, possibly, be there, but the spirit of art has, at all events, not been killed. In all the great qualities of literature ***Jude the Obscure*** seems to me the greatest novel written in England for many years.

It is interesting to compare ***Jude*** with a characteristic novel of Mr. Hardy's earlier period, with ***A Pair of Blue Eyes,*** or ***The Return of the Native***. On going back to these, after reading ***Jude,*** one notes the graver and deeper tones in the later book, the more austere and restrained roads of art which Mr. Hardy has sought to follow, and the more organic and radical way in which he now grips the individuality of his creatures. The individuals themselves have not fundamentally changed. The type of womankind that Mr. Hardy chiefly loves to study, from Cytherea to Sue, has always been the same, very human, also very feminine, rarely with any marked element of virility, and so contrasting curiously with the androgynous heroines loved of Mr. Meredith. The latter, with their resolute daring and energy, are of finer calibre and more imposing; they are also very much rarer in the actual world than Mr. Hardy's women, who represent, it seems to me, a type not uncommon in the south of England, where the heavier Teutonic and Scandinavian elements are, more than elsewhere, modified by the alert and volatile elements furnished by earlier races. But if the type remains the same the grasp of it is now much more thorough. At first Mr. Hardy took these women chiefly at their more obviously charming or pathetic moments, and sought to make the most of those moments, a little careless as to the organic connection of such moments to the underlying personality. One can well understand that many readers should prefer the romantic charm of the earlier passages, but—should it be necessary to affirm?—to grapple with complexly realized persons and to dare to face them in the tragic or sordid crises of real life is to rise to a higher plane of art. In *Jude the Obscure* there is a fine self-restraint, a complete mastery of all the elements of an exceedingly human story. There is nothing here of the distressing melodrama into which Mr. Hardy was wont to fall in his early novels. Yet in plot *Jude* might be a farce. One could imagine that Mr. Hardy had purposed to himself to take a conventional farce, in which a man and a woman leave their respective partners to make love to one another and then finally rejoin their original partners, in order to see what could be made of such a story by an artist whose sensitive vision penetrated to the tragic irony of things; just as the great novelists of old, De la Sale, Cervantes, Fielding, took the worn-out conventional stories of their time, and filled them with the immortal blood of life. Thus *Jude* has a certain symmetry of plan such as is rare in the actual world—where we do not so readily respond to our cues—but to use such a plot to produce such an effect is an achievement of the first order. . . .

But I understand that the charge brought against *Jude the Obscure* is not so much that it is bad art as that it is a book with a purpose, a moral or an immoral purpose, according to the standpoint of the critic. It would not be pleasant to admit that a book you thought bad morality is good art, but the bad morality is the main point, and this book, it is said, is immoral, and indecent as well.

So are most of our great novels. . . .

. . . It seems, indeed, on a review of all the facts, that the surer a novel is of a certain immortality, the surer it is also to be regarded at first as indecent, as subversive of public morality. So that when, as in the present case, such charges are recklessly flung about in all the most influential quarters, we are simply called upon to accept them placidly as necessary incidents in the career of a great novel.

It is no fortuitous circumstance that the greatest achievements of the novelist's art seem to outrage morality. *Jude the Obscure* is a sufficiently great book to serve to illustrate a first principle. I have remarked that I cannot find any undue intrusion of morality in the art of this book. But I was careful to express myself cautiously, for without doubt the greatest issues of social morality are throughout at stake. So that the question arises: What is the function of the novelist as regards morals? The answer is simple, though it has sometimes been muddled. A few persons have incautiously asserted that the novel has nothing to do with morals. That we cannot assert; the utmost that can be asserted is that the novelist should never allow himself to be made the tool of a merely moral or immoral purpose. For the fact is that, so far as the moralist deals with life at all, morals is part of the very stuff of his art. That is to say, that his art lies in drawing the sinuous woof of human nature between the rigid warp of morals. Take away morals, and the novelist is *in vacuo,* in the region of fairy land. The more subtly and firmly he can weave these elements together the more impressive becomes the stuff of his art. The great poet may be in love with passion, but it is by heightening and strengthening the dignity of traditional moral law that he gives passion fullest play. When Wagner desired to create a typically complete picture of passion he chose the story of Tristram; no story of Paul and Virginia can ever bring out the deepest cries of human passion. Shakespeare found it impossible to picture even the pure young love of Romeo and Juliet without the aid of the violated laws of family and tradition. 'The crash of broken commandments,' Mr. Hardy once wrote in a magazine article, 'is as necessary an accompaniment to the catastrophe of a tragedy as the noise of drum and cymbals to a triumphal march;' and that picturesque image fails to express how essential to the dramatist is this clash of law against passion. It is the same in life as in art, and if you think of the most pathetic stories of human passion, the profoundest utterances of human love, you probably think most readily of such things as the letters of Abélard and Héloise, or of Mlle. de Lespinasse, or of the Portuguese nun, and only with difficulty of the tamer speech of happier and more legitimate emotions. Life finds her game in playing off the irresistible energy of the individual against the equally irresistible energy of the race, and the stronger each is the finer the game. So the great artist whose brain is afire with the love of passion yet magnifies the terror and force of moral law, in his heart probably hates it.

Mr. Hardy has always been in love with Nature, with the instinctive, spontaneous, unregarded aspects of Nature, from the music of the dead heatherbells to the flutter of tremulous human hearts, all the things that are beautiful because they are uncontrolled by artificial constraint. The progress of his art has consisted in bringing this element of nature into ever closer contact with the rigid routine of life, making it more human, making it more moral or more immoral. It is an inevitable progression. That love of the spontaneous, the primitive, the unbound—which we call the love of 'Nature'—must as it becomes more searching take more and more into account those things, also natural, which bind and constrain 'Nature.' So that on the one side, as Mr. Hardy has himself expressed it, we have Nature and her unconsciousness of all but essential law, on the other the laws framed merely as social expedients without a basis in the heart of things, and merely expressing the triumph of the majority over the individual; which shows, as is indeed evident from Mr. Hardy's work, that he is not much in sympathy with Society, and also shows that, like Heyse, he recognizes a moral order in Nature. This conflict reaches its highest point around women. Truly or falsely, for good or for evil, woman has always been for man the supreme priestess, or the supreme devil, of Nature. 'A woman,' said Proudhon—himself the incarnation of the revolt of Nature in the heart of man—'even the most charming and virtuous woman, always contains an element of cunning, the wild beast element. She is a tamed animal that sometimes returns to her natural instinct. This cannot be said in the same degree of man.' The loving student of the elemental in Nature so becomes the loving student of women, the sensitive historian of her conflicts with 'sin' and with 'repentance,' the creations of man. Not, indeed, that any woman who has 'sinned,' if her sin was indeed love, ever really 'repents.' It is probable that a true experience of the one emotional state as of the other remains a little foreign to her, 'sin' having probably been the invention of men who never really knew what love is. She may catch the phrases of the people around her when her spirit is broken, but that is all. I have never known or heard of any woman, having for one moment in her life loved and been loved, who did not count that moment as worth all other moments in life. The consciousness of the world's professed esteem can never give to unloved virtue and respectability the pride which belongs to the woman who has once 'sinned' with all her heart. One supposes that the slaves of old who never once failed in abject obedience to their master's will mostly subdued their souls to the level of their starved virtues. But the woman who has loved is like the slave who once at least in his life has risen in rebellion with the cry: 'And I, too, am a man!' Nothing that comes after can undo the fine satisfaction of that moment. It was so that a great seventeenth-century predecessor of Mr. Hardy in the knowledge of the heart, painted Annabella exultant in her sin even at the moment of discovery, for 'Nature' knows no sin.

If these things are so, it is clear how the artist who has trained himself to the finest observation of Nature cannot fail, as his art becomes more vital and profound, to paint morals. The fresher and more intimate his vision of Nature, the more startling his picture of morals. To such an extent is this the case in *Jude the Obscure,* that some people have preferred to regard the book as a study of monstrosity, of disease. Sue is neurotic, some critics say; it is fashionable to play cheerfully with terrible words you know nothing about. 'Neurotic' these good people say by way of dismissing her, innocently unaware that many a charming 'urban miss' of their own acquaintance would deserve the name at least as well. In representing Jude and Sue as belonging to a failing family stock, I take it that Mr. Hardy by no means wished to bring before us a mere monstrosity, a pathological 'case,' but that rather, with an artist's true instinct—the same instinct

that moved so great an artist as Shakespeare when he conceived *Hamlet*—he indicates the channels of least resistance along which the forces of life most impetuously rush. Jude and Sue are represented as crushed by a civilization to which they were not born, and though civilization may in some respects be regarded as a disease and as unnatural, in others it may be said to bring out those finer vibrations of Nature which are overlaid by rough and bucolic conditions of life. The refinement of sexual sensibility with which this book largely deals is precisely such a vibration. To treat Jude, who wavers between two women, and Sue, who finds the laws of marriage too mighty for her lightly-poised organism, as shocking monstrosities, reveals a curious attitude in the critics who have committed themselves to that view. Clearly they consider human sexual relationships to be as simple as those of the farmyard. They are as shocked as a farmer would be to find that a hen had views of her own concerning the lord of the harem. If, let us say, you decide that Indian Game and Plymouth Rock make a good cross, you put your cock and hens together, and the matter is settled; and if you decide that a man and a woman are in love with each other, you marry them and the matter is likewise settled for the whole term of their natural lives. I suppose that the farmyard view really is the view of the ordinary wholesome-minded novelist—I mean of course in England—and of his ordinary critic. Indeed in Europe generally, a distinguished German anthropologist has lately declared, sensible and experienced men still often exhibit a knowledge of sexual matters such as we might expect from a milkmaid. But assuredly the farmyard view corresponds imperfectly to the facts of human life in our time. Such things as 'Jude' is made of are, in our time at all events, life, and life is still worthy of her muse. . . .

To sum up, *Jude the Obscure* seems to me—in such a matter one can only give one's own impressions for what they are worth—a singularly fine piece of art, when we remember the present position of the English novel. It is the natural outcome of Mr. Hardy's development, along lines that are genuinely and completely English. It deals very subtly and sensitively with new and modern aspects of life, and if, in so doing, it may be said to represent Nature as often cruel to our social laws, we must remark that the strife of Nature and Society, the individual and the community, has ever been the artist's opportunity. 'Matrimony have growed to be that serious in these days,' Widow Edlin remarks, 'that one really do feel afeard to move in it at all.' It is an affectation to pretend that the farmyard theory of life still rules unquestioned, and that there are no facts to justify Mrs. Edlin. If anyone will not hear her, let him turn to the Registrar-General. Such facts are in our civilisation to-day. We have no right to resent the grave and serious spirit with which Mr. Hardy, in the maturity of his genius, has devoted his best art to picture some of these facts. In *Jude the Obscure* we find for the first time in our literature the reality of marriage clearly recognized as something wholly apart from the mere ceremony with which our novelists have usually identified it. Others among our novelists may have tried to deal with the reality rather than with its shadow, but assuredly not with the audacity, purity and sincerity of an artist who is akin in spirit to the great artists of our best dramatic age, to Fletcher and Heywood and Ford, rather than to the powerful though often clumsy novelists of the eighteenth century.

There is one other complaint often brought against this book, I understand, by critics usually regarded as intelligent, and with the mention of it I have done. 'Mr. Hardy finds that marriage often leads to tragedy,' they say, 'but he shows us no way out of these difficulties; he does not tell us his own plans for the improvement of marriage and the promotion of morality.' Let us try to consider this complaint with due solemnity. It is true that the artist is god in his own world; but being so he has too fine a sense of the etiquette of creation to presume to offer suggestions to the creator of the actual world, suggestions which might be resented, and would almost certainly not be adopted. An artist's private opinions concerning the things that are good and bad in the larger world are sufficiently implicit in the structure of his own smaller world; the counsel that he should make them explicit in a code of rules and regulations for humanity at large is a counsel which, as every artist knows, can only come from the Evil One. This complaint against *Jude the Obscure* could not have arisen save among a generation which has battened on moral and immoral tracts thrown into the form of fiction by ingenious novices. The only cure for it one can suggest is a course of great European novels from *Petit Jehan de Saintré* downwards. One suggestion indeed occurs for such consolation as it may yield. Has it not been left to our century to discover that the same hand which wrote the disordered philosophy of *Hamlet* put the times into joint again in 'The New Atlantis,' and may not posterity find Thomas Hardy's hand in 'Looking Backward' and 'The Strike of a Sex?' Thus for these critics of *Jude* there may yet be balm in Utopia.

Arthur Mizener (essay date 1940)

SOURCE: "*Jude the Obscure* As a Tragedy", in *Southern Review,* Vol. 6, 1940-41, pp. 193-213.

[*In the following essay, Mizener argues that* Jude the Obscure *is not a tragedy in the sense that it represents the contrast between the ideal life and the "permanently squalid real life of man," but rather a "history of a worthy man's education."*]

> ... *who cannot see*
> *What Earth's ingrained conditions are.*
> —*"Seventy-four and Twenty."*

I suppose no one will question Hardy's right to the title of "the first great tragedian in novel form," taking *tragedy* in its looser sense. Yet there seems to be a general feeling that somehow his novels are not successful, are not, for all their deep sense of the horror of ordinary life, really tragic. "There is," as Mr. E. M. Forster says, "some vital problem that has not been answered, or even posed, in the misfortunes of Jude the Obscure." The cause of that feeling is, I think, an attitude which is probably more the product of his age than of Hardy's own understanding. In a sense the courage of Hardy's profoundest conviction failed him, precisely as Tennyson's did, under the pressure of the reasoning of his age.

Hardy, to be sure, refused to identify what he called "the ideal life" with the conventional views of his times, and this refusal saved him from the superior fatuousness of people like Tennyson and Browning at their worst. He could, indeed, be devastating about these conventional views: "How could smug Christian optimism worthy of a dissenting grocer find a place inside a man [Browning] who was so vast a seer and feeler when on neutral ground?" Yet at bottom Hardy's attitude suffered from the same kind of fault as Browning's. Browning tried to convince himself that because God was in his heaven all must be right with the world. Hardy's objection to this view of things was that it believed in heaven at all; for Hardy, using Browning's logic in reverse, tried to convince himself that because all was obviously not right with the world, there could be no heaven. The only source of hope left him, therefore, was the belief that the world would, by a process of moral evolution, become a kind of heaven in time. This kind of hope was the only kind Hardy could discover, once he had denied any independent reality to the dream of perfection, and without some hope not only tragedy but life itself is impossible.

The trouble with this view, for tragedy, is that its possessor is incapable of facing squarely the paradox of evil. Browning felt that, having accepted the proposition that God is the all-great and the all-loving too, he had committed himself to a denial of evil; life was therefore an exhilarating battle in which one proved his worth for heaven—

> Only they see not God, I know,
> Nor all that chivalry of his,
> The soldier-saints who, row on row,
>
> Burn upward each to his point of bliss—
> Since, the end of life being manifest,
> He had burned his way thro' the world to this.

Hardy, feeling profoundly the ingrained evil of human and animal life, thought that feeling committed him to a denial of heaven. Thus both Browning and Hardy found it impossible not to deny, for the sake of a smaller consistency, one of the realities which must be recognized and accepted for the larger consistency of tragedy. Both found it impossible to believe in "the goodness of God" and "the horrors of human and animal life"; neither, in Keats's phrase, was "capable of being in uncertainties, mysteries, doubts, without any irritable reaching after fact and reason." They felt called upon either to explain the real life as a logical corollary of the ideal life, or to explain the ideal life as a logical corollary of the real. They were thus incapable of representing in the same fiction the meaning and splendor of both lives and of using each to illuminate the limitations of the other.

But this inability to escape the smaller consistency was the central weakness of late nineteenth-century literature as a whole: "there is the assumption that Truth is indifferent or hostile to the desires of men; that these desires were formerly nurtured on legend, myth, all kinds of insufficient experiment; that, Truth being known at last in the form of experimental science, it is intellectually impossible to maintain illusion any longer, at the same time that it is morally impossible to assimilate Truth." It is in this sense that Hardy's attitude is more the product of his age than of his own understanding. It is probably more remarkable, under the circumstances, that he came as close as he did to escaping from the trap his age unconsciously set for itself than that he was, in the end, caught.

The code Hardy evolved as a description of the ideal life is a secularized version of the Sermon on the Mount, a thoroughly fumigated New Testament morality. The real subject of *Jude* is the evolution of this code in Jude's mind ("a species of Dick Whittington, whose spirit was touched to finer issues than a mere material gain"). In so far as this code is a statement of the potentialities of humanity, it is the possibility of their realization somewhere, somehow, which gives Jude's death meaning. In so far as it is not a statement of the potentialities of humanity Jude is mad and his death meaningless: this alternative was obviously no part of Hardy's intention. But Hardy had no place outside of the actual world of time where he could visualize these potentialities as being realized; he saw no possibility that the nothing of death itself, when the long sickness of health and living begins to mend, would bring all things. So he ended by implying the realization of these human potentialities in this world; ended, that is, by denying his most profound conviction, that earth's conditions are ingrained. And if it is difficult to believe that life is evil and God good, it is even more difficult to believe that the evil of life is ingrained and that it will nevertheless presently come unstuck.

That Hardy produced such powerful novels, in spite of his inability to conceive an ideal life with an existence either very strong or outside of time and in spite of the formal limitations which this attitude inevitably imposed on him, is a tribute to his profound rectitude: The power of Hardy's novels is the power of Hardy's character; the consistency and purity of the feeling throughout both the novels and the poems proves that his vision of evil is, quite simply, what he saw. Such feeling cannot be faked. This power makes itself felt in spite of Hardy's fumbling inability to think his way through to an understanding of his personal impressions or to a form which would organize them in terms of their meaning.

2

About his idea in *Jude* Hardy was quite explicit: *Jude* was "to show the contrast between the ideal life a man

wished to lead, and the squalid real life he was fated to lead. . . . [This] idea was meant to run all through the novel." It was to be a tragedy "of the WORTHY encompassed by the INEVITABLE." Such an idea requires for its successful representation a form which is consciously an artifice, a verisimilar and plausible narrative which the novelist values, not for its own sake, but as the perfect vehicle for his idea. He must keep his narrative alive at every turn with his idea, for he cannot, once committed to it, afford the luxury of a meaningless appeal to his reader's delight in recognition and suspense. The characters of such a novel, as Aristotle said of the characters in the tragedy of his day, are there for the sake of the action, and the action or fable is there, ultimately, for the sake of the idea—*is* the idea.

Yet Hardy, with such an essentially tragic idea never freed himself wholly from the naturalistic assumption that narrative must be significant historically rather than fabulously. In the case of *Jude* this assumption forced him to identify himself as author with his hero instead of with the action as a whole. Jude is not a character in a larger composition, the dramatization of one of several presented points of view which go together to make up the author's attitude, because Hardy's attitude was not complex and inclusive but simple and exclusive. He therefore sought to contrast the ideal life with the real life, not of man but of *a* man. That is to say, he wrote a naturalistic novel, a history of his hero, in which the hero is the author, for Jude is obviously autobiographical in the general sense. The essential meaning of his fiction for Hardy is its narrative or "historical" meaning, and Jude's understanding of that history is Hardy's. All that the narrative which is a perfect artifice ever proves according to Hardy is the historical existence of a "consummate artist"; all that it even tempts us to believe in is the historical reality of the events it presents. Hardy never really faced the possibility that a great work of art aims at a kind of truth superior (but not necessarily contradictory) to a scientific and historical verisimilitude. For Hardy, therefore, the true narrative was one which conformed to a historical conception of the truth from which the fabulous was very carefully excluded; and the truest of these was, in the general sense, autobiographical, since only the man who had lived through experiences generally like those described in the narrative could represent with historical accuracy not only the external events but the thoughts and opinions of a participant in these events.

Yet because Hardy had an idea he was not content simply to tell a story. If that idea was not finely enough conceived to drive him to discard the naturalistic form, it was strong enough to make him stretch that form to the breaking point by the use of devices which have no place in his kind of novel. There is, for example, nothing to be said against the use of a certain amount of coincidence in the novel which is consistently an artifice, but it only weakens a novel which depends for its acceptance on the reader's conviction of the distinguishably historical truth of its hero's career. In the same way Hardy's carefully devised contrasts fail of their full purpose because he is writing a novel at whose center there is no final contrast. These contrasts are not, therefore, means for enriching a central contrast between a vision of the ideal life and a vision of the real life; they are but means for contrasting a single view of things, which is true, with all other views of things, which are false. And this is the contrast of melodrama rather than of tragedy. In the same way, too, Hardy's use of symbolic incident, for all its immense immediate effectiveness, remains a kind of desperate contrivance in a novel which is not itself a symbol but "a true historie." These incidents do not, that is, have in them implications of contrasted views of experience; they are merely poetic projections of the hero's view of things. The result of all this is a novel which is formally neither fish, flesh, nor good red herring, a novel whose tremendous verisimilar life is constantly being sapped by a series of irrelevant devices and yet remains, as a systematic artifice, "a paradise of loose ends."

3

The nearest Hardy came to escaping from the strangling limitations of his attitude and the naturalistic form to which it committed him was in his pastoral idealization of the life of his Wessex peasants. He might, by completing this idealization, have produced profound romantic comedy; for he could see so clearly that "it is the on-going—*i.e.,* the 'becoming'—of the world that produces its sadness. If the world stood still at a felicitous moment there would be no sadness in it. The sun and the moon standing still on Ajalon was not a catastrophe for Israel, but a type of Paradise" *(The Early Life)*. It is his feeling that the world had come perceptibly closer to standing still at a felicitous moment for his Wessex peasants in the old days which tempted him to see their life as a type of Paradise.

Yet he did not know how to subdue the rational fact of the matter. The on-going of the world worked among the Wessex people too, if more slowly; and even if it did not, only the illusion of nostalgia could make one who knew that earth's conditions are ingrained suppose there had even been a felicitous moment in the past. The life of these peasants can be, for Hardy, only a charming anachronism; and their comments, though Hardy uses them chorically in his novels, are really irrelevant to any meaning which is possible for him. When Mrs. Edlin comments on Sue's marriage—"In my time we took it more careless, and I don't know that we was any the worse for it!" (438) [Page citations are from the Modern Library edition of *Jude*]—or when she is to be heard "honestly saying the Lord's Prayer in a loud voice, as the Rubric directed" (333), she is only an example of how much simpler and easier life was before man had progressed in the hands of inescapable time to his present high state of nervous and emotional organization. She cannot be, as Hardy's use of her sometimes seems to imply she is, an image from a timeless and ideal pastoral world, an Arden to which his hero will escape from the squalid real world of Duke Frederick's court. For much

as Hardy longed, however unconsciously, to make out of the world of his Wessex peasants an ideal pastoral world, the weary weight of its unintelligible actuality so burdened him that he was never able to see it as a type of Paradise, to make it a part of his means for "holding in a single thought reality and justice." It was indeed Hardy's tragedy as a writer that he never found any such means. Mrs. Edlin and the rest of his peasants remain meaningful only at the level of history; they are samples of the simpler and easier way of life in the past, preserved for Hardy's day by an eddy in time.

The moments of happiness which come in most of Hardy's novels just before the catastrophes are particular instances of his inability to make the country life a type of Paradise. Grace and Giles in Sherton Abbey while they still believe the divorce possible, Tess and Angel between the murder of Alec and the arrest at Stonehenge, Jude and Sue at the Wessex Agricultural Show, these felicitous moments are always moments when the protagonists believe they have won their way back to the Garden of Eden, to purity of heart and to a kindly country world which will be a satisfactory home for the pure in heart. Only a rather staggering amount of coincidence in the narrative or naïveté in the characters can provide moments of such delusion in the real world as Hardy knew it; and because Hardy was committed to a naturalistic form he not only had to produce these moments by coincidence and naïveté, but to demonstrate that, except as faint foreshadowings of a reformed humanity, they were fool's paradises. Thus Hardy's time-bound universe and the naturalistic form which it forced on him as a novelist prevented his imagining or presenting an artificial world which contained both reality and justice.

Committed as he was to the truth of abstract reason rather than the truth of imagination, Hardy therefore had no choice but to conceive his ideal life as a felicitous moment some place in the future of the real life, since this ideal life was the only kind which could be reached by strict reason from his premise. Hardy's faith in this kindly country world to which humanity would win in the course of history is seldom explicit in the novels, since to make it explicit is to make explicit also the contradiction between this faith and Hardy's overwhelming conviction that Earth's conditions are ingrained. That faith is, however, of necessity everywhere implicit in his presentation of the events of human and natural life; it is his only source for the light which reveals the horror of these events.

In that Hardy's novels rest, in this indirect fashion, on a belief in the world's progress toward a felicitous future, their meaning is the meaning of sentimental pastoral. They are what *As You Like It* would be without Jaques to remind us and the senior Duke that "the penalty of Adam" was not merely "the season's difference" but the knowledge of good and evil, without Touchstone to show us that weariness of the legs is as significant in its way as weariness of the spirit in its, and his love of Jane Smile as real as Silvious's love of Phebe or Orlando's of Rosalind. For however much Hardy failed to recognize it, his whole view of things was based on the assumption that the world of *The Woodlanders* without Fitzpiers and Mrs. Charmond and an educated Grace would be an ideal world, a world of

> *Men surfeited of laying heavy hands*
> > *Upon the innocent,*
> *The mild, the fragile, the obscure content*
> *Among the myriads of thy family.*
> *Those, too, who love the true, the excellent,*
> *And make their daily moves a melody.*
> > [*The Dynasts*, Fore Scene]

The success of such poems as **"In Time of 'The Breaking of Nations'"** depends on the implication that the life of the man harrowing clods and the maid and her wight is not only eternal—a world that stands still; but felicitous—a world which knows only the sweet adversity of "the season's difference" and not the adversity of evil. Such a pastoral vision of a still point of the turning world was the source of Hardy's sense of the squalid evil of real life. But because he refused to use the life of his Wessex peasants, or any other life, to body forth his forms of things unknown, he was unable to turn those forms to shapes at all.

But if Hardy's combination of half-despairing, scientific humanitarianism, and the naturalistic form which he thought it committed him to, was incapable of pastoral, it was even more incapable of tragedy. Hardy's feeling that the evil of this world was incurable is tragic. But because he was unable to place the source of the idealism by which he measured the world and found it wanting outside of time and therefore, *faute de mieux,* came to believe "in the gradual ennoblement of man," his attitude is such as to preclude a formal structure which pits the idealist against the practical man in equal combat. There is no basic, unresolvable tragic tension between the real and the ideal in his attitude, and there is as a consequence no tragic tension in the formal structure it invokes as its representation. The objection to Hardy's form for tragedy is, therefore, not a matter of his occasional awkwardness or carelessness; it is radical.

The assumption which justifies the naturalistic novel is that there can be only one kind of reality, and this is Hardy's assumption. But if there is only one kind of reality there can be also only one kind of truth, and that truth, in *Jude,* is the melioristic view of the world which is the only belief Hardy can find. As author Hardy is therefore unable to represent justly in *Jude* those kinds of men according to whose ideas the world must be run if earth's conditions are ingrained. In his fictional world such people can be shown only in the light of the single true view of things which Hardy and Jude share. It is as if Shakespeare had first made Hamlet altogether incapable of believing the evil of the world incurable and had then shown us Claudius only as Hamlet saw him. Hardy's Claudiuses are not mighty opposites; they are inexplicable villains. At best he can give them credit for

being better adjusted to the world as it is at the moment. And for the same reason the only irony he can direct against his hero is the irony to be derived from a demonstration of his temporary maladjustment in a world which, if it is not meaningless, will presently realize that hero's ideal. There is thus neither permanent justification in Hardy for the Arabellas nor permanent irony for the Judes. *Jude* cannot display the very real if limited truth of Claudius's

> For what we know must be, and is as common
> As any the most vulgar thing to sense,
> Why should we in our peevish opposition
> Take it to heart? Fie! 'tis a fault to heaven,
> A fault against the dead, a fault to nature,
> To reason most absurd . . .

nor the very real if terrible absurdity of Hamlet's "Go to, I'll no more on't; it hath made me mad. I say, we will have no moe marriage: . . ."

But if the actions of the Arabellas are seen only as Jude saw them, they must remain for the reader what they were for Jude, the consequences of an inexplicable and brutal stupidity rather than of a different kind of wisdom to Jude's. Thus Hardy's attitude and the form it invoked excluded from his representation, despite the fact that no one knew them better than he did, the point of view of those men and women for whom "the defence and salvation of the body by daily bread is still a study, a religion, and a desire." It excluded, too, an understanding of how a woman like Sue might, not in weakness but in strength, deny the validity of Jude's humanitarian idealism. It is one thing, that is, for Jude to preach to Sue the horror of her final surrender to Phillotson and conventional conduct or for Hamlet to preach to his mother the horror of surrender to Claudius and a "normal" life. It is quite another for Hardy, who does, or Shakespeare, who does not, to commit himself completely as author to this sermon.

At the same time, however, that Hardy presents the almost universal opposition to Jude as inexplicably cruel, he is forced to present people and animals—of which there are a great many in Hardy—in such a way as to support Jude's view of them. In other words, Hardy presents the same kinds of objects at once unjustly and sentimentally. And this is the manifestation in the "verbal correlative" of Hardy's attitude of the contradiction inherent in that attitude. Because he can see only a single reality, that of the time-bound actual world, the life of that reality has to be at once incurably evil and potentially good.

4

Jude the Obscure is, then, the history of a worthy man's education. Part One, for example, is primarily an account of Jude's youth up to the moment he departs for Christminster in search of learning. From the very beginning, however, Jude and the world through which he moves are presented as they appear to the eyes of one who has accepted the view of things which will be the end-product of Jude's education. In so far as Jude understands this view of things, he is not dramatized; he is the author. In so far as, in his innocence, he ignores the necessities and their implications which this view sees, he is dramatized, objectified by Hardy's irony. Hardy's narrative is, then, secondarily, a demonstration of the consequences of Jude's innocent ignorance of "Nature's logic"—in Part One in the matter of sex. Nature takes its revenge by entangling Jude irretrievably with Arabella. Hardy gives this demonstration a complex poetic elaboration, and it is easy to suppose as a consequence that his narrative is fundamentally symbolic, the pitting of two different views of experience—Jude's and Arabella's—against each other in a neutral arena. That it is not is evident from the fact that Hardy as the narrator takes advantage of every opportunity to support Jude's attitude. Furthermore, this part cannot, as symbolic narrative, be fitted into any pattern which runs through the book as a whole, for the only pattern *Jude* has is the pattern of history.

Nevertheless the poetic elaboration of this episode is interesting as an example, characteristic of the procedure of the book as a whole, of how Hardy's idea, striving to establish a form which will make sense of it, is constantly breaking through the limits of the naturalistic form. The meeting of Arabella and Jude, for example, is brought about by Arabella's hitting Jude with a pig's pizzle. No better image for what drew Arabella and Jude together could be found, and, a symbol of their meeting, the pig's pizzle hangs on the bridge rail between them throughout their first meeting. Thereafter, Arabella scarcely appears in this part unaccompanied by pigs. In the same way Jude's dream of an education which will take him through Christminster to a career as a philanthropic bishop is associated with a vision of Christminster as seen from the roof of the old Brown House against the blaze of the setting sun, like the heavenly Jerusalem, as the child Jude says solemnly to the tiler. It is also associated with the New Testament. The New Testament, in its strictly moral aspect, is the textbook of Hardy's humanitarian morality, and in so far as Jude values its morality he is demonstrating his instinctively humanitarian feelings. But Jude's Testament represents for him also religion and, in that it is a Greek text, learning; and in valuing it on these counts he is demonstrating his illusions.

During the wooing of Arabella by Jude there are sporadic recrudescences of these symbols. For example, Hardy is constantly bringing the two lovers back to the rise on which the old Brown House stands, from which Jude had once seen his vision of the heavenly Jerusalem and where, under the influence of an impulse rather awkwardly explained on the narrative level, he had also once knelt and prayed to Apollo and Diana, the god and goddess of learning and chastity (33). Under the influence of Arabella, Jude "passed the spot where he had knelt to Diana and Phoebus without remembering that there were any such people in the mythology, or that the sun was

anything else than a useful lamp for illuminating Arabella's face" (46). Hardy carefully notes, too, that a picture of Samson and Delilah hangs on the wall of the tavern where the two lovers stop for tea but instead, partly at Arabella's suggestion, drink beer (48, 79, 451). The linkage of Arabella and liquor (she had been a barmaid) is valuable to Hardy not only as a piece of naturalism but because it makes Arabella an incarnation of what Jude later calls "my two Arch Enemies . . . my weakness for women and my impulse to strong liquor" (420).

Yet these symbols, effective as they are, are sporadic and unsystematized. Hardy never deserts his naturalistic narrative and commits his meaning to them completely, and so the reader never feels to the full in him what Henry James once so beautifully called the renewal "in the modern alchemist [of] something like the old dream of the secret of life." Hardy never thought of himself as a modern alchemist but only as a historian. This fact is plain enough in the climactic scene of this part, the pig-killing scene, for here the pig is not primarily a symbol but an object at the naturalistic level. Arabella takes toward it, as such, an attitude perfectly consistent with the attitude she has maintained throughout. Her concern is for the salableness of the meat, and even her urging that Jude kill the pig quickly when it cries out is determined by her conventional fear lest the cry reveal to the neighbors that the Fawley's have sunk to killing their own pig. "Poor folks must live," she says when Jude protests against the inhumanity of slowly bleeding the pig to death (72). And though Hardy's description of the incident precludes any sympathy for Arabella, this statement is profoundly true within the limits of the world Arabella is aware of.

In direct contrast to Arabella's practical view of this killing, Hardy sets Jude's idealistic view of it: "The white snow, stained with the blood of his fellow-mortal, wore an illogical look to him as a lover of justice, not to say a Christian; . . ." (73). There is irony here, of course, but it is directed solely to the point that Hardy "could not see how the matter was to be mended" (73), not at all to the point that in one very real sense—the sense that Arabella understood—it could and ought never to be mended. This is so because Hardy is in fact and, as a consequence, by the form he has chosen committed to Jude's view of this incident. That commitment is clear in every word Hardy himself writes about the pig; for example: "The dying animal's cry assumed its third and final tone, the shriek of agony; his glazing eyes rivetting themselves on Arabella with the eloquently keen reproach of a creature recognizing at last the treachery of those who had seemed his only friends" (71).

The consequence of the author's putting the full weight of his authority in this way behind one of the conflicting views of the events is to take the ground out from under the other. The events are presented only as Jude saw them, so that Arabella's view of them seems to the reader simply inexplicably hard-hearted, however commonplace. Hardy can see that Arabella's attitude, in its complete ignorance of Jude's, is grimly funny: "'Od damn it all!' she cried, 'that ever I should say it! You've over-stuck un! And I telling you all the time—'" (71). But he cannot see that it is in any sense justified. The result of this commitment of the author is that the scene as a whole becomes sentimental; and it is difficult to resist the temptation to read it as "a burlesque of the murder of Duncan" with the pig substituted for the king ("Well—you must do the sticking—there's no help for it. I'll show you how. Or I'll do it myself—I think I could." [70]).

This pig-killing scene is of course meant to connect in the reader's mind with the earlier episode where Farmer Troutham whips Jude for allowing the rooks to eat his corn. For Jude the rooks "took upon them more and more the aspect of gentle friends and pensioners. . . . A magic thread of fellow-feeling united his own life with theirs. Puny and sorry as those lives were, they much resembled his own" (10). Here again Hardy presents these birds and Jude only as Jude sees them. For all his knowledge of "the defence and salvation of the body" he signally fails to do justice to Farmer Troutham's view of them, just as he fails to do justice to Arabella's view of Jude and the pig, because he cannot present two kinds of truth in a naturalistic novel. Hamlet, to say nothing of Shakespeare, could understand and yet defy augury both for himself and the sparrow, since he knew well in the end from experience what was well enough known to him from his reading from the start, that there is a "special providence" in these matters, so that "the readiness is all." Hardy, like Jude and Jaques, could only weep, knowing no providence at all. Shakespeare could therefore write "The Phoenix and the Turtle," Hardy only **"Compassion: An Ode in Celebration of the Centenary of the Royal Society for the Prevention of Cruelty to Animals."**

Part Two (at Christminster) brings Hardy's spiritual Whittington to his London where he is taught that his desire for learning had been only "a social unrest which had no foundation in the nobler instincts; which was purely an artificial product of civilization" (151). At the very beginning he catches a glimpse of the truth: "For a moment there fell on Jude a true illumination; that here in the stone-yard was a centre of effort as worthy as that dignified by the name of scholarly study within the noblest of the colleges" (96). Apart from his narrative function, Phillotson is used in this part to foreshadow Jude's discovery of this truth and to reveal what happens to a weaker person at such a disappointment (116-17). Arabella's temporary conversion after Cartlett's death has the same kind of formal relation to Sue's conversion, with the additional irony that Sue's conversion involves a return to active sexual life which she hates, Arabella's a loss of it which she cannot endure (373). Jude's discovery of the fraudulence of learning leaves him only his Christianity; that he will discover this too is "as dead as a fern-leaf in a lump of coal" Hardy tells us directly (96-7). That it has been replaced by a German-Gothic fake he suggests by his references to the tearing down of the "hump-backed, wood-turreted, and quaintly hipped"

Marygreen church and to the "tall new building of German-Gothic design" erected in its place (6, 146).

Meanwhile Jude meets his cousin Sue, whom Hardy always keeps before the reader as Jude first saw her in the picture at Marygreen, "in a broad hat, with radiating folds under the brim like the rays of a halo" (88), not only because she remains always for Jude a saint but because, by a terrible irony, she literally becomes one at the end of the book. Sue has twice Jude's quickness of wit and half his strength of character. She therefore saw from the beginning that there was nothing in the universe except "Nature's law"; but because of her lack of real profundity, she thought also that it was "Nature's . . . *raison d'être,* that we should be joyful in what instincts she afforded us . . ." (403). When she discovered that nature had no *raison d'être* and that paganism was as false as Christianity had seemed to her, she did not have the strength to face it and went back to conventional wifehood and conventional Christianity. All this, even the impermanence of Sue's paganism (the figures of Venus and Apollo are plaster and come off on her gloves and jacket), is implicit in the episode of the images in Chapter II and in the recollections of Sue's childhood in Chapter VI. By a fine piece of irony—since Sue is, while her strength lasts, a saint of Hardy's humanitarian faith— Hardy has Jude focus not only his physical but his religious feelings on Sue. Gradually he learns from her and experience the omnipotence of Nature's law. But meanwhile Jude sees this imperfect saint of humanitarianism as an Anglican saint. Of the irony of this illusion Hardy makes much (e.g., 123), and in incident after incident, until Jude unlearns his Christianity, he reëmphasizes the irony of this love between the pagan and delicately sexed Sue and the Christian and passionate Jude.

In Part Three Jude, having realized that learning is vain and that only his "altruistic feeling" had any "foundation in the nobler instincts," goes to Melchester, partly because it is "a spot where worldly learning and intellectual smartness had no establishment" (152), partly because Sue is there. There follows a series of episodes which represent the conflict between Sue's daring humanitarian faith and her weak conventional conduct, on the one hand, and Jude's "Tractarian" faith and courageously honest conduct, on the other. In the end, of course, Hardy arranges events so as to demonstrate the omnipotence of "the artificial system of things, under which the normal sex-impulses are turned into devilish domestic gins and springes to noose and hold back those who want to progress" (257), and Sue marries Phillotson. In Part Four Jude's education is almost lost sight of in the welter of narrative detail. Occasionally its progress is marked for the reader, as when Jude replies to Sue's question whether she ought to continue to live with Phillotson: "Speaking as an order-loving man—which I hope I am, though I fear I am not—I should say yes. Speaking from experience and unbiassed nature, I should say no" (248). Though Sue and Jude determine to sacrifice their love to right conduct, their coming together on the occasion of their aunt's death at Marygreen finally forces Jude to recognize the evil of the church's marriage system and Sue to realize that she must leave Phillotson for Jude. Sue tries at first to avoid marriage and an active sexual life, but Arabella's return, ironically, forces her to yield to Jude in order to hold him.

There follows in Part Five a period when "the twain were happy—between their times of sadness . . ." (341). Hardy shows them as devoted lovers at the Great Wessex Agricultural Show, where they are carefully contrasted with the conventional married couple Arabella and Cartlett (Chapter V). But the pressure of the conventional world on them as unmarried lovers forces them down and down until Jude, "still haunted by his dream" (395), brings Sue and the children to a "depressing purlieu" of Christminster. Here Jude makes a speech, from the cross, as it were, to the Roman soldiers of Christminster in which he states the result of his education: "I perceive there is something wrong somewhere in our social formulas: what it is can only be discovered by men or women with greater insight than mine—if, indeed, they ever discover it—at least, in our time" (388).

It is here at Christminster that Hardy makes the most extreme use of his one completely symbolic character, Father Time. All through Part Five he has been used to strike the ominous note which reminds us that Sue and Jude's moderate happiness is a snare and a delusion. Now, under the influence of his perfectly arbitrary melancholy and the misinterpretation of something Sue says, he kills all the children, including himself. Father Time is Jude and Arabella's son brought up by Jude and Sue, in order that Hardy may say (400):

> On that little shape had converged all the inauspiciousness and shadow which had darkened the first union of Jude, and all the accidents, mistakes, fears, errors of the last. He was their nodal point, their focus, their expression in a single term. For the rashness of those parents he had groaned, for their ill-assortment he had quaked, and for the misfortunes of these he had died.

The effect of this incident on Jude and Sue is to place each of them in the position from which the other had started at the beginning of the book (409):

> One thing troubled him more than any other, that Sue and himself had mentally travelled in opposite directions since the tragedy: events which had enlarged his own views of life, laws, customs, and dogmas, had not operated in the same manner on Sue's. She was no longer the same as in the independent days, when her intellect played like lambent lightning over conventions and formalities which he had at that time respected, though he did not now.

Sue returns to Christianity and Phillotson as a consequence of this change; and Jude, partly because of a kind of stunned indifference (he takes to drink), and partly because of Arabella's predatory sexuality, returns to his

first wife. It is perfectly apparent that in Hardy's opinion Sue has done an unforgivably inhuman thing to save a perfectly imaginary soul.

But Hardy is at least willing to suggest a conflict in Sue between her affection for Jude and her religious belief, even if he is capable of seeing only one right in that conflict. Thus, when Jude departs from their last meeting, to which he had gone knowing that he was committing suicide, "in a last instinct of human affection, even now unsubdued by her fetters, she sprang up as if to go and succor him. But she knelt down again, and stopped her ears with her hands till all possible sound of him had passed away" (466). On his way home Jude feels "the chilly fog from the meadows of Cardinal as if death-claws were grabbing me through and through" (469); Hardy catches the whole complex of "stern reality" in this symbolic statement by Jude. College, church, social convention, the very things which Jude had at the beginning believed in as the representatives of his ideal, have killed him, either by betraying him directly or by teaching Sue to betray him.

When Hardy comes to Jude's actual death, he also presents Arabella with a choice, the choice of staying with the dying Jude or going to the Remembrance games. The representation of her here is perhaps the best brief illustration in the book of the melodramatic effect which resulted from Hardy's exclusive attitude toward his material. There is not the slightest sign of conflict in Arabella over her choice; she goes without question to the games, flirts with the quack physician Vilbert, and is upset only by the thought that "if Jude were discovered to have died alone an inquest might be deemed necessary" (485). As in the pig-killing scene, Arabella is shown as feeling only brute passion and fear of convention; she is the parody villainess of melodrama, not the mighty opposite of tragedy. Thus the immediate pathos of Jude's death in part derives from Arabella's villainous neglect of him; like the cheers of the Remembrance day crowd which are counterpointed against Jude's dying quotation from *Job,* however, this neglect illustrates only the complete indifference of society to Jude's dream of an ideal life. The rest of the pathos derives from Jude's uncertainty as to why he had been born at all. But the meaning of his death, in so far as it has one, derives from such conviction as Hardy can muster that Jude's life has not been in vain, but the unfortunate life of a man who had tried to live the ideal life several generations before the world was reformed enough to allow him to. Jude's death is not, therefore, in our ordinary understanding of the word, tragic; since it is the result of a conflict between the ideal life a man wished to lead and the only temporarily squalid real life which he was forced to lead.

Jude the Obscure is then, not a tragedy, not a carefully devised representation of life the purpose of which is to contrast, at every turn, the permanently squalid real life of man, with the ideal life (or, if you will, man's dream of an ideal life). It is the history of how an obscure but worthy man, living a life which Hardy conceived to be representative, learned gradually "that the social moulds civilization fits us into have no more relation to our actual shapes than the conventional shapes of the constellations have to the real star-patterns" (242), learned what the true morality of "unbiassed nature" is. In the process of learning this optimistic morality he discovered also that neither nature nor society even recognized it, to say nothing of living by it. In so far as Hardy gave him hope at the end that in time they would, he denied what he otherwise saw so clearly, that earth's conditions are ingrained; in so far as he did not give Jude this hope he denied the possibility of the only ideal life he could conceive and made his hero's life and death essentially meaningless.

The instructive comparison to *Jude* is of course *Hamlet.* For Shakespeare too saw most profoundly the horror of life's ingrained conditions. But because he could also understand and represent the attitude of those who sought to adjust themselves to life's conditions, he saw that the only hope he could give his hero was for that consummation he so devoutly wished, and death is the only felicity Hamlet ever deems possible. Hamlet's death is not death in a universe in which there is no place without bad dreams; neither is it a death justified by a hope that some day the world's ingrained conditions will come unstuck. Jude's death is a little bit of both.

Hardy says in the preface to *Jude* that it "is simply an endeavor to give shape and coherence to a series of seemings, or personal impressions, the question of their consistency or their discordance . . . being regarded as not of the first moment." In that the feeling of the presented life in *Jude* has a powerful coherence this is a justified defense of it. But it is precisely because Hardy never really posed for himself the question of how the meaning of his impressions could be coherent without being consistent that *Jude,* for all the power of its presented life, is not a tragedy.

Frederick P. W. McDowell (essay date 1960)

SOURCE: Hardy's "Seeming or Personal Impressions: The Use of Image and Contrast in *Jude the Obscure*", in *Modern Fiction Studies,* Vol. 6, No. 1, 1960, pp. 233-50.

[*In the following essay, McDowell explores the symbolism of* Jude the Obscure, *contending that the novel's images "parallel events and deepen realistic and psychological aspects of the narrative" and afford the work a "richer texture" and greater depth of meaning.*]

I

Sixty years after publication, Thomas Hardy's *Jude the Obscure* still elicits controversial judgments. The majority of recent critics, such as William R. Rutland, Lord David Cecil, R. A. Scott-James, Douglas Brown, and Evelyn Hardy, have judged the book a relative failure because of its violations of probability, its morbidity, or

its philosophical pretentiousness.[1] Other critics, such as Lascelles Abercrombie, H. C. Duffin, Joseph Warren Beach, Arthur McDowall, and Albert Guerard, have acclaimed the book as possibly Hardy's best.[2] I agree with the most recent critic in this group, Albert Guerard, who finds *Jude the Obscure,* despite the "naturalistic paraphernalia," a haunting symbolic rendition of the modern age as it appeared to a compassionate pessimist.[3] In order to arrive at a sound approach to the novel, I have had recourse less to book-length studies of Thomas Hardy—except for Abercrombie and Guerard these are disappointing—than to articles and incidental treatments of Hardy in more general books.

Though I disagree with them in part, two of the most perceptive of these accounts—Arthur Mizener's and Walter Allen's—can serve as basis for further discussion.[4] These critics maintain that Hardy's naturalistic technique in *Jude* sets it off from his earlier fiction. More than in his preceding books, Hardy does stress the effects both of heredity and environment upon his characters, the conviction that social laws operate like natural laws, the presence of a strong if still incomplete determinism in human affairs, the need to present the unsavory and animalistic aspects of experience, the sense that primitive and eruptive forces are part of human nature, the insistence that Darwinian postulates underlie any modern world view, the belief that individualistic force is needed to break from an inherited morality, and the view that ethics are inductively derived from experience. Granted that these premises obtrude with greater force in *Jude the Obscure* than in the other novels, still Thomas Hardy primarily remained faithful in *Jude the Obscure* to his earlier defined, more fluid theory of the art of fiction.

Thomas Hardy departed from naturalistic convention in *Jude the Obscure* in being unable to efface his temperament from his work. *Jude the Obscure* thus illustrates Hardy's view that a writer should be free to select his materials, to give shape and form to them, to explore their poetical and metaphysical implications, and to declare his belief, however tentative or qualified, in values which he deems to have some permanent validity in experience.[5] Hardy felt that "scientific" novelists were to be commended for their desire to present the full truth and for their hatred of the false and hypocritical; but he also felt that artistic effectiveness derived more from a "sympathetic appreciativeness of life in all its manifestations" than from a sensitive eye and ear alone.[6] He alleged, therefore, that "art" in poetry and novel writing results in an illumination of subject material, going beyond mere reportage.[7] The mission of poetry, he said, is to record impressions and not convictions;[8] in the preface to *Jude the Obscure* he expressed himself similarly upon the art of the novel. This book, he maintained, was like former productions of his in being "simply an endeavor to give shape and coherence to a series of seemings, or personal impressions, the question of their consistency or their discordance, of their permanence or their transitoriness, being regarded as not of the first moment."[9]

Disregard or misconstruction of this statement has led Mizener and Allen to emphasize too completely the realism of *Jude the Obscure*. Mr. Mizener contends that its symbolic embellishments, which represent Hardy's attempt to give order to his impressions, are ineffective, and represent "a kind of desperate contrivance" in a basically naturalistic novel.[10] The symbolism in *Jude the Obscure*, I feel, is not adventitious but organic; it prevades the whole and provides those shades of ineffable and expanded significance which Mizener finds absent.

Allen's view that the power and impressiveness of the novel derive from "Hardy's very refusal to employ his great poetic talents in it" is, I think, similarly debatable.[11] It is just his exercise of these gifts in concentrated form which gives the book its full life. Allen apparently views the symbolism of *Jude the Obscure* as almost wholly ironic, existing primarily to provide implicit rational commentary upon incident, character, and value. Such is indeed the case, but most of the images in the novel haunt the imagination as well as gratify the mind. In an ineffable and poetic dimension, they give nuance, resonance, and intensity to action, psychology, and idea, and carry the fabric—of which they form part—away from an objectively rendered and obviously typical reality. In *Jude the Obscure* we have a naturalistic novel, but a naturalistic novel with a difference. Thus when *Jude the Obscure* is compared with *A Mummer's Wife* or *The Nether World,* its imagined universe stands out in far sharper relief.

Norman Holland, in his important "*Jude the Obscure:* Hardy's Symbolic Indictment of Christianity,"[12] has developed Guerard's insight that *Jude* is primarily a symbolic depiction of the chaotic modern age. Holland also admirably illustrates Morton D. Zabel's related insight that Hardy is a realist "developing toward allegory" and, in the process, getting away increasingly from "slavery to fact."[13] If anything, Holland errs in an opposite direction from Mizener and Allen, and concludes that *Jude the Obscure* is more allegorical than realistic. In the images of the novel Holland finds a pattern through which Hardy denies the relevance of Christianity to the modern world. The hanging by Father Time—a modern Jesus Christ—of himself and the two Fawley children is, in Holland's view, an atonement which is not efficacious in a spiritually barren society. Holland's interpretation is perhaps extreme: Hardy not only indicts Christianity, but by inference throughout the novel also condemns modern society for its failure to exemplify Christian ethical values. Furthermore, Father Time is "an enslaved and dwarfed Divinity" (p. 336) and in his narrow wilfulness becomes a parody upon, as well as counterpart to, the Christian Saviour. My purpose is to approach the novel with a method similar to Holland's but to give my discussion a less allegorical focus. Thus I shall endeavor to relate, more closely than Holland has done, the images and clusters of images in the novel to the actual lives of Sue Bridehead and Jude Fawley in society.

I wish also to develop the importance of one aspect of Hardy's technique, which Guerard has dismissed with slighting comment: his purposeful use of contrast.[14] All the contrasts in *Jude* are not so purely factitious and geometrical as Guerard indicates. Many of the parallel incidents provide a symbolic and metaphysical commentary upon the characters and their problems, just as the characters in parallel situations throw light upon one another and the action as a whole. In short, the ramifications and contortions of plot are in themselves provocative, and open up unexpected ranges of meaning. My examination of Hardy's marshalling of images and symbols in the novel, in conjunction with his skilled use of significant contrasts, will, I think, amplify Guerard's view that the lasting impression produced by *Jude* is its spiritual "trueness" for a time of moral, intellectual, and spiritual dislocation.[15]

II

The first function of the images, symbols, and symbolic or parallel incidents in *Jude the Obscure* is to deepen and reinforce the realistic and psychological aspects of the narrative, our impressions of the characters who figure in it, and the various developments arising from it. A number of images, first encountered in the early part of the novel, operate in this way. There is, for example, the well at Marygreen into whose depths Jude peered as a boy. Its "long circular perspective" indicates the path of Jude's own existence which many times converges circularly upon Marygreen. In somewhat the same manner, the schoolmaster Phillotson returns recurrently to Marygreen, where he had first been a teacher. The well also suggests infinity, and conveys an impression of the continuity of nature and of life itself. It hints at psychic and spiritual renewal and acts, therefore, as a counterweight to many of the death-connoting images in the novel. The well is in part a natural phenomenon and as such will survive man-made objects: thus it has outlasted the old church which has been supplanted by a newer, less aesthetically pleasing structure. Along with the suggestion of infinity, the well had given to the young Jude intimations of sadness and of the inscrutability of life; these impressions are, of course, heightened in him and us by his destiny.

The well has possible sexual connotations, too, and suggests the darkness, the mystery, the security, and the fertile energies of the womb. It thus reinforces the animal imagery which betokens physical sexuality and which is especially prominent in the early part of the novel.[16] There are the copulating earthworms which Jude as a boy tries to avoid crushing in a wet pasture. They are responding to the same natural force motivating the peasant youths and maidens who make love in upland privacy and populate thereby the neighboring villages. Somewhat later, Jude and Arabella become such lovers themselves. Arabella is, of course, associated with pigs throughout the novel; she is twice referred to as a "tiger," and at the Aldbrickham hotel when Sue visits her, she springs from bed like a beast from its lair. The most celebrated of the animal images is the pig's pizzle which Arabella throws at Jude to attract his attention when, at the brookside, she is washing a slaughtered pig for her father. One of the most arresting scenes is the subsequent flirtation on the bridge, after Arabella hangs on the rail the pizzle which Jude surrenders to her in a ritualistic yielding of his own virginity to her. The coarse and sensual nature of their soon developing affair is explicit, then, from its outset.

The first of a group of images and incidents relating to music appears early in the book. In the opening section Phillotson has difficulty getting a piano moved which he has never learned to play. His failure to master it is linked with his inability to play, subtly and potently, upon the keyboard of a woman's sensibility; with the defeat of his other aspirations, social, intellectual, and spiritual; and with the absence of emotional depths in his nature. While Sue is Phillotson's wife at Shaston, she and Jude are brought together when he plays upon this piano a newly written hymn which appeals with power to both of them. Almost from the first, then, Sue and Jude share, to Phillotson's detriment, experiences from which he is excluded. In addition to his sexual magnetism, Jude has greater spiritual reserves, in general, than Phillotson. Thus Jude achieves considerable distinction in church music at Melchester, singing with deep feeling the church chants while he accompanies himself with ease on a harmonium.

Events at Christminster are often subtly developed by references to music. Jude is greatly moved by the Gregorian chant which he hears at the cathedral church of Cardinal College: "Wherewithal shall a young man cleanse his way?" (p. 106). At this point he has begun struggling against his feeling for Sue, and the chant seems to have a special significance for him as sinner. His feeling of guilt disappears when he sees Sue in the cathedral and becomes conscious that they are both steeped in the same exalted harmonies. As Jude leaves Christminster in despair at the defeat of his intellectual ambitions, he cannot respond to the gay promenade concert. Some years later upon his return to Christminster he is much more susceptible to the spirited music which, on Remembrance Day, peals from the theater organ. The spell exerted by Christminster upon Jude is greater, therefore, than the bitterness engendered in him by his failure to become part of the university. In ironic counterpoint to the tragedy at Christminster when little Father Time hangs himself and the Fawley children is the joyous tumult of the organ sounding from a nearby chapel ("Truly God is loving unto Israel," [p. 412]) after the bodies have been discovered. The same incongruity obtrudes on the second Remembrance Day when the lilting strains of a waltz from Cardinal College penetrate the chamber where Jude has just died. Sue's early view of ultimate reality, in part Hardy's own, is expressed by a musical metaphor. She had thought that "the world resembled a stanza or melody composed in a dream" (p. 418), full of ineffable suggestion to the half-perceiving mind but "absurd" to the completely awakened intelligence. Sue's later distress, of course, involves a retreat

from this position to a less aesthetically satisfying concept of God as an anthropomorphic being who does not hesitate to punish those who flout convention.

Images in the novel drawn from the Bible also serve to intensify its realism and the psychic impulses of its characters. The relationship between Jude and Arabella is given by the picture of Samson and Delilah at the inn where the lovers decide to get tea during their courtship and are forced to get beer instead. As Holland observes, Arabella thereby combines the two forces which undermine Jude, his passion for women and his developing taste for strong drink.[17] When he is duped a second time into marrying Arabella, she appropriately thinks of him as "her shorn Samson" (p. 464). Biblical and ecclesiastical images are also associated with Sue Bridehead, who looks like a saint with a halo of light in her portrait at Marygreen and who is engaged in an apparently saintly occupation at Christminster. She is an artist for an ecclesiastical warehouse and is designing, when Jude first sees her through the shop window, the word *Alleluia* in zinc. Without knowing her "Voltairean" propensities, he feels that she would be a sweet companion for him in the Anglican worship, opening for him new social and spiritual possibilities and soothing him "like the dew of Hermon" (p. 107). In her marital difficulties she identifies herself with the Christian drama in Eden. Writing to Phillotson from her school room, she wishes that Eve had not fallen, so that a more delicate mode of reproduction than sex might have peopled Paradise. In her developing asceticism after the death of her children, she regards the flesh as "the curse of Adam" (p. 421). If, as she had said previously, she was "the Ishmaelite" as a result of her disregard of convention, she feels still more of an outcast after she tries to expiate her tragedy by mortification of the flesh.

In view of his devotion to Christianity in the first half of the novel, Jude is linked even more firmly with Biblical incident than is Sue. At Shaston Sue describes Jude as "Joseph, the dreamer of dreams" (p. 247) and as "St. Stephen who, while they were stoning him, could see heaven opened" (pp. 247-248). Here Sue refers, at least by implication, to Jude's scarcely practicable dreams, first of entering Christminster and then of becoming an altruistic licentiate, to his early vision of Christminster as a "heavenly Jerusalem," and to the scorn merged with indifference which his unusual ambition arouses among his Marygreen and Christminster acquaintances. When Jude gets to Christminster, he is fascinated by a model of ancient Jerusalem while Sue as a skeptic is indifferent to it. This model of Jerusalem anticipates that made by Jude and Sue some years later of his "new Jerusalem," Cardinal College, for the Great Wessex Agricultural Show at Stoke-Barehills.

The completeness of Jude's defeat at Christminster is implied when he climbs into the octagonal lantern of the theater and sees the city spread out before his eyes as if it were a Pisgah view of the Promised Land which he is never to reach. He then leaves the town, broken in spirit, and returns to Marygreen, "a poor Christ" (p. 147). When he comes back to Christminster in the last part of the novel, he lingers nostalgically outside the theater where he had first realized that study at Christminster was impossible for a man of his resources. Like Jude, the New Testament scribe who sought to reclaim his lapsed contemporaries to the love of Christ by citing the punishments meted to those in the Old Testament who defied God, Jude Fawley is a prophetic figure, seeing further than most of his contemporaries and deploring the placid indifference of most of them to the demands of Christian charity. As a stranger, too, to people in his own class, he is likened the last time at Christminster to Paul among the Lycaonians. Jude at this point is translating a Latin inscription and describing a carving to assembled strangers from the town side of Christminster. Jude, "the Tutor of St. Slums," had been thrust out of Christminster as Paul had been from Lystra; and like Paul, who returns to the city after persecution to preach again his gospel, Jude later comes back to Christminster to voice his radical social ideas to the crowd. On this return to his old haunts, he observes that leaving Kennetbridge for Christminster was like going from Caiaphas to Pilate. There is, by implication, no place anywhere for a man of his talents from his humble class.

Images drawn from pagan and classical sources also heighten character and incident. Pagan allusions gather around Sue early in the novel: the atmosphere surrounding her "blew as distinctly from Cyprus as from Galilee" (p. 107). A vivid scene occurs when she is walking on a hill outside Christminster and sees some statuary of classical deities, carved by an itinerant foreigner, spread out before her and half obliterating the distant towers of the city. Sue's pagan skepticism gets between her and the Christian traditions of the city which from the first secure Jude's allegiance. Her Pisgah view of the city shows her that the secular is fast encroaching upon the religious and indeed must continue to do so if the University is ever to recover intellectual leadership.

A pagan in her sympathies, Sue purchases statues of Venus and Apollo which upon nearer view seem to her embarrassingly large and naked. In theory, then, she embraces a pagan abandon which, in the actuality, discomposes her. She wraps the statues in leaves and brings her "heathen load" into the Christian city, much to the later horror of Miss Fontover, Sue's pious employer, who grinds one of the images with her heel and breaks its arm. Like ecclesiastical Christianity, then, pagan humanism is an incomplete philosophy for the modern age and its survival even more precarious, since its enlarged perspectives so often go counter to convention. Sue's own paganism is imperfect, possibly transient: the clay of the statues rubs off easily. At night she places candles before them as before Christian icons and communes with them raptly. At one such time she reads Swinburne, who expresses her own regret that "the pale Galilean" has conquered. While she peruses Swinburne and Gibbon, Jude in his lodging is studying the Greek New Testament. In the diffused light the statues stand out commandingly

against the wall ornaments: Christian texts, pictures of martyrs, and a gothic framed Latin cross, the figure on which is shrouded by shadows. This obscurely seen cross, which signifies the present abeyance of Christian sentiment in Sue, is in complete contrast to the brightly jeweled Latin cross in the church of St. Silas under which Jude finds Sue toward the end of the novel when, as a result of personal tragedy, Christian conventions become prominent in her life.

After Sue escapes from the training school at Melchester, where she had previously appeared "nunlike" to Jude, she seems to him "clammy as a marine deity" (p. 171) from having forded the river behind the school. Like a latter-day Venus Anadyomene, she seems to have materialized spontaneously out of the waters. If in this sequence she brings to mind the pagan goddess of love, Sue is no sensual Pandemos-like deity but the Venus Urania of heavenly love with whom she somewhat later identifies herself. Her garments also cling to her "like the robes upon the figures in the Parthenon frieze" (p. 171). In her most expansive moods, she seems to Jude, after they live together at Aldbrickham, to be a serene Roman matron or an enlightened woman from Greece who may have just been watching Praxiteles carving his latest Venus. Later, of course, Sue renounces Greek joyousness for Christian asceticism, and "the pale Galilean" in actuality does conquer.

Although Jude is most often seen in a Christian ambience, he is sometimes described in terms of the pagan past. As a devout young aspirant to intellectual culture who momentarily forgets his Christianity before his first sojourn at Christminster, he repeats the "Carmen Saeculare" and invokes on his knees the gods of moon and sun in parallel sequence to Sue's later worship of her statues at night. When Jude returns defeated from Christminster, he is described as a Laocöon contorted by grief; the pagan image implies that the bonds of Christian orthodoxy are loosening even now, primarily as a result of his unpermitted passion for Sue. He is also sensitive to the pessimistic, as well as to the harmonious aspects, of classical antiquity. After the Widow Edlin in Aldbrickham has told the lovers of their ill-fated ancestor who had been hanged as the ultimate result of a marital quarrel, Sue feels that the curse of the house of Atreus hangs over the family, and Jude then compares its doom to that haunting the house of Jeroboam. Later in the novel, however, it is Jude who resorts to the *Agamemnon* to demonstrate that Sue's premonition concerning the ancestral curse hanging over the Fawleys had been correct: "Things are as they are, and will be brought to their destined issue" (p. 415). After their tragedy, the lovers are seen to be, as they move through the Christminster fog, "Acherontic shades" (p. 440). When the seriously ill Jude perceives the ghosts of the Christminster worthies a second time (after his final trip to Marygreen), he poignantly quotes *Antigone* to signify his own anomalous and wretched situation: "I am neither a dweller among men nor ghosts" (p. 483). Despite his discouragement and enervation, Jude's persisting moral force resembles that of a stolid, stoic man of antiquity. This is suggested when he is described on his final trip to Marygreen as being "pale as a monumental figure in alabaster" (p. 476), or when he is seen by Arabella to be "pale" and "statuesque" in death with his features like "marble."

Another group of symbolic incidents is concerned with action taking place at windows or casements. At Melchester, Sue jumps from a window at the training college in order to escape the hateful discipline imposed there; at Shaston she jumps from a window to escape from Phillotson and the regimentation imposed by marriage. When Sue springs from the window at the Melchester school and wades neck-deep through the river to escape, she is making a sharp break with her past and is being borne into another life with Jude at its center. Her break for freedom takes her to the lodgings of the man she loves, but destiny prevents her then from seeing where her affections are centered. Hearing from Jude that he had been married previously, she is precipitated into her union with Phillotson, an impulsive action toward Phillotson in contrast with her later bold jump through the window away from him at Shaston. When Jude comes to visit her at Shaston, she talks to him from a casement, strokes his forehead, and calls him a dreamer; a similar episode takes place at Marygreen a few weeks later after Jude mercifully kills a maimed rabbit caught in a gin. She then leans far out of the window at Mrs. Edlin's and lays her tear-stained face on his hair. Seen so often from a relatively inaccessible casement, Sue is in part the immured enchanted maiden, also a kind of inverted Juliet talking to her ardent lover from the safety of a balcony, to which she does not invite him. Somewhat later Jude, living at Aldbrickham with Sue, talks to Arabella from an upper window of the house when she comes to tell him of the existence of the child, Father Time. Whereas Sue had to this time kept the passionate Jude at a distance, the walls of this house—primly erected upon Sue's inconsistent adherence to the conventions she affects to despise—are hardly proof against Arabella's frankly competitive, more direct animal energies. Afraid of losing Jude to Arabella, Sue yields at last to his ardor to possess her.

Other images or symbolic episodes give the novel a richer texture than that usually found in a realistic narrative. Thus the agonies of jealousy experienced by Sue's lovers at various points in the novel gain strength by being counterpointed with each other. Jude is tortured after the marriage at Melchester by the thought that any children born to Sue would be half Phillotson's. After Sue's visit to him in an illness following her departure from him, Phillotson himself is in jealous agony at the thought of Jude as Sue's physical lover (at this point he is not, so Phillotson's jealousy is wasted). Sue also experiences momentary discomfiture when she first sees Father Time, the child of Jude and Arabella, and thinks that he is as much Arabella's as Jude's. In his distressing final interview with Sue at Marygreen, what sustains Jude is her declaration that she is a wife to Phillotson only in name, whereas what later breaks him down is the Widow

Edlin's report to him that Sue has physically become Phillotson's wife as a punishment for having returned Jude's kisses with passion. Sue's statement that she was the only mourner to attend the funeral of her early Christminster lover gathers poignancy when one remembers her absence from the deathbed of the man whom she has loved even more. When she excludes Jude from their bedroom at Christminster, the scene is made intense by his ritualistic gesture of farewell: he flings his pillow to the floor, an act which signifies, he says, the rending of the veil of the temple of their marriage.

Sue, in effect, says farewell to the passions of the flesh in a similarly poignant scene toward the end of the novel. By mistake she had brought with her to Marygreen a beautifully embroidered nightgown. She impulsively tears it and throws the tatters into the fire, thus figuratively eliminating from her nature all stain of unpermitted earthly passion. In its place she will wear a plain nightdress, which impresses the Widow Edlin as similar to the sackcloth which Sue, in her passion for self-centered suffering, would now like to wear. The destruction of the nightgown also recalls another strong incident, Jude's burning his divinity books on a kind of funeral pyre to his religious aspirations when he realizes at Marygreen that he can no longer be licentiate in the church and continue to love Sue. In burning the nightgown Sue aspires, almost successfully, to invalidate the flesh; in burning the books, Jude relinquishes, to the stronger call of the flesh, his aspirations. He decides that he will give up all for love, but he later finds with a kind of hopeless irony that Sue has not fully reciprocated. Jude's destruction of his books also anticipates Arabella's thrusting her religious pamphlets into the hedge when as Cartlett's widow she decides she is still in love with Jude; in both cases, formal religion is unable to restrain a powerful passion. Arabella, moreover, seems to act as a kind of catalyst in the varying relationships between Sue and Jude. The effect of her first visit to the married couple at Aldbrickham is to thrust Sue into Jude's arms and to bring about the consummation of their union. Her second visit to the couple, after the tragedy to the children, confirms Sue in her opinion that she is no longer Jude's and must return to Phillotson, since she has come to the orthodox view that her early marriage is indissoluble.

III

The images and symbolic patterns in the novel not only deepen its significance, but give it scope and amplitude. The full and extended representations of locale help give the novel its broadened perspectives and take it again beyond the unadorned content of most naturalistic novels. In Hardy's evocation the physical Christminster is replete with Gothic grace and charming if irregular architectural harmonies. Shaston, "the ancient British Palladour," is described as "the city of a dream" (p. 239) and its past glories are suggested as they would now appeal to the sensitive beholder of the picturesque town. Melchester with its towering cathedral is presented with similar immediacy, though no set description of town or cathedral is given.

Although Marygreen is a desolate and remote spot, Hardy savored its uniqueness and quaintness. In particular, the features of the spacious countryside nearby are assimilated effectively into the action of the novel. The highway ascending the downs from Alfredston to Marygreen is one of the most consistently used topographical images in the novel. This is the road that Jude walks with Arabella in the early days of their relationship, it is along this road that the newly married pair settle, and it is by this road that Jude returns several times to his native village. Along this road occurs the fateful kiss between Jude and Sue; here Arabella, as the "volupshious widow" of Cartlett, relives the early days with Jude and determines to get him back. Phillotson's history is also intimately connected with the highway. The surrounding landscape is full of associations for Jude: the field where he chased the crows for Farmer Troutham, the Brown House from which he first had his view of Christminster in the distance, the milestone upon which he carved the word *thither* and an arrow pointing toward Christminster, and the gibbet upon which one of his ancestors was reputed to have been hanged. The sequence at Melchester when Jude and Sue climb the downs about Wardour Castle inevitably recalls the courtship walks with Arabella across the heights near Marygreen. One instance of Hardy's skilled use of these topographical images occurs at the novel's close. Jude's inscription on the milestone at Marygreen has now been almost effaced by moss: the implication is that Jude's aspirations have been slowly undermined with the years and are soon to be extinguished in his approaching death.

Other types of nature imagery similarly enlarge the realistic framework of the novel by suggesting that the life of nature underlies the social life of man even when that life is led in urban rather than in rural surroundings. Thus weather becomes as important as the terrain in establishing the emotional impress of *Jude the Obscure*. The Christminster fog, for example, hangs over the last sequences of the novel and adds to their chill and depressing effect. In one of these scenes, Jude in effect commits suicide by going back to Marygreen in a driving rain after he has begun to show symptoms of consumption. He also lies down to rest by the milestone near the Brown House where wind and rain are fiercest and coldest. Wind and storm continue when Sue that evening forces herself to yield to her husband. In ironic counterpoint to the brilliance of the sun and to the happy Remembrance Day games going on outside, Jude comes to his solitary shadowed end at Christminster. The classical and Biblical allusions, previously analyzed, also give the novel wider reference than a chronicle of contemporary events would normally possess, by suggesting that situations in the present somehow reach back through time and are comparable to conditions at remote dates in the history of humanity.

Both Sue and Jude live in a world of personal fantasy and illusion. The descriptions of their mental reactions and the images used to define them go counter to a strict realism by suggesting that an individualistic life in the mind is often fully as intense as life in society. Jude's inspiriting view of Christminster which his later experience cannot dispel, the lovers' enthusiasm for each other's company as a kind of paradisal union before tragedy strikes, and Jude's imaginative summoning of the spirits of the departed worthies that still haunt the university are all instances in Sue and Jude of concentrated mental vision, related only tangentially to the verisimilar life recorded in the book. Jude at times feels that he is as much a disembodied spirit as a struggling young man, upon occasion a "self-spectre" (p. 91) who is "spectre-seeing always" (p. 180); at the same time he regards Sue, despite her physical beauty, as ethereal and bodiless. Sue and Jude at various times see one another as naive and enthusiastic children; other spectators like Phillotson and Arabella comment upon their childlike quality. Emma Clifford has shown convincingly that part of the imaginative universe of *Jude the Obscure* consists of a childlike realm of fantasy.[18] She has demonstrated, moreover, that this realm of fantasy sometimes becomes malignant and approaches nightmare. The malevolence of life is epitomized, for example, by the obtrusive policeman who always acts as a kind of censor whenever the characters are at their most spontaneous. The aged and ageless child, Father Time, with his warped view of life, contributes, too, to the grim fantasy in the novel. Existence seen through the eyes of this precocious and humorless boy becomes a sinister and sick horror, at its most unrelieved, of course, in the hanging of his half-brother, his half-sister, and himself.

IV

The metaphors and metaphorical incidents in the novel often illustrate Hardy's philosophical ideas and values. The indifference of God, or the powers that control the universe, to man and his destiny are indicated figuratively at many points. The hard life of the crows which Jude must scare from Farmer Troutham's field leads him to think that "mercy towards one set of creatures was cruelty towards another" (p. 15); and the selling of her pet pigeons to the poulterer at the removal from Aldbrickham prompts Sue likewise to ask, "Oh, why should Nature's law be mutual butchery!" (p. 376). The imagery deriving from sickness reveals the futility of the characters' lives, their basic neuroticism, and the indifference of the cosmic powers to them. At the close of the novel when Sue as the source of his life's meaning is withdrawn from him, Jude gradually loses the desire to live. In despair he goes to a part of Christminster "where boughs dripped, and coughs and consumption lurked" (p. 444). His life becomes increasingly fevered and reaches a climax of desperation after the sordid saturnalia behind Donn's Christminster sausage shop which leads to his remarriage to Arabella. Subsequently, he is in physical pain from his loss of health and in mental pain from his loss of Sue and from his sense of degradation in having abandoned himself again to Arabella. After his farewell journey to Marygreen, "a deadly chill" penetrates his bones; back in Christminster he totters "with cold and lassitude," and becomes more fevered still. The inescapable conclusion is that only in a malignant universe could there be so much undeserved suffering.

The theme of modern restlessness, which Hardy had hitherto explored in *The Return of the Native,* is also dominating in his last major novel. This theme is not only explicitly stated several times but illustrated through the imagery. Early in the action Jude is described as "a tragic Don Quixote" (p. 247) and as a "Dick Whittington, whose spirit was touched to finer issues than a mere material gain" (p. 89)—the man, in other words, who will give over the ordinary securities and rewards to seek the all but unattainable. In serene Christminster the very buildings seem engaged in an insensate struggle for survival and comment implicitly upon the restlessness and the lack of ideal harmonies in modern society. At Christminister the angularity and precision of the stones cut by modern masons are deceptive. Modern thought is chaotic, less orderly and ordered by far than medieval, even if the relics of medievalism do not have the surface sharpness of modern stones. Jude's social unrest has its counterpart in the vagrancy of the itinerant show people who hibernate at Shaston. Sue, moreover, describes herself as a woman "tossed about, all alone, with aberrant passions and unaccountable antipathies" (p. 248). When Sue and Jude leave a settled life at Aldbrickham for a nomadic existence despite Sue's giving birth thereafter to two children, we may conclude that the social and domestic roots of the couple have dissolved. They spend two and a half years wandering from place to place and finally get back to Christminster. At this juncture Jude describes himself to bystanders as lost in "a chaos of principles—groping in the dark—acting by instinct and not after example" (p. 399). Thus, like Sue, he is symbolic of spiritual malaise and lacks a firm substratum of moral and intellectual values.

The opposition of the forces of life and death, fundamental to the complete meaning of the novel, is conveyed through appropriate images. Thus the past is seen both as a positive and a negative influence. Jude feels the vital energy emanating from Christminster infused into him when he strokes the stones of the buildings during his first night there. Though the university at night is a haunt of the dead, their spirits whisper a message of light and hope to him in these days. Jude remains loyal to the spiritual effluence of the university even when intellectual assent to its values is no longer complete. Jude's continued idealization of the Christian city would, in fact, imply that Christianity can still exert an authentic appeal to the imagination and the moral sensibilities even in a skeptical age. In his early vision of Christminster as a heavenly Jerusalem, he sees its topaz lights go out like "extinguished candles" as he looks toward the city. This image prefigures Jude's own later relation to Christminster, as its Christian influence dwindles over him and as his own hopes for matriculating disappear. His first vision of the lighted city through the

momentarily lifted fog also emphasizes his own difficulties in his attempt to reach it and to become identified with its life-giving spirit. The later associations of Christminster with fog indicate that it is not quite the clear intellectual center that Jude felt it to be in his early days. Jude becomes aware, moreover, that he is further away from Christminster when he is living in the town than he had been previously. The division between what he is and what he wants to be is the greater now that only a "wall" lies between him and the colleges. On Jude's final return to Christminster, this image of a separating wall is used again when only a wall quite literally divides his family's temporary lodgings from the college at the back of the house.

The precious spiritual heritage from the past is all present in Christminster but it has been greatly dissipated by inertia and decay. This is the belief of Sue who is oppressed by Sarcophagus College with its "four centuries of gloom, bigotry, and decay" (p. 406). As if to confirm her insight, "the quaint and frost-eaten stone busts" (p. 400) encircling the theater look down with disdain upon intruders like Jude and his family as an affront to their rock-bound conservatism. As an "outsider" to the end of his days (see Sue's earlier description of herself as an Ishmaelite), Jude daily repairs the colleges he will never enter and the windows he will never look from.

The images connected with Sue reveal her as an ambiguous moral force, and illustrate Hardy's conviction that positive and negative energies can be exerted, almost simultaneously and often unconsciously, by a gifted and unusual person. At first she seems to Jude to be a part of the atmosphere of light characterizing Christminster, and the fact that she is in the city helps determine him to come there. At this time she is a figure of mystery and suggestion; when Jude finally sees her he is impressed by her vibrancy and by her graciousness. She possesses "a kindling glance"; and later Jude refers to her intellect in these years as "a shining star" or as "lambent lightning." Phillotson, too, refers to her intellect as sparkling "like diamonds."

In the Melchester sequences before her marriage to Phillotson, her influence becomes more ambivalent. Generally a focus of light and life, she wishes "to ennoble some men to high aims" (p. 182) by infusing into them some of her intellectual energy. Like some women who wish to exert undue control over the destinies of men, she ends by destroying or depressing three men instead of exalting any of them. In the exercise of her vitality she is also curiously irresponsible. Thus she revels in new sensations, irrespective of their influence upon others. An "epicure in emotions" (p. 207), she visits in Jude's company the chapel in which she is to be married at Melchester, little thinking of the torture that this experience entails for the cousin who loves her but who is unable to marry her himself.

Jude's desire to live survives the death of his children; and, despite the horror of the occurrence, he feels that tragedy has enlarged his views while it has narrowed Sue's. Sue's latent revulsion from life, indicated in her Schopenhauerian conviction expressed at Aldbrickham that people in the future may will the extinction of the race, is intensified by the family tragedy. More given to depression than Jude, Sue had felt from the first greater spontaneous sympathy with little Father Time. As a result of his disruption of their family life, Sue embraces the negations that had previously warped the child's nature. Her children's deaths, in part the result of her indiscreet and evasive confidences to Father Time, symbolize her failure to emancipate herself from tradition and, incidentally, her death-bringing influence. The Widow Edlin recalls Sue's uncanny ability as a child to actualize the presence of the raven of death when she recited Poe's poem. Thus Sue, a vessel of the life-force, was also from her early years a potential force for death. Her secret wishes also carry her, she confides to Jude, backward to the security of infancy—ostensibly to the peace of the womb—rather than forward into life: "I like reading and all that, but I crave to get back to the life of my infancy and its freedom" (p. 164).

Jude's comment after the death of the children reveals how delicately balanced the conflicting energies of life and death are in Sue. She is mistaken in feeling that she is an ascetic, he says; rather she is healthy in her emotional responses, delicate but not inhumanly sexless. He does accuse her of never having loved him as he has loved her: her "heart does not burn in a flame" (p. 432), whereas he had been earlier seen with "his ardent affection for her burning in his eyes" (p. 288). In essence, he perceives that she has drained him of his life energies, at the same time that she is their all too volatile source. Now that the cosmic powers seem bent on vengeance, she is deaf to Jude's entreaty for her to stay with him and offers herself in a sacrificial rite to Christian convention by going back to Phillotson. At this point one recalls Sue's own pitying attitude toward the bride at Aldbrickham: Sue had then felt that the woman, bedecked with flowers, was a lamentable sacrifice on the altar of custom, answering a purpose similar to the sacrifice of bedecked heifers on Grecian altars to gods and principles now seen to be superstitions.

Possibly the characters in *Jude the Obscure* are relatively static, and possibly incident is for the most part contrived, since both men and society alike are controlled by deterministic natural law. Yet this is only one impression produced by the novel, I feel, and not the most important one. If *Jude the Obscure* possesses some of the stationary quality which often characterizes realism in the graphic arts, still as in the masterworks of realistic painting and sculpture the details of the composition and the relationships among them are not immediately available to the critic. Similarly the full ramifications of pattern emerge in *Jude the Obscure* only after these details have been studied, that is, only after an exhaustive analysis has been made of the images and parallel situations in it. New chains of connection among these subsidiary and component elements of the book are continually being suggested to the contemplative, inquiring intelligence. In

spite, then, of its somewhat rigid structural lines and philosophical framework, *Jude the Obscure,* as a pulsating organism within such limits, is continually alive with ever-expanding significance. This novel is, as it were, a kind of kaleidoscope: the pattern formed by image, event, character, and idea continually changes with the angle from which it is viewed. The fluid contours of the novel reform and reshape to furnish changing vistas of meaning; new impressions of the whole which are yet related to our previous impressions continually emerge.

[1] *Thomas Hardy: A Study of His Writings and Their Backgrounds* (New York, 1938), pp. 256-257; *Hardy the Novelist* (New York, 1943), pp. 172-173, 189-192; *Thomas Hardy* (New York, 1951: *Writers and Their Work,* No. 21), p. 26; *Thomas Hardy* (New York, 1954), pp. 98-100; *Thomas Hardy: A Critical Biography* (London, 1954), pp. 246, 253.

[2] *Thomas Hardy: A Critical Study* (London, 1912), p. 161; *Thomas Hardy: A Study of the Wessex Novels* (New York, 1916), p. 173; *The Technique of Thomas Hardy* (Chicago, 1922), pp. 242-243; *Thomas Hardy: A Critical Study* (London, 1931), p. 88; *Thomas Hardy: The Novels and the Stories* (Cambridge, Mass., 1949), p. 159.

[3] *Thomas Hardy: The Novels and the Stories,* p. 82.

[4] "*Jude the Obscure* as a Tragedy," *Southern Review,* VI (Summer 1940), pp. 193-213; and *The English Novel* (New York, 1954), pp. 285-304.

[5] See the essays "The Profitable Reading of Fiction" and "The Science of Fiction," reprinted in *Life and Art,* ed. Ernest Brennecke, Jr. (New York, 1925).

[6] "The Science of Fiction," p. 89.

[7] Florence E. Hardy, *The Early Life of Thomas Hardy, 1840-1891* (New York, 1928), p. 150.

[8] Florence E. Hardy, *The Later Years of Thomas Hardy, 1892-1928* (New York, 1930), p. 178.

[9] *Jude the Obscure,* 1895 text as reprinted in The Modern Library Edition, p. vi. Page references in my article are to this edition.

[10] *Southern Review,* VI (Summer 1940), p. 197.

[11] *The English Novel,* p. 302.

[12] *Nineteenth Century Fiction,* IX (June 1954), pp. 50-61.

[13] "Hardy in Defense of His Art," *Craft and Character: Texts, Method, and Vocation in Modern Fiction* (New York, 1957), p. 94.

[14] *Thomas Hardy: The Novels and the Stories,* p. 82.

[15] *Ibid.,* p. 33.

[16] The patterns of animal imagery in the novel are more fully analyzed in Holland's article, note 12 above.

[17] *Nineteenth Century Fiction,* IX (June 1954), p. 51.

[18] "The Child: The Circus: and *Jude the Obscure,*" *Cambridge Journal,* VIII (June 1954), pp. 531-546.

A. Alvarez (essay date 1961)

SOURCE: *Jude the Obscure,* in *Beyond All This Fiddle: Essays 1955-67,* Penguin Books, Ltd., 1968, pp. 178-87.

[*In the following essay, originally published in 1961, Alvarez claims that "the power of* Jude the Obscure *is . . . fictional rather than poetic" and sees the novel as essentially a study of loneliness rather than of character or of the workings of fate.*]

Jude the Obscure is Hardy's last and finest novel. Yet its publication in 1896 provoked an outcry as noisy as that which recently greeted *Lady Chatterley's Lover.* The press attacked in a pack, lady reviewers became hysterical, abusive letters poured in, and a bishop solemnly burnt the book. The fuss may seem to us, at this point in time, incredible and even faintly ridiculous, but its effect was serious enough: ' . . . the experience', Hardy wrote later, 'completely cured me of further interest in novel-writing.' After *Jude* he devoted himself exclusively to his poetry, never returning to fiction.

What caused the uproar? It was not Hardy's fatalism; after *Tess* his public had learned to live with that and even love it. Nor was his attack on social and religious hypocrisy particularly virulent, though there was certainly a good deal of entrenched resentment of his criticism of those two almost equally venerable institutions: marriage and Oxford. Zola's name was invoked by one or two reviewers, but not seriously. The real blow to the eminently shockable Victorian public was the fact that Hardy treated the sexual undertheme of his book more or less frankly: less frankly, he complained, than he had wished, but more frankly than was normal or acceptable.

Despite the social criticism it involves, the tragedy of *Jude* is not one of missed chances but of missed fulfilment, of frustration. It is a kind of *Anna Karenina* from the male point of view, with the basic action turned upside down. Where Anna moves from Karenin to Vronsky, from desiccation to partial satisfaction, Jude, swinging from Arabella to Sue, does the opposite. For all his—and Hardy's—superficial disgust, Jude and Arabella are, physically, very much married: their night at Aldbrickham after years apart is made to seem the most natural thing in the world; Jude's subsequent shame is prompted less by the act itself than by his anger at missing Sue and fear that she will somehow find out. On the other hand, his great love for Sue remains at its high pitch of romance and fatality largely because she never

really satisfies him. Hardy himself was quite explicit about this in a letter he wrote after the novel was published:

> One point . . . I could not dwell on: that, though she has children, her intimacies with Jude have never been more than occasional, even when they were living together (I mention that they occupy separate rooms, except towards the end, and one of her reasons for fearing the marriage ceremony is that she fears it would be breaking faith with Jude to withhold herself at pleasure, or altogether, after it; though while uncontracted she feels at liberty to yield herself as seldom as she chooses). This has tended to keep his passion as hot at the end as at the beginning, and helps to break his heart. He has never really possessed her as freely as he desired.

So Jude's tragedy, like every true tragedy, comes from inner tensions which shape the action, not from any haphazard or indifferent force of circumstance. Jude is as frustrated by Sue, his ideal, intellectual woman, as he is by Oxford, his equally shining ideal of the intellectual life. Frustration is the permanent condition of his life.

I am not, of course, suggesting that the book has no theme beyond the sexual relations of Jude, Sue, Arabella, and Phillotson. That was D. H. Lawrence's interpretation in his wonderfully perceptive, startlingly uneven *Study of Thomas Hardy.* But then Lawrence was writing not as a critic but as an imaginative artist who owed a great personal debt to Hardy. His critical method was simply to retell Hardy's plots as though he himself had written them, isolating only what interested him. The result was considerable insight and an equally considerable shift of emphasis away from the novel Hardy actually wrote.

Obviously, *Jude the Obscure* does have its declared social purpose: to criticize a system which could, for mainly snobbish reasons, keep out of the universities 'one of the very men', as Sue says, 'Christminster was intended for when the Colleges were founded; a man with a passion for learning, but no money, or opportunities, or friends. . . . You were elbowed off the pavement by the millionaires' sons.' A figure who for Thomas Gray, a Cambridge don elegizing in his country churchyard, was an object of mildly nostalgic curiosity, became in Hardy's work a living, tragic hero. And by this shift of focus Hardy helped make the issue itself live. In his postscript of 1912 he wrote 'that some readers thought . . . that when Ruskin College was subsequently founded it should have been called the College of Jude the Obscure'. Hardy may not have had as direct an influence on social reforms as Dickens; but he helped.

Yet *Jude the Obscure* is clearly more than a criticism of the exclusiveness of the major English universities. Surprisingly early in the book Jude realizes that his Christminster ambitions are futile. After that, though the University remains an obsession with him, it plays very little part in the novel itself. Instead, it is a kind of subplot echoing the main theme in slightly different terms, just as Gloucester and his sons repeat on a smaller scale the tragedy of King Lear and his daughters. But with a crucial difference: Jude is the hero of both the main plot and the sub-plot. Christminster may drop out of the major action, but his continuing obsession with it repeats, in another tone of voice, his obsession with Sue. In the beginning, both Sue and the university seem objects of infinitely mysterious romance; both, in the end, land Jude in disillusion. Both seem to promise intellectual freedom and strength; both are shown to be at bottom utterly conventional. Both promise fulfilment; both frustrate him. All Jude's intellectual passion earns him nothing more than the title 'Tutor of St Slums', while all his patience and devotion to Sue loses him his job, his children and finally even his title of husband.

Hardy himself knew perfectly well that the Christminster, social-purpose side of the novel was relatively exterior to its main theme. Years later, when there was talk of turning *Jude* into a play, he wrote: 'Christminster is of course the tragic influence of Jude's drama in one sense, but innocently so, and merely as a crass obstruction.' There is, however, nothing exterior in the part Sue plays in Jude's tragedy. At times, in fact, she seems less a person in her own right than a projection of one side of Jude's character. Even Phillotson remarks on this: 'I have been struck', he said, 'with . . . the extraordinary sympathy, or similarity, between the pair. He is her cousin, which perhaps accounts for some of it. They seem to be one person split in two!' And, in harmony with the principle by which all the major intuitions in the novel are given to the men, Jude himself perceives the same thing: when he lends Sue his clothes after she has escaped from the training college and arrived, soaking wet, at his lodgings, 'he palpitated at the thought that she had fled to him in her trouble as he had fled to her in his. What counterparts they were! . . . Sitting in his only arm-chair he saw a slim and fragile being masquerading as himself on a Sunday, so pathetic in her defencelessness that his heart felt big with the sense of it.' The situation, in which the hero dresses in his own clothes his wet, lost, desperate double, is exactly the same as that of the masterpiece of double identity, Conrad's *The Secret Sharer*.

Considering the ultimate differences between Sue and Jude, Hardy perhaps thought that their similarities merely emphasized the contrasts of which, he wrote, the book was full: 'Sue and her heathen gods set against Jude's reading the Greek testament; Christminster academical, Christminster in the slums; Jude the saint, Jude the sinner; Sue the pagan, Sue the saint; marriage, no marriage; etc. etc.' But the geometrical neatness of Hardy's plan does not make his psychological insight any less profound or compelling. All through the book Sue is Jude 'masquerading as himself on a Sunday'. As even her name implies (Sue, Hardy says himself, is a lily, and Bridehead sounds very like maidenhead), she is the untouched part of him, all intellect, nerves and sensitivity, essentially bodiless. That is why her most dramatic and

typical appearances have always something ghostly about them. When, for example, Jude suddenly and guiltily comes across her after his night with Arabella at Aldbrickham, 'Sue stood like a vision before him—her look bodeful and anxious as in a dream'. Or, when she unexpectedly returns to Phillotson in his illness, and does her odd, characteristic conjuring trick with the mirror: 'She was in light spring clothing, and her advent seemed ghostly—like the flitting in of a moth.' It is this combination of non-physical purity with exaggeratedly sharp intellect and sensitivity which preserves her for Jude as an object of ideal yearning, hopeless and debilitating. It is a yearning for his own lost innocence, before his Christminster ambitions were diverted by Arabella. Even when he finally rounds on her, after all their years and tragedies together, he can still only call her 'a sort of fey, or sprite—not a woman!' Despite everything he can do, she remains a bodiless idea, an idea of something in himself.

Sue and Arabella are, in fact, like the white and black horses, the noble and base instincts, which draw Plato's chariot of the soul. But because Hardy too had a passion for Sue's kind of frigid purity ('She is', he wrote, 'a type of woman which has always had an attraction for me'), he exaggerated the case against Arabella almost to the point of parody. Lawrence wrote:

> He insists that she is a pig-killer's daughter; he insists that she drag Jude into pig-killing; he lays stress on her false tail of hair. That is not the point at all. This is only Hardy's bad art. He himself, as an artist, manages in the whole picture of Arabella almost to make insignificant in her these pig-sticking, false-hair crudities. But he must have his personal revenge on her for her coarseness, which offends him, because he is something of an Angel Clare.

Where Hardy thought Arabella 'the villain of the piece', Lawrence tried to make her out the heroine. Both views are wrong, not because Sue is any more or less of the heroine than Arabella, but because *Jude the Obscure* is fundamentally a work without any heroines at all. It has only a hero. I will return to this. Lawrence was, however, right when he said that Arabella survives Hardy's deliberate coarsening of her. The artist does her justice against the grain of his tastes. So it is she, not Sue, who shows flashes of real intelligence:

> 'I don't know what you mean,' said Sue stiffly.
> 'He is mine if you come to that!'
>
> 'He wasn't yesterday.'
>
> Sue coloured roseate, and said 'How do you know?'
>
> 'From your manner when you talked to me at the door. Well, my dear, you've been quick about it, and I expect my visit last night helped it on. . . .'

And it is also she, not Sue, who really wants Jude:

> In a few moments Arabella replied in a curiously low, hungry tone of latent sensuousness: 'I've got

him to care for me: yes! But I want him to more than care for me; I want him to have me—to marry me! I must have him. I can't do without him. He's the sort of man I long for. I shall go mad if I can't give myself to him altogether! I felt I should when I first saw him!'

With fewer exclamation marks and without the moralizing qualification of 'latent sensuousness'—as though that were so reprehensible!—Arabella's words would sound more frank and serious than any protestation Sue manages in the whole book. Similarly, despite everything, it is Arabella whom Jude really wants physically. There is no doubt about this from the moment when, without a flicker of distaste, he picks up the pig's pizzle she has thrown at him:

> . . . somehow or other, the eyes of the brown girl rested in his own when he had said the words, and there was a momentary flash of intelligence, a dumb announcement of affinity *in posse,* between herself and him, which, so far as Judy Fawley was concerned, had no sort of premeditation in it. She saw that he had singled her out from the three, as a woman is singled out in such cases. . . . The unvoiced call of woman to man, which was uttered very distinctly by Arabella's personality, held Jude to the spot against his intention—almost against his will, and in a way new to his experience.

This may have in it none of the refinement of Jude's passion for Sue, but it is considerably more human and spontaneous. Jude, after all, fell in love with Sue's photograph before he fell in love with Sue herself; and the first time she saw him 'she no more observed his presence than that of the dust-motes which his manipulations raised into the sunbeams'. So they are never really married because the connection between them is of the sensibility, not of the senses. The only real moment of ecstasy Jude shares with Sue is bodiless, precipitated by the scent and brilliance of the roses at the agricultural show. 'The real marriage of Jude and Sue was', as Lawrence said, 'in the roses.' So it is Arabella who gets the last word; however much Hardy may have disliked her in principle, artistically he acknowledged the sureness of her physical common sense, to the extent at least of allowing her to make the final, unqualified judgement of the tragedy:

> 'She may swear that on her knees to the holy cross upon her necklace till she's hoarse, but it won't be true!' said Arabella. 'She's never found peace since she left his arms, and never will again till she's as he is now!'

Yet although his final attitude to Sue may have been ambiguous, in creating her Hardy did something extraordinarily original: he created one of the few totally narcissistic women in literature; yet he did so at the same time as he made her something rather wonderful. Her complexity lies in the way in which Hardy managed to present the full, bitter sterility of her narcissism and yet tried to exonerate her.

Bit by bit, even Jude is made to build up the case against her: she is cold, 'incapable of real love', 'an epicure of the emotions', and a flirt; she wants to be loved more than she wants to love; she is vain, marrying Phillotson out of pique when she learns that Jude is married, and going to bed with Jude only when Arabella reappears on the scene; she is even cruel, in a refined way, her deliberate, 'epicene' frigidity having killed one man before the novel even starts. Yet despite all this, Jude loves her. Part of his love, of course, is rooted in frustration: he wants her endlessly because he can never properly have her. And he loves her, too, because he loves himself; he has in himself a narcissism which responds to hers, a vanity of the intellectual life, of his ideals and ambitions, of the refinement of intellect and sensibility which he had first projected on to Christminster.

But the truth and power of the novel lie in the way in which Jude, in the end, is able to understand his love for Sue *without lessening it.* Until the closing scenes, he manages to make her conform to his ideal by a kind of emotional sleight of mind: he dismisses his glimpses of the unchanging conventionality below the bright surface of her non-conformity by invoking both his own worthlessness and that vague marriage-curse which has been the lot of his family. The turning-point is the death of the children.

> One thing troubled him more than any other; that Sue and himself had mentally travelled in opposite directions since the tragedy: events which had enlarged his own views of life, laws, customs, and dogmas, had not operated in the same manner on Sue's. She was no longer the same as in the independent days, when her intellect played like lambent lightning over conventions and formalities which he at the time respected, though he did not now.

Where Jude matures as a man, reconciling himself to the endless tragedies and disappointments until he can accept them more or less without self-pity, Sue remains fixed in her narcissism. She does not change, she simply shapes her outer actions to the commonplaces which at heart have always ruled her. Convention—which she calls High Church Sacramentalism—is simply a way of preserving her vanity intact. To break her self-enclosed mould would mean laying herself open to the real tragedy of her relationship with Jude—of which she, not Fate, is the main instrument and thus giving herself to him completely. Because she is unable to do this, she denies the true marriage between them and perverts it to fit a conventional idea of matrimony. Arabella may occasionally have turned whore for practical ends—that presumably, is how she raised the money to make Jude drunk before remarrying him—but it is Sue whom he accuses, when she returns to Phillotson, of 'a fanatic prostitution'. What began as intellectual freedom ends as prostitution to an idea. So when Jude finally turns on her with the cry 'Sue, Sue, you are not worth a man's love!', he is passing judgement not only on her but also, because he never once denies that he loves her, on something in himself. That cry and Arabella's closing words represent a standard of maturity which Jude only slowly and painfully attains.

There is something puzzling about *Jude the Obscure* as a work of art: in impact it is intensely moving; in much of its detail it is equally intensely false. The dialogue, for example, is, with very little exception, forced and awkward. Even granted the conventional formalities of the time, no character ever properly seems to connect with another in talk. Despite all the troubles they have seen together, Jude and Sue speak to each other as though they had just been introduced at a vicarage tea-party. As a result, their grand passion becomes, on their own lips, something generalized, like the weather or religion or politics. They are, in Sue's own words, 'too sermony'. Conversely, Arabella, apart from her few moments of truth and an occasional, ponderous slyness, is reduced to a kind of music-hall vulgarity of speech. Widow Edlin is archly folksy and Father Time is almost a caricature of Hardy at his most Hardyesque. The only people who seem able to talk more or less naturally to others are the solitaries, Phillotson and, in a slighter way, Vilbert.

It may be that Hardy had very little ear for dialogue; it is something he rarely does well. But his clumsiness in *Jude* is more than a fault, it is part of the nature of the work. For the essential subject of the novel is not Oxford, or marriage, or even frustration. It is loneliness. This is the one condition without which the book would show none of its power. When they are together the characters often seem amateurishly conceived, and sometimes downright false. But once they are left to themselves they begin to think, feel, act and even talk with that strange poignancy which is uniquely Hardy's. The brief, almost cursory paragraph in which Jude tries to drown himself after the failure of his first marriage is a far more effective and affecting scene than, for example, the elaborately constructed pig-killing—and largely, I think, because nothing is said. None of the emotional impact is lost in heavy moralizing or awkwardness. When Jude is on his own, as he is for a great deal of the novel, walking from one village to the next, one Christminster college to another, then he emerges as a creation of real genius.

The novel's power, in fact, resides in that sustained, deep plangency of note which is the moving bass behind every major incident. This note is produced not by any single action but by a general sense of tragedy and sympathetic hopelessness which the figure of Jude provokes in Hardy. And the essence of his tragedy is Jude's loneliness. He is isolated from society because his ambitions, abilities and sensibility separate him from his own class while winning him no place in any other. He is isolated in his marriage to Arabella because she has no idea of what he is about, and doesn't care. He is isolated in his marriage to Sue because she is frigid. Moreover, the sense of loneliness is intensified by the way in which both women are presented less as characters complete in themselves than as projections of Jude, sides of his character, existing only

in relation to him. In the same way, the wonderfully sympathetic and moving treatment of Phillotson in the scene at Shaston—his surprising delicacy and generosity and desolating loneliness—is essentially the same as the treatment of Jude. The two men, indeed, are extraordinarily alike: they are both in love with the same woman, both fail in much the same way at Christminster, both inhabit the same countryside and suffer the same loneliness. Their difference is in age and ability and passion. Phillotson, in short, is as much a projection of Jude as are the two women. He is a kind of Jude Senior: older, milder, with less talent and urgency, and so without the potentiality for tragedy. In one sense, the entire novel is simply the image of Jude magnified and subtly lit from different angles until he and his shadows occupy the whole Wessex landscape. And Jude in turn is an embodiment of the loneliness, deprivation and regret which are both the strength and constant theme of Hardy's best poetry. Hardy may have been perfectly justified in denying that the book was at all autobiographical, but it is a supremely vivid dramatization of the state of mind out of which Hardy's poetry emerged.

This is why Father Time fails as a symbol. He is introduced in one of the most beautiful passages of the novel:

> He was Age masquerading as Juvenility, and doing it so badly that his real self showed through crevices. A ground-swell from ancient years of night seemed now and then to lift the child in this his morning-life, when his face took a back view over some great Atlantic of Time, and appeared not to care about what it saw.

And he is finally left in a paragraph of equal force:

> The boy's face expressed the whole tale of their situation. On that little shape had converged all the inauspiciousness and shadow which had darkened the first union of Jude and all the accidents, mistakes, fears, errors of the last. He was their nodal point, their focus, their expression in a single term. For the rashness of those parents he had groaned, for their ill-assortment he had quaked, and for the misfortunes of these he had died.

But in between these two points, his ominous remarks, desolation, and self-consciously incurable melancholy are so overdone as to seem almost as though Hardy had decided to parody himself. Even the death of the children, and Father Time's appalling note—'Done because we are too menny'—is dangerously close to being laughable: a situation so extreme, insisted on so strongly, seems more appropriate to *grand guignol* than to tragedy. But Hardy, I think, was forced to overdraw Father Time because the child is redundant in the scheme of the novel. What he represents was already embodied in fully tragic form in the figure of Jude. There was no way of repeating it without melodrama.

The power of *Jude the Obscure* is, then, less fictional than poetic. It arises less from the action or the fidelity of the setting than from the wholeness of the author's feelings. It is a tragedy whose unity is not Aristotelian but emotional. And the feelings are those which were later given perfect form in Hardy's best poetry. The work is the finest of Hardy's novels because it is the one in which the complex of emotions is, despite Father Time, least weakened by melodrama, bad plotting, and that odd incidental amateurishness of detail by which, perhaps, Hardy, all through his novel-writing period, showed his dissatisfaction with the form. It is also the finest because it is the novel in which the true Hardy hero is most fully vindicated, and the apparently fascinating myth of immaculate frigidity is finally exploded. But I wonder if Hardy was not being slightly disingenuous when he claimed that the treatment of the book by the popular reviewers had turned him, for good, from the novel to poetry. After *Jude the Obscure* there was no other direction in which he could go.

Robert B. Heilman (essay date 1966)

SOURCE: "Hardy's Sue Bridehead", in *Nineteenth Century Fiction*, University of California Press, Vol. 20, No. 4, 1966, pp. 307-23.

[*In the following essay, Heilman examines Hardy's complex portrayal of the character of Sue Bridehead, calling it "an imaginative feat" that expresses Hardy's perception of modern human reality.*]

In *Jude the Obscure,* a novel in which skillful characterization eventually wins the day over laborious editorializing, Thomas Hardy comes close to genius in the portrayal of Sue Bridehead. Sue takes the book away from the title character, because she is stronger, more complex, and more significant, and because her contradictory impulses, creating a spontaneous air of the inexplicable and even the mysterious, are dramatized with extraordinary fullness and concreteness, and with hardly a word of interpretation or admonishment by the author. To say this is to say that as a character she has taken off on her own, sped far away from a conceptual role, and developed as a being whose brilliant and puzzling surface provides only partial clues to the depths in which we can sense the presence of profound and representative problems.

Sue's original role, of course, is that of counterpoint to Arabella: spirit against flesh, or Houyhnhnm against Yahoo. Sue and Arabella are meant to represent different sides of Jude, who consistently thinks about them together, contrasts them, regards them as mutually exclusive opposites (e.g., III, 9, 10; IV, 5). Early in their acquaintance he sees in Sue "almost an ideality" (II, 4), "almost a divinity" (III, 3); the better he gets to know her, the more he uses, in speech or thought, such terms as "ethereal" (III, 9; IV, 3; VI, 3), "uncarnate" (III, 9), "aerial" (IV, 3), "spirit, . . . disembodied creature . . . hardly flesh" (IV, 5) "phantasmal, bodiless creature" (V, 1), "least sensual," "a sort of fay, or sprite" (VI, 3). She herself asks Jude to kiss her "incorporeally" (V, 4), and she puts Mrs. Edlin "in mind of a sperrit" (VI, 9).

The allegorical content in Hardy's delineation of Sue has also a historical base: she is made a figure of Shelleyan idealism. When Phillotson describes the rather spiritualized affinity that he perceives between Jude and Sue, Gillingham exclaims "Platonic!" and Phillotson qualifies, "Well, no. Shelleyan would be nearer to it. They remind me of Laon and Cythna" (IV, 4), the idealized liberators and martyrs in *The Revolt of Islam* (which is quoted later in another context—V, 4). Sue asks Jude to apply to her certain lines from Shelley's "Epipsychidion"—" . . . a Being whom my spirit oft / Met on its visioned wanderings far aloft. . . . A seraph of Heaven, too gentle to be human" (IV, 5)—and Jude later calls Sue a "sensitive plant" (VI, 3).

Deliberately or instinctively Hardy is using certain Romantic values as a critical instrument against those of his own day, a free spirit against an oppressive society, the ethereal against commonplace and material. But a very odd thing happens: in conceiving of Sue as "spirit," and then letting her develop logically in such terms, he finds her coming up with a powerful aversion to sex—in other words, with a strong infusion of the very Victorianism that many of her feelings and intellectual attitudes run counter to. On the one hand, her objection to allegorizing the Song of Solomon (III, 4) is anti-Victorian; but when, in refusing to have intercourse with Jude, she says, "I resolved to trust you to set my wishes above your gratification," her view of herself as a supra-sexual holder of prerogative and of him as a mere seeker of "gratification" is quite Victorian. She calls him "gross," apparently both for his night with Arabella and for desiring her physically, and under her pressure he begs, "Forgive me for being gross, as you call it!" (IV, 5) Again, he uses the apologetic phrase, "we poor unfortunate wretches of grosser substance" (V, 1). All of Sue's terms for Arabella come out of middle-class propriety: "fleshy, coarse woman," "low-passioned woman," "too low, too coarse for you," as does her argument that Jude should not go to help her because "she's not your wife. . . ." Jude is not entirely pliant here; in fact, there is some defiance in his saying that perhaps he is "coarse, too, worse luck!" But even while arguing against her refusal of sex he can say that "your freedom from everything that's gross has elevated me," accepting the current view of the male as a lower being who needs to be lifted up to a higher life (V, 2). Even when, near the end, he is vehemently urging Sue not to break their union, he can entertain the possibility that in overturning her proscription of sex he may have "spoiled one of the highest and purest loves that ever existed between man and woman" (VI, 3); the "average sensual man" all but gives up his case to a conventional opinion of his own time. Other aspects of Sue's vocabulary betray the Victorian tinge: when she first calls marriage a "sordid contract" (IV, 2) it seems fresh and independent, but the continuing chorus of "horrible and sordid" (V, 1), "vulgar" and "low" (V, 3), "vulgar" and "sordid" (V, 4) suggests finally an over-nice and complacent personality. The style is a spontaneous accompaniment of the moral elevation which she assumes in herself and which in part she uses—Hardy is very shrewd in getting at the power-sense in self-conscious "virtue"—to keep Jude in subjection.

There is a very striking irony here: perhaps unwittingly Hardy has forged or come upon a link between a romantic idea of spirit (loftiness, freedom) and a Victorian self-congratulatory "spirituality"—a possibly remarkable feat of the historical imagination. He has also come fairly close to putting the novel on the side of the Houyhnhnms, a difficulty that he never gets around quite satisfactorily. But above all he has given a sharp image of inconsistency in Sue, for whatever the paradoxical link between her manifestations of spirit, she nevertheless appears as the special outsider on the one hand and as quite conventional on the other. In this he continues a line of characterization that he has followed very skillfully from the beginning. Repeatedly he uses such words as "perverseness," "riddle" (III, 1), "conundrum" (III, 2), "unreasonable . . . capricious" (III, 5), "perverse," "colossal inconsistency" (III, 7), "elusiveness of her curious double nature," "ridiculously inconsistent" (IV, 2), "logic . . . extraordinarily compounded," "puzzling and unpredictable" (IV, 3), "riddle" (IV, 4), "that mystery, her heart" (IV, 5), "ever evasive" (V, 5). With an inferior novelist, such an array of terms might be an effort to do by words what the action failed to do; here, they only show that Hardy knew what he was doing in the action, for all the difficulties, puzzles, and unpredictability have been dramatized with utmost variety and thoroughness. From the beginning, in major actions and lesser ones, Sue is consistently one thing and then another: reckless, then diffident; independent, then needing support; severe, and then kindly; inviting, and then offish. The portrayal of her is the major achievement of the novel. It is an imaginative feat, devoid of analytical props; for all of the descriptive words that he uses, Hardy never explains her or places her, as he is likely to do with lesser characters. She simply is, and it is up to the reader to sense the inner truth that creates multiple, lively, totally conflicting impressions. With her still more than with the other characters Hardy has escaped from the allegorical formula in which his addiction to such words as "spirit" might have trapped him.

From the beginning her inconsistency has a pattern which teases us with obscure hints of an elusive meaningfulness. Her first action characterizes her economically; she buys nude statues of classical divinities, but "trembled," almost repented, concealed them, misrepresented them to her landlady, and kept waking up anxiously at night (II, 3). She reads Gibbon but is superstitious about the scene of her first meeting with Jude (II, 4). She criticizes unrestrainedly the beliefs of Jude and Phillotson, but is wounded by any kind of retort (II, 5); repeatedly she can challenge, censure, and deride others but be hypersensitive to even mild replies, as if expecting immunity from the normal reciprocities of argument and emotion (III, 4; IV, 5; VI, 3, 4, 8). She reacts excessively to the unexpected visit of the school inspector, snaps at Phillotson "petulantly," and then "regretted that she had upbraided

him" (II, 5). Aunt Drusilla reports that as a girl Sue was "pert . . . too often, with her tight-strained nerves," and an inclination to scoff at the by-laws of modesty; she was a tomboy who would suddenly run away from the boys (II, 6).

These initial glimpses of Sue prepare for the remarkable central drama of the novel: her unceasing reversals, apparent changes of mind and heart, acceptances and rejections, alternations of warmth and offishness, of evasiveness and candor, of impulsive acts and later regrets, of commitment and withdrawal, of freedom and constraint, unconventionality and propriety. She is cool about seeing Jude, then very eager, then offish (III, 1). She escapes from confinement at school but appears increasingly less up to the exploit already concluded (III, 3-5). She tells Jude, "You mustn't love me," then writes "you may," quarrels with him, and writes, "Forgive . . . my petulance. . . ." (III, 5) Before and after marriage she resists talking about Phillotson ("But I am not going to be cross-examined . . .") and then talks about him almost without reserve (III, 6, 9; IV, 2). Again she forbids Jude to come to see her (III, 9), then "with sweet humility" revokes the prohibition (III, 10), is changeable when he comes, invites him for the next week (IV, 1), and then cancels the invitation (IV, 2). She "tearfully" refuses to kiss Jude, and then suddenly kisses him (IV, 3). Hardy identifies, as a natural accompaniment of her shifting of attitude and mood, a tendency to shift ground under pressure. Since she dislikes firm reply, argument, or questioning from others, she may simply declare herself "hurt." Another ploy is to make a hyperbolic statement of desolation or self-condemnation. "I *wish* I had a friend here to support me; but nobody is ever on my side!" (III, 5) "I am in the wrong. I always am!" (IV, 3) "I know I am a poor, miserable creature" (IV, 5). Another self-protective, situation-controlling move is to fall back directly on her emotional responsiveness to a difficult moment. She will not sleep with Jude but is jealous of Arabella; so she simply tells Jude, " . . . I don't like you as well as I did!" (IV, 5) When she will not acknowledge loving him and he remarks on the danger of the game of elusiveness, her reply, "in a tragic voice," is, "I don't think I like you today so well as I did . . ." (V, 1). For all of her intellectual freedom, she seems to accept the ancient dogma of "women's whims" (IV, 5) and calls Jude "good" because "you give way to all my whims!" (V, 4)

Through all the sensitiveness, fragility, and caprice there appears an impulse for power, for retaining control of a situation, very delicately or even overtly, in one's own terms. The Victorian acceptance of woman's pedestal implies a superiority to be acknowledged. Early in the story, just after Jude sees "in her almost a divinity" (III, 3), Sue states candidly that she "did want and long to ennoble some man to high aims" (III, 4)—which might be pure generosity or an idealism infected with egoism. She trusts Jude not to pursue her with a desire for "gratification" (IV, 5). She would rather go on "always" without sex because "It is so much sweeter—for the woman at least, and when she is sure of the man" (V, 1). The reappearance of Arabella so disturbs Sue's confidence in ownership that she tries to get rid of Arabella without Jude's seeing her, and when that fails, accepts the sexual bond only as a necessary means of binding Jude to her (V, 2). This gives her new confidence—"So I am not a bit frightened about losing you, now . . ."—and hence she resists marriage (V, 3). Behind this near-compulsion to prescribe terms is a need which Sue states three different times: "Some women's love of being loved is insatiable" (IV, 1); "But sometimes a woman's *love of being loved* gets the better of her conscience . . ." (IV, 5); "the craving to attract and captivate, regardless of the injury it may do the man" (VI, 3). Here again Hardy avoids both allegory and that idealizing of a character whom her own associates find it easy to idealize.

At the center of hypersensitivity he perceives a self-concern which can mean a high insensitivity to others and hence a habit of hurting them which may actually embody an unconscious intention (another version of the power-sense). Despite her formal words of regret and self-censure, Sue seems almost to relish the complaint of the student that she "was breaking his heart by holding out against him so long at such close quarters" (III, 4). Though she resents criticism of or even disagreement with her, all that Jude believes in and holds dear she attacks with an unrestraint that ranges from inconsiderateness to condescension to an outright desire to wound—the church, the university, and their traditions (III, 1, 2, and 4). Always careless of Phillotson's feelings, she does not even let him know about her expulsion from school (III, 6). Hardy presents her desire to leave Phillotson as understandable and defensible, but at the same time he portrays her style with Phillotson as fantastically inconsiderate. For instance, as he "writhed," she upbraided him in a doctrinaire style for not having a free mind as J. S. Mill advised (IV, 3); later, he lies "writhing like a man in hell" (IV, 6) as she lets him think that her relation with Jude is adulterous. She is indifferent to Jude's feelings when she refuses to have sexual intercourse with him. She insists that Jude must "love me dearly" (V, 3), but when he gives her an opening for speaking affectionately to him, she says only, "You are always trying to make me confess to all sorts of absurdities" (V, 5). She moves variously toward self-protection, self-assertion, and self-indulgence. One of the most remarkable cases of giving way to her own feelings in complete disregard of their impact on others is her telling Father Time, "vehemently," that "Nature's law [is] mutual butchery!" (V, 6)—a view that with any imagination at all she would know him utterly unfitted to cope with. It prepares for her thoughtless reply of "almost" to his statement that it "would be better to be out o' the world than in it" and her total ineptitude in dealing with his surmise that all their trouble is due to the children and with his desperation in finding that there is to be another child. Sue actually provides the psychological occasion, if not the cause, of the double murder and suicide (VI, 2)—the disasters that, with massive irony, begin her downward course to death-in-life.

The final touch in Sue as Victorian is her "I can't explain" when Father Time is driven frantic by the news that there will be another child. This is a lesser echo of Sue's embarrassment in all matters of sex—a disability the more marked in one who enters into otherwise intimate relations with a series of men. In her feeling free to deny the very center of the relationship what looks like naiveté or innocence masks a paradoxical double design of self-interest: she wants to be sexually attractive and powerful but to remain sexually unavailable. Sue has something of La Belle Dame Sans Merci, leaving men not "palely loitering" but worse off than that: of the three men who have desired her, one finally has her but only as a shuddering sacrificial victim, and the other two die of "consumption," which modern medical practice regards as predominantly of psychosomatic origin. She does give in to Jude, indeed, but immediately begins campaigning against marriage, and in terms so inapplicable—she repeatedly argues from the example of their earlier marriages, which are simply not relevant (e.g., V, 4)—that they exist not for their own sake but as a symbolic continuation of the resistance to sex. They secretly help to prepare us for her eventual flight from Jude, and to keep us from crediting her later statement that she and Jude found a pagan joy in sensual life (Hardy's belated effort to do something for sex, which he has hardly moved an inch from the most conventional position). True, she declares, just before resuming sexual relations with Phillotson, "I find I still love [Jude]—oh, grossly!" (VI, 9), but at this time the words seem less an intuition of truth than a reaction from the horror of her penitential life; and it is noteworthy that, in whatever sense they may be true, they are spoken by her only when the action they imply is now finally beyond possibility.

La Belle Dame Sans Merci cannot practice mercilessness without being belle—beautiful, or charming, or fascinating. Though Sue may be, as Arabella puts it, "not a particular warm-hearted creature" and "a slim, fidgety little thing" who "don't know what love is" (V, 5), even Gillingham feels what the three men in her life respond to, her "indefinable charm" (VI, 5). She is always spontaneous, often vivacious, occasionally kindly and tender. More important, Hardy has caught a paradoxical and yet powerful kind of charm: the physical attractiveness of the person who seems hardly to have physical existence and hence evokes such terms as "aerial" and "ethereal." The possibility that she unconsciously holds out to men in the enrichment of the ordinary sensual experience by its very opposite: all modes—or rather, the two extremes—of relationship are present at once in an extraordinary fusion. But this special charm is tenuously interwoven with the much more evident charm, the sheer power to fascinate, of an unpredictable personality. Though Sue may, as she herself theorizes, get into "these scrapes" through "curiosity to hunt up a new sensation," she does not have in her very much of the cold experimenter. Jude senses sadistic and masochistic elements in her (elements much noted by more recent critics). He theorizes that she "wilfully gave herself and him pain" for the pleasure of feeling pity for both, and he suspects that she will "go on inflicting such pains again and again, and grieving for the sufferer again and again" (III, 7). Her selfishness is never consistent; she can be virtually ruthless in seeking ends, and then try to make reparation. She can be contemptuous and cutting, and then penitent and tearful. She can be daring and then scared ("scared" and "frightened" are used of her repeatedly); inconsiderate, and then generous: self-indulgent, and then self-punishing; callous, and then all but heartbroken—always with a kind of rushing spontaneity. Such endless shifts as these, which Hardy presents with unflagging resourcefulness, make Jude call Sue a "flirt" (IV, 1). Jude merely names what the reader feels on page after page: the unconscious coquetry that Sue practices. The novel is, in one light, a remarkable treatment of coquetry, for it implicitly defines the underlying bases of the style. The ordinary coquette may tease and chill by plan, invite and hold off deliberately, heighten desire by displaying readiness and simulating retreat: the piquant puzzle. This is what Arabella offers with great crudity in the beginning: Hardy's preparation, by contrast, for the brilliant unconscious tactics of Sue.

The true, ultimate coquette, the coquette in nature, has no plans, no deliberations, no contrived puzzles. Her inconsistency of act is the inconsistency of being. She goes this way, and then that way, for no other reason than that she cannot help it. She acts in terms of one impulse that seems clear and commanding, and is then pulled away by another that comes up and, though undefined, is not subject to her control. On the one hand, she freely puts conventional limitations behind her; on the other, she hardly comes up to conventional expectations. She has freedom of thought but not freedom of action and being. She is desirable but does not desire. She wishes to be desirable, which means making the moves that signify accessibility to desire; the cost of love is then a commitment from which she must frantically or stubbornly withdraw. She is thoughtless and even punitive, but she has pangs of conscience; yet to be certain that she has conscience, she must create situations that evoke pity for others and blame of self. Hardy catches very successfully the spontaneity of each of her acts and gestures; they are authentic, unprogrammed expressions of diverse elements in her personality. Coquetry is, in the end, the external drama of inner divisions, of divergent impulses each of which is strong enough to determine action at any time, but not at all times or even with any regularity. The failure of unity is greater than that of the ordinary personality, and the possibilities of trouble correspondingly greater. If the coquette is not fortunate in finding men with great tolerance for her diversity—and ordinarily she has an instinct for the type she needs—and situations that do not subject her to too great pressure, she will hardly avoid disaster.

The split that creates the coquette is not unlike the tragic split; the latter, of course, implies deeper emotional commitments and more momentous situations. Yet one might entitle an essay on Sue "The Coquette as Tragic Heroine." Because she has a stronger personality than Jude, has more initiative, and endeavors more to impose her will, she is closer to tragic stature than he. Like traditional tragic heroes, she believes that she can dictate terms and clothe herself in special immunities; like them, she has finally to reckon with neglected elements in herself and in the order of life. If the catastrophe which she helps precipitate is not in the first instance her own, nevertheless it becomes a turning point for her, a shock that opens up a new illumination, a new sense of self and of the moral order. After the death of the children Sue comes into some remarkable self-knowledge. She identifies precisely her errors in dealing with Father Time (VI, 2). Her phrase "proud in my own conceit" describes her style as a free-swinging critic of others and of the world. She recognizes that her relations with Jude became sexual only when "envy stimulated me to oust Arabella." She acknowledges to Jude, " . . . I merely wanted you to love me . . . it began in the selfish and cruel wish to make your heart ache for me without letting mine ache for you." Such passages, with their burden of tragic self-understanding, predominate over others in which Sue looks for objects of blame, falls into self-pity, or frantically repeats her ancient self-protective plea, "Don't criticize me, Jude—I can't bear it!" (VI, 3)

But the passages that indicate growth by understanding are predominated over, in turn, by others in which Sue violently and excessively blames herself and pronounces on herself a life sentence of the severest mortification that she can imagine. Under great stress the precarious structure of her divided personality has broken down, and it has been replaced by a narrow, rigid unity under the tyrannical control of a single element in the personality— the self-blaming, self-flagellating impulse which Sue now formulates in Christian terms but which has been part of her all along. In place of the tragic understanding there is only black misery. Hence she ignores all Jude's arguments; Hardy may sympathize with these, but he knows what development is in character for Sue. A basic lack of wholeness has been converted, by heavy strains, into illness. Not that an imposition of a penalty is in itself pathological; we see no illness in the self-execution of Othello, or, more comparably, in the self-blinding of Oedipus. Facts become clear to them, and they accept responsibility by prompt and final action. Sue not only judges her ignoble deeds but undiscriminatingly condemns a whole life; she converts all her deeds into vice, and crawls into an everlasting hell on earth. Remorse has become morbid, and punishment seems less a symbolic acknowledgement of error than the craving of a sick nature.

The problem is, then, whether the story of Sue merely touches on tragedy, with its characteristic reordering of a chaotic moral world, or becomes mainly a case history of clinical disorder, a sardonic prediction of an endless night. As always, the problem of illness is its representativeness: have we a special case, interesting for its own sake, pitiable, shocking, but limited in its relevance, or is the illness symbolic, containing a human truth that transcends its immediate terms? There is a real danger of reading Sue's story as if its confines were quite narrow. If she is simply taken as an undersexed woman, the human range will not seem a large one. If she is simply defined as "sado-masochistic," we have only an abnormality. If she appears only as the victim of conventions which the world should get rid of, the romantic rebel unjustly punished, the intellectual range will seem too narrow, wholly without the comprehensiveness of George Eliot, who could see at once the pain inflicted by, and the inevitability of, conventions. If she seems simply a person of insufficient maturity—and Hardy used the words *child* and *children* repeatedly of Jude and Sue, and makes Sue say, " . . . I crave to get back to the life of my infancy and its freedom" (III, 2)—we will seem to have only the obvious truth that it is risky for a child to be abroad in a man's world. If she seems simply an innocent or idealist done in by a harsh world, the story will seem banal, if not actually sentimental. A Christian apologist might argue that her history shows the inescapability of Christian thought; an anti-Christian, that she is the victim of wrong ideas without which she would have been saved. The answer to the former is that such a Christian triumph would be a melancholy and hardly persuasive one, and to the latter that Sue's nature would find in whatever system of values might be available, religious or secular, the doctrinal grounds for acting out her own disorder.

She does not strike us, in the end, as of narrow significance. She is the rather familiar being whose resources are not up to the demands made upon them. This is not so much a matter of weakness and bad luck as it is of an impulsiveness and wilfulness that carry her beyond her depth; even as a child she shows signs of strain and tension. She has many of the makings of the nun, but she wants the world too; she is peculiarly in need of protection, but she wants always to assert and attack. She works partly from an unrecognized egotism, sometimes from an open desire to wound and conquer; her aggressiveness leads her into injurious actions not unlike those of tragic protagonists. Aside from inflicting unfulfilled relationships upon three men, she does a subtler but deeper injury to Jude: with a mixture of the deliberate and the wanton she helps undermine the beliefs that are apparently essential to his well-being; she cannot stand that he should have any gods but her own. She has the style of the blue-stocking who has found a new key to truth and is intolerant of all who have not opened the same door. Though she is sympathetic with Jude in many ways, she lacks the imagination to understand the real needs of his nature; instead of understanding either him or her substantial indifferences to his well-being, she volubly pities him because the university and the world are indifferent to him. Having lost his faith and hope, he leans heavily on her; then she takes that support away when her own needs set her on another course. Symbolically, she comes fairly close to husband-murder.

In them Hardy activates two important, and naturally hostile, strains of nineteenth-century thought and feeling. Jude is under the influence of the Tractarian Movement, which, appealing to some of the best minds in university and church, displayed great vitality in pursuing its traditionalist and anti-liberal aims. Yet his allegiance does not hold up under the blows of Sue's modernist criticism; she looks at Jude as a sort of archaeological specimen, "a man puzzling out his way along a labyrinth from which one had one's self escaped" (III, 2) and refers sarcastically to his "Tractarian stage" as if he had not grown up (III, 4). So he falls into a secular liberalism which simply fails to sustain him. Sue, on the other hand, has felt the influence of utilitarianism (she quotes Mill to Phillotson very dogmatically); but her skepticism wilts under catastrophe, and she falls into an ascetic self-torment which utterly distorts the value of renunciation (the reduction of hubris to measure). Sue often talks about charity, but, despite her moments of sweetness and kindliness, it is hardly among her virtues; as a surrogate for charity to others she adopts a violent uncharitableness to herself.

Hardy may be intentionally commenting on the inadequacy of two important movements, perhaps because neither corresponds enough to human complexity. But as novelist he is rather exhibiting two characters who in different ways fail, despite unusual conscious attention to the problem, to find philosophical bases of life that are emotionally satisfactory. They like to think of themselves as ahead of their times, but this is rather a device of self-reassurance in people who are less ahead of their times than not up to them. One suspects that in the twentieth century, which has done away with the obstacles that loomed large before their eyes, they would be no better off—either because they lack some essential strength for survival or because they elect roles too onerous for them. Hardy, indeed, has imagined characters who could hardly survive in any order less than idyllic.

In Sue the inadequacy of resources is a representative one that gives her character great resonance. The clue is provided by a crucial experience of her intellectual hero, John Stuart Mill: under the strain of a severe logical discipline he broke down and discovered the therapeutic value of poetry. Sue, so to speak, never finds a therapy. In all ways she is allied with a tradition of intellect; she is specifically made a child of the eighteenth century. She dislikes everything medieval, admires classical writers and architecture, looks at the work of neo-classical secular painters, conspicuously reads eighteenth century fiction and the satirists of all ages. Jude calls her "Voltairean," and she is a devotee of Gibbon. She is influenced, among later figures, by Shelley as intellectual rebel, by Mill's liberalism, and by the new historical criticism of Christianity. Rational skepticism, critical intelligence are her aims; in his last interview with her, Jude attacks her for losing her "reason," "faculties," "brains," "intellect" (VI, 8). Much as she is an individual who cannot finally be identified by categories, she is a child of the Enlightenment, with all its virtues and with the liabilities inseparable from it. Hardy was very early in intuiting, though he did not expressly define it, what in the twentieth century has become a familiar doctrine: the danger of trying to live by rationality alone.

In Sue, Hardy detects the specific form of the danger: the tendency of the skeptical intelligence to rule out the nonrational foundations of life and security. Sue cuts herself off from the two principal such foundations—from the community as it is expressed in traditional beliefs and institutions and from the physical reality of sex. The former she tends to regard as fraudulent and coercive, the latter as "gross"; in resisting marriage she resists both, and so she has not much left. Her deficiency in sex, whatever its precise psychological nature (we need not fall into the diagnositis of looking for a childhood trauma), is a logical correlative of her enthroning of critical intellect; thus a private peculiarity takes on a symbolic meaning of very wide relevance. The rationalist drawing away from nonrational sources of relationship creates the solitary; Sue is that, as she implies when, considering marriage because of the arrival of Father Time, she remarks, sadly, ". . . I feel myself getting intertwined with my kind" (V, 3). Precisely. But she is unwilling to be quite the solitary, and for such a person, the anchorite in search of an appropriate society, the natural dream is a private utopia—an endless unconsummated idyl with a single infinitely devoted lover.

At the heart of the drama of Sue is the always simmering revolt of the modes of life which she rejects, the devious self-assertion of the rejected values. Hence much of her inconsistency, of the maddening reversals that constitute a natural coquetry, the wonderfully dramatized mystery that simply stands on its own until the clues appear in the final section. Sue cannot really either reject or accept men, and in attempting to do both at once she leaves men irritated or troubled or desperate, and herself not much better off. She revolts against conventions, but never without strain; and here Hardy introduces an inner drama of conventions far more significant than the criticisms leveled by Jude and Sue. He detects in conventions, not merely inflexible and irrational pressures from without, but a power over human nature because of the way in which human nature is constituted. Sue is one of the first characters in fiction to make the honest mistake of regarding a convention as only a needless constraint and forgetting that it is a needed support, and hence of failing to recognize that the problem admits of no easy pros or cons. As a social critic Hardy may deplore the rigidity of conventions or the severity of their impact, but as an artist he knows of their ubiquity in human experience and of their inextricability from consciousness. They are always complexly present in the drama. At first Jude thinks that there is "nothing unconventional" in Sue (III, 2); then he decides that "you are as innocent as you are unconventional" (III, 4); still later he accuses her of being "as enslaved to the social code as any woman I know" (IV, 5). The Sue who is devastatingly witty about institutions finds herself constantly acting in terms of traditional patterns. On one occasion she assures Jude that "she despised herself for having been so conventional" (III, 10); on another she has to acknowledge, "I perceive I have said that in mere convention" (IV, 1); and above all she says to Phillotson, ". . . I, of all people, ought not

to have cared what was said, for it was just what I fancied I never did care for. But . . . my theoretic unconventionality broke down" (IV, 3). Then Jude, shocked when she joins him but will not sleep with him, finds relief in the thought that she has "become conventional" rather than unloving, "Much as, under your teaching, I hate convention . . ." (IV, 5). Here she is not clear herself, and she falls back mainly upon a concept whose conventionality she appears not to recognize, "woman's natural timidity." It is then that Jude accuses her of being "enslaved to the social code" and that she replies, "Not mentally. But I haven't the courage of my views . . ." Her words betray the split between reason and feeling, between the rational critique of the forms and the emotional reliance upon them. This steady trail of comments, clashes, and partial acknowledgments leads up to the key event: in Christminster, she catches sight of Phillotson on the street, and she tells Jude, " . . . I felt a curious dread of him; an awe, or terror, of conventions I don't believe in" (VI, 1). It is the turning point; her suppressed emotions, her needs, so long harried by her "reason," are seriously rebelling at last. "Reason" can still phrase her assessment of the event: "I am getting as superstitious as a savage!" Jude can lament the days "when her intellect played like lambent lightning over conventions and formalities" (VI, 3) and somewhat complacently attack her for losing her "scorn of convention" (VI, 8). But the defensiveness behind these criticisms soon emerges: as the defender of reason, Jude has also failed to find emotional anchorage, and his new independence of mind has provided him with no sustaining affirmations; and so he must blame Sue for deserting him.

Hardy has faithfully followed the character of Sue and has not let himself be deflected by his own sermonizing impulses. From the beginning he senses the split in her make-up—between rejections made by the mind, and emotional urgencies that she cannot deny or replace. If she is an "epicure in emotions," it may partly be, as she says apologetically, because of a "curiosity to hunt up a new sensation" (III, 7), but mostly it is that a turmoil of emotions will not let the mind, intent on its total freedom, have its own way. Much more than he realizes Jude speaks for both of them when he says "And [our feelings] rule thoughts" (IV, 1). Sue's sensitivity, her liability to be "hurt," is real, but she uses it strategically to cut off Jude's and Phillotson's thoughts when they run counter to those that she freely flings about; understandably Jude exclaims, "You make such a personal matter of everything!" (III, 4) Exactly; what appears to be thought is often personal feeling that must not be denied. Answerability, in ordinary as well as special situations, shakes her. On buying the Venus and Apollo she "trembled" and at night "kept waking up" (II, 3). When the school inspector visits, she almost faints, and Phillotson's arm around her in public makes her uncomfortable (II, 5). Repeatedly her feelings are very conventional: her embarrassment when Jude comes into the room where her wet clothes are hanging (III, 3), her discomfort after rebelling at school (III, 5), her jealousy of Arabella (III, 6; V, 2, 3). She is "evidently touched" by the hymn that moves Jude, she finds it "odd . . . that I should care about" it, and she continues to play it (IV, 1). She is "rather frightened" at leaving Phillotson (IV, 5). When she refuses to sleep with Jude, it is less that she is "epicene" and "boyish as a Ganymede" (III, 4) or that her "nature is not so passionate as [his]" (IV, 5) than that joining Jude is an act of mind, of principled freedom, that does not have emotional support. Hence her singular scruple that "my freedom has been obtained under false pretences!" (V, 1)—a rationalizing of feelings that, for all of her liking of Jude, run counter to their mode of life. Hardy rightly saw that only some very powerful emotional urgency could get her over the barrier between Jude and herself, and he supplies that in her jealousy of Arabella. It is a common emotion that her mind would want to reject: and it is notable that after giving in to Jude she give voice to another conventional feeling—assuring him, and herself, that she is "not a cold-natured, sexless creature" (V, 2).

In a series of penetrating episodes whose cumulative effect is massive. Hardy shows that her emotions cannot transcend the community which her mind endeavors to reject. With a deficiency of the feeling needed to sustain the courses laid out by the detached critical intellect, she would predictably return under pressure, to whatever form of support were available, to those indeed to which, while professing other codes, she has regularly been drawn. Though it would not take too much pressure, Hardy serves several ends at once by introducing the violent trauma of the death of the children. From here on he has only to trace, as he does with devastating thoroughness and fidelity, the revenge of the feelings that, albeit with admirable intellectual aspirations, Sue has persistently endeavored to thwart. They now counter-attack with such force that they make her a sick woman. Although her self-judgments take the superficial form of tragic recognition, what we see is less the recovery that accompanies the tragic anagnorisis than the disaster of a personality distorted by the efforts to bear excessive burdens and now blindly seeking, in its misery, excessive punishments. Illness is something other than tragic.

Whatever Hardy may have felt about the course ultimately taken by Sue, he was utterly faithful to the personality as he imagined and slowly constructed it. That is his triumph. His triumph, however, is not only his fidelity to the nature of Sue, but the perception of human reality that permitted him to constitute her as he did. We could say that he envisaged her, a bright but ordinary person, attempting the career that would be possible only to the solitary creative intellect, the artist, the saint, whose emotional safety does lie in a vision somewhere beyond that of the ordinary community. Sue does not have that vision; she is everyman. She is everyman entirely familiar to us: her sense of the imperfections around her leads her into habitual rational analysis that tends to destroy the forms of feeling developed by the historical community and to be unable to find a replacement for them. The insistence on the life of reason has become increasingly emphatic in each century of modern life, and Sue as the relentless critic of institutions incarnates the ideal usually held up to us in abstract terms. On the other hand, as if in defiance of rationalist aspirations, the twentieth century has seen destructive outbreaks of irrational force that would have been supposed incredible in the nineteenth. But a still more impressive modern phenomenon, since it entirely lacks the air of aberration, is a growing concern with the threat of intellect to the life of feelings and emotions. From some of the most respected guides of modern thought come warnings against arid rationality, and visions of a reconstructed emotional life essential to human safety and well-being. The present relevance of such cultural history is that it contributes to our understanding of Hardy: in *Jude the Obscure,* and primarily in the portrayal of Sue, he went to the heart of a modern problem long before it was understood as a problem. Yet the "modern" is not topical, for the problem is rooted in the permanent reality of human nature. Neurotic Sue gives us, in dramatic terms, an essential revelation about human well-being.

Richard Benvenuto (essay date 1970)

SOURCE: "Modes of Perception: The Will to Live in *Jude the Obscure*", in *Studies in the Novel,* Vol. 11, No. 1, 1970, pp. 31-41.

[*In the following essay, Benvenuto observes two differing modes of perception in* Jude the Obscure: *an objective, amoral mode that is indifferent to humanity and Jude's idealist, personalizing mode wherein lies the stonecutter's desire to live.*]

The Fury that greeted the first appearance of *Jude the Obscure* has long since subsided, yet we are no closer than its reviewers were to an agreement upon Hardy's intent in the novel or the caliber of his performance in it. *Jude* is not an especially difficult novel; it continues to divide its readers, however, because it imposes upon them what are, by Victorian standards, rigorous and unusual demands. Until the final chapters of *Jude,* Hardy commits himself and the reader to the life of his hero and to the high-minded courage and independence Jude shows in adversity. His character is one of Hardy's strongest arguments for the value and dignity a man can possess in a world that is alien to the ideals of humanity. When Jude says, "Well—I'm an outsider to the end of my days," not knowing how close he is to the end, he brings down the novel's condemnation on a system that behind its walls isolates itself from intelligence and integrity.[1] At the end of the novel, faced with what amounts to a reversal of judgment, our sense of identification with Jude is strained to the critical point. Jude curses himself and bitterly denounces those ideals and actions that made up his life and gave it tragic power and won him our approval and respect. We can understand Jude's vision of himself as a modern Job, but I cannot agree with him that it would have been better had he never lived. If *Jude the Obscure* has anything to say to us, it is that the world needs more Judes, not fewer or none at all.

When he curses the day of his birth, Jude speaks out of a broken spirit and in a semi-delirium. We would as a matter of course see in his last words the tragic fall and defeat of a man who is no longer a reliable witness for himself or the novel's norms and vision of life. Surely Hardy is not telling men that it would have been better for them if they had not been born. But we cannot assume even that much, because we cannot readily dissociate Jude's summation of his life from the novel's pervasive image of life. Early in the novel, the narrator spoke of Jude's "weakness of character"—his sensitivity to cruelties inflicted on life—which "suggested that he was the sort of man who was born to ache a good deal before the fall of the curtain upon his unnecessary life should signify that all was well with him again" (p. 13). The narrator combines an ironic with a literal mode of discourse and implies two perspectives from which man can be viewed and judged. The narrator speaks ironically about Jude's "weakness" of character, but his conclusion that Jude's life is "unnecessary" is the exact corollary of his recognition that the general scheme of life does not conform to man's scale of values. We understand Jude's "weakness" to be a strength of character, because we see Jude's sensitivity from another, more humanizing perspective than that of the general scheme for which it is a defect. The humanizing perspective, if it is expanded to cover all of Jude's life, reveals the necessity of his life, just as it recognizes the value of his sympathy for the birds in Troutham's fields. To hold to that perspective is to read irony where the narrator does not intend it. The narrator switches his mode of discourse when he passes from a part to the whole of Jude's life, and he concludes that life is meaningless because it must be lived in a scheme of things that turns moral resources into physical hardships. Essentially the same reason leads Jude to conclude that his life has been meaningless, and Hardy's critics have split into two camps which dispute whether pleasure or knowledge is possible from a novel with that conclusion. By taking the general perspective as the only one that matters in *Jude,* neither side attends to Hardy's vision of life from within its own frame of reference or feels the weight of his argument against the wish not to live.

The two perspectives in *Jude* are revealed through two modes of perception which elicit contrary values and meanings from human life. The perceptual modes are perhaps different in degree rather than in kind—a character at any given moment may occupy a point midway between the two—but they are easily distinguishable as extremes; and it is upon the polarity of the two that Hardy expresses his sense of human life in *Jude*. The mode of perception that sees Jude's life to be "unnecessary" is objective and universal in its frame of reference. It has accurate knowledge of the laws governing life and recognizes that the general scheme of things—the universal forces that act as laws in a man's life—is amoral and indifferent to man. To see man objectively is to see him as minute and isolated within the general impersonality of existence. This is Father Time's mode of perception: "The boy seemed to have begun with the generals of life,

and never to have concerned himself with the particulars." He does not see "houses," "willows," or "fields," but rather "human dwellings in the abstract, vegetation, and the wide dark world" (p. 334). He sees "the particulars" of life, and especially individual happiness, to be an illusion. He concludes that "All laughing comes from misapprehension. Rightly looked at there is no laughable thing under the sun" (p. 332). From the objective mode of perception, which for Father Time is "right," human life is an irrelevant anomaly from the general scheme of things, and it is therefore a hardship he can find no reason to endure. He tells Sue on the evening before his suicide, "I wish I hadn't been born!" (p. 402). He wishes not to live with a horrendous insistence that does not let him wait for the curtain of death to fall on its own and signify to him that all is well for his unnecessary life.

Father Time is wrong to kill himself and the other children, of course, just as Jude is wrong about himself on his death bed. The child's objective awareness of the insignificance of life has led him to treat people as though they were no more significant in themselves than they are for the conditions in which they live. He sees himself and others as superfluous, or as his note explains: "*Done because we are too menny*" (p. 405). In direct contrast to his son, Jude refused to kill "a single one" of the "scores" of earthworms covering the road between Troutham's field and his aunt's cottage (p. 13). Jude's mode of perception is individualistic and emotive; its frame of reference is composed of specific living things, which are as important for Jude as the abstract scheme is for Father Time. Jude's perception personalizes the world: it makes what he sees an extension of himself and endows it with human values. "He could scarcely bear to see trees cut down or lopped, from a fancy that it hurt them . . ." (p. 13). Father Time makes his image of self conform to his conception of the universe. Jude makes his conception of the universe conform to his image of self. His initial perceptions of Christminster project his individual yearnings and desires outward with such force that for his mind the scheme of things becomes as personal and as morally fitted to man as for Father Time's mind it is indifferent and inhumane. Jude perceives even inanimate nature as a reflection of human personality and emotions: "You," he said, addressing the breeze caressingly, 'were in Christminster city between one and two hours ago . . . touching Mr. Phillotson's face, being breathed by him; and now you are here, breathed by me—you, the very same'" (pp. 21-22). Though Jude is eventually disillusioned by Christminster and comes to see it and external nature more objectively the mode of vision which he possessed on top of the Brown House remains as a part of his consciousness, and it operates within the novel as a corrective against the a priori disillusionment of Father Time.

Neither the personal nor the objective mode of perception perceives life completely, and both Jude and Father Time suffer because of their limitations. Their perceptions, moreover, take shape within a larger mental pattern or system of beliefs about life. When Jude sees

Christminster as "a city of light," and when Father Time watches his fellow passengers laughing in the absence of any cause for laughter "under the sun," they convert their perceptions into judgments of life. The mode in which they see life becomes for each a basis for evaluating life. Perception and judgment become one and the same act. The Christminster that Jude perceives as a child is simultaneously a moral standard, a criterion by which he measures conditions in Marygreen and to which he, as an individual, aspires. He yearns for Christminster to be a place "which he could call admirable" (p. 24), and he immediately concludes, with no further evidence than what he can supply from within himself, that "It would just suit me" (p. 25). His vision of Christminster shapes what it sees according to what it values. It is ambiguous, therefore, whether the Christminster, that Jude sees is more truly an object of perception—a spot on the landscape—or an emanation of his moral sensibility. "It was Christminster, unquestionably," that Jude saw, "either directly seen, or miraged in the peculiar atmosphere" (p. 10). It is both: "directly seen" by Jude's personalized mode of vision, whose medium is the "peculiar atmosphere" of Jude's moral values.

Jude is an idealist, but he is not thereby guilty of an illusionistic fantasy of which his growing up or the real world only can cure him. His mode of perception does not disguise truth from him. It enables him to see individual existences as real and to respect them as valuable. It keeps Hardy's novel from reducing itself to Father Time's wish not to live.[2] Father Time's perception is objectively accurate for a world which, when seen as a whole, has many sorrows and little joy, but it is no less than Jude's an act of evaluation as well as of vision. And the consequences of Father Time's perceptual judgment pose a far greater threat to human life than do those of Jude's. Father Time's perception corrupts his appreciation of even those few joys which sensitive minds can experience. The pavilion of flowers at the great Wessex Agricultural Show is "an enchanted palace" to the "appreciative taste" of Sue and Jude. It provides the single glimpse of unalloyed happiness the reader has of them. The lovers press their faces to the flowers and speak of "Greek joyousness" and escape from sorrow. Father Time, the only shadow on the scene, refuses to participate with them. "'I am very, very sorry, father and mother,' he said. 'But please don't mind—I can't help it. I should like the flowers very very much, if I didn't keep on thinking they'd be all withered in a few days!'" (p. 358). The words condense the issues of the entire novel to an image or a tableau. Father Time's perception of the conditions of mortal life is correct: the flowers will wither and die like all other forms of life. But because the flowers will decay, they are as good as dead for Father Time even while they are in bloom and beautiful. He denies value to individual life because he perceives the flowers not as they are in themselves, but as they are subject to universal laws. His perception and his judgment take place in the abstract, while the flowers exist in a specific moment. The point is not that one mode of perception is to be preferred, but that there are two

modes of perception and two value systems by which *Jude the Obscure* sees and assesses human life. By contraposing the personalized to the objectifying mode of vision, the pavilion scene reveals life to be a source of joy and value as well as an object of despair.

In showing us the flowers before they wither, the pavilion scene stands out from the novel, and at the same time it heightens the dilemma in which Hardy places his human beings. Hardy is not content to divide human experience into two opposing perspectives. Rather, he suggests the need for syncretization of the two. It is clearly important to his design that we see the validity of Sue's conclusion that "Nature's law" is "mutual butchery" (p. 371), and that we share the narrator's "perception of the flaw in the terrestrial scheme, by which what was good for God's birds was bad for God's gardener . . ." (p. 13). The novel's recurrent perception of life is from the objective mode, which sees men trapped on the one side by the forces of evolutionary nature and on the other by the rigid systems of social conformity. It is equally important to Hardy's design that we see the significance of men themselves and of individual living things, apart from the forces enclosing them.[3] Given "the flaw in the terrestrial scheme," the flowers are beautiful at the time Sue and Jude enjoy them. If to know life fully one must perceive the general laws governing life, to be willing to live he must perceive individual lives as sources of value. To disregard either mode of perception is to oversimplify Hardy's vision of life and to reduce considerably the tension of emotions in *Jude*. The issue is whether man can will to live when he knows that life does not mean anything to the powers unaffected by his will—whether Jude in particular can sustain the mode of perception evoking his will to live as he acquires the mode that negates it. Because perceptions take on a normative function, moreover, it is vital for each mode of perceptual judgment to adhere to its own frame of reference—the personalized or the objective—and not transgress the other's. Jude made his frustration inevitable by taking the Christminster of his personalized perception for an objective standard of value in the universe. He seeks outside of himself the "heavenly Jerusalem" his vision created. Father Time is equally, if not more mistaken. He allows his objective knowledge of an inhuman universe to dehumanize all value out of individual lives and to be a sentence of death upon himself.

His verdict—"It would be better to be out o' the world than in it . . ." (p. 402)—applies to the personal perspective of life the reductive logic of Father Time's objective mode of perception. Because he can see no meaning for life in a transcendent pattern of existence, Father Time denies any possibility for value in the act of living itself, and he does so with horrifying consistency: "I think that whenever children be born that are not wanted they should be killed directly, before their souls come to 'em, and not allowed to grow big and walk about!" (p. 402). The immediate causes of Father Time's despair are his father's having to take lodgings in another house and the family's economic peril. As is manifest in his violent reaction to the news of Sue's pregnancy, the actual cause is his judgment that life is not a sufficient reason for the suffering men incur while living. The universe which reduces men to isolated, suffering units becomes Father Time's moral reference, the basis from which he argues for the direct killing of children "that are not wanted. . . ." Because it dehumanizes men into conformity with the inhumane, his proposal is an outrage against humanity and human values and a direct challenge to the personalized mode of perception. It is, therefore, critically important to know whether the novel makes an adequate reply.

In so far as it is informed by the narrator's mode of perceptual judgment, the novel does not reply. The narrator, though not to the unrelieved exclusiveness of Father Time, sees the world from the objective mode and is aware of personalized values only as ironically incongruous to the general scheme of things. He is sensitive to Jude's ambition to become a classical scholar, but his perspective reduces Jude to a helpless, pathetic figure waiting for guidance in a world where nobody came to guide him because "nobody does . . ." (p. 32). Though he speaks frequently in his own person elsewhere, the narrator makes no comment on Father Time's suicide or on his method of dispensing with unwanted children. Like Father Time, the narrator cannot see the particulars of life fully in their own light, because of his concern with "the generals of life . . ." (p. 334). Father Time's refusal to enjoy the roses that are beautiful and living, because they are doomed to decay, converts an accurate perception from the objective perspective into a false evaluation in the personalized perspective. An abstracting perception of what will be conditions his judgment of what is. When referring to Jude's "unnecessary life," the narrator blinds himself to the particular beauty and impact of that life because he perceives that it will have no account in the cosmic sum of things. Of course it will not; yet this does not prevent Hardy from considering Jude a very important man. The narrator speaks for what we know Hardy's cosmic vision to have been, but he should not be taken for what Wayne Booth calls a novel's "implied author."[4] His consciousness of life's meaning and value does not delimit the novel's portrait of life. The narrator tends to reduce the details of life to theorems about life and to see particular events in the light of what one can generally expect from life. His portrait of life is sometimes a stereotyped one.

This is true of the way he sees marriage, which shows the influence of objective realities upon the narrator's perceptual judgment of specific experience. Hardy wanted the marriage laws reformed, and he expressed his views of the general state of matrimony through the narrator's indignation at a society that calmly accepted the first exchange of vows between Jude and Arabella (pp. 65-66). But the narrator seldom sees more of marriage than what a stereotype of marriage would condition him to see. In this respect, he is very like Sue, who convinces herself of what marriage is before she marries. For both, marriage is fatal to love, as though by universal law. Hence, the narrator singles out Arabella and Cartlett

as illustrating "the antipathetic, recriminatory mood of the average husband and wife of Christendom" (p. 357)—a judgment he does not corroborate with evidence drawn from their married life, the typicalness of which we have no way of knowing. Jude and Arabella's landlord "doubted if they were married at all, especially as he had seen Arabella kiss Jude one evening when she had taken a little cordial; and he was about to give them notice to quit, till by chance overhearing her one night haranguing Jude in rattling terms, and ultimately flinging a shoe at his head, he recognized the note of genuine wedlock; and concluding that they must be respectable, said no more" (pp. 465-66). It is a bad marriage, but equally bad is the logic that makes affection dependent upon alcohol and equates respectability with violence.[5] This is not to say that Hardy's logic was flawless and easily distinguishable from his narrator's. It is to point out that the narrator, Sue, and Father Time have fixed, undeviating minds. Once they seize the general law, they feel qualified to judge as though they knew all the particulars.

We need to be more cautious of identifying the discursive commentator in Hardy's fiction with the novelist who created him, and especially because, as most critics have noted, the commentary of the novels is usually inept beside the dramatic power of their scenes. The pig killing, with its open conflict between Arabella's pragmatism and Jude's idealism, is particularly successful in relating perceptual mode to moral judgment. Arabella and Jude reveal what they are by how they perceive inhuman conditions. Jude sees the killing as "a hateful business"; Arabella replies simply that "Pigs must be killed" (p. 75). Taken in context, their contrary modes of perception extend to the inevitable death awaiting all living things. For Arabella the pig is merely an object with no value independent from its subjugation to the domain of general law: "Poor folks must live" (p. 75). Her perception neither falsifies things as they are nor comprehends them fully. Objectively, there is no inherent value in the pig, but Arabella recognizes no value in man's ability to personalize his world in a way that defines the ethical norms of his humanity. In effect, she denies value to men as well as to pigs, to those who perceive as well as to what they perceive. Perceiving the world to be a collection of objects governed only by the law of self-preservation, she gets rid of the inconvenient presence of her child, and she reacts to Jude's death in precisely the same way as she did to the pig's. Her mode of perception makes no distinction between the two. She gives the love-philter to Vilbert while Jude is dying, because "Weak women must provide for a rainy day" (p. 485). As with its parallel, "Poor folks must live," the objective conformity of this perception to general law corrupts and dehumanizes specific human values. It results in a fixed judgment of life in a world of objects, between which and itself the perceiving mind sees no qualitative difference. Like Father Time's and the narrator's, Arabella's mode of perception does not confer value upon men.[6]

Jude's mode of perception does, though he suffers because of it. Indeed, his greatness derives in large measure from the suffering he endures because he does not dehumanize his vision into conformity with the impersonal laws of nature. The spilled pail of pig's blood formed "a dismal, sordid, ugly spectacle—to those who saw it as other than an ordinary obtaining of meat" (p. 75), to a Jude, that is, who sees the spectacle as emblematic of his moral responsibility to life.[7] The necessity of the killing outrages his emotions and ideals; and though he was "aware of his lack of common sense," he "felt dissatisfied with himself as a man at what he had done . . ." (p. 76). His common sense and his feelings relate to the different perspectives in which a given event may be seen. By placing himself under the judgment of his feelings despite his common sense, he makes moral standards relevant to an event that has only pragmatic meaning to the morally indifferent Arabella. Without denying his common sense or submitting to it, Jude by personalizing the world spiritualizes it. As his common sense develops and as he becomes more objectively aware of the world, his feeling for life intensifies and the perception which spiritualizes life becomes more active and urgent within him. He pities Arabella as an "unreflecting fellow-creature" (p. 319), though he knows how she has used him; he has deep compassion for Father Time before he has seen the boy (p. 330). He perceives that Sue is "not worth a man's love" (p. 470), but he continues to love her. The truth of one mode of perception does not alter the importance of his love.[8] Neither his pity nor his love is ever repaid, but that does not mean he was foolish because he loved. It is precisely because Jude's ideals exist nowhere else but in his personalizing vision that Hardy stresses its importance as a mode of perception.

Critics too often give Hardy the role of grim realist dissecting the idealistic fallacies of self-deluded men. What he reveals through Jude is that under the grim reality of an indifferent universe only a human mind can value specific, living things and perceive their reality, as Jude does with the pig, the earthworms, and the people he loves. Christminster is not the "heavenly Jerusalem" Jude once thought it. But Jude's continuing to value the city that should have been is as important to his character as his getting to know the city as it is. The indifferent universe does not dehumanize his spiritualizing vision. Rather, in a world without value, Jude's way of seeing becomes the only source of value. As he did with Sue, he continues to love Christminster, though he knows the city is not worth his love. He continues to value his own powers of thought and feeling, though he learns the incongruity of human consciousness to the general scheme of things. He knows that to succeed in the world one must adapt to the world's general conditions, and "be as coldblooded as a fish and as selfish as a pig to have a really good chance of being one of his country's worthies." Jude attempted instead to "re-shape his course" to his own "aptness or bent"; he sought by his living to achieve his personalized image of life. Rather than condemn Jude's attempt as a misguided idealism, Hardy allows Jude to point out the common error of judging ways of life "not by their essential soundness, but by their accidental outcomes" (p. 393). Objectively a failure and

knowing himself so, Jude still affirms the essential soundness of his life.

He has a will to live, which is something other than a grasping at survival, or what Jude calls a "save-your-own-soulism" (p. 330), because it questions the universe and the laws by which the universe functions. Jude does not deny or ignore the universal law by which men blindly struggle to survive; he refuses to accept that kind of law as a basis for his actions or as the measure of his ideals. When he returns to Christminster, totally enlightened as to the scheme of things, he delivers an impassioned defense of the spiritualizing, self-emanating mode of perception. He says he is "in a chaos of principles—groping in the dark—acting by instinct and not after example." The "fixed opinions" of his youth have "dropped away," and the further he goes the less sure he is—but not of himself. He has lost the certainty of a mind that rests upon "fixed opinions." The principles that seemed to apply to life are "in a chaos." But he does not replace the principles which he has lost from his personalized mode of vision with principles that belong to the objective mode of vision. He accepts the necessity of living without "fixed opinions" and replaces principles with feelings, "inclinations which do me and nobody else any harm, and actually give pleasure to those I love best" (p. 394). It is not a stunning victory for the spirit of man, but neither is it one that we can afford to overlook. To be sure, Christminster is the obsolescent, corrupt institution that Sue ridicules, but it also remains an ideal within Jude's consciousness, which creates value by virtue of Jude's capacity for love. "Why should you care so much for Christminster," Sue asks him. "Christminster cares nothing for you. . . ." Jude answers simply, "I love the place . . ." (p. 386). Like the guilt that he feels for killing the pig, Jude's love is illogical. It also keeps him from despair in a life without hope. It is his commitment to the little that remains to humanity in the midst of the inhumane.

Jude's love is the shaping force behind his personalizing vision, and it is what Father Time and the narrator leave out of their perceptions of life. " . . . if children make so much trouble," Father Time asks Sue, "why do people have 'em?" (p. 402). It is the question of the reason for existence and the value of life that Hardy poses through all of **Jude**. Sue's answer, "O—because it is a law of nature," generalizes the meaning of life and reduces men to the status of creatures swept along in the struggle for survival. Jude's love suggests another answer because it affirms the independence of human value, if not the independence of man's fate, from natural law and cosmic scheme. In his Christminster speech, Jude accepts his own obscurity, from the objective point of view, as irrelevant to the spiritual experience and value of life; and he sees that external laws and abstract norms do not constitute a fixed design for living. In "a chaos," he must find rules to live by within his own individuality. After the "senseless circumstance" of the children's death, his spiritual independence of self contrasts strongly to Sue's self-destructive acceptance of "something external to us which says, 'You shan't!'" (p. 407). Jude shows the finest qualities of his love as a way of seeing when he comforts Sue, though he mourns for his children himself, though he watches her withdraw from him and destroy him. He is destroyed, but only when he stops loving, when his emotions lose their individualizing power and submit to the reductive logic of the objective universe. It is a tragic loss not only of "unfulfilled aims," as Hardy states in his "Preface," but of a vision of life that had fulfilled a man's essential humanity. In his death-bed despair, Jude is as wrong about himself as he was about Christminster in his idealism. We cannot agree that he should not have been born—we do not regret his failure to jump through the ice on the night Arabella left him. That impulse is part of the paternity of Father Time, but Jude outgrew his son and his son's logic of what to do with unwanted life. If we think of his last visit to Sue as a symbolic and successful return to the frozen pond, we grasp the tragic loss of a man whose soul came to him, who in his maturity and clearest senses spoke and acted as one who possessed, against the odds of logic, the will to live.

NOTES

[1] *Jude the Obscure* (London, 1965), p. 396. Subsequent references to *Jude* are to this edition, called The Greenwood Edition.

[2] A wide sentiment among Hardy's critics is summed up in Evelyn Hardy's remark that *Jude* is "a denial of life as we know it," although not all would agree with her that it "verges on the pathological. . . ." For Kathleen R. Hoopes, Jude's idealism is in conflict with the true and the real: "With the vanishing of his most precious ghosts, his will to live disintegrated, for he could not exist in the world of men." See *Thomas Hardy: A Critical Biography* (London, 1954), pp. 253, 246; and "Illusion and Reality in *Jude the Obscure*," *Nineteenth-Century Fiction*, XII (September 1957), 157. In one of the better articles on *Jude*, "The Child: The Circus: and *Jude the Obscure*," *The Cambridge Journal*, VII (June 1954), 531-46, Emma Clifford recognizes that Jude's vision "remains a glorious vision . . . that is both sustained and destroyed in the garish atmosphere of Thomas Hardy's special kind of hell" (542).

[3] Hardy often shrinks his characters to mere dots in a vast panorama, yet he does not treat them or the particulars of their lives as though they were insignificant. His "Preface" to *Two on a Tower* states that his aim was to set "the emotional history of two infinitesimal lives against the stupendous background of the stellar universe, and to impart to readers the sentiment that of these contrasting magnitudes the smaller might be the greater to them as men." In *Jude*, Hardy's art has matured and no longer needs a stupendous background, but his "sentiment" is fundamentally the same.

[4] *The Rhetoric of Fiction* (Chicago, 1961), pp. 71-77.

[5] Reviewing *Jude* for *Harper's Weekly* on December 7, 1895, William Dean Howells advanced a moderate and sensible reading of Hardy's view of the marriage problem: "If the experience of Jude with Arabella seems to arraign marriage, and it is made to appear not only ridiculous but impious that two young, ignorant, impassioned creatures should promise lifelong fealty and constancy when they can have no real sense of what they are doing, and that then they should be held to their rash vow by all the forces of society, it is surely not the lesson of the story that any other relation than marriage is tolerable for the man and woman who live together." Howells' review has been reprinted in *Thomas Hardy and His Readers: A Selection of Contemporary Reviews,* ed. Laurence Lerner and John Holmstrom (London, 1968), pp. 115-17, esp. p. 117.

[6] Arabella's undeniable will to survive is more mechanical than vital, a predatory instinct and not a human alternative to the wish not to live. She is as destructive to life as Father Time is, and in the egotism which preserves her, she is the most spiritually impoverished of the main characters in *Jude*. Defenders of Arabella tend to exaggerate the health and freedom of her spirit as compared with Sue's neurotic indecisiveness, and they obscure her close affinities with the unscrupulous Vilbert.

[7] Cf. Arthur Mizener, "*Jude the Obscure* As A Tragedy." *The Southern Review,* VI (1940), 205-6. The mighty opposites of tragedy that Mizener does not find in Jude and Arabella exist in the differing modes of perception that constitute the novel.

[8] As A. Alvarez observes in his "Afterword" to *Jude the Obscure* (New York: Signet Classics Edition, 1961), ". . . the truth and power of the novel lie in the way in which Jude, in the end, is able to understand his love for Sue *without lessening it*" (p. 410, original italics).

Shalom Rachman (essay date 1972)

SOURCE: "Character and Theme in Hardy," in *English*, Vol. 22, No. 110, Summer, 1972, pp. 45-53.

[*In the following essay, Rachman perceives two major themes in* Jude the Obscure—*those relating to the flesh and those relating to the spirit—and describes how these two themes come into conflict in the novel.*]

Whether it be **The Return of the Native, Tess of the D'urbervilles,** or **Jude the Obscure** that is Hardy's best, all-round achievement in the field of the novel is a matter not yet indisputably settled. Divided opinion in this respect can only lead to further fruitful critical discussion. What needs to be recognized however, is that **Jude** has a particular importance, not only among Hardy's own novels but among all English novels of the close of the nineteenth century. This importance confers upon **Jude** a singular position, not so much in terms of the developing craft of fiction as in the history of the novel as a reflection of man in society and in the cosmos. Both in date of publication, 1895, and in the vision of the world it embodies, *Jude* marks the point of division between nineteenth-century moderate optimism and twentieth-century pervasive gloom. The book looks back to early nineteenth-century Romanticism, and foreshadows the restlessness, the isolation of the individual, the collapse of old values, and the groping towards new ones, all of which have become the hall-marks of serious twentieth-century fiction. Jude himself is the last full-blooded romantic. In his passionate nature and in his high aspirations he shares much with Dorothea Brooke, but his world is shot through with elements utterly unknown in hers. The causes for this century's change in the conception of human nature are many, but if we want to look for some of them in the field of the novel, one of the books that will be most rewarding for such a study is *Jude*. When Hardy wrote the book he had never heard of any Freudian theories, and certainly did not think a world war likely, and yet somehow the book anticipates these two turning-points which have left indelible imprints on the consciousness of this century. After reading the book many developments of the twentieth century seem hardly surprising.

In what is to my mind one of the most perceptive essays on Hardy's novels, Eugene Goodheart makes the following remarks:

> 'Hardy's novels are in a sense demonstrations of the inadequacy of the Romantic conception . . . Hardy, though possessing the old Romantic feeling for personality, shared the Victorian burden of society . . . The dates of his birth and death, 1840-1928, dramatise the situation. By temperament a Romantic, he was born too late to be one. Born too early to be a modern, he lived too far into the modern period, sharing to some extent its awareness, to be considered a true Victorian.'[1]

The peculiar characteristics of Hardy, the man and his times, are suggested here, and these are particularly demonstrated in *Jude* since, as Walter Allen says, *Jude* 'is his one attempt to write a novel strictly of his own times'.[2] Hardy's temperament was fundamentally poetic, and this accounts not only for his achievement in poetry but also for the special quality of his fiction. Nature, time, society, institutions, religion, heredity, all engaged his interest. In *Jude* he held nothing back and projected his total awareness of man and his universe. The handling of a multiplicity of issues poses for the artist the basic problem of the organization of his material, and partly because of the variety of issues dealt with, partly because he was more a feeler than a thinker, the question of organization was beyond Hardy's ability to solve satisfactorily.

To introduce all the themes into the novel and to bring it to its envisaged end, Hardy found it necessary to create coincidences and manipulate events in a manner that is unsuited to what is essentially a realistic novel. The case of Little Father Time is often cited as the most glaring example of an artistic blunder, but the objections raised on this account are not completely justified. J. I. M.

Stewart's stricture that 'his [Father Time's] final deed has no more substance than last night's nightmare, and in the whole book it is perhaps this small epitome of woe that chiefly gives the game away' is, I think, questionable, and betrays a lack of patience in understanding what Hardy is doing or what he is trying to say. Stewart goes on to say that 'we are having foisted on us as human life a puppet show that is *not* human life; and this is something which neither tragedy nor comedy—and far less anything bearing the credentials of realistic fiction—ought to be'.[3] But it is precisely because of its human life, the characters in it, that *Jude* for all its shortcomings remains a considerable achievement.

In the preface to the first edition of the book, Hardy wrote:

> ' . . . *Jude the Obscure* is simply an endeavour to give shape and coherence to a series of seemings, or personal impressions, the question of their consistency or their discordance, of their permanence or their transitoriness, being regarded as not of the first moment.'[4]

It is here that the crux of a critical assessment of *Jude* is to be found. I take it that the coherence of the 'seemings' and the 'personal impressions' has to do with the characters. However, the explicit problematic aspects of *Jude* and the intrinsic states of Jude and Sue are not always consistently harmonized. The above statement is evidence enough that Hardy was aware of the dissonant notes struck in the book, and that his interest predominantly lay in the personal, human predicament rather than in the complex of forces introduced, in respect of which he was not quite sure of his stand. No wonder then that the book has fared poorly at the hands of the critics.

Albert J. Guerard's study of Hardy is generally a highly competent and accomplished piece of work. About *Jude*, however, he starts off by stating that it is 'an impressive tragedy in spite of its multiplicity of separated and detachable problems',[5] repeats later that 'it is not realism but tragedy, and like all tragedy is symbolic',[6] and finally says that 'Jude is not . . . a tragic hero—if only because he is a modern',[7] and that 'the cosmos, whether just or unjust or indifferent, necessarily dwarfs tragedy'.[8] Guerard also argues that Jude's dying words are a condemnation of the cosmos and that the tragic attitude lays the blame not on the stars but on ourselves. Obviously there is some inconsistency here. If Jude's dying words can be taken as a condemnation of the cosmos, they can equally be taken as a condemnation of his own nature as part of the cosmos. If the novel is an 'impressive tragedy', it cannot at the same time be a dwarfed one. The so-called cosmic forces in *Jude* are not conceived of as the sole determinants of Jude's fate, and why does the cosmos necessarily dwarf the tragedy? Why cannot it enhance it? Hardy's intention, as stated in his preface to the first edition, was 'to point the tragedy of unfulfilled aims'. If what is basic to all conceptions of tragedy is the opposition of an individual human being to some huge undefeatable force or forces, then *Jude* is a tragedy. It is not of the Greek type, as Lascelles Abercrombie points out.[9] It is not of the Shakespearian type, by which standard Arthur Mizener examines it and finds it wanting.[10] It is a tragedy of the romantic temperament frustrated in all the spheres in which it seeks to express itself. It is an awakening of the consciousness to all the contradictory aspects of the combined forces, inner and outer, which evoke the desire of complete fulfilment and yet, at the same time, thwart and defeat it. The only attainable wish which remains is death.

In the speech Jude makes to the crowd of people around him at Christminster on his return there with Sue and their children he says, 'I am in a chaos of principles—groping in the dark—acting by instinct and not after example' (p. 337). Earlier in the book in a conversation with Sue, he tells her that feelings rule thoughts (p. 211). The book as a whole reflects the state of perplexity of its characters, of its time, and of its author. The inconsistency in Hardy's 'impressions' is, to no small extent, the reason for the 'chaos of principles'. There is greater certainty as regards feeling and uncertainty as regards thought. This is not to suggest that there is a paucity of thought in the book. On the contrary, there is a good deal of thought in it, but the difficulty arises out of the contradictory aspects seen in each issue, and the impossibility of reconciling the contrarieties. Thought, therefore, loses its authority and feeling alone is left as a guide. Yet to resolve the perplexity it is necessary for feeling and thought to harmonize.

At one point in the book Hardy makes the following statement:

> 'The purpose of a chronicler of moods and deeds does not require him to express his personal views upon the grave controversy above given (p. 298).'
> [The grave controversy has to do with the indeterminate attitudes of Jude and Sue in regard to their marriage.]

Hardy records not only moods but also the conditions out of which the moods arise. In *Jude* he makes little direct authorial comment. The characters' deeds are given in the narrative; their moods and views are presented either through internal analysis or in dialogue. The author's view emerges indirectly from the combined statements of the action and reaction of the characters. Action and reaction are of course related to the problems with which the characters are concerned, and the problems involve the numerous themes. The various images introduced are used to help express character and theme, and to establish the connection between them. Each group of images is related to a theme, but it also forms a facet of a character.

Arabella, we are told, is a 'female animal', and she is very often associated with pigs and strong drink. The pig's pizzle that Arabella throws at Jude is the direct cause for the beginning of the relationship between them.

Critics point out that no better image could be found to hint at the nature of the attraction that brings the two together. Pigs, pizzle, strong drink, the picture of Samson and Delilah at the inn where Jude and Arabella have a drink, masculine strength and passion, and female sexuality and treachery, all bring out Jude's susceptibility to fall prey to physical desire, female wiles, and drink. This is perhaps the simplest illustration of the manner by which a cluster of images centre on a theme—the flesh—and at the same time serve as a means by which the character is created. A more complex example is the theme of Christminster worked out through Jude's and Sue's subjective vision of it and through the actual events of indeed the whole novel.

Marriage is another theme that is used to qualify the intrinsic qualities of the characters. Whilst Jude and Sue discuss the legal questions of marriage or its religious implications, it is primarily their personal states that are revealed. Their views on the subject as such, unorthodox as they may have seemed at the time of the book's publication, are of secondary importance. Sue's and Jude's involvement in marriage is part of the method by which their characters are established. We may say that Hardy weaves his themes into the very fibres of his characters. Hence it is necessary to examine the themes and how they are presented.

Two contradictory and irreconcilable aspects of Nature are put forward in the novel. On the one hand, there is what we may call the romantic view of nature, nature as the source of freedom, joy, and happiness. On the other hand, we have a growing awareness of the indifference and even inimical tendencies in Nature towards those elements with which, it would seem, she must most be in accord. After Jude gets a thrashing from Farmer Troutham for letting the birds eat off the soil from which he should have kept them away, he reflects that 'Nature's logic was too horrid for him to care for. That mercy towards one set of creatures was cruelty towards another sickened his sense of harmony' (p. 23). A few lines later we read, 'Then, like the natural boy, he forgot his despondency, and sprang up'. Nature's logic is horrid and incomprehensible, yet she works in a manner that conduces to further growth and is favourable to existence.

Nature has her own laws, 'People go on marrying because they can't resist natural forces . . .' (p. 268). Sue explains to little Father Time that people have children 'because it is a law of nature' (p. 344). When Jude returns to Melchester, a place near Shaston, where Sue, now married to Phillotson, lives, we are told that he did not remember that 'insulted Nature sometimes vindicated her rights' (p. 201). The rights seem to be vindicated and the two, Jude and Sue, are united, and for a short while live in relative happiness. After the disaster of the death of the children, Sue says this to Jude:

> 'We said—do you remember?—that we would make a virtue of joy. I said it was Nature's

intention, Nature's law and *raison d'être* that we should be joyful in what instincts she afforded us— instincts which civilisation had taken upon itself to thwart' (p. 350).

There is considerable irony here. The instincts Nature afforded Sue are not at all what is normally taken as 'Nature's intention'. But what she says is fully applicable to Jude. Later, he implores her not to think ill of their union, pleading, 'Nature's own marriage it is, unquestionably!' (p. 363) and that 'human nature can't help being itself' (p. 365), thus attempting to justify his own conduct.

As against all this, we have Sue saying, upon realizing that her sold pigeons are destined to be slaughtered, 'O, why should Nature's law be mutual butchery' (p. 318), and Jude telling Sue that she had been intended by Nature to be left intact. Most of all, as things go ill for Jude from the start, he soon comes to realize 'the scorn of Nature for men's finer emotions, and her lack of interest in his aspirations' (p. 185). This is an awareness Sue arrives at later. She ends her speech about Nature's law and *raison d'être* quoted above by saying, 'And now Fate has given us this stab in the back [the children's death] for being such fools as to take Nature at her word'. What Jude interprets as Nature's scorn, Sue sees as the working of Fate. Finally, we have Phillotson making the following statement when he considers Sue's and his own misfortunes: 'Cruelty is the law pervading all nature and society' (p. 329). Nature's laws are disharmonious. Nature and Fate conspire against men. Human nature is part of Nature, yet Nature is in opposition to it. Society is much more in accord with the cruelty in Nature than the individual with either, though Phillotson's remark implies that the individual too may not altogether be free of cruelty. The unadulterated, romantic sensibility of the early nineteenth century has been disturbed by the impact of Darwinism, and recent social theories, and there is a growing awareness that the old, established standards are no longer adequate to sustain belief of any sort. What is to be noted is that the conflicting views are not presented as objectively observed experience, but arise out of and define specific, personal states.

Nowhere is the inconsistency Hardy alludes to in the preface to the first edition of the book more apparent than in the treatment of the marriage theme. Marriage *qua* institution is much abused by both Jude and Sue, but if we take the numerous protests against the marriage laws at their face value, we shall most probably overlook what really happens to the characters. Sue considers that marriage is no sacrament (p. 174), that in fact it is a sordid contract (p. 218), a hopelessly vulgar institution. She says to Jude, 'I think I should begin to be afraid of you, Jude, the moment you had contracted to cherish me under a Government Stamp, and I was licensed to be loved on the premises by you' (p. 267). This is not a view she holds as a result of her previous, unfortunate experience with Phillotson. Whilst she was still in Phillotson's house as his wife, she confided to Jude that

'the social moulds civilisation fits us into have no more relation to our actual shapes than the conventional shapes of the constellations have to the real star-patterns' (p. 214).

Sue's actual shape, her delicate, disproportionate make-up, will not really fit into even the most flexibly conceived social mould, so long as it is a matrimonial mould. Her saying, 'It is none of the natural tragedies of love that's love's usual tragedy in civilised life, but a tragedy artificially manufactured for people' (p. 224) is a statement contrary to the evidence of events in the novel. What is actually shown in the novel is that love's tragedy is not at all artificial tragedy, but natural tragedy. It is Sue's fastidious and weak sexuality, or in other words her frigidity, that is the basic cause of love's tragedy in *Jude*. Sue's idea of having domestic laws made according to classified temperaments is fanciful and impracticable. In short, all Sue's pronouncements on marriage are a highly skilful camouflaging on her part of the fact which, put plainly as Jude puts it once to her, is her incapability of real love (p. 250). Had Hardy written the novel a decade or two later, he would most probably have made Sue's utterances carry allusions to modern psychological theories. As it is, she inveighs against conventions, institutions, and laws of her time to state a condition which, though not unrelated to them, is fundamentally not caused by them. Sue is not deliberately and coldly decrying the institution of marriage. She is simply making use of concepts and images at her disposal to construct her defensive arguments.

Similar instances are to be found in Jude's thoughts and utterances, in his case revealing a different aspect of character. Jude's thinking

'Is it that the women are to blame; or is it the artificial system of things, under which the normal sex-impulses are turned into devilish domestic gins and springes to noose and hold back those who want to progress?' (p. 226).

is no more than putting to himself a purely rhetorical question, for this is what he has come to believe. Although the domestic springes have noosed him, he has not been held back by them. His marriage to Arabella had only been a brief interlude after which he resumed his intended course, and what stands in his way to progress has, in the main, little to do with any domestic gins. The effect of couching Jude's reflections in such images is that the intellect of a man entertaining scholastic ambitions is somewhat blunted. At the same time his thought reveals that the momentary trouble is not progress, nor his own marital state, but his need of love, the sort of love Sue can never give him, though at this stage he does not know it yet.

Ostensibly there is a strong protest against the marriage laws of the time, but we are actually shown that what matters most is compatibility, and since in *Jude* we have both conditions—marriage and the 'natural state'—both leading to unhappiness, the edge of the protest is taken off. Marriage itself is much less of a problem than the way people go about it. Divorce is not unobtainable, and in fact is granted in both cases—Jude and Arabella; Sue and Phillotson; but the problem of compatibility remains, and it is the crucial aspects of the characters' different needs of fulfilment and the concomitant personal difficulties that are delineated through the associated theme and images.

Another central theme in *Jude* is that of Time. Jude's tragedy is occasioned by problems arising at a certain point of time as well as by timeless dilemmas. In so far as Jude is defeated by the prevailing conditions of his own time, he is a victim of forces against which the future may hold a remedy, but in so far as his fortunes are thwarted by the very fact of his existence in an unfriendly and inscrutable universe, there can never be a complete solution to man's predicament on this earth. The awareness that man is subject to time-bound and timeless agencies both of which happen to be in opposition to one's self, is overwhelming and tends to undermine the will to live.

The tragedy of Tess starts with her going to Alec D'urberville to claim kin, and there is good reason to believe that but for that step forced upon her by the economic difficulties of her family, all may have turned out well for her. In Jude's case there is no apparent reason for his turning away from the station of life in which he finds himself placed. At one point, whilst at Christminster at his work, he experiences 'a true illumination'—'that here in the stone yard was a centre of effort as worthy as that dignified by the name of scholarly study within the noblest of the colleges. But he lost it under stress of his old idea' (p. 91). His old idea of learning is partly due to his own characteristic bent, but for the greater part it is somehow induced by the spirit of his time, and we are told that the fact that he regards his trade as a provisional means only is 'his form of the modern vice of unrest'. Sue's tremulous psyche and Jude's high aspirations are seen as products of their time.

The spirit of the time conducing to change and displacement is everywhere at work, affecting people in different ways. Jude feels that a mere interest in books is not enough to gain 'rare ideas'. Every working man has now a taste for books, he thinks (p. 73). What he wants is the scholarly study he believes Christminster can offer him. It is not any new idea that stirs people to action; it is a general fret that sends them in quest of a better lot, without knowing exactly where and how it can be found. All four principal characters keep moving from place to place, and never find any rest. The direction of the impetus is from the lower social stratum upwards, but the energy is dissipated by the endless misadventures and no one reaches a rung higher.

When Jude realizes that he does not stand a chance in Christminster and contemplates entering the Church as a licentiate, he wonders whether his initial, more ambitious scheme 'had degenerated to, even though it might not

have originated in, a social unrest which had no foundation in the nobler instincts; which was purely an artificial product of civilisation' (p. 135). As already observed above, Jude's desire for learning springs from his nobler instincts, but it is also related to his time. The social unrest is an artificial product of civilization but it is also the force that sets off Jude to seek fulfilment of his ambition. Are we then to take Jude's intent as a vice? And if it is a vice, how can it be connected with the nobler instincts? The book does not provide an answer to such questions. Jude perceives in the stone yard that his trade is as dignified an effort as any, but from his childhood there are tendencies in his nature that make him the sort of man that could never really be content with the work of a stonemason.

Although Jude's thirst for knowledge is shared by thousands of young men, and although all are characteristic of the trend of the time, Jude's personal quest stands apart from the general stream. Whereas the mass of young men are 'self-seeking', Jude aims chiefly at altruism, at doing good and benefiting others. This is like facing in the opposite direction from the way things go. Soon after his arrival at Christminster, we are told that 'the deadly animosity of contemporary logic and vision towards so much of what he held in reverence was not revealed to him' (p. 91). It does not take him long to find that out, and though conditions change and the colleges of Christminster become accessible even to such as he later in his own days, his logic and his vision remain out of accord with contemporary tendencies. It is possible to trace the pattern of the changing trends. The widow Edlin, who is used as a choric figure, is there to remind us of a calm and simple past contrasted with the turmoil of the present, and there are two contradictory visions of the future. While Sue considers that in fifty or a hundred years people will act and feel still worse than she and Jude do (p. 296), Jude, on the other hand, lying on his death-bed, says that the time was not ripe for him and Sue—'Our ideas were fifty years too soon to be any good to us' (p. 414). The note of uncertainty as regards the future is unmistakable, but whatever the future may hold, the sombre undertones of the whole novel as well as its ending give little support to Jude's optimistic belief. To give substance to such a view it is necessary to consider Little Father Time, the only truly symbolic figure in the book.

Little Father Time is the embodiment of all the ill winds that have put the time out of joint, a sensitive creature sapped of the joy of life by his perception of the antagonistic turn of events that makes for a denial of life, not for an encouragement of it. When his experience of adversity reaches a new peak upon Jude's and Sue's return to Christminster, and when he hears from Sue, who is pregnant, of a new life that is to come to share the misery, he protests according to his own logic by killing himself and the two other children. In himself, Little Father Time is not incredible. Aged-looking and weird boys or girls are fortunately not representative of childhood even in the most calamitous of times. The vital force usually asserts itself in the early years of life at least. But such children do exist in all times. The boy has inherited from his father a hypersensitivity which engenders an unwillingness to grow up, and when circumstances heighten instead of allaying such a disposition, the death-wish forces itself into consciousness. The monstrous deed is not a fanciful invention on Hardy's part. If we read the column of *faits-divers* in the daily newspapers with attention, we shall come across such astonishing realities at one time or another. In the novel the boy's suicide is jarring because his act, which is an unrepresentative reality, is introduced into the reality of Jude and Sue which, in spite of the differences that mark them as individuals, is representative. The disaster also serves to provide a tangible cause for the next development in Sue's and Jude's affairs. This development is the result of a latent condition in their relationship which is basically unrelated to the boy's deed, but the extremity he creates helps make the latent overt. In short, on the realistic level of the book, the figure of Little Father Time seems very much like a *deus ex machina*.

However, on the symbolic level his creation is not a failure at all. Little Father Time is the concrete expression of the impersonal dislocating forces of the time and of the very personal and conscious reaction to the problem of existence of his father, a man whose impulses have been thwarted and whose lurking wish the boy enacts. The boy looks old, partly because the problem of existence is old and timeless, and partly because he as well as Jude never really experienced the joy of youth. His death foreshadows the equally untimely death of his father, but more important still it signifies the end of Jude's brand of idealism as well as the end of the race of Judes. The name Little Father Time is another way of pointing to the agency that is most responsible for the tragedy. Jude's recounting to Sue that according to the doctor the boy's death is a sign of 'the beginning of the coming universal wish not to live' (p. 348), may be taken as a prophetic vision on Hardy's part. For though the World War is in one sense an indication of the determination to live, in another it is also a sign of the 'wish not to live'. The theme of time is used by the author to create individual character as well as general atmosphere.

Christminster (Oxford), both as theme and image, is of major importance in *Jude*. In a sense, Jude's life-story is presented as a challenge to the citadel of learning. The outcome of the 'deadly war waged between flesh and spirit' might be different if the architects of man's soul dealt less with phantoms and grappled more with the realities of human existence. Jude's spirit is enkindled from the start with the idea of Christminster, and he dies in the city of his dreams with its sounds re-echoing in his ears. Illusion and reality alternate in the complex image of Christminster. Jude's illusions of the place are part of his reality, and his own existence is immaterial to Christminster. Similarly, a preoccupation with the remote, the spectral, is the reality of Christminster academical, whereas the real life of the city is unsubstantial to its scholars. The tendency of man's spirit

is to take flight from the real and build its abode in the shadowy. The true need, however, is to apply the intellect to the actual and fashion its moulds accordingly. The proper study of man is Man, that is, the whole of Man, the whole of his life. The pursuit of chimeras and of what ought to be leads to distortion and unhappiness. Only regard for what is and what can be may conceivably reduce human misery.

Jude's arrival at the city of his dreams at night, and his communing with the spirits of its departed, eminent sons is one of the most beautiful passages in the book. An isolated 'self-spectre' himself, he wanders about the medieval colleges, recalling the words of the men of heart and the men of head who had spent their lives within them. The following morning the perfect and ideal apparitions of the night are replaced by the imperfect real. His realization that his presence in Christminster has in no way brought him nearer to his goal does not alter his view of the place as 'the centre of thought and religion—the intellectual and spiritual granary of this country' (p. 120). It is Sue who introduces a dispassionate and more realistic view of Christminster, realistic both from the point of view of its relevance to the spiritual questions of the time and its attitude to people like Jude. Sue has had a platonic relationship with a Christminster graduate, is witty and well read, and has lived in the city long enough without being emotionally attached to it. She tells Jude that 'the mediaevalism of Christminster must go' (p. 157), and that 'at present intellect in Christminster is pushing one way, and religion the other; and so they stand stock-still, like two rams butting each other' (p. 158), that 'it is a place full of fetichists and ghost-seers'. Jude answers that he too is fearful of life, 'spectre-seeing always'. Parallel to the picture of Christminster as abstracted from reality there is the picture of the actual life of the city, and Jude is involved in both pictures. He notices the wide gap that exists between the gown life and the town life and that the latter is a compendious book of humanity little scrutinized by students or teachers. Tinker Taylor, a local labourer and a casual acquaintance of Jude, half mocking his scholastic pursuit tells him that 'there is more to be learnt outside a book than in' (p. 128), and Sue too is of the opinion that the townspeople see more life as it is than the college people do (p. 158). Though Jude perceives that there is much truth in all this, it is also because of this that his desire for learning remains unshaken throughout. He believes that Christminster is the place for him and such as he, and that instead of its scorning and excluding the so-called self-taught, it should be the first to acknowledge the efforts of men ambitious of learning and offer them the opportunity of fulfilling their aims. However, this is far from being the case.

A number of years later, by which time Jude has realized that his life has been a complete failure, he comes back to Christminster with Sue and the children on the day of its festivities. Standing in the crowd among whom are some of his old acquaintances, who remark that he has not made the grade, Jude says to the people around him:

'I may do some good before I am dead—be a sort of success as a frightful example of what not to do; and so illustrate a moral story' (p. 337).

This is an ambiguous statement. Does Jude mean that he ought not to have set his heart on learning, and because of his having done so, he has ruined his life? Such a view is not borne out by the novel. Other factors, not directly related to learning, have been much more detrimental to his happiness than his disappointed hopes of study. In any case, he had not deliberately chosen his aim; it had sprung directly from his nature and was enhanced by the spirit of the time. Does he mean that poor people like him, who are not 'cold-blooded' and 'selfish', ought not to pursue goals the achievement of which depends on the possession of such inhumane qualities? This is not an unlikely meaning, though it contradicts other views of his and Sue's, namely that Christminster is just the place for men with a passion for learning. Or does Jude mean that the whole pattern of his life, everything that has gone into the making of it, should serve as an example, not to other men like him—since they, like him, are inevitably bound to set their feet on the same path as he has—but to the colleges of Christminster and what they ought not to do? They ought not to shut out men desirous of knowledge; they ought not to ignore the reality of the time and hold on to outworn modes of thought. It seems to me that the general drift of the novel would justify such an interpretation.

In the same speech Jude goes on to say:

'I perceive there is something wrong somewhere in our social formulas; what it is can only be discovered by men and women with greater insight than mine—if, indeed, they ever discover it—at least in our time' (p. 338).

The social formulas have to do with the sum total of designs that make up the fabric of society. They set the patterns of economics, educational opportunities, jurisdiction, public opinion, and conventions, but more important still they are conditioned by religion and intellectual accomplishment, and it is from these two spheres, of which Christminster is the centre, that the regeneration of the formulas must come. Jude's appeal, and we may say Hardy's, is made to the authority in whose power it is to control that part of man's fortunes that is given to man to control. For his own part, Jude vows never to care any more about the 'infernal, cursed place'. The disaster of the children's death that befalls him in Christminster is a fateful event underscoring the 'example', but it also points to a power which by its incomprehensibility sets limits to human endeavour.

When Jude returns from his last visit to Sue, now back with Phillotson, he walks with Arabella through the streets of the city, seeing the spirits of the dead as he did on his first arrival in the place. He explains to Arabella:

'I seem to see them and almost hear them rustling. But I don't revere them as I did. I don't believe in

half of them . . . All that has been spoiled for me by the grind of stern reality . . . They seem laughing at me . . . The phantoms all about here . . .' (p. 406).

To this Arabella retorts: 'Come along do! Phantoms! There's neither living nor dead hereabouts except a damn policeman!' Kathleen R. Hooper remarks that 'Arabella gave the final, earthly comment of a world which Jude never understood'.[11] On the contrary, Jude has learnt from his bitter experience to look at his world with disillusioned eyes and to understand what is wrong with it and what hopes may be entertained as regards it. Lying on his death-bed, his mind is still preoccupied with the dream that has for ever haunted him. He tells Arabella that he has heard there are schemes to make the University less exclusive and to extend its influence (p. 413), but he knows only too well that for him it is too late.

Essentially there are only two major themes in *Jude:* one relating to everything connected with the flesh, and the other relating to everything connected with the spirit. Hardy dramatizes the conflict between these two themes, and stresses the need for their integration. Ideally the flesh should inform the spirit and the spirit the flesh. Jude would not have been completely happy if he had been given the opportunity of fulfilling his dreams of learning, but proper studies could have better equipped him to cope with 'stern reality'. One might argue that such studies were not available in his time, but towards such at any rate he aspired. The characters are created through the themes and in a sense they are the themes. They interpret the world and themselves in terms of old systems and outworn modes of thought, whereas their situation cries out for new terms of reference, new concepts, new values. Jude foresaw that the new was bound to come, and it cannot be said that his 'example' was to go unheeded, but the new formulas that were to emerge and the influence they were to spread were not to be of the kind to foster that good in life, that type of fulfilment at which he had originally aimed. In other words, in *Jude* Hardy laments the passage of an age and adumbrates the attitudes, or if we want, 'the formulas', that were to characterize the first half of the present century: formulas the latter-day Judes, battering against the walls of the establishment, hope to change.

[1] Eugene Goodheart, 'Thomas Hardy and the Lyrical Novel' in *Nineteenth Century Fiction,* no. 3, December 1957.

[2] Walter Allen, *The English Novel,* Penguin Books, 1958, p. 255.

[3] J. I. M. Stewart, *Eight Modern Writers,* Clarendon Press, 1963, p. 45.

[4] Thomas Hardy, *Jude the Obscure,* Macmillan, London, 1957, p. 1 (all further references will be to this edition).

[5] Albert J. Guerard, *Thomas Hardy: The Novels and Stories,* O.U.P., London, 1949, p. 32.

[6] Ibid., p. 110.

[7] Ibid., p. 152.

[8] Ibid., p. 153.

[9] Lascelles Abercrombie, *Thomas Hardy: A Critical Study,* Martin Secker, London, 1912, p. 26.

[10] Arthur Mizener, '*Jude the Obscure* as Tragedy', in *Modern British Fiction,* ed. Mark Schorer, O.U.P., N.Y., 1961.

[11] Kathleen R. Hooper, 'Illusion and Reality in *Jude the Obscure*', in *Nineteenth-Century Fiction,* no. 2, September 1957, p. 157.

Mary Jacobus (essay date 1975)

SOURCE: "Sue the Obscure," in *Essays in Criticism,* Vol. XXV, No. 3, July, 1975, pp. 304-28.

[*In the following essay, Jacobus accepts Hardy's contention that* Jude the Obscure *is a novel of contrasting ideas, and thus analyzes the work by focusing on the character of Sue Bridehead, rather than that of Jude.*]

Hardy's account of *Jude the Obscure* raises the problem at once:

> Of course the book is all contrasts—or was meant to be in its original conception. Alas, what a miserable accomplishment it is, when I compare it with what I meant to make it!—*e.g.* Sue and her heathen gods set against Jude's reading the Greek testament; Christminster academical, Christminster in the slums; Jude the saint, Jude the sinner; Sue the Pagan, Sue the saint; marriage, no marriage; &c., &c.

The degree of Hardy's success in executing these strongly-marked contrasts remains the central question about *Jude*. The bare bones of its design lie dangerously close to the surface, and the urgency of Hardy's commitment constantly threatens its imaginative autonomy. Its realism and its diagrammatic plotting pull in opposite directions, and Hardy's disconcerting tendency to translate ideas into physical realities sometimes leave us uncertain of the intention behind his effects. This apparent discrepancy between intention and achievement is at its most acute in the character of Sue. What did Hardy mean by her, and what in the end did he create? Above all, with what success are Sue and the issues she raises integrated into the novel as a whole?

'The first delineation in fiction of the woman who was coming into notice in her thousands every year—the woman of the feminist movement.' This was one reviewer's response to Sue Bridehead, recalled in the 1912 postscript to *Jude*. Hardy himself was non-commit-

tal; and although Sue has much in common with the 'New Woman' of the 1890s ('the intellectualized, emancipated bundle of nerves that modern conditions were producing'), she strikes us less as a specimen than as an individual whose vivid fictional life springs from and is defined by the novel itself. Hardy elsewhere wrote of her simply as 'a type of woman which has always had an attraction for me', adding that 'the difficulty of drawing the type has kept me from attempting it till now'. For most readers, this unique and painful individuality—at once confused and distinct, fragile and sharply etched—constitutes Hardy's main achievement; Sue is pitied, blamed, puzzled over, or mourned, as if she were a living woman. The difficulty lies in reconciling this fictional vividness with Hardy's elusive intention. To regard Sue primarily as a psychological portrait diminishes the importance of the ideas Hardy makes her express. It is particularly difficult to know where Hardy stands in relation to her feminism. In one sense his refusal to offer an unambiguous diagnosis, either within or outside the novel, contributes to our belief in Sue: she continues to haunt and perplex us long after we have finished reading because she is neither case-history nor propaganda. She too is 'obscure'. But Hardy's careful non-alignment also means that he can be accused of dodging or bungling the very issues he has raised. Kate Millett, for instance, sees in Sue's muddle ('by turns an enigma, a pathetic creature, a nut, and an iceberg') a reflection of her creator's intellectual uncertainty: '*Jude the Obscure* is on very solid ground when attacking the class system, but when it turns to the sexual revolution, Hardy himself is troubled and confused' (*Sexual Politics,* 1969, pp. 133-4). The accusation is an important and damaging one. *Jude* stands or falls on the coherence of its tragic protest, and Hardy's art as well as his clarity is in question. If he fails in dealing with Sue's sexual revolt, then the structure of contrasts on which the novel depends is weakened where it should be strongest—in the power of Sue's tragedy to complement and illuminate Jude's.

The most influential account of Sue's character is pseudo-psychological. In his *Study of Thomas Hardy,* D. H. Lawrence sees Jude as divided between the male and the female within himself; his tragedy lies in

> over-development of one principle of human life at the expense of the other; an over-balancing; a laying of all the stress on the Male, the love, the Spirit, the Mind, the Consciousness; a denying, a blaspheming against the Female, the Law, the Soul, the Senses, the Feelings. (*Phoenix,* 1936, p. 509)

In Lawrentian terms (the terms of 1914 and *The Rainbow*), Sue embodies the male principle: 'She was born with the vital female atrophied in her: she was almost male'. Her literary genealogy is that of the 'Amelias and Agneses, those women who submitted to the man-idea'—who betrayed the female within themselves in order to become 'the pure thing'. For such a woman, marriage can only be 'a submission, a service, a slavery', while the suppressed female within continually threatens to destroy her precarious equilibrium (pp. 496-7). Lawrence conveys his sense of her instability and inner division by an image of dizzy exposure:

> She had climbed and climbed to be near the stars. And now, at last, on the topmost pinnacle, exposed to all the horrors and magnificence of space, she could not go back. Her strength had fallen from her. Up at that great height, with scarcely any foothold, but only space, space all round her, rising up to her from beneath, she was like a thing suspended, supported almost at the point of extinction by the density of her medium. Her body was lost to her, fallen away, gone. She existed there as a point of consciousness, no more, like one swooned at a great height, held up at the tip of a fine pinnacle that drove upwards into nothingness. (pp. 503-4)

Since Lawrence's Sue is at once self-possessed and self-divided, sexual consummation can only bring desecration to her and negation to Jude:

> if it was death to her, or profanation, or pollution, or breaking, it was unnatural to him, blasphemy. How could he, a living, loving man, warm and productive, take with his body the moonlit cold body of a woman who did not live to him, and did not want him? It was monstrous, and it sent him mad. (p. 505)

Lawrence recreates the novel with such imaginative intensity that it is easy to substitute his version for Hardy's. To return to *Jude* itself is to confront an imagination no less powerful, but radically different in its emphases. More sympathetic, less diagnostic, Hardy also gives weight to ideas which the *Study of Thomas Hardy* entirely ignores.

Although Lawrence's blueprint does violence to the artistic and intellectual complexity of *Jude,* the Lawrentian view of Sue remains surprisingly current. Her crimes, ranging from frigidity to husband-murder, make her the villain of the piece in a number of recent critical accounts. And for Kate Millett—criticizing Hardy rather than Sue—she is 'the victim of a cultural literary convention (Lily and Rose) that in granting her a mind insists on withholding a body from her' (*Sexual Politics,* p. 133). Cast in this way as 'the frigid woman', the lily of her name, Sue becomes less a tragic figure in her own right than an aspect of Jude's tragedy. Of course, there can be no mistaking the depth of Hardy's sympathy for Jude, but has the novel been read too exclusively from his point of view?

To an extent which often goes unnoticed, Hardy offers us a dual focus which valuably modifies the literary convention identified by Kate Millett. We see Sue as she appears to Jude and Phillotson—lovable, ethereal, inconsistent, capable of inflicting great pain, and, for Jude at least, ultimately unforgivable. But during the course of the novel, Hardy also allows us to enter into Sue's consciousness—to hear her point of view at first hand, and, when we no longer do so, to speculate about it. Dialogue

plays a central part in *Jude,* translating its underlying ideas into subjectively-perceived truths. [Edmund] Gosse's complaint that Sue and Jude talk 'a sort of University Extension jargon' is fair. But the novel does concern education—education through the testing of ideas against experience. That sense of life which in Hardy's earlier novels sprang from rural activity or landscape derives in *Jude* from conversation. Sue's attempts to articulate her changing consciousness—whether exploratory or penetrating, tailing off into uncertainty or toppling into neurotic self-blame—make her a vital counterpart to Jude. When we no longer hear her voice, it is because Sue is alienated from herself as well as us. Her retreat from emancipation to enslavement, from speech to silence, balances Jude's progress from idealism to bitter, articulate disillusion in a double movement which intensifies the novel's protest. 'What are my books but one long plea against "man's inhumanity to man"—to woman—and to the lower animals?' asked Hardy; *Jude the Obscure* is just such a plea.

On its appearance in the mid-'90s, *Jude* was inevitably linked with Grant Allen's *The Woman Who Did* (1895) as another contribution to 'the marriage question'; for Mrs. Oliphant, it was a sign that Hardy had joined 'The Anti-Marriage League'. But Hardy himself pleaded innocence:

> It is curious that some of the papers should look upon the novel as a manifesto on 'the marriage question' (although, of course, it involves it). . . . The only remarks which can be said to bear on the *general* marriage question occur in dialogue, and comprise no more than half a dozen pages in a book of five hundred.

The 1912 postscript to *Jude* clarifies the implications of its epigraph ('The letter killeth'): 'My opinion at that time, if I remember rightly, was what it is now, that a marriage should be dissolvable as soon as it becomes a cruelty to either of the parties—being then essentially and morally no marriage'. But the novel itself says something both more disturbing and more radical, since the 'cruelty' bears particularly on the sensibility with which Hardy endows Sue. It is true that marriage has proved a trap to Jude, ensnared by the time-worn ruse of Arabella's fake pregnancy, but his disillusion with Arabella's artificial dimples and tresses brings neither the distress nor the personal discovery which marriage brings to Sue. ' "O Susanna Florence Mary! . . . You don't know what marriage means!"' (Wessex ed., 1912, p. 203) laments Jude to himself, when she marries Phillotson in a tangle of pique, muddle, obligation, and ignorance. We watch her gradual awakening. Her views on the marriage service come first, wryly conveyed in a letter to Jude—as yet unquestioning of conventional religion: ' "my bridegroom chooses me of his own will and pleasure; but I don't choose him. Somebody *gives* me to him, like a she-ass or a she-goat, or any other domestic animal. Bless your exalted views of woman, O Churchman!"' (p. 204). What she discovers in marriage itself is the independent sexual identity which survives this property transaction. Her aversion to Phillotson (an aversion endorsed by the traditional wisdom of Aunt Drusilla and Widow Edlin) is essentially a discovery about herself, tearfully and haltingly confessed to the more experienced Jude:

> 'though I like Mr. Phillotson as a friend, I don't like him—it is a torture to me to—live with him as a husband! . . . there is nothing wrong except my own wickedness, I suppose you'd call it—a repugnance on my part, for a reason I cannot disclose, and what would not be admitted as one by the world in general! . . . What tortures me so much is the necessity of being responsive to this man whenever he wishes, good as he is morally!— the dreadful contract to feel in a particular way in a matter whose essence is its voluntariness! . . .
> (p. 255)

In the last phrase, Sue is partly being Shelleyan; but she is also protesting, as Mill had done in *The Subjection of Women* (1869), at 'the lowest degradation of a human being, that of being made the instrument of an animal function contrary to her inclinations' (p. 57). More important, she no longer expresses a feminism that is only intellectually related to herself. She has now experienced, in a way too personal to tell anyone else, what 'belonging' to Phillotson actually means. As so often in the dialogue he gives Sue, Hardy holds the balance between her beliefs (the echoes of Shelley and Mill) and feelings which she has to articulate for herself—guiltily owning up to a sexual repugnance which 'the world in general' would refuse to recognize. Later the same night, when she and Jude have been woken by the cry of a trapped rabbit, Hardy stresses the change that has taken place in her consciousness; and again the mournful yet impatient speech rhythms authenticate Sue's new perception of herself:

> 'before I married him I had never thought out fully what marriage meant, even though I knew. It was idiotic of me—there is no excuse. I was old enough, and I thought I was very experienced . . . I am certain one ought to be allowed to undo what one has done so ignorantly! I daresay it happens to lots of women; only they submit, and I kick. . . .'
> (p. 258)

We are left with the image of the rabbit writhing in the gin. It is Sue's special tragedy that she has enough life to kick, but not enough strength to escape.

The image is picked up in the following chapter, when Jude reflects on his own experience of ' "the artificial system of things, under which the normal sex-impulses are turned into devilish domestic gins and springes"' (p. 261). Both he and Sue are released by partners who acknowledge other laws than 'the artificial system of things'—Arabella, impelled by an animal instinct when Jude has served her need; Phillotson, by genuine compassion. But Hardy shows us that more is at issue than the freedom to choose another partner. He is not simply advocating divorce, but—as Mrs. Oliphant detected—questioning the institution of marriage itself. Again, it is primarily through Sue's consciousness that the novel explores the tyranny of sexual orthodoxy, implying the doubt elsewhere explicitly expressed by Hardy, 'whether marriage, as we at present understand it, is such a desirable goal for all women as it is assumed to be'. Sue's time with Phillotson has taught her to recognize the gap between the identity imposed by society, and her real inner self: 'I am called Mrs. Richard Phillotson, living a calm wedded life with my counterpart of that name. But I am not really Mrs. Richard Phillotson, but a woman tossed about, all alone, with aberrant passions, and unaccountable antipathies. . . . ' (p. 247) To be called Mrs. Jude Fawley would be no less a denial of the troubled individual who is Sue Bridehead. The central aspect of Sue's character is not that in her the female is atrophied, as Lawrence maintained, but that in her the individual is highly developed. Havelock Ellis put it well, writing of 'the refinement of sexual sensibility with which this book largely deals':

> To treat Jude, who wavers between two women, and Sue, who finds the laws of marriage too mighty for her lightly-poised organism, as shocking monstrosities, reveals a curious attitude in the critics who have committed themselves to that view. Clearly they consider human sexual relationships to be as simple as those of the farmyard. They are as shocked as a farmer would be to find that a hen had views of her own concerning the lord of the harem. If, let us say, you decide that Indian Game and Plymouth Rock make a good cross, you put your cock and hens together, and the matter is settled; and if you decide that a man and a woman are in love with each other, you marry them and the matter is likewise settled for the whole term of their natural lives. (*Savoy*, 6 October 1896, p. 46.)

Sue is not a hen with views of her own, but a woman for whom the laws of the farmyard spell oppression. Institutionalized sex takes as little account of her 'lightly-poised organism' as it does of Jude's wavering between two women. Hardy told Gosse that Sue's sexuality was 'healthy as far as it goes, but unusually weak and fastidious'. Jude, by contrast, is aroused rather than repelled by the pig's pizzle which Arabella flings at him, and easily deflected from his dream of Christminster by her dimples. But the opposition between his need for sexual fulfilment and Sue's reserve is never presented simply in terms of Jude's frustration. Sue is allowed to state her own case when she speaks of her platonic relationship with the Christminster undergraduate who is responsible for many of her unorthodox ideas: ' "People say I must be cold-natured—sexless—on account of it. But I won't have it! Some of the most passionately erotic poets have been the most self-contained in their daily lives"' (pp. 178-9); later in the same conversation, she defends the Song of Songs against its Christian allegorists (' "I *hate* such humbug as could attempt to plaster over with ecclesiastical abstractions such ecstatic, natural, human love as lies in that great and passionate song!"', p. 182). Hardy sets her passionate imagination against Jude's unthinking passion—and then tests each against the claims of the other, using a specific sexual relationship to intensify the novel's wider vision of human frustration and defeat.

From Jude's point of view, Sue's religion of pagan joy is a bitter irony; she first liberates him from his religious asceticism, then refuses to satisfy him. Seen from Sue's point of view, however, her paganism is primarily an expression of revolt. When she sets up statues of Venus and Apollo in her bedroom and chants Swinburne, she is striking a private blow at the self-denying spiritual fervour which at the same moment inspires Jude's plain living and high thinking in another part of Christminster. What stands out is not Sue's comical blaspheming against the ethos of Miss Fontover's ecclesiastical knick-knack shop, but her inner refusal to conform. It is this area of personal freedom she tries to retain in her relationships. She will live with the Christminster undergraduate—but on her terms, not his. She is happy to go to Philotson 'as a friend'; it is as a husband, with rights over her body, that she rejects him. In the same way—as critics have often noted—she is at her most forthcoming to Jude when she has put between them an engagement, or a marriage, or a window, or simply man's clothes, as on the evening of her flight from the Melchester teachers' training college. When she asks the bewildered Phillotson to let her go, she has found in John Stuart Mill the intellectual basis for her instinctive assertion of individuality:

> 'And do you mean, by living away from me, living by yourself?' [asks Phillotson].
>
> 'Well, if you insisted, yes. But I meant living with Jude.'
>
> 'As his wife?'
>
> 'As I choose.'
>
> Phillotson writhed.
>
> She continued: 'She, or he, "who lets the world, or his own portion of it, choose his plan of life for him, has no need of any other faculty than the ape-like one of imitation". J. S. Mill's words, those are. I have been reading it up. Why can't you act upon them? I wish to, always.'
>
> 'What do I care about J. S. Mill!' moaned he. 'I only want to lead a quiet life!' (p. 269)

Confronted by Sue's blithe application of theory to life, we are likely to have some sympathy with Phillotson. Yet the force of ' "As I choose"' remains. Sue takes her text from the third chapter of *On Liberty* (1859), 'Of Individuality':

> There is always need of persons not only to discover new truths, and point out when what were once truths are true no longer, but also to commence new practices, and set the example of more enlightened conduct, and better taste and sense in human life . . . exceptional individuals, instead of being deterred, should be encouraged in

acting differently from the mass. . . . In this age the mere example of non-conformity, the mere refusal to bend the knee to custom, is itself a service. (pp. 106, 115, 120)

With this persuasive plea as a context, we may be less inclined to smile at Sue's earnestness. But ' "Who were we,"' she laments at the end of the novel, ' "to think we could act as pioneers!"' (p. 425).

Elsewhere, Sue's timidity, irresolution, and inconsistency often strike us more forcibly than her knowledge of Mill. The split between belief and instinctive behaviour is most acutely analyzed in the scenes leading up to the consummation of her relationship with Jude. Till she leaves Phillotson, Sue has successfully held out for the right to give or withhold herself as she chooses; the Christminster undergraduate dies unfulfilled, and Phillotson lets her go when her leap from a first-floor window convinces him of her aversion. The question which hangs over her third relationship is: will it prove a new departure, or only a repetition? a victory or a defeat? Hardy charts her surrender to Jude's more urgent sexuality with a mixture of acerbity and tenderness. The complexity of his sympathy is nowhere more enriching. He himself had known Mill's *On Liberty* 'almost by heart' as a young man, as well as sharing Sue's taste for Shelley and Swinburne. But *Jude the Obscure* belongs to a period thirty years later, and its absolutes are qualified by experience. Moreover, Mill had been largely concerned with the relation of individual to society; Hardy is also concerned with the relation of individual to individual—with the conflict between personal freedom and human commitment. When Sue comes to Jude, she begins by re-enacting the pattern of advance and retreat, of boldness followed by flight, which had characterized her even as a child at Marygreen. By chance and authorial design, she and Jude go for their first night together to the same hotel, the same room even, in which Jude had spent a night with Arabella not long before. Sue's tearful indignation at this discovery (' "Why are you so gross! *I* jumped out of the window!"', p. 293) is only dispelled by extorting a rueful tribute to her own contrasting spirituality. The words she puts into Jude's mouth, from Shelley's *Epipsychidion,* have an additional irony when one recalls Hardy's mistrust of Shelleyan individuals such as Angel Clare and Eldred Fitzpiers:

> ' "There was a Being whom my spirit oft
> Met on its visioned wanderings far aloft.
> A seraph of Heaven, too gentle to be human,
> Veiling beneath the radiant form of woman. . . . "
>
> O it is too flattering, so I won't go on! But say it's me!—say it's me!'
>
> 'It *is* you dear; exactly like you!' (p. 294)

Sue thus wins the first round at Jude's expense (he, apparently, must love only her, but she need not commit herself to him); and as he goes off sighingly to another room, the balance of our sympathy is surely with him.

But the balance is short-lived. Hardy is imaginatively generous towards both sides of the struggle, but as always his most intense feeling is for the loser. Sue's chief weapons are her undoubted attraction for Jude and her moral advantage (' "Why are you so gross!"'): Jude's weapon is simply his ability to take himself elsewhere. When Arabella returns to upset their precarious equilibrium (Jude pressing for marriage, Sue evasive as ever), she reveals to Sue that the price she pays for withholding herself is insecurity—that the complement of personal freedom must be self-reliance. Jude justifies his refusal to turn away his former wife in humane terms; but Sue's piteous entreaties show her tacit recognition of the sexual threat posed by Arabella: ' "Don't go now, Jude! . . . O, it is only to entrap you. . . . Don't, don't go, dear! She is such a low-passioned woman. . . ."' (p. 318). Jude seizes this chance to make his protest against the conditions of intimacy which Sue had earlier forced him to celebrate:

> ' . . . Please, please stay at home, Jude, and not go to her, now she's not your wife any more than I!'
>
> 'Well, she is, rather more than you, come to that,' he said, taking his hat determinedly. 'I've wanted you to be, and I've waited with the patience of Job, and I don't see that I've got anything by my self-denial. I shall certainly give her something, and hear what she is so anxious to tell me; no man could do less!' (p. 318)

' "No man could do less"' opposes charitable humanity to Sue's ungiving chastity. Yet her meekness in the face of his resolve, her child-like distress when he goes out into the night to find Arabella, and her undisguised relief when he returns without having seen her, give poignancy to Sue's capitulation. She succumbs to Jude, but it is under duress: ' "I ought to have known you would conquer in the long run, living like this!"', she tells him; ' "I give in!"' (p. 321). The blend of pleasure and regret which we feel in her defeat is beautifully caught in the kisses she exchanges with Jude the following day—kisses, Hardy tells us, returned by Sue 'in a way she had never done before. Times had decidedly changed. "The little bird is caught at last!" she said, a sadness showing in her smile.' (p. 322) Jude's reply (' "No—only nested"') consoles both her and us; but this time our sympathy is with her.

Hardy wrote that Jude had 'never really possessed [Sue] as freely as he desired'. But although she remains elusive to the last, 'That the twain were happy—between their times of sadness—was indubitable' (p. 348). Hardy subtly conveys the extent of her sexual awakening, and we gain enough sense of a shared sexual happiness to make its betrayal by Sue herself, at the end of the novel, a tragic one. In a central scene we see the two together, now lovers, visiting the Great Wessex Agricultural Show with Little Father Time in tow. It is a scene singled out by Lawrence—perhaps because, as in many of his own most sexually-charged scenes, flowers provide the catalyst:

> when they went to the flower show, her sense of the roses, and Jude's sense of the roses, would be most, most poignant. . . . The roses, how the roses glowed for them! . . . the real marriage of Jude and Sue was in the roses. Then, in the third state, in the spirit, these two beings met upon the roses and in the roses were symbolized in consummation. The rose is the symbol of marriage-consummation in its beauty. (*Phoenix*, pp. 506-7)

Lawrence may be right that Sue and Jude never know 'actual, sure-footed happiness'; there is always a sense of precariousness in their lives, as there is always a sense of rootlessness. But his insistence that this is a communion of minds which sexual consummation can only violate misses the vibrancy of fulfilment in the scene as Hardy presents it. The day of holiday has brought Arabella and her husband—'the average husband and wife'—to the show along with Sue and Jude. While one couple are sullen and indifferent, the other ('the more exceptional') reveal 'that complete mutual understanding' which makes the cynical Arabella doubt that they are actually married. What kind of happiness theirs is emerges from an incident in the flower tent:

> the more exceptional couple and the boy still lingered in the pavilion of flowers—an enchanted palace to their appreciative taste—Sue's usually pale cheeks reflecting the pink of the tinted roses at which she gazed; for the gay sights, the air, the music, and the excitement of a day's outing with Jude, had quickened her blood and made her eyes sparkle with vivacity. She adored roses, and what Arabella had witnessed was Sue detaining Jude almost against his will while she learnt the names of this variety and that, and put her face within an inch of their blooms to smell them.
>
> 'I should like to push my face quite into them— the dears!' she had said. 'But I suppose it is against the rules to touch them—isn't it, Jude?'
>
> 'Yes, you baby,' said he: and then playfully gave her a little push, so that her nose went among the petals.
>
> 'The policeman will be down on us, and I shall say it was my husband's fault!'
>
> Then she looked up at him, and smiled in a way that told so much to Arabella. (pp. 357-8)

The roses are indeed symbolic, as Lawrence asserts—but they are symbolic of more than spiritual communion. The rose which complements the lily in Sue has been brought into flower by Jude; it is he who gives her the playful push into contact with her own sensuous nature, making her fully and joyously responsive here. The 'cultural literary convention (Lily and Rose)' has been realistically blurred. What Arabella sees makes her jealous enough to accept Vilbert's love-philtre, and her lowering presence, like that of Satan spying on Adam and Eve in their pre-lapserian garden, accentuates the innocence of their sexuality.

Nevertheless, Sue and Jude are childlike here—'The Simpletons' of the novel's original title. ' "Silly fools—like two children!"' (p. 365), grumbles Arabella in the background. Their vulnerability is heightened by the exaggerated sense of transience voiced by Little Father Time—unable to enjoy the flowers because he knows they will soon be withered. What he foresees, in a parody of Hardy's own vision, Sue and Jude are to experience. 'The more exceptional couple', they also prove least able to withstand what time brings. Three years later, Arabella is a prosperous widow while Sue ekes out the family income selling Christminster cakes; Jude is sick and out of work, and Sue, already the mother of two children, is expecting a third. In the interval has come their restless movement from place to place, in search of work and the right to live by a private code of morals. They recoil from the cynical forms of civil marriage and the unthinking bourgeois ritual enacted in the name of religion; they are turned off from the job of restoring the Ten Commandments painted on the wall of a country church, in an episode which makes the point of Hardy's epigraph—the difference between Old Testament law and New Testament charity—with graphic plainness. In Mill's words, 'the strongest of all the arguments against the interference of the public with purely personal conduct, is that when it does interfere, the odds are that it interferes wrongly, and in the wrong place' (*On Liberty,* pp. 149-50).

But Hardy is not simply concerned to show the tragic defeat of exceptional individuals at the hands of society—what he elsewhere calls 'the triumph of the crowd over the hero, of the commonplace majority over the exceptional few'. Nature also conspires against them. Fulfilling natural laws, they have to face natural consequences—children. Mill had written of a scheme of things that 'cannot have had, for its sole or even principal object, the good of human or other sentient beings. Sue echoes his opinion of parenthood when she tells Arabella that ' "it seems such a terribly tragic thing to bring beings into the world"' (p. 375)—

> The fact itself, of causing the existence of a human being, is one of the most responsible actions in the range of human life. To undertake this responsibility—to bestow a life which may be either a curse or a blessing—unless the being on which it is to be bestowed will have at least the ordinary chances of a desirable existence, is a crime against that being. (*On Liberty,* p. 194)

This is the view of life that prematurely overwhelms Little Father Time; for him, his parents have committed a crime in bringing children into the world, not he who commits one in taking them out of it. Hardy's engineering of the novel's tragic crisis may lack tact; but the urgency of his protest against the double tyranny of society and Nature over 'the exceptional few' gives classic inexorability to his modern theme.

Like the flinging of the pig's pizzle (showing 'the contrast between the ideal life a man wished to lead, and the squalid real life he was fated to lead'), the death of the children brings the novel's underlying metaphors into the open. The family's doomed return to Christminster confronts us with more than just the death of Jude's hopes and his inevitable exclusion from Arnold's city of lost causes (' "I'm an outsider to the end of my days!"', p. 396). We also witness in Christminster the collapse of the couple's struggle for happiness on a purely personal level; as Mill had promised, 'from him that hath not, shall be taken even that which he hath'. The death of the children is the price Sue and Jude have to pay for their sexual fulfilment, in the face of a hostile society and the absence of contraception. Mrs. Oliphant jeered at Hardy for what she called his 'solution of the great insoluble question of what is to be the fate of children in such circumstances': 'Does Mr. Hardy think this is really a good way of disposing of the unfortunate progeny of such connections?' The episode is indeed grotesque; but the idea which underlies it, as often in *Jude,* is more powerful and more valid than the means used to express it. Its true force emerges less from the clumsily-contrived massacre than from the painful conversation which precipitates it. Pregnant and encumbered by children, Sue has has only found lodgings in Christminster on condition that Jude goes elsewhere; even so, the landlady's husband refuses to let them stay beyond the next day. It is in this context that Sue and Little Father Time, deeply depressed, talk together:

> 'It would be better to be out o' the world than in it, wouldn't it?'
>
> 'It would almost, dear.'
>
> ''Tis because of us children too, isn't it, that you can't get a good lodging?'
>
> 'Well—people do object to children sometimes.'
>
> 'Then if children make so much trouble, why do people have 'em?'
>
> 'Oh—because it is a law of nature.'
>
> 'But we don't ask to be born?'
>
> 'No indeed.' (p. 402)

The gap between adult's and child's perception is deceptively narrowed (Little Father Time groping to express what Sue knows too well); and—like Jude when Sue blames herself afterwards—we can comprehend her mistaken honesty in breaking the news that another child is on the way:

> The boy burst out weeping. 'O you don't care, you don't care!' he cried in bitter reproach. 'How *ever* could you, mother, be so wicked and cruel as this, when you needn't have done it till we was better off, and father well!—To bring us all into *more* trouble! No room for us, and father a-forced to go away, and we turned out tomorrow; and yet you be going to have another of us soon! . . . 'Tis done

o'purpose!—'tis—'tis!' He walked up and down sobbing. (p. 403)

All Sue can reply is ' "I can't explain, dear! But it—is not quite on purpose—I can't help it!"' (p. 403), and indeed she can't. What Little Father Time understands is already too much for him (' "I wish I hadn't been born!"', p. 402); what he can't understand accentuates Sue's helplessness. After the tragedy, she expresses with terrible clarity her sense of the forces massed against them: ' "There is something external to us which says, 'You shan't!' First it said, 'You shan't learn!' Then it said, 'You shan't labour!' Now it says, 'You shan't love!"' (p. 407). 'The coming universal wish not to live', portentously diagnosed by the doctor, objectifies Sue's feelings here and anticipates Jude's final, death-bed negation of life: ' "*Let the day perish wherein I was born . . .*" ' (pp. 406, 488).

The death of the children is the most flagrant instance of Hardy's preparedness to sacrifice verisimilitude to his diagrammatic design, but we are never allowed to forget that *Jude* is a novel of contrasting ideas. The culminating and most crucial of them is that between Sue's unbalance and Jude's disillusion. Throughout the book, however, the rigid ironies of Hardy's scheme have been translated into the changing consciousness of his characters. Hence the unexpected effect of a novel at once fixed and fluid, over-emphatic and true to life. Events which seem contrived precipitate inner changes which are painfully authenticated. The peculiar modernity of *Jude* lies in the weight it gives to such changes. The sturdy Wessex world of Hardy's earlier novels has been ousted by 'the ache of modernism'; no longer sustained by an enduring rural context, Sue and Jude have nothing to fall back on but their ideas, and one by one these fail them. Jude's mental education reveals the limitations of Christminster and evangelical Christianity. Sue's education—her experience as a woman—brings her from clarity to compromise, from compromise to collapse. The birdlike, white-clothed figure at the Great Wessex Agricultural Show becomes a heap of black garments sobbing and abasing herself beneath the cross in the Church of St. Silas of Ceremonies. Arnold's Christminster, for all its sweetness and light, gives Jude only his bitter sense of exclusion: Newman's Christminster—its Victorian complement—gives Sue her sense of guilt. She begins with Hellenic intellect as her light, and ends with Hebraic conscience as her yoke. Jude (increasingly the recording consciousness of the novel) underlines the tragic reversal of their positions:

> 'she was once a woman whose intellect was to mine like a star to a benzoline lamp: who saw all *my* superstitions as cobwebs that she could brush away with a word. Then bitter affliction came to us, and her intellect broke, and she veered round to darkness. Strange difference of sex, that time and circumstance, which enlarge the views of most men, narrow the views of women almost invariably.' (p. 484)

It is precisely Sue's femaleness which breaks her. When she loses her unborn child—her last stake in the future—

we can only find Lawrence's psychic interpretation appallingly inappropriate: 'She was no woman. And her children, the proof thereof, vanished like hoarfrost from her' (*Phoenix,* p. 507).

Sue's self-mortification after the death of her children (' "We should mortify the flesh—the terrible flesh—the curse of Adam!"', p. 416) is psychologically plausible; we recall the self-punishing impulse hinted at earlier in her pre-enactment with Jude of the wedding ceremony which will bind her to Phillotson. But it is too easy to write off her return to Phillotson as a morbid recurrence of this 'emotional epicureanism', the 'colossal inconsistency', noted by Jude years before. The tragic implications of her return emerge from Hardy's insistence that Sue is both the same person and significantly different. The woman who remarries Phillotson is not the girl who had married him long before:

> She had never in her life looked so much like the lily her name connoted as she did in that pallid morning light. Chastened, world-weary, remorseful, the strain on her nerves had preyed upon her flesh and bones, and she appeared smaller in outline than she had formerly done, though Sue had not been a large woman in her days of rudest health. (p. 445)

The oblique reminder of Sue's sprite-like insubstantiality gives pitying perspective to this second wedding; the burden has been too heavy, the bearer too frail. But it is not just that Sue is worn out by suffering. A younger Sue had denied her sexuality in ignorance: the older Sue does so knowingly. As we see from her reunion with Jude, three months later, she does still love him as passionately and physically as she is able. When Jude upbraids her (' "Sue, Sue, you are not worth a man's love!"') she bursts out:

> 'I can't endure you to say that! . . . Don't, don't scorn me! Kiss me, O kiss me lots of times, and say I am not a coward and a contemptible humbug—I can't bear it!' She rushed up to him and, with her mouth on his, continued: 'I must tell you—O I must—my darling Love! It has been—only a church marriage—an apparent marriage I mean!' (pp. 470-1)

Afterwards, she confesses to Widow Edlin: ' "I find I still love him—O, grossly"' (p. 476)—applying to herself the word she had once used disapprovingly of Jude. But ' "I've got over myself now"', she tells him, reminded of their dead children. We see the lengths she is prepared to go in getting over herself in the ritual reparation which is our last direct sight of Sue. Sex with love has brought only the death of her children: sex without love now brings the death of her deepest self. Earlier she had rent her embroidered nightgown, symbol of her shared joy with Jude, replacing it by a sacrificial, shroud-like calico garment in which to act out this penance. Hardy spares us nothing that matters of the harrowing scene in which she offers up her body on the altar of conventional morality, as she has earlier offered up her mind to a repressive form of Christianity. We overhear the conversation at Phillotson's bedroom door, gain a glimpse of his impatience ('There was something in [his] tone now which seemed to show that his three months of re-marriage with Sue had somehow not been so satisfactory as his magnanimity or amative patience had anticipated', p. 479); we witness Sue's oath of self-denial, her irrepressible repugnance (' "O God!"'), and her final submission—the subjection of the female to a covertly sadistic sexual code which demands the total surrender of her consciousness, individuality, and specialness:

> Placing the candlestick on the chest of drawers he led her through the doorway, and lifting her bodily, kissed her. A quick look of aversion passed over her face, but clenching her teeth she uttered no cry. (p. 480)

As silence falls, Widow Edlin offers her choric comment on this life-denying consummation: ' "Ah! poor soul! Weddings be funerals 'a b'lieve nowadays"' (p. 481).

The reviewer who identified Sue as a 'New Woman' also recorded his regret that 'the portrait of the newcomer had been left to be drawn by a man, and was not done by one of her own sex, who would never have allowed her to break down at the end'. Hardy was writing less to celebrate her revolt than 'to point the tragedy of unfulfilled aims' (p. viii); and while his sex did not prevent him doing justice to the anguish of Sue's tragedy, he did in one important respect subordinate it to Jude's. Sue's break-down accentuates Jude's strength and his fidelity to the values which originally inspired their struggle. As she blinds and shackles herself, he grows ever more clear-sighted. Though she is enslaved in body, and he enslaved by his own, he at least retains his intellectual freedom, railing against the state of things to the end. This contrast means that the complaint that *Jude the Obscure* is not fully tragic—that its hero remains a muddler, a man dragged down by his own weakness—is unjustified. Her submission to doctrine may be paralleled by his drunken re-marriage to Arabella (gin-drunk as she is creed-drunk); but as his body grows weaker, his mind grows stronger. What Sue betrays, he cleaves to. In the painful scene in which she abjures their sexual relationship, Jude is spokesman for a humane code which she is unable to sustain. Jude's anguished accusation, ' "You have never loved me as I love you—never—never!"' is no more than the truth, and there is poetic justice when he turns back on Sue the Shelleyan tribute she had once forced him to make: ' "You are, upon the whole, a sort of fay, or sprite—not a woman!"' (p. 426). Jude's plea, ' "Stay with me for humanity's sake"', seeks to transcend differences of sex and creed, binding them together in their common humanity. His symbolic action is the more moving because his belief in the sacredness of their bond remains: ' "Then let the veil of our temple be rent in two from this hour!". He went to the bed, removed one of the pair of pillows thereon, and flung it to the floor' (pp. 427-8). When he goes to see Sue for the last time, he reproaches her with ' "I *would* have died game!"' (p. 470), and the reproach signals his tragic determination to

remain true to his values even in death. His last, suicidal visit to Sue springs from a consciously undertaken resolution. He tells the scornful and incredulous Arabella:

> 'You think you are the stronger; and so you are, in a physical sense, now. . . . But I am not so weak in another way as you think. I made up my mind that a man confined to his room by inflammation of the lungs, a fellow who had only two wishes left in the world, to see a particular woman, and then to die, could neatly accomplish those two wishes at one stroke, by taking this journey in the rain. That I've done. I have seen her for the last time, and I've finished myself—put an end to a feverish life which ought never to have been begun!' (p. 473)

' "I meant to do for myself"', he asserts, and he succeeds. Like Henchard in *The Mayor of Casterbridge,* Jude wills himself out of existence; his act of self-obliteration is also self-affirming because he heroically refuses to betray what he believes—Samson-like, not only in his weakness for women, but in his final strength of purpose. However bitter, however despairing, he does die game, and Sue remains unforgiven.

But the last word in the novel goes to Sue, as Arabella and Widow Edlin talk beside Jude's open coffin to the sound of another Remembrance Day celebration:

> 'Did he forgive her?' [asks Widow Edlin]
>
> 'Not as I know.'
>
> 'Well—poor little thing, 'tis to be believed she's found forgiveness somewhere! She said she had found peace!'
>
> 'She may swear that on her knees to the holy cross upon her necklace till she's hoarse, but it won't be true!' said Arabella. 'She's never found peace since she left his arms, and never will again till she's as he is now!' (pp. 493-4)

In the end, Sue's tormented consciousness haunts us more than Jude's bitter oblivion. What her life with Phillotson can be we are left to imagine—' "Quite a staid, worn woman now. 'Tis the man—she can't stomach un, even now!"' (p. 493), reports Widow Edlin—but it is clearly a living death. Arabella, with the crude insight which characterizes her throughout, offers Phillotson her own cynical view of the Mosaic law under which Sue suffers: 'There's nothing like bondage and a stone-deaf taskmaster for taming us women. Besides, you've got the laws on your side. Moses knew . . ." Then shall the man be guiltless, but the woman shall bear her iniquity."' (p. 384)

Thus the novel's thesis—'The letter killeth'—is worked out in the interlocking tragedies of a man and a woman; and Hardy's attempt 'to deal unaffectedly with the fret and fever, derision and disaster, that may press in the wake of the strongest passion known to humanity' (p.

viii), comprehends Sue's specialized suffering along with Jude's. In one of those astonishing leaps of sympathy which occur in his own novels, Lawrence voices the novel's central plea for Sue:

> Sue had a being, special and beautiful. . . . Why must man be so utterly irreverent, that he approaches each being as if it were a no-being? Why must it be assumed that Sue is an 'ordinary' woman—as if such a thing existed? Why must she feel ashamed if she is specialized? (*Phoenix*, p. 510).

'She was Sue Bridehead, something very particular. Why was there no place for her?' is indeed the question Hardy leaves us asking at the end of *Jude the Obscure*. This overwhelming sense of Sue's specialness is at once the basis of Hardy's protest on her behalf, and a measure of his imaginative achievement. The cogency of his general plea combines with his portrayal of Sue's individual 'obscurity'; the realistic sense of the gap between what she thinks and what she does, between belief and behaviour, imparts unique complexity and life to the static contrasts of the novel's original conception. Through Jude's obscurity Hardy exposes 'the contrast between the ideal life a man wished to lead, and the squalid real life he was fated to lead': through Sue's obscurity he probes the relationship between character and ideas in such a way as to leave one's mind engaged with her as it is engaged with few other women in fiction. Hardy's intention in *Jude* may be incompletely realized, but the novel is not less suggestive, and its protest not less eloquent, for that.

Kathleen Blake (essay date 1978)

SOURCE: "Sue Bridehead: The Woman of the Feminist Movement," in *Studies in English Literature: 1500-1900*, Vol. XVIII, No. 4, 1978, pp. 703-20.

[*In the following essay, Blake probes Hardy's portrayal of the feminine in* Jude the Obscure, *noting that Sue Bridehead, in repressing her sexual urges as part of a "deliberate effort at widening her possibilities" represents "a daring and plausible try at personal liberation."*]

> Curiously enough, I am more interested in the Sue story than in any I have written.

> Sue is a type of woman which has always had an attraction for me, but the difficulty of drawing the type has kept me from attempting it till now.

Hardy's fascination with Sue Bridehead has been shared by many readers, some of whom feel she takes over *Jude the Obscure* from Jude. She is complex to the point of being irresistible, mystifying, or for some exasperating. She seems to Yelverton Tyrell, writing in 1896, "an incurably morbid organism," and to Desmond Hawkins, more than half a century later, "just about the nastiest little bitch in English literature."

Sue Bridehead will be more fascinating than frustrating to those who can find a thread that makes her windings worth following, and who can recognize in her mazes something more than the uniqueness of neurosis. Tyrell asks, "Why dwell on this fantastic greensickness?" Albert Guerard answers for the "minute responsibility" of Hardy's characterization, and Michael Steig argues her psychological coherence in clinical terms. Havelock Ellis and Robert Heilman carry the argument for our interest beyond the psychological consistency of what looks odd in Sue, to its representative importance.

Clearly Hardy thought Sue represented a type, however brilliantly individualized. She herself says that she is not such an exception among women as Jude thinks, particularly on the subject of marriage. She also says that she and Jude are not alone in their peculiarities (pp. 300, 327 [citations are from the 1912 Wessex edition of *Jude the Obscure*]). An important passage in Hardy's postscript of 1912 to the preface of *Jude* pinpoints Sue's type as "the woman of the feminist movement—the slight, pale 'bachelor girl'—the intellectualized, emancipated bundle of nerves that modern conditions are producing" (p. 50). By including it in his postscript, Hardy seconds the opinion of a German critic who wrote to him on Sue's feminism. No one seems to know who this German critic was. In fact the passage has been pretty much ignored. Some contemporary reviewers, such as Tyrell, classed *Jude* with "the fiction of Sex and the New Woman." And Hardy seems to have seen the novel in similar terms. When he contemplated dramatizing it, his projected titles were "the New Woman" or "A Woman With Ideas." But this view of the novel fell rather quickly from sight. Only recently has it begun to reappear, as in Lloyd Fernando's *'New Women' in the Late Victorian Novel* and A. O. J. Cockshut's *Man and Woman, A Study of Love in the Novel*. An essay by Mary Jacobus recognizes the conflict between Sue's desire to be an individual and the "femaleness that breaks her" but sets the struggle in rather narrowly personal terms so that her feminism remains disconnected from a wider Victorian framework. A similar lack of contemporary ideological framework causes Kate Millett to doubt Sue's coherence as a character because in her the new woman is at odds with the "frigid woman." I think that to place Sue in relation to Victorian thought on the woman question is to reveal the coherence of this "woman of the feminist movement," whose daring and precise logic of emancipation also produces its rending tensions. The feminism by which Sue frees her brilliant individuality makes her a "frigid woman" at the same time that it keeps her in constant peril of the "femaleness that breaks her."

Most criticism may have steered clear of feminist analysis of the novel because it is widely agreed that Hardy was doctrinaire in no cause or philosophy. He himself disclaims in a letter to Edmund Gosse that *Jude* is simply a problem novel on the marriage question. While not an avowed feminist, he knew something about feminist ideas. For instance, he quotes Tennyson's *Princess* in *The Mayor of Casterbridge* (1886). His library contained such examples of late-century new-woman fiction as Olive Schreiner's *Story of An African Farm,* Sarah Grand's *The Heavenly Twins,* and Grant Allen's *The Woman Who Did.* He sympathized with certain feminist views. If the divorce issue is not all there is to *Jude,* it is part. Hardy also knew and cared about certain women who were touched by the cause.

His first wife Emma was interested in women's rights, but the two models usually proposed for Sue Bridehead are Tryphena Sparks and Florence Henniker. While Robert Gittings' biography of Hardy shows that Tryphena Sparks must have been at least what Victorians called a "strong-minded woman," Florence Henniker was the more demonstrably an "enfranchised woman." Hardy's letters characterize her in these terms. One letter indicates that he plans to get the *Subjection of Women.* This directly implies Mrs. Henniker's feminist interests and their influence on Hardy. However, she was apparently not cut to any stock pattern. Hardy says that he is surprised at her agreeing with Mill. This response is difficult to interpret. But it seems of a piece with his disappointment that a woman in some senses "enfranchised" should be in others conventional, for instance in her religious beliefs. A woman emerges contradictory in her views—like Sue—with the contradictions of a new type. Florence Henniker herself wrote fiction, and one of her heroines called forth Hardy's admiration—"the girl . . . is very distinct—the modern intelligent mentally emancipated young woman of cities, for whom the married life you kindly provide for her would ultimately prove no great charm—by far the most interesting type of femininity the world provides for man's eyes at the present day." This sounds like Sue's type. The heroine's mistake, the conventional marriage, reflects what for Hardy was the similarly mistaken conventionality sometimes shown by her creator and, presumably, prototype.

Lloyd Fernando contrasts *Jude* to other new-woman fiction of the period whose heroines' perfection is made out of theories, not psychological probability. Hardy shows how and why Sue Bridehead is a free woman but a repressive personality, sophisticated but infantile, passionate but sexless, independent but needing men, unconventional but conventional, a feminist but a flirt. He observes her with such undogmatic exactness, with such pure fascinated tenacity, that he shows us how this "bundle of nerves" works, and how her nerves go wrong.

Sue Bridehead wants to free herself of the worst of a woman's fate. Hardy outlines that fate in the section on the young women at the Melchester Training School:

> they all lay in their cubicles, their tender feminine faces upturned to the flaring gas-jets . . . every face bearing the legend 'The Weaker' upon it, as the penalty of the sex wherein they were moulded, which by no possible exertion of their willing hearts and abilities could be made strong while the inexorable laws of nature remain what they are. (p. 183)

Hardy gives two versions of the reason for women's hard lot. One is social. When Sue compares a bride to a sacrificial heifer, Jude answers that women should not protest against the man but against the conditions that make him press her (p. 328). But the narrator charges masculine nature itself when he says that Sue is ignorant of "that side of [men's] natures which wore out women's hearts and lives" (p. 218). Hardy is able to have his sexual disaster both ways by piling one on top of the other. When Sue says "it is none of the natural tragedies of love that's love's usual tragedy in civilized life, but a tragedy artificially manufactured" (p. 257), he implies that, even take away the artificial, the natural tragedy would still remain.

The tragedy begins with sex. Hardy describes the students in the Melchester School with tender nostalgia: their hurry to shed the temporary immunity from the "deadly war" of passion provided by their "species of nunnery" only gives them longer to regret its loss (p. 47, 182). The young women are preoccupied with last year's seduction, young men who may turn out not to be cousins, late hours, and interesting delinquencies. They are safe, but restless, in the blockaded sexuality of their college regimen:

> They formed a pretty, suggestive, pathetic sight, of whose pathos and beauty they were themselves unconscious, and would not discover till, amid the storms and strains of after-years, with their injustice, loneliness, child-bearing, and bereavement, their minds would revert to this experience as to something which had been allowed to slip past them insufficiently regarded. (p. 183)

Hardy's position is clear. Women suffer by the operations of sexuality—injustice, loneliness, child-bearing, and bereavement. Children bring suffering, Mrs. Yeobright says to little Johnny Nunsuch in *The Return of the Native* (1878). Mother woe is one's personal suffering and the knowledge of having given birth only to suffering. *The Well-Beloved* (1897), written just before *Jude,* expresses another liability of motherhood, that it stunts as well as afflicts. Mrs. Pine-Avon illustrates the rule that the "advance as girls [is] lost in their recession as matrons." Why? "Perhaps not by reason of their faults as individuals, but of their misfortune as child-rearers." By the same token marriage offers no great advantage to a woman. Hardy thinks it is wrong for Florence Henniker's advanced young heroine to marry. There is an interesting late letter recounting the news of his sister-in-law's successful confinement. He responds to the glad tidings with an opposite sentiment: "if I were a woman I should think twice before entering into matrimony in these days of emancipation when everything is open to the sex."

The Training-School students enjoy temporary immunity from sexual disaster. Enforced from without, it is, with all of its repressiveness, yet a haven to be missed later. Sue Bridehead enjoys a more sustained immunity, though still inherently and tragically unstable, enforced from within. Hers is sexual self-repression in the interest of personal emancipation, not doctrinaire in its expression in the novel but capable of analysis in the context of nineteenth-century feminism.

Sue is a woman seeking self-determination. A strong phase of her personality is contained in the phrase, "I shall do just as I choose!" (p. 197). She often does it, buying the forbidden statues, leaving the school, throwing over Phillotson and Jude turn and turn about. She says she wants "an occupation in which I shall be more independent" (p. 147). She quotes Mill on liberty.

Her model of freedom comes from childhood. However, old Miss Fawley's intriguing account of Sue as a girl pictures her not in the full freedom of infancy but in moments of crucial consciousness of the threats to freedom, so that the childish Sue comes across more as a rebel than a free spirit. She was a good student and accomplished in other ways. "She could do things that only boys do, as a rule." But she was "not exactly a tomboy," partly it seems because she was already aware of gender and its divisions. She would suddenly refuse to play the boys' games. Yet she defied the limits placed on girls. She, who could hit and slide into the pond with the best of the boys, was once cried shame upon by her aunt for wading into that pond with her shoes and stockings off. She answered with twelve-year-old awareness of sexual roles and rebellion against them: "Move on, aunty! This is no sight for modest eyes!" (pp. 154-155).

Jean Brooks is one of the few critics willing to comment on the meaning of Sue's childhood. She compares her infantilism, her longing for childhood, with Catherine Earnshaw's, calling it "a death-wish longing." In my view neither Catherine nor Sue exhibits a death-wish so much as a life-wish. They hark back to a time before the split into sexual and thereby limited beings. Catherine comes to grief by being made a lady of, losing Wuthering Heights, the moors, Heathcliff, her heaven. For an androgynous union as of brother and sister in the panelled bed at the Heights is substituted the division and violence of adult love. Catherine dies in childbirth.

A catalog might be made of brilliant girl children of Victorian literature who stand to lose by growing up and do. Many say that Jane Eyre and Maggie Tulliver are less at their ends than their beginnings. Jane is rather diminished to a happy marriage with her "master." Maggie embraces self-renunciation and death. A classic instance of a fascinating girl's growing up to be a not-very-interesting woman is Paulina Bassompierre in Charlotte Brontë's *Villette*. In the brilliant opening chapters the six-year-old Polly threatens to take the novel away from its heroine, she is so complex, bizarre, above all so individual. But she comes to learn that she must bear a great deal at the hands of men, her father and her eventual husband, because she is a girl. She profits by the lesson, and the result is a happy marriage and the forfeiture of our attention in favor of the unhappy and unmarried Lucy Snowe. One of the most consistently engaging and admirable female characters of Victorian fiction, whose interest lies in her capability, not its defeat, is Alice. She is intelligent, resourceful, strong-minded, aggressive in a polite way that pleases by contrast to the outrageousness of the creatures she meets. She will stand no nonsense at the end of *Wonderland* and wins her game at the end of *Looking-Glass*. Lewis Carroll is often suspiciously regarded for liking little girls. The liking was eccentric insofar as it tended towards exclusiveness, but is it in itself incomprehensible? May not girls have something that they lose in growing up, especially in growing up to be Victorian ladies? Carroll said that he ceased seeing much of a child-friend after about the age of twelve because in most cases she ceased to be interesting. This may be taken as a comment on Carroll or on the girls. It is usually taken the first way, but I think the second way may be equally illuminating. It sheds an indirect light on Sue Bridehead's desire to "get back to the life of my infancy and its freedom," "to remain as I began" (pp. 181, 191).

Her method is to remain a virgin. The account of her relationship with the Christminster undergraduate is an important outline of the method. Contact with this young man represents educational "advantages" for Sue, opportunity beyond the usual girl's education. Jude says to her, "you don't talk quite like a girl,—well, a girl who has had no advantages" (p. 189). This is because of her exposure to masculine learning, to books that she would never have gotten hold of without the undergraduate. Sue chooses to be part of a wider world, instead of being cut out of it as out of the boys' games.

In this sense she follows the line of what George Moore calls in his *Drama in Muslin* one of the two representative types of emancipated woman in the later nineteenth century. This is the woman who gravitates toward men more than ever before because masculine contact, in contrast to her constrictive feminine circle, means "light, freedom, and instruction." Yet in another sense Sue belongs to the apparently opposite type of Moore's analysis, the woman who rejects men because of their reduction of women to merely sexual beings. Sue attempts a daring and dangerous combination of gravitation and rejection. This is her method. She says that she owes all of her advantages to a certain peculiarity that has shaped her life. It is that she has no fear of men and can mix with them freely. She removes the sexual barrier by as much as possible removing the sexual element from the relationship. This she does by repressing sexual invitation in herself. "Until [a woman] says by a look 'Come on' he is always afraid to, and if you never say it, or look it, he never comes" (p. 190).

I say that Sue represses her sexuality in an almost deliberate effort at widening her opportunities, but this analysis depends on her having sexual impulses to repress. I think she does, though many would not agree. Gosse says that "the *vita sexualis* of Sue is the central interest of the book," but later critics usually locate the interest in her *lack* of a sexual life. She is often taken at Jude's estimate on those occasions when he calls her sexless, a disembodied creature, incorporeal as a spirit, though it is to be noticed that he takes it all back when, for instance, she shows sexual jealousy over Arabella. Hardy explains in a letter to Gosse that Sue's oddity is sexual in origin, but not perversion and not entire lack. He says that her sexual drive is healthy as far as it goes but weak and fastidious. Michael Steig and Mary Jacobus are in the minority in giving her a significant sexual side. Wayne Burns says that critics have been led astray in denying it by the classic analysis of D. H. Lawrence.

Lawrence finds the woman in Sue Bridehead atrophied. He does not find her completely defunct. However he does assume that she was born thus atrophied, whereas I think it makes a difference that Hardy gives strong evidence of an originally passionate nature self-restrained and so debilitated. This is the force of her purchase of the statues of Venus and Apollo, her reading of Swinburne, her interpretation of the Song of Solomon as a paean to "ecstatic, natural, human love" (p. 195). She says herself that she loves Jude "grossly" (p. 434), and Arabella, who knows about these things, has the last word in the novel when she says Sue will never find peace outside of Jude's arms. It is true that Hardy's picture of Sue's sexual basis is so complex that it sometimes seems contradictory. For instance, one perplexing passage says she is "unfitted by temperament and instinct to fulfill the conditions of the matrimonial relation with Phillotson, possibly with scarce any man" (p. 260). This seems to imply inborn coldness; but then again is it sexual relations as such that instinct unfits her for, or their conditions, that is, their enforced nature in marriage? Also the ambiguity of the "possibly" is increased by the fact that two pages before Sue has kissed "close and long" with Jude, running spontaneously to meet his embrace and leaving it with "flushed cheeks."

I think when Hardy describes Sue at the Melchester School as "a woman clipped and pruned by severe discipline, an under-brightness shining through from the depths which that discipline had not yet been able to reach" (p. 175), we may understand both the under-brightness and the discipline as sexual in nature. Central to the treatment of the Training School is its powerful but repressed sexual charge. But unlike the other young women's discipline, Sue's is not only externally laid on. Hers is also a matter of herself neither saying or looking "Come on." The likeliest way to accomplish this over the long run would be to stop *feeling* "Come on."

A number of critics say that beneath her unconventionality Sue is really conventional. Heilman and Emmett call her sexual standoffishness a giveaway of ordinary Victorian prudishness. Millett suggests the same thing. But it is not ordinary. There was more than one tradition of female chastity. The ordinary one may be represented by the rule in Charlotte Yonge's complete Victorian lady's guide, *Womankind*—that a young lady must exercise self-restraint since "in almost all men there is a worse part which makes them willing to incite a girl to go as far as she will with them, and is flattered at the approaches to indiscretion which all the time make her forfeit their respect." Less ordinary is the specialized version of certain feminists. In fact Victorian feminists were responding to the same thing that Victorian prudes were—the noticeable disadvantages of being seen in a sexual light by men.

It is a commonplace of male literary treatment of emancipated women in the century to picture them like Tennyson's Princess Ida, walled off from the masculine world in a sort of convent-college of militant chastity, over whose gates stands written, death to any man that enters. It is a scientific commonplace to infer, like Herbert Spencer, flatchestedness in intellectually advanced women. The image of the new woman who rejects men appears often in the journals, for instance in the anti-feminist *Saturday Review,* which in an article of 1896 opposes the granting of university degrees to women because "it ministers to the new aspiration of some women for 'living their own lives'—that is, in fact, getting rid of the fetters of matrimony and maternity." I will cite George Moore again on this emancipated type:

> women who in the tumult of their aspirations, and their passionate yearnings towards the new ideal, and the memory of the abasement their sex have in the past, and still are being in the present, subjected to, forget the laws of life, and with virulent virtue and protest, condemn love—that is to say, love in the sense of sexual intercourse—and claim a higher mission for woman than to be the mother of men.

There may be a question whether this reflects mainly masculine presuppositions or new women as they actually lived and thought. This is also the question where Hardy gets Sue. We should turn to what some of the feminists themselves said.

A classic illustration of feminist ambivalence about sex is Mary Wollstonecraft's *Vindication of the Rights of Women.* Wollstonecraft lavishes outrage on the demeaning of women as the sexual objects of men, so that their whole training is towards the arts of enticement at the expense of every other reasonable human endeavor. Wollstonecraft was herself a passionate woman, tempestuous even; she attempted suicide twice for deserted love. She expresses as little attraction to the Houyhnhnms as the Yahoos. She defends healthy physicality in women—an appetite that is not puny and ladylike, unconstrained exercise in sport, dancing even to the point of hot faces and sweat. "Women as well as men ought to have the common appetites and passions of their nature, they are only brutal when unchecked by reason." But the point is that they ought to be checked. A heavy emphasis of the *Vindication* is to devalue passionate love. It is a romantic interlude and not the sine qua non, to be made the object of a woman's whole life. Wollstonecraft insists on the extremely short life of passion, cooled in weeks or months to be replaced by rational married comradeship. "In a great degree, love and friendship cannot subsist in the same bosom." She is in a hurry to get to the friendly stage and to dilate on its virtues. "A master and mistress of a family ought not to continue to love each other with passion." Since Wollstonecraft and virtually all feminists after her lay the blame for a woman's oppression and incapacity on her rearing first and foremost as man's sexual object, it is no wonder that many of them feel some reservation about sexuality, at the very least demoting it from the top rank of importance. So Wollstonecraft devotes a chapter to modesty, she praises Diana, she is disgusted by women's habits of bodily intimacy, she is very sensible of the "gross" and "nasty," and sounds distinctly puritanical. She does not denounce motherhood. In fact she says it is a woman's noblest function and that instead of being trained for the harem she should be trained for the nursery. But a number of later feminists wanted to escape both. For instance, in her *Morality of Marriage* Mona Caird says, "the gardener takes care that his very peach-trees and rose-bushes shall not be weakened by overproduction . . . valuable animals are spared in the same way and for the same reason. It is only women for whom there is no mercy." She asks, "do we not see that the mother of half a dozen children, who struggles to cultivate her faculties, to be an intelligent human being, nearly always breaks down under the burden, or shows very marked intellectual limitations?" Such feminists had twice as much reason for sharing Wollstonecraft's low estimation of sex, and their position helps to explain Sue Bridehead.

A valuable book by J. A. and Olive Banks treats later nineteenth-century feminist doctrine as part of an investigation of *Feminism and Family Planning in Victorian England*. Its discussion of feminists' sexual attitudes helps explain their silence on birth control, controversial in the 1870s. The Banks conclude that silence meant nonsupport, the reason being suspicion of contraceptive methods for offering further sexual license to men, to which women owed so much of their oppression. Feminist journals like the *Englishwoman's Journal*, the *Englishwoman's Review*, and the *Victorian Magazine* were not silent on another controversial issue of the 1870s and 1880s. This was Josephine Butler's campaign against the Contagious Diseases Act, which took prostitutes under state regulation and enforced their medical examination in order to stem the spread of venereal disease. The Act was seen by most feminists as condoning the double standard by treating men's philandering as a venial sin, a mere hygiene problem. The law was considered offensive since it detained prostitutes while their customers went free, and offered no guarantee against indiscriminate detention. The Banks illustrate the feminist position by citing a speech in favor of the Act's repeal that attacks "the assumption that indulgence is a necessity of man." The attitude held after the Act fell. A writer in the early twentieth-century *Freewoman* finds "sex-intercourse—otherwise subjection to man" and concludes that "women are forced to crush down sex, but in doing so, they are able to use the greatest dynamic, passion, for the liberation of women." According to the feminists, the solution to the problem of venereal disease,

among other problems, was chastity for men, as women already practiced it. The Banks sum up this line of thought with the suffragist slogan, "Votes for Women and Purity for Men." One of their most bizarre evidences of feminist antagonism to sexuality is a poem by Ellis Ethelmer, "Woman Free" of 1893, which looks to the equalization of the sexes for respite from menstruation by removal of its cause, men's undue sexual demands on women.

Some did support both contraception and women's rights. George Drysdale's *Elements of Social Science, or Physical, Sexual, and Natural Religion* argues the benefit of "venereal exercise" for women and men alike, to be enjoyed without Malthusian disaster by the use of birth control. He says that maladies of sexual frustration are in fact worse for a woman (from iron deficient blood to hysteria). She needs relief even more than a man because she is, under "our unfortunate social arrangements, far more dependent on love than man." We can see the feminism in the phrase "unfortunate social arrangements," and also foresee the parting of the ways between him and other feminists. His argument for sexual fulfillment partly concedes to the "unfortunate social arrangements" that make a woman's life destitute without it. The opposite tack is to minimize the need for love so as to reduce women's dependence on men in this as in other ways. The latter line of thought represents the feminist mainstream according to the Banks.

Feminist uneasiness about sex could be more or less encompassing. A review would have to include in addition to Wollstonecraft's asceticism, Margaret Fuller's denial of the Byronic axiom that love is a woman's whole existence and her glorification of virginity in *Woman in the Nineteenth Century,* and Christabel Pankhurst's salvaging in *The Great Scourge and How to End It* of the one valuable lesson—chastity—from women's history of subjection. J. S. Mill identifies the wife's duty of submission to her husband's desire as the ultimate form of slavery.

Hardy explicitly says in a letter to Gosse what he felt he must leave circumspectly implied in his novel, that part of Sue's reluctance to marry is her reluctance to relinquish the right to "withhold herself at pleasure, or altogether." This is behind Sue's aversion to being "licensed to be loved on the premises" (p. 300). As Fernando points out, the link between women's rights and the right over one's own body expressed in withholding it casts Sue in a distinctly feminist light.

Certainly she speaks of sex and marriage as the opposite of freedom. When she finally sleeps with Jude it is giving in, being conquered, being caught (pp. 307-308). She doesn't want to have children. She wishes "some harmless mode of vegetation might have peopled Paradise" (p. 267). A bride, to her, is the heifer brought to the sacrifice (p. 328). Jude reflects this attitude when he greets her, newly married to Phillotson, as a woman still free, with an individuality *not yet* squashed and digested by wifedom (p. 232).

Living fifteen months with her undergraduate friend, Sue remains as she began. Jude congratulates her on her innocence, but she responds rather unexpectedly. She says that she is not particularly innocent. In fact, she has a bad conscience about her method. She says a "better woman" would not have held off (p. 192). Sue is uneasy about her inhibition of sexuality. This ambivalence again shows her distance from merely ordinary attitudes on female purity. Neither is she a feminist programmatically heart-whole in her principles because she is simultaneously a believer in "ecstatic, natural, human love."

Her division roughly reflects the division in feminist theory, which had its hedonist along with its stronger ascetic impulse. For instance, Wollstonecraft's writings after the *Vindication* show her recognition of the strength of female passion, however heavily fraught with problems, and there were a few true erotic enthusiasts among the advocates of free love discussed by Hal Sears in *The Sex Radicals, Free Love in High Victorian America,* though the larger number of them stressed a woman's right of refusal, restraint, abstinence, continence, and varieties of quite stringent sublimation. A good spokesman for the feminism of erotic liberation is Edmund d'Auvergne in the *Freewoman.* Where Christabel Pankhurst endorses chastity in the cause of women, d'Auvergne finds it a male imposition and thinks Penelope should have enjoyed herself with the suitors as Odysseus did with Circe and Calypso.

"Better women" would have slept with their house-mates. Though it seems to be altogether necessary, holding out is not altogether good, which is why Sue Bridehead reflects about her life with the undergraduate, "men are— so much better than women!" (p. 191). There is an irony in her method of liberation. It allows her to mingle freely with men and to share their advantages, eliminating the barrier of gender by as much as possible eliminating gender. Sue is "almost as one of their own sex" (p. 190). Almost but not quite. It is significant that she is described as boyish, dressed in Jude's clothes, a Ganymede (p. 196). The liberating strategy makes her in a sense a boy rather than a man. It rules out exactly that aspect of masculinity that makes men "better."

Throughout the novel Sue suffers oddly excessive guilt culminating in her desire at the end to prick herself all over with pins to bleed the badness out (p. 385). I think the double source of her bad conscience can be traced to her relation with the undergraduate which prefigures that with Jude. She combines Moore's two types of liberation, to live with men and to escape them. This program involves injury to herself and to the man. She stunts her own nature and frustrates her lover.

There is evidence that Sue knows that sexual repression means loss as well as gain. She is defensive against people's idea that she is sexless—"I won't have it!" (p. 192). On occasion she seems to regret her coldness, even to Phillotson—"I am so cold, or devoid of gratitude, or

so something" (p. 280). She suspects that Jude will hold her in "contempt" for not loving Phillotson as a husband. She feels some "shamefacedness" at letting Phillotson know of her incomplete relations with Jude (pp. 254, 294). She shows herself the reverse of proud when she says, "I know I am a poor miserable creature. My nature is not so passionate as yours" (p. 282). She knows she makes others miserable as well. She helps kill the undergraduate, wounds Phillotson in career and spirit, tortures Jude—"O I seem so bad—upsetting men's courses like this!" (p. 280).

Sue attempts a compromise. But to mitigate the first sort of injury is the more certainly to impose the other. That is, the more she allows her sexual nature to survive in self-protective permutations, the more vulnerable she makes her lover. Bad conscience is a distinguishing feature of her attempt to live a free woman. The compromise is essentially Platonic in theory, or more specifically Shelleyan. She enunciates it in the passage on her life with the undergraduate. "Some of the most passionately erotic poets have been the most self-contained in their daily lives" (p. 192). This justifies both eroticism and self-containment. It is a doctrine of sublimation quite Freudian in its assumption of the importance of sexual drive to higher mental or spiritual attainments. Implied also is the perpetuation of the drive by obstacle and deflection, so that it is not quelled by satiation. This idea runs all through Hardy, as brilliantly demonstrated by J. Hillis Miller in *Thomas Hardy, Distance and Desire.* The theory of augmenting desire by distance gives Sue part of her brief against marriage. If married people were forbidden each other's embrace instead of locked into it by contract, she says, "there'd be little cooling then!" (p. 300).

The concrete illustration of Sue's Platonic/Shelleyan love theory is her fondness for windows. Her escape from the Training School window seems to represent sexual liberation, since she goes to Jude's lodging, but the jump from Phillotson's bedroom window represents quite another kind, one which Jude comes to experience himself in a milder version when Sue sends him to sleep by himself. The two modes resolve into Sue's favorite disposition of the sexes, making spiritual love with a window in between. Jude and Sue have a tender talk through a window at Marygreen (p. 256), and their interview at Shaston becomes more tender once Jude is outside the casement. She says, "'I can talk to you better like this than when you were inside' . . . Now that the high window-sill was between them, so that he could not get at her" (p. 247).

If Sue's project for liberation is in good part one of inhibited sexuality, it by no means aims at total extirpation, or total rejection of men. The reasons are that she needs men for the advantage they offer, the undergraduate's books, for instance, and just as important, she needs them for their sexual stimulus. This sounds paradoxical for the repressive Sue, but the more repressed she is, the more stimulus does she need, for sublimation must have something to work on. I think Lawrence shows the finest insight of anyone who has written on Sue Bridehead when he says that she needs Jude to arouse the atrophied female in her, so as to stimulate the brightness of her mind.

Jude calls her a flirt (p. 246), which she is, and the novel is a classic formulation of flirt psychology, all the more remarkable for linking the flirt to the feminist. If we think these roles mutually exclusive, as Cockshut does, we are cast back on the idea that Sue is not a new woman but an ordinary old one after all. This misses a lot. Heilman's is a good analysis of Sue as coquette. He observes that the coquette wants to attract and yet remain unobtainable. He gives the reason that she needs to exert power. It seems to me that this is validly observed from a man's point of view, Jude's say, who feels his helplessness under a woman's sway, and it may be part of the picture on the woman's side too. It is commonly said that flirts use men, but less commonly said what they use them *for*. I think a great deal of Sue's use of men comes from her feminist double bind. She needs to keep alive in herself a sexuality in danger of being disciplined all the way down to the source.

Men may feel that a woman triumphs in the power of frigidity by remaining untouchable while making a man know his own vulnerability, but it should also be understood that she may freeze in her own cold. She may need, even desperately, for a man to warm her. Masculine impotence is widely understood to spawn in the sufferer psychological complications of the most fascinating pathos. Feminine impotence is usually understood as the man's suffering more than the woman's. But Hardy goes a great deal beyond the usual, that is, beyond the masculine perspective. He shows the impulse behind Sue's "love of being loved," which is the more insatiable for her own difficulty in loving (p. 246, 284). This impulse owes less to the power of the strong than to the need of the much weakened.

In *Jude the Obscure,* more than in any of his other novels, Hardy investigates the potential liability of the doctrine of distance and desire, that is, of desire stretched to farther and farther distances from direct satisfaction, so that it begins to attenuate, until it is in danger of losing itself. The novel also examines what such a loss would mean. Sue Bridehead is like a reinvestigation from the inside of Marty South of *The Woodlanders,* published seven years before (1887). Marty and Giles Winterborne enjoy the most serene love in the book because it dispenses with sex. In *Jude* Hardy still depicts passion as virulent, and so Sue defends herself against it. But the novel also shows, intimately, dismayingly, what it would mean to try to be like Marty South, "a being who had rejected with indifference the attribute of sex for the loftier quality of abstract humanism."

Sue's inhibition of sexuality, though not beyond her uneasy consciousness, is beyond her control. Hardy shows that it is there to be drawn out, but only if Jude takes the initiative. "By every law of nature and sex a kiss was the

only rejoinder that fitted the mood and the moment, under the suasion of which Sue's undemonstrative regard of him might not inconceivably have changed its temperature" (pp. 200-201). He does not kiss her, and his acquiescence in her sexlessness reinforces it in her.

However, her attenuated sexual nature does remain alive in alternative and bizarre forms. There is her jealously, which proves to Jude that she is not; after all a sexless creature (p. 319). There is her disgust, which she cherishes in an odd way. The only thing worse than her shrinking from Phillotson would be to get used to him, for then it would be "like saying that the amputation of a limb is no affliction, since a person gets comfortably accustomed to the use of a wooden leg or arm in the course of time!" (p. 254). To feel repugnance is at least not to accept being an amputee. The oddest form of Sue's rerouted sexuality is her device of provoking pain in order to feel pity, as when she makes Jude walk up the church aisle with her just before she is to marry Phillotson. She later says that her relation to Jude began in the wish to make his heart ache for her without letting hers ache for him (p. 393). But Hardy shows that her feeling is really much more complicated. In fact, Sue goes out of her way to induce in herself pain, long-suffering, and pity. In so doing she is "an epicure in emotions," satisfying her "curiosity to hunt up a new sensation" (pp. 215-216). Far from triumphing in lack of feeling, Sue strains after sensation of some sort. Since she does not feel desire directly, she invents original and "perverse" substitutes.

A curious technique for stimulating sensation in herself is to pose obstacles which will produce pain, which she can then pity. What makes this curious is that the obstacles are sometimes social conventions that she does not believe in. For instance, she plans to punish Jude by letter for making her give way to an unconventional impulse and allow a kiss. Of course she is usually highly unconventional, on both the subject of religion and the subject of marriage, so that in theory it should not matter to her that the future parson kisses a woman who is not his wife. Yet she turns around to make it matter, according to the extraordinary logic that "things that were right in theory were wrong in practice." This is not simple illogic but a quite orderly psychological maneuver for the production of sentiment: "Tears of pity for Jude's approaching sufferings at her hands mingled with those which had surged up in pity for herself" (p. 260).

It is important to understand Sue's unexpected invocations of convention. These have led some to think hers an unconventionality of the surface only; according to this interpretation her prostration to the letter of the law at the end is simply a true showing of the ordinary stuff she has been made of all along. A woman's succumbing to convention is a repeated idea in Hardy, as in **"The Elopement":** "in time convention won her, as it wins all women at last." He gives several explanations for Sue's succumbing. One does support the view that she has a conventional stratum to fall back on, when courage or reason fails, or circumstances become too strong. That is, Phillotson explains her return to the idea of the indissolubility of marriage by her soaking in Christminster sentiment and teaching (p. 398), in spite of all she has said against them. There is in this sense some credence to Lawrence's analysis that Sue is the product of ages of Christianity in spite of her proclaimed paganism. Sue herself often blames her timidity for the breakdown of her theoretic unorthodoxy. Jude questions whether the demise of her advanced views is accountable to a defect in women's reason: "Is a woman a thinking unit at all?" (p. 391). Later he attributes the narrowing of her views to the way that "time and circumstances" operate on women (p. 440). Hardy seems to accept Jude's idea of "strange difference of sex"; he calls women "The Weaker" himself. But in what sense weaker? Of course one way of answering would be as Jude implies, that men's views enlarge while women's narrow in adversity because men are made of stronger stuff. Another way of answering would be, less that men are stronger than that "time and circumstances" are less strong against them, which turns out to be the case in the novel. "The woman mostly gets the worst of it, in the long run!" says Jude. "She does," says Sue (p. 394).

In giving so many accounts of what weakens Sue, Hardy comes across as less dogmatic than any isolated passage may suggest. He is true, in the aggregate, to a complexity in her character beyond the simple explanations that he has his characters, as it were, try out on her. Above all, he shows that even when Sue appears to act conventionally, she often does so out of the most unconventional of motives. This makes inadequate the idea that she exposes at the end an ordinariness that has only been covered over with daring theories. Sue may be overpowered, she may fall short of her promise, she may buckle to the letter of the law, but she is never ordinary. Just as her sexual repression comes from her feminism, more than from the Victorian commonplace of feminine purity which it externally resembles, so does much of her behavior represent tactics in a highly individualized feminist program, sometimes just when it looks the most externally conventional.

We have seen how Sue uses convention unconventionally to induce sensation. Another way she uses it is to shield herself from sex, for reasons very much her own, as we have also seen. For instance, she goes to visit Phillotson in his illness after she has left him. He shows signs of warming from friend to husband, and Sue, in her "incipient fright" shows herself ready to seize on "*any line of defense* against marital feelings in him" (p. 294, my emphasis). She claims her own wickedness in leaving, so that he can't possibly want her back. There is no question of her believing this; she grasps at it willy-nilly. Another instance of Sue's self-defense with any odd weapon that comes to hand is her tortured reasoning to show why she cannot marry Jude. She invokes the letter of the law in its very finest print. Her argument goes like this: since she did not commit adultery with Jude, her divorce from Phillotson was obtained under false pretenses; it is no divorce, so she cannot marry Jude,

which she clearly does not want to do for personal reasons quite other than legal (p. 298).

Sue's contradictoriness has depth and coherence. It represents an impressively original experiment in life and freedom. It also fails of its own divisions. Lawrence comes closest to explaining how this is, though his explanation must be disentangled from his sometimes offensive definitions of what it means to be a woman or a man, and from his idea that Sue was born with an unhealthy overbalance of the masculine. He recognizes that Hardy is concerned with something more complex than the pioneer's defeat by the simple retribution of an outraged society. He proposes the analysis that the pioneer breaks down through inability to bear the isolation. But I think he goes beyond this too, by suggesting that Sue's breakdown inheres in her very method of pioneering. He says, "It was a cruelly difficult position. . . . she wanted some quickening for this atrophied female. She wanted even kisses. That the new rousing might give her a sense of life. But she could only *live* in the mind . . . She could only receive the highest stimulus, which she must inevitably seek, from a man who put her in constant jeopardy."

This accords with my own view. Sue's method of emancipation is sexual repression, but by no means total repudiation of sex or men. In addition to wanting what men have to offer intellectually, she needs men to keep alive the driving force of feeling, sexual at its root, recognized as essential in her Platonic/Shelleyan theory of sublimation. A man stimulates her sexual nature, which she directs into relatively safe channels, jealousy, disgust, and epicurean emotions, thereby evading the worst of the "inexorable laws of nature" for women. But the safety is precarious because the man must feel desire direct, to satisfy her "love of being loved." He is always there with his desire, reminding her of the comparative debility of her own, and of the injury she causes in leaving him unsatisfied. She feels guilt on both counts. She feels herself a kind of stand-out to the life force which she values and needs in him, even though she knows it would also sweep her away from her individuality and her freedom. The man is always there, always insisting, which she wants, but he is also blaming her, as it is clear Jude does. In spite of his protestations of love to her as an incarnate spirit, when he sees his chance, he presses for what he really wants by complaining of the "poor returns" he gets from her on his love (p. 306). Using Arabella's reappearance he pressures Sue into sleeping with him. Her balance is precarious because it rests upon a difference between what she feels and what Jude feels, a difference at the same time necessary to her purposes and dangerous to them. She "gives in," she sleeps with him, and the balance is upset.

Yet Sue and Jude are happy together for a certain unspecified number of years. Hardy moves very quickly over this period, which leaves some readers in doubt of their happiness. Neither Lawrence nor Heilman can believe that Sue could have adjusted to a normal sexual relationship. Though the picture remains sketchy, I think it is important for an interpretation of Sue to take Hardy at his word: "that the twain were happy—between their times of sadness—was indubitable" (p. 329). Sue's reservation is overcome, as charmingly symbolized by Jude's pushing her face into the roses at the Great Wessex Agricultural Show, which she had thought the rules prohibited her to touch. "'Happy?' he murmured. She nodded."

The flower scene represents a return to "Greek joyousness" (pp. 337-338). Sue explains later that they lived according to a new theory of nature—to "make a virtue of joy . . . be joyful in what instincts she afforded us" (p. 379). She says that with whatever coolness on her side her relation with Jude began, she did get to love him after Arabella's arrival pushed them together, and that this love is passionate we gather from the way she returns his kisses even after she has renounced him to return to Phillotson. Arabella notices that if she is cooler than Jude, "she cares for him pretty middling much" (p. 333). Sue is able to love and she does. She puts her Platonic theory behind her and lives for a time by a new code. Yet Hardy shows that the self-protectiveness of the old code was against real dangers, which descend upon Sue when she abandons it, making her revert to an extreme version of the sexual renunciation which had been her original position. But now instead of being self-creative, it is self-destructive.

The liability of love is made flesh in children. Sue is not ashamed of her passion during her happy time with Jude, especially since she still protects her freedom from being married and licensed to be loved on the premises. But she does question the result of passion. Since the woman bears the children, she bears the question more heavily. This is especially true for this pair, since Sue has more of herself—a star to Jude's benzoline lamp—to lose (p. 440). When Father Time first calls Sue mother, she begins to feel herself "getting intertwined with my kind." She feels she must give over "struggling against the current" (p. 320). Sue is someone who had tried to live by Mill's doctrine—"who lets the world, or his own portion of it, choose his plan of life for him, has no need of any other faculty than the ape-like one of imitation" (p. 265). For her, to give up the struggle is to give up her higher faculties. The children make compromise necessary, to which Sue and Jude add compromise on the compromise, so that they give up some of their own freedom without providing their family complete respectability. They can laugh when Jude is fired for carving the ten commandments while breaking the seventh, but laughter is less possible when looking for lodgings for a family of five when the landlady wants to know, "Are you really a married woman?" (p. 370). Sue must either be true to her principles by saying she isn't, or to her children by saying she is. Given the social structure, children represent a conflict between personal liberty and concession to one's kind. But Hardy goes beyond blaming society. Sue says, "it seems such a terribly tragic thing to bring beings into the world—so presumptuous—that I question my

right to do it sometimes!" (pp. 352-353). Her guilt at bearing children seems well-founded in view of the Hardy world that awaits them—in Phillotson's summary, "cruelty is the law pervading all nature and society" (p. 359). The joy-in-instinct theory of nature by which Sue had tried to live is revealed as partial through the crucial episode of little Father Time's murder-suicide.

Father Time is so broadly symbolic that he is rather hard to take and hard to pin down. What makes him, for one thing, Sue's and Jude's "nodal point, their focus, their expression in a single term" (p. 377)? Does he enact the interior necessity of their love's disruption and Sue's about-face, or is he only one of Hardy's supernumeraries of nemesis? I think the catastrophe he brings about is not coincidental, because he acts out what Sue already feels, that she should not have had children. Having them is something she tells little Jude she must be "forgiven" for (p. 374). Sue explains that a "law of nature" brought them to birth (p. 373), and in killing them and himself he repudiates this law of nature.

Sue had originally sought to sidestep the law, before rather than after the fact. Then for a time she had allowed herself to imagine that the law is joy-in-instinct. But it turns out to be the inexorable law of nature, as it is called in the early passage on the women students. Women live out this law intimately, in their own bodies, and it means "injustice, loneliness, child-bearing, and bereavement." "The woman gets the worst of it." Jude blames himself for having disrupted the precarious equilibrium of their relationship, which had allowed evasion of the worst of nature's law (pp. 383, 394). Sue agrees that she should have remained as she began. Circumstances have persuaded her that she was right in her original position.

Hardy seems to support by the catastrophic fact Sue's analysis that "there is something external to us which says, 'you shan't,'" including "'you shan't love'" (p. 377). However precarious, there seems to be some reasonableness in her original attempt to evade this external "you shan't" by means of an internally imposed "you shan't." The latter allows a semblance of volition and self-determination which harnesses instinct to safer ends, at least, than hanging.

Sue's reaction to the decimation of her family is understandable. It is a return to an extreme form of her original position, self-mastery, self-renunciation. But no longer does she try to control her fate; she places it utterly outside her own hands. She now wishes to "mortify the flesh, the terrible flesh—the curse of Adam" (p. 384). This sounds like the sexual repression she started out with, except that then she never denied the force for possible good of sexuality. The contrast can be seen in that before she counted men "better" for their desire, while at the end she counts women "superior" for never instigating, only responding (p. 392). Before she had thought that instinct could be made the drivewheel of personal development. She had not wanted to accept amputation and was glad even of disgust as a sign that the flesh could still feel its loss. The burning of the night-gown worn with Jude and the forcing of her nature to go to Phillotson represent, in contrast, a terribly complete amputation.

In trying at the end to utterly eradicate instinct in herself, she gives up all forward motion. She says she wants to die in childbirth. Spiritually, she makes her sexual nature into death, whereas before in its paradoxical way it had been life. So Sue is described as a person bereft of will. She is "cowed," feels "creeping paralysis." "I have no more fighting strength left, no more enterprise." "All initiatory power seemed to have left her." Self-suppression is now "despairing" (pp. 382, 369, 400).

Hardy says in a letter to Florence Henniker, "seriously I don't see any possible scheme for the union of the sexes that w[ou]ld be satisfactory." This attitude turns *Jude* into something quite different from a social-problem novel, since the problem goes deeper than society. It renders doubtful much optimism for what might have been had Sue and Jude not been fifty years before their time. The law of nature would still remain. To inhibit nature is not the answer. It causes some loss and some guilt. It also doesn't work very well, since instinct cannot be totally stultified if it is to remain at call for redirection. The love of being loved is actually a clamor-ing need. Instinct must feed on the stimulus of a lover's direct desire, with all the disequilibrium that implies. But to act on natural impulse is not the answer either. The law of nature is "inexorable," and procreation brings guilt and retribution both. Sue's precarious balance is an impressive experiment in self-creation. The experiment might have continued to work after its fashion, but the internal pressure is great, so that it is no surprise or final blame to her when the upset comes.

The German reviewer whom Hardy credits in his preface with calling Sue "the woman of the feminist movement," also says that if she had been created by a woman she would never have been allowed to break down at the end (p. 50). Not all who say that Hardy is great on women say that he is kind to them. Lascelles Abercrombie calls his treatment "subtle, a little cruel, not as tolerant as it seems." He often shows a woman character weak, changeable, and in the wrong, and he is quick, often distressingly so (the earlier the novel the more distress-ingly) to generalize from the woman to women, while the man is allowed to represent only himself. He character-izes women straightforwardly as "The Weaker" in *Jude*. However, I do not think this weakness comes across in the richly detailed portrait of Sue Bridehead as weakness in animal force, intellect, drive, venturesomeness, origi-nality, or accomplishment. The explanations Hardy offers for her weakness become less definitive as they multiply. If *Jude* sometimes seems a paradise of loose ends, in Arthur Mizener's nice phrase, I think it never seems more so than when we hear that Sue's collapse comes from her indoctrination in conventions, or that women lack cour-age, or is it reason, or is it that they contract as men expand? No doubt a woman author, that is, a feminist

woman author, would not have had Sue break down for these reasons. But I don't think they are Hardy's essential reasons either.

Rather in Sue Bridehead he dramatizes a daring and plau-sible try at personal liberation which runs into problems, reflective of the times but by no means yet altogether superceded, that a woman gains freedom as she gains access to a man's wider world while ceasing to be his sexual object. She sets about to mix with men freely, but neither to say or look or feel "Come on," rather to redi-rect that impulse to safer channels. But once the premise is acted on, she runs afoul of universal law, which touches women so closely, and which dictates that if it is dangerous to act naturally, so is it dangerous to inhibit nature. Sue's breakdown is not a judgment on her. It is a judgment on the way things are between the sexes ac-cording to Hardy, and that is a war that probably can't be won.

John Goode (essay date 1979)

SOURCE: "Sue Bridehead and the New Woman," in *Women Writing about Women,* edited by Mary Jacobus, Croom Helm, 1979, pp. 100-13.

[*In the following essay, Goode concentrates on the char-acter of Sue Bridehead as he examines* Jude the Obscure *in terms of late nineteenth-century feminism, and ex-plores the means by which the novel exposes the mysti-fications of ideologically structured reality.*]

I

Criticism of *Jude the Obscure* usually takes it to be a *representation;* hence, however hard such analysis tries to come to terms with the novel's radicalism, it is inevi-tably ideological. Criticism of this kind necessarily dis-solves the specific literary effect of the text, the author's 'production', into its component sources which are situ-ated in 'reality'—that is to say, the ideological structure of experience by which we (including Hardy) insert our-selves into the hegemony. But *Jude* is such a truly radical novel precisely because it takes reality apart; that is, it doesn't merely reproduce reality, even as a 'series of seemings', but exposes its flaws and its mystifications. You cannot come to terms with the novel either as a moral fable or as an exhibition of social reality because it is the very terms of those structures, their ideological base, that it interrogates. After the death of her children, before she has, as they say, *broken down,* Sue tells Jude: 'There is something external to us which says, "You shan't!" First it said, "You shan't learn!" Then it said, "You shan't labour!" Now it says, "You shan't love!"' (VI. ii) This very precisely defines the overdetermined form of the novel. Learning, labour and love—the three human activities on which bourgeois ideology bases its libertarian pride—are shown to be denied by 'something external'. In most novels, including Hardy's own earlier work, these three are accommodated within 'the interstices of a mass of hard prosaic reality' (*Far from the Madding Crowd,* LVI); even Tess is left free finally to love. Here it really doesn't matter what the external is, whether nature's inexorable law or social oppression. What matters is that it is external; it might as well be God. But although Jude comments that this is bitter, he does not answer when Sue replies that it is true. Because he cannot answer, he has no way to stop her from seeking to propitiate this external with the mortification of the flesh, the terrible flesh. A further precision is needed in our reading of this passage. Sue can say this because she is more articulate than Jude, who has *already broken down* by returning absurdly to the centre of his dream (Christminster). That is why he is horrified by her denial of love. Jude on his own account, even with Sue's aid, can confront and articulate what forbids learning and labour (and confront it as ideological). But it is only Sue who can demystify love and identify its determinants. And that is what most critics cannot take, and why criticism of the novel tends to sprawl from fiction to reality when it comes to Sue.

Most accounts of *Jude the Obscure* cannot cope with Sue except by reference to some ideologically structured reality. This usually enables the critic to say one of two things, both of which are demonstrably false representations of the text: either that Hardy's presentation of Sue is inconsistent, or that she is a neurotic type of the frigid woman. The most extreme version of the second reading is, of course, Lawrence's, which sees Sue as 'no woman' but a witch, whose attraction to Jude in the first place is in reaction to the incomprehensible womanliness of Arabella:

> And this tragedy is the result of over-development of one principle of human life at the expense of the other; an over-balancing; a laying of all the stress on the Male, the Love, the Spirit, the Mind, the Consciousness; a denying, a blaspheming against the Female, the Law, the Soul, the Senses, the Feelings.[1]

I don't need to stress the sexism of Lawrence's account; it is remarkably like that of the reactionary reviewers such as Mrs Oliphant and R.Y. Tyrell whom Havelock Ellis implicitly rebuked when he said that to describe Sue as neurotic was to reveal an attitude which considers 'human sexual relationships to be as simple as those of the farmyard'.[2] But I think that Lawrence is important because what he identifies as Sue's 'maleness' is her articulateness:

> That which was female in her she wanted to consume within the male force, to consume it in the fire of understanding, of giving utterance. Whereas an ordinary woman knows that she contains all understanding, that she is the unutterable which man must forever continue to try to utter.

What is unforgivable about Sue is her utterance, her subjecting of experience to the trials of language. Lawrence, underneath the hysterical ideology, seems very acute to me, for he recognises that Sue is destructive because she utters herself—whereas in the ideology of sexism, the woman is an image to be uttered. That is to say, woman achieves her womanliness at the point at which she is silent and therefore can be inserted as 'love' into the world of learning and labour; or rather, in Lawrence's own terms, as the 'Law' which silences all questions.

The most available feminist inversion of Lawrence's ideology makes the inconsistencies of Sue's character part of the limitations of the novelist himself. Kate Millett on the one hand affirms Sue's rationality ('Sue is only too logical. She has understood the world, absorbed its propositions, and finally implemented that guilt which precipitated her own self-hatred. Nothing remains to her but to destroy herself')[3]; but on the other hand she clearly feels that Hardy loads the dice against Sue because of his own uncertainty, so that a woman who can be articulated by the feminist as 'an intelligent rebel against sexual politics' is presented to us as "by turns an enigma, a pathetic creature, a nut, and an iceberg'. She complains that we are never allowed to see Sue's motivation and processes of change, but decides that the clue to Sue, as to Arabella, is that they both despise womanhood, and that in Sue's case, this makes her hold sexuality in terror. It is not that Millett doesn't recognise the validity of Hardy's representation; it is rather that Hardy himself doesn't understand what defeats her.

I want to try to show that both approaches to Sue are wrong, but more than this, that a significant silence in both critics indicates the way in which they are wrong—and that this, in turn, indicates where the fictive effect of the novel displaces its own ideology in a mirror. For it is quite remarkable how many critics either despise Sue or blame Hardy for the confusion without ever asking whether the difficulty resides in the ways in which we articulate the world. Perhaps the most revealing recent account is John Lucas's.[4] Lucas finds *Jude* a less achieved novel than *Tess,* because by making Sue so unrepresentative, and failing to place her against some concept of womanhood ('we need more in the way of women than the novel actually gives us') Hardy fails to enable us to decide how much of the tragedy resides in the artificial system of things, and how much in the 'inexorable laws of nature' which make women what they are. Hardy, it is true, had already created a 'pure woman', but maybe we should ask whether the woman in *Jude* isn't precisely the question that is posed against that strange creation. Tess is the subject of the novel: that makes her inevitably an object of the reader's consumption (no novel has ever produced so much of what Sontag required in place of hermeneutics, namely, an erotics of art). But Sue is not the centre of the novel, she exists as a function of Jude's experience, hence as an object for him. It is surely possible that the questions come from her inability to take shape as that object. Lucas says that while we can understand why Sue shies away from Phillotson, the fact that she shies away from Jude makes her pathological, for although sex can be oppressive, it *'is, or ought to be* mutual' (my italics). Millett, we have noticed, says that Sue hates her sexuality; Lawrence, that she is sexless. First of all, as I shall show, this is not really true. What is true, however, is that Sue exposes the ideology of Lucas's statement. You can't, I think (as Millett says), be solid about the class system and muddled about sexual politics. These critics are muddled about both, and they are muddled because neither Hardy nor Sue will let go of the questions.

II

When Sue has retreated back into her marriage with Phillotson, Jude poses what I take to be the fundamental ideological question posed by the novel and found unforgivable by the critics who cannot take Sue:

> 'What I can't understand in you is your extraordinary blindness now to your old logic. Is it peculiar to you, or is it common to woman? Is a woman a thinking unit at all, or a fraction always wanting its integer?' (VI. iii)

If this question is asked in the novel it is surely naïve to ask it of the novel. What is more important is that this question should be asked; it poses for Sue only one of two possibilities—that the nature of her blindness to her own logic must be explained either by her 'peculiarity', or by her belonging to womanhood. Either way, she is committed to being an image, and it is this that pervades the novel. Nobody ever confronts Jude with the choice between being a man or being peculiar. The essential thing is that Sue must be available to understanding. We might want to deduce that Hardy feels the same way as Jude at this point, but I think to do so would go both against the consistency of the novel and against Hardy's whole career as a writer. Twenty years before he wrote *Jude,* Hardy had made Bathsheba Everdene say: ' "It is difficult for a woman to define her feelings in language which is chiefly made by men to express theirs'" (*Far from the Madding Crowd,* LI). He built a career as a writer out of the very mediations that woman as subject has to create to define her own subjectivity. The plots that turn on caprice, the scenes which reach outside the interaction of manners, the images which embody contradiction, are all constructs made by the novelist to articulate those unspeakable (though not unutterable) feelings. In *Jude,* for the first time in his major fiction, the woman is no longer the vessel of those mediations, but the object of male understanding. Sue not only speaks for herself because she is an intelligent rebel; she is called on to speak for herself—to place herself in relation to other woman and to their ways of feeling. She several times has to relate her particularity to what all women are like 'really'. In other words, she has to affirm that she is *a woman,* or admit her ethereal nature—her 'peculiarity'. If we think about the novel naturalistically, without any ideological idyllicising of love (it *'is or ought to be* mutual'), we might ask ourselves about the absurdity of Jude's lack of understanding. Sue has been driven around the country by prejudice and poverty, she is stuck in Christminster by Jude's obsession, and now all her chil-

dren have been killed by Jude's son whom she has made her own. Our perfect union, she tells Jude, is stained with blood. But of course we don't consider it naturalistically, because we don't ever ask what is happening to Sue; because it is rather a question of Sue happening to Jude. So what matters is where this reaction puts her, rather than why it comes about.

Sue is more than anything an image; that is literally how she comes into Jude's life, as a photograph, and how she is continually represented to us throughout the novel— dressed in Jude's clothes, walking in the distance with Phillotson, looking like a heap of clothes on the floor of St Silas's church. But if she is an image, it is a vital part of this image that it has a voice, and hence a logic. Although logic and image play contrasting and reinforcing roles in relation to one another at different points in the novel, it is the relationship between them which calls in question the ideological alternative between peculiarity, on one hand, and the nature of woman, on the other. Sue thus has an instrumentality which makes it irrelevant to ask what kind of ordeal she is undergoing, at least until the novel moves towards the shared experience of Jude and Sue in the Aldbrickham section. For example, at the very beginning Jude sees her haloed in the Christminster ecclesiastical art shop, while we see her buying pagan statues: a relatively simple juxtaposition of false image and conscious decision. But although Hardy presents her logic as having a potential subjectivity (that is, Sue's purchase of the statue is private, tentative, naïve and confused—it could be the frail start of an emancipation), by the time this logic has come to Jude's notice it is formed and decisive, something for him to understand and adjust his own attitude by. I don't think that this confusion entails confusion on Hardy's part, for it is as a confusing image that Sue is effective in breaking down Jude's illusions. Nor do I think that it is because she is in some way pathological. Sue has a potential coherence which is kept at bay by her function. If she is in any sense to be seen as abnormal, it is only in the sense that neurosis becomes normative in Freud because it exposes what a 'healthy' state of mind represses.

The question of her sexuality is crucial in this. It isn't an easy question. Jude himself calls her sexless before the consummation, then explicitly withdraws it when she gives in, only to repeat it in the last section when he is confronted with her return to Phillotson. And that seems to me what we are supposed to feel—an extreme confusion. But this confusion is not seen to reside in her personality; rather, it resides in the insertion of her dual role of image and logic into the world experienced by Jude. From the start this opens up a gap between what she actually says and the way that it is taken. When she tells Jude about the undergraduate who is supposed to have died of unrequited love, she cites it as an example of ' "what people call a peculiarity in me'" but immediately goes on to affirm that her peculiarity lies merely in having no fear of men because she knows they are not always out to molest you. The differentiation here is cultural: ' "I have not felt about them what most women are taught to feel." Jude makes it biologistic. Equally there is no mystery about why she never became the undergraduate's mistress: ' "He wanted me to be his mistress, in fact, but I wasn't in love with him"' (III. iv). It seems very straightforward, and the undergraduate's claim that he died of a broken heart is surely intended to be preposterous. That is, until Jude's reception of the story is defined: 'Jude felt much depressed; she seemed to get further and further away from him with her strange ways and curious unconsciousness of gender' (III. iv). The only sexual terror in this seems to me to be Jude's— the sense that there must be something unnatural in a woman who won't give way to a man she doesn't love. And yet at the same time, what Sue affirms seems to offer very different possibilities: ' "I suppose, Jude, it is odd that you should see me like this and all my things hanging there? Yet what nonsense! They are only a woman's clothes—sexless cloth and linen"' (III. iii). It seems to suggest, if only fragmentarily (though it goes with Aunt Drusilla's story of Sue as a child, her resistance to invidious comparison with Arabella, the adoption of Jude's son, and 'that complete mutual understanding' between her and Jude at the fair), a repressed version of a sexuality not possible in the novel itself.

That is all very well, but it is still true that Sue clearly doesn't want to consummate her relationship with Jude, and that she retreats into the most conventional guilt about their sexual relationship when the children are dead. But I think that if we take Sue's function into account, we cannot make the mistake of thinking that there is some inherent inconsistency in her characterisation. Again it is a question of the relationship of the image to the logic. For what seems to me to be most truly radical about this novel is that sexuality is not left as a kind of idyllic enclave within the oppressive social system. Loving is subject to that external denial too. We have to bear in mind what the meaning of the marriage to Phillotson is. It comes out of that dislocation between logic and image which Sue enacts and which Jude never emancipates her from. Marriage has to do, as Phillotson makes clear, with the regularisation of the sentiments, the ordering of sexuality in terms which will be socially effective. The evocation of Mill in this context is not, as Eagleton says, bourgeois liberalism;[5] it is rather the taking of that affirmation into the area at which the ideology works most opaquely, the point at which the artificial system of things leagues itself with the laws of nature. Lucas quotes as an example of Hardy's muddle the passage about the young women in the dormitory:

> their tender feminine faces upturned to the flaring gas-jets which at intervals stretched down the long dormitories, every face bearing the legend 'The Weaker' upon it, as the penalty of the sex wherein they were moulded, which by no possible exertion of their willing hearts and abilities could be made strong while the inexorable laws of nature remain what they are. (III. iii)

Strictly theoretically, this might constitute an evasion (is it social oppression or the laws of nature that make

women the weaker sex?), but the same point has to be made about this that is made about Sue's representativeness: it is the area of confusion between the two which constitutes the basis of the novel's question. Does Hardy mean to suggest the possibility that the laws of nature might change? Surely to do so calls into question the whole phenomenology of the narrative. This is a 'pretty, suggestive, pathetic sight', like the sleeping young women, an arena of understanding that slips out of our grasp as soon as it is glimpsed. Such contiguity of nature and society is exactly what constitutes the ideology of marriage. Sue's challenge to marriage is a challenge to the social structure itself, as Gillingham realises: ' "if people did as you want to do, there'd be a general domestic disintegration. The family would no longer be the social unit"' (IVol. iv). The Shelleyan counter to this is not marked by its sexlessness. *Epipsychidion,* which Sue invokes shortly after this, is about a love which evolves itself in transcendence of a prison, as some of the lines she omits make clear.

> High, spirit-wingèd Heart! who dost forever
> Beat thine unfeeling bars with vain endeavour,
> Till those bright plumes of thought, in which arrayed
> It over-soared this low and worldly shade,
> Lie shattered; and thy panting, wounded breast
> Stains with dear blood its unmaternal nest!
>
> (11. 13-18)

The last line surely reminds us of the blood-stained perfect union. Physical sexuality is continually implicated with marriage, and those early chapters in Aldbrickham are about the subject of marriage and 'the other thing' (sexuality) together, because sexuality is blood-stained. Once they have children, Jude and Sue have to live the economic life of the couple. In a sense Sue is right to see the children's death as retribution. It is the payment for a return to 'Greek joyousness'. Throughout the novel, what Jude and Sue aspire to is comradeship. This has to define itself against marriage, and thus against 'sexuality'. And yet, there can be no doubt that the real making of this comradeship comes in those few pages between the consummation and the return to Christminster. It is just, however, that it cannot descend into the world of actuality without being destroyed. And that is what Sue recognises in her mortification at the end. She and Jude were wrong to make their relationship physical because you cannot be comrades in a world of domestic gins.

As I have argued, Sue has to perform the function of articulating all this. The pattern of openness and retreat recognises the war between logic and image. But that is to put it too metaphysically; Sue is only bodiless in so far as the body of the woman is a basis of capitalist reproduction, and therefore not her own. At this point I should stress that I am not trying to find an apologetic for Sue. It is not a question of discovering a psychology or making her representative. What makes Sue effective is her function in the novel, which is the function of an exposing image—that is to say, of an image carrying its own logic which is not the logic of the understandable, comprising both what she utters and what she seems, the gap between them and the collusion they make. As this image she destroys the lives of the order-loving individuals who aspire out of their loneliness through her. It is this destruction, however, that uncovers the determinants of both their aspiration and their loneliness. The sexual fascination of Sue and its demand for comradeship exposes the very impossibility of sexuality. Outside the field of possibility which she calls attention to, there is always the external that limits the field. Where I think we can go so wrong in this novel is to treat it in terms of a representation which we then find incomprehensible. It is the incomprehensibility that constitutes the novel's effect; the incomprehensibility of Sue (who as an image is offered for comprehension) is one way at least in which the incomprehensibility of the world (i.e. bourgeois ideology) is offered. To seek to tie her down to representativeness, or to the explicable, would be to postulate that ideology is 'false consciousness'. But we are talking about a literary effect and it is the literary function of Sue as part of what Hardy produces in this novel that constitutes the basis of our understanding. And the case of Sue is relatively specific.

III

Hardy in the 'Postscript' of 1912 cites, perhaps disingenuously, a German critic who said that Sue was the first delineation in fiction of the woman of the feminist movement. In fact, as Elaine Showalter establishes, feminism is dominant in fiction already by the time Hardy writes *Jude*.[6] And more than this, Sue clearly belongs to a literary variant of the feminist heroine which became fashionable in English fiction after the first performance in England of *Hedda Gabler* in 1891, and which came to be known as the New Woman. A. R. Cunningham gives an informative account of this variant in 'The "New Woman Fiction" of the 1890s',[7] showing how other texts before *Jude* have heroines who cite Mill and Spencer and aspire to the emancipation which is doomed 'either through personal weakness or social law', and who even in some cases retreat like Sue into Christianity. While the better-known writers such as Grant Allen and Sarah Grand celebrate the New Woman largely as a figure of purity, other writers (most notably George Egerton) use the type as a means of confronting the displaced sexuality of woman. What I think characterises Hardy is that he uses this literary device not as a subject offered to the reader's amazement, but as an active force within the novel which answers to the buried ideology of the questing hero. In other words, whereas Arabella limits Jude's dream, Sue translates his dream into questions, taking him beyond the bewilderment of 'the artificial system of things' into the bewilderment of nature's inexorable law. Nevertheless she does this as an image, and what makes for her coherence is neither her consistency nor Hardy's, but the persistent way in which she exposes the limits of meaning. Although this is clearly a subject requiring elaboration, I want (rather than placing Sue in her immediate context as the New Woman) to see the novel in terms of the larger context of feminist literature at the end of the nineteenth century by relating it briefly to the best feminist text of that period, *The Story of An African Farm*.

Olive Schreiner's novel appeared in 1883 and there was a first edition in Hardy's library, though I have no idea whether he read it, and I am not trying to claim that it influenced him. More importantly, it seems to me, the relationship of Schreiner's novel to ideology shares a great deal with that of Hardy's. It is not accidental that Schreiner's text gets treated in very similar ways to Hardy's. Even Elaine Showalter says that matters of plot and construction were beyond Schreiner, and that what marks her writing is its ardour rather than its art. Schreiner as a writer, in fact, gets treated rather like Sue as a character—the talented neurotic who was unable to keep up any significant level of productivity. Of course there isn't much after *The Story of An African Farm*, but to have achieved that much seems fairly remarkable, and it is clear to me at least that it is a carefully structured text, positing many voices against one another, not—obviously—in a way that makes for an identifiable coherence or for a comfortably distanced fiction. But the relationship of Waldo to Lyndall is a liaison of speech, each of them stimulated into thought and given voice by a 'stranger' (the traveller who interprets Waldo's carving, the lover through whom Lyndall experiences the conditions of female sexuality); they are only able to communicate because they do not get entrammelled in sexuality: ' "I like you so much, I love you." She rested her cheek softly against his shoulder. "When I am with you I never know that I am a woman and you are a man; I only know that we are both things that think." '[8] As well as this possibility of a comradeship making language the bridge which 'reality' denies to both of them, what is also important in relation to *Jude* is that Lyndall should define the difference between man and woman as the difference between expecting to work and being expected to seem:

> 'It is not what is done to us, but what is made of us,' she said at last, 'that wrongs us. No man can be really injured but by what modifies himself. We all enter the world little plastic beings, with so much natural force perhaps, but for the rest—blank; and the world tells us what we are to be, and shapes us by the ends it sets before us. To you it says— *Work;* and to us it says—*Seem*! To you it says— As you approximate to man's highest ideal of God, as your arm is strong and your knowledge great, and the power to labour is with you, so you shall gain all that human heart desires. To us it says— Strength shall not help you, nor knowledge, nor labour. You shall gain what men gain, but by other means. And so the world makes men and women.

> 'Look at this little chin of mine, Waldo, with the dimple in it. It is but a small part of my person; but though I had a knowledge of all things under the sun, and the wisdom to use it, and the deep loving heart of an angel, it would not stead me through life like this little chin. I can win money with it, I can win love; I can win power with it, I can win fame. What would knowledge help me?

The less a woman has in her head the lighter she is for climbing. I once heard an old man say, that he never saw intellect help a woman so much as a pretty ankle; and it was the truth. They begin to shape us to our cursed end,' she said, with her lips drawn in to look as though they smiled, 'when we are tiny things in shoes and socks. We sit with our little feet drawn up under us in the window, and look out at the boys in their happy play. We want to go. Then a loving hand is laid on us: "Little one, you cannot go," they say; "your little face will burn, and your nice white dress be spoiled." We feel it must be for our good, it is so lovingly said; but we cannot understand; and we kneel still with one little cheek wistfully pressed against the pane. Afterwards we go and thread blue beads, and make a string for our neck; and we go and stand before the glass. We see the complexion we were not to spoil, and the white frock, and we look into our own great eyes. Then the curse begins to act on us. It finishes its work when we are grown women, who no more look out wistfully at a more healthy life; we are contented. We fit our sphere as a Chinese woman's foot fits her shoe, exactly, as though God had made both—and yet He knows nothing of either. In some of us the shaping to our end has been quite completed. The parts we are not to use have been quite atrophied, and have even dropped off; but in others, and we are not less to be pitied, they have been weakened and left. We wear the bandages, but our limbs have not grown to them; we know that we are compressed, and chafe against them.'[9]

That is what constitutes the unattainability of the woman; being expected to seem, she cannot talk unless she is able not to be a woman. In that gap between talking and seeming exists not only the character of Lyndall, but also the very form of the novel. The reality of the novel is more highly fragmented than many other texts of the period, and yet the writing itself acts out its ideological commitment to the Emersonian unity which is so often noticed in *The Story of An African Farm*—noticed, without its being seen as the instrument which makes possible the novel's own particular version of comradeship. Formally, this Emersonian unity comes to a head when Waldo's life is suddenly presented as phases of our life. In terms of the novel's meaning it is there in the final consolation of the hunter (a feather from the white bird of Truth) and the commitment Waldo makes to dreams. The form of the novel, that is to say, is instrumental.

But the instrumentality which the text achieves through its form must be defined in terms of its ideological recognition. When the stranger is telling Waldo of the hunter's search for truth, he makes it a precondition of that search that the hunter releases the birds of certain concepts from their cage: 'He went to his cage, and with his hands broke down the bars, and the jagged iron tore his flesh. It is sometimes easier to build than to break.'[10] The Emersonian commitment has to be seen in the context of this total demystification. Patiently the novel erodes all the ideological supports of the characters, so that it is the very fracturing of form that gives the novel

its instrumentality. Now a fiction is a representation—it is itself an image, so that to provide a text which is a coherent representation would be the same as being understandable. And I have tried to show what constitutes Sue's effectivity is that she isn't—that she constitutes an image which breaks down the certainties through her own logic. This is, self-consciously, the aesthetic of *The Story of An African Farm*: the preface to the second edition clearly foreshadows the 'series of seemings' which follow ('the method of the life we all lead [where] nothing can be prophesied', as opposed to 'the stage method'). Significantly, both Schreiner and George Egerton move towards fragmented form. An Egerton story is not only short, it is chopped. And it is also strictly speaking incomprehensible. The heroine of 'A Cross Line', for example, is able to speak to the stranger, but what she says is enigmatic and she only goes to him because he accepts the enigma. The account of woman here picks up all the themes—image, enigma, liar:

Then she fancies she is on the stage of an ancient theatre out in the open air, with hundreds of faces upturned towards her. She is gauze-clad in a cobweb garment of wondrous tissue. Her arms are clasped by jewelled snakes, and one with quivering diamond fangs coils round her hips. Her hair floats loosely, and her feet are sandal-clad, and the delicate breath of vines and the salt freshness of an incoming sea seems to fill her nostrils. She bounds forward and dances, bends her lissom waist, and curves her slender arms, and gives to the soul of each man what he craves, be it good or evil. And she can feel now, lying here in the shade of Irish hills with her head resting on her scarlet shawl and her eyes closed, the grand intoxicating power of swaying all these human souls to wonder and applause. She can see herself with parted lips and panting, rounded breasts, and a dancing devil in each glowing eye, sway voluptuously to the wild music that rises, now slow, now fast, now deliriously wild, seductive, intoxicating, with a human note of passion in its strain. She can feel the answering shiver of feeling that quivers up to her from the dense audience, spellbound by the motion of her glancing feet, and she flies swifter and swifter, and lighter and lighter, till the very serpents seem alive with jewelled scintillations. One quivering, gleaming, daring bound, and she stands with outstretched arms and passion-filled eyes, poised on one slender foot, asking a supreme note to finish her dream of motion. And the men rise to a man and answer her, and cheer, cheer till the echoes shout from the surrounding hills and tumble wildly down the crags. The clouds have sailed away, leaving long feathery streaks in their wake. Her eyes have an inseeing look, and she is tremulous with excitement. She can hear yet that last grand shout, and the strain of that old-time music that she has never heard in this life of hers, save as an inner accompaniment to the memory of hidden things, born with her, not of this time.

And her thoughts go to other women she has known, women good and bad, school friends, casual acquaintances, women workers—joyless machines for grinding daily corn, unwilling maids grown old in the endeavour to get settled, patient wives who bear little ones to indifferent husbands until they wear out—a long array. She busies herself with questioning. Have they, too, this thirst for excitement, for change, this restless craving for sun and love and motion? Stray words, half confidences, glimpses through soul-chinks of suppressed fires, actual outbreaks, domestic catastrophes, how the ghosts dance in the cells of her memory! And she laughs, laughs softly to herself because the denseness of man, his chivalrous conservative devotion to the female idea he has created blinds him, perhaps happily, to the problems of her complex nature. Ay, she mutters musingly, the wisest of them can only say we are enigmas.[11]

The point about this passage is that it is a self-communing—it offers what the understanding of the good husband leaves out, what is inexplicable to the new lover. I'm here trying to talk about form and content at once: both the structure and the portrayal move towards that inconsistency which constitutes Sue's effectiveness. The New Woman is most effective in that sense, not because she reads John Stuart Mill, has reservations about the exploitation of her sexuality, or submits to the external (death, the lover, God), but because that dance opens up the ideological structure of reality. The end of *Hedda Gabler* sums up the challenge to intelligibility: ' "People just don't do things like that." '

NOTES

References in the text are to the chapter divisions of Hardy's novels.

[1]'Study of Thomas Hardy' in E. D. McDonald (ed.), *Phoenix: The Posthumous Papers of D. H. Lawrence* (London, 1967), p. 509.

[2]R. G. Cox (ed.), *Thomas Hardy: The Critical Heritage* (London, 1970), p. 311.

[3]Kate Millett, *Sexual Politics* (London, 1972), pp. 130-4.

[4]*The Literature of Change: Studies in the Nineteenth-Century Provincial Novel* (Hassocks, Sussex, 1977), pp. 188-91.

[5]Introduction to *Jude the Obscure*, New Wessex edn. (London, 1975), p. 15.

[6]Elaine Showalter, *A Literature of Their Own: British Women Novelists from Brontë to Lessing* (London, 1977), pp. 182-215.

[7]*Victorian Studies*, vol. xvii (1974), pp. 177-86.

[8]Olive Schreiner, *The Story of An African Farm*, 2 vols. (London, 1883), vol. ii, p. 94.

[9]Ibid., vol. ii, pp. 39-42.

[10]Ibid., vol. i, p. 301.

[11]George Egerton, *Keynotes* (London, 1893), pp. 19-21.

Elizabeth Langland (essay date 1980)

SOURCE: "A Perspective of One's Own: Thomas Hardy and the Elusive Sue Bridehead," in *Studies in the Novel*, Vol. XII, No. 1, Spring, 1980, pp. 12-28.

[*In the following essay, Langland investigates Hardy's portrayal of Sue Bridehead in* Jude the Obscure, *concluding that she is an "unevenly conceived character" riddled with inconsistencies, but that these flaws point to the novel's "distinctly modern" narrative sensibility.*]

Form and content are inseparable. Story depends on technique, depends, Henry James claimed, on "every word and every punctuation point." Although Thomas Hardy could be expected to resist his contemporary's strict attention to minutiae, James's broad point about the interdependence of idea and form nonetheless helps explain problems in Hardy's *Jude the Obscure* and particularly in that elusive character, Sue Bridehead, who is a touchstone for many of the difficulties posed by Hardy's final novel. Critics have called this character childish, selfish, sadistic, masochistic, narcissistic, and frigid, all in explanation of what has been defined as her dominant trait: inconsistency. But these conclusions have not satisfied even their authors, among whom Irving Howe is representative in cautioning: "Yet one thing, surely the most important, must be said about Sue Bridehead. As she appears in the novel itself, rather than in the grinder of analysis, she is an utterly charming and vibrant creature." Perhaps a character can be so fluid and complex that she eludes the combined critical efforts to capture her. But, before despairing of analysis altogether, we should consider Sue's inconsistency and elusiveness in light of formal difficulties in Hardy's last novel.

That Sue Bridehead has resisted satisfactory analysis points both to problems in the formal conception of *Jude* and to the inadequacies of its point of view in conveying a growing sensitivity to other versions of the novel's central experiences. An omniscient narrator, such as Hardy offers in *Jude,* should be a guarantee of reliability, but Hardy's final narrator eludes and evades. And, for the first time, Hardy lets the perspective of a single character, Jude Fawley, dominate the story. To complicate matters further, it is not clear to what extent Jude's perspective is judged by the narrator, or even, as criticism has made clear, to what extent Hardy himself is involved in his narrator's and character's perspectives. In light of these complications, inconsistencies in Sue Bridehead's character and behavior call for reassessment.

We must disentangle Sue's character from the problematic narrative point of view which presents her—a point of view primarily Jude's, but buttressed by the narrator's. To do so, we confront questions of character autonomy and the matrix for judging character. As James saw, we cannot simply wrest character from the context of narrative technique and point of view. In discussing Sue's character, we must continually account for the novel's point of view which is closely allied with Jude's experience and with a man's perspective on an unconventional woman. And, any effort to resolve questions about Sue's personality must take into account the relationships among mimesis, narrative technique, and character development.

In this larger context, we recognize that Jude's primacy in the novel must shape Sue's role in it, much as in *Tess of the D'Urbervilles* the eponymous character determines and limits the representation of Alec D'Urberville and Angel Clare. In *Jude the Obscure,* Arabella and Sue clearly have as one primary function their appeal to opposite poles in the protagonist's nature: the fleshly and the spiritual. Such an observation has become commonplace, but its consequences for character representation have great importance. Hardy's last novel does not imitate Sue and Jude equally. It imitates the way in which one credulous and naive, but well-intentioned, man, Jude, confronts a world which he sees as increasingly inimical to his desires and goals. He is limited by the society in which he finds himself, by what Hardy calls the "hereditary curse of temperament," and by the conventionality of his own nature. Thus, one of Sue Bridehead's other narrative functions is to unmask the deep-seated assumptions which baffle Jude's hopes. That we come to recognize his personal limitations is essential to a tragic denouement which finds him partially responsible for his fate, not merely a pawn in society's or the universe's machinations. His share of responsibility gives Jude a tragic stature.

This imitation, with its focus on Jude's experience and his point of view, accords with the subject Hardy initially anticipated, the story of a young man "'who could not go to Oxford'—His struggles and ultimate failure. Suicide." But, in correspondence with Edmond Gosse after completing the work in 1895, Hardy admits his subject has broadened, stating that his novel is concerned first with the "labours of a poor student to get a University degree, and secondly with the tragic issues of two bad marriages. . . ." The new subject, now added to the original topic, potentially conflicts with full examination of the first, since it calls for examination of the positions and perspectives of both personalities in a marriage. Clearly feeling the increasing interest of his Sue plot, Hardy confessed to Florence Henniker in August 1895, "Curiously enough, I am more interested in the Sue story than in any I have written." Furthermore, dissatisfaction with his representation of Sue kept Hardy tinkering with her character through several revisions of the novel. Robert C. Slack has documented the textual changes in *Jude the Obscure* between the 1903 and 1912 Macmillan editions, and he finds them mainly concerned with revising passages which deal with Sue. Hardy's revisions alter the "affective meaning of a detail or of a passage . . . to give [Sue] more human sympathy." And, Slack adds, this group of revisions has "a consistent direction."

But the effect of such revisions must remain superficial when one considers both the force of Jude's controlling perspective on Sue and the continuing influence of the novel's original intention. A narrative technique focusing on Jude's perspectives is perhaps adequate to the story Hardy had initially envisioned but inadequate to the novel's subsequent development and to Hardy's growing interest in Sue. What had happened seems clear enough. Hardy's original story took on a new direction—or, perhaps it might be fairer to say, that a subplot of the envisioned original assumed greater importance in writing. A narrative technique which focused on Jude's perspective was perfectly adequate to depict the Sue of the story Hardy first envisioned, but not to depict the personality Hardy had become interested in as he wrote.

That Sue is enmeshed in Jude's limited point of view, then, helps account for our sense of inconsistencies in her character. We attempt to judge as a personality in her own right a figure intended to serve merely to define another personality. Often, when Jude looks at his cousin, he in fact gazes into a mirror which reflects the image of his own ambivalence. He finds Sue "almost an ideality" (p. 114 [Page references are to *Jude the Obscure,* the Wessex edition, 1912], "almost a divinity" (p. 174), "vision" (p. 223), "ethereal" (p. 224), "uncarnate" (p. 224), "disembodied creature" (p. 294), "sweet, tantalizing phantom" (p. 294), but he cannot ask whether this perceived spirituality is a reflection of her essence or an image of his fear that the fleshliness embodied in Arabella will once again ensnare him. It is Jude who tells us Sue is unpredictable and inconsistent: "her actions were always unpredictable" (p. 211), or "Possibly she would go on inflicting such pains again and again . . . in all her colossal inconsistency" (p. 210), or he "decided that she was rather unreasonable, not to say capricious" (p. 190), a "riddle" (p. 160), "one lovely conundrum" (p. 162).

His tendency to blame his cousin in this "gentle" way often reveals Jude's rationalizations of his own failures to act decisively as well. Jude has a keen eye for Sue's departures from candor, but he does not question his own consistency or honesty in concealing his marriage to Arabella from Sue. Interpretations of Jude's interview with his cousin, Sue, after she has run away from Melchester Boarding School focus on the radical inconsistency of her behavior, yet that behavior appears in a different light when we remember that Jude, too, is withholding information—his marriage to Arabella—and consequently behaving inconsistently. He cannot respond to Sue in expected ways, failing to kiss her when "by every law of nature and sex a kiss was the only rejoinder that fitted the mood and the moment. . . . [But Jude] had, in fact, come in part to tell his own fatal story. It was upon his lips; yet at the hour of this distress he could not disclose it" (p. 189). Jude chides Sue for her frigidity, but never questions the conventional attitudes which underlie his assumption that it is all right to sleep with Arabella despite his relationship with Sue, or that mere sexual intimacy makes Arabella more his wife than Sue with whom he shares intimacies of a more substantial kind.

If we see Sue as merely a narrative device to reveal Jude, we need not trouble ourselves with these "inconsistencies" in her character. But Sue refuses to be read as a device. Although the critical literature acknowledges limitations in Jude's point of view, it rarely accounts for the resultant distortions in its judgment of Sue. Its failure to do so leads to the problematic conclusion that Sue is what Jude, despite his limitations, thinks she is.

The novel's narrator, whose omniscience seems a guarantee of his reliability, tends sporadically to confirm Jude's conclusions. But close examination reveals inconsistencies even in that supposedly omniscient perspective. When the narrator offers comment, he does little to establish a viewpoint more dispassionate and reliable than Jude's. In such cases, his remarks are often confusing rather than definitive. So, Dale Kramer has recently made an effort to "clarify the nature of the narrator's self-contradictoriness." Kramer considers the striking example of a narrative comment which occurs after Sue and Jude kiss passionately for the first time—"Then the slim little wife of a husband whose person was disagreeable to her, the ethereal, fine-nerved, sensitive girl, quite unfitted by temperament and instinct to fulfill the conditions of the matrimonial relation with Phillotson, *possibly with scarce any man*"—and concludes that the italicized words show a "temporal perspective [in the narrator] as limited as that of any human character." The remark is typical of a series of narrative comments which ultimately pose problems for readers. As in this case, the narrator's observations do not substantiate conclusions drawn from our interpretation of incident and character. In evident despite of the narrator's remarks, Sue has just kissed Jude passionately. And, Aunt Drusilla's remark about Phillotson ("there be certain men here and there that no woman of any niceness can stomach. I should have said he was one" [p. 229]) helps support the perfectly natural aversion of Sue to her husband. Both Sue's actions and Aunt Drusilla's observation afford a more coherent view of Sue's character than the narrator offers.

Not only do Jude's and the narrator's perspectives present problems for our interpretation of Sue, but the continuing influence of the novel's original intention creates uncertainty over Sue's scope and purpose in the novel. The problem resolves itself into two main questions: what roles or role as fictional construct does Sue play in the novel, and in what ways does her "reality" seem to exceed these roles? In answer to the first, many critics have identified Sue's several functions: she is a double to Jude who, in formal terms, changes place with him in the course of the novel; she is the spiritual woman who contrasts with Arabella, the sensual woman; she represents the "sceptical voice of the present age"; she re-

veals the need and failure to make reason accord with feeling; she expresses the excess of selfishness and the lack of charity, of loving-kindness. In these interpretations, Sue is a schematic character, not a whole personality. She is one half of an equation: spirit/flesh, ego/alter ego, reason/feeling, intellect/emotion, selfishness/selflessness. Hardy encourages this interpretive bias in his claim, "Of course the book is all contrasts—or was meant to be in its original conception."

But Hardy's own reservation about the fulfillment of his original conception leads us to the second question, one more difficult but more essential to our problem here. To what extent does Sue become a cohesive personality and exceed the boundaries of those narrative functions intended for her? More particularly, to what extent does Sue become equal in significance to Jude and therefore exceed the capacities of the single perspective technique to reveal her adequately? And to what extent does she, as woman, not share Jude's problems, facing problems unique to her position in society and history instead? Finally, to what extent does Sue's role introduce larger contemporaneous issues of the "woman question" which ultimately cannot find resolution within the scope of the novel's subject.

The fullness of her role—a function of the developing story—and the slimness of her presentation—a function of the technique—have led critics to search beyond the novel's presentation to psychological interpretations of this character as being masochistic, narcissistic, frigid, or hysterical. Some of her comments seem to support such constructions. We hear narcissism in Sue's laments: "'Some women's love of being loved is insatiable . . .'" (p. 245), "'But sometimes a woman's *love of being loved* gets the better of her conscience'" (p. 290), or "'my liking for you is not as some women's perhaps. But it is a delight in being with you, of a supremely delicate kind . . .'" (p. 289). A masochism seems to dominate her tendency to self-blame: "'Everything is my fault always!'" (p. 189), or "'I am in the wrong! I always am!'" (p. 268), or "'I know I am a poor miserable creature'" (p. 288). And finally, frigidity suggests itself in the characterizations of her as "spirit . . . disembodied creature . . . tantalizing phantom" whose normal sexuality is asexuality:

> A seraph of Heaven too gentle to be human,
> Veiling beneath that radiant form of woman . . .
>   (p. 294)

When Sue's character is not drawn along psychological lines, it is perceived along sociological lines. Sue is a "type" or the "type" of new woman, as flat and stereotypical in her own way as some of Charles Dickens's pure heroines. She is the "Bachelor girl" heralded by the reviewer Hardy cites in his "Postscript" to *Jude*. She grafts a new independence and intellectuality onto woman's traditional dependence and emotionalism, and in this grafting major inconsistencies necessarily result. This new feminist, in the words of Lloyd Fernando,

[*"New Women" in the Late Victorian Novel,* 1977], "does not merely defy law and convention, she has put herself so far beyond them in spirit in the pursuit of individual independence that her personality has become grievously impoverished." Fernando continues, Sue "personifies the extreme refinement of sexual sensibility, the extreme moral fastidiousness toward which idealizing young feminists unwittingly tended." Robert Gittings concurs in seeing Sue as a type but disagrees as to which one. For Gittings, [in *Young Thomas Hardy,* 1975], Sue is not the "New Woman" of the 1890s, but "The Girl of the Period" in the 1860s. He bases his conclusions on the quality of Sue's intellectualism: her typical loss of faith and substitution of Positivism. Hardy himself encourages such interpretations since he spoke of Sue as a "type of woman which has always had an attraction for me," seeming to refer to her spirituality and intellectuality.

It is reasonable to assume that Hardy's original intention for the novel did envision Sue in these comparatively one-dimensional ways—spiritual, new woman, girl of the period. But as the character gained prominence and complexity, her personality did not necessarily evolve along those lines. Indeed, as the novel and the character change tack, Sue gains dimensions which are incompatible with Hardy's original scheme.

Lest we appear simply to be affirming the old inconsistencies—sometimes Sue is one thing, sometimes another—we need to make some distinctions. A personality can be defined as inconsistent in a novel; if his portrayed nature is to be flighty, spasmatic, or impulsive, we are aesthetically comfortable with expecting the unexpected from him. Most critics have seen Sue's inconsistency in this way. But as we have seen, the consequences of this perspective is a sense that the grinder of analysis is an inadequate tool for capturing Sue's character. A more radical inconsistency emerges when the character is inconsistent with her own personality; that is, the creator has failed to create a completely credible individual; or the creator finds those adhesive tapes of shopworn philosophy—this time about women—easier to apply than to reexamine the premise of his narrative framework.

Although the presentation of Sue is already difficult because of the novel's point of view and changing intentions, that presentation is further complicated by the terms for character evaluation. We have trouble crediting Sue with a cohesive, healthy personality because of the novel's deep ambivalence over the proper terms for evaluation of her. Whereas Jude and the narrator are increasingly clear that the source of Jude's tragedy is not the wrath of God "'only . . . man and senseless circumstance'" (p. 413), neither is quite sure about the source of Sue's tragedy. Hardy himself seems uncertain. The wild card of evaluation is Sue qua Woman, the innate disposition of this mysterious sex.

Katharine Rogers has explored the pervasive, though subtle, bias against women—with Sue standing for "typical woman"—in her "Women in Thomas Hardy" [*Cen-* tennial Review 19 (1975)]. Rogers points out that, even though they may "conscientiously" qualify such conclusions, both Jude and the narrator tend to blame Sue/ Woman for their own failures and pain. A characteristic passage captures the tensions:

> Strange that [Jude's] first aspiration—towards academical proficiency—had been checked by a woman, and that his second aspiration—towards apostleship—had also been checked by a woman. "Is it," he said, "that the women are to blame; or is it the artificial system of things, under which the natural sex-impulses are turned into devilish domestic gins and springes to noose and hold back those who want to progress?" (p. 261).

The second cause—inadequate social mechanisms—asks for a serious consideration, but the first, less unbiased, conviction that "women are to blame"—holds an equal attraction for Jude and the narrator.

This pervasive tendency to blame women's innate dispositions rather than to examine the social mechanisms which coerce them is mirrored on the individual level in Jude's tendency to search for the cause of Sue's behavior in the nature of her sex rather than in her situation. Jude speculates, giving Sue in marriage to Phillotson, "Women were different from men in such matters. Was it that they were, instead of more sensitive, as reputed, more callous, and less romantic. . . . Or was Sue simply so perverse . . ." (p. 209). When Jude belatedly reveals his marriage to Arabella, he terms Sue's outrage and betrayal the "exercise of those narrow womanly humors on impulse that were necessary to give her sex" (p. 200). Readers aware of Jude's duplicity must find such reductive generalizations either revelatory of Jude's failures or indicative of a sudden narrowing of the novel's meaning and significance, not to mention its humane vision. The narrator, too, joins Jude in these generalizations: "With a woman's disregard of her dignity when in the presence of nobody but herself, she also trotted down, sobbing articulately as she went" (p. 319). These words describe Sue's response to Jude's departure to visit Arabella, and they force us to contemplate the character not as an individual in anguish and indecision, but as a gender performing according to its innate nature.

The explanation of Sue's behavior by gender is echoed in more subtle ways. For example, Phillotson, discovering that Sue is avoiding him by sleeping in the clothes closet under stairs, speculates, "'What must a woman's aversion be when it is stronger than her fear of spiders!'" (p. 266). Or Phillotson tries to decide, "What precise shade of satisfaction was to be gathered from a woman's gratitude that the man who loved her had not been often to see her?" (p. 193). Obviously Hardy is heightening the sexual significance of these scenes by referring to genders, but "the man who loved her" is an epithet for Phillotson, whereas the periphrases "a woman's aversion" and "a woman's gratitude" have a broader scope. They talk about more than Sue's particular behavior. Each invokes a class norm about women's response to general situations by which the character seeks to measure Sue. The effect, is, again, to evaluate Sue's behavior in terms of sex rather than in terms of individual character or particular situation.

Even Sue is made to participate in these generalizations either seriously, as when she explains her refusal to become Jude's lover as "a woman's natural timidity when the crisis comes" (p. 288), or in self-mockery, as when she comments on Phillotson, "'According to the rule of women's whims I suppose I ought to suddenly love him, because he has let me go so generously and unexpectedly'" (p. 286).

Finally, at the conclusion of the novel, Jude questions whether Sue's "extraordinary blindness . . . to [her] old logic is . . . common to woman. Is a woman a thinking unit at all, or a fraction always wanting its integer?" (p. 424). He claims, "I would argue with you if I didn't know that a woman in your state of feeling is quite beyond all appeals to her brains" (p. 470). Or, Jude ponders, "events which had enlarged his own views of life . . . had not operated in the same manner on Sue's" (pp. 415-16) and then, to explain her behavior, generalizes, "Strange difference of sex, that time and circumstance, which enlarge the views of most men, narrow the views of women almost invariably" (p. 484). This reductive interpretation of a complex tragedy will hardly satisfy readers who have been attracted by the complex side of Hardy's vision.

On the other hand, when Sue judges Jude, she always ascribes his failure to inadequate social mechanisms or to his personal biases rather than to his nature as "Man." No comparable concept "Man" emerges in the novel, except in occasional comparisons between a man's and a woman's sexual appetites. Rather, the novel in its judgments of Jude, asks us to consider the interaction of the individual with social possibility, so that we recognize with Jude that "there is something wrong somewhere in our social formulas" (p. 394). The ease with which we might dismiss Sue's *social position and perspective as woman* need not disturb us if Sue remains a minor character; but, as she achieves increasing prominence through the marriage plot, the inadequacies of a judgment by gender emerge. As Sue becomes more prominent in the novel, we tend to accord to her the same terms for evaluation we accord to Jude, recognizing that her "inconsistencies," as well as Jude's, can be traced to the discrepancies between social pressure and individual needs, between individual ideals and quotidian realities.

Despite the plenitude of social analysis regarding Jude's fate, the novel is relatively lacking in equivalent analyses of Sue's. The pressures she must face as a woman of conviction in the 1890s far outweigh Jude's, yet they are, within the confines imposed by the novel's techniques, largely ignored. The reader can speculate on Sue's problems in light of such famous contemporaneous works as Ibsen's *Doll's House*. And George Eliot's novels also have much to say about the social hobbles on women of talent and aspiration. But in *Jude the Obscure,* Hardy, the narrator, and Jude have not finally decided on the cause of Sue's failures.

That Sue is Woman is of enormous importance to the novel's tensions, even though neither Jude nor the narrator can perceive much of what must be Sue's inner struggles. Jude aspires beyond his class; Sue aspires beyond her class and her sex. Jude's aspirations accord with his nature as man. Although society's "freezing negative" tells him to stay in his place, we do not conclude he has a fragmented or inconsistent personality because he aspires. Males have always aspired; aspiration against social restrictions is expected and normal. So, the class conflict Jude experiences in no way undermines the cohesiveness of his personality. Sue's is not simply a class conflict; it is a conflict of genders, a conflict finally between what woman can and is expected to do. The sociological and psychological analyses of Sue miss this point. They see her as a type and assume that the inevitable fragmentation of her personality follows. In this view, her aspirations are merely symptoms of her fragmented personality. The novel—albeit unevenly—suggests another possibility, that of a coherent, cohesive personality give the *appearance* of fragmentation by conflicting demands on her as individual and by reductive generalizations about her as Woman.

Hardy finally cannot decide by what standard to judge Sue. Indeed, his problems increase as Sue becomes more prominent because her problems are partly a function of the all-obscuring fact that she is a woman. That fact is important, not as an explanation of *innate disposition* but as it explains Sue's particular circumstances, not as it reveals a "type," but as it sharpens an individual's dilemma. What is missing from the novel, then, are counterpoints to the generalizations about woman's nature, vivid depictions of what it means *as a social and historical fact* to be a woman in Jude's world. We are missing the analogues for Sue to the novel's frequent explanations of what it means to be a poor man of humble origins. One brief scene does touch on that meaning. It occurs just after Sue flees Melchester Boarding School and the focus reverts momentarily to Sue's seventy young peers:

> Half-an-hour later they all lay in their cubicles, their tender feminine faces upturned to the flaring gas-jets which at intervals stretched down the long dormitories, every face bearing the legend "The Weaker" upon it, as the penalty of the sex wherein they were moulded, which by no possible exertion of their willing hearts and abilities could be made strong while the inexorable laws of nature remain what they are. They formed a pretty, suggestive, pathetic sight, of whose pathos and beauty they were themselves unconscious, and would not discover till, amid the storms and strains of after-years, with their injustice, loneliness, child-bearing, and bereavement, their minds would revert to this experience as to something which had been allowed to slip past them insufficiently regarded (p. 168).

The narrator still reverts to Nature—"the inexorable laws of [woman's] nature"—as explanation for "injustice, loneliness, child-bearing, bereavement," but the dramatized scene itself is sensitive to the chains social convention has forged for women. Women are locked in veritable prisons to safeguard their chastity of mind and body; by such lights, Sue has become a fallen woman. But the narrator's sense that social institutions imprison women is rare in *Jude,* the "laws of nature" being a more convenient view.

Conflicts of presentation and evaluation continue as we turn to a more pointed discussion of the distance between Sue's social position and her expectations and personal aspirations as articulated in the action of the novel but little understood by Jude, the novel's center of perception. Sue herself recognizes the obvious contradictions between intellect and emotion, statement and action. And her understanding articulates a consistency not superficially apparent. She tells Phillotson that she married him when her "theoretic unconventionality broke down" (p. 267), acknowledging her desire to be accepted socially at the same time that she cannot intellectually endure the terms of that acceptance. So, when Jude reproaches her for the "affectation of independent views" and accuses her of being "as enslaved to the social code as any woman I know," she does not admit the justice of his claim and argues, "'Not mentally. But I haven't the courage of my views, as I said before'" (p. 290). To identify Sue's rejection of tradition with a rejection of emotion and to see her intellect and ideas as divorced from her feelings is an oversimplification. Beneath both rejection and espousal lie deep feelings: a human desire to be accepted and loved and the passionate resistance of a cohesive personality to the self-suppression and loss of identity traditional love dictates and to the demands made on women in that contract. In this light, Sue suffers from a commitment to complexity of feeling rather than from an impoverishment of emotion.

Sue has integrity. Initially, she does not feel she should submit to anyone or anything against her feelings. She does not want to suffer, arguing with Phillotson, "'Why should I suffer for what I was born to be . . .'" (p. 268). The integrity of her life—in the face of enormous pressures from Jude and Phillotson—is remarkable. Jude is certainly incapable of the same strength of will in his relationship with Arabella. Sue wishes to make a life for herself not dependent on a man, and, even after she joins Jude, she insists on contributing her share of work with the result that Jude himself becomes more independent. She has the courage and self-respect not to bind Jude in marriage, and her pronouncements on this institution are consistently illuminating, intelligent, and rational. Hardy has, in fact, made Sue, not Jude, the mouthpiece for his own feelings expressed in the "postscript" to the novel.

Sue's attitudes toward sex and marriage provide the clearest measure of the distance separating her ambitions and desires from social possibilities shaping her self-realization. They provide the clearest measure of her cohesive personality. Her feelings about marriage and sex derive from a sense of her individuality and independence, which seem to her threatened by sexual or formal commitments. Sue wants an identity of her own. She does not see marriage as her ultimate goal in life. She is fearful of submerging her identity in that of another or worse, of becoming a kind of chattel. Before marrying Phillotson, she laments to Jude, "my bridegroom chooses me of his own will and pleasure; but I don't choose him. Somebody *gives* me to him, like a she-ass or a she-goat, or any other domestic animal" (p. 204). And Jude echoes her unconventional opinion after her marriage by saying that she is still "'dear, free Sue Bridehead. . . . Wifedom has not yet squashed up and digested you in its vast maw as an atom which has no further individuality'" (p. 227). Partly in acknowledgment of Sue's feelings, Jude adopts the trade of monument mason: "it was the only arrangement under which Sue, who particularly wished to be no burden on him, could render any assistance" (p. 314).

In wanting an identity of her own, an identity through work and financial contribution, Sue is asking for something which men take for granted and which conventional women by and large reject. Arabella, for example, is always looking for a man to keep her, and she finally promises her father that she will take herself off his hands if he will help her snare Jude. Sue is torn between the conventional expectations that she needs to snare a man and essentially imprison him in marriage— a position so crudely expressed by Arabella—and her own understanding which teaches her to esteem herself. Her decision to avoid marriage is, by her lights, a mark of respect for herself and Jude, not an instance of flirtation, frigidity, childishness, or self-enclosure.

In the novel marriage does indeed emerge as a grotesque trap, a gin to maim the creatures caught in it. Arabella tricks Jude into marriage twice, once with a pretended pregnancy and once with liquor. When married, she complacently remarks, "'Don't take on, dear. What's done can't be undone,'" while Jude wonders "what he had done . . . that he deserved to be caught in a gin which would cripple him, if not her also, for the rest of a lifetime?" (p. 71). If Sue demands her own freedom, she secures as much for Jude as well; living in their simple way, Jude is "more independent than before" (p. 314).

Neither Sue nor Jude can persuade themselves to marry. On this issue they share similar fears, although Sue again is more articulate than Jude. Kramer argues [in *Thomas Hardy: The Forms of Tragedy,* 1975] that the "only condition of the matrimonial relationship that she [Sue] is unfitted to fill is its coerciveness." And, in fact, here Sue's sexuality appears perfectly healthy. As lovers, she and Jude remain in a "dreamy paradise" (p. 328), and the advent of the child, Father Time, "rather helped than injured their happiness" because it brings into their lives "a new and tender interest of an ennobling and unselfish kind" (p. 348). Still, Sue fears the "iron contract" of marriage because it exacts certain behavior from the participants; it "licenses" love. And Arabella's blunt advice that Sue should "coax" Jude to marry her so that she has legal remedies and protection against his possible brutality only confirms Sue in her feelings that marriage is a "hopelessly vulgar" (p. 326) institution, "a sort of trap to catch a man" (pp. 323-25). Her pride will not let her act in ways repugnant to her self-esteem. She adopts a courageous position, made the more courageous by the lack of understanding support.

The issues go deeper. Jude shares her fears: "though he thought they ought to be able to do it, he felt checked by the dread of incompetency just as she did" (p. 345). Jude seems to realize a possibility that he might lapse into indifference, and such a fear is not without validity since, as we have seen, Jude is very conventional about human relationships. What freedom he attains seems principally a reflex of Sue's vision. Arabella calls him a "baby" because he is so gullible to conventional appeals. He, of course, marries Arabella because she says she is pregnant. Once married, Jude, of course, regards the arrangement as lifelong. Arabella suggests divorce. Once Sue joins him, they should, of course, have sexual relations because men and women do. And once divorced from their first spouses, they should, of course, marry. And when Arabella returns, she is more his wife than Sue since Arabella and Jude have had sexual relations. Even at the end of the novel, when Jude remarries Arabella, he claims hotly, the conventional blinkers still on: "'I said I'd do anything to—save a woman's honour . . . And I've done it!'" (p. 464). Never does Jude see the tension between sex and friendship, between marriage and identity, although he initially thought that "if he could only get over the sense of her [Sue's] sex, . . . what a comrade she would make" (p. 184). Jude's complicated initial responses to Sue reveal the confusions in his attitude toward woman as friend and woman as sexual object. Conventional in his instincts, Jude here reminds us of Hardy's Angel Clare, whose instincts betrayed him back to a rigid conventionality in his response to Tess. Sue is justified in fearing that, in a conventional relationship, Jude might well behave in totally conventional ways. He himself senses and fears it.

This is not to blame Jude for the tragedy. Rather it argues that we conclude something more than that "Jude's choice of Sue is what dooms him" Unfortunately the novel's conclusion once again limits the complexity and cohesiveness we have afforded Sue's character and, in so doing, encourages rather simplistic explanations. The stereotypic case study of a masochistic, narcissistic, hysterical, or intellectual-but-emotionally-impoverished woman is fulfilled in Sue's decision to return to Phillotson. Yet that conclusion, beginning with the death of the children, is curiously attenuated. The children exist in the novel principally to die. They have no convincing life; they do not engage us as personalities. Jude, who has come to Christminster still dominated by his early illusions, finally "sees," whereas Sue blinds herself.

The final acts of Hardy's drama are ritualistic; the dancers simply change places. Sue—a complex personality—

is relegated to "Woman": "was woman a thinking integer at all"; "Strange difference of sex, that time and circumstance . . . narrow the views of women. . . ." Aspects of her character—independence from traditional form and beliefs, emotional integrity, her sparkling intellect—are lopped off as if they had never existed. Her grief becomes her undoing in the narrator's eyes, but that final sketch of Sue seriously reduces, even contradicts, the character we have come to know through the novel's action. If we compare her with Angel Clare, whose narrative role in *Tess* is analogous to Sue's in *Jude,* we discover great differences. Angel's liberal notions are tested by Tess's revelation of her relationship with Alec, and his ideas are immediately found incompatible with his instincts. Sue's ideas, especially about marriage, have been consistently supported by her instincts and feelings. The action shows her to be what she believes she is—until the end.

The critical need to construct a coherent and logical character out of Sue—consistent even in her inconsistencies—has led to portraits which often, as the critic stands back to survey his work, must be qualified by the statement that she is really much more wonderful than this. Perhaps the only way to explain the contradiction between a critic's and a reader's Sue is finally to acknowledge that the artist's conception itself is inconsistent and flawed, that because of Hardy's change of subject, there is an imbalance in the narrative technique never compensated for despite revision. And that imbalance is heightened by ambivalent and incomplete evaluation of Sue. Sue remains an unevenly conceived character. Hardy, sensitive to ambiguity in his final novel, has extended his narrative art to its limits. But if the narrative technique complicates the portrait of Sue, it partially compensates for these problems in rendering the pathos of limited human understanding and so anticipates narrative experimentation in the twentieth century. The flaws in Sue's presentation and the limits of the novel's evaluation of her seem to mirror Jude's partial understanding, the partial understanding which underlies and baffles all human intercourse, attempts at meaning, and strivings for self-realization. Despite the typically nineteenth-century attempt at an omniscient narrator, then, the narrative sensibility underlying *Jude the Obscure* is distinctively modern.

Problems of individual limitations are at the heart of Hardy's last novel. His former tendency to find the tragic source in malevolent forces or inimical nature is more muted. In *Jude,* we have nothing comparable to Egdon Heath, and the choric voice of previous novels finds a thin and unconvincing substitute in Aunt Drusilla's warnings to Jude and Sue about the doom of hereditary temperament. They are destroyed by the gins and nets of a society very imperfectly tuned to their individual needs and by their own failures to understand each other.

Seen in this light, it is not surprising that *Jude the Obscure* is Hardy's last novel. It is the novel in which judgments and pronouncements are not so easy. Point of view is problematic. The complexities of the world Hardy depicts are not easily placed in a large philosophical perspective. And Jude, unlike Tess in her moments at Stonehenge, seems incapable of tragic transcendence and cathartic understanding. In earlier works, Hardy is genuinely comfortable in the philosophical, tragic mode. As his narrative vision and techniques become increasingly sensitive to the ambiguity of personal desire, social expectation and individual responsibility, his novelistic art becomes mature and subtle. But Thomas Hardy seems unhappy with the novelistic vision which stresses the ambiguity of experience, and he turns to a more congenial mode—poetry—which plays with the ambiguity of idea and which does not engage one in the painful complexities and failure of lived lives. Nonetheless, his final novel, *Jude,* stands as a testimony to Hardy's understanding of the painful immediacy of experience and the terrible ways in which personal limitations combine with social limitations to produce a disaster which no philosophy can redeem.

David Sonstroem (essay date 1981)

SOURCE: "Order and Disorder in *Jude the Obscure,*" in *English Literature in Transition: 1880-1920,* Vol. 24, No. 1, 1981, pp. 6-15.

[*In the following excerpt, Sonstroem focuses on Jude's at times "disorderly, random, [and] repetitive" migrations within the structured course of* Jude the Obscure *to illustrate the thematic implications of Hardy's framing of chaos in "intricate order."*]

In his thought-provoking "A propos de la construction de *Jude the Obscure,*"[1] Fernand Lagarde presents Hardy's novel as a rigidly balanced quasi-architectural construction, within which characters dance an intricate "ronde" or quadrille. In support of his view he points to the symmetrical disposition of chapters within each Part of the novel and among the six Parts, to the placement of a crisis at the precise center of each Part, and to many other such structural harmonies. He notes, too, the extensive network of similarities and contrasts among the personalities and careers of the four leading characters—implicit relationships that Hardy carries into even minute details: "Le roman tout entier est un subtil entrelacs de correspondances" (211); "On n'en fimirait pas de dresser une liste de ces rapprochements, de ces répétitions de l'expérience" (208). In short, for Lagarde *Jude the Obscure* is a thoroughgoing "recherche de la symétrie" (191).

At least one critic takes issue with his reading, finding it "remarkable" but "ultimately resistible."[2] I suspect that Michael Millgate's wariness is due to the abiding impression of disorganization conveyed by *Jude*—an impression of messy randomness that no skillful, extensive demonstration of order can dispel. Nor is he alone in sensing a chaotic streak: Ward Hellstrom, for example, has noted that "Jude's movement from place to place is a dramatic

illustration of 'the modern vice of unrest,'" and Ian Gregor has similarly observed, "our sense of the form of the novel in reading it, is of something . . . turbulent, a sense not of imposed design but of vexed movement. . . . "[3]

For my part, I find Lagarde's reading of *Jude* irrefutable but incomplete. The intricate design that he describes is demonstrably present in the novel, and he deserves thanks for opening our eyes to the remarkable extent of it. But in discerning narrative symmetries and thematic designs, he scants the erratic emotional, intellectual, and especially physical vagaries of the leading characters, those of Jude especially. At one point Lagarde does recognize a strain of disorder in this aspect of the book: referring to Vilbert, he remarks, "sa ronde immuable, placée comme elle l'est au début et à la fin du roman, vient à point nommè souligner la déroute de ceux qui osent tenter d'organiser à leur guise leur destinée." But within a few lines even Jude's peregrinations are included in what Lagarde calls "les mouvements de la danse" (199). I would maintain that Lagarde is at his weakest in considering simple movement of characters from place to place—the aspect of the novel from which other readers gain their impression of it as chaotic. To right the balance, I wish to examine Jude's itinerary in detail. I shall then proceed to a brief consideration of the relationship between the extraordinary order and the extraordinary disorder that Hardy depicts in *Jude the Obscure.*

Jude's journeys take place in and about "Wessex"—southwestern England overlaid with Hardy's fictive place-names, contracted somewhat, and suffused with his significances. We are led to assume that Jude is born in Marygreen. After his mother's death he lives for a time with his father in Mellstock, South Wessex. When his father, too, dies, the ten-year-old orphan returns to Marygreen to be reared by his great-aunt Drusilla. In this drab hamlet Jude reaches young manhood while nursing an obsessive, unrealistic vision of Christminster, the university town he worships from a distance as "the heavenly Jerusalem" (I, iii, p. 18). Jude's next move is to Alfredston, where he learns stone-masonry to support himself while preparing for entrance to Christminster. On one of his weekly walks between Alfredston and Marygreen he encounters Arabella Donn. An onrush of animal passion prevails, and shortly he finds himself married to her and living in a cottage between Alfredston and Marygreen. Even in geographical terms he has taken a backward step on his way to Christminster. But Arabella soon leaves him, and he returns to Alfredston. Three years later he finally goes to Christminster, taking a room in a suburb nicknamed "Beersheba" (the original Beersheba, we remember, was at a great remove from Jerusalem, being on the very outskirts of the Promised Land). In Christminster Jude comes to know his cousin, Sue Bridehead, to whom he has felt a rarefied attraction even before meeting her. In the course of their first interview they walk from Christminster to nearby Lumsdon to call on his old schoolmaster, Richard Phillotson, under whom Sue promptly takes a position as pupil-teacher. Jude journeys at least twice to Lumsdon to see her and once to Marygreen to visit his aunt, now in failing health. Discouraged by his inability to gain access to the university or to Sue's affections, Jude eventually returns to Marygreen. But soon he moves to Melchester to be near Sue, now attending the Melchester Normal School in preparation for marrying Phillotson. When she anticipates her rustication and flees to Shaston, Jude visits her there. After Sue weds Phillotson, Jude revisits his sick aunt in Marygreen and then continues to Christminster. There he happens upon Arabella, with whom he goes to Aldbrickham to spend the night. Returning the next day to Christminster, he is sought out by Sue, and he goes with her to Marygreen to visit their aunt yet again. Thence he reverts to his old quarters and employment at Melchester. After a disillusioning round trip to Kennetbridge to meet the composer of a hymn that has moved him, Jude journeys to Shaston to see Sue. Within a week he is called from Melchester to Marygreen upon the death of his aunt. There he again sees Sue and then goes back to Melchester.

When Sue forsakes Phillotson for Jude, Jude boards her train at Melchester, and they proceed to Aldbrickham—the first stage on their travels as a couple. There the discordant keynote of their relationship is struck: they quarrel when Jude inadvertently takes Sue to the very hotel to which he had brought Arabella a month before. Nevertheless, they remain together in Aldbrickham for some time. When gossip over their irregular domestic connection hinders Jude from finding work, they leave Aldbrickham to lead a nomadic life, driven for several years from place to place. Hardy mentions Sandbourne, Casterbridge, Exonbury, Stoke-Barehills, Quartershot, and Kennetbridge as typical stations in their wayfaring, and he pauses to present the couple in more detail at fairs at Stoke-Barehills and Kennetbridge. Eventually they return to Christminster, where after much difficulty they find lodgings for Sue and the children in one place and for Jude in another. The catastrophic death of the children ensues, and a chastened Sue returns to Phillotson, now teaching at Marygreen. Still at Christminster, Jude remarries Arabella in the carelessness of his despair and contracts consumption. He recklessly travels to Marygreen in a driving rain for a final meeting with Sue. Then he returns to Christminster and Arabella, where after a time he dies, utterly discouraged and embittered, at the dismal locus of his brightest dreams. . . .

[A map of Jude's migrations would indicate] a course remarkable for its length, its frequent shifts in direction, and its asymmetry—remarkable, too, for its repetitious revisitings, yet its apparent randomness. What do these qualities signify? The peculiar purport of Jude's itinerary emerges when we compare it on the one hand with the direct course of the protagonist in a shapelier novel and on the other hand with the utterly random course of the protagonist in a loosely organized novel.

Although Jude's path is probably an accurate condensation of that which most human beings actually take through life, it is extraordinarily elaborate and ungainly for the protagonist of a novel. Compare it, for example, with that of Jane Eyre. In *Jane Eyre* each place has its own meaning, and Jane's path is one of progress. Jane proceeds from Gateshead to Lowood, Thornfield, Marsh End, and finally Ferndean. Every new locale marks a stage in her growth, presenting her with a more advanced opportunity or challenge, as geographical movement reenforces personal development. Although Jane revisits Gateshead once and once Thornfield, Charlotte Bronte permits her to do so largely to show the reader that Jane cannot in fact reenter a situation she has outgrown. As Jane develops, she suffers her full share of dilemmas, but the relatively limited number of stages in her trim itinerary and their sharp differentiation bespeak the sureness of her growth.

In comparison with Jane's course or any other typical protagonist's, Jude's is much more extensive and far untidier. Others may log more miles than Jude does, but it would be hard to find a protagonist who changes direction so often. Jude's course is unusual, too, in its lack of economy—its turns and returns that bring about no real changes. Melchester, Lumsdon, and especially Marygreen and Christminster draw Jude time and again but to no significant effect. He leaves as he arrives, no happier and little wiser. None of the many removals marks an advance or makes a big difference.[5] Indeed, much of the poignancy of the novel hinges on Jude's expectation, which dies hard, that a change of place will bring about an improvement in his circumstances: his very last words to Sue are "Let us . . . run away together!" (VI, vii, p. 309). Jude never fully learns that the novelist's convention is not true to life: a change of place is not accompanied by a change in the human condition.

On the other hand, Jude's path through life is extensive and erratic enough to be that of a picaro, yet again there are telling differences. Unlike a picaresque novel, *Jude the Obscure* is not episodic. Jude holds to the same or at least related goals as he moves from place to place, and he suffers in one place the consequences of his behavior in another. In other words, Jude's world is uniform and interconnected, as the picaro's is not. Furthermore, the picaro instinctively comprehends and makes the most of the world in which he finds himself, whereas Jude mistakes the nature of his world, to his greater sorrow. The typical picaro, an unreflective creature, has no goal in life other than random adventure; he attends utterly to the here and now. Never bored because everything that concerns him changes as he goes, he lives on the difference between place and place, each locale appearing to him as a fresh and self-contained world. One might say that he is reborn with every removal. Not so Jude. Jude is never satisfied with the here and now, looking always beyond immediate circumstances for fulfillment. Unlike the picaro, he is always disappointed: as he moves, the world stays the same at base, and his past hounds him. His constant revisiting of Christminster and, to a lesser degree, Marygreen and Melchester (whereas Jack Wilton, for example in Thomas Nash's *The Unfortunate Travel-ler* visits no place twice) is a sign of the dreary uniformity of Jude's world. Unwilling to give up the premise that things are different elsewhere, Jude compulsively returns again and again to the sites of his greatest expectations in the hope of finding something fresh and better that he has overlooked. He never finds any such thing. His failure is especially galling because of the presence in the novel of Arabella and the itinerant Vilbert (a well-matched pair indeed), both of whom operate on picaresque assumptions and thrive in so doing. In short, the extensive, random path of the picaro signifies the vibrant exploration of a perpetually varying world, whereas Jude's extensive path—sometimes repetitive, sometimes random—signifies a wearisome struggle to escape a world teasingly diverse in superficial appearance but always ultimately noxious to decent, sensitive humanity.

Comparing *Jude the Obscure* both with the conventional novel and with the picaresque novel, we find it differing from both in the same basic way. Whereas both assume the fictive convention that change of situation is accompanied by important changes in the human condition, *Jude* contradicts the assumption. In any respect that matters, one place is like any other.

Hardy makes his point by means of Jude's travels and also by subsidiary means. For instance, the second chapter shows Jude in the middle of Farmer Troutham's field, a "wide and lonely depression in the general level of the upland." In this "vast concave"

> the brown surface of the field went right up towards the sky all round, where it was lost by degrees in the mist that shut out the actual verge and accentuated the solitude. The only marks on the uniformity of the scene were a rick of last year's produce standing in the midst of the arable, the rooks that rose at his approach, and the path athwart the fallow. . . . The fresh harrow-lines seemed to stretch like the channellings in a piece of new corduroy, lending a meanly utilitarian air to the expanse, taking away its gradations, and depriving it of all history beyond that of the few recent months. . . . (I, ii, p. 13)

The field in all its ugly uniformity is the world writ small, and the map of Jude's wanderings might well be scored into its soil.

Another way in which Hardy develops the meaninglessness of situation is to show Jude pursuing more than one goal. Jude is attracted not only to Christminster but also, of course, to Arabella and Sue, human counterparts to his geographical desires. The easily won Arabella and the skittish Sue promise, like Christminster, a fulfillment that proves chimerical. Life with each of them, like life in Christminster, is ordinary and distressing after all. By having Jude pursue several unsatisfying goals—companions as well as locations—Hardy leads us beyond questioning the individual objects of Jude's aspirations to

questioning the assumption common to them all, namely, that a better situation is somewhere to be found. Hardy encourages this more radical consideration by taking every opportunity to show, in the latter half of the book especially, how very much the earthy Arabella and the aetherial Sue resemble each other. Sue winces when Arabella remarks, "Bolted from your first [husband], didn't you, like me?" (V, ii, p. 213) but the parallel is justly drawn. Again Arabella tells a grating truth in saying of Sue, "she's took in a queer religious way, just as I was in my affliction at losing Cartlett . . ." (VI, iVol. p. 282). The cumulative effect of these and many other such passages is a drastic reduction, in the reader's eyes, of the distinction between the two women. At first glance they seem remarkably dissimilar, but we come at last to see them as sisters under the skin. Hardy's masterstroke in this regard is having Arabella and Sue trade places at the end. Early in the novel we find Jude with Arabella in Marygreen, where he is hindered from going to Christminster and to Sue, who lives there and is associated with the place. At the close of the novel we find Jude with Arabella in Christminster, where he is hindered from going to Marygreen and to Sue, who now lives there.[6] Having the two women exchange the places with which they are first associated blurs the distinctions on which Jude's quest depends. We are led to feel that, whatever Jude may think or do, any change in situation—from place to place, companion to companion—makes no real difference at all.

In sum, Jude's itinerary is an important part of a gruelling demonstration that situation does not matter; wherever he happens to be, "Jude stands alone and in the open. . . ."[7] The broadest, most telling irony of the book is that in a physical sense Jude *does* achieve his goal: born in Marygreen, he dies in Christminster; his tortuous path does lead to the city of his desires. But the bitter irony is that Christminster proves merely another clod or stone upon the expanse of earth. Jude might just as well have saved himself the trouble and stayed where he began.

To be sure, easy acceptance of his surroundings would diminish Jude's stature. We respect him for the dogged pursuit of his visionary ideals. But because he cannot begin to approach the ideal he pursues, he remains in effect a creature in a tormenting snare. The tale told by Jude's course is one of entrapment in circumstance. His protracted, errant path through life betokens neither progress nor even fresh adventure, as in a more typical narrative, but the sometimes repetitive, sometimes erratic, always futile writhings of an animal in a springe— a recurrent image in the novel. Unlike the pig he kills, Jude bleeds all too slowly. His long, contorted path through life and the imagery of entrapment it represents are admirably suited to Hardy's high argument; the exquisite misfit between the external world and the individual mind, and the painful meaninglessness of human existence.

We must now make what sense we can of the fact that the path of Jude winds through a novel that is nevertheless an extensive "recherche de la symétrie." How can we reconcile the erratic course of the protagonist with the dance-like disposition of the four leading characters and with the ornate architectural symmetries of the novel as a whole? We can only speculate on Hardy's deepest intentions. We can, however, recognize a similar pattern in other works by Hardy. Moreover, we can note a common effect produced by all such works and tentatively infer a purpose behind that effect.

Everyone knows that after writing *Jude,* Hardy quit novels to write poems instead. In one respect, though, he did not change his course, for the poems tend to reproduce in miniature the aesthetic pattern of *Jude.* By and large, the poems, too, are one shapely presentation after another of things gone awry. In the incidents related in the poems—example after example of "life's little ironies"—we repeatedly find the random or unexpected subsumed by a larger order. **"The Convergence of the Twain"** (1912) aptly illustrates the process:

> And as the smart ship grew
> In stature, grace, and hue,
> In shadowy silent distance grew the Iceberg too.
>
> Alien they seemed to be:
> No mortal eye could see
> The intimate welding of their later history,
>
> Or sign that they were bent
> By paths coincident
> On being anon twin halves of one august event[8]

The "path" of the iceberg seems determined by physical laws; that of the Titanic, by the allied aspirations of its builders and passengers. Disparate in almost every way, the two enormous objects seem quite "alien," worlds apart. From this perspective their collision appears a freakish, meaningless disaster, an absurd, inexplicable disruption of natural and human order. But Hardy presents it instead as supremely orderly—as the climax of an elaborate cosmic practical joke. "The Immanent Will that stirs and urges everything" choreographs the seemingly independent courses of the two objects into a shocking union.

The speaker of the poem clearly takes grim pleasure in this mock marriage arranged by the Immanent Will. The speaker justifies the prank on the grounds that it is a suitable punishment for human pride. What makes the moralizing ring false is the speaker's (and, through him, the Immanent Will's) relishing the scheme. Life's disasters seem due far less to human pride than to the Immanent Will's penchant for contriving. The poem suggests that Hardy preferred an orderly world, even one governed by gloating sadism, to an absurd one, subject to meaningless, random calamities.

Hardy's very metrics turn apparent chaos into larger harmonies. His preoccupation with meter is evident and often noted. He experiments with stanzaic form especially, seldom using a scheme for more than one poem. In a typical poem of his, a line will vary greatly from other lines in the stanza in its number of feet, yet the lines do always obey a rhyme scheme, and later stanzas do faithfully repeat the peculiar pattern of the initial stanza. What at first seems random and even chaotic is finally incorporated into a larger, rigid pattern. In **"The Convergence of the Twain,"** for example, we find two rhyming three-stress lines followed by an "irregular" line of six stresses; the incipient pattern of trimetric couplets is disrupted. It is replaced, however, by a new pattern, which serves as metric analogue to the actual convergence: two lines go their separate ways so to speak, until in the third line they are unexpectedly mated. The triple rhyme blesses the union of the whole. And as stanza follows stanza, we meet with an unbroken series of converging twains. In this way, too, Hardy schematizes the irregular.

I have glanced at the poems to establish that *Jude the Obscure* is not unique among Hardy's works for framing chaotic randomness within an intricate order. The aesthetic disposition is apparently a habit of mind, not a local stratagem. With respect to this disposition, *Jude* differs from the poems in at least two ways. The first is, of course, the sheer extent to which the two aspects are developed. *Jude* would be remarkable simply for its "subtil entrelacs de correspondances," traced by Lagarde, or for the protagonist's lengthy, tangled path, traced above. How much more remarkable it is, therefore, that Hardy painstakingly worked both these extensive linear configurations into the same novel. His doing so is especially intriguing because the two are contradictory in purport, one set of lines describing a messy, meaningless world, the other a harmonious one. Why Hardy would dwell thus on a contradiction may be implied in the second difference between novel and poems: in *Jude* the disruptive element is far more prominent than it is in the poems. The poems, their tidy schemas visible for all to see, are finally not so disturbed or disturbing as *Jude,* whose structural symmetries, once noted, can seem merely an elaborate game, quite beside the point of the tale told by Jude's path of pain and confusion. Millgate's resistance to Lagarde's essay is evidence that the symmetries of the novel can seem irrelevant to it.

The two linear configurations are demonstrable aspects of *Jude;* the significance of their relationship is open to interpretation and conjecture. To me the conjunction of the two patterns suggests the following possibility. The path of Jude drew Hardy to the brink of universal shapelessness—to nihilism. Courageous enough to mark the path and its purport thoroughly and clearly, Hardy remained profoundly unwilling to follow his protagonist to its end. The artist in Hardy manifested this unwillingness in the elaborate symmetries that Lagarde details. When the path of Jude nevertheless overwhelmed Hardy's attempts to resist its implications, Hardy turned to poetry, the most conspicuously orderly of genres. There the conflict between absurd chaos and design could be resumed on grounds more favorable to the latter element. Hardy proceeded to write poem after poem revealing both the continuance of the conflict within him and the preference for an orderly universe, even a malicious one, over one without underlying shape or purpose.

[1] Fernand Lagarde, "A propos de la construction de *Jude the Obscure,*" *Caliban,* III (Jan 1966), 185-214.

[2] Michael Millgate, "Thomas Hardy," in *Victorian Fiction: A Second Guide to Research,* ed by George H. Ford (NY: Modern Language Association of America, 1978), p. 329.

[3] Ward Hellstrom, "Hardy's Use of Setting and *Jude the Obscure,*" *Victorian Newsletter,* No. 25 (Spring 1964), 11; Ian Gregor, *The Great Web: The Form of Hardy's Major Fiction* (Totowa, NJ: Rowman & Littlefield, 1974), p. 207.

[4] Most commentators have assumed that Jude was born in Mellstock. They do so on the basis of Drusilla Fawley's remark, p. 12 (I, ii), that Jude "come from Mellstock, down in South Wessex, about a year ago . . . where his father was living. . . . " But they overlook I, xi, where Drusilla says that, when Jude was a baby, his parents left each other permanently near the Brown House barn, on the outskirts of Marygreen: "Your mother soon afterwards died—she drowned herself, in short, and your father went away with you to South Wessex, and never came here any more" (p. 58).

Quotations are taken from Thomas Hardy, *Jude the Obscure,* ed by Norman Page (NY: Norton, 1978). The many editions of the novel lead me to refer to part and chapter as well. All subsequent references are given in parentheses in my text.

[5] See Jean R. Brooks, *Thomas Hardy: The Poetic Structure* (Ithaca, NY: Cornell UP, 1971), p. 268: "The return to certain places connected with significant action is a well-tried narrative technique, which Hardy does not disdain to use in his most modern novel to mark the ironies of human progress." Here Brooks underestimates Hardy's originality. Hardy uses an old technique to new effect: Jude's returns measure no progress at all, except, perhaps, a painful, slow awakening to grim realities—if that be progress.

[6] Although he does not interpret it as I do, the reversal of place is pointed out by Bert G. Hornback, *The Metaphor of Chance: Vision and Technique in the Works of Thomas Hardy* (Athens, Ohio: Ohio State UP, 1971), p. 137.

[7] J. Hillis Miller, *Thomas Hardy: Distance and Desire* (Cambridge, Mass: Harvard UP, 1970), p. 3.

[8] *The Complete Poems of Thomas Hardy,* ed by James Gibson (NY: Macmillan, 1978), pp. 306-7.

Alexander Fischler (essay date 1981)

SOURCE: "An Affinity for Birds: Kindness in Hardy's *Jude the Obscure,*" in *Studies in the Novel,* Vol. XIII No. 3, 1981, pp. 250-65.

[*In the following essay, Fischler comments on the bird motif in* Jude the Obscure *and its relation to the theme and structure of the novel.*]

Though the manuscript evidence concerning the first pages of **Jude the Obscure** is still open to differing interpretations, those who have considered it agree on two points: (1) that the opening of the novel as we have it is not part of Hardy's original draft; and (2) that Hardy composed it, obviously with great care, after deciding that his heroine, Sue, should not be Jude's prime attraction to Christminster. The "deadly war" (p. 23) [all page references are to the New Wessex edition of **Jude the Obscure,** 1977] that Hardy set out to present, according to his Preface, required that Jude follow alternately the call of the spirit and the call of the flesh. Clearly, it was more appropriate to make the call to a place like Christminster spiritual. In the new opening, as a result, it is the schoolmaster, Phillotson, who invites Jude to visit him in the Heavenly Jerusalem, and it is his figure, not Sue's, that appears to Jude in the halo which glows over the city on the horizon (pp. 42-43). Yet, although he is possibly the best that out-of-the-way Marygreen has to offer, Phillotson is an uninspiring representative of spirit. He commands the affection of only one pupil, Jude, not one of the "regular day scholars, who came unromantically close to the schoolmaster's life . . ." (p. 29). He appears pathetic, in fact, standing by the "cumbersome" piano, a witness to his readily waning "enthusiasm," telling the boy about his "scheme or dream . . . to be a university graduate, and then to be ordained," a dream that might become reality at Christminster, "headquarters, so to speak," or near it (p. 29). It is obviously a key initial absurdity that the boy's own schemes and dreams should have crystallized on this figure and been nurtured by such stuff as his farewell address: "I shan't forget you, Jude," he said, smiling, as the cart moved off. "Be a good boy, remember; and be kind to animals and birds, and read all you can. And if ever you come to Christminster remember you hunt me out for old acquaintance' sake" (p. 29).

In the rook episode which follows and in its aftermath, Hardy illustrates the risk involved in kindness to birds; he also points out that the boy was predisposed to kindness by oversensitivity and "born to ache a good deal" for it (p. 36). The mentor's high-minded advice at the beginning of his career is like the milestone on which Jude inscribes his goal, "THITHER," in that it inspires him for a while, then turns into an ironic commentary on his endeavors, on the vanity of trying to improve or merely to "be good." When Jude reaches Christminster, Phillotson loses "at one stroke the halo which had surrounded" him as an incarnation of spirit; the mentor lives in humble quarters on the edge of town; he does not remember his pupil "in the least," and he is understandably reluctant to speak of his former ambitions (pp. 121-22).

Hardy asserted that the clash of spirit and flesh was the key to **Jude the Obscure,** but he neglected to add that in order to bring up to date the traditional conflict he had distorted its traditional form: he had seldom given spirit the nobler part; he had made the issue uncertain throughout; and he had even allowed the opponents to switch sides in mid-clash. Just as he chose for his first representative of spirit a rather dispirited type, he let one of the two representatives of flesh turn out to be an epicene "sprite." He was playing. Despite or perhaps precisely because of his intense personal involvement in the story, Hardy allowed himself unprecedented detachment in tone and levity in treatment. His original title for the novel, *The Simpletons,* implied an ironic perspective on the protagonists; after the first serial installment this was modified to *Hearts Insurgent,* which sounded a more positive note. The third and final title, *Jude the Obscure,* for the restored manuscript in book form, suggested no attitude whatever; yet the tone remained set from the start. After building a reputation for "good men" (the stock of Gabriel Oak and Giles Winterbourne) and then trying their virtue in Tess, "a pure woman," Hardy was offering the modern Job, a man who naively follows conventional advice or traditional wisdom, attempting to "be good." He was of course no biblical Job. In Hardy's universe, there is neither a devil to try nor a god to authorize the trial and, eventually, vindicate suffering and offer compensators; here, defeat is attributable mostly to character, that is, individual weakness or flaw, and, to a lesser extent, to such forces as an inimical social environment, inflexible conventions or laws, inexplicable family curses, and an arbitrary fate. It is not really the way in which defeat comes about that is new in *Jude,* but the manner in which it is expressed: happenstance and "life's little ironies" are overwhelmed by words, by disputes, reflections, broodings, by painfully extended attempts to explain and to justify. The novel itself would succumb were it not for brilliant characterization, meticulous structuring, and an apparently new and, no doubt, reckless way with words. "The letter killeth," says the epigraph (omitting that "the spirit giveth life"). Indeed, it has been suggested that in *Jude* Hardy is well on his way to abandoning prose and shifting to an exclusively poetic use of language. Name and word games, of course, go back to his earliest literary efforts; but the persistence evident here suggests a new manner if not a new purpose that is readily illustrated by the mentor's farewell words in the opening scene, words which set Jude on his hopeless quest and, eventually, allow the reader to trace a lifetime of adversity back to an inherent (and possibly inherited) weakness—kindness to birds.

Hardy's lifelong concern for animals in general and birds in particular is well documented. His biographers usually trace his own extreme sensitivity to an episode recalled in *Later Years,* a winter walk during which his father "idly" felled with a stone a half-frozen field fare; "and the child Thomas picked it up and it was as light as a feather, all skin and bone, practically starved. He said he had never forgotten how the body of the field-fare felt in his hand: the memory had always haunted him" (*LY,* p. 263). "The most persistent symbolism in Hardy is connected with birds," says F. B. Pinion [in *A Hardy Companion*]. Birds, indeed, abound in the novels and stories, as well as in the poetry, symbolizing most frequently what Pinion has called "the Frost's decree," the harshness of life and the vulnerability of living creatures. But in Hardy, birds are also the scarcely noticed witnesses of human activity, offering comment by word or presence; sometimes they provide a traditional, symbolic extension for the characters; at other times, they allow very personal metaphoric or metonymic descriptions to be set against the traditional background. Hardy knows his birds well and chooses among them carefully; in *Jude* alone, which is not his *birdiest* novel, references are made to the rook, sparrow, nighthawk, robin, raven, cock, pigeon, ringdove, and screech owl. In a materialistic world where protagonists are distinguished by their sensitivity to animals, birds offer the suggestion, deliberately left vague, of another dimension and of a broader scale to gauge human endeavors.

During the twenty-five years which spanned his career as a novelist, Hardy had thoroughly individualized the traditional bird-woman motif. His first heroine, Cytherea Gray, in *Desperate Remedies* (1871), was fairly conventionally singled out for birdlike gracefulness in her initial presentation and was said to possess a sense of perfect balance (tragically absent in her architect father!); the melodramatic plot then turned her, just as conventionally, into a "terrified, . . . panting and fluttering . . . little bird . . ." (*DR,* XII, 5, p. 252). Subsequent heroines, from Fancy Day to Fanny Robin, Ethelberta, Elizabeth-Jane, Suke Damson, Tess, and the three Avices, are more and more specifically associated with birds. Yet even in these associations, Hardy never goes far beyond the conventional. In *Jude the Obscure,* with Sue, the device becomes a technique of characterization, used deliberately, consistently and in conjunction with key themes; the traditional bird suggestions of gracefulness and pathos are used little and then, often, mockingly. Tess had been consistently associated with birds, but without detracting from her chief role as incarnation of womanhood; as pure woman, she had to be thoroughly grounded, even when Angel Clare set her among the gods in the peculiar role of Artemis-Demeter (*Tess,* III, xx, p. 115). Sue, on the other hand, is not only called a bird, but a mass of detail concerning her appearance and comportment suggests she is a bird in the specific as well as the general and colloquial sense; her idiosyncrasies almost invariably elicit pejorative reflections about women.

All evidence suggests that the decade which culminates in the publication of *Jude the Obscure,* 1885-1895, was a time when Hardy for personal as well as professional reasons was much concerned with women. (In this decade he also completed *The Mayor of Casterbridge, The Woodlanders, Wessex Tales, A Group of Noble Dames, Tess of the D'Urbervilles, Life's Little Ironies,* and *The Well-Beloved* in its original version.) His biographers agree that, partly because of domestic problems, he was driven more and more during these years to enjoy the notoriety of a daring novelist among the fashionable ladies. He attracted admirers and readily assumed with them the literary counselor role. Notable among them were Rosamund (Ball) Tomson, who inscribed to him her poem collection *The Bird Bride* in 1889, and Florence Henniker, frequently considered one of the models for Sue, with whom Hardy began a long friendship in 1893. During the composition of *Jude,* entries from his notebooks and comments in the "biography" he prepared record not only his personal musings about women's inability "to manage an *honest* man" (*LY*, p. 22), but indications that he thought and acted like an authority on feminine matters. He participated in sophisticated debates with "beautiful women" on marriage laws (*LY*, p. 23). He reflected on the difference between coquetting and flirting (*LY*, p. 24), the effects of natural selection on women (*LY*, p. 25), and the mores of country servants in London (*LY*, p. 30). He went to the music halls and noted subsequently that the girls "owe their attractions to art" (*EL*, p. 296), or that "They should be penned and fattened for a month to round out their beauty" (*LY*, p. 14). Writing about a conversation on hypnotism, concerning the possibility "of willing, for example, certain types of women by speech to do as you desire," he commented that, "If true, it seems to open up unpleasant possibilities" (*LY*, p. 34). His chief biographer, Robert Gittings, understandably finds this sexual blossoming of a man in his fifties intriguing.

It is of course impossible to indicate at which point personal preoccupation with women combined with Hardy's realization of the potential for verbal play yielded the bird motif in *Jude*. The suggestions were readily available. The woman-bird-bride association, according to the *Oxford English Dictionary,* goes at least as far back as the fourteenth century; the first instance cites dates from about 1300, and refers to Delilah, "that birde [var. bride, bryde, bruyd] was biddande bald." Connotations were not necessarily pejorative for a long time; by the end of the century, Chaucer still uses "bird" merely to designate a maid. Hardy himself played on bird-bride as early as 1866, in the poem **"Postponement,"** in which, according to J. O. Bailey, he probably represents himself in the role of the lover who loses his bird-bride for lack of money:

> "Ah, had I been like some I see,
> Born to an evergreen nesting-tree,
> None had eyed and twitted me,
>   Cheerily mating!"

During the same year, in the uncollected **"To a Bridegroom,"** he refers to the bride as a "fine-feathered jay."

From the start, Hardy's heroines first and flit, particularly on the point of betrothal, but until we meet Sue Bridehead, we have little to mark the evolution of a specific type which might be called the bird-bride. A specific source, could have been Rosamund Tomson's title ballad, "The Bird-Bride," which Gittings connects with Tess's "vision of the weird Arctic birds." It is based on a common folk motif. Tomson's bird-bride is a grey

gull who, having assumed human shape, is abducted by an Eskimo hunter; she responds to his love and, eventually, bears him three children. Except for an occasional impulsive response to the call of the wind, she accepts exile. When, however, he breaks his word to her and, driven by hunger, slays four gulls, she turns bird again and flies off, taking the children along. It is quite likely that, while devising Sue Bridehead's character, giving her the oft-noted affinity with Shelley's blithe spirits, Hardy remembered also Rosamund Tomson's exiled bird-bride, and that he eventually decided to make this heroine into a bird, dubiously exiled and dubiously blithe.

Between **"Postponement"** (1866) and *Jude* (1895), Hardy is evidently groping for a particular elusive and coquettish type of heroine and reaching beyond conventional bird associations to suggest it. Just before turning to Sue, he had offered in *The Well-Beloved* (1894) the three Avices, whose bird name, as Michael Millgate pointed out, also "may have been a punning allusion to *The Bird-Bride.* . . ." Yet, by comparison these too were superficial character studies. "Sue is a type of woman," Hardy writes to Gosse, "which has always had an attraction for me, but the difficulty of drawing the type has kept me from attempting it till now" (*LY*, p. 42). In the concluding lines of *Under the Greenwood Tree* (1872), Fancy Day, having at last decided to marry Dick Dewey, is shown reflecting on the "secret" she will never tell him, while the nightingale overhead calls, "come hither, come hither, come hither." Fancy's secret is actually fairly innocent, and her nightingale merely evokes Arden and the fragility of human bliss. Twenty-one years later, however, coyness has yielded to pathological reticence in Hardy, and birds no longer invite men to the heart of Wessex for a carefree life. In April 1893, while working on *Jude,* Hardy notes that "a clever thrush and a stupid nightingale sing very much alike" (*LY*, p. 16). This introduces the tale of "Nat C——'s good-for-nothing grandson [who] 'turned ranter'—*i.e.* street-preacher" but was easily made to revert to type by "a girl he used to carry on with . . ." (*LY*, p. 16). A parallel in *Jude,* is Arabella's brief flirtation with the Chapel, ended when she flings away the tracts to be herself again (p. 335). We recall that her first achievement on the old course is to instruct the schoolmaster, Phillotson, about the ways of women and make him yearn for Sue's return, so that she herself might lure Jude once more. Hardy, who had chosen to associate Arabella with pigs, could not identify her as a bird also; yet she nonetheless assumed the role of the nightingale, in the colloquial sense of whore, far from stupid, calling "come hither" in a world where pastoral no longer offers an escape.

By 1893, pretty associations of maids and birds having long lost their place in his fiction, Hardy returns to them with a vengeance, creating Sue Bridehead and building, largely on what she says and does, a case against the ways of birds with men. Whatever she might owe to live models, to a certain "H. A." in the London of **"Postpone-**

ment" days, to the Sparks sisters, notably Tryphena in the Weymouth of 1870, or to Florence Henniker in the London of 1893, Hardy saw in her a chance to draw a type to which the name bird-bride might indeed apply and with which his earlier heroines had relatively innocent affinities. Sue remains forever a bride, as has been pointed out, and she is a bird from the moment we first see her flitting through Christminster till we last hear her "tears resounding through the house like a screech-owl" (p. 384) on the eve of her remarriage to Phillotson, near the end of the novel.

Hardy's design was to make the book "all contrasts . . . in its original conception" (*LY*, p. 42). Sue was to be opposed to the substantial Arabella, and, indeed, as bird, she would seem almost fleshless: "light and slight"; "There was nothing statuesque in her; all was nervous motion. She was mobile, living . . ." (p. 109); a "pretty liquid-eyed, light-footed young woman" (p. 113) whom Jude was at first content to worship from afar. On close observation, however, most of what seemed ethereal turns out to be based upon exceptional emotionality. "The voice, though positive and silvery, [was] tremulous" (p. 120). "She was so vibrant that everything she did seemed to have its source in feeling. An exciting thought would make her walk ahead so fast that he could hardly keep up with her; and her sensitiveness on some points was such that it might have been misread as vanity" (p. 122). Sue, in fact, tends to live on the verge of hysterics and to keep on an elevated plane by dramatizing the commonplace (her dramatic talent as a child in recitation of "The Raven" is one of the things noted about her: "She'd bring up the nasty carrion bird that clear . . . that you could see un a'most before your eyes" [p. 131]). But whether hysterical or merely fussy in nature, Sue's characteristic behavior pattern suggests birds: after flitting about erratically, she plunges headlong on a course, generally associated with freedom in her mind, then, timorous or exhausted, she seeks protection nearby. Hardy establishes this pattern most clearly in conjunction with her escape from the Melchester training school (duplicated later in Shaston): having flown out of the window, forded the river, and "rustle[d]" up Jude's dark stairs, Sue begs piteously for a place by his fire (p. 164). She appears "a slim and fragile being . . . pathetic in her defenselessness . . . (p. 164); as she warms up, however, she talks challengingly of herself and her life with the London undergraduate and offers her views on sex and religion. She becomes characteristically defensive. Jude notes the fact that many of her arguments are shallow, supported by an ever-ready supply of tears and tragic modulations of her voice; she has a tendency to "make such a personal matter of everything!" (p. 172). As usual, he allows himself to be dominated by feelings of tenderness toward her, but when his "faulty and tiresome little Sue" resolves they are "going to be *very* nice with each other" and looks up trustfully, her voice "trying to nestle in his breast," Jude "looked away, for that epicene tenderness of hers was too harrowing" (p. 173).

As Sue Bridehead becomes bride, her birdlike attributes assert themselves even more pronouncedly. Her flighti-

ness in the events leading to her marriage with Phillotson is defined as "perverseness": Jude must not only give her away, but satisfy her momentary whim and serve as surrogate groom. When he meets her again, after a night with Arabella, she seems by contrast his "good angel," "so ethereal a creature that her spirit could be seen trembling through her limbs . . ." (p. 207). In fact, Sue is downcast, but she will not confess to unhappiness, even when Jude confronts her with it at their aunt's funeral: "I can see you through your feathers, my poor little bird!" (p. 231). She admits her marriage was a mistake only after the rabbit episode, blaming her "cock-sureness" in the midst of ignorance (p. 236). They part on a peck, "a scarcely perceptible little kiss upon the top of his head," impulsively offered although deemed improper. For Jude, this is a turning point: "his kiss of that aerial being had seemed the purest moment of his faultful life," proof that he is ill-suited for a religious vocation (p. 237). Characteristically, he burns his theology books and veers on a new course. No less characteristically, the kiss makes Sue retreat or, rather, flutter about: she reviews the incident "with tears in her eyes" (p. 239), then, applying what Hardy calls her "extraordinary" logic to it, she takes the blame on herself, readies punishment for Jude, and, very contrite, offers her husband a partial confession by way of atonement (p. 240). The meeting with Jude, nonetheless, let her face up to her situation. By midnight, she has deserted the conjugal chamber and "made a little nest for herself in the very cramped quarters" of a closet under the stairway which she refuses to vacate (p. 241). The next morning, looking at the spider webs over the "little nest where she had lain," Phillotson realizes how great her aversion to him must be "when it is stronger than her fear of spiders!" (p. 242). He first offers her separate quarters but, eventually, agrees to let her go after she once more takes the avian way out, leaping out of the window when he mistakenly comes to her room (p. 247). Their last meal together leaves a permanent image "imprinted upon his vision; that look of her as she glided into the parlour to tea; a slim flexible figure; a face, strained from its roundness, and marked by the pallors of restless days and nights . . ." (p. 254).

Hardy repeatedly underlines Sue's pathological aversion to her husband and offers it as grounds for her flight out of the window in Shaston. Sue herself, however, attributes it to fright caused by a bad dream, to being awakened suddenly in a large house whose doors will not lock. . . . She sublimates this very rapidly. By the time she stands in The George, having learned it is the hotel where Jude recently spent the night with Arabella, she claims to have been betrayed and repeats: "*I* jumped out of the window!" (p. 264); her flight asserted commitment to higher values, whereas he merely yielded to base passions.

One finds only a slight departure from the bird analogy when Hardy presents a "ghostly" Sue, flitting in like a moth (p. 269), to the bedside of the ailing Phillotson and fussing about him "with a childlike, repentant kindness, as if she could not do too much for him" (pp. 270-71); on leaving, "she put her hand in his—or rather allowed it to flit through his; for she was significantly light in touch" (p. 271). The bird analogy returns dominant, however, when Arabella's reappearance on the scene determines Sue to share Jude's bed. "'The little bird is caught at last!' she said, a sadness showing in her smile. 'No—only nested,' he assured her" (p. 287). Nesting, for Sue, merely implies settling down, as opposed to marriage which would mean reentering the cage. Against Arabella's advice, she talks Jude out of marriage, and, as they walk away from the parish-clerk's office, she recites to him the end of Thomas Campbell's "Song":

> Can you keep the bee from ranging,
> Or the ring-dove's neck from changing?
> No! Nor fettered love [from dying
> In the knot there's no untying]
>
> (p. 291).

(The last line, which Hardy used as a recurrent theme throughout his works, is left implied in *Jude*.)

Talk of marriage and a permanent bond invariably elicits a frightened, birdlike response from Sue. Thus, before leaving one more time to marry Jude at the Superintendent Registrar's Office, her "nervousness intensified": "'Jude, I want you to kiss me, as a lover, incorporeally,' she said, tremulously nestling up to him, with damp lashes. 'It won't be ever like this any more will it!'" (p. 302). But even when free of stress, at idyllic moments like their visit to the Great Wessex Agricultural Show, she is a bird: "Sue, in her new summer clothes, flexible and light as a bird, her little thumb stuck up by the stem of her white cotton sunshade, went along as if she hardly touched ground, and as if a moderately strong puff of wind would float her over the hedge into the next field" (p. 311). Arabella, who observes her unseen, calls her, with matronly disdain, "a slim fidgetty little thing . . . (p. 313); and Hardy underlines the contrast: whereas Sue fidgets and flits, Arabella and Cartlett "saunter" (pp. 310, 315).

Even in her own mind, Sue associates herself with the trapped little bird. Characteristically, she keeps a pair of pigeons for pets, and when they are sold at the auction to a butcher, for "a nice pie," she frees them, then regrets her act: "It was so foolish of me! O why should Nature's law be mutual butchery!" Jude, who early in his career had similarly questioned the natural scheme over the rooks, and learned it was to no avail, now knows he can only try to compensate the butcher (p. 327). Little Father Time, however, takes careful note of the "law," and when he later hears from Sue confirmation of his own suspicion that "It would be better to be out o' the world than in it" (p. 352), he acts on the information. While he is hanging the younger children, then himself, his father, who had failed to nest his brood the previous night and who must meet with Sue in separate quarters, is addressing her as kindly as ever: "Have breakfast with me now you are here, my bird. . . . There will be plenty of time to get back and prepare the children's meal before they wake" (p. 354).

When Sue overcomes the initial shock of her children's death and substitutes unquestionable dogma for her "enlightened" views, she is not as inconsistent as Jude claims. To the contrary, by temperament, she had all along been better suited for Victorian constraints than for rebellion against them; she had clung to Mill with almost religious fervor, and a great deal of fetishism had already attended her rituals to Venus and Apollo in defiance of the "pale Galilean" (p. 115). Despite her occasional flight for freedom, she had been all along a timorous type of bird, savoring the retreat at least as much as the adventure and ever-ready to assume a contrite and pathetic stance to gain sympathy. Her ultimate choice of the safety of a confining marriage, that is, of the cage which she had still then sought to escape, is not surprising, and it is probably not altogether condemnable in Hardy's view; one recalls his note on April 25, 1893, during the composition of *Jude,* wondering why Fear should not be idealized, "which is a higher consciousness, and based on a deeper insight" than courage (*LY,* p. 17). She is actually very lucid in the process of retreat and, like Jude, she is apt to generalize from her own predicament to the condition of women as a whole. He contrasts her "old logic" with her present "extraordinary blindness" and wonders: "Is it peculiar to you, or is it common to woman? Is a woman a thinking unit at all, or a fraction always wanting its integer?" (p. 371). Sue, however, argues that she has merely come to "see the light at last" (p. 371), and generalizes from her own frigid reticence to the relative position of the sexes: "An average woman is in this superior to an average man—that she never instigates, only responds. We ought to have lived in mental communion, and no more" (p. 372). Yet she admits she knew all along that assuming a submissive posture is in itself an exercise of powers.

> "At first I did not love you, Jude; that I own. When I first knew you I merely wanted you to love me. I did not exactly flirt with you; but that inborn craving which undermines some women's morals almost more than unbridled passion—the craving to attract and captivate, regardless of the injury it may do the man—was in me; and when I found I had caught you, I was frightened. And then—I don't know how it was—I couldn't bear to let you go—possibly to Arabella again—and so I got to love you, Jude. But you see, however fondly it ended, it began in the selfish and cruel wish to make your heart ache for me without letting mine ache for you" (p. 373).

Instead of justifying her behavior in terms of personal preference or, as she had increasingly tended to do, in terms of her "wickedness," Sue now attributes it to women in general. Again, she is not inconsistent, and she does not differ much from Jude in recognizing overwhelming forces in nature and society and unbreakable laws that govern intercourse among men and women; she is only more ready than ever to accept and to justify them. Oddly enough, but very much in keeping with her repentant stance, she now presents herself not as the freedom-loving little bird whom Jude and others would catch and confine, but as the one who herself had an inborn "craving to attract and captivate" and who, though frightened, could not stop preying or let the prey go once he was caught.

As indicated, Sue's career as bird goes on until the end of the novel. Even as she is crying "like a screech-owl" on the eve of her remarriage to Phillotson, we hear, Gillingham, nearby, reminding his friend that he had always objected to "opening the cage-door and letting the bird go in such an obviously suicidal way" (p. 385). Then following her last flutter before Jude in the Marygreen church, Sue comes to her husband's chamber bringing her body as ultimate offering, in order to reverse, as she says, her flight out of the window at Shaston (p. 415).

Hardy claimed to have written a novel about the conflict between flesh and spirit; yet the thought that he was exposing the awesome and often nefarious powers of women must have crossed his mind, as evidenced by the epigram for the first part of the book:

> "Yea, many there be that have run out of their wits for women, and become servants for their sakes. Many also have perished, have erred, and sinned, for women. . . . O ye men, how can it be but women should be strong, seeing they do thus?"— ESDRAS

Every one of the epigrams Hardy set at the beginning of the sections prior to publication in book form was carefully chosen. This particular one he abstracted from Esdras 4:26-32, which is the account of a contest among Darius's bodyguards to identify the greatest power in the land. The first guard argues for wine, the second for the King; the winner is the third, Zerubbabel, who argues that women have the most awesome strength, overwhelmed only by Truth.

The wiles of women, however, and their abuse of their power over men are not only the subject of the novel's first part: they are discussed all along, just as advice on how to deal with women is offered throughout. One is sometimes tempted to view *Jude* as Hardy's contribution to the bourgeois side in the *querelle des femmes,* an illustration of the ways of maids with men, bearing an undeniably misogynous bias. It is as though at some rudimentary level he had sought to balance out the sufferings of Tess, his "pure woman," at the hands of villainous men, by offering the sufferings of his good man and "simpleton" at the hands of bad women.

Though obviously no simple attitude emerges, the perspective offered in *Jude* is not flattering, and the rather pejorative association of women with birds is precisely what it seems to suggest. Women are flighty, deceptive, self-centered; they exploit mercilessly the passions which they arouse in men; and they are guided solely by their narrow self-interest. As indicated already, Hardy's heroines had been coquettes from the first: even the most innocent, like Tess and Marty South, had their moments of vanity. Very early, with Bathsheba in *Far from the Madding Crowd* (1874), women's games with men revealed their lethal potential. Hardy's women had feigned helplessness to achieve their ends long before Sue, and they had arrayed seductive devices long before Arabella (one needs only recall Mrs. Charmond, who enhances her charms with false locks in *Woodlanders*). Sue and Arabella, however, become incarnations of women's power over men. Sue, the epicene, is the promise followed only by frustration; Arabella responds, but knows only her own interest. Sue adopts evasion as a life style; Arabella makes seduction into a crude profession. The coquette turns *cocotte*. In *Woodlanders,* Suke Damson (a nighthawk) still makes a pretence of confused identities and intended escape; but Arabella, with her cochin's egg, makes none whatever. Hardy presents her as the modern Delilah who sublimates neither her appetite nor her self-interest: Phillotson becomes a pawn in her hands, and, seated next to her, the obscure Jude can only ironically be likened to sunlike Samson. Jude as a victim of his kindness to women elicits sympathy; but he is characterized by "weaknesses" of a kind that topples no Philistine temples.

Had it been published a century earlier, Hardy's novel might have been entitled *Jude or the Rewards of Kindness*. It is fashionable to read into it innovation and to demonstrate how Hardy was ahead of his time. But it is just as easy, and probably more accurate, to note that his last novel was very traditional, not only because it used an Everyman for protagonist and his progress for story, but because it developed episodically around a simplistic argument: kindness does not pay. Jude is pronounced fatally weak from the start because he cannot hurt anything, because he has kindness to excess. To be sure, kindness is not his only weakness of character, but it is chief, and the others are generally made to seem related. Jude is unable to overcome it for reasons which Hardy suggests are temperamental and hereditary. Indeed, even after losing nearly all in his disastrous marriage to Arabella, and after renouncing Sue and giving her away to a man she cannot possibly love, Jude wonders about the order of things but does not doubt his own actions: "Is it," he said, "that the women are to blame; or is it the artificial system of things, under which the normal sex-impulses are turned into devilish domestic gins and springes to noose and hold back those who want to progress?" (p. 238). Though seemingly aware now of his vulnerability before women, he remains unwilling and unable to turn his back on their plight: he takes in the escaping Sue, and, a while later, he rushes to help Arabella, because "she's a woman . . . an erring, careless, unreflecting fellow-creature" (pp. 284-85). For his troubles, he earns a fairly contemptuous appreciation from the latter: "Never such a tender fool as Jude is if a woman seems in trouble and coaxes him a bit! Just as he used to be about birds and things" (p. 289). He confirms this very soon by relieving her of the burden of Little Father Time. Eventually, he even accepts Sue's fastidiousness in everything relating to marriage and sex; and though it makes him wonder about women's intellectual capacity, he accepts her retreat into religion and her return to Phillotson, agreeing that "The woman mostly gets the worst of it in the long run" (p. 373). Then, when Arabella stands beneath his window asking to be taken in, out of the rain, and saved from prostitution or the workhouse, Jude consents, as he will consent to marry her again, most ironically, to save her "honor." Even drunk, he rants about kindness and duty to birds: "I'd marry the W——of Babylon rather than do anything dishonourable! . . . I have never behaved dishonourably to a woman or to any living thing. I am not a man who wants to save himself at the expense of the weaker among us!" (pp. 401-2). On his deathbed we still hear him making excuses for women in general and for Sue in particular: "Strange difference of sex, that time and circumstance, which enlarge the views of most men, narrow the views of women almost invariably" (p. 419). The excuses, of course, must serve him as well: "the time was not ripe for us!" (p. 419). Ironically, while he consoles himself and delights Mrs. Edlin with musings on the ways of birds, Arabella pours Vilbert his own "distillation of the juices of doves' hearts," telling herself in the process: "Well! Weak women must provide for a rainy day" (p. 421).

Hardy sets Arabella's views and most of her actions in direct opposition with those of Jude. He even allows her to elevate practical crassness to the level of doctrine, and to preach it to a very humble and attentive student, Phillotson. It turns out that Jude's former mentor, who had practiced kindness with Sue and then defended his acts so vehemently in Shaston that he was dismissed from his post and forced back to the Marygreen schoolhouse from where he had started, has not fatally committed himself to being good. Even though he still argues he had done "only what was right, and just, and moral" (pp. 336-37), he is in fact ready to learn from Arabella, especially after she tells him he had "dirt[ied his] own nest" (p. 337). "There's nothing like bondage and a stone deaf taskmaster for taming . . . women," she tells him, adding that in imposing bondage he would even have had divine law on his side. Phillotson must admit that, indeed, "Cruelty is the law pervading all nature and society; and we can't get out of it if we would!" (p. 338). He still claims ignorance of womankind on parting, but, when the opportunity arises, he shows that Arabella's teaching was not wasted on him: he has learned to seek out his interests above his convictions and, hence, to "make use" of Sue's new "views," even though they are not his (p. 378). He will "let crude loving-kindness take care of itself" (p. 379) and be wary of women since they "are so strange in their influence, that they tempt you to misplaced kindness" (p. 386). Indeed, his friend Gillingham, who had all along advised against "opening the cage-door," now wonders whether "the reactionary spirit induced by the world's sneers and his own physical wishes would make Phillotson more orthodoxly cruel to [Sue] than he had erstwhile been informally and perversely kind" (p. 386).

Kindness and cruelty, which on a simplistic level are consistently opposed in the novel, are also shown to be ill-defined and easily reversible in weak men like Phillotson. In Hardy's view of evolution, likewise, the thrust to altruism is forever threatened by reversion to egotism. What is remarkable in *Jude the Obscure* is that, despite a very rudimentary philosophy and psychology for background, and despite the intrusion of petty biases growing out of personal experience, Hardy was able to write a novel in which the reader's impulse to classify and to judge, which is encouraged by the presentation, is frustrated at every turn by the obvious complexity of the issues and the depth of the characters. The device of pairing that Hardy acknowledged is, in fact, largely effective because it makes for comparisons and contrasts which are so facile that they must seem inadequate. As has often been pointed out, the contrast between Arabella and Sue, Jude and Arabella, Jude and Phillotson, or any other pair in the novel, is undermined by close resemblance between them. Similarly, the thematic pair of kindness and cruelty would seem to be parallel with the pair of spirit and flesh; yet spirit, throughout, proves unkind, and cruelty of flesh is made hard to condemn; always, "what was good for God's birds was bad for God's gardener . . ." (p. 36).

The bird motif examined here belongs to the whole array of devices used by Hardy to schematize his plot. They simplify only on the surface. The reader is confirmed in what he anticipates from the ambiguous designation of bird as it is applied to Sue; and yet he finds himself uncomfortable with the conventionally misogynous views suggested. Sue and Arabella appear to share a common ground as birds, and even as brides, but they obviously differ in their main personality traits; and Jude's kindness to them is misplaced only in a very narrow sense, that is, to the extent that we can identify kindness with naiveté and hence condemn it. On the whole, in the interaction between humans and birds, conventional associations seem to hold, but they often do so ironically, and, as a rule, what they suggest is too complex to formulate. The child, Jude, who robs nests but then lies awake until he can return, also feels fatefully akin to birds. The rook episode demonstrates that this kinship means vulnerability. Indeed, birds will eventually allow themselves to be caught by the adult Jude, but they will trap him in the process. A cochin hen's egg, "hatching" in Arabella's bosom, confirms his seduction and a feigned pregnancy clinches his marriage. The distinction between "caught" and "nested" is tenuous here. Sue yields to Jude only before the threat of Arabella. But even Vilbert, a professional bird catcher devoid of kindness, allows himself to be caught by Arabella, using for excuse the efficacy of his own dove philtre (p. 315). Like the Aeschylean world of the *Agamemnon,* which is never far back in Hardy's mind, the world of *Jude the Obscure* is inhabited by men and women, who, although they are vaguely aware of being caught in the net of fate, plot their way through life either by setting traps for others or by figuring out ways for getting out of the trap in which they find themselves. Taking kindness to birds for a theme, Hardy may well have tried to offer the fabulist's view to mitigate this spectacle.

Carol Edwards and Duane Edwards (essay date 1981)

SOURCE: "*Jude the Obscure*: A Psychoanalytic Study", in *University of Hartford: Studies in Literature,* Vol. 13, No. 1, 1981, pp. 78-90.

[*In the following essay, Edwards and Edwards interpret the unconscious motivations of Jude, arguing that he "fails ultimately because he is too rational and too controlled."*]

When Thomas Hardy wrote *Jude the Obscure,* he hoped that the novel would be "cathartic," but it isn't. Despite the fact that Jude becomes increasingly rational and, in some important ways, comes to know himself, the ending offers no consolation, no purgation. Instead, it fizzles out before Jude can discover answers to the questions which baffle him. So the elevation of feeling which accompanies Oedipus's discovery of the awful truth is replaced, in *Jude the Obscure,* with depression.

Attempts to explain Jude's string of failures and, consequently, the depressing ending, generally focus on Jude's passion or on what Hardy himself called "the opposing environment." Both are overwhelming and destructive, many critics maintain; both practically guarantee that Jude will fail. But in reality Jude escapes from his environment repeatedly; he leaves Marygreen, leaves Christminster, leaves Melchester, leaves Shaston, and leaves Aldbrickham. And he is by no means the victim of his passion. In fact, the very opposite is true. Jude fails ultimately because he is too rational and too controlled.

Of course the opposing environment is important. Victorian morality, rigid divorce laws, Jude's poverty, family background, and rules governing entrance to Christminster all contribute something to Jude's unhappiness. And Jude does have several outbursts which seem to be the expression of emotion. He gets drunk, fornicates, and tries to commit suicide. But drinking is Jude's defense against his real feelings; fornication with Arabella is drive discharge only: it is not accompanied by tenderness or any other personal feeling; and even the attempted suicide is carried out with virtually no affect—that is, with a lack of the emotional response appropriate to the situation. In fact, Jude does little more than muse over the fact that he tried to take his own life.

Of course Jude has other outbursts. For example, he is fervent when he addresses the crowd on Remembrance Day (392-94) and angry when he recites the Nicene Creed in a bar (142-45) [page numbers refer to the Anniversary edition of *Jude the Obscure,* 1920]. But such outbursts should not be confused with those expressions of emotion which are curative or at least therapeutic. As Oedipus demonstrates, anger and suffering can purge when they are the emotional working through of repressed thoughts and impulses. But Jude's outbursts are not authentic: they have virtually nothing to do with what Jude consciously believes prompts them. Instead, they

are the result of an accumulation of memories and produce what is called, in psychoanalytic terms, "flooding in the ideational field." As such they are defense mechanisms rather than healthy expressions of feeling. Consequently, these outbursts leave Jude frustrated and depressed, but they do not subvert reason. In fact, they leave Jude free to exercise reason again and again, often to his disadvantage.

Although Jude reasons well and even assesses his position in life with extreme accuracy a number of times, he suffers a great deal, remains confused and depressed, experiences defeat frequently, and dies at an early age. Nevertheless, Hardy's readers persist in assuming that reason always works to an individual's advantage and passion to his disadvantage in the Wessex novels. Consistent with this, F. B. Pinion says [in *Thomas Hardy: Art and Thought,* 1977]: "Only when a person is not swayed by emotions or prejudices, when he is open to reason, is he capable of exercising freedom of choice." But *Jude the Obscure* illustrates that reason, like passion, can distort the truth and, furthermore, that an idea (or ideal) untainted by affect can be a prejudice. The novel also illustrates that an individual cannot make the choices that are right for him unless he is influenced by his mind and his emotions simultaneously, unless he is able to express not only his ideas (motives) but also the feelings that should accompany these ideas.

Since *Jude the Obscure* is a novel that Hardy began during the 80s, but published five years after *Tess of the d'Urbervilles,* it is easy to understand why Hardy's readers generally assume that Jude is destroyed by passion. After all, Tess succumbs to "reveries" repeatedly. In doing so, she ceases to use reason or exert her will, she is ruled by passion, and subsequently suffers. But Jude is not Tess. He is, in fact, as ideal as she is passionate. For this reason he sees Sue as "almost an ideality" (114) and has no difficulty rationalizing his relationship with her. He calls her "a kindly star, an elevating power, a companion in Anglican worship, a tender friend" (105). He is the victim of reason, of his ability to deal rationally with what is essentially a matter of passion.

There can be no doubt that Jude is attracted to Sue physically. He himself knows that his interest in her is "unmistakably of a sexual kind" (114). But this does not mean that Jude is overwhelmed by lust or even that his feeling for Sue is strong and healthy. In fact, Jude believes that his passion is "unauthorized" and requires a "cure" (114). He also describes his developing interest in Sue as "immoral" (114). As a result, he checks his impulses. For long periods of time he abstains entirely from sex. His interest in Sue continues to be physical, but his control is so strict and his conscience so severe that he does not act on his instincts. Even during those periods when they do make love, Jude continues to desire Sue not because he is so passionate but because she withholds herself even during love-making and, as a result, never satisfies him.

Why, then, does Jude tolerate Sue? To begin with, she is an intelligent, attractive, and unique person. At the same time she is very much like Jude. Detecting this, Phillotson says: "'They seem to be one person split in two!'" (276). And later the narrator observes that their "complete mutual understanding, in which every glance and movement was as effectual as speech for conveying intelligence between them, made them almost the two parts of a single whole" (352). But both the narrator and Phillotson fail to observe that Jude does not distinguish mentally between the two halves, between Sue and himself. In fact, Sue's wishes become his. At one point he tells her that they will marry whenever she chooses (331) and, later, says: "'Still, *anything* that pleases you will please me'" (343). In brief, Jude does not distinguish clearly between himself and the object of his love. He must, therefore, tolerate her indifference and cruelty since to reject her is to reject a portion of himself.

Jude's failure to distinguish sharply between himself and Sue suggests that his love for her is essentially narcissistic. This is reinforced in the novel in a number of ways. To begin with, Jude loves a cousin rather than someone who is in no way like him. Secondly, even when he barely knows her, he dreads being separated from her: "A cold sweat overspread Jude at the news that she was going away" (116). Fearful of losing a part of himself, he experiences anxiety. Finally, like the typical narcissist, he relies heavily on vision, sustains a belief in its power, and seeks to control his environment by means of sight.

Jude's reliance on sight is especially obvious in his relationship with Sue. Initially he prefers only to look at her, "to gain a further view of her" (106). In fact, he is "glad" that he can look at her without being detected, so he decides that "To see her, and to be himself unseen and unknown, was enough for him at present" (106). Of course he confronts her eventually, but he continues to watch her from a distance at times, from a window for example (247-48). Furthermore, even after his relationship with her has developed considerably, "his ardent affection for her" burns, significantly, "in his eyes" (284).

Why does Jude rely so heavily on seeing? The answer to this question is complicated. To begin with, Jude is ambivalent about sex. He wants sexual intercourse because his abstinence creates a strong need; however, because sex makes him feel disgusted, guilty, and ashamed, he also does not want it. He adjusts to this ambivalence by selecting Sue, a sexless woman he regards as "bodiless" (313), "almost a divinity" (174), and "a sort of fay, or sprite—not a woman" (426). But his natural desire to have sex asserts itself despite Sue's lack of physicality. As a result, Jude needs a substitute for sex. As the following passage illustrates, this substitute is seeing:

> Jude left in the afternoon, hopelessly unhappy. But he had seen her, and sat with her. Such intercourse as that would have to content him for the remainder of his life. The lesson of renunciation it was proper that he, as a parish priest, should learn (190).

Acting in character, Jude is ready, perhaps even eager, to be celibate and to accept looking at Sue as the only "intercourse" he will have for the rest of his life.

Jude's reliance on sight is stressed often in the novel. He reads a great deal, strains his eyes, sees Arabella initially with his "intellectual eye" (46), and climbs a tower to gaze at Christminster, the city of his dreams. Furthermore, as a result of gazing at various objects, he derives what is called, in psychoanalytic terms, "libidinous gratification." Thus even before he sees Sue, he sees Christminster and reacts in the following way:

> He was getting so romantically attached to Christminster that, like a young lover alluding to his mistress, he felt bashful at mentioning its name again (22).

His response to Christminster is similar to his response to Sue. Not surprisingly, then, Jude sees a halo above Christminster and above Sue's photograph when he looks at them. Both the city and the woman are idealized—even spiritualized—by young Jude. But Sue is a female nevertheless and, as an old man tells Jude, "'there's wenches in the streets [of Christminster] o'nights'" (23). So Jude will have to work hard to accomplish what he accomplished during the early stages of his affair with Arabella when he kept "his impassioned doings a secret almost from himself" (54).

He tries and he succeeds. Using idealization and rationalization, he is able to tolerate anticipated "instinctual experience." In fact, he is able to control all feelings to the extent that control itself becomes his problem. Eventually he is unable to express feelings which are appropriate to a given situation or person. He cannot resent Arabella (223, 473). He wants to "annihilate" his rival Phillotson but, the narrator says, "his action did not respond for a moment to his animal instinct" (196). In brief, Jude is eventually so rational, so controlled, that he responds without affect. Governed exclusively by reason, he decides logically and, it seems, inevitably, to let himself die. In doing so, he does what at one level he wanted to do all the while. As D. H. Lawrence observed, "That was his obsession. That was his craving: to have nothing to do with his own life."

And yet, in one sense, Jude, like Oedipus, approaches the truth about himself more and more closely as the novel progresses. In fact, Hardy's narrator emphasizes that in a number of ways. He cites Jude's rally or recovery after each setback and, more important, records Jude's "mental estimates" of himself and his situation in life. In fact, the novel is centered on a series of "estimates" which are more accurate, more nearly founded on fact and the eventual revealed truth, than are Oedipus's appraisals of his own condition. For example, at the end of Part Fifth, Jude acknowledges that he will never enter Christminster but admits, too, that the university remains "the centre of the universe" to him because of his early dream (386). Here and elsewhere he courageously accepts the awful truth about himself.

But Jude's responses differ from Oedipus's in ways that explain why Jude declines and Oedipus rises to heroic stature. To begin with, Oedipus confronts Creon, Teiresias, and the shepherd. As a result, he, like a patient being psychoanalyzed, learns to acknowledge and to express his emotions with an intensity he could not experience at the beginning of the play. In contrast, Jude makes each "mental estimate of his progress so far" either to himself or to a crowd and is not challenged. Not surprisingly, he speaks without affect, deflects his real feelings with rhetoric, and makes mental leaps from an unrecovered past into an unrealized future. In doing so, he escapes from the present and, consequently, from the need to acknowledge or act on his real feelings. Relying on facts, he does not interpret.

Since Jude does not interpret, he fails to recover his repressed feelings. He becomes more and more conscious of himself and his surroundings but fails to develop emotionally. As Lawrence said [in *Phoenix,* 1936], Jude "dragged his body after his consciousness. But change is theoretically possible all the while. So at given moments in the novel it appears that Jude could, but won't, free himself from what plagues him; however, in retrospect it seems that Jude was fated all the while to suffer and to die.

Significantly, Jude feels he is destined to fail and to be unhappy. And no wonder. After all, his Aunt Drusilla tells him repeatedly that he (like Oedipus) is part of a doomed family, and people such as Farmer Troutham convince him that he is worthless. So Jude learns to anticipate failure and is even "piqued" into action (33) and "illuminated" by it (80). Consistent with this, he aims for success only in the distant future. For example, he prepares for Christminster by going through the long process of studying Greek and Latin and later establishes 30 as the proper age for becoming a clergyman. So the possibility of success does nothing except enervate him in the present. Furthermore, he cannot receive stimulation from outside sources since he does not distinguish between himself and the external world. The world is a projection of his own mind. In fact, when he is only eleven, the landscape is already an emblem of his mind and the birds seem, "like himself, to be living in a world which did not want them" (11). He even identifies with trees that are cut down and earthworms that are stepped on (13). In brief, Jude projects his own pessimistic fatalism onto the physical world. Thus he is trapped from within and without. As a result, that change which is theoretically possible becomes, in actuality, impossible.

Jude's relationship with his parents helps to explain why he is so hopelessly trapped. To begin with, his mother abandoned him when he was a baby and shortly afterwards committed suicide. As a result, Jude does not learn to relate tenderness and sensuality. That's why he responds without affection to sensual Arabella and without passion to spiritual Sue.

Jude's relationship with his father is more difficult to explain. Jude lived with him for a while in South Wessex

and can recall that his father did not speak of his mother "till his dying day." But virtually nothing else is known about Mr. Fawley. Nevertheless, it's clear that Jude needs a male to emulate. This need is reflected in his imitation of Phillotson and in his desire to follow in the footsteps of an uncle he has never met (37).

Significantly, Jude does not attempt to emulate his father. He simply does not want to compete with him. (This is consistent with his unconscious desire to fail or at least to delay success.) But he does feel rivalry. Speaking to Sue at Melchester, he reveals his conflict. Like his father, he wants to be a parent, but he does not want to be involved in the act of procreation. He tells Sue that he would "gladly" live with her "as a fellow-lodger and friend, even on the most distant terms" (211), but there would be children nevertheless. Behaving characteristically, Jude "projected his mind into the future, and saw her with children more or less in her own likeness around her" (212). Rationalizing, he decides that such children would be a "continuation of her identity," but he reiterates that he would like a child that is "hers solely." Then the narrator says: "And then he again uneasily saw, as he had latterly seen with more and more frequency, the scorn of Nature for man's finer emotions, and her lack of interest in his aspirations" (212).

Clearly Jude is again rationalizing. He views his reluctance to have sex with Sue as one of "man's finer emotions." Furthermore, searching for the cause of his failure, he blames Nature which, like fate or bad luck in general, is a substitute for the rivalrous father in the male child's mind.

But of course Jude is unconscious of all this as, perhaps, Hardy himself was. Then, too, because Jude merely fantasizes, he cannot recover repressed feeling. After all, the person who fantasizes is responding purely intellectually; he is thinking without becoming involved bodily; he is using intellectualizing as a defense mechanism—as the means of fleeing from reality. And, all the while, he reinforces repression.

So Jude makes accurate mental estimates of his progress in life, makes shrewd comments about the human condition in general, and rationalizes in a consistent, coherent manner. But he does not express the emotion that is appropriate to his ideal love for Sue. He does not because he cannot: he is the victim of too much thought, too much reason, too much conscious control. This, not passion, is his affliction.

William R. Goetz (essay date 1983)

SOURCE: "The Felicity and Infelicity of Marriage in *Jude the Obscure,*" in *Nineteenth-Century Fiction,* Vol. 38, No. 2, 1983, pp. 189-213.

[*In the following essay, Goetz explores elements of* Jude the Obscure *that form a critique of marriage.*]

Matrimony have growed to be that serious in these days that one really do feel afeard to move in it at all. In my time we took it more careless; and I don't know that we was any the worse for it!

—the Widow Edlin in *Jude the Obscure*

When *Jude the Obscure* was published in 1895, it was interpreted in many quarters as Hardy's contribution to the growing contemporary debate on the "marriage question." The prominence of the public debate, as well as Hardy's candid and even sensational treatment of marriage and sex in his novel, tended to draw attention to this aspect of the work rather than to the other theme that Hardy apparently had in mind when he first conceived *Jude,* the educational one. In a letter of 10 November 1895 to his friend Edmund Gosse, Hardy expressed surprise at the way the novel was being received: "It is curious that some of the papers should look upon the novel as a manifesto on 'the marriage question' (although of course, it involves it)." Hardy's suggestion here that *Jude* is not *about* marriage as a social theme in the way the reviewers understood, yet does "involve" marriage, is amplified in his 1912 "Postscript" to the novel, which requires lengthier quotation:

> The marriage laws being used in great part as the tragic machinery of the tale, and its general drift on the domestic side tending to show that, in Diderot's words, the civil law should be only the enunciation of the law of nature (a statement that requires some qualification, by the way), I have been charged since 1895 with a large responsibility in this country for the present "shop-soiled" condition of the marriage theme (as a learned writer characterized it the other day). I do not know. My opinion at that time, if I remember rightly, was what it is now, that a marriage should be dissolvable as soon as it becomes a cruelty to either of the parties—being then essentially and morally no marriage—and it seemed a good foundation for the fable of a tragedy. (Norton *Jude,* pp. 6-7)

By calling the marriage laws his "machinery," Hardy suggests, as he did in the letter to Gosse, that the institution of marriage is important to the novel but only as a means, not as an end; the end is "tragedy" itself. The statement does admit, though, that the novel's theme has to do with marriage laws, and specifically that the novel seeks to call into question the institution of marriage on the grounds of natural morality. Hardy's opinion that a marriage based on "cruelty" is "essentially and morally no marriage" implies that the novel refers to two different notions of marriage. Civil marriage sanctioned by society may find itself at variance with a more natural form of marriage, one that does not depend on social conventions to validate it. This implicit distinction between two conceptions of marriage is based on the explicit distinction between "civil law" and the "law of nature." Ideally, the relation between these two laws is not so much one of opposition as of "enunciation," wherein the human code of law articulates or speaks the law of nature, which remains dumb. We must not, however, overlook Hardy's

parenthetical comment that this model of enunciation, attributed here to Diderot, is in need of "some qualification"—a qualification that Hardy does not supply but which the novel itself, as I shall argue, will supply for him. The Postscript, in any case, promptly forgets the need for "qualification" and proceeds to an attractively straightforward conclusion concerning the novel's theme. If civil marriage deviates from the law of nature by becoming cruel, it "should be dissolvable," presumably through divorce or annulment. The novel would demonstrate the perversion of a marriage that strays from the laws of nature into cruelty and yet cannot be corrected through divorce. Paradoxically, it would be the very lack of authority, or the groundlessness, of such a marriage that would provide the "foundation" for Hardy's own tragic work.

But this is, of course, far from an accurate description of what happens in *Jude,* and Hardy is certainly justified in arguing that his novel is no manifesto of this kind. What is striking in the novel is precisely the rapidity with which both Jude's and Sue's marriages are terminated at the beginning of Part v (though, as we shall see, one of these divorces is based on a mistake). This availability of divorce sets *Jude* off from Hardy's earlier treatment of the same problem in *The Woodlanders* (1887), where Grace's inability to obtain a divorce from Fitzpiers turns a potentially comic ending into a much more somber one. In *Jude,* Hardy goes one step farther by allowing divorce to occur, but then shows that it offers no lasting solution, so that the novel can conclude only after both protagonists have reentered marriages with their original partners in a sort of grotesque parody of the conventionally happy ending of the earlier English novel. Instead of chronicling a reassuring move from a corrupt civil state back to a natural one, then, the novel insists on the instability of both these states, and on the seemingly necessary return to a condition of marriage whose spiritual bankruptcy and cruelty have already been conclusively exposed.

Thus the opposition between marriage and divorce, in which divorce is seen as the antidote to a cruel marriage, already breaks down, and the relation between the two states becomes much more problematic. The whole novel, Hardy wrote to Gosse, was to be constructed on "contrasts," the foremost of which the author defined in his original preface as "a deadly war waged between flesh and spirit" (Norton *Jude,* p. 5). These contrasts, though, as we shall see, are not so much relations of mutual exclusion, when one term is to be preferred to the other, as they are double binds, when the inadequacy of one term gives way only to the inadequacy of the other. Such will be the structure of Hardy's "tragedy." Marriage finds its place in this tragedy not only as a social theme but as an institution whose form lends itself to the shape of the novel Hardy is trying to write.

To see how the structure works, and specifically to see how marriage functions, let us return to the basic opposition between "civil law" and "law of nature." Throughout the novel Jude and Sue will dwell in a constant state of tension between these two terms, debating the significance and the viability of both from the standpoint they occupy at the moment. Their continual dialogue on these questions is itself a reflection of the fact that the civil law may be nothing but an "enunciation" of the law of nature. The civil law is represented primarily in the form of a *language,* and as such it both sets itself off from but also (ideally) connects itself to the law of nature, which it articulates. What does it mean for human law, and especially the marriage laws, to be conceived as a language? In this novel it means at least two distinct things.

First, it means that the law is literally a kind of language that names its objects—"literally," as when we speak of "the letter of the law." The law here is associated with denomination and literalism. Most importantly, it becomes the "letter [that] killeth," the letter from II Corinthians 3:6 that Hardy chose as epigraph for his novel. Interestingly, the second half of this quotation— "the spirit [that] giveth life"—is omitted by Hardy both when it appears as epigraph and when Jude quotes it again toward the close of the novel (VI, 8). Hardy's refusal to quote the redemptive half of Paul's formula may well prove significant, but if for the moment we take the epigraph to be pointing to the familiar opposition between letter and spirit, then we have a new version of an opposition which is almost identical to that between "flesh" and "spirit" and which also seems to link up to that between the state of civil society and the state of nature. In this scheme the positive value is ascribed to the spirit and to the state of nature, while the letter of the law becomes the emblem of what is wrong with institutionalized society.

Acting as a letter, the law names its objects: persons and forms of behavior. But the law also functions linguistically in a second way: it not only names but dictates, prescribes, or constitutes its objects. As is well known, legal language lends itself readily to a *speech act* theory of language, because it is so frequently performative, rather than constative, in its function. Legal language—or again, for our purposes, the language of the marriage contract in particular—is so clearly performative that it furnishes the very first example of a speech act in J. L. Austin's *How To Do Things With Words,* the work that founded speech act theory:

> Examples:
>
> (E. *a*) "I do (sc. take this woman to be my lawful wedded wife)"—as uttered in the course of the marriage ceremony.

According to Austin's initial definitions, a performative utterance, for which the marriage oath furnishes the paradigm, is a kind of language that does not point to a state of affairs (as a "constative" utterance does) but *creates* or constitutes the state of affairs through the act of the utterance itself. Consequently, performatives cannot be judged to be true or false (since they do not correspond to any reality outside of themselves) but can only be judged "felicitous" or "infelicitous," depending upon whether they are appropriate or not to bring about the event they claim to perform. Their success or "felicity" will depend upon their fulfillment of a certain set of *conventions* that are both necessary and sufficient for the performance of the speech act in question.

Insofar as marriage furnishes the "machinery" for *Jude the Obscure,* the novel becomes an exploration of the marriage contract considered both as "letter" and as speech act. These two aspects of marriage, and especially the latter one, constitute the basis for Hardy's critique of marriage as an institution. Indeed, the unhappiness that all the main characters encounter in their marriages is to some extent analyzed as a consequence of the various "infelicities," in Austin's special sense, to which the act of marriage can succumb. Certain episodes in the novel can practically be read as textbook examples of "infelicity" in performative acts. Such is the mock marriage that Sue and Jude perform just hours before her real wedding to Phillotson (III, 7). Placing her arm in his for the first time, "almost as if she loved him," Sue insists on walking up the church nave to the altar railing and back down, "precisely like a couple just married." The act is infelicitous, of course, because of the absence of both an officiating minister and a marriage oath spoken by the two parties. Jude finds Sue's rash mimicking of the marriage act irresponsible, and says to himself, "She does not realize what marriage means!" Sue's toying with the wedding ceremony is, among other things, an instance of her ability to hurt the feelings of Jude, who finds her behavior here "merciless." Another example of an irresponsible tampering with the convention of marriage is given by Arabella when she consents to marriage with the man in Australia even though she is already married to Jude. This entire subplot, which includes Arabella's divorce from Jude and her remarriage, now within the proper forms, to the man she met in Australia, exemplifies a speech act that "misfires" (a subcategory of "infelicity" for Austin) and is then rectified by a return to the required conventions.

But Hardy is interested not only in showing such casual floutings of the marriage laws, which in themselves may seem isolated and accidental occurrences dependent upon individual willful acts. Instead of simply showing how the act of marriage can be infelicious, his real goal is to show that even when it is apparently felicitous—that is, when the recognized conventions governing the act of marriage have been properly invoked and performed— marriage is doomed to failure, because it promises to deliver something it cannot. This he demonstrates through the two main marriages in the novel. Although it is in Parts III and IV, with Sue's marriage to Phillotson, that the marriage question is brought to a head, the case against marriage as a misguided convention is already fully articulated in Part I, apropos of Jude's particularly infelicitous (in the common sense) marriage with Arabella. What is noteworthy about their wedding is the way in which Hardy's narrator undercuts the meaning of the act at the very moment it is being solemnized:

> And so, standing before the aforesaid officiator, the two swore that at every other time of their lives till death took them, they would assuredly believe, feel, and desire precisely as they had believed, felt, and desired during the few preceding weeks. What was as remarkable as the undertaking itself was the fact that nobody seemed at all surprised at what they swore. (1, 9)

The narrator treats the act of marriage essentially as the exchange of an oath or a promise (an important category of performatives in speech act theory). The most obvious kind of infelicity to which a promise can fall victim is of course insincerity, something J. L. Austin identifies as one of the possible "abuses" of a performative.

The narrator of *Jude the Obscure* does not, however, accuse either Jude or Arabella of insincerity or bad faith (even though bad faith has been involved in Arabella's entrapment of Jude in marriage on the false grounds of her alleged pregnancy), because this would again point only to an intentional, personal abuse of the convention. Rather, the narrator's comment strongly implies that the convention of the marriage oath is *intrinsically* infelicitous because of the nature of promises and the nature of human emotions. As one critic has written, the novel is here illustrating "the inappropriateness and the superficiality of conventional language." A few chapters later, a reflection attributed to Jude confirms the earlier narrative comment: "Their lives were ruined, he thought; ruined by the fundamental error of their matrimonial union: that of having based a permanent contract on a temporary feeling which had no necessary connection with affinities that alone render a lifelong comradeship tolerable" (I, II). Marriage fails not because of suspect intentions in the participants but because of an "error" contained in the convention itself. The convention suffers, in fact, from two distinct confusions: the confusion of the temporary with the "life-long" (a momentary oath supposedly binding one for life), and that of a "feeling" with an "affinity"; that is, a purely physical or sexual attraction is confused with the "spiritual" union that marriage should ideally represent. The two confusions are of course aligned in that sex is implicitly said to be a necessarily temporary feeling while spiritual "affinities" are lasting. There are problems here, not the least of which is that sex, which is here criticized as offering an inadequate basis for marriage, forms (as we shall see) an integral part of the definition or "letter" of marriage. But this particular problem will prove more of a difficulty for Sue than for Jude and Arabella. We have just seen that the latter's marriage is doomed to failure even as it begins, a failure not primarily attributable to the personal characters of the partners involved (though Arabella's duplicity undoubtedly adds to the sense of the inevitable wreck) but to a defect inherent in the convention of the marriage oath.

Sue's response to her marriage will both confirm and amplify the critique already made of Jude's marriage. In her fiercely unconventional, even antinomian, spirit, Sue attacks marriage as an institution and as a "letter," a dead letter to her, but one which nonetheless has the power to impose a new name on her:

> "the social moulds civilization fits us into have no more relation to our actual shapes than the conventional shapes of the constellations have to the real star-patterns. I am called Mrs. Richard Phillotson, living a calm wedded life with my counterpart of that name. But I am not really Mrs. Richard Phillotson, but a woman tossed about, all alone, with aberrant passions, and unaccountable antipathies. . . . (IV, I)

Sue's thinking is based on a radical opposition between social forms and a private self whose ineffable, unique quality must forever remain "unaccountable" in the terms of those social conventions (an opposition more drastic than Hardy's distinction between the "laws of nature" and "civil law"). The marriage law necessarily generalizes something that is in essence particular, and makes contractual a feeling that should be voluntary. Later, when Sue is arguing against the idea of a marriage between herself and Jude, she hints that her lack of feeling for Phillotson was actually the result of her contractual bond with him: "Don't you dread the attitude that insensibly arises out of legal obligation? Don't you think it is destructive to a passion whose essence is its gratuitousness?" (V, 3). Sue's critique of marriage is an even stronger one, then, than that made by the narrator on the occasion of Jude's marriage to Arabella. The narrator had argued only that the marriage oath is inconsistent with the ephemeral nature of human desires, while Sue claims that the oath, or the contract it establishes, actually *destroys* those desires. This would be the ultimate degree of infelicity for any performative, that through its very commission it should perform the exact opposite of what its "letter," or literal formula, claims to achieve.

Of course, as many critics of the novel have judged, Sue's theoretical arguments against marriage can be read in large part as rationalizations for what she finds to be the truly objectionable aspect of marriage, the sexual one. This does not mean that those arguments, in the context of the novel, are invalid, but it does mean that for Sue marriage is not only a verbal convention but is above all the occasion for the sexual act. It is Sue's ignorance of sex before her marriage to which Jude may be referring when he thinks to himself, "She does not realize what marriage means!" (III, 7). Later, after Sue's marriage to Phillotson has taken place, and has presumably been consummated, she admits to Jude: "Jude, before I married him I had never thought out fully what marriage meant, even though I knew" (IV, 2). The full "meaning" of marriage, then, is still more complicated than its status as a verbal act has indicated. Beyond constituting a legal state, marriage refers to an act of physical union, without which, as its "consummation," it is null and void. If the "spirit" of marriage seems to be contained in its verbal contract, its "letter," and arguably its true *referent,* is found in the sexual act. This is the letter that almost "killeth" Sue.

What Sue, with her sharp eye for conventions and their absurdity, had failed to see was the paradox that the conventionally defined act of marriage can be validated only through the physical, "raw" or noninstitutional act of sex. In Part VI, when little Jude asks her why babies come into the world, she will reply that it is "a law of nature" (VI, 2). The paradox is that the most natural of all acts should be inscribed within a verbal contract, made to subserve this contract and given a new meaning in reference to it. In other words, there is here a *crossing* of concepts that had previously seemed to belong to the distinct categories of the civil and the natural. Sue's disgust at this crossing is reflected in her language when she contemplates a new marriage to Jude: "I think I should begin to be afraid of you, Jude, the moment you had contracted to cherish me under a Government stamp, and I was licensed to be loved on the premises by you— Ugh, how horrible and sordid!" (V, I).

Sue may be offended by the logic of the marriage contract, but she is also capable of using the logic of conventions to her own ends, exploiting and undermining its terminology through an appeal to a more "natural" law. This is the way she frames her argument when she is trying to persuade Phillotson to allow her to live apart from him: "For a man and woman to live on intimate terms when one feels as I do is adultery, in any circumstances, however legal" (IV, 3). Sue's own crossing of categories here, in the oxymoronic notion of a "legal adultery," rests upon her interjection of a natural morality into the discussion of a contractual relation. Seen through the eyes of nature, Sue and Phillotson's marriage is adulterous—as if nature recognized marriage, and therefore adultery, at all. For Sue to call her own marriage adulterous represents a more radical attack on the institution of marriage than her engaging in an act of adultery could ever represent because it implies that adultery can happen not just outside of marriage but *inside* it as well.

Similarly, the solution Sue offers to Phillotson would, arguably, undermine marriage even more than a formal divorce. By proposing to live apart from him while remaining nominally his wife, Sue is proposing to preserve the appearance of their legal, contractual relationship while ceasing to fulfill its letter. Far from being dictated by a concern for appearances, though, Sue's suggestion is actually prompted by her total indifference to convention: the continued legal relationship with her husband would mean nothing to her as long as she were rid of the torment of physical intimacy. Her lack of respect for the marriage contract becomes even more apparent when she suggests that they terminate their marriage through a new verbal contract, this one sanctioned not by positive law but by natural morality: "Why can't we agree to free each other? We made the compact, and surely we can cancel it—not legally, of course; but we can morally, especially as no new interests, in the shape of children, have arisen to be looked after" (IV, 3). Sue is willing, as usual, to resort to conventional behavior when it suits her purposes, but what she appeals to now is a merely personal promise that cannot have the force of a legally recognized divorce. What she is proposing, then, is to under-

mine her marriage by a new speech act which is, however, not strictly symmetrical with the oath that created the marriage in the first place.

Of course, Sue's plan for this particular kind of separation from her husband—a separation that would leave her marriage intact as a legal contract and yet strangely void for lack of consummation—will work only temporarily, and soon we shall have to consider how the divorce Phillotson obtains from her alters her situation. But the arguments of Sue I have just cited, with their subtle undermining of the institution of marriage through a strange, mixed recourse to both natural and conventional forms of behavior, represent a distinct climax in the plot of the novel. The climactic sense comes in part from the way that Sue's reasoning so closely echoes Hardy's reasoning in his Postscript of 1912, namely "that a marriage should be dissolvable as soon as it becomes a cruelty to either of the parties—being then essentially and morally no marriage." Hardy's statement seems to support the action of his heroine at this critical juncture of the novel, and when Phillotson too, rather less expectedly, gives consent to it, the novel enters into a new phase.

This new phase would seem to be grounded in the principle that has permitted the judgment that a cruel marriage is "morally no marriage." It seems to presuppose the ideal of a relationship which is not sanctioned by the law and which can be sustained without cruelty to either partner. Such a relationship would be based on a natural affinity between two people who have no need even to "enunciate" their natural desire for each other through the language of the civil law. The relationship that this novel suggests might fulfill such an ideal is, of course, that between Jude and Sue. It is largely (though not exclusively) in reference to their relationship that the novel invokes a Romantic vocabulary of natural correspondences, elective affinities, and "magnetism" (II, 3). The narrative is establishing these links between Jude and Sue even while Sue's acquaintance and later marriage with Phillotson are driving her inexorably away from a union with Jude; it is in part Sue's already established attraction to Jude (along with her revulsion from her husband) that will rapidly make her marriage unviable. All of this would make it seem that Sue's marriage need only "dissolve" to enable her to rush into Jude's arms and find happiness. But this kind of clear-cut alternative is precisely what this novel is working against. Instead, even while the narrative has been instilling the idea that Sue and Jude are meant for each other, it has been complicating that idea by putting into question the notion of natural affinities altogether.

By one of those touches, ironic and fitting at the same time, of which the novel is full, it is Phillotson who supplies some of the strongest statements of the natural bond that exists between Sue and Jude. To his friend Gillingham he says: "I have been struck with these two facts; the extraordinary sympathy, or similarity, between the pair. He is her cousin, which perhaps accounts for some of it. They seem to be one person split in two!" (IV,

4). As he goes on to describe their extraordinary affinity, or sympathy, Phillotson adds to this Platonic myth the Shelleyan one of Laon and Cythna, the lovers from *The Revolt of Islam*—an allusion that links this passage to Hardy's **Well-Beloved,** which borrows its epigraph from the same poem. In both novels Plato's mythic explanation for the attraction between two people is supplemented by a characteristically Romantic hint of incest in the relations between two cousins. The otherwise prosaic Phillotson turns out to be a surprisingly Romantic reader of human relations.

But this Romantic interpretation has already been put into question before the disappointed husband enunciates it. It already informs the language the narrator uses to describe the first glimpses that Jude catches of Sue after his arrival at Christminster. On the first of these occasions Jude enters the shop where she is working and watches her silently until he hears her speak, whereupon "he recognized in the accents certain qualities of his own voice; softened and sweetened, but his own." This faintly incestuous affinity is based on the most spiritual and interior of all qualities, the living voice. But, as the text immediately asks, "What was she doing?" Working with a zinc scroll, Sue "was designing or illuminating, in characters of Church text, the single word ALLELUJA" (II, 2). Sue's work involves the letter, the written text, in its most material quality—its materiality underscored in Hardy's text by the word's being spelled out in Gothic lettering. The soft tones of Sue's voice are already opposed by the resistant physicality of the religious "letter," an emblem of the letter which, in the form of the religiously sanctioned marriage law, will later be Sue's enemy.

What remains as implicit commentary in this first scene, inscribed tacitly in the environment in which Sue is found, becomes explicit during Jude's next encounter with her. This meeting takes place in church, and this time the spiritual vehicle supposedly expressing the affinity between the two is again the voice, now supported by music. The chanting of a psalm for organ and choir, heard by the two cousins in the audience, is interpreted as the expression of a harmonic link between them. Although they are not seated together and Sue is not even aware of Jude's presence, he imagines her "ensphered by the same harmonies as those which floated into his ears; and the thought was a delight to him." The shared music encourages Jude to think that Sue "had, no doubt, much in common with him," and his fantasy culminates in a state of "ecstasy." Cutting this ecstasy short, however, the narrator immediately remarks: "Though he was loth to suspect it, some people might have said to him that the atmosphere blew as distinctly from Cyprus as from Galilee" (II, 3). "Some people," of course, might be wrong; yet the effect of this remark is to undercut Jude's own belief in the idealism (and religious purity) of his attraction to Sue and to replace it by a more carnal desire. This opposition between a genuine, ideal affinity and a merely sexual one is the same opposition the narrator had already used for his critique of Jude's marriage with Arabella, and it is therefore a particularly ominous presage of the future relations between Jude and Sue.

This erroneous grounding of a natural affinity between persons in a shared experience of church music has a curious parallel later in the novel. Shortly after Sue's marriage to Phillotson in Part III ("At Melchester"), Jude hears a newly composed hymn by a Wessex musician and is greatly impressed by its beauty. Jude promptly attributes the qualities of the music to its composer: "What a man of sympathies he must be! . . . 'He of all men would understand my difficulties,' said the impulsive Jude. If there were any person in the world to choose as a confidant, this composer would be the one, for he must have suffered, and throbbed, and yearned" (III, 10). Like Proust's Swann after hearing for the first time the sonata of Vinteuil, Jude resolves to meet the composer. But when he does—spending an entire Sunday journeying by rail to a small village and back—he is greatly disappointed. Far from exhibiting the same spiritual qualities as his music, the composer turns out to be petty and materialistic, interested only in the financial returns of his art, and thinking of changing from composing into the wine business. This disillusioning encounter, which Jude narrates to Sue when they meet again at the start of Part IV, has no further consequences for the main plot of the novel; it is a completely extrinsic episode. Its inclusion in the novel can be explained only by its reinforcement of the theme of wrong or deceptive affinities that had already been illustrated by Jude and Sue.

It is under the shadow of such hints as these that Sue deserts Phillotson and embarks on her free, unauthorized relationship with Jude (IV, 5). This is one reason why their new relations begin on an inauspicious note. Another reason concerns the way in which Sue and Jude both finally extricate themselves from their first marriages. When Sue begins to live with Jude, both are still married, so that their cohabitation gives the appearance of adultery. Yet **Jude the Obscure** is not a novel of adultery: no adulterous act ever occurs between the hero and heroine. If Sue refuses at first to have carnal relations with Jude, however, her refusal can hardly be ascribed to a respect for the convention of marriage. We have already seen that she was perfectly willing to undermine that convention from within by refusing to have sex with Phillotson, even while living with him as his wife. Beyond the reason of her lack of physical passion, she may decline to have sex with Jude also because, as an act of adultery, that act would *confirm* the legal claims of marriage in the way that any transgression confirms the existence of the law it transgresses against. Adultery is the "other" of marriage in the sense that it is the other side of the same coin. Disillusioned as she now is with marriage, Sue is seeking, whether consciously or unconsciously, a way out of what she sees as the false alternative between legal and illegal acts of sex. A radical putting into question of marriage will no longer acknowledge the relevance of the opposition between acts that occur "within" marriage and acts that occur "outside" of it.

There is yet another twist to Sue's undermining of the institution of marriage. Although she is unwilling to commit an act of adultery, she is willing to practice a deception and give the *appearance* of engaging in adultery. It is this appearance, as she must know, that will move Phillotson to seek and obtain a divorce from her. Their divorce is announced in the novel at the same time as Jude's divorce from Arabella (V, 1). In each case the wronged husband has successfully sued for divorce on the grounds of his wife's infidelity. Arabella's adultery has been real, but Sue's is only feigned. When her divorce is announced, she expresses to Jude her doubts as to its validity, since it has been obtained under "false pretences":

> "Well—if the truth about us had been known, the decree wouldn't have been pronounced. It is only, is it, because we have made no defence, and have led them into a false supposition? Therefore is my freedom lawful, however proper it may be?" (V, 1).

Jude is thrust into the position of the interpreter of the law, and he responds with what is no doubt the correct interpretation, especially from the point of view of speech act theory: "One thing is certain, that however the decree may be brought about, a marriage is dissolved when it is dissolved" (V, 1). Phillotson's divorce from Sue is "felicitous" because it has been pronounced by the court that has the institutional power to bring it about. A mere inconsistent fact like Sue's innocence, especially since it has been concealed from general knowledge, cannot get in the way of the workings of justice. In any case Sue finds it in her interest now to let the divorce proceed. Yet her question does raise a disturbing point about the validity of the divorce. In a sense Sue has undermined the convention of divorce through her feigning of adultery just as much as she undermined the convention of marriage by merely pretending to live in physical union with her husband. Though her divorce is valid in the eyes of the public, Sue knows that it is based on a misapplication of the letter of the law.

Consequently there is much ambiguity in her question as to whether her newly won freedom is "lawful." Most simply, she is asking whether divorced people return to the state of freedom they knew before marriage: "Are we—you and I—just as free now as if we had never married at all?" (V, 1). But clearly the freedom of being divorced is not the same as the freedom of never having been married, if only because the freedom one has now is "lawful." The free relation into which Sue is about to enter with Jude, supposedly based on a natural affinity, should exist prior to, or outside of, the law altogether. Instead, Sue's question implies—whatever the response to it may be—that their relationship is already inscribed within the law. (And it was obviously part of Hardy's tragic design that the two should not even meet until Jude was already bound in marriage to Arabella.) Moreover, because of the irregularity in Sue's divorce, there is the implication that her relationship with Jude, far from being pristine, is based on a misunderstanding, a legal error. This new phase of the novel, then, which according to a more reassuring scheme would have signaled the vindication of Hardy's view on the dissolubility of marriage, begins on a distinctly false note—a note that will

only get more strident as Sue and Jude persist in trying to make a life for themselves.

It does not take the narrative long to establish that divorce offers no solution to Jude's and Sue's problems. The freedom supposedly won through divorce does not emancipate them but only increases the awkwardness of their situation. Jude, indeed, takes it for granted that they should now regularize their relationship by marrying each other. His argument in favor of a new marriage, however, is scarcely persuasive: "People go on marrying because they can't resist natural forces, although many of them may know perfectly well that they are possibly buying a month's pleasure with a life's discomfort" (V, 1). He has obviously absorbed the lesson that Hardy already sought to drive home at the time of Jude's wedding with Arabella. The appeal to the "natural forces" of sexual desire is not calculated to convince Sue, who, as we have seen, is particularly repelled by the image of a sexual activity enforced by a code of law. The argument that Sue presently hears from Arabella—that she should marry because to be a wife is a social and economic convenience—has just as little appeal for the unconventional Sue.

There follow the agonizing chapters in which Sue and Jude persuade themselves to be married and go so far as to publish banns and even go to the registrar's office on the morning appointed for their wedding, only to be scared away by the sight of another, obviously ill-suited couple (V, 3, 4). After this they arrive at a compromise, which is to let others believe that they are married even while really remaining free of "the sordid conditions of a business contract":

> The result was that shortly after the attempt at the registrar's the pair went off—to London it was believed—for several days, hiring somebody to look to the boy. When they came back they let it be understood indirectly, and with total indifference and weariness of mien, that they were legally married at last. Sue, who had previously been called Mrs. Bridehead, now openly adopted the name of Mrs. Fawley. (V, 6)

Once again, Sue is subtly subverting the institution of marriage. Earlier she had lived with Phillotson as man and wife but had refused him the sexual intimacy that would consummate the letter of their contract; now she lives with Jude, granting him the sexual relationship (after she is driven to do so by jealousy of his relations with Arabella) and claiming to be his wife but declining the contractual oath that would really make her such. By "adopting" his name, Sue mimics that very consequence of the marriage contract that she resented in her marriage to Phillotson. Yet this adoption of the name is "infelicitous" in the absence of the marriage ceremony; her calling herself Mrs. Fawley is not the same as the law's calling her by that name. As she later admits to the landlady in Christminster: "though in [Sue's] own sense of the words she was a married woman, in the landlady's sense she was not" (VI, 1). What Jude and Sue consider they have done is to enter into a "natural" marriage, just as binding on them as a civil one would be but with less potential for cruelty. Yet it is significant that this natural union must immediately mask itself by adopting the forms of civil marriage.

The problem for Jude and Sue is precisely how to find a way to retreat, to recover a state of existence that is outside of, or prior to, the civil law of society. The latter stages of *Jude the Obscure* show that their attempt to do so inevitably fails, for two reasons: first, because their continuing ties to society make it impossible for them to escape society's laws, and second, because even an escape back to a putative state of nature would only reveal that nature too already articulates itself in terms of "laws," laws that offer only a false alternative to those of society.

It has often been observed that *Jude,* the last of Hardy's novels, portrays a world that is more social and less natural than the world of any of the earlier novels. Jude's profession is strictly an urban one, unlike the agricultural occupations prominent in most of the novels through *Tess of the d'Urbervilles.* Not only are Sue and Jude obliged to continue living in towns but his work brings him forcibly up against the very incarnation of social law. The episode Hardy chooses to illustrate this confrontation occurs in Aldbrickham, when Jude receives the commission to repair the lettering of the Ten Commandments in a small church. When Sue begins to assist him in the work of relettering the biblical phrases, this scene becomes the exact counterpart of that early scene when Jude first saw Sue in the act of illuminating the word "ALLELUJA." Sue herself notes the irony in their new employment: "that we two, of all people, with our queer history, should happen to be here painting the Ten Commandments" (V, 6). The two of them are working to restore the very "letter" of the law that neither of them now believes in, and which seems at least to admonish their own conduct in the form of the seventh Commandment.

Their full relationship to this letter, however, is suggested only by means of the story that the churchwarden tells (within their hearing) to some women who have entered the church and have begun to gossip about Sue and Jude. This gossip prompts the warden to narrate his anecdote, almost a legend, concerning a similar restoration of the text of the Ten Commandments in a nearby church about one hundred years earlier. This task, too, had been assigned to workers who were unfit because they drank on the job. After drinking themselves into a stupor, they woke up to find a thunderstorm raging and a "dark figure," an image of the devil himself, completing their work for them. Only the next day did the workers learn that "a great scandal had been caused in the church that Sunday morning, for when the people came and service began, all saw that the Ten Commandments wez painted with the 'Nots' left out" (V, 6).

The anecdote suggests that Jude and Sue, like the devil, are capable of removing the negatives from the injunc-

tions that stand at the source of the Judaeo-Christian religion. This suggestion has a certain plausibility, not only because Jude and Sue's immorality, at least in the eyes of the public, makes their work on the Ten Commandments subversive but also because they in fact are striving to live outside of all enunciated codes of law. For them, the Ten Commandments serve as a symbol of the social constraints under which they live. Sue will remark later to Jude: "There is something external to us which says, 'You shan't!' First it said, 'You shan't learn!' Then it said, 'You shan't labour!' Now it says, 'You shan't love!'" (VI, 2). Sue images the social (and the religious) law as a voice issuing negative commands. This voice cannot be the simple "enunciation" of the law of nature, as Hardy's Postscript to the novel suggests it should be, because nature, like the Freudian unconscious, knows no negatives. The idea of Sue's and Jude's removing the "nots" as they reletter the Ten Commandments, then, points to their desire to rewrite the social and theological laws in order to make them conform better to the law of nature. Yet such an attempt, the novel is suggesting, would be doomed. For removing the negatives from the commands still leaves them as commands—positive commands now but no less arbitrary and peremptory.

Jude and Sue, of course, through most of the novel, continue to harbor hope for a way of life that lies outside of, and prior to, the "letter" of the social law that is persecuting them. Their regressive impulse to recapture a putative state of nature is felt, most obviously, in their association with and concern for wild animals: the birds that Jude is punished for trying to feed in the second chapter of the novel, the rabbit caught in a gin that he puts out of its misery (IV, 2), the pigeons that Sue sets free as she and Jude prepare to leave Aldbrickham (V, 6). These trapped and suffering animals become, in the protagonists' minds, emblems of their own victimization at the hands of society, as when Jude calls Sue "my poor little bird" (IV, 2) or when, just a few pages after the incident of the caught rabbit, he converts the trap into a metaphor for his own condition: "is it the artificial system of things, under which the normal sex-impulses are turned into devilish domestic gins and springes to noose and hold back those who want to progress?" (IV, 3).

Despite the appeal of this figurative equation between man's treatment of animals and society's treatment of the individual, Jude is guilty here of nostalgic self-deception. As was the case in *Tess of the d'Urbervilles,* the protagonists in this novel also find themselves struggling against the cruelty not only of social laws but of the natural law as well. This cruelty is in fact already present in the nature or animal scenes that *Jude* offers. As early as Part I, in the scene in which Jude is supposed to be protecting the farmer's fields from the rooks, those fields are described as the site of a quite different natural or "lawless" activity:

> Love-matches that had populated the adjoining
> hamlet had been made up there between reaping
> and carrying. Under the hedge which divided the

field from a distant plantation girls had given themselves to lovers who would not turn their heads to look at them by the next harvest; and in that ancient corn-field many a man had made love-promises to a woman at whose voice he had trembled by the next seed-time after fulfilling them in the church adjoining. But this neither Jude nor the rooks around him considered (I, 2)

This indiscriminate lovemaking, in the scenarios the narrator proposes, can remain free and illegal or can lead to marriage; either way the result is usually cruel. Though Jude is oblivious to such cruelty at this early point, later episodes will educate both him and Sue into a tragic consciousness of man's and animal's inability to escape victimization. The rabbit caught in the gin cannot be freed by Jude but only put out of its misery quickly. Sue's later reflection on the pigeons she frees is, "O why should Nature's law be mutual butchery!" (V, 6). Shortly after this, Phillotson will remark to Arabella: "Cruelty is the law pervading all nature and society; and we can't get out of it if we would!" (V, 8).

These ruminations on nature's law reach their climax, of course, in Sue's conversations with Little Father Time, conversations that lead directly to the latter's suicide, the catastrophe of Part VI. When Father Time, with characteristic lugubriousness, asks Sue why children are born, she replies, "because it is a law of nature." When she goes on to tell him she is pregnant once again, the boy responds, "How *ever* could you, mother, be so wicked and cruel as this, when you needn't have done it till we was better off, and father well!" This speech is Father Time's last in the novel. Two pages later, Jude tries to alleviate the guilt Sue feels for Father Time's murder of their children and his subsequent suicide by saying, "It was in his nature to do it" (VI, 2).

Having rejected marriage, Jude and Sue are thrown back upon the laws of nature. But these laws turn out to have a cruelty of their own. In fact, the cruelty resulting from the laws of nature resembles the cruelty brought about by laws of man: both kinds of law have a relentless universality, an indifference to the fate of the individual. When Sue attributes her pregnancy to the law of nature, she is not so much finding a positive explanation as she is evading an admission of her own sexuality. Jude had earlier cited the natural sexual drive as the primary reason why most people marry. It is as if the laws of nature can be used to motivate any kind of behavior, social or nonsocial. In their monolithic, universal quality, the laws of nature become arbitrary, cruel, and machinelike. We are reminded that Hardy in his postscript had called the marriage laws the "tragic machinery" of his tale. Nature's law, as the novel represents it, is no less a part of Hardy's machinery, and it is between these two machines that the tragic hero and heroine find themselves squeezed.

It is left to Sue to draw the most important consequences from the new situation which is brought about by Little Father Time's murder-suicide. The boy's act is a response to his reflection on the law of nature, and Sue's own response to that act will take the form of a reinterpretation of the laws of marriage. It is the conclusion of the novel from this point on that many readers have felt to be unbearable, both because of the overwhelming pessimism implied in the events of the denouement and because of the strain placed on our credulity by Hardy's apparent manipulation of the catastrophe, and also, perhaps, by Sue's swift psychological turnabout. It is hard to deny that Hardy is here manipulating the plot for his tragic effect—but, then, he has been manipulating it since the beginning. To deplore Sue's conduct here as being either perverse or inexplicable, which is the reaction of practically all the other characters in the novel, is to miss the centrality of that conduct to the novel's main theme. The importance of the ideas Sue begins to articulate after the death of her children is suggested by the fact that even Hardy's narrator seems to disapprove of them. Sue is becoming the spokesman for the tragic design of the novel itself, a design that is more profound than the opinions of the other characters, the narrator, or even the "author" Hardy, who spoke optimistically in his postscript about the "dissolubility" of marriage. Sue almost single-handedly accomplishes the tragic conclusion to the novel by denying the view that marriage is dissoluble.

Sue's new position is all the more remarkable because it hardly seems to be the inevitable or logical response to Little Jude's murders. Her sense of guilt for the children's deaths, if that is what it is, appears misplaced. Little Jude's famous suicide note, "Done because we are too menny," with its pun on "men," accuses the natural order of reproduction and the human condition itself. Sue, however, is unwilling to assign blame either to the human condition in general or to the explanation Jude proposes, that is, that the boy was the harbinger of a "coming universal wish not to live" (VI, 2). Rejecting historical and existential explanations, Sue seeks a legalistic one: she chooses to interpret the deaths as the punishment for the infraction of a religious law that is embodied in a social code, and she sees her own sole chance for atonement in a conscious "submission" to that code—indeed, in a ringing reaffirmation of it (VI, 3).

When Sue first announces her new views on the indissolubility of marriage, the ensuing argument between her and Jude seems to take the form of a blocked dialectic. Jude argues that their relationship is "Nature's own marriage," and Sue responds, "But not Heaven's" (VI, 3). The terms of the dichotomy, at least, are new. Whereas both the protagonists had earlier appealed to nature as a positive law in contrast to society's negative one, nature is now being contrasted, to its disadvantage, with religious law. Now that Sue recognizes the religious underpinning of the marriage ceremony, she sees the ceremonial act as having an absolute, inviolable "felicity" that makes it indissoluble. Their debate centers, once again, on the question of performative speech acts and their binding quality. Jude pleads: "We still love. . . . Therefore our marriage is not cancelled." Sue not only denies this but insists that her marriage to Phillotson has never been interrupted: it is the divorce act that for her now becomes "infelicitous," totally without authority. Hence, the new wedding with Phillotson is not strictly necessary, except in society's eyes: "[Phillotson] is going to marry me again. That is for form's sake, and to satisfy the world, which does not see things as they are. But of course I *am* his wife already. Nothing has changed that" (VI, 4). There is indeed something extreme and perverse about Sue's new adherence to the law of conventional acts. Formerly, she had undermined convention by going along with the outward forms of marriage even while refraining from the behavior that would give meaning to the ceremony; now she has become a formalist holier than the Pope, willing to perform a redundant, repetitive ritual only because society at large has reneged on its faith in the binding force of the original act.

Sue's actions from now on constitute a careful reversal of all her previous actions and ways of thinking, which, as she now believes, led to catastrophe. Her acts are not only a reversal but also a repetition—repetition being the necessary mode of the tragedy Hardy is composing. Sue now insists on an almost maniacal enactment of the letter of the law that she had previously flouted. And Jude says in protest: "Sue! we are acting by the letter; and 'the letter killeth!'" Jude's interpretation is just as correct as Sue's action is necessary. At first, perhaps she herself is not aware of how absolute is the process of repetition that she is instigating. After her second marriage to Phillotson, when Jude gets out of his sick bed to visit her, she is capable of equivocating to the extent of telling him it is "only a church marriage—an apparent marriage I mean. . . . a nominal marriage" (VI, 8). In fact, she has up to now refused sexual relations with Phillotson, thus undermining their second marriage just as she had their first. But right after this scene, and as a consequence of it, Sue forces herself to the most painful act of penance of all (painful for both her and the reader) as she enters Phillotson's bed (VI, 9). In the meantime, one final act of repetition has occurred, more ridiculous than sublime: Jude's remarriage to Arabella has provided a wrenching parody of Sue's new union with Phillotson.

The two weddings at the end of the novel do not, of course, reestablish the legitimacy of marriage as an institution. The arguments Hardy has made against marriage through his narrative voice and his plot continue to hold, and perhaps even gain in force. Yet Sue's stated reasons for returning to Phillotson suggest that the state of marriage is in a sense inevitable for all the characters, and that the alternative between marriage and a state of natural freedom is a false one. Sue's actions reveal that finally the social law *is* only an "enunciation" of the natural law—but what it also enunciates is the latter's cruelty. The stalemate, or indeed regression, that characterizes the last phase of the plot, and which is the source of the novel's tragedy, arises from the exposure of the false alternative between the dictates of a social and of a natural way of life.

What happens to the opposition between social and natural law by the end of *Jude the Obscure* can be compared to what happens to the opposition between performative and constative utterances by the end of Austin's *How To Do Things With Words*. At the outset, Austin treats constative utterances as the norm and performatives as a special case. Before the end of his short work, however, he has decided that constatives are only a special case of illocutionary speech acts, all of which are in a sense performative; as Stanley Fish puts it, "the class of exceptions thus swallows the normative class." In *Jude the Obscure* the natural law initially seems to be prior to the social law, which must be interpreted either as an "enunciation" or a deformation of it. By the end of the novel, these two laws are threatening to collapse into one, or rather they become two versions of a system of determinism that governs human fate. There is no real alternative to living in the domain of performative speech acts such as commands (the Ten Commandments) and promises (the marriage oath). The marriage laws become Hardy's "tragic machinery" for conveying man and woman's plight; the ultimately false options between marriage, adultery, and divorce represent the false options (which nonetheless continually entice Jude and Sue) between a life in society and a life in nature. There is no authentic possibility of a life outside of the law in *Jude;* even the animals in this novel are caged, confined, or regulated. The theoretical possibility of a natural way of living—the kind of life associated with the theory of the elective affinity binding Jude and Sue—has disappeared, along with the natural landscape of Wessex that played such a great role in Hardy's earlier novels but is no longer visible in *Jude*.

It is this dilemma that Hardy is indicating in the epigraph to his novel: "The letter killeth." It is significant that Hardy did not go on to quote the rest of the biblical phrase, "but the spirit giveth life." *Jude* is depicting a new world, one in which the opposition between the letter and the spirit no longer operates; it is the world of the letter alone. It is Sue who in the novel best recognizes this world for what it is, Sue who is first seen engraving the word "ALLELUJA," and who is last seen reentering the marriage bed of her lawful husband.

Ramón Saldívar (essay date 1983)

SOURCE: "*Jude the Obscure*: Reading and the Spirt of the Law", in *ELH,* Vol. 50, No. 3, 1983, pp. 607-623.

[*In the following essay, Saldívar probes the nature of meaning and referentiality in relation to Hardy's novel, contending that "the narrative of* Jude the Obscure, *while telling the story of Jude's and Sue's unhappy marriages, also dispels the illusion of a readable truth."*]

> The letter killeth, but the spirit giveth life.
> —II Corinthians

Concern for the nature and response of an author's audience is, in some respects, one of the original tasks of literary criticism. Over the past decade, however, attempts to incorporate rhetorical, linguistic, and cognitive theories into literary criticism have led to the development of a hefty bibliography on the nature of the reader's role in the communication network of author, text, and reader. These reader-oriented studies stress, from their various perspectives, that the reader, as much as any character, contributes to the shaping of the novel's fictive world through his interpretive actions.

The value of this recent emphasis on the reader's role in fiction and of "reception history" in general could very well be tested by a text such as the author's "Postscript" to *Jude the Obscure*. There, the reading public is accused of "curing" the novelist of all desire to write prose fiction. In this case Hardy would seem to have us question the reader's role in the *destruction* of texts, for in no uncertain terms, it is the reader, in his incapacity to read, who is the problem. Since we cannot read his meaning properly, even when there has been no "mincing of words" in its enunciation, complains Hardy, he will spare himself and the reader by simply ceasing to write novels.

Yet readers often find this and Hardy's later comment that he expected *Jude the Obscure* to be read as "a moral work" (ix) somewhat disingenuous. We can hardly imagine, after the reception of *Tess* and after his attempt to cancel his contract with Harper & Brothers for *Jude,* that Hardy would not have anticipated the "shocked criticisms" (ix) that the publication of the novel evoked. In fact, when Hardy announces in the "Preface to the First Edition" that the novel will "deal unaffectedly with the fret and fever, derision and disaster, that may press in the wake of the strongest passion known to humanity" (viii), and then denies that "there is anything in the handling to which exception can be taken" (viii), he raises the very real possibility that the novel will be misread.

And it was misread. Angry reviewers and a solemn bishop saw in it, among other things, a cynical attack on the sacrament and institution of marriage. In a letter of November 1895 to Edmund Gosse, Hardy continued to express his concern for the proper reading of his novel by indicating that *Jude* was not merely "a manifesto on 'the marriage question' (although, of course, it involves it)," but was more the story of the tragic result of two marriages because of "a doom or curse of hereditary temperament peculiar to the family of the parties." The fact is, of course, as critics have convincingly argued, that the novel *is* concerned with the marriage laws in more than just a casual way. And Hardy himself points out that the plot of *Jude* is "geometrically constructed" around the marital realignments of the four principal characters. They repeatedly change their relationships through their alternately prospective and retrospective visions of one another and of the options society and nature allow them.

Poised between a desire for natural freedom and the need for a stabilizing social order, Hardy's characters try to act within their "geometrically constructed" system of marital and symbolic associations to accommodate their desires and needs. Hardy is clear about this. He tells us that *Jude the Obscure* dramatizes the sociological effect of the Victorian failure to reconcile the antithetical realms of culture and nature: "The marriage laws [are] used . . . to show that, in Diderot's words, the civil law should be only the enunciation of the law of nature" ("Postscript," x). But the difficulty of reading *Jude* properly may well stem from the fact that the novel is more than a realistic analysis of the historical condition of marriage in late Victorian England. I would like to suggest that the ambiguous status of the act of reading in the author's prefatory statements is only an indicator of a more radical investigation concerning reading and interpretation. By considering the interplay between "natural" and "civil" law, and by examining the nature of Hardy's "geometrically constructed" plot, we will be able to reflect on the possible relation of these issues to the apparent ease with which, according to Hardy, the novel can be misread. A reading of *Jude* that attempts to account for this cluster of formal and thematic elements can, I think, provide a new perspective on Hardy's conception of the realistic novel.

A first difficulty in understanding the novel is thematic and stems from the portrayal in the text itself of numerous cases of misreading. From the beginning, for instance, Jude sees in Christminster and its university the image of an attainable ideal world. His desire for this ideal vision involves a rejection of reality. For his own sporadically controlled, partially understood world, he substitutes the image of a unified, stable, and understandable one. Beguiled by his desire for order, the young Jude thus turns initially to language study both as a means of entering university life and as a possible course of stability. The narrator tells us:

> Ever since his first ecstasy or vision of Christminster and its possibilities, Jude had meditated much and curiously on the probable sort of process that was involved in turning the expressions of one language into those of another. He concluded that a grammar of the required tongue would contain, primarily, a rule, prescription, or clue of the nature of a secret cipher which, once known, would enable him, by merely applying it, to change at will all words of his own speech into those of the foreign one. . . . Thus he assumed that the words of the required language were always to be found somewhere latent in the words of the given language by those who had the art to uncover them, such art being furnished by the books aforesaid.
>
> (I.iVol.30-31)

Jude feels betrayed, consequently, when in his attempt to learn Latin he finds that "there was no law of transmutation, as in his innocence he had supposed" (31). Jude's desired "law of transmutation," the "secret cipher" to a system of translation, could exist only if a prior permanent code existed to allow a free substitution of signifiers for one autonomous signified. The metaphor of translation at this early point in the novel is doubly interesting. It both reveals Jude's desire for a serenely immobile text whose content might be transported without harm into the element of another language, and alludes to the relation Hardy establishes in the "Postscript" of 1912 between civil and natural law, making one the "enunciation" (x) of the other. These will continue to be decisive issues throughout the novel. At this point, Jude has no doubt that the voice of nature can, indeed, be read and translated, for when he "address[es] the breeze caressingly," it seems to respond: "Suddenly there came along this wind something towards him—a message . . . calling to him, 'We are happy here!'" (I.iii.22). By imposing single terms on the disparate variety of experience, we come to know and control our environment. Early on, however, Jude intuits that language is not a fixed system through which meaning can be "transmuted" from one system to another. Yet this is precisely the insight that Jude refuses to apply to his other readings of the world around him.

As he proceeds into the countryside, where the markings that hint at the limitations already imposed on his life stand to be deciphered, Jude's readings continue: "The only marks on the uniformity of the scene were a rick of last year's produce . . . and the path . . . by which he had come. . . . [To] every clod and stone there really attached associations enough and to spare—echoes of songs . . . of spoken words, and of sturdy deeds" (I.ii.10). History, echoing across the generations, seems to focus on Jude at the bottom of "this vast concave" field (I.ii.9), but he does not yet understand its voice. The substance of this discourse latent in the countryside is the essential dimension of the tradition into which he has been born. These "marks" and "associations" in the landscape of Wessex are "signs" inscribed by the force motivating all events, which Hardy was in *The Dynasts* to name the "Immanent Will." Thus, long before his birth, long before the story of his family has been inscribed, this tradition has already traced the pattern of behavior within which are ordered the possible changes and exchanges that will occur in Jude's short life. Each crucial event in Jude's life seems to invite the reader to interpret Jude's actions as an attempted reading of the role ascribed to him in some determining book of fate.

Initially, the young orphan Jude seems to see the schoolmaster, Phillotson, as an embodiment of his controlling "dreams" (I.iii.20), and as a symbolic substitute for the absent "real" father. Accordingly, when Phillotson leaves Marygreen, Jude replaces him with an ideal representation. Jude reads that ideal presence into the natural landscape of Wessex as Christminster, "that ecclesiastical romance in stone" (I.Vol.36):

> Through the solid barrier of cold cretaceous upland to the northward he was always beholding a gorgeous city—the fancied place he likened to the new Jerusalem. . . . And the city acquired a tangibility, a permanence, a hold on his life, mainly from the one nucleus of fact that the man for whose

knowledge and purposes he had so much reverence was actually living there.

> (I.iii.20)

In this ecstatic vision, Christminster, whose mark is "a halo or glow-fog" (I.iii.21), seems to send that "message" (I.iii.22) I mentioned earlier, but it is a message that must be translated from natural to human terms with all the inherent errors of language and its "figures" (I.iii.25). In a moment of revelation, George Eliot's narrator in *Adam Bede* comments that "Nature has her language, and she is not unveracious; but we don't know all the intricacies of her syntax just yet, and in a hasty reading we may happen to extract the very opposite of her real meaning." Now, as Jude attempts to learn the "syntax" of nature's "message," Christminster, through Phillotson, becomes the organizing center of his life: "It had been the yearning of his heart to find something to anchor on, to cling to—for some place which he could call admirable. Should he find that place in this city if he could get there?" (I.iii.24). The phrasing of his question in the rhetorical mode produces a grammatical structure that implies the existence of freedom of choice, when in fact, the pattern of choices has already been established for Jude by his own propensity for misreading. As he answers the questions posed in indirect discourse, beguiled by the transformation his mind has imposed on the scene through figurative language, Jude takes literally his own metaphors of the "new Jerusalem," "the city of light," and "the castle, manned by scholarship and religion" (I.iii.24-25).

Sue Bridehead is also presented in the metaphoric language that names Christminster. Jude has seen, for example, "the photograph of [her] pretty girlish face, in a broad hat, with radiating folds under the brim like the rays of a halo" (II.i.90). In fact, the metaphoric process by which Sue will later replace Christminster and Phillotson in Jude's dreams has been facilitated by the nature of Jude's language long before he is even conscious of Sue: earlier, he had become "so romantically attached to Christminster that, like a young lover alluding to his mistress, he felt bashful at mentioning its name" (I.iii.22). The transfer from Phillotson, to Christminster, and finally to Sue as metaphors of that sustaining vision is thus a simple, determined step. Jude's false reading of Sue at a chapel in Christminster as being "ensphered by the same harmonies as those which floated into his ears" leads him to conclude that he has "at last found anchorage for his thoughts" (II.iii.107). When Jude finally meets Sue, he approaches her cautiously and speaks to her as he has spoken of Christminster, "with the bashfulness of a lover" (II.iVol.117). At each step in the evolution of his story, his controlling dream is a fiction that he imposes on wayward circumstances.

From the beginning then, the object of desire is not "real" in any sense, but is a "phantasmal" (II.ii.97) creation of Jude's own mind, as are the "ghosts" that haunt Christminster. For Jude, however, the ghosts of his desires disappearing into the "obscure alleys" (II.i.92) of

Christminster are as real as Arabella's "disappearance into space" (II.i.92). Constituting himself as a whole subject by an identification with another who repeatedly disappears, "A hungry soul in pursuit of a full soul" (III.x.233), Jude is accordingly threatened by the possibility of disappearing too: "Jude began to be impressed with the isolation of his own personality, as with a self-spectre . . . seeming thus almost his own ghost" (II.i.92). Phillotson, Christminster, Arabella, and most strikingly, Sue, thus become the figures of an ideal paradise, which is fundamentally inaccessible, insofar as it is one more metaphor in a structuring system of substitutions and exchanges of phantasmal dreams. The displacement of desire among the various characters points out the existence of a symbolic order, which creates the idea of autonomy when, in fact, the characters exist determined by their propensity for interpretive error.

As an exegetic scholar, "divining rather than beholding the spirit" of his texts (I.Vol.34), Jude can never resist the temptation to read deep meanings, the "assemblage of concurring and converging probabilities" of "truths," into a scene (II.i.95). Yet it is less "absolute certitude" (II.i.95) that lies hidden beneath the manifest content of human experience in the novel than it is a mystified, but nonetheless threatening, organization of that content. When Jude thereafter looks into Sue's "untranslatable eyes" (II.ii.104) and immediately begins to interpret her character, he is only repeating the established pattern of error. Despite the difference in the agency that produces it, Jude manifests again the desire for that earlier "law of transmutation." Here, Sue's eyes reveal a text to be translated; but, as with the Greek and Latin grammars, no master code exists to guarantee the authority of Jude's translation. The rules governing the metonymic transfer, the figure Latin rhetoric calls *transmutio,* belong to the same illusion of a metaphysics of presence in the word, and to the same hallucination of a language determined on the basis of a verbal representation. Just as language is constituted through repetition, so too does Jude's life acquire a narratable consistency. But the symbolic "inscription" of Jude's desires upon the surface of Wessex as he travels its roads from Christminster to Shaston, to Aldbrickham and back again, constitutes only the provisional creation of meaning through a process of deferment. As Jude's dreams are transmuted from Arabella to Christminster, and to Sue, the fantasy of stability creates an apparently meaningful and readable text. It is always only in retrospect, however, that Jude's perceptions of those illusions of totality and stability can be organized and lived as an aesthetically coherent *meaning.*

But it is more the inner tensions produced by the characters' shifting relations that shape the action than haphazard or indifferent circumstance. And it is not entirely coincidental that the act of reading surfaces again to indicate these changes in connection with the constant letters that reaffirm the importance of writings, signs, inscription, and marks in the lives of these characters. Altogether there are at least thirty-two letters indicated or implied in the novel, ranging from one-line suicide notes (*"Done because we are too menny"*) to full-sized "carefully considered epistle[s]" (VI.iVol.433), directly or indirectly narrated, delivered or not delivered. The numerous instances of inscriptions and carvings reinforce the importance of the "letter" in the text as the emblem for the force of illusion.

The first of these letters between Jude and Sue had simply called for their initial meeting, but it was "one of those documents which, simple and commonplace in themselves, are seen retrospectively to have been pregnant with impassioned consequences" (II.iVol.115-16). By the time Sue is engaged to Phillotson, Jude is receiving sudden "passionate" letters (III.i.153) from her that seem to close the psychic distance between them in a way that they can never quite imitate in person. "'It is very odd—'" Jude says at one point, "'That you are often not so nice in your real presence as you are in your letters!'" "'Does it really seem so to you?'" asks Sue, who then replies, "'Well, that's strange; but I feel just the same about you, Jude'" (III.vi.197). A letter is a medium that effectively separates the writer from the effects of the message, while the message received is often one created by the reader himself. Even in their coldest tones, Sue's letters, while banishing Jude, nevertheless constantly summon him to her by the very fact that they establish a link of communication between them. Similarly, Phillotson's letter relinquishing Sue paradoxically begins reestablishing his hold on her; for the "shadowy third" (IVol.Vol.288), like the substantial couple, is always primarily constituted by this act of communication.

Moreover, when Sue writes a letter, she simultaneously removes and retains her absence and distance. This simultaneity of absence and presence is primarily an outcome of written discourse and is indicative of Jude's more general mystification concerning the existence of a stabilizing meaning. Sue is an eminently desirable woman, but she also becomes a sign in Jude's mind for an absent source of meaning. Accordingly, the act of writing becomes a bolster for the illusion of presence and wholeness within a discourse that appears innocent and transparent. Sue's letter can never replace her, but, conversely, her "real presence" is never identical with the original self promised in the letter. The written word does not allow access to the thing in itself, but always creates a copy, a simulacrum of it that sometimes moves the reader of the word more strongly than can the actual presence of the represented thing. Thus, the curious result is that the graphic sign, rather than the actual presence, of the desired becomes the cause of emotive energy. For Jude, the desire for this originary "anchoring point" becomes an indispensable illusion situated in the syntax of a dream without origin.

The intersubjective complex that structures the novel ***Jude the Obscure*** offers us some version of the following schema:

(1) dreams that fail—Jude, Phillotson, Sue;

(2) marriages that fail—Jude and Arabella; Sue and Phillotson; Jude and Sue; Arabella and Cartlett; both sets of parents; the legendary ancestor (mentioned in Vol.iVol.340);

(3) returns to original failures—Jude and Arabella at Christminster; Sue and Phillotson at Marygreen.

We began, remember, with Jude and Arabella at Marygreen, and with Sue and Phillotson at Christminster. The intervening movements in the plot that lead to the present renewal of the characters' former relations thus trace the pattern that characterizes the narrative structure. It is a *chiasmus,* the cross-shaped substitution of properties: the original couples are reunited, but in reverse locales. Hardy had referred to this structure more obliquely as the "geometric construction" behind his novel. Elsewhere he calls it the "quadrille" that puts in motion the opposing qualities of the four main characters. But it turns out that the very process of "construction" that the characters' actions enact is really one more reversal of earlier misguided "constructions." Would it not follow then that this new turn should restore the characters to their "proper" places? That is, if Jude and Sue have been improperly associated at Christminster, might we not recover a measure of truth by simply restoring her to Phillotson at Marygreen? Since this structure of reversal is not only at work on the thematic level of the story, within the marital relationships among the characters, but also animates the greater structure of the narrative, the plot itself, the deconstruction of its pattern has significant implications for the novel's concept of a readable, constructive, integrating process in general.

Jude's idea of a synthetic "anchoring point" of semantic stability originates as the effect of a prior requirement, namely, the requirement that the elements of that synthesis can themselves be permanently fixed in relation to stable qualities. Failing to integrate the ideal and the real with Sue, Jude is no more likely to do so with Arabella. Sue's situation with Phillotson and Jude is even more complex, for the two are versions of the same in different registers. Further reversals, consequently, promise only continued instability. And, I would say, it makes little difference in this novel whether one calls the trope governing the structure of the narrative metaphor, metonymy, chiasmus, or simply a "geometric construction," for from the first, the characters' roles have been inscribed in the determining contextual system defined by the marriage laws.

In the Victorian novel marriage is preeminently the foundation of social stability. As a quasi-contractual agreement, it sets up the participants as a center for other integrating relationships. These relationships are not simply necessary for society; they constitute it. And that larger social and historical life, the world of symbolic relationships, forms in dialectical turn the structure that orders individual behavior in Hardy's novels. In a moment of pure poetic insight Sue comments on the nature of those relations:

> I have been thinking . . . that the social moulds civilization fits us into have no more relation to our actual shapes than the conventional shapes of the constellations have to the real star-patterns. I am called Mrs. Richard Phillotson, living a calm wedded life with my counterpart of that name. But I am not really Mrs. Richard Phillotson, but a woman tossed about, all alone, with aberrant passions, and unaccountable antipathies.
>
> (IVol.i.246-47)

With remarkable clarity Sue recognizes that the social woman is a representation, transposed and supplemented by desire, of her real self. But the relation between her natural and social selves is like the relation between "real star-patterns" and traditional interpretations of the "conventional" constellation shapes, like that between a referent and its linguistic sign—that is, *aesthetic* and hence *arbitrary.* The concept of the self is the product of an aberrant substitution of rhetorical properties. Sue here clearly understands that this rhetorical operation is at best a metaphorical, interpretive act—one that is necessarily open to a variety of figural misreadings.

We have seen that the law that regulates marriage ties in this novel superimposes the kingdom of *culture* on that of *nature.* Following its dictates, Jude artificially imposes a vision of organic totality (figured at different times by Phillotson, Christminster, Sue, etc.) onto nature and accords it a moral and epistemological privilege. In contrast, the narrator's ironic comments show Jude's substitutions and realignments within the marriage system and within the pattern of metaphors for his vision of an "anchoring point" to be purely formal, analogous only by contingency, and hence without privilege. When the value of those associations is questioned, when the notion of Sue as the representation of Jude's dreams is made problematic, the possibility of a simple relation between signified and signifier is also questioned.

That formerly unquestioned assumption is the original moment of illusion that the narrative demystifies. The narrator reveals to us that Jude's and Sue's notion of a privileged system of law is an hypothesis, or a fictional construct (a *doxa*), that makes the orderly conduct of human affairs possible. It is not a "true" and irrefutable axiom based on knowledge (an *episteme*). Their tendency, as revealed by the metaphorical rhetoric of their desires, is always to abide by the lawful order of "natural" logic and unity: "'It is,'" Sue says at one point, "'none of the natural tragedies of love that's love's usual tragedy in civilized life, but a tragedy artificially manufactured for people who in natural state would find relief in parting!'" (IVol.ii.258). But if the order of "natural" law is itself a hypothetical construct rather than a "natural" occurrence in the world, then there is no necessary reason to suppose that it can, in fact, provide "relief." And it is Sue once again, who, after the tragic deaths of their children, perceives that possibility when she says to Jude:

> "We said . . . that we would make a virtue of joy. I said it was Nature's intention, Nature's law and

raison d'être that we should be joyful in what instincts she afforded us—instincts which civilization had taken upon itself to thwart. . . . And now Fate has given us this stab in the back for being such fools as to take Nature at her word!"

(VI.ii.408-09)

Jude, who likes to think of himself "as an order-loving man" of an "unbiased nature" (IVol.ii.252), can only stand by helplessly as he hears Sue destroy the basis of their "natural" marriage.

Hardy's novel situates itself explicitly within the context of the marriage laws that establish Victorian society. It portrays, as Hardy tells us, the attempted translation of the law of nature into civil terms. The characters, however, cannot legitimately perform this translation without confusing the names of two such divergent semantic fields as those covered by "natural law" and "civil law." Confusion arises because the terms designate contextual properties, patterns of integration and disintegration, and not absolute concepts. In Hardy's Wessex, the "law of nature" designates a state of relational integration that precedes in degree the stage of "civil law" since civil law only "enunciates" what is already present in nature to be read. The undoing of a system of relations codified in "civil law" will always reveal, consequently, a more fragmented stage that can be called "natural." This prior stage does not possess moral or epistemological priority over the system that is being undone. But Jude always does assign it priority.

Remembering that "his first aspiration—towards academical proficiency—had been checked by a woman, and that his second aspiration—toward apostleship—had also been checked by a woman," Jude asks himself ungallantly "'Is it . . . that the women are to blame; or is it the artificial system of things, under which the normal sex-impulses are turned into devilish domestic gins and springs to noose and hold back those who want to progress?'" (IVol.iii.261). The weight of the second clause of the question makes it simply rhetorical: the women are of course not to blame. Although the "natural" pattern that Jude and Sue attempt to substitute for the accepted "civil" one is itself one system of relations among others, they see it as the sole and true order of things and not as an artifice like civil structure. But once the fragmentation of the apparently stable structure of civil law is initiated, endless other versions of "natural law" might be engendered in a repeating pattern of regression.

The decisive term characterizing Jude's and Sue's relationship, "natural law," thus presents itself to be read as a chiastic pattern also. Natural law deconstructs civil law; but natural law is then itself open to the process of its own analysis. Far from denoting a stable point of homogeneity, where they might enact the mythic integration of their "one person split in two" (IVol.iVol.276), the "natural law" of Hardy's Wessex connotes the impossibility of integration and stability. Any of Hardy's texts that put such polarities as natural and civil law, desire

and satisfaction, repetition and stability into play will have to set up the fiction of a synthetic process that will function both as the deconstructive instrument and as the outcome of that deconstruction. For Hardy, dualisms are never absolute. Deconstruction, however, is the process that both reveals the deluded basis of the desire for the synthesis of dualism, and also creates the elements necessary for a new and equally deluded desire for integration. *Jude the Obscure* thus both denies the validity of the metaphor that unites "natural" and "civil" law, and elaborates a new metaphor to fulfill the totalizing function of the original binary terms. This new metaphor of life as an organic and orderly process now allows the narrative to continue by providing a myth of a future moment when, as Phillotson's friend Gillingham says, Jude and Sue might make "their union legal . . . and all would be well, and decent, and in order" (VI.iVol.433). This mythic moment, however, never comes.

It is crucial, then, that the basic conflicts of the novel occur within the "give and take" of marriage, for it situates the issue directly in the referential contexts of ethics and legality. Civil law, in fact, can be conceived as the emblem of referentiality *par excellence* since its purpose is to codify the rules for proper social intercourse. But to abide by the law, we must be able to read its text; ignorance is after all, in English common law, no excuse. Attempting to read it, Jude concludes that "we are acting by the letter; and 'the letter killeth'!" (VI.viii.469). Jude thus interprets the Pauline dictum, "The letter killeth but the spirit giveth life," as an injunction against a *literal* reading of the codes governing ethical action. Yet his *figural* reading leads to no spiritual truth either. On the contrary, Jude's illusions result from a figurative language taken literally, as with Sue he takes "Nature at her word." For Jude and Sue, then, there is no text present anywhere that is yet to be transmuted, yet to be translated from natural to civil terms. There is no *natural* truth written anywhere that might be read without being somehow altered in the process. The text of associations Jude fabricates around him is already woven of interpretations and differences in which the meaning of dreams and the desire for illusions are unnaturally coupled. Everything in Wessex "begins" with repetition, with secondary images of a meaning that was never present but whose *signified* presence is reconstituted by the supplementary and belated word of Jude's desires.

I am saying, of course, that the narrative of *Jude the Obscure,* while telling the story of Jude's and Sue's unhappy marriages, also dispels the illusion of a readable truth; that the novel gains its narrative consistency by the repeated undoing of the metaphor of life as organic unity. But the story that tells why figurative denomination is an illusion is itself *readable* and *referential* to the negative truth that Jude never perceives, and the story thus relapses into the very figure it deconstructs. The structure of the narrative as chiasmus, the cross-shaped substitution of properties, also tells, therefore, another story in the form of allegory about the divergence between the literal and figural dimensions of language. That the text reverts to doing what it has claimed to be impossible is not a sign of Hardy's weakness as a novelist, for the error is not with the text, nor with the reader who attempts to understand it. Rather, I would say that with Jude we find that language itself, to the extent that it attempts to be truthful, necessarily misleads us about its own ability to take us outside its own structures in search of meaning.

The myth of a stabilizing natural or civil law, then, is actually the representation of our will to make society seem a unified and understandable organism. But Hardy's novel persists in showing society's laws as open to subversion by the actions of the individuals who make up society. In everyday life, there is an ever possible discontinuity between the word of the law, its spirit, and the practice, the letter, of the law. And the necessary failure of the law to enforce its monologic interpretations of the infinite variety of human behavior can lead to the subversion of the entire relational system. This explains why Jude, by his actions, constantly and unintentionally subverts the Word that he figures in Sue and in his dreams of a university career.

In applying the accepted social law to themselves, Jude and Sue constitute a version of the law, but in applying the general law to their particular situation, they instantaneously alter it. Rather than serving as a source of universal order from which social relations might be stabilized and unified within a social totality, the accepted social law exhibits its inability to constrain the heterogeneity of social relations. The law, then, is always shown to be grammatically structured, since it always engenders only a contingent, contextual meaning. Jude's revolutionary attempt to establish a ground for authentic meaning thus produces an anarchy of mutually exclusive readings of the one piece of language, "The letter killeth." This discontinuity between the "letter" and the "spirit" of the law, between a literal and a figural reading of its sign, is what constitutes Hardy's break with referentiality. Although the law indicates that "The letter killeth," Jude finds it impossible to decide what is the *letter* and what the *spirit* of the law. In each reading, whether within a "natural" or a "civil" system, the law is transposed, altered, and led to produce the conditions for its own undoing. Like Sue's ambiguous letters, the law is consequently only a promise (which cannot be kept) of a future stability and is never adequate to deal with the instability of the present moment.

The repetitions in the novel put at stake not only the relation between Jude's present actions and his family's history, but also the very readability of the initial text of that history. Everywhere about him, history calls out to be read, but Jude consistently fails to do so properly. Because he cannot read it, his actions are never simply a representation of that past, but are an interpretation that has gone awry. Since the novel is itself a kind of history, it too is open to all the errors of interpretation of which it speaks. Hardy's "Postscript," which calls attention to the decisive issues of reading and interpretation, must

thus be seen in retrospect as an ironic repetition of the situation dramatized in *Jude* concerning the impossibility of authoritative readings, for it accuses the reader of partaking in Jude's error. We cannot read the novel as Jude reads the motto of his life, that is, with the expectation of encountering an ideally sanctioned stable truth.

But how *are* we to read it then? If the notion of representation is to be at all meaningful, we must presuppose the stability of subjects with stable names who are to be represented, and a rapport between the sign and the referent in the language of the representation. Yet both conditions are absent from this text (notoriously so in the allegorical figure of little Father Time). We can, of course, discern similarities among the characters' various actions. And as we read, attempting, in Hardy's words, "to give shape and coherence to this series of seemings" (viii), we too must rely on Jude's example in constructing an interpretive model. But we cannot accept his model of metaphoric synthesis as an absolute. Jude's model of metaphor (governing the patterns of idealization and substitution) is erroneous because it believes in its own referential meaning—it believes that the inwardly desired "anchoring point" can be concretely encountered in the external world as Phillotson, as Christminster, as Arabella, or as Sue. It assumes a world in which literal and figural properties can be isolated, exchanged, and substituted. For the reader and the narrator, metaphoric synthesis persists within the interpretive act, but not as the ground of ultimate reconciliations. Jude himself, however, remains caught in the error of metaphor. But it is an error without which reading could not take place.

We thus find that Hardy's narrative puts the assurance of the truth of the referent into question. But in making this situation thematic, it does allow a meaning, the text, to exist. We are not dealing simply with an *absence* of meaning, for if we were, then that very absence would itself constitute a referent. Instead, as an allegory of the breakdown of the referential system, *Jude the Obscure* continues to refer, to its own chiastic operations. This *new* referentiality is one bounded strictly by the margins of textuality. In our courses on the nineteenth-century novel we find it convenient to use *Jude* as a "transitional" text; it is either the last of the Victorians or the first of the Moderns. Morton Zabel has written, [in *Thomas Hardy,* edited by Albert Guerard], for instance, that Hardy was "a realist developing toward allegory . . . who brought the nineteenth century novel out of its slavery to fact." This seems to me fine, as far as it goes. But I would add that this allegorical pattern manifests itself in *Jude* primarily through the subversive power of the dialogic word, which refuses to be reduced to the single "anchoring point" of a transcendent and determining Will, Immanent or otherwise.

As Hardy came to see early on, the function of realistic fiction was to show that "*nothing* is as it appears." It is no wonder, then, that Hardy's last novel was misread. The suggestive and poetic force of *Jude* arises less from its positive attempt to represent appearance than from its rejection of any vision pretending to convey the totality and complexity of life. Accordingly, in *Jude* Hardy repudiates the notion that fiction can ever be Truth, that it can ever "reproduc[e] in its entirely the phantasmagoria of experience with infinite and atomic truth, without shadow, relevancy, or subordination." He dramatizes, instead, the recognition that in narrative "Nothing but the illusion of truth can permanently please, and when the old illusions begin to be penetrated, a more natural magic has to be supplied." To be realistic, the text must proceed as if its representing systems correspond to those in the world; it must create a new illusion of reference to replace the old of representation.

But this transmutation of illusions modifies the original considerably. Like Sue's "real presence," perpetually deviating from the ideal figure of Jude's dreams, the letter of the text, "*translat*[*ing*] the qualities that are already there" in the world, contains after all only the inadequate ciphers of the spirit of meaning, not the "thing" itself. The deconstruction of the metaphorical model of substitution and translation (operating in Jude's various desires for Christminster, Sue, natural law, etc.) is performed by the rhetorical structure of chiasmus, whose own figural logic both asserts and denies referential authority. From the reader's point of view, the results of each of the figural movements can then be termed "meanings," but only by forgetting that the resulting sociological, ethical, legal, or thematic categories are undone by the very process that creates them.

It may well be, therefore, that Hardy's final novel does not "mean"; but it does signify to a redoubtable degree. It signifies the laws of language over which neither Hardy nor his readers can exercise complete control. To read those laws is to undermine their intent. This is why Hardy, like Jude who adds to the textual allegory of Wessex and generates its history while marking its closure, is bound to allegorical narratives: he creates the fiction of an ideal reader while he constructs a narrative about the illusion of privileged readings. On this level of rhetorical self-consciousness, prose fiction is on the verge of becoming poetry.

Sherilyn Abdoo (essay date 1984)

SOURCE: "Hardy's Jude: The Pursuit of the Ideal as Tragedy," in *The Existential Coordinates of the Human Condition: Poetic-Epic-Tragic,* D. Reidel Publishing Company, 1984, pp. 307-18.

[*In the following essay, Abdoo maintains that* Jude the Obscure *is a tragic novel in the classical tradition.*]

> All tragedy is grotesque. (Thomas Hardy, *Life,* August 13, 1898)

INTRODUCTION

Virginia Woolf's tribute to Thomas Hardy was written shortly after his death on January 11, 1928. In it she said:

"if we are to place Hardy among his fellows, we must call him the greatest tragic writer among English novelists." She goes on to assert that although it is "the most painful" and "pessimistic" of his novels, *Jude the Obscure* "is not tragic." Hardy, himself, in the 1895 Preface to the First Edition of the novel referred to *Jude* as "simply an endeavor to give shape and coherence to a series of seemings, or personal impressions . . . not of the first moment." Superseding, however, is his later statement, which under the stimulus of the early critical attacks on *Jude,* identifies the novel's central interest for him:

> the greater part of the story—that which presented the shattered ideals of the two chief characters, and had been more especially, and indeed most exclusively, the part of interest to myself— practically ignored by the adverse press.

The purpose of this paper is exegesis, a critical analysis of Thomas Hardy's last and greatest novel. My aim is a comprehensive interpretation of the novel, a look into its heart—to the origins—of Hardy's view of the human situation: the inevitable defeat of the human spirit by a powerful force which allows no redemption, whether in this life or elsewhere.

In *Jude,* Hardy recapitulates and interweaves the major themes of his prior novels: idealization of the beloved; man's alienation from himself and isolation from others; God as unknowable; that man's fate—puppet-like—is controlled by a capricious hand; that life, particularly marriage, is a trap from which death is the only escape; the self-proclaimed believers are among the most impious members of the human community, wherein modern religion is itself an hypocrisy; the injustice of a social order favoring a privileged class—while, others, the working classes most especially, must strictly adhere to conventional propriety in order to retain even an aura of respectability; the juxtaposition of the ordinary with the grotesque; Pride, the dominant human character trait of Hardy's protagonists, as major contributor to their tragic ends; and finally, the immense living presence of Nature as She provides both a backdrop to and a reflection of, the unredemptive human tragedy, which is simply, being alive.

The primary issues this paper addresses and tries to resolve are the following: (1) whether *Jude the Obscure* is, in fact, a tragic novel; (2) the ways that the novel's tragedy is supported by Hardy's antecedent prose writings and extant biographical materials, including Florence Emily Hardy's *Life of Thomas Hardy* (which we now know he wrote himself), and the recently published *Personal Notebooks* and *Letters*; (3) how Hardy's preoccupation with the heroic man and the idealistic feminine became objects of his intellectual pursuit; (4) the degree to which Thomas Hardy, as poet/novelist, pursued the elusive, ideal woman of his dreams (much to the distress of his two wives) in his novels and poetry—and, in so doing, he became his own hero; (5) the alliance in Hardy's novels between Evil and the grotesque; (6) the metaphor for Life itself in Hardy's novels is the Greek "web," the inexorable pattern that binds his characters to their doom; and finally (7) "tragedoia," the "goat-song"—as the primary factor in the origin of tragic genre—is, at its most primitive, raw, excruciating, half-mad sense, the mimetic impulse that Hardy's dramas were created to express.

This paper's position is based on the premise that with *Jude* Hardy had ultimately fulfilled his purpose as a novelist; he had given full expression to his understanding of the tragic in the human condition; and that his abandonment of novel-writing for poetry, therefore, was an artistic necessity. As A. Alvarez comments: "After *Jude the Obscure* there was no other direction in which he could go."

Many have tried since Aristotle's *Poetics* to explain what the tragic experience is. At best, we can expect only to receive a second- or third-hand description. However, what we can hope to gain in understanding through art, is a moment's glimpse—an approximation—of individual suffering which may help us bear our own loneliness and fear.

To begin at the beginning necessitates a return to the Greek origins of tragedy, in this case primarily to the understanding of Hardy's sources as he was an avid, life-long student of Greek tragedy. But first let's consider some of his own thoughts on tragedy and identify those aspects of his earlier novels which are particularly relevant to Jude's tragedy. His early note (November, 1885) that: "tragedy exhibits a state of things in the life of an individual which unavoidably causes some natural aim or desire of his to end in a catastrophe when carried out" (*Life,* p. 176), became, just three years before *Jude* (October, 1892) more specific: "The best tragedy—highest tragedy in short—is that of the WORTHY encompassed by the INEVITABLE" (*Life,* p. 251).

Jude's tragedy is bound to his two failures: (1) failure to achieve admittance to Balliol College, Christminster, and the education he desires, and (2) failure to achieve complete possession of Sue Bridehead, the woman he successively idealizes, loves, pursues, loses, regains, lives with, has children by and finally loses again, forever. Throughout the course of the novel Jude is psychially sustained by his concurrent struggles to achieve education and to win Sue's love. His efforts with these involvements provide both the impetus and the reasons for his continuing to live. Jude's ineligibility for a university education, when he is finally rejected, is due not to his lack of scholarly ability, but to his low social status; he is, after-all, a laborer, a restorer of churches. And while he finally loses Sue altogether because of her overwhelming guilt after the hangings of their children, Jude *never* derived full satisfaction from their sexual life together. Sue was incapable of completely giving herself to him. To do so would have made her totally dependent on Jude for her identity, a state of being that her already too fragile self-image could not tolerate. In short, Sue Bridehead is terrified of losing her self-identity in Jude—of becoming a non-existent personality.

Jude's frustration remains unabated while he has hope of realizing his goals and he doggedly struggles to achieve them. But when his idealizations are denied him Jude's will to live evaporates and he dies. Obtaining a university education and possessing Sue Bridehead are identified here as idealizations in the Platonic sense. For Jude education represents knowledge, the ultimate achievement that will open the door to worldly success; possessing Sue is the possession of something especially fine, a quality above his rough experience. To claim Sue for his own is for Júde equivalent to touching the ethereal or other-worldly—similar in fact to experiencing a transcendent religious experience. In Sue's case, her lack of sexual desire and her inability to love Jude completely creates a barrier beween them. Jude is forced to live out his Platonic idealization of the feminine, while Sue's denial keeps "his passion as hot at the end as at the beginning, and helps to break his heart" (*Life,* p. 272). On the other hand, Jude's struggles to educate himself in preparation for the university are, in the face of his desperate situation, only keeping alive his hope for a better time. Had it been more than a dream, would he have waited so long to find out the truth? Was it not then the struggle against adversity, the struggle towards education, towards possession of the most beautiful, wonderful woman he knew that keeps Jude alive?

Hardy's original idea for Jude's story was as follows: "A short story of a young man—'who could not go to Oxford'—His struggles and ultimate failure. Suicide" (*Life,* pp. 207-8). And in a letter to an unidentified friend after its publication, Hardy comments on the novel's reviews and tries, retrospectively, to clarify his original thesis:

> It is curious that some of the papers should look upon the novel as a manifesto on "the marriage question" (although, of course, it involves it), seeing that it is concerned first with the labours of a poor student to get a University degree, and secondly with the tragic issues of two bad marriages, owing in the main to a doom or curse of hereditary temperament peculiar to the family of the parties. (*Life,* p. 271)

Now that we are closer to Hardy's purpose, let's consider the actual sequence of events. The boy Jude lives with his maiden aunt and is inspired by his teacher, Phillotson, to advance himself by studying so that he will eventually be accepted to the university at Christminster. Suffering the rough indifference of his aunt, Jude grows up to become a stone mason—all the while teaching himself Latin and Greek and looking towards a brighter future, a time when he would be in Christminster—the "heavenly Jerusalem" (*JO,* p. 18). [all page references are to the Wessex editions of Hardy's novels]. Along the way he becomes temporarily distracted by his awakened sexuality and marries Arabella Donn. But she soon tires of Jude and leaves him. When he finally does reach Christminster it is to meet his cousin, Sue Bridehead, the woman he fell in love with when he saw her photo at his aunt's house. But he also again meets Phillotson, his old teacher, and introduces him to Sue. Sue becomes attracted to Phillotson when he offers her a job as pupil teacher if she will attend a teacher's college to become qualified. Instead Sue runs away from the college and shortly thereafter Phillotson marries her, nonetheless. The marriage is an altogether excruciating event for Jude who is forced, by virtue of the fact that he is Sue's only living relative besides Aunt Drusilla who is against marriage, to give her away at the ceremony. Sue goes off with Phillotson, but their marriage is never consummated. Meanwhile Aunt Drusilla dies, Jude meets Arabella again and in his despair has a brief affair with her, becomes inspired by religious music and begins ecclesiastical studies. Sue, having met Jude at Aunt Drusilla's funeral and knowing she cannot stay with Phillotson, who is getting impatient with her excuses, declares her love for Jude and runs away to live with him. At this point Jude abandons his religious studies. Eventually Jude and Arabella divorce as do Sue and Phillotson; Phillotson's teaching career is, meanwhile, ruined by the results of his disastrous liaison with Sue. But it is Sue's fear that Arabella will win Jude back that compels her to agree to marry Jude for convention's sake. Circumstances arise, however, which cause postponement until they abandon the idea. At this time Jude learns of the existence of his child by Arabella—Little Jude, nicknamed "Little Father Time . . . because [he] looked so aged" (*JO*, p. 221). The child arrives to live with Sue and Jude and three years pass. Sue by this time has succumbed to Jude's physical desire, has borne him two children and is pregnant with a third. When Little Father Time learns of Sue's pregnancy he is horrified with what seems to him her irresponsible fecundity. He chides her remorselessly and in a fit of despair hangs the two infants and himself. Sue's remorse and guilt drives her away from Jude and back to Phillotson who she has convinced herself is her only true husband. Arabella now a widow, seduces the ill, distraught Jude and tricks him into marrying her for the second time. Jude's last unsuccessful attempt to get Sue back is preceded and followed by a suicidal walk in the freezing rain. He dies reciting Job while Sue lives in self-punishment, submitting to Phillotson's lust.

The connective thread running between Jude, Sue and his educational pursuits is Phillotson. Jude's initial desire for university education is stimulated by Phillotson's early interest in him as his boyhood teacher and friend. Ironically, it is the same Phillotson—the only male figure who takes an interest in him—that frustrates the boy Jude by promising but not immediately sending the Latin textbooks, who marries the woman he loves and then after Jude has won Sue back and they have produced several children, takes her away from him again. Thus, Phillotson is the menacing, powerful father figure who must prevent the threatening son from replacing him. It is Phillotson's inner weakness, though, that keeps him, like Sue and Jude, isolated and dependent on others for his own sense of personal identity. Phillotson's role (whether or not consciously known to Hardy) is that of the castrating

father in competition with the son. Similarly, Sue's relationship with Phillotson is an Oedipal one; for her he also at first becomes a father figure by virtue of his age (he is forty-five when they marry, "old enough to be the girl's father" [*JO*, p. 86]). Her instinctive revulsion for his physical person is a self-protecting act against incest.

The novel's structure is largely constructed around the tensions of the couplings and separations that take place among the participants of two sets of love triangles: Jude-Sue-Phillotson, and Arabella-Jude-Sue. But this pattern is an already familiar one to Hardy; he used it in virtually *all* his prior novels. In fact, we can state that in Hardy's case the love triangle is a compulsive, repetitive literary device. But this device is more than a convenient structure. It is the portrayal of Hardy's own inner neurotic state, whether or not he ever realized it. The similarities between Hardy and Jude, despite his disclaimer that "no book he had ever written contained less of his own life" (*Life*, p. 274), must be considered before the central problem can be revealed and resolved.

To move on to this paper's central premise that ***Jude the Obscure*** is a tragic novel, we must recognize that Jude is also St. Jude, martyr and patron saint of hopeless causes; his goal is Christminster, "the home of lost causes" (*JO*, p. 66). Jude is the sacrificial scapegoat of both the pagan and Christian ethos. The novel's progression travels historically from the pagan sacrifice to the Christian sacrifice, but in neither case is redemption achieved. The first sacrifice comes with the discontent and break-up of Jude's first marriage to Arabella. It is the death of erotic love that is so vividly portrayed in the pig-killing scene. Arabella, after-all, threw the pig's pizzle that first captured Jude's attention. So it is the agonized death of the dumb creature, so clearly representing their earthy, natural coupling, that appropriately joins Jude's fate to the pig's: "the white snow, stained with the blood of his fellow-mortal" (*JO*, p. 55). And later, when he and Sue discover their two children hanging on garment hooks and "little Jude . . . in a similar manner" (*JO*, p. 265), Jude cries out in recognition: "O my comrade, our perfect union—our two-in-oneness—is now stained with blood" (*JO*, p. 267)! The children's deaths are virtual sacrifices; the three little bodies a crude emulation of the crucifixion and the result is Sue's final desertion of Jude for Phillotson in an attempt she says, to "mortify the flesh—the terrible flesh—the curse of Adam" (*JO*, p. 272)! The pagan sacrifice of the pig marks the death of Jude's marital relation to Arabella and the physical expression of his nature; the Christian sacrifice of the children marks the death of Jude's relation to Sue and the spiritual/redemptive hope that he lives for. He dies finally neither pagan nor Christian, but identifying totally with the suffering Job:

> Let the day perish wherein I was born, the night in which it was said, there is a man child conceived. . . . Why died I not from the womb? Why did I not give up the ghost when I came out of the belly? . . . For now should I have lain still and been quiet. I should have slept: then had I been at rest!

. . . Wherefore is light given to him that is in misery, and life unto the bitter in soul? (*JO*, p. 320)

Hardy's juxtaposition of the pagan, Christian and Old Testament sources as only briefly noted here, reveals his ambivalence about religion. The issue at hand is basically to identify those elements of Greek tragedy beginning with Aristotle's definition in the *Poetics* that **Jude** incorporates, and to show that despite the later consequences of Christianity vis-à-vis Darwin's *Origin of Species,* **Jude the Obscure** is nonetheless a tragedy following in the classical tradition.

From Plato who identified the tragedian as "an imitator, whose product is at least three removes from nature . . . and the truth," we can consider first Aristotle's initial statement towards a definition of tragedy:

> Tragedy, then, is an imitation of an action that is serious, complete, and of a certain magnitude; in language embellished with each kind of artistic ornament, the several kinds being found in separate parts of the play; in the form of action not of narratives; through pity and fear effecting the proper purgation of these emotions.

Jude's tragedy, then, arising from Hardy's imagination, is an imitation twice removed from the experiences of his personal life and three times removed from the experiences of friends, relatives and strangers as related to him second- or third-hand, and common hearsay embellished and altered to fit the situation. The dramatic agents of the tragedy are principally Jude Fawley and Sue Bridehead. Their actions reveal the arrangement of incidents—in short, the plot. The novel's action is certainly "serious, complete and of a certain magnitude," if by "serious" we mean that it deals with issues or events that can alter the course of a life, result in poverty, physical disability, or death, "complete" because it relates a single story or statement with a beginning, middle and end, and "of a certain magnitude" because of the powerful emotional effects it has on the reader—due to reversal (or turn of the plot) and recognition by the hero/protagonist of his true situation and the consequences thereof. In **Jude,** the elements of surprise triggering the plot's reversal are several. First of all Arabella tricks Jude into marrying her with a false claim of pregnancy; second, Sue Bridehead's sudden decision to marry Phillotson when she discovers that Jude is already married; third, the appearance of Little Father Time; and fourth, the grotesque hangings of Jude's and Sue's children. Jude's recognitions dealing with his erotic nature are two; in each case he sees the human failings of the two women in his life and realizes that they do not measure up to his original idea of them. In Arabella's case: "He knew well, too well, in the secret center of his brain, that Arabella was not worth a great deal as a specimen of womankind." But, in an effort to repress the true state of his feelings he "kept up a fictitious belief in her. His idea of her was the thing of most consequence, not Arabella herself, he sometimes said laconically" (*JO*, p. 48). And later, Jude accuses Sue in

a moment of revelation: "Sue sometimes . . . I think you are incapable of real love" (*JO*, p. 192). He recants almost immediately though, accepting in place of the passion and warmth that he craves, the Sue he imagines her to be: "you spirit, you disembodied creature, you dear, sweet, tantalizing phantom—hardly flesh at all; so that when I put my arms round you I almost expect them to pass through you as through air!" (*JO*, p. 195).

Just as important is Jude's recognition of the value of his work as a stone-cutter in light of his ambition for obtaining a university education:

> For a moment there fell on Jude a true illumination; that here in the stone yard was a centre of effort as worthy as that dignified by the name of scholarly study within the noblest of the colleges. But he lost it under stress of his old idea. (*JO*, p. 69)

To continue, Hardy identified the tragic hero as one who was the "WORTHY encompassed by the INEVITABLE" (*Life*, p. 251)—one whose misfortunes and suffering inspired in the reader not only feelings of fear and pity, but by association to one's own situation, results in a therapeutic purgation of the emotions. We may question why our feelings of fear and pity are aroused? We feel fear because of the closeness of the protagonists' situation to our own and pity because of the undeserved misfortunes that plague a decent man. Purgation is a temporary cleansing of our emotions through weeping and lamentation. It is precisely because of this temporary relief to our emotional tensions that the entire process of purgation must be repeated again and again. Hence, the significance of repetitious or cyclical ritual sacrifice. It is the spectacle of watching someone else suffer, the sadistic satisfaction (sometimes amounting to lust) we feel in knowing that it is not us doing the suffering, and the exhilaration of having survived yet another test of time that we enjoy. Again, a public display of grief allows the spectator to empathize with the slain or suffering hero and expiates the guilt he feels. The realization that death is so close to the living experience intimately joins us to the pathos of the victim's plight. It is the survival of the fittest that counts, or perhaps more accurately, the struggle between the will-to-live undermined by the subconscious death-wish. Here again, the idea of a sinless hero is an important distinction; for, while a despicable, worthless hero would inspire neither feelings of fear or pity, nor can we share our most profound experiences with a perfect man/god who has the power to control his own destiny. Rather, he must be like us, a human man with feelings and flaws.

Hardy's concept of nature and man's place in the universe obviously deviated from the traditional acceptance of a Christian God who offered redemption from sin in an afterlife beginning only with death. Darwin's *Origin of Species* appeared when Hardy was a young man; its impact when he read it was immediate and so affected his beliefs that when Darwin died Hardy attended his funeral. Though his family was long a church-going one,

Hardy nevertheless found it difficult to continue believing in a Christian God who could allow good people so much earthly suffering. Of God's existence he says: "I have been looking for God 50 years, and I think that if he had existed I should have discovered him" (*Life,* p. 224).

In addition, his early and continued study of Greek literature introduced him to an alternate view of the universe and man's relation to its nature. His search for a cosmological order led him, an avowed agnostic, to devise a plausible answer to the question of what force, if not God, determined the natural order of things?

His search carried him through the writing of fifteen novels, two volumes of poetry and one volume of short stories (***Wessex Tales***) before he could offer the explanation he finally gives in ***The Dynasts***. In ***The Dynasts*** Hardy creates the Immanent Will or the Prime Cause as the force in nature which determines the course of events. Humanity for Hardy was an immense creature, "a monster whose body had four million eyes and eight million heads" (*Life,* p. 136). It is a "collective personality" (*Life,* p. 416), "one great network or tissue which quivers in every part when one point is shaken, like a spider's web if touched" (*Life,* p. 177). And man, compelled by his own nature, marches his path blindly until he is woven so tightly into his fate as the threads of a carpet, that he becomes trapped like the fly in a spider's web. No amount of struggling will undo or dislodge him from the pattern that the Immanent Will has created by pulling the strings of the men/puppets to weave the tapestry of its universe.

The structure, then, of Hardy's universe, this giant tapestry of humanity and nature, allows no deviation. Once Jude has chosen his path, he is compelled to follow it to the end of his life, which he does. It is no accident that Hardy had a cobweb phobia. He would search the corners of his house every night before retiring so that he wouldn't sleep in the vicinity of them. The importance of the web image in Greek tragedy is the symbol of entanglement; it is what binds Agamemnon to his fate—it is the carpet that Clytemnestra uses to capture and disable him with. In trying to understand the workings of a universe in which the Christian God's existence was for him unknowable, Hardy borrowed from Aeschylus a metaphor, the web or net, which he then translated into a whole fabric of nature into which each man weaves his own destiny.

To return at last to the original mimetic impulse that Hardy was trying to express in his tragedies, we must consider "tragedoia," the Greek word for tragedy, meaning "goat-song." As we know the goat was used as a sacrificial animal in primitive ritual to represent the slain god Dionysus and helped promote the theory that the cult of Dionysus lamenting over its ritual slaying of its dead god was the root of tragic drama. Here I am concerned with the 'song' aspect of "goat-song," the threnody, the lamentation, the agonized inhuman scream of Oedipus when he puts his eyes out. In ***Jude the Ob-***

scure there are at least two instances when Hardy connects Jude's suffering to this primitive expression of tragic song, the vocal expression of pain and grief.

The first example is found in the well-known pig-killing scene early in the novel. As Arabella ties the pig down in preparation, its "repeated cries of rage . . . changed. . . . It was . . . now . . . the cry of despair; longdrawn, slow and hopeless." After Jude stabs the pig in its neck, "The dying animal's cry assumed its third and final tone, the shriek of agony" (*JO,* p. 54). And secondly, after Jude's marriage to Arabella failed and he is then discouraged from applying to the university, his mental suffering caused by these two failures is compared to the agony of Virgil's Laocoön when he is squeezed to death by serpents in punishment for violating the sacred wood:

> And twice about his gasping throat they fold.
> The priest thus doubly chok'd, their crests divide,
> And tow'ring o'er his head in triumph ride.
> With both his hands he labors at the knots;
> His holy fillets the blue venom blots;
> His roaring fills the flitting air around.

The parallel passage in ***Jude*** is:

> If he had been a woman he must have screamed under the nervous tension which he was now undergoing. But that relief being denied to his virility, he clenched his teeth in misery, burying lines about his mouth like those in the Laocoön, and corrugations between his brows. (*JO,* p. 152)

Jude the Obscure is a tragedy not because Hardy created it for the purpose of giving "shape and coherence to a series of seemings, or personal impressions . . . not of the first moment." It is a tragedy because he has offered a post-Darwinian cosmological structure in which humanity is a "collective conscious"; he offers an unChristian, unredemptive conclusion to his novel, in fact an ending totally without hope; he borrows the Greek/pagan metaphor of the web or net of entrapment to express his idea of the human situation; and finally, he gives us, through first the pig-scream and second the suffering Laocoön, an imitation only of Jude's agony. For these reasons I must disagree with Virginia Woolf's statement that ***Jude the Obscure*** "is not tragic," and declare that it is most definitely a tragedy, particular to and coincident with Hardy's own life experience.

Phillip Mallett (essay date 1989)

SOURCE: "Sexual Ideology and the Narrative Form in *Jude the Obscure,*" in *English,* Vol. XXXVIII, Autumn, 1989, pp. 211-24.

[*In the following essay, Mallett discusses the relation between the confines of language and those of gender ideology in* Jude the Obscure; *he observes that "through its interruptions, silences, and juxtapositions, the narrative form of the novel dramatises and echoes the predicament of its heroine."*]

Critical discussion of *Jude the Obscure* has quite properly concentrated on Sue Bridehead. There have been two main points of departure: the first is Hardy's own account of her in 1912 (teasingly offered as the opinion of an 'experienced reviewer' from Germany) which sees her as the first delineation in fiction of 'a woman of the feminist movement' who represents 'the intellectualized, emancipated bundle of nerves that modern conditions were producing'. The second major departure-point is the pseudo-psychological reading offered two years later by Lawrence in his *Study of Thomas Hardy,* which is in effect an attack on what he sees as Sue's denial of her true female nature ('that which was female in her she wanted to consume within the male force'). But in running these two lines of inquiry—Sue as in some way representative, Sue as a warped individual—critical accounts of the novel have seemed to echo the question, or accusation, with which Jude confronts her as she breaks down at the end of the novel: 'What I don't understand is your extraordinary blindness now to your old logic. Is it peculiar to you, or is it common to Woman?' John Goode has detected a sexist bias, or at least an element of confusion, in the kind of critical interrogation which follows Jude in demanding that Sue must be 'available to understanding'; as Goode points out [in *Women Writing and Writing about Women,* edited by Mary Jacobus, 1979], no such demand is made of Jude, or any other male character. Penny Boumelha goes further [in *Thomas Hardy and Women: Sexual Ideology and Narrative Form,* 1982], and accuses the narrator of acting in 'collusion' with Jude, with the result that Sue is made the instrument of his tragedy rather than the subject of her own. Boumelha goes on to argue, however, that because Sue is distanced from the reader by being seen first through Jude's eyes and then through Arabella's, what we are offered in the novel is 'openly a man's picture of a woman': Sue is 'resistant to appropriation by the male narrator.' But this is an awkward argument which involves the narrator (assumed to be male), Jude and Arabella working together to produce an image of Sue which is simultaneously disavowed within the novel (how?) as 'a man's picture of a woman'. And 'appropriation' is surely tendentious: as if the attempt by a male novelist to imagine a female character were intrinsically improper. (It is, after all, Jude, and not Hardy, who speaks of capitalised 'Woman'.) But it is precisely here that Boumelha's description of *Jude* as a novel pressing against the limits of realism is so useful. The nineteenth century realist novel allows and indeed invites the reader to regard the text as a kind of unseen window, opening directly onto reality. *Jude* is not in these terms a realist novel: or, more exactly, it is not realist in the presentation of Sue. The narrative form of the novel is organised to show how Sue is taught to see herself first of all as a woman, second as Sue Bridehead/Phillotson/Fawley, and finally again as a woman: it does this to reveal the operation of sexual ideology, not to claim that Hardy (or his narrator) has been able to transcend ideology. *Jude the Obscure* is, as Rosemarie Morgan has recently argued [in *Women and Sexuality in the Novels of Thomas Hardy,* 1988], Hardy's most heterodox novel,

but not simply because his sexual politics had become more radical by the 1890s. What distinguishes *Jude* from Hardy's earlier novels is that here the moral iconoclasm which had always characterised his work is no longer inhibited by fictional conventions at odds with his purpose.

Late in the novel (V,v) the narrator denies any obligation to express his 'personal' views on what had become known as 'the Marriage Question', but Hardy was well aware that he was entering this debate, as were the reviewers, whether broadly sympathetic like Edmund Gosse or, like Mrs Oliphant, vehemently hostile. It could hardly have been otherwise in a novel which follows the marriage, divorce, and remarriage of not one but two ill-matched couples, and which has at its centre the painful relationship of Jude and Sue, each registering with extreme sensitivity and as it were seismographically the shocks of the age. And, despite his disclaimers, the narrator's sympathies (like Hardy's own) are clearly with those who saw marriage in the late nineteenth century as an institution which needed to be questioned. In this novel, for example—as not in *The Woodlanders* (1887)—divorce is apparently easy to come by. Yet in each case it is the *woman* who seeks to end the marriage, but the *man* who has to instigate the divorce. The Matrimonial Causes Act of 1857 provided for a husband to divorce his wife on the simple grounds of her adultery, whereas a woman was asked to prove adultery aggravated by desertion (for a period of two years), or by cruelty, incest, rape, bestiality or sodomy. It was, in effect an Act enabling men to divorce their wives. Consequently, Jude must divorce Arabella, and Phillotson divorce Sue, and the women must become the 'guilty' parties. Sue's divorce is the case of Phillotson *versus* Phillotson and Fawley; she is named as the property appropriated, and Jude as the man who has wrongfully taken her. By an irony characteristic of this novel, it was Jude, at the time Sue's nearest married relation, who originally 'gave her away' in marriage—'like a she-ass, or she-goat, or any other domestic animal', as Sue reflects indignantly (III,vii). And while the narrator at times confesses uncertainty about Sue's feelings and motives, he never challenges her protests.

To take a second example from the same area of the novel. For reasons deliberately left unclear, Sue finds it a 'torture' to live on sexually responsive terms with Phillotson, and tells him so: 'For a man and woman to live on intimate terms when one feels as I do is adultery . . . however legal' (IV,iii). Here Sue (and Hardy) enter still more controversial areas of nineteenth century sexual politics. The Act of 1857 had been framed in terms of a man's need to ensure that his property would pass to an heir guaranteed to be his: hence the emphasis on the fidelity of the wife. But contemporary discussion about the Act had highlighted the male desire for the exclusive possession of women as a main element in the double standard—both as enacted in the divorce law, and as allowed by custom: that is, the rule of chastity for middle-class women, sexual license for middle-class men. The passing of the Contagious Diseases Acts (1864, 1866, and 1869), providing for the compulsory medical examination of suspected prostitutes in certain areas of the country, but not (of course) the examination of their male clients, and the defence of these Acts by the medical and military establishments, served to underline the way women's sexuality was being defined, in law, not as their own, but in terms of male demands upon it. Feminists such as Mona Caird (who was known to Hardy) began to speak of 'the twin system of marriage and prostitution', arguing that women were compelled on economic grounds to sell their sexuality, either unofficially and temporarily, in prostitution, or, where the man wanted to transmit either his name or his property, officially and more or less permanently within marriage. Here again it seems that Hardy's narrator adopts the radical position. There is no animus, no show of disgust, against Arabella when she begins to prepare for herself a possible match with the quack physician Vilbert; her sexuality is her best hope of security, and as she has already said, 'poor folks must live' (I,x). More significantly, however, Sue's need *not* to give herself to Phillotson, married though they are, is also treated sympathetically by the narrator. Sue has earlier assured Jude that 'no man short of a sensual savage' will molest a woman: 'Until she says by a look "Come on", he is always afraid to, and if you never say it, or look it, he never comes' (III,iv). But Sue has reckoned without marriage. Phillotson is hardly a sensual savage, but he tells her 'You are committing a sin in not liking me' (IV,iii). His friend Gillingham takes a still harsher view: 'she ought to be smacked, and brought to her senses—that's what I think!' (IV,iv). Phillotson's initial refusal to accept such advice leads to his dismissal from his post, and his 'returning to zero, with all its humiliations' (V,viii). What the 'sensual savage' took by force the husband could claim by law as his 'right', and Sue's wish to avoid this 'torture' is allowed in the novel the full force of that word. It is for this reason, surely, that we are allowed to feel *both* that Sue's reluctance is more general than commonly recognised, *and* to attribute it either to some peculiarity in Phillotson (which her great-aunt intuits, and Sue admits but refuses to explain), or alternatively to an exceptional fastidiousness on Sue's part. Whatever the reason, Sue ought not to be compelled to undergo 'torture'; the reason itself is immaterial, and it is deliberately left unclear. Sue's final capitulation and return to Phillotson's bed, however legal, is felt as a violation: 'a fanatic prostitution', as Jude says (VI,iv).

What these instances illustrate is Hardy's (novelistic) ability to reconstruct what is written in the law, or identified in contemporary polemic, as part of the lived experience of his characters, and especially of course of Sue as moment by moment she endures, explores, seeks to evade, or to exploit, the ways in which she is made to inhabit her gender: to be aware of herself as first and last a 'woman'. 'Made to inhabit her gender' because Hardy does not present Sue as 'having' a 'woman's nature' which she then seeks to express—as if 'woman's nature' were an ahistorical 'given'. Rather, he shows how she constantly has to adapt to being seen by others, and indeed to see herself, in terms of the ideology of womanhood. Here again Hardy is in the middle of the sexual-political battlefield. When John Stuart Mill insisted in *The Subjection of Women* (1869) that 'what is now called the nature of women is an eminently artificial thing', and so should not be made the basis for a theory of their social role as wives, mothers, and managers of households, he was attacking those who too readily identified the 'natural' with the merely 'customary'—as for example slave-owners thought it natural that blacks should be enslaved—and not proposing his own account of women's 'nature'. With the Utilitarians' boundless faith in the efficacy of education to bring about change, Mill did not regard women's nature as a given, one day finally to be disclosed and recognised. But those who opposed Mill from the high ground of late Victorian science took exactly this view. Menstruation, for example, was a fact of nature, and the principle of the conservation of energy was a law of nature. Dr Henry Maudsley explained what resulted from the conjunction of these two 'givens': if women expended their energies on higher education, they must expect to find their reproductive abilities stunted, if not destroyed—to become the mothers of 'a puny, enfeebled, and sickly race': 'When Nature spends in one direction, she must economise in another direction.' Nature, then, and not history, the 'given' of the female body, and not the putatively malleable structures of society, was the site of women's disabilities. They were the prisoners of their biology, and could not 'rebel . . . against the tyranny of their organisation'. The science, or quasi-science, which developed from Darwin's work on evolution and on sexual selection was quick to argue that women's natures were indeed just as they had been described, or prescribed, by the conservative theorists Mill had sought to challenge. What was *now* called 'the nature of women' was natural, *pace* Mill, and not to be changed by human endeavour.

Jude the Obscure resists this position: specifically, it moves away from women's nature as given, and re-sites Sue in particular in history. We see her learning how she is seen, what is demanded of her, the ways in which she is to represent and articulate herself—embraced, as it were, in the ideology of 'woman'. To see how complete and entangling this embrace is, and better to understand Sue's struggles within it, it is necessary to stand back a little and consider the three leading themes of the novel. There is first the exploration of a woman's self-awareness in a patriarchal society—the Marriage Question, though it involves a good deal more than marriage alone. Second, there is the interest in Jude's attempts at self-education, and his failed academic hopes—the story of the young man who could not go to Oxford. Third, there is the account of the (diminishing) role of Christian belief in late Victorian society; Jude's desire to go to Oxford/ Christminster derives in part from its reputation as a place where clergymen are grown like radishes in a bed. Both Christminster education and Christminster religion are shown to be irrelevant to the real needs of Jude and Sue. Jude's learning, remarkable as it is, is also fragmented, his expression of it often stilted, his quotations at first innocently and later deliberately and perversely mis-applied. Orthodox Christian teaching is similarly discredited. Jude's 'dogmas' tell him that it is Sue's duty to overcome the 'pruderies' which prevent her from submitting to sexual intimacy with the man she has married, but 'experience and unbiased nature' contradict his theological judgment (IV,ii). Later in the novel, his own relationship with Sue, loving but illicit, leads to their persecution by other dogmatic believers, and dismissal from their work at Aldbrickham; as they await the inquest on their children the chapel organ plays 'Truly God is loving unto Israel', while two clergymen debate 'the eastward position' (VI,ii). Jude's academic books are spattered with pig-grease, and he burns his theological books; in both cases the reader's sympathy with his distress is modified by doubts about the value of what he is seeking.

All this is familiar. But it is important to recognise the interpenetration of these three themes, signalled in the way each draws on the same pool of vocabulary, opposing *spirit* and *flesh, noble* and *gross, high* and *low*. For example, the orthodox language of sexuality sees Arabella as 'low'; the narrator refers to her 'low and triumphant laugh of a careless woman,' and Sue describes her as a 'low-passioned woman'. But this is simultaneously the language of class; it's a matter for remark that Jude, who has kept himself 'up' with his academic ambitions, has now 'descended so low' as to walk with Arabella, and Sue goes on to describe her as 'too low, too coarse' for Jude's company (I,vii, V,ii). Jude has 'high' academic hopes: he wants to join the 'high thinkers' of the University, to enter the 'soul' of the Colleges instead of working outside on their 'carcases'; simultaneously, and necessarily, he wants to 'rise' socially, and to earn his £5,000 a year. But this desire to 'rise', to become less 'rough' and more 'refined', all in class terms, leads back to the language of sexuality. That Sue seems sexually reticent and 'refined' appeals to 'all that's best and noblest' in Jude, and her 'freedom from everything that's gross' has 'elevated' him: the terms are of course social as well as moral (V,ii). When Sue tells Jude that she has always longed to 'ennoble some man to high aims' we can't separate out the acquisition of the higher knowledge, the access to a higher class, and the refusal of the 'low' vices of sexual desire and drunkenness to which Jude thinks himself subject, and which inhibit his belief in his ability to rise (III,iv). It is eventually Jude's doubts about his ability to subordinate the 'low' and 'fleshly' aspect of his nature to the 'high' and 'spiritual' side that persuade him to give up his ambition to enter the Church as a licentiate.

The dominant language of the book, then, though it is not one that is *approved* in the novel, privileges, or appears to privilege one set of terms over another: spirit, soul, noble, high, etc., over flesh, body, gross, low, etc.; and in the process suggests that whatever the ostensible topic of their discussions—religious belief, academic aims, sexual behaviour—Jude and Sue will have to encounter the same all-pervading dualism. Two points, I think, follow from this. First, it suggests the lines on which Hardy might have answered D. H. Lawrence's charge that he failed sufficiently to support his characters in their war against the age. Lawrence argues that in the tragic drama of Sophocles or Shakespeare the characters are pitted against 'the vast, uncomprehended and incomprehensible morality of nature or of life itself', and their defeat is inevitable. In the novels of Tolstoy and Hardy, however, it is merely 'the lesser human morality, the mechanical system' which is transgressed; accordingly, Sue and Jude (or Anna and Vronsky) ought to have won, to have come through: 'they were not at war with God, only with Society.' But this is to suppose that 'society' is one identifiable target, as it were 'out there', separate from the characters; what Hardy suggests is that the values of the society are not 'out there', distinct from the consciousness of Jude and Sue, but permeate their language and their being. This point is central to our understanding of the novel. However bracing Lawrence's energy in repudiating his society, we need to recognise that Hardy's vision of his characters' relation to society is entirely different: less romantic, but perhaps more persuasive. There is no rainbow vision, no world elsewhere, for Jude and Sue.

The second point is closely related. To show how all-encompassing and how damaging this dualism is, Hardy needed a double focus. Jude's may be the central consciousness of the novel, but Sue's is the central experience, and the two are mutually re-inforcing. They inhabit the same ideological world, and this helps to reveal the coercive power of the language they also inhabit. The natural comparison is with Hardy's own novel, *The Return of the Native* (1878), which also has a double focus. Here the two exceptional members of the community are Clym, filled with dreams of educating and improving his community, and Eustacia, who dreams of passionate love and sexual fulfilment. They are naturally drawn together, but to what purpose in the novel is unclear. Both are filled with Promethean fire and rebellion; both are defeated. But while Clym learns to take a grim satisfaction in the 'oppressive horizontality' of the heathland around him, Eustacia struggles to remain vertical until she is finally dragged down as if by 'a hand from beneath'. Clym, despite his early ambitions, becomes an agent of the force which destroys Eustacia; Eustacia, seeking her own fulfilment, helps bring Clym to his mood of grim acceptance. We are left uncertain: how are we invited to feel about rebellion and resignation, about acceptance and aspiration, when the two leading protagonists seem to belong each to a separate moral universe? In *Jude* Hardy avoids this confusion. Although the focus is in one case on class, and in the other on gender, Jude and Sue do share the same ideological world, the same language. Their every attempt to speak to each other exposes them to the same ideological forces, and exposes these forces to us as readers.

From here it is possible to see more clearly what it means to say that Sue is 'made to inhabit her gender', and how Hardy reveals sexual identity not as 'natural' or 'given' but as made or ideologically constructed. Early in the novel Jude as a boy dreams of an idealised Christminster, a 'city of light', a 'heavenly Jerusalem' (I,iii). The narrator quickly warns us that Jude's dreams 'were as gigantic as his surroundings were small'; the dream of Christminster takes its origin in the ugliness of the meanly utilitarian fields of Marygreen. And when Jude reaches Christminster, he ignores the palpable city before his eyes, and sees a visionary one still: 'when he passed objects out of harmony, . . . he allowed his eyes to slip over them' (II,i). The narrator is compassionate, but does not for a moment share Jude's obsessive love of the city; wiser than his hero, he forewarns us that Jude will eventually discover 'the deadly animosity' of all modern thought to what he holds dear in Christminster. Precisely this pattern of an idealising dream, and the narrator's refusal to share it, is used to introduce Sue. Even before they meet Jude is enough in love with her to kiss her photograph. When he sees her working in a shop selling religious articles, he thinks hers 'a sweet, saintly, Christian business', and imagines how she would be to him 'a kindly star, an *elevating* power' (italics added)—much as he had seen Christminster as his 'Alma Mater' and himself as her 'beloved son' (II,ii). Already Jude has begun to insert Sue in this dominant idiom; and in order to reveal how arbitrary this is, the narrator allows us one of our very few glimpses of Sue outside the perceptions of the other characters. Here she is seen buying her plaster statuettes of Venus and Apollo, reading Gibbon on Julian the Apostate, and then turning to Swinburne's 'familiar poem' ('Thou hast conquered, O pale Galilean'): far from the sweet and saintly girl of Jude's imaginings, she is so stirred by her adventure that after she has 'unrobed' her figures, and undressed herself, she lies 'tossing and staring' through the night (II,iii). This palpable Sue, her clothes soiled by plaster from her statuettes, is not to be seen by Jude, any more than he sees the palpable Christminster. Just as his dream of the city was conceived against the ugliness of village life, so his dream of an ethereal Sue is conceived in opposition to the physicality of his marriage to Arabella. As she was a 'female animal', so Sue must be a female angel.

From the beginning of their relationship, then, Jude, 'sees' Sue in the dualistic, ideological terms noted earlier. But even as a child, we learn from Drusilla Fawley, Sue was taught to see herself in a gendered way. She would play happily on a slide among a group of boys, but her performance would be applauded; she would accuse the boys of being 'saucy'—i.e., of addressing her through an awareness of gender—and flee indoors; they would follow, and plead with her to return (II,vi). The pattern here is of advance; insertion into gender; retreat; discovery of the self as desired. To this we must add a sense of guilt: Sue, we are told, was often smacked for her 'impertinence' or immodesty—i.e., for failing to stay within the boundaries of her gender. This pattern is repeated with the three men in her adult life, beginning with the Christminster graduate with whom she tried to form a friendship as if they were two male friends or 'comrades'. He attempted to make her his mistress; she retreated; he responded with the claim that his desire for her was killing him. With both Phillotson and Jude Sue again looks for comradeship; is at once seen as a possible sexual partner; seeks to retreat, while still relishing the sense of being valued and approved; and eventually, trapped both by the guilt they produce in her, and by her own fear of losing their approval, allows herself to be caught in a sexual relationship. Denied the possibility of a gender-free comradeship, Sue must either leave the relationship, and forfeit friendship and approval, or surrender to a sexual role, guiltily, not freely, as the price to be paid for being approved. Refused what she asks for—a non-sexual love—she wishes at least to keep the sexual love she shares with Jude free from the constraints of a formal marriage. But as the novel makes clear, this affords her a merely token increase in freedom; she accepts the name 'Mrs Fawley', bears Jude's children, becomes economically dependent on Jude, and sees her fortunes fall with his.

Jude's revulsion from the low and physical Arabella, and his aspiration towards the high and spiritual Christminster, encourages him to see Sue as 'ethereal', 'refined', 'uncarnate': in short, as all but 'sexless'. Sue's desire to be approved, loved but not possessed, is inevitably reinforced by Jude's response. Here the contradictions within this dominant idiom begin to emerge. The narrator notes that Jude briefly has 'a true illumination': that the real centre of Christminster life is with the people who live and work in the town, and not within the Colleges (II,ii). Sue at times urges on him the same recognition. But this runs against the dominant high-low idiom. To embrace this 'low' life, which maintains the 'carcases' of the buildings, at the expense of the 'high' intellectual life of the spirit, would be to undermine Jude's project of self-improvement, and Sue's role as the ennobling and elevating presence in his life. So long as Jude privileges such words as 'elevated' and 'ethereal', bound up as they are with his class position and his academic dreams, he must structure Sue's sexuality in the same terms: 'grossness', sexually and socially, is the only alternative within the idiom. And so long as Sue needs his approval, and sees that it depends on his valuation of her as elevated, she is necessarily inhibited from urging on him the value of the *in*carnate 'real life' of Christminster, as against the unreal and *un*carnate life of his academic visions. 'Real life' in Christminster, as we see it in the novel, is never celebrated; it is either the occasion for, or the analogue to, Jude's vices of drunkenness or sexuality. With the sardonic humour so frequent in this work, Jude and Sue are seen as trapped between the 'high' world of the University dons of Christminster, and the 'low' world of Arabella, née Donn, of here, there and everywhere.

There is another way of describing the contradictions felt here in the language used by Jude and Sue. Sexual life is problematic for Sue, but not, it appears, for Arabella, who in the course of the novel marries two men twice each, one of these marriages being bigamous. For Arabella, sexual life means the satisfaction of her physical desires, or the exchange of her favours in return for economic security. This is sex without mystery. For Sue, however—in part because of the pressure from Jude—sex is made, not one experience, but the defining experience: the ultimate personal act. One sees these two views clashing when she discovers that Jude has again slept with Arabella: Jude dismisses the act as 'nothing', because it was without emotional meaning; Sue calls it 'gross' for the same reason (IV,v). Yet the act Jude describes as 'nothing' is also, when imagined as between himself and Sue, everything, and her denial of it all but unbearable. Sue, free from all that's gross, must participate in the act in order to keep Jude loyal to her, yet—if she is to retain his approval—she must be separate from it. On the one hand, as she realises with increasing distress, sexual love has been secularised, made subject to the law, to written contracts, and the involvement of courts, forms and registrars; on the other, it has been sacralised, made a mystery. It has become simultaneously the defining private act, and a matter for public legislation. Sue thus finds herself in an intolerable position: sexual love is 'nothing', and it is everything; it is 'gross', and it is the mark of an ultimate commitment; it belongs to a world that is high and elevated, and it is carried out to complete an official contract between two 'parties' of stated age, rank and condition.

This dominant language, at once coercive and contradictory, needs to be further related to the narrative form of the novel. In the Preface to the 1895 edition, Hardy described the novel as 'a series of seemings', and the question of 'their consistency or discordance' as 'not of the first importance'. This is to understate his position. In opposition to those who saw women's 'nature' as effectively fixed and immutable, Hardy chose to show how Sue's identity is constructed in language, and to trace the way in which that language is entangled with questions of social class, and sanctioned by the authority of the Church. He shows no desire to reconcile Sue's experience of contradiction by making her fully intelligible to us, while not so to herself. Instead, he leaves deliberate gaps in his narrative. Most notably, we only rarely see Sue away from Jude and Phillotson, the two men who most often ask her to be intelligible to them, or who seek to mould her into their own favoured idioms. Constantly the novel allows Jude and Phillotson to interrogate Sue; again and again they are refused entry into her mind. Jude speculates that his confessions about Arabella may have prompted Sue's engagement, but neither she nor the narrator confirms the suspicion. After her wedding to Phillotson she enters Jude's house for a moment, and Jude is convinced she is about to speak: but 'whatever she had meant to say remained unspoken' (III,vii). Sue argues that a person unhappy in marriage has a right to proclaim the fact 'even . . . upon the housetops', but she attributes her own misery to 'a reason I cannot disclose' (IV,ii). The apparent confidence of the narrator's account of her as 'quite unfitted by temperament and by instinct to fulfil the conditions of the matrimonial relation with Phillotson' is immediately qualified: 'possibly with scarce any man' (IV,iii). This is characteristic. 'Possibly', says the narrator, or 'perhaps', but rarely more:

'perhaps she knew that [Phillotson] was thinking of her thus' (II,v); 'that was just the one thing [Jude] would not be able to bear, as she probably knew' (III,i). The narrative can disclose the pressures operating on Sue, but does not allow us to suppose that she has some essential self, separate from these, but available to our understanding, as if we observed her from some neutral ground.

The sense that Sue is situated in language, and is not to be reached by some means other than language, and the fact that there is no 'objective' language in which to reach her, explains two other features of the text. It explains firstly what Mary Jacobus has described [in *Essays in Criticism* 25 (1975)] as the 'diagrammatic' plotting of the novel: the highly visible pattern of contrasts, repetitions and echoes, and their frequent grotesqueness. Hardy himself wrote to Gosse that 'the book is all contrasts . . . e.g. Sue and her heathen gods set against Jude's reading the Greek testament; Christminster academical, Christminster in the slums; Jude the saint, Jude the sinner; Sue the Pagan, Sue the saint; marriage, no marriage; &c, &c'. To these one might add: Sue as a heap outside Phillotson's window, Sue as a heap on the floor of St Silas' church; Arabella's two seductions of Jude; the clergyman's view that Sue has been 'saved as by fire' by her re-marriage to Phillotson, Jude's sense that he is giving his body to be burned in re-marrying Arabella; and so on. These 'contrasts' should not be dismissed as examples of Hardy's supposed heavy-handedness. Their effect is to remind us of the fictionality of the novel; if one mark of the 'classic realist text' is that it tends to conceal its literary character, *Jude the Obscure* should perhaps be described as an anti-realist novel. Hardy eschews all claim to the sort of finality and authority associated with realist fiction (and, to a still greater extent, with Victorian 'scientific' accounts of women's nature); he explores the clash of languages around Sue, within which her identity is constructed, but does not pretend to offer a 'metalanguage' granting direct access to her being.

The paraphernalia of quotations and allusions that litter the pages of the novel may be understood in the same way: the narrator, the epigraphs, and the characters, all remind us of the fictionality of the work. Many of the allusions in the novel are distorted. In I,vi Jude imagines his future: 'Yes, Christminster shall be my Alma Mater, and I'll be her beloved son, in whom she shall be well pleased.' The reference here is to Matthew 3:17, and in the gospel a dove appears at this point; in the novel, a pig's-pizzle bangs against Jude's face, discrediting rather than confirming the words. After the death of their children, Sue quotes I Corinthians 4:9: 'We are made a spectacle unto the world, and to angels, and to men!' (VI,ii); Paul's words form part of his assertion of the imminence and supreme importance of divine judgment, but Sue's bitterness thrusts aside this context. The narrator too quotes inappropriately: for example, from William Barnes and Michael Drayton in IV,iv, as Phillotson makes his way in torment to see his friend Gillingham. The epigraphs interact uneasily with the sections of narrative they introduce. To take one example, that to Part Third ('At Melchester') is from Sappho: 'For there was no other girl, O Bridegroom, like her!' Sappho's poem is from a group of *epithalamia* and bridal songs, celebrating just that erotic joy which Sue does not find with her husband; the quotation is wrenched out of context, and made instead to anticipate the 'fastidiousness' by which Sue feels singled out. Numerous texts move through the pages of *Jude the Obscure:* the Bible, and the Nicene Creed; Horace, Ovid and Marcus Aurelius; Burns, Wordsworth, Byron, Shelley, Browning, Swinburne, Barnes, Longfellow, Poe; the 'spectres' who address Jude as he arrives in Christminster. The effect is to insist on the fictionality of the novel, to draw attention to its status as a construct. The language of the fiction, like the language of sexual identity, is being exposed as made, not given; the novel, that is to say, is not presented as a revelation, an uncovering of what is demonstrably 'there', but confesses itself the result of human action: imperfect therefore, and implicated in those forms of language in which Sue is seen to be entrapped. Through its interruptions, silences and juxtapositions, the narrative form of the novel dramatises and echoes the predicament of its heroine.

Jeffrey Berman (essay date 1990)

SOURCE: "Infanticide and Object Loss in *Jude the Obscure,*" in *Narcissism and the Novel,* New York University Press, 1990, pp. 176-98.

[*In the following essay, Berman examines the bleak psychology of parents and children that appears in* Jude the Obscure.]

Little Father Time's suicide in *Jude the Obscure* (1895) is the turning point of a novel demonstrating the cruelty that pervades nature and society. As if the boy's suicide is not terrible enough, Hardy has him hang his younger half-brother and half-sister, the three children suspended from closet hooks. Located near Father Time's body is a note with the victim's last words: "*Done because we are too menny.*" The suicide letter reveals the boy's belief that his father, Jude Fawley, and stepmother, Sue Bridehead, would be better off without the children, who only add to the couple's woes in a Malthusian world. Jude sees his son's suicide as symbolic of an impending universal death wish, and he mournfully reassures Sue that she could not have averted the tragedy. "It was in his nature to do it. The doctor says there are such boys springing up amongst us—boys of a sort unknown in the last generation—the outcome of new views of life." These boys, adds Jude, see all the terrors of life before they are strong enough to resist them. "He says it is the beginning of the coming universal wish not to live. He's an advanced man, the doctor: but he can give no consolation to—" (406) [all page references are to the Macmillan edition of *Jude the Obscure,* 1971].

Curiously, although no subject is more important to society than the nurture of its children, the double murder and

suicide in *Jude the Obscure* have elicited virtually no literary commentary—a scholarly neglect confirming Father Time's judgment that the world would be better off without the children. The dearth of criticism is more surprising in light of the fact that the violent deaths of the three children represent, in Ian Gregor's words [in *The Great Web: The Form of Hardy's Major Fiction,* 1974], the "most terrible scene in Hardy's fiction, indeed it might be reasonably argued in English fiction." Nearly all readers have agreed with Irving Howe's conclusion [in *Thomas Hardy,* 1967] that the suicide is aesthetically botched: "botched not in conception but in execution: it was a genuine insight to present the little boy as one of those who were losing the will to live, but a failure in tact to burden him with so much philosophical weight." Howe consigns this observation to a parenthesis, however, and Hardy's critics have condemned Father Time's suicide without investigating the underlying causes.

There are, admittedly, several objections that may be raised to a psychological interpretation of the double murder and suicide. Father Time is clearly an allegorical, not a realistic, character. Few literary children have appeared so relentlessly morbid and fatalistic, and his melodramatic entrance and exit strain credibility. To take seriously his fears and vulnerability may strike some readers as misplaced critical attention. Does it matter how Hardy disposes of the three shadowy children, two of whom are neither named nor described?

Despite these criticisms, *Jude the Obscure* remains one of the most psychologically rich novels in our language, as the published criticism confirms. However artistically contrived Father Time's ending may be, the fictional suicide reveals many of the characteristics of real-life suicides. More importantly, Father Time's actions foreshadow the murderous impulses culminating in Sue's grim return to her former husband, Richard Phillotson, and Jude's own self-destruction. Father Time is not biologically related to Sue, but he is the true heir to the gloomy philosophy of his father and adoptive mother. Although Jude and Sue attribute Father Time's death to his "incurably sad nature," the suicide is the logical result of a series of narcissistic injuries involving defective parenting. This is a more disturbing interpretation of Father Time's suicide, since it implicates the parents in the children's deaths.

To be sure, from the beginning of the novel, Hardy seems to be indicting nature, specifically, the brutality of a scheme in which the living are condemned to a woeful existence. Nature itself appears to be a defective parent, allowing one species to survive, temporarily, at the expense of another. An early incident, young Jude's identification with a flock of rooks scavenging for food, evokes Hardy's pessimistic naturalism. "They seemed, like himself, to be living in a world which did not want them" (11). Instead of scaring away the birds to prevent them from devouring the produce destined for human consumption, as Farmer Troutham has paid him to do, Jude allows them to feed off the land. He is swiftly punished for the act. The narrator remarks upon the "flaw in the terrestrial scheme, by which what was good for God's birds was bad for God's gardener" (13). To be alive is to be victimized, the novel suggests, and the Tennysonian belief in nature "red in tooth and claw" pervades Wessex. Jude cannot walk across a pasture without thinking about the coupled earthworms waiting to be crushed on the damp ground. "Nature's logic was too horrid for him to care for. That mercy towards one set of creatures was cruelty towards another sickened his sense of harmony" (15).

Although the narrator ascribes these gloomy thoughts to Jude's "weakness of character," reflective of an unusually sensitive disposition, the other major figures in the story echo the awareness of injustice. Jude's dismay during the pig-killing scene with Arabella foreshadows Sue's horror at the thought of pigeons intended for Sunday dinner. "O why should Nature's law be mutual butchery!" she exclaims (371). Phillotson similarly observes to Arabella that "Cruelty is the law pervading all nature and society; and we can't get out of it if we would!" (384). *Jude the Obscure* "fluctuates between two opposing views of 'nature,'" Robert B. Heilman notes, [in his Introduction to *Jude the Obscure,* Harper and Row, 1966], "between a romantic naturalism . . . and the pessimistic aftermath of scientific naturalism." Nature itself appears to be fundamentally defective, perpetuating suffering and death.

To demonstrate the unfortunate consequences of nature, Hardy introduces Little Father Time into the novel. He is the accidental product of the ill-fated marriage between Jude and Arabella. Born eight months after Arabella left England for Australia, the boy spends his early years with her. Arabella hands over the unwanted child to her parents, who in turn decide they no longer wish to be "encumbered" with him. Arabella then turns him over to Jude. Symptomatic of Father Time's past treatment is the fact that he was never christened, because, he explains, "if I died in damnation, 'twould save the expense of a Christian funeral" (337). His mother and grandparents name him "Little Father Time" because of his aged appearance. He is, the narrator states, "Age masquerading as Juvenility, and doing it so badly that his real self showed through crevices" (332). Sue observes that his face is like the tragic mask of Melpomene, the muse of tragedy. A younger and more extreme portrait of Jude, Father Time is obsessed with death and indignant over the inevitable termination of life. His response to flowers seems almost pathological, especially coming from a child. "I should like the flowers very very much, if I didn't keep on thinking they'd be all withered in a few days!" (358). By the same logic he might have concluded that the flowers' fragility compels us to admire their beauty and vitality. The lively exchange in *Sons and Lovers* on how to pick flowers is missing from *Jude the Obscure*. Unlike Jude, Father Time makes no effort to escape his surroundings or pursue a better life; for this reason he remains pathetic, not tragic, defeated too easily and quickly.

Jude agrees to accept his newly discovered son, telling Sue: "I don't like to leave the unfortunate little fellow to neglect. Just think of his life in a Lambeth pothouse, and all its evil influences, with a parent who doesn't want him, and has, indeed, hardly seen him, and a stepfather who doesn't know him" (330). Jude recognizes that a child's healthy development depends upon loving parents and a friendly environment. Sue intuitively empathizes with Father Time's situation, and she is moved to tears when he calls her "mother." But she is distressed by the physical resemblance between Arabella and Father Time, which causes Jude to exclaim: "Jealous little Sue!" (335). Ironically, Little Father Time shares his adoptive mother's gloomy temperament. A number of years pass, with Father Time bringing unexpected joy into his parents' lives. Even though Jude and Sue live together without marrying, consequently suffering social ostracism, they are portrayed as loving, conscientious parents. Jude's decision to move elsewhere for employment prompts Sue to reaffirm her allegiance to Father Time. "But whatever we do, wherever we go, you won't take him away from me, Jude dear? I could not let him go now! The cloud upon his young mind makes him so pathetic to me; I do hope to lift it some day!" (361). Jude reassures her that the family will remain intact.

The crucial scene preceding the children's deaths takes place in Part Sixth, ii, when Sue and Father Time are together in a cheerless room of a lodging house from which they have just been ordered to leave. Opposite the lodging house stands Sarcophagus College, whose outer walls "threw their four centuries of gloom, bigotry, and decay into the little room she occupied" (401). Despondent over the loss of lodgings and Jude's declining prospects for employment, Sue mirrors this gloom to Father Time. When he asks her if he can do anything to help the family, she replies: "No! All is trouble, adversity and suffering!" (402). As the dialogue continues, it becomes increasingly clear that Sue's despair exacerbates the boy's innately melancholy temperament:

> "Father went away to give us children room, didn't he?"
>
> "Partly."
>
> "It would be better to be out o' the world than in it, wouldn't it?"
>
> "It would almost, dear."
>
> "'Tis because of us children, too, isn't it, that you can't get a good lodging?"
>
> "Well—people do object to children sometimes."
>
> "Then if children make so much trouble, why do people have'em?"
>
> "O—because it is a law of nature."
>
> "But we don't ask to be born?"
>
> "No indeed." (402)

Instead of heeding the child's cry for help, Sue validates Father Time's worst fears—namely, that he and the other two children are responsible for the family's desperate situation. Sue repeatedly misses the opportunity to allay his suspicion of being unwanted and unloved. In the next line Father Time expresses the fear of becoming a burden to his family, a fear intensified by the fact that Sue is not his biological mother and, therefore, under no obligation to care for him. "I oughtn't to have come to 'ee—that's the real truth! I troubled 'em in Australia, and I trouble folk here. I wish I hadn't been born!"

Here is the perfect moment for Sue to reassure Father Time that he is indeed loved by his parents. If they didn't want him, she could have truthfully said, they never would have consented to adopt him. With luck and determination, she might have added, their lives will improve. However allegorical Father Time's role may be in the novel, during this scene he acts and talks like a scared child. The reader responds to him as if he is fully human, deserving of sympathy. Father Time needs simply to be reassured that the family's circumstances will improve in the future. Indeed, he expects only a reasonable reassurance, not a rosy promise of future happiness. He certainly does not need to hear that unwanted children are responsible for their parents' suffering. How does Sue respond to his wish never to have been born? "You couldn't help it, my dear."

Sue's empathic failure triggers Father Time's inner violence, and his statements become increasingly frantic. "I think that whenever children be born that are not wanted they should be killed directly, before their souls come to 'em, and not allowed to grow big and walk about!" (402). These unwanted children are Father Time and his two siblings. Father Time contemplates infanticide because Sue has already given up on him; she does nothing to diminish his despair because she shares it fully. The narrator similarly regards Father Time's pessimism as philosophically justified and, hence, beyond disagreement. "Sue did not reply" to the boy's accusations, the narrator tell us, since she was "doubtfully pondering how to treat this too reflective child" (402). Father Time *is* too reflective, but that is not the issue. His thinking remains morbid, obsessional, and frighteningly simplistic in its solution to suffering.

Mary Jacobus refers to Sue's "mistaken honesty" in telling Father Time that another child is on the way, but Sue's real mistake lies in her failure to understand her child's needs. She equates Father Time's pessimism with profundity, resolves silently to be "honest and candid" with him, as if he were a mature adult rather than a terrified child, and then informs him that she is pregnant again. The information predictably drives him into a frenzy. The dialogue closes with the distracted boy vowing that "if we children was gone there'd be no trouble at all!" Sue answers, "don't think that, dear" (403). Even when she tries to be reassuring, she succeeds only in confirming his fears. The next time she sees him, the three children are hanging from their necks. Devastated

by the sight, Sue prematurely goes into labor and suffers a miscarriage.

Jude and Sue adopt Father Time to avoid exposing him to further parental neglect, yet, as the final dialogue between mother and son indicates, it would be hard to imagine a more chilling family environment for the child. Sue is not an abusive or overcontrolling mother, as Mrs. Joe and Miss Havisham are in *Great Expectations,* and she does not deliberately intend to harm Father Time. She is a depressed mother, not a sadistic one, and since she cannot help herself, readers may reasonably ask how she can be expected to help others, especially someone intent upon killing himself and his two siblings. And yet, unlike Father Time, Sue is an adult, therefore, responsible for the consequences of her actions. However much we empathize with Sue, we cannot suspend our judgment of her.

Jude the Obscure implies that suicide runs in families, like a defective gene passed from one doomed generation to another, but a more plausible explanation for this family curse lies in environmental and interactional causes. Sue remains only partly aware of this. She reads Father Time's suicide letter and breaks down, convinced that their previous conversation has triggered his violence. Sue and Jude plausibly conjecture that upon waking from sleep, Father Time was unable to find his mother and, fearing abandonment, committed the double murder and suicide. Sue accepts responsibility for Father Time's actions, but her explanations mitigate her complicity in the boy's suicide. Perhaps she should have told him all the "facts of life" or none of them, as she says. Nevertheless, the disclosure of the pregnancy is less wounding to Father Time's self-esteem than her failure to convince him that he is wanted and loved.

By projecting her morbidity onto Father Time and confirming his infanticidal fantasies, Sue effectively places a noose around the child's neck. Father Time's inability to enjoy flowers because they will be withered in a few days has its counterpart in Sue's rationalization of the children's deaths. "It is best, perhaps, that they should be gone.—Yes—I see it is! Better that they should be plucked fresh than stay to wither away miserably!" (409). Jude remains supportive, agreeing that what has happened is probably for the best. "Some say that the elders should rejoice when their children die in infancy" (409). Jude does not rejoice at the children's deaths, but he remains unaware of how his statements here and elsewhere mirror the self-destructive philosophy that has victimized the Fawleys. Even the attending physician's interpretation of Father Time's suicide—"the beginning of the coming universal wish not to live"—contains a subtle rationalization. If nothing could have been done to prevent the three deaths, then no one is to blame for the tragedy.

Sue's empathic failure is striking. Her inconsistency of love and self-distraction overwhelm Father Time, as they later do Jude. The defective maternal mirroring represents Father Time's final narcissistic injury. By treating Father Time as an extension of herself, Sue acts out her own unresolved inner conflicts. Moreover, by reinforcing Father Time's suspicion that all children are monstrous, she repeats Victor Frankenstein's abandonment of the Creature. Sue is the opposite of the healthy mother Alice Miller writes about in *Prisoners of Childhood:* "If a child is lucky enough to grow up with a mirroring mother, who allows herself to be cathected narcissistically, who is at the child's disposal—that is, a mother who allows herself to be 'made use of' as a function of the child's narcissistic development, . . . then a healthy self-feeling can gradually develop in the growing child." The issue is not whether Sue is a perfect mother, but whether she is a good enough mother who can prepare her children for the vicissitudes of life.

In suggesting that Sue is implicated in her children's deaths, I raise several questions. How is her abandonment of Father Time related to other conflicts in her life? Why does she forsake Jude, the man she loves, for Phillotson, whom she does not love? How does she enact the roles of both Narcissus and Echo?

Sue's contradictions are dazzling. Intellectually liberated but emotionally repressed, she claims to reject the church's outmoded teachings but then embraces reactionary dogma. Refined and ethereal—Jude calls her a "phantasmal, bodiless, creature" with hardly any "animal passion" (312)—Sue arouses men mainly to reject them. Torn between the conflicting claims of body and mind, she sacrifices the integrity of both in a futile quest for self-absolution. The pattern of her behavior suggests defiance, guilt, self-punishment, and abject submission. "There was no limit to the strange and unnecessary penances which Sue would meekly undertake when in a contrite mood" (322). Early in the story she buys two plaster statuettes of Venus and Apollo, symbolic of her attraction to classical beauty and wisdom, respectively, but when the landlady asks her to identify the objects, she dissembles, claiming they are casts of St. Peter and Mary Magdalene. She cannot tell the truth to Jude, not even after the landlady has spitefully shattered the pagan objects.

To understand the origins of Sue's conflicts, we must examine her childhood, but unfortunately, Hardy passes over this period, as Albert J. Guerard points out [in *Thomas Hardy: The Novels and Stories,* 1949]. "The origin of Sue's epicene reticence lies somewhere in her childhood, of which Hardy tells us almost nothing; the origin of her moral masochism lies there also." Hardy gives us an important clue, though, about her history before introducing her into the story—a "friendly intimacy" with a Christminster undergraduate. Sue accepted his invitation to live with him in London, but when she arrived there and realized his intentions, she made a counterproposal—to live with him in a sexless union. Sue's relationship with the Christminster undergraduate remains ambiguous. Was she aware of the sexual implications of his invitation to live with him, and, if so, for

what reasons did she decline a passionate romance? Several possibilities come to mind, including fear of pregnancy and threat of social ostracism. The friends shared a sitting room for fifteen months, until he was taken ill and forced to go abroad. Although the shadowy episode represents part of her struggle to emancipate herself from repressive social conventions, Sue blames herself for the undergraduate's death. It remains unclear whether she actually intended to hurt him. In narrating the student's account of their relationship, she seems to accept his version of reality, including his censure. "He said I was breaking his heart by holding out against him so long at such close quarters; he could never have believed it of woman. I might play that game once too often, he said. He came home merely to die. His death caused a terrible remorse in me for my cruelty—though I hope he died of consumption and not of me entirely" (177-78).

We have no way to authenticate what actually happened between Sue and the Christminster undergraduate, but we can analyze the transference implications of Sue's narrating style. Just as patients' stories in psychoanalysis repeat the themes and conflicts of their past, so do fictional characters' narrating styles represent "memorializations of their unresolved pasts." Expressing the hope that the student died of consumption and not from herself, Sue reveals a tendency to hold herself responsible for all the failures in her relationships. In characterizing the young man as a victim of love, she depicts herself as a victimizer. She feels remorse for her cruelty but also satisfaction over her power, even though in hurting others, she hurts herself. Jude is understandably horrified by Sue's story, which provokes her to say, with a "contralto note of tragedy" in her voice: "I wouldn't have told you if I had known!" (178). But Sue knows how Jude will react to the story. Like Estella, who repeatedly warns Pip that she will break his heart if he becomes romantically involved with her, Sue forewarns Jude about the dangers of intimacy with her—a heeding he fatally disregards.

Sue's relationships with Phillotson and Jude are replays of the unhappy union with the Christminster undergraduate. Phillotson is a hardworking school teacher whose name evokes his conventional social views and stolid character. Eighteen years older than Sue, he is a father figure to her, a fact that troubles his rival, Jude. Despite the temperamental and age differences between teacher and student, they enter into a chilling marriage and wisely agree to a divorce when their incompatibility becomes apparent. Sue moves in with Jude and bears two children. After their deaths, Sue inexplicably returns to Phillotson and remarries him. As Mrs. Edlin observes at the end, "Weddings be funerals a' b'lieve nowadays" (481).

Sue marries Phillotson largely to seek revenge on Jude, who she incorrectly believes has betrayed her. The engagement and marriage to Phillotson follow Jude's disclosure of his imprudent marriage to Arabella. As if to hurt Jude further, Sue asks him to give her away at the wedding. She even teases him by calling him "father," a term for the man who gives away the bride. The rejected suitor represses his response to the word: "Jude could have said 'Phillotson's age entitles him to be called that!' But he would not annoy her by such a cheap retort" (206). During a morning walk, Sue and Jude find themselves in front of the church where the scheduled marriage is to take place. She holds Jude's arm "almost as if she loved him," and they stroll down the nave as if they are married. Sue defends her provocative behavior by saying that she likes "to do things like this." Shortly before the wedding ceremony, Jude reflects on Sue's cruelty toward him, concluding that "possibly she would go on inflicting such pains again and again, and grieving for the sufferer again and again, in all her colossal inconsistency" (210).

Sue's wish to captivate men has Oedipal and pre-Oedipal implications. By marrying Phillotson, she may hope to repair the troubled relationship with her own father. By calling Jude "father," she projects the same complicated symbolism onto him. But if Sue sees Phillotson and Jude as variations of Oedipus, she seems to view herself as a female Narcissus, exerting fatal attraction over men. "I should shock you by letting you know how I give way to my impulses, and how much I feel that I shouldn't have been provided with attractiveness unless it were meant to be exercised! Some women's love of being loved is insatiable; and so, often, is their love of loving" (245). Sue's infatuations end in disillusionment and failure. She later expands upon the reasons for her marriage to Phillotson. "But sometimes a woman's *love of being loved* gets the better of her conscience, and though she is agonized at the thought of treating a man cruelly, she encourages him to love her while she doesn't love him at all. Then, when she sees him suffering, her remorse sets in, and she does what she can to repair the wrong" (290).

Like Narcissus, Sue seems to be in love with the unobtainable, the elusive, the spectral; like other narcissistic lovers, she proceeds from idealization to devaluation. Sue is also an Echo, denying her own independence and free will. Toward the end of the novel, she admits that she began her relationship with Jude in the "selfish and cruel wish" to make his heart ache for her. "I did not exactly flirt with you; but that inborn craving which undermines some women's morals almost more than unbridled passion—the craving to attract and captivate, regardless of the injury it may do the man—was in me; and when I found I had caught you, I was frightened" (426). Although she has grown to love Jude, she abruptly abandons him, causing anguish to them both. "And now you add to your cruelty by leaving me," Jude says, to which she replies: "Ah—yes! The further I flounder, the more harm I do!" (426).

Significantly, Sue's need to be loved by men has little to do with the wish for sexual gratification. She is so horrified at the possibility of intercourse with her husband that she throws herself out of the bedroom window when he accidentally enters her room. Jude calls her return to Phillotson, with whom she has never had sexual

relations, a "fanatic prostitution" (436). Sue returns to her former husband presumably to punish herself and Jude for their nonconformist behavior. The "wickedness" of her feelings at the end of the novel is the same self-revulsion she experiences scarcely eight weeks into her first marriage to Phillotson. Denying there is anything wrong with her marriage, Sue delivers to Jude one of the most revealing speeches in the book:

> "But it is not as you think!—there is nothing wrong except my own wickedness, I suppose you'd call it—a repugnance on my part, for a reason I cannot disclose, and what would not be admitted as one by the world in general! . . . What tortures me so much is the necessity of being responsive to this man whenever he wishes, good as he is morally!— the dreadful contract to feel in a particular way in a matter whose essence is its voluntariness! . . . I wish he would beat me, or be faithless to me, or do some open thing that I could talk about as a justification for feeling as I do! But he does nothing, except that he has grown a little cold since he has found out how I feel. That's why he didn't come to the funeral. . . . O, I am very miserable— I don't know what to do! . . . Don't come near me, Jude, because you mustn't. Don't—don't!" (255-56)

Sue's speech reveals a multitude of defenses gone awry. The middle sentences confirm the need for outside intervention denied in the beginning and end. Her cry for help anticipates Father Time's appeal for assistance preceding his suicide. Through displacement, Phillotson becomes the hated object, a projection screen for Sue's inner conflicts. Phillotson is not a brutal man; when he releases her from marriage, he shows enlightened judgment. Sue's first marriage to Phillotson may be attributed in part to naïveté and inexperience, but her second marriage suggests an unconscious need to continue her self-punishment. Her sexual surrender takes on the appearance of the "fanatic prostitution" Jude has sadly prophesied.

In remarrying Phillotson, Sue chooses to act out rather than analyze her conflicts. Unable to divorce herself from the institution of marriage she no longer believes in, she falls back upon martyrdom. Even as she punishes herself by returning to a husband she has never loved, she abandons the lover who has remained devoted to her. Sue occupies a dual role in the novel, victim (of Phillotson) and victimizer (of Jude). The roles are interrelated. In terms of ego psychology, she identifies with the aggressor—a process, Anna Freud remarks, in which passive is converted to active. "By impersonating the aggressor, assuming his attributes or imitating his aggression, the child transforms himself from the person threatened into the person who makes the threat." Sue invokes an unsound social code to rationalize an unhealthy psychological situation. The repressive institution of marriage—repressive to Hardy because its rigidity did not allow a relationship to be dissolvable as soon as it became a cruelty to either party—legitimizes her self-punishment. Sue's second marriage thus becomes a more sinister replay of her first marriage, an example of a repetition compulsion principle that dominates *Jude the Obscure*.

In acting out their parents' broken marriages, Sue and Jude demonstrate how the present repeats the past. Sue's family background is almost identical to that of Jude, her first cousin. In endowing them with similar family backgrounds, Hardy intimates their unity of character. "They seem to be one person split in two," Phillotson remarks (276), vexed by his failure to understand either of them. To this extent, Sue and Jude resemble Catherine and Heathcliff in *Wuthering Heights,* who struggle to regain lost unity. The products of broken marriages, Jude and Sue have lost one or both parents at an early age and are raised by indifferent caretakers. According to Arabella, Jude's father ill-used his wife in the same way that Jude's paternal aunt (Sue's mother) mistreated her husband. Both marriages are doomed. After Jude becomes involved with Arabella, his great-aunt, Drusilla Fawley, informs him that his parents never got along with each other, parting company when he was a baby. Jude's mother, continues Arabella, drowned herself shortly afterwards. Drusilla makes no effort to soften the revelation or anticipate its terrible impact upon Jude. Drusilla's empathic failure repeats his mother's earlier rejection of him and foreshadows Sue's rejection of Father Time. After hearing the details of his mother's death, Jude attempts suicide in a similar way by walking on a partly frozen pond. The cracking ice manages to sustain his weight, temporarily thwarting his self-annihilation.

Hardy does not elaborate on the reasons for Jude's half-serious suicide attempt, but the painful repetition of the past cannot be ignored. As with most suicide attempts, including Father Time's, the motivation is overdetermined. Jude's attempt to repeat his mother's suicide is unmistakable, recalling John Bowlby's observation that children who suffer early maternal loss are vulnerable to suicide. Jude's suicide attempt suggests a wish for reunion with the lost mother, a desire for revenge, a need to punish himself for harboring murderous feelings toward the lost love object, and a feeling that life is not worth living. Both Jude and Father Time attempt or commit suicide following maternal loss; they are mirror images of each other, portraits of the same abandoned child. After his mother's death, Jude is raised by a father about whom he never speaks, not even after he has grown up and become a father himself. As with *Frankenstein* and *Wuthering Heights, Jude the Obscure* remains preoccupied with the consequences of defective parenting but gives little information about absent parents. After his father's death, Jude is taken in by his great-aunt, who makes it clear that he would have been better off dead, like his parents. "It would ha' been a blessing if Goddymighty had took thee too, wi' thy mother and father, poor useless boy!" (8-9).

Against a background of parental loss, Jude develops into a compassionate and idealistic man. Nothing in his family history accounts for his remarkable sensitivity, and for a time it seems as if he has escaped his past. His willing-ness to adopt Father Time demonstrates his generosity of spirit, and he remains devoted to his wife and children. Jude is a better parent to his newly discovered son than presumably his own parents were to him. Nevertheless, Jude is absent when Father Time most needs him, during the moments preceding the suicide. Although his role in Father Time's suicide is more ambiguous than Sue's, Jude readily accepts the inevitability of his son's death.

Sue's background reveals a similar pattern of parental loss. According to Drusilla, Sue's father offended his wife early in the marriage, and the latter "so disliked living with him afterwards that she went away to London with her little maid" (81). We never discover the length of time she lives with her mother in London or the circumstances of their life. Sue is then brought up by her father to hate her mother's family. Like Eustacia Vye in *The Return of the Native,* another motherless daughter raised by a remote male guardian, Sue grows up to reject conventional society. Her rebellion, no less than Eustacia's, is singularly unsuccessful. Sue's defiance as a twelve-year-old girl, boldly exhibiting her body as she wades into a pond, reveals a spiritedness that contrasts her later inability to be touched by her husband. Her craving for conformity culminates in her sexual surrender to Phillotson. In a novel filled with agonizing self-inflicted deaths, Sue's decision to remarry is one of the most horrifying moments—in effect, another suicide. She returns to her former husband, not to seek a better life, but to punish herself for the past. Sue can survive, paradoxically, only through self-debasement. *Jude the Obscure* reflects a closed system in which loveless marriages, restrictive social conventions, and unmerciful superegos thwart the possibility of a fulfilling life.

Sue's pattern of defiance followed by blind submission suggests, clinically, the child's ambivalence toward the parents: the rejection of the mother, the original love object, followed by the need to recover the lost unity of infancy. Sue and Jude return to the wrong marital partners, and the attempt toward reparation is doomed. From the viewpoint of object relations, Sue and Jude's inner world is precarious and turbulent. Each returns to a despised marital partner, suggesting the child's inability to separate from a defective caretaker. Phillotson and Arabella represent the omnipotent parents who can never be defied successfully. They offer punishment, not love, to the returning child, humbled and broken. Sue's submission to Phillotson parallels Jude's submission to Arabella. Both Sue and Jude regress to infantile modes of behavior (one is creed-drunk, the other is gin-drunk), obliterating themselves in a fatal union with hated love objects.

Object loss is a central theme in *Jude the Obscure,* and Freud's seminal essay "Mourning and Melancholia" (1917) casts light on many of the baffling psychological dynamics of Hardy's characters. Freud's definition of melancholia (depression) [in "Mourning and Melancholia," 1917] describes many of Sue's conflicts: "a profoundly painful dejection, cessation of interest in the outside world, loss of the capacity to love, inhibition of all activity, and a lowering of the self-regarding feelings to a degree that finds utterance in self-reproaches and self-revilings, and culminates in a delusional expectation of punishment." In depression, Freud suggests, "dissatisfaction with the ego on moral grounds is the most outstanding feature" (248). This is especially true of Sue's self-punishing tendencies. Freud argues that the self-recriminations characteristic of depression are "reproaches against a loved object which have been shifted away from it on to the patient's own ego" (248). Depression is related to object loss in that the sadism directed initially against the object is converted to masochism. In both mourning and depression, the loss of an object deprives a person of the love necessary for growth and nurture. Unlike mourning, which is usually a temporary phenomenon, depression may last permanently. Freud viewed depression as arising from hostile feelings, initially directed toward parents, that are internalized, producing guilt and low self-esteem.

Depression is widely regarded as one of the most common of psychiatric illnesses, but there is disagreement over its origin and treatment. Analysts distinguish object-related depression from narcissistic depression. The sense of helplessness and lowered self-esteem are common to both forms of depression, but their origins appear to be different. Object-related depression, which Freud had in mind, awakens virulent aggression toward the disappointing love object. Narcissistic depression, by contrast, originates from disappointments in achieving fantasized or idealized states. For object relations theorists like Otto Kernberg, depression represents the internalization of aggression originally directed toward the rejecting love object. The major conflicts in object-related depression involve aggression: the fear of one's own destructive rage and the fear of retaliation by the object. For theorists like Heinz Kohut, on the other hand, depression represents the inability to merge with the idealized object. The major conflicts in narcissistic depression involve unrealistic or unobtainable goals, such as the pursuit of a perfect relationship.

Elements of both forms of depression appear in *Jude the Obscure*. The family backgrounds of Sue and Jude reflect a long history of parental neglect and abandonment. Both suffer object loss as children and parents. Their sadomasochistic relationship represents a defense against further object loss. That is, the sadist and masochist "play out both sides of the pain-inducing/pain-suffering object relationship." Masochism represents a bond—or, more accurately, a bondage—to the early sadistic object. Contrary to their separation at the end, Sue and Jude remain symbiotically bonded, just as sadism and masochism are inextricably conjoined. The narcissistic element of their depression appears in their failure to merge with healthy, empathic selfobjects. Neither Jude nor Sue can sustain former ambitions, goals, ideals; both fall victim to bitter disillusionment. Sue's movement from social rebellion to repressive conformity parallels Jude's journey from unquestioning acceptance of life to embittered rejection.

Nowhere is Jude's idealizing power more evident than in his desire to pursue a university education at Christminster. The novel opens with Phillotson telling Jude why a university degree is important. "It is the necessary hall-mark of a man who wants to do anything in teaching" (4). Jude invests Christminster with mystical significance, transforming it into a radiant city of light, a "heavenly Jerusalem" (18). The eleven-year-old Jude associates his esteemed schoolteacher with holy Christminster, and he is understandably distressed by Phillotson's departure. Jude's infatuation with Christminster has erotic significance. "He was getting so romantically attached to Christminster that, like a young lover alluding to his mistress, he felt bashful at mentioning its name again" (22). At the same time, Jude speaks of his devotion to Christminster in terms of a son's devotion to his mother. "Yes, Christminster shall be my Alma Mater; and I'll be her beloved son, in whom she shall be well pleased" (41). Before leaving Jude, Phillotson invites him to Christminster, promising never to forget him. The promise is broken years later when Jude visits Phillotson and discovers that the teacher cannot remember him. Jude thus experiences his rejection by Christminster and Phillotson as repetitions of maternal and paternal abandonment.

Jude's lofty idealization of Christminster becomes a deadly mirage, as elusive as Narcissus' reflection. Jude's idealization is really an attempt to compensate for disappointment over parental abandonment. But on discovering the reality of university life, he is dismayed by its hypocrisy, rigidity, and narrowmindedness. Jude suffers other setbacks: he is deceived by the quack Vilbert, who reneges on the promise to supply him with Greek and Latin grammars; he is disillusioned at learning that Phillotson has given up the scheme to receive a university degree; and he is distressed upon receiving a letter from a Christminster professor advising him to renounce intellectual aspirations. We feel Jude's crushing rejection, his outrage at the collapse of his hopes for a university education. And yet, given Jude's impossible idealization of Christminster, we sense that he would have been disillusioned by any university system.

Jude comes to perceive, with Hardy's approval, that "there is something wrong somewhere in our social formulas: what it is can only be discovered by men or women with greater insight than mine,—if, indeed, they ever discover it—at least in our time" (394). Jude does not perceive, however, the narcissistic meaning of his idealizing tendencies. As Kernberg and other analysts point out, defensive idealization conceals fundamentally ambivalent feelings toward the love object, feelings that arise in the early mother-child relationship. The repetitive and compulsive nature of idealization suggests the continual effort to deny the disappointment and aggression associated with early object loss. Jude is eloquent in his social criticism and knowledge of literary and political history, but he is less convincing in his understanding of psychology. Wounded by early narcissistic injuries, Jude is rendered finally into a pining Echo, and his last words echo Job's: *"Let the day perish wherein I was born"* (488).

We can now see more clearly the parallel between Father Time's infanticide and the defective nurturing Jude and Sue received as children. A shadowy bad parent haunts *Jude the Obscure,* linking three generations of Fawleys. Each generation executes a death sentence in the name of the parents. Sue interprets her children's deaths as a sign of divine punishment for her wicked union with Jude. "I see marriage differently now. My babies have been taken from me to show me this! Arabella's child killing mine was a judgment—the right slaying the wrong. What, *What* shall I do! I am such a vile creature—too worthless to mix with ordinary human beings!" (422-23). The reversal is astonishing. She now views Father Time, the murderer of her own children, as an agent of divine retribution, while the two innocent children are evil, like herself. Sue submits herself to a vindictive God, a reflection of her bad father. She seems close to psychotic, lost in a terrible delusion. The violent self-hatred revealed in her speech to Phillotson conceals her infanticidal fantasies, now rationalized in the name of religious purification. "My children—are dead—and it is right that they should be! I am glad—almost. They were sin-begotten. They were sacrificed to teach me how to live!—their death was the first stage of my purification. That's why they have not died in vain! . . . You will take me back?" (439). By splitting the children into good and bad objects, Sue denies her ambivalence toward them, thus preserving her psychic life from massive extinction.

Jude and Sue miss the most terrifying insight of all, the realization that their ambivalence has slain the children. Sue's key admission, that she is "glad—almost" of the children's deaths, betrays an unconscious wish. This explains her complicity in Father Time's decision to annihilate the unwanted children of the world. The boy obediently carries out her wishes. Long before she brings children into the world, Sue has been punishing herself relentlessly for feelings of wickedness. The murders objectify her repressed wishes. By endorsing Father Time's infanticidal actions, Sue reveals herself as the abandoning parent, determined to destroy the hated child within herself. At the same time, she is the abandoned child, intent upon merging with the hated father, Phillotson. Although Jude, Sue, and Father Time refuse to name the bad parent, they create situations in which they punish themselves and the parental surrogates who have failed them. For the tragic protagonists of *Jude the Obscure,* the present repeats the nightmarish past. Hardy's symmetrical plot demonstrates his deterministic view that "What's done can't be undone" (70).

Jude the Obscure portrays Nature as a deficient mother, the law as a repressive father, the two antagonists locked in a deadly, indissolvable marriage. "Radical disorder in the universe is finally matched by radical disorder in human personality," Heilman has remarked about the novel. Hardy's philosophical pessimism cannot be reduced to a single biographical determinant; yet the "Gen-

eral Principles" behind his artistic vision reflect the defective parenting, empathic failure, and object loss implicit in *Jude the Obscure*. In *The Life of Thomas Hardy,* ostensibly written by his second wife, Florence Emily Hardy, but largely ghost-written by the novelist himself, there is an important passage that evokes the spirit of the Fawleys:

> General Principles. Law has produced in man a child who cannot but constantly reproach its parent for doing much and yet not all, and constantly say to such parent that it would have been better never to have begun doing than to have *over*done so indecisively; that is, than to have created so far beyond all apparent first intention (on the emotional side), without mending matters by a second intent and execution, to eliminate the evils of the blunder of overdoing. The emotions have no place in a world of defect, and it is a cruel injustice that they should have been developed in it.

Although it is unlikely that Hardy intended this passage either as a criticism of his own parents or as a commentary on *Jude the Obscure,* the novelist's world view reflects the philosophical pessimism in Father Time's farewell speech. It would be misleading, of course, to identify Hardy with a single fictional character, especially with a boy who ends his life before he has a chance to live it. Nevertheless, despite the claim of objectivity in *Jude the Obscure*—"The purpose of a chronicler of moods and deeds does not require him to express his personal views" (348)—the narrator is implicated in the characters' gloomy vision. To give but one example, early in the novel the narrator asks why no one comes along to befriend the young Jude, already disillusioned by his hopeless struggle to master Greek and Latin. "But nobody did come, because nobody does; and under the crushing recognition of his gigantic error Jude continued to wish himself out of the world" (32). In *"I'd Have My Life Unbe"* (1984), Frank Giordano traces the pattern of self-destructive characters in Hardy's world, concluding that, for the novelist, "the desire never to have been born was far more than a traditional poetic trope, while the wish to have his life 'unbe' seems to have recurred often and been very powerful at certain stages."

It is now possible to inquire into the biographical elements of Hardy's novel. Not surprisingly, Hardy insisted that "there is not a scrap of personal detail" in *Jude the Obscure*. There is little in his biography to indicate overt object loss, certainly nothing like the early traumatic loss experienced by Jude and Sue. One fascinating detail emerges, however, about Hardy's entry into the world. When the infant was born, he was presumed dead and cast into a basket by the surgeon in order to attend to the mother, herself in distress. "Dead! Stop a minute: he's alive enough, sure!" the midwife exclaimed (*The Life of Thomas Hardy,* 14). The incident has a tragicomic quality entirely befitting Hardy's later vision of life. As a child, he was extremely delicate and sickly, often cared for by a neighbor. Hardy's biographers acknowledge his inauspicious beginning in life, suggesting a possible link between his early deprivation and life-long bouts of depression. Robert Gittings speaks about an "early thread of perverse morbidity in Hardy, something near abnormality," [in *Young Thomas Hardy,* 1975] while Michael Millgate observes [in *Thomas Hardy,* 1982] that Hardy's parents took little interest in him because they believed he would die in childhood.

James W. Hamilton, a psychoanalyst, has suggested that the actual circumstances of Hardy's birth burdened him "with profound guilt for having damaged and almost killed his mother," as revealed in his first poem, "Discouragement." An incident in *Tess of the D'Urbervilles* reveals a mother's underloving and overloving tendencies. Hamilton speculates that Tess's ambivalence toward her infant son, aptly named Sorrow (corresponding, perhaps, to the allegorical Father Time in *Jude the Obscure*), may well reflect Jemima Hardy's feelings toward her own child. "When the infant had taken its fill," Hardy writes in *Tess of the D'Urbervilles,* "the young mother sat it upright in her lap, and looking into the far distance dandled it with a gloomy indifference that was almost dislike; then all of a sudden she fell to violently kissing it some dozens of times, as if she could never leave off, the child crying at the vehemence of an onset which strangely combined passionateness with contempt." Sorrow's death, like Father Time's, implicates both nature and nurture: "So passed away Sorrow the Undesired—that intrusive creature, that bastard gift of shameless Nature who respects not the social law" (*Tess,* 81).

Hardy's acknowledgement that the fictional portrait of Mrs. Yeobright in *The Return of the Native* was closely based upon his own mother is also revealing. Closely resembling Mrs. Morel in Lawrence's *Sons and Lovers,* Mrs. Yeobright is an intimidating woman, alternating between moods of gentleness and anger. Like Paul Morel, Clym Yeobright is implicated in his mother's death. Michael Millgate points out in his biography that while Jemima Hardy always commanded the unquestioning devotion of her children, she could be "cold in her manner, intolerant in her views, and tyrannical in her governance" (21). The same could be said about nearly all parents at one time or another, but Mrs. Yeobright, like Mrs. Morel, is particularly overbearing.

To what extent did Hardy suffer narcissistic injuries as a consequence of erratic maternal care? Giordano notes that Hardy was plagued by feelings of low self-esteem, referring to himself on his forty-seventh birthday as "Thomas the Unworthy" (*The Life of Thomas Hardy,* 200). Although we do not usually think of Hardy as a mother-fixated novelist, as we do of D. H. Lawrence, Gittings observes that he repeatedly fell in love with women (in particular, with several maternal cousins) who reminded him of his mother. "More than most mother-fixed youths, Hardy was falling in love with his own mother over and over again, in a physical and consistent way that was a typical part of his almost literal-minded nature" (*Young Thomas Hardy,* 64). Hardy's attraction to his cousin, Tryphena Sparks, one of the chief sources of

Sue Bridehead, has generated intense biographical speculation. Whatever actually happened between Hardy and his mysterious cousin, Jude and Sue reflect the novelist's fascination with incestuous love and its elusive, forbidden nature. Hardy's tragic heroes and heroines repeatedly find themselves pursuing the unobtainable. Like Narcissus, they discover the bittersweet quality of infatuation, ending their lives defeated and broken, unable to recover lost primal unity.

Hardy's little-known novel *The Well-Beloved* (1897) powerfully confirms the narcissistic infatuation to which his characters are particularly vulnerable. Hardy wrote *The Well-Beloved,* subtitled "A Sketch of a Temperament," at about the same time he was working on *Jude the Obscure.* Both novels explore spectral love. Critics generally agree that *The Well-Beloved* is Hardy's most autobiographical novel in its revelations of his unhappy love life. Jocelyn Pierston is a sculptor, not a writer, but like Hardy he is blessed and cursed by a seemingly endless series of blinding infatuations that end in bitter disillusionment. Pierston tires of his lovers as soon as he knows them well, and only one aspect of his life remains constant: the instability of his love. Unusually introspective, Pierston meticulously analyzes his infatuations, lamenting the havoc they wreak upon his life:

> To see the creature who has hitherto been perfect, divine, lose under your very gaze the divinity which has informed her, grow commonplace, turn from flame to ashes, from a radiant vitality to a relic, is anything but a pleasure for any man, and has been nothing less than a racking spectacle to my sight. Each mournful emptied shape stands ever after like the nest of some beautiful bird from which the inhabitant has departed and left it to fill with snow.

Pierston's pursuit of the Beloved One, as he calls his elusive love object, suggests defensive idealization, concealing hostility toward women. "Each shape, or embodiment, has been a temporary residence only, which she has entered, lived in awhile, and made her exit from, leaving the substance, so far as I have been concerned, a corpse, worse luck!" (33). Like Narcissus, Pierston realizes that he is doomed to pursue phantoms who vanish upon close approach. Poetic justice catches up with him when he finds himself infatuated hopelessly with a young woman (the daughter of the woman he rejected earlier) who, driven by the same psychology, tantalizes and finally spurns him. Pierston is in love with the idea of love, as Sue Bridehead is. Indeed, Sue's revealing admission, that sometimes her love of being loved gets the better of her conscience, causing her to treat a man cruelly, applies equally well to Pierston. Both Sue and Pierston fail in their reparative efforts to undo the harm they have caused others.

In an illuminating article on *The Well-Beloved* [in *Thomas Hardy after Fifty Years,* edited by Lance St. John Botler, 1977] that reveals as much about the creative source of his own fiction as it does about Hardy's, John Fowles has identified the real object of Pierston's hopeless quest. "The vanished young mother of infancy is quite as elusive as the Well-Beloved—indeed, she *is* the Well-Beloved, although the adult writer transmogrifies her according to the pleasures and fancies that have in the older man superseded the nameless ones of the child— most commonly into a young female sexual ideal of some kind, to be attained or pursued (or denied) by himself hiding behind some male character." Intrigued by an interpretation of *The French Lieutenant's Woman* published by the Yale psychoanalyst Gilbert Rose, Fowles posits in Hardy and other novelists an unconscious drive toward the unobtainable. Fowles accepts Rose's thesis that the wish to reestablish unity with the lost mother of infancy is an important motive behind the creative impulse. Behind Tryphena Sparks and the other incarnations of the Well-Beloved, including Sue Bridehead and Tess, both of whom Fowles calls in *The French Lieutenant's Woman* "pure Tryphena in spirit," lies the pre-Oedipal mother, the muse behind all creativity.

Yet Hardy's maternal muse was profoundly paradoxical, both creative and destructive. *Jude the Obscure* remains his bleakest novel, arguably the bleakest in English literature. Of all Hardy's great tragic novels, *Jude the Obscure* alone lacks convincing affirmation. Despite Hardy's sympathy toward Jude and Sue, he casts them into an indifferent world and then shows, in a novel at once beautiful and terrible, the tragedy of their self-extinction. "How cruel you are," Swinburne wrote to Hardy in an otherwise glowing review the novelist cites in his biography. "Only the great and awful father of 'Pierrette' and 'l'Enfant Maudit' was ever so merciless to his children" (270). Speaking like a disillusioned parent renouncing further children, Hardy observes, in the "Postscript to the Preface" to *Jude the Obscure,* that the experience of writing the book cured him completely of the wish to write additional novels. The novel provoked so much hostility, in fact, that he later referred to a book-burning incident in which the real object of the flames was the novelist himself. It may seem extravagant to compare Father Time's infanticide to Hardy's decision to silence forever his fictional voice. The fact remains, however, that although Hardy published a voluminous amount of poetry in the remaining thirty-three years of his life, he repudiated the art of fiction, perhaps believing, like Father Time, that the world would be better off without him. In that decision lies the greatest loss of all.

Mary Ann Kelly (essay date 1992)

SOURCE: "Individuation and Consumption in Hardy's *Jude the Obscure*: The Lure of the Void," in *The Victorian Newsletter,* No. 82, Fall, 1992, pp. 62-64.

[*In the following essay, Kelly studies Jude's existential separation from society and his desire for "a sense of belonging and integration."*]

"He could not *realize himself.*"
(*Jude the Obscure* 60)

The peripatetic motif in *Jude the Obscure,* Hardy's final novel, is obvious to any reader confronted with Jude's wanderings in Hardy's six Parts: from Marygreen to Christminster; from Melchester to Shaston; from Aldbrickham and "Elsewhere"—back to Christminster again, where Jude chooses finally to die, to become *unreal.* The fact of Jude's rootlessness clearly enhances his isolation from community, his obscurity (read worthlessness) in society's eyes, and his pain in existing as an individual—his rootlessness demonstrating Everymodern-man's predicament: the struggle to overcome disconnectedness and fragmentation. Jude's isolation, separateness, and obscurity remit only suffering. In Jude's struggle to flee the isolation and the void, he learns, eventually, and paradoxically, that the void is in fact home, a state which he need no longer flee. Though Hardy insisted he was conveying only his impressions of existence, the philosophical basis of Jude's desperate and aimless search for a "home," a feeling of completeness, belonging, and connectedness (a search demonstrated in the degradations of sexual longing which lead him to Arabella; in his compulsion to drink himself into oblivion; in his obsessive attempts at transcendence through learning and idealizing Sue Bridehead; and, finally, in death itself), is informed greatly by a knowledge of Hardy's appreciation of Schopenhauer's dictum that, in this life, "*determinism* stands firm." According to Schopenhauer, the real world of phenomena is simply illusory, and an individual discovers who he is only after he has acted since will manifests itself before understanding. Individuals are merely manifestations of the blind, impulsive Will to live. Further, if birth itself is original sin, if consciousness is an evolutionary mistake, and if human behavior is essentially irrational, willful compulsion thinly disguised by the vanity and denial inherent in human reason, then the conscious existence of each individual is a kind of imprisonment from which we all, to some degree, yearn to escape. Escape from illusory *reality* as we know it, from individuation, becomes necessity. In Schopenhauer, Hardy found a philosopher who attempted to explain (not merely justify) existence: consciousness was evolutionary error, and so, in a sense, was individuation, the separation of the individual from the mass. Jude's initial attempts to realize himself by connecting with the phenomenal world are shown to be misguided. His final attempt to realize himself by connecting with the noumenal world, the void, is shown to remit peace.

Jude the Obscure opens with a separation—Phillotson, Jude's teacher and inspiration, leaving him behind. Jude's history is an account of a series of these kinds of separations which throw him back upon himself, separations from: his father; his mother; his aunt; Arabella; Sue; the world of academics; his children; and, finally, his faith in God. Jude's history of being left an orphan, from his earliest days, primes him to expect that loss, isolation, and solitude are his lot—and yet, his "lot" feeds a tremendous compensatory urge for community which he sublimates in his affinity with Nature and in his attraction to the role of caretaker and protector of wild birds, rabbits, and the domesticated pig. In these specimens of Nature, Jude, not necessarily consciously, but certainly intuitively, recognizes himself; in his sympathy for suffering creatures, victims, outcasts, he gives what he longs to receive: sympathy, compassion, and a sense of community with others—or, *an* other. Jude's attempts at integration with something beyond himself—community—whether it be with the natural world, with the family represented by his aunt, or with the family always potentially represented in his marriages—repeatedly fail. Hardy demonstrates his misguided effort to experience consummation, communion, in the world of phenomena. Jude's longing therefore increases in strength and immediacy until he is driven largely by this compulsion for reintegration—with something beyond himself—for the duration of his life.

The need for a sense of oneness with this world, or with an other, points to the truth that no man can live happily and be autonomous. Autonomy is a version of hell. Yet Jude's fate, above all, is to feel obscure, isolated, and rejected in the corporeal world; and the obsessive desperation of his psychological need to belong (which is correct in Nature, according to Schopenhauer), coupled with repeated repudiation, becomes his tragic flaw. In turn, this cycle of desperate need and insistent repudiation becomes his informant, a significant signpost on the path to truth.

Jude's yearning to travel, to roam, to escape, literally and philosophically, is the result of an unmet need in Hardy's eyes—a hunger for consummation, oneness, belonging, peace—denied Jude most obviously by society—but even moreso by his own nature—human nature, which according to Schopenhauer, is purblind Will. In one sense, then, Jude's "groping in the dark" (258) [page references are to the Houghtan, Mifflin edition of *Jude the Obscure,* 1965] can be seen as a dramatization of Schopenhauer's irrational and impulsive Will to live: incessantly seeking contentment through connection but more often finding pain in thwarted connections.

Schopenhauer's fatalism, his view of consciousness as a painful evolutionary blunder, fascinated Hardy and explained his own sense of the needless pain and futility of existence. Schopenhauer's solution to the "quieting" of the will, informed by Buddhist asceticism, Franciscan transcendence, as well as Kantian idealism, provided Hardy with a philosophical explanation for the moments wherein Jude (and, of course, Hardy himself, according to his autobiography) felt a longing to liberate his spirit from the imprisonment of his body: to travel in the realms occupied by the dead, as he does early in Part Second at night among the ghosts of Christminster. The wish or yearning to self-destruct, or rather the wish not to be imprisoned in the flesh, could be understood by Hardy in Schopenhauerian terms, not as simple suicide, but rather as a yearning for the freeing of one's will, the ultimate escape into will-lessness and, simply, consummation, a sense of belonging and integration.

The lure of the void is increasingly for Jude an enticement toward integration which yields promise in contrast to his life of segregation. This variety of nothingness is, as Robert Adams describes it [in *Nil: Episodes in the Literary Conquest of the Void in the Nineteenth-Century,* 1966], an

> ominous and preparatory Nothing, as a sudden hush before the storm; there is a Nothing of *completion,* the void which follows on a cycle fully worked out. It is the clear intent of many tragic actions to clear the moral atmosphere by reducing their viewers to this pure simplicity, all passion spent. (13-14)

Thus, the void paradoxically promises Jude the re-union with a larger entity, even if this entity, which so promises a completion and reintegration, is Nothing, oblivion.

Early on, Jude exhibits repeated death wishes—from jumping on the frozen ice, to the slow disintegration of himself through drinking. In the disintegration of the self, there is the paradoxical promise of integration with the whole. Above all, this need for consummation, obliteration of self, integration of self with the entirety of Nature and the cosmos, overtakes Jude's motivations to *realize himself* (60) in the more traditional meaning of enhancing one's individuality. The will to self-destruct in order to belong transcends Jude's will to live as a separate being.

In this interpretation, Jude's peripatetic wandering; his self-destructive tendencies in alcoholism; his ruinous, desperate, and clutching attraction to Sue Bridehead; and finally his "suicidal" walk in the rain, can be seen as attempts to travel beyond the veil and to experience consummation, a communion with all others in Nature, with *an* other represented by Sue, and even communion with the dead which Jude longs for from the early pages of the novel. In philosophical terms, Jude's "groping in the dark—acting by instinct and not after example" (258) is ended when he lets go and chooses no longer to will to live:

> *"Let the day perish wherein I was born, and the night in which it was said, There is a man child conceived."*
>
>   . . . . .
>
> *"For now should I have lain still and been quiet."* (321)

The aimless, frenetic travel characterized by Jude's search for quiet ends with Jude's last trip to Christminster, at least in part, because Hardy found philosophical explanations for the inherent aimlessness and rootlessness and discontent at the quick of Jude's (and everyman's) being—and because he found a spiritual, though nihilistic, alternative to Jude's compulsive search for consummation; Hardy demonstrated this alternative in Jude's final, simple, passive, and peaceful acquiescence; and, even more importantly, in Jude's willing not to live among those symbols of learning in Christminster which he long believed to be the only things worth living for. In death, Jude travels beyond the veil in a way which can be interpreted in Schopenhauerian terms not as simply despairing and suicidal. Jude exits this life with dignity and grace, and even an oddly uplifting serenity, under pressure—and in that, his demise can be seen as a transcendental and even fulfilling re-integration with the void.

The loss of the surrogate father, mentor, and caretaker in Phillotson in line one of the novel becomes a reverberating motif in Jude's wretched history. Even the beacon represented by the lights of Christminster is surely tied to Jude's need to be reconnected to the parent Phillotson represents. Jude's search for the parent, the father, God, the Truth, manifests itself in ways hidden to his conscious deliberation—yet this search compels all Jude's choices in life.

For example, in Christminster Jude makes associations in the dark shadows of the walls surrounding the college which attest to his desperate need to discover lost "fathers":

> "Meanwhile I will read, as soon as I am settled in Christminster, the books I have not been able to get hold of here: Livy, Tacitus, Herodotus, Aeschylus, Sophocles, Aristophanes—"
>
> . . . . .
>
> —Euripedes, Plato, Aristotle, Lucretius, Epictetus, Seneca, Antoninus. Then I must master other things: *the Fathers* thoroughly:
>
> . . . . .
>
> Yes, Christminster shall be my *Alma Mater*; and I'll be her beloved son, in whom she shall be well pleased.
>
> (32, emphasis added)

Of course, the loftiness of Jude's aim for this ideal re-creation of a sense of belonging is undercut by his substitution of Arabella, "a complete and substantial female animal—no more, no less" (33) as a sexual conduit or shortcut to a lesser variety of temporary consummation—that satisfied by the sexual urge. But the need to "belong," to feel attached, and to be part of and lost in another persists inexorably in Jude, so desperate is his longing and so magnificent is his spiritual deficit. Varieties of the botched marriage, thus, become a central concern in the novel, and also become incidents which teach Jude by default the true route to communion.

The spiritual destitution Jude embodies renders his search for some variety of consummation a compulsion. And the degree of dependency manifested in his most depleted moments echoes through the novel:

> Onward he still went, under the influence of a

child-like yearning for the one being in the world to whom it seemed possible to fly—an unreasoning desire, whose ill judgment was not apparent to him now.

. . . . .

> "I am so wicked, Sue—my heart is nearly broken, and I could not bear my life as it was! So I have been drinking and blaspheming, or next door to it, and saying holy things in disreputable quarters. . . . O, do anything with me, Sue—*kill me*—I don't care! *Only don't hate me and despise me like all the rest of the world!*"
>
> (99, emphasis added)

The ultimate consummation, symbolized by Jude's repeated wish for death, lurks always in the recesses of his mind. Death, extinction, is a subliminal and unconscious, yet tenacious and persistent, possibility. Ironically, the ultimate remedy to Jude's "obscurity" is for him to "belong" in a final consummation so complete in Death that he cannot be separate, individuated again. In the end, Jude, who is a "chaos of principles" (258) enters the larger chaos, the cacaphony and silence behind the veil, which finally entices him in his search for safety more than the "real" world he inhabits. Jude *realizes himself* in death because he is finally integrated, connected—albeit in a noumenal realm whose ghostly inhabitants have "called" to him since childhood. As Hardy discovered in Schopenhauer, birth may well be tantamount to original sin, and death may be the fulfilling correction of a mistake.

In one sense, *Jude* is the tragedy of "unfulfilled aims" which Hardy refers to in his Preface. But, in another sense, the novel is a curiously fulfilling demonstration of the disquieting emotions which set Jude on the road to pursue a geographical cure for a disease of the spirit: there is beauty in Jude's final ticket to oblivion because it attests to his learning an important lesson in his journey through life, a lesson he has sensed intuitively and more acutely than others since his boyhood days: that oneness with his fellows, living and dead, is his ultimate destiny; and that in obliteration of the individual, sublimation manifests itself most completely. Jude achieves the state of percipience without volition ascribed to Tess at the end of her plight. He recognizes that

> Quietism, *i.e.* surrender of all volition [and] asceticism, *i.e.,* . . . consciousness of the identity of one's own nature with that of all things . . . , stand in the closest connection.
>
> (Schopenhauer)

Elizabeth Langland (essay date 1993)

SOURCE: "Becoming a Man in *Jude the Obscure*," in *The Sense of Sex: Feminist Perspectives on Hardy,* edited by Margaret R. Higonnet, University of Illinois Press, 1993, pp. 32-48.

[In the following essay, Langland evaluates Jude's dilemma of identity in terms of his struggles with the social ideologies of class and gender.]

Because Thomas Hardy's representations of women, by and large, exceed the simple stereotypes scholars initially identified as characteristic images of women, feminist critics early turned to his novels. While those first studies opened up possibilities of a rewarding feminist approach to Hardy, recent work looks more broadly at gender, exploring the problem of masculinity as well as femininity. Poised between centuries (nineteenth and twentieth), between cultures (rural and urban), and between classes (peasantry and middling), Hardy engaged profound social dislocations in ways that disturbed the stability of gender classifications. His representation in *Jude the Obscure* of the social and material construction of masculinity and femininity reveals something that feminist and gender critics are only beginning to explore: the extent to which patriarchal constructions of masculinity become constrictions and, when inflected by class, create contradictions for individual males. To speak of "patriarchy" in this way exposes a basic truth. Patriarchy (like the resistance to it) is not only outside but also inside, structuring language, logic, our very understanding of human subjectivity. Part of the novel's brilliance derives from Hardy's ability to represent Jude's battle with the class and gender self-constructions his culture offers him. His embattlement gives the novel its richness and generates its tragic denouement.

The novel articulates Jude's dilemma of identity largely through his conflicting responses to his cousin, Sue Bridehead. This interpretation of *Jude the Obscure* turns attention away from questions of the authenticity of Sue's character—where it has often focused—and queries instead Sue's place in the construction of Jude's masculinity, her role as catalyst for the text's trenchant critique of gender and class paradigms. In an earlier article, I have demonstrated that Sue as character is filtered almost entirely through Jude's perspective. Thus, she is known to us through his experience and interpretations of her. I will argue here that Jude increasingly embraces relationship with his cousin as a means of self-fulfillment. He seizes upon her as an answer to the difficulty of "growing up," his feeling that "He did not want to be a man" (1.2.15) [page references are to the New American Library edition of *Jude the Obscure*, 1961]. Through kinship and twinship with Sue, Jude seeks an alternative to the frustrating constructions of his masculinity that his culture holds out.

By linking issues of self-definition to cultural practices, discourses, and institutions, Teresa de Lauretis and Linda Alcoff provide a way of thinking about a human subject [in *Signs* 13 (Spring 1988)] "constructed through a continuous process, an ongoing constant renewal based on an interaction with the world . . . [defined] as experience. 'And thus [subjectivity] is produced not by external ideas, values, or material causes, but by one's personal, subjective engagement in the practices, discourses, and institutions that lend significance (value, meaning, and affect) to the events of the world.'" Alcoff goes on to note that this is the process "through which one's subjectivity becomes en-gendered."

We may merge this concept of subjectivity with a Bakhtinian distinction between authoritatively persuasive and internally persuasive discourses that interact in the historical and cultural construction of a subject. Often, Bakhtin explains [in *The Dialogic Imagination: Four Essays*, 1981],

> an individual's becoming, an ideological process, is characterized precisely by a sharp gap between these two categories: in one, the authoritative word (religious, political, moral; the word of a father, of adults and of teachers, etc.) that does not know internal persuasiveness, in the other internally persuasive word that is denied all privilege, backed up by no authority at all, and is frequently not even acknowledged in society (not by public opinion, not by scholarly norms, nor by criticism), not even in the legal code. The struggle and dialogic interrelationship of these categories of ideological discourse are what usually determine the history of an individual ideological consciousness.

Bakhtin offers an important dialogical model of an individual's engagement with the world, the struggle between the authoritatively persuasive and the internally persuasive word. In the wide gap between the two, however, he locates idealistically the possibility of individual choice and control over one's destiny.

In contrast, I would agree with Alcoff that authoritative discourse often takes on the aspect of the internally persuasive word, if not at first then at last. De Lauretis explains further [in *Feminist Studies / Critical Studies*, edited by De Lauretis, 1986]: "Self and identity, in other words, are always grasped and understood within particular discursive configurations. Consciousness, therefore, is never fixed, never attained once and for all, because discursive boundaries change with historical conditions." Such a theory allows us to account for Jude's initial embrace, rejection, and final recuperation of his culture's religious, political, sexual, and moral discourses: the authoritative word of a father, of adults, of teachers. Jude's longing for Sue Bridehead is culturally embedded within this dynamic: he interprets her as that which his culture forbids. As an alternative to authoritative discourses, she embodies the internally persuasive voice.

It is a striking detail of the novel that Jude longs for Sue before he sees her, before he has even seen a picture of her. Why? Sue is introduced early in the novel in Aunt Drusilla's comments to a neighbor overheard by Jude. She links her two foster children through their love of books—"His cousin Sue is just the same" (1.2.9). Yet, she also contrasts Sue, a "tomboy," to Jude, a "poor useless boy," who has the sensibility and frame of a girl. Slender and small, Jude weeps easily and feels pain keenly: "he was a boy who could not himself bear to hurt anything," a tendency the narrator terms, only half-ironically, a "weakness of character" (1.2.13). Jude feels the assaults of his life so sharply that he wishes "he could only prevent himself growing up! He did not want to be a man" (1.2.15). Jude's desire to evade the constraints of manhood leads him to posit an alternative that he reifies in the character at once like and unlike him, his cousin, Sue.

The problem of becoming a man and the prohibition of Sue Bridehead are linked in Jude's mind by the early events at Marygreen and Aunt Drusilla's comments on the tragic issue of Fawley marriages. If marriage is fatal to one Fawley, the same blood flowing through two linked individuals must culminate in tragedy. Sue is, therefore, forbidden to Jude. Hardy encodes that prohibition as a function of fate or nature. Aunt Drusilla warns: "Jude, my child, don't *you* ever marry. Tisn't for the Fawleys to take that step any more" (1.2.9). Hardy himself defined his concern in the novel as "the tragic issues of two bad marriages, owing in the main to a doom or curse of hereditary temperament peculiar to the family of the partners." The idea of hereditary taint reproduces in the narrator's attitudes the same conflicts that doom Jude. Such fatalistic discourse disguises the extent to which actual institutions coerce and thwart individuals, a process traced throughout the novel, which contemporaneous critics rightly recognized as a trenchant attack on authoritarian social practices and institutions.

That attack begins in the early events of the novel when Jude is hired to scare away the rooks come to peck the grain in Farmer Troutham's field. "His heart grew sympathetic with the birds' thwarted desires" (1.2.11), and he lets them feed until surprised by his angry employer who beats him. That beating, which chastens desire, initiates Jude's reluctance to become a man, at least a man fashioned after the class models most readily available to him.

In the process of formulating his identity, Jude fastens on Christminster and becoming a "university graduate," "the necessary hallmark of a man who wants to do anything in teaching" (1.1.4). Both are associated with Mr. Phillotson, his early model, and both are utterly distinguished from his current life, substituting as they do a middle-class for a lower-class model of manhood. Ironically, his aunt puts the idea in his head that such an occupation might suit her "poor boy." After Troutham fires Jude, she complains: "Jude, Jude, why didsn't go off with that schoolmaster of thine to Christminster or somewhere?" (1.2.14). He reverently anticipates that "Christminster shall be my Alma Mater; and I'll be her beloved son, in whom she shall be well pleased" (1.6.41). Although the Latin makes the school his mother, in fact, by entering Christminster, Jude would embrace an established patriarchal tradition, a fact underscored in the Biblical passage that Jude's rhetoric echoes: "This is my beloved Son, in whom I am well pleased" (Matthew 3:17).

Hardy frames the larger issue of Jude's struggle with social codes by stressing his desire to learn the languages of the past. Jude will master Latin and Greek with the goal of ultimately being authorized to speak as an educated, middle-class man. Latin, in particular, holds power over him even before he knows anything about it except its ascribed value. His longing for that authority culminates in a fanciful idea of Christminster as a "new Jerusalem" (1.3.20) and as a "mistress" (1.3.22) who is beckoning him to his fulfillment. The intensity with which Jude applies himself to these dead languages reveals their power, which is not simply the authoritatively persuasive word of his "fathers" and of the past, but quickly becomes an internally persuasive word guiding Jude's first major struggle toward self-definition. His ability to use Latin and to understand Latin will determine his behavior at later moments of crisis.

Until he is nineteen, Jude's sexual impulses are held completely in abeyance by his infatuation for the scholastic life. But Jude's encounter with Arabella Donn temporarily displaces the authority of intellectual discourse with another ideology. Generally, Jude's distraction has been interpreted as a capitulation to his natural sexual instincts, what the narrator characterizes as "The unvoiced call of woman to man, which . . . held Jude to the spot against his intention—almost against his will" (1.6.44). But sexual desire is not, in fact, what traps Jude. Notably, he is never the sexual aggressor with Arabella; she sees all his advances as "rather mild!" (1.7.52), and she has to plot rather cleverly to bring him to the point.

Two cultural paradigms of masculinity motivate Jude's divided drives. The first dictates that a "natural" man will find the stimulus of a proximate woman sufficient to arouse strong sexual desire, and it cuts across classes. The second involves the rhetoric of chivalric or honorable love and courtship and belongs more properly to the middle and upper classes. According to the first essentialist discourse, men are sexually different from women. Even Phillotson, a middle-aged, staid scholar, can consummate and reconsummate his marriage with a rigid and unresponsive Sue Bridehead. He, after all, is a "man." Thus, although the rhetoric of the novel presents Jude's weakness for women as a fault, it also insists on that "weakness" or susceptibility as important evidence of manliness. When Jude fails to live up to other discursive formulations of his masculinity, this one never fails him, as we shall discover in the crucial final scenes of the novel.

Surprisingly, this rhetoric of manliness is not undercut by the behavior of Arabella Donn, who is always equally ready to engage in sexual relations. We may attribute that curious gap to the presence of the second authoritative discourse we have identified. When Jude becomes sexually involved with Arabella, he simultaneously becomes entangled in another discourse of manliness whose hallmark is romance, chivalry, and honor: "It was better to love a woman than to be a graduate, or a parson; ay, or a pope!" (1.7.53). These two discourses cooperate to construct the "gentle-man," a middle-class ideal. Notably, Phillotson is as bound by the second discourse as Jude; it initially determines his decision to let Sue leave him to go to Jude. He justifies his decision to Gillingham in the following way: "I don't think you are in a position to give an opinion. I have been that man, and it makes all the difference in the world, if one has any manliness or chivalry in him" (4.4.278).

Jude's susceptibility to the chivalric code of helpless women and protective and honorable men allows Arabella to use her claim of pregnancy to trap him into marriage. In spite of the fact that Jude knows too well "that Arabella was not worth a great deal as a specimen of womankind," "he was ready to abide by what he had said, and take the consequences" and "save [her] ready or no" (1.9.65, 70). His susceptibility to this discourse—a function of his middle-class aspirations—distinguishes Jude's "finer" aspirations and sensibilities from the "peasant cynicism" of country women like Arabella and Aunt Drusilla. According to their discourse, he is a "simple fool" (1.9.65) and "poor silly fellow" (1.9.66). When Arabella's plot is revealed, Jude vaguely ponders not his own folly, but "something wrong in a social ritual" (1.9.70). In fact, Jude's construction of manliness betrays him because he applies a middle-class ethic to Arabella's classic peasant ruse.

After Jude should have learned the bankruptcy of this patriarchal code of male honor and female victims—in its inapplicability to his relationship with Arabella where he is the defenseless innocent and she the practiced seducer—it seems inexplicably naive of him to persist in it. Yet such persistence provides another example of the ways in which authoritative discourses becomes internally persuasive. Indeed, Jude clings to such constructions both because they define him as middle-class and because they define him as masculine (not simply as male). Jude learns from Arabella *not* to question the adequacy of such formulations but only to "feel dissatisfied with himself as a man at what he had done" (1.10.76).

Such class and gender constructions of his masculinity come to seem essential to Jude's identity. When Arabella and Jude separate at her instigation, Jude returns to his dream of education in Christminster, motivated by another pair of self-images. First, he reaffirms his dream of modeling his manhood and *embourgeoisement* on the schoolteacher, Phillotson. In addition, he pursues an elusive superiority and gender neutrality figured by his middle-class cousin, Sue Bridehead, whom he has seen only in a photograph. The narrator explains this new motive as "more nearly related to the emotional side of him than to the intellectual, as is often the case with young men." It really is surprising that Jude should be led to Christminster by a photograph, especially after his disastrous marriage. But we accept the motive, I believe, because we recognize that Sue offers an alternative version of his problematic self. She is like Jude, after all, also "of the inimical branch of the family" (2.1.90).

Entering Christminster at evening, Jude immediately feels himself in the presence of "those other sons of the place" (2.1.93), a kind of patrillineage that seems to promise accommodation for a humble laborer. But in the morning, "he found that the colleges had treacherously changed their sympathetic countenances. . . . The spirits of the great men had disappeared" (2.2.97). Although Jude is momentarily impressed by the dignity of manual labor, what the narrator calls a "true illumination"—that the "stone yard was a centre of effort as worthy as that dignified by the name of scholarly study within the noblest of colleges"—he soon loses this impression "under the stress of his old idea" (2.2.98). Ironically, this discourse of manual labor's dignity stems from the middle-class intellectual elite, and the very condescension implicit in the perspective undermines its validity. So the narrator reproduces in his own rhetoric the conflicts that will doom Jude. Because Jude will *be* a manual laborer denied access to scholarly pursuits, the gap opened up will lead him increasingly to Sue as an authentic alternative. Not surprisingly, then, no sooner is Jude aware of the gap between his aspirations and his pursuits than his passion for Sue intensifies. He insists his aunt send his cousin's portrait, "kissed it—he did not know why—and felt more at home. . . . It was . . . the one thing uniting him to the emotions of the living city" (2.2.99).

This extraordinary scene of alienation and "at homeness" makes Sue pivotal to the construction of Jude's identity. Jude's claim of blood and emotional kinship (she "belongs" to him) suggests that his investment in her is deeply tied to his gender identity (2.2.103). Before meeting her, Jude has already internalized Sue's being as essential to his own subjecthood, a process intensified by his aunt's prohibition that "he was not to bring disturbance into the family by going to see the girl" (2.2.99). Sue represents what is in him but also what he is not to seek in himself, which is here coded as the feminine. His desire to discover that alternative, of course, results from his frustrations with both lower-class social definitions of manhood and the conflicts introduced by middle-class codes. When he first locates Sue, he "recognized in the accents certain qualities *of his own voice*." (2.2.103) [my emphasis]. Later Jude sees Sue, dressed in his clothes, as "a slim and fragile being masquerading as himself on a Sunday" (3.3.173). He affirms, "You are just like me at heart!" (4.1.243). Phillotson corroborates the "extraordinary sympathy, or similarity, between the pair. . . . They seem to be one person split in two!" (4.4.276). Jude appropriates Sue to ground his floundering self in her "social and spiritual possibilities" (2.3.107).

Jude alternates between reflections on Sue as an "ideality" or a "divinity"—totally divorced from the coarse Arabella—and sexual longings for her. The tension in Jude's view has often been interpreted as stemming from Sue's "inconsistency"—her waxing hot and cold, her frigidity coupled with her desire for attention. But this approach to her character as a charming neurotic tends to ignore her fictional, cultural, and tendentious construction. I propose, instead, that the tension within the narrator's depiction of Sue reflects Jude's complex investment in her, which also causes him to hide from her his marriage to Arabella.

The urgent need Jude feels for Sue stems from his increasingly precarious sense of masculine identity and social significance. Comparing Christminster's "town life" to its "gown life" (2.6.139), he characterizes the former as the "real Christminster life" (2.7.141). The text implies that, if Jude were not possessed by "the modern vice of unrest" (2.2.98), not a "paltry victim of the spirit of mental and social restlessness" (6.1.393-94), he might be able to have a more authentic existence, that is, one grounded in a secure sense of who and what he is. At such moments, the narrator seems implicated in the same ideological illusions and conflicts that condemn Jude. The idea of an authentic existence is problematic in the text. Thus, Jude flounders among social markers for masculine identity and increasingly turns to Sue as the source of his meaning, finally concluding, "with Sue as companion he could have renounced his ambitions with a smile" (2.6.137). Of course, Jude is naive to believe he can easily renounce his ambitions; they are already too important to his self-concept, as we shall see.

In the novel's first half, Jude progresses from would-be intellectual, to honorable young husband (Marygreen), to would-be intellectual again (Christminster), to would-be ecclesiastic (Melchester)—each stage dominated by a particular authoritative discourse that promises to make a man of Jude. All the while Jude keeps in reserve his dream of Sue as a means to construct a self outside unsatisfactory patriarchal models: "To keep Sue Bridehead near him was now a desire which operated without regard of consequences" (2.4.121). Only the force of his need explains why Jude cannot tell Sue of his marriage to Arabella and must instead project his failure and secretiveness onto her as *her* inconsistency. When he finally and belatedly informs her and lamely excuses himself— "It seemed cruel to tell it"—she justly rebukes him, "To yourself, Jude. So it was better to be cruel to me!" (3.6.198).

When Jude finally reveals his marriage to Arabella, he also begins to generalize about Sue as a "woman." Such generalizations characterize the two points in the narrative when Jude must defend himself against separation from Sue, first here and then at the end of the novel. Previously, Sue has been represented in a more gender-neutral way, as a "tomboy," who joins boys in their exploits, or as a "comrade" with a "curious unconsciousness of gender" (3.4.179), who mixes with men "almost as one of their own sex" (3.4.177). Impelled to defend his own sexuality, Jude now stresses Sue's need to exercise "those narrow womanly humours on impulse that were necessary to give her sex" (3.6.200). Sue both is and is not a typical woman depending on Jude's psychosocial investment in her. At those points when he fears he will lose her, he tends to brand her typical of her sex to distance himself from his need for her. He repeats this distancing act at Susanna's marriage to Phillotson:

"Women were different from men in such matters. Was it that they were, instead of more sensitive, as reported, more callous and less romantic?" (3.7.209).

Sue's self-generalizations as woman have a somewhat different textual function. She says, for example, in reference to herself, "some women's love of being loved is insatiable" (4.1.245). Such comments reinforce Jude's characterizations of Sue as asexual "spirit," a "disembodied creature," a "dear, sweet, tantalizing phantom— hardly flesh at all" (4.5.294). The spiritualization preserves her as the endlessly desired object, a Shelleyan Epipsyche. The text demands, above all, "the elusiveness of her curious double nature" (4.2.251).

The last half of the novel focuses the tension between Jude's need to be the man his culture demands and his desire to locate a more fulfilling existence outside custom and convention. When Jude argues his similarity to his cousin—"for you are just like me at heart"—she demurs, "But not at head." And when he insists, "we are both alike," she corrects him, "Not in our thoughts" (4.1.243). Their disagreement arises because Sue's attractiveness disrupts but cannot displace the categories of masculinity Jude has already internalized. Jude is drawn in two directions because he can never fully abandon the categories of thought he has imbibed from his culture.

Constructed as an outsider to patriarchal culture, Sue can articulate social tensions that Jude can then increasingly recognize. She argues, "the social moulds civilization fits us into have no more relation to our actual shapes than the conventional shapes of the constellations have to the real star-patterns" (4.1.246-47). When Sue asks Jude, hypothetically, if a woman with a repugnance for her husband ought "to try to overcome her pruderies," he responds in contradictory ways, "speaking as an order-loving man . . . I should say yes. Speaking from experience and unbiased nature, I should say no" (4.2.252). Shortly thereafter, under pressure of his love for Sue, Jude announces, "my doctrines and I begin to part company" (4.2.258). After he passionately kisses Sue, Jude realizes that "he was as unfit, obviously by nature, as he had been by social position, to fill the part of a propounder of accredited dogma." Yet barred by Sue's marriage to Phillotson and his own marriage to Arabella, Jude has recourse to the category of "woman" to explain his difficulties: "Strange that his first aspiration—toward academic proficiency—had been checked by a woman, and that his second aspiration—toward apostleship—had also been checked by a woman. 'Is it,' he said, 'that women are to blame.'" (4.3.261).

The conclusion, "women are to blame," lodges Jude's reasoning within a traditional framework that takes him back to the Garden of Eden, Genesis, and Eve's temptation and fall. Although Jude should reject a discourse so inadequate to his experience, instead he reauthorizes its tenets on women. Such constructions are so essential to his subjectivity that they cannot be completely abandoned. Indeed, it is important to Jude that "he might go on *believing* as before but he *professed* nothing" (4.3.262, my italics).

The role of women as temptresses in this narrative corresponds to an ideology of masculinity that suggests sex is, for a man, a snare that leads first to entrapment, then disillusionment, and even damnation. As we have seen, a deep ideological subtext of the novel argues that a "man" is inherently disposed toward sexual relations and will find women a lure to physical intimacy. The fact that sexual familiarity may culminate in contempt does not prevent his being ready to behave sexually on the next encounter. A companion ideology stipulates that, whatever his feelings, a "gentle-man" will then behave honorably toward the "victimized" woman. The logic of these interlocking ideologies supports Jude's sexual relations with Arabella, both initially and following a chance encounter after several years' separation.

Jude's embrace of the gentlemanly ethic allows the lower-class Arabella repeatedly to exploit him. Similarly, when Arabella later appeals to Jude to follow her to her hotel to hear her story, and Sue objects, Jude argues: "I shall certainly give her something, and hear what it is she is so anxious to tell me; no man could do less!" (5.2.318). Arabella pronounces, "Never such a tender fool as Jude is if a woman seems in trouble" (5.2.324).

All of Jude's justifications of his behavior produce essentialist views of men and women. When Sue asks, "Why should you take such trouble for a woman who has served you so badly," he responds, "But, Sue, she's a woman, and I once cared for her; and one [a man] can't be a brute in such circumstances" (5.2.319). In response to Sue's accusation that his behavior is "gross," Jude replies, "You don't understand me either—women never do!" (4.5.293). By generalizing from "you"—Sue—to "women," Jude also implicitly generalizes from "me"—Jude—to "men." Women do not understand men or male sexuality.

Jude's determination to fulfill a "man's" obligations to Arabella exerts a sexual coercion on Sue, who precipitously agrees to sleep with Jude to erase Arabella's claims on him. When Sue capitulates, Jude transfers to her his sexual allegiance and chivalric code. Arabella is no longer "a woman" but her clever self: "You haven't the least idea how Arabella is able to shift for herself" (5.2.322).

The sexual possession of Sue marks a crux in the novel and in Jude's self-construction. It permits him to define his male "nature" as one given to sensual indulgence— wine, women, and blasphemy. But he also aspires to a value outside a carnal construction of his masculinity that he locates in his relations with Sue. He tells her: "All that's best and noblest in me loves you, and your freedom from everything that's gross has elevated me, and enabled me to do what I should never have dreamt myself capable of, *or any man,* a year or two ago" (5.2.320, my italics). The kinship Jude feels for this female self allows

him to move beyond the patriarchal imprimatur, defining an identity he had not believed accessible to himself or any man. In the "nomadic" phase of their life together, Jude "was mentally approaching the position which Sue had occupied when he first met her" (5.7.373).

Their kinship will be undermined by the cultural codes that define Jude's masculinity. Although Jude is represented as sharing Sue's anxiety about the constraints of marriage, his behavior is simultaneously shaped by Biblical injunctions on manhood: "For what man is he that hath betrothed a wife and hath not taken her?" (5.4.338). And although the couple is exquisitely happy in their life together—returned, in Sue's words, to "Greek joyousness" (5.5.358)—Jude reveals his continuing attraction to Christminster in the Model of Cardinal College he and Sue have made for the Wessex Agricultural Show. Despite the narrator's insistence on Jude's independence of thought, he chooses to bake "Christminster cakes" when he is pressed for employment after his illness. Arabella neatly pinpoints his continuing obsession and slavery to his former ideals: "Still harping on Christminster—even in his cakes. . . . Just like Jude. A ruling passion." Sue admits: "Of course Christminster is a sort of fixed vision with him, which I suppose he'll never be cured of believing in. He still thinks it a great centre of high and fearless thought, instead of what it is, a nest of commonplace schoolmasters whose characteristic is timid obsequiousness to tradition" (5.7.376).

Arabella's accidental meeting with Phillotson, immediately following her rencontre with Sue, sets the stage for the series of reversals or "returns" that conclude the novel. Her crude invocation of Old Testament law and learning as a model for contemporary behavior prepares us for the way in which Jude, as well as Phillotson, will be drawn back to the authority and consequence held out to them as men in a patriarchal society. Arabella states: "There's nothing like bondage and a stone-deaf taskmaster for taming us women. Besides, you've got the laws on your side Moses knew. . . . 'Then shall the man be guiltless; but the woman shall bear her iniquity'" (5.8.384). Arabella's addendum—"Damn rough on us women; but we must grin and put up wi' it!"—comfortably accepts a damaging gender bifurcation that Jude and even Phillotson have struggled to overcome in their response to Sue Bridehead. When Sue questions, "Why should you care so much for Christminster?" Jude replies: "I can't help it. I love the place. . . . it is the centre of the universe to me, because of my early dream. . . . I should like to go back to live there—perhaps to die there!" (5.8.386). Part 5 culminates with the realization of his dream to return there; Part 6 culminates with the realization of his dream to die there.

We, too, ask Sue's questions: why does Jude suddenly develop a passionate desire to return to Christminster for this Remembrance Day, and why does he return in a way so entirely forgetful of Sue and his children? Then, why does Jude persist in his resolve to seek work in Christminster after it has become the scene of his grotesque tragedy and can serve only as a reminder of that tragedy? In fact, the text occludes these questions and shifts focus to Sue Bridehead's intellectual, sexual, and emotional degradation. But there are significant ideological implications in that textual strategy. These breaks and shifts reveal their inner logic if we keep our eye on Jude's alternating evasion and pursuit of manhood.

Jude's return to Christminster spells a rejection of Sue and a reembrace of the patriarchal discourse that originally attracted him. Whereas on one level it seems absurd to say that Jude has rejected Sue since he pleads for her emotional and physical return to him, the subtext of the novel argues differently. By returning to Christminster, Jude privileges a hierarchic order in opposition to his more egalitarian relationship with Sue. Indeed, by delaying the search for housing, he shifts the burden of their relationship onto Sue, who bears the visible evidence of their three children and her pregnancy while he again becomes, in effect, the unencumbered novice who first entered the city several years earlier. When he again seeks lodging in his old quarter, Beersheba, he continues to replicate his earlier patterns. The unbearable poignancy of the novel's last section derives not only from the representation of Sue's collapse but also from the painful tension between Jude's embrace and rejection of Sue, a rejection that demands the collapse of her textual function as a significant alternative.

Jude longs for the spirit of the law, but is drawn to the letter as primary ground of his identity. Jude finally seeks an authority to define the meaning of his life, and he must do that from within the system, from a position that validates the system and its judgments of him as a failed man who has "missed everything." This final need for authority explains Jude's return to Christminster. Jude wants that intellectual milieu to frame the tragic limitation of his manhood. *If,* as Sue says, Christminster is only a "nest of commonplace schoolmasters," then Jude's life is a relative success. To give his life the tragic cast he favors, he must reauthorize Christminster. Relationship with Sue originally provided a focal point for a critique of authoritative discourse. Now that relationship, in its domestic and quotidian aspects, cuts away the ground of meaning necessary to Jude's "tragedy." The triumphant tragedy of Jude's life is only apparent when inscribed within the dominant, authoritative discourse of Christminster. It is under that authority that he can echo Shakespeare's *Romeo and Juliet* in summarizing his life: "However, it was my poverty and not my will that consented to be beaten. It takes two or three generations to do what I tried to do in one" (6.1.393).

The narrative sequence supports a reading of Jude's return to Christminster as a rejection of Sue Bridehead. First, Jude chooses to return on Remembrance Day when the city is teeming with visitors. Upon arrival he initially insists that "the first thing is lodgings," but he quickly abandons that goal in his desire to hurry to the procession, ignoring Sue's demurral: "Oughtn't we to get a house over our heads first?" Although "his soul seemed

full of the anniversary," Jude announces that Remembrance Day is really "Humiliation Day for me!" a "lesson in presumption," an image of his own "failure" (6.1.390). Of course, to see his failure is also to see the possibility of success, to see that he might have become "a son of the University." The Alma Mater as pater familias. As it begins to rain and "Sue again wished not to stay," Jude grows more enthusiastic as he rediscovers old friends and reevaluates his life. He says he is "in a chaos of principles—groping in the dark—acting by instinct and not after example" (6.1.394), thereby grounding his identity in the context of Christminster and its definitions of success. Through that prism he reexamines his life, granting to Christminster authority to write his "romance," the middle-class tragic romance of the common man: "I'm an outsider to the end of my days!" (6.1.396).

Throughout the entire day, through thunderstorms and drenchings, Jude ignores his pale, reluctant wife and his several children to bask once more in the reflected glory of Christminster, "to catch a few words of the Latin," and so, in spirit, join the fraternity that has otherwise excluded him. He may tell Sue that "I'll never care any more about the infernal cursed place," but as they belatedly begin to search for lodgings, Jude is drawn to "Mildew Lane," close to the back of a college, a spot he finds "irresistible" and Sue "not so fascinating" (6.1.396). She is finally housed outside Sarcophagus and Rubric Colleges, Hardy's symbolically appropriate names, and she contemplates "the strange operation of a simple-minded man's ruling passion, that it should have led Jude, who loved her and the children so tenderly, to place them here in this depressing purlieu, because he was still haunted by his dream" (6.2.401). Jude's pursuit of his "dream" has left Sue and the children terribly exposed, and the events culminate in Father Time's suicide and murder of the other two children. Sue claims responsibility for these tragic events and neither the narrator nor Jude disputes her interpretation, yet responsibility really belongs to Jude who, in returning to Christminster, rejected Sue and his children for his old "dream."

Sue now takes on the narrative function of justifying Jude: "My poor Jude—how you've missed everything!—you more than I, for I did get you! To think you should know that [the chorus of the *Agamemnon*] by your unassisted reading, and yet be in poverty and despair!" (6.2.409). There is nothing in the narrative that contradicts Sue's assessment. Thus the text can endorse the position that Jude "missed everything" while Sue, in getting Jude, apparently "got" what she wanted. It is ironic that she, who was supposed to be what he wanted, now stands debased, as the coin he received for his labors, an emblem of what riches he has missed.

It is a further irony that the only blame Jude accepts is for "seducing" Sue, a grotesque reinterpretation of his desire for Sue. He claims, "I have seemed to myself lately . . . to belong to that vast band of men shunned by the virtuous—the men called seducers. . . . Yes, Sue—that's what I am. I seduced you. . . . You were a distinct type—a refined creature, intended by Nature to be left intact" (6.3.414). The idea of Jude as seducer presents an absurd reduction of their complex relationship with its twin fulfillments of independence and happiness. But a reconstruction of the scenario with himself as seducer serves the function of reconstructing yet another social aspect of Jude's manhood.

As Jude adopts these conventional, middle-class gender terms, he deprives Sue of any meaningful textual role outside parallel gender stereotypes, which dictate that the chaste but violated female move toward self-sacrificing, punitive, masochistic degradation. We return, once more, to the generalizations about women that were absent during the long emotional and sexual intimacy between Jude and Sue: "Is woman a thinking unit at all, or a fraction always wanting its integer?" (6.3.424). The text's positioning of comments like this one suggests that Sue's function as desirable other, a space free from the socially coded and rigid definition of manhood, has been exhausted or used up. In order for Jude to reclaim the construction of his manhood implicit first in Christminster and then in his relationship with Arabella, Sue must be reinterpreted as merely a pathetic woman whose mind has become unhinged. Hence, her "inconsistency."

This strict sexual bifurcation figures in the novel's closing rhetoric. Sue says to Jude, "Your wickedness was only the natural man's desire to possess the woman" (6.3.426). And, on Sue's return, Phillotson says ominously, "I know woman better now" (6.5.442). Sue accounts for her own role in the relationship by admitting to an "inborn craving which undermines some women's morals. . . . the craving to attract and captivate, regardless of the injury it may do the man" (6.3.426).

Jude returns to the twin evils of his life, his "two Arch Enemies . . . my weakness for womankind and my impulse to strong liquor" (6.3.427). He embraces in his Christminster dreams and the cruel reality of marriage to Arabella the same constricting construction of his manhood which figured prominently in the opening pages of the novel. Although drunk, Jude calls up the established discourse of manliness to justify remarrying Arabella: "I'd marry the W——of Babylon rather than do anything dishonourable. . . . marry her I will, so help me God! . . . I am not a man who wants to save himself at the expense of the weaker among us!" (6.7.461-62). By sacrificing himself to the sham of this "meretricious contract with Arabella," Jude, of course, preserves a definition of manhood essential to his identity.

The honor, the rectitude, the righteousness, and the learning that Jude claims as the hallmarks of his middle-class manhood allow him to die with the words of Job on his lips: "Let the day perish wherein I was born, and the night in which it was said, There is a man child conceived" (6.11.488). Such an invocation accords well with the other discourses Jude has previously embraced.

In *Jude the Obscure,* Hardy has given us a novel in which the authoritatively persuasive word ultimately becomes the internally persuasive one in the construction of one man's subjectivity. In the process, Hardy has revealed masculinity as a cultural and social class construct, one that coerces and limits individuals even as it holds out the irresistible promise of conferring definitive meaning on their lives. In Jude's longing for Sue, Hardy has made us feel the poignant desire for a self free from such coercive definitions, the need for some more flexible way to confront the problem of "growing up . . . to be a man," for some way to feel satisfied with himself as a man (1.2.15). In Sue's emotional and intellectual collapse, which proleptically justifies Jude's return to the Christminster way, he has made us feel the virtual impossibility of any individual defining himself in opposition to the dominant culture of his or her society. Jude's death and Sue's degradation, the events concluding the novel, arrest but do not resolve the text's testing of discursive formulations of gender paradigms. The anticipated unfolding of a subject proves to be an involution, a collapse inward resisted only by social practices and discourses that mock the idea of individual self-determination and locate self-fulfillment in death.

Early in her relationship with Jude, Sue Bridehead claims that, "We are a little beforehand, that's all" (5.4.345). In fact, she is only partly right; Jude and Sue are constructed by the very terms they seek to transcend. The lingering sadness of this novel lies in its apprehension of the ways destructive cultural self-constructions ultimately reach out to claim them, the ways, indeed, they are always already within, crucial to the formation and development of individual subjecthood and therefore perilous to reject. This modern understanding of the problematic subject and the material basis for subjectivity allows Hardy to give us a trenchant interrogation of the cultural construction of gender paradigms and their often contradictory inflections by class. It also allows him to generate a new form of tragic irony in the disparity between what we can understand and aspire to and what we can ultimately become—undermined, as we are, from within. Hardy's depiction of this ineluctable dilemma of identity gives him a distinctive place in the Victorian canon and suggests significant links with a modern sensibility, which has been acknowledged in his poetry but not so readily in his novels. In this regard, we may recognize Hardy as both the most modern of Victorians, and, in the poignancy of his final novel, the most Victorian of moderns.

FURTHER READING

Criticism

Adelman, Gary. *Jude the Obscure: A Paradise of Despair.* New York: Twayne Publishers, 1992, 137 p.
  Summarizes the historical context and critical reception

of *Jude the Obscure*, followed by an interpretive reading of the novel that highlights its prevailing mood of despair.

Alden, Patricia. "A Short Story Prelude to *Jude the Obscure*: More Light on the Genesis of Hardy's Last Novel." *Colby Library Quarterly* XIX, No. 1 (March 1983): 45-52.
Observes the "germ" of *Jude the Obscure* in Hardy's short story "A Tragedy of Two Ambitions."

Bloom, Harold, ed. *Thomas Hardy's 'Jude the Obscure.'* New York: Chelsea House Publishers, 1987, 152 p.

Collection of nine critical essays on *Jude the Obscure*.

Dellamora, Richard. "Male Relations in Thomas Hardy's *Jude the Obscure*." *Papers on Language & Literature: A Journal for Scholars and Critics of Language and Literature* 27, No. 4 (Fall 1991): 453-72.
Studies the juxtaposition of erotic and ambitious male desire in *Jude the Obscure*.

Freeman, Janet H. "Highways and Cornfields: Space and Time in the Narration of *Jude the Obscure*." *Colby Library Quarterly* XXVII, No. 2 (June 1991): 161-73.
Argues the ultimate congruence of "space, time, and narrativity in *Jude the Obscure*."

Giordano, Frank R., Jr. "*Jude the Obscure* and the *Bildungsroman*." *Studies in the Novel* IV, No. 4 (Winter 1972): 580-91.
Seeks "a unifying formal principle in *Jude the Obscure* by examining the novel in relation to . . . the *Bildungsroman*, the novel of development and education."

Hassett, Michael E. "Compromised Romanticism in *Jude the Obscure*." *Nineteenth-Century Fiction* 25, No. 4 (March 1971): 432-43.
Contends that the lives of Jude Fawley and Sue Bridehead form a critique of "the Romantics' faith in the power of transcending or transforming imagination."

Ingham, Patricia. "Introduction." In *Jude the Obscure*, by Thomas Hardy, pp. xi-xxii. Oxford: Oxford University Press, 1985.
Percieves *Jude the Obscure* as critical of the three major forces operating in late Victorian society: class, patriarchy, and Christianity.

Kincaid, James R. "Girl-watching, Child-beating and Other Exercises for Readers of *Jude the Obscure*." In *The Sense of Sex: Feminist Perspectives on Hardy*, edited by Margaret R. Higonnet, pp. 132-48. Urbana: University of Illinois Press, 1993.
Studies the topics of homicidal voyeurism and sadism directed toward children in *Jude the Obscure*.

Lodge, David. "*Jude the Obscure*: Permission and Fictional Form." In *Critical Approaches to the Fiction of Thomas Hardy*, New York: Barnes and Noble, 1979, pp. 193-201.
Presents several key scenes in the novel as evidence that the form of *Jude the Obscure* "works to articulate and reinforce the pessimism of its vision of life."

Millgate, Michael. "*Jude the Obscure*." In *Thomas Hardy: His Career as a Novelist*, pp. 317-35. New York: Random House, 1971.
Evaluates the narrative technique and structure of *Jude the Obscure*.

Paterson, John. "The Genesis of *Jude the Obscure*." *Studies in Philology* 57, No. 1 (January 1960): 87-98.
Uses manuscript evidence to suggest the development of *Jude the Obscure* from a critique of the Victorian educational system into a work that takes "an equally critical examination of the sacrament and institution of marriage."

Schwartz, Barry N. "*Jude the Obscure* in the Age of Anxiety." *Studies in English Literature 1500-1900* X, No. 4 (Autumn 1970): 793-804.
Analyzes *Jude the Obscure* as a "modern epic" that endeavors to explore "the realities of twentieth-century life."

Steig, Michael. "Sue Bridehead." *Novel: A Forum on Fiction* 1, No. 3 (Spring 1968): 260-66.
Offers a psychoanalytic interpretation of Sue Bridehead and proposes that she is an aesthetically coherent example of the "hysterical character."

Watts, Cedric. *Thomas Hardy: 'Jude the Obscure.'* London: Penguin Books, 1992, 132 p.
Provides extensive biographical, textual, critical, and contextual information relating to *Jude the Obscure*.

————. "Hardy's Sue Bridehead and the 'New Woman.'" *Critical Survey* 5, No. 2 (1993): 152-56.

Investigates Hardy's depiction of Sue Bridehead as a proto-feminist 'New Woman,' a "young woman who is educated, intelligent, emancipated in ideas and in morality, and who is resistant to the conventional notion that marriage and maternity should be the goal of any normal female's progress."

Kenji Mizoguchi

1898-1956

Japanese film director and scriptwriter.

INTRODUCTION

During the three decades of his career as a film director, Mizoguchi was one of the most distinctive and dominant figures in the Japanese motion picture industry. In the early 1950s he achieved breakthrough success in the international art film market, and was hailed by European critics as one of the world's great cinema artists. Both praise and criticism of Mizoguchi centers on his trademark style and themes: his preference for panoramic long shots over closeups; his tendency to let entire scenes play out in one uninterrupted take; his preoccupation with downtrodden women; and his meticulous recreation of historical settings.

Biographical Information

When Mizoguchi was growing up in Tokyo, his father lost everything in a failed business venture; as a result, Mizoguchi's beloved older sister Suzu was sold into prostitution. According to biographers, this trauma determined Mizoguchi's lifelong personal fascination with sexually exploited women, reflected in many of his films, including *Gion no shimai* (*Sisters of the Gion*), *Saikaku ichidai onna* (*The Life of Oharu*), *Ugetsu monogatari*, and *Akasen chitai* (*Street of Shame*). Denied an education by his penurious father, he eventually attended art school with Suzu's financial help, and worked as a commercial artist before obtaining a job as a low-level functionary at the Nikkatsu film studio in 1922. He quickly rose through the ranks and got an opportunity to direct films, the first of which, *Ai ni yomigaeru hi* (*The Resurrection of Love*), was released in 1923. Mizoguchi negotiated his career with care and flexibility, managing to maintain his characteristic style and subject matter through changing cultural fashions and political demands, first from the Fascist Japanese government during the 1930s and early 1940s, and then from the occupying American forces following Japan's defeat in World War II.

Major Works

At the start of his filmmaking career, Mizoguchi distinguished himself with such commercial and critical successes as *Kaminingyo haru no sayaki* (*A Paper Doll's Whisper of Spring* and *Tokai kokyogaku* (*Metropolitan Symphony*. However, he regarded his silent and early sound films as essentially apprentice work. With studio contracts that allowed him greater creative control, he achieved what he considered his mature style, starting in the mid 1930s with *Sisters of the Gion* and *Naniwa ereji*

(*Osaka Elegy*) and culminating with the internationally acclaimed *Life of Oharu*, *Ugetsu*, *Sansho dayu* (*Sansho the Bailiff*), and *Street of Shame*. Although Mizoguchi wrote the scripts or original scenarios for some of his early films, most of his more well-known works are based on screenplays written by others, such as Matsutaro Kawaguchi and Yoshikata Yoda. However, Mizoguchi worked closely with his screenwriters and took an active part in shaping scripts to meet his artistic standards. He earned a repuation as a zealous perfectionist who required lengthy research and preparation for both his historical dramas, such as the nationalistic samurai epic *Genroku chushingura* (*The Loyal Forty-Seven Ronin*), and his naturalistic modern-day depictions of geishas and other lower-class characters. Altogether he made approximately ninety films, only about a third of which were still in existence by the end of the twentieth century.

Critical Reception

From the 1920s through the 1940s, Mizoguchi's films were seldom seen in the West, and his reputation rested primarily with Japanese audiences and critics. Although he scored several popular hits in the 1920s and 1930s, esteem for his work lessened as his artistic signatures, such as the meticulously authentic period piece and the single-take long shot, began to seem stale. Perception of his career changed radically when he entered the world cinema scene with *The Life of Oharu*, which won him the grand prize at the 1952 Venice Film Festival. The highly influential critics and filmmakers of the French New Wave movement established his enduring international public image as one of Japan's greatest directors. During the 1980s, retrospective showings of his films stimulated new scholarly writings and critical appreciations of his works.

PRINCIPAL WORKS

Ai ni yomigaeru hi [*The Resurrection of Love*] (film) 1923
Chi to rei [*Blood and Soul*] (film) 1923
Furusato [*Hometown*] (film) 1923
Haikyo no naka [*Among the Ruins*] (film) 1923
Haizan no uta wa kanashi [*Failure's Song is Sad*] (film) 1923
Joen no chimata [*City of Desire*] (film) 1923
Seishun no yumeji [*Dream of Youth*] (film) 1923
Yoru [*The Night*] (film) 1923
Kanashiki hakuchi [*The Sad Idiot*] (film) 1924
Kanraku no onna [*A Woman of Pleasure*] (film) 1924
Toge no uta [*The Song of the Mountain Pass*] (film) 1924
Gakuso o idete [*Out of College*] (film) 1925
Doka o [*The Copper Coin King*] (film) 1926
Kaminingyo haru no sayaki [*A Paper Doll's Whisper of Spring*] (film) 1926
Kane [*Money*] (film) 1926
Nihonbashi [*The Nihon Bridge*] (film) 1929
Tokai kokyogaku [*Metropolitan Symphony*] (film) 1929
Gion matsuri [*Gion Festival*] (film) 1933
Jinpuren [*The Jinpu Group*] (film) 1933
Gion no shimai [*Sisters of the Gion*; with Yoshikata Yoda] (film) 1936
Naniwa ereji [*Osaka Elegy*; with Yoshikata Yoda] (film) 1936
Naniwa onna [*Woman of Osaka*] (film) 1940
Genroku chushingura [*The Loyal Forty-Seven*] (film) 1941-42
Saikaku ichidai onna [*The Life of Oharu*] (film) 1952
Ugetsu monogatari [*Tales of the Rainy Moon*] (film) 1953
Sansho dayu [*Sansho the Bailiff*] (film) 1956

CRITICISM

Andrew Sarris (essay date 1973)

SOURCE: "Ugetsu: A Meditation on Mizoguchi," in *Favorite Movies: Critics' Choice,* edited by Philip Nobile, Macmillan Publishing Co., Inc., 1973, pp. 61-9.

[*In the following essay, explains why Mizoguchi's* Ugetsu *is one of his favorite films, noting the continuing mystery and inaccessibility of Mizoguchi's work.*]

When I was asked to contribute to [*Favorite Movies: Critics' Choices*], I had two options: I could have said yes or I could have said no. If I had said no, that would have been the end of the affair. My integrity, my scruples, my sanctity, my aversion to the hysteria of hyperbole would have remained inviolate. I could then scoff at colleagues who participated in such blatantly promotional enterprises as a "favorite film anthology." Having said yes, however, I would seem to be morally obligated to play by the rules of the game. And these rules do not allow setting one's self up as a paragon of critical virtue or as a being of supreme fastidiousness. In this, as in many other matters, a simple yes or no will suffice. Nonetheless, I am willing to bet that at least one contributor to this anthology will take the opportunity to demean the others. In sports parlance that would be called a cheap shot, since no one is more vulnerable than a critic flushed with enthusiasm. And especially a film critic. Indeed, mere superciliousness still masquerades as profundity in the culturally insecure realm of cinema. And so I say in advance to the nitpickers among us: Humbug! Play the game as it is supposed to be played, or go stand on the sideline with the other kibitzers.

But as much as my participation in this anthology obliges me to accept its premises, I must make it clear at the outset that in my estimation, there is not a single film or a single director that towers over the rest. I have never been a desert-island man in the sense that I could make up a list of ten or a hundred or even a thousand films that could content me for the rest of my life. I need the constant challenge of rediscovery and renewal in a cosmopolitan, moviegoing life style. As Claude Chabrol once observed, there are no waves, new or otherwise, there is only the ocean. Similarly, there are no peaks in the cinema, only a series of plateaus, and on the highest of these (in my view) is Kenji Mizoguchi and a score or more directors from various places and periods. I could have written about a great many other films and about a great many other directors. It just so happens that of all the directors I admire most highly, Mizoguchi remains the most mysterious and inaccessible. I have never before made a sufficient effort to justify my admiration for Mizoguchi. Of the eighty or ninety films he directed in a thirty-five-year career, I have seen only a dozen, but I am finally satisfied that I have seen the bulk of his finest work. Perhaps I have nothing more substantial to go on than Mizoguchi's own self-appraisal in a 1950 interview with a Japanese film critic: "Born in 1898, I shall be fifty-two in May this year. For a Japanese film-maker, I am perhaps not quite so young any more. As you see, I am in excellent health. I still find myself greatly attracted to women. I admit to feeling very envious of Matisse when I read in an article the other day that, when he was seventy, he had a child by a young woman of twenty. In any case, I think the true work of an artist can only be accomplished after he is fifty, when he has enriched his life with accumulated experiences."

Mizoguchi's self-prophecy took form on the screen with *The Life of Oharu* (1952), *Ugetsu Monogatari* (1953), *Sansho the Bailiff, The Crucified Woman, Chikamatsu Monogatari* (1954), *The Empress Yang Kwei Fei* and *The Taira Clan* (1955). Mizoguchi died in Kyoto on August 24, 1956 at the height of his powers and popularity. He left behind a heritage of sublime achievement that his admirers in the West would ponder on for years and years to come. I am grateful to Peter Morris, Donald Richie and J. L. Anderson for all the material they have compiled in English on Mizoguchi's life and career.

Ugetsu Monogatari is but one of five "favorite" Mizoguchi films I might have chosen for this anthology. *The Empress Yang Kwei Fei* or *The Life of Oharu* or *The Taira Clan* or *Sansho the Bailiff* can be said to merit as extended and as ecstatic an appraisal as does *Ugetsu Monogatari,* which I have chosen partly because it is the most familiar of Mizoguchi's films, and partly because it is the most delicately balanced between the mystical and humanistic tendencies in the director's personality.

The title *Ugetsu Monogatari* has been translated as *Tales of the Pale and Silvery Moon After the Rain*. The film's official credits indicate that the scenario is by Mizoguchi, Yoda Yoshikata and Kawaguchi Matsutaro, and has been adapted from a novel by Veda Akinari. Not only am I totally unfamiliar with the novel, I am not even sure that the novel is the sole literary source of the screenplay. Peter Morris's invaluable monograph *Mizoguchi Kenji* (published by the Canadian Film Institute) is somewhat ambiguous on this point: "Inspired by the classic tale of the sixteenth century, the story is an amalgam of a Chinese legend often called 'The Lewdness of the Female Viper' (twenty times adapted to films in Japan and China) and a novel, *The House in the Broken Reeds*."

Unfortunately, Morris never makes clear how much of the anecdotal material of the film is derived from the "classic tale of the sixteenth century," how much from "a Chinese legend," and how much from the novel. Or to what extent the various literary sources diverge or overlap as they flow to their ultimate destination on the screen. Perhaps it would have required another monograph merely to resolve this issue. No matter. The only point I wish to make is that my appreciation of *Ugetsu* is not based on the same proportion of overall cultural awareness as my appreciation of, say, *The Magnificent Ambersons*. As it happens, I neither read nor speak Japanese. Hence I cannot evaluate the readings of the dialogue in *Ugetsu*. I must either accept these readings on faith, or judge them deductively in terms of the parallel sensibility revealed in the supposedly universal language of the visual component.

"It is interesting to note," Morris tells us further on, "that the story on which *Ugetsu* was based was also used in a 1927 Japanese film, *The Obscenity of the Viper*, directed by Thomas Kurihara, who had been a cameraman for Thomas Ince in the U. S. A. By all accounts, this film showed considerable atmosphere. It would be interesting to know if Mizoguchi ever saw this earlier version."

It would, indeed; but again we are compelled to proceed with insufficient information. Beyond *Ugetsu* is a vast, shadowy configuration of cultural influences not only on Mizoguchi, but also on his collaborators and on his audiences. We must therefore defer any definitive appraisal of the literary origins of *Ugetsu* until some future unknown—if not, indeed, inconceivable—date. What is left to contemplate is a screen spectacle endowed with supposedly internationalizing and universalizing subtitles.

The two story lines that have been fashioned into the narrative fabric of *Ugetsu* may be said to be parallel but unequal. Involved in this rickety duplex structure are two obviously counterposed couples in a sixteenth-century Japanese village menaced by rampaging armies of one feudal lord or another. Genjuro (Mori Masayuki) is a potter so obsessed by his craft and the income it represents that he risks his own life and that of his wife (Tanaka Kinuyo) and little boy to keep his ceramics from being charcoaled in the untended kiln. Genjuro is assisted by a neighboring farmer (Ozawa Sakae) who dreams of becoming a great samurai warrior as an escape from both the drudgery of his work and the imprecations of his shrewish wife.

Successful in both rescuing his pots and evading the raping, recruiting and requisitioning soldiers, the two families set off for the city in a small boat to sell their wares and find their fortune. If I may pause at the bend of the river, it is to be noted that already Mizoguchi's contemplatively fluid camera work has cast a spell of stylistic conviction comparable to F. W. Murnau's in the boat trip of *Sunrise*. From the very first sustained traveling shot of villagers scurrying hither and yon across a brooding landscape, Mizoguchi establishes a tension between the essential wholeness of the world and the existential restlessness of its inhabitants.

By not cutting up visual reality into conceptual fragments à la Eisenstein and his devoted disciples, the nonmontage Mizoguchi, like Murnau before him, preserves the illusion that the world extends beyond the arbitrary frames of the screen. In this sense, a taste for Mizoguchi can be associated with a certain period of polemical aesthetics, a period in which the good guys of mise-en-scène were somewhat carelessly lumped together against the bad guys of montage. That is to say that if you liked Mizoguchi and Murnau, you were obliged to like also Ophuls and Renoir and Rossellini and Welles. It was a time in which deep focus contained hidden depths, and a camera movement could be construed as a moral statement. Indeed, the great aesthetic hero of that era was not a director at all, but that late great critic's critic, André Bazin, and it was Bazinian aesthetics as much as anything else that influenced many of us to turn irrevocably away from the more fashionable fierceness of Kurosawa to the relatively serene meditations of Mizoguchi. I once remarked (with more generosity toward Kurosawa than was expressed by fellow *cahierists* of that epoch) that Mizoguchi was to Kurosawa as Sophocles was to Euripides. Nowadays, among Mizoguchi's own country's filmmakers, it is Ozu who poses the most formidable aesthetic challenge to the West with an antithetical expression of existence as a waiting for death through rigidly static compositions photographed at the tatami level in contrast to Mizoguchi's dreamlike movement toward death through a stream of atmospheric adventure. Mizoguchi's is thus a cinema of perpetual anticipation, whereas Ozu's is a cinema of perpetual anticlimax.

Perhaps if Bazin were alive today, he could resolve the Mizoguchi-Ozu dialectic as charitably and as eloquently as he once resolved the Mizoguchi-Kurosawa dialectic in the days when *la politique des auteurs* prescribed an aesthetic Manicheanism. As Truffaut quotes from a personal letter from Bazin in that passionate period:

> I'm sorry I couldn't see Mizoguchi's film again with you at the Cinémathèque. I rate him as highly as you people do and I claim to love him more because I love Kurosawa too, who is the other side of the coin: would we know the day any better if there were no night? To dislike Kurosawa because one loves Mizoguchi is only the first step towards understanding. Unquestionably, anyone who prefers Kurosawa must be incurably blind, but anyone who loves only Mizoguchi is one-eyed. Throughout the arts there runs a vein of the contemplative and mystical as well as an expressionist vein.

Returning to the bend of the river, we find our varied protagonists drifting in a sea of stylistic ambiguity. Through the mists of Mizoguchi's classical mise-en-scène another boat appears as in a dream of death, but it is nonetheless a real boat with a dying voyager, a victim of the violence lurking just beyond the arbitrary frames of the film. Whereas a similar encounter of the living and the dead on the metaphorical waters is expressed merely on the single level of self-conscious symbolism in Ingmar Bergman's *Shame*, Mizoguchi operates on the additional level of wide-awake reality. Hence the flotsam and jetsam of dead bodies in *Shame* merely confirm that the ostensibly living characters are actually sleepwalking through the nightmare of a sensually senseless history. By contrast, the single corpse in *Ugetsu* galvanizes the living characters into decisive action. The potter decides to leave his wife and son behind on land, and the poignancy of parting is reinforced with the premonition of permanent separation by the expressive intensity of a sustained camera movement of the wife and child as they make their way along the shore to the outermost extremity of ground from which to wave their final good-byes.

We have now reached the first convulsive rupture in the narrative, and henceforth the emotional and spiritual inequality of the two parallel plots becomes increasingly apparent. We could actually detach the inferior plot from our discussion without appreciably affecting the ultimate implications of the work. The ambitious farmer and his nagging wife are a relatively sordid pair. What happens is that the farmer is granted his wish to become a samurai after a Grand Guignol episode with the severed head of an enemy chieftain. The risen samurai's abandoned wife wanders into the woods where she is raped by ubiquitously passing soldiers, after which she returns to the city to consolidate her new status in a house of prostitution. Who should then pop up at his wife's temple of shame but the preening peacock of a husband at the head of his band of warriors? The irony of the reunion of husband and wife is difficult enough to digest. What is worse is the husband's unconvincing abandonment of his lifelong ambition as an act of contrition. Mizoguchi himself complained of the facile resolution of the secondary plot: "The man played by Ozawa should not change his mind at the end, but continue, regardless, with his ambitious social climb. But Daiei didn't want this ending and forced me to change it. I don't like this brand of commercialism."

However, even if one could imagine Mizoguchi's implied ending, the rising samurai and his fallen wife would remain excessively schematic characterizations, existing not so much for their own sakes as for their ability to illustrate a rather elementary anti-militaristic thesis. They end up padding out the film with a spurious social significance without really expanding its more crucial concerns. That *Ugetsu* could become a landmark in film history with such a disabling subplot is itself something of a miracle.

Which means we must follow the path of Genjuro the potter and the two women who lead him beyond life itself before he finds his way back to the truth of his existence. But how does one describe an aesthetic experience in which meaning and mise-en-scène are fused together in one steady stream of luminosity? For example, the first entrance of the phantom princess Wasaka (Kyo Machiko) is effected not at night in her haunted habitat by the reeds and the marshes, but instead in broad daylight, amid the hustle and bustle of a crowded marketplace. Indeed, we do not yet know that she is a ghost, but there is something unsettling about her just the same. Mizoguchi's first shot of her is actually a rearview shot of a very regally expansive sunhat making its way almost autonomously toward Genjuro's pottery stall. When we finally see a face emerging magically from this chrysalis of a hat, it is the face of the Japanese cinema's most beautiful actress (Kyo Machiko, often billed in the West as Machiko Kyo, and first recognized as the wife in Kurosawa's *Rashomon*), and the face also of one of the screen's most profoundly ambiguous temptresses. She ensnares Genjuro by treating him less as a man seeking diversion than as an artist seeking recognition. She lures him quite literally from the open marketplace of the humble craftsman to the closed palace of the coterie artist. Could Mizoguchi have seen in Genjuro just a little of himself, that strangely uprooted creature who became an annual apparition at the Venice Film Festival through the early fifties? No matter. The princess Wasaka initiates Genjuro into pleasures he never knew existed. His seduction is almost complete, but the spell is abruptly broken one day by a passing monk who sees death in Genjuro's face, and not only death, but evil decadence. Genjuro finally awakens from his morbid bewitchment, and thinks once more of his wife and son.

Meanwhile we have witnessed a harrowing scene with Genjuro's wife and a ravenously hungry straggler who stabs her for the food she is carrying for her child. Mizoguchi's intuitive flair for expressing spectacle in terms of integral space comes to the fore here as he shows us within one frame the parallel movements of the desperately wounded wife, with child in hand, and her demented attacker staggering along the wavering line of his own lunacy.

Genjuro returns to the village, peers into his hut through a dark window, sees nothing, cries out and hears no sound in response, and walks around the walls of his hut past other windows leading toward the door. And as the camera follows his movement, it captures almost in passing the suddenly luminous image of the wife sewing by a lamp. I have seen *Ugetsu* a dozen times or more, and this literally and figuratively moving shot of epic serenity never fails to shatter me emotionally. (That its scale of nobility is perhaps closer to Homer than to Joyce may be attributable to the greater affinity of Mizoguchi's narrative style with myth than with psychology.)

Genjuro awakens the next morning to learn that his wife, seemingly alive by lamplight the night before, has been dead for several weeks, having died only after bringing Genjuro's son safely home to the village. Thus Genjuro has awakened from two fantasies—one embracing the phantom princess Wasaka and her sensuous intimations to his vanity of fame, fortune and fashion; and the other a reverie of supernatural domesticity based on Genjuro's wish-fulfillment of his wife's physical indestructibility, a necessary illusion for his realization of her spiritual immortality. The film ends with Genjuro's speaking to his wife's spirit as he works at his craft, and his boy's placing flowers at her grave as the camera rises slowly to show the farmers in the fields beyond in a harmonic invocation of space and time as the stuff of community in nature and of humanity in history.

I would never suggest that a critique, evaluation, description, appreciation or even synopsis of *Ugetsu* is in any way equivalent to the film itself. A film is one thing, and a piece of writing is another. Hence *Ugetsu* exists apart from my appraisal of it, and should not be compromised by my meager contribution to the body of criticism inspired by it. As I have noted, *Ugetsu* came before me at a time when I was especially susceptible to the mystical wholeness of its mise-en-scène, to the nobility of its central characters, and to the contemplative calm of its director's gaze. Even the deliberate slowness that seems to irritate many of my students nowadays worked in favor of the film as it did for the films of Dreyer, Bresson and

Antonioni. Who needed Mickey-Mouse pacing when souls were at stake (and with Dreyer and Bresson even on the stake)? But *Ugetsu* (unlike *Odd Man Out* and *Citizen Kane*) has outlived and outgrown my more naive standards of aesthetic appraisal.

For example, the poetry that Mizoguchi fashions from the potter's wheel cannot be ascribed simply to the allegorical equation: Pottery equals Art. What I never knew until very recently but always vaguely sensed in *Ugetsu* was that Mizoguchi was as obsessed artistically with ceramics as with cinema. It is only when an urn, Asian or Grecian as the case may be, is incontestably itself that it can suggest anything else.

Another recent discovery I have made about Mizoguchi helps explain his inexhaustible fascination with the mystique of the female. An associate recalls that Mizoguchi was once grievously stabbed in the back by a former mistress, and that his films became darker and more reflective from that time on. This incident occurred years before *Ugetsu,* but somehow it helps me to understand the metaphysical helplessness Mizoguchi expresses in his confrontation with all forms of human passion. For Woman, especially, he shows his love, not by paternalistic understanding of her little secrets, but by passionate acceptance of her great mysteries.

Robin Wood (essay date 1976)

SOURCE: "The Ghost Princess and the Seaweed Gatherer: Ugetsu Monogatari and Sansho Dayu," in *Personal Views: Explorations in Film,* Gordon Fraser Gallery Ltd., 1976, pp. 225-48.

[*In the following essay, Wood analyzes Mizoguchi's style of direction and camera work in* Ugetsu *and* Sansho Dayu.]

A colleague told me recently that he would not feel qualified to talk about Ozu and Mizoguchi; that he would not know how to approach them; that he could do so only in terms of *mise-en-scène*. In the context of the conversation it was clear that this was a covert reprimand rather than an expression of humility: my colleague meant that he did not know enough about the circumstances of production within which the films were made (the Japanese film industry, social-political-cultural conditions at the time) or about the conventions on which they draw and the cultural tradition within which those conventions developed; and he implied (correctly) that I knew no more than he. I think we were both aware that fundamental principles were involved, though neither of us pursued them: fundamental questions about the nature and function of art and the status of individual works: art as art, or art as social process. My own position with regard to movies from 'alien' cultures is implicit in earlier essays. . . . I think any knowledge one might acquire about cultural background and circumstances of production is potentially useful, but also potentially dangerous: useful, as a test of one's own perceptions; dangerous, because such knowledge of a culture which must necessarily remain alien however much information we acquire, can easily influence our reading of individual works disproportionately: we begin to see 'Japanese culture' instead of Mizoguchi. A 'realized' work of art will, by and large, carry its explanation within itself, for anyone willing to trust (however provisionally) his instincts and imagination.

Around the same time, one of my students told me, during a seminar, about Yin and Yang. Yin and Yang are, in Japanese tradition, the passive and active principles respectively; they correspond to the moon and sun, woman and man, water and fire. My student applied them (resourcefully, I thought) to the water and fire imagery of *Sansho Dayu*. I like Yin and Yang; I find them immensely reassuring. They confirm for me that I had understood *Sansho Dayu* before I heard of either of them. They figure, I think, in most mythologies (e.g., Diana and Apollo) and in the novels of D. H. Lawrence (e.g., *The Rainbow*). They help me to make my point: that (give or take a few details) the essential significance of *Sansho Dayu* can be deduced from the specific realization of the film; that, at most, one needs a knowledge of a few other Japanese films from the same period in order to confirm one's deductions. How many westerns must one see before one can confidently interpret *Rio Bravo* or *The Searchers?* A few, I think: perhaps four or five. I am aware (and could, I think, have deduced without being told) that the styles of Ozu and Mizoguchi derive from various traditional elements in Japanese art—particularly drama and painting. I cannot imagine how a more detailed knowledge of these elements than I have would significantly affect the way in which I read the films.

An attempt to define the art of Mizoguchi can usefully take as its starting-point comparison with his great contemporary Ozu. It must be said at once that any general definition must be tentative in the extreme, being based on only a small proportion of each director's work: about a dozen Mizoguchis and only half as many Ozus, mainly late works in both cases. The enterprise is further complicated by the great range of subject-matter and expression within Mizoguchi's work. Rather than attempt to offer generalizations that would cover even all his accessible films, I am limiting this essay to only two, though they seem to me the greatest and most completely representative of those I have seen: *Sansho Dayu* and *Ugetsu Monogatari*. They are closely related to each other, and the other late works—including those with a modern setting like the magnificent *Uwasa No Onna* (*Woman of Rumour*) and even a film as different in obvious ways as *Street of Shame*—can be seen to relate significantly to them: one might reasonably claim that they represent, together, a central core within Mizoguchi's late period, though others might wish to make similar claims for *Shin Heike Monogatari* or *Yang Kwei Fei*.

Although Ozu and Mizoguchi, when juxtaposed, appear in many ways polar opposites, both have been placed in opposition to the more western- (and 'western'-) influenced Kurosawa. Kurosawa's work is studded with adaptations of western literature; his films not only show the influence of the western cinema but lend themselves in turn to adaptation, so that at least four have been re-made in Hollywood or Italy. No one seems to be rushing to remake *Tokyo Story* or *Sansho Dayu* in an American setting, though the subject-matter of neither would present insuperable difficulties. The films' tone and style are felt as somehow indigenously Japanese, though it is difficult to link them beyond a somewhat loose application of the adjective 'contemplative'. Mizoguchi's style shows greater affinities with that of Ophuls on the one hand and Rossellini on the other than with that of any other Japanese director within my experience, yet one does not think of him as in any sense deriving from European cinema: any resemblances seem fortuitous, a matter of spiritual affinity rather than influence in either direction. One guesses that the late styles of both Mizoguchi and Ozu are the product of a long period of evolution within the Japanese cinema, and, beyond it, within Japanese culture.

Ozu's visual compositions are dominated by the square and the rectangle; Mizoguchi's are characterized by an equally striking and pervasive emphasis on diagonals. The tendency of Ozu's cinema is towards a series of 'stills'. His characters either face the camera directly or sit or stand at right angles to it. The square or rectangular patterns of the décor—walls or doorways or windows—often frame them as if to enclose each in his or her separate compartment. Each image takes on the quality of a framed picture, as if cut off from any outer world beyond the confines of the screen. When characters enter or leave the frame during a shot, they do so behind an intruding screen or partition; the unity of the image and enclosedness of the frame are carefully preserved. The spectator's eye is directed always towards the figure at the centre of the composition, almost never towards the periphery.

The composition even of static dialogue scenes in Mizoguchi is habitually built on diagonals cutting across the screen. The characters are placed at oblique angles to the camera, and so are the mats on which they sit; where Ozu tends to place his actors squarely against walls or doorways, Mizoguchi typically uses a corner as focal point. However beautifully organized the composition (and there are no more beautiful compositions anywhere in the cinema), the diagonals invariably lead the eye outwards, always implying a world beyond the frame. What is true of interiors is equally so of exteriors. Paths cross the screen diagonally; in *Ugetsu* the boat bearing the dying fisherman emerges through the mist at an oblique angle to the boat poled by Ohama; in *Madame Yuki* a speedboat and its wake cut a diagonal line across the image.

This contrast is reinforced by the totally opposed camera styles of the two directors. In late Ozu the camera virtually never moves; to cut from static image to static image is to detach and separate little segments of the world as objects of contemplation. In late Mizoguchi the camera moves in the great majority of shots, and the movements are frequently long and elaborate; to move the camera so that one part of the world is excluded while another is framed, is to unite, to make connections. If 'Cinema of Contemplation' is a phrase applicable to the work of both directors, it is a much more adequate description of Ozu than of Mizoguchi: the contemplative aspect of the latter's work is continually balanced, and at times superseded, by its dynamism. Ozu's characters (in the late films) almost never touch—an abstention that confers great importance on even the simplest hand-clasp, by virtue of its rarity. Mizoguchi's characters, on the other hand, always relate to one another physically, often with great intensity: witness any of the emotional climaxes in his films. And a general observation about the content of their respective *oeuvres* is relevant here. Both deal recurrently with the theme of the Family; but where characteristically Ozu's people are finally separate, alone, Mizoguchi's move almost invariably towards union, mystical rather than physical, even when some of them are dead. The stylistic differences are clearly related to—if not actually expressive of—this opposition in overall movement.

An example will help to clarify the part played by the contemplative in Mizoguchi's style. Consider (as representative rather than exceptional) the brief scene in *Sansho Dayu* where Zushio, seeking redress for the horrors Sansho has perpetrated, attempts to confront the minister with a petition and is overcome and dragged away to prison by guards. The tracking-shot that accompanies Zushio's desperate efforts to be heard is far from contemplative: it involves the viewer very directly in the scene's hectic movement, in the urgency and near-hysteria of the young man. Mizoguchi does not cut away to show us the guards approaching—they suddenly irrupt into the frame from all sides. This is immediately recognizable as a recurrent motif in Mizoguchi's films: other striking examples are the mother's attempted escape from the island of Sado in *Sansho* and the rape of Ohama in *Ugetsu*. The sudden intrusion of hostile, menacing forces into the foreground of the image, surrounding and overwhelming the protagonist, forcefully expresses the director's sense of the precariousness of things, the continual imminence of disaster, his characters' terrible vulnerability. It also suggests the dynamic nature of his style, the sense of a world beyond the frame, the compositions never final, subject to continual variation and modification. But equally striking, and equally typical, is the sudden cut to long-shot at the climactic moment as Zushio is overcome, the action abruptly distanced, the foreground of the shot occupied by a large, decorative, bushy tree. The violence, and the hero's frenzied screams, are suddenly placed in a context of stillness and serenity. The opposition is central to Mizoguchi's art, and to his vision of life.

Or consider the shot, after Ohama's rape in *Ugetsu,* of her sandals (which have fallen off in the struggle) on the beach. It is in some ways a fairly close equivalent to those series of shots of landscapes or townscapes that punctuate Ozu's films, generally used as transitions from scene to scene or from one time of day to another, having something of the function of establishing shots, but serving primarily as points of meditation, the action of the film suspended, the eye and mind given an emotionally neutral view—or, at least, a view not directly related to the immediate narrative—on which to rest for a moment. But herein lies an important difference: the shot of the sandals provides, certainly, a still point of meditation after the emotional and physical turmoil that have preceded it, yet it is by no means divorced from the action nor emotionally neutral. The stillness and emptiness of the shot emphasize, by contrast, the journey structure on which the film is built; its desolate effect arises from a complex of contextual implications, chief among which is our sense of her husband Tobei's responsibility for Ohama's fate. Where Ozu's 'punctuating' shots are still points of pure contemplation, the shot of the sandals encourages in the spectator that precise balancing of contemplation and involvement characteristic of Mizoguchi.

The vivifying impulse in Mizoguchi's late films is towards wholeness and unity, and this is expressed in stylistic detail as surely as in overall movement. It is an impulse that necessitates the maintenance of a certain emotional distance between artist and material, the purpose of which is not to deny or diminish the emotional intensity inherent in the action, but to place it in a wider context, a context both spatial and temporal. An event in a Mizoguchi film is never felt as isolated. We are not allowed to respond simply, with the immediate emotional reactions the event might provoke: we are encouraged to view the event within a cosmic perspective. If this sounds mystical (and we are perhaps too ready, in the west, to distrust mysticism, or confuse it with mere vagueness), it can be pinned down in the concrete detail of Mizoguchi's *mise-en-scène.* Consider two scenes where the emotional content is inherently very powerful, the kidnapping in *Sansho,* the mortal wounding of Miyagi in *Ugetsu.* Both can stand as representative of Mizoguchi's method, though they are in some respects stylistically dissimilar: the underlying assumptions about life, about values, about the function of art, about the relationship between the spectator and the action on the screen, are the same.

Sansho: Tamaki and her two children Zushio and Anju, on their way to join their exiled husband/father, are sheltered and fed by an elderly priestess who persuades Tamaki to continue the journey by boat. She in fact betrays them: Tamaki and the children's old nurse are carried off in the boat while the priestess and another boatman hold the children; the nurse, too old to be a valuable commodity, is thrown overboard and drowns, the children break away and rush to the water's edge but are swiftly recaptured. Stylistically three aspects stand out: dynamic movement, whether of the camera or within the frame, communicating the intensity of the protagonists' struggle against separation; a preponderance of long-shots that place the violence, grief and turbulence of the action in a context of natural tranquillity—smooth water, still sky, motionless rushes and bare tree; superb deep focus images. At the beginning of the sequence the boatmen are introduced in an image dominated by the leafless, thorny tree left of screen but centred on the fire, beside which the men rouse to sinister alertness as they become aware of the family's approach: the juxtaposition of fire and water is a unifying motif to which I shall return.

The emotional distance implied by the use of long-shot has nothing of coldness or complacency: the extraordinary intensity with which the action is staged amply testifies to Mizoguchi's readiness to enter fully into his characters' anguish. The use of long-shot is of course inseparable from the use of deep focus. The effect is to hold the action at a distance while consistently emphasizing its reality. Nowhere in the cinema has the reality of physical space been used to more eloquent effect. Mizoguchi cross-cuts between boat and shore, but never fragments, never destroys our sense of the unity of the action: from the boat, Tamaki in the foreground, we can see the children struggling to escape, straining towards her; from the shore, children in the foreground, Tamaki's frantic efforts to return are shown in crystalclear long-shot. From shot to shot, the widening of the distance separating them is rendered with scrupulous precision, and the distance is always physically there on the screen, shore and boat in the same image. The style here implies the essential theme of the film, the tension between physical separation and spiritual unity, the family forcibly held apart yet united by Mizoguchi within the frame.

Ugetsu: Miyagi, trying to return home with her child, is attacked on a mountain path by three starving outcasts (perhaps deserters) who steal the rice-cakes she has been given. When she protests, one of them drives a spear into her. Her little boy still on her back, she staggers on, supporting herself on a stick. Here, there is no cutting: the scene is a classic example of what the French call the *plan-séquence,* the 'sequence' organized within a single shot. But the preservation of spatial reality within the image, and the preservation of the spectator's distance from the action, are again crucial to the total effect.

For the great majority of directors, the temptation here would be to go for impact: one 'could invent a breakdown of the scene into twenty or so shots—close-ups of the men emerging from the hut, of Miyagi's frightened face, of the spear driven in, of the screaming, terrified child, of the woman in agony, of the men, showing their callous indifference—which could be immensely powerful in its force and directness. Mizoguchi's long take holds the spectator at a distance throughout, preserves the unity and continuity of the action, and preserves the sense of environment—of the action situated in a real world governed by the realities of time and space. We are not asked to respond simply and directly to the physical horror of a spear entering a woman's belly, but to an event existing in a context. The detachment with which the camera compels us to watch the action makes the emotion it evokes much less immediate and overwhelm-

ing, but also much finer and deeper: we are free to contemplate the scene's wider implications, to reflect on the events that have preceded it and its likely consequences.

The organization of the complex action over a large area within a single take is remarkable: one would call it virtuoso did not the word carry connotations of display, the technique here being self-effacing in the extreme. The staging has many of the features one thinks of as characteristically Mizoguchian. The camera position is slightly above the action, in the interests of clarity: from it, we can see not only the path and the hut, but down into the valley below. The path crosses the screen diagonally. As Miyagi walks along it, the child on her back, the men emerge from the sides of the screen, eventually surrounding her—our minds are led back to the parallel scene of the rape of Ohama. The men steal the food, one of them wounds Miyagi, they disappear down the slope. Miyagi struggles to her feet and staggers on; the camera tracks with her, revealing the stick she takes to support herself, which lies at right angles to the path, hence making another diagonal to the frame—all the composition's main lines point outwards to the world beyond the screen. As Miyagi and the camera move on, we can see the men again in extreme long-shot in the valley, quarrelling and fighting over the meagre bits of food, their movements providing a strong if distant visual counterpoint to Miyagi's. The pain of the woman is placed in a context of universal disorder and suffering; our horror at the men's indifference is qualified by a sense of a world in which human beings starve to death and are degraded to an animal-like struggle for survival.

It is known that Mizoguchi had problems with *Ugetsu:* specifically, he was forced for box-office reasons to change his conception of the sub-plot. Originally, Tobei and Ohama were to have progressed, ironically, to great material prosperity and worldly fame as samurai and courtesan respectively; the ending would therefore have balanced worldly gain/spiritual loss (Tobei and Ohama) against worldly loss/spiritual gain (Genjuro and Miyagi). The film's actual ending provides a contrast that is much less sharp. In material terms, both men are back to square one, but Genjuro has developed spiritually while Tobei has merely accepted his lot; Genjuro and Miyagi achieve ideal union, though on opposite sides of the grave, while Tobei resigns himself guiltily to the aggressive domination of a very much alive Ohama. The resolution of the action works well enough, but the last-minute alterations in the scenario may be at least partly responsible for one's sense that the two plots are not very successfully integrated in the second half of the film. A worse flaw seems to me the awkward and arbitrary introduction of the Buddhist priest who 'sees' Genjuro's fate in his face, though it is not impossible that there is a cultural barrier here, a convention operating to which Japanese audiences would know how to respond. Relative to *Sansho,* one must judge *Ugetsu* structurally flawed, though it is still possible to value it above almost every other work in the cinema. Two elements in the film seem to me to demand attention if one is to offer some justification for so high an estimate: Mizoguchi's magical evocation of the supernatural in the central scenes, and the reconciliation with reality, with 'normal' human experience, towards which the whole film moves.

No film-maker in my experience—not even Tourneur or Dreyer—has treated the supernatural with such delicacy and respect, with such subtle force of suggestion and so rigorous a refusal to sensationalize or vulgarize. Strikingly, the treatment involves the complete eschewal of all camera trickery and 'special effects': Mizoguchi refuses to tamper with the reality within the image, restricting his eerie effects to what décor and lighting can achieve and the camera record. Hence the suggestion that the Princess Wakasa's mansion exists in a world outside time is conveyed by our being shown it, unobtrusively and without comment, in three different conditions: first, derelict and decaying, the garden overgrown, the broken gate swinging on its hinges; second, magically restored and revivified by Genjuro's entry into it, the garden neat, the walls, windows and panels as new, servant-girls emerging with candle-flames; third, as ruins, a few blackened sticks and struts (over which lie the kimonos Genjuro bought for Wakasa) rising out of apparently uncultivated grass. The film's other great 'supernatural' effect—the apparition of Miyagi to welcome her husband home—is even more remarkable. The camera is inside the house as Genjuro approaches, looks in at the window, opens the door and enters. The room is quite bare and unkept. He walks across it hesitantly, calling Miyagi, and the camera pans left with him, excluding the right hand part of the room. He goes out through another door, left, and we see him through windows walking round outside, back to the front entrance. The camera accordingly moves back with him; but this time, as the rest of the room comes back within the frame, we see that its décor has been miraculously restored and that Miyagi is in the middle of it, cooking over a fire, awaiting Genjuro, who sees her as he re-enters, the camera now having returned to its original position. The *frisson* this moment excites is due largely to the simple technical fact that there has been no cut, no dissolve, no ending of any kind: the impossible has happened before our eyes.

The respect Mizoguchi accords the supernatural stylistically, also involves rejecting any temptation to rationalize it. If we are led to find symbolic meaning in *Ugetsu*'s ghosts, it is by a process of suggestion that never destroys or undermines our sense of wonder. The 'meaning' is suggested, I think, by the parallel my above description implies. In both scenes, the house is, as it were, brought back to life by the man's entry into it. The scene with the ghost Miyagi clearly associates this with the restoration of marital and family union; but the ghosts of the central sequences, Wakasa and her nurse, were also motivated by the desire that Wakasa be fulfilled through marriage. The resemblances encourage us to connect the scenes in our minds, but the purpose of the parallel is clearly to make us aware of major oppositions. The Wakasa world, outside time, is associated with illusion, with the dream-fulfilment of unrealizable aspirations (the pottery vessels

that Genjuro recognizes, somewhat hesitantly, as his own, were clearly never made by him in the 'real' world), and ultimately with death—the only condition wherein the desire to escape from the stresses and responsibilities of reality can be fulfilled. Mizoguchi creates its seductive beauty in a style that contrasts with that of the rest of the film while remaining recognizably Mizoguchian: the compositions are still built on diagonals, the camera still moves fluently, but the images look much more consciously and artfully composed, the camera moves away from one such beautiful composition precisely to frame another. We are also, here, brought in much closer to the actors than elsewhere in the film: even in the culminating erotic scene on the lawn, there is a sense of oppressiveness. Wakasa urges Genjuro to stay with her and perfect his art—the art represented by the delicate objects she has presented as his creations, 'art for art's sake', rarefied and out of touch with the outside reality where Miyagi suffers. At the end of the film Genjuro, mystically united with his dead wife, is turning a pot under her spiritual guidance, a pot as different from the *objets d'art* of the Wakasa world as it is from the crudely functional, mass-produced 'commercial' vessels we saw Genjuro making and selling earlier. The new dedication he brings to the work comes across as the outcome of assimilated experience: the artisan has become an artist, in the full Mizoguchian sense, the sense, that is, defined by the style, structure and significance of the late films. The fineness and depth of Mizoguchi's sensibility can be gauged from the way in which, having created for us the Wakasa dream-world with such richness of sensuous beauty, he can lead us to find greater beauty in Genjuro's ultimate reconciliation with the real world and the processes of life-in-time.

From the film's last sequence I want to single out two shots in which the assimilative impulse of Mizoguchi's art finds perfect expression. One is the shot of Genjuro at Miyagi's grave. He asks why she had to die; her voice tells him softly that she is there beside him. The camera has already begun to track back, and as Miyagi speaks we see first the empty space beside Genjuro and then their son, kneeling at the graveside—the child in whom both parents are reunited, who represents what is perhaps the only immortality to which men should presume to aspire: immortality through continuity, and through what is transmitted. The second shot is the last of the film. In the background, Genjuro is tending his kiln, the pots so lovingly created, conceived as the joint work of man and wife, are baking; in the foreground, Ohama gives the child a bowlful of the rice she has been cooking. He runs off to the right, and the camera tracks with him to Miyagi's grave. He places the rice before the grave as if his mother were still alive, and the camera cranes up away from him to reveal again the landscape with which the film opened, with two men in the distance at work in the fields. Several factors contribute to making this one of the most poignantly beautiful last shots of any film. First, the continuity of camera movement that connects all the components of the scene: the pots baking, the child moving between father and mother, the underlying sense communicated of the triumph of the spirit over death, of the family mystically reconstituted and reunited, new life developing out of this reaffirmed unity. Second, the sense of continuity hinted at in the two labourers (for the film opened with Genjuro and Tobei leaving for the town), the sense of other lives being lived, similar to those whose progress we have watched yet different, each unique. Third, the shot formally reverses the opening shot of the film, which started on the same landscape and moved left and downwards to show Genjuro with his cart. It is not just a case of a satisfying formal symmetry: having shown us Genjuro's story, Mizoguchi turns us outward, to the world, and the potentialities for experience it offers every individual. The total effect is to universalize the action, to suggest that the narrative we have watched unfold is at once unique and typical, that the path towards spiritual acceptance and assimilation is there for each man to tread in his own way.

I have hinted that in certain respects *Ugetsu* can be read as Mizoguchi's artistic testament. The three kinds of pottery with which Genjuro is associated, and more particularly his attitudes to them and the personal developments with which each is linked, are very suggestive from this viewpoint, especially in conjunction with the stylistic contrast I have noted within the film. Mizoguchi through his narrative rejects commercialism (the pursuit of easy money separated Genjuro from Miyagi) on the one hand, and 'ivory tower' aestheticism (the claustrophobic though alluring world of Wakasa) on the other, in favour of a progress towards an art that will truly express the assimilated experience of life, art that resolves the dichotomy of 'personal' and 'impersonal' by growing out of experience yet commanding that experience through understanding and acceptance. *Sansho Dayu,* made a year after *Ugetsu,* can be regarded as the perfect equivalent for the pottery Genjuro is making at the end of the earlier film. The parallels between the two films are in some ways very close. If one regrets the absence from *Sansho* of the supernatural dimension that gives *Ugetsu* its uniquely haunting and suggestive quality, this is more than compensated for by the later film's undeniable superiority in structure and by the poetic density its structural perfection makes possible; for by 'structure' here I wish to imply not only something that could be schematically worked out on paper but the delicate inter-relationship of all the parts down to the smallest details.

The inter-relationships are so intricate, so much the product of a supreme creative genius at its most alive (the aliveness a matter of the free intercourse between the conscious and the intuitive), that complete analysis seems neither possible nor desirable: it would quickly become unwieldy. Looking for some way into the film that will make it possible to suggest its nature without laborious over-explicitness, I fasten on its recurrent fire and water imagery, as an aspect conveniently limited yet clearly central. I use the word 'imagery' (rather than 'symbolism') advisedly: the most cursory consideration of the film should suggest at once the undeniable unifying significance of fire and water and the lack of any rigid sche-

matic meaning attaching to them. Water is frequently associated with the women, and with the concepts of patience and passive endurance; fire is often linked with violence and active cruelty. But the opposition is by no means inflexible. The sea is associated naturally with danger ('Is the sea safe?' Tamaki asks the treacherous priestess the night before the kidnapping), separation (Tamaki helplessly calling to her children from the cliff on the island of Sado) and natural disaster (the tidal wave that has drowned great numbers of people referred to at the end of the film). Mizoguchi never imposes symbolism on the action. Accordingly, the significance of the recurrent imagery is to be interpreted flexibly, in relation to the events with which it is linked; as the film progresses, it accumulates complex emotional overtones from the shifting juxtapositions, until by the end the visual presence of the sea makes emotionally present for us all the past events with which fire and water have been associated, becoming one of the means by which Mizoguchi deepens and intensifies our response to the last scene as the point to which every impulse in the film has moved. At the beginning, mother and young children are walking beside a stream; at the end, mother and adult son are reunited in view of the sea.

The scene of Anju's suicide—visually, among the most exquisite (I mean the word in no pejorative sense) things the cinema has given us, the visual beauty being the expression of spiritual depth—offers a convenient point of entry. It is a perfect example of Mizoguchi's ability to create images that are at once intrinsically beautiful and expressive, and rich in accumulated resonances. His characteristic delicacy and reticence are there in the choice of long-shot and the sharply focused tracery of foliage that part-frames, part-screens the girl's slow progress to the water. The cross-cutting between Anju and the old woman who has helped her bring in another recurrent and complexly treated motif of the film, the opposition between enclosure and openness, slavery and freedom: the old woman is standing in the gateway to the slaves' compound as Anju descends to the freedom of death. That 'freedom' is not entirely ironic. The tranquillity of the setting and the sense of ceremony in Anju's gesture of obeisance to her old helper confer serenity upon her action. At first, in long-shot, the water looks like mist, into which Anju seems to merge, suggesting a gentle dissolution into the harmony of nature, the soul diffused into its native element. We may connect the stillness of the water with the name Anju was given in the compound: Shinobu, which means patience. Anju's death is dignified—in Mizoguchian terms, or in the film's total context, made sacred—by its purpose. She sacrifices herself to facilitate Zushio's escape, and because she knows she would reveal his whereabouts under torture, and the aim of his escape is to reunite the dispersed family (and incidentally save the life of Namiji, the sick slave-woman who was kind to them earlier because they reminded her of her own lost children—the ramifications of the family theme and its extension into loyalty-to-the-past reach everywhere in the film). The water into which Anju disappears links her with her mother: Tamaki is consistently associated with water, from the image early in the film of her scooping it from the stream to drink (which inaugurates one of the flashbacks showing her unity with her husband) to the final reunion with Zushio by the sea. The image, inevitably, recalls the scene of the kidnapping (the dispersal of the family), but it also, less obviously, anticipates the scene of Zushio's visit (his escape successful) to the father's grave in Tsukushi, shot against a background of distant water. Our sense of interconnectedness is intensified by Mizoguchi's use of Tamaki's song ('Zushio, Anju, I long for you. . . . ') on the soundtrack as fitting accompaniment to the girl's suicide, half-ironic, profoundly poignant. Her descent into the water is framed between a flourishing bamboo to her left and a leafless, stunted shrub to her right. The last shot of the scene sums up its emotional ambivalence, that characteristic fusion of the tragic and affirmative: the water has closed over the girl's head, but the ripples are still widening across the surface, Anju's sacrifice is both an end and a beginning. The scene seems very close, in its economy, lucidity and complexity, its extreme concreteness of imagery and its mysterious aura of suggestivity, to the spirit of the haiku.

The essential difference is that a haiku exists in isolation, self-sufficient, while a detail in *Sansho* reverberates subtly through the whole structure. The final image of the water dissolves to the darkness around the temple where Zushio has sought refuge, a darkness almost immediately penetrated by the flaming torches of his pursuers. The progression is repeated later: from the scene of Zushio at Anju's memorial by the water, after the overthrow of Sansho, Mizoguchi takes us directly to the freedom celebrations of the released slaves, around a bonfire which eventually burns down Sansho's mansion. The fire imagery is more consistent in significance than the water imagery, though the visual artist in Mizoguchi is always ready to seize on fire simply as the focal point for a composition. In general, fire is associated with violence and evil: the boatmen-kidnappers are introduced huddled around a fire, and earlier our first view of the priestess has been introduced by a flame appearing disturbingly out of the darkness. In particular, fire is linked with Sansho, the principle of active cruelty and tyranny, as against Tamaki's endurance, Anju's patience, and the strength of memory and fidelity. Almost every scene in which he appears has a fire blazing; his habitual punishment for slaves is branding with a red-hot iron; his house is consumed by fire. Zushio's spiritual development in the central part of the film is from his brutalization under Sansho's dominance to his resolution to escape and reunite the family when a combination of circumstances recalls him to himself by making his sense of family real to him again. It can be traced from his acceptance of the duty of branding the old man who attempted to run away, to his decision to run away himself and take Namiji with him: in the shot where he lifts her to carry her off, water-drops suggesting tears of compassion are splashing from a spring at the left of the image. One may comment here in passing on the consistent purity of Mizoguchi's treatment of violence on the screen, which avoids the opposite pitfalls of sadism and softening. The horror of the brandings is by no means diminished by the fact that in both cases they are just off-screen. The scene in which the brothel-keepers cut Tamaki's Achilles' tendon to prevent further attempts at escape is especially reticent visually (the act concealed behind trellis-work), yet extraordinarily powerful: like the other women present, we want to avert our gaze, despite the fact that nothing horrible is shown on screen. But the crucial point here is the treatment of Sansho's downfall. Mizoguchi refuses to indulge any vindicative desire we might feel to watch this monster meet a violent, messy death: he is simply denounced, bound and sent into exile.

As in *Ugetsu,* the essential movement of *Sansho* is towards the assertion of spiritual triumph over time and space, towards that poignant fusion of affirmation and tragic loss. This movement, centred on the theme of family unity, is implicit in the film from the beginning, finding especially beautiful expression in the introductory flashbacks. Mizoguchi implies the continuing presentness of the past by dissolving from Zushio as adolescent to Zushio as child, running in the same direction from the camera. Even more beautiful is the linking of wife and husband across time: from Tamaki scooping water from the stream we are carried back to her husband making the same gesture as he raises a drinking vessel to his lips. Most beautiful of all is the sense that the memories are shared. The last of the flashbacks, showing the father's farewell, his gift of the symbolic statuette (the goddess of mercy) to his son, and his passing on of precepts about the brotherhood of human beings, begins as Tamaki's memory, but at its close we are returned to Zushio, handling the statuette around his neck and repeating the precepts. What we took to be the mother's memory of the father proves to be simultaneously his: the spiritual communion of the family could scarcely be more subtly or more tellingly expressed.

I want to examine the last sequence of *Sansho* in some detail: no scene is richer in accumulated resonances. First, however, it is important to have clear the film's political implications. Learning of his father's, then of Anju's death, Zushio renounces the power he has achieved—which he has in any case jeopardized by his grand gesture of overthrowing Sansho and freeing the slaves, a gesture that affronts the entire social and ideological structure of the time. The treatment of authority and rebellion in the film is characteristically complex and comprehensive. While the film's ideology is clearly traditionalist and aristocratic (much is made of inheritance and continuity; progress is achieved by the heroic actions of individuals of noble descent), it is also progressive and even, within limits, revolutionary. One is invited to compare and contrast its three father-figures: Zushio's father, Sansho (who almost becomes an alternative father to him), and the minister to whom Zushio presents the petition. Mizoguchi offers no simple explanation of human goodness: Zushio, the son of a humane and noble father, is corruptible, and *almost* becomes a second Sansho; Taro, Sansho's son, has an innate humanity inexplicable in terms of heredity. Yet Zushio's strength is seen as at least partly derived from, and sustained by, parental example: when he frees the slaves, he is conscious of 'following father's path'. Taro has no such example to give his actions force and conviction: though outraged by his father's behaviour, he can never stand up to him—can only depart surreptitiously; he fails to right Sansho's iniquities, and retires into the passive, contemplative life of a monastery. The minister, another compassionate figure, reminds one of Zushio's father—a connection underlined by the respect he expresses to Zushio; yet his humanity functions only within the limits determined by the *status quo*; he is an essentially conservative figure, his passivity contrasting with the defiant progressive acts of father and son. Because of this, he is able to retain power and to continue doing limited good of the kind that will never being about radical change; Zushio and his father both go into exile.

The film implies a further distinction between the radical acts of the father and son. Zushio's action in freeing the slaves (which the film unequivocally—though not simplistically—endorses) is much more extreme and outrageous, more overtly passionate and defiant, than his father's support of the peasantry; as in *Shin Heike Monogatari,* the strength the son draws from allegiance to an inherited moral code enables him to go much further than his father would have done. His renunciation is correspondingly more extreme: where the father rode into exile in his ministerial robes and remained a venerated authority-figure in Tsukushi (the peasants there keep his grave fresh with flowers), Zushio casts off all outward signs of authority and leaves for Sado as a pauper, alone. The attitude to Zushio's action, while complex, is very precisely defined. He achieves no widespread transformation of society, and the implications of his resignation are, on the socio-political level, extremely pessimistic; yet his action destroys one petty tyranny, ends the 'earthly hell' of Sansho's estate, makes more bearable the lives of a few individuals. His revolutionary gesture, therefore, is presented as neither futile nor reprehensible; and I do not feel that the treatment of the slaves' freedom-celebrations—the clumsy, drunken dance filmed in a single tracking-shot in which the camera serenely surveys the chaos and wreckage, finally rising slightly to look down on it—radically contradicts this. The sequence-shot here exemplifies that constant tension between style and content that characterizes Mizoguchi's late work: the presentation of a violent, disordered world from a viewpoint of compassionate contemplation and an achieved serenity totally devoid of complacency. It marks a realistic acknowledgement that the liberation of a people kept in ignorance, squalor and misery (the old man Zushio branded is prominent in the scene, personalizing the general conception) cannot produce instant utopia. Someone told me that Zushio resigns because he realizes that his action has merely led to further disorder, and that the despair implicit in this (a despair seen as going with, and justifying, an inherent conservatism) represents Mizoguchi's position, but this is a demonstrably incorrect reading: Zushio has already written his resignation when

he is told that Sansho's house is burning. It is clear, I think, from his words to his mother at the end of the film, that he *must* resign: the prevailing system cannot tolerate the sort of radical action he has performed.

The effect of the final scene is partly dependent on the socio-political pessimism: Zushio has gone as far as he can go in terms of political action; the system will close its ranks, there will be (doubtless *are*) other Sanshos; the final emphasis is less on the limited social good Zushio has achieved than on the personal integrity, the triumph of humane feeling, the achievement confirms. The apparently very different conclusions of *Ugetsu, Sansho* and *Shin Heike*—the first essentially conservative, the third defiantly radical, *Sansho* offering a point of balance between them—are doubtless partly determined by their historical contexts and source material; that maturity should be associated in *Ugetsu* with resignation and contentment with one's lot, in *Shin Heike* with active and passionate defiance, can be explained by the fact that the hero of the former is a peasant (hence quite unable to affect destiny on a political level), of the latter a samurai. Yet, beneath the differences, the three endings are consistent in their emphasis on self-determination within the available possibilities—on the protagonist's achievement of awareness of the world, awareness of self, on his definition of his own identity which is also a definition of relationship to the past. It is this achievement of awareness—present ubiquitously in the style of the late films—that represents the supreme value of the Mizoguchian universe.

The last sequence is prefaced by a sequence-shot without dialogue whose immediate narrative function is simply to record Zushio's progress towards his mother, but which is rich in emotional associations. Having enquired for Tamaki in the brothel district of Sado, where he learns (though reports conflict) that she was drowned in the tidal wave that devastated the area two years previously, he nevertheless presses on around the cape, impelled either by desperation (for if she too is dead, the entire progress of his life, and of the film, is merely towards the discovery of futility) or by some profound, quasi-mystical instinct: the two are not incompatible, and the context (which is no less than the entire film) makes both relevant. It is that context, indeed, that the sequence-shot evokes. The camera records Zushio's progress along the cliff from which, earlier, Tamaki, lamed, called to her children across the sea. Her crying of their names echoes through the film, the very first shot of which (after the 'foreword') established two of its main motifs: the journey towards reunion (as the family moved through the forest towards the exiled father and the boy Zushio ran forward along a fallen tree that cut the screen diagonally) and the mother calling to her son (the first word of dialogue). The 'call' motif was taken up in the sequence where the children gathered brushwood for the night's shelter, and it was the enacted repetition of that scene (when, as adults and slaves, Zushio and Anju gathered sticks and reeds to build a shelter for the dying Namiji) that was crucial in recalling Zushio to himself after his

Sansho-dominated lapse into brutalization—the scene that culminated in the moment where brother and sister heard, or seemed to hear, the mother's voice calling to them across space and time. The visual presence of the cliff—again, we are facing out to sea—evokes all these associations, making real for us the notion of spiritual journey. What is lacking is the melody of Tamaki's song—the song that, sung by the young girl-slave from Sado in Sansho's compound, became the children's one intimation that their mother might still be alive. The melody accompanied Tamaki's cries across the sea; it also accompanied Anju's suicide. Now, at the point where we would logically expect a further recapitulation of it (to the extent that I actually invented one in the original version of this essay), the silence is broken only by a strange (to western ears) flute-cry. In *Ugetsu,* when Genjuro, on his way to deliver his pots at the Wakasa mansion, paused before a cloth salesman's to imagine Miyagi admiring the fine kimonos, a holy man passing in the background played an instrument that emitted similar sounds, so the flute-cry may have religious overtones. But it also (one can say more confidently) 'stands in' for the cries of Tamaki in the earlier scene; and our expectations of the accompanying melody are aroused here so that their delayed fulfilment may be, when it eventually comes, the more moving. The sequence-shot ends with the camera turning to show Zushio moving down towards the little bay that was the scene of Tamaki's attempted escape, when, desperate to rejoin her children, she tried to bribe a boatman to take her away, before being recaptured by her pursuers from the brothel. The fact that the two earlier scenes (the cliff, the bay) are evoked here in reverse order subtly intensifies the sense that Zushio is moving *back* towards reunion with Tamaki.

The last scene of the film, to which this evocation of the past is the necessary prelude, consists of eleven shots marked as a sequence by the near-symmetry of the first and last, both of which link the three participating characters in a single camera-movement, the first moving left to right, the last right to left. The sequence uses every camera position from extreme close-up to extreme long-shot, and every kind of camera movement (as well as the static camera)—panning, tracking, craning: the fact suggests Mizoguchi's stylistic flexibility and command of expression. The action can be broken down as follows: (Shot 1) It is low tide; Zushio questions an old man who is spreading seaweed out to dry from a large pile he has collected. The old man has just told Zushio that Tamaki is certainly dead when her song, faint to the verge of inaudibility, drifts across in a frail, cracked voice. (2-7) Zushio makes himself known to his mother, who is now blind as well as lame, but she rejects him, preferring hopeless resignation to the further dashing of vain hopes: she has been deceived too many times. (8-10) Zushio convinces her that he is indeed her son by giving her the little figure of the goddess of mercy; he tells her of the deaths of his father and Anju; after a moment of bitter grief, the two cling together, reunited.

The overall effect of the last scene, like that of *Ugetsu,* is to balance the sense of loss and tragic waste with an affirmation of spiritual unity; if in *Sansho,* the effect is somewhat more desolate, the affirmation more penetrated by irony, this is partly accountable for by the absence of a child, though I shall argue that concepts of continuity and renewal are subtly present in other ways. The obvious comparison is with the late plays of Shakespeare (and their great forerunner, the father/daughter reconciliation scene of *King Lear*), and Mizoguchi is perhaps the only film-maker who would not suffer from such a juxtaposition; the recognition scene of *Pericles,* in which the presence of the sea is also crucial, offers the closest parallels. We see Zushio, like Marina with her father, restore Tamaki to life by reawakening within her the desire to live: a movement expressed in the action, the editing and the imagery. Tamaki's blindness (unlike the lameness, given no narrative explanation) has a symbolic dimension: she has withdrawn into herself, away from life and light; her almost tuneless chanting of the song ('Zushio, Anju, I long for you. . . . ') has become automatic, expressing fantasy without hope, lacking all outgoing purpose, as ineffectual as her feeble beating with the switch in her hands. Like Lear ('You do me wrong to take me out o'the grave'), she resists Zushio's revelation of his survival, scornfully rejecting him: the paralysed despair in which she exists is easier. The sequence opposes two backgrounds, each dominating four shots of the eleven: the sea (1, 3, 7, 11), associated now with Zushio and life, open, calm and bright, gleaming in the gentle sunlight; the hovel (4, 5, 8, 10) into which Tamaki tries to withdraw, merely a dark enclosure (we make out nothing of its interior).

Central to the action and significance of the sequence (hence of the whole film) is the figure of the goddess of mercy, whose special status is underlined by a cut in to close-up (shot 9) that echoes the earlier cut-in of Zushio's written resignation (both objects lying diagonally across the image). The figure evokes particular associations for Tamaki (the father, his moral precepts, past family unity) and more for the spectator (the saving of Namiji, the recognition of Zushio by the minister); its accumulated significance, as well as its intrinsic meaning, draws together all the threads of the film at this climactic point. Tamaki's fingers, in the close-up, trace its outlines as, in the next shot, they will trace the features of Zushio's face—as if she were tracing there the features of the child who was dragged from her or the husband whom she was following into exile. The significance of the statuette as a life-renewing emblem is defined very exactly by the *mise-en-scène:* in the eighth shot of the sequence, Tamaki hobbles into the darkness of the hut, almost disappearing from view; Zushio follows her (their backs are towards us) and as a last resort gives her the figure; clutching it, she turns, and moves out again into the sunlight, towards the camera, where she examines it with her fingers.

The force of affirmation is partly derived from the contextual sense of the spiritual presence of the father and

Anju: in performing a noble, altruistic deed (but one in which family feeling—the desire to rescue Anju—also played its part) before renouncing temporal power, Zushio has indeed followed his father's path (as the film's first scenes showed him doing literally), and Anju's death has contributed to the reunion of mother and son. Although two members of the family are dead and a third blind, lame and decrepit, the sense of loss and waste (the devastation of the tidal wave, the monstrousness of human cruelty) is counter-balanced by that of achieved mystic unity, the past alive in the present, the dead living on in the survivors, the transmitted values reaffirmed and validated: 'You followed father's words', Tamaki tells her son in the film's last line of dialogue; 'that is why we can meet here like this.' In the world of conflicts, cruelty and violent disorder that Mizoguchi so vividly creates for contemplation, the survival of humane, *human* feeling ('Without compassion, man is but a beast'—one of the father's precepts), defined in terms of a complex and living relatedness to family and tradition, is itself a triumph to be celebrated.

There remain for consideration the two shots involving the seaweed-gatherer, the sequence's symmetrical framework and culmination. The symmetry, it is important to note, is not exact: in shot 1 the camera tracks and cranes, in shot 11 it cranes and *pans*. The distinction is not merely pedantic. In the first shot, the tracking camera carries us along *with* Zushio, emotionally participating in his movement; in the last shot, the camera cranes up from the embracing mother and son, revealing sea and sky, a world opened up to us as if re-created, and pans to show the old man still at work, laying the seaweed out to dry. The seaweed, a reminder of the sea's power and potential for devastation, will be used either as food or fertilizer, to sustain life and foster new growth: the symbolism, quite unobtrusive, is profoundly satisfying as a summation of the film's progress, implying continuity and renewal wrested out of disaster; and this effect is underlined by the fact that the action has reached the point of completion, the pile of seaweed has disappeared. The crane up (to a greater height than the first shot, giving us a more panoramic view) communicates most movingly, like the last shot of *Ugetsu,* a sense of spiritual uplift; the fact that the camera now pans detaches us from the characters, conveying a sense of a heightened, contemplative and serenely accepting perspective on life that is wholly lacking in sentimentality. Style in *Sansho Dayu* is the convincing embodiment of the cinema's supreme intelligence and sensibility.

Joan Mellen (essay date 1976)

SOURCE: "Mizoguchi: Woman as Slave," in *The Waves at Genji's Door: Japan Through Its Cinema,* Pantheon Books, 1976, pp. 252-69.

[*In the following essay, Mellen discusses Mizoguchi's portrayal of women within the confines of traditional Japanese society, arguing that in his best films women* rebel—although their efforts are futile—against the system of oppression, usually dying for their cause.]

Those directors protesting against the oppression of the Japanese woman believe that even the failed rebellion is worth the effort. The finest films of Mizoguchi, who of the older directors best understood how the Japanese patriarchy demeans women, are those in which his women fight the hardest against their fate. The men in Mizoguchi's films are always weaker than the women, not because he was unable to characterize men, but because their childishness is meant to be an analogue to moral emptiness. The assertions of women in a patriarchy where they have no power, where they can be summoned as concubines to a daimyo—or sold by parents to a whorehouse—are acts more worthy of representation than those of a *bushi* participating in his daily willful abuse of the weak.

Mizoguchi's films reveal that it is absurd to speak about the relations between men and women in the context of the social role of the Japanese woman as long as she remains victim of the Confucian obediences to father, husband and son. The implicit argument behind his portrayal of the relations between men and women is that women are forced to sacrifice themselves simply by existing. Revolution against one's condition as a slave, which also demands sacrifices, is then infinitely preferable to passive submission to an enslaving fate. Osan, in his *Story from Chikamatsu,* riding off to her crucifixion (the punishment for a woman's adultery during the Tokugawa period), achieves a level of humanity she could never have enjoyed as the acquiescent wife of the merchant Ishun. In *White Threads of the Waterfall (Taki no Shiraito,* 1933) Mizoguchi bitterly satirizes the utter hostility of Meiji society toward women who, day after day, were sacrificing themselves to its prosperity. He scorns the entire Meiji concept of success. The society in which Kinya, the young man the heroine Taki puts through school, rises to prominence is unworthy of Taki's sacrifice because it is incapable of showing her mercy. Reduced to whoredom and then murder by the superhuman task she has undertaken, Taki finally has no recourse but suicide. Through his treatment of women Mizoguchi very early makes the same point directors like Imamura would later make for Koreans, *burakumin,* pollution victims, and others whose lives have been sacrificed to Japan's postwar development. Japan emerges strong after the Restoration, according to Mizoguchi, only by using and then discarding those who mistakenly sacrifice themselves in the belief that to be successful in the new society and to dedicate oneself to its economic growth is worth any effort.

In 1936 Mizoguchi made his most brilliant pre-war film, *Osaka Elegy (Naniwa Hika),* shot in twenty days and banned after 1940 for "decadent tendencies," a euphemism barely concealing the military government's fear of the radicalism of Mizoguchi's satire of the ruthless, all-pervasive Osaka capitalism. In this film the mature Mizoguchi style emerges for the first time as he creates, entirely through visual means, a balance between the fate of the heroine Ayako and the corrupt, degenerate values of Osaka. The plot concerns the seduction of Ayako, a switchboard operator, by her boss. In the background, however, is an equally important theme: the destruction of the individual by the greed of a boundless laissez-faire capitalism and its hostility toward anyone too weak to compete in the jungle of Social Darwinism that was Osaka—and Japan. Rhetoric about the dawning of an era of "freedom" fills the air, and Ayako even reads an article about "women's liberation." Mizoguchi reveals both to be a sham in this Osaka where money rules all and "freedom" is the province only of the businessmen frantically attempting to build mini-, if not authentic, *zaibatsu.*

Ayako is corrupted (she becomes a prostitute) not only by her boss but also by her family's need for money, the symbol of Osaka. As a woman, her role is to sacrifice herself to the needs of her family. The twentieth century has brought no amelioration of the traditional function of the Japanese woman. At first, Ayako tries to borrow from a weak and spineless fiancé, a typical Osaka company-man-to-be. He refuses her. Behind them in the shot is a construction site, bespeaking the rapid progress that is Osaka's *raison d'être.* At home, money is the main topic of conversation; Ayako's brother, having lost all connection with the traditional Japanese value of austerity, is obsessed by greed, a passion difficult to satisfy in the fiercely competitve society of the thirties.

Beset by the prevailing family pressure for her to help them, Ayako accepts the liaison with her boss and is transformed into a *"moga"* or modern girl. Her entire personality undergoes a change, as Mizoguchi portrays the psychic price a woman must inevitably pay for selling herself. Ayako now smokes, listens to Western music, and files her fingernails à la Mae West. Temporarily, the camera assumes the point of view of her boss climbing the stairs, ending outside the curtained window of the room where Ayako awaits him. Later, Ayako and her boss attend a performance of *Double Suicide* at the Bunraku Puppet Theater, where the traditions of the play and the strong passion of Jihei and Koharu for each other contrast with the loveless relationship between Ayako and her lover, and with the deflated mock-heroics of life in the present. The boss's wife discovers them, and intercut with a tumultuous Bunraku scene is her expression of rage, an indecorous fury which, by its very disruptiveness, provides a further judgment on the destructiveness of Ayako's affair.

Ayako nevertheless pursues this relationship with her boss because of unrelenting family pressures. Brother and sister conspire against her, a sister pleading that the older brother needs money while the camera tracks behind Ayako's back until she is left standing, alone and frightened, on subway stairs. A shot of the empty stairs after she has gone is followed by a low-angle shot of the tall buildings and speeding cars of Osaka, the city that will overwhelm her. In a fine, three-layered, deep-focus

shot Mizoguchi reveals three family members occupying different levels of being, the need for money having so alienated them that, although they are in the same room, it is as if they occupy wholly separate universes. The indolent older brother lies in bed, drinking tea, in the left foreground of the shot. The father is in the background, the period of his influence having ceased. Ayako is in the right foreground, now the only means by which the family can still compete in the struggle for financial survival in the new Japan.

In the climactic scene Ayako blames her callow and weak boyfriend for not having given her the money so that she need not have sold herself to her boss. Mizoguchi accepts this assessment. In the society of her time Ayako has had no choice but to become a *"moga."* A second lover, finding her with this cowardly fiancé, demands the return of the money he had given Ayako. Bravely, she suggests that she and her boyfriend work hard to pay him back. Encouraged by the possibility that she can do something about her fate, she begins to whistle. Disconsolate, her fiancé looks on. A moment later, Ayako is being arrested for having stolen the money, the camera tracking back and forth from her to the boyfriend, who is accused of using her to get money for himself. His wish not to become involved has resulted only in his being implicated, the thing he feared most.

At the end, Ayako returns home from the police station, still cheerful and glad to see her family: "It's a long time since we've eaten together." But rather than with welcome, she is greeted only with recriminations. Even her younger sister whines that she will no longer go to school, so humiliated is she by the "disgrace." Ayako walks out alone and stands on a bridge, while debris floats to the surface of the water below, as aimless as herself. The doctor of her boss passes by, but he, as a representative of this society, has no answer to her question: "What can you do for a woman who has turned into something like this?" Like the society which condemned Taki, Ayako's Osaka treats her as human debris. The doctor walks one way, Ayako the other. Prostitution is her final fate.

In the last shot of *Osaka Elegy* Ayako walks full into the camera in the film's only close-up; it suggests her heroism but also a hopelessness shared by the director, as overwhelmed as she by the values of this Osaka. Except for this last shot, Ayako has always been portrayed in relation to others, reflecting Mizoguchi's judgment that her "choices" have all been the result of pressures from without. Through his shot compositions in which Ayako has always been seen with boss, father, brother, or boyfriend, Mizoguchi has revealed, paradoxically, her profound isolation and total inability to locate an avenue for resistance, let alone rebellion.

Throughout his career Mizoguchi saw in his country of the double standard the prostitute as symbol of the oppressed Japanese woman. His married women sell themselves as well, and he certainly would have lamented the fate of Ozu's independent-minded Noriko in *Early Summer*. At twenty-eight Noriko, who has said that she would prefer to remain single, finally yields to family pressure and marries a neighboring widower about to take up work in cold, rural Akita. A theoretical opponent of marriage, Noriko consents to marry this man, whom she clearly does not love, because she is needed and can build a life with him. He is acceptable primarily because he was the best friend of her younger brother who died in the war, as well as being a colleague of her elder brother who is a doctor; a family bond already exists between them. Passion between these two seems inconceivable; Noriko herself seems to choose this man precisely because she, disliking what she clearly recognizes as the serfdom of marriage, will be more secure in an arrangement between friends rather than lovers.

Mizoguchi, however, would have viewed Noriko's decision as a sacrifice and would have challenged the association between marriage and service as if these terms were identical. Ozu accepts as natural a dutiful marriage based upon a mild feeling of companionship between two people. Mizoguchi always views the relations between men and women as invariably involving the man's using the woman as an object to satisfy his needs—a practice he deems absolutely indefensible. He would liberate the Japanese woman from the duplicitous contract wherein, in exchange for sacrificing her abilities and her very identity, she gains "control" of a household. Taken as a whole, Mizoguchi's body of films about women subtly equates the traditional wife with the prostitute. Each sacrifices all that she has, all that she is. The life of the Japanese woman, for Mizoguchi, is symbolized by a prostitution of the spirit.

Mizoguchi depicted a group of prostitutes in his last film, *Red-Light District* (*Akasen Chitai*, 1956), mistakenly translated in the American version as *Street of Shame*, with inappropriate pejorative and moralistic connotations. The setting is a seedy, desperate, run-down Yoshiwara (prostitute quarter) at the moment in 1956 when prostitution is about to be outlawed in Japan. The "heroine" is the prostitute, represented by five very different women, all of whom are portrayed as valuable human beings whose suffering would only be exacerbated by the outlawing of their "profession."

In the last scene, the young maid of the house is about to lose her virginity. Her mother's frequent demands for money, after a mining accident suffered by the father, have left her no choice. As she passively succumbs, her face is powdered. "Discard it with good grace," advises a rebellious Mizoguchi heroine, offering a tidbit to sweeten the pain. When this child ventures a glance outside, the street is filled with soliciting women. A whistling, eerie music merges with their cries. Barely able to speak, she hides behind a post in a brief, temporary respite. The final slow fade spares us and Mizoguchi the agonies of viewing her final fall.

In *A Picture of Madame Yuki* (*Yuki Fujin Ezu*, 1950) Mizoguchi offers an analysis of the psychology of a woman he could not achieve in films like *Utamaro And His Five Women, Women of the Night* (*Yoru no Onnatachi*, 1948), or *Red-Light District*—films primarily concerned with a group of women within a social context that was of equal concern to the director. Mizoguchi made *Madame Yuki* for Shintoho Takimura Productions on the condition that the producer Takimura would then permit him to do a film based on the stories of Saikaku. *The Life of Oharu* (*Saikaku Ichidai Onna*) was indeed made in 1952, but for another company, Daiei.

Mizoguchi's theme in *Madame Yuki* is the prostitution of the wife, a role often no less redolent of degradation than that of the whore. Yuki (Michiyo Kogure) is a woman of great beauty, her room filled with the aura of incense and mystery. Yet she remains enslaved to a vulgar, loutish husband. Yuki is forever prey to this man's sensuality. Even when he brings home his cabaret-singer mistress, whose dark lipstick bespeaks her vulgarity, Yuki can still yield to him. A *koto* player who is a neighbor (Ken Uehara) admires Yuki but, passive and unmanly as he is, Yuki cannot view him as man enough to free her of her husband. Instead, he hovers in the background of her life. Yuki does go so far as actively to consider divorce, but she always succumbs to her husband's advances. In one scene the maid, surprised, comes in upon the husband reposing in Yuki's room. Yuki's fallen kimono lies in view, a symbol of the collapse of her will to resist him, as is her obi buckle with a Noh mask imprinted on it. "A devil lives inside woman," says Yuki. It is the same devil tormenting Luis Buñuel's *Belle du Jour*, a woman who could be aroused only by the perverse, and never by her gentle, considerate husband.

At the end, Yuki kills herself, lacking the strength to overcome the indecision and humiliation which are the alternatives to a frightening struggle for freedom. Uehara tells her that to be saved she must solve the problem for herself, something a Japanese woman of gentility who has been conditioned to passivity simply cannot do. Uehara plays modern music on the piano, as if Mizoguchi were saying that we must find the means to cope with the postwar world as it is, instead of living among idle dreams.

But Yuki is a woman whose personality has been shaped by centuries of conditioning which taught the Japanese girl from childhood on that she must accept the conditions of her life. Although Mizoguchi sees the need for the Japanese woman to change radically, he is also very aware of how difficult this will be. Speaking for the director, Uehara becomes impatient with Yuki's passivity: "You never try to struggle against your suffering. You're a human being. You must have the confidence to live as a human being. Become strong!" Yet Mizoguchi also believes in the truth of Yuki's reply: "You tell me to do what I cannot."

Yuki disappears. Her clothes once more lie discarded on the floor. The camera tracks with the husband as he searches for her. But she is already in the misty woods, small against the landscape. When Yuki's body is found (she has drowned herself), the maid who had admired her so much throws Yuki's obi and the buckle with the Noh mask into the lake in anger. "You coward, you coward," she screams as Mizoguchi dollies *down* for his final shot, to the lake waters rippling and moving. The maid speaks for the angry Mizoguchi, as if he had been finally betrayed by a character so unworthy of his passionate anger over the oppression of the Japanese woman. The heroine of *The Life of Oharu* will not so disappoint him.

After *A Story from Chikamatsu, The Life of Oharu* is Mizoguchi's greatest film. It opens as an aged prostitute recalls for her friends the history of her life, a story that embodies the fate of all women in feudal Japan. Huddled in the cold beside a fire under a bridge are Oharu and her fellow prostitutes, all well past fifty and suffering hard times. A priest unfeelingly objects to their illegal lighting of a fire in the vicinity of the temple, while in the background we hear monks chanting Zen sutras, of little solace or relevance to these abandoned women.

Organized religion emerges in this film as one of the most sinister oppressors of the Japanese woman. As the camera tracks, following the wizened Oharu moving away from the scene, the chanting grows louder and louder. The camera increases its motion, as if in competition with the chanting voices. By contrasting camera movement with sound, Mizoguchi seems to be presenting two forces at eternal war: suffering women and institutionalized religion, which turns a deaf ear to their cries of pain.

Oharu enters a Buddhist Temple of the Rakans, filled with statues of life-sized monks, each with a unique and individualized visage. Mizoguchi pans these figures until Oharu's eyes focus on one face, which dissolves to that of the actor Toshiro Mifune, meant to remind Oharu of the first man who loved her. A flashback now removes us to 1686, when Oharu's story properly begins, and she is a very young woman attached to the court. The irony is that once we enter the flashback, the young man who loves Oharu, a page at the Old Imperial Palace, is not played by Mifune at all. Many years later she remembers him as a man much more handsome, vital, and energetic than he really was, one of the tricks life plays on lonely women. Her error is recorded by the camera without comment and in the understated manner that has made Mizoguchi one of the greatest directors in the history of world cinema.

Another dissolve takes us to the court, where Oharu's troubles begin when she accepts the advances of this man of lower rank than herself. Obedient to the norms upholding a rigid class structure, she is at first outraged when he sends her a poem declaring his love. In order to meet her at all, so bound by convention are those chosen to serve at court, he must use deception and pretend to be delivering a message from their superior.

"Who would read a letter from a mere page?" says Oharu when they meet in the graveyard. Katsunosuke's reply teaches her the meaning of life as Mizoguchi would have us see it. There are values that transcend those defined as *giri* or obligation by the class society. "I'm loyal and sincere," says this page, Katsunosuke, "you can despise my low rank, but you can't ignore my devotion." He asks who among the nobility would care enough to marry Oharu and make her happy: "a woman can be happy only if she marries for true love."

Within the context of the feudal society of the time, this is an outrageous, revolutionary idea, one that requires the breaking of laws, the punishment for which is death for the rebel. The class boundaries of Japanese society as a whole would have to be broken were marriage to be based upon love. For no matter how much Oharu and Katsunosuke care for each other, neither the Imperial Court nor her father would ever permit them to marry.

Still in the graveyard, Oharu embraces Katsunosuke, with Mizoguchi employing a variation on his famous one-shot, one-scene technique, in which an entire scene is conveyed in one shot with no cuts to vary the angle or change the point of view. Mizoguchi employs this technique at the most intense psychological moments in his films, even at times photographing a scene for five minutes from a single point of view. "During the course of filming a scene, if an increasing psychological sympathy begins to develop," he has said, "I cannot cut into this without regret. I try rather to intensify and prolong the scene as long as possible." This take between Oharu and Katsunosuke in the graveyard is very long, a sign that Katsunosuke's words have been experienced by Oharu as truth.

As she falls to the ground in passion, amidst the dying autumn leaves, Katsunosuke lifts and carries her out of the frame. The camera, remaining, tilts down ever so slightly to reveal two graves side by side, a foreshadowing of the fate of this forbidden love. Another long take focuses on the scene now empty of human beings, the length of the shot expressing the power of an environment that cares nothing for the feelings of people. The long take which Mizoguchi uses so frequently often asserts a problem admitting of no easy resolution. It is the cinematic opposite of rapid cutting which suggests change, hope, progress, and development, and which characterizes the film style of Kurosawa. The long take, in Mizoguchi's hands, bespeaks the recalcitrance of the outside world, the difficulty of change, the spuriousness of optimism.

At the inn where they have gone to be alone, the police burst in upon Oharu, the daughter of a samurai, and Katsunosuke, a mere retainer. A rapid fade-in and fade-out at once removes us to a long shot in which Oharu is being sentenced for her crime. Her parents are simultaneously punished; she is an extension of them and not a separate individual, the very term an anachronism in feudal Japan. According to Tokugawa justice, the parents are as guilty as she.

As we view the scene in long shot, Oharu's "crime" is read out loud. She is guilty of misconduct with a person of low rank. To emphasize their powerlessness, Mizoguchi stubbornly reveals only the backs of their heads as she and her parents are told that they are to be exiled from Kyoto. They bow in obedience. To debate the question would constitute a further crime.

A dissolve within the scene to the crowd waiting outside is employed not to indicate the passage of time (the more frequent use of this technique), but to express the shame of this family before those who know them, as much a part of the punishment as the exile itself. The camera remains at a very low angle as Oharu and her parents cross a bridge into the next phase of their lives. From under the bridge, in extreme long shot, Mizoguchi shoots three tiny figures on the horizon. They are indeed insignificant. Before the fade ending the sequence, on a sloping horizon remain one bare tree and three tiny silhouettes. The shot composition itself contains a protest against feudalism.

In exile, Oharu is upbraided by her father for destroying family honor and causing them to live in shame. She replies with the truth she has by now fully assimilated: "Why is it immoral if a man and woman love each other?" But the high angle looking down at Oharu is from the point of view of her father, and reinforces only her powerlessness, despite her growing awareness.

Oharu and her family suffer the pain of exile. But Katsunosuke, a male, and an inferior who violated the laws governing rank, must be executed. He sends Oharu a message she will find it very difficult to fulfill: "Please find a good man. Be sure to marry only where there is mutual love." He hopes for a time when there will be no such thing as social rank and people can marry for love. The steel of the sword raised over his head glints in the sun. We are permitted to see the sword in close-up, but not the death blow, because Mizoguchi wishes us to remember Katsunosuke in his strength. Unlike Kurosawa, Mizoguchi, in a much more traditionally Japanese approach to characterization, rarely uses facial expressions to reveal personality. A kimono obscures Oharu's face when she learns of Katsunosuke's death. Her emotions are revealed, instead, in the next action she takes. She makes an unsuccessful attempt at suicide.

Oharu now begins her descent, a plunge unapparent because there is first a seeming rise in her fortunes. The retainer of Lord Matsudaira arrives in town bearing a scroll painting of the ideal woman whose likeness is to be approximated by the concubine he will select for his Lord. Lady Matsudaira is barren and the clan will be ruined unless a woman is found to bear Matsudaira a child.

Mizoguchi satirizes the prevailing standards of beauty. The ears of this paradigm must not stand out; her feet can be only twenty-one or twenty-two centimeters long; she must have neither odor nor moles. The camera tracks down the line of assembled beauties, as if they were cattle at auction, while the fat retainer, ruler in hand, examines them for imperfections. A deep-focus shot reveals the whole line reaching back into oblivion, as if all women in Japan were every day being subjected to the inhumanity of such scrutiny, reduced to sexual objects. None pleases him until he discovers Oharu at dancing school. Somehow she had escaped the public inspection, a further hint of her rebellious nature and unwillingness to be humiliated. Before she can say a word, Matsudaira's retainer rushes in on the scene and announces to all, "I'll buy her!"

Oharu's parents, particularly her father, are delighted by the opportunity to sell their daughter. The father promises no longer to curse her for their exile. But Oharu's rebellion continues. She now announces that she doesn't wish to be a concubine: "Katsunosuke won't permit me to." But physical violence will be employed against any woman who defies the wishes of her superiors—lord, father, or husband. Oharu's father throws her brutally to the ground. In the next sequence she is in a sedan, arriving at Edo to become Matsudaira's concubine.

Lady Matsudaira, whom Oharu very much resembles, is told to subordinate her own feelings "for the sake of the clan." Women are set against each other in a society where each day marks a struggle for survival. In deep focus, a performance of the Bunraku at court finds the puppets acting out Oharu's arrival and the jealousy it engenders. The play is a means by which those sympathetic to Lady Matsudaira are to be reconciled to the change in her circumstances. With such subtlety, harmony is enforced without public dissension and malcontents are silently ordered to conform.

When Oharu bears a son, she is told that she has not "borne" a child, but that she has been "caused to bear" one. The child is immediately removed to be nursed by someone else, and, of course, belongs—as did all male children at the time, regardless of class—to the father and his family. While Oharu's father is profligately buying silk in the hope of becoming a merchant, she is banished because Lord Matsudaira loved her so much that he was expending all his energy on their relationship. In the clan system, even the powers of an individual lord are limited. Oharu, as a woman, cannot please whether she is deemed adequate or inadequate. She is given five ryo for her trouble, an incredibly paltry sum, but a measure of a woman's worth. In anger, her father hurls her against the sedan in which she arrives home.

Oharu is next sold as a courtesan to the Shimabara whorehouse, where her rebelliousness, ever endorsed by Mizoguchi, expresses itself as she flings the money of an arrogant customer back into his face. "I'm not a beggar," she proudly asserts, a forehadowing of her final fate. "But you are no different from a fish," she is told, "we can prepare and dispose of you as we wish." As her merchant customer is unmasked as a counterfeiter, Oharu stands in one of the finest deep-focus shots in the film, a small, lonely figure on a balcony observing the chaos of the man's apprehension in the courtyard below. She is almost unnoticed by us, just as her rebellion is temporarily overlooked by her superiors in the urgency of the moment.

Rapidly descending the social scale, Oharu becomes servant to a merchant. As soon as the man discovers that she has been at Shimabara, he attempts to seduce her. The religious satire enters the film once more as the merchant begins his approach to Oharu while pretending to be engaged in Buddhist prayers. Meanwhile, his jealous wife torments Oharu, who achieves her revenge by sending a cat late at night to pluck off the woman's wig to which Oharu, as the woman's hairdresser, has applied an appropriate odor. Thus is the wife's baldness revealed to her husband, a revelation that she has feared would ensure his leaving her. Women who might be natural allies destroy each other, while men are aided in the oppression of women by the competition among them for men, their only means of survival.

Only once does Oharu marry. Her husband is a fan-maker who is devoted to her. In a rather crude manipulation of plot, Mizoguchi has him attacked by thieves and murdered. In his final moment he is shown holding an obi, a gift destined for Oharu. Although he loved her for herself, the world separated them anyway. Oharu becomes a nun, but when the merchant of the bald wife pursues her at the temple and she rebels, she is condemned by the head nun for licentiousness in a brilliant satire on the hypocrisy of religious orders.

The merchant arrives at the temple, demanding the cloth she has not yet paid for. Oharu insists that she has already converted it into a kimono and begins stripping herself as if to return the goods. The nun, viewing the kimono on the floor (an image of sexual relations, as in *A Portrait of Madame Yuki*) and the naked Oharu, immediately casts her out. But the nun is angry, not because of Oharu's violation of the rules of the Buddhist order, but because she herself has been sexually aroused. "Do you provide me with a visual demonstration, hoping I would join you?" she demands of Oharu, indicating a barely concealed desire to do just that: "I can't be tempted by a whore like you." Oharu is now punished for the nun's own repressed feelings. Religious orders offer no refuge for the oppressed but, rather, cooperate in their oppression.

The only kindness shown Oharu in her long travail is by the old prostitutes of the first sequence; as the most demeaned of women, they have known the same pain. And they have learned that "whatever we do, it doesn't make any difference to the world." Oharu joins them and, unfortunately, is selected by a pilgrim in Mizoguchi's final thrust at organized religion for its failure to offer compassion to the suffering. This pilgrim drags Oharu into the light, where he uses her as a means of convincing his followers to renounce the evil of sexual intercourse. "Take a good look at this witch," he leers, "do you still want to lie down with a woman?" Oharu becomes an example of the sinner. In bitterness she protests, "you'll always be able to remember you came face to face with a real witch!" But her rebellion now falls short because she has no choice; she must retrieve from the floor the coins they have thrown her way.

Religious hypocrisy is paralleled by that of the political structure. The Matsudaira clan would accept her back, except that, by becoming a courtesan, she has not kept her loyalty to those pompous and cruel "descendants of Ieyasu Tokugawa," as they term themselves. Mizoguchi now offers his full contempt for class superiority, and for those who claim to be valuable on the ground of family connection. In her last rebellion, Oharu breaks free of the clan elders to have one look at her stuffed-shirt of a son. As he passes with his entourage, his face bespeaks what he is—an adolescent, callow and empty, a scion of those who have long ceased to have any claim to humane emotion, an emblem of a dying aristocracy.

In the last sequence, an aged Oharu, now a beggar, seeks alms. In a house where a woman holds a baby, she is treated kindly; at another, a man waves her away, a symbol of his sex's treatment of women. Oharu looks toward a pagoda in the distance; raising her eyes in prayer, she walks out of the frame. And the camera is left in this last shot to focus on the pagoda, as if Mizoguchi were blaming it for her suffering. Only Yuki, a woman of modern Japan, but never Oharu, is told by the director that she ought to have shown greater strength. In this, perhaps the finest film ever made in any country about the oppression of women, the director, shunning didactic moralizing, can only echo her pain.

One "mistake," even when it is based purely on a misunderstanding, can ruin a woman forever, a fact equally true for Ayako of the 1930s in *Osaka Elegy* and Osan of Mizoguchi's *A Story from Chikamatsu* in Tokugawa Japan. At first Osan is only grateful to Mohei, her husband's worker, for standing by her. She neither loves nor desires him. Rather, they are brought together only by the circumstance of having to flee through mud and swamps, fugitives like runaway slaves in the American South. Should they be caught, the punishment would be crucifixion, with no one stopping to inquire whether or not they had in fact been lovers. Osan "belongs" to her husband as a serf would to a feudal lord. Only extremes of social chaos, brought on by the merchant's rapid ascent to power, have led her to such impropriety, to what she calls so "strange" a fate.

From choosing death through suicide on ironically calm Lake Biwa, Osan moves, for the sake of an authentic love, to a willingness to defy the society's highest laws defining a woman's behavior. In four cuts Mizoguchi develops her emotions. Lake Biwa appears with a solitary temple in long shot against the sky. The boat from which Osan and Mohei plan to drown themselves then rows into the frame, still in long shot. A dissolve next brings the edge of the boat close to us but in very shallow focus. A closer shot reveals Mohei tying Osan's legs together, readying her for the suicide.

Mizoguchi then turns to his characteristic one-shot, one-scene technique. The long take in the beautiful Lake Biwa scene begins as Mohei declares his love for Osan. The rowboat in which the two have been drifting is now anchored firmly in the center of the shot. When Osan's feelings become impossible to contain and she announces to Mohei "your confession [that he loves her] has made me change my mind. I don't want to die," both are standing in the precariously rocking boat. It is a moment of extreme transcendence, perhaps the first in Osan's life in which she has expressed what she feels as a unique, separate human being. She grabs Mohei and the boat begins to move, the camera remaining static, as if fully endorsing Osan's choice of *ninjo,* or, rather, of a higher *giri,* a duty to the growing love between herself and Mohei. Mizoguchi at last need not intervene. He dissolves to the empty boat on the lake, now interpolating a very short take. His woman has achieved her humanity, defined always for Mizoguchi in terms of an act of rebellion against feudal norms.

But the rebellion of one individual does not a revolution make. The moment of Osan's greatest happiness is rapidly followed by a descent leading to her crucifixion. Mohei, knowing that this is the fate awaiting them, would send her back to "the Master." It is she who becomes the stronger of the two, insisting that she cannot live without Mohei. The first taste of freedom strengthens one's character. It transforms us from passive acceptance to active insistence upon controlling our own destinies. And it is at such triumphant moments in their development that Mizoguchi loves his women best.

Class differences recede, as if a liberation for women in Japan would mean a simultaneous social emancipation for all. "You're no longer my servant," Osan tells Mohei, "you're my beloved husband, my master." That she calls Mohei, the man she has chosen, her "master" in no way invalidates Osan's achievement. Choosing whom to love, in the context of the life of a woman under feudalism, constitutes the highest degree of revolutionary struggle.

The world, of course, conspires against Mohei and Osan. It could not do otherwise. Her brother, outraged at her persistent refusal to return to Ishun, says that Osan should be "cut to pieces." It is he who turns her in to the police at the house of her mother, where Mohei, inspired by Osan's own resilience, had claimed her. Their destinies are finally resolved in a last one-shot, one-scene in which a slowly panning camera reveals to us Osan and Mohei tied together, riding off to be crucified. Osan looks serene, Mohei cheerful. The camera remains still as they ride off into long shot, as if satisfied at having told a story so full of nobility. Each camera set-up has seemed determined by Osan's movements on her path to liberation, as if guided by the magnificence of a Japanese wife triumphantly escaping her bondage. Death is a small enough price to pay for spiritual transcendence. It has

awaited all revolutionaries. Mizoguchi would urge us, finally, that it need not be feared.

As a coda to his films about the oppression of women, Mizoguchi made his first color film, *The Princess Yang Kwei Fei (Yokihi),* in 1955, the year before his death. The story is not properly that of a woman, but of the Emperor Hui Sung, who falls in love with a scullery maid named Kwei Fei, and then loses her in an execution necessitated by political upheaval over which he has no control. It is a testament to the undying love aroused by Kwei Fei and of the capacity for such love in a man. *The Princess Yang* is thus a paean to the feelings between men and women that should be possible, but which the world rarely permits. It is a much weaker film than *A Story from Chikamatsu,* which immediately preceded it, perhaps because Mizoguchi is at his best when he is absorbed in a struggle against oppression. In *The Princess Yang,* when forces separate the lovers, rebellion is assumed to be impossible, despite the man's being an Emperor!

The Emperor finally comes to the close of his troubled life. He calls the dead Kwei Fei's name, and in a metaphysical moment that becomes Mizoguchi's argument for a Buddhist-oriented renunciation of the possibility of happiness in this world, she replies, having waited faithfully in the next world for his arrival: "I've come to take you. I have been waiting for this moment for years. Give me your hand. Let me guide you . . . no one will ever disturb us this time." At last Kwei Fei can offer the Emperor a "happiness that has no ending." Together they join in uproarious, joyous, cosmic laughter, as curtains blow in the now empty room, a sign of the presence of the supernatural. It is Mizoguchi meeting the moment of his own death, and welcoming his departure from a world that has offered only grief to woman—and to man as well. Rebellion has achieved little; death and the unchangeable offer the final and only relief.

If in *The Life of Oharu* Mizoguchi lived inside his heroine, a Flaubert to his personal Madame Bovary, in *The Princess Yang Kwei Fei* his is the point of view of the besieged, imprisoned Emperor. At the end of a long and distinguished career in which he directed more than eighty films (the exact number is unknown), Mizoguchi experiences a sense of exhaustion. Instead of rebellion against feudal norms, he now prefers communication with a world beyond the tawdry, blemished land of the living. It would remain for younger directors like Susumu Hani to take up with renewed vigor the theme of the oppression of the Japanese woman.

Robert Cohen (essay date 1978)

SOURCE: "Mizoguchi and Modernism: Structure, Culture, Point of View," in *Sight and Sound,* Vol. 47, No. 2, Spring, 1978, pp. 110-18.

[*In the following essay, Cohen discusses Mizoguchi's place in the Japanese modernist movement, stressing the necessity of critical contextualizing when analyzing the artistic efforts of other cultures.*]

It is twenty-two years since Donald Richie and Joseph Anderson's first major article on Kenji Mizoguchi appeared in *Sight and Sound;* and twenty since Anderson stated: 'The Japanese cinema has been established as long as the cinema has existed anywhere. In the past thirty years or so it has been much in need of discovery.' In the light of recent structural criticism in *Screen* which claims to have found traces of modernism in the films of Ozu, there is a touch of *déjà vu.* Mizoguchi, like Ozu, made fully matured films before World War II, and both directors have been considered quite traditional by Japanese critics and by the majority of non-structural Western critics. The new evaluation of Ozu, therefore, seems to suggest one of three things: first, that the structuralists have been able to reinterpret what is meant by the traditional; or that they have been able to recast much of the cultural information we have had about Japan into a modernist mode; or that structural criticism has really found an authentic new substance in the work of Ozu. It is the contention of this essay, however, that recent criticism of the Japanese film has indeed jumped too far ahead in labelling Ozu a modernist precisely because it has not sufficiently made use of the Japanese context. In following its lead, we find ourselves back at the stage which Anderson refers to, and the Japanese film looks merely exotic once again.

For structural criticism to be consistent and to claim the attention of the wider, non-academic film community, it must make use of culturally specific information. Certain elements of any alien culture must be understood, to be able to recognise historical details and social customs, to better understand character motivation and to appreciate subtleties of imagery and language. There is really no such thing in criticism as description apart from interpretation; and like the deciphering of a dream, the critic continually shifts back and forth between the elements of the work and the mechanism which created it. It is much like the old example of a conversation between two Japanese, where yes means no and vice versa. If one does not know the convention, or the language, one cannot describe the encounter or interpret the relationship.

In looking at the point of view structure of Mizoguchi's films, this essay is an attempt to lay a foundation on which we may eventually build a more accurate picture of Japanese modernism. It is contended that Mizoguchi, along with Ozu, Gosho, Kinugasa and Yasujiro Shimazu, helped to create a cinema of classical realism closer to the Western model than to anything which has only recently been accomplished in a cinema of modernism in Europe. The classical realism of the Japanese film is indeed a system of representation in the same way that Hollywood movies are a system: they are both essentially formal tendencies rather than hard and fast rules for the definition of space and the control of causal relationships. Japanese realism, however, differs from the Western model primarily in two ways: it employs an editing

system of 90 and 180 degrees utilising a 360 degree rule rather than Hollywood's 180; and the Japanese system tends to use a moving camera with the long take to photograph dialogue scenes instead of the shot/reaction shot preferred in the West. When this system is placed within the specific context of Mizoguchi's films, we will see that it functions with great economy to create spatial and temporal coherence different from but analogous to that found in Western classical realism.

In the *Screen* articles on Ozu (Vol. 17, No. 2), these characteristics of Japanese film structure are corroborated. The difficulty is not so much that the critics misunderstand the Japanese system as that they impose on it too many Western assumptions. This effort would perhaps lead directly to an understanding of Japanese modernism if it were true that in Japan the 19th century European novel had determined the use of filmic codes without having been radically altered; if Renaissance perspective had been responsible for organising a humanistic subject within the structure of discourse and graphic arts; and these structural assertions would perhaps be true if Japanese linguistic and psychoanalytical structure were uniformly responsible for developing art forms which are clearly subject-centred. These ideas have become the basis for most structural studies of film; but debatable as they are even in Western criticism, there has yet to be any analysis of these concepts in Japanese terms. Conclusions, therefore, about the nature of Japanese modernism based on these tentative assumptions are without adequate foundation.

There is also a distinction to be made between the modern and the modernistic. As a modern, post-industrial society, Japan interacts with other such societies. There is an affinity with the 20th century mental attitude of the West, and in art this interrelationship is manifest in a borrowing and adaptation of cultural forms and models. The purely modern has, thus, been influential for the Japanese. For an artist, this has been both a liberation and a liability. It has meant a degree of freedom from convention and from the restrictive use of genre, while it has meant a form of personal isolation already acute for the Japanese artist.

In literature, the so-called modern novel when specifically referred to in Japanese means the *shosetsu*. It designates an approximation of the term 'novel' in the West, but it was a literary form adopted full blown as it were rather than a phenomenon which evolved in Japan over centuries. To be sure there were precedents in various kinds of writing, but it was not until the Meiji Restoration that a truly modern international age began. There was at the turn of the last century a great hunger for European modernistic technique; but more often than not the effects of adaptation came very close to expressing classical Japanese aesthetic ideas. As Masao Miyoshi has indicated (*Accomplices of Silence: The Modern Japanese Novel*), the Japanese surrealists could have found what they were looking for in the *waka* and *haiku*. Kawabata and the Neo-Perceptionists could have used these forms in their attempts to modernise written Japanese. What this indicates is that, despite talk of foreign influence by the Japanese themselves, the form in which the work finally appears must be evaluated in both its intent and its effect.

A similar point can be made about Mizoguchi's films in terms of their use of Western editing techniques. Mizoguchi was one of the first in Japan to make fully realised sound films by assimilating the Western model. His system differed in the ways already mentioned, but it came about because of his understanding of European and American films. It was considered progressive for a Japanese film-maker to accept foreign influence during the silent period, and Mizoguchi was a leader with the progressives. The fact remains, however, that when sound came to Europe the continuation of classical realism with further emphasis on the relative correspondence between sound and image was generally a conservative manoeuvre. It becomes clear that, depending on context, the Western codes were either progressive or conservative depending on their function, and that they were certainly modern for the Japanese. What they accomplished, however, within the system of representation already established is another story.

The term modernism itself seems to be used more by critics who understand it least. The ubiquity of the term is confirmed when we see it applied to such diverse film-makers as Godard, Resnais, Antonioni, the Straubs and Paul Sharits. But the aspect of modernism with which we will deal involves the notion of the 'deconstruction' of classical realism. The interplay between first person shots (point of view associated with a character, but not necessarily a 'subjective shot') and the third person/authorial view is said by structuralists to be the privileged form of classical realism. Since the narrative film dominates the Western feature industry, this alternation of points of view creates an imaginary time and space whose purpose it is to reinforce the illusion of the reality of the story. Modernist works subvert the 'natural' causality that such a form is made to imply. It is said to break the imaginary closed nature of realist illusionism in its refusal to resolve in its plastic form the enigma of its content. What is often called the 'invisibility' of realist editing ensures the contrary; that the illusion to which the film refers outside the film becomes more real to the audience than the screen images themselves. It is because the systematic portrayal of point of view is central to this concept of realism that it is used to discuss the modernism of Mizoguchi.

Since all films are forced to use some form of representation to record their images on celluloid, it is through the representative function that modernism arises. It has often been a structural dictum that while the realist film can question reality through representation, only the modernist text can question the very act of representation. *Last Year at Marienbad* is the prototype, because the juxtaposition of past and present is never resolved into one coherent imaginary whole. The expectation for

precise causality is thwarted; the film therefore becomes a puzzle, and this enigma and its working out is more central and real than any imaginary referent. The danger of this conception of modernism is of course that such a host of other concerns becomes secondary that the primary theme of all modernistic works becomes the problem of representation.

Any formal element which appears not to fit within the realist system is potentially a modernistic component. These have two aspects. They can merely signify a gap in the film's design, and as Barthes has shown, these features are often key dimensions to gain us entry into the illusionism of a fictional work. The second possibility is that the element will signify a break with the realist conception, and in this case other components will be sought to verify the assertion. When a consistent structural arrangement is found that does seem to de-emphasise the causal connections between images, then we may have a case for a complete modernist film. In both cases, however, intelligibility depends on an awareness of the conventions which are being contradicted and on the analysis of the film on a proper conceptual level.

It is on the question of levels and the notion of convention that the Japanese film is most problematic. A situation exists analogous to one found in Japanese literature. The poetic tradition in Japan has been dominated for almost a thousand years by the lyric form, and elements of lyricism inform the Japanese novel in a much stronger, more direct way than was the case in Europe, where the antecedent would perhaps be the epic poem. It is possible, therefore, that in the Japanese novel the creation of atmosphere or a rather disjointed stream of thoughts and digressions will take precedence over the creation of a flesh and blood character. It is equally the case that a book with more than a minimum of emphasis on action will merely juxtapose events of secondary importance and leave out the primary action (Nagai Kafu's *Geisha in Rivalry,* for example). It is partly a consequence of knowing convention and partly having expectations at all which gears the reader towards his own level of interest. It is also a question of finding consistency on any level which offers a work its overall intelligibility. If we, therefore, apply Western notions of narrative to Japanese films, we most likely will find appropriate gaps; but for those elements to subvert illusionism (i.e. to hint at or reflect a different world from that created on the screen), they must do so in terms of the Japanese system itself.

There is a tendency of film structuralism to isolate specific cinematic figures—the shot/reaction shot, for example—and attribute to them one particular function without considering the range of possible identities they may have for an audience. Terms like modernism and realism, therefore, are often solely derived from what Georges Poulet calls 'the exclusive interdependence of the objective elements' (*The Structuralist Controversy,* 'Criticism and the Experience of Interiority'). This objectification of form has often meant that the range of subjective responses one has in any one film are considered secondary. We know there are as many reasons for identifying with a film as there are people, and that every film offers a special case. Systematising special structures of identification, however, seems to lead to acute problems when we consider films from alien cultures.

Japanese films use forms of catharsis, as do most Western films, but in doing this they exhibit a causal structure quite different from Hollywood. They also employ a system of characterisation which produces strong protagonists but not as complete individuals; a lack of psychological depth is compensated for in the pathos of a character's actions. There is self-consciousness in Japanese art, and there are forms of self-reflexivity in literature and film. There is a precedent for the multi-view rather than perspective, and this too throws into question the idea of subjective identification.

All this is not to say that in the uniqueness of Japan we are able to see objective structures based on acceptance of a clear, unproblematic classical realism; but that the Japanese system itself exhibits analogous tensions to those of Hollywood realism when we try to affix a label to any element, whether the reaction shot or the long take. This essay only aspires to highlight a number of areas previously taken for granted.

Point of view, besides being a series of precise visual strategies, is also a product of a certain orientation towards subject matter. The most consistent themes which we find in nearly all Mizoguchi's surviving films (thirty-two out of an estimated eighty) are those associated with women. Before 1936 and the start of his successful collaboration with the screenwriter Yoshikata Yoda, Mizoguchi made a number of films based on stories by Izumi Kyoka. These stories, written as romantic treatments of troubled domesticity, seem to be the first major source for Mizoguchi's preoccupation with women. Izumi was extremely popular, and some of Mizoguchi's adaptations were no doubt true to the spirit of the author in being over-sentimental. But a few serious literary critics recognised Izumi's perception of a number of real certainties within male/female relationships as they were perceived just after 1900. The central one was the fact that Japanese women were continually called on to sacrifice themselves and their own needs for their lovers; according to Tadao Sato, these stories usually centred on the husband's career taking precedence over the wife. An equally common Izumi situation found an older woman involved with a student, usually as lover and patroness. This is the background of two of Mizoguchi's earliest surviving films, *White Threads of the Waterfall* (1933) and *The Downfall* (1935).

This theme of woman as sacrificial lamb expanded throughout Mizoguchi's career to attack misogyny in general. Because we must begin looking at his films of the 1930s without the luxury of seeing his earlier development, it appears that he very quickly broke with Izumi's romantic mould and entered into a mode of realism. In describing *Sisters of the Gion* (1936), Richie and

Anderson see that the film poses a question of choice for the Japanese audience: the film condemns both sisters for their actions, but is more sympathetic to the traditional older sister. That it at least presents two sides of an issue separates the film from earlier notions of the romantic.

It is less important to decide whether these early films or the later ones meet all the requisites for the realist label. There are enough indications that the setting up of a thematic duality in their subject matter tends to confirm the Japanese notion of a general style of realism. A series of issues are opposed to each other, and at least part of the resolution of a Mizoguchi film is left up to the audience. For point of view in general, this means that the narrator, the author of the film, will have an equalising influence on the perspectives of the characters. Rather than have characters function in opposition, in these films we find parallelism. This is a rhetorical device found obviously in other cultures, but in Mizoguchi's films the characters are so often identified with obverse aspects of a common series of themes that they almost appear as doubles.

We find some version of the parallel in almost all the films. The varied lives of prostitutes is a particularly clear picture of the parallel as microcosm in *Women of the Night* (1948) and *Street of Shame* (1956). The most frequent parallel involves two women embodying complementary or conflicting characteristics, or one showing a later stage towards which the other is headed. Fifteen films make obvious use of this device, from the good girl devotion versus bad girl status and money parallel of *Hometown* (1930), to the older/younger geisha conflict of *Gion Festival Music* (1953); the mother/daughter in *A Woman of Rumour* (1954), and the famous Miyagi/Wakasa, wife versus vampire, structure of *Ugetsu* (1953). Parallelism is not confined to women. There is the student versus non-student form in *Song of a Hometown* (1925); the rival tenors in *Hometown* and the clan rivalries in *The 47 Ronin* (1941 and 1942); Oharu's series of lovers in *The Life of Oharu* (1952), and the contrasting patrons of the women in *Street of Shame*. This type of parallelism does not set up polar opposites; and in these contrasts, the characters usually have more in common than they have differences.

Parallelism provides that there will be at least two central character points of view. These are ideal forms of identification. There is also an element of choice, which is of course gratuitous because the audience is given only very special information. We note that these general tendencies of Mizoguchi's films are perhaps no more than tendencies. These features—the use of two strong central characters, the two points of view and the elements of gratuitous choice—can be found in films from any number of cultures. It is only when they combine in a specific way and for a specific reason that they create a unique something which we call a film by Mizoguchi; therefore, in conjunction with the above characteristics, we find another figure, that of a detached observer. In virtually every film there are characters, some important and others merely peripheral, who see the action as it unfolds; and the audience sees these characters as they watch.

The function of these observing figures is naturally determined by the film itself. Often they are in the scene from the beginning, but equally camera movement reveals them after some particularly dramatic moment, or they walk before the camera at the exit of some more central character. This adds a possible third point of view to the action, and we can often draw an analogy between these people and the audience in relation to the screen. If the audience watches a series of actions, and simultaneously sees another character in frame observing the same activity, there is a tendency to believe the truth of the action. This is also the case when either by eyeline or physical proximity an observer is implied even though not actually visible on the screen. This is most important, because in Mizoguchi's films characters have only a limited number of choices for their action. Their behaviour is conventional, and in Japan especially that means there are very few possibilities.

As already stated, Mizoguchi's visual style is characterised by the infrequent use of the one-shot, shot/reaction shot in dialogue scenes. There is a preference for the two-shot, or shots in which all the protagonists appear together in frame. If one character is framed by himself, this is followed more often by a pan or track than by a cut; or if there is a cut, then it is followed by a pan or track to more dialogue involving the same or different characters. This procedure reinforces the objectifying function of the observer, and gives most action its communal character. Action appears as a shared experience when the audience is generally given an additional view which seems to match its own.

This objectivity is itself an illusion, the Bazinian ideal, but it is a specific formal arrangement distinct from the general classical realism of the West. Even directors like Wyler, who match the long take, deep-focus model, still regularly use close-ups and first person point of view shots. Mizoguchi uses these devices, but not as regular units of his 'most typical' style. His later films often look more Western in using tighter character framing, but they still rely on the pan and track instead of cutting during dialogue. They create an overriding third person perspective like that of Hollywood, but it is accomplished by a different technique. The objective illusion is taken to more of an extreme in Mizoguchi's films precisely because of the observer. Space is defined with few first person shots and with a moving camera combined in extreme cases either with no cutting in the scenes composed with one shot (more consistent in the 40s) or with one 180 degree cut (the technique dominant in the 30s). In most films, all sides of any room in which dialogue occurs are shown either quickly through cutting when one first sees the area or later after considerable action has taken place. Scenes of the first type occur during the opening dialogue between the policeman and the madam in *Street of Shame* (a series of cuts) and in the watermelon cutting scene in the kitchen during the 1939 *Story*

of the Late Chrysanthemums (one 180 degree cut). The latter definition of space is used with the sisters' home in *Sisters of the Gion* and the Western-style apartment in *Osaka Elegy* (1936). The observers who look on during these scenes or who are present in these rooms at other times testify to the concreteness of the setting and help to create an objectified illusion of continuity.

Seeing all sides of any spatial area raises the question of the camera position, and in Mizoguchi's films there is a continuous series of so-called 'impossible shots'. We see areas of walls or objects positioned in the same places where the camera must also be. Sometimes this is obvious, as in the kitchen scene from *Chrysanthemums* or the shot between two mirrors in *Sisters of the Gion*. Generally, however, the impossible shot occurs as in Western films when there is a high or low angle, and we accept the fact that a directorial presence is 'naturally' in evidence. These devices create continuity for cinematic fiction when they do not call attention to themselves; and because we accept convention, we rarely notice the impossibilities. It is not quite the same for Mizoguchi, because on the way towards continuity there are usually a number of temporary spatial uncertainties. In the young woman's apartment in *Osaka Elegy,* it takes repeated viewings to put the floor plan together because there are so many scenes which take place in smaller areas. (This apartment must be one of the oddest ever created, a Japanese art deco version perhaps of something Mizoguchi saw in a European film.) Mizoguchi uses a number of devices to create intermittent spatial ambiguity (offscreen space and sound being primary); but because these are always resolved, they seem to be more classical than modern.

There is a final aspect to the general consideration of point of view. This is the use of motifs organised around moments of ritualised observation. These moments include the many uses of the theatrical experience; references to particular spatial possibilities of the *kabuki* theatre; references to performances of various kinds, from the musical recital to the duel; and the uses of *seppuku* or ritual suicide. In all these, there is a clear distinction between performing and observation, and the event itself at the centre is socially defined. It has specific dramatic functions in its varied contexts, but it also reinforces the general impetus we find in Mizoguchi's films towards objectifying the action. The performance as socially defined is generally a time of repose, in which interaction between observer and performer is abstract but direct. The reality of the performance is absolutely objective in the sense that it happens for so many people; but during these moments, the subjectivity of the events becomes more important. These moments are therefore privileged, because they both heighten and subdue all the various points of view which converge in any one Mizoguchi film.

These motifs range from the uses of the world of the theatre itself in *The Straits of Love and Hate* (1937), *Late Chrysanthemums, White Threads of the Waterfall* and *The Love of the Actress Sumako* (1947), to the use of theatregoing to create a particularly dramatic climax in *A Woman of Rumour*. In *Osaka Elegy,* the public nature of attending the theatre provides a dramatic turn in which being seen is as important as seeing; and in *The 47 Ronin* (both parts) the *noh* performance creates historical authenticity and metaphoric intensity. Other moments in which observation is formalised include the final river parade in *Chrysanthemums* and the challenge sword fight in *Musashi Myamoto* (1944); the courtroom scenes in *White Threads* and *The Victory of Women* (1946); the election rally in *My Love Has Been Burning* (1949); the classroom scenes in *Song of a Hometown, The Poppy* (1935) and *The Lady from Musashino* (1951); and the musical performances in *Hometown, The Empress Yang Kwei-Fei* (1955), *Ugetsu* and *Miss Oyu* (1951). In these examples, the process of seeing and being seen produces certain individual thematic patterns and provides a number of moments when various points of view (not the least important being that of the audience) seem to merge into one.

The other prominent motif of ritualised observation is *seppuku,* and this is the most important because of its implications. This form of suicide was the favoured way of death for the samurai (second only to dying in battle) because it preserves the honour there is in paying for the death of one to whom one has been in debt, or in regaining the honour that one has lost. To accomplish *seppuku,* one follows a number of very precise steps, from assuming the proper position, to cutting open one's stomach with a particular blade, to the cutting off of the head by a second. The procedure is very slow, and it is perhaps one of the most painful ways one could die. *Seppuku* today is generally reserved for fanatics (like Yukio Mishima) and for history.

There are no graphic portrayals of the act of *seppuku* in Mizoguchi's films; nothing of the irony in a film like Kobayashi's *Harakiri*. Even though ritual suicide in its historical form appears only in *The 47 Ronin,* it has important consequences in the many other suicides in Mizoguchi's films. The common element is the observing figures. The second whose function it is to sever the head is also responsible for seeing that the suicide itself is carried out correctly. In part II of *The 47 Ronin,* Lord Hosokawa and his men are responsible for the ceremony, and they oversee each of the deaths of Oishi and his men. They are the seconds, the observers and the upholders of the shogun's law. In Part I, however, Lord Asano's suicide is supervised by another lord, and even though Asano's men take no legal responsibility for his original act of violence, they are denied the privilege of watching the ceremony.

The scene of Asano's walk to his death is one of the most striking in either part. The camera dollies back as a retainer walks with Asano, then cranes up as Asano enters the ceremonial yard. The retainer is left outside, and the high angle shot places Asano in the interior with the retainer separated from him by the courtyard wall. The shot is held as the retainer collapses and Asano disappears at the top of the frame. (The use of off-screen space at the top and bottom of the frame is a frequent Mizoguchi device.) In this scene, the denial of observation is paradoxically tragic and at the same time a form of self-preservation. The retainer knows it is his duty both to avenge his lord's death and to kill himself in return. He is denied the privilege of seeing Asano die, but he is also spared the resultant agony. Much like the ritual of communion, *seppuku* for the observer celebrates both a triumph over one's own immediate death (one's sins are relieved by the death of another), and one feels remorse over not having been able to spare the other's life in the first place. When the retainer is kept from being a direct observer, the pathos of his predicament is that much more intense.

There are other forms of suicide in Mizoguchi's films, and although most involve drowning, they also make use of observing figures. In *Portrait of Madame Yuki* (1950) and in *Sansho the Bailiff* (1954), women drown themselves in a lake; in the former the death is an act of weakness, while the latter is a show of strength. Madame Yuki's death shows Hama how false her illusions have been. Her final words to the dead woman are, 'You coward!' and it is fairly certain that Hama has finally come out from under the older woman's influence. In *Sansho,* the old woman says nothing after Anju sacrifices herself so that her brother can escape from Sansho's bondage. It is as much sorrow at the girl's fate as joy in her final release from the misery of slavery that the old woman must feel. In both instances there is a palpable sense of ambivalence towards death. This combination of antithetical attitudes is at the core of the *seppuku* tradition; and in both cases there is more than a little resemblance to the Freudian interpretation of the ritual of mourning.

These examples, ranging from parallel construction to the observer and then to forms of ritual, are general patterns which tend to provide in turn general contexts which determine point of view. Point of view itself, of course, has a dual nature: it includes both what characters see and how the narrator/author presents them and the action. There is a bridge, however, in Mizoguchi's films which narrows this potential distance. This is accomplished not by alternating first and third person shots, but by generally alternating (if there is any cutting at all) the third person view. Even with the implied continuity of scenes done in one shot, Mizoguchi still seeks to deny all potential discontinuity. This is a direct result of the use of recurrent motifs which involve seeing and observation.

When we discuss specific points of view, we find there are a number of shots which do correspond to a character's subjective viewpoint. In *The Downfall* (1935) and in *The Noted Sword* (1945), there are superimpositions which reflect character subjectivity, but these are not rendered through the eyes of the character in the form which shows us exactly what he or she sees. These scenes include both the characters and what they see within the same shot. Only in *The Life of Oharu* is there a precise subjective superimposition, when Oharu sees her former lover's face in place of a Buddhist statue. In a film like *Oyuki, the Virgin* (1935), there is crosscutting of first person shots in a dialogue, but they only occur once in a scene of particularly charged emotion. The same is true in *Yang Kwei-Fei,* but it is generally used only for effect. It is present in the coach scene in the opening flashback of *White Threads,* but the rest of the film eschews its use. There is another formal pattern, however, which seems problematic, and is the closest example which on the surface may suggest a modernist label. In *White Threads, The Downfall, Sisters of the Gion* and *Ugetsu,* there are specific shots which are first presented as subjective, first person character views, but which eventually include within the shot (by camera movement) the characters whose view we have ostensibly been given.

This apparent mixing of points of view defies the clarity and obviousness of Western realism because it blurs the distinction between first and third person perspectives. As we have said, the interplay between these viewpoints has been considered the privileged structural feature of the classical model. With this type of device, one shot includes both a third and a first person view. In realist films (as defined by structuralists), a first person shot can approximate a third person shot and vice versa; but one can not be graphically shown to be simultaneously both. There can be overlapping, but it must be accomplished by implication. We also often find in realism a cut from a first or third person point of view to a similar shot closer to the action. Even when we see that the relationship between characters is unchanged, we accept the cut as an element of a director's personal style, or as some formal way of intensifying the action. In either case, there is usually no contradiction posed in terms of the individual shot. The one-shot contradiction must, therefore, either be considered a mistake or one must search for its function in thematic or generic terms.

In considering specific structural arrangements in Mizoguchi's pre-war films, one must be specially careful because of the fact that others have re-edited some of these features, and 'complete' versions of some prints circulated in the West only remain in a single Japanese copy. (The suicide of the heroine in *White Threads* exists only in one print held in Kyoto.) There is the additional possibility that some sequences were put together rather arbitrarily, as the seemingly illogical editing of the long bridge scene in *White Threads*. Yoshikata Yoda's explanation for this scene is that its apparent monotony forced Mizoguchi to change camera positions as a concession to the viewer. Be that as it may, there is still in the early films a general consistency in creating unambiguous spatial relationships; and Yoda's explanation remains merely a warning to those over-zealous for great paradoxes. The opening sequence of *The Downfall* at the stormy railway station is meticulous in placing the major characters on the platform in an unambiguous relationship to each other. They are directly linked by camera movement and eyeline matching. The contradictory shot appears in the

first flashback sequence as does the same device in *White Threads,* and, therefore, the contrast is striking. There are other matching problems in *The Downfall*, however, and because of the film's age, it is difficult to find a function for these devices which is not in some sense still unclear.

In *White Threads,* the heroine in her flashback sees herself in the coach which is being driven by the young man who has subsequently become her lover. There is a medium shot of the woman, Taki, as she sits motionless inside the coach and gazes forward and down to screen left. There is a cut which because of her glance implies that the next shot will be her point of view. The shot is a tight medium shot of the driver as he bends over to fix the wheel. The camera tilts up and we see Taki in the background looking forward at him. The sequence in *The Downfall* is much the same. In the flashback the heroine, Osen, is shown in a tight medium shot at night in the yard of a shrine. She is looking for the hero, Sokichi, and she looks down and to screen left. She squats and her gaze is directed back into the frame and to the left. There is a cut to a close-up of Sokichi's sandals, and the camera tilts up to reveal Osen squatting in the background.

Because both these examples occur in flashback when subjectivity is crucial, there is some truth to the assertion that this contradictory device is a 'structural principle . . . of the fantastic genre' (Mark Nash, *Screen,* Vol. 17, No. 3). There is further evidence of this in its use in *Ugetsu;* but Nash concludes his study of Dreyer's *Vampyr* with the following: 'The fantastic text is not modernist in the sense of say Robbe-Grillet's *L'Immortelle* . . . but it is progressive in that in it the category of the real is at least under scrutiny.' In this context, reality refers to two things: the first is the expectation for classical continuity in which first and third person views are intercut but remain separate. The interruption of this convention by a director as conscious of form as Dreyer indicates some kind of explicit interpretation; structure will become a direct indicator of meaning. Secondly, reality is the knowledge of fantastic genres, either of other vampire movies or of extra-filmic elements such as the fantastic archetypes in literature or the science and folklore of vampires themselves. In the specific mode of the fantastic (as defined by Tzvetan Todorov), the reality of a central action cannot be determined by any one explanation; and therefore a formal point of view device which does not clearly indicate whose perspective is shown does produce an unresolvable dilemma. It is of course possible that when Mizoguchi includes these sequences within flashbacks, he is negating completely the point of view question. Still in *The Downfall* the lead-in shot to one flashback is from one character, and the return shot focuses on the other. There is an indication that this is therefore a shared flashback, and once again ambiguity enters. This is even intensified when action occurs in Sokichi's flashback which he could not have known.

It is ridiculous to call any of Mizoguchi's films discussed so far fantastic. To be more than arbitrary, the label must take note of a significant number of other features. Nash and others have no doubt isolated crucial patterns of editing and camera movement which have great influence over determining the relationship between style and content. The structuralist label for any element, however, does not mean that the feature cannot be found in other contexts and with additional functions. In Nash's analysis of *Vampyr,* the indeterminate viewpoint (or rather the confusion of a consistent view) near the opening of the film (in which an apparent point of view shot from Gray of the weathervane then reveals Gray in the shot) becomes primary only after it relates to other points of view later on. The fantastic label for the film is possible only after this connection. Likewise, the same problem in **The Downfall** and **White Threads** can only be put into perspective after it is given its proper place within the entire film. When these comparisons are made, we find ourselves not simply with an empirical method of analysis, but within the more speculative process of interpretation. A procedure is what it is only because it does what it does. Being conservative at this point, we can say that Mizoguchi was very conscious of the need for a consistent point of view, and he knew the means which were available to manipulate it.

When Nash brings in information outside the film itself to explain the film's formal arrangement, he is explaining how certain themes are worked out in terms of structure. The crucial point of view which is made ambiguous calls attention to itself as a theme. Since we know from fantastic literature that seeing is a central problem, the obfuscation of point of view fits well into showing how *Vampyr* works as a fantastic work. The fact that seeing is the key to the believability of the fantastic means that the act of representing what one sees, or what the director wishes the audience to see, becomes integral to the film and to the genre. It could be argued that the fantastic is the only genre (if that is what it is) which has the same general preoccupation as the larger question of modernism itself. This is one of the reasons Nash does not call *Vampyr* a modernist work. It is possible, therefore, that certain of Mizoguchi's films also make use of the themes of seeing but only for specific effect. This is indicated by the overall point of view structure we have already discussed in terms of the observer and ritualised observation.

One sequence in *Ugetsu* is a particularly clear example of Mizoguchi's control over point of view, and it illustrates the viability of considering this device as an economic means of creating significant themes. The film divides in half rather neatly with the first part dealing with the potter and his wife, Miyagi; the second shows his infatuation and subsequent terror in his confrontation with the ghost, Wakasa. The scene of a contradictory point of view occurs conveniently between the two halves. If we accept this division, we note that in all the scenes in each half between the potter, Genjuro, and both women, spatial continuity is maintained, and the reality of the women in each of their domains is created with conventional imagery. Miyagi is associated of course with the home, family

and security. Even the lake scene in the first part, while ghostly because of being dark and unpredictable, is still a metaphor of foreboding within the story. There is talk of spirits and supernatural danger, but there are no formal devices which key us to the fact that anything will occur which is perhaps beyond imagination. Lady Wakasa also appears at first without fanfare, and her non-human form is only hinted at by use of shadows and imagery associated with neglect and decay. The entire second half in fact can be explained as either pole which circumscribes the fantastic (either the 'marvellous' or the 'uncanny'), but there are no internal structural elements which undercut the fact that the actions could have happened if only in Genjuro's mind.

After the initial impersonal exchange at the market-place between Genjuro and Lady Wakasa, the potter ventures for the first time in search of the woman. Immediately preceding their reunion, and before the three (Genjuro, Wakasa and the old nurse) approach the family mansion, Genjuro stops at a kimono shop. In the first shot the camera is at the back of the shop, and Genjuro is seen in a long shot as he walks forward toward the camera and the proprietor, who is seated on screen left. The potter looks up and forward at the hanging kimono material, and the camera cuts 180 degrees to Genjuro's point of view. The camera pans from right to left, but we see neither the shop owner nor the material previously seen at the front of the store. There is a cut to a two-shot of the owner and Genjuro, the camera again at the back of the shop. Cut to a medium close-up of Genjuro, then to a medium shot of kimonos from his point of view; cut back to a one-shot of the potter; then as he looks forward at kimonos, harp music begins and there is another cut back to his p.o.v. [point of view]. From the left background enters Miyagi carrying a tray of pottery. She stops and looks at the material, puts down the tray, and walks forward to admire the kimonos. She glances at the camera, and then a dolly out reveals Genjuro in the shot as he stares at his wife with his back to the camera. As she recedes out of sight, there is a cut to a medium shot of Genjuro entranced; he shakes his head as if he cannot believe what he has seen. He hears a voice calling him; he looks off-screen right; cut to a full shot of Wakasa and the nurse.

The point of view contradiction of this scene (the potter brought into his own subjectivity) is marked off by several keys. We are led into it by the first subjective shot which does not include the proprietor, and by the harp music which seems to match Genjuro's evident reverie just before he sees Miyagi. His wife disappears from the frame as if she were only going to reappear any moment trying on another kimono. When there is a cut back to the last reaction shot of the potter, he blinks as if he also is not sure whether she will return or not. He hears a voice off-screen, and for a moment he is further confused. The potter looks screen right, and the cut to Wakasa and the nurse reinforces the 'realistic' associations attached to a reaction shot motivated by the preceding directional glance. The two figures that Genjuro sees are, therefore, more real in this sequence than Miyagi even though we know (or will realise shortly) that they are apparitions. By following this editing pattern, we see how subtly and carefully the points of view are creating a crisis within the potter's perception and at the same time within the viewer's.

This sequence is so carefully detailed that the dolly back to include Genjuro is merely one signpost in calling attention to the precarious nature of Genjuro's perception of his exploits. The point of view of the film, therefore, revolves around Genjuro. Lady Wakasa is never shown apart from him, and thus exists only for him. Miyagi on the other hand is shown in her death, and the entire Tobei/Ohama relationship is also shown apart from Genjuro (another parallel). In this way, the realness of the people in the potter's family (Tobei is Genjuro's brother) is affirmed over Wakasa's dependence for her existence on Genjuro being with her. In one scene the apparent reality of Wakasa is emphasised when we see her rise while Genjuro is still asleep. This is a third person viewpoint, and it makes Wakasa seem to exist apart from Genjuro's observation. Mizoguchi avoids in the second half of the film the direct trickery of the distorted first person shot; and therefore, when we hear that Wakasa is a ghost, we are somewhat less prepared for the shock. The mysterious mansion with its torn paper walls on the outside and its mended interior causes a sense of foreboding, but only the voice of the old patriarch really denotes the supernatural. Even the *noh* inspired architecture (the exterior-like stage with the surrounding pine trees) only reinforces the antique quality of the scenes in the mansion. It does not specifically challenge the reality of the episode.

There are actually no ways of explaining the contradictory point of view shot; it does combine a first person view with a third. There are, however, within the context of the film, many explanations for the sequence in terms of seeing and perception. *Ugetsu* was taken from two stories of the supernatural by Akinari Ueda, and we can quite legitimately talk of certain fantastic impulses within the work. In using the point of view device Mizoguchi is totally aware of what he is doing; but the film as a whole does not remain an enigma, nor is there a real crisis in its overall formal design.

The modernist notions we have been using would require that the entire film be recast in the mould of its enigma. The contradiction of *Ugetsu*, however, is reinforced only on a thematic level and not by further formal arrangements of the contradiction. It is used for an effect—to throw into obscurity the authenticity of Genjuro's view—but it does not force us to re-evaluate all Genjuro's relationships. His sojourn with Wakasa can even be considered a dream, but it does not negate either the fact of Miyagi or the entire enterprise of his life. The contradictory points of view occurring in one shot can indeed be the 'structural principle of the fantastic', but it is also a device which can be used in other contexts to undercut character believability. Because it subverts our expectations for absolute causality, it shares a modernist pale, but it is not inexorably modernistic.

The closeness between *Ugetsu* and fantastic stories is primarily due to Mizoguchi's handling of Ueda's original tales. While this genre is particularly close to the problems of seeing and memory, there are other examples in Mizoguchi's films where a similar form suggests analogous crises. One of the opening sequences of *The Portrait of Madame Yuki* is perhaps the most audacious use of the obfuscation of time and space within a quite conventional modern Japanese melodrama. The fact that *Madame Yuki* preceded *Ugetsu* shows also how Mizoguchi was perhaps working toward the perfection of the later film. Both share common elements, the largest being the disillusionment of both central characters, and the difficulty portrayed of reconciling past and present.

After her initial arrival at Madame Yuki's home in Atami, the young girl, Hama, is framed in a tight medium shot as she takes a bath. She gazes screen right, and the camera pans in this direction, taking her out of frame and settling on a close-up of water overflowing the side of the tub. (Water imagery abounds in Mizoguchi, particularly associated with sexuality in *Madame Yuki* and in *Ugetsu*.) Hama's voice-over begins recounting her earliest memories of what she has been told about Madame Yuki, and there is a cut to a panning shot from left to right. We see a Japanese room with curtains, an open *shoji*, a small table before the *tokanoma* (an inset portion of the traditional room where flower arrangements and calligraphy are displayed), and there is a lap dissolve to another panning shot in the same direction. This is another room with trees visible outside, and as the narration continues we see a woman's dressing area. The pan stops on a mirror in long shot with the words, 'that face', and a male voice interrupts saying that this is Yuki's room. There is a cut, and Hama and the boy Seitaro are shown seated in the room from which the pan has just come.

The voice-over in this sequence, which marks temporal continuity, is contradicted by having the narration interrupted and then showing Hama in a different place and with an obvious time lapse from when it began. Not only is this interval unaccounted for, but the two pans in Yuki's rooms are of unknown areas until we are later told what they are. The ambiguity is of course heightened by the contrast of Mizoguchi's maintaining the left to right movement originally motivated by Hama's look. He is playing on spatial and temporal conventions to posit a crisis in Hama's point of view. Through the rest of the action, Hama is the primary observer of Yuki's weaknesses and her desire for suicide; and Hama is continually confronted with the falsity of her first romantic ideals. This particular device, therefore, posits the contradiction in a way that is specifically thematic. Hama's voice-over describes what she has been told in the past, while the images we see can be either past, present or future.

These brief words of explanation do not explain away this device, and it remains an explicit contradiction in the structure of the film. It is there for a purpose, however, and like the potter's return home in *Ugetsu,* where the house is first empty and then Miyagi appears by a fire, it is here a type of trick for producing an effect. It has the immediate function of opening up the film for a variety of readings. It brings forward Hama's subjectivity to a prominent position, and intimates that her point of view will be central. As with *Ugetsu,* the contradictory device is modern, but it does not throw into question perception or reality. Hama comes to grips with her ruined expectations, and because she is so compassionate over Yuki's senseless suicide, she is a strong progressive character.

The last example of a contradictory point of view occurs in *Sisters of the Gion*. Near the beginning of the film, the bankrupt merchant, Furusawa, visits his mistress, the older sister, Umekichi. As she hustles him on his way to the bath, Omocha, the younger sister, watches the couple while brushing her teeth. There is a one-shot, medium shot of her looking toward screen right which is followed by a cut to Umekichi and Furusawa by the doorway. In this shot, the camera is placed where Omocha stands, and we are therefore in a position to see her point of view. As Furusawa leaves, the camera pans right with Umekichi as she re-enters the outer room and frames her as she meets Omocha there; the younger girl has changed positions unbeknownst to the viewer.

In this example and in *Madame Yuki,* the movement of the characters reveals a temporal ellipsis. The extreme continuity of the action in *Sisters,* however, seems to make this ambiguity almost nebulous. In *Madame Yuki,* as we have seen, it is an aural device primarily which is responsible for the contradiction. The device is not one which obscures the relationship between characters, but only the relation between the narrator and the characters. Because this occurs in Mizoguchi's films in a variety of contexts, it is not a device we can associate specifically with any one genre over another. It occurs in *Sisters* in the historical present, in *The Downfall* and *White Threads* in flashback, in *Madame Yuki* as a bridge between present and future and in *Ugetsu* as a moment of fantasy within what seems to be the present. There is thus a decided link between point of view and time; and this distinction is the most general mark of a narrator's imprint on any fictional work.

In Mizoguchi's use of the contradictory point of view, we can see illusion being undercut—the illusion of an absolute separation between narrator and character point of view. In the West, first and third person shots often overlap, but they do not as a rule appear openly contradictory. In Japan, however, the fictional narrator is built into most modern works by a process of self-effacement. This is only secondarily a result of modern convention and the illusionism of classical realism. Its centre expresses the closeness in Japan between the subject and object. Every allusion to the subject whether as subject of discourse or of the text or of speech is suspect because it asserts the independence of the self. The fact that in both Japan and the West there are forms of illusionism does not mean that they were created by the same means and for the same reasons. In Western realism, the nature of the con-

figuration, *post hoc ergo propter hoc* does as much to affirm the individual as it does to mask a guiding intelligence. The same is perhaps true in Japan, except that the Japanese have continually tried to break down this distinction between subject and object, self and other, while the West has attempted to conceal it. Neither enterprise has been successful, and the points at which both intersect are those filled with the most ambiguity.

What has seemed like an obvious incompatibility in these contradictory point of view structures seems actually in the Japanese context to suggest a negation of difference. These formal relationships are much like the simple first person shots which if held for a considerable time begin to appear like objective, third person views. In *The Life of Oharu,* fully three-quarters of the film occurs in flashback from Oharu's point of view; at the end of her recollection, however, the opening shots are repeated. Oharu's rendition of her past is thus objectified, and her perspective is made to correspond with the author's in a manner which is conspicuous. This circularity is true in a sense to the original (Saikaku's *The Life of an Amorous Woman*), in that it too is told by a narrator but through the woman's own words. Once he disappears, he never returns, and her comments merge with his in an implied agreement. We ultimately cannot tell who is telling the story, and this is also true of Mizoguchi's film.

It is true that the contradictory point of view occurs infrequently if we can only find five instances in thirty-two films. It is, therefore, quite narrow to suppose that in uncovering some common ground between the films in which the devices occur, we have 'explained' Mizoguchi. It is also true, however, that a film which blurs a consistent point of view can be modernist in one context and classical in another. This possibility is certainly a problem in Japanese literature, when the 20th century novel often has more in common with the *nouveau roman* than with Hemingway or George Eliot. Does this mean that Japanese writers have assimilated the 19th century novel to such an extent that they can reject it by creating new evolutionary forms? Or is there something within the Japanese understanding of the novel in general which allows them to create something new but based on their own theories of aesthetics? Is this modernism or neoclassicism?

In Japan it is most likely that critics will not notice these contradictions in Mizoguchi, or if they do, they are not very concerned with them. This does not mean that filmmakers themselves are unaware of them, or that the more modest, audience-pleasing directors will not carefully avoid contradictions and potential ambiguity. Still, there is some phenomenon in Japanese culture that makes both these observations true; and it seems important to understand what this is so that we can discuss point of view with some kind of authority.

Part of the solution lies in Mizoguchi's iconoclasm. It is reported how he argued with Shochiku that in the interest of realism he would be obliged actually to kill the actors in *The 47 Ronin*. His persuasion was in part responsible for his using a recent *kabuki* version of the story in which there were none of the usual expansive action sequences. Of course many of his films were among the most popular of their day, but a number were evidently hard for audiences to follow. He is now considered an 'art' director, and this means in Japan approximately what it does in the West.

The greater part of explaining Mizoguchi's use of contradiction is perhaps better seen as expressing the conciliatory function of the Japanese artist. Whether this is looked on as a reconciliation between nature and culture or some other such abstraction, it does denote a particular mediating function of artists in Japan. (The distinction between serious and popular is often meaningless for the creator of Japanese fiction.) Similarly, in most of Mizoguchi's films, there are characters who function as go-betweens within the stories. They either mediate between other characters or manipulate the action by themselves. This figure has a real counterpart in Japanese society (formalised in arranged marriages or informal industrial mediation) and it is a permanent fixture of consensus democracy. It is therefore possible to see Mizoguchi's presence as narrator marked into a few of his films by the contradictory device. He organises film continuity in a way which is similar to the manner in which his characters attempt to manipulate their realities.

This analogy is different from a non-Japanese equivalent because of the emphasis placed in Japan on formalism. This leads to further speculation that only by calling attention to form can art in Japan really be separated from life. If Mizoguchi did perceive point of view to be the essential construction of film, then his making it into a contradiction is a form of his self-consciousness. It makes his films more real than reality by seeming less autonomous and less illusory; however, the myth of no illusion can be just as binding as the myth of total illusion.

Audie Bock (essay date 1978)

SOURCE: "Kenji Mizoguchi," in *Film Directors,* Kodansha International Ltd., 1978, pp. 33-68.

[*In the following essay, Bock provides a biographical overview of Mizoguchi's work, focusing especially on the director's ambiguous political sympathies and their reflection in his work.*]

As evasive as he was redoubtable, Kenji Mizoguchi has left behind him not only some of the most pictorially exquisite films in the world, but lingering questions about the relationship between his personal life and ideals and these haunting masterpieces. One of the earliest Japanese filmmakers, with a directing career that began in 1923, at the time of his death in 1956 he had made 85 films of which only 30 are extant today. His works from 1952 on made him one of the first Japanese directors to be reckoned with internationally.

After *The Life of Oharu* won him the International Director's Prize at the 1952 Venice Film Festival, "Mizo" became an idol of the incipient French New Wave. Young critics such as Jacques Rivette adored Mizoguchi for his mastery of mise-en-scène, Jean-Luc Godard eulogized his elegance, metaphysics and instinct as a director, Philippe Sablon admired his scorn for logical exposition and the laws of drama and his preference for a more painterly or musical structure. These qualities in fact emerge in those post-1952 works of Mizoguchi that were winning prizes year after year at Venice— *Oharu* was followed by *Ugetsu* in 1953 and *Sansho the Bailiff* in 1954—and for the avant-gardist French his films constituted symbols of purity and personalism that rendered Mizoguchi a hero and the haplessly logical, more montage-oriented Kurosawa a villain (Godard unabashedly dismissed Kurosawa as "second-rate"). There were even suggestions by the influential André Bazin that Mizoguchi represented a more authentic Japaneseness, while Kurosawa was quite obviously influenced by the west, as was Mizoguchi.

The juxtaposition of Kurosawa and Mizoguchi in the *mise-en-scène* over montage battle cry of the New Wave undoubtedly had a political value in the imbroglios of developing a new aesthetic at the time. But the standoff is an artificial one when one considers Kurosawa's reverence for Mizoguchi and his avowed indebtedness to his methods. The most obvious influence Kurosawa has felt is Mizoguchi's unflinching realism in the application of the past to the present, the portrayal of personal drama in a broad and fully detailed historical milieu. Even today he muses on the model of directorial perfectionism and individualism that Mizoguchi, referred to by many who worked with him as the "demon," set for him to follow. It was, after all, Kurosawa who said, " . . . in the death of Mizoguchi, Japanese film lost its truest creator."

Kurosawa has also pointed out the fact that the realms handled best by Mizoguchi were those concerning the merchant class and women, subject matter glossed over by the New Wave French and one of the sources of Mizoguchi riddles. Fluid camera movement, superb long-shot, long-take photography and intricate use of sound and framing provide a veneer of aestheticism to an ambivalent attitude toward women and an enigmatic political stance toward oppression, poverty, and even the Japanese family. In following Mizoguchi's career one finds disturbing reversals of affiliation, a consistent love of novelty, and an attitude of mixed adulation, pity and fear toward women. The keys to some of these problems lie embedded in the vicissitudes of his personal life.

POVERTY, PAINTING, POETRY, FILM

Mizoguchi was born in Tokyo in 1898, middle child of a roofer-carpenter of rather distinguished lineage. His father was an erratic, alternately stubborn and kindly dreamer of the type portrayed as the heroine's father in Mizo's 1936 *Osaka Elegy*. His mother was the daughter of not very successful dealers in Chinese herbal medicine. The family was poor at the outset, but their situation became desperate when Kenji's father tried to make a killing in selling raincoats to the military during the 1904-05 Russo-Japanese War. By the time he had borrowed money, set up a factory and produced the coats, the brief war had ended and the family was forced to move. Since there was not enough food for the entire family, Kenji's older sister Suzu was given up for adoption at the age of 14. Her foster parents sold her a few years later to a geisha house, but she had the rare good fortune of finding a wealthy aristocratic patron who not only redeemed her and provided her with a house and income, but later married her when his wife died. Mizoguchi bitterly resented his father all his life for the treatment of the women in his family (his mother, whom he loved dearly, and who saw to the family's needs throughout his father's caprices, died when he was 17), yet he himself later became fully dependent on his sister without the slightest compunction.

Before completing elementary school Kenji was also sent away to live as an apprentice in cold northern Iwate Prefecture with relatives who owned a pharmacy. There he was able to finish his primary education, and in 1912 he returned to Tokyo hoping to attend middle school. There were an additional two or three adopted children to feed at home, and his father refused permission. Soon after, his father began to suffer from rheumatism, and it was Suzu who came not only to support the whole family but to get Kenji his first job. At 15 he became apprentice to a textile designer of *yukata,* light summer kimonos.

Evidently it was through this apprenticeship, and another immediately following it in the same work, that Mizoguchi began to develop a love of painting. A year later he entered the Aohashi Western Painting Research Institute run by Seiki Kuroda, the first importer of European oil painting techniques of the French plein-airist school. It is the aesthetics of these early days that marks the shimmering landscapes of Mizoguchi's latest films. Through the Aohashi Institute Mizoguchi not only came to relish taunting schoolgirls by showing his nude sketches to them, but also to appreciate western opera, operetta and dance revues, for which productions the institute did stage design. But he soon realized, as Akira Kurosawa would many years later, that he would not be able to make a living from painting.

Suzu again aided her brother in finding employment as an illustrator for a progressive newspaper in the southwestern port city of Kobe. After a very short abortive attempt of one day to go into porcelain design in Nagoya following another introduction by his sister he seemed to settle into newspaper work fairly happily. He made a relatively good salary for the time, and busied himself with publishing his own poems. He would later claim to be more interested in literature than in painting, and put his own poetry on a par with that of the illustrious Takuboku Ishikawa. The quality of his own work aside, a deep love of literature, both western and Japanese, marked his poor but leisurely life from his art school days. He felt a spe-

cial affinity for Kyoka Izumi, whose work would be the basis for his lost 1929 *Nihonbashi* and 1934 *Downfall of Osen,* set in neighborhoods where he lived, Hongo and Kanda, and he also devoured the poetic, brooding Soseki Natsume, the melodramatic Koyo Ozaki, and the lover of unadorned femininity, Kafu Nagai. These Japanese authors were supplemented with extensive reading of Tolstoy, Zola and Maupassant. Nevertheless, Mizoguchi soon tired of his work in Kobe, and after a year returned to Tokyo because of acute homesickness.

He moved in with his disconcerted sister and showed no signs of seeking employment. But he began to see a teacher of the *biwa,* Japanese lute, and became acquainted with one of the students, a movie actor from the Nikkatsu company. The impressionable and erratic 20-year-old Mizoguchi soon succumbed to the glamorous lure of the budding film industry, and after visits to the studio fancied that he too could become an actor. This never happened, but he did have his actor friend introduce him to the rising director Osamu Wakayama, and he was hired as an assistant director in 1922.

NOVELTY LOVER

By 1923 Mizoguchi became a full-fledged director because one of Nikkatsu's oldest directors walked out with the actors of female roles who struck the company in 1922. In a desperate flurry, the oldest major film studio in Japan, established in 1912, began to realize that to keep its audience it had not only to begin using actresses, but to move away from its standard Shimpa tragedy material—slow-moving melodramas portraying middle-class Meiji Period (1868-1912) life in opposition to the period dramas of the Kabuki stage. Apparently no one knew what Mizoguchi was up to, for his first film was a denunciation of economic class differences that was completely foreign to either film or stage at the time. Labeled as a "puro-ide" (proletarian ideology) piece, there was so little left of it when the censors finished that continuity had to be fabricated with *biwa* music.

This film, long since lost along with all but two that Mizoguchi made in his most prolific years before 1930, marks the debut of a director who appeared fully committed to the left as well as to new inspirations and new techniques. Although Mizo later had so many confrontations with police and censors that he became utterly paranoid about authority figures, his commitment to the left would prove shallow. But his commitment to new art would be borne out immediately and consistently throughout his career. Mizo overturned Shimpa apolitical conventions in his first film, and he also attacked—whether through inexperience or intention is not known—film conventions in the personage of the narrator. Neglecting the script that was always produced for the off-screen live narrator (*katsuben* or *benshi*), the 25-year-old Mizoguchi made flagrant use of intertitles, even for dialogue, and the narrators protested to the company.

Mizoguchi's enthusiasm for novelty was even more pronounced in his 1923 *Blood and Soul,* which made use of the exaggerated sets, makeup and shadows of German expressionist films such as *The Cabinet of Dr. Caligari,* which had been released in Japan in 1921. He was also using French and American sources for his stories at this time, launching an Arsene Lupin fad with *813* and the beginnings of his flair for atmospheric settings with *Foggy Harbor,* based on O'Neill's *Anna Christie.*

In 1923 the Great Kanto Earthquake devastated Tokyo and the surrounding areas. Mizoguchi rushed into the ruins with a camera crew and filmed all he saw. His documentary footage was sent to America, but he also used the event to produce a feature called *In the Ruins* before the whole contemporary drama staff of Nikkatsu's Mukojima studios was sent to Kyoto.

In Kyoto Mizoguchi entered his first slump—the fact that in 1953 he could remember few of the films he made in 1924 and 1925 may well be an indication of their poor quality. He spent his free time drinking and frequenting the Gion and Pontocho geisha districts. He had been rebuffed by a geisha in Tokyo and was leading a relatively celibate life until he fell in love with a Kyoto waitress and began living with her in 1925. This relationship lasted only two months before the woman came after him with a razor and slashed his back in a widely publicized jealousy scene. Years later when he first showed his scar to his screenwriter Yoshikata Yoda, he admonished, "Yoda, women are terrifying." The raging jealous woman would be part of the realism of Mizoguchi's later films, notably in the 1946 *Utamaro and His Five Women,* which Yoda wrote using Mizo as the real-life model for Utamaro. Mizoguchi forgave his mistress, however, and quit work to go to Tokyo and find her. They were reconciled, and he lived off her income as a maid in a Japanese inn until an acquaintance warned him he was wasting his life. He returned to Kyoto and pursued his filmmaking with a vitality that had been lacking prior to his encounter with the animal viciousness of a neglected woman. His lost film, the 1926 *Paper Doll's Whisper of Spring,* which was set in his native downtown Tokyo and showed the miserable life of the working poor, marks the moment of "my own direction beginning to be set." The mistress he left behind in Tokyo disappeared into prostitution.

From his first film Mizo had shown a sympathy for the poor that irked the censors. In 1929, however, he burst into the full-fledged leftist "tendency film" (*keiko eiga*) fad begun that year with *Metropolitan Symphony.* Before drastic censorship, this lost film, based on the work of several proletarian writers, contained scenes in which the benevolent rich make pigs of themselves in a slum area where they go to exhort and chastise the unemployed. Summoned by the police, a cowering Mizoguchi begged the company to look after his new wife, a former dance-hall girl, but he received only an order to show the poor as more cheerful: this he meekly set about doing. The "tendency" films decrying the living conditions of the poor, however, were squelched almost as soon as the

movement began, due to the rise of fascist militarism, and Mizoguchi's last in the genre, the lost 1931 *And Yet They Go* would bring him back to the subject matter that was so much a part of his life: the woman who runs away with a man who then deserts her, leaving her with no means of livelihood but prostitution.

By 1932 Mizoguchi had reluctantly become involved in making a piece of militarist propaganda, *The Dawn of Manchukuo and Mongolia.* Such works are a great disappointment to those who would like to see him as the champion of the left, but his so-called proletarian films themselves reveal a political ambiguity rather than a commitment. Questioned on why he went into the "tendency" genre he said it was simply because he was a full-blooded Tokyoite and therefore a lover of novelty, but there may also have been considerable influence from his own poverty-stricken past and his association with leftist writers and theater people in Kobe and Osaka. Mizoguchi's remarks were always flippant, bragging or whining, but no matter what his "tendency" motivation was, his forays into proletarianism laid the groundwork for a more fully developed, far more poignant social realism in his great mid-1930s works about oppressed women.

FEMINISM

Mizoguchi falls within the strong tradition of "feminists" in Japanese film, literature and drama. However, this English loan word has nuances in Japan that differ considerably from its western usage. Aside from its predictable meaning, "proponent of women's rights, equality or liberation," it has a second, more popular usage: "a man who is indulgent toward women; a worshiper of women." In the arts such men with a marked fascination with women are epitomized by one of Mizoguchi's favorite writers, Kafu Nagai (1879-1959), whose portrayals of the downtrodden women of the prostitutes' quarters are among the most famous in Japanese literature. However, these finely drawn portraits, in Mizoguchi's case as well as Kafu's, do not necessarily imply a political concern with the improvement of women's status in society. The fascination becomes an end in itself.

In this respect Mizoguchi's feminine portraits reveal inherent contradictions, as does the Japanese use of the word "feminist" and the director's attitude toward the women in his own life. His hatred for his father is hardly vindicated by his behavior toward Suzu, who continued to give him money until well after he had become a director at Nikkatsu. He neglected his Kyoto mistress, protected her from the police after she tried to murder him, quit work to look for her, lived off her when he found her and finally abandoned her to prostitution. He went through complex machinations to secure his wife, who was still married to someone else, and proceeded to neglect her. She in turn refused to cook for him at unusual hours, allowed him not a penny of his own salary, and was occasionally dragged around by the hair by Mizo during bursts of sadistic vengeance. When she went insane in 1941 due to "hereditary syphilis" in Mizoguchi's words, he had her institutionalized for the rest of her life. After the Pacific War, he took his wife's widowed sister and her two daughters into his home out of pity. He lived with his sister-in-law as a wife, but proposed marriage to his leading actress, Kinuyo Tanaka, around 1947. She refused him and from 1953 on would have nothing further to do with him because he tried to prevent her from directing her first film. In short, Mizo was "unusual in the extent to which he suffered at the hands of women. He hated women; he was contemptuous of women. On the other hand, when he fell in love, it was with the sincerity of a little boy." All of the admiration, exploitation, fear and pity concerning women shown in his life would find expression in his films.

In the mid-1930s Mizoguchi reached a peak of what has been dubbed social realism through his deepening portrayals of women on the screen. The two types of heroines he developed during this period would reappear in slightly varying incarnations throughout his films to the end of his life. His reason for selecting the social and psychological position of women as the prevailing theme of his work may be seen as a logical progression from the concerns of his late 1920s to the early 1930s "tendency" films, for "He had long thought that after Communism solved the class problem, what would remain would be the problem of male-female relationships." Nevertheless, the story content of his films shows not a positive call for active revolution on the part of women, but a bleak condemnation to the status quo. What his two types of heroine have in common is a singular pathos—the fate of the long-suffering ideal woman is as grim as that of the spiteful rebel. It has been suggested that Mizoguchi himself was too deeply implicated in the psycho-social system that ensured the oppression of women to be able to cast them as revolutionaries, and that his life work consisted rather of the "purification of a national resentment" regarding women's tragic role.

Mizoguchi's ideal woman is the one who can love. This love consists, however, of a selfless devotion to a man in the traditional Japanese sense. She becomes the spiritual guide, the moral and often financial support for a husband, lover, brother or son. The prototype of his self-sacrificing ideal is Taki, the heroine of the 1933 *Takino Shiraito, the Water Magician*. Her pride of self-realization consists of her ability to ensure her lover's worldly and moral success, and his financial and spiritual dependence on her is her proof of his love. She is driven to the point of stealing and inadvertent murder in order to keep her promise of financial provision for him, and the reward for her perseverance appears in her chance to see him dressed in his judicial robes, handing down the just verdict that condemns her. Her eyes shine with pride and admiration at the image of his achievement, and never does she for a moment blame him for the cruel judgment. We do not actually see her forgive him for doing what the law demands, but her devotion is compensated by the guilt that drives him to commit suicide.

Taki's relationship with her lover expresses a value system that remains very much a part of Japanese life. Not only is she the feminine ideal of the Meiji and Taisho periods (1868-1926), when speedily modernizing Japan subscribed to the democratic theory that anyone can get ahead by subordinating women's achievements to the worldly success of their men, but she represents the classic mother-son interaction in which the parent shows her suffering to induce guilt on the part of the child who is absolved only by achieving and fulfilling the mother's expectations. The fact that Taki and her lover resemble a mother-son relationship more than an egalitarian male-female love relationship in the western sense reveals the lingering cultural definition of love in Japan as dependence, entailing a man's expectations of continual indulgence, forgiveness and encouragement by a woman. In Mizoguchi's own life the model who most obviously corresponds to the image of Taki is his older sister Suzu, but a generous lacing of his uncomplaining mother may well be part of this saintly ideal.

The women who embody Mizoguchi's ideal often live in a time too far in the past to be role models for today, a quirk of which Mizoguchi seems to have been aware. He once said of himself that he portrayed "what should not be possible as if it should be possible," a statement that most aptly describes the virtues of his period heroines. Otoku, the devoted maid in his 1939 *Story of the Last Chrysanthemum,* is, like Taki, a Meiji Period woman. She loses all for the sake of her man's success on the Kabuki stage, sees him through years of hardship, and dies alone at the moment he fulfills her hopes for him. Mizoguchi felt that he was saying what he really wanted to say in this picture made when suppression of free speech was already the rule. His wartime goal would be the celebration of the Japanese virtues of self-sacrifice and dedication, expressed not only in the revenge and suicide of *The Loyal 47 Ronin,* but also in his four-film cycle on performing artists beginning with *The Story of the Last Chrysanthemum*.

Mizoguchi's ideal postwar women show the same self-sacrificing characteristics, but they move yet farther into the past while developing a spiritual power to transcend their physical suffering. Oharu, the court lady in *The Life of Oharu* who declines into prostitution because she once allows herself to love a man beneath her station, moves out of our view, not living comfortably in a temple and prattling glibly to a couple of curious young men as in Saikaku's original late seventeenth-century story, but alone and homeless, reciting sutras from door to door with a begging bowl. The seriousness of Mizoguchi's treatment of Oharu's ever intensifying social decline, poverty and humiliation leaves no doubt in the spectator's mind that her final rejection of worldly concerns is total and sincere. Behind the flippant amorality of Saikaku's fiction, Mizoguchi read his own deep resignation. Oharu blames no one for her fate; she prays for all humanity.

Miyagi, the murdered wife in *Ugetsu* (1953), lives on despite death in her sixteenth-century setting. When her deluded husband has returned to fulfill her ideal, her voice encourages him, her spirit turns his potter's wheel. Anju, the devoted sister in the eleventh-century world of *Sansho the Bailiff* (1954), commits suicide to help her brother escape from their slave compound. Their aristocratic mother, after years of forced labor as a prostitute, crippled and blind, rejoices at reunion with her son, whose return to humanitarian values was brought about by a supernatural summons from her spirit. But the most remote feminine ideal is Mizoguchi's last and most maudlin, *Princess Yang Kwei Fei* (1955). The eighth-century Chinese scullery maid turned imperial concubine molds herself into the distracted ruler's image of perfection, and then walks calmly to her death to save his life. The voice of her dead spirit remains to reassure the broken, powerless emperor of a love that transcends death.

In all of these paragon portayals, the vision of society remains the same. The dramatic form is tragic, and spiritual success brings death and worldly defeat. Even in the 1954 *Story from Chikamatsu,* where love is the only goal, the lovers must die for their adultery according to the feudal code. The society of every age is pictured as vicious, greedy, unfeeling. Worldly ambitions, though often encouraged by women for their men, bring spiritual loss if they are fulfilled. All ideals are envisioned in societies where the basic problems of economic class structure, abusive power and avarice have not been solved.

The other side of the paragon is the rebel. She is often a prostitute or geisha or similar social outcast, and most often a contemporary woman. She resents the abuses of fathers, employers, and men who buy her and leave her, and attempts to lash back. But her solitary, proud, spiteful opposition does nothing to change the system, and in fact she usually subscribes to its corrupt values, using seduction, deceit and financial exploitation as her methods for revenge. She has nothing spiritual with which to replace the consuming love relationship, and in rejecting it she condemns herself to a life of self-seeking bitterness. She often appears with a meek woman counterpart who underscores the unviability of either stance in the modern world.

Ayako, the innocent switchboard operator of the 1936 *Osaka Elegy,* seeks the financial help of her poor boyfriend. Rejected, she turns to exploiting the system that exploits her. By letting herself be set up as a mistress she attains financial security, but loses love, and in the end is cast out onto the street by her apprehended patron, her horrified boyfriend, and her ashamed family.

Omocha (literally "toy"), the modern geisha in *Sisters of the Gion* (1936), resents the way men treat women as objects and mocks her older sister's devotion to a bankrupt former patron. Setting out to beat men at their own game, she deceives and ruins a sincere young store clerk and has his employer provide her with what she wants: money, pretty clothes and fancy restaurant meals. But as surely as her sister's old patron returns to his wife and a new business opportunity, the clerk takes revenge on Omocha, and she ends up in a hospital bed decrying the institution of geisha while her abandoned sister sits sobbing at her side.

Women like Omocha and her sister reappear in Mizoguchi's postwar films about prostitutes and geisha from the 1946 *Utamaro and His Five Women* to the 1948 *Women of the Night,* the 1953 *Gion Festival Music* and his last work, the 1956 *Street of Shame.* In this last film, Yasumi, the callous young woman who steals men from and lends money at usurious rates to her fellow-prostitutes, is as spiritually defeated in her economic success as Hanae, the middle-aged woman who sells her body to provide for her family, is admirable in her honest, devoted poverty.

In Mizoguchi's life these vivacious, volatile, condemned women were the geisha and prostitutes of Kyoto's Pontocho and Gion, Tokyo's Tamanoi and Ueno, of Osaka and every other city in which he dallied. They were also his razor-wielding mistress and the wife who went insane. These and the enduring spirit mother-sister ideals were what he knew best, and his lack of understanding for any other type of woman is best shown in his own work. The accusation that he did not really grasp the new postwar humanism proves itself in the similarity of the prostitute's dismal fate in the 1948 *Women of the Night* to that in his 1931 *And Yet They Go.* His attempts to portray feminist movement heroines like Sumako Matsui (*The Love of Sumako the Actress,* 1947) and Hideko Kageyama (*My Love Burns,* 1949) show them as confident and good only as long as they have a man to whom they can devote themselves. They end by discovering they are "only women." Perhaps the most ironic of his portraits of successful women is the severe, pedantic, lonely heroine of the 1946 *Victory of Women* who shows precious little that is attractive in her encouragement of others to follow her lead.

Yet there is one heroine who retains both love and moral courage in life. Fumi, the country stage entertainer of the recently rediscovered 1937 *Straits of Love and Hate,* survives male abuse, poverty and the temptation to sell out. When the wealthy student who abandoned her with a child asks her to come back to him years later, she decides to stay with her stage partner, the man who has been her moral support through the years. She grabs the baby away from his indolent, proud father and the grandfather who has accused her of avarice in returning, realizing that the advantages her son would receive in their rich home are not worth the humiliation she would have to endure. The last shot shows her back on the stage doing comic skits with the partner who had stepped back to let her do what was best for her, and we are assured that her son will grow up poor but with people who love him and each other. One cannot help but wonder if, had the war not intervened—by the following year Mizoguchi was already making propaganda films—the director might not have developed this more positive view of love and high ethical standards into a truly modern feminism.

THE "DEMON" AT WORK

During the course of his long career Mizoguchi formulated a style peculiarly his own and an authoritarian perfectionism that both terrorized and rewarded his staff. He bounced from company to company and back and forth between Tokyo and Kyoto looking for total artistic control. When a company forced him to make something he hated, such as the 1938 military propaganda film *Song of the Camp,* he would leave. When he had a project he wanted to do, such as *The Life of Oharu,* which was planned in 1949, and the company would not accept it, he would leave. In this way he worked with seven different production companies in his lifetime, often following the relocation of his friends, producer Masaichi Nagata, who became president of the Daiei company, for which Mizo made most of his late films, and Matsutaro Kawaguchi, an elementary school friend who over the years would provide scripts, original stories and a place to work when he became a studio head.

A crucial aspect of Mizoguchi's creativity was his close relationship with scriptwriters, notably Yoshikata Yoda, who was responsible for virtually all of his extant masterpieces from the 1936 *Osaka Elegy* on. Together they would forge out the eloquently literary scripts that drew on such a wide variety of sources. It was Yoda who at the beginning of his career wanted to do Maupassant, Molière, and above all Junichiro Tanizaki, his favorite author (he would do Tanizaki in the 1951 *Miss Oyu,* and though Mizoguchi had already done Maupassant in the 1935 *Oyuki the Madonna,* a Maupassant story would figure into the ideas for Yoda's *Ugetsu* script in 1953). It was Mizoguchi who forced him to read Kafu Nagai and Saikaku, the ribald portraitist of the feudal period merchant class and demimonde. Yoda has written with deep affection, close to adoration, of the blustering tyrant who trained him, and the character that emerges is both a petulant child and a visionary genius. "He never told me anything concrete about the scenario. He simply said, 'This is no good.'" Mizoguchi would rant, rave, insult and reject until he got what he wanted from Yoda, which was a synesthetic essence of humanity: " . . . you must put the odor of the human body into images . . . describe for me the implacable, the egoistic, the sensual, the cruel . . . there are nothing but disgusting people in this world." Yoda's first script for *Osaka Elegy* was returned to him more than ten times for revision, but when the film was completed he felt elation and appreciation for Mizo's strictness. Later in his career the director would take to writing out his criticisms of the script in letters, leaving an enlightening record of a visual perfectionist who constantly guided Yoda's dialogue away from banality, sentimentality and commentary on the action and toward a language of poetry, drama and, above all, emotion. Yet Mizoguchi's perfectionism regarding dialogue characterization, a perfectionism that carried over into art direction, acting and cinematography, created problems with the very emotion it sought to create.

Mizoguchi's famous "one-scene, one-shot" technique was facilitated largely through his demand for completely detailed sets. He began employing the long take as early as 1930 in the lost *Mistress of a Foreigner,* supposedly influenced by King Vidor's 1929 *Hallelujah!* and the theories of his friend psychologist Kojiro Naito, but the mark of Joseph von Sternberg's moving camera technique is unmistakable in films such as the 1937 *Straits of Love and Hate,* which plagiarizes the hero's entry into the smoky, crowded bar in the 1928 *Docks of New York.* In 1936 a reverent Mizo dragged a grumbling Sternberg to see one of his own films in Kyoto, only to have him disown it because of the poor condition of the print. The long-take style became fully established as Mizoguchi's own, however, through his association with art director Hiroshi Mizutani who worked with him for 20 years beginning from the lost 1933 *Gion Festival.* From 1939, with *The Story of the Last Chrysanthemum,* Mizutani did not only the detailed, massive sets for Mizoguchi's films, but also the costumes, for he found the courage to tell the director that his interpretation of Meji period clothing was inaccurate. Through his art directors and other period specialists summoned to consult on his films, Mizoguchi developed the overwhelming atmosphere of his films. His passion for "exact size replica," which became an important element of his films beginning with the 1941-42 *The Loyal 47 Ronin,* assumed an intensity that nearly dwarfs the human dramas taking place in these marvelous environmental constructions.

As with his scripts, never once, according to Mizutani, did the director give a specific order for his sets, but relied totally on his art director to create a full atmosphere appropriate to the delivery of the actors' lines. His method was to demand the complete performance of a particular scene, and in order not to interrupt the emotional continuity, he would follow the actors relentlessly with the camera. While he never gave instructions to actors either—a method Kurosawa later claimed is the only way to train them properly—he would demand acting that "broke the barriers of the frame. Cutting and composing the frame were the staff's responsibilities, and a drama played with attention paid to the width of the frame was 'no good.'" This centrifugal force applied to the edges of the frame would be a rallying cry of the New Wave French, and Mizo's long-take, moving camera one of the models for development of their hand-held camera techniques.

One of the finest examples of Mizoguchi's dramatic continuity in the long take appears in the otherwise uninspiring 1951 *Miss Oyu,* for which Mizutani designed the sets. It is a 5-minute-45-second take showing the highest emotional moment of the story: the young wife is accusing her husband of having married her solely to be near her more attractive older sister. The actors move through three rooms and seven different positions, away from each other and back together again three times, rising and sitting, as the wife finally breaks into sobs and falls prostrate to the floor while her husband stands helplessly by with his back to the camera. The scene illustrates not only his weakness, but a point Mizutani has made about all of Mizoguchi's highly emotional moments: "On the set the staff were often moved to tears, but when the scene became a filmed image no one could cry." The effect of Mizoguchi's insistence on the long or medium shot, long-take method is to endistance the viewer from deep emotional involvement in the action. Kurosawa has said that Mizoguchi's camera movement serves to "animate a static composition that could become monotonous . . . the actors are fixed and the camera moves for them." By the standards of fast action in Kurosawa's films, Mizoguchi's are by comparison indeed slow, but certainly not static. They move at the pace of the merchant class rather than samurai life, and the camera moves to incorporate all of the details in the surroundings of that life, the atmosphere itself, contemporary or historical, assuming its own effect on the drama and the spectator. In explaining why he rejected closeups, Mizoguchi said, "It is enough that there be a lyrical ambience in the whole of the film," and this is what his technique achieves.

UGETSU

The inspiration for the 1953 film that best expresses Mizoguchi's elegant lyricism was, as with the majority of his works, literary. Two stories from Akinari Ueda's 1776 collection of the supernatural, *Ugetsu Monogatari* (*Tales of the Rainy Moon*), and a Maupassant character study, *La Décoration* (*How He Got the Legion of Honor*), form the basis of a film that becomes completely Mizoguchi's own. The spirit of Maupassant emerges not only in the story of Tobei (Eitaro Ozawa), the farmer who so aspires to the glories of samurai status that he neglects his wife, but in the vanity and greed of the main character, Genjuro the potter (Masayuki Mori). Mizoguchi's own recurrent themes appear in the fate of the two men's wives, Miyagi (Kinuyo Tanaka), who is murdered and becomes the spiritual guide of the reawakened Genjuro at the end, and the abandoned Ohama (Mitsuko Miura), who sinks to surviving by prostitution after being raped while searching for her husband. Throughout the film, a fidelity to the eeriness of Akinari resides in the tension between illusion and reality, while a transcendent environmental lyricism informs *Ugetsu* with a value beyond the pathos of human drama.

As in many of Mizoguchi's late films, including *Sansho the Bailiff, Princess Yang Kwei Fei, The Woman of the Rumor* and *A Story from Chikamatsu, Ugetsu* takes a circular form, beginning and ending with a landscape that places all of the human events and emotions of the narrative in the subsuming context of nature. The camera travels from fields and woods to alight on the dwelling where Genjuro and his family are busying themselves with making pottery, and the narrative begins. Closing the film, the camera moves away from the little boy offering rice at Miyagi's grave near the same dwelling to rise again to the woods and fields, where a farmer can be seen at work in the distance. Like a classic Chinese ink painting with a tiny human figure dwarfed by towering mountains, the endings of these violent dramas restore a sense of proportion to human affairs: people are barely significant entities that live, work, love, suffer and die within the greater immutable order. These enclosing moments of Zen-like space remove the viewer from the exhausting human passions and remind him of his role as spectator at a performance and as contemplator of life.

The presentation of the supernatural enhances the transcendental quality of the opening and closing shots. Mizoguchi's original impulse to do the film with surrealistic decor "à la Dali" was never realized, and instead he and Yoda brought the supernatural into the narrative structure, using devices that resemble the classical Japanese Noh drama. The mist-enshrouded trip by boat across Lake Biwa, during which the protagonists encounter a dying boatman, was invented by Mizoguchi with a view to preparing the mysterious atmosphere that would dominate the whole central dream interlude of Genjuro's love affair with the phantom Lady Wakasa (Machiko Kyo). As in the structure of Noh, the entry into the supernatural is a journey, corresponding to the *jo* (introduction) section of a play. The central emotional event of the Noh, *ha* (destruction), is the protagonist's recollection or dream presented in stylized form, corresponding to Genjuro's entire experience with Wakasa, and her danced expression of her own feelings. In Noh the protagonist finally reveals his true identity, often as a ghost or demon, in the most dramatic *kyu* (fast) movement of the play. In *Ugetsu* Wakasa is gradually exposed as a vengeful ghost in the dangerous love affair, and Miyagi also proves to have only a spiritual presence at the end of the film. Together with these structural devices, however, lighting and camerawork lend a haunting air to *Ugetsu*.

The dream setting of Wakasa's mansion appears first as an isolated, dilapidated residence of the type sheltering neglected beauties in *The Tale of Genji*, the entrance choked by weeds and shrubbery, the walls cracked and crumbling. Genjuro sits waiting for the Lady to emerge from the inner depths of the house, and as a servant lights the oil lamps, the walls are transformed into well-kept opulence; the potter falls deeper under the unearthly spell. He drinks and converses with the lovely Wakasa, who flatters him for his humble pottery and completes his final enthrallment. When she sings and dances her love for Genjuro, coquettish looks embellishing her stately Noh-like movements, the voice of her dead father joins in with a muffled, rumbling recitation that seems to emanate from the warrior's helmet displayed in the room. We the audience by now accept these manifestations of the supernatural along with the spellbound potter because they are so subtle—no superimposed transparent phantoms, no dissolves and fades, no Dali-influenced decor calls attention to the otherworldliness of Genjuro's experience. All is kept in a supreme tension through affective lighting, sourceless sound and realistic sets combined with the corporeality of the forms of Wakasa and her nurse. Even when Genjuro has had a Sanskrit incantation inscribed on his back by a Buddhist priest to thwart the demon's powers, it is only through gradual, shot-by-shot alterations in

Kyo's makeup that her demonic nature is revealed. Then rather than make her disappear through photographic tricks, Mizoguchi moves the camera away from her, following Genjuro's frenzied sword slashing from behind as she and her maid retreat into the darkness of the mansion's interior and he falls exhausted into the garden.

An equally delicate cinematic assertion of the supernatural within the real carries though the remainder of the film and Genjuro's return to his country home. The camera follows him through the dark house, passing the cold hearth as he leaves the house through the back door. The camera pans back to the right along the interior wall, following the sound of his voice as he calls for Miyagi outside, and as the hearth comes into view a second time in the same shot, it burns brightly. Miyagi, whom the audience knows to be dead, sits cooking supper and welcomes Genjuro as he reappears at the front door. Everything in the scene looks perfectly real, but since we have seen it empty and dark and then fully inhabited within a single take of a few seconds, the effect is one of tremendous shock, much greater shock than if the transformation had been effected through a montage.

Characteristically for late Mizoguchi, the abandoned wife forgives immediately, refusing even to listen to apologies and excuses, in a departure from the original, where she demands to know all and then states, " . . . you should know that a woman could die of yearning, and a man can never know her agony." Miyagi's supernatural, forgiving presence remains even after her dawn disappearance in a further departure from the original story. In the last scenes Genjuro resumes his work at the wheel, and when Miyagi's voice assures him "Now at last you have become the man I wanted you to be," she speaks as the completely fulfilled woman. In a setup recalling one of the earliest shots in the film, Genjuro sits in profile at his wheel fashioning a pot; to the right is the pump that Miyagi had operated to drive the wheel; it stands still but the wheel spins. The fusion of the real and the supernatural culminates in this final scene, and we accept the life-in-death of Miyagi that exists in Genjuro's mind because of a cinematic presentation that is at once startling and unobtrusive.

Mizoguchi's sought-after lyrical ambience permeates the whole film through the treatment of the human drama in environmental long shot, but it assumes its greatest strength when it moves away from the human beings altogether. This occurs not only in the opening and closing coda of the film, but in the midst of Genjuro's delusion. The camera travels through the woods to fix on a medium long shot of Genjuro and Wakasa cavorting at a sumptuous outdoor hotspring bath. Wakasa coyly teases the enraptured Genjuro, and as she makes a movement to disrobe and join him in the water, the camera moves off again through the woods. As it travels it turns downward to the barren ripples of the ground, a dissolve occurs, the ground shifts slightly, and the camera momentarily edges past the circular grooves of a raked gravel Zen garden, rises, and shows the couple disporting themselves in a distant picnic on a lawn. Not only has time passed through the dissolve (in the original story Genjuro fails to return to his native village for seven years), but the viewer has passed through an unpeopled space that brings to mind emptiness and the transiency of human life. This moment of emptiness is of the sort that would be more frequently exploited by Mizoguchi's younger contemporary and friend, Yasujiro Ozu, but it is used for the same effect. Opposing Ozu's montage details of, for example, the famous stone and gravel Ryoanji Zen garden in the 1949 *Late Spring,* Mizoguchi skims his camera over the Zen symbol as part of the larger landscape of which the characters in the story are unaware. It is the spectator alone who feels the silent, transcendental reality between and beyond the drama of mortals on the screen, and *Ugetsu* becomes one of Mizoguchi's most profound statements on the delusions of ambition, vanity, eroticism and the achievement of even so simple a goal as domestic tranquility. (In the original script, the would-be samurai Tobei never returns to his wife, but the production company would not allow such a bleak ending.) *Ugetsu* is the "chronicle of a dream disappointed, of a hope deceived," and the suggestion of the beyond in the lyricism of nature surrounding the tragic mortals in a small aesthetic redemption from their fate.

INTERNATIONAL MIZO

By the time Mizoguchi, Yoshikata Yoda and Kinuyo Tanaka were taking *Ugetsu* to the Venice Film Festival in 1953, the director's life had passed through astounding metamorphoses of faith. The man who made leftist tendency films in 1931 and lost his younger brother in 1938 to the militarists' suppression of Communism became a member of the Cabinet Film Committee in 1940 and published statements on the role of film in promoting the nationalistic spirit. The man who traveled to China in 1943 for the purpose of making an army propaganda film, who attempted to carry a sword and demanded to be treated as a general, in the same year the war ended became head of the Shochiku studio's first labor union which he inaugurated with the opening speech, "From now on I will give the orders. I expect you to be prepared to receive them." By 1946 he was devising arguments to persuade the U.S. Occupation authorities to let him make a period film, which was forbidden as a glorification of feudal values. He was successful; his film portrayed the late eighteenth-century woodblock printmaker Utamaro as an artist of the people, a libertarian democrat who despised the samurai class and the police oppressors. The author of the original story was outraged at Mizoguchi's betrayal of the purely erotic, libertine spirit in his work's faithfulness to Utamaro's time.

An analysis of Mizoguchi's political behavior shows simply that he never understood politics. He used his various positions of political authority to make the films he wanted to make, and if blame is to be cast, it must fall upon those who were foolish enough to grant authority to a political innocent. His direction was set well before the war and never changed: he wanted to make "real" period films true to the spirit of particular eras, as he said in a speech offending many in 1949, and he wanted to make films about women, especially prostitutes. He succeeded in doing both in the postwar era, but not without opposition. When the period film he had fought to make about the Saikaku court lady who declines into prostitution at last won him the Director's Prize at Venice in 1952, after placing only ninth in the Best Ten at home, Mizoguchi's reaction was spiteful: "It seems that the Japanese do not understand movies." His success at Venice would give him new energy and inspiration in his last years.

Though his political views may have lacked sophistication and commitment, Mizoguchi's late films are suffused with a view of life that transcends politics. Even his ambivalent view of women and their oppression becomes acceptable because all is cast in an aestheticism bespeaking the ephemeral quality of human suffering. The heroines of Mizoguchi's films of the 1950s all rush headlong into destruction or death, but the beauty of his presentation of their tragedies takes the viewer beyond, to the Zen garden of *Ugetsu,* to the voice of the guardian spirit of *Princess Yang Kwei Fei,* to the quiet ripples in the lake where Anju has drowned herself in *Sansho the Bailiff,* to the smiles on the lovers' faces as they ride to their crucifixion in *A Story from Chikamatsu*. In 1953 Mizoguchi took a votive image of the thirteenth-century Buddhist saint Nichiren with him to Venice. He prayed to win, swearing he could not return to Japan unless he did. He had become, in his own inimitable capricious fashion, a follower of the Nichiren sect, as his detested father had done after the trauma of the 1923 Great Kanto Earthquake. Mizo's discovery of the Japanese faith that would give him personal solace coincided with his portrayal of his first transcending woman, Oharu, who unsuccessfully seeks refuge from men and the bitter world in a Buddhist nunnery, and in the end becomes a solitary, sutra-chanting itinerant nun. It coincided also with his debut as an international director, for his late, pictorially exquisite, contemplative tragedies were those that made him the New Wave darling. It also may well have coincided with the onset of the leukemia that would take his life in the midst of rewriting the script for his first postwar comedy, *Osaka Monogatari,* in 1956. In 1954 with *A Story from Chikamatsu*, Mizoguchi ceased to be a demon of perfectionism; the picture was finished in 28 days. A lover of novelty, worshiper and hater of women, inventor of authentic period films and fully played emotion in a distanced, lyrical long take, whimsical in politics and love, Mizoguchi died a devout Buddhist.

Keiko I. McDonald (essay date 1983)

SOURCE: "Atmosphere and Thematic Conflict in Mizoguchi's 'Ugetsu,'" in *Cinema East: A Critical Study of Major Japanese Films,* Fairleigh Dickinson University Press, 1983, pp. 103-22.

[*In the following essay, McDonald analyzes Mizoguchi's use of varying points of view in* Ugetsu *to capture the conflicting emotions brought on by civil war.*]

It has been said that the strength of Japanese film lies in its creation of mood or atmosphere by presenting characters in their setting. Kenji Mizoguchi's major films exemplify this feature of Japanese cinema. Early examples in Mizoguchi's films include the final, nocturnal scene of the bridge from *Osaka Elegy* [*Naniwa Ereji,* 1936], the frequent takes of the small alley from *Sisters of the Gion* [*Gion no Shimai,* 1936], and the moon-viewing festival scene from *Miss Oyu* [*Oyusama,* 1951]. *Ugetsu* [*Ugetsu Monogatari,* 1953], the 1953 Venice Festival Silver Lion Prize winner, is, however, the best example of his assiduous evocation of mood. In this film Mizoguchi knows exactly how to put atmosphere to work at both thematic and stylistic levels.

The central theme of *Ugetsu* evolves around the question: "How should one come to terms with life in the midst of civil war?" This is clearly indicated in Mizoguchi's letter to Yoshikata Yoda, the screenwriter of *Ugetsu:*

> Whether war originated in the ruler's personal motive or public concern, how violence disguised as war oppresses and torments the populace both physically and spiritually! However, they have to keep living in direct confrontation with this violence. I want to emphasize this as the main theme of the film. . . .

This theme is of highly realistic, political concern, and it entails two conflicting ways of confronting the war. Through the creation of mood, Mizoguchi makes sure that we see the thematic conflict at different levels of perception. He invests the harsh reality of war with mood. Through his control of the camera, mood incites or invites us to absorb ourselves right in it and feel it. Especially when mood reflects the inner reality of the individual character, it helps us to feel his predicament as our own felt experience. In other words, mood provides variation in our rhetorical stance. In *Ugetsu* we must basically remain detached observers of the opposing choices of action in adapting to the civil war, because our perspective on the individual character's action is much wider than his own. However, mood leads us to vacillate between detachment and empathy.

Furthermore, the film treats a dual reality grounded in the supernatural and the natural; the supernatural represented by the world of ghosts, and the natural most tangibly represented by a world at war. The epigraph on the screen at the onset of the film illustrates this: "Strange incidents and supernatural existence in *Tales of Moonlight and Rain* (*Ugetsu Monogatari*) evoke in a contemporary man's mind various fantasies. This film was made in order to visualize those fantasies."

The fusion of the supernatural aura or atmosphere with realistic setting becomes increasingly dominant in the second part of the film, which focuses on Genjuro's infatuation with the ghost, Princess Wakasa. Here, a highly stylized lyricism, provided by the supernatural mood, contrasts with the crude realism of war. Visions of integration again make us see the individual character's conflict in a more enriching way, because we oscillate between indulgence in illusion and reflection upon social reality.

Significantly, mood largely contributes to the aesthetic presentation of the thematic conflict that becomes more evident in the middle of the film. Scenes such as the boat sequence and the lawn sequence could well stand alone as proof of Mizoguchi's superb mastery of formal pattern. There Mizoguchi employs to the fullest what is considered to be the core of his style: the one-scene, one-shot method (the long take), the long shot, the dissolve, and low-key photography.

The film's action examines two ways of confronting the civil war. The first, represented by Genjuro, Tobei, and to a certain extent Ohama, Tobei's wife, is the way of opportunistic greed. It ensures geographic mobility. The second, represented by Miyagi, Genjuro's wife, is the way of optimistic endurance. It involves commitment to her community and orientation toward the future.

The first way would seem impossible, given the rigid socioeconomic structure of feudal Japan where geographic mobility was not allowed the common people, but the turmoil of the sixteenth-century civil war that shook the foundations of feudalism itself provided enough dislocation to permit it. The first part of the film concentrates on the clash of these dichotomous values and the resultant dissolution of the family. The second part shows Genjuro's obsession with illusion and the restoration of the family.

The film opens with the epigraph, which establishes both the historical and geographic settings of the film, elements that are indispensable to the thematic conflict. The time is the end of the sixteenth-century, a time when feudal lords constantly vied with one another for military supremacy. The location is the north shore of Lake Biwa in Omi Province. It is very close to the capital (Kyoto) and is thus subject to the ravages of civil war at any time.

At this early stage, we already witness Mizoguchi's intricate camera work, moving slowly from the general to the particular. First, the camera captures an entire small community at the foot of the mountain. Then, it slowly travels across the field past a stand of trees, pans 360 degrees, and finally stops, displaying a potter and his wife in front of their small house. They are loading pottery onto a wagon. Suddenly, sharp reports of rifles in the distance disturb the serene atmosphere of the village. Throughout the film rifles and guns reverberate on the sound track; they constantly remind us of the fact of war as a tangible reality which the characters confront, a phenomenon distinctly opposed to the supernatural reality which they must also experience.

In the next scene, Mizoguchi lets the individual characters verbalize their choice of action in adapting to the war. Two potters—Genjuro and his brother, Tobei—insist on taking a wagonful of pottery to the nearest town, risking the danger of the battles raging near the village. Tobei claims that he should become a samurai since he "is fed up with poverty." Both men are ambitious enough to captalize upon the war. They are, in fact, obsessed with money.

Next, the camera follows Genjuro and Tobei pushing the wagon along a mountain path until a dissolve quickly returns us to the village they had just left. The chief of the village, radiating serenity and wisdom, comments that both Genjuro and Tobei should know that money obtained through profiteering cannot last. Significantly, he subtly forewarns the audience of the ill fortune that will befall the brothers.

Tobei and Genjuro return from the town with great profits from their trade. It is here that Mizoguchi dramatically expresses the dichotomy of the two options, aided by atmosphere. A long take captures the happy mood of Genjuro, Miyagi and his son. They gather around the hearth, enjoying the things which Genjuro has brought back. The family is placed together in the center of the screen. The cozy, peaceful mood largely depends upon the stable camera and the visual image of the smoke from the cooking fire. Genjuro shows Miyagi a new kimono, saying: "I wanted to buy you a kimono all these years, and at last my dream came true." His wife gratefully answers: "I rejoice in this dress but only because it expresses your love." Mizoguchi lulls us into this peaceful mood; we begin to share in this obvious contentment. Since what we see in front of us is an extension of our ordinary world—the universal, empathy is our spontaneous reaction.

However, this moment of solidarity and contentment is suddenly broken both thematically and visually when Genjuro starts showing off his purchases. Our empathetic mood vanishes as he brags about his new wealth: "Dried fish, oil, flour and rice cakes—all bought with money. With money there is no suffering. Without money hope flies." He goes to a corner of the kitchen, leaving his wife. She silently checks the cooking pot hung over the hearth.

This visual separation marks the beginning of the dissolution of the family: it not only signifies a division between the two options (represented by husband and wife respectively) but also foreshadows the husband's choice of geographic mobility. Now Mizoguchi wants us to take the inside view of Miyagi and give her values the benefit on a sympathetic hearing. He does this by focusing the camera on her. The husband, now out of focus in the corner of the kitchen, indicates his intention to capitalize on the war: "War has brought us profit and a business boom." Miyagi protests: "Next time it won't do."

The subsequent scene shows a greater tension between the two options. The marriage of Genjuro and Miyagi is to be endangered. They are now making pottery, and the irritable husband asks his wife to turn the potter's wheel faster. The little boy's cry for his mother's milk is ignored. We are now alert viewers who, with detachment, contemplate and reflect on the clash of the two value systems. Irony contributes to this rhetorical stance: the light, rhythmic music, which is in complete harmony with the rotating wheel, is in contrast with the visual dissolution of the family. Miyagi sighs, saying: "All I want is that we work together, praying to be happy together—the three of us."

In Tobei's family, Mizoguchi presents choices of action in another light. Tobei's strong inclination toward social mobility is parallel to Genjuro's obsession with financial gain. Tobei's ambition is to become a samurai, which, he thinks, will liberate him from the drudgery of the life of a farmer. When he goes to the town, Tobei realizes that the financial power to buy a sword and a suit of armor can secure his ascent to samuraihood in the war. Tobei, who is too poor to realize his ambition, goes home and faces his wife, who has been waiting in Genjuro's house, worrying about him.

When Mizoguchi shifts the geographic focus of the film from the interior of Genjuro's house to the exterior, he increases our sense of the contrast between these four persons' motives, again aided by mood. Genjuro, Miyagi, Tobei, and Ohama are now busy with pottery making. The bright fire from the kiln diffuses the darkness of the night surrounding the four. This meeting of light and dark intensifies the quiet nocturnal atmosphere, which could be disturbed at any time by the arrival of soldiers. Genjuro and Tobei's allusions to money became more frequent. Profiteering has been firmly established as chief among their ambitions. Mizoguchi proceeds to expose us to a more realistic view of the historical milieu. First, through Miyagi's speech, he expresses disapproval of Genjuro and Tobei's new ambition: "Is this a man's way? Up to now he [Genjuro] has been steady. War has changed men." On the contrary, Ohama defends both men's motives, saying: "They have thrown everything into this kiln, body and soul." Then, the war itself arrives with the roar of the Shibata army approaching the village.

The villagers' fears of the ransacking army are rendered through the appropriate mood created by the combined effect of low-key photography, and many long and medium shots. Only the entrances of the houses are illuminated. All else—the rest of the houses and the street—is dim. Against this backdrop, Mizoguchi presents a series of long shots of the villagers, who scatter. Here Mizoguchi does not cut to a close-up of a single villager, because he wants to emphasize collective, not individual, fear. Furthermore, the oppressive mood articulates the villagers' relationship with their environment, and again we are drawn right into this dark texture to feel their suffering as something immediate to our experience. The villagers show their fear for their property, since the rapacity of soldiers is notorious. When one of the farmers is caught in a small storage shed by two soldiers, they drag him out to put him to work, ignoring his wife's

desperate pleas. The light comes through the entrance of the shed while the rest of it is again captured in darkness. The gloomy atmosphere thus persistently encourages us to experience the villagers' fear as our own felt reality.

Significantly, throughout this sequence, Mizoguchi introduces a close-up only once and that extremely effectively. While the villagers flee toward the mountain, Miyagi rushes into the house to get her boy out of bed and holds him in her arms. Suddenly, Mizoguchi presents a close-up of her face. He thus calls our attention to her genuine love for her family, which remains intact throughout the calamity of war.

Mizoguchi keeps portraying the collective misery that war has brought to the villagers all the way through this sequence. One of the most vivid, general depictions of suffering occur toward the end of this sequence. This time Mizoguchi's camera slowly dollies along a group of villagers making their way up the mountain. First, the camera, in a long-shot take, moves with the villagers pushing a wagon up the slope. Next, in a medium shot it travels with the group crossing the mountain path and then once more it follows them reaching the summit.

After Genjuro discovers that the pottery they fired during the attack of the Shibata army is undamaged, Genjuro, Miyagi, their son, Tobei and Ohama start with it across the lake in a small boat. It is here that we are introduced to a prime example of Mizoguchi's supernatural mood, so highly acclaimed by so many critics. The mood is created by four cinematic devices: the almost static camera; low-key photography; a combination of long and medium shots; and acoustic effects. Furthermore, Mizoguchi lets the natural and the supernatural interact so that we are shifted back and forth between two levels of reality.

The scene starts with a long shot of their boat emerging from the mist and approaching the camera. This in itself engenders a supernatural mood, which is also enhanced by Ohama's monotonous singing and by vibrant drumbeats in the background. The drum is intermittently interrupted by the sounds of distant rifles and guns, which echo the tangible reality of war as experienced by the passengers. The boat, turning ninety degrees, shows its side to us. At this point, Mizoguchi introduces the one-scene, one-shot method, fixing a static camera on the four sitting in the boat. As the supernatural atmosphere wanes gradually, the film takes on a realistic dimension both visually and aurally. The men in the boat, drinking sake, again begin to speak of money. Genjuro says: "We'll be rich." Tobei responds: "I'll buy a set of armour after we sell the pottery." On the other hand, Miyagi nibbles food in silence, her face revealing sad resignation. We are again reminded of the options in conflict.

Then, all of a sudden, the one-scene, one-shot method is dropped and the realistic texture recedes. The supernatural atmosphere reasserts itself as a point-of-view shot from the passengers' perspective reveals a strange boat approaching from the distance. The mist still hovers over the lake. Although the frame Mizoguchi uses is an open one, the effect of this dark texture is that of close framing. It steeps our senses in a kind of supernatural ambiance, and we actively experience the passengers' sense of approaching danger. The drumbeats grow louder and louder, as Ohama's singing diminishes. A long shot of the two boats almost stern to stern quickly gives way to a medium shot of both. The party of five thinks that the mysterious boat is haunted by a ghost. However, the supernatural yields to the natural again, when a man in the boat explains to them that he has been attacked by pirates. The boatman adds that the pirates will take everything, especially women. Then the camera swiftly cuts to the two women's faces in anxiety, reinforcing the image of women as war's greatest victims. The boatman is now dying. A medium shot of all concerned gathering in consternation around him, aided by the repeated sinister drumbeats, expresses their horrified apprehension of the dangers that lie ahead on their journey. Now the supernatural has completely gone; all they feel is the immediacy of war.

Throughout the film Mizoguchi uses his favorite cinematic punctuations: the dissolve and the fade. Both techniques not only show the passing of time but make a transition between two contrasting scenes much smoother, by virtue of the soft texture they create. For example, a dissolve of the boat turning back to the shore concludes the scene described above, and prepares us for what follows.

The scene cuts to the passengers back on shore. Genjuro, Tobei, and Ohama are ready to venture the journey on the lake once more while Miyagi is advised to stay behind with her little boy.

This scene reflects the central problem of the film in three ways. First, just as in the earlier take of husband and wife busy with the pottery, it signifies the division between the two options: opportunism and resignation. While those who stay in the boat gamble on mobility, Miyagi adheres to a more traditional value of geographic fixty. Second, crosscutting, a convenient method for rendering individual relationships, elucidates the mutual caring of husband and wife, which will be at stake in the latter part of the film. The camera first focuses on the husband, who says: "In ten days, I'll come back. . . . " Then, it shifts to the wife, who replies: "God will protect you." The camera next sweeps back to the husband and the other passengers in the boat, and then captures all parties involved on board and ashore. Finally, through very subtle camera work, Mizoguchi projects his own view of the conflicting options: his sympathies lie with the value system represented by Miyagi. After the boat glides off the screen, Mizoguchi does not intercut between the passengers and Miyagi. Instead, he lets the camera slowly dolly along with her as she walks along the shore with her boy on her back to see the party off. When she stops, the camera stops, too, and in the subsequent long shot we see her still standing among the tall grass watching the boat in the distance. Mizoguchi has moved his camera as if he were compassionately watching this poor woman's plight. He has employed no close-up for directly transmitting her emotions to the audience. Rather, he has let us watch her plight with him from the perspective of omnipotent, empathetic observers. Furthermore, the complete absence of the traveling boat from the screen conveys the sense of the irreconcilable chasm between the two options. A fade follows the long shot of Miyagi, investing it with an elegiac mood that is appropriate to her sorrow.

The second half of the film reveals Mizoguchi's pervasive evocation of mood for the dramatization of the thematic conflict. One of the focal points is the way Mizoguchi presents Ohama as a helpless prey of the war. We come to learn that the way of opportunism, as taken by her, is worse than fruitless. While she is looking for her husband, who has disappeared to buy a set of armor, she becomes the target of the roaming samurai's lust. Their assault on her takes place in front of the sacred goddess of mercy in a devastated temple. While the feet of the ruthless samurai, standing about in dirty shoes, dominate the entire screen, the statue is set far off in a corner of the hall.

This take, buttressed by low-key photography, symbolizes the moral impotence among the populace in the face of gross social disorder. As before, Mizoguchi projects his sympathy for woman's plight—this time, Ohama's—with subtle camera movement. As Ohama bursts into tears, surrounded by the lecherous samurai, the camera swiftly cuts back to the outside of the temple as if the director could not bear to see her raped. In turn, he presents a close-up of Ohama's straw sandals left on the road. Mizoguchi seems to be asking us to imagine what is happening inside the temple. From this point on, the film dignifies Ohama's sufferings with a sensitive and sympathetic portrayal of them. When Ohama comes out after the samurai leave her, the *Noh* chorus vocalizes her sorrow and indignation. Just as in Miyagi's case, the camera follows straightforwardly, taking its cues from her motions. In the next shot, we see a fine example of Mizoguchi's employment of mood. A low-angle long shot shows Ohama standing in the door of the temple; she is looking up at the sky absentmindedly with her back to us. Her disheveled figure fits in with the desolate surrounding: the ruined temple and the gloomy sky with a waning moon. This fusion creates the despondent mood, and externalizes Ohama's emotional quandary as articulated by the *Noh* chorus. Even though a close-up of her face is absent, this typical Mizoguchi mood helps draw us into her mind. Moreover, this entire filmic composition, especially the low-angle shot, makes it appear as though Mizoguchi were looking up at Ohama, admiring her for her courage to struggle through her life; it looks as if he, the conscious eye of the camera, were saying: "Ohama, you fought against these ruthless men desperately, and though you finally had to succumb to them, I praise you for your moral courage and sympathize with your predicament."

A similar technique was used by Mizoguchi in an equally sophisticated way in *The Life of Oharu* [*Saikaiu Ichidai Onna,* 1952], the film that preceded *Ugetsu* (1953). It occurs when Oharu and her family are ordered to leave the capital. The camera is first immobile as they travel along the bank of a river. Then, when the party is just about to disappear from the screen, Mizoguchi's camera quickly dollies across the screen and then looks up at the party from underneath the bridge at this side of the bank. The effect is one of exquisite pity taken on the unhappy travelers.

After the rape sequence in *Ugetsu,* Mizoguchi lets us see how Ohama, who initially encouraged the opportunism of both Tobei and Genjuro, begins to relinquish her sense of morality. In the brothel scene, from the perspective of Tobei, her husband, who happens to be a customer, we see Ohama haggling with her own customer for her proper share of money. The subsequent reunion of husband and wife takes the audience to the exterior. It is in this scene that we realize Ohama's genuine caring for her husband, the intrinsic quality of her femininity, unchanged despite her moral degradation. Above the sounds of the entertainment from inside the brothel, Ohama's crying becomes resonant: "How many times I thought of dying! But I thought I must see you first." Husband and wife then fall together to the ground, embracing each other. Mizoguchi's soft fade terminates this take, evoking the pathos of a husband and wife who have suffered such a painful and complex ordeal.

This final scene convinces us of Tobei's realization that his social ascendancy has been achieved at his wife's expense. But it becomes all the more convincing only when we consider the subtle way in which Mizoguchi has repeatedly stressed the futility of Tobei's social climbing. Tobei has taken advantage of the war, and through good timing, he has taken the head of an enemy general and been accorded a horse and attendants. He assumes that the measure of his success proves the value of the way of opportunism.

Along with this social advancement the filmic composition shifts. In earlier parts of the film, the camera repeatedly pans down on Tobei groveling, the butt of samurai's ridicule and the thief of a spear. In contrast, later in the film a low-angle shot is pervasively used for Tobei as he absurdly and proudly mounts a horse, accompanied by his retainers. This radical shift in camera work ironically brings to the surface the suspicion that his climbing up the social ladder is not to be seen as "success" at all but the mere illusion created by his vanity. The suspicion is further reinforced by his bragging in the brothel. Here, he gets his comeuppance, discovering that his own wife, because of the fortune of war, is a fallen woman.

In the latter part of the film, Miyagi's way of resignation turns out to be equally futile. After presenting her husband's infatuation with Princess Wakasa at a supernatural level, Mizoguchi quickly cuts to Miyagi at home. He presents Miyagi's confrontation with death at a realistic level. Her village is attacked by a number of hungry samurai and Miyagi flees from her house. Here again we see Mizoguchi's subtle camera movement registering the woman's emotional dilemma. The camera dollies along with her running along the mountain path with her boy on her back. It stops when she starts struggling with the samurai, begging them for the little boy's sake, not to take her scraps of food. Miyagi is stabbed. When she starts struggling forward, with her son still on her back, the camera slowly moves with her. Then it again stops with her when she finally staggers on to die while behind her in the field two samurai are fighting each other for the food. Again through this camera movement Mizoguchi suggests his sympathy for her crisis. Again, no close-ups are employed, nor is any mood conveyed that corresponds to Miyag's feelings. A long shot predominates, emphasizing the environmental forces that overwhelm her.

As previously stated, the latter half of *Ugetsu* is mainly centered on Genjuro, whose way of opportunism takes a radical turn in the middle of the film. He moves from commonplace greed to the passion of love. Accordingly, the filmic texture shifts from the matter of social realism to a supernatural lyric mood corresponding to this thematic conflict. At this turning point we see Genjuro torn between family obligation and individual freedom. However, his conjugal affection for Miyagi gradually replaces his purely sexual attraction to Princess Wakasa. Then his discovery that Wakasa is a ghost prompts him to return to his wife.

Genjuro's first encounter with Wakasa takes place in the busy market of the town. He is surprised at her mysterious beauty; her face is made up to resemble a half-smiling *Noh* mask evoking a sense of the supernatural. A medium close-up of his face looking up at hers articulates his admiration for her beauty and foreshadows his gradual infatuation with her. However, at this stage, Genjuro's love for Miyagi is still unchallenged. He comes to a kimono shop and looks at the wares displayed there. One white kimono, which he wants to buy for his wife, is presented in close-up, demonstrating his yearning for her. The subsequent shots portray Genjuro's fantasy, in which Miyagi comes through the door of the shop and tries the kimono on. Japanese harp music on the sound track intensifies this happy mood in which Genjuro indulges himself.

However, the following scene shows Genjuro's love for his wife being put to the test. When he comes out from the shop, Wakasa's attendant calls Genjuro and tells him that both Wakasa and his wife will guide him to their mansion to which he is supposed to deliver pottery. The supernatural aura, which is to be more fully explored later, is already here: the princess's face again resembles the female *Noh* mask, and her stride is of an unearthly lightness like that of a ghost in a *Noh* play. Mizoguchi employs an unusually long dolly shot to show the three going down the street and through the field and garden of Wakasa's mansion. This method keeps us in suspense, preparing us for the coming glimpse into the supernatural.

When they arrive at the mansion, Mizoguchi begins to reinforce our sense of the supernatural through the combined effects of long and medium shots, low-key photography, and textural contrast. After Genjuro is guided down the long corridor and shown to a back room, there is a slow crosscutting between his room and other rooms along the corridor. First, darkness prevails, and then yields to a soft illumination as Wakasa's servants light and set candles in the other rooms. Now the cinematic action is all set for Wakasa's seduction of Genjuro. She again comes in like a *Noh* actor appearing on the stage, with her face made up like a female *Noh* mask. Genjuro sits between her and her aged attendant. Sinister chimes—perhaps of a bell for Buddhist prayers—are heard intermittently. The attendant, attired in a black kimono, sits closest to the camera, showing her back to the audience. In contrast, Wakasa clad in a white kimono, is placed farthest from the camera, facing it. The imposing stature of the old attendant, like that of the alluring Wakasa, is used to block Genjuro, as if to predict his subsequent entrapment by these women.

As Wakasa takes a drink of sake from a small wine cup, we hear the chime, and when Genjuro drinks from the same cup, we hear it again. By this time we are convinced that the chime occurs at each stage of Genjuro's moral quandary. We also know that drinking sake from the same sake cup symbolizes the marriage bond, and indeed, the attendant later suggests that Genjuro marry Wakasa. After this suggestion, the princess stands up and tries to corner Genjuro, who, in turn, rises to flee. The following long shot, enhanced by the acoustic effects of the chime, a flute, and a *koto,* presents the chase. It evokes a sinister claustrophia, finalizing Genjuro's entrapment in Wakasa's snare. The long shot turns into a medium shot, when Genjuro is finally captured by Wakasa and collapses to the floor with her. By presenting this final shot slightly askew, Mizoguchi suggests his silent condemnation of the lovers' illicit relationship. By this time, Mizoguchi's persistent evocation of a sense of encirclement and oppression has made us aware of some element of doom in their love.

In the following scene, the acoustic effects are fully realized in order to accent the supernatural aspect of this vignette. Wakasa sings in tune with the *samisen:* "The best of silk of choicest hue / May change and fade away, / As would my life, beloved one . . ." Her singing gradually merges with what appears to be a priest's low-toned prayer from a *Noh* play, accompanied by the sounds of a wooden drum being beaten for prayers. The camera quickly dollies from the center of the room to the corner and stops on a suit of black armor, the source of the mysterious incantation. We then learn from the princess's attendant that the voice is the spirit of Wakasa's father still haunting the mansion and that he is pleased with her betrothal. Thus, the merging songs of Wakasa and the spirit conjure up an image of death in connection with this love affair.

The subsequent sequence that presents the lovers' bathing and their repose on the lawn thematically demonstrates the culmination of Genjuro's passion. Mizoguchi's cinematic rubric of the mood, enhanced by his elaborate camera movement and pictorial filmic composition, helps him to aestheticize this mood. Genjuro is soaking himself in the spring while Wakasa is still ashore. Holding her hands, he says: "I have never had such a wonderful experience in my life." The camera then follows Wakasa, who momentarily leaves Genjuro. She steps into the woods, takes off her clothes, and comes back to him. Now they share the bath, and just when they are about to embrace, Mizoguchi's camera becomes, as Joan Mellen also points out, very disturbing. It quickly moves away from them along a diagonal and ends with a dissolve, as if to say that the director himself is averting his eyes from this spectacle and moral disarray. This sweeping pan is in strong contrast with the earlier slow dolly, which implied Mizoguchi's sympathy for both Ohama and Miyagi.

After the dissolve the camera dollies across the bushes of a garden with raked white sand and then moves up to show a long shot of Genjuro and Wakasa on the lawn. The garden looks like the stone garden of Ryoanji or that of Daitokuji Temple. If Mizoguchi's intention is to let this uninhabited landscape serve as a stasis, its effect is that of a sudden illumination, a kind of shock. The garden presented for only a second is charged with significant meaning: it stands by itself, transcending all petty human affairs.

Now we see Genjuro and Wakasa having a picnic on a blanket spread on the lawn. It is flooded by warm spring sunlight. A long shot persists. Genjuro starts to chase her, and the couple, clad in very light silk kimonos, look like two fluttering butterflies, the symbol of spring. This take is cited by many critics as one of the most memorable examples of Mizoguchi's atmospheric rendition. However, it soon becomes tinged again with an ominous undertone when Genjuro catches Wakasa. The camera approaches them and the next moment we see a medium shot of him kissing her and saying: "I don't care if you are a demon. I will not let you go." On the sound track, the chime sounds again, marking for us another stage of Genjuro's moral crisis, which is further reinforced by the combination of the discordant harp music and the intermittent chime. The final shot in this scene presents Wakasa kissing Genjuro who is lying on the lawn. A soft fade that terminates the scene again speaks for Mizoguchi, expressing his grief for those who are lost in unbridled passion.

In order to keep the two lines of argument distinct, and yet in balance, Mizoguchi frequently crosscuts between scenes depicting Genjuro's encounters with the blandishments of the supernatural, and the more down-to-earth trials and tribulations of the other three characters. The prime example of this crosscutting is the contrast between the love scenes of the bathing and the picnic in which Genjuro is shown discarding social conventions, and the hazards of war and scenes like that depicting Miyagi's death.

After Miyagi's death, we are shifted back to the supernatural reality of Genjuro's final confrontation with Wakasa. A priest has discovered that Genjuro is haunted by evil spirits. Following the priest's advice, Genjuro has his back painted with a prayer inscription to exorcize the spirits. He goes back to the mansion to face Wakasa and her attendant. In the following scenes, the supernatural aura is evoked through a combination of low-key photography, versatile camera work, gestures of individual characters, and, to a significant extent, acoustic effects.

Wakasa tells Genjuro that he must not go out, that they should move away to live together happily. While enticing him, Wakasa first corners him from the left and then from the right. Genjuro confesses that he is married. Very low discordant music evokes the tension between the two. Genjuro is accused by both the princess and her attendant of breaking a vow of love. He cries: "Please forgive me!" While the discordant music continues, a high-angle shot focuses on Genjuro cornered by the two sinister-looking women, all of them in low exposure. The overall effect of these combined techniques expresses the still persistent snare, in which Genjuro has been trapped by these women. The culmination of his attempt to free himself from them occurs when the back of Genjuro, who is lying on the floor, is shown in close-up with the two women reproachfully looking down at the sutra painted on his back. Wakasa's face goes through a metamorphosis. Through shot-by-shot alterations, Mizoguchi gradually reveals her true identity. Genjuro must do battle with the demon who is now revealed to him. He picks up a sword lying on the floor and starts chasing the women. He extinguishes the candles and darkness prevails. Then, the supernatural atmosphere in which Genjuro faints in the end of his battle suddenly transports us back to everyday reality. This abrupt shift in "realities" puts us in a state of shock.

Now we see only the potter Genjuro amidst the ruins of the mansion in the grass. The police inspectors awaken him and leave with the sword, which has turned out to be a sacred relic belonging to a nearby shrine. Genjuro, now alone, starts wandering among the ruins. He recalls Wakasa's song: "The best of silk of choicest hue / May fade away. . . . ." As Joan Mellen points out, the camera starts following Genjuro diagonally as he walks away from it. This shot is counterpoised with the earlier sweeping away from Genjuro and Wakasa engaged in their love affair. It emphasizes his psychological transformation, his repentance over his moral degradation—repentance of which Mizoguchi registers his approval. The fade, which Mizoguchi has consistently employed thus far to convey the elegiac tone, again concludes this take, stressing the omnipotent director's pity for the pathos of the human condition. Genjuro's face is not facing the camera, but Mizoguchi's camera movement has said enough about the potter's feelings.

The following scene depicts Genjuro's return to his home. Here, the conjugal bond between Genjuro and Miyagi is reasserted through his realization that the way of opportunism was the wrong way. Genjuro begs his wife's forgiveness. Gradually, this scene reassumes the supernatural aura. As Audie Bock points out, the transition from the natural to the supernatural is made in such a way that the audience is again put in the state of shock. When Genjuro comes home, he enters the dark, uninhabited house. He goes out through the back door and when next the camera cuts to the interior, we are surprised to see Miyagi sitting near the brightly burning hearth. A fine example of Mizoguchi's evocation of mood occurs after the husband and the child are put to sleep. The slow camera movement and extremely low-key photography yield a mixture of tenderness and eeriness: the typical Mizoguchi mood. Only a tiny spot of light from Miyagi's candle moves from place to place as she moves around the house, while the rest of the screen is dominated by darkness. We next see Miyagi starting to patch her husband's kimono, her slightly smiling face meeting the darkness. The supernatural atmosphere completely recedes when the villagers visit Genjuro to tell him that his wife was killed during the war.

Mizoguchi cuts back to Tobei and Ohama trudging home. On the bridge near their village Tobei tosses his sword into the river. The implication is clear: his rejection of his social ambition.

We are now prepared for the final scene of the film, which recaptures the exterior of Genjuro's house and the entire community. The camera moves here from the particular to the general, in contrast to its movement in the opening sequence.

The exterior of the potter's house, which used to be barren, is presented first. It is now a farm that Tobei is tilling. The camera then follows the little boy going toward his mother's tomb and stops as he kneels before it. Next, it pans up to, and then sweeps across the field to show us the entire community. The movement of the camera thus provides a movement for reflection on war and how it has complicated the lives of the four persons and indeed the whole village.

We have seen the conflicting "ways" finally brought to resolution and witnessed also a complex theme worked out through the use of mood as a rhetorical device. We have come to accept that in time of civil war both "ways" were equally impossible to realize. The world view that the film reveals is ironic: no matter how an individual character internalizes his motive, he cannot win. His survival is simply dependent upon chance. Miyagi's option, with which Mizoguchi seems to sympathize most, is less rewarding than the option chosen by either of the rest. Although, Tobei, Genjuro, and Ohama have been defeated in their motives, they have survived the war, and their very defeat has shown them the futility of their options. This knowledge itself is their only reward as they must transform it into a guiding principle for the future.

We have also observed in Miyagi and Ohama the prototype of Mizoguchi's women—those who sacrifice themselves for the needs of men and the family. The supernatural realm in which Genjuro's conjugal relationship is finally consummated indicates the impossibility of genuine love on this earth. Only in defeat do Genjuro and Tobei learn the virtue of female love, which can sustain their own existence.

The sweeping shot of the entire village in the last scene seems to convey a deeper philosophical idea, the concept of *mujo* (the mutability of all earthly phenomena), which must emerge from the film's final analysis. There are two important elements that suggest this. One is Wakasa's singing, introduced twice in the film. At the wedding Wakasa sings, "The best of silk of choicest hue / May change and fade away,/ As would my life, beloved one, / If thou shouldst prove untrue." Roaming around the rampart of the mansion, Genjuro recalls the same song. Wakasa's song invokes the transitoriness of all human affairs, which underlies much of traditional Japanese art. Different aspects of life—interactive human motives, love and fame—that we have witnessed are ephemeral as symbolized by the rotating wheel. This wheel, the other important image, is also introduced twice, aided by the director's subtle presentation of mood. In the earlier scene, which is permeated by the cozy domestic atmosphere, both Genjuro and Miyagi start spinning the wheel in tune with some rather light music. In the latter scene, which yields the serene, peaceful mood after the turmoil of the civil war, Genjuro alone rotates the wheel, while his deceased wife's voice, heard on the sound track, encourages him to make good pottery. Time, symbolized by the rotating wheel, transcends all these human affairs, whether or not they seem individually or publicly significant. In a large span of time they comprise only one insignificant spot.

At the very end of the film we see the hitherto uninhabited landscape of the field with a few farmers tilling the soil. The complete harmony of these farmers with their environment/surroundings thus evokes a sense of regeneration. The tension of the war and the possibility of coming peace in the future are thus presented as a cyclic pattern in the passage of time.

Dudley Andrew (essay date 1984)

SOURCE: "The Passion of Identification in the Late Films of Kenji Mizoguchi," in *Film in the Aura of Art,* Princeton University Press, 1984, pp. 172-92.

[*In the following essay, Andrew examines the ways in which Mizoguchi's later films showcase a worldview of stoic contemplation and acceptance through revolt against injustice.*]

Representative both of artistic grace and social rebellion, women are at the center of virtually every film Kenji Mizoguchi made, pursuing the values of futile revolt and tragic acceptance which he himself prized. He filmed them implacably with unblinking eye until they would stare back accusingly as at the end of *Sisters of the Gion* and *Osaka Elegy*. But he also filmed them sympathetically in pathetic surroundings and with unquestionable feeling in the movement of his camera.

How can we put together the rebellious social side of Mizoguchi with the nearly stoic metaphysical side? When Okita, at the conclusion of *Utamaro and His Five Women,* murders her lover and his mistress and then prepares to end her own fated existence, she tells Utamaro that she has practiced in her life what he developed in his art, a refusal of all compromise and a drive to go to the end of an action no matter what its consequence. If women have revolted against the system of prohibitions, exchanges, and hierarchies established by men with the congenital blindness suited to the self-centered banality of their ambitions, it is because women alone see right through to the end of this system, sensing its futility. If they have anything to teach us, it is the transpersonal, transhistorical, essentially artistic comprehension of the absurdity of such existence. Their vision goes well beyond those responsible for their personal plights. They see through the system, through the audience, and into the structure of an impersonal cosmos. Revolt thus leads the way to a kind of stoic contemplation which in his late films Mizoguchi pursued with fanaticism.

While certain male characters embody one or the other of these functions (think of the "sacrilegious hero" of the Taira clan saga or of the essentially passive artist-hero of *Ugetsu*), only Mizoguchi's females unite these impulses and do so to a degree that is beyond expression. As artist and iconoclast, Mizoguchi takes his inspiration from the stories he tells and the actresses who portray these stories for him. His least heroine, we feel, has gone further than reform or art. In their very way of walking is asserted a comprehension not even a lifetime of art could equal. Mizoguchi was obsessed with the gait of women, with their swoons, with their averted or penetrating gaze.

The dual nature of his women, and Mizoguchi's fluctuating attitude toward them (recording them naturalistically only later to identify with them), pose special requirements for the viewer. At the same time this offers a potential and rare reward by providing an interval in time and space within which the spectator can move, oscillate. This is the interval between the borders of *identification* and *interpretation,* an interval that encourages us to rethink some of the key aesthetic issues of our era.

It is precisely the absence of such an interval that contemporary philosophers and critics have tried to expose in western fiction and film. Identification has been analyzed as an effect of a text striving to produce the illusion of presence and plenitude with the emptiness of differential signs. Under the banner of deconstruction contemporary criticism has waged a war against the illusions of identification and of full representation, whereby the spectator is overwhelmed by an undeniable picture of reality. Against such standard art a tradition of modernism is promoted: Lautréamont over Zola, Mayakovsky over Gorki, Vertov over Vidor, Oshima over Kurosawa. Modernism has come to mean the arbitrary play of signs in a text that promotes the free construction of meaning. The viewer or reader's relation to such a text is one of strong reading ("rewriting" in Roland Barthes' vocabulary), the absolute contrary of the slavish passivity of identification.

Among film scholars Noël Burch has long been in the vanguard of the deconstructionist project. Not only has he tried to expose the mechanisms of illusion and representation, he has actively proposed alternative models of filmic signification: specifically the silent era before 1920, the current avant-garde, and, most important for us, the prewar cinema of Japan. Mizoguchi is a key figure in Burch's view of Japanese cinema. Before the war he, along with Ozu, developed and sustained a totally non-Hollywood narrative film tradition. After the war he can be cited as among those Japanese directors who not only succumbed to western modes of representation, but who pandered to western tastes, groveling for the lucrative export market.

Burch's rhetorical project leads him to bisect the world of texts into those complicit with a dominant (Hollywood) version of reality, featuring illusion and identification, and those other texts that ascetically abjure the temptations of this method and its obvious rewards. Its moralism aside, Burch's view of Japanese cinema and of Mizoguchi in particular remains crudely on the surface. Mizoguchi's postwar films may indeed have reached an export market and may indeed employ the lure of identification, not to mention a compellingly delicious pictorialism, but these devices don't exhaust the project of his films. That project might best be termed a "cinema of responsiveness." A machine of recording, the camera can also become an instrument of response to what is recorded. This mélange of objectivity and affect situates Mizoguchi's aesthetic within the problematic of reading and interpretation. Specifically, Mizoguchi treats his subjects as texts whose illusions promote in him the need to respond in such and such a way. Identification with the illusion, then, is only the first part of an arc that ends in productive interpretation. Hence his films, especially the late ones, never pretend to touch ground and always point to themselves as textual experiences. While this should attract Burch and the deconstructionists, Mizoguchi's responses, his readings, have nothing of the anarchic about them. His films are disciplines in reading, the results of which, as every viewer of *Ugetsu* will attest, are as compelling and inevitable as the most tightly plotted Hollywood film.

While we do not go through Mizoguchi to something seemingly solid beyond, he gives us the solidity of his response to a text that hovers as an illusion before him. In Mizoguchi (and, Barthes has argued, in Japan generally) there is never a question of pure reality to transmit nor of some independent Nature which the heroic artist may journey to and bring back to share with his spectators; instead there can only be the purity of the reading of a text about reality, that is, the productive reaction to an illusion. Every reading produces a reaction which in turn can be read as a text. Thus eddies out the infinite text of culture. The curiously mixed feelings of Mizoguchi's films are a measure of this intermediate stance between illusion and interpretation, the product of the "full emptiness" we are made present to, especially in *Ugetsu, Sansho the Bailiff, The Life of Oharu,* and *Miss Oyu.*

The concluding camera "fixation" in each of these films transcends the drama that leads up to it. This is not the authorial transcendence of the tidy rhetorical flourish, nor an ironic comment on the action, but the completion of another action which has been operative throughout the film, that of the filmmaker's sympathetic reading of the destiny of his characters. Identification, in the generic sense of the term, acts as a relay between separate levels of the text, essentially between separate texts. At the first level the character is created via actor identification with the role or circumstance of the script. To assure this, Mizoguchi's actresses were forced, for months before their role, to wear the costume of the period, to frequent museums, and to listen to the music of the time.

His well-known refusal to cut within an action can in part be attributed to the respect he accorded the player's identification with her role. One might be tempted to suppose that the camera struggles to follow and amplify the actress's reading of the role if it were not for the fact that Mizoguchi's most elaborate movements are those that, though beginning with an actor's movement, continue until they reach a new, distinct, and settled composition all their own. And so although characters control the framing of shots, always finish the actions they begin, and usually initiate whatever movements the camera does make, the audience soon identifies with the camera via its quasi-independence. This independence is also attributable to the aestheticized compositions of many scenes and to the noticeable ellipses between actions. To put this all together, the viewer must read the camera's response to an actress's response to her situation. Nor does it stop here, for the presumably originary situation she identifies with is often itself a textual response (in the form of legend, story, poem) to a hypothetical reality so far back it is literally out of the picture.

The Life of Oharu suitably exemplifies these strata and the movement of identification that interrelates them. The camera watches Kinuyo Tanaka come to terms with the role of Oharu, derived from one of Japan's greatest literary classics, Saikako's *Life of an Amorous Woman.* This seventeenth-century tale, essentially satiric and picaresque, chronicles the foibles of an easy woman who stumbles morally over and over to the delight of the reader. Tanaka, reading this tale from the perspective of postwar Japan, projects a tragic pathos in the grace of her falls, a grace so transcendent that she is permitted to escape society altogether in a final fall to the role of an indifferent mendicant nun.

This notion of role operates beyond the obvious technical requirements of the cinema, for the character, Oharu herself, conceives of her life as a series of roles in which she has participated. The flashback structure of the film guarantees this attitude of "reinhabiting" situations, allowing feelings to well up out of memory. In the opening segment she enters a temple to stare at a constellation of statues of famous Bodhisattvas. Focussing on one of these, she sees in its stony face the visage of Toshiro Mifune, her former lover executed for love of her. A glance-object structure (including the film's single close-up shots) underlines the primacy of this moment as trigger for the film to follow. She identifies, if not with Mifune, then with the past in which he played the decisive role. More important, her hallucination not only produces the image that permits the film of her life to unroll, it produces as well a reaction from her. In one of cinema's most gracefully telling gestures, her head cocks sadly and she slowly pulls the scarf from her hair. The liquid slipping of this silk down the side of the screen is her response to the reading of the image before her. It is the prototype for numerous falls she will have throughout the film and for the equally numerous camera descents by which Mizoguchi will sympathize with her plight (after the family's exile at the bridge, after the beheading of Mifune, after the suicidal run of Oharu). We can go so far as to say that just as Oharu's reactions to her situation are more important than the events that produced them, so Mizoguchi's reaction to Oharu transcends her tale. That tale begins with the distant camera set before a carefully raked palace garden while Oharu and her small entourage pass before us in extreme long shot. It ends with Oharu continuing to pass screen left out of frame, this time alone, as the camera remains still on the elegiac temple in the distance. She has entered and passed completely through Mizoguchi's view, our view. We have used her as the pretext for our own movement, just as Tanaka, as actress, used Saikaku's novel as pretext for her performance. Thus goes the dialectic of identification and interpretation.

Oharu may be Mizoguchi's most rigorous and complex film, but in terms of the question of identification it is far simpler than some of the later masterworks. It clearly exhibits the paradox of distance and involvement which defines the experience of his films. The *distance* comes not merely from camera placement but from Mizoguchi's determination to let every action run its course and to separate each action with tangible intervals. The *involvement* derives from Mizoguchi's peculiar timing which insists on a certain view of an action and waits for it to erupt, as though the camera itself were a bellows stirring the embers of the dramatic interplay to ignite in sudden flame. Each scene has its own dramatic structure and runs to its own fiery conclusion. The camera flourish which concludes so many of these scenes is an expression of the involvement that demands and results from this kind of obsessive uninterrupted look.

Sansho Dayu forthrightly takes up the questions of identification and sympathy in relation to the status of texts. Instead of a single character with whom we and the camera must come into relation, *Sansho* presents us with a family who exchange sympathy via identification through texts. In the first sequence mother and son exchange a memory about the father's trauma of exile. The mother recalls their last moments together when the son received an heirloom from his father along with the sacred text, "Be merciful to all men." A dissolve returns us not to the mother but to the son wearing the heirloom and speaking of his father. His spirit and love is thus shared. In the film's closing scene this same mother and son will again merge in repeating the father's text. The route which the film follows to permit this conclusion involves a set of exchanges too intricate to detail here. What is crucial to note, however, is that these exchanges occur as the passing on of texts. The mother's plaintive song from the island of Sado is brought to the daughter via a slave girl. The memory of the mother's cry "Anju, Zushio" wells up when the siblings repeat the cutting of the branch. Mizoguchi's camera here insists on the textualizing of this scene, making it not an action but the record of a meaning. This scene becomes a theatrical scene, read by its actors who change their lives in relation to the meaning it holds.

Sansho Dayu is a film about the emergence of morality out of a state of natural brutality. It is also about the centrality of texts and textuality in an illiterate and, consequently, unreadable world. When Zushio recognizes meaning in the text of a song, a dramatic reenactment, or the saying of his father, he frees himself from the meaningless activity of the slave camp, activity which by its very nature is unmemorable. Because they intone a text (the father's dictum), this forlorn couple, huddling alone on the beach out of sight even of the oblivious seaweed gatherer, rekindles the lost flame of culture and an idea of humanity.

Mizoguchi's position in this film is more direct and explicit than it was in *Oharu*. He actively joins scenes and memories. He himself memorializes and textualizes the activity of the family. Consciously the film participates in the proliferation of the father's text. The credits are themselves supered over two ancient sacred markers, present-day traces of the birth of meaning. When the slave girl from Sado sings the mother's song, she spins wool from wheel to wheel. Likewise the film unwinds in creating the fabric of the same plaintive hymn, passed on not directly but through the countless retellings the tale of Sansho has undergone, culminating in Mori Ogai's sensationally popular novel, the credited source of the movie.

If Mizoguchi's film seems disturbingly empty in the end, it is because he has audaciously placed his legend within the indifference of undramatic time. The seaweed gatherer exists in the state of nature, while the legend, dramatic and consequential, institutes cultural time, progress, and hope in the future. In identifying with Mizoguchi's weaving cinema we identify not with the success of culture and legend, but with the effort of textuality in an otherwise unreadable world. This is not a question of comedy versus tragedy since both of these are cultural constructions. In *Sansho* we participate in the eloquence of a meaningful gesture thrown up in the face of the indifference to which it arises in response. Once again identification is the key to the film and to our experience, but it is a knowing identification which places a burden of sympathy on the subject, refusing the consolation of fullness or presence. We are asked to identify with the difference of a text in the indifferent emptiness of the cosmos.

Can we continue to call this operation, by which an artist creates an image of a prior text, "identification," especially when the distance between the image and its subject is sadly insisted upon as it is at the end of all the films we have discussed so far? This kind of sympathetic participation by an observer in a primary scene is part of Japanese aesthetics generally and, therefore, lifts it out of the category of illusionism and passive identification.

Recall the horizontal panel paintings of the feudal era. Seldom is a scene of natural beauty rendered without the presence of an observer visibly meditating on or reacting to the view before him. The summer mountain scene may suggest or express "majesty" or "tranquility" or any of the highly coded moods permitted in Japanese art, but it will do so through an observer moved by this experience. Nature itself either cannot be trusted to deliver feeling or, more probably, is thought to express feeling only in the presence of a spectator.

Haiku poetry concentrates this same convention through the sequence of its rigid lines. A scene or action is presented in the first two lines, whereas the third line suddenly introduces a particular perspective, a human view or feeling. Listen to Basho:

> The sound of a water jar
> Cracking on this icy night
> As I lie awake.

Coming closer to Mizoguchi's own interests and to the cinema, one would do well to start with the various aesthetics embodied in the *no, kabuki, bunraku,* and *shinpa* theater. Many instances of each of these dramatic forms crop up in his films and we know that he was an addicted spectator all his life. A catalogue would contain many straightforward adaptations and even more instances of the partial inclusion of a theater performance in his films.

More important than direct reference to these forms of theater, however, is the model they provide for a kind of mediated artistic experience. Mizoguchi was to shape this model into his own complex narrative stance. At the very least he took from traditional theater the absolute separation of action and telling. Here most importantly, narration is sung from the side of the stage, accompanied by instrumental music which provides the scene with added aural mimesis (the sound of rain or of a battle), but which can also respond to the action or reflect upon it. In *bunraku,* of course, the visible presence of the puppeteers further mediates the performance and the tale it

represents. In addition to these aspects of narration, the stories, sets, and acting in *kabuki* theater readily serve to accentuate heightened moments through a kind of concentration and counterpoint which Eisenstein was the first to recognize as a potential the cinema might adopt but which few filmmakers have dared to emulate. In his own way Mizoguchi did dare, so much so that one might speak of his work as *performances* in film, including the performance of his actors which he was loath to interrupt through cutting, the performance of his camera which, in quasi-independent fashion, responds to the actors, and the performance of the music which both participates in the drama and reacts pathetically to its consequences.

The route of this aesthetic leads directly to Japan's unique contribution to early cinema practice, the *benshi*. Audiences came to watch not just a film, but a professional response to that film. The *benshi's* commentary related the tale, to be sure, but from a distinct style and personal repertoire. This Japanese penchant for separate but simultaneously presented texts, linked by mood and thought, finds its champion in Mizoguchi. He treated each of his collaborators as the maker of a finished text which it was up to him, Mizoguchi, to play out in his own medium and in his own way. This accounts for the stony silence that notoriously signaled his dissatisfaction with a writer's draft, a decorator's sketch, or an actress's run-through of a scene. Refusing to impose his will in an area that didn't belong to him, he nevertheless forced all to repeat and rework their particular "texts" until they had surpassed themselves and given him something at the peak of intensity and expressiveness, something with which he could identify and begin to interpret. Hence the paradox: Mizoguchi, at once the most feared and exacting of directors, was also the one who gave to his co-workers the fullest responsibility for creating an acceptable artifact in their own fields of expertise.

This view of the artist as disciplined craftsman infuses Mizoguchi's most personal and sustained meditation on the vocation of the artist, his portrait of Utamaro, the greatest of the *ukiyo-e* printmakers of the eighteenth century. Mizoguchi clearly admires the way the mass-produced aspects of the *ukiyo-e* do not in the least detract from its instrumentality as a means of refined expression. Utamaro is at once a popular hero and an artist whose genius is capable of challenging the greatest practitioners of graphics living in Japan. He works in a frenzy for art equalled only by the passion for life which his subjects, beautiful courtesans, play out to the fullest. He exists within the heat of history and event, only he does so with a calculated distance. His works immortalize the history they seek to express, the passions that are so strong and sublime that it is at once inevitable and inconceivable that they should pass away. The final credits roll over a torrent of prints that rain down from above, each landing on and replacing the one beneath, each memorializing a passionate scene from the lives of the women who lived not with but around him. What obsesses Utamaro and, through him, Mizoguchi, is not the fleeting lives of the women, nor even the prints he makes of them, prints that are disposable and mass-produced; rather it is the activity of expression which through repetition and discipline is the way to vision and serenity.

The primacy of discipline and activity, that is, of artwork over artifact, lends prestige to popular arts and crafts, to pottery, printmaking, and the cinema. Mizoguchi surrendered himself to this ethic and this aesthetic, and sought to bring out in his films the fleeting vestige of such discipline. The Japanese critic Tadao Sato has demonstrated how intimately related to traditional Japanese arts is this Zen attitude of Mizoguchi, an attitude that crystallizes in the peculiarly Japanese effect of "impermanent posturing." Unlike the classics of western cinema, Mizoguchi's films deliver neither clear statement, nor well-constructed drama, nor stable outline. Instead, he presents us with the *process* of coming to a peak of meaning, only to slip off in search of something further. This eloquently describes the feelings conveyed by his famous crane shots which, at the appropriate moment in the drama, glide into a perfectly expressive composition and then fall away after holding this posture for as long as is seemly.

The Zen philosophy that this camera strategy is said to express and the peculiar texture of his films that it helps describe are of less interest to us than its function as an important and challenging sort of identification. For this gesture of his camera carves out an intangible space which has no meaning of its own but rather is linked to a pretext that develops and itself disappears. This act of response, this co-expression, completes itself in the spectator from whom is demanded neither understanding nor judgment, but the permanent readiness of a distinct yet parallel response. Mizoguchi's films are not objects to be observed but textual acts putting in motion correlative acts of response.

In what way is this style and aesthetic complicit with western representational models? What we have described as "impermanent posturings" and "fixations" of response, Burch accuses of mere pictorialism, catering to the West's facile understanding of Japan as a land of mystery and vague beauty where philosophers and artists wistfully ponder the evanescence of life. Certainly the overwhelming popularity in Europe and America of films such as Kinugasa's *Gate of Hell* with its pastel view of a traditional past gives substance to Burch's charge that Japan in the 1950s cashed in on an international hunger for delicious illusions. Over against the more dialectical, analytical films of the thirties whose subject matter was often socially relevant, these export "festival" films seem escapist and precious, exciting western audiences for that very reason.

But in his blanket condemnation of the rejuvenated Japanese industry, Burch blinds himself to the peculiar use Mizoguchi makes of the pictorialism his films undeniably include and the seductive illusions they just as undeniably tempt the viewer to succumb to. What Burch finds to be "academically decorative" and "opportunistic" is in fact a working past "decoration" in search of its authority

and its value. What he claims is only a "contrived laying of certain traits of [Mizoguchi's] earlier system over the framework of Hollywood codes" might better be thought of as a meditation via those traits on the kind of suffering he explored in his social films of the thirties.

To see this at work one should begin with the first of these late films, **Miss Oyu**. Burch can hardly complain about Mizoguchi cashing in on a ready-made audience, for this film, a critical and box-office flop, sought to revive quite an unpopular genre, the Meiji period film. The project of this revival led him to give Mizutani's set design a most prominent function in the overall effect of nostalgia indicated by the story. More important still, **Miss Oyu** marks the first collaboration between Mizoguchi and Kazuo Miyagawa and initiates the studied use of the elegiac camera movements that enthralled the West in **The Life of Oharu** and that might be said to characterize the late films in general. **Miss Oyu** is the first in a line of films to take aestheticism to the limit in order to peer beyond it.

The source of the film goes a long way in distinguishing Mizoguchi's project from the norm, for **Miss Oyu** derives from one of Junichiro Tanizaki's most famous stories of his "art for art's sake period," *Ashikari*. Tanizaki in the 1930s represented precisely the sort of Japanese artist scorned by Burch. Westerners have always felt at home in his delicious sensual refinement, and in his evocative nature descriptions which invariably are seasoned with the metaphysical. His is a literature of small but stunningly subtle effects.

Ashikari is a perfect example of Tanizaki's philosophy of art for it begins and ends in search of nearly indescribable effects. The story of **Miss Oyu,** which is the narrative heart of this novella, actually comprises but one-half its pages. The remaining half is an elaborate introduction in which a tourist encounters a traveler on the evening of the traditional moon-viewing ceremony by the River Yoda. Tanizaki has carefully given over his narrative voice to an aimless pleasure-seeker, out to relish the landscape and enjoy the country cooking. The story of Oyu has no direct connection to him (or to us) except as a prop to heighten the sensual and psychological effects which he has sought that evening.

Indeed, the introduction is even further contrived by the fact that the interior narrator who tells our tourist the story is himself also an observer at a distance. Although we surmise (and are eventually told) that he is the issue of the romantic tragedy he recounts, his knowledge of that tragedy comes not from direct experience but from his father who told him of Miss Oyu years ago when father and son made their annual pilgrimage to gaze not just at the moon but at a noble lady playing the koto on the porch of her lakeside estate.

And so we approach the tableau of the revered figure, Miss Oyu, through Tanizaki, through the tourist, through the traveler he meets, and that traveler's memory of his father's tale. Oyu is indeed a hazy moon of a lady casting her glow coolly and from afar.

The tale surrounding Oyu only heightens her inaccessibility. A woman of rare independence, she has smitten the heart of Shinosuke, but being a recently widowed mother she is in fact unavailable. Through a uniquely Japanese web of allegiances, duties, and self-sacrificings, Shinosuke marries Oyu's young sister Oshizu and the three establish an unconventional menage. This arrangement outlasts the scandal it causes, but when Oyu learns that because of her, the married couple are living like brother and sister, she is filled with remorse and marries lovelessly. The couple disappears into a Tokyo slum where Oshizu dies in childbirth; Oyu retreats to the lovely villa by Lake Ogura passing her days in an atmosphere of melancholy elegance. Everyone is drawn into this atmosphere: Shinosuke, his son, and now even the tourist whose general sense of sadness is defined and deepened by the story he has heard. To this Tanizaki adds a characteristically haunting coda. Our tourist looks from the moonlit landscape back to his interlocutor. "But where he had been sitting, there was nothing to be seen save the tall grasses swaying and rustling in the wind. The reeds which grew down to the water's edge were fading from sight, and the man had vanished like a wraith in the light of the moon."

The novella stops here, for our guide has succeeded in his search; he has been surprised by the moonscape he went out to see, a moonscape whose "haunting" beauty doubtless contains within it myriad ghostly tales. By this blurring of narrative and spectacle the "framed" tale of Oyu is not the novella's ultimate treasure, for it, too, has been used as a frame, a narrative frame within which the landscape can evoke its peculiar effects.

Tanizaki's effects are precious because they are invariably directed to the single observer. The tourist's highly tuned sensibility is meant to lead our own into an atmosphere that floods us with that eerie feeling of ghostly loss. It is precisely this concentration, cultlike, on private sensation and mystification, which contributes to the suspicions of critics like Noël Burch who indict this aesthetic for its frivolity and uselessness. Neither art nor society is improved, disrupted, or even affected by such stories which nevertheless masquerade as serious.

In adapting *Ashikari* and particularly in enhancing the misty pictorialism of its already evocative imagery, Mizoguchi seems liable to Burch's charges. Yet his is by no means an "art for art's sake" aesthetic; rather it is art for the sake of peering past art's limit to that which precisely but namelessly bounds it. First of all, if Tanizaki aimed to manipulate private sensations, we must say that Mizoguchi's goal is to convey the *impersonal* character of emotion. To begin, he approaches the tale directly, eliminating all three interior narrators and (uncharacteristically) maintaining complete chronological sequence from the moment Shinosuke lays eyes on Oyu to his disappearance into the reeds beyond her lakeside manor.

Furthermore, he distributes viewer identification among the three main characters by offering support through camera movement and point of view to Shinosuke, Oyu, and Oshizu in succession. This keeps us at bay, juggling our sense of the complex feelings involved and reserving our fullest identification for the camera view which outlasts its convergence with the views of any one character.

After the unraveling of the menage toward the end of the film, when Oyu retires to her manor and the couple moves to their Tokyo slum, the camera view asserts its full independence, almost lifting itself beyond the pathetic drama to a general view of human passion and suffering. The style associated with this project borders on the ritualistic. The sequence showing the couple's decline in Tokyo, for instance, opens and closes with symmetrical descriptive shots of the slum, where in the distance a steaming locomotive passes first left (nudging the camera to move aside) and then screen right. Within these temporal and spatial brackets Oshizu dies in childbirth wrapped in Oyu's ceremonial kimono. This instance of dramatic economy is more than a case of understatement to quiet the audience before an explosive finale. It establishes the cool and measured tone with which Mizoguchi brings this potentially torrid melodrama to its end, generalizing rather than cashing in on its sentimental effects.

The final sequence opens with an elaborate tracking shot approaching a picturesque lakeside villa. Circling up to a moon-viewing party, we gradually distinguish Oyu and her retinue of maidservants and artists as they perform sad music, consonant with the night [12]. A baby's cry sends her servants out into the garden where they find Oshizu's infant and a letter from Shinosuke. While Oyu reads this letter commending the baby to her for life, the camera tracks from her face and down across the full length of the koto lying next to her. Never has a film insisted so literally on its own lyrical project. Although nestled in nature, Oyu's villa is utterly artificial, as the delicate shape of the koto, cut off from all background, testifies. Oyu responds to this moment, the culmination of her life's sole passion, in the only way she knows how, by asking her music teacher to play a composition to welcome the new child brought to her by the moon.

In a most daring coda, Mizoguchi frames a fully traditional moonscape, his own "composition" responding to the drama: on the misty moonlit lake, a boatman in the distance rhythmically rows to deposit on the shore a silhouetted passenger. A final tableau, the most painterly of Mizoguchi's entire career, places the hazy moon above a marsh full of rushes. Shinosuke (for it is he) moves *no*-like into the reeds singing the traditional air he had shared in happier times with Oyu:

> Without you here
> Every time I think on it
> All seems melancholy
> Osaka and my life

All the more unbearable.
Don't think badly of me
Our love was wrong.

Shinosuke recedes completely into the reeds leaving us in a landscape which signifies bleakly the passing of man and of love, and yet which signifies this so pathetically that it simultaneously insists on the presence of human feeling in the earth itself [13-16].

Nature has become a sign that Mizoguchi both employs and reads, a crucial paradox that takes us back to a remark Oyu made in an early moment of triumph. After her exquisite koto recital during which she had gone to great lengths to create the proper atmosphere (with candles and incense), she confesses that she barely enjoys her instrument. Instead it is the pomp of the performance that she adores, particularly the ornate Heien era kimono which she wears at once pretentiously and seriously.

Mizoguchi likewise overdoes the atmosphere, cloaking this tale in an ancient, formal pictorial style and nudging its dramatic progression along in a hieratic rhythm. Music, light, composition, and such traditional *topoi* as a boat, the hazy moon, and the rushes of a marsh, concentrate the pathos of the tale in the coda. But just as Oyu felt an authentic rapport with an environment of her own construction, so Mizoguchi can seriously respond to the desolate scene not just of spent human passions but of their dissolution into a pictorial drama of nature: moonlight on a somber marsh.

Here we can measure Mizoguchi's distance from Tanizaki, for the filmmaker has obviously sought to reproduce the elements of the novel's final sentence "The reeds which grew down to the water's edge were fading from sight, and the man had vanished like a wraith in the light of the moon." The sudden break which this passage signals in the novel between a tale and the status of the teller (is he a ghost?) strikes us with an icy eeriness. This is that singular effect which Tanizaki, following Poe, sought to produce in his narrator and in his reader. But Mizoguchi's presentation of the same tableau in no way seeks such a narrative twist. Instead this is the fullest and baldest exposition of the aesthetic strategy that has controlled the entire film, a strategy based once again on identification at a distance. The emotions that these final compositions indisputably arouse are so transpersonal in character (opposed to the sensualism of Tanizaki) that we must question the power and use of identification.

The traditional garb of the moonscape, just like the Heien kimono, bears a definite feeling that we can neither resist nor call our own. Oshizu is happy to end her life enfolded in Oyu's gown, just as Oyu could feel most authentically herself in that gown's ancient aura, an aura, by the way, that Shinosuke and his sister claim belonged to their mother as well. In the same way, Mizoguchi is not being facile, as Burch no doubt would have it, when he calls up these ancient images out of his story; nor is he inventing a personal expression or one suitable to his characters.

Instead, he is invoking an ancient ghost of nature, artificially bringing it up via the magnificent labor of actors, designers, and cameraman. Thus nature is a traditional and an exquisite mask through which paradoxically another nature appears, the bleak nothingness that outlasts the drama that produced it as an image. Transpersonal, even apersonal, emotion in Mizoguchi's aesthetics is a fact of nature, not of individuals, and his film produces out of the artifice of passion (a love story) a truly passionate artifice, this picture.

Mizoguchi's impersonal and indifferent mode of identification must make us question the concept itself. If we insist on defining identification as an illusion, we must do so now in relation to the "real illusion" of the cosmos as Mizoguchi saw it. If we only know reality through texts and only act in relation to our reading of them, then we must become adequate to the texts that precede us. Textuality is not arbitrary. The illusions of life have specific and developing contours and Mizoguchi succeeded in identifying some of those contours through the passion/action of his films.

Surely the proof of Mizoguchi's success in this method is the conclusion of *Ugetsu*. There his camera explicitly participates in the duping of the hero Genjuro who hallucinates the appearance of his dead wife upon his return to his empty home. But Genjuro retires to bed and the camera remains with the vision it has conjured up, with Miyagi who kneels before the fire and sadly does her mending. For several minutes we watch and sympathize with the ghost of Miyagi, waiting for the dawn sadly to sublime her into its white haze. What is remarkable here is not merely the paradox of presence and absence which the film has created, but Mizoguchi's willingness to learn from that paradox, his ability to adjust his sensibility to the sensibility of a phantom of his own creation.

Is this identification? And do the phantoms of his films likewise demand from us an identification that makes us adjust our sensibilities to them? I think they do, yet this is a very particular kind of identification indeed. Richard Wollheim, in his essay on identification in Freud, distinguishes between the empathic and the sympathetic imagination, noting that we may suffer the same things as the subject of imagination or we may suffer in response to what we imagine the character to feel. Wollheim's explicit incorporation of the term "internal audience" within his notion of the imagination has even broader implications for film theory. Identification in his scheme can only be the name of a certain form of psychic potency, one in which our internal audience coincides with the subject of the imagination, as when I imagine my father and respond as I feel certain he would respond. Mizoguchi's method is quite other than this, coming much closer to sympathetic imagination wherein the internal audience is free to respond in its own way to a subject it nevertheless imagines in the strongest possible manner.

I have argued that this mode of identification is represented by the activity of reading, wherein two consciousnesses come together without coincidence across the body of a text. The results of this encounter are not pathological, locking us into the view of another; they are potentially therapeutic, expanding our range, shifting perspectives, allowing what Ricoeur aptly calls a complete redescription of reality from the parallactic vision that our crossover has made possible.

But while avoiding the trap of pathological identification, Mizoguchi, we have seen, does not enter the camp and campaign ruled over by Barthes, Burch, and all the apostles of modernism who preach an ultimately solipsistic (de)constructivism. Mizoguchi provides a third way of dealing with a character, a text, and by extension with life itself. Through a studied discipline that permits the crossing over to another (a text, a person, a point of view) and a return to oneself, he imagines sympathetically in order to respond personally to the encounter. The object of imagination provides the rule for the response in much the way that, in Ricoeur's view, the semantic and syntactic aspects of a metaphorical combination provide a rule for interpretation. This doesn't mean that they point to a final or correct meaning; instead they invite us to roam in a new field of meaning but one that has been purchased for us by a pre-text.

In this way Mizoguchi's cinema performs the function that I consider most crucial for art in our epoch. Through the physicality and otherness of a set of signifiers, we are urged to entertain a new range of thoughts that promise to affect us. Captive neither of the artwork (traditional illusionism) nor of our own constructions (modernism), we adjust our sensibilities and potentially our lives to the rightness of something standing before us and inviting our imagination, inviting our sympathy, in short, inviting the gesture of our reading.

Robert N. Cohen (essay date 1992)

SOURCE: "Why Does Oharu Faint? Mizoguchi's 'The Life of Oharu' and Patriarchal Discourse," in *Reframing Japanese Cinema: Authorship, Genre, History*, edited by Arthur Nolletti, Jr., and David Desser, Indiana University Press, 1992, pp. 3-55.

[*In the following essay, Cohen interprets Mizoguchi's portrayal of the plight of women in Japan in his film* The Life of Oharu *using the Western concept of patriarchal control, concluding that Mizoguchi created a "fractured" character in Oharu, which strengthens rather than weakens the patriarchy he set out to question.*]

There is little doubt today in the West that Mizoguchi's most important subject has been the plight of the Japanese woman. At the same time, we realize that Mizoguchi was a director of commercial films, and consequently, that his work represents an institutional discourse, the structure and ideology of which inform this subject matter. Thus in view of the general feeling that the women in his films are essentially powerless to affect their lives in

the narratives, the concept of patriarchy offers a way to discuss the limitations placed on them at the level of discourse. It is here that we can approach the apparent ambiguities of his films and ask questions concerning the sources of pleasure in his texts, the function of women as object and icon, and the subjective positioning of both male and female characters.

It is, therefore, the purpose of this essay to apply the Western theory of patriarchy to one of Mizoguchi's most prominent films about women, *The Life of Oharu* (*Saikaku ichidai onna,* Shin Toho, 1952). This late film seems especially suited for such an analysis, not only because the common interpretation of the film becomes increasingly doubtful under such scrutiny, but also because *Oharu* is an example of Mizoguchi's film style at its most enigmatic. It is largely a work in the director's characteristic style (long takes, great camera-to-subject distances, editing strategies based on a ninety-degree rule), but more important, it also includes several instances of the shot/reverse shot, which establishes a specific character point of view, and which is almost nonexistent in Mizoguchi's other films. What is most significant, of course, is that the reverse shot is the linchpin of classical Western film and the most fundamental structure of patriarchal discourse as it has been defined in Western film theory. Therefore, an evaluation of the ways the reverse shot functions in *Oharu* will tell us how well the film either confirms or contradicts the patriarchal implications underlying the Western film, whose conventions the Japanese understood so well.

The fate of Mizoguchi's heroine, for example, at the end of *Oharu* exemplifies the precarious interpretation that critics have offered for Oharu's becoming the itinerant priest. It is the consensus of opinion that Oharu triumphs in her unwitting battle to overcome an oppressive society. She is said to "transcend" her life on earth, and in Audie Bock's phrase, as the priest Oharu "prays for all humanity." Clearly this spiritual victory is one that is exclusively reserved for women in Mizoguchi, and in a revealing passage Dudley and Paul Andrew associate it with the woman's special vision.

> Most frequently, the women in Mizoguchi's films scream with their glance. . . . They see through the system, through the audience, into the structure of an impersonal cosmos. Revolt thus leads the way to a kind of stoic contemplation, which in his late films Mizoguchi seemed to prize beyond all other goals.

The woman's access to vision notwithstanding, it is one of the functions of patriarchy to position women as objects of contemplation, as symbols for what they lack in the signifying structures of the narratives. Men, Dudley Andrew and Paul Andrew tell us, "initiate the actions . . . carry on the way of the world . . . are suited for action, progress." According to the theory of patriarchy, however, it is as active subjects of the discourse that men become the controllers of the look and vision that functions to objectify women as passive objects. It is, therefore, hard to maintain the view that Oharu triumphs at the end of the film when to achieve this position she is kept passive in the discourse, denied a sexual identity at the end of the film, and made to assume the guilt of others.

In the West, patriarchy has been a major subject of feminist theory for at least fifteen years. For this study, however, the works of two authors are especially important: Laura Mulvey and her pioneering essay "Visual Pleasure and Narrative Cinema," and Mary Ann Doane, particularly *The Desire to Desire*. The former essay and its subsequent elaborations have established the "system of the look" as the basic cinematic figure by which patriarchy structures male desire in the Western film and positions women as both "masculine spectators" and feminine objects of the screen spectacle. It is the essential instability of such structures of subject positioning and desire which has led feminist critics particularly to the issues that Doane addresses—namely, the characteristics of melodrama conceived as a specific kind of patriarchal discourse where women are defined primarily in relation to forms of narcissism and neurosis. Doane's work in this area is exemplary for what it allows us to observe about Oharu's psychopathology and in relation to the unique tension between the forms of audience identification and distance that characterize many of the director's films.

Since psychoanalysis forms the basis of these concepts and their application, it is important to point out initially that there are at least two related aspects of Mizoguchi's film that have profound psychoanalytic consequences: Oharu's failed search for a stable identity, and the fact that she faints three times over the course of the narrative. *Oharu* traces the fall of the title character from her exalted life as a court lady through the separate strata of seventeenth-century Japanese society until she lands as a common street prostitute. Told largely in flashback from Oharu's point of view, the story portrays her life as a series of crises in which she is unable to establish herself in any socially defined role, whether it be as mother, daughter, wife, geisha, concubine, or nun. The flashback of these events culminates in Oharu's fainting for the last time. The convergence of these two occurrences thus authorizes an interpretation based on their cause-effect relationship, whereby Oharu's fainting must be seen as a reaction to the form and the content of her memory. Such a radical response on the woman's part suggests a desire to avoid deep-seated anxieties caused by the knowledge that her sense of self is not stable or secure. In Freudian terms, Oharu's predicament is succinctly described by Philip Rosen in the following passage:

> Primary experiences of identity are constructed against a radical anxiety, summarized as castration anxiety. Processes of desire, sexuality, and fantasy are intertwined with consciousness of self, which is produced to counter against the founding anxiety and is always in dialectic with it. As a result, the normal experience of identity occurs only on condition that its basic processes are hidden from the "I" thus constructed. This is an essential Freudian point: There is always a fundamental

*mis*recognition involved in the individual's desire to find—or recognize—his or her self as stable and secure.

Accordingly, Oharu's fainting at the end of the flashback represents the failure of this process of "misrecognition." Since fainting itself is often taken as a corollary for blindness where the individual displaces a perceived psychic threat onto the site of the body, Oharu's fainting can be taken as a neurotic response to her memory where castration anxiety threatens to enter the text at the end of the flashback. The woman's narration of her past therefore can be analyzed as Oharu's Oedipal journey, and her fainting suggests its irresolution. Patriarchy, however, has a stake in the outcome of the discourse, and it is through this influence that the Hollywood film regularly represses the full expression of woman's sexual identity. Similarly, in Mizoguchi's film we will try to apprehend an analogous system of patriarchal influences that can explain the repression of the Japanese woman and the conversion of her body into the symptoms of her cinematic illness.

In the Hollywood film, patriarchy asserts itself most conspicuously through the subordination of the female characters by the controlling gaze of the male. According to Laura Mulvey, because men are the central characters of most Hollywood films, it is through an identification with the male protagonist that the spectator enters the action of a film. Point of view, and particularly the shot/reverse shot, place men in a position to control the narrative by possessing the gaze that marks them as subjects who look and women as objects to be looked at. Pleasure is established for the character, and by identification for the spectator, in looking at women as objects of a male desire. Men thus actively control women and the narrative by controlling the look.

In *Oharu,* there are two series of reverse shots that position Oharu as the subject of the look, and both bracket the woman's flashback. In the opening sequence in the famous hall of Buddhas, there are four shots of Oharu looking at the statues intercut with three point-of-view shots of what she sees. In the last, her gaze rests on one statue, and over this figure the face of Katsunosuke, her first lover, is superimposed twice. At the end of the flashback, we have a similar series of POV [point of view] shots that establish Oharu in relation to the statues. From a medium long shot of Oharu inside the hall, there are two shots of her looking at the statues and two POV shots of what she sees. In the second, the statues go out of focus, and in the following shot of recognition, Oharu projects a great sense of fear and then she faints.

In these examples Oharu assumes the position of the subject, whose look objectifies the man, Katsunosuke. According to these series of shots, we have two potentially subversive moments within the discourse if it is actually being governed by the laws of patriarchy. According to Mulvey's characterization of the woman in patriarchy as possessing a "to-be-looked-at-ness," Oharu's active look constitutes a reversal. There are several issues, however, in **Oharu** which govern the woman's access to the look and foreground her essential "to-be-looked-at" position. Most of these center around the polarities set up in the text between the possibilities of seeing and being seen.

First off, the interior of the temple acts as a certain haven for Oharu, given the fact that throughout the film she is forever being banished from place to place, turned out, as it were, from areas associated with stability and belonging to those scarcely offering safe repose. It is in this inner chamber that Oharu has her fullest access to vision. It is here, too, that she has access to her memory, which recalls her past and her relationship with Katsunosuke, the retainer of lesser rank, who is beheaded for his affair with her. Therefore, there is little doubt that Oharu's gaze inside the temple is an erotic look that sets up her pleasure as a major signifying element of the text. Simultaneously, it is Oharu's very access to vision and the accessibility of her past, of Katsunosuke, and her self, which are rendered problematic throughout the film. This is clearly specified in Oharu's gesture of ceremoniously removing her scarf during the first temple scene, at the precise moment she realizes that one of the Buddhist statues reminds her of Katsunosuke. Here she reveals herself openly and freely for the first time in contrast to the opening shots of the film where, as a common street prostitute, Oharu conspicuously keeps her face hidden.

The contrast further reveals not only that the film will be about Oharu's inner journey, but also that her desire for knowledge will take precedence over her relations with the world around her. This is clearly specified through the inner/outer dichotomy where outside the temple Oharu recoils from her feminine position as someone who is seen—the prostitute who shuns revealing her face—but inside, she actively positions herself as the subject who sees. Since the text establishes that this latter desire is indistinguishable from Oharu's desire for Katsunosuke, her self-image is inexplicably bound up with him. Oharu's position in the text at the threshold of memory thus places her as the voyeur, as someone who wishes to see without being seen. This position, which is denied to women in terms of psychoanalytic theory, points to the possible explanation that Oharu suffers in the film because she possesses a desire forbidden by its overriding patriarchy. It is almost as if her gesture of removing the scarf is the key which unlocks a Pandora's Box of memories that inauspiciously culminate in her fainting at the end of the flashback.

Additionally, the shot/reverse shot preceding the flashback is characterized by Katsunosuke's fundamental absence from the film's historical present. He is objectified only within Oharu's imagination. Oharu, therefore, retains an essentially feminine position by becoming the subject of a daydream. Doane raises this issue in her discussion of what she calls the "medical discourse films" of the Hollywood cinema during the 1940s, in which she refers to Freud and Breuer and their study of female hysteria: "For it is daydreaming which instigates the illness in the first place—an uncontrolled and addressee-less daydreaming."

Oharu thus seems to have access to a subject position only in relation to Katsunosuke as an object of fantasy. It is consequently only in this position that Oharu as the woman may become active within the discourse. Throughout the rest of the film, in both the flashback and the action after she faints, Oharu is represented passively, as the object of the desire of others.

Oharu's subjectivity in this early scene also suggests another of Doane's observations. Like the illnesses which play a part in medical discourse films, Oharu's fainting, "implicat[es] woman's entire being." She is not merely an object of spectacle possessing a body that functions only to be looked at by men. When her entire being is at stake, the woman's body, in Doane's phrase, becomes "fully a signifier" of that which is invisible, by which she means that the woman's body signifies an illness. Her status in the discourse thus shifts from the "spectacular" to the "symptomatic." Likewise, Oharu can assume a subject position normally reserved in the classic cinema for the male subject without provoking a crisis in the film's overall patriarchy. This implies that patriarchy can be operating in **Oharu** even though Oharu's body escapes being "entirely" signified as "an object of male vision." Equally, it is possible that Oharu has access to the look in this early sequence only on condition that she remain castrated and other throughout the remainder of the film.

In the system of the look, as Mulvey first proposed, the woman is constituted as an icon for the pleasure of the male, but it is ultimately an ambiguous pleasure, for the woman in the classic text represents the threat of castration for the male spectator. To determine whether or not Oharu as an image represents such a threat requires an examination of two aspects of Mizoguchi's film. One is that Oharu is totally objectified during the course of the flashback, turned into an object of pleasure for a succession of male characters. The second stems from the fact that Oharu is treated differently under the law than her first lover. For the crime of sleeping with someone of a differing rank, Katsunosuke is condemned to die by beheading, while Oharu is banished. Both sentences are established in the narrative as legal consequences of the patriarchal law in Japan that seeks to maintain the rigid vertical hierarchy of social relationships. Within the parameters set up in the discourse, the woman's "fall" is thus represented as a series of lesser banishments, where each time a relationship "fails," she is sent away, put, as it were, out of sight. In this way, Oharu receives special but unequal treatment and is punished by a law that is characterized by treating the woman's whole body as the offending object. Oharu is thus identified as a woman who, like her counterpart in the classic Western text, is represented as being "overpresent."

Being constituted as the female and singled out for special treatment and punishment, Oharu therefore symbolically represents that which must be repressed. As she moves through and is moved by the narrative during the flashback, she is "read" by each of the male characters after Katsunosuke's death as a feared object. Her banishment then becomes a series of textual positions that identify Oharu as the object of a desire whose goal is "not to see" the woman as a threatening presence. This goal is clearly the sole possession of the patriarchal forces that structure the text. What is demanded of Oharu by the male characters is in effect a complete silencing of her femininity and her complete exclusion from collective life. Oharu is thus compelled to give up her access to the look, thereby taking on the guilt of others and repressing her sexuality. All of this is played out against a series of conflicting positions centered around Oharu as both the desired and the feared object.

Each of these general tendencies of the Mizoguchi text suggests that Oharu's image in fact does represent sexual difference, and consequently the castration threat for the male spectator. Its clearest expression occurs in the next-to-last episode of her flashback. Earlier, on the same night that Oharu enters the temple as the aging prostitute, she is stopped by a man, who she thinks is a customer. She carefully covers her face to keep him from seeing her true age. They enter a cheap inn, and the man then leads her near a back room where several young pilgrims sit around a table. They all crane their necks to get a glimpse of Oharu's face, which she still keeps conspicuously hidden. With all male eyes toward her, the man removes Oharu's scarf and raises his lantern to give the others a clearer view of her. He says, "You want a girl. Take a look at this witch." The men stare and then look away self-consciously while the man tells them that if they wish, Oharu will lead them in a life of sin. He then thanks her and pays her off. She looks at the coins and then stops. Returning to the men, Oharu suddenly hisses at them with a demented air, hunches her back, and assumes the pose of a cat, clawing at them as if to pluck out their eyes. The men recoil from her, when again she stops, looks back at the money, laughs, and thanks them. She then leaves with the men's voices nervously laughing offscreen.

The first thing to notice is that this scene is consciously ironical. For this man, who so unabashedly uses Oharu as an object, is one of the few throughout the entire film to acknowledge Oharu for what she is now: a ridiculous aging courtesan. He restates her own self-knowledge about what she has become in order to survive. He therefore acknowledges her true feminine identity, but not only does he do it for the wrong reason, he does it too late. This fact is of primary significance because as Doane makes clear, "mistiming" is one of the fundamental requirements of pathos, part of what Franco Moretti calls the "rhetoric of the too late." The depth of Oharu's humiliation in this scene is a result of this mechanism which is "related to a certain construction of temporality in which communication or recognitions take place but are mistimed."

It is not only the man's "too late" recognition of Oharu that distinguishes this scene, but also the heroine's self-recognition of what she has become. This explains Oharu's sense of irony, while at the same time it provides her motivation for assuming the pose of the cat. This position refers back to the sequence where Oharu turns a cat loose on the merchant's wife, who has humiliated her by forcing her to cut off her long, beautiful hair. The moment in both scenes thus represents Oharu's castrating desire for revenge. The nervous laughter of the pilgrims in the inn signifies their half-realization of this threat. However, Oharu quickly realizes the futility of her gesture in the later scene, which suggests a further reference to Doane's comments on female narcissism:

> In his article, "On Narcissism: An Introduction," Freud compares the self-sufficiency and inaccessibility of the narcissistic woman to that of "cats and the large beasts of prey" (as well as that of the child, the criminal, and the humorist). The cat is the signifier of a female sexuality which is self-sufficient, and, above all, objectless.

Oharu's primary position throughout her narration as the object of repression thus undercuts her aggressive stance as the cat. Her sexuality, which the man singles out for special consideration, offering it as a lure and a trap for the young men under his care, becomes blunted and "inaccessible." The viewer is made aware of these conflicts and their effects on Oharu's character precisely because of the pathos of the scene, and the distance separating Oharu from her original desires.

The scene's importance in the discourse, however, as the culminating episode of Oharu's reminiscence comes from the power of the woman to take over the control of vision. She is taken into the inn and used by the man as a visual sign of the forbidden object. In this way, she is offered to the pilgrims as an aberration of their sexual desires. Once Oharu sees the bitter irony of the situation, however, she sizes control and flaunts her "to-be-seen-ness," turning the men's aggressiveness back on them and mocking her position as the object of the look. To some extent, she thus holds out the threat of castration as a desirable position both for the pilgrims and for the male spectator. This ambivalence, however, is immediately dissipated again through Oharu's control of vision as she looks down at the money in her hand and laughs. The men's eyes follow her gesture, moving from the woman's body to the money. Through this move their discomfort is assuaged.

This gesture in effect relates Oharu to the money as a commodity which increases the pathetic nature of her degradation. It also represents an additional feature of pathos characterized by Doane as "a sense of disproportion—between desires and their fulfillment or between the transgression . . . and the punishment associated with it." Any sympathy the viewer may feel at this point in the text is derived from this sense of the disproportion between Oharu's original "sin" and these obvious consequences. These associations link Oharu through her aggressive behavior not only to the merchant's wife, but also to her liaison with Katsunosuke. Thus her whole life as portrayed in the flashback comes to bear on these few gestures, and it is Oharu's control of the trajectory of vision that makes this possible even without a shot/reverse shot structure.

Even though it remains an oversimplification to see Oharu's figure in itself throughout the film as an icon for the castration threat, the text acknowledges her sexual difference in this scene through the laughter of the men, which is kept off-screen. As Oharu walks away in silence, she comes to embody that difference and lack which the discourse sets up through the *mise-en-scène* and its sound track. Through a unique form of suture, the men's voices create the perception of absence, which, like the suturing effect of the shot/reverse shot, stimulates, as Kaja Silverman says, a desire "to see more."

According to orthodox suture theory, the breaking up of scenographic space into character point-of-view shots forces the spectator to become aware of the frame, and thus the limitations on his ability to control what he sees. "He discovers that he is only authorized to see what happens to be in the axis of the gaze of another spectator, who is ghostly or absent." This "absent one" is conceptualized as the "speaking subject," which is a position in the classic narrative that is never acknowledged within the film.

In the Mizoguchi text, which generally eschews the point-of-view shot, there are invariably elements of the *mise-en-scène* that force an awareness of the frame onto the spectator and the limits it poses on what he can see. Without articulating an absent gaze, the Mizoguchi text continually marks absence as a function of the controlling third-person view. Characters stand just off-screen during dialogue scenes which continue across the frame line or, as in the scene at the inn above, character voices emanate from an off-screen space before, during, and after the central action. In none of these constructions is there an explicit subject who is articulated as different from the speaking subject of the film.

We can theorize a difference, however, that is set up through the absence which is signified through off-screen space. The voices of the pilgrims at the inn signify this absent field, and it is the text's refusal to return to them that implies the existence of an absent, speaking subject. As Silverman shows in her reading of Hitchcock's *Psycho*, "The whole operation of suture can be made more rather than less irresistible when the field of the speaking subject is continually implied." This implication, I would argue, constitutes an essential structural tension that underlies a great many of Mizoguchi's most idiosyncratic scenes in terms of their difference from Western classical film. Held within the third-person, nondifferentiated shot, the movement and framing of characters continually articulates a system of discourse predicated on presence

and absence, "unmediated, 'unsoftened' by the intervention of a human gaze."

An extreme example of this process occurs in Katsunosuke's beheading scene, in which the sword itself functions to center vision and structure absence without a human subject. In this one-shot scene, Katsunosuke dictates his final message to Oharu, and then the camera leaves the man and centers the sword in the frame as the executioner prepares to carry out the sentence. Through a series of camera and object movements, the blade enters and exits the frame as the central identifying presence until the camera pans up with it, and the blade slashes out of frame, leaving an almost blank sky to mark its absence. The executioner then steps back into frame, the sword with him, at which point the camera reframes the blade and then pans down its length until the scene fades to black.

Here there is no mistaking the symbolic power invested in the sword merely by its central presence in the discourse. Its movements establish its link to the castrating power of the law. Not only is the actual beheading accomplished offscreen, with the movements of the sword standing for Katsunosuke's death, but the articulation of excessive absences in such a scene of heightened spectacle no doubt intensifies the spectator's anxiety concerning what is kept off-screen. Without a shot/reverse shot, the scene powerfully manipulates the viewer's frustrated desire to see in such a manner that only the fade to black can reassert the viewer's right to control.

Not all of **Oharu**'s reverse shots are as radical as this example. In fact, the initial scene inside the hall of Buddhas essentially duplicates the orthodox suturing process which introduces the field of the Absent One. Whenever we have a one-shot of Oharu looking at the statues, Katsunosuke, whose face has been superimposed there, becomes the signifier of absence. His absence from the frame alternated with hers creates this conventional suturing effect. What is further evident, however, is that at the end of the scene, Mizoguchi organizes the images so that they disavow this absence and lack as in the Western cinema, by producing again this desire to see more. In this case, the "more" is not another shot of Katsunosuke but the entire content of the flashback, which Mizoguchi places immediately after a final shot of Oharu looking. Her fantasy/daydream is thus tied to the hermeneutic code associated with Katsunosuke's presence in this early scene, and the spectator's desire to learn Oharu's story is substituted for Katsunosuke's absence in the last shot of the reverse-field figure.

The motivating forces behind the film's long flashback can thus be ascribed to those elements of patriarchy that function to disavow absence and lack, which, Mulvey proposed, imply the castration threat for the male spectator. Her two proposals for disavowal have to do with the ways narratives progress and the ways they are interrupted through fetishizing the female as an icon. Both strategies have their place in **Oharu**.

In the first instance, what Mulvey calls voyeurism, the patriarchal text attributes to the heroine characteristics that establish her guilt. In Oharu's memory of the events of her life, this is indeed the case. Katsunosuke offers her personal devotion and the promise of a true loving relationship through marriage. He first says to her, "I want to make you happy," and in his final message, he urges, "Please find a good man and have a good life with him. But, be sure to marry only when there is true mutual love." Then to the executioners, he says, "I hope the time will come when there is no social rank." This is the message Oharu takes away, when she questions her father, "If we love each other, what if our ranks are different?" Oharu, therefore, explicitly believes in the philosophy which Katsunosuke voices, and her response to it is to faint in the man's arms the first time she hears it, thereby giving herself to him. In this way, with a show of feminine overemotionalism, she expresses her femininity, which makes her more susceptible to the ideal he represents. Throughout the flashback, Oharu is continually reminded of this ideal, if only in an abstract way. Only once does she again refer to Katsunosuke, even though the ideal he represents to her colors the spectator's response to her fall by its pathos. As indicated before, a sense of disproportion informs the pathetic discourse, a distinction "between desires and their fulfillment." Oharu's suffering and her "tragedy" throughout the subsequent episodes thus evolve in her memory as a consequence of her uncompromising moral stance and the restrictive social laws which make her liaison with Katsunosuke a "just" crime.

In contrast to this reading of the flashback, Oharu is not punished simply for being gullible, or for actually marrying a man of inferior rank, but for sleeping with him, for committing an error in conduct. Therefore, even though the disparity in their social ranks signifies the violation of the law, it is her sexual nature specifically for which she is punished. The patriarchal law exerts its control over her by banishing her from Kyoto and, consequently, by contributing to her loss of parental esteem, which has the effect of converting Oharu into an object of exchange. She is returned to her family in exchange for giving up her feminine "to-be-looked-at" nature. She is reconstituted as a daughter, and her return to her family, characterized by her father as the destruction of family honor, is the text's mark of the denial of her sexual nature. The text pushes her into a regressive position, and her words to her father, which combine the concepts of love and social rank, further deflect the spectator's attention away from Oharu's sexual guilt. Her "moral" crime and its extension in the betrayal of her father are thus the marks of disavowal characteristic of the voyeuristic strategy.

Oharu's return to the family's provincial home closes the opening sequence of the film and constitutes an essential paradigm for the subsequent action of the flashback. In each of the following episodes, Oharu enters into a new relationship as the object of an exchange, the purpose of which can be ascribed to the desire of patriarchy to control Oharu and her sexuality. In the sequence preceding Oharu's sojourn with Lord Matsudaira, for example, the "search for the ideal beauty" episode, Oharu is discovered dancing with a group of provincial daughters. In the only male point-of-view shot of the flashback, Oharu is singled out and taken away from the other dancing women. To cover over the immediate threat of castration this suturing instance signifies in classical narrative, Matsudaira's messenger falls to his knees and proclaims, "I'll buy her." Immediately, the merchant agrees to act as intermediary, and the narrative resumes with Oharu's father selling his daughter to the lord. In this way, the lack enunciated through the "Absent One" in the reverse shot of Oharu dancing is disavowed by the resumption of narrative which converts the woman into an object of exchange. She is selected for this position, as in each of the following episodes, because her femininity meets the needs of the men who purchase her. Likewise, she is eventually banished from each relationship when this femininity seeks expression and recognition through a sexuality that is invariably problematic.

This view of Oharu as a commodity is structured by the discourse itself, whose logic determines the actions and thoughts of the woman throughout the flashback. Thus in each episode of her fall, Oharu's problematic sexuality is expressed primarily through the woman's body. Most often it is her inherent "to-be-looked-at" nature which puts Oharu's social position into jeopardy, when the mere sight of her elicits a male desire that ultimately forces her away and down to the next level of degradation. Often, however, individual parts of her body are singled out for special treatment. Her hair is cut by the jealous wife of the merchant as a way to erase the visual attraction Oharu holds for her husband. In the Matsudaira sequence, it is the uterus, the center of female reproduction, which is the focus of her appeal—she is brought there to have a child—and when she is no longer needed, she is pathetically separated from the lord and her child. As a commodity, therefore, Oharu is represented exactly like the typical woman in the Western maternal melodrama, where

> the texts bring into play the contradictory position of the mother within a patriarchal society—a position formulated by the injunction that she focus desire on the child and the subsequent demand to give up the child to the social order. Motherhood is conceived as the always uneasy conjunction of an absolute closeness and a forced distance.

This distance between Oharu and her child dominates the last part of the narrative and creates the great pathos of the film. We can see that the text, therefore, contains two major narrative threads: one which involves the social law and Oharu's relation to it, and another, the patriarchal law that controls her sexuality and her reproductive identity. Significantly, it is the commodification of the heroine through the discourse that transforms the first into the second. After Katsunosuke is beheaded, there is almost no mention of the social law and rank that he represents in Oharu's explicit memory. She becomes no social crusader for societal reform, no activist trying to make a martyr out of Katsunosuke and his courageous stance for the rights of the individual. Instead she devotes herself to the simple pursuits of happiness and personal satisfaction as a woman, and the fact that she acknowledges herself as a commodity in these pursuits represents the deflection of her desire from an identification with others to an identification with herself. To extend the former into the action of the flashback would mean a critique of the patriarchal basis of Japanese society. Since we can argue that the purpose of the flashback is to uphold the patriarchy of the discourse, it is the woman who is put at fault and not society.

This explains why Oharu's memory is overwhelmingly preoccupied with feelings and experiences associated with being victimized. This too explains why Oharu is kept from her son at the end of the film. She is guilty, not, as Matsudaira's vassals contend, because Oharu has humiliated the clan by her life of degradation, but simply because she has lived her life as a Japanese woman.

At the same time the patriarchy of Mizoguchi's text invokes the mechanism of voyeurism to control the heroine during the extended flashback, investigating her guilt and meting out punishment, it simultaneously establishes the beauty of Oharu's position, overvaluing her through the mechanism Mulvey describes as fetishistic scopophilia. This form of disavowal converts the woman into a fetish object for the male spectator whereby her beauty is substituted for the threat she invariably poses as the signifier of sexual difference.

In many ways, the description of this mechanism in *Oharu* takes us to the heart of one of the most idiosyncratic aspects of Mizoguchi's style: the tension so often displayed in all his films between identification and distance. These are the moments when Mizoguchi's camera will hold the characters in long shots during moments of great emotional significance. In *Oharu,* these examples occur in an extreme form, sometimes functioning like a coda for the preceding action, and often followed by a fade to black. There are four instances of the technique: the scene of Oharu's attempted suicide after Katsunosuke's parting note, the last shot of the geisha house sequence, the last shot of Oharu playing the samisen after catching a glimpse of her son, and the last shot in the film of Oharu as the traveling priest. The examples are similar to but somewhat different from Mizoguchi's overall tendency to maintain a generally large camera-to-subject distance and do not indicate the full range of meanings that the technique entails. Their usage in *Oharu,* therefore, is a unique instance of Mizoguchi's style which functions to fetishize the figure of the woman within the specific patriarchal context of this film.

Most commentators on this aspect of Mizoguchi's work hold the concepts of identification and distance as binary oppositions. The typical features of Mizoguchi's distanciation are thought to weaken the spectator's identification with the characters on the screen, thereby increasing the viewer's autonomy and powers of discrimination. The Mizoguchi distance is thus assumed to be Brechtian in being a critical strategy which deconstructs the transparency of the traditional classical codes. These codes, in turn, are believed to support the fact that Mizoguchi's films are most often intense melodramas of extreme pathos. Distance is considered an antidote to the overemotionalism that his films constantly approach, but which often fails to materialize because of the lack of audience involvement with the characters. Conversely, however, as the examples from *Oharu* show, it is the very foundations of melodrama, its great emotionalism and its pathos, that the Mizoguchi distance intensifies in this film. Based on the concepts of disproportion and mistiming, these scenes make the woman into a fetish object, not by emphasizing distance over identification but by combining the two processes.

In each of the four scenes we take to correspond to Mulvey's second category of patriarchal disavowal, a sense of disproportion characterizes Oharu's relationship with something she lacks. It is this distance between Oharu and the object of her desire that provides the pathos of each scene. In the suicide attempt, it is Katsunosuke that Oharu mourns, and whom she attempts to join in death by trying to kill herself. The camera keeps her and her mother in long shot as they run through the bamboo grove, and their dialogue informs the viewer directly about these issues. The subject of the scene is thus Katsunosuke's death and Oharu's distant response to it. Likewise, in the geisha house, the subject of the entire preceding segment is money, its power to corrupt, and Oharu's refusal to succumb to its lure. In the last shot of this scene, Oharu stands in the extreme background as the counterfeiter is led away by the police. The restaurant owner and the others who are left in the frame throw down the bogus coins in disgust while Oharu stands above in all her geisha finery, representing her distance from money and power. Outside the temple after Oharu has been thrown out of the nunnery, it is her child from whom she has been separated. She watches him from afar, and then she sits in front of her samisen and cries. And in the final shot of the film, the long shot frames Oharu as the priest, her distance from any identifiable sexuality marked through her ambiguous dress.

In each of these cases, the spectator's ability to understand the emotions in the scene without the use of close-ups comes from the relationship established in the text between the character and the explicit intent of the scene expressed through either dialogue or action. At times this relationship is easier to read than at others. In the suicide attempt, it is Oharu's loss of Katsunosuke that determines her emotions. In the scene following Oharu's viewing of her son, it is her separation from him that motivates her depression. At the geisha house, it is Oharu's lack of money in relation to the rest of her life; in the final shot, it is her lack of a feminine identity and more. It is less important, however, in Mizoguchi's discourse to know exactly what the character feels, because knowing less does not make the shot less emotional. In fact, the scenes often become unbearably emotional because of the distance that is represented between Oharu and what she desires. This emotion is, therefore, intensified through the mistiming that the sense of disproportion signifies. As Doane again observes, "Moving narratives manifest an unrelenting linearity which allows the slippage between what is and what should have been to become visible. What the narratives demonstrate above all is the irreversibility of time." It is this aspect of *Oharu* that results from its general picaresque form with its precise cause/effect structure punctuated by these "interruptions" which heighten and foreground Oharu's position as the one who suffers. It is at these moments that the temporal aspect of Mizoguchi's film as melodrama functions to create the most intense feelings of pathos.

The lack of closeness between the spectator and Oharu in these scenes represents the lack that Oharu represents as a woman, and thus her position as the fetish object. This is established through the distance and temporality that are specific marks of the Mizoguchi text as melodrama. Simultaneously, the beauty of the compositions and the position bestowed on Oharu as an aesthetic object mark her as a fetish for the male viewer. Oharu becomes appealing both as a signifier of suffering and as an aesthetic object, "satisfying in itself," as Mulvey says. In this position, the woman comes closest to representing a sign of disavowal for the male spectator.

Significantly, Mizoguchi's brand of fetishism does not break up Oharu's body into parts through separate shots, dwelling on her face or figure. Instead, it frames her whole body, which emphasizes its completeness, but places it against a background which seems more complete, more narratively significant than the immediate action implies. Noel Burch has commented on the "surplus of iconographic signs" in Mizoguchi's distancing shots where the environment included in the frame signifies elements seemingly extraneous to the narrative. Far from diluting the narrative at these points, however, Mizoguchi's distance intensifies it, especially in scenes such as the above, where what the heroine lacks in the fiction implies its completion through the overdetermined environment which contains her. Her whole body then takes on this symbolic aspect of absence and lack, and it is only through the long shots, through the various distancing devices, that Mizoguchi is able to accomplish this unique form of disavowal. More significant still is the fact, as Doane admirably demonstrates, that an identification between the woman and her body signifies a narcissism that is a specific pathological condition of women caught up in the male desire of most mainstream narratives.

By the logic that patriarchy imposes on Oharu's character, her memory gains the force of a psychic trauma which triggers her fainting as a hysterical attack. In Freudian terms, "the nucleus of an hysterical attack . . . is a memory, the hallucinatory reliving of the scene which was significant for the illness." This return of the repressed, again according to Freudian theory, takes the form of the projection onto others of the guilt an individual feels over the events in memory. This kind of distortion in the memories of victims of hysteria conforms to the pattern of guilt that places Oharu as the one who is wronged by others in her own personal narrative. The crucial point is, nevertheless, that "the returning portions of the memory are distorted by being replaced by analogous images from contemporary life; thus they are distorted only in one way—by chronological shifting but not by the formation of a substitute."

This explanation underscores Katsunosuke's prominence in Oharu's memory. Her relations with him, placed in her memory as the initial cause of her suffering, become the founding relationship of her psychic life and function as the paradigm for all Oharu's future relations with others. Katsunosuke becomes her ego ideal, which is a position in the actual chronology of her life that should be taken over by her father. In the logic of her "distorted" memory, however, Katsunosuke is substituted for her father, and his loss comes to represent her failed search for happiness, pleasure, and identity. Oharu's flashback, therefore, must represent her Oedipal journey, and its chronological distortions signify the fact that it remains unresolved. Her memory takes on the forces of a defense in which Oharu projects all her neurotic fears onto Katsunosuke. The social wrongs which plague her throughout memory become projections of her own internal fear that she has been wronged. It is this anxiety concerning Oharu's unresolved Oedipal conflicts, as well as her fear of having been castrated, which threatens her at the conclusion of the flashback and which motivates her fainting. Her defense is unsuccessful, however, for as Freud commented, "with the return of the repressed in a distorted form, the defense has failed."

This failure of Oharu's defenses suggests that Oharu's narration of her life as a memory is directly responsible for her fainting, and thus for the woman's illness. Doane's analysis of the medical discourse films, however, tells us that when a heroine becomes the narrator of her memories, the process can have one of two functions: it can be therapeutic or "disease-producing." In the American films, which so often include psychoanalysis within the narratives, the former is characterized by the presence of a doctor who listens to the woman's narration and interprets her illness, while the latter, as we have seen before, is associated with daydreaming. According to Doane, the daydream

> feeds that narcissistic self-sufficiency to which women are always prey. The woman's narrative acumen is thus transformed into the symptom of illness. Her narrative cannot stand on its own—it must be interpreted. Narration by the woman is therefore therapeutic only when constrained and regulated by the purposeful ear of the listening doctor.

Oharu's narration thus seems disease-producing, while at the same time it is contained within a controlling discourse which "constrains and regulates" it. It therefore combines both functions. Her fainting after the flashback confirms her illness, while the signs of patriarchy within the discourse suggest how it is being controlled.

The containing discourse that regulates the woman's memory need not be the courtroom setting, the psycho-analytic session, or the hospital bed, which are the typical institutional arenas in the medical discourse films which guarantee that the male doctor will discover the "truth" of the woman's illness. As Doane makes clear, the controlling discourse is much more an issue of who controls the image. In *Oharu,* we remember that just preceding the flashback Oharu is positioned as the subject of the discourse, whose specific point-of-view shots project Katsunosuke's image onto the Buddhist statue. It is from this enunciating position that the woman's narration follows. It would seem, therefore, that Oharu's flashback controls the image, thus authorizing her point of view as the controlling presence of the memory; nevertheless, this is not altogether the case.

First there is the fact that Oharu's point-of-view shots, as well as the flashback, are framed by the film as a whole. In the classic text, the seemingly narratorless aspect of the discourse provides the "reality effect" of the film when the diegesis is introduced in the third person. This is the case in *Oharu,* which begins with the shot of Oharu walking alone on the grounds outside the temple. The flashback in such a context must be marked in some way differently from this surrounding enunciation. In Mizoguchi's film, as in the medical discourse examples, however, the woman's subjective point of view never returns as an explicit mark of enunciation once the flashback has begun. Thus the events of Oharu's memory are accorded the same value in the discourse as the surrounding action and are granted the same truth as the overall discourse itself; in effect the surrounding discourse validates the truth which it contains. This validation is strengthened by the fact that the last action Oharu remembers is a repetition of the opening shot of her on the temple grounds. It is marked in her memory, however, with an absence of sound—the words of the couple Oharu observes no longer appear on the sound track—and the implication arises that the woman's memory is somehow incomplete, lacking in relation to its more powerful, authoritative surrounding context.

The second mark of the discourse which devalues the authority of Oharu's subjectivity occurs in the last one-shot of her just preceding the flashback. After Oharu is positioned as the subject of the look, and Katsunosuke is established as the object of her glance, there follows the shot of Oharu removing the scarf. This tight medium shot, the closest to an American shot in Mizoguchi, is characterized by an extremely self-conscious attitude on the part of the heroine. Her eyes focus inward after she slides off the scarf, and then she leans against a pillar in a repose of passive contemplation, her eyes falling downward. Simultaneously, the shot contains an overaccumulation of filmic codes, which, while signifying the transition to the past that takes place in Oharu's

mind, also establishes the power of the discourse itself to place Oharu in this position. At the beginning of the shot, *gagaku* music is inserted to represent not only the transition into the flashback, but equally the courtly role that Oharu assumes in the following sequence. Second, the camera slightly reframes the character as the scarf slides off her head with an almost gratuitous movement, the beauty and elegance of which serve again to prefigure Oharu's courtly role and sensitivity. Third, there is a dissolve that punctuates the shift back in time.

The accumulation of these filmic effects marks the author's presence within the discourse and signifies the presence of the "speaking subject" of the text. Oharu's ability to control her flashback is thus undercut by this sign of her lack of power which keeps her as a symbol of difference and lack for the male spectator. Her memory is, therefore, a daydream by Doane's definition, but one which is itself subject to the control of the text's inherent patriarchy, the purpose of which, we can assert, is to confirm Oharu's basic narcissism. Her fainting at the end of the flashback thus authenticates her basic illness as a mark of disavowal. Like the woman's film in America during the 1940s, Oharu's illness is inscribed onto her body, and similar to her portrayal in the Western film, "the trauma of the woman is total."

The patriarchy that controls Oharu during the flashback also determines the course of the action after she faints by reactivating what Silverman has called patriarchy's "compulsory narrative of loss and recovery." After Oharu faints in the hall of Buddhas, the narrative resumes with her reunion with her mother, the news that her father is dead, the final recovery of her son, their separation, and her transformation into the traveling priest. All of the events are portrayed not only using the familiar motifs of visibility and invisibility, but also by invoking the logic of Oharu's guilt at it has been portrayed during her recollection.

The penultimate sequence of the film is Oharu's reunion with the Matsudaira clan. She returns to them in hopes of being reunited with her son, who has now become their leader. Instead, she is chastised by the Matsudaira vassals for behavior inappropriate for the mother of their new lord and is pronounced guilty of shirking her social obligations. She is again sentenced to banishment after being allowed one last look at her son. Her attempt to get near him is played out in a grand spectacle as Oharu rushes toward the boy, only to be restrained by the men, who are both horrified of her power and afraid of their own vulnerability. With koto rhythmically punctuating their chase, the men lose Oharu somewhere on the castle grounds. The sequence ends in a stunning deepfocus shot of the vassals charging back and forth in the background, while in the center of the frame sits Oharu's palanquin, the "mysterious basket," to borrow from Proust, which will presumably carry her off into a life in exile. Oharu has thus finally escaped her ultimate "to be looked at" position. Therefore, the film should end with this last shot of the sequence: Oharu, unseen, her whole body hidden from the gaze of the spectator, away from the eyes of the Matsudaira vassals, submerged in herself, in the basket, symbol of prison and the womb.

Oharu's complete banishment from the text, however, despite the fact that it is based on the logic of the feminine within the discourse, must be disavowed by its underlying patriarchy. This explains the necessity of the final scene, which places Oharu as the begging priest, to fulfill the desire of the narrative that she repent for her guilt. Her lack of sexual identity is thus made beautiful and "satisfying in itself" as Oharu is transformed and overvalued as the priest. Religion in this case becomes the mark of denial for the woman's narcissistic wound. She becomes a religious object only as a substitute for what she lacks as a woman in the discourse. Her so-called transcendence is thus an imaginary concept forced on the spectator, who must assume the position of the male subject.

There is still an ambivalence here that comes from the pathos of the scene. While Oharu's religious conversion signifies the male desire to disavow her ultimate castrated condition and by association his own, the use of *gagaku* music tends to undercut this position. When Oharu sees the pagoda in the distance after she leaves the houses where she begs, she stops to pray, and the music recalls her past life specifically with Katsunosuke. This aural signifier brings back Oharu's original transgression as an element of the discourse and serves as a reminder to the male spectator of the inescapability of Oharu's past. This juxtaposition of past and present, a result of the text's pathos, reaffirms, as we have previously seen, the "slippage between what is and what should have been" and solidifies the spectator's own position as lacking.

The composition of the scene substantiates Oharu as the beautiful object, the self-sacrificing woman, who is captured within an environment whose symmetry is meant to represent her completeness. The melodramatic requirements of the narrative, however, keep reminding the spectator of what has come before and what might have been in a manner that contests Oharu's completeness as a traveling priest. What comes back to the spectator is the sense of what Oharu now lacks, of what has become absent through her fetishized conversion into a religious object.

The beauty of such a position and the artistic consequences of Oharu's conversion finally tend to fetishize the distance Mizoguchi establishes between the spectator and the screen. This seems an inevitable mark of a Japanese desire that patriarchy control its own ambivalence. As Doane again observes, "In a patriarchal society, to desexualize the female body is ultimately to deny its very existence." Since women do exist in Mizoguchi and in Japan, but remain, at least in *The Life of Oharu,* representations of lack and desire, they are subject to procedures of disavowal which elevate them into symbols of suffering and beauty. Beautiful but lacking, whole yet fractured, women in Mizoguchi signify the fundamental misrecognition at the heart of the director's patriarchal discourse.

FURTHER READING

Bibliography

Andrew, Dudley and Paul Andrew. *Kenji Mizoguchi: A Guide to
References and Resources*. Boston: G. K. Hall, 1981, 333 p.
> Includes film credits, references in English and Japanese, and essays on Mizoguchi's life and works.

Criticism

McDonald, Keiko. *Mizoguchi*. Boston: Twayne Publishers, 1984, 187 p.
> Critical survey of Mizoguchi's works.

Sato, Tadao. "Mizoguchi." In *Japanese Cinema*, pp. 178-84.
New York: Kodansha International, 1982.
> Examines Mizoguchi's use of the camera.

Tucker, Richard N. "Mizoguchi: A Woman's Man." In *Japan: Film Image*, pp. 57-64. London: Studio Vista, 1973.
> Discussion of Mizoguchi's style and themes.

Ugetsu: Kenji Mizoguchi, Director, edited by Keiko I. McDonald. New Brunswick: Rutgers University Press, 1993, 176 p.
> Anthology of materials related to *Ugetsu*; includes the stories that served as the film's original source material, the continuity script, and selected critical commentary on the film.

Arthur Morrison

1863-1945

English novelist, journalist, and short story writer.

INTRODUCTION

Morrison's literary reputation is for the most part based on his realistic novels and short stories about London slum life, of which the most prominent was *A Child of the Jago*. In addition, much of his body of work is detective fiction that is openly derivative of Arthur Conan Doyle's Sherlock Holmes stories. Possessed of a wide and free-ranging curiosity, Morrison wrote both fiction and nonfiction works on diverse subjects, from Japanese art to occultism, and participated in the life of English belles lettres well into the Second World War.

Biographical Information

Morrison was born in London's East End slums on 1 November 1863. While he apparently wanted to live down his working-class origins, and never gave any specific accounting of his early years, this never prevented him from displaying his penetrating and thorough understanding of slum life in his work. Commentators consider it likely that he was largely, if not entirely self-educated. In 1886, at the age of twenty-three, Morrison began working as a clerk for the "People's Palace," a social-improvement charity organized by novelist and critic Walter Besant. By 1889, Morrison was working as an editor for Besant's *Palace Journal,* and made a brief appearance on the editorial staff of the *Globe* as well. His East End sketch, "A Street," published in *Macmillan's Magazine* in 1891, brought him some popular attention and the interest of William Ernest Henley, editor of the *National Observer*. Through Henley, Morrison met Rudyard Kipling, Thomas Hardy, Robert Louis Stevenson, J. M. Barrie, and other literary figures of the time, and his work began to appear in the *Observer* regularly, with a collection of his short stories about London slum life, *Tales of Mean Streets,* appearing in 1894. In that same year, at a time when Conan Doyle had apparently ceased writing Sherlock Holmes stories, Morrison inaugurated a detective series of his own. The stories appeared in the *Strand* and *Windsor* and were collected in four volumes over the next few years. Morrison's career as a noted author who was engaged with the literary trends of his time was founded on his 1896 novel, *A Child of the Jago,* the first of three novels based on East End slum life. By 1910, Morrison's interest in literature had fallen off. Through Henley, he acquired a taste for Eastern art, especially Japanese painting and printmaking. Morrison assembled an extensive collection of Japanese and other Eastern art, as well as works by a number of English masters, including William Hogarth, Thomas Gainsborough, John Constable, and J. M. W. Turner. His literary output continued to dwindle, even as he was elected to the Royal Society of Literature and went on to serve on its council for a time, and Morrison eventually became a professional art dealer. He died in 1945 at the age of eighty-two.

Major Works

Morrison's works are best understood as falling into three main categories: realistic East End chronicles, detective stories, and nonfiction studies on various subjects. Morrison's first fiction collection, *Tales of Mean Streets,* brought him to the attention of Reverend A. Osborne Jay, a priest who invited him to visit his East End parish and witness the conditions there for himself. Out of this series of visits Morrison produced his most famous and best-received novel, the unsentimental *A Child of the Jago,* a bleak account of the plight of the urban poor trapped in crime-ridden slums by social forces beyond their control or understanding. Its appearance fed into the ongoing controversy over literary realism, a debate involving such authors as Stephen Crane and Emile Zola. Morrison went on to produce two more East End novels: *To London Town,* about middle-class life on the outskirts of London, and the much-praised *The Hole in the Wall,* set in a public house on the lawless Radliffe Highway. The next major category of Morrison's works, his detective fiction, began in 1894, when Morrison responded to the death of Sherlock Holmes (in Conan Doyle's story "The Final Problem") with a sleuth of his own, the private investigator Martin Hewitt, whose various adventures were published in the *Strand* (occasionally with illustrations by Sidney Paget, illustrator for Doyle's Sherlock Holmes stories) and in *Windsor Magazine*. The Hewitt stories were collected in four volumes: *Martin Hewitt, Investigator, Chronicles of Martin Hewitt, Adventures of Martin Hewitt,* and *The Red Triangle* . Hewitt, while as perceptive, reserved, unsentimental, and eclectically erudite as Holmes, was much more a man of the crowd, average in appearance, temperament, and demeanor, a former solicitor's clerk who found his personality and inclination better suited to private investigation. Nonetheless, Hewitt's cases were just as bizarre and exotic as any of Holmes's: Hewitt hunts up clues underwater in a diving suit in "The Nicobar Bullion Case"; solves "The Case of the Lost Foreigner," in which anarchists are out to destroy civilization with bombs concealed in loaves of bread, by interpreting the doodles of an aphasic and agraphic character; and, in "The Case of the Missing Hand," puts his knowledge of Romany, the language of the Gypsies, to good use. Morrison made two other forays into the detective field, the first: *The Dorrington*

Deed-Box, which introduces the quasi-criminal antihero Dorrington, and *The Green Eye of Goona,* a pastiche of Wilkie Collins's *The Moon-Stone* (1868). The third main category of Morrison's works comprise a series of non-fiction works, several of which reflected his growing interest in Japanese art, including *Exhibition of Japanese Screens Painted by the Old Masters, The Painters of Japan,* and *Guide to an Exhibition of Japanese and Chinese Paintings.* Of these, his two-volume *Painters of Japan* was a primary reference work for decades to follow.

Critical Reception

Although he was accused of morbidly overemphasizing the gloomier and more fatalistic side of East End life, Morrison received considerable praise and attention for his collection *Tales of Mean Streets,* considering how little-known was his previous work. Similarly, *A Child of the Jago* figured significantly in an ongoing debate about literary realism and was both esteemed and criticized for its grimly vivid depictions of the bleakness and the squalor of his characters' lives. Of all his realistic novels, only *The Hole in the Wall* received unreserved critical approval, which was matched by popular success. Morrison's detective fiction suffered by inevitable comparison with Sherlock Holmes, but enjoyed moderate popularity all the same. As far as modern critics are concerned, many have observed that Morrison's work has fallen into undeserved obscurity and merits serious reconsideration.

PRINCIPAL WORKS

The Shadows around Us, Authentic Tales of the Super-natural (nonfiction) 1891
Martin Hewitt, Investigator (short stories) 1894
Tales of Mean Streets (short stories) 1894
Chronicles of Martin Hewitt (short stories) 1895
Zig-Zags at the Zoo (short stories) 1895
Adventures of Martin Hewitt (short stories) 1896
A Child of the Jago (novel) 1896
The Dorrington Deed-Box (short stories) 1897
To London Town (novel) 1899
Cunning Murrell (novel) 1900
The Hole in the Wall (novel) 1902
The Red Triangle: Being Some Further Chronicles of Martin Hewitt, Investigator (short stories) 1903
The Green Eye of Goona (novel) 1904; also published as *The Green Diamond*
Divers Vanities (short stories) 1905
Green Ginger (short stories) 1909
Exhibition of Japanese Screens Painted by the Old Masters (criticism) 1910
The Painters of Japan. 2 vols. (criticism) 1911
Guide to an Exhibition of Japanese and Chinese Paintings (criticism) 1914

Fiddle O'Dreams (short stories) 1933
Short Stories of Today and Yesterday (short stories) 1929

CRITICISM

The Bookman (essay date 1895)

SOURCE: A review of "Tales of Mean Streets," in *The Bookman,* Vol. 1, No. 1, February, 1895, pp. 121-22.

[*The following review praises Morrison's* Tales of Mean Streets.]

[*Tales of Mean Streets*] is an unmistakably strong book. The East End and its dwellers have never before been painted from the same standpoint, nor in so vigorous and independent a fashion. That it gives the inevitable picture which sojourners in the neighbourhood must carry away, we certainly do not assert. It is distinctly limited, but limited because its point of view is individual, its purpose scrupulously truthful. Mr. Morrison's intention has been to tell just what he has seen, idealising nothing and keeping back little. He has carried it out with a frankness which no doubt some readers will term brutal, and which certainly wants some courage to face. They are pictures of misery, cruelty, sordidness, he gives us for the most part, pictures rather than descriptions; the moral show-man never appears at all to pull a long face, or shake his head, or say "How pitiful!" or "How wrong!" The reader is left to make his own reflections, and they will not be comfortable ones, on **"Lizerunt," "Without Visible Means,"** and **"On the Stairs."** Mr. Morrison has plainly a bias; and who has not? With the right or wrong of that bias literary criticism has nothing to do, provided he give it logical and forcible expression. It is, however, perfectly legitimate to take objection to the long monotony of dreariness, which the slight facetiousness of **"The Red Cow Group,"** the comic mixture of rascality and hysteria in **"A Conversion,"** the patient pluck in **"Three Rounds,"** and the grim independence of **"Behind the Shade,"** are not enough, and hardly of a kind, to relieve. It is fair to say that there is something wanting in his picture—something pertaining to rational happiness and unselfish endeavour, which experience has led one to expect in streets however mean. We need not accept his as the whole picture, but who will dare to say it is not true in great part? The book is far from heartless; indeed, possibly it is just because the observer's feelings were not of that easy kind that can be relieved by mere words of pity that his stories are so grim and so ungenial. So much for the effect of the tales on our emotions. Regarded merely from the point of fiction, they are the work of an unusually vigorous writer, whose vision is clear and whose dramatic sense is vivid, and who, in putting his scenes and pictures into words, invariably takes the best and shortest way. An introduction has been written for the American edition; and a portrait of Mr. Morrison will be found among our News Notes.

The Spectator (essay date 1895)

SOURCE: A review of "Tales of Mean Streets," in *The Spectator,* Vol. 74, No. 3480, March 9, 1895, pp. 329-30.

[*In the following review, critic praises* Tales of Mean Streets, *but contends that Morrison's characters are not typical of London's East End dwellers.*]

These tales [*Tales of Mean Streets*.] paint with a marvellous literary skill and force the life which the author by implication alleges to be the normal life of the London poor. Were this the East-End, the whole of the East-End, and were the East-End nothing but this, then indeed are we of all men most miserable. If the squalor, the cruelty, the drunkenness, the deadly and grinding monotony, the total lack of all that is wholesome and loveable in human nature, here so vividly depicted, were really typical of the poorer streets of London, we should have to admit that we are face to face with a moral situation as awful and as terrifying as any that the world has ever encountered. If "Lizerunt," the factory girl, and Billy, the man who lives on her and his mother, truly represented the people of the mean streets, and if the social and political forces now at work were giving us such people as their normal product, one must feel that our society is rotten to the core, and that the sooner it is smashed to atoms the better. But we do not believe that the life here set forth is typical, or that Billy is a normal character, and we venture to say that those who know the East-End at first hand, and who most deplore its miseries, would be the first to endorse this denial. We do not say that Mr. Morrison has not drawn from the life. He may have done so and yet not painted the typical East-Ender. What we assert is that he has taken the worst characters in Mr. Booth's Class A—the class of the semi-criminals and the morally and physically degraded—and has set them up, or appeared to set them up, as if they were truly representative of East London. But Class A, as Mr. Booth showed us, is only some 9 per cent. of the East End.

Let us show by quotation what sort of people are Lizerunt and Billy. Lizerunt (Elizabeth Hunt) worked in a pickle factory. She married late, *i.e.,* at seventeen, Billy Chope, who supported life by taking from the widowed mother with whom and on whom he lived, the proceeds of her mangling. When he married Lizerunt, after a courtship in which knocking her down and kicking her was an episode, he had two women to provide money for him instead of one, and this suited him exactly. He grudged Lizerunt her babies, however, as they kept her from work. At last his mother began to sicken, and, as the poor will, developed the instinct of saving enough money to bury her. Billy found the little hoard and seized it—

"'No, Billy, don't take that—don't!' implored his mother. 'There'll be some money for them things when they go 'ome—'ave that. I'm savin' it, Billy, for something partic'ler: s'elp me Gawd, I am, Billy.'—'Yus,' replied Billy, raking diligently among the clinkers, 'savin' it for a good ol' booze. An' now you won't 'ave one. Bleedin' nice thing, 'iding' money away from yer own son!'—'It ain't for that, Billy—s'elp me, it ain't; it's case anythink 'appens to me. On'y to put me away decent, Billy, that's all. We never know, an' you'll be glad of it t'elp bury me if I should go any time—'—'I'll be glad of it now,' answered Billy, who had it in his pocket; 'an' I've got it. You ain't a dyin' sort, *you* ain't; an' if you was, the parish 'ud soon tuck *you* up. P'raps you'll be straighter about money after this.'—'Let me 'ave *some,* then—you can't want it all. Give me some, an' then 'ave the money for the things. There's ten dozen and seven, and you can take 'em yerself if yo like.'—'Wot—in this 'ere rain? Not me! I bet I'd 'ave the money if I wanted it without that. 'Ere—change these 'ere fardens at the draper's wen you go out: there's two bob's worth an' a penn'orth; I don't want to bust my pockets wi' them.'"

That is how Billy treated his mother. How he treated his wife while she was expecting her first baby, is told in the previous chapter. Billy kicks Lizerunt because she will not give him money, and then goes out. By the time he comes back the baby is born. After looking at it he asks, "Where's my dinner?"—

"'I dunno,' Lizer responded hazily. 'Wot's the time?'—'Time? Don't try to kid me. You git up; go on. I want my dinner.'—'Mother's gittin' it, I think,' said Lizer. 'Doctor had to slap 'im like anything 'fore 'e'd cry. 'E don't cry now much. 'E—'—'Go on; out ye git. I do'want no more damn jaw. Git my dinner.'—'I'm a-gitting of it, Billy,' his mother said, at the door. She had begun when he first entered. 'It won't be a minute.'—'You come 'ere; y'aint alwis s' ready to do er' work are ye? She ain't no call to stop there no longer, an' I owe 'er one for this mornin.' Will ye git out, or shall I kick ye?'—'She can't Billy,' his mother said. And Lizer snivelled and said, 'You're a damn brute. Y'ought to be bleedin' well booted.' But Billy had her by the shoulders and began to haul; and again his mother besought him to remember what he might bring upon himself. At this moment the doctor's dispenser, a fourth-year London Hospital student of many inches, who had been washing his hands in the kitchen, came in. For a moment he failed to comprehend the scene. Then he took Billy Chope by the collar, hauled him pell-mell along the passage, kicked him (hard) into the gutter, and shut the door. When he returned to the room, Lizer, sitting up and holding on by the bed-frame, gasped hysterically: 'Ye bleedin' makeshift, I'd 'ave yer liver out if I could reach ye! You touch my 'usband, ye long pisenin' 'ound you! Ow!' And, infirm of aim, she flung a cracked teacup at his head. Billy's mother said, 'Y'ought to be ashamed of yourself, you low blaggard. If 'is father was alive 'e'd knock yer 'ead auf. Call yourself a doctor—a passel o' boys—! Git out! Go out'o my 'ouse or I'll give y'in charge!'"

This is no doubt in one sense a true description, but is only true of a small and exceptional class in the East-

End. It requires, however, a certain effort not to regard it as typical as well as true. If we read a vivid account of the cruel and savage husband in Mayfair we recognise easily enough that he is not a type of the West-End husband. We know, however, so little of East-End life at first-hand that we are apt to treat everything depicted with an East-End atmosphere as typical. It is the mistake of the traveller also who goes to the East and happens, as he well may, on some accidental and occasional piece of humanity or cruelty, as the case may be. Down it goes in his note-book as an instance of normal Arab goodness or wickedness, and unless he is able to live down this impression he is apt to think of "all Eastern peoples" as tinged with the particular vice or virtue which he came across in so sensational a way. But it may be said that Mr. Morrison does not merely paint East London by striking and sensational stories. In his introduction, he gives us a general description of the moral atmosphere of the mean streets. True, the effect of this general description seems hardly less appalling than that produced by the more dramatic portions of the book. Here is the description of the normal day in the street, and every day is normal. First comes the calling of the men by the policeman:—

> "The knocking and the shouting pass, and there comes the noise of opening and shutting of doors, and a clattering away to the docks, the gasworks and the shipyards. Later, more door-shutting is heard, and then the trotting of sorrow-laden little feet along the grim street to the grim Board School three grim streets off. Then silence, save for a subdued sound of scrubbing here and there, and the puny squall of croupy infants. After this, a new trotting of little feet to docks, gasworks, and shipyards with father's dinner in a basin and a red handkerchief, and so to the Board School again. More muffled scrubbing and more squalling, and perhaps a feeble attempt or two at decorating the blankness of a square hole here and there by pouring water into a grimy flower-pot full of dirt. Then comes the trot of little feet toward the oblong holes, heralding the slower tread of sooty artisans; a smell of bloater up and down; nightfall; the fighting of boys in the street, perhaps of men at the corner near the beer-shop; sleep. And this is the record of a day in this street; and every day is hopelessly the same."

The children of the street and the life they lead wail in undertone in Mr. Morrison's description:—

> "There is no house without children in this street, and the number of them grows ever and ever greater. Nine-tenths of the doctor's visits are on this account alone, and his appearances are the chief matter of such conversation as the women make across the fences. One after another the little strangers come, to live through lives as flat and colourless as the day's life in this street. Existence dawns, and the doctor-watchman's door knock resounds along the row of rectangular holes. Then a muffled cry announces that a small new being has come to trudge and sweat its way in the appointed groove. Later, the trotting of little feet and the school; the mid-day play hour, when love peeps even into this street; after that more trotting of little feet—strange little feet, new little feet—and the scrubbing, and the squalling, and the barren flower-pot; the end of the sooty day's work; the last home-coming; nightfall; sleep."

Mr. Morrison will not even let us hope that his mean street is the exception. It is the rule—

> "Where in the East End lies this street? Everywhere. The hundred-and-fifty yards is only a link in a long and a mightily tangled chain—is only a turn in a tortuous maze. This street of the square holes is hundreds of miles long. That it is planned in short lengths is true, but there is no other way in the world that can more properly be called a single street, because of its dismal lack of accent, its sordid uniformity, its utter remoteness from delight."

So convincing and so excellent is Mr. Morrison's art, that it requires no small effort to pull oneself together, and ask again,—Is this true, and is it indeed a fact that all East London has upon it the weight of twenty Atlantics of grim, grimy, sordid, impenetrable, hopeless, helpless misery? We believe that it is not true. We shall be told that we are drugging a middle-class conscience in denying its truth, but we deny it. We believe that Mr. Morrison, like so many men before him, has painted his mean street in these hues of gloom and wretchedness, because he has imported into it the ideas of his own class. What the highly-educated and cultivated man of letters at this century's end dreads above all things is dull monotony. A life which does not run glittering like a brook in the open sunshine is not merely unblest, but the most terrifying, the most awful of earthly ills. Than that, he would rather face anything. But the plain men and women of this workaday world, though they may like a holiday and a spree, have no such horror of monotony. Their nerves are not shaken with wild vibrations by the dread of a yesterday, a to-day, and a to-morrow, which know no change. Besides, A's monotony is always more appalling to B than B's own. X, a head-clerk in the City, goes to the Bank every day by the same 'bus, and will do so till the unknown day on which each and every City man hails his last 'bus. This is monotony indeed; yet that very man heartily pities the eating-house waiter who spends his life calling out "a sausage on mash." Examine Mr. Morrison's account closely, and it is clear that the monotony is what horrifies him. But that monotony Providence has inexorably fixed on the shoulders of ninety-nine-hundredths of the human race. Can the results achieved by the one man in a hundred who escapes the monotony of existence be said to prove that life is necessarily better when unmonotonous?

But we must not seem to write as if we thought the life of the mean streets a desirable one. God knows there is much there to be morally and physically mended. The ugliness and griminess of life in the East-End is a great and terrible evil. We have no sort of sympathy with those who talk as if the ugliness and the grime did not matter.

They do matter; and it is not too much to say that the men and women who are reared, not in the woods and fields, but in the East-End as it is at present, cannot grow to perfection. For that reason we would do everything that communal effort can do to combat the dirt and the sordidness. And, first, the fog and the smoke. While London pours coal grit on its own head day after day, the poorer Londoners can never know the pleasure of cleanliness and fresh air. By all means let us abate the evils of London life, but do not let us delude ourselves into imagining that half London is inhabited by a race of Yahoos.

A last word as to Mr. Morrison's book as a whole. What we have said must not be taken in the least as said in depreciation of his art. He is a writer of great power. Again, we have not the least wish to speak as if he were deluding consciously the public into taking too black a view of the East-End. He is merely a painter who draws sombre subjects and works in sombre colours. To point this out, and to add that nevertheless the world is not a place without light and sunshine, is not to impeach either his art or his sincerity.

H. G. Wells (essay date 1896)

SOURCE: "A Slum Novel," in *The Saturday Review,* New York, Vol. 82, November 28, 1896, p. 573.

[*In the following essay, Wells notes the shortcomings of* A Child of the Jago, *yet praises it as "admirably conceived and excellently written."*]

The son of the alcoholic proletarian, the apparently exhausted topic of Dr. Barnardo, has suddenly replaced the woman with the past in the current novel. We have had him clothed in Cant as with a garment in the popular success of *Cleg Kelly,* and we have had him presented, out Mr.-Henry-James-ing Mr. Henry James in pursuit of the *mot juste,* in the amiable *Sentimental Tommy.* And two men of knowledge as well as ability have been dealing with him in the new spirit of sincerity. No doubt this is, as yet, but a beginning. Next year the artful publisher will be asking his young authors for books about poor boys born in sin and vermin and displaying with infinite pathos the stunted rudiments of a soul, and the still more artful bookseller will be passionately overstocking himself with innumerable imitations. It is indisputable that the rediscovery of Oliver Twist is upon us. The imitator, that pest of reviewers, that curse of literature, will catch him and keep him. After the fashion of these latter days, we shall all be heartily sick of him long before we are allowed to hear the last of him. So far, however, he has been a fairly interesting person.

A Child of the Jago is indeed indisputably one of the most interesting novels this year has produced. We have admired Mr. Morrison already for his **"Lizer'unt"**; we have disliked him for his despicable detective stories; and we will frankly confess we did not think him capable of anything nearly so good as this admirably conceived and excellently written story. It deals with a well-known corner of the East End, not only with extraordinary faithfulness, which indeed is attainable to any one reasonably clear of cant and indolence, but also with a really artistic sense of effect. It is beyond doubt that Mr. Morrison must be full of East End material, and never once through this book does he drop into the pitfall of reporting. *A Child of the Jago* is one of those rare and satisfactory novels in which almost every sentence has its share in the entire design.

The design, it must be confessed, is a little narrow. It is as if Mr. Morrison had determined to write of the Jago and nothing but the Jago. It is the Jago without relativity. The reader will remember the spacious effect at the end of Mr. Conrad's *Outcast of the Islands,* when Almayer shook his fist at the night and silence outside his sorrows. Mr. Morrison never gets that spacious effect, although he carries his reader through scenes that would light into grandeur at a glance, at the mere turn of a phrase. The trial scene of Josh Perrott for the murder of Weech, and the execution scene that follows, show this peculiar want of breadth in its most typical manner. Mr. Morrison sticks to Josh Perrott, hints vaguely at the judge, jerks with his thumb at the Royal Arms, moves his head indicative of policemen, as though he was uneasy in such company. The execution is got off in three pages with a flavour of having been written in a hurry, is, indeed, a mere sketch of one of the characters for the fuller picture there should have been. It seems all the slighter, because it comes immediately after an elaborately written murder, action as finely executed as one could well imagine, and just before the equally stirring concluding chapter, the killing of Dick Perrott in a street faction fight. Moreover, by this brevity the latter chapter is brought too close to the murder chapter. Instead of crest and trough, a rise and cadence of emotion, we end in a confusion, like water breaking on a rocky beach. Had the father and son been presented in antagonism with some clearly indicated creative and destroying force, with Destiny, with Society or with human Stupidity, the book might have concluded with that perfect unity of effect it needs and does not possess.

But this want is not a failure with Mr. Morrison so much as the expression of his peculiar mental quality. He sees the Jago, is profoundly impressed by the appearance of the Jago, renders its appearance with extraordinary skill. But the origin of the Jago, the place of the Jago in the general scheme of things, the trend of change in it, its probable destiny—such matters are not in his mind. Here, perhaps, is his most fundamental utterance, *à propos* of a birth:—

> Father Sturt met the surgeon as he came away in the later evening, and asked if all were well. The surgeon shrugged his shoulders. 'People would call it so,' he said. 'The boy's alive, and so is the mother. But you and I may say the truth. You know the Jago far better than I. Is there a child in all this place that wouldn't be better dead—still better unborn? But does a day pass without bringing

you just such a parishioner? Here lies the Jago, a nest of rats, breeding, breeding, as only rats can; and we say it is well. On high moral grounds we uphold the right of rats to multiply their thousands. Sometimes we catch a rat. And we keep it a little while, nourish it carefully, and put it back into the nest to propagate its kind.'

Father Sturt walked a little way in silence. Then he said: 'You are right, of course. But who'll listen, if you shout it from the housetops? I might try to proclaim it myself, if I had time and energy to waste. But I have none—I must work, and so must you. The burden grows day by day, as you say. The thing's hopeless, perhaps, but that is not for me to discuss. I have my duty.'

The surgeon was a young man, but Shoreditch had helped him over most of his enthusiasms. 'That's right,' he said, 'quite right. People are so very genteel, aren't they?' He laughed, as at a droll remembrance. 'But, hang it all, men like ourselves needn't talk as though the world was built of hardbake. It's a mighty relief to speak truth with a man who knows—a man not rotted through with sentiment. Think how few men we trust with the power to give a fellow-creature a year in gaol, and how carefully we pick them! Even damnation is out of fashion, I believe, among theologians. But any noxious wretch may damn human souls to the Jago, one after another, year in and year out, and we respect his right—his sacred right.'

There speaks Mr. Morrison. It is practical on the face of it, and quite what would occur to a man looking so nearly at Whitechapel that the wider world where the races fight together was hidden. But the fact is that neither ignorance, wrong moral suggestions, nor parasites are inherited; the baby that survives in the Jago must needs have a good physique, the Jago people are racially indistinguishable from the people who send their children to Oxford, and the rate of increase of the Jago population is entirely irrelevant to the problem. The Jago is not a "black inheritance," it is a black contagion—which alters the whole problem. And Mr. Morrison knocks his surgeon's case entirely to pieces by his own story; for he shows, firstly, in Mrs. Perrott that to come into the Jago is to assimilate one-self to the Jago; and, secondly, in Kiddo Cook, that a vigorous, useful citizen may come out of it.

Blackwood's Edinburgh Magazine (essay date 1896)

SOURCE: A review of "A Child of the Jago," in *Blackwood's Edinburgh Magazine*, Vol. 160, December, 1896, pp. 841-44.

[*In the following essay, the critic questions why the reading public would want to expose itself to the "den of horrors" detailed in* A Child of the Jago.]

Mr Arthur Morrison's work [*A Child of the Jago*] is [a] development of the New School. It is not a piece of de-liberately constructed pessimism (which is the fashionable word), like the horrible story of the Carissima, in which there is so little trace of a real story to tell, or any natural impulse, and so much of elaborate manufacture. Mr Morrison's method is different. He does not attempt to horrify us by the sudden apparition of the demon under an exterior made up of all the attractive graces. There is nothing attractive at all in the world which he opens to our gaze. It is a world without hope or desire of any fair or pleasant thing, knowing nothing but the foullest sediment of existence, unable to conceive of anything better—brutal, filthy, miserable, yet in a measure content. The "Mean Streets" of his former work were meaner, more squalid and horrible even, than the reality, terrible to contemplate, and madding to think of. It is strange to think upon what rule it is that pictures like these please the imagination, and are received by so many in the character of an entertainment, a portion of the relaxation of life. It may be well that we should see how another part of the world lives; and indeed the reports of some benevolent societies afford here and there similar stories, told without skill, as bare records of fact, which make little impression, and which we may glance over for duty, but certainly not for refreshment. In these publications, however, the "cases" are generally exceptional, and we are not called upon to accept them as the ordinary level of life.

But Mr Morrison's narratives are professedly on that level, and the scenes he puts before us are too foul for any imagination, and, in all their horrible details, must either be fact or a lie, since no one, we imagine, could invent them. What are they for? to make us all a kind of missionaries, impelled by disgust and horror, if by no better motive? If that were so, they might be justified—nay, might be better than the most weighty and powerful arguments. But we know that at least in many dens of London, if not in the particular Mean Streets here illustrated, the missionaries, whether of religion, or of scrutiny, or of benevolence, jostle each other already, and send out appeals and demands without cease. Are we then to take these doubtful tales for amusement? France has accepted a similar kind of amusement from M. Zola; but only when highly spiced with vice and the peculiar kind of garbage upon which the French novel-reader has chosen to feed. Seldom, however, does the historian of the Jago bring in this element to make his horrors palatable. He shows us all the uncleannesses of the streets excepting that. So far as we can recollect the appalling sketch called **'Leizerunt in the Mean Streets,'** in which the brutality becomes tragic and so almost justifies itself, is the only one in which the great pollution of all is so much as referred to. Sheer filth, misery, blows, and bloodshed, hunger, squalor, nakedness, cold, and filth again—the lowest depths to which human creatures can fall—are the subjects, the atmosphere, the meaning of these tales. To read *A Child of the Jago* is voluntarily to place yourself in a spot reeking with every odious smell and sight, among savages whose sole instruction is how to thieve, and whose children are as proud of their first efforts in stealing as others are of a successful lesson or a prize won. What can be more extraordinary than that we should receive these disclosures as a source of recreation and relaxation to our own minds, to occupy our lighter hours and charm our weariness? In the days which are now old-fashioned we used to be warned against the "sensibility" which wept over fictitious distresses, but rarely, so said our mentors, was moved thereby to any act of charity. What shall we say for the fictitious horrors which are now pressed upon us for pleasure? But perhaps Mr Morrison will say that he does not wish to please, but only to exhibit another phase of life.

We are glad to say that we have been assured, by an authority very well qualified to speak on the subject, that such a den of horrors as the Jago is so little common that she, with an immense experience of the slums, finds it difficult to believe in its existence,—from which so much comfort as is practicable may be taken. Mr Morrison, however, gives us a map of the district in which that region of utter lawlessness, intestine warfare, crime, and savagery is to be found; where two factions, men and women, fight to the death periodically without interposition of the police, sometimes even killing, often wounding and maiming, each other, quite unchecked by the law. He even gives us chapter after chapter descriptive of these illustrious fights, and the Homeric encounters of the Ranns and the Learys, with wild interludes of single combat led by the bleeding furies Norah Welsh and Sally Green. In the midst of all these horrors there arises a little boy, an imp so far contradictory of his "environment" that, though the commandment has been read to him, Thou shalt steal, and he feels the excitement of his first achievement in this way, and of the pursuit and flight that follow, to be glorious,—is all the same a fresh little dutiful soul out of heaven, knowing no evil, and full of love, obedience, and trust. Dicky is born to steal and fight, as other boys are to be good and get on in the world. He knows no other way, until it is suddenly revealed to him that there is such a thing as working and getting wages, an alternative which he embraces with his whole heart, though without any sort of conviction that it is more virtuous; but thieving is precarious and its rewards irregular, and the serving of the shop, and its protection from all predatory prowlers, is infinitely elevating and delightful. Poor Dicky is slandered by a diabolical "fence," or receiver of stolen goods, who fears his talents are to be lost to his natural profession, and thus is plunged again into the vile current from which he has almost escaped; but he is no less an innocent and naturally honest child, because he is a poor little thief, bound by both hatred and love, such love as is possible in the Jago, to its horrible lot. This strange problem Mr Morrison has worked out very tenderly and pathetically. His little hero is in no way superior to his surroundings, has no aspirations after excellence, no dreams of either cleanliness or godliness; yet the little soul in that human hell has still a faint trail of the light that came with him from a brighter world.

It is a pity that Josh Perrott, the father, should follow so closely in the steps of Bill Sykes, who did it better—both

the flight over the housetops and the rest. But the murder for a moment raises the Jago and its dreadful inhabitants into something like humanity. We cannot say very much for the Parson, whose figure is visionary, and whose muscular Christianity seems somehow out of date, a thing which has gone by, which indeed is quite true, though perhaps a pity. Let us hope that Father Sturt will yet get possession of his uneasy parish, and, aided by all the new lodging-houses, succeed in clearing out the Jago. But it will be to little purpose, we fear. The rooks disturbed will cluster anew in some other rookery. They will find the half-ruinous houses, the familiar dirt, in some other quarter, and the new tenements will receive another class. Will it ever be possible, driving them thus out of one hole of misery into another, to wear away these dreadful tribes altogether? Who can tell? But the prospect seems an unlikely one.

We have an apology to make to Mr Morrison. His motto shows that it is not without purpose that he has taken up this subject. But perhaps when a writer quotes from the prophet Ezekiel to show his motive, it would be better for him to put his work in another form. Fiction is scarcely the medium for a lesson taught in such miserable detail, and in colours so dark and terrible. It is a gruesome book to sit down to by the fireside after a day's work, when our minds require repose rather than stirring up to a consideration of the most bitter of problems. Perhaps he thinks it is the best way to seize the attention of the frivolous public; but we think he is mistaken, and that, however much he may secure it, very little practical service will come from the people who are thus beguiled into a lesson, and that of the most serious kind, when they expected entertainment. It is not in this way, we fear, that any practical good is to be done. And in these days the public is not by any means exclusively devoted to fiction as the sort of sugar adapted to coat a pill. On the contrary, the gentlest of readers prefers to be seen with Nordau, or Kidd, or Pearson, quite superior kinds of literature, upon her table. And there is a great future before the man who will expound to us with all the guarantees of fact, and for some real purpose, those scenes to which we highly object when they are served up for our amusement. Then Mr. Morrison will no longer need to give point to his story with an episode *à la* Bill Sykes.

But we advise him in the meantime to study the Parson of to-day with diligence. He is by no means the Parson of yesterday, but a very different person. Muscular Christianity has, we fear, much disappeared from the Mean Streets; but there are other powers at work of much potency and well worth expounding. Do they accomplish as much as the cost of personal outlay and endurance warrants? We know not. When Mr Rudyard Kipling with his keen eyes descended into the slums, of which, indeed, in the nature of things (so far as that is of any avail with a born See-er) he ought to have known nothing, he found there a Catholic priest, an Anglican curate, and certain women, all fighting the devil in their several ways. Was it merely from the exigencies of art that he placed them there? Is it with respect to the exigencies of another kind of art that Mr Morrison keeps them out? Facts apparently, so far as we are able to get at them, and with our imperfect means of sifting and verifying them, are on the side of the angels, so to speak, and reveal a web of closely woven agencies penetrating everywhere, or almost everywhere, in that dark world. Fiction has the great disadvantage as an expositor that we never can be quite sure that it does not add a light, or heap on a darkness, almost involuntarily in the interest of its picture. We should very much like to know which is true.

V. S. Pritchett (essay date 1947)

SOURCE: "An East End Novelist," in *The Living Novel & Later Appreciations,* revised edition, 1964. Reprint by Vintage Books, 1967, pp. 206-12.

[*In the following essay, which was first published in 1947, Pritchett praises Morrison's realistic storytelling.*]

"And the effect is as of stables." My eye has been often baffled by lack of the word which would define the poor streets of the East End, as they used to be before the last war; and here in Arthur Morrison's *Tales of Mean Streets* which were written in 1894, I find it. Those acres of two-story houses which lay below the level of the railway arches of Bethnal Green and which stood like an alien stretch of unfeatured plowing beyond the Commercial Road, are particularized at last. The mind has won a foothold in a foreign city.

For, east of Aldgate, another city begins. London flattens and sinks into its clay. Over those lower dwellings the London sky, always like a dirty window, is larger; the eyes and hands of people are quicker, the skins yellower, the voices are as sharp as scissors. Every part of London has its smell, and this region smells of rabid little shops, bloated factories, sublet workrooms and warehouse floors; there is also the smell of slums, a smell of poverty, racy but oftener sour; and mingling with these working odors, there arises an exhalation of the dirty river which, somewhere behind these streets and warehouses and dock walls, is oozing toward the flats of the Thames estuary like a worm. The senses and the imagination of the stranger are so pricked by this neighborhood that he quickly gets a fevered impression of it; it will seem dingier or more exotic than it really is. And when we turn to literature for guidance, we are even less sure of what we see. For the literature of the East End is very largely a stranger's literature. It lies under the melodramatic murk and the smear of sentimental pathos, which, in the nineteenth century, were generated by the guilty conscience of the middle classes. They were terrified of the poor who seethed in a trough just beyond their back door. The awful Gothic spectacle of hunger, squalor and crime was tolerable only as nightmare and fantasy—such as Dickens provided—and the visiting foreigner alone could observe the English slums with the curiosity of the traveler or the countenance of the anthropologist. And there was another difficulty. Philanthropy, for all its humbug, did slowly

have its effect on the public conscience in every generation, so that it was genuinely possible to say "things have changed." The Ratcliffe Highway went. Limehouse had been purged, and there arose a romantic literature of the East End, based on a riotous evocation of the bad old times. The stranger's literature was the literature of a time which first strengthened morale by giving the reader a fright, and then went on to make the fright pious, sentimental and picturesque.

But what of the literature written from within the East End, the really saturated literature which has been lived before it has been written? For many years now, in accounts of the realism which came into fashion at the time of Gissing, I had noticed a recurring title: *Tales of Mean Streets,* by Arthur Morrison, and lately I have been put on to *The Hole in the Wall* and *Child of the Jago* by the same author. They are written from the inside and they have extraordinary merit; *The Hole in the Wall* strikes me as being one of the minor masterpieces of the last sixty years. It has the kind of fidelity to scene that the modern documentary writers have sought, yet is never flattened, as their work is, by concern for conditions; let us not allow "conditions" to deflate the imagination or argue away the novelist's chief delight and greatest difficulty: the art of constructing and telling a story complete in itself. For unless he learns this art, a novelist neutralizes his power of observation, his power to observe more than one thing at a time, his power of writing on different planes and varying perspectives, and discriminating among the accumulated incrustations of fact that clog an impressionable mind. Arthur Morrison had this power. "Conditions" were in his bones; his books stand apart from the worthy and static pathos of Gissing, from the character albums of the writers of low comedy, from the picturesque and the nightmare schools. Mr. Morrison's early novels and sketches are often modest in their art, like the work of someone learning to write, but they have an anthropological drama of their own, and, at any rate, are not more awkward than Bennett's *Tales of the Five Towns.* What is missing from these novels is the modern novelist's sardonic exposure of the economic rackets which make the poor man poor; the brutality of poverty is subject enough for Mr. Morrison. A book like *Child of the Jago,* the story of a young thief in Bethnal Green, shows a sharp-eyed and intimate knowledge of how East End society used to behave as a society, of how it used to deploy its cunning and uphold its customs. Injustice is done and the President of the Immortals has already abandoned the hopeless scene to the human instinct of self-preservation when Mr. Morrison comes in to record it. Out comes the cosh, the street wars begin, the half-naked harpies run at each other with broken bottles, the pimps and fences step over the bodies of the drunks who lie, pockets turned inside out, in the gutters. It's a world of sullen days in backrooms with the baby lying half dead on the bed and the hungry women gaping listlessly at the empty cupboards, while the men go out in search of loot and drink and come back with their eyes blackened and their belts ready to flay the undeserving family. I have picked out the seamier side of *Child of the*

Jago not to gloat over the horrors but to indicate the material. Such incidents are not raked into the book without discrimination; these novels are not pools of self-pity in the Gissing manner; nor are they worked up with that sadistic touch of angry ecstasy which Dickens brought to his pictures of poverty. In Mr. Morrison's book slum life is the accepted life, a dirty but not a turgid stream. In their position, you say—as one ought to say of all human beings—these people have lived, they've kept their heads above water for a spell. Man is the animal who adapts himself.

Child of the Jago describes the brutal, drunken, murderous London of the late nineteenth century which used to shatter the visiting foreigner and send him home marveling at English violence and English hypocrisy. Its picture of the street wars is unique. *The Hole in the Wall* raises this material to a far higher plane of narrative. Here is a thriller set in Dockland, where the filthy river, its fogs and its crimes, stain the mind as they did in *Our Mutual Friend*. Every gas-lit alley leads abruptly to some dubious business. The average thriller takes us step by step away from probability. It strains away from likelihood. *The Hole in the Wall* belongs to the higher and more satisfying kind, which conducts us from one unsuspected probability to the next. Mr. Morrison has employed what is, I suppose, the classical method of writing this kind of book; he shows us the story mainly through the eye of a young boy. The child goes to live with his grandfather who keeps a pub at Wapping and there he gradually discovers that his heroic grandfather is really a receiver of stolen goods. The old man comes by a wallet containing £800 which has been robbed from a defaulting shipowner—who has been murdered—and the plot is made out of the attempts of various criminal characters to get this money back. The merit of the book lies in its simple but careful reconstruction of the scene—the pubs and gin shops of the Old Ratcliffe Highway, the locks and swing bridges, the alleys and gateways of Dockland with their police notices, the riverside jetties and their lighters, the way over the marshes to the lime kilns. I take it to be a mark of the highest skill in this kind of novel that nothing is mentioned which will not have, eventually, an importance to the tale; and that the motives for action arise in the characters and are not imposed on them by the need of working up a mystery and creating suspense. We do not know what their next step will be, because these people are still ruminating upon it themselves. Marr, the absconding shipowner, disguises himself as a sailor, but forgets that he will blab if he gets drunk; Dan Ogle who merely intends to take his watch, gradually sees that murder will be necessary if the £800 is to be taken; the blind fiddler who does not mind very much being double-crossed, thinks otherwise when he is assaulted and ridiculed as well as cheated. And Mr. Morrison succeeds with them because he shows them to us, first of all as ordinary shady characters muddling along the path of shifty illegality, and then suddenly faced by a new, a more terrible temptation and jumping at it.

The Hole in the Wall moves calmly from one major scene to the next; there is no sagging of the narrative. We see Marr, stunned and tottering, led like a broken marionette between his murderers. They are bawling at the tops of their voices so that, in the night, passersby will think they are drunken sailors helping a pal, instead of murderers, dragging an almost lifeless body to the river. We see the body fished out—and what a remarkable piece of description that is. It "tells"—as Henry James used to say—because of the very homeliness of the boy's narrative. (There is a lesson to the modern tough writers here. They lose their effect because they are tough all the time. They do not allow us to have the homely, frightened, law-abiding emotions. They do not allow us the manly fear, and they lose the interest of moral conflict.) And then there is the tremendous scene where the blind fiddler takes his revenge on Ogle, the murderer. He is hiding in a lime quarry. At night the fiddler gropes across the marshes to the shed where Ogle is sleeping:

> He had been gone no more than a few seconds, when the snore stopped. It stopped with a thump and a gasp, and a sudden buffeting of legs and arms; and in the midst arose a cry; a cry of so hideous an agony that Grimes the wharf-keeper, snug in his first sleep fifty yards away, sprang erect and staring in bed, and so sat motionless for half a minute ere he remembered his legs and thrust them out to carry him to the window. And the dog on the wharf leaped the length of its chain, answering the cry with a torrent of wild barks.

> Floundering and tumbling against the frail boards of the shed the two men came out at the door in a struggling knot; Ogle wrestling and striking at random, while the other, cunning with a life's blindness, kept his own head safe and hung as a dog hangs to a bull. His hands gripped his victim by ear and hair, while the thumbs drove at the eyes the mess of smoking lime that clung and dripped about Ogle's head. It trickled burning through his hair and it blistered lips and tongue, as he yelled and yelled again in the extremity of his anguish.

The blind man had blinded his persecutor.

One puts the book down looking back on the ground it has covered, seeing how economically it implanted that sinister Dockland of the eighties on the mind, with a simple warmth and precision; how it mocked the little criminals, and then, suddenly, struck out into the squalor behind the drink in the snug bar and the bawling songs in the upper room; and how finally it pierced one with human fear and horror, without once cutting adrift from probability and an identifiable daily life. It is a masterly course, sustained, calm and never exaggerated. The style is a little old-fashioned, but it never scuttles away for safety into period dress. There was a London like this—we are convinced—mean, clumsy and hungry, murderous and sentimental. Those shrieks were heard. There were those even more disturbing silences in the night. Dockland, where the police used to go in threes, has its commemoration.

Jocelyn Bell (essay date 1952)

SOURCE: "A Study of Arthur Morrison," in *Essays and Studies,* Vol. 5, 1952, pp. 77-89.

[*In the following essay, Bell provides a biographical survey of Morrison's writing.*]

At a distance of half a century an age is no longer dismissed as old-fashioned; its historical importance and period singularity are recognized. The Victorians and Edwardians are reappearing, freshly presented in reprints and radio serials and revalued in biography and criticism. Arthur Morrison is among them. Born in 1863, he belongs in literature to the 1890's and the turning century, finishing his best work by 1902 but writing throughout the Edwardian reign until he retired in 1913. He was one of those contemporary best-sellers who could be found on every Edwardian bookshelf, but who vanished in the Great War and were unknown to the new and changed generation which followed; and now that, once again, the novels which made his name are in the bookshops, it is not out of place to attempt an assessment of his literary talent, to determine how much he achieved, and why he did not achieve more.

The 1890's were brilliant, chaotic years: gay, sombre; irresponsible, earnest; years which saw Lottie Collins at the Gaiety and Mrs. Pat Campbell as Paula Tanqueray; which saw Keir Hardie's first Labour Party and the Diamond Jubilee; the Sidney Webbs, Beardsley, and the trial of Oscar Wilde. The literary world introduced its own novelties, from the "incomparable Max" to George Bernard Shaw, and the dramatic explosion of Ibsen had been preceded but a few years previously by that of Zola, when in the 1880's his novels were first translated into English, immediately suppressed, and their publisher imprisoned. If it was an age of aesthetic adventure, it was also an age of moral revolution.

The translations of the French "realistic" novelists, Zola and Flaubert, the Goncourts and Maupassant, had raised a sharp and violent controversy in the English periodical press as to the place of frankness in literature, an outcry which had been countered successfully by prominent critics like Edmund Gosse and lesser known pioneers like Hubert Crackanthorpe, and by 1894 the "new" realistic fiction, though still experimental, was recognized in literary circles and developed by major writers like George Moore and George Gissing, and by minor ones like Henry Harland, "George Egerton", Crackanthorpe, and Grant Allen. Taking its main inspiration from the French writers, it was concerned with the direct portrayal of the social conditions and moral problems of contemporary life, and novelists, claiming broader horizons for their art, asserted their right to deal with any subject, fine or ugly, beautiful or sordid, which was a genuine aspect of human existence. Arthur Morrison belongs to the forefront of this realistic movement, and his *Tales of Mean Streets* which appeared in 1894, were not only the first examples of "mean street" studies, but also a collection of best-sellers which provided a neat generic title for the subsequent studies of slum life which followed in rapid succession from other writers. Morrison's "mean street" realism, however, is in a different category from that of George Moore or Gissing, who used such surroundings as background to the main play of character and moral problem, for he is not a moralist, nor does he attempt studies of psychology and temperament; he presents the slum surroundings, not as the background, but as the main theme. It is a serious theme, too, plainly spoken. Slums and poverty were not, of course, new to literature; they were in Dickens, Mrs. Gaskell and Charles Kingsley, or, nearer to hand, in books like Walter Besant's *Children of Gideon*—a romance in the dismal East End setting of Hoxton which is at the same time a plea for social reform; and in Gissing's *The Nether World* there are descriptions of Pennyloaf Candy's wretched home in Clerkenwell which foreshadow Morrison's **Child of the Jago.** But Morrison was the first to set out deliberately to record slum life as it really was: "In my East End stories," he said, "I determined that they must be written in a different way from the ordinary slum story. They must be done with austerity and frankness, and there must be no sentimentalism, no glossing over. I felt that the writer must never interpose himself between his subject and his reader. I could best bring in real life by keeping myself and my . . . moralizings out of it. For this I have been abused as hard and unsympathetic, but I can assure you it is far more painful for me to write stories than for you to read them." How far in this attitude he saw himself as part of a literary trend it is difficult to say, for he was undoubtedly aware of the realistic movement and had seen its possibilities; he belonged to his time. Yet he was a journalist rather than a man of letters, and literary historians are sometimes prone to over-emphasize "influences"; however much he may have read of contemporary English and French realism, his primary inspiration came without question direct and at first hand from his own experience in the East End.

The People's Palace, founded by Walter Besant, had been opened at Mile End in 1887, and Morrison worked for many years as Secretary of the People's Palace Trust, being a close friend of its Chairman, Sir Edmund Currie, and living, as he said, "in the very heart of that part of London". When he turned to journalism it was from these days that he drew material for his tales. The publication of the first of them in *Macmillan's Magazine* attracted the attention of W. E. Henley, then editing the famous *National Observer*. Morrison wrote, at Henley's request, further short stories which appeared in the *National Observer* and were later collected into the one volume: *Tales of Mean Streets*. Henley was an exacting editor; he demanded brevity, incisiveness and finish from his contributors, and Morrison, though he wrote many more stories, does not again achieve the variety and skill of these sketches and descriptive incidents, drawn objectively, but with a strong undercurrent of feeling, and detailing facets of East End life—its brutality, its heartlessness, its shoddy gentility and grey monotone. The first tale: **"A Street"**—where he tries to paint the empty sameness of average slum life, is perhaps the least successful, though it struck an original note when it was written, but there is a touch of genuine drama ending the story **"In Business"**, as the patient, stupid husband, driven at last to protest against his wife's nagging victimization, walks out quietly one morning and leaves her; a touch of comedy in the lighter treatment of a similar relationship in **"That Brute Simmons"**—a tale which he afterwards dramatized. There is the stringent cynicism of **"Conversion"**, in which light-fingered Scuddy Lond slips neatly back to iniquity after an emotional spasm of grace in the local mission hall; or the unblinking horror of **"Lizerunt"** (once christened, but long forgotten as, Elizabeth Hunt), her courtship and marriage. They are plain tales in plain language, in which, from a present-day vantage-point, it is easier to see omissions than achievement, since there is neither subtlety nor sophistication, depth of character study nor creation of mood, no sensuous appeal nor lyric grace. They possess, on the other hand, a firm and even economy of line, etched with a dry restraint which can deepen into caustic terseness; the subject-matter is genuine, the treatment honest, and, while in accordance with his purpose he sternly avoids emotionalism and sensationalism, he is never detached— the pressure of his own keen feeling is perceptible, strengthening his style.

The short story was becoming a popular form, and realism was a new vogue; *Tales of Mean Streets,* in addition to their intrinsic merit, came appropriately. Critics were impressed, and the author's reputation was established. Other writers like W. Pett Ridge and Edwin Pugh pursued the "mean street" theme in sketches of suburban types—shop girls, clerks, domestic servants, but played for Cockney comedy rather than serious comment. Nearer to Morrison in spirit were Richard Whiteing, who wrote *No. 5. John Street* as a picture of life in a London tenement, and Somerset Maugham, whose first novel, *Liza of Lambeth,* was in 1897 considered shockingly daring and quite improper for young ladies, since it told of an illicit love affair followed by a miscarriage. The style in its immature simplicity is tepid beside Morrison's, although the gift of sharp and accurate observation, the acute interest in people and their behaviour, which were ultimately to make him a more accomplished writer, are already apparent. Morrison took his own East End studies further two years later in a full-length novel, *Child of the Jago*. The Jago was his name for that part of Shoreditch known as the Nichol, from the name of Old Nichol Street, and it comprised the Boundary Lane area skirted by the Shoreditch High Street and the Bethnal Green Road. Nothing of it remains today except the faded name-plate of Old Nichol Street; there is merely a commonplace agglomeration of shops, houses, prefabs, and bomb damage, buttressed by the stolid barrack-like buildings of the L.C.C. housing estate. Contemporary nineteenth-century reports, however, described it as "a nest of vice and disease" comprising "congeries of filthy and insanitary courts and alleys", and it was a notorious slum. It is claimed by those who know Morrison's book and something of the background against which it was written, that

its publication was finally responsible for urging the London County Council to act and clear this district; unfortunately the compliment is without foundation, for the facts disprove it. The L.C.C. had been formed in 1889, and had started slum clearance in this part of Shoreditch as a pressing priority in 1891. Morrison himself stated, in a long interview in the *Daily News* for December 12th, 1896, that when he first went to the Nichol it was "on the point of being pulled down", although encroachment was slow. He lived in the Nichol, working and talking with the inhabitants, for eighteen months, and his novel is a record of his experience, which he completed in 1896 "just as the last houses were coming down". Building of the new estate began immediately, and it was opened by the Prince of Wales in 1900. Yet, although Morrison could not be credited with instigating the reform, he did receive tribute for commemorating it, for the Prince when speaking at the opening ceremony said that "few, indeed, will forget this site who have read Mr. Morrison's pathetic tale of *Child of the Jago*." Certainly the book made its mark, and its frank honesty may have influenced later housing schemes. It is as a sidelight on social history rather than as a novel that it is now valuable; the Jago, though vanished, is as symptomatic as Gin Lane. As a novel, the book is but average, but as a documentary it is illuminating. Critics complained, not without reason, of the technical faults in construction, and deplored the unpleasantness of the subject-matter, shifting a little uneasily, no doubt, before such an uncompromising statement of the facts, while Morrison in reply agreed that the Nichol was one of the isolated plague spots and not typical of the sheer dreariness of most East End life, which was "respectable to the gloomiest point of monotony"; on the other hand, he rewarded his critics with chapter and verse for the origin of some of the incidents they had picked out as improbable: "Critics have considered that Sally Green, my fighting heroine, was exaggerated. Indeed she is not. She is alive now, and her particular mode of fighting . . . is spoken of to this hour." Glass bottles, deliberately broken and jagged, were "quite a feature of East End life" as aggressive weapons. Those who argued that he had "nothing new to say" and that in any case the evil he exposed was already being remedied were answered in the preface to a later edition of the novel, as well as in newspaper articles: "I have remarked in more than one place the expression of a foolish fancy that because the houses of the old Jago have been pulled down the Jago difficulty has been cleared out of the way. That is far from being the case. The Jago, as mere bricks and mortar, is gone. But the Jago in flesh and blood still lives. . . ." Slum clearance was only the first step in social reform, which would not be really effective until organized and authoritative action was taken for dealing with the human problem which the slums produced.

Morrison's intention in writing the book can also be given in his own words. It was "to tell the story of the horrible Nichol . . . and of a boy who, but for his environment, would have become a good citizen". The tale is of Dicky Perrott, whose parents, though once boasting an honest if shabby livelihood, have sunk to Jago level. The mother is an inert weakling, the father a thief. Dicky, too, shows an early aptitude for theft which is promptly exploited by the cunning fence, Aaron Weech, while his childish gropings towards a better way of life are fostered by the local missionary, Father Sturt, who finds him a job as a shop boy in the Bethnal Green Road. The evil Mr. Weech, however, thereby losing a client, negotiates the boy's dismissal, and Dicky, bewildered and only half-comprehending the forces stronger than himself, returns to his old haunts, accepting the Jago dictum: "Spare nobody and stop at nothing, for the Jago's got you, and it's the only way out, except the gaol and the gallows." The father, Josh Perrott, does end on the gallows for murdering Aaron Weech, but Dicky is knifed in a street brawl and so is spared the worst excesses of Jago life.

Morrison had excellent narrative skill, and could reproduce all the pert pungency of the Cockney dialect. His style is swift and direct, his descriptions forceful. Yet one of his critics put the paradoxical view that, in spite of the realistic immediacy, the final effect of the book was one of unreality, which led him to suggest that Morrison could succeed better within the compass of the short story than in the full-length novel. That the latter was not the case Morrison was to prove when he wrote *The Hole in the Wall,* but the paradox holds, and can be explained. As in *Tales of Mean Streets* the author was writing from deep conviction about what he knew, but what in the former work was a source of strength is here a source of weakness. His very feeling about his subject blunts his vision, leading him to record rather than interpret his experience. He is too near to be able to shed irrelevancies and distil the essential features, or to illuminate the heart of his story by throwing it into relation with a broader background. His emotions are too violent to be a creative inspiration; they break through, upsetting poise and perspective, leading him into acid sarcasm, or over-description. He seeks to emphasize by repetition rather than selection. He portrays facts, but not the motives which underlie them, and material circumstance alone does not make a living novel any more than genuine cups and saucers on the stage made a living drama; it is the old confusion between realism and reality. We are led ingeniously on through a series of vivid incidents, but one street fight follows another very like it—Morrison was an expert boxer himself, and no doubt enjoyed describing what he understood so well—but in the end we have arrived nowhere; we have experienced movement without progression. In the same way, his characters live in sharp and convincing outline, but they do not grow; they are solid enough when in action, but revert to pasteboard stuff when they have to think or feel. Dicky Perrott is a real child when he steals the Bishop's watch or runs for his life from his pursuers, but when faced with an emotional experience tends to become mawkish or theatrical. Morrison's ability to create character was limited to what was outwardly visible; had he had George Eliot's penetrating insight into character he might have drawn a child as memorable as Maggie Tulliver, for he had a theme full of potentialities.

Morrison had been introduced to the Nichol by the Reverend Osborne Jay, Vicar of Holy Trinity, Shoreditch, a man for whom he had profound affection and respect, and he dedicated the book to him, incorporating him in the Jago story as Father Sturt. Jay must indeed have been a man of fine and powerful character, for since his appointment to the living in 1886 he had carried out reforms in the face of heartbreaking odds which eventually won the acknowledgement even of the Jagos: "He had an influence among them such as they had never known before. . . . The mean cunning of the Jago, subtle as it was, and baffling to most strangers, foundered miserably before his relentless intelligence, and crafty rogues . . . soon gave up all hope or effort to deceive him. . . . Thus he was respected. . . . Then there became apparent in him qualities of charity and loving-kindness, well-judged and governed, that awoke in places a regard that was in a way akin to affection." Offset against this are sarcastic criticisms of the church mission and popular philanthropy, whether justified or not it is not easy to say at this distance; certainly the Shoreditch Committee of the London Charity Organization Society was admitting defeat in 1888: "An examination of cases has shown a great mass of hopeless poverty, with which private charity is not strong enough to cope. . . . In many instances efforts were made to help, but the results have not been encouraging. . . . " In face of the dire need for drastic and official social reforms, Morrison had no use for fashionable "slumming" or for genteel charity operated from a safe distance, and he had seen the futility of the methods of the sentimental pietist in a district like the Nichol where poverty bred crime and criminal bred criminal in rapid and progressive deterioration. "The false sentiment of the day is the curse of the country", he wrote in one newspaper article, and he aimed to show that "Father Jay's method is the only one it is possible to employ in such a district". If the book is a social indictment, it is also a tribute to a man's work.

Those who did not care for hard facts in fiction could choose elsewhere, and the choice was wide and varied. There were the early stories of Kipling, glowing with unfamiliar colour; the gentler mood of Barrie, or Kenneth Grahame; *The Time Machine* had appeared in 1895 and was quickly followed by more of Wells's scientific romances, while those who preferred historical romance could turn to Anthony Hope, Gilbert Parker, or Stanley Weyman, and Marie Corelli's unique sensationalism was drawing its own readers—*The Sorrows of Satan,* produced in 1895, reached its fortieth reprint within a few years. Emerging as a new genre was the detective story, for Arthur Conan Doyle had won immediate popularity with the first Sherlock Holmes stories in the late 1880's and early 90's, and readers who had enjoyed these could turn back to Arthur Morrison for further adventures in the same vein. He came as a quick successor to Conan Doyle, and alongside *Tales of Mean Streets* in 1894 came a close imitation of *The Adventures of Sherlock Holmes* in *Martin Hewitt, Investigator*. This in turn was continued in further volumes as the *Adventures* and *Chronicles* of the same hero. The comparison with

Conan Doyle, who is still good entertainment, is an amusing one. Hewitt and his staunch friend, Brett, replace Holmes and the blunt-witted Watson, and Brett, like Watson, acts as the chronicler of his brilliant friend's exploits. Hewitt, like Holmes, is encyclopaedic. As Holmes has only to see a Chinese tattoo mark to launch into a description of the art, so Hewitt is equally fluent on Chinese seals or the chemical decomposition of burnt boot buttons, and proves himself just as instantaneous in decoding a cypher or summing up a character's past history from his personal appearance. In short, "Hewitt's infallible intuition", as his *Times* critic phrased it, "is positively stupefying". Morrison copied Doyle's method of exposition by explanatory narrative dialogue which is long and sometimes unwieldy, though Morrison could write good dialogue when on his own ground, as his Cockney stories show. Conan Doyle's style in general is crisper than Morrison's, and the incidents he invents are more bizarre and exotic. Hewitt does not possess Holmes's exceptional flair for disguises, nor is he ever called in to help the crowned heads of Europe out of their intrigues. Sherlock Holmes's creator endowed him with an eccentric personality: a tall, spare figure with pipe and silk dressing-gown, aquiline features and long, nervous fingers, with moody and unpredictable habits and a fondness for solving his problems by sitting up all night smoking, cross-legged on a pile of silk cushions. Morrison, on the contrary, insists on the ordinariness of his detective; Hewitt is just a plain fellow, an ex-barrister enjoying a hobby, a "pleasant and companionable" chap, of ordinary height and even inclined to stoutness; in detective literature he marks a distinct break-away from the established eccentric type of crime-investigator. Working in a plainer style than Holmes, he deals with more homely crimes, which, in fact, recur a little monotonously, as do the attendant circumstances of burnt papers, forged cheques and locked doors. Morrison is not very inventive, and does not stray far from jewel robberies, forgery and simple murder, although in a later sequence, *The Red Triangle,* Hewitt does have to pit his wits against a dangerous hypnotist, and Morrison gives the genre a new twist in *The Dorrington Deed-box,* where the unravelling of crime is done by Dorrington as a fake inquiry-agent who turned his talents to his own profit. Moreover, he avoids cheap sensationalism, and the incident in *The Dorrington Deed-box* where the dupe wakes up to find himself drowning in an iron tank and is rescued miraculously at the last minute by a workman providentially employed next door, is a rare lapse from his usual good sense. To modern readers these early detective stories seem unsubtle in their directness and one-sided in their purely intellectual exercise, forerunners in period dress of what is now an ingenious and intricate literature; yet they have their assured place in the history of detective fiction. Sherlock Holmes has become immortal, and though Martin Hewitt will not be known to many readers, the historian recognizes that Morrison's sound style and good craftsmanship was a solid contribution to a genre which was too readily debased by third-rate hack-writing.

Detective stories were a diversion. Morrison returned at the close of the century to an authentic background of an entirely different kind from the East End of London in his next two novels: *To London Town* and *Cunning Murrell.* The former is competent but undistinguished, employing his knowledge of Epping Forest and the stretch of country through Leytonstone into north-east London to Blackwall Cross and Harbour Lane, where the widowed Mrs. May comes to find a livelihood in shopkeeping while her son Johnny is apprenticed as a ship engineer. *Cunning Murrell* is well worth remembering as a real record of witchcraft in Essex in the 1850's, against a background of smuggling around the coast of Leigh and Hadleigh, which were then quiet rural backwaters. It is incredible but true that in such parts of Essex belief in witchcraft lingered throughout the nineteenth century and even into the twentieth. Contemporary newspapers provide evidence of actual cases brought before the local courts from time to time, as near our own day as 1908. The real James Murrell, the original of Morrison's novel, belongs to the mid-nineteenth century period, and he lived in Hadleigh as a shoemaker by trade, who made an additional income by telling fortunes, casting spells, and discovering witches, and, as a practising herbalist, by administering drugs and potions. He was widely known and feared for his occult powers, and when he died in 1860 a large number of letters and papers were disclosed which revealed the extent of his practices and influence. Morrison had seen these—he mentions them in his foreword—and it is from them that he weaves this tale of how Murrell casts out an innocent old woman as a witch, with the intricate train of events which follow. In spite of its unusual and potentially sinister theme, it is more genial in tone and better-made as a novel than *Child of the Jago* and with descriptions of Hadleigh, its castle and Essex landscape as a background the story flows with just sufficient movement, mystery and suspense to keep the reader turning the next page, the next chapter, to the end.

Morrison knew his Essex as intimately as he knew his East End. He had married in 1892 and probably settled at Loughton soon afterwards, for we find him giving an address there in 1896, though of course he continued for many years to work in London. His connection with the People's Palace Trust ended in 1902 when Sir Edmund Currie resigned the chairmanship, and he devoted all his time to journalism, working on the editorial staff of a London newspaper. Later his Essex address changes to High Beech, in the heart of Epping Forest, where W. W. Jacobs also lived. No doubt his best writing went into newspaper articles which were often unsigned or written under an assumed name, for although in the Edwardian period he published further collections of short stories: *Divers Vanities, Green Ginger* and *The Green Eye of Goona,* they do not disclose any development of talent, but repeat, albeit skilfully, the same patterns grouped round earlier East End characters, or those Essex characters which appeared in *Cunning Murrell*. His former trenchancy has gone, and here comedy is uppermost, resting on Cockney humour which exploits situation and dialogue, in which there is much genuine comedy in spite of a tendency to jauntiness. One misses the warmer, more human, quiet comedy of Jacobs.

He did, however, write one more full-length novel, which V. S. Pritchett has claimed to be "one of the minor masterpieces of this century". This is a just estimate of *The Hole in the Wall,* though out of focus, for the book belongs to its period and it would be a truer definition to call it a "minor Edwardian masterpiece". The Hole in the Wall is a public-house, in the notorious Radcliffe Highway of the mid-nineteenth century, which by 1902, when the book was written, had been purged and re-named St. George Street. The tale is of the small orphaned boy, Stephen, who is brought up there by his grandfather, and surrounded by murder, violence and swindling. Morrison can be trusted to deal with a sensational theme unsensationally, and the economy and quiet forcefulness with which the sinister plot unfolds produce a vivid, concise narrative; indeed, this narrative gift, always his first asset, is here seen at its best. Instead of the unrelieved sordidness which marred the after-effect of *Child of the Jago,* the dark episodes are lightened by comedy, derived from the flowing Cockney dialogue with which he is always at home, and in particular from the character of Mr. Cripps, the scoundrel artist who haunts the pub for what he can gain and who cannot resist interfering—to his own ultimate discomforture—in other people's affairs. Such moments are among Morrison's most enjoyable, and one remembers the incident in the otherwise tepid story of *To London Town* where the pretentious Mr. Butson is accosted on dockside by the half-drunk Emma Pacey and badgered to lend her twopence. It is broad, simple comedy, but effective.

Morrison's device of telling the **The Hole in the Wall** story partly as "Stephen's tale" and partly as direct narrative is an imaginative stroke which heightens the effect considerably. Intensity and perspective vary as the angle of vision shifts from the child's personal story to the author's, lighting the stage now this way, now that, as, for example, where the screams of the woman who has fallen over a certain dead body which she dreaded finding in the dark, are heard in Blue Gate by the last pubstragglers and at the same time by Stephen, lying in bed listening with innocence but apprehension to the creaking house. The honest simplicity of the child's nature throws an even murkier shadow over the evil which surrounds him.

The central theme is the change wrought in Grandfather Nat—by no means a virtuous character—by his incurred responsibility towards the child, and by the child's unquestioning affection for him. It has already been suggested that Morrison's ability to draw character was limited, and that although his people live and move with enough conviction to propel the story, they do not develop, but then portrayal of temperament and personal relationship was not his first concern. He draws types rather than individuals, and having drawn them, tends to repeat the pattern, or he will draw a slightly eccentric personality by emphasizing one feature at the expense of the rest, so giving characters like Aaron Weech in **Child of the Jago** or Long Hicks in **To London Town** a superficial Dickensian resemblance—superficial, because the two authors have little really in common except their social anger and London background. In **The Hole in the Wall** however, he achieves a much closer interrelation of character and event than hitherto, and attempts to show, at least in the case of Grandfather Nat, a character modified by experience. Furthermore, action springs from character as well as from incident: it is Mag's devotion to Dan Ogle—her one virtue—which ironically focuses suspicion on him; it is Mr. Cripps's officious self-importance which precipitates the unmasking of Mrs. Grimes; it is the enraged vanity of Blind George, who, malicious as he is towards others, cannot bear taunts about his own blindness, which incenses him to blind Dan Ogle in revenge, and indirectly to change the end of the story. In the other novels characters were either good or bad; here at times they suggest a deeper complexity, with moods of doubt and fear.

The author's descriptive method is direct photography—a recording of things as they are. That this is not always successful is illustrated by his description of the notorious pub, for he devotes a page to drawing its twisted geometry, whereas a few significant strokes and a touch of imagery would have created for the reader a less exact but more impelling impression. But such instances are few, and are more than offset by the controlled incisiveness of such scenes as Mag's journey across Limehouse flats, the blinding of Dan Ogle, or the fire which destroys the public-house. These, and passages from his other East End books, leave memorable pictures of the London river with its docks and wharfs, its warehouses and murky dockside streets, its marshy flats and sullen skies, of slum squalour and the humdrum traffic of poverty.

After the excellence of *The Hole in the Wall* Morrison's failure to develop as an Edwardian novelist is disappointing, and possible reasons for this are by now apparent; he was, in the final count, a skilled craftsman rather than a creative artist, and lacked the imaginative power to sustain original work; moreover, he was a busy practising journalist and perhaps had neither the time nor the ambition to attempt literary eminence. One further reason may have lain in the fact that he was at this time compiling a work of very different dimensions. Morrison devoted his spare time to the collection of works of art, and he was a keen connoisseur not only of English painting, but also, and of more importance, of Oriental art. His last published work before he retired in 1913 was a two-volume survey of the painters of Japan, which became, and is still regarded as, a leading work on the subject, while his fine collection of Chinese and Japanese drawings was acquired by the British Museum on his retirement.

His career as a writer was therefore over, but his interest in literature by no means waned. After the 1914-18 war he returned from Epping Forest to live in London, and settled in Cavendish Square, off Regent Street. In December, 1924, through his close friendship with Sir

Henry Newbolt, he was elected a member of the Royal Society of Literature by unanimous invitation of its Council. Eleven years later he was invited to join the Council itself, on which he served as a keen and active member until his death in his Buckinghamshire home in 1945.

It was perhaps the circumstance of his death, together with the returning taste for this period of literature, which brought about the re-issue of his best work, and present-day readers owe much to publishers like Eyre and Spottiswoode, whose Century Library series is designed to save such authors as Morrison from oblivion, for they deserve to be reinstated on our bookshelves. Yesterday's best-sellers can be more than today's curiosities; with an assured and honest craftsman they exhibit talents which both inform and entertain.

Vincent Brome (essay date 1965)

SOURCE: "Arthur Morrison," in *Four Realist Novelists,* Longmans, Green & Co., 1965, pp. 7-20.

[*In the following essay, Brome discusses the realism of Morrison's novels that depict the lives of London's poor.*]

A cloud of self-induced obscurity surrounds the life of Arthur Morrison, that small master among the group of English novelists who concentrated their attention on the working classes in their East End *milieu* during the late nineteenth century. The *Times* obituary about him is a bewildered piece of writing. A few lines giving the barest bones of his life are overwhelmed by a laboured examination of his work. According to Morrison himself, he was born in Kent in 1863, but his birth certificate places him immutably in the East End of London. His father he described as an engineer, but he was in fact an engine fitter. Professionally, he identified himself, later in life, as a civil servant and this may be considered a legitimate extension of the fact that he helped to run the People's Palace, a charitable 'mission' founded by Walter Besant in the East End of London in 1887. It was almost as if the man who so vividly evokes the horror, the poverty, the seaminess of late nineteenth century London, wanted to forget or run away from his roots.

His personality is similarly masked. Few interviews or sketches worthy of the name remain, and none reveals what manner of man he was, but there are hints in his contemporaries' comments of a touch of snobbery which might complicate his reasons for concealing his origins. He tired very soon of his life as 'a civil servant' and turned to journalism, becoming a member of the staff of a London daily newspaper. He married in 1892 Elizabeth Adelaide, the daughter of a Dover man. Their one son, Guy, died in 1921 of 'maladies consequent on his war service'. Morrison himself served as an inspector of special Constabulary during World War I, and had the curious distinction of telephoning the warning of the first Zeppelin raid on London. Little else of a personal nature has been recorded.

In 1892-3 he drew on his experiences of the East End to write a number of short stories the first of which, published in *Macmillan's Magazine,* attracted the attention of W. E. Henley, who was then steadily building up the reputation of the famous *National Observer.* Morrison wrote, at Henley's request, a number of new short stories which were gathered and published in one volume under the title *Tales of Mean Streets* in 1894, the year when Henley also discovered H. G. Wells. Perhaps it is irrelevant to ask for subtlety or depth of character in stories which set out brutally and bluntly to depict the darker side of life in the East End of London, but these early stories are not so effective as Morrison's first novel, *A Child of the Jago,* which appeared in 1896.

Morrison's intention in writing *A Child of the Jago* can be given in his own words: 'To tell the story of the horrible [Jago] . . . and of a boy who, but for his environment would have become a good citizen.' He sets the scene rapidly in the opening paragraphs:

> It was past the mid of a summer night in the Old Jago. The narrow street was all the blacker for the lurid sky. . . . Below, the hot heavy air lay, a rank oppression, on the contorted forms of those who made for sleep on the pavement; and in it, and through it all, there rose, from the foul earth and grimed walls, a close, mingled stink—the odour of the Jago . . . there the Jago, for one hundred years the blackest pit in London, lay and festered.

Carefully avoided by most of those who came from the West End of London, the Jago was an awful Gothic spectacle of squalor, brutality and crime, which actually existed under another name in the East End of London, and many of its inhabitants knew what it meant to be driven by hunger into extreme behaviour.

A small boy, Dicky Perrott, streaks across this scene with the hunted vitality of a child whose wits have been sharpened beyond anything childhood should know, and whose spindly body is alive with the nervous tensions of desperate need. One day he stealthily insinuates himself into the ceremony of opening the new wing of the Institute, a procedure which allows Morrison fine scope for satirizing those West End eminences, including a Bishop, who come to witness the results of their own charity and congratulate themselves on the wonderful effects of 'Pansophic Elevation' among the degraded classes. The canker in their midst, Dicky Perrot, hides himself behind the curtains of the room wherein the Bishop and other Eminences will retire to take tea after the ceremony. Presently the amiable Bishop, 'beaming over the tea-cup . . . at two courtiers of the clergy, bethought him of a dinner engagement and passed his hand downward over the rotundity of his waistcoat. "Dear, dear" said the Bishop glancing down suddenly, "Why—what's become of my watch".'

When Dicky Perrott bursts in on his family ten minutes later crying: 'Mother—Father—look! I done a click. I got a clock—a red un!'—he expects praise, but his father, carefully pocketing the watch, up-ends and beats him. From now on the horror of double-dealing, of dirt, crime and brutality grows as the novel unfolds scene after scene where gangwarfare outdoes in violence anything known today:

> Down the middle of Old Jago Street came Sally Green: red-faced, stripped to the waist, dancing, hoarse and triumphant. Nail-scores wide as the finger striped her back, her face, and her throat, and she had a black eye; but in one great hand she dangled a long bunch of clotted hair, as she whooped defiance to the Jago. It was a trophy newly rent from the scalp of Norah Walsh, a champion of the Rann womanhood who had crawled away to hide her blighted head and be restored with gin.

Against this background, rendered with horrific detail, Dicky Perrott finds himself torn between Aaron Weech, the cunning fence who can dispose of anything so long as it is stolen, and Father Sturt, who gets Dicky a job as a shop-boy in the Bethnal Green Road and sets him on the path to respectability. Furious because he has lost a skilful child operator, Weech engineers the boy's dismissal and Dicky, once more the bewildered victim of forces he only dimly comprehends, drifts back to his old haunts and his old ways. Once again the Jago teaches him: 'Spare nobody and stop at nothing, for the Jago's got you, and it's the only way out except the gaol and the gallows.' In due course Josh Perrott, the father, murders Aaron Weech and Dicky is knifed in a street brawl. One solitary principle comes through the murk and the muck. When Dicky is dying Father Sturt asks him—'who did it?'—and he replies, 'Dunno Fa'er'. The lie—the staunch Jago lie. Thou shalt not nark.

Arthur Morrison developed into a distinguished practitioner of a new school of realism in English fiction which derived from Zola, Dickens and Gissing but in his hands became different from any of their work. Descriptions of slums and low life occur in Dickens, Charles Kingsley, Walter Besant and many others but Morrison disdained the quaintness of Dickens's slum characters and recoiled from any attempt to romanticise East End lives. He wanted to record the reality as it was.

Gissing in *The Nether World* gave a description of Pennyloaf Candy's terrible home in the East End of London which leads directly into Morrison's work, but Morrison carefully avoided the self-pity evident in much of Gissing's work:

> In my East End stories I determined that they must be written in a different way from the ordinary slum story. They must be done with austerity and frankness, and there must be no sentimentalism, no glossing over. I felt that the writer must never interpose himself between his subject and his reader. I could best bring in real life by keeping myself and my moralizings out of it. For this I have been abused as hard and unsympathetic, but I can assure you it is far more painful for me to write stories than for you to read them.

There was no *explicit* moral anger in Morrison's work as there was with Dickens, and the French naturalism of Zola gave place to the empirical realism of England. The character which dominates *A Child of the Jago* is really the Jago itself. But it is presented without social comment, and for all the remorseless accuracy with which the author reveals every corner of this black and hopeless pit, he seldom suggests any explicit concern for its inhabitants. On the surface, Morrison seems to shrug his shoulders. Conditions are like this. Slum life has to be accepted and the destiny of those born within its precincts is played out under Morrison's direction with a dreadful inevitability. Take the dialogue in the first chapter of *A Child of the Jago* between Kiddo Cook and the stranger:

> 'Ah-h-h-', he said, 'I wish I was dead; and kep a cawfy shop.'
>
> Kiddo Cook felt in his pocket, and produced a pipe and a screw of paper. 'This is a bleedin unsocial sort o'evenin' party, this is', he said. 'An ere's the on'y real toff in the mob with 'ardly a pipeful left, an' no lights. D'y'ear me lord',—leaning towards the dozing neighbour—'got a match?'
>
> 'Go t'ell.'
>
> 'O wot 'orrid langwidge . . . '
>
> 'Go t'ell.'
>
> A lank elderly man who sat with his back to the wall, pushed up a battered tall hat from his eyes, and producing a box of matches exclaimed:
>
> 'Hell? And how far's that? You're in it . . . '
>
> 'Ah', Kiddo Cook remarked, as he lit his pipe in the hollow of his hands, 'that's a comfort Mr. Beveridge, anyhow.'

There is another element implicit in the book which tends to qualify its external realism. A black despair which verges upon hatred appears in over-emphasized descriptions, and bursts of emotion are sometimes expressed in acid sarcasm. For all his protestations, there are times when Morrison cannot keep his own feelings out of the book. Philanthropy and its half-sister charity may have brought about changes in the Jago, but they were full of smugness and humbug which Morrison exposes. His general method is to describe the surface reality in detail. He gets his effects by selecting and reiterating melodramatic episodes, but occasionally he goes beyond this naturalistic approach and ventures a moral judgement.

He did not create in Dicky Perrott a child as memorable as George Eliot's Maggie Tulliver because he deliberately foreswore insight into the hidden workings of character. In his view nature reacted on nature and produced a series of conditioned reflexes in Dicky Perrott. That was sufficient for him. The power of environment was more important than any hidden complex in the psychological makeup of the child.

It is possible to charge the method with superficiality. The wellsprings of human nature are subject to many complicated influences of which topographical environment is only one, if a major one, but it now becomes necessary to explore the theory of English realism in nineteenth-century fiction and its ancestor French naturalism.

One of the most repetitive and confused pieces of writing of which Zola was ever guilty, his prolonged essay, or series of interlocking essays, on 'The Experimental Novel' tries to relate the naturalistic school to the scientific method. It is a pity that no-one at that stage of critical history took the trouble to define clearly the differences between the words naturalistic, realistic and scientific, for the result was that the labels could sometimes be interchanged to the confusion of the whole scene. The main distinguishing feature between French 'naturalism' and English 'realism' was that French writers saw character and event as shaped by environment and other processes which could be scientifically defined. English writers tended to be interested in character as something essentially idiosyncratic, an end in itself, and action as often determined by the operations of chance.

What Zola meant by the *école naturaliste* can be stated fairly simply. Zola saw the late nineteenth century as an age of science, and believed that no subject which was not studied and developed according to the scientific method could claim attention as a serious branch of knowledge. The essence of the scientific method was centred on experiment, and as the scientist had passed from experiment in chemistry and physics to experiment in physiology, so the novelist must pass from the traditional novel to the experimental novel. He saw the novel partly as a means to social reform, and a moral element must therefore prevail in this new approach. The experimental novelist 'must do for man as a whole what the experimenting physiologist does for his body'. He would probe into inherited characteristics, take account of the influence of environment, dissect every action to discover its cause and effect and then, acknowledging the laws of scientific determinism, give an account from beginning to end of the interaction of mind, body and environment.

Strictly speaking, Zola was describing not the application of the scientific method to novel-writing but simply a new departure from an old creative tradition. Granted an overwhelming reverence for the new science, Zola wanted to make it part of literature, but there were only two points where they really met. First the rejection of the romantic tradition and the substitution of a realism which recorded what it saw no matter how nasty or sordid that reality turned out to be, and second, the belief that

life and events were mechanistically determined. An experiment carried out under controlled conditions in the laboratory was very different from telling a story in a new way with more realistic observation. Zola wanted novels in future to be closely based on the realities of life and the underlying philosophy of scientific determinism. Henry Norman summed up the desired change in technique in the *Fortnightly Review* for 1 December 1883:

> Do not contrive a complicated family or social puzzle of which your novel is to exhibit the process of solution, exhausting your ingenuity in making people misunderstand one another, and in placing obstacles in their way; but take a piece of real life for your basis and let your motives and means be those of our common existence.

The first translations of Zola's novels in England were received with disgust, and a public outcry led to the imprisonment in 1889 of his publisher, Vizetelly. For English readers, with their uneasy Victorian conscience, Zola had overstepped the borderline between the sordid and the pornographic. Always fascinated by the raw material of life, Zola had in fact set out to explore this in a series of novels telling the story of the Rougon-Macquart family and its enormous ramifications during the second Empire. This was intended to be not merely a picture of French life and society but also a study in heredity.

Arthur Morrison read *La Terre,* included in the second half of the series. It is almost certain that he also read Zola's rambling attempt to make a science of literature in *The Experimental Novel,* which was translated into English in 1893, the year before *A Child of the Jago* appeared. Literary periodicals in England also paid attention to the new French school and novels like George Moore's *Esther Waters* were stamped as naturalistic, but the growth of English realism had several distinguishing characteristics. It did not concern itself with science or the scientific method and in the hands of Morrison it had nothing to do with moralizing. Dickens had given it a peculiarly English twist by concentrating on 'characters' but neither Morrison nor Dickens accepted the assumption on which Naturalism as a literary movement was based—that man and his societies can be explained entirely in mechanistic or deterministic terms.

When challenged to explain the precise nature of his brand of realism, Morrison produced a rambling essay in the *New Review* for March 1897 which lost its way in an outburst of pique and failed to answer the question. Stung by an article in the *Fortnightly,* Morrison declared:

> I decline the labels of the schoolmen and of the sophisters; being a simple writer of tales who takes whatever means lie to his hand to present life as he sees it; who 'insists' on 'no process' and who refuses to be bound by any formula prescription prepared by the cataloguers and pigeon-holers of literature.

He then gives his definition of realism:

It seems to me that the man who is called a 'realist' is one who, seeing things with his own eyes, discards the conventions of the schools and presents his matter in individual terms of art.

This, of course, will not do. It is not a definition of a realist; it merely describes a particular kind of artist. A man who sees things with his own eyes and presents them in individual terms too often imposes his own vision on the scene observed and loses the documentary quality which is a prime element in realism. Dickens ceases to be a realist when his Cockney characters are converted by his vision into comical caricatures and his slums take on a picturesque or quaint air. Trade unionism in *Hard Times* ceases to be an instrument of working class organization and becomes a form of pointless intimidation, which is very unrealistic.

Not so in the work of Arthur Morrison. If anything he tended to make the Jago more appalling than it was—if that were possible—by over-emphasizing its depravity and squalor. Certainly the London to which he was born provided him with a wealth of realist material. The rabid region east of Aldgate was a catacomb of evil-smelling alleys and tiny shops, of crumbling warehouses and sub-let rooms, of a rancid river slithering furtively to the sea and mud flats which oozed into the city carrying their sour exhalation to the railway arches of Bethnal Green and the grim blackness of the Commerical Road. Thousands of people lived out their pallid lives without leaving the precincts of the slums and many died before they were forty of disease, malnutrition and the hazards of everyday life in places like the Jago. Of course, there were music halls, pubs and gaiety. Of course, on Saturday nights a zest for living burst through all the horrors and insisted on a coarse form of—was it happiness? Arthur Morrison did not deal in the reverse side of the coin. He was concerned with slums, poverty, hardship, to the exclusion of joy, and to that extent could be accused of being an inverted romantic rather than a realist.

He had a second very precise purpose in his writing, which made it necessary to exercise a special technique of selection. Before Gissing and Arthur Morrison, the literature of the East End of London was a stranger's literature seen from the outside. As V. S. Pritchett has written:

> It lies under the melodramatic murk and the smear of sentimental pathos, which in the nineteenth century were generated by the guilty conscience of the middle classes. They were terrified of the poor who seethed in an abyss just beyond their back door. The awful Gothic spectacle of hunger, squalor and crime was tolerable only as nightmare and fantasy—such as Dickens provided—and the visiting foreigner alone could observe the English slums with the curiosity of the traveller or the countenance of the anthropologist.

Gissing and Arthur Morrison broke into this convention to write from *within* the slums, to make internal what had always been external. They looked out through the eyes of men, women and children living in places like the Jago and faithfully recorded what it meant to be involved, day in, day out, in a kind of poverty which was far removed from anything to do with the picturesque. Gissing's novels are full of misery and worthy pathos. Arthur Morrison's dispense with the pathos and convey the impression of a species adapting itself to horrors which should have overwhelmed it. His novels are different from picturesque or nightmare novels and different again from the 'character albums of the writers of low comedy'.

His second novel, *London Town* (1899), another Tale of East End Life 'among the better sort of people in those parts' was not very successful. Dealing with the extremities of East End life Morrison emerged supreme. When he tried to convey a slice of less extravagant life where people were not so hard-pressed and even the beauties of Epping Forest had their place, the note was less urgent, the descriptions less vivid, the narrative rambling.

The powerful colours of squalor and violence inevitably had an impact far greater than the quieter colours of the semi-respectable. It is a severe test of any writer to make the commonplace as interesting as the melodramatic. Morrison did not match up to it. He said, in a note which prefaced this second novel:

> I designed this story, and, indeed, began to write it, between the publication of *Tales of Mean Streets* and that of *A Child of the Jago,* to be read together with these books: not that I pretend to figure in all three—much less in any one of them—a complete picture of life in the eastern parts of London, but because they are complementary, each to the two others.

Aware that his first novel had splashed down one kind of East End life in fierce colours, he tried to redress the balance by evoking more neutral scenes which would justify his claim to realism. He did not succeed. As if aware of this his third novel, *Canning Murrell,* was a total departure from what had gone before. It dealt with the activities of a witch doctor in rural Essex in the early 19th century.

Morrison's fourth novel—*The Hole in the Wall*—is his best and stands out among the novels of working class life in the late nineteenth century as a minor masterpiece. It returns once more to the techniques of *A Child of the Jago.* The Hole in the Wall was a public house in the notorious Radcliffe Highway of the East End, and the novel centres upon an orphaned boy, Stephen, brought up by his grandfather in an atmosphere of filth, murder, deception and theft. The viewpoint of the novel shifts from Stephen the boy to the omniscient novelist, one chapter being seen through Stephen's eyes, another taking the wider, third person perspective. It is a clumsy device. It breaks the consistency of the novel and the shifting viewpoint occasionally threatens verisimilitude. It would have been a far more severe test of Morrison as a novelist if he had limited himself to Stephen's viewpoint and seen everything through the boy's eyes. Indeed there are many indications that he intended to do just that, but the intractable material did not easily surrender to the single viewpoint and particularly to the viewpoint of a boy. In an attempt to bring the activities of all the characters into a cohesive whole he was driven to step out of Stephen's shoes.

The central theme of the novel is the effect on Grandfather Nat of the boy's relationship with him. The child is 'sheltered' by Nat, and as he observes the murky life of the pub, he gradually discovers that his grandfather is a receiver of stolen goods. Marr, a defaulting ship owner, disguises himself as a sailor to escape with £800 which eventually comes into the hands of Grandfather Nat. Marr gets drunk and is murdered by Dan Ogle, who at first intended no higher flight of theft than stealing a watch. There is a terrifying scene in which Marr, stunned and tottering between the two men, is dragged towards the river while they sing and bawl at the tops of their voices, pretending they are drunken sailors helping a pal to keep his feet. It is a pity, in one sense, that Morrison introduced that *cliché* character, a blind fiddler, because it modifies the austerity of his realism, but the fiddler finally indulges a form of brutality which lifts him clean away from any romantic tradition. While the wallet with the stolen £800 passes mysteriously to Grandfather Nat, the blind man is double-crossed, assaulted and ridiculed by Dan Ogle. He sets out to track Ogle down across the marshes and when he finds him asleep in a shed concealed by a lime quarry, he attacks him:

> Floundering and tumbling against the frail boards of the shed the two men came out at the door in a struggling knot; Ogle wrestling and striking at random, while the other, cunning with a life's blindness, kept his own head safe and hung as a dog hangs to a bull. His hands gripped his victim by ear and hair while the thumbs still drove at the eyes the mess of smoking lime that clung and dripped about Ogle's head. It trickled burning through his hair and it blistered lips and tongue, as he yelled and yelled again in the extremity of his anguish.

The blind man has blinded his enemy. Just one word seems out of place in a description which is much longer and more powerful in the original; the word 'yelled'. It does not adequately convey the reaction of a man whose head is burning from lime and whose eyes are being put out by another man's hands. Such a man undergoing such an experience would have screamed.

The clash between the innocent boy's view of the events he witnesses and the depravity of most of the remaining characters, including Grandfather Nat, gives the novel the tension of moral conflict. As in *A Child of the Jago,* where the clash occurs between the evil of the Jago which itself becomes one of the main characters and the social goodness of Father Sturt, here the child's innocence and unquestioning affection modify Grandfather

Nat's degenerate character. The people in *A Child of the Jago* tend to be good or bad, black or white, but in *The Hole in the Wall* they are more complex and the novel, in consequence, more sophisticated.

Once again the River Thames, dragging through its murkiest reaches, the wharves with cranes wheeling a-tiptoe, the marshy flats, sullen skies and the ghastly traffic in human beings trapped in one squalid conspiracy after another, combine to leave a memorable picture of one side of East End life conveyed in the most realistic terms. Only Stephen and Grandfather Nat emerge with any hope for the future:

> Dan Ogle, blinded and broken, but silent and saving his revenge; Musky Meg, stricken and pitiable but faithful even if to death; Henry Viney, desperate but fearful and urgently needy; these three skulked at bay in dark holes by Blue Gate.

It remains to guess that Stephen and Dicky Perrot were both embodiments of the shy sensitive boy Arthur Morrison, who had been born into an East End jungle which he wanted to dissociate from his new and cultured life as a writer.

Following *The Hole in the Wall,* Morrison failed to develop as a novelist and produced nothing worthy of comparison. There are obvious reasons for this. In the first place, as a busy journalist his spare time was limited, and another powerful preoccupation had arisen to challenge his interest in creative writing. After the first four novels much of his spare time was spent studying Oriental painting. He left a fine collection of Chinese and Japanese drawings to the British Museum, and wrote a two-volume study of Japanese painting which is still respected by scholars in the field. He also wrote, as early as 1894, a series of detective stories which began with *Martin Hewitt, Investigator.* Within his work itself, however, lay the major reason for his failure to develop. Morrison was a craftsman who rose occasionally to the heights of original creation, but these experiences could not be sustained. Moreover he had stated and re-stated his particular message. He did not have the boundless creative energy of great novelists like Dickens and Zola, and the range of his interests was much more limited. His was a brilliant but minor talent which could not reach beyond the area it had already illumined.

Michel Krzak (essay date 1979)

SOURCE: "Arthur Morrison's East End of London," in *Victorian Writers and the City,* edited by Jean-Paul Hulin and Pierre Coustillas, Publications de l'Université de Lille III, 1979, pp. 147-82.

[*In the following essay, Krzak describes Morrison's personal and professional connections to London's East End.*]

Arthur Morrison, who died in December 1945 at the age of 82, is still described as a native of Kent in many reference books—for instance in the 1974 edition of the *Encyclopaedia Britannica*—despite new data found notably in P. J. Keating's introduction to the 1969 edition of *A Child of the Jago*. Such an indication is unfortunate since it may lead readers to think that his was an outsider's picture of London.

We may wonder what prompted Arthur Morrison to provide false information about his origins to *Who's Who's* first biographical enquiry in 1897, at a time when he was an established short-story writer and the novelist of *A Child of the Jago*. If we dismiss ignorance on his part—although we can understand why he chose Kent, his mother's native country, rather than Essex which he had adopted as his home—, we are faced with a riddle, only partially and unsatisfactorily solved by charges of deceit or social snobbery. Not that a deliberate wish to stand aloof was out of character in a man who, judging by the testimonies of acquaintances, was reserved and secretive. But there remains a mystery when we realize that this information would have provided an overwhelming argument to counter the fierce reactions and bitter attacks after the publication of *Tales of Mean Streets* and *A Child of the Jago,* especially during the controversy on realism initiated by H.D. Traill. Perhaps he felt that Victorian society could not acknowledge his rise from a working-class background. Whatever his true motives, personal and social, there is no need to capitalize on his mystification at this juncture. Indeed, we can reinstate him as a man of the people, born in Poplar, and the son of an engine fitter. Though we have no documents about his education, we know, from the 1871 census, that he was still in the East End at the age of eight; and, as he became an office boy at fifteen, he must have spent all his childhood east of Aldgate. Thanks to the encouragements of W.E. Henley, he made his way to realistic literature in the 1890s, via his secretaryship at the People's Palace in Mile End Road and journalism in Fleet Street.

The biography, as well as the historical and social context, underlines the significance of Morrison's work. In the closing decades of the nineteenth century, a new outlook on the environment of industrial cities prevailed—London being regarded as an epitome and a development of the basic traits of urban life. Special emphasis was laid on hidden features, and fresh evidence was brought forward to question society's achievement, notably its policy towards the poor. *The Bitter Cry of Outcast London,* which forcefully sounded the alarm in 1883, was by no means an isolated appeal for changes and reforms. Several other publications and reports— Walter Besant's *All Sorts and Conditions of Men* in 1882 and George Gissing's *The Nether World* in 1889 are prominent literary examples—exposed shameful facts and were instrumental in arousing acute concern for city slum dwellers in the 1880s and 1890s.

Naturally, Mayhew's studies of London labour, Chadwick's and Greenhow's investigations of the 1840s and 1850s should be kept in mind when examining Morrison's descriptions of the 1890s, even though their perspective was different. The image of the unknown country was still used to describe the poverty-stricken areas, but Morrison's main interest focused on the urban growth of London as the cause of severe negligence despite successive reports and subsequent reforms. His presentation can be seen as resulting from a long investigation into living conditions which started with an enquiry into the paupers of mid-century London to end with Booth's study of the submerged population. From the **"Cockney Corners"**, which appeared as early as 1888, through the trilogy *Tales of Mean Streets, A Child of the Jago* and *To London Town,* to *The Hole in the Wall,* published in 1902, Morrison followed a path leading from fact to fiction, from a factual account to a more elaborate description of city life, from journalism to naturalism and realism.

. . . . .

Morrison's earliest contribution to *The People* provides his first approach to a picture of London. As the announcement made it clear, this series of independent "sketches" was to "deal with localities and their peculiarities, rather than with individuals." Its aim was to introduce the reader to several districts of London and to pinpoint their characteristic traits—Poplar and its Saturday market, Clerkenwell and its clockmakers and jewellers, the French restaurants of Soho, Bow Street Police Court, Whitechapel with its rows of houses, its homecrafts and ethnical groups, Jacob's Island, and the contrapuntal areas of Greenwich Park and Epping Forest.

Morrison successfully gives the impression of a dense population at certain key points of the capital, on London Bridge for instance every Saturday at noon, when "the pavement is filled by two solid streams of steadily hurrying human beings" and when pedestrians must dodge an incessant flow of traffic. Similarly on Saturday nights another gathering of people busy shopping in the East End is depicted in these words: "The broad Whitechapel road swarms with laughing, shouting, noisy human life. Buyers and sellers, rogues and dupes, drinkers and fighters. Each for himself and the thought of the moment!" The struggle for life is felt all the more acutely as economic competition is magnified by the thick crowd and as London Hospital looms up in the vicinity, looking after those who "have come to grief in some of the thousand ways so easy among the dense population, the large works, and the traffic". Urban concentration is an unquestionable factor of accidents in this "great cosmorama of life and death, joy and sorrow, health, sickness, and pain". Morrison excels in drawing accurate sketches of people in the streets, but on the whole he sticks to a general description and watches with a critical eye both setting and city dwellers. His "explorer's mind" notices in Soho "bell-handles, thick on the door-posts, like stops on an organ, front door never shut, children rolling down the steps, dirty babies nursed by premature little women and 'Apartments to Let' everywhere", as so many signs of overcrowding, of the conditions of tenant and sub-tenant families, and of the corollary questions of child care and hygiene.

In contrast with city life and to balance or counter the effects of urban overcrowding and pollution, Epping Forest is a godsend, whose proximity and advantages should be realized by the busy population of London, for, as Morrison puts it in his sketch, "Epping Forest is a Cockney Corner, from Epping to Wanstead Flats, and from Walthan Abbey to Chigwell, but one without smoke, chimney pots, noise and dirt; with whispering thickets, noble trees, grassy hollows and cool waters; with singing birds, humming insects, all sweet sounds . . .". How surprising to find this quasi-lyrical description of nature coming from Morrison's pen! The author so appreciated this wholesome "lung" of the city, the benefits of which should fall to the working East Ender, that he settled on the outskirts of the forest, at Chingford, and later at Loughton. He publicly stated his marked preference for life in Essex, never far from London it is true, and was well aware of the threat of industrial or urban growth, of the continual encroachment of the town upon nature, upon the Hainault Forest for instance. The notion of an antithesis between town and country life, not original in itself, refers to a duality inscribed in Morrison's life and literary career. His emigration may be seen as corresponding to the typical aspiration of the East Ender he was. Rooted in the East End, he later developed a professional life in London and a private life in the country, chiefly in Essex. This parallel is present in the double current of his production—his East End studies and his Essex stories, united by the same insight into place and character, and an earnest commitment to faithful treatment. Besides, if his interest in oriental art lies beyond this duality, his commitments to the literature of detection, to journalism and to humorous short stories are essentially urban.

Whereas *Tales of Mean Streets* and *A Child of the Jago* are set in London only, *To London Town* depicts a migration to London from the country for economic reasons. Actually, several migratory movements, illustrating a general situation, are outlined in the plot. First, sons and daughters leave their rustic parents to come and work in the job-supplying East End of London; secondly, when an emergency arises, if the father dies for instance, the family returns to the parents or grandparents in the country; thirdly, when the latter source of supporting income becomes extinct, a new economic migration takes place—the industrious widow enters the labour market as head of the family while the elder son becomes an apprentice at the firm which used to employ his father. The facts and the events are exemplary in so far as the Mays are drawn by the centripetal force of London; the country is their native soil as well as a temporary refuge or source of comfort—it is motherly on both counts. Indeed, even though this orphaned family is uprooted and plunged into a highly competitive world, it is hardly touched by urban morality; only the younger generation represented by Johnny proves more adapted to a tougher milieu and more wary of city sharks or spongers. The Mays are still

endowed with sturdy rustic qualities; they have retained a filial love for the country of their forbears, which they semi-consciously uphold as their ideal.

Contrasted with a world ruled by the economic struggle for bread, the country is idyllically associated with the notions of peace and quiet. But this position is far from being immune to change. As London keeps expanding, nature is slowly and relentlessly the victim of urbanization and industrialization. If the air in Essex is still "healthier and cleaner" than in London, the country has become a "poorer hunting ground" for butterflies, a prey to "the great smoky province that lay to the south-west". London is a magnetic and tentacular force which draws the lifeblood from the provinces through migration and impairs the country's unadulterated state through pollution.

. . . . .

Apart from this image of the city threatening the countryside, Morrison's early descriptions of the outer environment of the poorer classes of London lay stress on the sameness of streets and houses. He notices in **"Jacob's Island"** a "very dull street" with "mean, black little dwelling houses", and draws attention to the depressing atmosphere pervading this dreary, matter-of-fact world:

> Back from the river, what a sorry blank is Jacob's Island! It is to-day, without exception, the saddest Cockney Corner we know. Not eminently crime-saddened, or poor or starved. Colourless, blank . . . Mean little houses, not old enough to be interesting and not new enough to be clean, cluster thick about Jacob Street, London Street, Hickman's Folly and their alleys (. . .) Jacob's Island is comparatively respectable, but, oh!, how fearsomely dull!

As in another sketch, **"On Blackwall Pier"**, which takes up the identical themes of sordid street monotony and hard living conditions, the crude facts are attended by pessimistic comment. This particular emphasis paves the way for his highly praised study entitled **"A Street"**, which dwells obsessively upon the drabness of surroundings.

If the setting in **"Cockney Corners"** can be regarded as a décor in the sense of a somewhat neutral visual presentation, in his subsequent work it loses its picturesqueness to assume social significance since it is directly, if negatively, related to its counterparts in more favoured districts. The architectural impression is strengthened by a parallel view of the inhabitants' way of life. Morrison establishes an inevitable link between outer appearance and actual existence, although this interpretation, which sets the tone for a realistic approach, is not borne out in all the "tales of mean streets", for life is not necessarily dreary where living conditions are grim.

Morrison was not the first nor the last of his generation to have observed the uniformity of the streets and houses in London. Hubert Crackanthorpe for instance depicts the monotony of "shabbily symmetrical" streets, with "a double row of insignificant, dingy-brick houses". In *To London Town* Morrison offers a similar description when the Mays come to the East End. If "the road narrowed and grew fouler, and the mouths of unclean alleys dribbled slush and dirty children across the pavements", they eventually reach "a place of many streets lying regularly at right angles, all of small houses, all clean, every one a counterpart of every other", Unlike some other areas, Shipwrights Row is renowned for its cleanliness and the colour pattern of the outside paintwork. Yet, monotony is spreading—the children travelling to Essex notice "close, regular streets of little houses, all of one pattern, (that) stared in raw brick, or rose, with a forlorn air of crumbling sponginess, amid sparse sticks of scaffolding"—as if London kept exporting a mass-produced housing pattern. The depressing monotony in certain quarters is intensified by overcrowding. Families gather near their places of work, in districts which soon become congested. These districts change character according to their inhabitants, whose number keeps increasing. People pile into quickly saturated lodgings—"eight, ten or a dozen human sleepers" in one room, in the extreme case of the Jago.

Foul nooks and crannies inevitably developed in the texture of Victorian London, as backhouses enjoyed the cheap rents a working-class family could afford. Different types of slum dwellings emerged as demands rose and rents altered, tenancy being more or less temporary. The poorer labourers had to resort to these lodging ghettos, motivated by proximity of work and their financial resources. The ironically named Pleasant Court in Crackanthorpe's *Vignettes* (1896) is a good example— "To find it, you must penetrate a winding passage, wedged between high walls of dismal brick". And Jago Court, the focal point in Morrison's novel, is a typical, though extreme, example of reclaimed backyards where all kinds of needy people have come to settle. Dr. Barnardo's article entitled "A Tale of a Mean Street" provides a parallel depiction of a narrow, ill-paved, East-End street and a dark cellar-like kitchen. An identical impression of an underground world pervades the crowded courts, typical of those built-in areas which have long passed saturation point, depicted by Octavia Hill in the 1870s. The spatial confinement becomes unbearable in the sultry atmosphere. In "a narrow paved court with houses on each side, the sun has heated them all day, till it has driven nearly every inmate out of doors". The children especially are "crawling or sitting on the hard hot stones till every corner of the place looks alive". The opening pages of *A Child of the Jago* offer an exact parallel. The Jago is the "blackest pit in London" and Jago Court, "the blackest hole in all that pit". In the sultry and smelly atmosphere of summer nights, it is filled with rat-like human shapes. Because the contemporary picture, with its rhetoric, is so consistent, we may infer that Morrison's fiction is based on reliable facts, and insist on his first-hand knowledge of the places he describes—a knowledge he repeatedly stressed in reply to criticisms. His four years as secretary to the People's Palace, his observations as a journalist, and his careful documentation prior to writing (notably his "intimate study" of the parish of Trinity Church at Shoreditch which lasted a year and a half), bear witness to the credibility of his account.

There is both a gradation and an evolution in presentment. **"A Street"** underlines the bleak monotony of city streets in Poplar, where spectacular aspects are deliberately discarded. Yet, his denunciation of false, biased views of the East End as "an evil plexus of slums that hide human creeping things", is contradicted by the image of the Jago in his first novel. Again, if the docks in *To London Town,* where the Mays used to live, are described in a subdued manner, and if the busy riverside at Blackwall Pier is less colourful, the dockland and Wapping area in *The Hole in the Wall* is much more picturesque and dangerous with its maze of "crooked lanes" and "small, ill-lighted streets". Off the notorious Ratcliff Highway, lies Blue Gate, hazardous and ill-famed, set in mid-nineteenth-century London.

Habitation and reputation varied according to the district and the economic situations of the inhabitants of the East End. While regular workers lived in rather characterless though clean lodgings, casual labourers and new immigrants had to be content with unsuitable dwelling places, for financial reasons. They had to join other urban categories—marginal groups such as criminal types—, running the risk, repeatedly stressed, of being contaminated. As for the densely crowded areas, or rookeries, inhabited by a fluctuating, unstable population, they were often considered dangerous quarters—a threat to civilized society. The traditional haunts of disreputable characters, thieves and criminals, such as Whitechapel, Limehouse, Ratcliff Highway, were often painted in this light.

In point of fact, as the slum dwellers had little inclination to stay confined in their small dingy rooms, they repaired to the street, which was the meeting place of natives and visitors, and a vantage point for the observant novelist. The streets in the East End were busy places at any hour, but on a number of regular and special occasions, people gathered in large numbers. While fun fairs, bank holiday rejoicing, and street fights tended to draw people from far and near, street markets assembled a more local crowd. Apart from adults, loafers or busy tradesmen and housewives, observers noticed the presence of a great number of children, which seemed to corroborate the idea of a prolific East End. Although school attendance was compulsory, it was seldom or inadequately enforced, so that, when unemployed, children were left on their own. Because of the absence of their fathers, ill or dead or in jail, which obliged mothers to rule the home, the children had to fend for themselves, unsupervised. As bread, not to mention money, was lacking, many of them became self-sufficient at an early age. They regarded the streets as a spectacle—witness the boys watching the clockmakers in a sketch called **"Clerkenwell"**—, but they were also on the lookout for a favourable opportunity—picking up an odd job like parcel carrying, or snatching things. Maturity soon fell upon their young shoulders, especially when, like Mother Sister Julia in Edwin Pugh's *A Street in Suburbia* (1895), the elder children helped to bring up little brothers and sisters, or when new family or social responsibilities prevailed. Early moral and economic independence was not a new fact in the late Victorian period, but a characteristic feature of the working-class children of East London. Dicky Perrott is the archetype of boys who, rather than playing games, were in search of food, or objects to exchange for bread, and who, like adults, had to rely on themselves only.

The documentary realism used by Morrison and some of his contemporaries to present a vivid description of the environment in East London also provided a basis for reflection. Many aspects of this environment seemed unworthy of a modern Victorian city; they were at variance with the ideals and principles expounded by contemporary society. These writers implicitly demanded that efforts should be made to relieve those shameful areas, those dark recesses which bore witness to obvious neglect in town planning, and also to abolish the actual and latent dangers of a marginal, segregated life to the population at large, but especially to children left without proper material care and moral support. If the later Morrison seems to have been more cautious about such possibilities, the young writer of the **"Cockney Corners"** did not hesitate to dwell on the positive merits of Epping Forest and public parks as essential lungs for oppressed East-Enders, just as he provided guidance in organizing the activities of young members when he was at the People's Palace.

. . . . .

Morrison reveals that there is a definite physical and moral pattern of life in the East End of London, people being identified with their streets and their districts. From his descriptions of the drab lives in mean streets and the violent life in the Jago, we can gather that urban structures had a direct bearing on the material and mental conditions of people.

A direct consequence of the sanitary conditions, already exposed by Edwin Chadwick in the 1840s, was the high death-rate in slum areas. Shoreditch is an exemplary case, even in 1898: "Nowhere else in London can you gaze on such a scene of wretchedness. Houses hardly fit to be dog-kennels, breeding disease which brings the children of Shoreditch to the grave with terrible rapidity and suddenness. Four graves are dug here for every one in any other part of London". Statistics showing population density and mortality rates were used to show the consequences of deplorable circumstances. Morrison did not fail to stress the phenomenon dramatically:

> Albeit the Jago death-rate ruled full four times that of all London beyond, still the Jago rats bred and bred their kind unhindered, multiplying apace and infecting the world.

Infant mortality was markedly more widespread in cities, and among poor urban working-class families. The death registers at Somerset House bear numerous mentions of still-born babies. Moreover, neglect and lack of food caused the untimely deaths of frail children, as we may observe in *A Child of the Jago,* in little Looey's case. Dicky Perrott's sister is soon replaced, however, by little Em and baby Josh, which demonstrates the high birthrate prevailing in East London. For the same environmental reasons, children like Dicky "would never get really tall". In those substandard lodgings and insanitary conditions, the children were the first to suffer, as poverty was the cause of undernourishment and malnutrition, which accelerated disease and death.

Poverty was also related to, and aggravated by, drinking. In view of the social context, it is not surprising that drinking should have been so popular. The public houses were attractive, brightly lit places which stood out against the dreary surroundings, and afforded an outlet, a release from outer struggles and family troubles. Octavia Hill clearly points out the effect of the close, stifling courts on people's behaviour—during the hot evenings "the drinking is wildest, the fighting fiercest, and the language most violent", while Robert Sherard indicates that "it is indeed rather on account of the physical exigencies of their work (and, we may add, of their lodgings) that these people, as a class, exceed and are intemperate". Naturally, drinking was considered an aggravating factor in those unfavoured districts of the East End. Not only did it divert money from more immediate needs, but it also brought people into contact with disreputable characters. The pubs were indeed places where shady business transactions were often settled. Apart from "The Hole in the Wall" which chiefly enjoys an underground activity, there are several types of public houses in the Jago. "The Feathers" is described as "the grimiest and vilest of the four", and in all of them there were frequent "bar riots". At Mother Gapp's, fighting and rejoicing alternate. On great occasions, such as the homecoming of a released convict—Josh Perrott in the novel—the public house fulfils a social function, in that it proclaims reintegration and asserts its communal feeling. Hannah Perrott has to "prove herself not unduly proud" and indulge in gin-drinking, lest she should incur her neighbours' rebukes.

Much of the money is spent on drinking—in poor districts shopping is done on Sunday morning after Saturday's drink, with what is left of the week's wages. The search for food and the basic necessities of life takes several forms, according to the ability of the housewife. Morrison points out in **"A Workman's Budget"**, published in 1901, that although generalization is difficult, the working-class woman is "commonly no fool and no idler". Yet, recalling his personal experience—"I have met with perfectly amazing cases of masterly household management on slender means; and brilliant instances aside, the average workman's 'missis' is a very good housewife"—, he implicitly infers that there are less happy cases. In fact, he acknowledges the existence of wide differences—"between the drunkard, whose household starves while he soaks away his wages, and the weakling, whose wife takes every penny and scarce gives him one back, there lie many degrees"—, between a Jago family and the Ropers or the Mays.

Hunting for the money necessary for subsistence and lodging involves a daily struggle. When illness strikes a working-class family, hardships increase. **"Chrisp Street, Poplar"**, after a picturesque description of the streets, introduces the reader to the pathetic story of a couple emerging from a pawnshop:

> Times have been hard with Joe and the missis. Joe has had rheumatic fever, and has spent his entire convalescence in hunting for a job. Day after day he has started out, good fellow, with a mendacious assurance to the missis that he didn't feel up to any breakfast, well knowing the little he left for her and the small Barkers even then. Evening after evening he has come home again—feetsore, hungry, disappointed, and well-nigh heartbroken—unsuccessful. And evening after evening his noble little missis has met him with a smile—poor soul, it gets harder to smile as the face grows thinner and the brain feels duller—with a smile and a kiss as warm and as true as even when she was a plump-faced nursemaid and he was a jolly 'prentice lad over on the island.

If the outlook is optimistic and the tone slightly sentimental, as the family is seen climbing uphill with courage and perseverance, this vignette depicting representatives of the "industrious poor" is nonetheless truthful enough.

To overcome adversity, pawning is the usual solution. From the **"Cockney Corners"** onwards, Morrison mentioned it in his works. When Josh Perrott is injured and is unable to work, his wife Hannah pawns a coat at a "leaving shop in a first floor back in Jago Row". In *To London Town,* Norah's dress is pledged as a direct consequence of the drinking habits of her mother. The same means was used to pay the rent. Otherwise, as a long term solution, it was possible to sub-let, or take in lodgers, but Hannah Perrott would not hear of this simply because "she doubted her ability to bully the rent out of them, or to turn them out if they did not pay"—which indicates that the practice was frequent.

Circumstances drove people along various paths, even beyond the limits of morality, to obtain basic necessities. Several methods were used to get money and clothing from the "profitable sentimentalist" in the Jago, although these methods were held in contempt by the "sturdier ruffians", who preferred stealing. One of the devices consisted of "a profession of sudden religious awakening", which reminds us of the study called **"A Conversion"**. Hesitant potential converts received "the boots, the coats, and the half-crowns used to coax weak brethren into the fold". Similar behaviour is seen in children who do not normally attend school except when free gifts—coal or food—are distributed. Dicky, for instance, goes to school "at irregular intervals", but "whenever anything was given away, he attended as a matter of course".

Hardships tend to favour a realistic approach to daily problems. Several examples of the suffering poor are given in **"Cockney Corners"**, especially in **"London Hospital"**, where disease or injury leads to crises. A bricklayer, who has fallen from his scaffolding, is happy to see his wife, courageous and smiling:

> His wife is sitting by him, with her little boy. See what a brave, bright face she keeps, and how gaily she reports her own well-doing, although the poor fellow himself well knows how few shillings there were in hand a month ago, when he first came in, and how she is charring hard for every mouthful she and the child eat.

The poignancy of the picture is enhanced if we are aware that Morrison's mother may have gone through a similar experience when his father was in hospital suffering from phthisis.

Diseases, death, brutal or violent events steel people to a stern, often stoic, attitude to life. Harsh realities and constant worries are not conducive to pleasure and laughter. Indeed, women with a tendency towards merriment or singing are regarded with suspicion and judged mercilessly, like the young countrywife in **"A Street"**. Lizerunt, in the opening "tale", hardly experiences any pleasure in her almost inevitable progression from work at a pickle factory to charring, mangling, and finally to forced prostitution. Robert Sherard, who also describes "the mean miseries of the very poor", insists on work as being their all-encompassing activity, which means that they have "no time for relaxation" and that "their entire energy is taken up in the hunting of the loaf".

Yet "the utter remoteness from delight", which closes **"A Street"** and sets the tone for the *Tales of Mean Streets,* must be qualified. Even in **"Lizerunt"** courting represents a pleasant, if brief, spell of comparative happiness before marriage. Elsewhere life is brightened up, if not illuminated, on a few rare occasions, especially when a little time or money can be spared. Drinking can be a special occasion, even in the Jago, when Josh Perrott wins his fight for instance. In more favoured spots, a funfair (as in **"Lizerunt"**), or a ball at the Institute (as in *To London Town,* though it comes to naught for the young pair), are events that lit up the dull, workaday routine. Brief, fleeting pleasures, with no time wasted in refinement, characterize life in the East End.

Socially, if anonymity prevails in all great cities and particularly in the urban pattern of the East End, there is also a definite sense of community. Neighbours, because of proximity and promiscuity, exert a more or less overt pressure on each other, seemingly inspired by both a sense of bondage in poverty and a desire to be protected against social annihilation. On the positive side we see in *To London Town* the exchange of paint as a mark of good neighbourly relationship and solidarity; on the negative, the compulsory leave-taking of the May family once the shame of quarrelling and the accusation of adultery and bigamy have stained the shop's good name and the family's character. Respectability varies according to districts, but, as often as not, the fear of scandal and loss of people's esteem are compelling forces in matters of behaviour. Even in a district like the Jago, the Ropers find it hard to preserve their working-class decency. Their presence in the Jago results from unemployment; they are not integrated. Mrs. Roper is disliked because of her neatness and cleanliness, and her "aloofness from gossip", just as her husband is rejected, for not drinking, or brawling, or beating his wife. This reluctance to comply with the Jago norm is a cause of antagonism; the Ropers are a disruptive example, or, as Morrison puts it, "a matter of scandalous arrogance, impudently subversive of Jago custom and precedent". The tension is so acute that the Ropers, who have complained of robbery, are accused of "assailing the reputation of the neighbourhood" and, because they are but "pestilent outsiders", are beaten up and plundered by their neighbours, only to be saved by the parson's timely intervention. The Ropers are in fact an alien graft and are physically and morally rejected by the community; they are fought as a threat to its identity. Brian Harrison gives corroborative evidence when he points out that "slum dwellers disliked working men" who "gave themselves airs", and that teetotallers were often insulted.

Hannah Perrott experiences similar difficulties at first, because her background is different and she is "an alien who has never entirely fallen into Jago ways". She neither drinks, nor gossips; nor is she beaten by her husband—a side reference to the normal relationship between husbands and wives. Her attitude is regarded as scornful aloofness and resented by other women, "irritated by such superiorities", to the point of causing her harm—she is in fact beaten up as she belongs neither to the Ranns nor the Learys, the two families in feud. Noncompliance thus exposes people to reprisal. In Hannah's case though, a slow process of acceptance and integration takes place, the physical preceding the moral change.

Respectability can be demonstrated in various ways. In **"Behind the Shade"**, two women, a widow and her daughter, live in a cottage at the end of "the common East End street", but the neighbours disapprove of the independence enjoyed by this one isolated family, and gossip over the "pianoforte lessons" advertised in the window. Gradually their situation deteriorates and rather than appeal to public charity, they let themselves die of hunger. Two features are revealed; on the one hand a sense of conformity to a general "code of morals" even if it is a warped one, and self-respect on the other. To starve rather than beg stems from an attitude of stoic defiance. Echoes of the same notion were common enough at the time: a commentator noted in 1898 that "the reticence and reserve of the respectable struggling poor, who would prefer to starve in a garret rather than apply for the charitable doles, was not understood". The idea expressed here establishes categories among the

poor and the destitute, and takes for granted that charitable money was there for the asking, though there undoubtedly were misuses. What Morrison and his contemporaries often insisted upon, was the extreme point to which self-respect could lead. Typical is the attitude towards funerals—everything becomes subservient to the profound, stubborn urge to stage a "handsome funeral". **"On the Stairs"** portrays an old mother who fails to help her dying son and keeps the money that could have brought him relief in order to procure the "mutes" and "plooms" required for a respectable departure, to be acknowledged by the whole neighbourhood. There are similar observations in **To London Town**, also in George Gissing's *The Nether World*. Elsewhere the characters express their horror of a cheap, plain coffin, and long for a "lovely" one—vainly in the case of Jack Randall in **"All That Messuage"**. Such an attitude may be the sign of imported middle-class notions, but it represents a characteristic outburst of self-respect or pride in the harsh life of the poor.

If we now return to the problem of the precarious existence of the working classes, we are led to note how often the chase for subsistence was frustrated, since work was insecure for the labourer whose hands were his sole property. In addition to the bad housing and sanitary conditions, the lack of security endangered the health and life of the working population. But unlike Sherard, who exposed the harsh and dangerous conditions in industry, Morrison did not dwell upon life in factories—except an engineering firm in **To London Town**. Instead, he depicted women at home, engaged in various occupations, such as rush-bag, sack or matchbox making. The latter especially enjoyed popularity among late Victorian observers. *A Child of the Jago* provides us with a well-documented picture—Morrison himself claimed to have assembled a few boxes. Hannah Perrott's case is typical in so far as "temporarily widowed" wives were numerous in the Old Nichol-Jago area since many men were "in the country", i.e. in jail. Several such activities, like shirt-mending, were in great demand, and were reserved for these more or less permanent widows. In the course of one of their removals, the Perrotts come to a room "wherein a widow had died over her sack-making two days before", leaving hungry children. She presumably tried to avoid going to the workhouse, to which her children were eventually sent. Hannah, like the other women, would rather be exploited by manufacturers, and work for a pittance, than depart to the "house". Dr. T.J. Barnardo, in an article on the East End working classes, described their dread of the workhouse:

> The workhouse? Ah! Well you hardly know, perhaps, the loathing and horror with which the industrious and decent poor contemplate the prospect of breaking up their little homes, of being separated from their children, and of committing themselves, without hope of deliverance, to the Union.

The "Union" or the "house" meant the break up of families, since the sexes as well as children and parents were separated, and imposed restrictions on the independence of the poor. Outdoor relief was rarely given, but even when people were entitled to it and even though they were at the end of their tether, they radically refused the provisions of the Poor Law. Individualism and self-respect prevailed again.

Thinking of the slum population in this light, sociologists have divided families into clear-cut categories. Mayhew proposed several divisions according to the "honesty" of the poor, and distinguished between those "who *will* work", those "who *can't* work", and those "who *won't* work", in other words, the "striving", the "disabled" and the "dishonest". The range of people presented by Morrison provides a parallel with this classification. Just as there were various types of slums, so there were different classes of East Enders, "working class" being an ambiguous or inadequate term when applied to the second and third categories. The third one also includes criminals of the Jago type, as well as spongers on charity organizations or even on women like Mr. Burton in *To London Town*. In the preface to this story, Morrison described his new novel on the East End as forming with *Tales of Mean Streets* and *A Child of the Jago* "a trilogy intended to paint a picture of a certain portion of life in the East End". Although he insisted on the limits of his representation, he claimed that "in these three books there is a fairly wide range, from thieves and blackguards, through decent workmen and their wives, to the best classes of workmen, the last of whom make up the characters in *To London Town*". P.J. Keating's distinction between the poverty-stricken, the criminals and the respectable artisans in Morrison's work is another convenient way of describing the same three classes.

Morrison tried to restore a truer perspective in an interview published in *Cassell's Saturday Journal,* stating that:

> The 'East-Ender' is, more often than not, a respectable, hard-working man, who does his duty to his wife and children, and goes cleanly and honestly through the world. The great majority of the men work regularly and live in decent houses.

Here, the pendulum undoubtedly swung too far the other way, but the author at least tried to justify his view by adding that:

> There is still in the East End an enormous multitude of people who seem almost of another race than ours, who bring up large families in poverty, live in dens rather than houses, and eat to-morrow what they earn to-day.

It is refreshing to see him leave aside moral characteristics, and stress physical and genetic as well as social and environmental features. No doubt his exposure of the daily life of representative sections of East End Londoners led to a wholesome and salutary reaction. The realistic portrayal of the living conditions of the poor and the working classes resulting from the urban environment in the East End was to disturb consciences and to challenge the unruffled complacency of the time. Characteristic of the contemporary reception of Morrison's studies was the enlightened appraisal in the *Literary Year Book* for 1898 which commended their direct sociological significance: "In his two studies of the East End, *Tales of Mean Streets* and *A Child of the Jago,* Mr. Morrison has made his mark both as an artist and as a sociological observer. He gives as it were the subjective side of one of Mr. Charles Booth's pictures".

. . . . .

Because of the complex interaction of several factors it is hard to assess exactly the negative influence of urban conditions upon people's lives. If overcrowding and poverty were sometimes perceived as leading to delinquency and crime, the mere association of urban and social evils was more often observed than their causality. The back streets and backyards in the slum areas of East London certainly created conditions which were conducive to crime. These blights in the urban fabric made it possible for people to evade both the Victorian sanitation and policing laws. In the crowded rookeries, criminals of all descriptions could find shelter, secure as they were from police interference, while the streets and main thoroughfares were regarded by them as hunting grounds. Jago Court is described by Morrison as "an unfailing sanctuary, a city of refuge ever ready, ever secure", to the extent that higher rents had to be paid for "the privilege of residence in the Jago", however questionable this advantage was in respect of sanitation and housing. Arthur Mee recalls Orange Court, in the Old Nichol area of Shoreditch, which "was approached by a tunnel from the street, and was on this account the favourite haunt of thieves", adding that "the police dare not enter the court, as the men would watch them emerge from the tunnel and throw bricks at them". It is not surprising in this context that people should have developed special norms of behaviour, verging on, if not altogether steeped in, criminality. Contagion did play a role. As J. J. Tobias points out in general terms, "groups of people, living in distinctive areas, had evolved a way of life of their own based on crime", which forced other people to adopt the "same techniques, habits and attitudes". A minority was thus capable of influencing a whole group and of giving a peculiar reputation to a given area.

Because of their unreachable recesses, the dockland and riverside areas of London, which play such prominent parts in *A Child of the Jago* and *The Hole in the Wall,* used to harbour and even favour dishonest deals and shady transactions performed by unscrupulous characters. The environment also palpably told on people's physical and mental health. William Booth insisted upon the "disease-breeding, manhood-destroying character" of congested housing, statistically involving about three million "submerged" people. Quite naturally, contemporary writers dwelt on the notion of degradation to bestiality, and resorted to animal imagery when depicting slum dwellers. Crowded courts would be compared to dens, unfit for human habitation. Morrison uses this image extensively in his description of the Jago, where people are debased into "slinking" rats living in foul dens.

The danger of contagion, previously mentioned, menaced young people especially. The children were often in the streets, and, for want of parental authority, were submitted to various harmful influences. R. L. Shoenwald, studying Chadwick's investigations in the 1830s, observes that exclusion of children from factories or reduced hours, has often turned them "out into the streets and swollen the ranks of juvenile delinquents". Even after the creation of School Board inspectors there were many ways of playing truant. Moreover, the milieu had such a powerful impact on the children that they could not improve in it. They were "schooled, not educated", as William Booth deplored. Many were born in workhouses, or were orphaned, experiencing, instead of a protective— though often inadequate—parenthood, the "competitive city life". In that context of indiscipline and laissez-faire, young minds were an easy prey to social determinism.

A prison chaplain, the Reverend W. D. Morrison, observed in 1896 that "Juveniles in all ranks of life are exceedingly sensitive to public opinion, and, unless gifted with great inborn force of character, are apt to become what the world in general considers them to be"—which pinpoints the pressure weighing on those young shoulders. The young were expected to behave the way their parents did; they had to bear the burden of their social origins as if they had committed unredeemable faults. Everyone was induced to follow the code of morals prevailing in his neighbourhood. Self-appropriation, for instance, was the means of defeating necessity in the Jago, and even "the one way to riches". Typical of this unwritten law is Dicky's reflection over his first theft, that "by all Jago custom and ethic it was his if only he could get clear away with it". For those quick-maturing, self-sufficient boys, who modelled their conduct on the general pattern, the atmosphere was conducive to delinquency.

Yet, the notion of determinism seems to be absent from the following statement by W. D. Morrison:

> There is a population of habitual criminals which form a class by itself. Habitual criminals are not to be confounded with the working or any other class; they are a set of persons who make crime the object and business of their lives; to commit crime is their trade; they deliberately scoff at honest ways of earning a living, and must accordingly be looked upon as a class of separate and distinct character from the rest of the community.

This viewpoint, which in 1891 was by no means new, reminds us of the distinction made in 1851 by Mary Carpenter between the "perishing classes", in danger of falling into crime, and the "dangerous classes", living by theft. Logically, all reformatory endeavours were directed towards the former, the latter being judged unredeemable. The moral distinction between the deserving and the underserving poor became a sociological one, so that, despite this clear-cut categorization, it was still thought possible to alter conditions and circumstances so as to salvage endangered people, without examining the direct correlation between poverty and crime.

The existence of a criminal class was so much taken for granted that it found its way into fiction. In *A Child of the Jago* the criminal class is inseparable from the milieu that gives it nurture and support, and, behind the apparently individualistic and empirical character of its actions, it has developed an internal discipline and a structure capable of stimulating the young. Dicky Perrott entertains two hopes—owning a shop, and achieving the status of a mobsman, i.e. a first class thief. In his eyes both objectives are praiseworthy; they would earn him consideration on the economic and social levels. A high mobsman, like the Mogul, commands general respect in the underground world—he is a tyrannical ruler exerting his sway over a given urban territory. He generally enjoys "suburban respectability" and police immunity because of his established position based on wealth, so that he can operate safely as the brain behind important swindles or robberies. He is the ruthless captain at the top of the criminal hierarchy, and there is intense rivalry among cabin-boys, or street urchins—young Dicky is a good example—to resemble most closely the man they at once admire and dread.

The actions performed are measured with a special yardstick which distinguishes several categories of crime, from pilfering to shoplifting, and from house-breaking to burglary, just as thieves fall into classes and are manipulated by fences and mobsmen. The latter control people, supervise fights and organize betting in the Jago. Once a young boy like Dicky has proved his worth, he may be contacted and engaged by a receiver—Aaron Weech uses food and flattery to coax the hungry boy into working for him. A whole substructure is thus revealed. When the chase after the thief becomes too hot, stolen goods are dropped into the fence's yard, conveniently concealed from the public eye. On the other hand, when Josh Perrott wants to sell the watch he has stolen from the Mogul, or King of the High Mobsmen, the news has already got abroad and he vainly goes from Mother Gapp to pawnbrokers and to Weech. The latter treacherously informs the Mogul in the hope of a reward from this powerful protector. This incident points to an active underground organization, which controls individuals to preserve its cohesion.

For a better understanding of environmental influences on young people, we may examine Dicky Perrott's exemplary case, and try to grasp the meaning of the rise and eventual downfall of a talented boy who could have made his way to the top. Forced to fend for himself at an early age, he soon realizes that "he must take his share, lest it fall to others". Necessity accelerates maturity and self-sufficiency. The lack of food in the cupboard and the fact that "there seemed nothing at home worth staying for", reduce him to loitering and pilfering, then to petty larceny with groups of other boys where he is noticed for his efficiency. He soon becomes an expert thief, and wins grades, the birchrod being part of his experience. This progression follows the lines traced by Old Beveridge in his advice to Dicky, when he urged him to become a high mobsman, "one of a thousand"—which implies that luck is necessary in the strife to find room at the top. All means are justified to reach this end—"Learn to read and write, learn all you can, learn cunning, spare nobody and stop at nothing, and perhaps"—Dicky might become one of the High Mob. "It's the best the world has for you, for the Jago's got you", Old Beveridge adds. The moral standard of behaviour directly originates from this East End corner.

The second pole of his potentiality is presented by Father Sturt, but it presupposes a transformation in outlook. No doubt Dicky senses that it is "a chance of life", but the dream of becoming "a tradesman, with a shop of his own and the name R. Perrott, with a golden flourish, over the door", is soon shattered by the jealous villainy of Weech the fence and the shopkeeper's prejudices. Old Beveridge's lessons and Weech's philosophy cannot be ignored, especially when life proves too firmly rooted in Jago reality. Dicky's defeat confirms his predestination— "He was of the Jago, and he must prey on the outer world, as all the Jago did"—and should not long after an impossible ideal. The other—and better—way out, somewhat artificially reiterated by the dying Dicky, is impossible. He feels further branded and rejected when his father is executed: "Now he went doubly sealed of the outcasts: a Jago with a hanged father . . . He was a Jago and the world's enemy". He is inexorably doomed: he is destined either for the Gallows or for the High Mob.

One is led to think that such children become outcasts because they are cast out by society, and restricted to their self-contained world of crime. Dicky's position is conditioned by two driving forces: hunger or necessity on the one hand—theft or crime are alternatives to starvation—, ambition on the other—the desire to reach a high criminal status. These forces, especially the second, must be related to pressures and influences stemming, not only from congested slums, but also from the jungle-like atmosphere people have been steeped in from their childhood. These are hereditary causes, not in the sense of genetic developments due to alcoholism for instance, though this factor is not to be neglected, but because criminal fathers, parents and neighbours are the models on which children frame their image of the world. The street is their school. Old Beveridge is Dicky's real teacher; Father Sturt only an occasional preceptor from the outside who has neither the time nor the influence necessary to alter the situation. Conditioning affects adults as well as children; because they are unable to bear physical or moral rejection, individuals are sucked under. The phenomenon that Jocelyn Bell calls "sinking to Jago level" reaches the Ropers—who are later offered a chance to escape—and also affects Hannah Perrott.

Social commentators seem to have been especially aware of the inversion or distortion of moral values, though criminality was seen as an inherent product of the environment. Of the same district in Shoreditch a writer observed: "There are men here whom it is impossible to convince that stealing is a crime. They were born into evil, bred on stealing, and it is their means of livelihood". In the fiercely competitive street life of late Victorian London, a certain type of class war was being waged. In Morrison's Jago, people not only take to plundering each other's property, but keep delivering attacks on the well-stocked shops in Meakin Street, and on wealthy passers-by—walking in some streets of East London was actually fraught with dangers for everyone. But their predatory instinct carries them further afield. Dicky ventures as far as St Paul's, while Josh takes the train to Canonbury to commit burglary, disturbing the suburban tranquillity enjoyed by a High Mobsman who directly exploits East End thieves. Warehouses are also visited—the "great goods depot of a railway company" at the end of Bethnal Green Road and the neighbouring tobacco factories are preyed upon by the Jagos. The "fat's a-running" industry, i.e. snatching goods from vehicles and running away, is part of the sport practised by the able-bodied and younger members. "To venture a load of goods up Luck Row" was perilous indeed, the narrator observes when describing the experience of a newly-appointed carman who rashly chases a thief into the Jago area. After plundering, the compromising objects are quickly disposed of. Other instances of stealing, burgling, peter-claiming, swindling are also depicted in *Divers Vanities* (1905). In *The Hole in the Wall,* fighting, smuggling, violence and murder flourish unhindered by the river. Dicky himself sometimes resorts to the riverside area, as well as to the market-places in Mile End and Stepney, or to Liverpool Street Station to do some bag-carrying, though the struggle is all the more savage as he intrudes upon territories where the local boys claim their hunting right. He is more secure in his own district and shares this feeling with his father. In the Jago's movement from exposure to shelter, from enemy territory to family or community (and *vice versa*), can be seen a pattern characteristic of hunters in primitive societies: the man roams abroad, till he finds the food or the articles necessary for his sustenance and that of his family.

As in tribal groups there is an endless feud between families, the Ranns and the Learys inside the Jago, but also an eternal feud, racial in character, between the Jago area and Dove Lane, with peaceful spells between the battles underlined by bouts of general rejoicing at Mother Gapp's. Nevertheless, they are united by a common feeling against the police: hostility and distrust. Their code of morals forbids them to "nark", and retaliation threatens informers—Aaron Weech is thus murdered by Josh Perrott when the latter is released from prison. As for Dicky, he refuses to tell the name of his young assassin. "Thou shalt not nark" is one of the first commandments of the Jago creed. Any police intervention is resented as a violation; people observe the law of silence or attempt to baffle any investigation. In Darkest England there can be no intrusion or trespassing.

This specifically urban type of criminality was partially due to the presence of uncleared, foul spots, notably in

East London. Distressing slum-dwelling conditions, coupled with destitution and disease, could not but sharpen the moral and social problem of criminality, which became all the more acute as urban growth gathered pace and as the rift between East and West, the poor and the rich, widened. Moreover those facts were variously perceived by the public. The existence of a hard core of criminals amidst a working class community did cast a shadow over the East End as a whole. Morrison's descriptions were sometimes misread and their actual bearing misinterpreted. A book reviewer went so far as to warn his readers: "let us not delude ourselves into imagining that half London is inhabited by a race of Yahoos". This sweeping statement prompted the author to react in a letter to the editor of the *Spectator* in which he insists on his personal knowledge of life in East London and rejects the unfair generalization. The concept of dangerous classes, mentioned above, was part of the prejudiced associations latent in the mind of the middle-class public. Though Morrison's work has no strictly statistical basis, it has sometimes been incorrectly judged, just as Mayhew's description of street folk has been made to encompass all the poor and working-class population of London. Despite his protests, Morrison may nonetheless have unwittingly contributed, through the very forcefulness of his East End studies, to lay an undue emphasis on the question of urban violence and criminality among the poor, east of Aldgate. His stories have given the city poor a metaphorical dimension which appears to be responsible for simplified modern visions of the "brutal, murderous London of the late 19th century", to cite V.S. Pritchett's words.

If determinism is sometimes blurred or hard to define, human behaviour proceeding both from a broadly genetic process and an environmental phenomenon, *A Child of the Jago* is clearly basically naturalistic in character. Théodore de Wyzewa, a contemporary French critic, perceived it to be so in his article entitled "Un naturaliste anglais", published in 1897. Although the English equivalent of Zola did not develop as a naturalist, his picture is sociologically significant. The existence of criminal rookeries was known, but a detailed description was needed to throw the issues into sharp relief, to shake the sensibilities and rouse the conscience of the middle-class. The demonstration agrees with J. J. Tobias's insistence on the strict relation between environment and crime when he writes: "These youngsters were criminal in England because of lack of work and because of the pernicious effects of a morally unhealthy urban environment". In Dicky Perrott's tragedy we find a striking exposure of society's sly ways of rejecting an individual's attempt to better his condition. Society maintains and safeguards its rigid hierarchy. In the same way as the Jago dictates its law to its immigrants, the world outside the ghetto keeps the *status quo*. The novel may in fact be seen as presenting a realistic and pessimistic view of urban and social mobility.

H. D. Traill, in his attack of the book in *The Fortnightly Review*, to which Morrison replied in *The New Review*,

asserted that it was not impossible to escape from the Jago, thus refuting Dicky's predicament. In an interview given in 1907, Morrison himself indicated this possibility if only in the form of a radical break—transplantation through the adoption of children for example. In the same interview the author expressed his intentions and expounded his views of the "curse of environment":

> In *A Child of the Jago* it was my desire to show that, no matter how good a boy might be, or how great his abilities, there was no chance for him if he was put in the wrong environment, and that if his lot was thrown among the habitual criminals, he was inevitably bound to become a criminal.

More explicit of the naturalistic nature of his picture is his earlier analysis published in 1900 where he stresses the fundamentally deterministic value of his demonstrative case:

> The root of the whole problem is the child, and it was to show this that I wrote the story of the Jago, one of the worst of all the districts in the East End. I took a boy through the whole of his life in the environment of the Jago, and tried to show how he was crushed at every turn, and how helpless any effort to uplift him was.

Upbringing and environment are powerful influences: "stealing became a moral habit" to the boy—which means that, as Dicky is morally determined, the moral debate is irrelevant and the social one is essential. "So criminals are made and paupers are brought into the world", Morrison concludes, implicitly accusing society.

If statistical data are rare in Morrison's novel—we know that there are seventy males on ticket of leave in Old Jago Street alone—, William Booth's work, *In Darkest England,* provides us with figures on criminality and suicide which substantiate his idea of the oppressing forces bearing on the population that is "partially, no doubt, bred to prison, the same as other people are bred to the army and to the bar". In his mind society is to blame for the existence of "the hereditary criminal", since in many cases such causes as poverty or "sheer starvation" are determining factors:

> Absolute despair drives many a man into the ranks of the criminal class, who would never have fallen into the category of criminal convicts if adequate provision had been made for the rescue of those drifting to doom. When once he has fallen, circumstances seem to combine to keep him there.

Dicky Perrott's life is a study in depth of the impossible emergence of a talented boy. Family education and experience in the street are too powerful to be discarded, so that, despite a brave attempt at improvement—through decent, honest work—, the criminal context proves the victor. The Jago frustrates his higher ambitions, plunges him into its murderous ways, and eventually, causes his death.

. . . . .

Morrison's presentation of East London constitutes a social indictment, a statement of failure on several counts, which spells out the crying need for adequate organization. As far as town planning is concerned, *A Child of the Jago* is a realistic story based on a slum clearance scheme. While the crowded, insanitary district moulds characters and shapes events, the transformation of the structure by demolition serves as a background to the crisis. Only at the end does the changed area defeat Josh Perrott who can no longer find a refuge in his flight. It is unquestionable that the destruction of rookeries cleared dangerous quarters where policing was difficult, besides providing more wholesome lodgings. But Morrison did not fail to highlight the contradictions and inadequacies of such schemes.

If the demolition of "the foul old lanes" and the "subterranean basements where men and women had swarmed, and bred, and died, like wolves in their lairs" can be regarded as a positive achievement, as it also served to deter criminality in that particular area, the planning scheme which intended to "wipe out the blackest spot in the Jago" was a partial failure. In the novel, Morrison mocks the eager philanthropic movement which intended to "abolish poverty and sin" in that part of the East End, and points out that people were very reluctant to leave the Jago. They devised all sorts of pretexts to postpone their eviction and, when they left, preferred to rent a room in another area. Morrison ironically notes this tendency to crowd neighbouring districts.

> They did not return to live in the new barrack-buildings; which was a strange thing, for the County Council was charging very little more than double the rents which the landlords of the Old Jago had charged.

The only successful case presented is Kiddo Cook, whose prosperity enables him to take *two* rooms in the new County Council dwellings. Similarly, H. J. Dyos and D. A. Reeder point to the paradox of these urban improvements, which were

> hailed as a means of clearing the slums, though they had hardly ever failed to aggravate them, for their effect always was to reduce the supply of working class housing, either absolutely or in terms of the kind of houses which those turned out of doors by their operations could afford or wish to occupy.

The complaint was not new in the 1890s though the range of it had altered: the lowest strata of slum-dwellers were the worst hit. Moreover, in the case of the Old Nichol Area, the number of people to be rehoused was gradually reduced, as indicated in *The Housing Question in London* (1900). On the one hand, town-planners were concerned, as they are to-day, with problems of expenditure and rent; on the other, people shrank from living in lodgings so rationally, or impersonally, laid out—they resented any interference. What was more subjective but nonetheless real was the ineradicable habits of the destitute deplored by Octavia Hill in *Houses of the London Poor* in 1875: "Transplant them to-morrow to healthy and commodious houses, and they would pollute and destroy them". She disbelieved in public intervention and favoured individual initiative, with good results in some cases only. Many medical officers were reluctant to act forcefully through the Sanitation Acts, because they rightly thought that expulsion meant further overcrowding. Also, though various bodies were conscious of the relation between rent-paying and wage-earning, it was not until the turn of the century that adequate solutions were realistically examined. The Public Health Act of 1875 was insufficiently enforced. Yet, on the credit side, some progress was made towards a better grasp of the social problems of overcrowding and slum-dwelling.

Even though the clearance scheme was already in progress when Morrison gathered his material in the district of the Old Nichol in Shoreditch, his novel had a definite, if tardy, influence, as testifies the reference made by the Prince of Wales in 1900 at the official opening of the new lodgings. It is no mean achievement on the author's part to have illustrated the problem so well. But Morrison's outlook was pessimistic. To the objection that the slums were slowly disappearing, he replied in 1900:

> Are you quite sure of that? You drive the people away by pulling down their houses, but you drive them to another place—that is all. One slum goes, another comes. The lower East-End, as we know it to-day, will disappear, but it will appear farther out (. . .). The same evils we are seeking to destroy in Central London are growing up in the suburbs. In many of the larger suburban towns the people are being crowded together, and some day Greater London will be face to face with the slum problem as we have it in the East-End to-day.

Starting from the observation that the load was merely transferred from one area to another, and that the movement generated from the centre, he reached the conclusion that the centrifugal shift would affect the suburbs. Fortunately the prophecy of an outgrowing housing problem was not to be realized in such terms.

Correspondingly the problem of criminality could not be solved simply by wiping out criminals' haunting places—the root causes could not be obliterated overnight. Young Dicky Perrott, as we have seen, inevitably relapses into his former habits despite the advice and protective support of a priest, which proves that moral precepts and honest living are defeated. In fact, harsh contact with daily reality has abated the ideals and the enthusiasm of both the surgeon and the missioner in the Jago. In an enlightening dialogue, the surgeon acknowledges the failure of medicine to deal with the consequence of the high birth rate, but advocates the right to curb the proliferation of children in such a dangerous environment:

> Is there a child in all this place that wouldn't be better dead—still better unborn? (. . .)

> Here lies the Jago, a nest of rats, breeding,
> breeding, as only rats can; and we say it is well.
> On high moral grounds we uphold the right of rats
> to multiply their thousands.

As for Father Sturt, he confesses that the situation is hopeless, while stoically insisting on the duty he has to perform.

These ideas are taken up in the *Saturday Journal* article where Morrison voices his private views on the impossibility of influencing the race of criminals and paupers. Because the latter frustrate any hope of improvement he proposes a strict control: "Personally I should be in favour of almost any means which would restrict the growth of such a race" in order "to eliminate danger to the community". And he suggests segregation and transportation. If this solution, and indeed the notion of a race apart, is rather unpalatable in the 1970s, it nevertheless stems from a keen wish to protect vulnerable individuals, and, first and foremost, children—"the care of the children is really of grave importance", he adds—, which may mitigate the brutality of the proposal.

Poverty increased certain types of criminal offence, because the Poor Law was inadequate and the workhouses were considered to be worse than prisons. They dissuaded needy people from applying for relief and were even regarded as schools for gaol-birds. As for the failure of penal measures, Morrison is more precise when he examines the problem of hooliganism. Condemning the leniency of justice, he recommends a deterrent punishment—the cat-o'-nine-tails in cases of violence. This proposition recalls two features in *A Child of the Jago*. When Josh Perrott weighs the pros and cons before committing his burglary, or robbery with violence, he shudders at the thought of the cat, like all the Jago toughs. Dicky Perrott, on the other hand, would rather take a whipping than go to a reformatory. Although Morrison's analysis is correct on the whole, the problem of urban hooliganism included elements and factors beyond his ken. His was a plea for an unsentimental, hence realistic, apprehension of the bankruptcy of religious, social and judicial measures.

Education was also inadequate in the East End. The Education Acts left loopholes in their regulations, and inspectors could not enforce the measures capable of schooling the young East Londoners. If the number of juvenile delinquents alarmed the authorities, compulsory education contributed in no negligible way to diminish the rate of criminality, if only because it kept young children from the streets where they were "learning their lessons of evil". Besides, the opening of Institutes proceeded from an attempt to find an appropriate cultural and educational means of reaching working-class people, and of catering for the masses in dense urban districts. In *To London Town,* Johnny attends evening courses at the Institute founded by a shipbuilder, which includes a gymnasium, a cricket club and activities like boxing, also cookery and dressmaking for girls. This recalls the example of the People's Palace as a way of educating the culturally underdeveloped working-class area of Poplar in the East End. Morrison, who had quitted the post of secretary to the Beaumont Trust administering this scheme after four years of active work, later criticized the development of the institution into a polytechnic, seemingly because it had ceased to fulfil its vaster cultural and social role. Yet this venture was not lost, it paved the way for the one University in East London, Queen Mary College, an outpost of culture and advancement set in this essentially working-class district.

In his article in the *Saturday Journal,* he reveals his disappointment at the non-realization of cultural plans for the masses: "Such places as the People's Palace, and a hundred others—excellent institutions all of them—do not reach the people they are started for". He also pinpoints the delusion, which affected outside visitors, of "imagining that these well-dressed people were once the dirty, ragged, vulgar people these institutions were built for", and then condemns the misdirection of otherwise praiseworthy endeavours. His purpose is clearly to debunk his contemporaries' dangerous complacency. "Let us be honest", he concludes, "and not pretend that we are reaching people who are quite beyond our influence". This is a statement of failure and incompetence, stemming from a pessimistic view of the possibility of social improvements. Equally pessimistic is the description of miscarried ventures in the rookeries. Slumming led to philanthropic blunders, which are satirized in *A Child of the Jago,* notably in the form of the East End Elevation Mission and Pansophical Institute. Superior or paternalistic attitudes were ill-suited to the character of the East-Ender; ill-adapted too, was the sentimental approach, mocked in the novel. Most charitable institutions fell short of their promises.

As positive evidence there remains Arthur Osborne Jay's (or Father Sturt's) example—a model of muscular approach to Christianity and to social problems. His down-to-earth principles, his iron discipline, his directness and singeing irony, seem to have had good results in his East End parish. Clubs could unite people, and boxing was a sport that suited their temperament and kept them away from street fights. But he refused to take advantage of their presence in the club to force religion into them. His was a new pedagogy, adapted to a tough milieu; it represented a breakaway from stale and sterile patronizing attitudes. Yet Jay was rather fatalistic as he noted only slight improvements in the Old Nichol area. Morrison probably inherited this pessimistic outlook on human nature. But both men wanted change. Jay wished to "wake up the authorities as to the state of the district". as he put it in the opening pages of *A Story of Shoreditch* (1896). and demanded reform for those who "enter life heavily handicapped". Morrison, too, still believed in social reform, if not in a social revolution:

> There is not likely to be any great upheaval. The
> East-End is no revolutionist. And in the main it is
> much better than its reputation. But there will
> always be room for the social reformer, as there

will be in every great city, and the most hopeful aspect of his work, I think, will be that which aims at the child.

This is an appeal to concentrate duly on the future generation in the city.

. . . . .

Arthur Morrison's record of East End life should be examined in relation to the sociological works of men like Booth and of social workers and reformers like Octavia Hill. Morrison is one of the few writers who wrote forcefully and convincingly of the **"People of the Abyss"** in the 1890s, to refer to the title of Jack London's social novel published in 1902. If Morrison's books had such an enduring impact, it is partly because his account of East London represented a shock treatment for the public, but also and essentially because his presentation supported as well as foreshadowed other descriptions and parallel images drawn by contemporary writers and social historians. His work both crystallized and perpetuated a portrayal of an East End calling for reform.

His exposure of the physical and moral degradation of the poor and working-class population in the East End implies that determinism of the environment should not prevail, and that alleviation if not complete eradication, of hardships and handicaps, are possible by eliminating the causal errors, the blameful shortcomings of social structures. If the Jago already represented an old battle when Morrison published his fictional account, the problems raised reach beyond its contemporary, documentary value. It is exemplary of the housing question whenever society relinquishes its responsibilities and fails to cater for its needy members—especially the children whose expectancies are frustrated.

Although W.C. Frierson correctly sees the naturalistic current in *A Child of the Jago,* one must question his conclusion that "Morrison draws no lesson and preaches a sermon" and that "he accepts the low creature's depravity". The author's quotation from Ezekiel, which heads the novel, is indicative of his intention to rouse public opinion. The message borne out by Morrison's work is the necessity for a solution to the larger issue of urban poverty and criminality—still a relevant problem to-day when unfavourable environment favours unsocial or delinquent attitudes. In Lizerunt's fate and in Dicky Perrott's tragic life, the reader may feel a desire for a truly equalitarian city, where equal opportunities should be made available to all its inhabitants, a plea for improving the material conditions and for raising the educational and moral standards of the disinherited through supporting bodies, which should be organized yet flexible. This desired urban therapy depends on a reform of social legislation, which ultimately rests on the politico-economic plane.

His social exposures paved the way for the welfare state, but there remain issues on which the battle to be waged is sure to be a long one. One can cite for example two present-day problems: the question of battered wives and the dockland redevelopment program in East London. The former is more universal in its bearing—with some reservation one is tempted to say that Lizerunt is with us still. It involves family morals as well as social legislation, whereas the second more specifically concerns town planning policy. In a pamphlet issued by the London Docklands Study Team in April 1973, one may read: "Some parts of the Area have interest and character, but the general impression of the physical environment is of drabness and deterioration". and one of the first alternatives proposed is "to provide housing for families living in overcrowding conditions or in dilapidated property". Mean streets and mean lodgings still. The East End has witnessed a radical alteration due to the closure of the docks; it is ironic that industry should now be asked to migrate to the East End to meet the labour supply of this essentially working-class community. In this period of economic crisis in Britain, redeployment has come to a head, though the long term programme will be carried to the nineties—the 1990s. As in Victorian times, there are housing problems and planning misjudgements, and social priorities are still matter for debate in East London.

Derek Severn (essay date 1980)

SOURCE: "The Damned and the Innocent: Two Novels by Arthur Morrison," in *London Magazine,* Vol. 19, No. 2, February, 1980, pp. 62-7.

[*In the following essay, Severn praises Morrison's work in* A Child of the Jago *and* A Hole in the Wall.]

Of the minor novelists who formed the 'realist' school at the turn of the century only Gissing has an established place in the literature of his time. Arthur Morrison, who at his best was a writer of greater power, has been forgotten. The reason is not far to seek: of his 15 volumes only one is truly distinguished, and one other notable enough to merit consideration.

Morrison was born in 1863, the son of an East End engine fitter (a background that he was at some pains to conceal), and spent some time in his twenties as a social worker in Walter Besant's People's Palace in Mile End Road. He turned then to journalism, joining the staff of a London daily newspaper, and presently published in *Macmillan's Magazine* a number of stories which attracted the attention of W. E. Henley, the distinguished editor of the *National Observer,* whose contributors included Barrie, Kipling, Hardy, Wells and Stevenson. In 1894 Morrison's contributions to these two periodicals were collected as *Tales of Mean Streets,* and with his next two volumes he joined the fairly considerable number of imitators of the Sherlock Holmes stories. In all he published seven novels and eight volumes of stories, but apart from *Selected Tales* (1929) and *Fiddle O'Dreams,* which appeared as late as 1933, he wrote no fiction after 1909. He had by then become an authority on Oriental painting, and published in 1911 a two-volume study, *The Painters of Japan,* which still holds a respectable place in its field; his collection of Chinese and Japanese paintings was bought by the British Museum in 1913. Morrison did not die until 1945, when his copyrights passed by bequest to the Westminster Hospital and the NSPCC.

His first novel is of no importance, but the second, *A Child of the Jago,* which Henley published in instalments in the *New Review* in 1896, is a work of horrifying power. In it he sets out 'to tell the story of the [Jago] . . . and of a boy who, but for his environment, would have become a good citizen'. But in that environment the boy is tricked into theft by a hymn-singing receiver of stolen property, for whose murder his father is hanged, and is eventually knifed in a street fight. It is a terrible story, and it is written from the inside: the Jago actually existed, though that was not its name, and Morrison had little need to draw on his imagination for his material. He sets the scene at once:

> It was past the mid of a summer night in the Old Jago. The narrow street was all the blacker for the lurid sky; for there was a fire in the farther part of Shoreditch, and the welkin was an infernal coppery glare. Below, the hot, heavy air lay, a rank oppression, on the contorted forms of those who made for sleep on the pavement: and in it, and through it all, there rose from the foul earth and the grimed walls a close, mingled stink—the odour of the Jago . . . There the Jago, for one hundred years the blackest pit in London, lay and festered; and half-way along Old Jago Street a narrow archway gave upon Jago Court, the blackest hole in all that pit.

> A square of two hundred and fifty yards or less— that was all there was of the Jago. But in that square the human population swarmed in thousands . . . What was too vile for Kate Street, Seven Dials, and Ratcliff Highway in its worst day, what was too useless, incapable and corrupt—all that teemed in the Old Jago.

The Jago itself is thus a major character in the novel. Old Beveridge points out to the boy the High Mobsmen, the big-time gangsters, 'swaggering in check suits and billycocks, gold chains and humpy rings':

> 'Now, Dicky Perrott, you Jago whelp, look at them— look hard. Some day, if you're clever—cleverer than anyone in the Jago now—if you're only scoundrel enough, and brazen enough, and lucky enough—one of a thousand—maybe you'll be like them: bursting with high living, drunk when you like, red and pimply. There it is—that's your aim in life—that's your pattern . . . It's the best the world has for you, for the Jago's got you, and that's the only way out, except the gaol and the gallows. So do your devilmost, or God help you, Dicky Perrott—though he won't: for the Jago's got you!'

It is an area where women lure strangers to their squalid rooms so that their men may cosh them for the contents of their pockets. The Ranns and the Learys with their factions fight savage street battles, but entertain their common enemies from Dove Lane with much punctilio. Cupboards are empty, the children are left to fend for themselves, the proceeds of theft are spent on drink. The only purpose is self-preservation, the condition of survival is cunning, the only commandment is 'Thou shalt not nark'.

Although it is somewhat old-fashioned in tone, Morrison's prose is spare and muscular. He has the journalist's eye for detail, the journalist's economy. He preaches no gospel. 'My East End stories,' he wrote, . . . 'must be done with austerity and frankness, and there must be no sentimentalism, no glossing over. I felt that the writer must never interpose himself between his subject and the reader. I could best bring in real life by keeping myself and my moralizings out of it.' The result is not Dickens's nightmare representation of the London slums: it is Hogarth's Gin Lane:

> Down the middle of Old Jago Street came Sally Green: red-faced, stripped to the waist, dancing, hoarse and triumphant. Nail-scores wide as the finger striped her back, her face, and her throat, and she had a black eye; but in one great hand she dangled a long bunch of clotted hair as she whooped defiance to the Jago. It was a trophy newly rent from the scalp of Norah Walsh, a champion of the Rann womanhood who had crawled away to hide her blighted head and be restored with gin.

The power of that passage is sustained throughout. The novel has three outstanding qualities—Morrison's steadiness of vision, his accuracy of observation, and the assurance with which he handles each of his major scenes. If *A Child of the Jago* fails as a work of art it is because he has not yet mastered his craft as he has certainly mastered his material. His characters are simply drawn— not lacking in conviction but lacking in depth; in the early chapters the quality of his imagination is not always matched by the quality of his narrative; the heavily ironical tone of several passages is an intrusive element; the concentration on squalor, crime and violence is too intense, the range of colour too restricted, so that there is not enough variation of texture, pace and tension; and the episodic nature of the story robs the theme of a little of its force. But if *A Child of the Jago* is something less than a masterpiece, it is much more than a work of mere promise. It is a substantial achievement by a writer with power in reserve, a necessary preparation for *The Hole in the Wall,* which was published in 1902 and has recently been reissued by the Folio Society, and is by any standards a masterpiece.

The scene is Dockland in (presumably) the 'eighties of the last century, and much of the action is presented through the half-comprehending eyes of another small boy, Stephen, who comes to live with his grandfather, a retired sea captain and a receiver, in a riverside pub which gives the novel its title. This is not an area for strangers to enter, though many unsuspecting seamen do, to be coshed and robbed and, if necessary, dropped in the river: the alley walls are plastered with police notices headed 'Found Drowned'. The whole life of the area is in this story, the seamen, the polluted, twisting, gas-lit alleys, the locks and wharves, the stink of stale beer and garbage, the dubious business in every corner and rathole. Plots are hatched, mouths closed by fear or the cosh, disappearances noted in silence. When Marr, an absconding ship-owner, is robbed of his wallet, which contains more than £800, the money comes by accident into the hands of Grandfather Nat, who determines to keep it for Stephen's education, since Marr was responsible for the death of the boy's father. But the hunt is on: not only Marr's partner, Viney, but every petty criminal in this warren is after it.

The material, then, is that of a thriller, and Morrison brings to it the swiftness and economy of a writer practised in that genre, sustaining the excitement with masterly control. Simply as an exercise in plotting *The Hole in the Wall* is superbly accomplished, and the story is strong enough not to be dislocated by the occasional shifts of viewpoint. Although there is nowhere any sense of constriction, there is not an incident, not a paragraph or a detail that fails either to advance the story or to develop the background. But the novel's strength lies not only in the unbroken chain of causality: it lies also in the unity of tone, which is sustained unfalteringly whether the narrator is the child Stephen or the omniscient novelist. Above all it lies in the remarkable skill with which Morrison ensures that every twist and turn of the plot derives from the characters of these stupid, blundering little criminals, who live from moment to moment, for ever plotting but unable to think more than one move ahead, and forced by every new development to change their plans. Nothing appears to be contrived, because the next move is always unforeseen. There is another element, too, which removes all possibility that the novel may degenerate into crude melodrama. The presentation of the story through Stephen's eyes is not a mere technical device to enhance the interest or elaborate the plot: it adds another dimension, implicitly and in every paragraph, by establishing the contrast between the rampant evil of the action and the child's innocence, a contrast made all the more effective by the steady progress towards redemption of Grandfather Nat.

Morrison's sense of place is acute, and his eye for detail so unerring that the story commands one's assent with absolute authority:

> Scarce eighty yards from Blue Gate stood Blind George, fiddling his hardest for a party dancing in the roadway. Many were looking on, drunk or sober, with approving shouts; and every face was ghastly phosphorescent in the glare of a ship's blue-light that a noisy negro flourished among the dancers.

So too with his characters, Blind George exuding evil, with his left eye 'horribly wide and white and rolling',

like the china marble in Stephen's pocket, and his 'flow o' language as would curl the sheathing off a ship's bottom'; little Cripps the sign-painter, with his dirty hands and lank dirty hair and his nose 'wide and bulbous and knobbed all over' under his greasy wideawake hat; Viney's 'yellow face, ever stretched in an uneasy grin, a grin that might mean either propitiation or malice, and remained the same for both'; the charwoman, Mrs Grimes, 'rusty and bony, slack-faced and very red-nosed', who 'swept the carpet and dusted the shelves with an air of angry contempt for everything she touched'. They have, every one of them, not only character but personality. Dickens might have drawn them, but he would have exaggerated the lighting, made them eccentric and romanticized them with his curious poetry. Morrison does no such thing. His characters are drawn to the life, and belong as ineluctably to this environment as do the rotting buildings, the lighters, the snug in the bar parlour to which come petty thieves with something to sell. They are more complex, more closely observed, more deeply understood than those of *A Child of the Jago*. In that novel the characters have always been what they are; but those of *The Hole in the Wall* have become what they are. Nothing about them, not a flicker of an eye or an inflection of the voice, escapes Morrison's notice. They are not controlled by the plot: they create it.

And yet the plot is inescapable, and Morrison moves his story steadily towards its climax through a succession of major scenes that are handled with masterly authority. Marr, already coshed and robbed, is dragged off between his murderers to be dropped in the river; they are singing at the tops of their voices, pretending to be two drunks helping another home. Ogle, the murderer, is blinded with slaked lime on the marshes where he is hiding by the blind man he has abused. Here is the finding of Marr's body:

> The rope came up from its entanglement with a spring and a splash, flinging some amazing great object up with it, half out of water; and the men gave a cry as this thing lapsed heavily to the surface.
>
> The man in the boat snatched his hook again and reached for the thing as it floated. Somebody threw him a length of line, and with this he made it fast to his boat, and began pulling towards the stairs, towing it. I was puzzled to guess what the object might be. It was no part of the lighter's rudder, for it lay in, rather than on, the water, and it rolled and wallowed, and seemed to tug heavily, so that the boatman had to pull his best . . . He brought up alongside the foreshore, and he and another hauled at the tow-rope. The thing in the water came in, rolling and bobbing, growing more hideously distinct as it came; it checked at the mud and stones, turned over, and with another pull lay ashore, staring and grey and streaming: a dead man. The lips were pulled tight over the teeth, and, the hair being fair, it was the plainer to see that one side of the head and forehead was black and open with a great wound. The limbs lay limp and tumbled, all: but one leg fell aside with so loose

a twist that plainly it was broken, and I heard, afterwards, that it was the leg that had caused the difficulty with the hawser.

That exactness and steadiness of observation, with its suggestion of yet more power in reserve, never falters. Without hurry, and without the least sign of strain, Morrison has achieved what few novelists ever achieve, a book in which all the elements—scene, action, character and moral problem—are woven into a seamless fabric. We know this area and these people as if we lived among them, we feel the fear that counterpoints the dreadful story at every turn; and when we have come through to safety with Stephen at the end, we salute the book with the satisfaction one always feels over something superbly well done. It is a work of classic quality, and deserves a permanent place in English literature.

Roger Henkle (essay date 1992)

SOURCE: "Morrison, Gissing, and the Stark Reality," in *Novel*, Vol. 25, No. 3, Spring, 1992, pp. 302-20.

[*In the following essay, Henkle discusses Morrison's portrayal of the urban poor in the context of the late nineteenth-century debate over realism and naturalism.*]

I.

Finally, in the early 1890s, the urban poor acquire a voice. Not the ventriloquized voice of Henry Mayhew, but the voice of one who was born in the East End of lower working-class parents, grew up there, worked there, and chose it as his subject. Arthur Morrison was born in Poplar in 1863, the son of an engine fitter who worked on the docks. His father died of consumption when Arthur was a boy, and his mother raised the three children by running a haberdasher's shop in Grundy Street. Arthur himself took a job early as office boy in the architect's department of the School Board of London at a weekly salary of seven shillings, and moved up to junior and then "third class" clerk in 1886, when he left to become secretary of the Beaumont Trust, which administered Besant's People's Palace. There he started a Dickensian kind of journalistic ascent, publishing pieces on the East End in the *Palace Journal,* honing his journalistic skills at the evening *Globe,* and finally attracting attention, like Boz, with the publication in *Macmillan's Magazine* (October 1891) of his sketch of **"A Street"** in the East End.

As his brief biography might suggest, Morrison underwent an *embourgeoisement* that took him beyond his East End roots. The dialogue that his writings create is with a middle-class reading audience. But he saw himself as an authentic voice of the urban slum experience, and his early works provided such a strikingly different version of the East End that they immediately created a small critical sensation. They were unlike the representations of the poor that had dominated the literature for half a century. Thus Morrison rejects the sentimental and the melo-

dramatic for a laconic, unmodulated prose that rarely rises to a dramatic climax. He portrays of world of gratuitous violence or enervating degradation which offers up no *meaning* to the middle-class reader; it cannot be integrated into the systems of value, psychology, or material relations of the middle class. Morrison's world seems to be of a different order altogether.

The bourgeois feminine sensibility, . . . [once] the site of affective connection between the middle class and the urban underclass, . . . no longer provides a focal point around which to construct even the effect of subjectivity. In **"Lizerunt,"** the most famous story in Morrison's first book, ***Tales of Mean Streets*** (1894), the protagonist Elizabeth Hunt differs significantly from the pure and "unexpressive" young women who became the channels for middle-class ethical projection. As the corruption of her name to **"Lizerunt"** signifies, she has scarcely any chance to assert her own integrity and separate identity. Her time as a saucy young flirt, playing off the boys against each other, proves to be short; she attaches herself to Billy Chope in spite of his viciousness, and descends quickly into a life of steadily increasing degradation, in which she gradually becomes coarsened. Morrison graphically renders the *relationships* of East End existence that had been missing from the earlier journalistic and sociological accounts. They are not uplifting.

> . . . Billy, rising at ten with a bad mouth, resolved to stand no nonsense, and demanded two shillings.
>
> "Two bob? Wot for?" Lizer asked.
>
> "Cos I want it. Non o' yer lip."
>
> "Ain't got it," said Lizer sulkily.
>
> "That's a bleed'n' lie."
>
> "Lie yerself."
>
> "I'll break y'in 'arves, ye blasted 'eifer!" He ran at her throat and forced her back over a chair. "I'll pull yer face auf! If y' don't give me the money, gawblimy, I'll do for you!"
>
> Lizer strained and squalled. "Le' go! You'll kill me an' the kid too!" she grunted hoarsely. Billy's mother ran in and threw her arms about him, dragging him away. "Don't Billy," she said, in terror. "Don't Billy—not now! You'll get in trouble. Come away! She might go auf, an' you'd get in trouble!"
>
> Billy Chope flung his wife over and turned to his mother. "Take yer 'ands auf me," he said: "go on, or I'll gi' ye somethin' for yerself." And he punched her in the breast by way of illustration.

Billy later tries to abuse Lizer within hours after she has given birth to their unwanted baby and has to be thrown out of the house by the attending medical student, who is then roundly attacked by both Lizer and Billy's mother for interfering. He is an outsider who clearly does not understand the codes of East End life, which follows its own brutal logic. When Billy's mother dies from overwork, too poor for a decent burial because he has stolen all her savings, Lizer then feels the full brunt of his meanness. And the story ends with him forcing her into prostitution.

"Lizerunt" follows Rudyard Kipling's remarkable story, "The Record of Badalia Herodsfoot," in detailing the "creed and law" that governs slum life. Badalia is recruited into service by the local curate to help distribute alms because she is streetwise enough to spot a fraudulent claim and because she is not above smashing the face of any woman who tries to steal food or money meant for those in need. The story tells of her struggle between maintaining the trust that has been placed in her and her adherence to the slum code of womanhood that says she will be faithful to her drunken husband to the end. The struggle proves fatal; her husband beats her mercilessly in an attempt to get the alms-money out of her. Yet even on her deathbed she refused to accuse him—thus keeping both "trusts."

Morrison and Kipling sketch out an East End that is more complexly—and fatalistically—coded than that of earlier accounts. It is no longer a land of shadows cast by the projections of middle-class subjectivity, no longer a terra incognita to be read in line with the dominant class anxieties and desires. It constitutes its own social order: a subsystem of gender relations that exert a power within their own domain that cannot be interpolated into bourgeois categories of self-agency. The slums of Morrison and Kipling acquire a density of customs and personal patterns that had rarely been observed in earlier accounts, as if, in Morrison's case especially, there were an effort to say that the East End is not simply an object of upper-class anxiety or domination, but an entity in and of itself. At the same time that he asserts this, Morrison also insists upon the enclosed, immobilizing fatality of that world: its immersion in violence, its deadened submission to poverty, its constricting social containment. The vicious circularity of the poor is symptomized by the frequent set pieces of Amazonian brawls between women, such as this one from a later Morrison work:

> Down the middle of Old Jago Street came Sally Green: red-faced, stripped to the waist, dancing, hoarse and triumphant. Nail-scores wide as the finger striped her back, her face, and her throat, and she had a black eye; but in one great hand she dangled a long bunch of clotted hair, as she whooped in defiance to the Jago. It was a trophy newly rent from the scalp of Norah Walsh, champion of the Rann womenkind, who had crawled away to hide her blighted head, and be restored with gin.

For all the efforts of social services to confirm the woman as the ethical center of lower-class life, she turns out, in many of these stories, to be as uncontrollable as the men, at her worst, or too passive to resist her own victimization, at her best. . . .

The conditions of Morrison's East End not only diminish the capacity of women to act as an ethical force in family and neighborhood; the economic isolation of the slums also eliminates them as figures of commodity desire. Ironically, the objectifying in the upper classes of women into fetishes of style, beauty, even spiritual worth, transposes them into symbols of social and economic status and advancement. Clearly this is a form of dehumanization, but it has the effect of masking or finessing whatever subjection of the women is occurring. In a subsociety such as Morrison's urban slums, in which women cannot be conceived as icons of aesthetic or ethical value because there is no role for such values in the social order—no possibilities for women to be the means of financial or social improvement, no function for them to fulfill as the conservers of money and ideals—their status will be severely reduced. Their subjection will be all the more evident.

Correspondingly, the diminishment of women refigures the literary form, for the heroine as the register of morality, and as the focal point at which aesthetic and social ideals were brought together, had been essential to the English novel itself. The great experiment in the naturalist novel of the lower classes—Emile Zola's *L'Assomoir,* Edmond and Jules de Goncourt's *Germinie Lacerteux,* and George Moore's *Esther Waters*—had been to dramatize the moral and emotional issues of poverty and struggle through women whose victimization, and in some cases, personal weaknesses, stripped them of much of the auratic power of the conventional heroine. Moore, in particular, compensated by sentimentalizing his heroine, and it is telling that the prominent English example relies on the bourgeois ethos of feeling to sustain a measure of attraction to his protagonist. Morrison will have none of that, and, as a consequence, his writing in **Mean Streets** has different rhetorical rhythms; it resembles in many respects the uninflected, neutral style of Margaret Harkness's *A City Girl.*

The circumstances of life in the slums affect the possibilities for writing a traditional masculine text as well. The wave of optimism that prevailed at the beginning of the Victorian period, and which allowed the writers of Mayhew's generation to balance all their misgivings about the rapaciousness of the new competitive order and the loss of scope for mythicized action in men's lives against the excitement of change and social mobility . . . has disappeared from the scene of lower-class London. The dynamism that converts the somewhat puerile fantasy of masculine adventure and power into a vibrant, if often bizarre, scene of small entrepreneurialism and vivid sensory impression is gone. In its place is misogyny. The lower classes had always been depicted as misogynist, and we are quite aware how poverty leads to abuse and the self-hatred that goes with it, but the East End of Morrison's and Kipling's streets is the logical deterioration of the propensities of the illusory, gender-fixed compensations of the 1840s and '50s representations of an alternative underworld. . . . The misogynist social texts that we get of the slums thus . . . undermine any attempt to construct a generative male subjectivity. Morrison's male protagonists are to a man unfulfilled, fated to frustration. Economic and social conditions force this upon them, but the inchoate natures of all the characters indicate that a full, mutually interdependent code of subject construction is absent. A system such as that of the middle class, in which a female ethical subject balances and validates the agency that is granted to the male, is missing in the nether world.

This is, after all, the primary reason that the myth of a realm of primarily male adventure and "freedom" cannot be represented except in the hermetic form of the boys' adventure story, in which the protagonist never has to come of age. There is something of the same limitation in Morrison's novels about the slums, all of which focus on boyhood and young adolescence. It is only natural, in a way, that Morrison should turn to some form of the *Bildungsroman* for his accounts of life in the East End, since the likely course that the slum culture would take would be to imitate the middle class in its effort to establish for itself a masculine-based, if not patriarchal, order. The *Bildungsroman* is the form that epitomizes that effort, and we can surmise that Arthur Morrison had in mind, as a kind of model, the century's best known book about poverty, Dickens's *Oliver Twist*. Morrison's most famous and most compelling book on East End life, *The Child of the Jago* (1896), and his later novels touching on the urban slums, *To London Town* (1899) and *The Hole in the Wall* (1902), focus, therefore, on the issue of the formation of the male in the slums: the classic patriarchal story. Tellingly enough, the protagonist in each of these novels is a boy, as if to indicate that mature or "full" subjectivity is never attained in lower urban existence.

Morrison selected as his setting for *A Child of the Jago* one of the most anarchic and violent quarters of the East End, the Old Nichol area in Bethnal Green, a nest of streets just to the east of what is now Shoreditch High Street (about ten blocks north of Liverpool Station). The Old Nichol (which Morrison calls "The Jago"), was known as the warren of some of the most impoverished and depraved wretches in London, a pocket of narrow streets and courts that was on the verge of being demolished by the London County Council in the 1890s. Morrison spent eighteen months there, gathering impressions under the tutelage of the Reverend Arthur Osborne Jay, a well regarded and intrepid slum minister. In a later interview with *The Daily News,* Morrison contended that the "majority of the Jago people are semi-criminal, and an ordinary respectable working man would quickly be hounded out. . . . " Morrison's Jago denizens eke out an existence in robbery, burglary, picking pockets, or "coshing" unwary strangers (a "cosh" is an iron bar); the women survive making match boxes or through other marginal activities. The men and women entertain themselves with massive and bloody brawls between rival gangs, and *A Child of the Jago* has several unforgettable accounts of the pitched battles between the Ranns and the Learys, which rage back and forth throughout the novel.

There is no quarter given to delicate Victorian sensibilities in *Jago,* and the popularity of the novel was matched only by the critical outrage over its alleged grossness. Yet the violence is so spectacular, and so emblematic of the ferocity that comes out of lives of depravity and idleness, that the pathology becomes *symbolic*. The opening chapter establishes an atmosphere in which the specific details—of the restlessness in the Jago on a typical night, as a victim is coshed and robbed—are transposed into a symbolic setting: "Old Jago Street lay black and close under the quivering red sky: and slinking forms, as of great rats, followed one another quickly between the posts in the gut by the High Street, and scattered over the Jago." Even the violated human body auratically conveys a social pathology:

> Out in the Jago the pale dawn brought a cooler air and the chance of sleep. From the paving of Old Jago Street sad grey faces, open-mouthed, looked upward as from the Valley of Dry Bones. Down by Jago Row the coshed subject, with the blood dry on his face, felt the colder air, and moved a leg.

The ostensible protagonist of the story is the Child of the Jago, Dickie Perrott, who roams its streets, participating in its random violence, its crime, and its occasional play. He is a lad of strong familial instincts, attached to his younger brother and sister, but he shares some of the community's meanness, especially toward a crippled boy, Bobby Roper, who becomes Dickie's nemesis and stands for the perverse crippling of Dickie's own conscience. Under the influence of Father Sturt (modeled after Arthur Osborne Jay), Dickie makes one effort to go straight, and work his way out of the Jago, but it is condemned to failure. Indeed, any effort to get out of the Jago, by virtuous work or crime, is doomed, and the "moral" of the story is intoned by old Beveridge, regarded . . . as a trifle 'balmy', though anything but a fool," who points to a gathering of the super-criminals, the High Mobsmen, and tells Dickie,

> "Now, Dickie Perrott, you Jago whelp, look at them—look hard. Some day, if you're clever—cleverer than anyone in the Jago now—if you're only scoundrel enough, and brazen enough, and lucky enough—one of a thousand—maybe you'll be like them: bursting with high living, drunk when you like, red and pimply. There it is—that's you aim in life—there's your pattern. Learn to read and write, learn all you can, learn cunning, spare nobody and stop at nothing, and perhaps—It's the best the world has for you, for the Jago's got you, and that's the only way out, except gaol and the gallows. So do your devilmost, or God help you, Dickie Perrott—though He won't: for the Jago's got you!"

If the only way out of the Jago is to emulate the High Mobsmen, it is a route through a parodic Jago-vision of the "better world" of money and power. "Those of the High Mob were the flourishing practitioners of burglar, the mag, the mace, and the broads, with an outer fringe of such dippers—such pickpockets—as could dress well, welshers, and snidesmen. These, the grandees of rascality, lived in places far from the Jago, and some drove in gigs and pony traps." The Mobsmen and their circle mimic and exaggerate upper-class clothing and upper-class airs—those with their gigs and pony traps—and parade before their inferiors a bizarre parody of privilege and grand manners. Their affectations transmit the felt presence of upper-class power—they play out a crude image of another realm of life—but they have the upper-class codes all wrong. . . . Swept up in the centrifugal vortex of its ignorance and self-violence, the Jago denizen cannot conceive of the alternative world in a way that would allow him or her psychological access to it (at least in any terms that are "real"). It is as if the two spheres—the urban slums and the social world above it—are sealed off from each other. . . .

A social formation so detached from the prevalent order can, however, be conceived symbolically. This was, as it turned out, the very thing that Morrison's middle-class reviewers refused to allow him to do. The minute they read the disquieting book, they called it a "realistic" novel. And by "realism" they meant the English literary establishment's conception of "naturalism," a literature that dealt with lower social orders, with distasteful and debasing material, and that was characterized by graphic detail, violence, and physicality.

II.

The late nineteenth-century English debate over realism and naturalism, then, involves much more than literary taste and style: it embodies the effort by the cultural establishment to assure that all depiction and expression of lower-class life will be kept within the power of the middle class to assimilate it and represent it. One of the major pitched battles occurred between Morrison and the prominent literary critic H. D. Traill and it is worth pursuing briefly because it focuses the issues at stake. Remarkably enough, Traill perceives at some level that *Jago* is a symbolic text, and it makes him so uneasy that he rushes to dismiss the possibility. He acknowledges that what "has most astonished" him "is the impression of extraordinary unreality which, taken as a whole, [the novel] leaves behind it. To a critic opposed to the theories and methods of so-called realism, this is naturally rather disconcerting." Girded to show that the realism of *Jago* has sacrificed art for a false and exaggerated naturalism, Traill "comes out from the Jago with the feelings, not, as he had expected, of a man who has just paid a visit to the actual district under the protection of the police, but of one who has just awakened from the dream of a prolonged sojourn in some fairyland of horror. This, to be sure, may be the effect which Mr. Morrison desired to produce: it is certainly not difficult, I think, to show that his methods are distinctly calculated to produce it; but then those methods cannot be exactly the methods which the realist professes to employ, nor that effect at which he is commonly supposed to aim." Traill insists that Morrison's work be treated as realism, that it be

measured by a truth-factor and be shown to be untrue to actuality. "But I will make bold to say that as described by Mr. Morrison—described, that is to say, as a place of which, with [a] half-dozen exceptions . . . every single inhabitant out of 'swarming thousands' is either a thief, or a harlot, or a 'cosher' or a decoy, or a 'fence,' or a professional mendicant—it never did and never could exist. . . . If it is not what you would have actually found in exploring the Jago, it is no doubt what you might have found if all London had happened to pour its manifold streams of corruption into that particular *sentina*."

Several things bother Traill here. First, he rejects Morrison's premise that the urban slums constitute a fully fleshed-out subsociety, with its own set of codes so antithetical to bourgeois norms for the lower classes. Second, he recoils from the notion that there might be a place where people live who cannot be reached and redeemed by either sentiment or economic "logic." Realism for Traill (and others of his time) means that characters will always stand in for human subjects, and by this he means figures whose sensibility are registered on terms readily associated with middle-class values: who desire what we desire. And finally, Traill's determination to categorize Morrison as a "realist" will assure that Morrison's vision will always be grounded in *material* terms. . . .

Morrison's Jago is not accessible to that scheme. The physical details in his novel attest, paradoxically, to the estrangement of the lower classes. Amy Kaplan has noted this in American realist works, saying that they "often assume a world which lacks solidity, and the weightiness of descriptive detail—one of the most common characteristics of the realistic text—often appears in inverse proportion to a sense of insubstantiality, as though description could pin down the objects of an unfamiliar world to make it real." The spareness of Morrison's prose, its starkness—held in place only by a half-Dickensian ironic narrative commentary—constitutes not realism, at least as the English and French middle-class literary culture knew it, but a symbolic text. So disturbing is his version of slum existence, so alien, so intractable is it to middle-class representation and hegemonizing, that he has to be content with the charges that what he describes *isn't there*.

Consequently, an almost absurd exchange took place between Morrison and his supporters and Traill and his. The publication of Traill's essay on Morrison in his book *The New Fiction* was accompanied by a letter from a Mr. Woodland Erlebach, "who speaks from a thirty years' acquaintance with the district (Mr. Morrison's Jago)," and who writes, "I boldly say that the district, though bad enough, was not even thirty years ago so hopelessly bad and vile as this book paints it." Traill then appends the names and addresses of eight other people who had written letters protesting Morrison's picture of the East End. Morrison, for his part, rallied Arthur Osborne Jay to his defense, and argued his bona fides in *Daily News* interview. In a separate article titled **"What Is a Realist?"** in the *New Review,* he summed up all the strategies used against him:

There is a story current in the East End of London, of a distracted lady who, assailed with a request for the loan of a sauce pan, defended herself in these words:—"Tell yer mother I can't lend' er the saucepan, consekince o' 'avin lent it to Mrs. Brown, besides which I'm a-usin' of it meself, an' moreover it's gone to be mended, and what's more I ain't got one." In a like spirit of lavish objection it has been proclaimed in a breath that I transgress:—because in the first place I should not have written about the Jago in its nakedness; next, that my description is not in the least like; moreover, that it is exaggerated; further, that though it may be true, it was quite unnecessary, because the Jago was already quite familiar, and everybody knew all about it; beyond this, that the Jago houses have been pulled down; and finally that there never was any such place as the Jago. . . .

When the journalist Clarence Rook tried to follow in the line of Arthur Morrison in his book *The Hooligan Nights* (1899), a reputedly first-hand account of the life of a young criminal named Alf from the slums of South London, he seemed prepared for some of the same objections to his "realism." Thus in the Preface, he stresses that [he has written] "neither a novel, nor in any sense a work of imagination. Whatever value or interest the following chapters possess must come from the fact that their hero has a real existence. . . . " Rook goes on, however, to paint a picture of a slum career with a romance to it that is a long way from Dickie Perrot's existence:

> When the Daily Chronicle published portions of the history of young Alf early in the year the editor received numerous complaints from well-meaning people who protested that I had painted the life of a criminal in alluring colours. They forgot, I presume, that young Alf was [a] study in reality, and that in real life the villain does not invariably come to grief before he has come of age. Poetic justice demands that young Alf should be very unhappy; as a matter of fact, he is nothing of the sort. And when you come to think of it, he has had a livelier time than the average clerk on a limited number of shillings a week. He does not know what it is to be bored. Every day has its interests, and every day has its possibility of the unexpected, which is just what the steady honest worker misses.

Young Alf is something of an original: he was trained as a boy by an acrobat to be able to creep about in absolutely complete silence; he modeled himself after South London's Patrick Hooligan, with whom, "as with the lives of Buddha and of Mahomet, legend has been at work"; and he apprenticed himself to the celebrated Billy the Snide, the most accomplished passer of false coin of his time. He lives a life along the undersides of society that often approaches, in Peter Keating's term, the "pastoral" in its freedom from moral self-doubt and in its removal from the harsh realities of the economic system. Alf glides in and out of Rook's view at times like a phantom, losing himself in back alleys, stairways, and the crowded stalls of the South London slums. He insinuates himself upon victims through his charm, and eludes cap-

ture by the same means; in one bold house burglary he saves a baby from choking to death on its night-dress and is toasted with wine by its grateful parents, the burglary victims. The Artful Dodger lives again.

A similar romanticism creeps into another Morrison-inspired novel, W. Somerset Maugham's early work *Lisa of Lambeth*. Liza, though a product of the margins of the slums and the lower working classes, charms the reader in ways that no denizen of the urban depths had done before her:

> It was a young girl of about eighteen, with dark eyes, and an enormous fringe, puffed-out and curled and frizzed, covering her whole forehead from side to side, and coming down to meet her eyebrows. She was dressed in brilliant violet, with great lappets of velvet, and she had on her head an enormous black hat covered with feathers. . . .
>
> Liza had been so intent on her new dress and the comment it was exciting that she had not noticed the organ.
>
> "Oo, I say, let's 'ave some dancin'," she said as soon as she saw it. "Come on, Sally," she added, to one of the girls, "you an' me'll dance togither. Grind away, old cock!"

Spirited, genial, fun-loving, engagingly flamboyant in dress and gesture, Liza is perhaps the most affecting figure in late nineteenth-century representations of the poor. Yet the dark futility of the slums quickly casts its shadow upon her. She proves vulnerable to the charms of a married man who will not leave his family to marry her, and she is turned into a pariah among the Lambeth lower working class. Caught up in an awful determinism, she slips into social ruin, finally beaten so severely by her lover's wife, in one of those celebrated fights among women which seemed to have become staples of the novel of the lower classes after Zola and Morrison, that she miscarries the child she is carrying, and dies of its complications. The paradigm is similar to that of a *Mean Streets* story, but the difference is that a winsome, vital figure emerges briefly in the portrait of Liza. A personality is created and possibilities for self-definition are suggested, as if in an effort to open up a space for a gentler, happier experience among the lowest of the working classes and the urban poor. Liza has time to dream, to fall in love, to play cricket in the streets with the neighborhood children, to go off with her boyfriend on a lively, pleasurable bank holiday excursion. Maugham, who observed many of the conditions of Lambeth poverty during his years there as a medical student and clerk to physicians, shared some of Morrison's pessimism about the bridging of social spheres—and Liza's death symbolizes the futility of it—yet the tenor of *Liza of Lambeth* differs greatly from that of **"Lizerunt."** A new element has been infused into the line of slum novels so dramatically begun by Morrison. Just as Alf's *joie de vivre* absolves us from the depressing fatality of poverty and petty criminality, so we can find solace in

Liza's sharing of the same desires that any lower middle-class girl might. Her instinctive good-heartedness can pass for a lower-class version of ethics; she is potentially redeemable, transformable within the system. The fact that she cannot rise above her blighted circumstances may make her, in an odd way, more comforting to the reader, for she enacts the myth that says that the lower class share bourgeois English traits and are resigned to exercise them in even the most unpromising of circumstances.

Rook's and Maugham's novels belong to the line of late nineteenth-century literature that Peter Keating categorizes as the Cockney School of novel. These novels generally dealt with the urban lower working class, and only occasionally with the hard-core poor, but they proved to have a greater influence on the nature of the fiction of the lower class than Morrison's graphic accounts, largely because they provide a means of appropriating the lower classes into formulas recognizable to the upper strata. The writers of the "cockney school" such as Henry Nevinson and Edwin Pugh created an individual subject that could be brought within the hegemonizing of middle-class English culture. "Because of [the cockney's] determination to remain free," Keating writes, "he has developed the ability to take whatever life has to offer without complaint; take it wittily, cheerfully or philosophically. Such a man is of inestimable use to a democratic society. So long as his wit, drunkenness, violence, sentimentality and love of freedom are expressed in individual terms, he is socially harmless; so long as these qualities are viewed from a distance he is even attractive and picturesque." He epitomizes, in Regenia Gagnier's words, the optimistic liberal view that the lower class individual is "an apparently autonomous and universal human spirit." The cockney is typecast as the English "common man" individualistic, spirited, jingoistic, hard-playing, blunt, beef-eating, beer-drinking, and for all that, ultimately law-abiding. Certainly the portrait has its truth value—all the visitors to the working-class areas in the East End attest to its vital popular culture and to the remarkable resilience of the people—but one is reminded of the critique by the Frankfurt School that mass culture transforms originally realistic accounts into representations that one can read as repetitive diversions which present no danger to the dominant system.

The separation of depictions of the lower orders of London that we noted before thus takes place. On the one hand, the Cockney Novel reiterates the redeemable nature of the working class; it can be hegemonized through its own yeoman image. While the culturalistic programs of Besant and the settlement house workers sought to absorb working-class popular culture into a more refined expression, the Cockney Novel makes use of the more raw versions of that culture to achieve the same ideological objectives. On the other hand, Morrison's *Jago* and *Mean Streets* . . . and George Gissing's *The Nether World* confront the reader with an essentially alienated domain.

John L. Kijinski (essay date 1994)

SOURCE: "Ethnography in the East End: Native Customs and Colonial Solutions in 'A Child of the Jago,'" in *English Literature in Transition: 1880-1920,* Vol. 37, No. 4, 1994, pp. 490-501.

[*In the following essay, Kijinski explicates the connection between London's nineteenth-century poor and native peoples of Africa in the time of colonization and the anxiety both groups produced in the English upper classes because of their foreigness and "degradation."*]

One sign of the anxiety that many British citizens felt at the end of the nineteenth century about England's future position as an imperial power was the widely shared concern over how poverty and urban living conditions were debilitating the working classes. Recruiting problems during the Boer War had been unnerving: an alarmingly large number of working-class recruits were found to be unfit for service. In 1904, an Interdepartmental Committee on Physical Deterioration was established to investigate this problem. The question had to be asked: had conditions in urban England created a generation of men unfit to protect the interests of the overseas empire? Worse than this, the homeland itself was placed in jeopardy; it appeared that within the very heart of the British Empire an alien and almost invisible group of "sub-standard" urban dwellers was coming into existence by a reverse process of evolution. As Harold Perkin comments, the presence of this group posed "a covert and insidious threat from poverty itself to the physical, intellectual and moral fitness of the nation."

One of the most important novels that allowed the middle-class public to envision these aliens within their midst was Arthur Morrison's *A Child of the Jago* (1896). The novel presented an examination of inhabitants of a particularly poor section of London's East End. Morrison, who had already gained a reputation as a chronicler of East End life with his *Tales of Mean Streets* (1894), had first-hand experience—both personal and professional—of life in the less-fashionable parts of London. Born and raised in the East End, he worked first as an office boy and then as a third-class clerk for the architect's department of the School Board of London. In 1886 he was selected to be the secretary to the Beaumont Trust, which funded the People's Palace. Putting into concrete form Walter Besant's ideas about educating the poor, the People's Palace offered opportunities for recreation and self-improvement to residents of the East End. Under Besant, Morrison became sub-editor of the Palace's publication, the *Palace Journal,* which featured news and information about the cultural activities offered by this institution.

Morrison's *Child of the Jago* is a fictional counterpart of such factual reports on London's poor as Andrew Mearns's *The Bitter Cry of Outcast London* (1883), William Booth's *In Darkest England and the Way Out* (1890), and A. Osbourne Jay's *Life in Darkest London*

(1891)—all written by men with a religious mission to the poor. Morrison, in fact, wrote his novel in response to a suggestion from Jay. Jay urged Morrison to use his talents as a literary artist to give the public a picture of the Old Nichol, a particularly poor and violent East End neighborhood where Jay worked as a pastor. The Old Jago is the name that Morrison would give to this area.

As the titles of Jay's and Booth's books indicate, these investigations of life among Britain's poor build upon contemporary interest in African exploration and colonization, as does Morrison's novel. The value of the African/British comparison is suggested by Booth, who notes that ethnographic accounts of "degraded" African people had won the attention of British readers: "This summer the attention of the civilised world has been arrested by the story which Mr. Stanley has told of 'Darkest Africa' and his journeyings across the heart of the Lost Continent." Booth suggests, however, that this interest in a "native other" could be focused on populations much closer to home:

> But while brooding over the awful presentation of life as it exists in the vast African forest, it seemed to me only too vivid a picture of many parts of our own land. As there is a darkest Africa is there not also a darkest England? Civilization, which can breed its own barbarians, does it not also breed its own pygmies? May we not find a parallel at our own doors, and discover within a stone's throw of our cathedrals and palaces similar horrors to those which Stanley has found existing in the great Equatorial forest?

Booth, Mearns, and Jay had alerted readers to the existence of this degraded and home-grown "native" through their compilation of factual reports on the lives of the London poor. Morrison, however, as a novelist, creates a fictional world that becomes a living urban jungle and presents his middle-class readers living subjects—"natives" who are surprisingly human but who live within a series of cultural structures that fall outside those norms taken for granted by the average British citizen of the late nineteenth century. Dwellers in the Jago are human and thus—like the inhabitants of the "prehistoric" world of Conrad's *Heart of Darkness*—particularly frightening, but they are also "natives," the regressive, devolving "other," living within a progressive, evolving culture, and thereby placing it in jeopardy.

Morrison's attempt to present middle-class readers with a vivid account of this alien population gained immediate—but controversial—popularity. H. G. Wells, for example, reviewing the novel for the *Saturday Review,* found it to be a powerful account of London slum life—although it was not didactic enough to satisfy Wells completely. The influential H. D. Traill attacked the novel as a representative of what he calls the "New Realism." Traill compares Morrison's novel to the work of another realist, Stephen Crane, and concludes that Morrison's work is much superior to that of Crane:

> Above all, Mr. Morrison wields a certain command of pathos, a power in which Mr. Crane is not only deficient, but of which he does not even appear to know the meaning; and were it not for a certain strange and, in truth, paradoxical defect, of which more hereafter, in his method of employing it, he would at times be capable of moving his readers very powerfully indeed. In a word, the English writer differs from the American by all the difference which divides the trained craftsman from the crude amateur, and he deserves to that extent more serious and detailed criticism.

But in spite of this favorable comparison with Crane, Traill attacks what he sees as the programmatic realism of the novel because, he claims, the method paradoxically renders Morrison's account of the Jago too unreal: "What, however, has most astonished one of Mr. Morrison's critics fresh from a perusal of *A Child of the Jago,* is the impression of extraordinary unreality which, taken as a whole, it leaves behind it." Roger Henkle, in a recent article on late-Victorian fictional accounts of the urban poor, perceptively comments on why Traill is unable to credit Morrison's portrait of the Jago: "First, he rejects Morrison's premise that the urban slums constitute a fully fleshed-out subsociety, with its own set of codes so antithetical to bourgeois norms for the lower classes. Second, he recoils from the notion that there might be a place where people live who cannot be reached and redeemed by either sentiment or economic 'logic'." As Henkle argues, Traill is unable to credit the existence of subjects within the heart of London whose basic cultural norms are outside the middle-class sense of experience.

It should be remembered that during the time Morrison was working on *A Child of the Jago,* British interest in systematic methods for describing "exotic" populations was at an all time high, as evidenced by the appearance of increasingly professional studies in ethnology, folklore, and urban sociology. All of these fields shared in common a method which involved exacting observation by an expert who had qualified himself to present new and systematically organized knowledge on the group being observed. In addition to his long personal acquaintance with the East End, Morrison further qualified himself to write this novel by systematic study of the Old Nichol. Jay commented on how carefully Morrison prepared himself before he began writing the book: "Mr. Morrison's laborious and persistent care amazed me. He would take nothing for granted; he examined, cross-examined and examined again as to the minutest particulars, until I began to fear his book would never be begun. Till then I never realised what conscientious labour art involved." Morrison prepared himself to produce a portrait of a native population in much the same way as an ethnographer of the time would have. Morrison's (and Jay's) hope that the novel would help to bring about public awareness and reform was also in keeping with the general tendency of Victorian ethnography. As George Stocking has noted in his discussion of E. B. Tylor's *Primitive Culture* (1871)—a key work of late-Victorian ethnography—ethnographers of the time worked to aid progress and promote reform by exposing elements of contemporary society that had not kept up with the process of cultural evolution: "Active thus both in 'aiding progress and removing hindrance,' Taylor's science of culture was 'essentially a reformer's science'."

With the care and aims of a late-Victorian ethnographer, Morrison brings us into the world of this novel, a world so alien to the reader that the guidance of a professional is required from the very first chapter. The reader is given the precise boundaries of the region that will stand at center focus of the book; Morrison even includes a map of this foreign territory, a "Sketch Plan of the Old Jago." But more importantly the reader is made to see that the Jago—though in the heart of London—is as foreign to the average Englishman as any region in Africa. Here is the reader's first glimpse of the Jago:

> It was past the mid of a summer night in the Old Jago. The narrow street was all the blacker for the lurid sky; for there was a fire in a farther part of Shoreditch, and the welkin was an infernal coppery glare. Below, the hot, heavy air lay a rank oppression on the contorted forms of those who made for sleep on the pavement: and in it, and through it all, there rose from the foul earth and the grimed walls a close, mingled stink—the odour of the Jago.

Morrison next places within this foreign atmosphere and geography a population which he describes in terms that place them outside any norms one would expect to operate in a civilized, modern city: "Old Jago Street lay black and close under the quivering red sky; and slinking forms, as of great rats, followed one another quickly between the posts in the gut by the High Street, and scattered over the Jago." Here and consistently throughout the novel, the natives of the Jago are referred to as rats, their neighborhood a network of breeding grounds. Nor does the language spoken by the Jagos do much to connect them to the middle-class reader. Here is the first dialogue that we are presented with in the novel:

> "Ah—h—h—h," he said, "I wish I was dead: an'kep' a cawfy shop." He looked aside from his hands at his neighbours; but Kiddo Cook's ideal of heaven was no new thing, and the sole answer was a snort from a dozing man a yard away.

> Kiddo Cook felt in his pocket, and produced a pipe and a screw of paper. "This is a bleed'n' unsocial sort o' evenin' party, this is," he said. "An 'ere's the on'y real toff in the mob with 'ardly'arf a pipeful left, an'no lights. D'y' 'ear, me lord"—leaning toward the dozing neighbour—"got a match?"

> "Go t"ell!"

Indeed, the language of the Jago so differs from the dialect of the middle-class reader that Morrison consistently feels compelled to offer narrative commentary on its

meaning and even provides the reader with a "Glossary of Slang and Criminal Terms."

Once these surface features of difference are established, Morrison goes on to examine the customary life of the natives of the Jago. What we find is a picture of the poor crucially different from those presented by mid-Victorian novelists—such as Dickens, Gaskell, Kingsley, and Disraeli—interested in the "condition of England" question. Morrison's poor are not simply normal people fallen on hard times. Instead, the very cultural structures by which they experience their lives put them outside the purview of all "advanced" norms of contemporary Christian culture. Morrison dramatizes this most emphatically through his exploration of what passes for normal domestic relations in the Jago. George Stocking notes that post-Darwinian Victorian ethnography focuses, far more than one might expect, on "two particular human institutions: religion and marriage. . . . " Further, he goes on to demonstrate Victorian ethnographers focused on native marriage customs and formalized relations between men and women as an index to the overall level of civilization of a people. As Stocking notes, Victorian ethnographers considered the treatment of women to be a key indicator of how far a given culture had traveled along the road of moral evolution:

> . . . the pedestal of Victorian domesticity was the high point of evolutionary progress. As Herbert Spencer put it, "the moral progress of mankind" was in no way more clearly shown than by contrasting the "position of women" among savage and civilized nations: "At the one extreme a treatment of them cruel to the utmost degree bearable; and at the other extreme a treatment which, in some directions, gives them precedence over men."

Morrison makes use of this formula to assign the most primitive status to the Jagos, making it clear that the abuse of wives is not randomly committed by less admirable members of this society but rather that it is the norm—ritualized and even insisted upon. For example, the mother of Dicky Perrot—the boy whose development the novel chronicles—is, in part, an outcast from the world of the Jago because her marriage includes no ritualized violence: "As for herself [Hannah Perrot], she was no favourite in the neighbourhood at any time. For one thing, her husband did not carry the cosh [an instrument used to bludgeon a victim who is to be robbed]. Then she was an alien who had never entirely fallen into Jago ways; she had soon grown sluttish and dirty, but she was never drunk, she never quarreled, she did not gossip freely. Also her husband beat her but rarely, and then not with a chair nor a poker."

The idea of what is *normal* behavior is crucial here. For the Victorian ethnographer, the existence of "criminal" behavior (as defined by middle-class standards) among a native people was not necessarily proof of the degraded state of that people. What marked a people as degraded was the acceptance of "criminal" or deviant behavior as normal. Ethnographers such as Tylor and Lubbock argued that the fact that what is seen as aberrant or criminal behavior in civilized nations is promoted as the norm in "savage" societies offers convincing evidence for the existence of *moral*—as well as material—evolution among European peoples. As Tylor notes, "a Londoner who should attempt to lead the atrocious life which the real savage may lead with impunity and even respect, would be a criminal only allowed to follow his savage models during his short intervals out of gaol." This is precisely what puts the Jagos beyond the pale: they have developed a society on savage principles within the very heart of metropolitan London. Consider, for example, this passage in which we are presented with what passes for a not only acceptable, but even admirable, domestic/business relationship between Jago men and women. A Jago denizen sees a young, respectable man being led into the district by a woman, and makes this comment: "There's Billy Leary in luck ag'in: 'is missis do pick 'em up, s'elp me. I'd carry the cosh meself if I'd a woman like 'er." The narrator then offers this explanatory comment:

> Cosh-carrying was near to being the major industry of the Jago. The cosh was a foot length of iron rod, with a knob at one end, and a hook (or a ring) at the other. The craftsman, carrying it in his coat sleeve, waited about dark staircase corners till his wife (married or not) brought in a well-drunken stranger: when, with a sudden blow behind the head, the stranger was happily coshed, and whatever was found on him as he lay insensible was the profit on the transaction. In the hands of capable practitioners this industry yielded a comfortable subsistence for no great exertion. Most, of course, depended on the woman: whose duty it was to keep the other artist going in subjects. There were legends of surprising ingatherings achieved by wives of especial diligence: one of a woman who had brought to the cosh some six-and-twenty on a night of public rejoicing. This was, however, a story years old, and may have been no more than an exemplary fiction, designed, like a Sunday School book, to convey a counsel of perfection to the dutiful matrons of the Old Jago.

Thus, criminal behavior is more than tolerated; it becomes an ideal.

What seals the case of the Jagos as a dangerous "other" within the heart of an advanced civilization, what makes colonial action against them necessary, is that ritualized violence as a community response to the environment around them has made the Jagos true aliens, even in such basic matters as physicality and response to pain. Throughout the novel Morrison develops a picture of residents of the Jago as physically degenerate. As I have noted, he consistently refers to the Jagos as rats; even Dicky Perrot, the boy on whom the reader's attention is primarily focused, is viewed by the narrator as a "ratling from the Jago." According to Morrison, Jago rats so greatly vary from the physical norms of Englishmen that an outsider would not even be able to determine with any

accuracy the age of a Jago child: "A small boy, whom they met full tilt at the corner, staggered out to the gutter and flung a veteran curse after them. He was a slight child, by whose size you might have judged his age at five. But his face was of serious and troubled age. One who knew the children of the Jago, and could tell, might have held him eight, or from that to nine." The outsider needs the ethnographer to interpret correctly even the bodies of these natives. The untrained observer must discover that even what one would think of as the universally understood sign of smiling needs reinterpretation in the Jago: "Now the Jago smile was a smile by itself, unlike the smiles in other places. It faded suddenly, and left the face—the Jago face—drawn and sad and startling by contrast, as of a man betrayed into mirth in the midst of great sorrow. So that a persistent grin was known for a work of conscious effort."

But even more important than the observable physical differences of the Jagos are the communal styles by which they inflict, observe, and endure violence to the body. The most memorable scenes of the novel present the ritualized violence which is part of the pattern of existence in the Jago. We see the continually smoldering feud that goes on indefinitely between two leading Jago clans—an example of native tribal warfare. Another source of communal violence is the ongoing war the Jagos wage against residents of neighboring Dove Lane. Morrison comments on the ritualized, normalized character of these sources of violence: "The feud between the Jago and Dove Lane was eternal, just as was that between the Ranns and the Learys; but, like the Rann and Leary feud, it had its paroxysms and its intervals." The narrator then goes on to examine the customs of violence among the natives. One of the most striking passages describes a woman warrior, much admired for her prowess as a street fighter:

> Once a succession of piercing screams seemed to betoken that Sally Green had begun. There was a note in the screams of Sally Green's opposites which the Jago had learned to recognise. Sally Green, though of the weaker faction, was the female champion of the Old Jago: an eminence won and kept by fighting tactics peculiar to herself. For it was her way, reserving teeth and nails, to wrestle closely with her antagonist, throw her by a dexterous twist on her face, and fall on her, instantly seizing the victim's nape in her teeth, gnawing and worrying.

Sally is fully described as a native warrior taking part in a ritual display of power:

> Down the middle of Old Jago Street came Sally Green: red-faced, stripped to the waist, dancing, hoarse and triumphant. Nail-scores wide as the finger striped her back, her face, and her throat, and she had a black eye; but in one great hand she dangled a long bunch of clotted hair, as she whooped defiance to the Jago. It was a trophy newly rent from the scalp of Norah Walsh, champion of the Rann womankind, who had

crawled away to hide her blighted head, and be restored with gin. None answered Sally's challenge, and, staying but to fling a brickbat at Pip Walsh's window, she carried her dance and her trophy into Edge Lane.

What is particularly damning, however, is not the existence of this woman, but the response of the Jagos to the violence that she embodies. What is absent in the Jago response to this violence is a normal fear of bodily pain or of any empathy for the physical suffering of others. Instead, periods of widespread violence are met with enthusiasm; members of the community become delighted observers or participants.

In this, and in many other ways, Morrison equates the residents of the Jago with natives of a "less advanced" culture. For example, he demonstrates that Jagos are able to work only for short periods of time, that they are unable to understand the laws of delayed gratification, and that they live exclusively in the present. He shows that the skillful "colonial" administrator—in this case an admirable Anglican pastor, "Father" Sturt, who actually lives and works among his poor parishioners—needs to treat the "natives" as one would treat large children. Through this procedure Sturt is able to keep order among the natives, when they enter the clubhouse that he has created for them, without their ever really understanding how completely they are under his control: they were "all governed with an invisible discipline, which, being brought to action, was found to be of iron." Morrison even demonstrates that, as natives, Jagos may be cunning but certainly not intelligent: "But it was the way of the Jago that its mean cunning saw a mystery and a terror where simple intelligence saw there was none."

It is not surprising, then, that Morrison, although attempting to present even this semi-criminal East End neighborhood with sympathy, offers the reader reasons to believe that drastic measures are to be taken toward places like the Jago, that the residents of these areas are not in any real sense English citizens but rather alien beings living according to alien cultural codes. Toward the end of the novel, Morrison records this conversation between "Father" Sturt and a young surgeon who has just overseen the birth of Dicky Perrot's brother:

> Father Sturt met the surgeon as he came away in the later evening, and asked if all were well. The surgeon shrugged his shoulders. "People would call it so," he said. "The boy's alive, and so is the mother. But you and I may say the truth. You know the Jago far better than I. Is there a child in all this place that wouldn't be better dead—still better unborn? But does a day pass without bringing you just such a parishioner? Here lies the Jago, a nest of rats, breeding, breeding, as only rats can; and we say it is well. On high moral grounds we uphold the right of rats to multiply their thousands. Sometimes we catch a rat. And we keep it a little while, nourish it carefully, and put it back into the nest to propagate its kind."
>
> Father Sturt walked a little way in silence. Then he said: "You are right of course."

One can almost hear muted echoes of "Exterminate all the brutes."

What is most troubling for Morrison is that the Jago cannot be destroyed simply by destroying the neighborhood. When the buildings making up the Jago are torn down, he comments on the ineffectiveness of simple slum clearance: "The dispossessed Jagos had gone to infect the neighbourhoods across the border, and to crowd the people a little closer. . . . And so another Jago, teeming and villainous as the one displaced, was slowly growing, in the form of a ring, round about the great yellow houses." Keating describes Morrison's bleak view of the possibility of reclaiming these marginal poor, and his chilling belief that, unless drastic measures were taken, they would simply continue to produce a criminal race: "That Morrison believed they could not be reformed is clear from *A Child of the Jago* and he later publicly endorsed Jay's proposal for the establishment of Penal Settlements which would solve the problem of heredity by wiping out the entire strain." Those sentenced to such penal settlements would remain there for life and would not be allowed to reproduce.

William Booth was particularly fascinated by Stanley's distinction between those African natives who would, and those who would not, conform to standards of industry: "Of these pygmies there are two kinds; one a very degraded specimen with ferret-like eyes, close-set nose, more nearly approaching the baboon than was supposed to be possible, but very human; the other very handsome, with frank open innocent features, very prepossessing. They are quick and intelligent, capable of deep affection and gratitude, showing remarkable industry and patience." In a sense, Morrison had given the middle-class reader the domestic equivalents of these two types of African native. In *Tales of Mean Streets* (1894) he had presented readers with portraits of mostly (but not exclusively) respectable East Enders. With *A Child of the Jago* he examines those who will not conform. Strangely human and at the same time alien, they pose a threat to the heart of the empire.

Morrison's ethnographic account of these natives that somehow have come to exist at home underlines the need for radical solutions on the colonial model. When we view this call for radical action in light of the lessons that the twentieth century has taught us about final solutions, the stance that Morrison takes toward the Jagos becomes particularly frightening. And yet Morrison was convinced that he was writing in the best interests of the working poor of London. He would go on to write two more working-class novels—*To London Town* (1899) and *The Hole in the Wall* (1902)—which offer more positive accounts of how the effects of urban poverty can be overcome. It is in contrast to these more sympathetic portraits of the poor that Morrison's willingness to classify the Jagos as totally alien becomes most problematic. Although Morrison calls for sympathy for all the people whose lives he chronicles, his insistence on the Jagos' difference, even in matters that pertain to such basic cultural codes as responding to physical suffering, marks them as a problem that needs to be dealt with in ways that would not be appropriate for dealing with "non-natives." The novel is particularly urgent because it suggests that this native other, which has come into existence within a seemingly civilized country, is not a closed category. The existence of such "natives" can serve as a catalyst that allows the process of reverse evolution to begin to degrade the respectable poor. Through this fully realized dramatization of alien subjects on home soil, Morrison demonstrates the need for an active "colonial" policy to be put into effect within the very heart of England.

FURTHER READING

Bibliography

Calder, Robert. "Arthur Morrison: A Commentary with an Annotated Bibliography of Writings About Him." *English Literature in Transition* 28 (1985): 276-297.
    Comprehensive secondary bibliography.

Criticism

"Review: *A Child of the Jago.*" *Athenaeum* 108 (12 December 1896): 832-833.
    Contemporary review, characterizing the novel as vivid but pointless and overly graphic.

Bleiler, E. F. Introduction to *The Best Martin Hewitt Detective Stories,* by Arthur Morrison, pp vii-xiv. New York: Dover, 1976.
    Sketch of Morrison's literary career with particular attention to his detective fiction, which Bleiler claims was only a trivial distraction for Morrison.

"Review: *A Child of the Jago.*" *Bookman* 5 (January 1897): 464-465.
    Praises Morrison's social responsibility and accuracy in *A Child of Jago* while deploring the novel's graphic violence.

"Review: *Tales of Mean Streets.*" *The Critic* 605 (15 June 1895): 436
    Contemporary American review summarizing the narratives of Morrison's stories in *Tales of Mean Streets.*

Greene, Hugh. Introduction to *The Rivals of Sherlock Holmes: Early Detective Stories*, edited by Hugh Greene, pp 9-20. New York: Pantheon, 1970.
    General introduction for the collection, which includes two Morrison stories, one involving Martin Hewitt, the other his anti-hero Dorrington. Greene presents Morrison's detective fiction within the broader context of the genre.

Krzak, Michael. Preface to *Tales of Mean Streets,* by Arthur Morrison, pp 7-17. Suffolk: Boydell Press, 1983.
    Provides a summary of Morrison's early career as a journalist and critical commentary on the stories in *Tales of Mean Streets.*

Santoka Taneda

1882-1940

(Pseudonym of Shoichi Taneda) Japanese poet.

INTRODUCTION

Santoka is considered a unique proponent of "free-style" haiku poetry, a mode that abandoned much of the customary form and subject matter of traditional haiku in favor of a direct and unadorned depiction of human experience. A wandering poet and ascetic Zen priest for the last fifteen years of his life, Santoka emphasized many of the essential qualities of Zen Buddhism in his verse, including *mujo* (impermanence), the necessity of *sabi* (solitude), the importance of simplicity in life, and the pervasive sadness that accompanies all human affairs. Many of his poems point toward the Zen goal of overcoming this ubiquitous melancholy by achieving spiritual enlightenment and serenity. To this view Santoka added his concern with what James Abrams called "the vital necessity of movement and the partial release it brings to the anguish of the soul."

Biographical Information

Santoka was born Shoichi Taneda in 1882, the son of a wealthy landowner from Hofu in western Japan. He studied literature at Waseda University in Tokyo, and while there began writing poetry. He adopted a pen-name, as is the custom among haiku poets, choosing the name Santoka, which can be rendered in English as "burning mountain peak." Excessive drinking and a severe nervous breakdown forced him to drop out of school in 1904, however. In the ensuing years he attempted to assist his father in running a sakè brewery, but this too failed in all respects and contributed to Santoka's growing alcoholism. His arranged marriage in 1909 proved yet another failure in Santoka's personal life. Still, he continued with his literary efforts, and by 1911 had produced translations of such writers as Ivan Turgenev and Guy de Maupassant. The forthcoming years witnessed the steady influence of the haiku poet Seisensui Ogiwara on Santoka. Leader of the so-called "new tendency" or "free-style" school of haiku poetry, Seisensui was also founder of the literary journal *Soun*, of which Santoka became poetry editor in 1916. Meanwhile, Santoka made half-hearted attempts to maintain employment and support his family when not succumbing to his addiction to sakè. In 1924 he attempted suicide by standing in front of an oncoming train. Before impact, however, the train's engineer saw him and was able to stop. After the incident Santoka was taken to a nearby Zen temple in order to recover. He stayed there for a year, studying Zen Buddhism, and in 1925 was ordained a priest and placed in charge of a small temple. But by the following year Santoka had forsaken his clerical duties and left the temple to wander as a mendicant priest. With the financial support of some friends he published his first collection of haiku poetry, *Hachi no ko,* in 1932. That year several of his friends also renovated an old hermitage for Santoka, which he named "Gochuan," or "Cottage in the Midst." He stayed at Gochuan only briefly, opting instead to spend the rest of his life as he had the prior six years: as an impoverished, itinerant poet-priest, begging for money and food. He made another failed attempt at suicide several years later—this time with sleeping pills—and went on to publish six more collections of haiku verse before his death in 1940.

Major Works

Santoka published seven small books of haiku poetry containing approximately 800 of the thousands of poems he composed during his lifetime. Based on his experiences while wandering Japan as a mendicant, the haiku are written in an unadorned style and rarely contain more than ten words—although Santoka often labored meticulously over each poem. Simple in form, Santoka's poems dispense with the seasonal imagery and constraining five-seven-five syllable pattern of their traditional predecessors. In them Santoka confronts manifold subjects, making observations on the natural world, Zen philosophy, the loneliness and isolation of his wanderings, art, death, and the joys of drinking sakè. The last of these forms a favorite topic for Santoka, both in his haiku and his life, the drink offers him a temporary release from his feelings of guilt, which inevitably would return, accompanied by a heightened sense of remorse over his dissipated life, with sobriety.

Critical Reception

Before his death Santoka was largely unknown outside of a small group of friends who read and circulated his poetry and at times supported him financially. By the 1970s, however, his verse had reached a point of remarkable popularity in Japan and elsewhere. The mass of his writings, including his published verse and unpublished journals and diaries, have since been collected in the seven-volume *Teihon Taneda Santoka Zenshu* (1972), and many of his haiku poems have now been translated into English and other languages. Scholars have since evaluated Santoka's place in the Japanese poetic tradition, seeing him as among the last in a lengthy line of wandering haiku poets. Others have begun to devote closer study to his break with tradition as a writer of "free-style" haiku and examine the intricacies of what J. Thomas Rimer has called his "laconic, deceptively simple" poetry.

PRINCIPAL WORKS

Hachi no ko (poetry) 1932
Somokuto (poetry) 1933
Sangyo suigyo (poetry) 1935
Zasso fukei (poetry) 1936
Kaki no ha (poetry) 1938
Kokan (poetry) 1939
Karasu (poetry) 1940
Teihon Taneda Santoka Zenshu. 7 vols. (poetry and prose) 1972
Mountain Tasting: Zen Haiku by Santoka Taneda (poetry) 1980

CRITICISM

R. H. Blyth (essay date 1964)

SOURCE: "Santoka," in *A History of Haiku,* Vol. II, The Hokuseido Press, 1971, pp.173-88.

[*In the following essay, which was originally published in 1964, Blyth studies Santoka's haiku poems, especially as they signify the poet's acceptance of more melancholy aspects of life.*]

To give a modern poet a whole chapter to himself, albeit a short one, may seem strange, but Santoka belongs to the small group of beggar-like haiku poets; Rotsu is another example, and Basho and Issa are not dissimilar. Santoka, was born in 1882 of a landowner in Yamaguchi Prefecture. After retiring from Waseda University on account of a nervous breakdown in 1904, he married, set up a brewery with his father, whose business had failed, and together with him went bankrupt in 1916. He had begun to write haiku already in 1911, under Seisensui. He separated from his wife in 1920, and tried various jobs, but did not continue in them. From 1926, with a kasa and a begging bowl, he wandered all over Japan for eight years, and then made a hermitage in 1932 back in Yamaguchi Prefecture, and yet another outside Miyukidera Temple. He ended his life of wandering and drinking in 1940.

Here are a few anecdotes of the life of Santoka, taken from *Haijin Santoka,* by Oyama Sumita. When the author visited Gochuan, the hut-hermitage where Santoka lived in 1938, Santoka asked him if he had had his midday meal. On hearing that he had not, he brought in an iron bowl of rice, and a single pimento, and put it on the tatami. Oyama began to weep, it was so hot. Santoka sat gazing at him, and on being asked, "Why don't you eat too?" told him, "I have only one bowl." Thinking of Ryokan, he finished his rice. Santoka took the bowl, filled it with rice (which was mixed with barley and other things) and ate it together with the remains of the pimento. Santoka washed the bowl in the water the rice was washed in, but did not throw away the water. He used it to wash the floor, and then as manure for his little garden.

One December, the author stayed the night with Santoka. There was only one quilt, so Santoka gave him this, and three magazines of Kaizo or Bungei Shunju for a pillow, and spread on the top of him his own underclothes and summer garments, and then everything that remained in the cupboard. As he was still cold, Santoka put his little desk over him, reminding us of what Thoreau says in *The Week on the Concord,* Tuesday:

> But as it grew colder towards midnight, I at length encased myself completely in boards, managing even to put a board on top of me, with a large stone on it, to keep it down.

At last he went to sleep, and when he woke at dawn he found Santoka still sitting by him doing zazen.

Even though he had no rice, he would buy sake to drink, being unable to keep money in his pocket. Someone gave him a *tombi,* a kind of coat used in the Meiji Era. He was very pleased, for two or three days, and then gave it to someone else. One autumn Seisensui came to see him, and gave him a piece of calligraphy, *Gochu ichinin,* referring to his hut-hermitage. Santoka had it framed, and for some time enjoyed it, but then gave it away.

One night Santoka came home at two o'clock in the morning, followed by a dog with a very big rice-cake in its mouth. He received this and roasted it and ate it.

Santoka loved weeds, like Clare, and wrote in his diary for the 19th of August, 1940:

> Those who do not know the meaning of weeds do not know the mind of Nature. Weeds grasp their own essence and express its truth.

He wrote many verses on weeds. His view of life is given in another entry in his diary:

> I do not believe in a future world. I deny the past. I believe entirely in the present. We must employ our whole body and soul in this eternal moment. I believe in the universal spirit, but the spirit of any particular man I reject. Each creature comes from the Whole, and goes back to it. From this point of view we may say that life is an approaching; death is a returning.

In these anecdotes about Santoka we see the naturalness of his life, his unattachedness to things, and his lack of plan in everything, like God's.

He put every ounce of his spiritual energy into his verses, which were often free as to form and season-word like those of his teacher Seisensui. He recalls to us Pascal, Kierkegaard, Kafka, Kraus, Rilke, and others of the "disinherited mind." The verses are a combination of Zen, Buddhism, and Japaneseness, the last word implying an innate appreciation of the transitoriness of life, the just-so-ness, the thus-ness of things, their existence value.

> *Ushiro-sugata no shigurete yuku ka*
>
> My back view as I go,
> Wetted with the winter rain?

We may compare this with Issa's verse on a picture of himself:

> *Ushiro kara mite mo samuge na atama kana*
>
> > Even seen from behind,
> > His head looks
> > Cold.

But Santoka's verse is better, I think, because it gives us the picture of himself as viewed by the friends who are seeing him off.

> *Itsumademo tabi wo suru koto no tsume wo kiru*
>
> Up to the very end, it is journeying,
> And cutting our (toe-) nails.

We must journey alone through life; and we must cut our toe-nails. These things are so, inevitably.

> *Furusato wa tokushite ki no me*
>
> My native place
> Far away:
> The buds on the trees.

When we are young, neither far nor near, youth nor age has any very deep meaning, but when we are old, distance and youth affect us beyond measure.

> *Tetsubachi no naka e mo arare*
>
> Into the iron bowl also,
> Hailstones.

Democracy is a weak word to express the universal, all-penetrating, indiscriminate, "religious" power of nature.

> *Kasa e pottori tsubaki datta*
>
> Plop on my kasa
> The flower of the camellia!

This verse is very good in its onomatopoeia, not merely the *pottori,* but the *datta* at the end.

> *Itadaite tarite hitori no hashi wo oku*
>
> I have gratefully received it;
> It was enough;
> I lay down my chopsticks.

This would make a good death-poem. We have received what we were born to receive. We have had enough. We used our own chopsticks and fed ourselves. We now lay them down. Compare Landor's "I warmed both hands," which is however the verse of a well-off, artistic, and self-satisfied man.

> *Shizukana michi to nari dokudami no me*
>
> The road became quiet and solitary;
> *Dokudami* is budding.

The *dokudami,* also called *shibuki,* is a small, ill-smelling weed with a four-petalled white flower that blooms in summer. The quietness of the road, and of his mind, is revealed to us by his noticing such a small and insignificant thing as the buds of this weed.

> *Karasu naite watashi mo hitori*
>
> A crow is cawing;
> I also am by myself.

Santoka wrote this verse in response to the following by Hosai:

> *Karasu ga damatte tonde itta*
>
> A crow flew by,
> In silence.

Hosai, 1885-1926, became head of a life insurance company, wandered in Manchuria, then, after some deep experience in 1923, sold all his belongings, became a monk in various temples, and died a year after his retirement from the world. He comes on page 200.

> *Wake-itte mo wake-itte mo aoi yama*
>
> Going further into them,
> And further into them,
> Still more green mountains.

There is in this verse a feeling of infinity in space, not beyond it, and something sad in it, as in the poetry of Christina Rossetti. It reminds us of lines in Wordsworth's *Stepping Westward:*

> > the thought
> > Of travelling through the world that lay
> > Before me in my endless way.

> *Shitodo ni nurete kore wa michishirube no ishi*
>
> This is the stone,
> Drenched with rain,
> That marks the way.

The poet also is wet, but feels a faint but deep thankfulness to the stone. Compare Issa's verse, which is much more direct, and to this extent less poetical, less religious:

> *Hito no tame ni shigurete hotoke sama*
>
> > Rained upon
> > For all our sakes,
> > *Hotoke Sama.*

Hotoke Sama is the stone statue of some Buddha of a wayside shrine.

> *Ko-no-ha chiru aruki-tsumeru*

> Leaves of the trees fall;
> Walking on and on.

This is hearing

> Time's winged chariot hurrying near,

in the falling of the leaves.

> *Sei-shi no naka no yuki furi-shikiru*

> The snow of life and death
> Falls incessantly.

Saigyo says:

> We know well
> That this cicada-shell body
> Is but an illusion,
> But when it snows,
> The days are chill.

> *Fumi-wakeru hagi yo susuki yo*

> Walking through
> The bush clover, the pampas grass,
> Walking on through them.

We see the beauty and pathos of the bush-clover and the pampas grass, the dew on them, and the sunlight on it, but we pass through and beyond them, not lingering with their beauty but going on with our life as they do with theirs.

> *Hyo-hyo to shite mizu wo ajiwau*

> Buoyantly we go
> Like the wind,
> Tasting water.

The *Rubaiyat* says that we come

> Into this Universe, and *Why* not knowing,
> Nor *Whence*, like Water willy-nilly flowing.

Tasting water is different from drinking it. The first has meaning, the second only use.

> *Hitori de ka ni kuwarete iru*

> I am bitten by mosquitoes,
> Quite alone.

There is something in the itching that intensifies, or rather brings out the meaning of the loneliness of a human being.

> *Kasa ni tombo wo tomarasete aruku*

> I walk along,

> Letting the dragon-fly
> Perch on my *kasa*.

The poet walks a little more steadily, so that the dragon-fly, which he hears perch on his *kasa*, is not frightened away from it. Compare Hosai's verse:

> *Tombo ga sabishii tsukue ni tomari ni kite kureta*

> The dragon-fly
> Kindly came and perched
> On this lonely desk.

> *Shigururu ya shinanaide iru*

> Cold winter rain;
> I am still alive.

This "verse" expresses something very simple but profound. This "not being dead" does not mean "not dead yet"; it does not mean that he is grateful for life. It is the mere, brute fact of not being dead, just like not being fine warm weather. The same applies to the following:

> *Do shiyo mo nai watashi ga aruite oru*

> I am walking;
> It cannot be otherwise.

> *Kare-kitta kawa wo wataru*

> Crossing over
> A dried up river.

This "verse" asks much from the reader, even more than the orthodox haiku. Though it is so short, 11 syllables instead of 17, its onomatopoeia is good,

> k r k t k w w w t r,

the *k* and *t* sounds expressing the dryness, the *w* and *r* sounds the water that is not there.

> *Sukkari karete mame to natte iru*

> Quite withered up,
> It is just beans.

Nothing could be barer than this verse, except the scene itself, just dried-up earth and yellow bean-pods, open, with the dry beans showing.

> *Sutekirenai nimotsu no omosa mae ushiro*

> I can't throw it away,
> But how heavy my pack,
> Before and behind!

This may be compared with what Basho says at the beginning of *Oku no Hosomichi*, about having to carry the things that his friends had kindly given him.

> *Ano kumo ga otoshita ame ni nurete iru*

> I am wet

By the rain
From that cloud.

The poet feels no more animosity towards the cloud than it does to him. He moves, and the cloud moves; and when they come together, a wetting takes place.

Aki to natta zasso ni suwaru

The grasses
That have become autumn,—
Sitting down in them.

The poet feels swallowed up in autumn,—not in a vague, mystical way, but that he is sitting on autumn, looking at autumn, breathing it, eating it, being it. The next verse seems a continuation of this:

Hoi konna ni yaburete kusa no mi

Seeds of grasses;
My monkish robe
Is so worn!

When he stands up, he finds all kinds of seeds have stuck to his clothes, and as he looks at them he notices how worn and old they are.

Toshi toreba kokyo koishii tsukutsuku-boshi

As I grow old,
I yearn for my native place:
Tsukutsukuboshi!

The cicadas are crying *tsukutsukuboshi*, which sounds somewhat like *kokyokoishi, kokyokoishi,* "I yearn for my native place." Old age, love of one's native place, the voices of the cicadas,—these are different manifestations of one thing. What is this One Thing?

Mizuoto to issho ni sato e orite kita

Together with the sound of the water,
I came down to my native village.

In Hermann Hesse's *Siddhartha* we feel the closeness of man and flowing water. What is man himself indeed but walking water, laughing, weeping, thinking, enlightened water?

Shimi-jimi taberu meshi bakari no meshi de aru

Intently
I eat my meal
Of boiled rice only.

Just like an animal, almost an animal, with what Huxley calls "animal grace," which is far from gracefulness.

Mattaku kumo ga nai kasa wo nugi

Not a single cloud in the sky;
I take off my *kasa.*

Hosai's verse is:

Ozora no shita boshi kaburazu

Under the vast sky
I have no hat on.

We may compare Mr Cronch, in Powys's *Lie Thee Down Oddity!* who takes off his hat as the great chimney falls on him. Also we may contrast Housman's "Shoulder the sky!"

Amadare no oto mo toshi-totta

The sound of the rain-drops also
Has grown older.

Hosai's verse:

Hisashiburi no ame no amadare no oto

We haven't had any rain for a long time:
The sound of the rain-drops.

To see youth in the rain-drops when we are young, age in the rain-drops when we are old, this is true wisdom, for the rain-drops are both young and old, and we ourselves but the rain-drops of a passing shower.

Mono kou ie mo naku nari yama ni wa kumo

No house more to beg from;
Clouds over the mountains.

This was composed in Kyushu in the afternoon of an Indian summer. Walking on and on, Santoka came to a vast plain. There were no more houses where he could beg his food. Only in the distance a long range of mountains, and the clouds piled upon them.

Kasa mo moridashita ka

Has my *kasa* too
Begun to leak?

When the only *kasa* he has begins to leak, the poet feels deeply the impermanence of things. The *kasa* is part of himself. The body itself is only lent like any other thing, and wears thin and old with the years.

Ate mo naku fumiaruku kusa mina karetari

The grasses I tread,
Uncertain and fickle,
Are all withered away.

There is a certain grimness here, a subjectivity that is nevertheless not unjustified in the works of nature. The poet walks, as chance (that is, destiny) wills it, over the brown and withered grasses. They too have followed their destiny, so out of accord with what he could have wished. Like Basho's morning-glory, these grasses could not be his friend. And yet, as deep as, or perhaps deeper than the instinct for the changeless is the instinct for change, since this changefulness is an aspect of the Buddha-nature of both man and grass.

*Yama-suso atataka na hi ni narabu haka sukoshi
    kana*

> In the warm sunlight
> At the foot of the hill, standing side by side,
>   A few graves.

What brings out the meaning of the scene is the fewness of the graves. Even death itself seems less significant under the sky that overarches the grassy mountains. This verse has twenty one syllables and no season word, for the word "warm" will apply to any season, even to winter, which would perhaps be most appropriate here. The "kana" is different from the ordinary stop-gap of the regular haiku. It signifies the poet's acceptance of the melancholy fact of life and death, abundance and paucity, nature and man. And this is all contained in the word *sukoshi*. A few graves stand in a line at the foot of the hill; the slope always receives the afternoon sun. They have chosen a warm spot for the last resting place of the dead. In life they worked and talked together; now they sleep an eternal sleep side by side. There is a mildness in the thought, the rhythm, the warmth of the place which makes it akin, in mood and treatment, to a verse from the *Elegy:*

> Beneath those rugged elms, that yew tree's shade
> Where heaves the earth in many a mouldering
>   heap,
> Each in his narrow place forever laid,
>   The rude Forefathers of the hamlet sleep.

But the Japanese poem is not so funereal; we have sunlight and warmth instead of darkness and gloom, yet the feeling is deeper and keener because of the contrast, and because of the word "few." What is unexpressed *and inexpressible* is what is expressed by Becquer, the Spanish Heine, in his poem *Los Muertos:*

> La picqueta al hombro,
> el sepulturero,
> cantando entre dientes,
> se perdió a lo lejos.
> La noche se entraba,
> reinaba el silencio;
> perdido en las sombras,
> medité un momento:
> *"¡ Dios Mio, qué solos
> se quedan los muertos!*

This is what the Japanese poet does not say.

*Ichi-nichi mono iwazu umi ni mukaeba shio
    michite kinu*

> I was silent all day:
>   Facing the sea,
>   The tide came up.

The poet was silent because there was nothing to say, no one to speak, no one to speak to. This is the silence of nature, of the moon and the stars, of night. And it is the silence that is in the thunder, in the tick of the clock. This is why Blake says that

> The roaring of lions . . . the raging of the stormy
> sea . . . are portions of eternity too great for the
> eye of man.

The full brimming tide is felt to be, for all its crash of waves, the same silent thing that has taken up its abode within his heart.

James Abrams (essay date 1977)

SOURCE: "Hail in the Begging Bowl: The Odyssey and Poetry of Santoka," in *Monumenta Nipponica,* Vol. XXXII, No. 3, Autumn 1977, pp. 269-302.

[*In the following essay, Abrams provides an overview of Santoka's life and work.*]

> *Into my metal bowl too,*
> *hail.*
>
>   Santoka

Taneda Santoka, 1882-1940, is one of the most recent and perhaps one of the last of a long and colorful line of priest-poets in Japanese literary history. An alcoholic and business failure who became a Buddhist priest after an attempted suicide at the age of forty-two, Santoka spent the last sixteen years of his life as a raucous itinerant monk who survived through begging and the good graces of his many acquaintances. Throughout this period he was a voracious observer of life, nature and self in his prolific free-verse haiku. When Santoka died in October 1940 he was still a penniless alcoholic whose years of wandering and solitude had only made him more acutely aware of how far he remained from happiness and personal salvation. He had published seven small books of poetry which had been well received by his poetic circle but were almost entirely unknown by the Japanese literary world.

It has only been in the last ten years, with the publication of several biographical sketches of his life, that a minor 'Santoka boom' has brought the poet a measure of fame and reputation. The reasons for his recent rise to acclaim are not difficult to discern. People are first of all attracted to his lifestyle, the vagabond existence in which the road and pace of one's life are chosen by day-to-day inclinations. It is a lifestyle that despite its inevitable mental and physical hardships has an alluring sense of romanticism and nostalgia for the majority of people burdened with the responsibilities of family and job.

The image of Santoka the man is also extremely appealing. A literate and garrulous man, he considered a good conversation and a bottle of *sake* to be the ultimate source of pleasure. He was welcomed with open arms into the homes of friends and strangers all over the country, despite the common knowledge that the priest would drink their *sake,* share their bed, and then cheerfully bid farewell the next morning without a word about repaying the hospitality. Photographs of the poet present us with an almost comic figure, large bamboo hat, priest's garb, thick spectacles, metal begging bowl, and two spindly legs supported on a pair of straw sandals. But if the pictures somehow epitomize the incongruity of his role as a priest and expose the eccentricity of the man, they also hint at a robust spirit, boundless curiosity, and a large capacity for friendship.

Then finally there are his poems, which for all their simplicity seem to have struck a harmonious chord with many Japanese. Sometimes as short as two words and seldom more than ten, Santoka's free-verse haiku possess a degree of sincerity and involvement that is often lacking in Japanese poetry so dominated by form and convention.

Sincerity, of course, does not necessarily make for great poetry, and Santoka certainly did not possess the poetic genius of itinerant nature poets such as Saigyo or Basho or the intellectual skills and polish of semi-recluses such as Kamo no Chomei or Buson. Yet the intricate relationship between his artistic and experiential lives, coupled with his training in Zen and Buddhist thought, gives his work an acuteness of expression and at times a striking freshness.

This essay will in the main be devoted to an introduction to Santoka's poetic works. To clarify his poems I have added a prefatory introduction to Santoka's life and have tried to arrange his poems to give a clear image of his physical and mental transitions after he entered the priesthood. The poems selected are grouped mainly by subject matter rather than time period. I have tried to picture the man and the poet by choosing poems that best represent his feelings toward the subjects that were of primary concern to him—nature, religion, travel, *sake,* poetry, solitude, and death. Excerpts from his diary are also included.

SANTOKA'S LIFE

Santoka was born as Taneda Shoichi, the oldest son of Takejiro and Fusa, on 3 December 1882 in Bofu, Yamaguchi prefecture, a rural area in western Japan. His father was a well-off landowner who kept two or three mistresses and seems to have been generally too busy with his affairs of the heart to properly manage his business. When Shoichi was ten years old, his mother, who had given birth to five children, committed suicide at the age of thirty-three by jumping into the family well. She was probably driven to the act by her husband's dissipation and neglect of the family. The children were thereafter raised by an aunt.

Shoichi was a good student who from an early age showed an interest in literature. At the age of nineteen he left home for Tokyo to prepare for entering university, and in the following year he was admitted into the Department of Literature, Waseda University. It was in this period that he first began to use the pen name Santoka. It was also at this time that Shoichi first began to drink heavily. His inability to keep up with his classes was doubtlessly in part a result of his drinking habits, and in

1904, at the age of twenty-two, he suffered a nervous breakdown, dropped out of school, and returned to his father's home. Takejiro, whose intemperate habits had not mellowed with age, was forced to sell his property in 1906, and in the same year father and son opened a *sake* brewery in a nearby village. However, from the start neither the womanizing father nor the drinking son showed much proclivity for running the business.

Unlike his father, Shoichi was throughout his life only minimally interested in women. He admits in his writings that the suicide of his mother had deeply wounded him and had left a void in his spirit which no other woman was ever able to fill. Despite his protests that he was determined to enter the priesthood and had no need for a wife, his father forced him into a marriage in 1909 with Sato Sakino, the oldest daughter of a man from a neighboring village. The new couple seem to have been on good terms for a few months, during which time Sakino became pregnant with their first and only child, Ken. But Shoichi began returning home drunk or staying out all night, and there was soon little or no intimacy between the two.

In 1911 Shoichi contributed translations of Turgenev and Maupassant to the literary journal *Seinen*. Two years later, at the age of thirty-one, he became a disciple of the poet Ogiwara Seisensui, a leader of the 'new tendency school' of haiku, which discarded the traditional use of seasonal words and the 5-7-5 syllables for a freer verse form. Shoichi, now using his literary name Santoka, at the same time began writing for Seisensui's poetry journal, *Soun*. In 1916, the same year in which he joined the staff of *Soun* as a poetry editor, the *sake* business went bankrupt after father and son had allowed the *sake* to go sour for two straight years. Taking his wife and child, Santoka moved to Kumamoto city, where poetry acquaintances helped him to set up a secondhand bookstore.

His attempt to settle down into a normal life was again disrupted in 1918 when his younger brother Jiro committed suicide and Tsuru, the aunt who had raised him after his mother's death, died. Santoka left the management of the bookstore and a later picture-frame shop to his wife, and more and more often had to be bailed out by his friends after running up drinking bills which he had no way of paying. In 1919 he left his wife to find work in Tokyo and in the following year Sakino obtained a divorce from him. Santoka found a job in Tokyo as a librarian, but after two years, in December 1922, he quit after another nervous breakdown. He stayed in Tokyo long enough to experience the devastating Great Kanto Earthquake in September 1923, soon after which he returned to Kumamoto.

On a night in December 1924 a very intoxicated Santoka tried to commit suicide by standing in the path of an oncoming train. The engineer spotted him in time and the train managed to pull up before hitting him. Santoka was taken to a Zen temple in Kumamoto to recuperate and it was there that he resolved to begin training for the priesthood. In the following months he underwent a great change, forcing himself into a rigidly fixed regimen, and in February 1925, at the age of forty-two, he was ordained as a priest and assigned as custodian of a small temple in rural Kumamoto. For a year he served faithfully at the temple, opening a Sunday school and a night school for the villagers, while concentrating on his poetry. But he was continually plagued by the idea that a man of his spiritual weakness was in no way qualified to minister to the souls of the villagers who fed him and paid for the upkeep of the temple. Finally, unable to bear the isolation and his spiritual turmoil, he gave up his post in April 1926 and set off as a mendicant priest on wanderings that continued almost uninterrupted for six years.

Santoka was to destroy the diary of his early years on the road, and there is no clear record of where the priest's wanderings took him. He apparently traveled throughout Kyushu, crossed over to Shikoku, and begged his way through most of the western end of the main island of Honshu. In 1929 and 1930 he returned briefly to Kumamoto and stayed with Sakino, helping in her store. He also again started to contribute to *Soun* and began publication of his own poetry journal, *Sambaku*.

By now his life had settled into a familiar pattern: an earnest attempt to lead a serious life, followed by a drinking and spending spree, deep repentance, and the start of another directionless, soul-cleansing journey. Santoka walked from village to village, chanting for alms at every farmhouse he passed by. He spent his nights in cheap lodging houses, which he paid for with his day's take of coins and rice. Increasingly in his later years he also used his pilgrimages as an excuse to visit his wide range of poetry colleagues in western Japan, staying for a few days of good food and abundant *sake* before setting off for the next village or the next friend.

In the autumn of 1932, with the financial assistance of his admirers he settled into a country hermitage he named 'Gochuan', literally, 'Cottage in that Midst', in the village of Ogori, Yamaguchi prefecture. In the same year he published his first book of poems, *Hachi no ko (Rice Bowl Child),* and put out a few more issues of *Sambaku.* He planted his first garden, and took pride in the fact that at least to a limited extent he could lead a self-dependent life. In the spring of 1934 the restless Santoka set off on a trip into the central mountains of Shinshu, but his fifty years of age were beginning to tell on him and he was hospitalized with acute pneumonia. Early in the following year, back at Gochuan, physically and mentally exhausted and increasingly obsessed with death, Santoka again tried to kill himself by taking a large quantity of sleeping pills. But by the following spring, 1936, he was back on the road, traveling to Tokyo for a meeting of *Soun* backers and then heading north into the Tohoku region.

The last few years of his life were spent in active writing and continual drifting. As he noted in his diary at that time, his only two purposes in life were 'to produce all the true poems that are within me' and 'to die a blessed death, without lengthy pain, without being a burden to others.' In 1938 he finally abandoned Gochuan, and after another trip eastward crossed over to Shikoku where, in December 1939, he settled down in a temple hermitage, again provided through the assistance of poetry colleagues, near the city of Matsuyama.

On 10 October 1940, his poetry companions gathered at the cottage for their regular discussion meeting and found Santoka in what seemed to be a drunken stupor, not an unusual condition. They left him sleeping and went ahead with their meeting, but after they had all returned home, a neighbor came by to check on him late that night and, finding his condition worsened, called a doctor. Santoka died early the next morning, shortly before his fifty-eighth birthday, of an apparent apoplexy.

MOTION

The resolution of spiritual doubts through physical movement is hardly a new phenomenon peculiar to Santoka or Japanese priest-poets. Moses wandered through the desert for forty years before finding the Promised Land. Parcival and his contemporaries in the Middle Ages discovered the secrets of the heart and spirit after years of wandering from one adventure to another. Kerouac and his generation made the highway the modern path to salvation. What Santoka in particular inherited was a deeply ingrained Japanese tradition of seeking in nature itself a release from worldly anxiety and an opening to spiritual enlightenment. Since ancient times the excursion into nature has been linked with, and to a large extent indistinguishable from, the religious pilgrimage.

In the Heian period emperors and nobles led their entourages down rivers and into mountains for the dual purpose of visiting shrines or temples and stimulating the poetic and aesthetic sensibilities of the court. In the Middle Ages Saigyo and Chomei, together with thousands of other priests and social outcasts, found that by retreating into nature they could to some extent relieve the burdens of living in a very troubled world. Yet while their Western counterparts have tended to seek wisdom and reason in their natural environment, Japanese nature-lovers asked of nature no more than to give them peace of mind. For some this meant silent and meditative absorption into nature; for others such as Santoka, it meant an exhausting physical experience, the positive and aggressive exposure of self to blazing suns, freezing rain, and endless roads of dust and mud.

What distinguishes Santoka in this long tradition is the almost desperate quality about his journeys. There were times when it was only motion, only day after day of walking, that maintained his sanity. As he notes in his diary:

> Wordlessly I cross mountain after mountain. To an almost overpowering degree I feel the loneliness and tranquility of isolation. Thus I continue to

walk, with questions of what will come next, what will I do, what ought I to do, and still I walk. There is nothing I can do but walk. To walk—that alone is far enough.

This idea of the vital necessity of movement and the partial release it brings to the anguish of his soul is a constant theme in his poems.

> There can be no other way,
> I keep walking.

> Seeking something,
> walking through the wind.

> There is no road but this road,
> a spring snow falls.

> Open to the wind,
> over and over condemning myself, I walk.

> The muddied waters flow on,
> clearing as they go.

> Laying on the grass,
> I open the wounds of this trip to the sun.

Santoka's literary mentor Seisensui commented, 'Santoka walks without purpose, walks like the clouds or the rivers, because he has to keep moving, because walking is living for him.' This life force that refused Santoka an end to his journey is best illustrated in one of his most famous poems:

> I push my way through,
> push my way through,
> green mountains.

Anyone who has ever climbed a mountain knows the experience of being certain that the ridge ahead must surely be the peak, only to discover that there is yet another ridge towering up behind it. For Santoka this feeling of frustration, mixed with determination to continue on, was not confined to one mountain top or one long day of traveling, but to years of wandering without finding his destination. He might scale one peak, find one moment of respite, but always with the final realization that there lay yet another road and another mountain in front of him.

Santoka was himself greatly concerned about the unproductive, unstable nature of his life. Both before and after becoming a priest he made furiously enthusiastic attempts to reform himself and take proper care of his family. Through the years 1930 and 1931 he spent considerable time with his former wife Sakino in Kumamoto, trying to convince himself that he could be satisfied helping her tend the store, looking after their son Ken, and occupying himself with his poetry journals and poetry acquaintances. In 1933 and 1934 he temporarily found some degree of peace and calmness in his country retreat at Gochuan. But in the end it was the very determination to settle down to a normal, secure life that led to his overpowering sense of guilt and self-condemnation when he found him-

self at the end of another drinking spree and forced him into yet another pilgrimage to cleanse his soul.

As Santoka left Gochuan in December 1935 after another suicide attempt, he wrote:

> Above the water passes the shadow of a cloud,
> something will not let me be at peace.

And on the same trip he expressed his feelings as the sweet exhaustion of movement began to warm his body and heal his battered soul:

> One more layer stripped off,
> from journey to journey.

SELF-INTERROGATION

It is essential to an understanding of Santoka's inner turmoil to remember that when he did finally turn to religion it was to Zen and not to another Buddhist or Christian sect. As the following quotations from his diary reveal, what Santoka sought was not a god who would embrace him or a faith that would soothe his spirit, but a frame of mind that would permit him to strip himself of all his hypocrisies and teach him to accept with tranquility his place in the universe.

> There is nothing so easy to say but so hard to do as 'give up'. Resignation is not self-abandonment, nor blind obedience. Resignation is the spiritual peace permitted only after one has exhausted the heart and mind of things.

It was through Zen, which teaches that salvation can be reached only through self-discipline and order, not doctrine or faith, that Santoka tried to achieve this resignation and spiritual peace that so eluded him.

The following excerpts from his diary may also help to illustrate the nature of his harsh self-interrogation:

> How can the man who cannot believe in himself possibly believe in God?

> One day's life resolves for that day alone one's doubts about the universe.

> Human life begins in conquest of one's self and it ends in conquest of one's self.

> A man who has consumed all his power and has never known a word of prayer is a hero free of illusions.

> If you find you must pray, turn toward yourself and pray.

> Self-love is not self-flattery, it is not tolerance toward oneself. The man who loves himself is the most severe, the most heartless toward himself.

> Weep not for seeking and not obtaining, but for seeking and not being fulfilled in what is gained.

The life of the weak is a continuing chain of acts of repentance. And this repentance is no more than repentance for its own sake.

In the strong too there are times of repentance, but there is no repentance of the kind that does not give rise to the bud of new life.

The truth is both full of mercy and at the same time brutal. Just as there is truth in God there is also truth in the devil.

To live the true life is to know suffering.

What we find in these aphorisms, a pursuit of Santoka's into which he put a great deal of effort in his middle years, is the image of a sick man determined to cure himself through naked exposure to the elements, an existentialist who must interminably suffer the recognition of his inability to cope with life. Santoka sought to overcome his spiritual weaknesses by negating any outer source of salvation and putting all his energy into self-interrogation and self-revelation. But in his pursuit of the truth about himself he was to find that his weaknesses became all the more apparent, that he was undeniably a bogus priest who was unable to control his physical appetites and lived off the good will of his friends. Thus the truth led to suffering, and suffering became almost an aesthetic virtue worthy of cultivation. He wrote:

> The honest man must suffer. The honest man becomes honest in proportion to his suffering. Pain deepens thought and strengthens life. Pain is the purification of life.

If the search for truth results not in the salvation of peace of mind but in the further accumulation of suffering, and if by choice or fate the final escape of death is not yet open, then suffering has to be recognized for its inextricable relationship to life.

> Even when he doubted god, doubted man, and even doubted himself, he could never doubt the fact of his own suffering. To that extent was his suffering deeply embedded and deeply rooted in his existence.

> Pain always comes from within, never from without. The seed of pain that we plant, we ourselves must harvest and drink of its fruit. Pain cannot be broken, it can only be embraced. We must grasp the dark power at the bottom of pain.

Yet Santoka was not unaware of the dangerously sentimental and masochistic nature of his excessive inclination to suffer. As noted above, he found his purposeless acts of repentance nothing more than an additional form of weakness, to be scorned and ridiculed.

> Just as there is seduction in pleasure, there is attraction in pain. Those people whose lives are nothing but pain yet have no fear of death often continue to live, not because of the will for existence but because they have grasped the sweetness at the bottom of pain.

To taste pain is valuable, but to become accustomed to pain is fearful.

The emptiness of those who torture their flesh in order to soothe their spirit.

This last statement reads like a condemnation of his entire course of life. The man who will walk thousands of miles to calm his spirit realizes even before the journey has begun that it will all be meaningless and futile. But it is also the only course left to him, and he must travel it with humility and dignity.

> The man who has come from hell does not shout and run. Silently, gazing fixedly at the earth, he walks.

NATURE AND SIMPLICITY

Santoka's path away from the established life of man into nature has been followed by numerous religious and intellectual figures in Japanese history. The world of nature has offered a limitless arena of serenity, inevitability, and unalterable flow for those who had been too caught up in the worldly affairs of man to contemplate mortal life and universal eternity.

But Santoka was also a priest who never believed in an eternal afterlife and who had despaired of ever achieving salvation. As a consequence his perception of the hundreds of mountains and rivers he crossed in his journeys was of a different dimension from the view of those who sought in nature a definition of life. Santoka never attempted to solve the divine pattern manifested in nature, nor did he try to find in nature a symbolic equivalent to human mortality.

While Santoka's poetry abounds in images from nature, he almost completely ignores such traditional images as the plum and cherry blossoms, the nightingale, wild geese, and maple leaves. He was consciously trying to break away from binding poetic conventions, and he was not interested in the well-established religious and philosophical connotations that they suggested. Santoka was to find expression for his own state of being in the growth and decay of nature, but he was far too involved in revealing his own individual soul to find universal truths in the scattering of blossoms or the falling of autumn leaves. His religious deference to nature is of a more undefinable, emotional quality, a sense of awe before the miracle and profundity of life:

> Sacredness,
> a pure white chicken.

> What is sown will grow,
> I tread firmly the calmness of the earth.

> Receiving the deep autumn waters,
> I return.

> A voice stirring above the wind,
> 'Praise to Kannon.'

The first of the above poems was written when Santoka spotted a chicken perched on the roof of a temple he was visiting. He finds that the strikingly white living animal is able to convey a deeper impression of sacredness than the temple and the religious images within it. The next two poems express a sense of joyful thanksgiving on experiencing the bountifulness of nature. Nature is a religious altar, offering worshipers myriad rewards. And in the final poem he hears a voice real or imagined, or perhaps his own, that seems to harmonize with the wind in an endless, amorphous chant to Kannon, the Goddess of Mercy.

But much more than the reverence for nature's mystery and profundity, it was the sense of serenity and in some instances joy in the simplicity and unequivocality of nature that sustained Santoka on his journeys and provided the source of his poetry. He approached nature in literally an almost naked state, carrying his alms bowl and one pair of chopsticks as his luggage. In his view, to protect himself from nature was a sacrilege against his self-proclaimed discipline of simplicity. He even went to the extent of refusing to wear false teeth after all his teeth had fallen out and, except in the most dire cases, declining the use of mosquito nets, both needless artifices for a man who has opened himself up to nature in its entirety. Santoka was rewarded while this tenacity of spirit lasted with a view of life and nature at its most basic and unadorned, and this view at times filled him with a joy as profound as his grief could be limitless.

> With a buoyant heart,
> I taste the water.

Santoka's love of cold, clear water was almost as great as his taste for *sake*. In this small but spirited verse the poet's heart surges with pleasure as the cool liquid circulates through his hot and tired body. He does not drink the water but tastes it, absorbs it into himself. Other poems with water as the theme include:

> The going gets late,
> how sweet this water tastes.

> Winter-withered mountain,
> all the water one can drink.

> Together with the sound of water
> I have descended to the village.

Santoka's poems expressing his real joy in the simplicity of his life on the road or at the hermitage, and the unambiguity with which the natural scene complements this joy, are among his very best. To give a small sampling:

> Ah, the sparrow dances,
> Ah, the dandelions scatter.

> Finally it has blossomed,
> the flower is white.

> Stretching out my legs
> to take in the day's last rays of sun.

> Evening sky,
> the silhouettes of farmers in their fields
>   deepen.

> Not a wisp of cloud,
> I take off my bamboo hat.

> The wind through the pines is cool,
> man eats,
> horse eats.

> As I walk, buttercups,
> as I sit, buttercups.

> The ground moist with morning dew,
> I go where I want.

> Suddenly,
> something grazing past in the wind.

> The hotness, sweetness of potato gruel,
> autumn has come.

> The sun's rays
> lingering on withered leaves—
> the color is sad.

Santoka tells of one small town in Kagoshima where the police would not allow him to beg. Buying a newspaper, he spent the day lounging in the sun, then checked into a cheap lodging house where he was quartered with a Korean peddler, a traveling masseur, and a stone polisher. After exchanging stories with these other men of the road, he wrote letters for both the illiterate masseur and polisher, and then when all had gone to bed he took out his diary and wrote of his day:

> At last they are all asleep,
> ah, it's a good, moonlight night.

He found particular attraction in the fertility and tenacity of weeds, writing in his diary, 'My existence is not different from that of wild grass. But in that alone I find satisfaction.' The following poem expresses the wild beauty and vitality of weeds:

> In its natural state
> as a weed,
> it shoots forth its buds.

Just as Santoka sang of the white chicken perched on the temple roof, he found in the whiteness and plainness of his main and often only food, rice, a constant source of celebration:

> The sweetness of rice,
> a blue, blue sky.

> The fallen leaves are warm,
> from the rice I chew a glow.

> Light fills the air,
> the rice is shining white.

> The sweet taste of rice,
> alone, chewing.

Crickets,
only enough rice for tomorrow.

A moonlight night,
polishing the only rice I have.

Another joy was a hot morning bath. Santoka loved the hot springs of Kyushu, and when he had the money he spent long days luxuriating at the baths:

Soaking in the quietness
of a brimming morning bath.

The pleasantness of a morning bath,
quietly waiting my turn in the steam.

My stark naked body,
revealed to the sun.

Even in the last year of his life, with his physical energy sorely reduced and in a deepened state of depression over his incorrigible lifestyle, he was able to write verses full of wonder at the beauty and simplicity of nature:

A persimmon resting on my palm,
fascinatingly red.

If Santoka denied an afterlife, he was still a firm believer in the perpetual present, and nature, always changing but always the same, was the manifestation of this tenseless world. In the preface to his poetry collection *Sanko Suiko* ('Mountain Travels, Water Travels'), he writes the poem,

When in the mountains,
I will watch the mountains,
On rainy days
I will listen to the rain,
Spring, summer, fall, winter,
Morning is good,
Evening is good.

This sense of the world of today, the reduction of life to a single object and a single moment, is also seen in these poems:

Today,
I pick butterbur flowers,
I eat butterbur flowers.

Today,
the roadside dandelions of this day
have blossomed.

Endlessness

Yet if there were moments of joy in his travels, there were also times when Santoka felt the endlessness of his trek and the vastness of the natural world draining his energy and weighing him down. The spatial and temporal infinitude of nature made him painfully aware of the insignificance and the futility of his attempt to confront nature in its rawest form. He wrote,

In the midst of life and death,
a steady fall of snow.

The poem could be translated more prosaically, 'The snow of life and death falls steadily'—a rather trite statement of the continuity of nature. A similar poem by the poetry master Saigyo offers a deeper insight into what Santoka was saying:

Though I know
this cicada-shell body
to be a trifling thing,
this day of falling snow
is bitter cold.

Like Santoka, Saigyo was continually struggling with the contradiction between his desire to come to grips with mortality and his attachment to life. And in both of their poems, they have come to the disheartening realization that their inner struggle is of so little significance in the face of the reality of a chilling winter snowfall. In Santoka this despair in the insignificance of his existence is often expressed in terms of the immeasurable vastness of the world in which he travels:

Waking from an afternoon nap,
whichever way I look,
mountains.

The shrikes cry,
there is no place to abandon myself.

My home is far away,
the sprout of a tree.

Picking up a stick in the wind,
I walk on.

The sound of water,
from afar, from near,
leading me on.

The crow crying,
the crow flying,
no place to settle down.

Sweltering heat,
train tracks straight into the distance.

A crow flies off,
I will cross the water.

Unending rain,
mountains,
more mountains,
unknown mountains.

My spirit is exhausted,
the mountains, the sea,
are too beautiful.

Filled with shades of night
the water flows on,
autumn lodgings.

The endless journey, and the insignificance Santoka attached to man-built monuments, are well expressed in the poem that he wrote after completing a long journey to the famous ancient city of Hiraizumi in the northern area of Tohoku in 1936. It was the farthest north Santoka ever traveled.

> I have come this far,
> a drink of water, and I am gone.

Several visits to the coast of the rough Japan Sea evoked similar sentiments of the vastness of nature:

> My heart empty,
> the surge and ebb
> of pounding waves.

> The sound of waves is unending,
> home is so far away.

> Thrusting my legs into the wild sea,
> a journey stretching into the past,
> into the future.

> Now I am here,
> the blueness of the sea is infinite.

There is also the short but difficult poem:

> I ford across
> a bone-dry stream.

One can only guess at the emotions of the poet as he wrote this last poem, but from his emphasis on 'bone-dry' (*karekitta*), it may well be imagined that Santoka here too felt the vitality of his journey seeping away, that the lifeless riverbed had again reminded him of the ultimate emptiness and terrible loneliness of his unending path.

LONELINESS

If a sense of insignificance before nature was the philosophical burden that Santoka had to carry, loneliness and a sense of isolation were the more visceral feelings he experienced in his life on the road. By temperament he was a man who loved good companionship, and his forays into unfamiliar regions where he knew no one were conscious acts of self-discipline and penitence for his frequent falls from grace. This forced separation heightened his awareness of the isolation and loneliness of being in a place where he suddenly had no one to talk to and fall back on. The intensity of this feeling is shown in some of his poems:

> A crow caws,
> I too am alone.

> Falling snow,
> alone, alone I go.

> Watching the moon begin to sink,
> I alone.

> On a straight road,
> so lonely.

> In the midst alone,
> always alone,
> the grass is bursting into bloom.

One can hardly doubt the depth of the poet's emotions in these poems, but they are perhaps too direct, too filled with pathos, to escape the charge of being uncomfortably sentimental. Santoka is better able to convey the feeling without the theatrical pose in his poems in which he uses a more classical approach of Japanese literature, such as expressing his loneliness in the sadness of autumn:

> Without a home of my own,
> the autumn becomes ever deeper.

> The road has disappeared,
> the leaves whisper of their fall.

> The snap of dried twigs,
> not a thought in my head.

> A single stream of water
> drawn down upon a solitary house,
> shades of autumn.

> The tips of reeds,
> walking on
> with the path of the wind.

There is also this moving poem written on returning to his empty hermitage after a long journey:

> Penetrating quiet,
> dust on the desk.

Various other poems aptly express this mood:

> The winter night that has left me here,
> in such a way.

> A whole day without a word,
> the sound of waves.

> Someone speaks
> in a voice like my father,
> this trip is filled with sadness.

> Walking through the autumn rains,
> a village where no one will let me in.

> Iron begging bowl,
> receiving a falling leaf.

> Into my metal bowl too,
> hail.

This last poem, one of Santoka's best known, was written on a cold January day as he walked companionless along a deserted seacoast. It calls on the reader to imagine both the scene and the sound of hail hitting the metal alms bowl. The dull metallic ring of the bowl shivers through the body of the solitary figure, increasing his coldness and sense of isolation.

Mention must also be made of Santoka's deep attraction to *shigure,* the long cold drizzles of autumn, as an image to describe the loneliness of the long journey, both in its figurative and literal sense. This subject is taken up in an essay on Santoka by the literary scholar Maruya Saiichi, and I will here present only a few of Santoka's poems on the subject:

> Autumn rains,
> walking deep into the mountains
> of the autumn rains.

> That sound—
> autumn rain?

> From morning an autumn drizzle,
> the beauty of persimmon leaves.

> Soaked in an autumn rain,
> the friend I await has come.

> A steady autumn drizzle,
> one road, straight ahead.

> A temple among the pines,
> the autumn rains have begun,
> here I will stay.

BEGGING AND SELF-RIDICULE

Another factor that made his journeys long and lonely was a strong inner resistance to the act of mendicancy which he demanded of himself as a monk on pilgrimage. He disliked begging, disliked staying in cheap, crowded, and noisy inns, and, in the tradition of many of the literary recluses of Japan, preferred when possible to accept the shelter provided by his friends and benefactors. He was also aware of the hypocrisy of justifying his purposeless wandering by the donning of a monk's garb, and he often thought himself nothing more than a dissipated beggar disguised as a holy man seeking enlightenment. His friends were in general agreement that Santoka was basically a poet and not a priest, and that his priest's robes were of secondary importance in his life and work, but Santoka had to convince himself that his pilgrimages were not in fact compounding the sinful nature of his life.

He justified his begging by telling himself that he did not presume to give sermons but did awaken the spirit of Buddha in people by receiving alms. He also lived by a fairly strict rule that when he had received enough for his daily living needs he would stop begging and return to writing or walking. There were times when he found satisfaction or at least resignation in this life, as in these poems:

> Tossed to me in offering,
> the shine of a single coin.

> No more houses where I can beg,
> clouds over the mountains.

More often he chose to see himself as a humorous and good-natured, if somewhat ridiculous, oddity. In a poem titled **'Self-image',** he describes himself as,

> Dressed in rags,
> bulging in padded winter-clothes,
> a face of innocent happiness.

He tried to put himself over as a foolish, harmless old man, not to be held responsible for his eccentricities:

> The heaviness of baggage
> I cannot bring myself to throw away,
> on my front, on my back.

In another poem, written in 1931 as he started out on another trip, he laughs at himself rather ruefully in a poem titled **'Self-ridicule'**:

> A receding figure,
> soaked in the autumn rains?

His complete lack of possessions, his primitive way of living, are laughed at in the poems about his teeth, of which only three remained by the time he was fifty:

> No money,
> no possessions,
> no teeth,
> alone.

> Something missing,
> another tooth fallen out,
> I heave it into the evening darkness.

But there were also times when humor would not sustain the weight of his self-abuse, as in the autumn of 1930 when, after drinking up his gains, he cried, 'It is truly shameful that the gifts I receive are converted directly into alcohol and nicotine.' It was at these times that his chanting and begging took on a more distracted, guilt-ridden quality.

> Walking into the wind,
> heaping abuse upon myself.

> Taking in the scorching sun,
> begging as I go.

> I go on soaked by the rain
> of my selfish, willful journey.

On his way back from a trip to northern Japan in 1936 he stopped wearing his priest's robes in penitence for indulging in an eating and drinking binge that he could not pay for and again having to be bailed out by a friend. In the last year of his life when his fortunes were at an ebb, he once more stripped off his robes and for a short time sought alms not as a priest but as a mere beggar:

> Once again the beggar that I was,
> a single towel.

As his life drew toward its end and he realized that he was as far away from any kind of enlightenment as ever, Santoka began to lose confidence in his begging, his efforts became half-hearted, and alms were often not enough for food and lodging. His despondency was reflected in a letter he wrote to a young poet who wanted to emulate his lifestyle, for he sharply rebuked the man for even thinking about leading such an irresponsible life.

In a short poem titled **'Regrets',** written in his later years, he asks himself:

> My bamboo hat—
> has it too begun to leak?

The wide-brimmed *kasa* that Santoka had worn for so many years had finally begun to rot and fall apart, and he rather wistfully ridicules his own tattered, worn-out body as it too gradually begins to waste away.

SECLUSION

In 1932, at the age of fifty, Santoka found temporary respite from his long journey when he began to live in the hermitage that his friends had renovated for him in the village of Ogori. He named it 'Gochuan', 'Cottage in that Midst', from a Kannon sutra which contains the phrase, 'In that midst a solitary man wrote, and this he sang.'

A friend who taught at a local agricultural high school mobilized his students to rebuild the abandoned cottage, and Santoka's closest friend, fellow *Soun* poet Kimura Rokuhei of Kumamoto, was put in charge of a modest fund to provide him with a periodic allowance. The money was entrusted to Rokuhei to prevent Santoka from spending it all in one drunken splurge. The first days at Gochuan were some of the most tranquil Santoka was ever to experience. After settling down there, he wrote:

> Finally I have returned to the world of existence; I feel that I can actually speak of 'returning home, meditating in peace'. For a long time I have wandered. Not only my body but my heart has wandered. I have suffered the fact that I must live. I have found anguish in the necessity of existence. Thus finally I have been able to find peace with existence, and through that I have discovered myself.

He busied himself in writing, keeping his few belongings in spotless order, visiting with neighbors, and receiving old friends and new acquaintances eager to listen to his endless stories and share with him a bottle of *sake*. For the first time he cultivated his own garden and received great satisfaction from watching the products of his labors:

> Over a red sunrise
> a rain is falling,
> I will plant radishes.

His contentment in this period is reflected in poems that show a genuine sense of harmony and optimism in life:

> The spider weaves his web,
> I affirm myself.

> This morning the sound of water,
> a feeling that good news will come.

> To live life in tranquility,
> a wren.

> Opening the window,
> a window full of spring.

> Every day naked,
> butterflies,
> dragonflies.

> Dusk,
> polishing a placid kettle.

> Receiving,
> contented,
> alone, I lay down my chopsticks.

Yet just as on the road Santoka was constantly battling the loneliness of being in a strange land, so also in his cottage life there was the oppressing loneliness of silence and long hours of inactivity. Loneliness is a theme with a long history in Japanese literature, but for Santoka it was something of a different dimension from the concept of courtiers such as Murasaki Shikibu or Ki no Tsurayuki, who found in it social refinement, or the *renga* masters Sogi and Shinkei, who made it into a standard of beauty. Loneliness continually gnawed at Santoka, depriving him of the peace of mind he so desperately sought and driving him to the bouts of self-oblivion and mindless wandering he so wanted to avoid.

Santoka tried to overcome the pain of loneliness at Gochuan. He urged himself to surrender to the very essence of solitude. 'We must bear the loneliness of isolation. We must overcome our own coldness. We must dig down into there and from that bottom lick the sweet taste of life oozing out.' He tried to discipline himself to accept solitude coolly, without emotion: 'Do not write in tears. The poem written in tears is both cowardly and superficial. Until the tears have completely dried, sit in silence, alone, and think.'

For the next few years he spent much of his time at the cottage, often in contentment and often in nearly unbearable restlessness, but always conscious of being alone.

> Snow settles upon snow,
> I am in the midst of quietude.

> Waking, the snow is falling,
> it is not lonely,
> and yet. . . .

> A crow on a withered tree,
> The New Year has come and gone.

> One flower on the desk,
> slowly opening.

> One day the longing for a friend,
> buds of trees, buds of grass.

> Always alone,
> a red dragonfly.

Feelings of joy,
and feelings of sadness,
thickly growing grass.

When I calm my heart,
the sound of water.

Today, too, all day,
no one has come,
fireflies.

This last poem is somewhat reminiscent of Saigyo's verse,

Deep in the mountains,
in this retreat
where no man comes,
the only sound
is the clamor of monkeys.

While dragonflies and monkeys are quite different as an
artistic image, both poets see or hear another living creature in their isolated world, and the fact that these living
things are beyond the realm of human communication
makes the solitude of the poet even more poignant.

No one to talk to,
I eat my dinner under the mosquito net.

The shadows subdued,
deep at night
I am eating.

At the tobacco shop
no cigarettes,
a cold rain falls.

No one is here,
the fallen leaves I swept away,
deep in the day.

Despite his sincere efforts to settle down to a peaceful and
moderate life, Santoka would still at times be found passed
out along the road after frantic drinking bouts. He occasionally received funds from his benefactors, but his drinking
kept him destitute most of the time. Leading a sedentary life,
he was unable to consume his excess energy and frustration,
and he came to feel more and more closed in:

Closed in, by myself,
an insect comes rapping
against the sliding door.

As time went by his need to travel again began to stir
him, and although he was not to abandon Gochuan for
good until 1938, his interests had long before started to
wander, and the cottage gradually fell into a state of dis-
repair.

The wall is crumbling,
vines creeping in.

FRIENDSHIP

I have nothing at all, nothing except friends. To
have such good friends is a source of pride for me.

It is yet another of the ironies of Santoka's life that the
man who put such faith in self-discovery was ultimately
to find his only real source of pleasure in the companionship of others. He asked much of his friends and at times
caused them a great deal of trouble, but it is a tribute
both to the irresistible warmth of his character and the
Japanese tolerance toward the failings of old friends that
they continued to greet him with genuine pleasure when
he appeared at their houses.

Santoka first visited Kimura Rokuhei, his longtime bene-
factor, in Kumamoto in 1918. After an evening of con-
vivial conversation Santoka left for home, but his good
spirits led him into a *sake* shop for one more round. The
next morning Rokuhei received a visit from the police,
who told him that Santoka had landed in jail for getting
drunk and being unable to pay his bill, and that he had
told the police to ask his new friend to bail him out.

Rokuhei did so, as he was to do many times during their
long friendship. It is possible, in fact, that Santoka might
have been a greater poet, of the caliber of Saigyo or
Basho, had he not been so well taken care of by his
friends. Santoka would feel deeply repentant after causing his friends such trouble, but would soon be calling on
them again, ready for yet another round. Some of his
friends' wives were less than overjoyed to see the be-
draggled monk turn up again for another disrupting three
or four days of eating and drinking, but few could be-
grudge the man who accepted their hospitality with such
sincere and ingenuous gratitude.

It would not be difficult to draw parallels between the
broken home life of the boy Shoichi and of the man
Santoka, who almost willfully formed relationships of
dependence in his friendships, but it is perhaps worthwhile emphasizing the deep craving Santoka had for
friendship and the real joy he derived from it.

People's compassion
touches my heart,
I stroke the warm brazier.

The quilt is long,
the night too is long,
I have been given this place to sleep.

A well-stuffed quilt,
dreams of home.

A grasped hand,
chaps.

[At the bath]
Naked,
talk jumps back and forth.

The sound of wind chimes,
at the time when you should come.

As the grass starts to stir,
for some reason I wait for a friend to come.

When the clouds of dusk are so beautiful,
I yearn for a friend.

The sound of voices approaching,
buds of trees brightly bearing.

I have nothing particular to wait for. . . .
In the fall of evening
the cry of cicada.

This last poem is similar to one written by the great *Shinkokinshu* poetess Shikishi Naishinno:

The fall paulownia leaves
have even now
made passage difficult,
though by no means
is there someone I would wait for.

Just as friendship was his greatest joy, parting was for Santoka the hardest of all acts. He tried to make farewells as painless as possible by exchanging quick, light goodbyes and then briskly setting out down the road. One poet acquaintance tells of the first time Santoka invaded his home, when the two drank and talked and slept together for three days; then at the time of parting, the monk murmured a word of thanks, and, contrary to Japanese custom, marched off down the road without a glance back at his host and new friend.

Departing, each on our separate ways,
I turn my face to the sun.

But if Santoka tried to make his partings as unemotional as possible, both his partings in life and by death left a deep impression on him.

Face to face we smile,
we who will never meet again.

So easily it darkens
in the reluctance of our parting,
a ten-day moon.

The road of our parting
runs straight ahead.

Drifting off from the water,
the lamp of the girl
dances in the dark.

Perhaps we will not meet again,
a blur of tree sprouts.

Since we parted,
every day the snow has fallen.

Both the snow on a distant mountain
and a friend who has gone away.

My cough won't stop,
no hand to beat my back.

Of course, the most difficult parting of all was that of death, not only because of the personal loss involved but also because the death of another made even more acute Santoka's sense of guilt in not fulfilling his obligations to the living and his despair over his inability to achieve a quick and graceful death.

The peach tree has begun to bear fruit,
you have already died.

With a tomato in my palm,
in front of Buddha,
in front of my father,
in front of my mother.

No trace left of the house of my birth,
fireflies.

SAKE

If there was only one thing that remained constant throughout Santoka's chaotic life, it was his weakness for *sake*. *Sake* was for him both an elixir and the source of his destruction; despite his periodic feeble attempts at abstinence, it played, as Santoka well realized, an integral role in determining the course of his life. His friends and acquaintances generally agree that Santoka was a confirmed alcoholic, and it would be difficult to find fault with that diagnosis. His drinking was certainly to some extent moderated by his constant lack of funds, but when he was treated by friends, he drank with a relish and abandon that filled people with amazement and consternation. That drink was another form of escape, a mental pilgrimage not essentially different in purpose from his constant urge to wander, is undeniable. *Sake* released him briefly from his unhappy childhood, his inability to take care of his family, and his guilt over his dissipated course of life.

His poetry mentor Seisensui said that as the years went by Santoka was no longer able to distinguish between the worlds of drunkenness and sobriety, that it was only through drinking that he was able to attain some level of sobriety. While Seisensui's theory may appear somewhat oversimplified, it seems to be true that when Santoka drank he enjoyed those few delicious moments in which the mental state which he had been seeking through Zen and through begging—a calm acceptance of life, a feeling of security, and confidence in himself and his relationships with people—were suddenly opened up to him. According to Santoka, 'Dreams are the *sake* of the consoled spirit. *Sake* is the dream of the anguished flesh.' The sense of transcendence brought on by *sake* may indeed be an illusion, a dream that makes the attainment of real enlightenment even more difficult, yet for Santoka this temporary respite from the anguished flesh was irresistible.

In his diary Santoka constantly lectures himself on how to drink in order to enjoy its many virtues without suffering from its many evils. For example, 'There is no crime in intoxicating *sake*. There is poison in *sake* that does not intoxicate.'

Also,

> The *sake* we drink is *sake* drunk for its taste; it is
> *sake* that we should sip, *sake* drunk with a smile.
> Do not drink in tears—drink laughing. Do not drink
> alone—drink shoulder to shoulder. Do not drink
> *sake* that, no matter how much you drink, cannot
> make you drunk; drink *sake* that intoxicates while
> the taste is still on the lips. Do not drink bitter
> *sake*—drink sweet *sake*.

> The man who cannot spontaneously become
> intoxicated must finally destroy himself.

> *Sake* ought not to be drunk in times of discontent.
> Drinking when we are not discontented, we can
> penetrate to the true taste of the liquid.

There were times when Santoka expressed the pure delight of drinking, as in his famous poem:

> A soft whirling drunk,
> a scattering of leaves.

The poem revolves around the adverb *horohoro,* which signifies a mellow, blissful, sentimentally happy state of drunkenness, and also describes the fluttering and dancing of falling leaves. The drunken poet is like the leaves—floating, weightless, carried aimlessly to and fro by the cool autumn breeze.

He also wrote about the mental and physical pain his drinking brought him:

> The pitifulness
> of not being able to get drunk,
> the crickets cry.

> Waking from drunkenness,
> the wind blows mournfully through.

In September 1940, just one month before his death, his body weakened but his thirst unabated, he wrote:

> No more *sake,*
> staring fixedly
> at the moon.

One of the best illustrations of Santoka's powerful craving for drink is an incident which took place when he came down with acute pneumonia while traveling in the snowy Japan Alps in early 1934. The hospital which took him in refused to accept his claim that alcohol was his 'best medicine', so the thirsty Santoka was obliged to sneak out in his hospital slippers to down a few hot *sake* drinks at a nearby restaurant. Feeling thoroughly recovered after this refreshment, he boarded the next train and began the long journey back to Gochuan.

WRITING

Santoka tends to leave the impression of a talented but undisciplined poet who did little more than jot down his tiny vignettes of life as they appeared before his eyes. He wrote thousands of poems and to a certain extent forces upon the reader the task of sifting through them to decide which are the 'better' works of art. Santoka admits in his diary, 'Rather than poetry produced skillfully, I desire the poem unskillfully born.' Just as he tried to reduce his way of life to its simplest elements, he believed that the good poem was one that arose out of the most pure and direct response to a scene or personal experience. He was an incorrigible romantic, who dreamed of taking all the artifice out of art and returning it to its 'natural' state. 'I want to make my poems sing like the floating clouds, like the flow of water, like a small bird, like the dancing leaves.'

While prizing the spontaneity of the poetic sentiment, however, Santoka also went to surprisingly great pains to polish the final poetic form. He worked laboriously on his poems, rewriting, discussing them with friends, and corresponding with other poets for advice. Like many haiku and short-verse poets in Japan, he was capable of long debates and considerable personal discomposure over a single grammatical particle or verb tense. The tremendous energy Santoka spent in reviewing and rephrasing his work is very much in the tradition of Japan's recluse writers, those poets and essayists such as Kamo no Chomei and Yoshida Kenko, who to various degrees withdrew from society and set about trying to communicate their views to that society in as fluent a manner as possible. This need for the 'detached' writer to express himself has its elements of irony, especially for such writers as Saigyo and Santoka who were making very conscious attempts to overcome their self-centered personalities. But writing, especially poetry, can also be a means of disciplining the mind and calming the raging spirit, and it was in this respect that Santoka, and Saigyo, found in poetry a possible road to salvation.

In preparing his poetry collections Santoka showed a meticulousness completely out of harmony with his ordinary drunken, unregulated life. In his collection *Sanko Suiko* he went through two thousand of his poems to select a mere 140 which he considered good enough to include in the work. As an example of his selection process we have his comments at the end of his collection titled *Kaki no ha (Persimmon Leaf):*

> When I walk,
> fruit-bearing grasses,
> when I sit,
> fruit-bearing grasses.

> When I walk,
> cuckoos,
> when I run,
> cuckoos.

> One or the other verse had to be discarded, but it
> was difficult for me to discard either of them. I
> traveled through the Tohoku region, and in constant
> surprise at the large number of cuckoos I listened
> to their song with great interest. And on the
> Shinano road for the first time in my life, I even
> caught a glimpse of the bird.

After all,
to be alone is good,
wild grasses.

After all,
to be alone is sad,
dried-up grasses.

I am for ever possessed by sentimental feelings of self-love, but considering that such feelings are not allowed in an individual collection of verse I arbitrarily chose one for the book. I believe that readers will be able to understand my frame of mind.

In both cases he chose the second poem for the collection, not so much on its own merits as an independent poem but on the degree of his personal involvement with its sentiments.

While living in his new hermitage in Shikoku during the last year of his life, Santoka wrote about the importance of poetry in his life:

I am pressed every day to meet the needs of life. I spent yesterday and today concerned about whether I eat or not. Probably tomorrow, too—no, it will be so until the day I die.

But every day, every night, I am writing. Even though I neither drink nor eat, I never neglect writing. In other words, though my stomach is empty I am able to write. Like the flow of water my poetic spirit bubbles up and spills over. Living for me is the writing of poetry. Poetry is my life.

It was the one great consolation of his life that when all else failed him, when he had hardly enough to eat, his physical strength broken, and his inability to come to terms with life still plaguing him, he could still obtain much personal gratification through his poetry.

DEATH

It may be appropriate to conclude this study of Santoka's life and work by examining his preoccupation and fascination with death. Death held great attraction for him as the final solution to his search for harmony with existence. Yet his several suicide attempts were all abortive, because his disaffection with life was tempered by his fear of what he believed was the finality of death.

In his study on Santoka, Kaneko Tota observes that Santoka's life was one of 'stoic decadence', resulting from his lack of value in life and lack of initiative toward death. Santoka spent his life in endless dissection of his own character, searching for 'realities' and inner truths that served little purpose except to further castigate his own restless soul.

After 1924, when he failed in his bid to get run over by a train and then entered the priesthood, Santoka seemed to have decided that the end of his life was not to be achieved by a positive act, and thus in a passive sense he came to accept the fact that his life was for the time being to continue. Like a man standing on a bridge trying to summon up the courage to jump into a river, he finally realized that it was not in him to make the leap, but that the energy he had consumed in the effort had made it impossible for him to return to the safety of dry land. In 1934 he wrote in the postscript to his collection *Sanko Suiko*:

I am now prepared to try to start out again, to re-acknowledge the 'world of existence'. I am reluctant to say whether that is good or bad; I only know that it comes neither from so-called resignation nor from what could be termed enlightenment.

What it did mean was that Santoka had tentatively accepted life but that at least indirectly, through extending his physical and mental powers of endurance to their limits, he would continue to keep his options open for leaving this world. He would not personally take the final plunge, but would lay himself bare before the forces of life and death in the hope that death would have no difficulty in snatching him away.

His attraction to death, and the loneliness of his search for death, is a frequent theme in his poems.

Again the autumn rains?
Death has yet to come.

In the face of death,
a cool wind.

Even the ring of the wind chimes,
the approach of death.

The sound of the waves
fading out, flowing in,
my life draws to its close.

The rain falls,
the sun shines,
I search for a place to die.

If this were to be my deathplace. . . .
The grass grows deeper and deeper.

A graveyard basks in warmth,
the poor children.

The quietness of death,
clear-skied, leafless tree.

The sound of raindrops,
I have become old.

As he became old, his unsettled way of life came to tax his physical strength more and more. The cold autumn rain penetrated his tired body and for perhaps the first time made death a reality to be directly confronted. But death still eluded him. On his last pilgrimage through Shikoku in 1939, he wrote:

I cannot seem to die,
on the other bank a red flower blooms.

The red flower (*higanbana*) is associated with *higan,* literally 'the other bank', the equinoctial week in which Buddhists pray for the souls of the dead, and Santoka sees there the beautiful flower which is still beyond his grasp.

He wanted above all to accept death as easily as the flowers and the insects followed their natural course of growth and decay.

This plant which at any time may die,
blossoms and bears fruit.

I plant a tree seed,
the fruit will someday die.

Peacefully, possessing the power of death,
grass is withering.

This is the dance of the butterflies
before death.

The Japanese for 'nirvana' is *jakumetsu,* the two Chinese characters of which translate as 'solitude' and 'annihilation'. In an analogous way, Santoka defined salvation as the destruction of an overactive ego that had isolated him from the natural order. He sought to merge his spirit with the universal process of the flower or the butterfly, for which to wither or to die was a natural act of no intrinsic difference from to blossom or to dance.

Yet in the end his efforts at self-annihilation did little more than accentuate the tenacity of his ego and his great distance from salvation. After struggling with his soul for year after year, he died in October 1940, no more settled, no more sober, and no more at peace with himself than when he began his odyssey of purification some fourteen years earlier.

That Santoka suffered is undeniable. That this suffering was motivated more by a masochistic cycle of dissipation and punishing acts of repentance than by the quest of some noble ideal is equally true. But Santoka also had a wonderful capacity to celebrate the joys and sorrows of life, the pure mountain waters, the fragile spring blossoms, the heights and depths of *sake,* the smell and taste of cooked rice, and most of all the warmth of human friendship. As a testimony to these emotions, his poetry is certainly worthy of attention.

John Stevens (essay date 1980)

SOURCE: In an introduction to *Mountain Tasting: Zen Haiku by Santoka Taneda,* translated by John Stevens, Weatherhill, 1980, pp. 9-29.

[*In the following excerpt, Stevens discusses Santoka's poetry, life, and worldview.*]

Recently, a remarkable interest in the life and poetry of the mendicant Zen priest Santoka Taneda (1882-1940) has developed in Japan. Collections of Santoka's haiku and accounts of his life are being published regularly. At present, more books on Santoka are available than perhaps on any other Japanese poet, ancient or modern. In addition, he is considered to be a great Zen master much like Ikkyu, Hakuin, and Ryokan. How is it that such an eccentric, drink-loving haiku poet came to be so highly regarded?

From a literary standpoint, Santoka's poems are generally admired for their unadorned style, representative of the "new haiku movement," but this does not explain his great popularity with all types of people, not only poets and scholars. Whatever the literary merit of his work, far more important are the special Zen qualities of simplicity (*wabi*), solitude (*sabi*), and impermanence (*mujo*) conveyed in a modern setting by his haiku. Poetry has often been nothing more than a pastime for many in China and Japan, so that portrayals of "poverty," "solitude," "meditation," and so on were mere conventions. In Santoka's case, however, such themes were absolute; no one was poorer, more alone, or more anguished. Hence his poems are alive, cutting to the marrow of existence. There is no dichotomy between poetry and poet, life and emotion.

Santoka's life embodies the Zen spirit in three ways. First, since his life and poetry were one, he represents the ideal of "no duplicity." In any art or discipline it is essential to unify thought, speech, and action. Second, he did not mimic anyone else. This is rare in any society. In Japan, the life of a wandering poet is considered the most impermanent, irregular, and individualistic of all occupations. It is a life of freedom from everything: material possessions, mental concepts, social norms. Third is Santoka's simplicity of expression. In his verses there is nothing extra, no pretense, no artificiality. They can be understood at once without analysis. Sharp and direct, Santoka's haiku epitomize Zen writing: pure experience, free of intellectual coloring.

Santoka's appeal is not limited to Japan. Haiku and Zen practice are established throughout the world. As a man of the twentieth century, Santoka is close to us in thought and temperament. Fortunately, his haiku lose little in translation, so with the publication of this collection of his poems, people of all countries will now be able to share in his unique "journey into the depths of the human heart."

SANTOKA'S LIFE

Shoichi Taneda—now better known as Santoka—was born in the village of Sabare in the Hofu district of Yamaguchi Prefecture on December 3, 1882. His father, a large and impressive figure, was a landowner and active in local politics but not very good at running his business or personal affairs. Shoichi was the second child, first boy, and one more sister and two more brothers were born in the next few years.

Shoichi was good at his studies and displayed an interest in literature as early as elementary school. Unfortunately, his father was a dissolute womanizer who carried on with several mistresses at a time. When he wasn't playing with the ladies he was politicking, so he was rarely home. While he was vacationing in the mountains with one of his mistresses, his wife committed suicide by throwing herself into a well on the family property. She was thirty-three years old. Shoichi, just eleven at the time, never completely recovered from the shock of seeing his mother's lifeless body being lifted from the well, and this tragic event affected him throughout his life. Afterwards he was raised by his grandmother.

In 1896 he entered middle school and began to write traditional-style haiku. In 1902 he enrolled in the literature department of Waseda University in Tokyo. There, following the custom, he took a pen name; from then on he called himself Santoka ("Burning Mountain Peak"). He began to drink heavily, suffered a nervous breakdown, and was unable to complete the first-year requirements. In addition, his father was in financial straits and could no longer afford the tuition, so Santoka had to return home.

Santoka arrived in his home town in July 1904 at the beginning of the Russo-Japanese War. His father sold off some of the family land and purchased a sakè brewery that he opened with Santoka in 1907. Two years later, at the insistence of his father, who thought a wife might help cut down Santoka's drinking, an arranged marriage took place with Sakino Sato, a pretty girl from a neighboring village. However, the union was troubled right from the beginning, and Santoka never adjusted to married life. The following year their only child, Ken, was born.

In 1911 Santoka came under the influence of Seisensui Ogiwara (1884-1976), the founder of the *jiyuritsu*, or free-style, school of haiku. Following the death of Shiki (1867-1903), who had revitalized and revolutionized the world of haiku, there were two main streams in the haiku world: one working in a more or less traditional form using modern themes, and the other, the *shinkeiko*, or new-development, movement, which abandoned the standard 5-7-5 syllable pattern and the obligatory use of a word to indicate the season, or *kigo*. In April 1911 Seisensui established the magazine *Soun* to expound the theory that it is necessary for a poet to express what is in his heart in his own language without regard to any fixed form. Seisensui felt that haiku should be an impression of one's inner experiences; individual symbolism is most important. Seisensui stressed *jiyu* (freedom), *jiko* (self), and *shizen* (nature), together with the elements of *chikara* (strength) and *hikari* (brightness), for his new haiku. Seisensui was influenced by European literature, especially Goethe and Schiller, and his poetry was essentially a combination of Japanese sensitivity and Western expressionism. However, it was neither agnostic nor scientific like much of the other new haiku. Haiku is a "way" rather than mere literature or art. Such a highly individu-

alistic and subjective theory was criticized by many traditionalists, but it greatly appealed to Santoka. Beginning in 1913, Santoka became one of the main contributors to *Soun* and the free-style school.

Seven of Santoka's verses were printed in 1913, and the following year Santoka met Seisensui for the first time at a poetry meeting. Santoka was active composing poetry and essays for the next few years and became an editor of *Soun* in 1916. In the meantime, however, the sakè brewery was turning into a disaster. The father continued to run around with women, and the son kept drinking up what little profit they occasionally made. More and more family property was sold off to prop up the brewery. In 1915 the entire stock spoiled, and in April the next year the brewery went bankrupt and the Taneda family lost everything. The father fled one night with one of his mistresses, while Santoka and his family moved to Kumamoto City, where one of his friends offered to help him.

Santoka originally planned to open a secondhand bookstore, but that failed to work out, so his wife took over and started a store specializing in picture frames. Santoka continued his heavy drinking, and the marriage deteriorated. In 1918 his younger brother Jiro committed suicide (his other brother had died in infancy), another shock for the high-strung poet.

Santoka and his wife drifted apart, and in 1919 he decided to go to Tokyo to seek work. His first job was a part-time position with a cement firm. Later he found a temporary position as a clerk in the Hitotsubashi municipal library. Santoka and his wife were legally divorced in 1920. Sakino continued to operate the store and raise their son. The following year Santoka's father died. Santoka was offered a permanent position at the library and he accepted. Unfortunately, he proved no better at this job than at making sakè. He suffered another nervous breakdown and was forced to retire a year and a half after he began. On September 1, 1923, the Great Kanto Earthquake struck Tokyo and destroyed much of the city. Santoka escaped injury, but his boardinghouse was reduced to rubble. He decided to return to Kumamoto, where he helped his former wife with the store.

Near the end of December 1924, Santoka, drunk and apparently intent on committing suicide, stood in the middle of some railroad tracks facing an oncoming train. The train screeched to a halt just in time, and Santoka was pulled out of the way. He was taken to a nearby Zen temple called Hoon-ji. The head priest there, Gian Mochizuki Osho, did not reprimand or question Santoka: he didn't even ask his name. The monk fed Santoka and told him he could stay at the temple as long as he wished.

Santoka had long been interested in Zen. He had attended several lectures of the famous Zen master Kodo Sawaki Roshi in Kumamoto and had spent most of his spare time at the library in Tokyo reading books on Buddhism. Under Gian's direction Santoka sat in Zen meditation, chanted sutras, and worked around the temple. In 1925, at the age of forty-two, Santoka was ordained a Zen priest under the name Koho after a Chinese Zen priest also named Taneda (Chung-t'ien in Chinese pronunciation) who was famous for cultivating a small rice field to raise enough food to support himself. Gian explained that Koho Taneda is one who plows and cultivates the field of his heart.

Santoka's ex-wife Sakino joined the Methodist Church and became an active member soon after Santoka entered the temple. She never remarried, and Santoka continued to visit her and help with the store from time to time for the rest of his life.

After Santoka was ordained, Gian arranged for him to stay at Mitori Kannon-do, a small temple on the outskirts of Kumamoto. Santoka supported himself by begging in the neighborhood, occasionally making longer trips to visit his friends in nearby towns. After a year of living alone in the temple, Santoka decided to make a pilgrimage. His first intention was to train at Eihei-ji, the head temple of the Soto Zen school, but he apparently realized it would be difficult for him as a forty-three-year-old man to practice with a group of priests in their early twenties, most of whom were putting in the required time in order to someday inherit their family temples. Santoka's monastery turned out to be the back roads and mountain paths of the countryside.

In April 1926 he started out on his first pilgrimage. His only possessions were his black priest's robe, his begging bowl, and his *kasa,* a large woven straw hat worn by traveling monks to shield them from the sun and rain. For the next four years Santoka was on a continual journey throughout southern Honshu, Kyushu, and Shikoku. He prayed at innumerable shrines and temples, visited famous sites, met with his friends, and attended poetry meetings. After a lapse of almost five years his poems began to appear in *Soun* again.

In December 1930 he returned to Kumamoto and rented a small room. With the help of some friends who were publishers, he put out three issues of a little magazine called *Sambaku,* named after his boardinghouse. Six months after moving into Sambakukyo he was taken into custody for public drunkenness. (This requires some effort, since Japanese are very tolerant of drunkards.) He stayed at the picture-frame shop for a few months and then began another series of trips. In 1932, his friends found a small cottage for him in the mountain village of Ogori in Yamaguchi Prefecture. Santoka called it Gochu-an after a verse in the *Lotus Sutra.* [This verse refers to one member of a large group telling the others to call on the name of Kanzeon Bosatsu, the goddess of compassion; then all will be saved from calamities.] The cottage was rather dilapidated yet spacious, with three rooms, a well, and a tiny field surrounded by many fruit trees. He posted this sign:

To All Visitors

—If you bring your favorite sweet or sour food with you
—And dance and sing unreservedly with the gentleness of the spring wind and autumn streams
—Without putting on airs or being downhearted, all will share great happiness.

This year also marked the publication of his first collection of haiku, *Hachi no ko (The Begging Bowl),* produced by a friend's small publishing house.

From 1932 to 1938 Santoka divided his time between Gochu-an and traveling. He made trips to Hiroshima, Kobe, Kyoto, and Nagoya. In 1934 he fell ill and returned to his hermitage, Gochu-an. Sick and penniless, he contemplated suicide for a time but abandoned the idea after regaining his health, and began an eight-month journey to northern Honshu, retracing much of the route taken by the famous haiku-poet Basho (1644-94) as described in *Oku no hosomichi* (Narrow Road to the Deep North). During this period he published more issues of his journal *Sambaku,* in addition to putting out four more collections of his poetry: *Somokuto (Grass and Tree Stupa,* 1933), *Sangyo suigyo (Flowing with Mountains and Rivers,* 1935), *Zasso fukei (Weedscapes,* 1936), and *Kaki no ha (Persimmon Leaves,* 1938).

When he was staying at Gochu-an, he often had visitors from all parts of the country. Occasionally poetry meetings were held there. However, in 1938 Gochu-an literally collapsed and Santoka moved to a small hut in Yuda Hot Springs about eight miles away. He remained there a few months, set out on another trip, returned briefly, and then was off again. In December 1939 he settled down in Matsuyama City, Ehime Prefecture, in a little cottage that he named Isso-an, One Blade of Grass Hut.

In 1940 an expanded version of *Somokuto* was published containing selections from his previous works, including a sixth collection entitled *Kokan* (Isolation) and published in 1939. His seventh and final collection, *Karasu* (Crows), was brought out in 1940 a few months after *Somokuto.*

Early in October 1940 a poetry meeting was held at Isso-an. The members of the group gathered at Isso-an, but found Santoka quite intoxicated, so they moved to a nearby member's house. They looked in on Santoka before they left and found him sleeping soundly. Uneasy, the wife of one of his friends went to see Santoka the next morning and discovered that he had departed on his final journey during the early morning hours of October 11, 1940.

THE WANDERING BEGGAR

Santoka is said to have walked more than twenty-eight thousand miles during his travels as a wandering monk. His initial trips, especially the first one to Shikoku to visit the eighty-eight shrines and temples associated with the Buddhist saint Kobo Daishi (Kukai; 774-835), were pilgrimages to pray for the repose of his mother's troubled spirit. Later on, however, many of his trips were made without any particular destination.

> *Sate dochira e iko kaze ga fuku*
> Well, which way should I go?
> The wind blows.

Renouncing the world, drifting here and there, living close to nature, settling now and then in a hermitage, and dying alone is a type of spirituality especially appreciated by the Japanese. Many of their favorite poets, priests, and artists were wanderers—Saigyo, Ippen Shonin, Basho, Sesshu, Enku, to name a few. A life of travel is an abandoning of all that seems permanent or stable; life is reduced to absolute essentials, in the present moment, free of ordinary restrictions or constraints.

Whenever Santoka attempted to settle down, he was unable to do so for more than a few months. He wrote: "Too much contact with people brings conflict, hatred, and attachment. To rid myself of inner conflicts and hatred I must walk."

> *Nigoreru mizu no nagaretsutsu sumu*
> As muddy water flows
> It becomes clear.

Walking through the mountains and along the seacoast accompanied by butterflies and dragonflies, he had a rhythm in his stride that made poetry writing easier—one breath, one step, one verse. In another sense, traveling is a continuous search for our real home, the *furusato* Santoka so often speaks of in his poems.

Santoka was seeking freedom: "To do what I want, and not to do what I don't—this is why I entered such a life." Japan was gearing toward the tragedy of World War II, and the government demanded conformity from all its citizens. Santoka passively resisted by letting his body and mind wander freely.

Once a reporter was interviewing one of Santoka's poet friends when Santoka happened to arrive unannounced. The reporter told Santoka: "If everyone lived like you, society would be in big trouble." Santoka smiled and said: "I'm one of society's warts, it's true. A big black wart on the face is hideous, but a small one is no problem. Sometimes people even have affection for their little blemishes. Please think of me like that."

Like Basho, Santoka noted that "when you travel you truly come to understand human beings, poetry, and nature." Santoka was more extreme than Basho, completely giving himself to *mujo* (impermanence) and *sabi* (solitude). Santoka was a beggar-monk who always traveled alone, flowing with the clouds and water.

He would generally beg for about three hours every day. Stopping to chant in front of a house, more often than not he would be chased away and verbally, and sometimes physically, abused. Usually he had to visit from fifteen to twenty homes (as the depression deepened he had to make thirty or more stops) before he had received enough for a day. As soon as he had received just enough rice and money for one day's food and lodging, he would stop immediately and go to the cheapest inn he could find. He never provided for the next day. "How can you be a beggar if you have extra money?" he asked.

Santoka would gratefully accept whatever was placed in his bowl, regardless of the quantity or quality. "Begging with a heart full of gratitude and respect, I hope to find the world of unlimited life and light. My pilgrimage is into the depths of the human heart. Begging is mutual gratitude and charity, the basis of society." Once an old woman mistakenly put a five-sen coin, a fairly large amount in those days, in Santoka's bowl. Later, after leaving the village, Santoka discovered the error; he walked back to the village, found the old woman, and returned the coin.

However, Santoka's begging was rather different from that of Ryokan Osho (1758-1831), the famous beggar-monk-poet of Echigo, who frequently left his begging bowl by the side of the road while he tossed a ball with the village children, played marbles with the local geishas, or picked flowers. When someone mentioned this contrast to Santoka, he replied: "My passions are too deep to do such a thing. If I don't have a begging bowl, I can't live. Therefore, I never forget my bowl."

It is rather remarkable that Santoka never fell seriously ill during his begging trips. When he did get sick, he recovered in one of two ways. Once when he developed a high fever, he was forced to lie down on the ground. An old woman came over to him and said: "I'll give you an offering if you recite the *Shushogi* (excerpts from the writings of Dogen Zenji) and the *Kannon Sutra*." Santoka staggered to his feet and began chanting. Totally absorbed in the words, he forgot about the old woman, his sickness, and the offering. After finishing forty minutes later, he felt completely recovered from his fever.

Another time in freezing weather he drank a great deal of sakè to keep warm and suddenly became violently ill, suffering from liver trouble. He was taken to a hospital and placed on a strict regimen of bitter medicine and no sakè. Santoka did not care for that, so he escaped from the hospital, went to the nearest shop, drank two cups of sakè, ate some *yudofu* (boiled soybean cake), and was restored.

On his trips Santoka rose at 4:30, bathed, chanted the morning service, ate a tiny breakfast, and started out on a begging trip. When he had received enough, he would either return to the inn or move on to the next place, depending on his mood. He might even stay as long as a month if he liked the area and if the food and lodging were cheap.

Santoka usually received about thirty-five sen from his begging. The charge for a room at an inn ranged from twenty-five to thirty-five sen. Anything extra went for sakè, small amounts of tobacco, or post cards to send to his friends. He often shared his meager take with other beggars. Santoka described one of his favorite places like this: "The food is very cheap here, the salvation of this old hobo. Raw fish is five sen a plate, tempura five sen, *yudofu* two sen. Even a drunkard like me can become a Buddha in this very body for thirty sen." He described his greatest happiness as "one room, one person, one light, one desk, one bath, and one cup of sakè."

Every evening he recorded in his journal the name of the inn, the sights he had seen, the money received from begging, his expenses for that day, and then the haiku he had written, together with his reflections. His journal was his self-portrait. In his travels he "touched this and that and recorded the mind's changing impressions." He poured his life into his haiku and journals, writing down his most intimate thoughts and arguing with himself. Occasionally he felt too attached to his journals; then he would burn them or throw them away. (Similarly, before he left Gochu-an he burned the few possessions he had accumulated.)

In his last journals we find these two entries that sum up his life: "This is the path I must follow—there is no other road for me to walk on. It is a path containing both pleasure and pain. It is far off yet definite. It is very narrow and steep. However, it is also a white path [of purity], full of amazing and wonderful things. It is not a cold and lifeless way.

"I am nothing other than a beggar-monk. There is nothing you can say about me except that I am a foolish pilgrim who spent his entire life wandering, like the drifting water plants that float from shore to shore. It appears pitiful, but I find happiness in this destitute, quiet life. Water flows, clouds move, never stopping or settling down. When the wind blows, the leaves fall. Like the fish swimming or the birds flying, I walk and walk, going on and on."

The day before his death Santoka went to visit a friend and told him: "After the poetry meeting tomorrow I'll be starting out on a journey. I want to throw myself into nature one last time. I haven't got long to live, and I want to be like the sparrows or wild elephants who die alone quietly in the fields."

SAKÈ, ZEN, AND HAIKU

> Days I don't enjoy:
> Any day I don't walk.
> Any day I don't drink sakè.
> Any day I don't compose haiku.

Sakè, Zen, and haiku were the three main elements of Santoka's life; they were always present together, often interchangeable and sometimes indistinguishable.

Santoka's Zen was not the sitting Zen (*zazen*) of Dogen or the koan Zen of Rinzai. It was "walking Zen." Santoka

was very much like the Chinese monks of old who practiced walking rather than sitting meditation, gaining realization through contact with nature on long pilgrimages from one mountain temple to another. Such monks were solitary figures, attached to no institution or master. Walking was their zazen:

> Without anger, without speaking,
> Without covetousness,
> Walk slowly, walk steadily!

while begging was the discipline of killing selfish desires:

> Pierce the poverty of the poorest man,
> Throw yourself into the most foolish foolishness.
> Rather than imitate anyone else
> Use the nature you were born with.

In his travels Santoka attempted to accept everything that came his way without clinging to ideas of self and others, true or false, good or bad, life or death. This was not easy. "Adherence to things material and spiritual prevents me from being as free as the wind or flowing water."

> *Sutekirenai nimotsu no omosa mae ushiro*
> Baggage I cannot throw off,
> So heavy front and back.

Although Gian was a priest of the Soto Zen school, which emphasizes zazen and careful attention to detail, he understood Santoka's character and did not try to direct him into any established routine or practice. He gave Santoka a copy of the *Mumonkan,* a collection of koans from Chinese Zen masters, to study on his travels. As it turned out, Santoka did meet many people (including the old woman that made him chant sutras when he was ill) who confronted him with various questions about Buddhism. One such dialogue went:

> "Where is the Way?" a fellow traveler demanded.
> "Under your feet. Straight ahead.
>
> You are standing on it right now," Santoka replied.
>
> "Where is the mind?"
>
> "Everyday mind is the Way. When tea is offered, drink it; when rice is served, eat it. Respect your parents and look after your children. Mind is not inside or outside."

Santoka made the following list, which might be entitled "My Religion":

> My Three Precepts:
> Do not waste anything.
> Do not get angry.
> Do not complain.
>
> My Three Vows:
> Do not attempt the impossible.
> Do not feel regret for the past.
> Do not berate oneself.

My Three Joys:
Study.
Contemplation.
Haiku.

The one traditional Zen practice that Santoka was very careful about was being satisfied with any amount and not wasting anything. There are two well-known stories about Santoka living by this precept told by Sumita Oyama, Santoka's close friend, editor, and biographer.

The first time Oyama saw some of Santoka's poems in *Soun* he immediately wanted to meet him. However, Oyama knew that Santoka was continually on the road and difficult to contact. When Oyama heard that Santoka was staying at Gochu-an, he wrote to him and arranged for a visit.

Soon after Oyama arrived at Gochu-an, Santoka said to him: "You must be hungry. Here, I've made some lunch for you." He gave Oyama a bowl of boiled rice and one hot pepper for seasoning. Santoka told Oyama to please begin eating. When Oyama suggested they eat together, Santoka said: "I have only one bowl."

After Oyama finished his meal, Santoka took the bowl and ate the remainder of the rice and hot pepper. He then rinsed out the bowl in a bucket of water, took the water to wash off the floor and entranceway, and then went out to the garden with the remaining water. He called out: "Onions! Spinach! It's been a long time since you had some good food. Here's some special fertilizer for you."

Another time Oyama had to spend the night at Gochu-an. There was naturally only one sleeping quilt, and Santoka insisted: "You are my guest. You use the quilt. I'll stay up." The quilt was little more than a ragged piece of cloth that would barely cover a child, let alone a full-grown man. As the winter wind blew in through the many holes in the walls and ceilings, Oyama became colder and colder and was unable to sleep. Santoka put his priest's robe, his summer kimono, and several other pieces of cloth on top of Oyama, but he was still cold. Finally, Santoka piled all his old magazines and even his little desk on top of his shivering friend. The next morning when Oyama awoke, Santoka was still sitting in zazen.

Santoka was used to sharing anything he had. One night, as Santoka prepared for another dinnerless evening, a large dog came to his door carrying a big rice cake in its mouth. Santoka had no idea where the dog or the rice cake had come from. He took the rice cake, split it in two and gave half to the dog, who then ran off into the darkness. As soon as the dog was gone a little cat came up to Santoka and begged for some of the rice cake. Santoka split it again.

Aki no yo ya inu kara morattari neko ni ataetari
  Autumn night—
    I received it from the dog
    And gave it to the cat.

These two *gathas* (Buddhist poems written in Chinese) describe Santoka's Zen:

  Spring wind, autumn rain;
  Flowers bloom, grass withers.
  Self-nature is self-foolishness.
  Walking on and on in the Buddha Land.

  Intoxication has come as I lie on a stone pillow;
  The sound of the valley stream never ceases.
  Everything within the sakè, completely used up:
  No self, no Buddha!

Sakè was Santoka's koan. He said that "to comprehend the true taste of sakè will give me satori." He attempted to completely efface himself through drinking, a practice not unknown among certain types of Zen monks. Sitting for hours in zazen in a monastery is difficult but perhaps not as difficult as wandering through distant villages without money or food. Casting off body and mind through sitting and solving koans is arduous training but so is truly using up everything within the sakè: "When I drink sakè I do so with all my heart. I throw myself recklessly into sakè drinking."

There is no point in romanticizing Santoka's alcoholism, however. He himself struggled with this problem for many years and never solved his greatest koan. On several occasions he was even arrested for public drunkenness and vagrancy. He owed all of his friends money. Yet despite this and all his other weaknesses, we still can find a profundity and clarity in his poems that speak of a certain measure of enlightenment. He had little self-pride, the last and greatest obstacle to satori.

Santoka admitted that he could do only three things: walk, drink sakè, and make haiku. Sakè and haiku were almost identical:

  Sakè for the body, haiku for the heart;
  Sakè is the haiku of the body,
  Haiku is the sakè of the heart.

Furthermore, haiku for Santoka was written Zen—spontaneous, sharp, clear, simple, direct. There must be nothing extra, no artifice, no straining. Haiku is like a *kiai,* the sudden resonant shout of a swordsman. ["When composing a verse let there not be a hair's breadth separating your mind from what you write; composition of a poem must be done in an instant, like a woodcutter feeling a huge tree or a swordsman leaping at a dangerous enemy."—Basho] Since haiku flows from the depths of one's being, how can we be overly concerned with predetermined structure or theme? The most important element in Santoka's haiku is self-expression: "Haiku is not a shriek, a howl, a sigh, or a yawn; rather, it is the deep breath of life. In poetry we constantly examine life, occasionally shouting but never groaning. Sometimes tears fall, other times sweat flows; at all times we must savor each experience and move on without being obstructed by circumstances.

"Real haiku is the soul of poetry. Anything that is not actually present in one's heart is not haiku. The moon glows, flowers bloom, insects cry, water flows. There is no place we cannot find flowers or think of the moon. This is the essence of haiku. Go beyond the restrictions of your era, forget about purpose or meaning, separate yourself from historical limitations—there you'll find the essence of true art, religion, and science."

We can see from the above that while others maintained haiku to be literature or art, Santoka felt that haiku was life itself. He carved himself into each verse; creating haiku was his *samadhi,* a transcendent state of total absorption in his surroundings. "Sometimes clear, sometimes cloudy. Clear or cloudy I compose each verse in a state of body and mind cast off (*shinjindatsuraku*)."

Just before his death he wrote: "Every day I find myself in great difficulty. I don't know if I'll eat today or not. Death is approaching. The only thing I am able to do is to make poetry. Even if I don't eat or drink I cannot stop writing haiku. . . . For me, to live is to make haiku. Haiku is my life."

WATER, WEEDS, MOUNTAINS

More than ten percent of Santoka's haiku concern water—being drenched with it, flowing with it, bathing in it, listening to it, drinking it. Japan is a wet, humid country surrounded by the sea and full of hot springs. Rain is the constant companion of Japanese travelers. Many of Santoka's verses describe the various possibilities of being soaked. Snowfall is rare in southern Japan, where Santoka spent most of his life, but winter rain is perhaps more chilling.

The water (in those days) was pure, good tasting, and abundant. Santoka's greatest joy was drinking cold water at the end of a day's journey and warm sakè at night. For a time he thought he even preferred water to sakè. His diet—water, rice, sakè, *umeboshi* (pickled plum), *takuan* (pickled radish), *yudofu*—consisted of the simplest, most common, and least expensive Japanese foods; yet when properly savored they are the most delicious and nourishing foods there are.

Water was a symbol of his life and poetry—ever-flowing, plain, simple, uncomplicated.

> *Hyohyo to shite mizu o ajiwau*
> Aimlessly, buoyantly,
> Drifting here and there,
> Tasting the pure water.

Santoka's next favorite theme was weeds and wild grasses. He often compared himself (and human beings in general) to weeds. "Sprouting, growing, blooming, seeding, and withering, just as weeds, nothing more—that is good." Weeds are everywhere, uncultivated, living with all their might, until they wither away, die, and are reborn again the following spring.

> *Shinde shimaeba zasso ame furu*
> When I die:

Weeds, falling rain.

If weeds represent human existence, mountains are the world of Buddha—vast, remote, sublime. Water and weeds are close to us, touchable, comprehensible; mountains appear mysterious, difficult to grasp.

> *Wake itte mo wake itte mo aoi yama*
> Going deeper
> And still deeper—
> The green mountains.

Although mountains seem to be impenetrably high and wide, Santoka threw himself into their depth. "Westerners like to conquer mountains; Orientals like to contemplate them. As for me, I like to taste the mountains."

FOOD FROM HEAVEN

> "Today my path was wonderful. I wanted to shout out to the mountains, the sea, and the sky. The sound of the waves, the birds, the pure water— I'm grateful for everything. The sun shone brightly and the number of pilgrims increases daily. The memorials, the bridges, the shrines, and the cliffs were so beautiful. My rice was like food from heaven."

Santoka centered his life on the things directly in front of him. "Truth is seeing the new in the ordinary. Settle in this world. There are hidden treasures in the present moment." In his poetry he concerned himself with the simplest and most commonplace materials, for he understood that while "rice won't make you drunk, the essence of the rice will."

For Santoka any subject was suitable for poetry. Consequently, we find poems on almost every conceivable theme—nature, society, life and death, weeds, sex, the human body and its functions, the taste of water, sakè, and rice. Everything but history: "Do not be attached to the past or wait for the future. Be grateful for each day, that is enough. I do not believe in a future world. I deny the past. I believe entirely in the present. Employ your entire body and mind in the eternal now."

J. Thomas Rimer (essay date 1988)

SOURCE: "The Poetry of Santoka (1882-1940)," in *A Reader's Guide to Japanese Literature,* Kodansha International, 1988, pp. 121-23.

[*In the following essay, Rimer discusses Santoka's life and "laconic, deceptively simple" haiku poetry.*]

The reader who believes that art transcends its own times will surely take solace and inspiration from the work of Taneda Santoka (1882-1940), a remarkable Zen priest and poet of our century who produced poetry as personal and profound as that of his illustrious predecessor and spiritual mentor, Ryokan (1758-1831). Like Ryokan's poetry, Santoka's work can best be understood as a record of his quest for spiritual enlightenment, the kind of voyage that can be undertaken in any era. Readers in our increasingly secular age may first be drawn to Santoka out of a sense of nostalgia, but in reading his poetry they will immediately come face to face with a strong will and the personality of a man who, whatever his personal weaknesses, appears quite unafraid to live on the very edge of society, far from its received values and expectations. Santoka explores, or re-explores, realms that are commonly believed no longer to exist.

Santoka (a pen name the translator John Stevens has rendered "Burning Mountain Peak") began his life as an ordinary young man with some interest in literature. His father was a local politician who owned a certain amount of property. Santoka began writing *haiku* in college, where he also slipped into a pattern of heavy drinking. Married, then separated, he drifted from job to job until, after what may have been a suicide attempt, he was sent to convalesce in a Zen temple. This proved the turning point in his spiritual life, and in 1925 he was officially ordained as a Zen priest. Santoka went here and there begging for his sustenance, short trips turning into longer pilgrimages. Sinking into drunkenness again, he was rescued by friends, who found him a small cottage to use as a hermitage. This served as a base for his walking trips, which took him through many parts of Japan, begging, writing, drifting. Some of these trips were undertaken in order to seek out certain traditional sites holy to Buddhists in Japan, some without apparent destination. A number of his poems were published during his lifetime, and indeed he achieved a degree of fame. But worldly attention was apparently of little interest. He once told a newspaper reporter, "I'm one of society's warts."

Santoka's free-style *haiku* poetry, like his life, appears stripped to the essentials.

> No path but this one—
> I walk alone.
> (trans. John Stevens)

> Walking into the wind,
> heaping abuse upon myself.
> (trans. James Abrams)

Walking, walking, he traveled on. Like his great poet predecessors, stretching back through Basho to Saigyo and beyond, Santoka perceived that movement, in and of itself, provided a sense of elevated awareness that might in turn lead to some higher level of understanding.

> Stretching out my feet;
> Some daylight still remains.
> (trans. John Stevens)

> A steady autumn drizzle,
> one road, straight ahead.
> (trans. James Abrams)

Laconic, deceptively simple, these brief vignettes allow the reader to penetrate special instants in the poet's journey, creating an empathy of strong feeling between poet and reader.

For all the timelessness of this spiritual landscape, Santoka is quite able to record our own century when he feels the need.

> At the tobacco shop
> no cigarettes,
> a cold rain falls.
> (trans. James Abrams)

> The deep, cool moon
> Appears between the buildings.
> (trans. John Stevens)

The moon, traditionally a Buddhist symbol for enlightenment, remains; only the milieu has changed.

Haiku being as difficult as they are to render into English, it sometimes helps to contrast translations of the same poem in order to uncover layers of implicit meaning. Here, for example, is a famous poem in which, by extension, walking may serve as a symbol for the difficult, unending search for self-understanding.

> Going deeper,
> And still deeper—
> The green mountains.
> (trans. John Stevens)

> I push my way through,
> push my way through,
> green mountains
> (trans. James Abrams)

There are few answers in Santoka's poetry, only signs of his continuing search. Success, failure, and frustration are courageously recorded.

> Thinking of nothing,
> I walk among
> A forest of withered trees.
> (trans. John Stevens)

Difficult as Santoka's life and art may be to describe, the reader who examines these *haiku* with care and sympathy can experience something of them both. The poems are so close to the heart of the man that one seems a reflection of the other. The reader's interest can begin with either.

Twentieth-Century Literary Criticism

Cumulative Indexes
Volumes 1-72

How to Use This Index

The main references

Calvino, Italo
1923-1985.....CLC 5, 8, 11, 22, 33, 39,
73; SSC 3

list all author entries in the following Gale Literary Criticism series:

BLC = *Black Literature Criticism*
CLC = *Contemporary Literary Criticism*
CLR = *Children's Literature Review*
CMLC = *Classical and Medieval Literature Criticism*
DA = *DISCovering Authors*
DC = *Drama Criticism*
HLC = *Hispanic Literature Criticism*
LC = *Literature Criticism from 1400 to 1800*
NCLC = *Nineteenth-Century Literature Criticism*
PC = *Poetry Criticism*
SSC = *Short Story Criticism*
TCLC = *Twentieth-Century Literary Criticism*
WLC = *World Literature Criticism, 1500 to the Present*

The cross-references

See also CANR 23; CA 85-88;
obituary CA 116

list all author entries in the following Gale biographical and literary sources:

AAYA = *Authors & Artists for Young Adults*
AITN = *Authors in the News*
BEST = *Bestsellers*
BW = *Black Writers*
CA = *Contemporary Authors*
CAAS = *Contemporary Authors Autobiography Series*
CABS = *Contemporary Authors Bibliographical Series*
CANR = *Contemporary Authors New Revision Series*
CAP = *Contemporary Authors Permanent Series*
CDALB = *Concise Dictionary of American Literary Biography*
CDBLB = *Concise Dictionary of British Literary Biography*
DLB = *Dictionary of Literary Biography*
DLBD = *Dictionary of Literary Biography Documentary Series*
DLBY = *Dictionary of Literary Biography Yearbook*
HW = *Hispanic Writers*
JRDA = *Junior DISCovering Authors*
MAICYA = *Major Authors and Illustrators for Children and Young Adults*
MTCW = *Major 20th-Century Writers*
NNAL = *Native North American Literature*
SAAS = *Something about the Author Autobiography Series*
SATA = *Something about the Author*
YABC = *Yesterday's Authors of Books for Children*

Literary Criticism Series
Cumulative Author Index

Abasiyanik, Sait Faik 1906-1954 ....
See Sait Faik
See also CA 123

Abbey, Edward 1927-1989 .... **CLC 36, 59**
See also CA 45-48; 128; CANR 2, 41

Abbott, Lee K(ittredge) 1947- .... **CLC 48**
See also CA 124; CANR 51; DLB 130

Abe, Kobo 1924-1993**CLC 8, 22, 53, 81; DAM
NOV**
See also CA 65-68; 140; CANR 24; DLB 182;
MTCW

Abelard, Peter c. 1079-c. 1142 ...... **CMLC 11**
See also DLB 115

Abell, Kjeld 1901-1961 .... **CLC 15**
See also CA 111

Abish, Walter 1931- .... **CLC 22**
See also CA 101; CANR 37; DLB 130

Abrahams, Peter (Henry) 1919- .... **CLC 4**
See also BW 1; CA 57-60; CANR 26; DLB 117;
MTCW

Abrams, M(eyer) H(oward) 1912- .... **CLC 24**
See also CA 57-60; CANR 13, 33; DLB 67

Abse, Dannie 1923- . **CLC 7, 29; DAB; DAM
POET**
See also CA 53-56; CAAS 1; CANR 4, 46; DLB
27

Achebe, (Albert) Chinua(lumogu) 1930-**C L C
1, 3, 5, 7, 11, 26, 51, 75; BLC; DA; DAB;
DAC; DAM MST, MULT, NOV; WLC**
See also AAYA 15; BW 2; CA 1-4R; CANR 6,
26, 47; CLR 20; DLB 117; MAICYA;
MTCW; SATA 40; SATA-Brief 38

Acker, Kathy 1948- .... **CLC 45**
See also CA 117; 122; CANR 55

Ackroyd, Peter 1949- .... **CLC 34, 52**
See also CA 123; 127; CANR 51; DLB 155;
INT 127

Acorn, Milton 1923- .... **CLC 15; DAC**
See also CA 103; DLB 53; INT 103

Adamov, Arthur 1908-1970**CLC 4, 25; DAM
DRAM**
See also CA 17-18; 25-28R; CAP 2; MTCW

Adams, Alice (Boyd)
1926- .... **CLC 6, 13, 46; SSC 24**
See also CA 81-84; CANR 26, 53; DLBY 86;
INT CANR-26; MTCW

Adams, Andy 1859-1935 .... **TCLC 56**
See also YABC 1

Adams, Douglas (Noel) 1952- .... **CLC 27, 60;
DAM POP**
See also AAYA 4; BEST 89:3; CA 106; CANR

34; DLBY 83; JRDA

Adams, Francis 1862-1893 .... **NCLC 33**

Adams, Henry (Brooks) 1838-1918 **TCLC 4,
52; DA; DAB; DAC; DAM MST**
See also CA 104; 133; DLB 12, 47

Adams, Richard (George) 1920-**CLC 4, 5, 18;
DAM NOV**
See also AAYA 16; AITN 1, 2; CA 49-52;
CANR 3, 35; CLR 20; JRDA; MAICYA;
MTCW; SATA 7, 69

Adamson, Joy(-Friederike Victoria)
1910-1980 .... **CLC 17**
See also CA 69-72; 93-96; CANR 22; MTCW;
SATA 11; SATA-Obit 22

Adcock, Fleur 1934- .... **CLC 41**
See also CA 25-28R; CAAS 23; CANR 11, 34;
DLB 40

Addams, Charles (Samuel) 1912-1988**CLC 30**
See also CA 61-64; 126; CANR 12

Addison, Joseph 1672-1719 .... **LC 18**
See also CDBLB 1660-1789; DLB 101

Adler, Alfred (F.) 1870-1937 .... **TCLC 61**
See also CA 119

Adler, C(arole) S(chwerdtfeger) 1932- . **C L C
35**
See also AAYA 4; CA 89-92; CANR 19, 40;
JRDA; MAICYA; SAAS 15; SATA 26, 63

Adler, Renata 1938- .... **CLC 8, 31**
See also CA 49-52; CANR 5, 22, 52; MTCW

Ady, Endre 1877-1919 .... **TCLC 11**
See also CA 107

Aeschylus
525B.C.-456B.C.**CMLC 11; DA; DAB; DAC;
DAM DRAM, MST; WLCS**
See also DLB 176

Afton, Effie
See Harper, Frances Ellen Watkins

Agapida, Fray Antonio
See Irving, Washington

Agee, James (Rufus) 1909-1955 **TCLC 1, 19;
DAM NOV**
See also AITN 1; CA 108; 148; CDALB
1941-1968; DLB 2, 26, 152

Aghill, Gordon
See Silverberg, Robert

Agnon, S(hmuel) Y(osef Halevi) 1888-1970
CLC 4, 8, 14
See also CA 17-18; 25-28R; CAP 2; MTCW

Agrippa von Nettesheim, Henry Cornelius
1486-1535 .... **LC 27**

Aherne, Owen
See Cassill, R(onald) V(erlin)

Ai 1947- .... **CLC 4, 14, 69**
See also CA 85-88; CAAS 13; DLB 120

Aickman, Robert (Fordyce) 1914-1981**CLC 57**
See also CA 5-8R; CANR 3

Aiken, Conrad (Potter) 1889-1973**CLC 1, 3, 5,
10, 52; DAM NOV, POET; SSC 9**
See also CA 5-8R; 45-48; CANR 4; CDALB
1929-1941; DLB 9, 45, 102; MTCW; SATA
3, 30

Aiken, Joan (Delano) 1924- .... **CLC 35**
See also AAYA 1; CA 9-12R; CANR 4, 23, 34;
CLR 1, 19; DLB 161; JRDA; MAICYA;
MTCW; SAAS 1; SATA 2, 30, 73

Ainsworth, William Harrison 1805-1882
NCLC 13
See also DLB 21; SATA 24

Aitmatov, Chingiz (Torekulovich) 1928-**CLC 71**
See also CA 103; CANR 38; MTCW; SATA 56

Akers, Floyd
See Baum, L(yman) Frank

Akhmadulina, Bella Akhatovna
1937- .... **CLC 53; DAM POET**
See also CA 65-68

Akhmatova, Anna 1888-1966**CLC 11, 25, 64;
DAM POET; PC 2**
See also CA 19-20; 25-28R; CANR 35; CAP 1;
MTCW

Aksakov, Sergei Timofeyvich 1791-1859
NCLC 2

Aksenov, Vassily
See Aksyonov, Vassily (Pavlovich)

Aksyonov, Vassily (Pavlovich)
1932- .... **CLC 22, 37, 101**
See also CA 53-56; CANR 12, 48

Akutagawa, Ryunosuke 1892-1927 **TCLC 16**
See also CA 117; 154

Alain 1868-1951 .... **TCLC 41**

Alain-Fournier .... **TCLC 6**
See also Fournier, Henri Alban
See also DLB 65

Alarcon, Pedro Antonio de 1833-1891**NCLC 1**

Alas (y Urena), Leopoldo (Enrique Garcia)
1852-1901 .... **TCLC 29**
See also CA 113; 131; HW

Albee, Edward (Franklin III)
1928-**CLC 1, 2, 3, 5, 9, 11, 13, 25, 53, 86; DA;
DAB; DAC; DAM DRAM, MST; WLC**
See also AITN 1; CA 5-8R; CABS 3; CANR 8,

See Mencken, H(enry) L(ouis); Nathan, George
Jean

Anderson, Jessica (Margaret) Queale **CLC 37**
See also CA 9-12R; CANR 4

Anderson, Jon (Victor) 1940- .. **CLC 9; DAM
POET**
See also CA 25-28R; CANR 20

Anderson, Lindsay (Gordon) 1923-1994 **C L C
20**
See also CA 125; 128; 146

Anderson, Maxwell 1888-1959 **TCLC 2; DAM
DRAM**
See also CA 105; 152; DLB 7

Anderson, Poul (William) 1926- .... **CLC 15**
See also AAYA 5; CA 1-4R; CAAS 2; CANR
2, 15, 34; DLB 8; INT CANR-15; MTCW;
SATA 90; SATA-Brief 39

Anderson, Robert (Woodruff) 1917- **CLC 23;
DAM DRAM**
See also AITN 1; CA 21-24R; CANR 32; DLB
7

Anderson, Sherwood 1876-1941 **TCLC 1, 10,
24; DA; DAB; DAC; DAM MST, NOV;
SSC 1; WLC**
See also CA 104; 121; CDALB 1917-1929;
DLB 4, 9, 86; DLBD 1; MTCW

Andier, Pierre
See Desnos, Robert

Andouard
See Giraudoux, (Hippolyte) Jean

Andrade, Carlos Drummond de .... **CLC 18**
See also Drummond de Andrade, Carlos

Andrade, Mario de 1893-1945 .... **TCLC 43**

Andreae, Johann V(alentin) 1586-1654 **LC 32**
See also DLB 164

Andreas-Salome, Lou 1861-1937 ... **TCLC 56**
See also DLB 66

Andrewes, Lancelot 1555-1626 .... **LC 5**
See also DLB 151, 172

Andrews, Cicily Fairfield
See West, Rebecca

Andrews, Elton V.
See Pohl, Frederik

Andreyev, Leonid (Nikolaevich) 1871-1919
TCLC 3
See also CA 104

Andric, Ivo 1892-1975 .... **CLC 8**
See also CA 81-84; 57-60; CANR 43; DLB 147;
MTCW

Angelique, Pierre
See Bataille, Georges

Angell, Roger 1920- .... **CLC 26**
See also CA 57-60; CANR 13, 44; DLB 171

Angelou, Maya 1928- **CLC 12, 35, 64, 77; BLC;
DA; DAB; DAC; DAM MST, MULT,
POET, POP; WLCS**

See also AAYA 7, 20; BW 2; CA 65-68; CANR
19, 42; DLB 38; MTCW; SATA 49

Annensky, Innokenty (Fyodorovich) 1856-1909
TCLC 14
See also CA 110; 155

Annunzio, Gabriele d'
See D'Annunzio, Gabriele

Anodos
See Coleridge, Mary E(lizabeth)

Anon, Charles Robert
See Pessoa, Fernando (Antonio Nogueira)

Anouilh, Jean (Marie Lucien Pierre) 1910-1987
CLC 1, 3, 8, 13, 40, 50; DAM DRAM
See also CA 17-20R; 123; CANR 32; MTCW

Anthony, Florence
See Ai

Anthony, John
See Ciardi, John (Anthony)

Anthony, Peter
See Shaffer, Anthony (Joshua); Shaffer, Peter
(Levin)

Anthony, Piers 1934- .... **CLC 35; DAM POP**
See also AAYA 11; CA 21-24R; CANR 28, 56;
DLB 8; MTCW; SAAS 22; SATA 84

Antoine, Marc
See Proust, (Valentin-Louis-George-Eugene-)
Marcel

Antoninus, Brother
See Everson, William (Oliver)

Antonioni, Michelangelo 1912- .... **CLC 20**
See also CA 73-76; CANR 45

Antschel, Paul 1920-1970 ....
See Celan, Paul
See also CA 85-88; CANR 33; MTCW

Anwar, Chairil 1922-1949 .... **TCLC 22**
See also CA 121

Apollinaire, Guillaume 1880-1918 **TCLC 3, 8,
51; DAM POET; PC 7**
See also Kostrowitzki, Wilhelm Apollinaris de
See also CA 152

Appelfeld, Aharon 1932- .... **CLC 23, 47**
See also CA 112; 133

Apple, Max (Isaac) 1941- .... **CLC 9, 33**
See also CA 81-84; CANR 19, 54; DLB 130

Appleman, Philip (Dean) 1926- .... **CLC 51**
See also CA 13-16R; CAAS 18; CANR 6, 29,
56

Appleton, Lawrence
See Lovecraft, H(oward) P(hillips)

Apteryx
See Eliot, T(homas) S(tearns)

Apuleius, (Lucius Madaurensis) 125(?)-175(?)
CMLC 1

Aquin, Hubert 1929-1977 .... **CLC 15**
See also CA 105; DLB 53

Aragon, Louis 1897-1982 .. **CLC 3, 22; DAM
NOV, POET**
See also CA 69-72; 108; CANR 28; DLB 72;
MTCW

Arany, Janos 1817-1882 .... **NCLC 34**

Arbuthnot, John 1667-1735 .... **LC 1**
See also DLB 101

Archer, Herbert Winslow
See Mencken, H(enry) L(ouis)

Archer, Jeffrey (Howard) 1940- ..... **CLC 28;
DAM POP**
See also AAYA 16; BEST 89:3; CA 77-80;
CANR 22, 52; INT CANR-22

Archer, Jules 1915- .... **CLC 12**
See also CA 9-12R; CANR 6; SAAS 5; SATA
4, 85

Archer, Lee
See Ellison, Harlan (Jay)

Arden, John 1930- .... **CLC 6, 13, 15;
DAM DRAM**
See also CA 13-16R; CAAS 4; CANR 31; DLB
13; MTCW

Arenas, Reinaldo 1943-1990 . **CLC 41; DAM
MULT; HLC**
See also CA 124; 128; 133; DLB 145; HW

Arendt, Hannah 1906-1975 .... **CLC 66, 98**
See also CA 17-20R; 61-64; CANR 26; MTCW

Aretino, Pietro 1492-1556 .... **LC 12**

Arghezi, Tudor .... **CLC 80**
See also Theodorescu, Ion N.

Arguedas, Jose Maria 1911-1969 **CLC 10, 18**
See also CA 89-92; DLB 113; HW

Argueta, Manlio 1936- .... **CLC 31**
See also CA 131; DLB 145; HW

Ariosto, Ludovico 1474-1533 .... **LC 6**

Aristides
See Epstein, Joseph

Aristophanes 450B.C.-385B.C. **CMLC 4; DA;
DAB; DAC; DAM DRAM, MST; DC 2;
WLCS**
See also DLB 176

Arlt, Roberto (Godofredo Christophersen)
1900-1942 **TCLC 29; DAM MULT; HLC**
See also CA 123; 131; HW

Armah, Ayi Kwei
1939- .... **CLC 5, 33; BLC;
DAM MULT, POET**
See also BW 1; CA 61-64; CANR 21; DLB 117;
MTCW

Armatrading, Joan 1950- .... **CLC 17**
See also CA 114

Arnette, Robert
See Silverberg, Robert

**Arnim, Achim von (Ludwig Joachim von
Arnim)** 1781-1831 .... **NCLC 5**
See also DLB 90

Arnim, Bettina von 1785-1859 .... **NCLC 38**
See also DLB 90

Arnold, Matthew 1822-1888**NCLC 6, 29; DA; DAB; DAC; DAM MST, POET; PC 5; WLC**
See also CDBLB 1832-1890; DLB 32, 57

Arnold, Thomas 1795-1842 .... **NCLC 18**
See also DLB 55

Arnow, Harriette (Louisa) Simpson 1908-1986 **CLC 2, 7, 18**
See also CA 9-12R; 118; CANR 14; DLB 6; MTCW; SATA 42; SATA-Obit 47

Arp, Hans
See Arp, Jean

Arp, Jean 1887-1966 .... **CLC 5**
See also CA 81-84; 25-28R; CANR 42

Arrabal
See Arrabal, Fernando

Arrabal, Fernando 1932-.... **CLC 2, 9, 18, 58**
See also CA 9-12R; CANR 15

Arrick, Fran .... **CLC 30**
See also Gaberman, Judie Angell

Artaud, Antonin (Marie Joseph) 1896-1948 **TCLC 3, 36; DAM DRAM**
See also CA 104; 149

Arthur, Ruth M(abel) 1905-1979 ...... **CLC 12**
See also CA 9-12R; 85-88; CANR 4; SATA 7, 26

Artsybashev, Mikhail (Petrovich) 1878-1927 **TCLC 31**

Arundel, Honor (Morfydd) 1919-1973**CLC 17**
See also CA 21-22; 41-44R; CAP 2; CLR 35; SATA 4; SATA-Obit 24

Arzner, Dorothy 1897-1979 .... **CLC 98**

Asch, Sholem 1880-1957 .... **TCLC 3**
See also CA 105

Ash, Shalom
See Asch, Sholem

Ashbery, John (Lawrence) 1927-**CLC 2, 3, 4, 6, 9, 13, 15, 25, 41, 77; DAM POET**
See also CA 5-8R; CANR 9, 37; DLB 5, 165; DLBY 81; INT CANR-9; MTCW

Ashdown, Clifford
See Freeman, R(ichard) Austin

Ashe, Gordon
See Creasey, John

Ashton-Warner, Sylvia (Constance) 1908-1984 **CLC 19**
See also CA 69-72; 112; CANR 29; MTCW

Asimov, Isaac 1920-1992 **CLC 1, 3, 9, 19, 26, 76, 92; DAM POP**
See also AAYA 13; BEST 90:2; CA 1-4R; 137; CANR 2, 19, 36; CLR 12; DLB 8; DLBY 92; INT CANR-19; JRDA; MAICYA; MTCW; SATA 1, 26, 74

Assis, Joaquim Maria Machado de

See Machado de Assis, Joaquim Maria

Astley, Thea (Beatrice May) 1925-... **CLC 41**
See also CA 65-68; CANR 11, 43

Aston, James
See White, T(erence) H(anbury)

Asturias, Miguel Angel 1899-1974 **CLC 3, 8, 13; DAM MULT, NOV; HLC**
See also CA 25-28; 49-52; CANR 32; CAP 2; DLB 113; HW; MTCW

Atares, Carlos Saura
See Saura (Atares), Carlos

Atheling, William
See Pound, Ezra (Weston Loomis)

Atheling, William, Jr.
See Blish, James (Benjamin)

Atherton, Gertrude (Franklin Horn) 1857-1948 **TCLC 2**
See also CA 104; 155; DLB 9, 78

Atherton, Lucius
See Masters, Edgar Lee

Atkins, Jack
See Harris, Mark

Atkinson, Kate .... **CLC 99**

Attaway, William (Alexander) 1911-1986**CLC 92; BLC; DAM MULT**
See also BW 2; CA 143; DLB 76

Atticus
See Fleming, Ian (Lancaster)

Atwood, Margaret (Eleanor) 1939-**CLC 2, 3, 4, 8, 13, 15, 25, 44, 84; DA; DAB; DAC; DAM MST, NOV, POET; PC 8; SSC 2; WLC**
See also AAYA 12; BEST 89:2; CA 49-52; CANR 3, 24, 33, 59; DLB 53; INT CANR-24; MTCW; SATA 50

Aubigny, Pierre d'
See Mencken, H(enry) L(ouis)

Aubin, Penelope 1685-1731(?) .... **LC 9**
See also DLB 39

Auchincloss, Louis (Stanton) 1917-**CLC 4, 6, 9, 18, 45; DAM NOV; SSC 22**
See also CA 1-4R; CANR 6, 29, 55; DLB 2; DLBY 80; INT CANR-29; MTCW

Auden, W(ystan) H(ugh) 1907-1973**CLC 1, 2, 3, 4, 6, 9, 11, 14, 43; DA; DAB; DAC; DAM DRAM, MST, POET; PC 1; WLC**
See also AAYA 18; CA 9-12R; 45-48; CANR 5; CDBLB 1914-1945; DLB 10, 20; MTCW

Audiberti, Jacques 1900-1965**CLC 38; DAM DRAM**
See also CA 25-28R

Audubon, John James 1785-1851 .. **NCLC 47**

Auel, Jean M(arie) 1936-**CLC 31; DAM POP**
See also AAYA 7; BEST 90:4; CA 103; CANR 21; INT CANR-21; SATA 91

Auerbach, Erich 1892-1957 .... **TCLC 43**

See also CA 118; 155

Augier, Emile 1820-1889 .... **NCLC 31**

August, John
See De Voto, Bernard (Augustine)

Augustine, St. 354-430 .... **CMLC 6; DAB**

Aurelius
See Bourne, Randolph S(illiman)

Aurobindo, Sri 1872-1950 .... **TCLC 63**

Austen, Jane 1775-1817 **NCLC 1, 13, 19, 33, 51; DA; DAB; DAC; DAM MST, NOV; WLC**
See also AAYA 19; CDBLB 1789-1832; DLB 116

Auster, Paul 1947-............................... **CLC 47**
See also CA 69-72; CANR 23, 52

Austin, Frank
See Faust, Frederick (Schiller)

Austin, Mary (Hunter) 1868-1934 . **TCLC 25**
See also CA 109; DLB 9, 78

Autran Dourado, Waldomiro
See Dourado, (Waldomiro Freitas) Autran

Averroes 1126-1198.......................... **CMLC 7**
See also DLB 115

Avicenna 980-1037 .... **CMLC 16**
See also DLB 115

Avison, Margaret 1918- **CLC 2, 4, 97; DAC; DAM POET**
See also CA 17-20R; DLB 53; MTCW

Axton, David
See Koontz, Dean R(ay)

Ayckbourn, Alan 1939- **CLC 5, 8, 18, 33, 74; DAB; DAM DRAM**
See also CA 21-24R; CANR 31, 59; DLB 13; MTCW

Aydy, Catherine
See Tennant, Emma (Christina)

Ayme, Marcel (Andre) 1902-1967 .... **CLC 11**
See also CA 89-92; CLR 25; DLB 72; SATA 91

Ayrton, Michael 1921-1975 .... **CLC 7**
See also CA 5-8R; 61-64; CANR 9, 21

Azorin .... **CLC 11**
See also Martinez Ruiz, Jose

Azuela, Mariano 1873-1952 . **TCLC 3; DAM MULT; HLC**
See also CA 104; 131; HW; MTCW

Baastad, Babbis Friis
See Friis-Baastad, Babbis Ellinor

Bab
See Gilbert, W(illiam) S(chwenck)

Babbis, Eleanor
See Friis-Baastad, Babbis Ellinor

Babel, Isaac
See Babel, Isaak (Emmanuilovich)

Babel, Isaak (Emmanuilovich) 1894-1941(?)
   TCLC 2, 13; SSC 16
   See also CA 104; 155

Babits, Mihaly 1883-1941 .... **TCLC 14**
   See also CA 114

Babur 1483-1530 .... **LC 18**

Bacchelli, Riccardo 1891-1985 .... **CLC 19**
   See also CA 29-32R; 117

Bach, Richard (David) 1936- **CLC 14; DAM NOV, POP**
   See also AITN 1; BEST 89:2; CA 9-12R; CANR 18; MTCW; SATA 13

Bachman, Richard
   See King, Stephen (Edwin)

Bachmann, Ingeborg 1926-1973 .... **CLC 69**
   See also CA 93-96; 45-48; DLB 85

Bacon, Francis 1561-1626 .... **LC 18, 32**
   See also CDBLB Before 1660; DLB 151

Bacon, Roger 1214(?)-1292 .... **CMLC 14**
   See also DLB 115

Bacovia, George .... **TCLC 24**
   See also Vasiliu, Gheorghe

Badanes, Jerome 1937- .... **CLC 59**

Bagehot, Walter 1826-1877 .... **NCLC 10**
   See also DLB 55

Bagnold, Enid 1889-1981 .... **CLC 25; DAM DRAM**
   See also CA 5-8R; 103; CANR 5, 40; DLB 13, 160; MAICYA; SATA 1, 25

Bagritsky, Eduard 1895-1934 .... **TCLC 60**

Bagrjana, Elisaveta
   See Belcheva, Elisaveta

Bagryana, Elisaveta .... **CLC 10**
   See also Belcheva, Elisaveta
   See also DLB 147

Bailey, Paul 1937- .... **CLC 45**
   See also CA 21-24R; CANR 16; DLB 14

Baillie, Joanna 1762-1851 .... **NCLC 2**
   See also DLB 93

Bainbridge, Beryl (Margaret) 1933- **CLC 4, 5, 8, 10, 14, 18, 22, 62; DAM NOV**
   See also CA 21-24R; CANR 24, 55; DLB 14; MTCW

Baker, Elliott 1922- .... **CLC 8**
   See also CA 45-48; CANR 2

Baker, Jean H. .... **TCLC 3, 10**
   See also Russell, George William

Baker, Nicholson 1957- **CLC 61; DAM POP**
   See also CA 135

Baker, Ray Stannard 1870-1946 .... **TCLC 47**
   See also CA 118

Baker, Russell (Wayne) 1925- .... **CLC 31**
   See also BEST 89:4; CA 57-60; CANR 11, 41, 59; MTCW

Bakhtin, M.
   See Bakhtin, Mikhail Mikhailovich

Bakhtin, M. M.
   See Bakhtin, Mikhail Mikhailovich

Bakhtin, Mikhail
   See Bakhtin, Mikhail Mikhailovich

Bakhtin, Mikhail Mikhailovich 1895-1975
   CLC 83
   See also CA 128; 113

Bakshi, Ralph 1938(?)- .... **CLC 26**
   See also CA 112; 138

Bakunin, Mikhail (Alexandrovich) 1814-1876
   NCLC 25, 58

Baldwin, James (Arthur) 1924-1987 **CLC 1, 2, 3, 4, 5, 8, 13, 15, 17, 42, 50, 67, 90; BLC; DA; DAB; DAC; DAM MST, MULT, NOV, POP; DC 1; SSC 10; WLC**
   See also AAYA 4; BW 1; CA 1-4R; 124; CABS 1; CANR 3, 24; CDALB 1941-1968; DLB 2, 7, 33; DLBY 87; MTCW; SATA 9; SATA-Obit 54

Ballard, J(ames) G(raham) 1930- **CLC 3, 6, 14, 36; DAM NOV, POP; SSC 1**
   See also AAYA 3; CA 5-8R; CANR 15, 39; DLB 14; MTCW; SATA 93

Balmont, Konstantin (Dmitriyevich) 1867-1943
   TCLC 11
   See also CA 109; 155

Balzac, Honore de 1799-1850 **NCLC 5, 35, 53; DA; DAB; DAC; DAM MST, NOV; SSC 5; WLC**
   See also DLB 119

Bambara, Toni Cade 1939-1995 **CLC 19, 88; BLC; DA; DAC; DAM MST, MULT; WLCS**
   See also AAYA 5; BW 2; CA 29-32R; 150; CANR 24, 49; DLB 38; MTCW

Bamdad, A.
   See Shamlu, Ahmad

Banat, D. R.
   See Bradbury, Ray (Douglas)

Bancroft, Laura
   See Baum, L(yman) Frank

Banim, John 1798-1842 .... **NCLC 13**
   See also DLB 116, 158, 159

Banim, Michael 1796-1874 .... **NCLC 13**
   See also DLB 158, 159

Banjo, The
   See Paterson, A(ndrew) B(arton)

Banks, Iain
   See Banks, Iain M(enzies)

Banks, Iain M(enzies) 1954- .... **CLC 34**
   See also CA 123; 128; INT 128

Banks, Lynne Reid .... **CLC 23**
   See also Reid Banks, Lynne
   See also AAYA 6

Banks, Russell 1940- .... **CLC 37, 72**

See also CA 65-68; CAAS 15; CANR 19, 52; DLB 130

Banville, John 1945- .... **CLC 46**
   See also CA 117; 128; DLB 14; INT 128

Banville, Theodore (Faullain) de 1832-1891
   NCLC 9

Baraka, Amiri 1934- **CLC 1, 2, 3, 5, 10, 14, 33; BLC; DA; DAC; DAM MST, MULT, POET, POP; DC 6; PC 4; WLCS**
   See also Jones, LeRoi
   See also BW 2; CA 21-24R; CABS 3; CANR 27, 38; CDALB 1941-1968; DLB 5, 7, 16, 38; DLBD 8; MTCW

Barbauld, Anna Laetitia 1743-1825 **NCLC 50**
   See also DLB 107, 109, 142, 158

Barbellion, W. N. P. .... **TCLC 24**
   See also Cummings, Bruce F(rederick)

Barbera, Jack (Vincent) 1945- .... **CLC 44**
   See also CA 110; CANR 45

Barbey d'Aurevilly, Jules Amedee 1808-1889
   NCLC 1; SSC 17
   See also DLB 119

Barbusse, Henri 1873-1935 .... **TCLC 5**
   See also CA 105; 154; DLB 65

Barclay, Bill
   See Moorcock, Michael (John)

Barclay, William Ewert
   See Moorcock, Michael (John)

Barea, Arturo 1897-1957 .... **TCLC 14**
   See also CA 111

Barfoot, Joan 1946- .... **CLC 18**
   See also CA 105

Baring, Maurice 1874-1945 .... **TCLC 8**
   See also CA 105; DLB 34

Barker, Clive 1952- .... **CLC 52; DAM POP**
   See also AAYA 10; BEST 90:3; CA 121; 129; INT 129; MTCW

Barker, George Granville 1913-1991 **CLC 8, 48; DAM POET**
   See also CA 9-12R; 135; CANR 7, 38; DLB 20; MTCW

Barker, Harley Granville
   See Granville-Barker, Harley
   See also DLB 10

Barker, Howard 1946- .... **CLC 37**
   See also CA 102; DLB 13

Barker, Pat(ricia) 1943- .... **CLC 32, 94**
   See also CA 117; 122; CANR 50; INT 122

Barlow, Joel 1754-1812 .... **NCLC 23**
   See also DLB 37

Barnard, Mary (Ethel) 1909- .... **CLC 48**
   See also CA 21-22; CAP 2

Barnes, Djuna 1892-1982 **CLC 3, 4, 8, 11, 29; SSC 3**
   See also CA 9-12R; 107; CANR 16, 55; DLB 4, 9, 45; MTCW

Barnes, Julian (Patrick) 1946-**CLC 42; DAB**
See also CA 102; CANR 19, 54; DLBY 93

Barnes, Peter 1931- ....**CLC 5, 56**
See also CA 65-68; CAAS 12; CANR 33, 34;
DLB 13; MTCW

Baroja (y Nessi), Pio 1872-1956**TCLC 8; HLC**
See also CA 104

Baron, David
See Pinter, Harold

Baron Corvo
See Rolfe, Frederick (William Serafino Austin
Lewis Mary)

Barondess, Sue K(aufman) 1926-1977 **CLC 8**
See also Kaufman, Sue
See also CA 1-4R; 69-72; CANR 1

Baron de Teive
See Pessoa, Fernando (Antonio Nogueira)

Barres, Maurice 1862-1923 .... **TCLC 47**
See also DLB 123

Barreto, Afonso Henrique de Lima
See Lima Barreto, Afonso Henrique de

Barrett, (Roger) Syd 1946- .... **CLC 35**

Barrett, William (Christopher) 1913-1992
CLC 27
See also CA 13-16R; 139; CANR 11; INT
CANR-11

Barrie, J(ames) M(atthew) 1860-1937 **T C L C
2; DAB; DAM DRAM**
See also CA 104; 136; CDBLB 1890-1914;
CLR 16; DLB 10, 141, 156; MAICYA;
YABC 1

Barrington, Michael
See Moorcock, Michael (John)

Barrol, Grady
See Bograd, Larry

Barry, Mike
See Malzberg, Barry N(athaniel)

Barry, Philip 1896-1949 .... **TCLC 11**
See also CA 109; DLB 7

Bart, Andre Schwarz
See Schwarz-Bart, Andre

Barth, John (Simmons) 1930-**CLC 1, 2, 3, 5, 7,
9, 10, 14, 27, 51, 89; DAM NOV; SSC 10**
See also AITN 1, 2; CA 1-4R; CABS 1; CANR
5, 23, 49; DLB 2; MTCW

Barthelme, Donald 1931-1989**CLC 1, 2, 3, 5, 6,
8, 13, 23, 46, 59; DAM NOV; SSC 2**
See also CA 21-24R; 129; CANR 20, 58; DLB
2; DLBY 80, 89; MTCW; SATA 7; SATA-
Obit 62

Barthelme, Frederick 1943- .... **CLC 36**
See also CA 114; 122; DLBY 85; INT 122

Barthes, Roland (Gerard) 1915-1980**CLC 24,
83**
See also CA 130; 97-100; MTCW

Barzun, Jacques (Martin) 1907- .... **CLC 51**

See also CA 61-64; CANR 22

Bashevis, Isaac
See Singer, Isaac Bashevis

Bashkirtseff, Marie 1859-1884 ...... **NCLC 27**

Basho
See Matsuo Basho

Bass, Kingsley B., Jr.
See Bullins, Ed

Bass, Rick 1958- .... **CLC 79**
See also CA 126; CANR 53

Bassani, Giorgio 1916- ....**CLC 9**
See also CA 65-68; CANR 33; DLB 128, 177;
MTCW

Bastos, Augusto (Antonio) Roa
See Roa Bastos, Augusto (Antonio)

Bataille, Georges 1897-1962 .... **CLC 29**
See also CA 101; 89-92

Bates, H(erbert) E(rnest) 1905-1974**CLC 46;
DAB; DAM POP; SSC 10**
See also CA 93-96; 45-48; CANR 34; DLB 162;
MTCW

Bauchart
See Camus, Albert

Baudelaire, Charles 1821-1867 .**NCLC 6, 29,
55; DA; DAB; DAC; DAM MST, POET;
PC 1; SSC 18; WLC**

Baudrillard, Jean 1929- .... **CLC 60**

Baum, L(yman) Frank 1856-1919 ... **TCLC 7**
See also CA 108; 133; CLR 15; DLB 22; JRDA;
MAICYA; MTCW; SATA 18

Baum, Louis F.
See Baum, L(yman) Frank

Baumbach, Jonathan 1933- ....**CLC 6, 23**
See also CA 13-16R; CAAS 5; CANR 12;
DLBY 80; INT CANR-12; MTCW

Bausch, Richard (Carl) 1945- .... **CLC 51**
See also CA 101; CAAS 14; CANR 43; DLB
130

Baxter, Charles 1947-**CLC 45, 78; DAM POP**
See also CA 57-60; CANR 40; DLB 130

Baxter, George Owen
See Faust, Frederick (Schiller)

Baxter, James K(eir) 1926-1972 .... **CLC 14**
See also CA 77-80

Baxter, John
See Hunt, E(verette) Howard, (Jr.)

Bayer, Sylvia
See Glassco, John

Baynton, Barbara 1857-1929 .... **TCLC 57**

Beagle, Peter S(oyer) 1939- .... **CLC 7**
See also CA 9-12R; CANR 4, 51; DLBY 80;
INT CANR-4; SATA 60

Bean, Normal

See Burroughs, Edgar Rice

Beard, Charles A(ustin) 1874-1948 **TCLC 15**
See also CA 115; DLB 17; SATA 18

Beardsley, Aubrey 1872-1898 .... **NCLC 6**

Beattie, Ann 1947-**CLC 8, 13, 18, 40, 63; DAM
NOV, POP; SSC 11**
See also BEST 90:2; CA 81-84; CANR 53;
DLBY 82; MTCW

Beattie, James 1735-1803 .... **NCLC 25**
See also DLB 109

Beauchamp, Kathleen Mansfield 1888-1923
See Mansfield, Katherine
See also CA 104; 134; DA; DAC; DAM MST

Beaumarchais, Pierre-Augustin Caron de 1732-
1799 ....**DC 4**
See also DAM DRAM

Beaumont, Francis 1584(?)-1616**LC 33; DC 6**
See also CDBLB Before 1660; DLB 58, 121

**Beauvoir, Simone (Lucie Ernestine Marie
Bertrand) de** 1908-1986 **CLC 1, 2, 4, 8,
14, 31, 44, 50, 71; DA; DAB; DAC; DAM
MST, NOV; WLC**
See also CA 9-12R; 118; CANR 28; DLB 72;
DLBY 86; MTCW

Becker, Carl (Lotus) 1873-1945 ..... **TCLC 63**
See also CA 157; DLB 17

Becker, Jurek 1937-1997 .... **CLC 7, 19**
See also CA 85-88; 157; DLB 75

Becker, Walter 1950- .... **CLC 26**

Beckett, Samuel (Barclay) 1906-1989 **CLC 1,
2, 3, 4, 6, 9, 10, 11, 14, 18, 29, 57, 59, 83;
DA; DAB; DAC; DAM DRAM, MST,
NOV; SSC 16; WLC**
See also CA 5-8R; 130; CANR 33; CDBLB
1945-1960; DLB 13, 15; DLBY 90; MTCW

Beckford, William 1760-1844 .... **NCLC 16**
See also DLB 39

Beckman, Gunnel 1910- .... **CLC 26**
See also CA 33-36R; CANR 15; CLR 25;
MAICYA; SAAS 9; SATA 6

Becque, Henri 1837-1899 .... **NCLC 3**

Beddoes, Thomas Lovell 1803-1849 **NCLC 3**
See also DLB 96

Bede c. 673-735 .... **CMLC 20**
See also DLB 146

Bedford, Donald F.
See Fearing, Kenneth (Flexner)

Beecher, Catharine Esther 1800-1878 **N C L C
30**
See also DLB 1

Beecher, John 1904-1980 .... **CLC 6**
See also AITN 1; CA 5-8R; 105; CANR 8

Beer, Johann 1655-1700 .... **LC 5**
See also DLB 168

Beer, Patricia 1924- .... **CLC 58**

See also CA 61-64; CANR 13, 46; DLB 40

Beerbohm, Max
See Beerbohm, (Henry) Max(imilian)

Beerbohm, (Henry) Max(imilian) 1872-1956
TCLC 1, 24
See also CA 104; 154; DLB 34, 100

Beer-Hofmann, Richard 1866-1945 **TCLC 60**
See also DLB 81

Begiebing, Robert J(ohn) 1946- .... **CLC 70**
See also CA 122; CANR 40

Behan, Brendan 1923-1964 **CLC 1, 8, 11, 15, 79; DAM DRAM**
See also CA 73-76; CANR 33; CDBLB 1945-1960; DLB 13; MTCW

Behn, Aphra 1640(?)-1689 **LC 1, 30; DA; DAB; DAC; DAM DRAM, MST, NOV, POET; DC 4; PC 13; WLC**
See also DLB 39, 80, 131

Behrman, S(amuel) N(athaniel) 1893-1973
CLC 40
See also CA 13-16; 45-48; CAP 1; DLB 7, 44

Belasco, David 1853-1931 .... **TCLC 3**
See also CA 104; DLB 7

Belcheva, Elisaveta 1893- .... **CLC 10**
See also Bagryana, Elisaveta

Beldone, Phil "Cheech"
See Ellison, Harlan (Jay)

Beleno
See Azuela, Mariano

Belinski, Vissarion Grigoryevich 1811-1848
NCLC 5

Belitt, Ben 1911- .... **CLC 22**
See also CA 13-16R; CAAS 4; CANR 7; DLB 5

Bell, Gertrude 1868-1926 .... **TCLC 67**
See also DLB 174

Bell, James Madison 1826-1902 ... **TCLC 43; BLC; DAM MULT**
See also BW 1; CA 122; 124; DLB 50

Bell, Madison Smartt 1957- ...... **CLC 41, 102**
See also CA 111; CANR 28, 54

Bell, Marvin (Hartley) 1937- **CLC 8, 31; DAM POET**
See also CA 21-24R; CAAS 14; CANR 59; DLB 5; MTCW

Bell, W. L. D.
See Mencken, H(enry) L(ouis)

Bellamy, Atwood C.
See Mencken, H(enry) L(ouis)

Bellamy, Edward 1850-1898 .... **NCLC 4**
See also DLB 12

Bellin, Edward J.
See Kuttner, Henry

Belloc, (Joseph) Hilaire (Pierre Sebastien Rene Swanton) 1870-1953 **TCLC 7, 18; DAM POET**
See also CA 106; 152; DLB 19, 100, 141, 174; YABC 1

Belloc, Joseph Peter Rene Hilaire
See Belloc, (Joseph) Hilaire (Pierre Sebastien Rene Swanton)

Belloc, Joseph Pierre Hilaire
See Belloc, (Joseph) Hilaire (Pierre Sebastien Rene Swanton)

Belloc, M. A.
See Lowndes, Marie Adelaide (Belloc)

Bellow, Saul 1915- **CLC 1, 2, 3, 6, 8, 10, 13, 15, 25, 33, 34, 63, 79; DA; DAB; DAC; DAM MST, NOV, POP; SSC 14; WLC**
See also AITN 2; BEST 89:3; CA 5-8R; CABS 1; CANR 29, 53; CDALB 1941-1968; DLB 2, 28; DLBD 3; DLBY 82; MTCW

Belser, Reimond Karel Maria de 1929- ....
See Ruyslinck, Ward
See also CA 152

Bely, Andrey .... **TCLC 7; PC 11**
See also Bugayev, Boris Nikolayevich

Benary, Margot
See Benary-Isbert, Margot

Benary-Isbert, Margot 1889-1979 .... **CLC 12**
See also CA 5-8R; 89-92; CANR 4; CLR 12; MAICYA; SATA 2; SATA-Obit 21

Benavente (y Martinez), Jacinto 1866-1954
TCLC 3; DAM DRAM, MULT
See also CA 106; 131; HW; MTCW

Benchley, Peter (Bradford) 1940- **CLC 4, 8; DAM NOV, POP**
See also AAYA 14; AITN 2; CA 17-20R; CANR 12, 35; MTCW; SATA 3, 89

Benchley, Robert (Charles) 1889-1945 **TCLC 1, 55**
See also CA 105; 153; DLB 11

Benda, Julien 1867-1956 .... **TCLC 60**
See also CA 120; 154

Benedict, Ruth (Fulton) 1887-1948 **TCLC 60**
See also CA 158

Benedikt, Michael 1935- .... **CLC 4, 14**
See also CA 13-16R; CANR 7; DLB 5

Benet, Juan 1927- .... **CLC 28**
See also CA 143

Benet, Stephen Vincent 1898-1943 . **TCLC 7; DAM POET; SSC 10**
See also CA 104; 152; DLB 4, 48, 102; YABC 1

Benet, William Rose 1886-1950 .... **TCLC 28; DAM POET**
See also CA 118; 152; DLB 45

Benford, Gregory (Albert) 1941- ...... **CLC 52**
See also CA 69-72; CAAS 27; CANR 12, 24, 49; DLBY 82

Bengtsson, Frans (Gunnar) 1894-1954 **TCLC 48**

Benjamin, David

See Slavitt, David R(ytman)

Benjamin, Lois
See Gould, Lois

Benjamin, Walter 1892-1940 .... **TCLC 39**

Benn, Gottfried 1886-1956 .... **TCLC 3**
See also CA 106; 153; DLB 56

Bennett, Alan 1934- **CLC 45, 77; DAB; DAM MST**
See also CA 103; CANR 35, 55; MTCW

Bennett, (Enoch) Arnold 1867-1931 **TCLC 5, 20**
See also CA 106; 155; CDBLB 1890-1914; DLB 10, 34, 98, 135

Bennett, Elizabeth
See Mitchell, Margaret (Munnerlyn)

Bennett, George Harold 1930- ....
See Bennett, Hal
See also BW 1; CA 97-100

Bennett, Hal .... **CLC 5**
See also Bennett, George Harold
See also DLB 33

Bennett, Jay 1912- .... **CLC 35**
See also AAYA 10; CA 69-72; CANR 11, 42; JRDA; SAAS 4; SATA 41, 87; SATA-Brief 27

Bennett, Louise (Simone) 1919- **CLC 28; BLC; DAM MULT**
See also BW 2; CA 151; DLB 117

Benson, E(dward) F(rederic) 1867-1940
TCLC 27
See also CA 114; 157; DLB 135, 153

Benson, Jackson J. 1930- .... **CLC 34**
See also CA 25-28R; DLB 111

Benson, Sally 1900-1972 .... **CLC 17**
See also CA 19-20; 37-40R; CAP 1; SATA 1, 35; SATA-Obit 27

Benson, Stella 1892-1933 .... **TCLC 17**
See also CA 117; 155; DLB 36, 162

Bentham, Jeremy 1748-1832 .... **NCLC 38**
See also DLB 107, 158

Bentley, E(dmund) C(lerihew) 1875-1956
TCLC 12
See also CA 108; DLB 70

Bentley, Eric (Russell) 1916- .... **CLC 24**
See also CA 5-8R; CANR 6; INT CANR-6

Beranger, Pierre Jean de 1780-1857 **NCLC 34**

Berdyaev, Nicolas
See Berdyaev, Nikolai (Aleksandrovich)

Berdyaev, Nikolai (Aleksandrovich) 1874-1948
TCLC 67
See also CA 120; 157

Berdyayev, Nikolai (Aleksandrovich)
See Berdyaev, Nikolai (Aleksandrovich)

Berendt, John (Lawrence) 1939- ...... **CLC 86**
See also CA 146

Blair, Eric (Arthur) 1903-1950 ....
See Orwell, George
See also CA 104; 132; DA; DAB; DAC; DAM MST, NOV; MTCW; SATA 29

Blais, Marie-Claire 1939-CLC **2, 4, 6, 13, 22; DAC; DAM MST**
See also CA 21-24R; CAAS 4; CANR 38; DLB 53; MTCW

Blaise, Clark 1940- .... **CLC 29**
See also AITN 2; CA 53-56; CAAS 3; CANR 5; DLB 53

Blake, Nicholas
See Day Lewis, C(ecil)
See also DLB 77

Blake, William 1757-1827 ....**NCLC 13, 37, 57; DA; DAB; DAC; DAM MST, POET; PC 12; WLC**
See also CDBLB 1789-1832; DLB 93, 163; MAICYA; SATA 30

Blake, William J(ames) 1894-1969 ...... **PC 12**
See also CA 5-8R; 25-28R

Blasco Ibanez, Vicente 1867-1928 **TCLC 12; DAM NOV**
See also CA 110; 131; HW; MTCW

Blatty, William Peter 1928-CLC **2; DAM POP**
See also CA 5-8R; CANR 9

Bleeck, Oliver
See Thomas, Ross (Elmore)

Blessing, Lee 1949- .... **CLC 54**

Blish, James (Benjamin) 1921-1975 . **CLC 14**
See also CA 1-4R; 57-60; CANR 3; DLB 8; MTCW; SATA 66

Bliss, Reginald
See Wells, H(erbert) G(eorge)

Blixen, Karen (Christentze Dinesen) 1885-1962

See Dinesen, Isak
See also CA 25-28; CANR 22, 50; CAP 2; MTCW; SATA 44

Bloch, Robert (Albert) 1917-1994 .... **CLC 33**
See also CA 5-8R; 146; CAAS 20; CANR 5; DLB 44; INT CANR-5; SATA 12; SATA-Obit 82

Blok, Alexander (Alexandrovich) 1880-1921 **TCLC 5**
See also CA 104

Blom, Jan
See Breytenbach, Breyten

Bloom, Harold 1930- .... **CLC 24**
See also CA 13-16R; CANR 39; DLB 67

Bloomfield, Aurelius
See Bourne, Randolph S(illiman)

Blount, Roy (Alton), Jr. 1941- .... **CLC 38**
See also CA 53-56; CANR 10, 28; INT CANR-28; MTCW

Bloy, Leon 1846-1917 .... **TCLC 22**
See also CA 121; DLB 123

Blume, Judy (Sussman) 1938- ... CLC **12, 30; DAM NOV, POP**
See also AAYA 3; CA 29-32R; CANR 13, 37; CLR 2, 15; DLB 52; JRDA; MAICYA; MTCW; SATA 2, 31, 79

Blunden, Edmund (Charles) 1896-1974 **C L C 2, 56**
See also CA 17-18; 45-48; CANR 54; CAP 2; DLB 20, 100, 155; MTCW

Bly, Robert (Elwood) 1926-CLC **1, 2, 5, 10, 15, 38; DAM POET**
See also CA 5-8R; CANR 41; DLB 5; MTCW

Boas, Franz 1858-1942 .... **TCLC 56**
See also CA 115

Bobette
See Simenon, Georges (Jacques Christian)

Boccaccio, Giovanni 1313-1375 ...**CMLC 13; SSC 10**

Bochco, Steven 1943- .... **CLC 35**
See also AAYA 11; CA 124; 138

Bodenheim, Maxwell 1892-1954 .... **TCLC 44**
See also CA 110; DLB 9, 45

Bodker, Cecil 1927- .... **CLC 21**
See also CA 73-76; CANR 13, 44; CLR 23; MAICYA; SATA 14

Boell, Heinrich (Theodor) 1917-1985 **CLC 2, 3, 6, 9, 11, 15, 27, 32, 72; DA; DAB; DAC; DAM MST, NOV; SSC 23; WLC**
See also CA 21-24R; 116; CANR 24; DLB 69; DLBY 85; MTCW

Boerne, Alfred
See Doeblin, Alfred

Boethius 480(?)-524(?) .... **CMLC 15**
See also DLB 115

Bogan, Louise 1897-1970 . **CLC 4, 39, 46, 93; DAM POET; PC 12**
See also CA 73-76; 25-28R; CANR 33; DLB 45, 169; MTCW

Bogarde, Dirk .... **CLC 19**
See also Van Den Bogarde, Derek Jules Gaspard Ulric Niven
See also DLB 14

Bogosian, Eric 1953- .... **CLC 45**
See also CA 138

Bograd, Larry 1953- .... **CLC 35**
See also CA 93-96; CANR 57; SAAS 21; SATA 33, 89

Boiardo, Matteo Maria 1441-1494 .... **LC 6**

Boileau-Despreaux, Nicolas 1636-1711 . **LC 3**

Bojer, Johan 1872-1959 .... **TCLC 64**

Boland, Eavan (Aisling) 1944- .. **CLC 40, 67; DAM POET**
See also CA 143; DLB 40

Bolt, Lee
See Faust, Frederick (Schiller)

Bolt, Robert (Oxton) 1924-1995CLC **14; DAM DRAM**
See also CA 17-20R; 147; CANR 35; DLB 13; MTCW

Bombet, Louis-Alexandre-Cesar
See Stendhal

Bomkauf
See Kaufman, Bob (Garnell)

Bonaventura .... **NCLC 35**
See also DLB 90

Bond, Edward 1934- **CLC 4, 6, 13, 23; DAM DRAM**
See also CA 25-28R; CANR 38; DLB 13; MTCW

Bonham, Frank 1914-1989 .... **CLC 12**
See also AAYA 1; CA 9-12R; CANR 4, 36; JRDA; MAICYA; SAAS 3; SATA 1, 49; SATA-Obit 62

Bonnefoy, Yves 1923-... CLC **9, 15, 58; DAM MST, POET**
See also CA 85-88; CANR 33; MTCW

Bontemps, Arna(ud Wendell) 1902-1973**C L C 1, 18; BLC; DAM MULT, NOV, POET**
See also BW 1; CA 1-4R; 41-44R; CANR 4, 35; CLR 6; DLB 48, 51; JRDA; MAICYA; MTCW; SATA 2, 44; SATA-Obit 24

Booth, Martin 1944- .... **CLC 13**
See also CA 93-96; CAAS 2

Booth, Philip 1925- .... **CLC 23**
See also CA 5-8R; CANR 5; DLBY 82

Booth, Wayne C(layson) 1921- .... **CLC 24**
See also CA 1-4R; CAAS 5; CANR 3, 43; DLB 67

Borchert, Wolfgang 1921-1947 .... **TCLC 5**
See also CA 104; DLB 69, 124

Borel, Petrus 1809-1859 .... **NCLC 41**

Borges, Jorge Luis 1899-1986CLC **1, 2, 3, 4, 6, 8, 9, 10, 13, 19, 44, 48, 83; DA; DAB; DAC; DAM MST, MULT; HLC; SSC 4; WLC**
See also AAYA 19; CA 21-24R; CANR 19, 33; DLB 113; DLBY 86; HW; MTCW

Borowski, Tadeusz 1922-1951 .... **TCLC 9**
See also CA 106; 154

Borrow, George (Henry) 1803-1881 **NCLC 9**
See also DLB 21, 55, 166

Bosman, Herman Charles 1905-1951 **T C L C 49**

Bosschere, Jean de 1878(?)-1953 ... **TCLC 19**
See also CA 115

Boswell, James 1740-1795 . **LC 4; DA; DAB; DAC; DAM MST; WLC**
See also CDBLB 1660-1789; DLB 104, 142

Bottoms, David 1949- .... **CLC 53**
See also CA 105; CANR 22; DLB 120; DLBY 83

Boucicault, Dion 1820-1890 .... **NCLC 41**

Boucolon, Maryse 1937(?)- ....

See Conde, Maryse
See also CA 110; CANR 30, 53

Bourget, Paul (Charles Joseph) 1852-1935
TCLC 12
See also CA 107; DLB 123

Bourjaily, Vance (Nye) 1922- ....**CLC 8, 62**
See also CA 1-4R; CAAS 1; CANR 2; DLB 2, 143

Bourne, Randolph S(illiman) 1886-1918
TCLC 16
See also CA 117; 155; DLB 63

Bova, Ben(jamin William) 1932- ...... **CLC 45**
See also AAYA 16; CA 5-8R; CAAS 18; CANR 11, 56; CLR 3; DLBY 81; INT CANR-11; MAICYA; MTCW; SATA 6, 68

Bowen, Elizabeth (Dorothea Cole) 1899-1973
CLC 1, 3, 6, 11, 15, 22; DAM NOV; SSC 3
See also CA 17-18; 41-44R; CANR 35; CAP 2; CDBLB 1945-1960; DLB 15, 162; MTCW

Bowering, George 1935- .... **CLC 15, 47**
See also CA 21-24R; CAAS 16; CANR 10; DLB 53

Bowering, Marilyn R(uthe) 1949- .... **CLC 32**
See also CA 101; CANR 49

Bowers, Edgar 1924- .... **CLC 9**
See also CA 5-8R; CANR 24; DLB 5

Bowie, David .... **CLC 17**
See also Jones, David Robert

Bowles, Jane (Sydney) 1917-1973 **CLC 3, 68**
See also CA 19-20; 41-44R; CAP 2

Bowles, Paul (Frederick) 1910- **CLC 1, 2, 19, 53; SSC 3**
See also CA 1-4R; CAAS 1; CANR 1, 19, 50; DLB 5, 6; MTCW

Box, Edgar
See Vidal, Gore

Boyd, Nancy
See Millay, Edna St. Vincent

Boyd, William 1952- .... **CLC 28, 53, 70**
See also CA 114; 120; CANR 51

Boyle, Kay 1902-1992**CLC 1, 5, 19, 58; SSC 5**
See also CA 13-16R; 140; CAAS 1; CANR 29; DLB 4, 9, 48, 86; DLBY 93; MTCW

Boyle, Mark
See Kienzle, William X(avier)

Boyle, Patrick 1905-1982 .... **CLC 19**
See also CA 127

Boyle, T. C. 1948-...
See Boyle, T(homas) Coraghessan

Boyle, T(homas) Coraghessan 1948-**CLC 36, 55, 90; DAM POP; SSC 16**
See also BEST 90:4; CA 120; CANR 44; DLBY 86

Boz
See Dickens, Charles (John Huffam)

Brackenridge, Hugh Henry

1748-1816 .... **NCLC 7**
See also DLB 11, 37

Bradbury, Edward P.
See Moorcock, Michael (John)

Bradbury, Malcolm (Stanley) 1932- **CLC 32, 61; DAM NOV**
See also CA 1-4R; CANR 1, 33; DLB 14; MTCW

Bradbury, Ray (Douglas) 1920-**CLC 1, 3, 10, 15, 42, 98; DA; DAB; DAC; DAM MST, NOV, POP; WLC**
See also AAYA 15; AITN 1, 2; CA 1-4R; CANR 2, 30; CDALB 1968-1988; DLB 2, 8; INT CANR-30; MTCW; SATA 11, 64

Bradford, Gamaliel 1863-1932 ...... **TCLC 36**
See also DLB 17

Bradley, David (Henry, Jr.) 1950- .. **CLC 23; BLC; DAM MULT**
See also BW 1; CA 104; CANR 26; DLB 33

Bradley, John Ed(mund, Jr.) 1958- .. **CLC 55**
See also CA 139

Bradley, Marion Zimmer 1930-**CLC 30; DAM POP**
See also AAYA 9; CA 57-60; CAAS 10; CANR 7, 31, 51; DLB 8; MTCW; SATA 90

Bradstreet, Anne 1612(?)-1672**LC 4, 30; DA; DAC; DAM MST, POET; PC 10**
See also CDALB 1640-1865; DLB 24

Brady, Joan 1939-............................... **CLC 86**
See also CA 141

Bragg, Melvyn 1939- .... **CLC 10**
See also BEST 89:3; CA 57-60; CANR 10, 48; DLB 14

Braine, John (Gerard) 1922-1986**CLC 1, 3, 41**
See also CA 1-4R; 120; CANR 1, 33; CDBLB 1945-1960; DLB 15; DLBY 86; MTCW

Bramah, Ernest 1868-1942 .... **TCLC 72**
See also CA 156; DLB 70

Brammer, William 1930(?)-1978 .... **CLC 31**
See also CA 77-80

Brancati, Vitaliano 1907-1954 .... **TCLC 12**
See also CA 109

Brancato, Robin F(idler) 1936- .... **CLC 35**
See also AAYA 9; CA 69-72; CANR 11, 45; CLR 32; JRDA; SAAS 9; SATA 23

Brand, Max
See Faust, Frederick (Schiller)

Brand, Millen 1906-1980 .... **CLC 7**
See also CA 21-24R; 97-100

Branden, Barbara .... **CLC 44**
See also CA 148

Brandes, Georg (Morris Cohen) 1842-1927
TCLC 10
See also CA 105

Brandys, Kazimierz 1916- .... **CLC 62**

Branley, Franklyn M(ansfield) 1915-**CLC 21**

See also CA 33-36R; CANR 14, 39; CLR 13; MAICYA; SAAS 16; SATA 4, 68

Brathwaite, Edward Kamau 1930- . **CLC 11; DAM POET**
See also BW 2; CA 25-28R; CANR 11, 26, 47; DLB 125

Brautigan, Richard (Gary) 1935-1984**CLC 1, 3, 5, 9, 12, 34, 42; DAM NOV**
See also CA 53-56; 113; CANR 34; DLB 2, 5; DLBY 80, 84; MTCW; SATA 56

Brave Bird, Mary 1953-....................................
See Crow Dog, Mary (Ellen)
See also NNAL

Braverman, Kate 1950- .... **CLC 67**
See also CA 89-92

Brecht, Bertolt 1898-1956**TCLC 1, 6, 13, 35; DA; DAB; DAC; DAM DRAM, MST; DC 3; WLC**
See also CA 104; 133; DLB 56, 124; MTCW

Brecht, Eugen Berthold Friedrich
See Brecht, Bertolt

Bremer, Fredrika 1801-1865 .... **NCLC 11**

Brennan, Christopher John 1870-1932**TCLC 17**
See also CA 117

Brennan, Maeve 1917- .... **CLC 5**
See also CA 81-84

Brentano, Clemens (Maria) 1778-1842**NCLC 1**
See also DLB 90

Brent of Bin Bin
See Franklin, (Stella Maraia Sarah) Miles

Brenton, Howard 1942- .... **CLC 31**
See also CA 69-72; CANR 33; DLB 13; MTCW

Breslin, James 1930-.......................................
See Breslin, Jimmy
See also CA 73-76; CANR 31; DAM NOV; MTCW

Breslin, Jimmy ....**CLC 4, 43**
See also Breslin, James
See also AITN 1

Bresson, Robert 1901- .... **CLC 16**
See also CA 110; CANR 49

Breton, Andre 1896-1966**CLC 2, 9, 15, 54; PC 15**
See also CA 19-20; 25-28R; CANR 40; CAP 2; DLB 65; MTCW

Breytenbach, Breyten 1939(?)- . **CLC 23, 37; DAM POET**
See also CA 113; 129

Bridgers, Sue Ellen 1942- .... **CLC 26**
See also AAYA 8; CA 65-68; CANR 11, 36; CLR 18; DLB 52; JRDA; MAICYA; SAAS 1; SATA 22, 90

Bridges, Robert (Seymour) 1844-1930**TCLC 1; DAM POET**
See also CA 104; 152; CDBLB 1890-1914; DLB 19, 98

Bridie, James .... TCLC 3
See also Mavor, Osborne Henry
See also DLB 10

Brin, David 1950- .... CLC 34
See also AAYA 21; CA 102; CANR 24; INT
CANR-24; SATA 65

Brink, Andre (Philippus) 1935- . CLC 18, 36
See also CA 104; CANR 39; INT 103; MTCW

Brinsmead, H(esba) F(ay) 1922- .... CLC 21
See also CA 21-24R; CANR 10; MAICYA;
SAAS 5; SATA 18, 78

Brittain, Vera (Mary)
1893(?)-1970 .... CLC 23
See also CA 13-16; 25-28R; CANR 58; CAP 1;
MTCW

Broch, Hermann 1886-1951 .... TCLC 20
See also CA 117; DLB 85, 124

Brock, Rose
See Hansen, Joseph

Brodkey, Harold (Roy) 1930-1996 .... CLC 56
See also CA 111; 151; DLB 130

Brodsky, Iosif Alexandrovich 1940-1996 ....
See Brodsky, Joseph
See also AITN 1; CA 41-44R; 151; CANR 37;
DAM POET; MTCW

Brodsky, Joseph 1940-1996 CLC 4, 6, 13, 36,
100; PC 9
See also Brodsky, Iosif Alexandrovich

Brodsky, Michael (Mark) 1948- .... CLC 19
See also CA 102; CANR 18, 41, 58

Bromell, Henry 1947- .... CLC 5
See also CA 53-56; CANR 9

Bromfield, Louis (Brucker)
1896-1956 .... TCLC 11
See also CA 107; 155; DLB 4, 9, 86

Broner, E(sther) M(asserman) 1930- CLC 19
See also CA 17-20R; CANR 8, 25; DLB 28

Bronk, William 1918- .... CLC 10
See also CA 89-92; CANR 23; DLB 165

Bronstein, Lev Davidovich
See Trotsky, Leon

Bronte, Anne 1820-1849 .... NCLC 4
See also DLB 21

Bronte, Charlotte 1816-1855 NCLC 3, 8, 33,
58; DA; DAB; DAC; DAM MST, NOV;
WLC
See also AAYA 17; CDBLB 1832-1890; DLB
21, 159

Bronte, Emily (Jane)
1818-1848 .... NCLC 16, 35; DA; DAB; DAC;
DAM MST, NOV, POET; PC 8; WLC
See also AAYA 17; CDBLB 1832-1890; DLB
21, 32

Brooke, Frances 1724-1789 .... LC 6
See also DLB 39, 99

Brooke, Henry 1703(?)-1783 .... LC 1
See also DLB 39

Brooke, Rupert (Chawner) 1887-1915 T C L C
2, 7; DA; DAB; DAC; DAM MST, POET;
WLC
See also CA 104; 132; CDBLB 1914-1945;
DLB 19; MTCW

Brooke-Haven, P.
See Wodehouse, P(elham) G(renville)

Brooke-Rose, Christine 1926(?)- .... CLC 40
See also CA 13-16R; CANR 58; DLB 14

Brookner, Anita 1928- CLC 32, 34, 51; DAB;
DAM POP
See also CA 114; 120; CANR 37, 56; DLBY
87; MTCW

Brooks, Cleanth 1906-1994 .... CLC 24, 86
See also CA 17-20R; 145; CANR 33, 35; DLB
63; DLBY 94; INT CANR-35; MTCW

Brooks, George
See Baum, L(yman) Frank

Brooks, Gwendolyn 1917- CLC 1, 2, 4, 5, 15,
49; BLC; DA; DAC; DAM MST, MULT,
POET; PC 7; WLC
See also AAYA 20; AITN 1; BW 2; CA 1-4R;
CANR 1, 27, 52; CDALB 1941-1968; CLR
27; DLB 5, 76, 165; MTCW; SATA 6

Brooks, Mel .... CLC 12
See also Kaminsky, Melvin
See also AAYA 13; DLB 26

Brooks, Peter 1938- .... CLC 34
See also CA 45-48; CANR 1

Brooks, Van Wyck 1886-1963 .... CLC 29
See also CA 1-4R; CANR 6; DLB 45, 63, 103

Brophy, Brigid (Antonia) 1929-1995 CLC 6,
11, 29
See also CA 5-8R; 149; CAAS 4; CANR 25,
53; DLB 14; MTCW

Brosman, Catharine Savage 1934- ..... CLC 9
See also CA 61-64; CANR 21, 46

Brother Antoninus
See Everson, William (Oliver)

Broughton, T(homas) Alan 1936- ..... CLC 19
See also CA 45-48; CANR 2, 23, 48

Broumas, Olga 1949- .... CLC 10, 73
See also CA 85-88; CANR 20

Brown, Alan 1951- .... CLC 99

Brown, Charles Brockden 1771-1810 N C L C
22
See also CDALB 1640-1865; DLB 37, 59, 73

Brown, Christy 1932-1981 .... CLC 63
See also CA 105; 104; DLB 14

Brown, Claude
1937- .... CLC 30; BLC; DAM MULT
See also AAYA 7; BW 1; CA 73-76

Brown, Dee (Alexander)
1908- .... CLC 18, 47; DAM POP
See also CA 13-16R; CAAS 6; CANR 11, 45;
DLBY 80; MTCW; SATA 5

Brown, George
See Wertmueller, Lina

Brown, George Douglas 1869-1902 TCLC 28

Brown, George Mackay 1921-1996 CLC 5, 48,
100
See also CA 21-24R; 151; CAAS 6; CANR 12,
37; DLB 14, 27, 139; MTCW; SATA 35

Brown, (William) Larry 1951- .... CLC 73
See also CA 130; 134; INT 133

Brown, Moses
See Barrett, William (Christopher)

Brown, Rita Mae 1944- CLC 18, 43, 79; DAM
NOV, POP
See also CA 45-48; CANR 2, 11, 35; INT
CANR-11; MTCW

Brown, Roderick (Langmere) Haig-
See Haig-Brown, Roderick (Langmere)

Brown, Rosellen 1939- .... CLC 32
See also CA 77-80; CAAS 10; CANR 14, 44

Brown, Sterling Allen 1901-1989 CLC 1, 23,
59; BLC; DAM MULT, POET
See also BW 1; CA 85-88; 127; CANR 26; DLB
48, 51, 63; MTCW

Brown, Will
See Ainsworth, William Harrison

Brown, William Wells 1813-1884 ... NCLC 2;
BLC; DAM MULT; DC 1
See also DLB 3, 50

Browne, (Clyde) Jackson 1948(?)- .... CLC 21
See also CA 120

Browning, Elizabeth Barrett 1806-1861
NCLC 1, 16, 61; DA; DAB; DAC; DAM
MST, POET; PC 6; WLC
See also CDBLB 1832-1890; DLB 32

Browning, Robert 1812-1889 NCLC 19; DA;
DAB; DAC; DAM MST, POET; PC 2;
WLCS
See also CDBLB 1832-1890; DLB 32, 163;
YABC 1

Browning, Tod 1882-1962 .... CLC 16
See also CA 141; 117

Brownson, Orestes (Augustus) 1803-1876
NCLC 50

Bruccoli, Matthew J(oseph) 1931- ... CLC 34
See also CA 9-12R; CANR 7; DLB 103

Bruce, Lenny .... CLC 21
See also Schneider, Leonard Alfred

Bruin, John
See Brutus, Dennis

Brulard, Henri
See Stendhal

Brulls, Christian
See Simenon, Georges (Jacques Christian)

Brunner, John (Kilian Houston) 1934-1995
CLC 8, 10; DAM POP
See also CA 1-4R; 149; CAAS 8; CANR 2, 37;
MTCW

NCLC 2, 12; DA; DAB; DAC; DAM MST, POET; PC 16; WLC
See also CDBLB 1789-1832; DLB 96, 110

Byron, Robert 1905-1941 .... **TCLC 67**

C. 3. 3.
See Wilde, Oscar (Fingal O'Flahertie Wills)

Caballero, Fernan 1796-1877 .... **NCLC 10**

Cabell, Branch
See Cabell, James Branch

Cabell, James Branch 1879-1958 .... **TCLC 6**
See also CA 105; 152; DLB 9, 78

Cable, George Washington 1844-1925 **T C L C 4; SSC 4**
See also CA 104; 155; DLB 12, 74; DLBD 13

Cabral de Melo Neto, Joao 1920- ... **CLC 76; DAM MULT**
See also CA 151

Cabrera Infante, G(uillermo) 1929-.. **CLC 5, 25, 45; DAM MULT; HLC**
See also CA 85-88; CANR 29; DLB 113; HW; MTCW

Cade, Toni
See Bambara, Toni Cade

Cadmus and Harmonia
See Buchan, John

Caedmon fl. 658-680 .... **CMLC 7**
See also DLB 146

Caeiro, Alberto
See Pessoa, Fernando (Antonio Nogueira)

Cage, John (Milton, Jr.) 1912- .... **CLC 41**
See also CA 13-16R; CANR 9; INT CANR-9

Cahan, Abraham 1860-1951 .... **TCLC 71**
See also CA 108; 154; DLB 9, 25, 28

Cain, G.
See Cabrera Infante, G(uillermo)

Cain, Guillermo
See Cabrera Infante, G(uillermo)

Cain, James M(allahan) 1892-1977 **CLC 3, 11, 28**
See also AITN 1; CA 17-20R; 73-76; CANR 8, 34; MTCW

Caine, Mark
See Raphael, Frederic (Michael)

Calasso, Roberto 1941- .... **CLC 81**
See also CA 143

Calderon de la Barca, Pedro 1600-1681 .. **L C 23; DC 3**

Caldwell, Erskine (Preston) 1903-1987 **CLC 1, 8, 14, 50, 60; DAM NOV; SSC 19**
See also AITN 1; CA 1-4R; 121; CAAS 1; CANR 2, 33; DLB 9, 86; MTCW

Caldwell, (Janet Miriam) Taylor (Holland) 1900-1985 .... **CLC 2, 28, 39; DAM NOV, POP**
See also CA 5-8R; 116; CANR 5

Calhoun, John Caldwell 1782-1850 **NCLC 15**
See also DLB 3

Calisher, Hortense 1911- **CLC 2, 4, 8, 38; DAM NOV; SSC 15**
See also CA 1-4R; CANR 1, 22; DLB 2; INT CANR-22; MTCW

Callaghan, Morley Edward 1903-1990 **CLC 3, 14, 41, 65; DAC; DAM MST**
See also CA 9-12R; 132; CANR 33; DLB 68; MTCW

Callimachus c. 305B.C.-c. 240B.C. **CMLC 18**
See also DLB 176

Calvin, John 1509-1564 .... **LC 37**

Calvino, Italo 1923-1985 **CLC 5, 8, 11, 22, 33, 39, 73; DAM NOV; SSC 3**
See also CA 85-88; 116; CANR 23; MTCW

Cameron, Carey 1952- .... **CLC 59**
See also CA 135

Cameron, Peter 1959- .... **CLC 44**
See also CA 125; CANR 50

Campana, Dino 1885-1932 .... **TCLC 20**
See also CA 117; DLB 114

Campanella, Tommaso 1568-1639 .... **LC 32**

Campbell, John W(ood, Jr.) 1910-1971 **C L C 32**
See also CA 21-22; 29-32R; CANR 34; CAP 2; DLB 8; MTCW

Campbell, Joseph 1904-1987 .... **CLC 69**
See also AAYA 3; BEST 89:2; CA 1-4R; 124; CANR 3, 28; MTCW

Campbell, Maria 1940- .... **CLC 85; DAC**
See also CA 102; CANR 54; NNAL

Campbell, (John) Ramsey 1946- **CLC 42; SSC 19**
See also CA 57-60; CANR 7; INT CANR-7

Campbell, (Ignatius) Roy (Dunnachie) 1901-1957 .... **TCLC 5**
See also CA 104; 155; DLB 20

Campbell, Thomas 1777-1844 .... **NCLC 19**
See also DLB 93; 144

Campbell, Wilfred .... **TCLC 9**
See also Campbell, William

Campbell, William 1858(?)-1918 ....
See Campbell, Wilfred
See also CA 106; DLB 92

Campion, Jane .... **CLC 95**
See also CA 138

Campos, Alvaro de
See Pessoa, Fernando (Antonio Nogueira)

Camus, Albert
1913-1960 **CLC 1, 2, 4, 9, 11, 14, 32, 63, 69; DA; DAB; DAC; DAM DRAM, MST, NOV; DC 2; SSC 9; WLC**
See also CA 89-92; DLB 72; MTCW

Canby, Vincent 1924- .... **CLC 13**
See also CA 81-84

Cancale
See Desnos, Robert

Canetti, Elias 1905-1994 **CLC 3, 14, 25, 75, 86**
See also CA 21-24R; 146; CANR 23; DLB 85, 124; MTCW

Canin, Ethan 1960- .... **CLC 55**
See also CA 131; 135

Cannon, Curt
See Hunter, Evan

Cape, Judith
See Page, P(atricia) K(athleen)

Capek, Karel 1890-1938 ... **TCLC 6, 37; DA; DAB; DAC; DAM DRAM, MST, NOV; DC 1; WLC**
See also CA 104; 140

Capote, Truman 1924-1984 **CLC 1, 3, 8, 13, 19, 34, 38, 58; DA; DAB; DAC; DAM MST, NOV, POP; SSC 2; WLC**
See also CA 5-8R; 113; CANR 18; CDALB 1941-1968; DLB 2; DLBY 80, 84; MTCW; SATA 91

Capra, Frank 1897-1991 .... **CLC 16**
See also CA 61-64; 135

Caputo, Philip 1941- .... **CLC 32**
See also CA 73-76; CANR 40

Card, Orson Scott 1951- **CLC 44, 47, 50; DAM POP**
See also AAYA 11; CA 102; CANR 27, 47; INT CANR-27; MTCW; SATA 83

Cardenal, Ernesto 1925- .... **CLC 31; DAM MULT, POET; HLC**
See also CA 49-52; CANR 2, 32; HW; MTCW

Cardozo, Benjamin N(athan) 1870-1938 **TCLC 65**
See also CA 117

Carducci, Giosue 1835-1907 .... **TCLC 32**

Carew, Thomas 1595(?)-1640 .... **LC 13**
See also DLB 126

Carey, Ernestine Gilbreth 1908- .... **CLC 17**
See also CA 5-8R; SATA 2

Carey, Peter 1943- .... **CLC 40, 55, 96**
See also CA 123; 127; CANR 53; INT 127; MTCW; SATA 94

Carleton, William 1794-1869 .... **NCLC 3**
See also DLB 159

Carlisle, Henry (Coffin) 1926- .... **CLC 33**
See also CA 13-16R; CANR 15

Carlsen, Chris
See Holdstock, Robert P.

Carlson, Ron(ald F.) 1947- .... **CLC 54**
See also CA 105; CANR 27

Carlyle, Thomas 1795-1881 . **NCLC 22; DA; DAB; DAC; DAM MST**
See also CDBLB 1789-1832; DLB 55; 144

Carman, (William) Bliss 1861-1929 **TCLC 7; DAC**

Cesaire, Aime (Fernand) 1913-. CLC 19, 32; BLC; DAM MULT, POET
See also BW 2; CA 65-68; CANR 24, 43; MTCW

Chabon, Michael 1963- .... CLC 55
See also CA 139; CANR 57

Chabrol, Claude 1930- .... CLC 16
See also CA 110

Challans, Mary 1905-1983 ....
See Renault, Mary
See also CA 81-84; 111; SATA 23; SATA-Obit 36

Challis, George
See Faust, Frederick (Schiller)

Chambers, Aidan 1934- .... CLC 35
See also CA 25-28R; CANR 12, 31, 58; JRDA; MAICYA; SAAS 12; SATA 1, 69

Chambers, James 1948- ....
See Cliff, Jimmy
See also CA 124

Chambers, Jessie
See Lawrence, D(avid) H(erbert Richards)

Chambers, Robert W. 1865-1933 ... TCLC 41

Chandler, Raymond (Thornton) 1888-1959 TCLC 1, 7; SSC 23
See also CA 104; 129; CDALB 1929-1941; DLBD 6; MTCW

Chang, Jung 1952- .... CLC 71
See also CA 142

Channing, William Ellery 1780-1842 NCLC 17
See also DLB 1, 59

Chaplin, Charles Spencer 1889-1977 CLC 16
See also Chaplin, Charlie
See also CA 81-84; 73-76

Chaplin, Charlie
See Chaplin, Charles Spencer
See also DLB 44

Chapman, George 1559(?)-1634 LC 22; DAM DRAM
See also DLB 62, 121

Chapman, Graham 1941-1989 .... CLC 21
See also Monty Python
See also CA 116; 129; CANR 35

Chapman, John Jay 1862-1933 .... TCLC 7
See also CA 104

Chapman, Lee
See Bradley, Marion Zimmer

Chapman, Walker
See Silverberg, Robert

Chappell, Fred (Davis) 1936- ..... CLC 40, 78
See also CA 5-8R; CAAS 4; CANR 8, 33; DLB 6, 105

Char, Rene(-Emile) 1907-1988 .... CLC 9, 11, 14, 55; DAM POET
See also CA 13-16R; 124; CANR 32; MTCW

Charby, Jay
See Ellison, Harlan (Jay)

Chardin, Pierre Teilhard de
See Teilhard de Chardin, (Marie Joseph) Pierre

Charles I 1600-1649 .... LC 13

Charyn, Jerome 1937- .... CLC 5, 8, 18
See also CA 5-8R; CAAS 1; CANR 7; DLBY 83; MTCW

Chase, Mary (Coyle) 1907-1981 .... DC 1
See also CA 77-80; 105; SATA 17; SATA-Obit 29

Chase, Mary Ellen 1887-1973 .... CLC 2
See also CA 13-16; 41-44R; CAP 1; SATA 10

Chase, Nicholas
See Hyde, Anthony

Chateaubriand, Francois Rene de 1768-1848 NCLC 3
See also DLB 119

Chatterje, Sarat Chandra 1876-1936(?) ....
See Chatterji, Saratchandra
See also CA 109

Chatterji, Bankim Chandra 1838-1894 NCLC 19

Chatterji, Saratchandra .... TCLC 13
See also Chatterje, Sarat Chandra

Chatterton, Thomas 1752-1770 . LC 3; DAM POET
See also DLB 109

Chatwin, (Charles) Bruce 1940-1989 CLC 28, 57, 59; DAM POP
See also AAYA 4; BEST 90:1; CA 85-88; 127

Chaucer, Daniel
See Ford, Ford Madox

Chaucer, Geoffrey 1340(?)-1400 LC 17; DA; DAB; DAC; DAM MST, POET; PC 19; WLCS
See also CDBLB Before 1660; DLB 146

Chaviaras, Strates 1935- ....
See Haviaras, Stratis
See also CA 105

Chayefsky, Paddy .... CLC 23
See also Chayefsky, Sidney
See also DLB 7, 44; DLBY 81

Chayefsky, Sidney 1923-1981 ....
See Chayefsky, Paddy
See also CA 9-12R; 104; CANR 18; DAM DRAM

Chedid, Andree 1920- .... CLC 47
See also CA 145

Cheever, John 1912-1982 CLC 3, 7, 8, 11, 15, 25, 64; DA; DAB; DAC; DAM MST, NOV, POP; SSC 1; WLC
See also CA 5-8R; 106; CABS 1; CANR 5, 27; CDALB 1941-1968; DLB 2, 102; DLBY 80, 82; INT CANR-5; MTCW

Cheever, Susan 1943- .... CLC 18, 48
See also CA 103; CANR 27, 51; DLBY 82; INT

CANR-27

Chekhonte, Antosha
See Chekhov, Anton (Pavlovich)

Chekhov, Anton (Pavlovich) 1860-1904 TCLC 3, 10, 31, 55; DA; DAB; DAC; DAM DRAM, MST; SSC 2; WLC
See also CA 104; 124; SATA 90

Chernyshevsky, Nikolay Gavrilovich 1828-1889 NCLC 1

Cherry, Carolyn Janice 1942- ....
See Cherryh, C. J.
See also CA 65-68; CANR 10

Cherryh, C. J. .... CLC 35
See also Cherry, Carolyn Janice
See also DLBY 80; SATA 93

Chesnutt, Charles W(addell) 1858-1932 TCLC 5, 39; BLC; DAM MULT; SSC 7
See also BW 1; CA 106; 125; DLB 12, 50, 78; MTCW

Chester, Alfred 1929(?)-1971 .... CLC 49
See also CA 33-36R; DLB 130

Chesterton, G(ilbert) K(eith) 1874-1936 TCLC 1, 6, 64; DAM NOV, POET; SSC 1
See also CA 104; 132; CDBLB 1914-1945; DLB 10, 19, 34, 70, 98, 149, 178; MTCW; SATA 27

Chiang Pin-chin 1904-1986 ....
See Ding Ling
See also CA 118

Ch'ien Chung-shu 1910- .... CLC 22
See also CA 130; MTCW

Child, L. Maria
See Child, Lydia Maria

Child, Lydia Maria 1802-1880 .... NCLC 6
See also DLB 1, 74; SATA 67

Child, Mrs.
See Child, Lydia Maria

Child, Philip 1898-1978 .... CLC 19, 68
See also CA 13-14; CAP 1; SATA 47

Childers, (Robert) Erskine 1870-1922 TCLC 65
See also CA 113; 153; DLB 70

Childress, Alice 1920-1994 .. CLC 12, 15, 86, 96; BLC; DAM DRAM, MULT, NOV; DC 4
See also AAYA 8; BW 2; CA 45-48; 146; CANR 3, 27, 50; CLR 14; DLB 7, 38; JRDA; MAICYA; MTCW; SATA 7, 48, 81

Chin, Frank (Chew, Jr.) 1940- .... DC 7
See also CA 33-36R; DAM MULT

Chislett, (Margaret) Anne 1943- ...... CLC 34
See also CA 151

Chitty, Thomas Willes 1926- .... CLC 11
See also Hinde, Thomas
See also CA 5-8R

Chivers, Thomas Holley 1809-1858 NCLC 49
See also DLB 3

See Westlake, Donald E(dwin)

Coetzee, J(ohn) M(ichael) 1940- **CLC 23, 33, 66; DAM NOV**
See also CA 77-80; CANR 41, 54; MTCW

Coffey, Brian
See Koontz, Dean R(ay)

Cohan, George M. 1878-1942 .... **TCLC 60**
See also CA 157

Cohen, Arthur A(llen) 1928-1986 . **CLC 7, 31**
See also CA 1-4R; 120; CANR 1, 17, 42; DLB 28

Cohen, Leonard (Norman) 1934- **CLC 3, 38; DAC; DAM MST**
See also CA 21-24R; CANR 14; DLB 53; MTCW

Cohen, Matt 1942- .... **CLC 19; DAC**
See also CA 61-64; CAAS 18; CANR 40; DLB 53

Cohen-Solal, Annie 19(?)- .... **CLC 50**

Colegate, Isabel 1931- .... **CLC 36**
See also CA 17-20R; CANR 8, 22; DLB 14; INT CANR-22; MTCW

Coleman, Emmett
See Reed, Ishmael

Coleridge, M. E.
See Coleridge, Mary E(lizabeth)

Coleridge, Mary E(lizabeth) 1861-1907**TCLC 73**
See also CA 116; DLB 19, 98

Coleridge, Samuel Taylor 1772-1834**NCLC 9, 54; DA; DAB; DAC; DAM MST, POET; PC 11; WLC**
See also CDBLB 1789-1832; DLB 93, 107

Coleridge, Sara 1802-1852 .... **NCLC 31**

Coles, Don 1928- .... **CLC 46**
See also CA 115; CANR 38

Colette, (Sidonie-Gabrielle) 1873-1954**T C L C 1, 5, 16; DAM NOV; SSC 10**
See also CA 104; 131; DLB 65; MTCW

Collett, (Jacobine) Camilla (Wergeland) 1813-1895 .... **NCLC 22**

Collier, Christopher 1930- .... **CLC 30**
See also AAYA 13; CA 33-36R; CANR 13, 33; JRDA; MAICYA; SATA 16, 70

Collier, James L(incoln) 1928-**CLC 30; DAM POP**
See also AAYA 13; CA 9-12R; CANR 4, 33; CLR 3; JRDA; MAICYA; SAAS 21; SATA 8, 70

Collier, Jeremy 1650-1726 .... **LC 6**

Collier, John 1901-1980 .... **SSC 19**
See also CA 65-68; 97-100; CANR 10; DLB 77

Collingwood, R(obin) G(eorge) 1889(?)-1943 **TCLC 67**
See also CA 117; 155

Collins, Hunt
See Hunter, Evan

Collins, Linda 1931- .... **CLC 44**
See also CA 125

Collins, (William) Wilkie 1824-1889**NCLC 1, 18**
See also CDBLB 1832-1890; DLB 18, 70, 159

Collins, William 1721-1759**LC 4; DAM POET**
See also DLB 109

Collodi, Carlo 1826-1890 .... **NCLC 54**
See also Lorenzini, Carlo
See also CLR 5

Colman, George
See Glassco, John

Colt, Winchester Remington
See Hubbard, L(afayette) Ron(ald)

Colter, Cyrus 1910- .... **CLC 58**
See also BW 1; CA 65-68; CANR 10; DLB 33

Colton, James
See Hansen, Joseph

Colum, Padraic 1881-1972 .... **CLC 28**
See also CA 73-76; 33-36R; CANR 35; CLR 36; MAICYA; MTCW; SATA 15

Colvin, James
See Moorcock, Michael (John)

Colwin, Laurie (E.) 1944-1992**CLC 5, 13, 23, 84**
See also CA 89-92; 139; CANR 20, 46; DLBY 80; MTCW

Comfort, Alex(ander) 1920-**CLC 7; DAM POP**
See also CA 1-4R; CANR 1, 45

Comfort, Montgomery
See Campbell, (John) Ramsey

Compton-Burnett, I(vy) 1884(?)-1969**CLC 1, 3, 10, 15, 34; DAM NOV**
See also CA 1-4R; 25-28R; CANR 4; DLB 36; MTCW

Comstock, Anthony 1844-1915 ...... **TCLC 13**
See also CA 110

Comte, Auguste 1798-1857 .... **NCLC 54**

Conan Doyle, Arthur
See Doyle, Arthur Conan

Conde, Maryse 1937- ...... **CLC 52, 92; DAM MULT**
See also Boucolon, Maryse
See also BW 2

Condillac, Etienne Bonnot de 1714-1780 **L C 26**

Condon, Richard (Thomas) 1915-1996**CLC 4, 6, 8, 10, 45, 100; DAM NOV**
See also BEST 90:3; CA 1-4R; 151; CAAS 1; CANR 2, 23; INT CANR-23; MTCW

Confucius 551B.C.-479B.C. . **CMLC 19; DA; DAB; DAC; DAM MST; WLCS**

Congreve, William 1670-1729 **LC 5, 21; DA;**

DAB; DAC; DAM DRAM, MST, POET; DC 2; WLC
See also CDBLB 1660-1789; DLB 39, 84

Connell, Evan S(helby), Jr. 1924-**CLC 4, 6, 45; DAM NOV**
See also AAYA 7; CA 1-4R; CAAS 2; CANR 2, 39; DLB 2; DLBY 81; MTCW

Connelly, Marc(us Cook) 1890-1980 .. **CLC 7**
See also CA 85-88; 102; CANR 30; DLB 7; DLBY 80; SATA-Obit 25

Connor, Ralph .... **TCLC 31**
See also Gordon, Charles William
See also DLB 92

Conrad, Joseph 1857-1924**TCLC 1, 6, 13, 25, 43, 57; DA; DAB; DAC; DAM MST, NOV; SSC 9; WLC**
See also CA 104; 131; CDBLB 1890-1914; DLB 10, 34, 98, 156; MTCW; SATA 27

Conrad, Robert Arnold
See Hart, Moss

Conroy, Donald Pat(rick) 1945- **CLC 30, 74; DAM NOV, POP**
See also AAYA 8; AITN 1; CA 85-88; CANR 24, 53; DLB 6; MTCW

Constant (de Rebecque), (Henri) Benjamin 1767-1830 .... **NCLC 6**
See also DLB 119

Conybeare, Charles Augustus
See Eliot, T(homas) S(tearns)

Cook, Michael 1933- .... **CLC 58**
See also CA 93-96; DLB 53

Cook, Robin 1940- .... **CLC 14; DAM POP**
See also BEST 90:2; CA 108; 111; CANR 41; INT 111

Cook, Roy
See Silverberg, Robert

Cooke, Elizabeth 1948- .... **CLC 55**
See also CA 129

Cooke, John Esten 1830-1886 .... **NCLC 5**
See also DLB 3

Cooke, John Estes
See Baum, L(yman) Frank

Cooke, M. E.
See Creasey, John

Cooke, Margaret
See Creasey, John

Cook-Lynn, Elizabeth 1930-.. **CLC 93; DAM MULT**
See also CA 133; DLB 175; NNAL

Cooney, Ray .... **CLC 62**

Cooper, Douglas 1960- .... **CLC 86**

Cooper, Henry St. John
See Creasey, John

Cooper, J(oan) California .... **CLC 56; DAM MULT**
See also AAYA 12; BW 1; CA 125; CANR 55

DRAM
See also CA 110; 152; DLB 7

Croce, Benedetto 1866-1952 .... **TCLC 37**
See also CA 120; 155

Crockett, David 1786-1836 .... **NCLC 8**
See also DLB 3, 11

Crockett, Davy
See Crockett, David

Crofts, Freeman Wills 1879-1957 .. **TCLC 55**
See also CA 115; DLB 77

Croker, John Wilson 1780-1857 .... **NCLC 10**
See also DLB 110

Crommelynck, Fernand 1885-1970 .. **CLC 75**
See also CA 89-92

Cronin, A(rchibald) J(oseph) 1896-1981**C L C 32**
See also CA 1-4R; 102; CANR 5; SATA 47;
SATA-Obit 25

Cross, Amanda
See Heilbrun, Carolyn G(old)

Crothers, Rachel 1878(?)-1958 ...... **TCLC 19**
See also CA 113; DLB 7

Croves, Hal
See Traven, B.

Crow Dog, Mary (Ellen) (?)- .... **CLC 93**
See also Brave Bird, Mary
See also CA 154

Crowfield, Christopher
See Stowe, Harriet (Elizabeth) Beecher

Crowley, Aleister .... **TCLC 7**
See also Crowley, Edward Alexander

Crowley, Edward Alexander 1875-1947 ....
See Crowley, Aleister
See also CA 104

Crowley, John 1942- .... **CLC 57**
See also CA 61-64; CANR 43; DLBY 82; SATA
65

Crud
See Crumb, R(obert)

Crumarums
See Crumb, R(obert)

Crumb, R(obert)
1943- .... **CLC 17**
See also CA 106

Crumbum
See Crumb, R(obert)

Crumski
See Crumb, R(obert)

Crum the Bum
See Crumb, R(obert)

Crunk
See Crumb, R(obert)

Crustt
See Crumb, R(obert)

Cryer, Gretchen (Kiger) 1935- .... **CLC 21**
See also CA 114; 123

Csath, Geza 1887-1919 .... **TCLC 13**
See also CA 111

Cudlip, David 1933- .... **CLC 34**

Cullen, Countee 1903-1946**TCLC 4, 37; BLC;
DA; DAC; DAM MST, MULT, POET;
WLCS**
See also BW 1; CA 108; 124; CDALB 1917-
1929; DLB 4, 48, 51; MTCW; SATA 18

Cum, R.
See Crumb, R(obert)

Cummings, Bruce F(rederick) 1889-1919 .....
See Barbellion, W. N. P.
See also CA 123

Cummings, E(dward) E(stlin) 1894-1962**CLC
1, 3, 8, 12, 15, 68; DA; DAB; DAC; DAM
MST, POET; PC 5; WLC 2**
See also CA 73-76; CANR 31; CDALB 1929-
1941; DLB 4, 48; MTCW

Cunha, Euclides (Rodrigues Pimenta) da 1866-
1909 .... **TCLC 24**
See also CA 123

Cunningham, E. V.
See Fast, Howard (Melvin)

Cunningham, J(ames) V(incent) 1911-1985
CLC 3, 31
See also CA 1-4R; 115; CANR 1; DLB 5

Cunningham, Julia (Woolfolk) 1916-**CLC 12**
See also CA 9-12R; CANR 4, 19, 36; JRDA;
MAICYA; SAAS 2; SATA 1, 26

Cunningham, Michael 1952- .... **CLC 34**
See also CA 136

Cunninghame Graham, R(obert) B(ontine)
1852-1936 .... **TCLC 19**
See also Graham, R(obert) B(ontine)
Cunninghame
See also CA 119; DLB 98

Currie, Ellen 19(?)- .... **CLC 44**

Curtin, Philip
See Lowndes, Marie Adelaide (Belloc)

Curtis, Price
See Ellison, Harlan (Jay)

Cutrate, Joe
See Spiegelman, Art

Cynewulf c. 770-c. 840 .... **CMLC 23**

Czaczkes, Shmuel Yosef
See Agnon, S(hmuel) Y(osef Halevi)

Dabrowska, Maria (Szumska) 1889-1965**CLC
15**
See also CA 106

Dabydeen, David 1955- .... **CLC 34**
See also BW 1; CA 125; CANR 56

Dacey, Philip 1939- .... **CLC 51**
See also CA 37-40R; CAAS 17; CANR 14, 32;
DLB 105

Dagerman, Stig (Halvard) 1923-1954 **T C L C
17**
See also CA 117; 155

Dahl, Roald 1916-1990**CLC 1, 6, 18, 79; DAB;
DAC; DAM MST, NOV, POP**
See also AAYA 15; CA 1-4R; 133; CANR 6,
32, 37; CLR 1, 7, 41; DLB 139; JRDA;
MAICYA; MTCW; SATA 1, 26, 73; SATA-
Obit 65

Dahlberg, Edward 1900-1977 .. **CLC 1, 7, 14**
See also CA 9-12R; 69-72; CANR 31; DLB 48;
MTCW

Dale, Colin .... **TCLC 18**
See also Lawrence, T(homas) E(dward)

Dale, George E.
See Asimov, Isaac

Daly, Elizabeth 1878-1967 .... **CLC 52**
See also CA 23-24; 25-28R; CAP 2

Daly, Maureen 1921- .... **CLC 17**
See also AAYA 5; CANR 37; JRDA; MAICYA;
SAAS 1; SATA 2

Damas, Leon-Gontran 1912-1978 .... **CLC 84**
See also BW 1; CA 125; 73-76

Dana, Richard Henry Sr. 1787-1879**NCLC 53**

Daniel, Samuel 1562(?)-1619 .... **LC 24**
See also DLB 62

Daniels, Brett
See Adler, Renata

Dannay, Frederic 1905-1982 . **CLC 11; DAM
POP**
See also Queen, Ellery
See also CA 1-4R; 107; CANR 1, 39; DLB 137;
MTCW

D'Annunzio, Gabriele 1863-1938**TCLC 6, 40**
See also CA 104; 155

Danois, N. le
See Gourmont, Remy (-Marie-Charles) de

d'Antibes, Germain
See Simenon, Georges (Jacques Christian)

Danticat, Edwidge 1969- .... **CLC 94**
See also CA 152

Danvers, Dennis 1947- .... **CLC 70**

Danziger, Paula 1944- .... **CLC 21**
See also AAYA 4; CA 112; 115; CANR 37; CLR
20; JRDA; MAICYA; SATA 36, 63; SATA-
Brief 30

Da Ponte, Lorenzo 1749-1838 .... **NCLC 50**

Dario, Ruben 1867-1916 .... **TCLC 4; DAM
MULT; HLC; PC 15**
See also CA 131; HW; MTCW

Darley, George 1795-1846 .... **NCLC 2**
See also DLB 96

Darwin, Charles 1809-1882 .... **NCLC 57**
See also DLB 57, 166

Daryush, Elizabeth 1887-1977 ...... **CLC 6, 19**

See also CA 49-52; CANR 3; DLB 20

Dashwood, Edmee Elizabeth Monica de la Pasture 1890-1943 ....
See Delafield, E. M.
See also CA 119; 154

Daudet, (Louis Marie) Alphonse 1840-1897 **NCLC 1**
See also DLB 123

Daumal, Rene 1908-1944 .... **TCLC 14**
See also CA 114

Davenport, Guy (Mattison, Jr.) 1927-**CLC 6, 14, 38; SSC 16**
See also CA 33-36R; CANR 23; DLB 130

Davidson, Avram 1923- ....
See Queen, Ellery
See also CA 101; CANR 26; DLB 8

Davidson, Donald (Grady) 1893-1968**CLC 2, 13, 19**
See also CA 5-8R; 25-28R; CANR 4; DLB 45

Davidson, Hugh
See Hamilton, Edmond

Davidson, John 1857-1909 .... **TCLC 24**
See also CA 118; DLB 19

Davidson, Sara 1943- .... **CLC 9**
See also CA 81-84; CANR 44

Davie, Donald (Alfred) 1922-1995 . **CLC 5, 8, 10, 31**
See also CA 1-4R; 149; CAAS 3; CANR 1, 44; DLB 27; MTCW

Davies, Ray(mond Douglas) 1944- ... **CLC 21**
See also CA 116; 146

Davies, Rhys 1903-1978 .... **CLC 23**
See also CA 9-12R; 81-84; CANR 4; DLB 139

Davies, (William) Robertson 1913-1995 **C L C 2, 7, 13, 25, 42, 75, 91; DA; DAB; DAC; DAM MST, NOV, POP; WLC**
See also BEST 89:2; CA 33-36R; 150; CANR 17, 42; DLB 68; INT CANR-17; MTCW

Davies, W(illiam) H(enry) 1871-1940**TCLC 5**
See also CA 104; DLB 19, 174

Davies, Walter C.
See Kornbluth, C(yril) M.

Davis, Angela (Yvonne) 1944- **CLC 77; DAM MULT**
See also BW 2; CA 57-60; CANR 10

Davis, B. Lynch
See Bioy Casares, Adolfo; Borges, Jorge Luis

Davis, Gordon
See Hunt, E(verette) Howard, (Jr.)

Davis, Harold Lenoir 1896-1960 .... **CLC 49**
See also CA 89-92; DLB 9

Davis, Rebecca (Blaine) Harding 1831-1910 .... **TCLC 6**
See also CA 104; DLB 74

Davis, Richard Harding 1864-1916**TCLC 24**

See also CA 114; DLB 12, 23, 78, 79; DLBD 13

Davison, Frank Dalby 1893-1970 ..... **CLC 15**
See also CA 116

Davison, Lawrence H.
See Lawrence, D(avid) H(erbert Richards)

Davison, Peter (Hubert) 1928- .... **CLC 28**
See also CA 9-12R; CAAS 4; CANR 3, 43; DLB 5

Davys, Mary 1674-1732 .... **LC 1**
See also DLB 39

Dawson, Fielding 1930- .... **CLC 6**
See also CA 85-88; DLB 130

Dawson, Peter
See Faust, Frederick (Schiller)

Day, Clarence (Shepard, Jr.) 1874-1935 **TCLC 25**
See also CA 108; DLB 11

Day, Thomas 1748-1789 .... **LC 1**
See also DLB 39; YABC 1

Day Lewis, C(ecil) 1904-1972 . **CLC 1, 6, 10; DAM POET; PC 11**
See also Blake, Nicholas
See also CA 13-16; 33-36R; CANR 34; CAP 1; DLB 15, 20; MTCW

Dazai, Osamu .... **TCLC 11**
See also Tsushima, Shuji
See also DLB 182

de Andrade, Carlos Drummond
See Drummond de Andrade, Carlos

Deane, Norman
See Creasey, John

de Beauvoir, Simone (Lucie Ernestine Marie Bertrand)
See Beauvoir, Simone (Lucie Ernestine Marie Bertrand) de

de Brissac, Malcolm
See Dickinson, Peter (Malcolm)

de Chardin, Pierre Teilhard
See Teilhard de Chardin, (Marie Joseph) Pierre

Dee, John 1527-1608 .... **LC 20**

Deer, Sandra 1940- .... **CLC 45**

De Ferrari, Gabriella 1941- .... **CLC 65**
See also CA 146

Defoe, Daniel 1660(?)-1731 . **LC 1; DA; DAB; DAC; DAM MST, NOV; WLC**
See also CDBLB 1660-1789; DLB 39, 95, 101; JRDA; MAICYA; SATA 22

de Gourmont, Remy(-Marie-Charles)
See Gourmont, Remy (-Marie-Charles) de

de Hartog, Jan 1914- .... **CLC 19**
See also CA 1-4R; CANR 1

de Hostos, E. M.
See Hostos (y Bonilla), Eugenio Maria de

de Hostos, Eugenio M.
See Hostos (y Bonilla), Eugenio Maria de

Deighton, Len .... **CLC 4, 7, 22, 46**
See also Deighton, Leonard Cyril
See also AAYA 6; BEST 89:2; CDBLB 1960 to Present; DLB 87

Deighton, Leonard Cyril 1929- ....
See Deighton, Len
See also CA 9-12R; CANR 19, 33; DAM NOV, POP; MTCW

Dekker, Thomas 1572(?)-1632 .. **LC 22; DAM DRAM**
See also CDBLB Before 1660; DLB 62, 172

Delafield, E. M. 1890-1943 .... **TCLC 61**
See also Dashwood, Edmee Elizabeth Monica de la Pasture
See also DLB 34

de la Mare, Walter (John) 1873-1956**TCLC 4, 53; DAB; DAC; DAM MST, POET; SSC 14; WLC**
See also CDBLB 1914-1945; CLR 23; DLB 162; SATA 16

Delaney, Franey
See O'Hara, John (Henry)

Delaney, Shelagh 1939-**CLC 29; DAM DRAM**
See also CA 17-20R; CANR 30; CDBLB 1960 to Present; DLB 13; MTCW

Delany, Mary (Granville Pendarves) 1700-1788 **LC 12**

Delany, Samuel R(ay, Jr.) 1942-**CLC 8, 14, 38; BLC; DAM MULT**
See also BW 2; CA 81-84; CANR 27, 43; DLB 8, 33; MTCW

De La Ramee, (Marie) Louise 1839-1908 ......
See Ouida
See also SATA 20

de la Roche, Mazo 1879-1961 .... **CLC 14**
See also CA 85-88; CANR 30; DLB 68; SATA 64

De La Salle, Innocent
See Hartmann, Sadakichi

Delbanco, Nicholas (Franklin) 1942- **CLC 6, 13**
See also CA 17-20R; CAAS 2; CANR 29, 55; DLB 6

del Castillo, Michel 1933- .... **CLC 38**
See also CA 109

Deledda, Grazia (Cosima) 1875(?)-1936 **TCLC 23**
See also CA 123

Delibes, Miguel .... **CLC 8, 18**
See also Delibes Setien, Miguel

Delibes Setien, Miguel 1920- ....
See Delibes, Miguel
See also CA 45-48; CANR 1, 32; HW; MTCW

DeLillo, Don 1936- **CLC 8, 10, 13, 27, 39, 54, 76; DAM NOV, POP**
See also BEST 89:1; CA 81-84; CANR 21; DLB 6, 173; MTCW

de Lisser, H. G.
See De Lisser, H(erbert) G(eorge)
See also DLB 117

De Lisser, H(erbert) G(eorge) 1878-1944
TCLC 12
See also de Lisser, H. G.
See also BW 2; CA 109; 152

Deloria, Vine (Victor), Jr. 1933- ..... **CLC 21;**
DAM MULT
See also CA 53-56; CANR 5, 20, 48; DLB 175;
MTCW; NNAL; SATA 21

Del Vecchio, John M(ichael) 1947- ... **CLC 29**
See also CA 110; DLBD 9

de Man, Paul (Adolph Michel) 1919-1983
CLC 55
See also CA 128; 111; DLB 67; MTCW

De Marinis, Rick 1934- .... **CLC 54**
See also CA 57-60; CAAS 24; CANR 9, 25, 50

Dembry, R. Emmet
See Murfree, Mary Noailles

Demby, William 1922- . **CLC 53; BLC; DAM**
MULT
See also BW 1; CA 81-84; DLB 33

de Menton, Francisco
See Chin, Frank (Chew, Jr.)

Demijohn, Thom
See Disch, Thomas M(ichael)

de Montherlant, Henry (Milon)
See Montherlant, Henry (Milon) de

Demosthenes 384B.C.-322B.C. ...... **CMLC 13**
See also DLB 176

de Natale, Francine
See Malzberg, Barry N(athaniel)

Denby, Edwin (Orr) 1903-1983 .... **CLC 48**
See also CA 138; 110

Denis, Julio
See Cortazar, Julio

Denmark, Harrison
See Zelazny, Roger (Joseph)

Dennis, John 1658-1734 .... **LC 11**
See also DLB 101

Dennis, Nigel (Forbes) 1912-1989 .... **CLC 8**
See also CA 25-28R; 129; DLB 13, 15; MTCW

Dent, Lester 1904(?)-1959 .... **TCLC 72**
See also CA 112

De Palma, Brian (Russell) 1940- .... **CLC 20**
See also CA 109

De Quincey, Thomas
1785-1859 .... **NCLC 4**
See also CDBLB 1789-1832; DLB 110; 144

Deren, Eleanora 1908(?)-1961 ....
See Deren, Maya
See also CA 111

Deren, Maya 1917-1961 .... **CLC 16, 102**
See also Deren, Eleanora

Derleth, August (William) 1909-1971 **CLC 31**
See also CA 1-4R; 29-32R; CANR 4; DLB 9;
SATA 5

Der Nister 1884-1950 .... **TCLC 56**

de Routisie, Albert
See Aragon, Louis

Derrida, Jacques 1930- .... **CLC 24, 87**
See also CA 124; 127

Derry Down Derry
See Lear, Edward

Dersonnes, Jacques
See Simenon, Georges (Jacques Christian)

Desai, Anita 1937- **CLC 19, 37, 97; DAB; DAM**
NOV
See also CA 81-84; CANR 33, 53; MTCW;
SATA 63

de Saint-Luc, Jean
See Glassco, John

de Saint Roman, Arnaud
See Aragon, Louis

Descartes, Rene 1596-1650 .... **LC 20, 35**

De Sica, Vittorio 1901(?)-1974 .... **CLC 20**
See also CA 117

Desnos, Robert 1900-1945 .... **TCLC 22**
See also CA 121; 151

Destouches, Louis-Ferdinand 1894-1961 **C L C**
9, 15
See also Celine, Louis-Ferdinand
See also CA 85-88; CANR 28; MTCW

de Tolignac, Gaston
See Griffith, D(avid Lewelyn) W(ark)

Deutsch, Babette 1895-1982 .... **CLC 18**
See also CA 1-4R; 108; CANR 4; DLB 45;
SATA 1; SATA-Obit 33

Devenant, William 1606-1649 .... **LC 13**

Devkota, Laxmiprasad 1909-1959 . **TCLC 23**
See also CA 123

De Voto, Bernard (Augustine) 1897-1955
TCLC 29
See also CA 113; DLB 9

De Vries, Peter 1910-1993 **CLC 1, 2, 3, 7, 10,**
28, 46; DAM NOV
See also CA 17-20R; 142; CANR 41; DLB 6;
DLBY 82; MTCW

Dexter, John
See Bradley, Marion Zimmer

Dexter, Martin
See Faust, Frederick (Schiller)

Dexter, Pete 1943- ... **CLC 34, 55; DAM POP**
See also BEST 89:2; CA 127; 131; INT 131;
MTCW

Diamano, Silmang
See Senghor, Leopold Sedar

Diamond, Neil 1941- .... **CLC 30**

See also CA 108

Diaz del Castillo, Bernal 1496-1584 .... **LC 31**

di Bassetto, Corno
See Shaw, George Bernard

Dick, Philip K(indred) 1928-1982 **CLC 10, 30,**
72; DAM NOV, POP
See also CA 49-52; 106; CANR 2, 16; DLB 8;
MTCW

Dickens, Charles (John Huffam) 1812-1870
NCLC 3, 8, 18, 26, 37, 50; DA; DAB; DAC;
DAM MST, NOV; SSC 17; WLC
See also CDBLB 1832-1890; DLB 21, 55, 70,
159, 166; JRDA; MAICYA; SATA 15

Dickey, James (Lafayette) 1923-1997 **CLC 1,**
2, 4, 7, 10, 15, 47; DAM NOV, POET, POP
See also AITN 1, 2; CA 9-12R; 156; CABS 2;
CANR 10, 48; CDALB 1968-1988; DLB 5;
DLBD 7; DLBY 82, 93, 96; INT CANR-10;
MTCW

Dickey, William 1928-1994 .... **CLC 3, 28**
See also CA 9-12R; 145; CANR 24; DLB 5

Dickinson, Charles 1951- .... **CLC 49**
See also CA 128

Dickinson, Emily (Elizabeth) 1830-1886
NCLC 21; DA; DAB; DAC; DAM MST,
POET; PC 1; WLC
See also AAYA 22; CDALB 1865-1917; DLB
1; SATA 29

Dickinson, Peter (Malcolm) 1927- **CLC 12, 35**
See also AAYA 9; CA 41-44R; CANR 31, 58;
CLR 29; DLB 87, 161; JRDA; MAICYA;
SATA 5, 62

Dickson, Carr
See Carr, John Dickson

Dickson, Carter
See Carr, John Dickson

Diderot, Denis 1713-1784 .... **LC 26**

Didion, Joan 1934- **CLC 1, 3, 8, 14, 32; DAM**
NOV
See also AITN 1; CA 5-8R; CANR 14, 52;
CDALB 1968-1988; DLB 2, 173; DLBY 81,
86; MTCW

Dietrich, Robert
See Hunt, E(verette) Howard, (Jr.)

Dillard, Annie 1945- **CLC 9, 60; DAM NOV**
See also AAYA 6; CA 49-52; CANR 3, 43;
DLBY 80; MTCW; SATA 10

Dillard, R(ichard) H(enry) W(ilde) 1937-
CLC 5
See also CA 21-24R; CAAS 7; CANR 10; DLB
5

Dillon, Eilis 1920-1994 .... **CLC 17**
See also CA 9-12R; 147; CAAS 3; CANR 4,
38; CLR 26; MAICYA; SATA 2, 74; SATA-
Obit 83

Dimont, Penelope
See Mortimer, Penelope (Ruth)

Dinesen, Isak .... **CLC 10, 29, 95; SSC 7**

See also Blixen, Karen (Christentze Dinesen)

Ding Ling .... CLC 68
See also Chiang Pin-chin

Disch, Thomas M(ichael) 1940- .... CLC 7, 36
See also AAYA 17; CA 21-24R; CAAS 4;
CANR 17, 36, 54; CLR 18; DLB 8;
MAICYA; MTCW; SAAS 15; SATA 92

Disch, Tom
See Disch, Thomas M(ichael)

d'Isly, Georges
See Simenon, Georges (Jacques Christian)

Disraeli, Benjamin 1804-1881 .... NCLC 2, 39
See also DLB 21, 55

Ditcum, Steve
See Crumb, R(obert)

Dixon, Paige
See Corcoran, Barbara

Dixon, Stephen
1936- .... CLC 52; SSC 16
See also CA 89-92; CANR 17, 40, 54; DLB 130

Dobell, Sydney Thompson 1824-1874 N C L C
43
See also DLB 32

Doblin, Alfred .... TCLC 13
See also Doeblin, Alfred

Dobrolyubov, Nikolai Alexandrovich 1836-1861
NCLC 5

Dobyns, Stephen 1941- .... CLC 37
See also CA 45-48; CANR 2, 18

Doctorow, E(dgar) L(aurence)
1931- .... CLC 6, 11, 15, 18, 37, 44, 65;
DAM NOV, POP
See also AAYA 22; AITN 2; BEST 89:3; CA
45-48; CANR 2, 33, 51; CDALB 1968-1988;
DLB 2, 28, 173; DLBY 80; MTCW

Dodgson, Charles Lutwidge 1832-1898 ....
See Carroll, Lewis
See also CLR 2; DA; DAB; DAC; DAM MST,
NOV, POET; MAICYA; YABC 2

Dodson, Owen (Vincent) 1914-1983 CLC 79;
BLC; DAM MULT
See also BW 1; CA 65-68; 110; CANR 24; DLB
76

Doeblin, Alfred 1878-1957 .... TCLC 13
See also Doblin, Alfred
See also CA 110; 141; DLB 66

Doerr, Harriet 1910- .... CLC 34
See also CA 117; 122; CANR 47; INT 122

Domecq, H(onorio) Bustos
See Bioy Casares, Adolfo; Borges, Jorge Luis

Domini, Rey
See Lorde, Audre (Geraldine)

Dominique
See Proust, (Valentin-Louis-George-Eugene-)
Marcel

Don, A

See Stephen, Leslie

Donaldson, Stephen R. 1947- CLC 46; DAM
POP
See also CA 89-92; CANR 13, 55; INT CANR-
13

Donleavy, J(ames) P(atrick) 1926-CLC 1, 4, 6,
10, 45
See also AITN 2; CA 9-12R; CANR 24, 49;
DLB 6, 173; INT CANR-24; MTCW

Donne, John 1572-1631LC 10, 24; DA; DAB;
DAC; DAM MST, POET; PC 1
See also CDBLB Before 1660; DLB 121, 151

Donnell, David 1939(?)- .... CLC 34

Donoghue, P. S.
See Hunt, E(verette) Howard, (Jr.)

Donoso (Yanez), Jose 1924-1996CLC 4, 8, 11,
32, 99; DAM MULT; HLC
See also CA 81-84; 155; CANR 32; DLB 113;
HW; MTCW

Donovan, John 1928-1992 .... CLC 35
See also AAYA 20; CA 97-100; 137; CLR 3;
MAICYA; SATA 72; SATA-Brief 29

Don Roberto
See Cunninghame Graham, R(obert) B(ontine)

Doolittle, Hilda 1886-1961CLC 3, 8, 14, 31, 34,
73; DA; DAC; DAM MST, POET; PC 5;
WLC
See also H. D.
See also CA 97-100; CANR 35; DLB 4, 45;
MTCW

Dorfman, Ariel 1942- ...... CLC 48, 77; DAM
MULT; HLC
See also CA 124; 130; HW; INT 130

Dorn, Edward (Merton) 1929- ... CLC 10, 18
See also CA 93-96; CANR 42; DLB 5; INT 93-
96

Dorsan, Luc
See Simenon, Georges (Jacques Christian)

Dorsange, Jean
See Simenon, Georges (Jacques Christian)

Dos Passos, John (Roderigo) 1896-1970 C L C
1, 4, 8, 11, 15, 25, 34, 82; DA; DAB; DAC;
DAM MST, NOV; WLC
See also CA 1-4R; 29-32R; CANR 3; CDALB
1929-1941; DLB 4, 9; DLBD 1, 15; DLBY
96; MTCW

Dossage, Jean
See Simenon, Georges (Jacques Christian)

Dostoevsky, Fedor Mikhailovich 1821-1881
NCLC 2, 7, 21, 33, 43; DA; DAB; DAC;
DAM MST, NOV; SSC 2; WLC

Doughty, Charles M(ontagu) 1843-1926
TCLC 27
See also CA 115; DLB 19, 57, 174

Douglas, Ellen .... CLC 73
See also Haxton, Josephine Ayres; Williamson,
Ellen Douglas

Douglas, Gavin 1475(?)-1522 .... LC 20

Douglas, Keith 1920-1944 .... TCLC 40
See also DLB 27

Douglas, Leonard
See Bradbury, Ray (Douglas)

Douglas, Michael
See Crichton, (John) Michael

Douglas, Norman 1868-1952 .... TCLC 68

Douglass, Frederick 1817(?)-1895NCLC 7, 55;
BLC; DA; DAC; DAM MST, MULT; WLC
See also CDALB 1640-1865; DLB 1, 43, 50,
79; SATA 29

Dourado, (Waldomiro Freitas) Autran 1926-
CLC 23, 60
See also CA 25-28R; CANR 34

Dourado, Waldomiro Autran
See Dourado, (Waldomiro Freitas) Autran

Dove, Rita (Frances) 1952-CLC 50, 81; DAM
MULT, POET; PC 6
See also BW 2; CA 109; CAAS 19; CANR 27,
42; DLB 120

Dowell, Coleman 1925-1985 .... CLC 60
See also CA 25-28R; 117; CANR 10; DLB 130

Dowson, Ernest (Christopher) 1867-1900
TCLC 4
See also CA 105; 150; DLB 19, 135

Doyle, A. Conan
See Doyle, Arthur Conan

Doyle, Arthur Conan 1859-1930TCLC 7; DA;
DAB; DAC; DAM MST, NOV; SSC 12;
WLC
See also AAYA 14; CA 104; 122; CDBLB 1890-
1914; DLB 18, 70, 156, 178; MTCW; SATA
24

Doyle, Conan
See Doyle, Arthur Conan

Doyle, John
See Graves, Robert (von Ranke)

Doyle, Roddy 1958(?)- .... CLC 81
See also AAYA 14; CA 143

Doyle, Sir A. Conan
See Doyle, Arthur Conan

Doyle, Sir Arthur Conan
See Doyle, Arthur Conan

Dr. A
See Asimov, Isaac; Silverstein, Alvin

Drabble, Margaret
1939- CLC 2, 3, 5, 8, 10, 22, 53; DAB; DAC;
DAM MST, NOV, POP
See also CA 13-16R; CANR 18, 35; CDBLB
1960 to Present; DLB 14, 155; MTCW;
SATA 48

Drapier, M. B.
See Swift, Jonathan

Drayham, James
See Mencken, H(enry) L(ouis)

Drayton, Michael 1563-1631 .... LC 8

Dreadstone, Carl
See Campbell, (John) Ramsey

Dreiser, Theodore (Herman Albert) 1871-1945 **TCLC 10, 18, 35; DA; DAC; DAM MST, NOV; WLC**
See also CA 106; 132; CDALB 1865-1917; DLB 9, 12, 102, 137; DLBD 1; MTCW

Drexler, Rosalyn 1926- .... **CLC 2, 6**
See also CA 81-84

Dreyer, Carl Theodor 1889-1968 ...... **CLC 16**
See also CA 116

Drieu la Rochelle, Pierre(-Eugene) 1893-1945 **TCLC 21**
See also CA 117; DLB 72

Drinkwater, John 1882-1937 .... **TCLC 57**
See also CA 109; 149; DLB 10, 19, 149

Drop Shot
See Cable, George Washington

Droste-Hulshoff, Annette Freiin von 1797-1848 **NCLC 3**
See also DLB 133

Drummond, Walter
See Silverberg, Robert

Drummond, William Henry 1854-1907 **TCLC 25**
See also DLB 92

Drummond de Andrade, Carlos 1902-1987 **CLC 18**
See also Andrade, Carlos Drummond de
See also CA 132; 123

Drury, Allen (Stuart) 1918- .... **CLC 37**
See also CA 57-60; CANR 18, 52; INT CANR-18

Dryden, John 1631-1700 **LC 3, 21; DA; DAB; DAC; DAM DRAM, MST, POET; DC 3; WLC**
See also CDBLB 1660-1789; DLB 80, 101, 131

Duberman, Martin 1930- .... **CLC 8**
See also CA 1-4R; CANR 2

Dubie, Norman (Evans) 1945- .... **CLC 36**
See also CA 69-72; CANR 12; DLB 120

Du Bois, W(illiam) E(dward) B(urghardt) 1868-1963 **CLC 1, 2, 13, 64, 96; BLC; DA; DAC; DAM MST, MULT, NOV; WLC**
See also BW 1; CA 85-88; CANR 34; CDALB 1865-1917; DLB 47, 50, 91; MTCW; SATA 42

Dubus, Andre 1936- **CLC 13, 36, 97; SSC 15**
See also CA 21-24R; CANR 17; DLB 130; INT CANR-17

Duca Minimo
See D'Annunzio, Gabriele

Ducharme, Rejean 1941- .... **CLC 74**
See also DLB 60

Duclos, Charles Pinot 1704-1772 .... **LC 1**

Dudek, Louis 1918- .... **CLC 11, 19**
See also CA 45-48; CAAS 14; CANR 1; DLB 88

Duerrenmatt, Friedrich 1921-1990 **CLC 1, 4, 8, 11, 15, 43, 102; DAM DRAM**
See also CA 17-20R; CANR 33; DLB 69, 124; MTCW

Duffy, Bruce (?)- .... **CLC 50**

Duffy, Maureen 1933- .... **CLC 37**
See also CA 25-28R; CANR 33; DLB 14; MTCW

Dugan, Alan 1923- .... **CLC 2, 6**
See also CA 81-84; DLB 5

du Gard, Roger Martin
See Martin du Gard, Roger

Duhamel, Georges 1884-1966 .... **CLC 8**
See also CA 81-84; 25-28R; CANR 35; DLB 65; MTCW

Dujardin, Edouard (Emile Louis) 1861-1949 **TCLC 13**
See also CA 109; DLB 123

Dulles, John Foster 1888-1959 .... **TCLC 72**
See also CA 115; 149

Dumas, Alexandre (Davy de la Pailleterie) 1802-1870 .. **NCLC 11; DA; DAB; DAC; DAM MST, NOV; WLC**
See also DLB 119; SATA 18

Dumas, Alexandre 1824-1895 **NCLC 9; DC 1**
See also AAYA 22

Dumas, Claudine
See Malzberg, Barry N(athaniel)

Dumas, Henry L. 1934-1968 .... **CLC 6, 62**
See also BW 1; CA 85-88; DLB 41

du Maurier, Daphne 1907-1989 **CLC 6, 11, 59; DAB; DAC; DAM MST, POP; SSC 18**
See also CA 5-8R; 128; CANR 6, 55; MTCW; SATA 27; SATA-Obit 60

Dunbar, Paul Laurence 1872-1906 . **TCLC 2, 12; BLC; DA; DAC; DAM MST, MULT, POET; PC 5; SSC 8; WLC**
See also BW 1; CA 104; 124; CDALB 1865-1917; DLB 50, 54, 78; SATA 34

Dunbar, William 1460(?)-1530(?) .... **LC 20**
See also DLB 132, 146

Duncan, Dora Angela
See Duncan, Isadora

Duncan, Isadora 1877(?)-1927 .... **TCLC 68**
See also CA 118; 149

Duncan, Lois 1934- .... **CLC 26**
See also AAYA 4; CA 1-4R; CANR 2, 23, 36; CLR 29; JRDA; MAICYA; SAAS 2; SATA 1, 36, 75

Duncan, Robert (Edward) 1919-1988 **CLC 1, 2, 4, 7, 15, 41, 55; DAM POET; PC 2**
See also CA 9-12R; 124; CANR 28; DLB 5, 16; MTCW

Duncan, Sara Jeannette 1861-1922 **TCLC 60**
See also CA 157; DLB 92

Dunlap, William 1766-1839 .... **NCLC 2**
See also DLB 30, 37, 59

Dunn, Douglas (Eaglesham) 1942- **CLC 6, 40**
See also CA 45-48; CANR 2, 33; DLB 40; MTCW

Dunn, Katherine (Karen) 1945- .... **CLC 71**
See also CA 33-36R

Dunn, Stephen 1939- .... **CLC 36**
See also CA 33-36R; CANR 12, 48, 53; DLB 105

Dunne, Finley Peter 1867-1936 ...... **TCLC 28**
See also CA 108; DLB 11, 23

Dunne, John Gregory 1932- .... **CLC 28**
See also CA 25-28R; CANR 14, 50; DLBY 80

Dunsany, Edward John Moreton Drax Plunkett 1878-1957 ....
See Dunsany, Lord
See also CA 104; 148; DLB 10

Dunsany, Lord .... **TCLC 2, 59**
See also Dunsany, Edward John Moreton Drax Plunkett
See also DLB 77, 153, 156

du Perry, Jean
See Simenon, Georges (Jacques Christian)

Durang, Christopher (Ferdinand) 1949- **CLC 27, 38**
See also CA 105; CANR 50

Duras, Marguerite 1914-1996 **CLC 3, 6, 11, 20, 34, 40, 68, 100**
See also CA 25-28R; 151; CANR 50; DLB 83; MTCW

Durban, (Rosa) Pam 1947- .... **CLC 39**
See also CA 123

Durcan, Paul 1944- **CLC 43, 70; DAM POET**
See also CA 134

Durkheim, Emile 1858-1917 .... **TCLC 55**

Durrell, Lawrence (George) 1912-1990 **CLC 1, 4, 6, 8, 13, 27, 41; DAM NOV**
See also CA 9-12R; 132; CANR 40; CDBLB 1945-1960; DLB 15, 27; DLBY 90; MTCW

Durrenmatt, Friedrich
See Duerrenmatt, Friedrich

Dutt, Toru 1856-1877 .... **NCLC 29**

Dwight, Timothy 1752-1817 .... **NCLC 13**
See also DLB 37

Dworkin, Andrea 1946- .... **CLC 43**
See also CA 77-80; CAAS 21; CANR 16, 39; INT CANR-16; MTCW

Dwyer, Deanna
See Koontz, Dean R(ay)

Dwyer, K. R.
See Koontz, Dean R(ay)

Dylan, Bob 1941- .... **CLC 3, 4, 6, 12, 77**
See also CA 41-44R; DLB 16

Eagleton, Terence (Francis) 1943- ....
See Eagleton, Terry
See also CA 57-60; CANR 7, 23; MTCW

Eagleton, Terry .... CLC 63
See also Eagleton, Terence (Francis)

Early, Jack
See Scoppettone, Sandra

East, Michael
See West, Morris L(anglo)

Eastaway, Edward
See Thomas, (Philip) Edward

Eastlake, William (Derry) 1917-1997 CLC 8
See also CA 5-8R; 158; CAAS 1; CANR 5; DLB
6; INT CANR-5

Eastman, Charles A(lexander) 1858-1939
TCLC 55; DAM MULT
See also DLB 175; NNAL; YABC 1

Eberhart, Richard (Ghormley) 1904- CLC 3,
11, 19, 56; DAM POET
See also CA 1-4R; CANR 2; CDALB 1941-
1968; DLB 48; MTCW

Eberstadt, Fernanda 1960- .... CLC 39
See also CA 136

Echegaray (y Eizaguirre), Jose (Maria Waldo)
1832-1916 .... TCLC 4
See also CA 104; CANR 32; HW; MTCW

Echeverria, (Jose) Esteban (Antonino) 1805-
1851 .... NCLC 18

Echo
See Proust, (Valentin-Louis-George-Eugene-)
Marcel

Eckert, Allan W. 1931- .... CLC 17
See also AAYA 18; CA 13-16R; CANR 14, 45;
INT CANR-14; SAAS 21; SATA 29, 91;
SATA-Brief 27

Eckhart, Meister 1260(?)-1328(?) ... CMLC 9
See also DLB 115

Eckmar, F. R.
See de Hartog, Jan

Eco, Umberto 1932- CLC 28, 60; DAM NOV,
POP
See also BEST 90:1; CA 77-80; CANR 12, 33,
55; MTCW

Eddison, E(ric) R(ucker) 1882-1945TCLC 15
See also CA 109; 156

Eddy, Mary (Morse) Baker 1821-1910T C L C
71
See also CA 113

Edel, (Joseph) Leon 1907- .... CLC 29, 34
See also CA 1-4R; CANR 1, 22; DLB 103; INT
CANR-22

Eden, Emily 1797-1869 .... NCLC 10

Edgar, David 1948- ... CLC 42; DAM DRAM
See also CA 57-60; CANR 12; DLB 13; MTCW

Edgerton, Clyde (Carlyle) 1944- ...... CLC 39
See also AAYA 17; CA 118; 134; INT 134

Edgeworth, Maria
1768-1849 .... NCLC 1, 51
See also DLB 116, 159, 163; SATA 21

Edmonds, Paul
See Kuttner, Henry

Edmonds, Walter D(umaux) 1903- ... CLC 35
See also CA 5-8R; CANR 2; DLB 9; MAICYA;
SAAS 4; SATA 1, 27

Edmondson, Wallace
See Ellison, Harlan (Jay)

Edson, Russell .... CLC 13
See also CA 33-36R

Edwards, Bronwen Elizabeth
See Rose, Wendy

Edwards, G(erald) B(asil) 1899-1976CLC 25
See also CA 110

Edwards, Gus 1939- .... CLC 43
See also CA 108; INT 108

Edwards, Jonathan 1703-1758 .... LC 7; DA;
DAC; DAM MST
See also DLB 24

Efron, Marina Ivanovna Tsvetaeva
See Tsvetaeva (Efron), Marina (Ivanovna)

Ehle, John (Marsden, Jr.) 1925- .... CLC 27
See also CA 9-12R

Ehrenbourg, Ilya (Grigoryevich)
See Ehrenburg, Ilya (Grigoryevich)

Ehrenburg, Ilya (Grigoryevich) 1891-1967
CLC 18, 34, 62
See also CA 102; 25-28R

Ehrenburg, Ilyo (Grigoryevich)
See Ehrenburg, Ilya (Grigoryevich)

Eich, Guenter 1907-1972 .... CLC 15
See also CA 111; 93-96; DLB 69, 124

Eichendorff, Joseph Freiherr von 1788-1857
NCLC 8
See also DLB 90

Eigner, Larry .... CLC 9
See also Eigner, Laurence (Joel)
See also CAAS 23; DLB 5

Eigner, Laurence (Joel) 1927-1996 ....
See Eigner, Larry
See also CA 9-12R; 151; CANR 6

Einstein, Albert 1879-1955 .... TCLC 65
See also CA 121; 133; MTCW

Eiseley, Loren Corey
1907-1977 .... CLC 7
See also AAYA 5; CA 1-4R; 73-76; CANR 6

Eisenstadt, Jill 1963- .... CLC 50
See also CA 140

Eisenstein, Sergei (Mikhailovich) 1898-1948
TCLC 57
See also CA 114; 149

Eisner, Simon
See Kornbluth, C(yril) M.

Ekeloef, (Bengt) Gunnar
1907-1968 .... CLC 27; DAM POET
See also CA 123; 25-28R

Ekelof, (Bengt) Gunnar
See Ekeloef, (Bengt) Gunnar

Ekwensi, C. O. D.
See Ekwensi, Cyprian (Odiatu Duaka)

Ekwensi, Cyprian (Odiatu Duaka) 1921-CLC
4; BLC; DAM MULT
See also BW 2; CA 29-32R; CANR 18, 42; DLB
117; MTCW; SATA 66

Elaine .... TCLC 18
See also Leverson, Ada

El Crummo
See Crumb, R(obert)

Elia
See Lamb, Charles

Eliade, Mircea 1907-1986 .... CLC 19
See also CA 65-68; 119; CANR 30; MTCW

Eliot, A. D.
See Jewett, (Theodora) Sarah Orne

Eliot, Alice
See Jewett, (Theodora) Sarah Orne

Eliot, Dan
See Silverberg, Robert

Eliot, George 1819-1880 NCLC 4, 13, 23, 41,
49; DA; DAB; DAC; DAM MST, NOV;
WLC
See also CDBLB 1832-1890; DLB 21, 35, 55

Eliot, John 1604-1690 .... LC 5
See also DLB 24

Eliot, T(homas) S(tearns) 1888-1965CLC 1, 2,
3, 6, 9, 10, 13, 15, 24, 34, 41, 55, 57; DA;
DAB; DAC; DAM DRAM, MST, POET;
PC 5; WLC 2
See also CA 5-8R; 25-28R; CANR 41; CDALB
1929-1941; DLB 7, 10, 45, 63; DLBY 88;
MTCW

Elizabeth 1866-1941 .... TCLC 41

Elkin, Stanley L(awrence) 1930-1995 CLC 4,
6, 9, 14, 27, 51, 91; DAM NOV, POP; SSC
12
See also CA 9-12R; 148; CANR 8, 46; DLB 2,
28; DLBY 80; INT CANR-8; MTCW

Elledge, Scott .... CLC 34

Elliot, Don
See Silverberg, Robert

Elliott, Don
See Silverberg, Robert

Elliott, George P(aul) 1918-1980 .... CLC 2
See also CA 1-4R; 97-100; CANR 2

Elliott, Janice 1931- .... CLC 47
See also CA 13-16R; CANR 8, 29; DLB 14

Elliott, Sumner Locke 1917-1991 ..... CLC 38
See also CA 5-8R; 134; CANR 2, 21

Elliott, William
See Bradbury, Ray (Douglas)

Ellis, A. E. .... CLC 7

Exley, Frederick (Earl) 1929-1992 **CLC 6, 11**
See also AITN 2; CA 81-84; 138; DLB 143;
DLBY 81

Eynhardt, Guillermo
See Quiroga, Horacio (Sylvestre)

Ezekiel, Nissim 1924- .... **CLC 61**
See also CA 61-64

Ezekiel, Tish O'Dowd 1943- .... **CLC 34**
See also CA 129

Fadeyev, A.
See Bulgya, Alexander Alexandrovich

Fadeyev, Alexander .... **TCLC 53**
See also Bulgya, Alexander Alexandrovich

Fagen, Donald 1948- .... **CLC 26**

Fainzilberg, Ilya Arnoldovich 1897-1937 .....
See Ilf, Ilya
See also CA 120

Fair, Ronald L. 1932- .... **CLC 18**
See also BW 1; CA 69-72; CANR 25; DLB 33

Fairbairns, Zoe (Ann) 1948- .... **CLC 32**
See also CA 103; CANR 21

Falco, Gian
See Papini, Giovanni

Falconer, James
See Kirkup, James

Falconer, Kenneth
See Kornbluth, C(yril) M.

Falkland, Samuel
See Heijermans, Herman

Fallaci, Oriana 1930- .... **CLC 11**
See also CA 77-80; CANR 15, 58; MTCW

Faludy, George 1913- .... **CLC 42**
See also CA 21-24R

Faludy, Gyoergy
See Faludy, George

Fanon, Frantz 1925-1961 **CLC 74; BLC; DAM
MULT**
See also BW 1; CA 116; 89-92

Fanshawe, Ann 1625-1680 .... **LC 11**

Fante, John (Thomas) 1911-1983 ..... **CLC 60**
See also CA 69-72; 109; CANR 23; DLB 130;
DLBY 83

Farah, Nuruddin 1945- **CLC 53; BLC; DAM
MULT**
See also BW 2; CA 106; DLB 125

Fargue, Leon-Paul 1876(?)-1947 ... **TCLC 11**
See also CA 109

Farigoule, Louis
See Romains, Jules

Farina, Richard 1936(?)-1966 .... **CLC 9**
See also CA 81-84; 25-28R

Farley, Walter (Lorimer) 1915-1989 **CLC 17**
See also CA 17-20R; CANR 8, 29; DLB 22;

JRDA; MAICYA; SATA 2, 43

Farmer, Philip Jose 1918- .... **CLC 1, 19**
See also CA 1-4R; CANR 4, 35; DLB 8;
MTCW; SATA 93

Farquhar, George 1677-1707 ... **LC 21; DAM
DRAM**
See also DLB 84

Farrell, J(ames) G(ordon) 1935-1979 **CLC 6**
See also CA 73-76; 89-92; CANR 36; DLB 14;
MTCW

Farrell, James T(homas) 1904-1979 **CLC 1, 4,
8, 11, 66**
See also CA 5-8R; 89-92; CANR 9; DLB 4, 9,
86; DLBD 2; MTCW

Farren, Richard J.
See Betjeman, John

Farren, Richard M.
See Betjeman, John

Fassbinder, Rainer Werner 1946-1982 **CLC 20**
See also CA 93-96; 106; CANR 31

Fast, Howard (Melvin) 1914- **CLC 23; DAM
NOV**
See also AAYA 16; CA 1-4R; CAAS 18; CANR
1, 33, 54; DLB 9; INT CANR-33; SATA 7

Faulcon, Robert
See Holdstock, Robert P.

Faulkner, William (Cuthbert) 1897-1962 **CLC
1, 3, 6, 8, 9, 11, 14, 18, 28, 52, 68; DA; DAB;
DAC; DAM MST, NOV; SSC 1; WLC**
See also AAYA 7; CA 81-84; CANR 33;
CDALB 1929-1941; DLB 9, 11, 44, 102;
DLBD 2; DLBY 86; MTCW

Fauset, Jessie Redmon 1884(?)-1961 **CLC 19,
54; BLC; DAM MULT**
See also BW 1; CA 109; DLB 51

Faust, Frederick (Schiller) 1892-1944(?)
TCLC 49; DAM POP
See also CA 108; 152

Faust, Irvin 1924- .... **CLC 8**
See also CA 33-36R; CANR 28; DLB 2, 28;
DLBY 80

Fawkes, Guy
See Benchley, Robert (Charles)

Fearing, Kenneth (Flexner) 1902-1961 . **C L C
51**
See also CA 93-96; CANR 59; DLB 9

Fecamps, Elise
See Creasey, John

Federman, Raymond 1928- .... **CLC 6, 47**
See also CA 17-20R; CAAS 8; CANR 10, 43;
DLBY 80

Federspiel, J(uerg) F. 1931- .... **CLC 42**
See also CA 146

Feiffer, Jules (Ralph) 1929- ..... **CLC 2, 8, 64;
DAM DRAM**
See also AAYA 3; CA 17-20R; CANR 30, 59;
DLB 7, 44; INT CANR-30; MTCW; SATA
8, 61

Feige, Hermann Albert Otto Maximilian
See Traven, B.

Feinberg, David B. 1956-1994 .... **CLC 59**
See also CA 135; 147

Feinstein, Elaine 1930- .... **CLC 36**
See also CA 69-72; CAAS 1; CANR 31; DLB
14, 40; MTCW

Feldman, Irving (Mordecai) 1928- ..... **CLC 7**
See also CA 1-4R; CANR 1; DLB 169

Felix-Tchicaya, Gerald
See Tchicaya, Gerald Felix

Fellini, Federico 1920-1993 .... **CLC 16, 85**
See also CA 65-68; 143; CANR 33

Felsen, Henry Gregor 1916- .... **CLC 17**
See also CA 1-4R; CANR 1; SAAS 2; SATA 1

Fenton, James Martin 1949- .... **CLC 32**
See also CA 102; DLB 40

Ferber, Edna 1887-1968 .... **CLC 18, 93**
See also AITN 1; CA 5-8R; 25-28R; DLB 9,
28, 86; MTCW; SATA 7

Ferguson, Helen
See Kavan, Anna

Ferguson, Samuel 1810-1886 .... **NCLC 33**
See also DLB 32

Fergusson, Robert 1750-1774 .... **LC 29**
See also DLB 109

Ferling, Lawrence
See Ferlinghetti, Lawrence (Monsanto)

Ferlinghetti, Lawrence (Monsanto) 1919(?)-
CLC 2, 6, 10, 27; DAM POET; PC 1
See also CA 5-8R; CANR 3, 41; CDALB 1941-
1968; DLB 5, 16; MTCW

Fernandez, Vicente Garcia Huidobro
See Huidobro Fernandez, Vicente Garcia

Ferrer, Gabriel (Francisco Victor) Miro
See Miro (Ferrer), Gabriel (Francisco Victor)

Ferrier, Susan (Edmonstone) 1782-1854
NCLC 8
See also DLB 116

Ferrigno, Robert 1948(?)- .... **CLC 65**
See also CA 140

Ferron, Jacques 1921-1985 .... **CLC 94; DAC**
See also CA 117; 129; DLB 60

Feuchtwanger, Lion 1884-1958 .... **TCLC 3**
See also CA 104; DLB 66

Feuillet, Octave 1821-1890 .... **NCLC 45**

Feydeau, Georges (Leon Jules Marie) 1862-
1921 .... **TCLC 22; DAM DRAM**
See also CA 113; 152

Fichte, Johann Gottlieb 1762-1814 **NCLC 62**
See also DLB 90

Ficino, Marsilio 1433-1499 .... **LC 12**

Fiedeler, Hans

See Doeblin, Alfred

Fiedler, Leslie A(aron) 1917- . **CLC 4, 13, 24**
See also CA 9-12R; CANR 7; DLB 28, 67;
MTCW

Field, Andrew 1938- .... **CLC 44**
See also CA 97-100; CANR 25

Field, Eugene 1850-1895 .... **NCLC 3**
See also DLB 23, 42, 140; DLBD 13; MAICYA;
SATA 16

Field, Gans T.
See Wellman, Manly Wade

Field, Michael .... **TCLC 43**

Field, Peter
See Hobson, Laura Z(ametkin)

Fielding, Henry 1707-1754 **LC 1; DA; DAB;
DAC; DAM DRAM, MST, NOV; WLC**
See also CDBLB 1660-1789; DLB 39, 84, 101

Fielding, Sarah 1710-1768 .... **LC 1**
See also DLB 39

Fierstein, Harvey (Forbes) 1954- ... **CLC 33;
DAM DRAM, POP**
See also CA 123; 129

Figes, Eva 1932- .... **CLC 31**
See also CA 53-56; CANR 4, 44; DLB 14

Finch, Robert (Duer Claydon)
1900- .... **CLC 18**
See also CA 57-60; CANR 9, 24, 49; DLB 88

Findley, Timothy 1930- . **CLC 27, 102; DAC;
DAM MST**
See also CA 25-28R; CANR 12, 42; DLB 53

Fink, William
See Mencken, H(enry) L(ouis)

Firbank, Louis 1942- ....
See Reed, Lou
See also CA 117

Firbank, (Arthur Annesley) Ronald 1886-1926
TCLC 1
See also CA 104; DLB 36

Fisher, M(ary) F(rances) K(ennedy) 1908-1992
CLC 76, 87
See also CA 77-80; 138; CANR 44

Fisher, Roy 1930- .... **CLC 25**
See also CA 81-84; CAAS 10; CANR 16; DLB
40

Fisher, Rudolph 1897-1934 . **TCLC 11; BLC;
DAM MULT; SSC 25**
See also BW 1; CA 107; 124; DLB 51, 102

Fisher, Vardis (Alvero) 1895-1968 ...... **CLC 7**
See also CA 5-8R; 25-28R; DLB 9

Fiske, Tarleton
See Bloch, Robert (Albert)

Fitch, Clarke
See Sinclair, Upton (Beall)

Fitch, John IV
See Cormier, Robert (Edmund)

Fitzgerald, Captain Hugh
See Baum, L(yman) Frank

FitzGerald, Edward 1809-1883 .... **NCLC 9**
See also DLB 32

Fitzgerald, F(rancis) Scott (Key) 1896-1940
**TCLC 1, 6, 14, 28, 55; DA; DAB; DAC;
DAM MST, NOV; SSC 6; WLC**
See also AITN 1; CA 110; 123; CDALB 1917-
1929; DLB 4, 9, 86; DLBD 1, 15; DLBY 81,
96; MTCW

Fitzgerald, Penelope 1916- ... **CLC 19, 51, 61**
See also CA 85-88; CAAS 10; CANR 56; DLB
14

Fitzgerald, Robert (Stuart) 1910-1985 **CLC 39**
See also CA 1-4R; 114; CANR 1; DLBY 80

FitzGerald, Robert D(avid) 1902-1987 **CLC 19**
See also CA 17-20R

Fitzgerald, Zelda (Sayre) 1900-1948 **TCLC 52**
See also CA 117; 126; DLBY 84

Flanagan, Thomas (James Bonner) 1923-
CLC 25, 52
See also CA 108; CANR 55; DLBY 80; INT
108; MTCW

Flaubert, Gustave 1821-1880 **NCLC 2, 10, 19,
62; DA; DAB; DAC; DAM MST, NOV;
SSC 11; WLC**
See also DLB 119

Flecker, Herman Elroy
See Flecker, (Herman) James Elroy

Flecker, (Herman) James Elroy 1884-1915
TCLC 43
See also CA 109; 150; DLB 10, 19

Fleming, Ian (Lancaster) 1908-1964 . **CLC 3,
30; DAM POP**
See also CA 5-8R; CANR 59; CDBLB 1945-
1960; DLB 87; MTCW; SATA 9

Fleming, Thomas (James) 1927- .... **CLC 37**
See also CA 5-8R; CANR 10; INT CANR-10;
SATA 8

Fletcher, John 1579-1625 .... **LC 33; DC 6**
See also CDBLB Before 1660; DLB 58

Fletcher, John Gould 1886-1950 .... **TCLC 35**
See also CA 107; DLB 4, 45

Fleur, Paul
See Pohl, Frederik

Flooglebuckle, Al
See Spiegelman, Art

Flying Officer X
See Bates, H(erbert) E(rnest)

Fo, Dario 1926- .... **CLC 32; DAM DRAM**
See also CA 116; 128; MTCW

Fogarty, Jonathan Titulescu Esq.
See Farrell, James T(homas)

Folke, Will
See Bloch, Robert (Albert)

Follett, Ken(neth Martin) 1949- ..... **CLC 18;**

DAM NOV, POP
See also AAYA 6; BEST 89:4; CA 81-84; CANR
13, 33, 54; DLB 87; DLBY 81; INT CANR-
33; MTCW

Fontane, Theodor 1819-1898 .... **NCLC 26**
See also DLB 129

Foote, Horton 1916- **CLC 51, 91; DAM DRAM**
See also CA 73-76; CANR 34, 51; DLB 26; INT
CANR-34

Foote, Shelby 1916- **CLC 75; DAM NOV, POP**
See also CA 5-8R; CANR 3, 45; DLB 2, 17

Forbes, Esther 1891-1967 .... **CLC 12**
See also AAYA 17; CA 13-14; 25-28R; CAP 1;
CLR 27; DLB 22; JRDA; MAICYA; SATA 2

Forche, Carolyn (Louise) 1950- **CLC 25, 83,
86; DAM POET; PC 10**
See also CA 109; 117; CANR 50; DLB 5; INT
117

Ford, Elbur
See Hibbert, Eleanor Alice Burford

Ford, Ford Madox 1873-1939 **TCLC 1, 15, 39,
57; DAM NOV**
See also CA 104; 132; CDBLB 1914-1945;
DLB 162; MTCW

Ford, Henry 1863-1947 .... **TCLC 73**
See also CA 115; 148

Ford, John 1895-1973 .... **CLC 16**
See also CA 45-48

Ford, Richard .... **CLC 99**

Ford, Richard 1944- .... **CLC 46**
See also CA 69-72; CANR 11, 47

Ford, Webster
See Masters, Edgar Lee

Foreman, Richard 1937- .... **CLC 50**
See also CA 65-68; CANR 32

Forester, C(ecil) S(cott) 1899-1966 ... **CLC 35**
See also CA 73-76; 25-28R; SATA 13

Forez
See Mauriac, Francois (Charles)

Forman, James Douglas 1932- .... **CLC 21**
See also AAYA 17; CA 9-12R; CANR 4, 19,
42; JRDA; MAICYA; SATA 8, 70

Fornes, Maria Irene 1930- .... **CLC 39, 61**
See also CA 25-28R; CANR 28; DLB 7; HW;
INT CANR-28; MTCW

Forrest, Leon 1937- .... **CLC 4**
See also BW 2; CA 89-92; CAAS 7; CANR 25,
52; DLB 33

Forster, E(dward) M(organ)
1879-1970 **CLC 1, 2, 3, 4, 9, 10, 13, 15, 22, 45,
77; DA; DAB; DAC; DAM MST, NOV;
SSC 27; WLC**
See also AAYA 2; CA 13-14; 25-28R; CANR
45; CAP 1; CDBLB 1914-1945; DLB 34, 98,
162, 178; DLBD 10; MTCW; SATA 57

Forster, John 1812-1876 .... **NCLC 11**
See also DLB 144

Fuchs, Daniel 1934- .... CLC 34
See also CA 37-40R; CANR 14, 48

Fuentes, Carlos
1928-CLC 3, 8, 10, 13, 22, 41, 60; DA; DAB;
DAC; DAM MST, MULT, NOV; HLC;
SSC 24; WLC
See also AAYA 4; AITN 2; CA 69-72; CANR
10, 32; DLB 113; HW; MTCW

Fuentes, Gregorio Lopez y
See Lopez y Fuentes, Gregorio

Fugard, (Harold) Athol 1932-CLC 5, 9, 14, 25,
40, 80; DAM DRAM; DC 3
See also AAYA 17; CA 85-88; CANR 32, 54;
MTCW

Fugard, Sheila 1932- .... CLC 48
See also CA 125

Fuller, Charles (H., Jr.) 1939-CLC 25; BLC;
DAM DRAM, MULT; DC 1
See also BW 2; CA 108; 112; DLB 38; INT 112;
MTCW

Fuller, John (Leopold) 1937- .... CLC 62
See also CA 21-24R; CANR 9, 44; DLB 40

Fuller, Margaret .... NCLC 5, 50
See also Ossoli, Sarah Margaret (Fuller
marchesa d')

Fuller, Roy (Broadbent) 1912-1991CLC 4, 28
See also CA 5-8R; 135; CAAS 10; CANR 53;
DLB 15, 20; SATA 87

Fulton, Alice 1952- .... CLC 52
See also CA 116; CANR 57

Furphy, Joseph 1843-1912 .... TCLC 25

Fussell, Paul 1924- .... CLC 74
See also BEST 90:1; CA 17-20R; CANR 8, 21,
35; INT CANR-21; MTCW

Futabatei, Shimei 1864-1909 .... TCLC 44
See also DLB 180

Futrelle, Jacques 1875-1912 .... TCLC 19
See also CA 113; 155

Gaboriau, Emile 1835-1873 .... NCLC 14

Gadda, Carlo Emilio 1893-1973 .... CLC 11
See also CA 89-92; DLB 177

Gaddis, William 1922- CLC 1, 3, 6, 8, 10, 19,
43, 86
See also CA 17-20R; CANR 21, 48; DLB 2;
MTCW

Gage, Walter
See Inge, William (Motter)

Gaines, Ernest J(ames)
1933- .... CLC 3, 11, 18, 86; BLC;
DAM MULT
See also AAYA 18; AITN 1; BW 2; CA 9-12R;
CANR 6, 24, 42; CDALB 1968-1988; DLB
2, 33, 152; DLBY 80; MTCW; SATA 86

Gaitskill, Mary 1954- .... CLC 69
See also CA 128

Galdos, Benito Perez
See Perez Galdos, Benito

Gale, Zona 1874-1938TCLC 7; DAM DRAM
See also CA 105; 153; DLB 9, 78

Galeano, Eduardo (Hughes) 1940-... CLC 72
See also CA 29-32R; CANR 13, 32; HW

Galiano, Juan Valera y Alcala
See Valera y Alcala-Galiano, Juan

Gallagher, Tess 1943- ...... CLC 18, 63; DAM
POET; PC 9
See also CA 106; DLB 120

Gallant, Mavis 1922-... CLC 7, 18, 38; DAC;
DAM MST; SSC 5
See also CA 69-72; CANR 29; DLB 53; MTCW

Gallant, Roy A(rthur) 1924- .... CLC 17
See also CA 5-8R; CANR 4, 29, 54; CLR 30;
MAICYA; SATA 4, 68

Gallico, Paul (William) 1897-1976 ..... CLC 2
See also AITN 1; CA 5-8R; 69-72; CANR 23;
DLB 9, 171; MAICYA; SATA 13

Gallo, Max Louis 1932- .... CLC 95
See also CA 85-88

Gallois, Lucien
See Desnos, Robert

Gallup, Ralph
See Whitemore, Hugh (John)

Galsworthy, John 1867-1933TCLC 1, 45; DA;
DAB; DAC; DAM DRAM, MST, NOV;
SSC 22; WLC 2
See also CA 104; 141; CDBLB 1890-1914;
DLB 10, 34, 98, 162

Galt, John 1779-1839 .... NCLC 1
See also DLB 99, 116, 159

Galvin, James 1951- .... CLC 38
See also CA 108; CANR 26

Gamboa, Federico 1864-1939 .... TCLC 36

Gandhi, M. K.
See Gandhi, Mohandas Karamchand

Gandhi, Mahatma
See Gandhi, Mohandas Karamchand

Gandhi, Mohandas Karamchand 1869-1948
TCLC 59; DAM MULT
See also CA 121; 132; MTCW

Gann, Ernest Kellogg 1910-1991 ...... CLC 23
See also AITN 1; CA 1-4R; 136; CANR 1

Garcia, Cristina 1958- .... CLC 76
See also CA 141

Garcia Lorca, Federico
1898-1936 . TCLC 1, 7, 49; DA; DAB; DAC;
DAM DRAM, MST, MULT, POET; DC 2;
HLC; PC 3; WLC
See also CA 104; 131; DLB 108; HW; MTCW

Garcia Marquez, Gabriel (Jose)
1928- ...... CLC 2, 3, 8, 10, 15, 27, 47, 55, 68;
DA; DAB; DAC; DAM MST, MULT, NOV,
POP; HLC; SSC 8; WLC
See also AAYA 3; BEST 89:1, 90:4; CA 33-
36R; CANR 10, 28, 50; DLB 113; HW;
MTCW

Gard, Janice
See Latham, Jean Lee

Gard, Roger Martin du
See Martin du Gard, Roger

Gardam, Jane 1928- .... CLC 43
See also CA 49-52; CANR 2, 18, 33, 54; CLR
12; DLB 14, 161; MAICYA; MTCW; SAAS
9; SATA 39, 76; SATA-Brief 28

Gardner, Herb(ert) 1934- .... CLC 44
See also CA 149

Gardner, John (Champlin), Jr. 1933-1982
CLC 2, 3, 5, 7, 8, 10, 18, 28, 34; DAM NOV,
POP; SSC 7
See also AITN 1; CA 65-68; 107; CANR 33;
DLB 2; DLBY 82; MTCW; SATA 40; SATA-
Obit 31

Gardner, John (Edmund) 1926-CLC 30; DAM
POP
See also CA 103; CANR 15; MTCW

Gardner, Miriam
See Bradley, Marion Zimmer

Gardner, Noel
See Kuttner, Henry

Gardons, S. S.
See Snodgrass, W(illiam) D(e Witt)

Garfield, Leon 1921-1996 .... CLC 12
See also AAYA 8; CA 17-20R; 152; CANR 38,
41; CLR 21; DLB 161; JRDA; MAICYA;
SATA 1, 32, 76; SATA-Obit 90

Garland, (Hannibal) Hamlin 1860-1940
TCLC 3; SSC 18
See also CA 104; DLB 12, 71, 78

Garneau, (Hector de) Saint-Denys 1912-1943
TCLC 13
See also CA 111; DLB 88

Garner, Alan 1934-CLC 17; DAB; DAM POP
See also AAYA 18; CA 73-76; CANR 15; CLR
20; DLB 161; MAICYA; MTCW; SATA 18,
69

Garner, Hugh 1913-1979 .... CLC 13
See also CA 69-72; CANR 31; DLB 68

Garnett, David 1892-1981 .... CLC 3
See also CA 5-8R; 103; CANR 17; DLB 34

Garos, Stephanie
See Katz, Steve

Garrett, George (Palmer) 1929-CLC 3, 11, 51
See also CA 1-4R; CAAS 5; CANR 1, 42; DLB
2, 5, 130, 152; DLBY 83

Garrick, David 1717-1779 .... LC 15; DAM
DRAM
See also DLB 84

Garrigue, Jean 1914-1972 .... CLC 2, 8
See also CA 5-8R; 37-40R; CANR 20

Garrison, Frederick
See Sinclair, Upton (Beall)

Garth, Will
See Hamilton, Edmond; Kuttner, Henry

Giraudoux, (Hippolyte) Jean 1882-1944
TCLC 2, 7; DAM DRAM
See also CA 104; DLB 65

Gironella, Jose Maria 1917- .... CLC 11
See also CA 101

Gissing, George (Robert) 1857-1903 TCLC 3, 24, 47
See also CA 105; DLB 18, 135

Giurlani, Aldo
See Palazzeschi, Aldo

Gladkov, Fyodor (Vasilyevich) 1883-1958
TCLC 27

Glanville, Brian (Lester) 1931- .... CLC 6
See also CA 5-8R; CAAS 9; CANR 3; DLB 15, 139; SATA 42

Glasgow, Ellen (Anderson Gholson) 1873(?)-1945 .... TCLC 2, 7
See also CA 104; DLB 9, 12

Glaspell, Susan 1882(?)-1948 .... TCLC 55
See also CA 110; 154; DLB 7, 9, 78; YABC 2

Glassco, John 1909-1981 .... CLC 9
See also CA 13-16R; 102; CANR 15; DLB 68

Glasscock, Amnesia
See Steinbeck, John (Ernst)

Glasser, Ronald J. 1940(?)- .... CLC 37

Glassman, Joyce
See Johnson, Joyce

Glendinning, Victoria 1937- .... CLC 50
See also CA 120; 127; CANR 59; DLB 155

Glissant, Edouard 1928- . CLC 10, 68; DAM MULT
See also CA 153

Gloag, Julian 1930- .... CLC 40
See also AITN 1; CA 65-68; CANR 10

Glowacki, Aleksander
See Prus, Boleslaw

Gluck, Louise (Elisabeth) 1943- CLC 7, 22, 44, 81; DAM POET; PC 16
See also CA 33-36R; CANR 40; DLB 5

Glyn, Elinor 1864-1943 .... TCLC 72
See also DLB 153

Gobineau, Joseph Arthur (Comte) de 1816-1882 .... NCLC 17
See also DLB 123

Godard, Jean-Luc 1930- .... CLC 20
See also CA 93-96

Godden, (Margaret) Rumer 1907- ... CLC 53
See also AAYA 6; CA 5-8R; CANR 4, 27, 36, 55; CLR 20; DLB 161; MAICYA; SAAS 12; SATA 3, 36

Godoy Alcayaga, Lucila 1889-1957 ....
See Mistral, Gabriela
See also BW 2; CA 104; 131; DAM MULT; HW; MTCW

Godwin, Gail (Kathleen) 1937- CLC 5, 8, 22, 31, 69; DAM POP
See also CA 29-32R; CANR 15, 43; DLB 6; INT CANR-15; MTCW

Godwin, William 1756-1836 .... NCLC 14
See also CDBLB 1789-1832; DLB 39, 104, 142, 158, 163

Goebbels, Josef
See Goebbels, (Paul) Joseph

Goebbels, (Paul) Joseph 1897-1945 TCLC 68
See also CA 115; 148

Goebbels, Joseph Paul
See Goebbels, (Paul) Joseph

Goethe, Johann Wolfgang von 1749-1832
NCLC 4, 22, 34; DA; DAB; DAC; DAM DRAM, MST, POET; PC 5; WLC 3
See also DLB 94

Gogarty, Oliver St. John 1878-1957 TCLC 15
See also CA 109; 150; DLB 15, 19

Gogol, Nikolai (Vasilyevich) 1809-1852 NCLC 5, 15, 31; DA; DAB; DAC; DAM DRAM, MST; DC 1; SSC 4; WLC
See also DLB 198

Goines, Donald 1937(?)-1974 CLC 80; BLC; DAM MULT, POP
See also AITN 1; BW 1; CA 124; 114; DLB 33

Gold, Herbert 1924- .... CLC 4, 7, 14, 42
See also CA 9-12R; CANR 17, 45; DLB 2; DLBY 81

Goldbarth, Albert 1948- .... CLC 5, 38
See also CA 53-56; CANR 6, 40; DLB 120

Goldberg, Anatol 1910-1982 .... CLC 34
See also CA 131; 117

Goldemberg, Isaac 1945- .... CLC 52
See also CA 69-72; CAAS 12; CANR 11, 32; HW

Golding, William (Gerald) 1911-1993 CLC 1, 2, 3, 8, 10, 17, 27, 58, 81; DA; DAB; DAC; DAM MST, NOV; WLC
See also AAYA 5; CA 5-8R; 141; CANR 13, 33, 54; CDBLB 1945-1960; DLB 15, 100; MTCW

Goldman, Emma 1869-1940 .... TCLC 13
See also CA 110; 150

Goldman, Francisco 1955- .... CLC 76

Goldman, William (W.) 1931- .... CLC 1, 48
See also CA 9-12R; CANR 29; DLB 44

Goldmann, Lucien 1913-1970 .... CLC 24
See also CA 25-28; CAP 2

Goldoni, Carlo 1707-1793 LC 4; DAM DRAM

Goldsberry, Steven 1949- .... CLC 34
See also CA 131

Goldsmith, Oliver 1728-1774 LC 2; DA; DAB; DAC; DAM DRAM, MST, NOV, POET; WLC
See also CDBLB 1660-1789; DLB 39, 89, 104, 109, 142; SATA 26

Goldsmith, Peter
See Priestley, J(ohn) B(oynton)

Gombrowicz, Witold 1904-1969 CLC 4, 7, 11, 49; DAM DRAM
See also CA 19-20; 25-28R; CAP 2

Gomez de la Serna, Ramon 1888-1963 CLC 9
See also CA 153; 116; HW

Goncharov, Ivan Alexandrovich 1812-1891
NCLC 1

Goncourt, Edmond (Louis Antoine Huot) de 1822-1896 .... NCLC 7
See also DLB 123

Goncourt, Jules (Alfred Huot) de 1830-1870
NCLC 7
See also DLB 123

Gontier, Fernande 19(?)- .... CLC 50

Gonzalez Martinez, Enrique 1871-1952
TCLC 72
See also HW

Goodman, Paul 1911-1972 ...... CLC 1, 2, 4, 7
See also CA 19-20; 37-40R; CANR 34; CAP 2; DLB 130; MTCW

Gordimer, Nadine 1923- CLC 3, 5, 7, 10, 18, 33, 51, 70; DA; DAB; DAC; DAM MST, NOV; SSC 17; WLCS
See also CA 5-8R; CANR 3, 28, 56; INT CANR-28; MTCW

Gordon, Adam Lindsay 1833-1870 NCLC 21

Gordon, Caroline 1895-1981 CLC 6, 13, 29, 83; SSC 15
See also CA 11-12; 103; CANR 36; CAP 1; DLB 4, 9, 102; DLBY 81; MTCW

Gordon, Charles William 1860-1937 ....
See Connor, Ralph
See also CA 109

Gordon, Mary (Catherine) 1949- CLC 13, 22
See also CA 102; CANR 44; DLB 6; DLBY 81; INT 102; MTCW

Gordon, Sol 1923- .... CLC 26
See also CA 53-56; CANR 4; SATA 11

Gordone, Charles 1925-1995 CLC 1, 4; DAM DRAM
See also BW 1; CA 93-96; 150; CANR 55; DLB 7; INT 93-96; MTCW

Gorenko, Anna Andreevna
See Akhmatova, Anna

Gorky, Maxim .... TCLC 8; DAB; WLC
See also Peshkov, Alexei Maximovich

Goryan, Sirak
See Saroyan, William

Gosse, Edmund (William) 1849-1928 TCLC 28
See also CA 117; DLB 57, 144

Gotlieb, Phyllis Fay (Bloom) 1926- .... CLC 18
See also CA 13-16R; CANR 7; DLB 88

Gottesman, S. D.
See Kornbluth, C(yril) M.; Pohl, Frederik

Gottfried von Strassburg fl. c. 1210- **C M L C 10**
See also DLB 138

Gould, Lois .... **CLC 4, 10**
See also CA 77-80; CANR 29; MTCW

Gourmont, Remy (-Marie-Charles) de 1858-1915... **TCLC 17**
See also CA 109; 150

Govier, Katherine 1948- .... **CLC 51**
See also CA 101; CANR 18, 40

Goyen, (Charles) William 1915-1983**CLC 5, 8, 14, 40**
See also AITN 2; CA 5-8R; 110; CANR 6; DLB 2; DLBY 83; INT CANR-6

Goytisolo, Juan 1931- . **CLC 5, 10, 23; DAM MULT; HLC**
See also CA 85-88; CANR 32; HW; MTCW

Gozzano, Guido 1883-1916 .... **PC 10**
See also CA 154; DLB 114

Gozzi, (Conte) Carlo 1720-1806 .... **NCLC 23**

Grabbe, Christian Dietrich 1801-1836**N C L C 2**
See also DLB 133

Grace, Patricia 1937- .... **CLC 56**

Gracian y Morales, Baltasar 1601-1658**LC 15**

Gracq, Julien .... **CLC 11, 48**
See also Poirier, Louis
See also DLB 83

Grade, Chaim 1910-1982 .... **CLC 10**
See also CA 93-96; 107

Graduate of Oxford, A
See Ruskin, John

Grafton, Garth
See Duncan, Sara Jeannette

Graham, John
See Phillips, David Graham

Graham, Jorie 1951- .... **CLC 48**
See also CA 111; DLB 120

Graham, R(obert) B(ontine) Cunninghame
See Cunninghame Graham, R(obert) B(ontine)
See also DLB 98, 135, 174

Graham, Robert
See Haldeman, Joe (William)

Graham, Tom
See Lewis, (Harry) Sinclair

Graham, W(illiam) S(ydney) 1918-1986**C L C 29**
See also CA 73-76; 118; DLB 20

Graham, Winston (Mawdsley) 1910-**CLC 23**
See also CA 49-52; CANR 2, 22, 45; DLB 77

Grahame, Kenneth 1859-1932**TCLC 64; DAB**
See also CA 108; 136; CLR 5; DLB 34, 141, 178; MAICYA; YABC 1

Grant, Skeeter

See Spiegelman, Art

Granville-Barker, Harley 1877-1946**TCLC 2; DAM DRAM**
See also Barker, Harley Granville
See also CA 104

Grass, Guenter (Wilhelm) 1927-**CLC 1, 2, 4, 6, 11, 15, 22, 32, 49, 88; DA; DAB; DAC; DAM MST, NOV; WLC**
See also CA 13-16R; CANR 20; DLB 75, 124; MTCW

Gratton, Thomas
See Hulme, T(homas) E(rnest)

Grau, Shirley Ann 1929-.. **CLC 4, 9; SSC 15**
See also CA 89-92; CANR 22; DLB 2; INT CANR-22; MTCW

Gravel, Fern
See Hall, James Norman

Graver, Elizabeth 1964- .... **CLC 70**
See also CA 135

Graves, Richard Perceval 1945- .... **CLC 44**
See also CA 65-68; CANR 9, 26, 51

Graves, Robert (von Ranke) 1895-1985 **C L C 1, 2, 6, 11, 39, 44, 45; DAB; DAC; DAM MST, POET; PC 6**
See also CA 5-8R; 117; CANR 5, 36; CDBLB 1914-1945; DLB 20, 100; DLBY 85; MTCW; SATA 45

Graves, Valerie
See Bradley, Marion Zimmer

Gray, Alasdair (James) 1934- .... **CLC 41**
See also CA 126; CANR 47; INT 126; MTCW

Gray, Amlin 1946- .... **CLC 29**
See also CA 138

Gray, Francine du Plessix 1930- ..... **CLC 22; DAM NOV**
See also BEST 90:3; CA 61-64; CAAS 2; CANR 11, 33; INT CANR-11; MTCW

Gray, John (Henry) 1866-1934 ...... **TCLC 19**
See also CA 119

Gray, Simon (James Holliday) 1936- **CLC 9, 14, 36**
See also AITN 1; CA 21-24R; CAAS 3; CANR 32; DLB 13; MTCW

Gray, Spalding 1941-**CLC 49; DAM POP; DC 7**
See also CA 128

Gray, Thomas 1716-1771**LC 4; DA; DAB; DAC; DAM MST; PC 2; WLC**
See also CDBLB 1660-1789; DLB 109

Grayson, David
See Baker, Ray Stannard

Grayson, Richard (A.) 1951- .... **CLC 38**
See also CA 85-88; CANR 14, 31, 57

Greeley, Andrew M(oran) 1928- .... **CLC 28; DAM POP**
See also CA 5-8R; CAAS 7; CANR 7, 43; MTCW

Green, Anna Katharine 1846-1935 **TCLC 63**
See also CA 112

Green, Brian
See Card, Orson Scott

Green, Hannah
See Greenberg, Joanne (Goldenberg)

Green, Hannah 1927(?)-1996 .... **CLC 3**
See also CA 73-76; CANR 59

Green, Henry 1905-1973 .... **CLC 2, 13, 97**
See also Yorke, Henry Vincent
See also DLB 15

Green, Julian (Hartridge) 1900- ....
See Green, Julien
See also CA 21-24R; CANR 33; DLB 4, 72; MTCW

Green, Julien .... **CLC 3, 11, 77**
See also Green, Julian (Hartridge)

Green, Paul (Eliot) 1894-1981**CLC 25; DAM DRAM**
See also AITN 1; CA 5-8R; 103; CANR 3; DLB 7, 9; DLBY 81

Greenberg, Ivan 1908-1973 ....
See Rahv, Philip
See also CA 85-88

Greenberg, Joanne (Goldenberg) 1932- **C L C 7, 30**
See also AAYA 12; CA 5-8R; CANR 14, 32; SATA 25

Greenberg, Richard 1959(?)- .... **CLC 57**
See also CA 138

Greene, Bette 1934- .... **CLC 30**
See also AAYA 7; CA 53-56; CANR 4; CLR 2; JRDA; MAICYA; SAAS 16; SATA 8

Greene, Gael .... **CLC 8**
See also CA 13-16R; CANR 10

Greene, Graham 1904-1991**CLC 1, 3, 6, 9, 14, 18, 27, 37, 70, 72; DA; DAB; DAC; DAM MST, NOV; WLC**
See also AITN 2; CA 13-16R; 133; CANR 35; CDBLB 1945-1960; DLB 13, 15, 77, 100, 162; DLBY 91; MTCW; SATA 20

Greer, Richard
See Silverberg, Robert

Gregor, Arthur 1923- .... **CLC 9**
See also CA 25-28R; CAAS 10; CANR 11; SATA 36

Gregor, Lee
See Pohl, Frederik

Gregory, Isabella Augusta (Persse) 1852-1932 **TCLC 1**
See also CA 104; DLB 10

Gregory, J. Dennis
See Williams, John A(lfred)

Grendon, Stephen
See Derleth, August (William)

Grenville, Kate 1950- .... **CLC 61**
See also CA 118; CANR 53

Grenville, Pelham
See Wodehouse, P(elham) G(renville)

Greve, Felix Paul (Berthold Friedrich) 1879-
1948 ....
See Grove, Frederick Philip
See also CA 104; 141; DAC; DAM MST

Grey, Zane 1872-1939 .. **TCLC 6; DAM POP**
See also CA 104; 132; DLB 9; MTCW

Grieg, (Johan) Nordahl (Brun) 1902-1943
TCLC 10
See also CA 107

Grieve, C(hristopher) M(urray) 1892-1978
CLC 11, 19; DAM POET
See also MacDiarmid, Hugh; Pteleon
See also CA 5-8R; 85-88; CANR 33; MTCW

Griffin, Gerald 1803-1840 .... **NCLC 7**
See also DLB 159

Griffin, John Howard 1920-1980 ..... **CLC 68**
See also AITN 1; CA 1-4R; 101; CANR 2

Griffin, Peter 1942- .... **CLC 39**
See also CA 136

Griffith, D(avid Lewelyn) W(ark) 1875(?)-1948
TCLC 68
See also CA 119; 150

Griffith, Lawrence
See Griffith, D(avid Lewelyn) W(ark)

Griffiths, Trevor 1935- .... **CLC 13, 52**
See also CA 97-100; CANR 45; DLB 13

Grigson, Geoffrey (Edward Harvey) 1905-1985
CLC 7, 39
See also CA 25-28R; 118; CANR 20, 33; DLB
27; MTCW

Grillparzer, Franz 1791-1872 .... **NCLC 1**
See also DLB 133

Grimble, Reverend Charles James
See Eliot, T(homas) S(tearns)

Grimke, Charlotte L(ottie) Forten 1837(?)-1914

See Forten, Charlotte L.
See also BW 1; CA 117; 124; DAM MULT,
POET

Grimm, Jacob Ludwig Karl 1785-1863**NCLC
3**
See also DLB 90; MAICYA; SATA 22

Grimm, Wilhelm Karl
1786-1859 .... **NCLC 3**
See also DLB 90; MAICYA; SATA 22

Grimmelshausen, Johann Jakob Christoffel von
1621-1676 .... **LC 6**
See also DLB 168

Grindel, Eugene 1895-1952 ....
See Eluard, Paul
See also CA 104

Grisham, John 1955- .... **CLC 84; DAM POP**
See also AAYA 14; CA 138; CANR 47

Grossman, David 1954- .... **CLC 67**
See also CA 138

Grossman, Vasily (Semenovich) 1905-1964
CLC 41
See also CA 124; 130; MTCW

Grove, Frederick Philip .... **TCLC 4**
See also Greve, Felix Paul (Berthold Friedrich)
See also DLB 92

Grubb
See Crumb, R(obert)

Grumbach, Doris (Isaac) 1918-**CLC 13, 22, 64**
See also CA 5-8R; CAAS 2; CANR 9, 42; INT
CANR-9

Grundtvig, Nicolai Frederik Severin 1783-1872
NCLC 1

Grunge
See Crumb, R(obert)

Grunwald, Lisa 1959- .... **CLC 44**
See also CA 120

Guare, John 1938- . **CLC 8, 14, 29, 67; DAM
DRAM**
See also CA 73-76; CANR 21; DLB 7; MTCW

Gudjonsson, Halldor Kiljan 1902- ....
See Laxness, Halldor
See also CA 103

Guenter, Erich
See Eich, Guenter

Guest, Barbara 1920- .... **CLC 34**
See also CA 25-28R; CANR 11, 44; DLB 5

Guest, Judith (Ann) 1936- **CLC 8, 30; DAM
NOV, POP**
See also AAYA 7; CA 77-80; CANR 15; INT
CANR-15; MTCW

Guevara, Che .... **CLC 87; HLC**
See also Guevara (Serna), Ernesto

Guevara (Serna), Ernesto 1928-1967 ....
See Guevara, Che
See also CA 127; 111; CANR 56; DAM MULT;
HW

Guild, Nicholas M. 1944- .... **CLC 33**
See also CA 93-96

Guillemin, Jacques
See Sartre, Jean-Paul

Guillen, Jorge 1893-1984 .... **CLC 11; DAM
MULT, POET**
See also CA 89-92; 112; DLB 108; HW

Guillen, Nicolas (Cristobal) 1902-1989 **C L C
48, 79; BLC; DAM MST, MULT, POET;
HLC**
See also BW 2; CA 116; 125; 129; HW

Guillevic, (Eugene) 1907- .... **CLC 33**
See also CA 93-96

Guillois
See Desnos, Robert

Guillois, Valentin
See Desnos, Robert

Guiney, Louise Imogen 1861-1920 **TCLC 41**
See also DLB 54

Guiraldes, Ricardo (Guillermo) 1886-1927
TCLC 39
See also CA 131; HW; MTCW

Gumilev, Nikolai Stephanovich 1886-1921
TCLC 60

Gunesekera, Romesh .... **CLC 91**

Gunn, Bill .... **CLC 5**
See also Gunn, William Harrison
See also DLB 38

Gunn, Thom(son William) 1929-**CLC 3, 6, 18,
32, 81; DAM POET**
See also CA 17-20R; CANR 9, 33; CDBLB
1960 to Present; DLB 27; INT CANR-33;
MTCW

Gunn, William Harrison 1934(?)-1989 ....
See Gunn, Bill
See also AITN 1; BW 1; CA 13-16R; 128;
CANR 12, 25

Gunnars, Kristjana 1948- .... **CLC 69**
See also CA 113; DLB 60

Gurdjieff, G(eorgei) I(vanovich) 1877(?)-1949
TCLC 71
See also CA 157

Gurganus, Allan 1947- . **CLC 70; DAM POP**
See also BEST 90:1; CA 135

Gurney, A(lbert) R(amsdell), Jr. 1930- . **C L C
32, 50, 54; DAM DRAM**
See also CA 77-80; CANR 32

Gurney, Ivor (Bertie) 1890-1937 ... **TCLC 33**

Gurney, Peter
See Gurney, A(lbert) R(amsdell), Jr.

Guro, Elena 1877-1913 .... **TCLC 56**

Gustafson, James M(oody) 1925- ... **CLC 100**
See also CA 25-28R; CANR 37

Gustafson, Ralph (Barker) 1909- ..... **CLC 36**
See also CA 21-24R; CANR 8, 45; DLB 88

Gut, Gom
See Simenon, Georges (Jacques Christian)

Guterson, David 1956- .... **CLC 91**
See also CA 132

Guthrie, A(lfred) B(ertram), Jr. 1901-1991
CLC 23
See also CA 57-60; 134; CANR 24; DLB 6;
SATA 62; SATA-Obit 67

Guthrie, Isobel
See Grieve, C(hristopher) M(urray)

Guthrie, Woodrow Wilson 1912-1967 ....
See Guthrie, Woody
See also CA 113; 93-96

Guthrie, Woody .... **CLC 35**
See also Guthrie, Woodrow Wilson

Guy, Rosa (Cuthbert)
1928- .... **CLC 26**
See also AAYA 4; BW 2; CA 17-20R; CANR
14, 34; CLR 13; DLB 33; JRDA; MAICYA;
SATA 14, 62

Gwendolyn
See Bennett, (Enoch) Arnold

H. D. .... CLC **3, 8, 14, 31, 34, 73; PC 5**
See also Doolittle, Hilda

H. de V.
See Buchan, John

Haavikko, Paavo Juhani 1931- .. CLC **18, 34**
See also CA 106

Habbema, Koos
See Heijermans, Herman

Hacker, Marilyn 1942- CLC **5, 9, 23, 72, 91;
DAM POET**
See also CA 77-80; DLB 120

Haggard, H(enry) Rider 1856-1925TCLC **11**
See also CA 108; 148; DLB 70, 156, 174, 178;
SATA 16

Hagiosy, L.
See Larbaud, Valery (Nicolas)

Hagiwara Sakutaro 1886-1942TCLC **60; PC
18**

Haig, Fenil
See Ford, Ford Madox

Haig-Brown, Roderick (Langmere) 1908-1976
CLC **21**
See also CA 5-8R; 69-72; CANR 4, 38; CLR
31; DLB 88; MAICYA; SATA 12

Hailey, Arthur 1920-CLC **5; DAM NOV, POP**
See also AITN 2; BEST 90:3; CA 1-4R; CANR
2, 36; DLB 88; DLBY 82; MTCW

Hailey, Elizabeth Forsythe 1938- ..... CLC **40**
See also CA 93-96; CAAS 1; CANR 15, 48;
INT CANR-15

Haines, John (Meade) 1924-.............. CLC **58**
See also CA 17-20R; CANR 13, 34; DLB 5

Hakluyt, Richard 1552-1616 .... LC **31**

Haldeman, Joe (William) 1943- .... CLC **61**
See also CA 53-56; CAAS 25; CANR 6; DLB
8; INT CANR-6

Haley, Alex(ander Murray Palmer) 1921-1992
CLC **8, 12, 76; BLC; DA; DAB; DAC;
DAM MST, MULT, POP**
See also BW 2; CA 77-80; 136; DLB 38;
MTCW

Haliburton, Thomas Chandler 1796-1865
NCLC **15**
See also DLB 11, 99

Hall, Donald (Andrew, Jr.) 1928- CLC **1, 13,
37, 59; DAM POET**
See also CA 5-8R; CAAS 7; CANR 2, 44; DLB
5; SATA 23

Hall, Frederic Sauser
See Sauser-Hall, Frederic

Hall, James
See Kuttner, Henry

Hall, James Norman 1887-1951 ..... TCLC **23**
See also CA 123; SATA 21

Hall, (Marguerite) Radclyffe 1886-1943
TCLC **12**
See also CA 110; 150

Hall, Rodney 1935- .... CLC **51**
See also CA 109

Halleck, Fitz-Greene 1790-1867 .... NCLC **47**
See also DLB 3

Halliday, Michael
See Creasey, John

Halpern, Daniel 1945- .... CLC **14**
See also CA 33-36R

Hamburger, Michael (Peter Leopold) 1924-
CLC **5, 14**
See also CA 5-8R; CAAS 4; CANR 2, 47; DLB
27

Hamill, Pete 1935- .... CLC **10**
See also CA 25-28R; CANR 18

Hamilton, Alexander
1755(?)-1804 .... NCLC **49**
See also DLB 37

Hamilton, Clive
See Lewis, C(live) S(taples)

Hamilton, Edmond 1904-1977 .... CLC **1**
See also CA 1-4R; CANR 3; DLB 8

Hamilton, Eugene (Jacob) Lee
See Lee-Hamilton, Eugene (Jacob)

Hamilton, Franklin
See Silverberg, Robert

Hamilton, Gail
See Corcoran, Barbara

Hamilton, Mollie
See Kaye, M(ary) M(argaret)

Hamilton, (Anthony Walter) Patrick 1904-1962
CLC **51**
See also CA 113; DLB 10

Hamilton, Virginia 1936- .... CLC **26; DAM
MULT**
See also AAYA 2, 21; BW 2; CA 25-28R;
CANR 20, 37; CLR 1, 11, 40; DLB 33, 52;
INT CANR-20; JRDA; MAICYA; MTCW;
SATA 4, 56, 79

Hammett, (Samuel) Dashiell 1894-1961 C L C
3, 5, 10, 19, 47; SSC 17
See also AITN 1; CA 81-84; CANR 42; CDALB
1929-1941; DLBD 6; DLBY 96; MTCW

Hammon, Jupiter 1711(?)-1800(?) ..NCLC **5;
BLC; DAM MULT, POET; PC 16**
See also DLB 31, 50

Hammond, Keith
See Kuttner, Henry

Hamner, Earl (Henry), Jr. 1923- ...... CLC **12**
See also AITN 2; CA 73-76; DLB 6

Hampton, Christopher (James) 1946- CLC **4**
See also CA 25-28R; DLB 13; MTCW

Hamsun, Knut .... TCLC **2, 14, 49**
See also Pedersen, Knut

Handke, Peter 1942-CLC **5, 8, 10, 15, 38; DAM
DRAM, NOV**
See also CA 77-80; CANR 33; DLB 85, 124;
MTCW

Hanley, James 1901-1985 ..... CLC **3, 5, 8, 13**
See also CA 73-76; 117; CANR 36; MTCW

Hannah, Barry 1942- .... CLC **23, 38, 90**
See also CA 108; 110; CANR 43; DLB 6; INT
110; MTCW

Hannon, Ezra
See Hunter, Evan

Hansberry, Lorraine (Vivian)
1930-1965 ...... CLC **17, 62; BLC; DA; DAB;
DAC; DAM DRAM, MST, MULT; DC 2**
See also BW 1; CA 109; 25-28R; CABS 3;
CANR 58; CDALB 1941-1968; DLB 7, 38;
MTCW

Hansen, Joseph 1923- .... CLC **38**
See also CA 29-32R; CAAS 17; CANR 16, 44;
INT CANR-16

Hansen, Martin A. 1909-1955 .... TCLC **32**

Hanson, Kenneth O(stlin) 1922- .... CLC **13**
See also CA 53-56; CANR 7

Hardwick, Elizabeth 1916- .... CLC **13; DAM
NOV**
See also CA 5-8R; CANR 3, 32; DLB 6; MTCW

Hardy, Thomas 1840-1928TCLC **4, 10, 18, 32,
48, 53, 72; DA; DAB; DAC; DAM MST,
NOV, POET; PC 8; SSC 2; WLC**
See also CA 104; 123; CDBLB 1890-1914;
DLB 18, 19, 135; MTCW

Hare, David 1947-........................ CLC **29, 58**
See also CA 97-100; CANR 39; DLB 13;
MTCW

Harford, Henry
See Hudson, W(illiam) H(enry)

Hargrave, Leonie
See Disch, Thomas M(ichael)

Harjo, Joy 1951- .... CLC **83; DAM MULT**
See also CA 114; CANR 35; DLB 120, 175;
NNAL

Harlan, Louis R(udolph)
1922- .... CLC **34**
See also CA 21-24R; CANR 25, 55

Harling, Robert 1951(?)- .... CLC **53**
See also CA 147

Harmon, William (Ruth) 1938-......... CLC **38**
See also CA 33-36R; CANR 14, 32, 35; SATA
65

Harper, F. E. W.
See Harper, Frances Ellen Watkins

Harper, Frances E. W.
See Harper, Frances Ellen Watkins

Harper, Frances E. Watkins
See Harper, Frances Ellen Watkins

Harper, Frances Ellen
See Harper, Frances Ellen Watkins

Harper, Frances Ellen Watkins 1825-1911
  TCLC 14; BLC; DAM MULT, POET
  See also BW 1; CA 111; 125; DLB 50

Harper, Michael S(teven) 1938- .... **CLC 7, 22**
  See also BW 1; CA 33-36R; CANR 24; DLB 41

Harper, Mrs. F. E. W.
  See Harper, Frances Ellen Watkins

Harris, Christie (Lucy) Irwin 1907- **CLC 12**
  See also CA 5-8R; CANR 6; DLB 88; JRDA; MAICYA; SAAS 10; SATA 6, 74

Harris, Frank 1856-1931 .... **TCLC 24**
  See also CA 109; 150; DLB 156

Harris, George Washington 1814-1869**NCLC 23**
  See also DLB 3, 11

Harris, Joel Chandler 1848-1908 ... **TCLC 2; SSC 19**
  See also CA 104; 137; DLB 11, 23, 42, 78, 91; MAICYA; YABC 1

Harris, John (Wyndham Parkes Lucas) Beynon 1903-1969 ....
  See Wyndham, John
  See also CA 102; 89-92

Harris, MacDonald .... **CLC 9**
  See also Heiney, Donald (William)

Harris, Mark 1922- .... **CLC 19**
  See also CA 5-8R; CAAS 3; CANR 2, 55; DLB 2; DLBY 80

Harris, (Theodore) Wilson 1921- ..... **CLC 25**
  See also BW 2; CA 65-68; CAAS 16; CANR 11, 27; DLB 117; MTCW

Harrison, Elizabeth Cavanna 1909- ....
  See Cavanna, Betty
  See also CA 9-12R; CANR 6, 27

Harrison, Harry (Max) 1925- .... **CLC 42**
  See also CA 1-4R; CANR 5, 21; DLB 8; SATA 4

Harrison, James (Thomas) 1937- **CLC 6, 14, 33, 66; SSC 19**
  See also CA 13-16R; CANR 8, 51; DLBY 82; INT CANR-8

Harrison, Jim
  See Harrison, James (Thomas)

Harrison, Kathryn 1961- .... **CLC 70**
  See also CA 144

Harrison, Tony 1937- .... **CLC 43**
  See also CA 65-68; CANR 44; DLB 40; MTCW

Harriss, Will(ard Irvin) 1922- .... **CLC 34**
  See also CA 111

Harson, Sley
  See Ellison, Harlan (Jay)

Hart, Ellis
  See Ellison, Harlan (Jay)

Hart, Josephine 1942(?)-**CLC 70; DAM POP**
  See also CA 138

Hart, Moss 1904-1961**CLC 66; DAM DRAM**
  See also CA 109; 89-92; DLB 7

Harte, (Francis) Bret(t) 1836(?)-1902**TCLC 1, 25; DA; DAC; DAM MST; SSC 8; WLC**
  See also CA 104; 140; CDALB 1865-1917; DLB 12, 64, 74, 79; SATA 26

Hartley, L(eslie) P(oles) 1895-1972**CLC 2, 22**
  See also CA 45-48; 37-40R; CANR 33; DLB 15, 139; MTCW

Hartman, Geoffrey H. 1929- .... **CLC 27**
  See also CA 117; 125; DLB 67

Hartmann, Sadakichi 1867-1944 ... **TCLC 73**
  See also CA 157; DLB 54

Hartmann von Aue c. 1160-c. 1205**CMLC 15**
  See also DLB 138

Hartmann von Aue 1170-1210 ...... **CMLC 15**

Haruf, Kent 1943- .... **CLC 34**
  See also CA 149

Harwood, Ronald 1934- .... **CLC 32; DAM DRAM, MST**
  See also CA 1-4R; CANR 4, 55; DLB 13

Hasek, Jaroslav (Matej Frantisek) 1883-1923 **TCLC 4**
  See also CA 104; 129; MTCW

Hass, Robert 1941- ... **CLC 18, 39, 99; PC 16**
  See also CA 111; CANR 30, 50; DLB 105; SATA 94

Hastings, Hudson
  See Kuttner, Henry

Hastings, Selina .... **CLC 44**

Hathorne, John 1641-1717 .... **LC 38**

Hatteras, Amelia
  See Mencken, H(enry) L(ouis)

Hatteras, Owen .... **TCLC 18**
  See also Mencken, H(enry) L(ouis); Nathan, George Jean

Hauptmann, Gerhart (Johann Robert) 1862-1946 .... **TCLC 4; DAM DRAM**
  See also CA 104; 153; DLB 66, 118

Havel, Vaclav 1936- ... **CLC 25, 58, 65; DAM DRAM; DC 6**
  See also CA 104; CANR 36; MTCW

Haviaras, Stratis .... **CLC 33**
  See also Chaviaras, Strates

Hawes, Stephen 1475(?)-1523(?) .... **LC 17**

Hawkes, John (Clendennin Burne, Jr.) 1925- **CLC 1, 2, 3, 4, 7, 9, 14, 15, 27, 49**
  See also CA 1-4R; CANR 2, 47; DLB 2, 7; DLBY 80; MTCW

Hawking, S. W.
  See Hawking, Stephen W(illiam)

Hawking, Stephen W(illiam) 1942- .. **CLC 63**
  See also AAYA 13; BEST 89:1; CA 126; 129; CANR 48

Hawthorne, Julian 1846-1934 .... **TCLC 25**

Hawthorne, Nathaniel 1804-1864 **NCLC 39; DA; DAB; DAC; DAM MST, NOV; SSC 3; WLC**
  See also AAYA 18; CDALB 1640-1865; DLB 1, 74; YABC 2

Haxton, Josephine Ayres 1921- ....
  See Douglas, Ellen
  See also CA 115; CANR 41

Hayaseca y Eizaguirre, Jorge
  See Echegaray (y Eizaguirre), Jose (Maria Waldo)

Hayashi Fumiko 1904-1951 .... **TCLC 27**
  See also DLB 180

Haycraft, Anna
  See Ellis, Alice Thomas
  See also CA 122

Hayden, Robert E(arl) 1913-1980 . **CLC 5, 9, 14, 37; BLC; DA; DAC; DAM MST, MULT, POET; PC 6**
  See also BW 1; CA 69-72; 97-100; CABS 2; CANR 24; CDALB 1941-1968; DLB 5, 76; MTCW; SATA 19; SATA-Obit 26

Hayford, J(oseph) E(phraim) Casely
  See Casely-Hayford, J(oseph) E(phraim)

Hayman, Ronald 1932- .... **CLC 44**
  See also CA 25-28R; CANR 18, 50; DLB 155

Haywood, Eliza (Fowler) 1693(?)-1756 **LC 1**

Hazlitt, William 1778-1830 .... **NCLC 29**
  See also DLB 110, 158

Hazzard, Shirley 1931- .... **CLC 18**
  See also CA 9-12R; CANR 4; DLBY 82; MTCW

Head, Bessie 1937-1986... **CLC 25, 67; BLC; DAM MULT**
  See also BW 2; CA 29-32R; 119; CANR 25; DLB 117; MTCW

Headon, (Nicky) Topper 1956(?)- ..... **CLC 30**

Heaney, Seamus (Justin) 1939- **CLC 5, 7, 14, 25, 37, 74, 91; DAB; DAM POET; PC 18; WLCS**
  See also CA 85-88; CANR 25, 48; CDBLB 1960 to Present; DLB 40; DLBY 95; MTCW

Hearn, (Patricio) Lafcadio (Tessima Carlos) 1850-1904 .... **TCLC 9**
  See also CA 105; DLB 12, 78

Hearne, Vicki 1946- .... **CLC 56**
  See also CA 139

Hearon, Shelby 1931- .... **CLC 63**
  See also AITN 2; CA 25-28R; CANR 18, 48

Heat-Moon, William Least .... **CLC 29**
  See also Trogdon, William (Lewis)
  See also AAYA 9

Hebbel, Friedrich 1813-1863**NCLC 43; DAM DRAM**
  See also DLB 129

Hebert, Anne 1916-**CLC 4, 13, 29; DAC; DAM MST, POET**
  See also CA 85-88; DLB 68; MTCW

Hudson, W(illiam) H(enry) 1841-1922 **T C L C 29**
See also CA 115; DLB 98, 153, 174; SATA 35

Hueffer, Ford Madox
See Ford, Ford Madox

Hughart, Barry 1934- .... **CLC 39**
See also CA 137

Hughes, Colin
See Creasey, John

Hughes, David (John) 1930- .... **CLC 48**
See also CA 116; 129; DLB 14

Hughes, Edward James
See Hughes, Ted
See also DAM MST, POET

Hughes, (James) Langston 1902-1967**CLC 1, 5, 10, 15, 35, 44; BLC; DA; DAB; DAC; DAM DRAM, MST, MULT, POET; DC 3; PC 1; SSC 6; WLC**
See also AAYA 12; BW 1; CA 1-4R; 25-28R; CANR 1, 34; CDALB 1929-1941; CLR 17; DLB 4, 7, 48, 51, 86; JRDA; MAICYA; MTCW; SATA 4, 33

Hughes, Richard (Arthur Warren) 1900-1976 **CLC 1, 11; DAM NOV**
See also CA 5-8R; 65-68; CANR 4; DLB 15, 161; MTCW; SATA 8; SATA-Obit 25

Hughes, Ted 1930- **CLC 2, 4, 9, 14, 37; DAB; DAC; PC 7**
See also Hughes, Edward James
See also CA 1-4R; CANR 1, 33; CLR 3; DLB 40, 161; MAICYA; MTCW; SATA 49; SATA-Brief 27

Hugo, Richard F(ranklin) 1923-1982 **CLC 6, 18, 32; DAM POET**
See also CA 49-52; 108; CANR 3; DLB 5

Hugo, Victor (Marie) 1802-1885**NCLC 3, 10, 21; DA; DAB; DAC; DAM DRAM, MST, NOV, POET; PC 17; WLC**
See also DLB 119; SATA 47

Huidobro, Vicente
See Huidobro Fernandez, Vicente Garcia

Huidobro Fernandez, Vicente Garcia 1893-1948 .... **TCLC 31**
See also CA 131; HW

Hulme, Keri 1947- .... **CLC 39**
See also CA 125; INT 125

Hulme, T(homas) E(rnest) 1883-1917 **T C L C 21**
See also CA 117; DLB 19

Hume, David 1711-1776 .... **LC 7**
See also DLB 104

Humphrey, William 1924- .... **CLC 45**
See also CA 77-80; DLB 6

Humphreys, Emyr Owen 1919- .... **CLC 47**
See also CA 5-8R; CANR 3, 24; DLB 15

Humphreys, Josephine 1945- ..... **CLC 34, 57**
See also CA 121; 127; INT 127

Huneker, James Gibbons 1857-1921**TCLC 65**

See also DLB 71

Hungerford, Pixie
See Brinsmead, H(esba) F(ay)

Hunt, E(verette) Howard, (Jr.) 1918- .... **CLC 3**
See also AITN 1; CA 45-48; CANR 2, 47

Hunt, Kyle
See Creasey, John

Hunt, (James Henry) Leigh 1784-1859**N C L C 1; DAM POET**

Hunt, Marsha 1946- .... **CLC 70**
See also BW 2; CA 143

Hunt, Violet 1866-1942 .... **TCLC 53**
See also DLB 162

Hunter, E. Waldo
See Sturgeon, Theodore (Hamilton)

Hunter, Evan 1926- . **CLC 11, 31; DAM POP**
See also CA 5-8R; CANR 5, 38; DLBY 82; INT CANR-5; MTCW; SATA 25

Hunter, Kristin (Eggleston) 1931- .... **CLC 35**
See also AITN 1; BW 1; CA 13-16R; CANR 13; CLR 3; DLB 33; INT CANR-13; MAICYA; SAAS 10; SATA 12

Hunter, Mollie 1922- .... **CLC 21**
See also McIlwraith, Maureen Mollie Hunter
See also AAYA 13; CANR 37; CLR 25; DLB 161; JRDA; MAICYA; SAAS 7; SATA 54

Hunter, Robert (?)-1734 .... **LC 7**

Hurston, Zora Neale 1903-1960**CLC 7, 30, 61; BLC; DA; DAC; DAM MST, MULT, NOV; SSC 4; WLCS**
See also AAYA 15; BW 1; CA 85-88; DLB 51, 86; MTCW

Huston, John (Marcellus) 1906-1987**CLC 20**
See also CA 73-76; 123; CANR 34; DLB 26

Hustvedt, Siri 1955- .... **CLC 76**
See also CA 137

Hutten, Ulrich von 1488-1523 .... **LC 16**
See also DLB 179

Huxley, Aldous (Leonard) 1894-1963 **CLC 1, 3, 4, 5, 8, 11, 18, 35, 79; DA; DAB; DAC; DAM MST, NOV; WLC**
See also AAYA 11; CA 85-88; CANR 44; CDBLB 1914-1945; DLB 36, 100, 162; MTCW; SATA 63

Huysmans, Charles Marie Georges 1848-1907

See Huysmans, Joris-Karl
See also CA 104

Huysmans, Joris-Karl .... **TCLC 7, 69**
See also Huysmans, Charles Marie Georges
See also DLB 123

Hwang, David Henry 1957- ... **CLC 55; DAM DRAM; DC 4**
See also CA 127; 132; INT 132

Hyde, Anthony 1946- .... **CLC 42**
See also CA 136

Hyde, Margaret O(ldroyd) 1917- ..... **CLC 21**
See also CA 1-4R; CANR 1, 36; CLR 23; JRDA; MAICYA; SAAS 8; SATA 1, 42, 76

Hynes, James 1956(?)- .... **CLC 65**

Ian, Janis 1951- .... **CLC 21**
See also CA 105

Ibanez, Vicente Blasco
See Blasco Ibanez, Vicente

Ibarguengoitia, Jorge 1928-1983 ..... **CLC 37**
See also CA 124; 113; HW

Ibsen, Henrik (Johan) 1828-1906 **TCLC 2, 8, 16, 37, 52; DA; DAB; DAC; DAM DRAM, MST; DC 2; WLC**
See also CA 104; 141

Ibuse Masuji 1898-1993 .... **CLC 22**
See also CA 127; 141; DLB 180

Ichikawa, Kon 1915- .... **CLC 20**
See also CA 121

Idle, Eric 1943- .... **CLC 21**
See also Monty Python
See also CA 116; CANR 35

Ignatow, David 1914- .... **CLC 4, 7, 14, 40**
See also CA 9-12R; CAAS 3; CANR 31, 57; DLB 5

Ihimaera, Witi 1944- .... **CLC 46**
See also CA 77-80

Ilf, Ilya .... **TCLC 21**
See also Fainzilberg, Ilya Arnoldovich

Illyes, Gyula 1902-1983 .... **PC 16**
See also CA 114; 109

Immermann, Karl (Lebrecht) 1796-1840 **NCLC 4, 49**
See also DLB 133

Inchbald, Elizabeth 1753-1821 ...... **NCLC 62**
See also DLB 39, 89

Inclan, Ramon (Maria) del Valle
See Valle-Inclan, Ramon (Maria) del

Infante, G(uillermo) Cabrera
See Cabrera Infante, G(uillermo)

Ingalls, Rachel (Holmes) 1940- .... **CLC 42**
See also CA 123; 127

Ingamells, Rex 1913-1955 .... **TCLC 35**

Inge, William (Motter) 1913-1973 . **CLC 1, 8, 19; DAM DRAM**
See also CA 9-12R; CDALB 1941-1968; DLB 7; MTCW

Ingelow, Jean 1820-1897 .... **NCLC 39**
See also DLB 35, 163; SATA 33

Ingram, Willis J.
See Harris, Mark

Innaurato, Albert (F.) 1948(?)- .. **CLC 21, 60**
See also CA 115; 122; INT 122

Innes, Michael
See Stewart, J(ohn) I(nnes) M(ackintosh)

Keith, Michael
See Hubbard, L(afayette) Ron(ald)

Keller, Gottfried 1819-1890 ...... **NCLC 2; SSC 26**
See also DLB 129

Kellerman, Jonathan 1949- ... **CLC 44; DAM POP**
See also BEST 90:1; CA 106; CANR 29, 51; INT CANR-29

Kelley, William Melvin 1937- .... **CLC 22**
See also BW 1; CA 77-80; CANR 27; DLB 33

Kellogg, Marjorie 1922- .... **CLC 2**
See also CA 81-84

Kellow, Kathleen
See Hibbert, Eleanor Alice Burford

Kelly, M(ilton) T(erry) 1947- .... **CLC 55**
See also CA 97-100; CAAS 22; CANR 19, 43

Kelman, James 1946- .... **CLC 58, 86**
See also CA 148

Kemal, Yashar 1923- .... **CLC 14, 29**
See also CA 89-92; CANR 44

Kemble, Fanny 1809-1893 .... **NCLC 18**
See also DLB 32

Kemelman, Harry 1908-1996 .... **CLC 2**
See also AITN 1; CA 9-12R; 155; CANR 6; DLB 28

Kempe, Margery 1373(?)-1440(?) .... **LC 6**
See also DLB 146

Kempis, Thomas a 1380-1471 .... **LC 11**

Kendall, Henry 1839-1882 .... **NCLC 12**

Keneally, Thomas (Michael) 1935- **CLC 5, 8, 10, 14, 19, 27, 43; DAM NOV**
See also CA 85-88; CANR 10, 50; MTCW

Kennedy, Adrienne (Lita) 1931- ..... **CLC 66; BLC; DAM MULT; DC 5**
See also BW 2; CA 103; CAAS 20; CABS 3; CANR 26, 53; DLB 38

Kennedy, John Pendleton
1795-1870 .... **NCLC 2**
See also DLB 3

Kennedy, Joseph Charles 1929- ....
See Kennedy, X. J.
See also CA 1-4R; CANR 4, 30, 40; SATA 14, 86

Kennedy, William 1928- .. **CLC 6, 28, 34, 53; DAM NOV**
See also AAYA 1; CA 85-88; CANR 14, 31; DLB 143; DLBY 85; INT CANR-31; MTCW; SATA 57

Kennedy, X. J. .... **CLC 8, 42**
See Kennedy, Joseph Charles
See also CAAS 9; CLR 27; DLB 5; SAAS 22

Kenny, Maurice (Francis) 1929- ..... **CLC 87; DAM MULT**
See also CA 144; CAAS 22; DLB 175; NNAL

Kent, Kelvin
See Kuttner, Henry

Kenton, Maxwell
See Southern, Terry

Kenyon, Robert O.
See Kuttner, Henry

Kerouac, Jack .... **CLC 1, 2, 3, 5, 14, 29, 61**
See also Kerouac, Jean-Louis Lebris de
See also CDALB 1941-1968; DLB 2, 16; DLBD 3; DLBY 95

Kerouac, Jean-Louis Lebris de 1922-1969 ...
See Kerouac, Jack
See also AITN 1; CA 5-8R; 25-28R; CANR 26, 54; DA; DAB; DAC; DAM MST, NOV, POET, POP; MTCW; WLC

Kerr, Jean 1923- .... **CLC 22**
See also CA 5-8R; CANR 7; INT CANR-7

Kerr, M. E. .... **CLC 12, 35**
See also Meaker, Marijane (Agnes)
See also AAYA 2; CLR 29; SAAS 1

Kerr, Robert .... **CLC 55**

Kerrigan, (Thomas) Anthony 1918- **CLC 4, 6**
See also CA 49-52; CAAS 11; CANR 4

Kerry, Lois
See Duncan, Lois

Kesey, Ken (Elton) 1935- **CLC 1, 3, 6, 11, 46, 64; DA; DAB; DAC; DAM MST, NOV, POP; WLC**
See also CA 1-4R; CANR 22, 38; CDALB 1968-1988; DLB 2, 16; MTCW; SATA 66

Kesselring, Joseph (Otto) 1902-1967 **CLC 45; DAM DRAM, MST**
See also CA 150

Kessler, Jascha (Frederick) 1929- ...... **CLC 4**
See also CA 17-20R; CANR 8, 48

Kettelkamp, Larry (Dale) 1933- .... **CLC 12**
See also CA 29-32R; CANR 16; SAAS 3; SATA 2

Key, Ellen 1849-1926 .... **TCLC 65**

Keyber, Conny
See Fielding, Henry

Keyes, Daniel 1927- **CLC 80; DA; DAC; DAM MST, NOV**
See also CA 17-20R; CANR 10, 26, 54; SATA 37

Keynes, John Maynard 1883-1946 **TCLC 64**
See also CA 114; DLBD 10

Khanshendel, Chiron
See Rose, Wendy

Khayyam, Omar 1048-1131 **CMLC 11; DAM POET; PC 8**

Kherdian, David 1931- .... **CLC 6, 9**
See also CA 21-24R; CAAS 2; CANR 39; CLR 24; JRDA; MAICYA; SATA 16, 74

Khlebnikov, Velimir .... **TCLC 20**
See also Khlebnikov, Viktor Vladimirovich

Khlebnikov, Viktor Vladimirovich 1885-1922
See Khlebnikov, Velimir
See also CA 117

Khodasevich, Vladislav (Felitsianovich) 1886-1939 .... **TCLC 15**
See also CA 115

Kielland, Alexander Lange 1849-1906 **TCLC 5**
See also CA 104

Kiely, Benedict 1919- .... **CLC 23, 43**
See also CA 1-4R; CANR 2; DLB 15

Kienzle, William X(avier) 1928- ..... **CLC 25; DAM POP**
See also CA 93-96; CAAS 1; CANR 9, 31, 59; INT CANR-31; MTCW

Kierkegaard, Soren 1813-1855 ...... **NCLC 34**

Killens, John Oliver 1916-1987 .... **CLC 10**
See also BW 2; CA 77-80; 123; CAAS 2; CANR 26; DLB 33

Killigrew, Anne 1660-1685 .... **LC 4**
See also DLB 131

Kim
See Simenon, Georges (Jacques Christian)

Kincaid, Jamaica 1949- .. **CLC 43, 68; BLC; DAM MULT, NOV**
See also AAYA 13; BW 2; CA 125; CANR 47, 59; DLB 157

King, Francis (Henry) 1923- **CLC 8, 53; DAM NOV**
See also CA 1-4R; CANR 1, 33; DLB 15, 139; MTCW

King, Martin Luther, Jr. 1929-1968 **CLC 83; BLC; DA; DAB; DAC; DAM MST, MULT; WLCS**
See also BW 2; CA 25-28; CANR 27, 44; CAP 2; MTCW; SATA 14

King, Stephen (Edwin) 1947- **CLC 12, 26, 37, 61; DAM NOV, POP; SSC 17**
See also AAYA 1, 17; BEST 90:1; CA 61-64; CANR 1, 30, 52; DLB 143; DLBY 80; JRDA; MTCW; SATA 9, 55

King, Steve
See King, Stephen (Edwin)

King, Thomas 1943- ... **CLC 89; DAC; DAM MULT**
See also CA 144; DLB 175; NNAL

Kingman, Lee .... **CLC 17**
See also Natti, (Mary) Lee
See also SAAS 3; SATA 1, 67

Kingsley, Charles 1819-1875 .... **NCLC 35**
See also DLB 21, 32, 163; YABC 2

Kingsley, Sidney 1906-1995 .... **CLC 44**
See also CA 85-88; 147; DLB 7

Kingsolver, Barbara 1955- **CLC 55, 81; DAM POP**
See also AAYA 15; CA 129; 134; INT 134

Kingston, Maxine (Ting Ting) Hong 1940- **CLC 12, 19, 58; DAM MULT, NOV; WLCS**
See also AAYA 8; CA 69-72; CANR 13, 38; DLB 173; DLBY 80; INT CANR-13; MTCW; SATA 53

See Tieck, (Johann) Ludwig

le Carre, John .... **CLC 3, 5, 9, 15, 28**
See also Cornwell, David (John Moore)
See also BEST 89:4; CDBLB 1960 to Present;
DLB 87

Le Clezio, J(ean) M(arie) G(ustave) 1940-
CLC 31
See also CA 116; 128; DLB 83

Leconte de Lisle, Charles-Marie-Rene 1818-
1894 .... **NCLC 29**

Le Coq, Monsieur
See Simenon, Georges (Jacques Christian)

Leduc, Violette 1907-1972 .... **CLC 22**
See also CA 13-14; 33-36R; CAP 1

Ledwidge, Francis 1887(?)-1917 .... **TCLC 23**
See also CA 123; DLB 20

Lee, Andrea 1953-**CLC 36; BLC; DAM MULT**
See also BW 1; CA 125

Lee, Andrew
See Auchincloss, Louis (Stanton)

Lee, Chang-rae 1965- .... **CLC 91**
See also CA 148

Lee, Don L. .... **CLC 2**
See also Madhubuti, Haki R.

Lee, George W(ashington) 1894-1976**CLC 52;
BLC; DAM MULT**
See also BW 1; CA 125; DLB 51

Lee, (Nelle) Harper 1926- .. **CLC 12, 60; DA;
DAB; DAC; DAM MST, NOV; WLC**
See also AAYA 13; CA 13-16R; CANR 51;
CDALB 1941-1968; DLB 6; MTCW; SATA
11

Lee, Helen Elaine 1959(?)- .... **CLC 86**
See also CA 148

Lee, Julian
See Latham, Jean Lee

Lee, Larry
See Lee, Lawrence

Lee, Laurie 1914-1997 **CLC 90; DAB; DAM
POP**
See also CA 77-80; 158; CANR 33; DLB 27;
MTCW

Lee, Lawrence 1941-1990 .... **CLC 34**
See also CA 131; CANR 43

Lee, Manfred B(ennington)
1905-1971 .... **CLC 11**
See also Queen, Ellery
See also CA 1-4R; 29-32R; CANR 2; DLB 137

Lee, Stan 1922-.................................... **CLC 17**
See also AAYA 5; CA 108; 111; INT 111

Lee, Tanith 1947- .... **CLC 46**
See also AAYA 15; CA 37-40R; CANR 53;
SATA 8, 88

Lee, Vernon .... **TCLC 5**
See also Paget, Violet
See also DLB 57, 153, 156, 174, 178

Lee, William
See Burroughs, William S(eward)

Lee, Willy
See Burroughs, William S(eward)

Lee-Hamilton, Eugene (Jacob) 1845-1907
TCLC 22
See also CA 117

Leet, Judith 1935- .... **CLC 11**

Le Fanu, Joseph Sheridan 1814-1873**NCLC 9,
58; DAM POP; SSC 14**
See also DLB 21, 70, 159, 178

Leffland, Ella 1931- .... **CLC 19**
See also CA 29-32R; CANR 35; DLBY 84; INT
CANR-35; SATA 65

Leger, Alexis
See Leger, (Marie-Rene Auguste) Alexis Saint-
Leger

**Leger, (Marie-Rene Auguste) Alexis Saint-
Leger** 1887-1975 **CLC 11; DAM POET**
See also Perse, St.-John
See also CA 13-16R; 61-64; CANR 43; MTCW

Leger, Saintleger
See Leger, (Marie-Rene Auguste) Alexis Saint-
Leger

Le Guin, Ursula K(roeber) 1929- **CLC 8, 13,
22, 45, 71; DAB; DAC; DAM MST, POP;
SSC 12**
See also AAYA 9; AITN 1; CA 21-24R; CANR
9, 32, 52; CDALB 1968-1988; CLR 3, 28;
DLB 8, 52; INT CANR-32; JRDA; MAICYA;
MTCW; SATA 4, 52

Lehmann, Rosamond (Nina) 1901-1990**CLC 5**
See also CA 77-80; 131; CANR 8; DLB 15

Leiber, Fritz (Reuter, Jr.) 1910-1992 **CLC 25**
See also CA 45-48; 139; CANR 2, 40; DLB 8;
MTCW; SATA 45; SATA-Obit 73

Leibniz, Gottfried Wilhelm von 1646-1716**LC
35**
See also DLB 168

Leimbach, Martha 1963- ....
See Leimbach, Marti
See also CA 130

Leimbach, Marti .... **CLC 65**
See also Leimbach, Martha

Leino, Eino... **TCLC 24**
See also Loennbohm, Armas Eino Leopold

Leiris, Michel (Julien) 1901-1990 ..... **CLC 61**
See also CA 119; 128; 132

Leithauser, Brad 1953- .... **CLC 27**
See also CA 107; CANR 27; DLB 120

Lelchuk, Alan 1938- .... **CLC 5**
See also CA 45-48; CAAS 20; CANR 1

Lem, Stanislaw 1921- .... **CLC 8, 15, 40**
See also CA 105; CAAS 1; CANR 32; MTCW

Lemann, Nancy
1956- .... **CLC 39**
See also CA 118; 136

Lemonnier, (Antoine Louis) Camille 1844-1913
TCLC 22
See also CA 121

Lenau, Nikolaus 1802-1850 .... **NCLC 16**

L'Engle, Madeleine (Camp Franklin) 1918-
CLC 12; DAM POP
See also AAYA 1; AITN 2; CA 1-4R; CANR 3,
21, 39; CLR 1, 14; DLB 52; JRDA;
MAICYA; MTCW; SAAS 15; SATA 1, 27,
75

Lengyel, Jozsef 1896-1975 .... **CLC 7**
See also CA 85-88; 57-60

Lenin 1870-1924.....................................
See Lenin, V. I.
See also CA 121

Lenin, V. I. .... **TCLC 67**
See also Lenin

Lennon, John (Ono) 1940-1980 . **CLC 12, 35**
See also CA 102

Lennox, Charlotte Ramsay 1729(?)-1804
NCLC 23
See also DLB 39

Lentricchia, Frank (Jr.) 1940- .... **CLC 34**
See also CA 25-28R; CANR 19

Lenz, Siegfried 1926- .... **CLC 27**
See also CA 89-92; DLB 75

Leonard, Elmore (John, Jr.) 1925-**CLC 28, 34,
71; DAM POP**
See also AAYA 22; AITN 1; BEST 89:1, 90:4;
CA 81-84; CANR 12, 28, 53; DLB 173; INT
CANR-28; MTCW

Leonard, Hugh .... **CLC 19**
See also Byrne, John Keyes
See also DLB 13

Leonov, Leonid (Maximovich) 1899-1994
CLC 92; DAM NOV
See also CA 129; MTCW

Leopardi, (Conte) Giacomo 1798-1837**NCLC
22**

Le Reveler
See Artaud, Antonin (Marie Joseph)

Lerman, Eleanor 1952- .... **CLC 9**
See also CA 85-88

Lerman, Rhoda 1936- .... **CLC 56**
See also CA 49-52

Lermontov, Mikhail Yuryevich 1814-1841
NCLC 47; PC 18

Leroux, Gaston 1868-1927 .... **TCLC 25**
See also CA 108; 136; SATA 65

Lesage, Alain-Rene 1668-1747 ....**LC 28**

Leskov, Nikolai (Semyonovich) 1831-1895
NCLC 25

Lessing, Doris (May) 1919-**CLC 1, 2, 3, 6, 10,
15, 22, 40, 94; DA; DAB; DAC; DAM MST,
NOV; SSC 6; WLCS**
See also CA 9-12R; CAAS 14; CANR 33, 54;

14, 161; JRDA; MAICYA; MTCW; SATA 7, 60

Livesay, Dorothy (Kathleen) 1909-**CLC 4, 15, 79; DAC; DAM MST, POET**
See also AITN 2; CA 25-28R; CAAS 8; CANR 36; DLB 68; MTCW

Livy c. 59B.C.-c. 17 .... **CMLC 11**

Lizardi, Jose Joaquin Fernandez de 1776-1827 **NCLC 30**

Llewellyn, Richard
See Llewellyn Lloyd, Richard Dafydd Vivian
See also DLB 15

Llewellyn Lloyd, Richard Dafydd Vivian 1906-1983 .... **CLC 7, 80**
See also Llewellyn, Richard
See also CA 53-56; 111; CANR 7; SATA 11; SATA-Obit 37

Llosa, (Jorge) Mario (Pedro) Vargas
See Vargas Llosa, (Jorge) Mario (Pedro)

Lloyd Webber, Andrew 1948- ....
See Webber, Andrew Lloyd
See also AAYA 1; CA 116; 149; DAM DRAM; SATA 56

Llull, Ramon c. 1235-c. 1316 .... **CMLC 12**

Locke, Alain (Le Roy) 1886-1954 .. **TCLC 43**
See also BW 1; CA 106; 124; DLB 51

Locke, John 1632-1704 .... **LC 7, 35**
See also DLB 101

Locke-Elliott, Sumner
See Elliott, Sumner Locke

Lockhart, John Gibson 1794-1854 .. **NCLC 6**
See also DLB 110, 116, 144

Lodge, David (John) 1935- .... **CLC 36; DAM POP**
See also BEST 90:1; CA 17-20R; CANR 19, 53; DLB 14; INT CANR-19; MTCW

Loennbohm, Armas Eino Leopold 1878-1926

See Leino, Eino
See also CA 123

Loewinsohn, Ron(ald William) 1937-**CLC 52**
See also CA 25-28R

Logan, Jake
See Smith, Martin Cruz

Logan, John (Burton) 1923-1987 .... **CLC 5**
See also CA 77-80; 124; CANR 45; DLB 5

Lo Kuan-chung 1330(?)-1400(?) .... **LC 12**

Lombard, Nap
See Johnson, Pamela Hansford

London, Jack . **TCLC 9, 15, 39; SSC 4; WLC**
See also London, John Griffith
See also AAYA 13; AITN 2; CDALB 1865-1917; DLB 8, 12, 78; SATA 18

London, John Griffith 1876-1916 ....
See London, Jack
See also CA 110; 119; DA; DAB; DAC; DAM

MST, NOV; JRDA; MAICYA; MTCW

Long, Emmett
See Leonard, Elmore (John, Jr.)

Longbaugh, Harry
See Goldman, William (W.)

Longfellow, Henry Wadsworth 1807-1882 **NCLC 2, 45; DA; DAB; DAC; DAM MST, POET; WLCS**
See also CDALB 1640-1865; DLB 1, 59; SATA 19

Longley, Michael 1939- .... **CLC 29**
See also CA 102; DLB 40

Longus fl. c. 2nd cent. - .... **CMLC 7**

Longway, A. Hugh
See Lang, Andrew

Lonnrot, Elias 1802-1884 .... **NCLC 53**

Lopate, Phillip 1943- .... **CLC 29**
See also CA 97-100; DLBY 80; INT 97-100

Lopez Portillo (y Pacheco), Jose 1920-. **C L C 46**
See also CA 129; HW

Lopez y Fuentes, Gregorio 1897(?)-1966**C L C 32**
See also CA 131; HW

Lorca, Federico Garcia
See Garcia Lorca, Federico

Lord, Bette Bao 1938- .... **CLC 23**
See also BEST 90:3; CA 107; CANR 41; INT 107; SATA 58

Lord Auch
See Bataille, Georges

Lord Byron
See Byron, George Gordon (Noel)

Lorde, Audre (Geraldine) 1934-1992**CLC 18, 71; BLC; DAM MULT, POET; PC 12**
See also BW 1; CA 25-28R; 142; CANR 16, 26, 46; DLB 41; MTCW

Lord Houghton
See Milnes, Richard Monckton

Lord Jeffrey
See Jeffrey, Francis

Lorenzini, Carlo 1826-1890 ....
See Collodi, Carlo
See also MAICYA; SATA 29

Lorenzo, Heberto Padilla
See Padilla (Lorenzo), Heberto

Loris
See Hofmannsthal, Hugo von

Loti, Pierre .... **TCLC 11**
See also Viaud, (Louis Marie) Julien
See also DLB 123

Louie, David Wong 1954- .... **CLC 70**
See also CA 139

Louis, Father M.

See Merton, Thomas

Lovecraft, H(oward) P(hillips) 1890-1937 **TCLC 4, 22; DAM POP; SSC 3**
See also AAYA 14; CA 104; 133; MTCW

Lovelace, Earl 1935- .... **CLC 51**
See also BW 2; CA 77-80; CANR 41; DLB 125; MTCW

Lovelace, Richard 1618-1657 .... **LC 24**
See also DLB 131

Lowell, Amy 1874-1925 .... **TCLC 1, 8; DAM POET; PC 13**
See also CA 104; 151; DLB 54, 140

Lowell, James Russell 1819-1891 .... **NCLC 2**
See also CDALB 1640-1865; DLB 1, 11, 64, 79

Lowell, Robert (Traill Spence, Jr.) 1917-1977 **CLC 1, 2, 3, 4, 5, 8, 9, 11, 15, 37; DA; DAB; DAC; DAM MST, NOV; PC 3; WLC**
See also CA 9-12R; 73-76; CABS 2; CANR 26; DLB 5, 169; MTCW

Lowndes, Marie Adelaide (Belloc) 1868-1947 **TCLC 12**
See also CA 107; DLB 70

Lowry, (Clarence) Malcolm 1909-1957**T CLC 6, 40**
See also CA 105; 131; CDBLB 1945-1960; DLB 15; MTCW

Lowry, Mina Gertrude 1882-1966 ....
See Loy, Mina
See also CA 113

Loxsmith, John
See Brunner, John (Kilian Houston)

Loy, Mina .... **CLC 28; DAM POET; PC 16**
See also Lowry, Mina Gertrude
See also DLB 4, 54

Loyson-Bridet
See Schwob, (Mayer Andre) Marcel

Lucas, Craig 1951- .... **CLC 64**
See also CA 137

Lucas, George 1944- .... **CLC 16**
See also AAYA 1; CA 77-80; CANR 30; SATA 56

Lucas, Hans
See Godard, Jean-Luc

Lucas, Victoria
See Plath, Sylvia

Ludlam, Charles 1943-1987 .... **CLC 46, 50**
See also CA 85-88; 122

Ludlum, Robert 1927-**CLC 22, 43; DAM NOV, POP**
See also AAYA 10; BEST 89:1, 90:3; CA 33-36R; CANR 25, 41; DLBY 82; MTCW

Ludwig, Ken .... **CLC 60**

Ludwig, Otto 1813-1865 .... **NCLC 4**
See also DLB 129

Lugones, Leopoldo 1874-1938 .... **TCLC 15**

See also CA 116; 131; HW

Lu Hsun 1881-1936 .... **TCLC 3; SSC 20**
See also Shu-Jen, Chou

Lukacs, George .... **CLC 24**
See also Lukacs, Gyorgy (Szegeny von)

Lukacs, Gyorgy (Szegeny von) 1885-1971 ....
See Lukacs, George
See also CA 101; 29-32R

Luke, Peter (Ambrose Cyprian) 1919-1995
CLC 38
See also CA 81-84; 147; DLB 13

Lunar, Dennis
See Mungo, Raymond

Lurie, Alison 1926- .... **CLC 4, 5, 18, 39**
See also CA 1-4R; CANR 2, 17, 50; DLB 2;
MTCW; SATA 46

Lustig, Arnost 1926- .... **CLC 56**
See also AAYA 3; CA 69-72; CANR 47; SATA
56

Luther, Martin 1483-1546 .... **LC 9, 37**
See also DLB 179

Luxemburg, Rosa 1870(?)-1919 ..... **TCLC 63**
See also CA 118

Luzi, Mario 1914- .... **CLC 13**
See also CA 61-64; CANR 9; DLB 128

Lyly, John 1554(?)-1606 .... **DC 7**
See also DAM DRAM; DLB 62, 167

L'Ymagier
See Gourmont, Remy (-Marie-Charles) de

Lynch, B. Suarez
See Bioy Casares, Adolfo; Borges, Jorge Luis

Lynch, David (K.) 1946- .... **CLC 66**
See also CA 124; 129

Lynch, James
See Andreyev, Leonid (Nikolaevich)

Lynch Davis, B.
See Bioy Casares, Adolfo; Borges, Jorge Luis

Lyndsay, Sir David 1490-1555 .... **LC 20**

Lynn, Kenneth S(chuyler) 1923- .... **CLC 50**
See also CA 1-4R; CANR 3, 27

Lynx
See West, Rebecca

Lyons, Marcus
See Blish, James (Benjamin)

Lyre, Pinchbeck
See Sassoon, Siegfried (Lorraine)

Lytle, Andrew (Nelson) 1902-1995 ... **CLC 22**
See also CA 9-12R; 150; DLB 6; DLBY 95

Lyttelton, George 1709-1773 .... **LC 10**

Maas, Peter 1929- .... **CLC 29**
See also CA 93-96; INT 93-96

Macaulay, Rose 1881-1958 .... **TCLC 7, 44**

See also CA 104; DLB 36

Macaulay, Thomas Babington 1800-1859
NCLC 42
See also CDBLB 1832-1890; DLB 32, 55

MacBeth, George (Mann) 1932-1992**CLC 2, 5,
9**
See also CA 25-28R; 136; DLB 40; MTCW;
SATA 4; SATA-Obit 70

MacCaig, Norman (Alexander) 1910-**CLC 36;
DAB; DAM POET**
See also CA 9-12R; CANR 3, 34; DLB 27

MacCarthy, (Sir Charles Otto) Desmond 1877-
1952 .... **TCLC 36**

MacDiarmid, HughCLC 2, 4, 11, 19, 63; PC 9
See also Grieve, C(hristopher) M(urray)
See also CDBLB 1945-1960; DLB 20

MacDonald, Anson
See Heinlein, Robert A(nson)

Macdonald, Cynthia 1928- .... **CLC 13, 19**
See also CA 49-52; CANR 4, 44; DLB 105

MacDonald, George 1824-1905 .... **TCLC 9**
See also CA 106; 137; DLB 18, 163, 178;
MAICYA; SATA 33

Macdonald, John
See Millar, Kenneth

MacDonald, John D(ann) 1916-1986 **CLC 3,
27, 44; DAM NOV, POP**
See also CA 1-4R; 121; CANR 1, 19; DLB 8;
DLBY 86; MTCW

Macdonald, John Ross
See Millar, Kenneth

Macdonald, Ross .... **CLC 1, 2, 3, 14, 34, 41**
See also Millar, Kenneth
See also DLBD 6

MacDougal, John
See Blish, James (Benjamin)

MacEwen, Gwendolyn (Margaret) 1941-1987
CLC 13, 55
See also CA 9-12R; 124; CANR 7, 22; DLB
53; SATA 50; SATA-Obit 55

Macha, Karel Hynek 1810-1846 .... **NCLC 46**

Machado (y Ruiz), Antonio 1875-1939**T C L C
3**
See also CA 104; DLB 108

Machado de Assis, Joaquim Maria 1839-1908
TCLC 10; BLC; SSC 24
See also CA 107; 153

Machen, Arthur .... **TCLC 4; SSC 20**
See also Jones, Arthur Llewellyn
See also DLB 36, 156, 178

Machiavelli, Niccolo 1469-1527**LC 8, 36; DA;
DAB; DAC; DAM MST; WLCS**

MacInnes, Colin 1914-1976 .... **CLC 4, 23**
See also CA 69-72; 65-68; CANR 21; DLB 14;
MTCW

MacInnes, Helen (Clark) 1907-1985 **CLC 27,**

39; DAM POP
See also CA 1-4R; 117; CANR 1, 28, 58; DLB
87; MTCW; SATA 22; SATA-Obit 44

Mackay, Mary 1855-1924 ....
See Corelli, Marie
See also CA 118

Mackenzie, Compton (Edward Montague)
1883-1972 .... **CLC 18**
See also CA 21-22; 37-40R; CAP 2; DLB 34,
100

Mackenzie, Henry 1745-1831 .... **NCLC 41**
See also DLB 39

Mackintosh, Elizabeth 1896(?)-1952 ....
See Tey, Josephine
See also CA 110

MacLaren, James
See Grieve, C(hristopher) M(urray)

Mac Laverty, Bernard
1942- .... **CLC 31**
See also CA 116; 118; CANR 43; INT 118

MacLean, Alistair (Stuart) 1922-1987**CLC 3,
13, 50, 63; DAM POP**
See also CA 57-60; 121; CANR 28; MTCW;
SATA 23; SATA-Obit 50

Maclean, Norman (Fitzroy) 1902-1990 **C L C
78; DAM POP; SSC 13**
See also CA 102; 132; CANR 49

MacLeish, Archibald
1892-1982 ..... **CLC 3, 8, 14, 68; DAM POET**
See also CA 9-12R; 106; CANR 33; DLB 4, 7,
45; DLBY 82; MTCW

MacLennan, (John) Hugh 1907-1990 **CLC 2,
14, 92; DAC; DAM MST**
See also CA 5-8R; 142; CANR 33; DLB 68;
MTCW

MacLeod, Alistair 1936-**CLC 56; DAC; DAM
MST**
See also CA 123; DLB 60

MacNeice, (Frederick) Louis 1907-1963**C L C
1, 4, 10, 53; DAB; DAM POET**
See also CA 85-88; DLB 10, 20; MTCW

MacNeill, Dand
See Fraser, George MacDonald

Macpherson, James 1736-1796 .... **LC 29**
See also DLB 109

Macpherson, (Jean) Jay 1931- .... **CLC 14**
See also CA 5-8R; DLB 53

MacShane, Frank 1927- .... **CLC 39**
See also CA 9-12R; CANR 3, 33; DLB 111

Macumber, Mari
See Sandoz, Mari(e Susette)

Madach, Imre 1823-1864 .... **NCLC 19**

Madden, (Jerry) David 1933- .... **CLC 5, 15**
See also CA 1-4R; CAAS 3; CANR 4, 45; DLB
6; MTCW

Maddern, Al(an)
See Ellison, Harlan (Jay)

Madhubuti, Haki R. 1942- CLC 6, 73; BLC;
DAM MULT, POET; PC 5
See also Lee, Don L.
See also BW 2; CA 73-76; CANR 24, 51; DLB
5, 41; DLBD 8

Maepenn, Hugh
See Kuttner, Henry

Maepenn, K. H.
See Kuttner, Henry

Maeterlinck, Maurice 1862-1949 ... TCLC 3;
DAM DRAM
See also CA 104; 136; SATA 66

Maginn, William 1794-1842 .... NCLC 8
See also DLB 110, 159

Mahapatra, Jayanta 1928- .... CLC 33; DAM
MULT
See also CA 73-76; CAAS 9; CANR 15, 33

Mahfouz, Naguib (Abdel Aziz Al-Sabilgi)
1911(?)- ....
See Mahfuz, Najib
See also BEST 89:2; CA 128; CANR 55; DAM
NOV; MTCW

Mahfuz, Najib .... CLC 52, 55
See also Mahfouz, Naguib (Abdel Aziz Al-
Sabilgi)
See also DLBY 88

Mahon, Derek 1941- .... CLC 27
See also CA 113; 128; DLB 40

Mailer, Norman 1923-CLC 1, 2, 3, 4, 5, 8, 11,
14, 28, 39, 74; DA; DAB; DAC; DAM MST,
NOV, POP
See also AITN 2; CA 9-12R; CABS 1; CANR
28; CDALB 1968-1988; DLB 2, 16, 28;
DLBD 3; DLBY 80, 83; MTCW

Maillet, Antonine 1929- .... CLC 54; DAC
See also CA 115; 120; CANR 46; DLB 60; INT
120

Mais, Roger 1905-1955 .... TCLC 8
See also BW 1; CA 105; 124; DLB 125; MTCW

Maistre, Joseph de 1753-1821 .... NCLC 37

Maitland, Frederic 1850-1906 .... TCLC 65

Maitland, Sara (Louise) 1950- .... CLC 49
See also CA 69-72; CANR 13, 59

Major, Clarence 1936- CLC 3, 19, 48; BLC;
DAM MULT
See also BW 2; CA 21-24R; CAAS 6; CANR
13, 25, 53; DLB 33

Major, Kevin (Gerald) 1949-.. CLC 26; DAC
See also AAYA 16; CA 97-100; CANR 21, 38;
CLR 11; DLB 60; INT CANR-21; JRDA;
MAICYA; SATA 32, 82

Maki, James
See Ozu, Yasujiro

Malabaila, Damiano
See Levi, Primo

Malamud, Bernard 1914-1986CLC 1, 2, 3, 5,
8, 9, 11, 18, 27, 44, 78, 85; DA; DAB; DAC;
DAM MST, NOV, POP; SSC 15; WLC

See also AAYA 16; CA 5-8R; 118; CABS 1;
CANR 28; CDALB 1941-1968; DLB 2, 28,
152; DLBY 80, 86; MTCW

Malaparte, Curzio 1898-1957 .... TCLC 52

Malcolm, Dan
See Silverberg, Robert

Malcolm X .... CLC 82; BLC; WLCS
See also Little, Malcolm

Malherbe, Francois de 1555-1628 .... LC 5

Mallarme, Stephane 1842-1898 NCLC 4, 41;
DAM POET; PC 4

Mallet-Joris, Francoise 1930- .... CLC 11
See also CA 65-68; CANR 17; DLB 83

Malley, Ern
See McAuley, James Phillip

Mallowan, Agatha Christie
See Christie, Agatha (Mary Clarissa)

Maloff, Saul 1922- .... CLC 5
See also CA 33-36R

Malone, Louis
See MacNeice, (Frederick) Louis

Malone, Michael (Christopher) 1942-CLC 43
See also CA 77-80; CANR 14, 32, 57

Malory, (Sir) Thomas 1410(?)-1471(?)LC 11;
DA; DAB; DAC; DAM MST; WLCS
See also CDBLB Before 1660; DLB 146; SATA
59; SATA-Brief 33

Malouf, (George Joseph) David 1934-CLC 28,
86
See also CA 124; CANR 50

Malraux, (Georges-)Andre 1901-1976CLC 1,
4, 9, 13, 15, 57; DAM NOV
See also CA 21-22; 69-72; CANR 34, 58; CAP
2; DLB 72; MTCW

Malzberg, Barry N(athaniel) 1939- ... CLC 7
See also CA 61-64; CAAS 4; CANR 16; DLB 8

Mamet, David (Alan) 1947-CLC 9, 15, 34, 46,
91; DAM DRAM; DC 4
See also AAYA 3; CA 81-84; CABS 3; CANR
15, 41; DLB 7; MTCW

Mamoulian, Rouben (Zachary) 1897-1987
CLC 16
See also CA 25-28R; 124

Mandelstam, Osip (Emilievich) 1891(?)-1938(?)
TCLC 2, 6; PC 14
See also CA 104; 150

Mander, (Mary) Jane 1877-1949 ... TCLC 31

Mandeville, John fl. 1350- .... CMLC 19
See also DLB 146

Mandiargues, Andre Pieyre de
.... CLC 41
See also Pieyre de Mandiargues, Andre
See also DLB 83

Mandrake, Ethel Belle
See Thurman, Wallace (Henry)

Mangan, James Clarence 1803-1849NCLC 27

Maniere, J.-E.
See Giraudoux, (Hippolyte) Jean

Manley, (Mary) Delariviere 1672(?)-1724L C
1
See also DLB 39, 80

Mann, Abel
See Creasey, John

Mann, Emily 1952- .... DC 7
See also CA 130; CANR 55

Mann, (Luiz) Heinrich 1871-1950 ... TCLC 9
See also CA 106; DLB 66

Mann, (Paul) Thomas 1875-1955 TCLC 2, 8,
14, 21, 35, 44, 60; DA; DAB; DAC; DAM
MST, NOV; SSC 5; WLC
See also CA 104; 128; DLB 66; MTCW

Mannheim, Karl 1893-1947 .... TCLC 65

Manning, David
See Faust, Frederick (Schiller)

Manning, Frederic 1887(?)-1935 ... TCLC 25
See also CA 124

Manning, Olivia 1915-1980 .... CLC 5, 19
See also CA 5-8R; 101; CANR 29; MTCW

Mano, D. Keith 1942- .... CLC 2, 10
See also CA 25-28R; CAAS 6; CANR 26, 57;
DLB 6

Mansfield, KatherineTCLC 2, 8, 39; DAB; SSC
9, 23; WLC
See also Beauchamp, Kathleen Mansfield
See also DLB 162

Manso, Peter 1940- .... CLC 39
See also CA 29-32R; CANR 44

Mantecon, Juan Jimenez
See Jimenez (Mantecon), Juan Ramon

Manton, Peter
See Creasey, John

Man Without a Spleen, A
See Chekhov, Anton (Pavlovich)

Manzoni, Alessandro 1785-1873 .... NCLC 29

Mapu, Abraham (ben Jekutiel) 1808-1867
NCLC 18

Mara, Sally
See Queneau, Raymond

Marat, Jean Paul 1743-1793 .... LC 10

Marcel, Gabriel Honore 1889-1973 . CLC 15
See also CA 102; 45-48; MTCW

Marchbanks, Samuel
See Davies, (William) Robertson

Marchi, Giacomo
See Bassani, Giorgio

Margulies, Donald .... CLC 76

Marie de France c. 12th cent. - .... CMLC 8

Mathews, John Joseph 1894-1979 .. **CLC 84; DAM MULT**
See also CA 19-20; 142; CANR 45; CAP 2; DLB 175; NNAL

Mathias, Roland (Glyn) 1915- .... **CLC 45**
See also CA 97-100; CANR 19, 41; DLB 27

Matsuo Basho 1644-1694 .... **PC 3**
See also DAM POET

Mattheson, Rodney
See Creasey, John

Matthews, Greg 1949- .... **CLC 45**
See also CA 135

Matthews, William 1942- .... **CLC 40**
See also CA 29-32R; CAAS 18; CANR 12, 57; DLB 5

Matthias, John (Edward) 1941- .... **CLC 9**
See also CA 33-36R; CANR 56

Matthiessen, Peter 1927-**CLC 5, 7, 11, 32, 64; DAM NOV**
See also AAYA 6; BEST 90:4; CA 9-12R; CANR 21, 50; DLB 6, 173; MTCW; SATA 27

Maturin, Charles Robert 1780(?)-1824**NCLC 6**
See also DLB 178

Matute (Ausejo), Ana Maria 1925- .. **CLC 11**
See also CA 89-92; MTCW

Maugham, W. S.
See Maugham, W(illiam) Somerset

Maugham, W(illiam) Somerset 1874-1965
CLC 1, 11, 15, 67, 93; DA; DAB; DAC; DAM DRAM, MST, NOV; SSC 8; WLC
See also CA 5-8R; 25-28R; CANR 40; CDBLB 1914-1945; DLB 10, 36, 77, 100, 162; MTCW; SATA 54

Maugham, William Somerset
See Maugham, W(illiam) Somerset

Maupassant, (Henri Rene Albert) Guy de 1850-1893**NCLC 1, 42; DA; DAB; DAC; DAM MST; SSC 1; WLC**
See also DLB 123

Maupin, Armistead 1944-**CLC 95; DAM POP**
See also CA 125; 130; CANR 58; INT 130

Maurhut, Richard
See Traven, B.

Mauriac, Claude 1914-1996 .... **CLC 9**
See also CA 89-92; 152; DLB 83

Mauriac, Francois (Charles) 1885-1970**C L C 4, 9, 56; SSC 24**
See also CA 25-28; CAP 2; DLB 65; MTCW

Mavor, Osborne Henry 1888-1951 ....
See Bridie, James
See also CA 104

Maxwell, William (Keepers, Jr.) 1908-**CLC 19**
See also CA 93-96; CANR 54; DLBY 80; INT 93-96

May, Elaine 1932- .... **CLC 16**

See also CA 124; 142; DLB 44

Mayakovski, Vladimir (Vladimirovich) 1893-1930 .... **TCLC 4, 18**
See also CA 104; 158

Mayhew, Henry 1812-1887 .... **NCLC 31**
See also DLB 18, 55

Mayle, Peter 1939(?)- .... **CLC 89**
See also CA 139

Maynard, Joyce 1953- .... **CLC 23**
See also CA 111; 129

Mayne, William (James Carter) 1928-**CLC 12**
See also AAYA 20; CA 9-12R; CANR 37; CLR 25; JRDA; MAICYA; SAAS 11; SATA 6, 68

Mayo, Jim
See L'Amour, Louis (Dearborn)

Maysles, Albert 1926- .... **CLC 16**
See also CA 29-32R

Maysles, David 1932- .... **CLC 16**

Mazer, Norma Fox 1931- .... **CLC 26**
See also AAYA 5; CA 69-72; CANR 12, 32; CLR 23; JRDA; MAICYA; SAAS 1; SATA 24, 67

Mazzini, Guiseppe 1805-1872 .... **NCLC 34**

McAuley, James Phillip 1917-1976 .. **CLC 45**
See also CA 97-100

McBain, Ed
See Hunter, Evan

McBrien, William Augustine 1930-.. **CLC 44**
See also CA 107

McCaffrey, Anne (Inez) 1926-**CLC 17; DAM NOV, POP**
See also AAYA 6; AITN 2; BEST 89:2; CA 25-28R; CANR 15, 35, 55; DLB 8; JRDA; MAICYA; MTCW; SAAS 11; SATA 8, 70

McCall, Nathan 1955(?)- .... **CLC 86**
See also CA 146

McCann, Arthur
See Campbell, John W(ood, Jr.)

McCann, Edson
See Pohl, Frederik

McCarthy, Charles, Jr. 1933- ....
See McCarthy, Cormac
See also CANR 42; DAM POP

McCarthy, Cormac 1933- **CLC 4, 57, 59, 101**
See also McCarthy, Charles, Jr.
See also DLB 6, 143

McCarthy, Mary (Therese) 1912-1989**CLC 1, 3, 5, 14, 24, 39, 59; SSC 24**
See also CA 5-8R; 129; CANR 16, 50; DLB 2; DLBY 81; INT CANR-16; MTCW

McCartney, (James) Paul 1942- **CLC 12, 35**
See also CA 146

McCauley, Stephen (D.) 1955- .... **CLC 50**
See also CA 141

McClure, Michael (Thomas) 1932-**CLC 6, 10**
See also CA 21-24R; CANR 17, 46; DLB 16

McCorkle, Jill (Collins) 1958- .... **CLC 51**
See also CA 121; DLBY 87

McCourt, James 1941- .... **CLC 5**
See also CA 57-60

McCoy, Horace (Stanley) 1897-1955**TCLC 28**
See also CA 108; 155; DLB 9

McCrae, John 1872-1918 .... **TCLC 12**
See also CA 109; DLB 92

McCreigh, James
See Pohl, Frederik

McCullers, (Lula) Carson (Smith) 1917-1967
CLC 1, 4, 10, 12, 48, 100; DA; DAB; DAC; DAM MST, NOV; SSC 9, 24; WLC
See also AAYA 21; CA 5-8R; 25-28R; CABS 1, 3; CANR 18; CDALB 1941-1968; DLB 2, 7, 173; MTCW; SATA 27

McCulloch, John Tyler
See Burroughs, Edgar Rice

McCullough, Colleen 1938(?)-**CLC 27; DAM NOV, POP**
See also CA 81-84; CANR 17, 46; MTCW

McDermott, Alice 1953- .... **CLC 90**
See also CA 109; CANR 40

McElroy, Joseph 1930- .... **CLC 5, 47**
See also CA 17-20R

McEwan, Ian (Russell) 1948- .... **CLC 13, 66; DAM NOV**
See also BEST 90:4; CA 61-64; CANR 14, 41; DLB 14; MTCW

McFadden, David 1940- .... **CLC 48**
See also CA 104; DLB 60; INT 104

McFarland, Dennis 1950- .... **CLC 65**

McGahern, John 1934-**CLC 5, 9, 48; SSC 17**
See also CA 17-20R; CANR 29; DLB 14; MTCW

McGinley, Patrick (Anthony) 1937- . **CLC 41**
See also CA 120; 127; CANR 56; INT 127

McGinley, Phyllis 1905-1978 .... **CLC 14**
See also CA 9-12R; 77-80; CANR 19; DLB 11, 48; SATA 2, 44; SATA-Obit 24

McGinniss, Joe 1942- .... **CLC 32**
See also AITN 2; BEST 89:2; CA 25-28R; CANR 26; INT CANR-26

McGivern, Maureen Daly
See Daly, Maureen

McGrath, Patrick 1950- .... **CLC 55**
See also CA 136

McGrath, Thomas (Matthew) 1916-1990**CLC 28, 59; DAM POET**
See also CA 9-12R; 132; CANR 6, 33; MTCW; SATA 41; SATA-Obit 66

McGuane, Thomas (Francis III) 1939-**CLC 3, 7, 18, 45**
See also AITN 2; CA 49-52; CANR 5, 24, 49;

Michelangelo 1475-1564 .... **LC 12**

Michelet, Jules 1798-1874 .... **NCLC 31**

Michener, James A(lbert) 1907(?)- **CLC 1, 5, 11, 29, 60; DAM NOV, POP**
See also AITN 1; BEST 90:1; CA 5-8R; CANR 21, 45; DLB 6; MTCW

Mickiewicz, Adam 1798-1855 .... **NCLC 3**

Middleton, Christopher 1926- .... **CLC 13**
See also CA 13-16R; CANR 29, 54; DLB 40

Middleton, Richard (Barham) 1882-1911
TCLC 56
See also DLB 156

Middleton, Stanley 1919- .... **CLC 7, 38**
See also CA 25-28R; CAAS 23; CANR 21, 46; DLB 14

Middleton, Thomas 1580-1627 **LC 33; DAM DRAM, MST; DC 5**
See also DLB 58

Migueis, Jose Rodrigues 1901- .... **CLC 10**

Mikszath, Kalman 1847-1910 .... **TCLC 31**

Miles, Jack .... **CLC 100**

Miles, Josephine (Louise) 1911-1985**CLC 1, 2, 14, 34, 39; DAM POET**
See also CA 1-4R; 116; CANR 2, 55; DLB 48

Militant
See Sandburg, Carl (August)

Mill, John Stuart 1806-1873 .... **NCLC 11, 58**
See also CDBLB 1832-1890; DLB 55

Millar, Kenneth 1915-1983 .... **CLC 14; DAM POP**
See also Macdonald, Ross
See also CA 9-12R; 110; CANR 16; DLB 2; DLBD 6; DLBY 83; MTCW

Millay, E. Vincent
See Millay, Edna St. Vincent

Millay, Edna St. Vincent 1892-1950 **TCLC 4, 49; DA; DAB; DAC; DAM MST, POET; PC 6; WLCS**
See also CA 104; 130; CDALB 1917-1929; DLB 45; MTCW

Miller, Arthur 1915-**CLC 1, 2, 6, 10, 15, 26, 47, 78; DA; DAB; DAC; DAM DRAM, MST; DC 1; WLC**
See also AAYA 15; AITN 1; CA 1-4R; CABS 3; CANR 2, 30, 54; CDALB 1941-1968; DLB 7; MTCW

Miller, Henry (Valentine) 1891-1980**CLC 1, 2, 4, 9, 14, 43, 84; DA; DAB; DAC; DAM MST, NOV; WLC**
See also CA 9-12R; 97-100; CANR 33; CDALB 1929-1941; DLB 4, 9; DLBY 80; MTCW

Miller, Jason 1939(?)- .... **CLC 2**
See also AITN 1; CA 73-76; DLB 7

Miller, Sue
1943- .... **CLC 44; DAM POP**
See also BEST 90:3; CA 139; CANR 59; DLB 143

Miller, Walter M(ichael, Jr.) 1923-**CLC 4, 30**
See also CA 85-88; DLB 8

Millett, Kate 1934-............................... **CLC 67**
See also AITN 1; CA 73-76; CANR 32, 53; MTCW

Millhauser, Steven 1943-............. **CLC 21, 54**
See also CA 110; 111; DLB 2; INT 111

Millin, Sarah Gertrude 1889-1968 ... **CLC 49**
See also CA 102; 93-96

Milne, A(lan) A(lexander) 1882-1956**TCLC 6; DAB; DAC; DAM MST**
See also CA 104; 133; CLR 1, 26; DLB 10, 77, 100, 160; MAICYA; MTCW; YABC 1

Milner, Ron(ald) 1938- **CLC 56; BLC; DAM MULT**
See also AITN 1; BW 1; CA 73-76; CANR 24; DLB 38; MTCW

Milnes, Richard Monckton 1809-1885**N C L C 61**
See also DLB 32

Milosz, Czeslaw 1911- **CLC 5, 11, 22, 31, 56, 82; DAM MST, POET; PC 8; WLCS**
See also CA 81-84; CANR 23, 51; MTCW

Milton, John 1608-1674 ..... **LC 9; DA; DAB; DAC; DAM MST, POET; PC 19; WLC**
See also CDBLB 1660-1789; DLB 131, 151

Min, Anchee 1957- .... **CLC 86**
See also CA 146

Minehaha, Cornelius
See Wedekind, (Benjamin) Frank(lin)

Miner, Valerie 1947- .... **CLC 40**
See also CA 97-100; CANR 59

Minimo, Duca
See D'Annunzio, Gabriele

Minot, Susan 1956- .... **CLC 44**
See also CA 134

Minus, Ed 1938- .... **CLC 39**

Miranda, Javier
See Bioy Casares, Adolfo

Mirbeau, Octave 1848-1917 .... **TCLC 55**
See also DLB 123

Miro (Ferrer), Gabriel (Francisco Victor) 1879-1930 .... **TCLC 5**
See also CA 104

Mishima, Yukio 1925-1970**CLC 2, 4, 6, 9, 27; DC 1; SSC 4**
See also Hiraoka, Kimitake
See also DLB 182

Mistral, Frederic 1830-1914........... **TCLC 51**
See also CA 122

Mistral, Gabriela .... **TCLC 2; HLC**
See also Godoy Alcayaga, Lucila

Mistry, Rohinton 1952- .... **CLC 71; DAC**
See also CA 141

Mitchell, Clyde

See Ellison, Harlan (Jay); Silverberg, Robert

Mitchell, James Leslie 1901-1935 ....
See Gibbon, Lewis Grassic
See also CA 104; DLB 15

Mitchell, Joni 1943- .... **CLC 12**
See also CA 112

Mitchell, Joseph (Quincy) 1908-1996**CLC 98**
See also CA 77-80; 152; DLBY 96

Mitchell, Margaret (Munnerlyn) 1900-1949
TCLC 11; DAM NOV, POP
See also CA 109; 125; CANR 55; DLB 9; MTCW

Mitchell, Peggy
See Mitchell, Margaret (Munnerlyn)

Mitchell, S(ilas) Weir 1829-1914 ... **TCLC 36**

Mitchell, W(illiam) O(rmond) 1914-**CLC 25; DAC; DAM MST**
See also CA 77-80; CANR 15, 43; DLB 88

Mitford, Mary Russell 1787-1855 ... **NCLC 4**
See also DLB 110, 116

Mitford, Nancy 1904-1973 .... **CLC 44**
See also CA 9-12R

Miyamoto, Yuriko 1899-1951 .... **TCLC 37**
See also DLB 180

Mizoguchi, Kenji 1898-1956 .... **TCLC 72**

Mo, Timothy (Peter) 1950(?)- .... **CLC 46**
See also CA 117; MTCW

Modarressi, Taghi (M.) 1931- .... **CLC 44**
See also CA 121; 134; INT 134

Modiano, Patrick (Jean) 1945- .... **CLC 18**
See also CA 85-88; CANR 17, 40; DLB 83

Moerck, Paal
See Roelvaag, O(le) E(dvart)

Mofolo, Thomas (Mokopu) 1875(?)-1948
TCLC 22; BLC; DAM MULT
See also CA 121; 153

Mohr, Nicholasa 1935-**CLC 12; DAM MULT; HLC**
See also AAYA 8; CA 49-52; CANR 1, 32; CLR 22; DLB 145; HW; JRDA; SAAS 8; SATA 8

Mojtabai, A(nn) G(race) 1938- **CLC 5, 9, 15, 29**
See also CA 85-88

Moliere 1622-1673 . **LC 28; DA; DAB; DAC; DAM DRAM, MST; WLC**

Molin, Charles
See Mayne, William (James Carter)

Molnar, Ferenc 1878-1952 .. **TCLC 20; DAM DRAM**
See also CA 109; 153

Momaday, N(avarre) Scott 1934- **CLC 2, 19, 85, 95; DA; DAB; DAC; DAM MST, MULT, NOV, POP; WLCS**
See also AAYA 11; CA 25-28R; CANR 14, 34; DLB 143, 175; INT CANR-14; MTCW;

NNAL; SATA 48; SATA-Brief 30

Monette, Paul 1945-1995 .... **CLC 82**
See also CA 139; 147

Monroe, Harriet 1860-1936............ **TCLC 12**
See also CA 109; DLB 54, 91

Monroe, Lyle
See Heinlein, Robert A(nson)

Montagu, Elizabeth 1917- .... **NCLC 7**
See also CA 9-12R

Montagu, Mary (Pierrepont) Wortley 1689-
1762 .... **LC 9; PC 16**
See also DLB 95, 101

Montagu, W. H.
See Coleridge, Samuel Taylor

Montague, John (Patrick) 1929- **CLC 13, 46**
See also CA 9-12R; CANR 9; DLB 40; MTCW

Montaigne, Michel (Eyquem) de 1533-1592
LC 8; DA; DAB; DAC; DAM MST; WLC

Montale, Eugenio 1896-1981**CLC 7, 9, 18; PC**
13
See also CA 17-20R; 104; CANR 30; DLB 114;
MTCW

Montesquieu, Charles-Louis de Secondat 1689-
1755 .... **LC 7**

Montgomery, (Robert) Bruce 1921-1978.......
See Crispin, Edmund
See also CA 104

Montgomery, L(ucy) M(aud) 1874-1942
TCLC 51; DAC; DAM MST
See also AAYA 12; CA 108; 137; CLR 8; DLB
92; DLBD 14; JRDA; MAICYA; YABC 1

Montgomery, Marion H., Jr. 1925- .... **CLC 7**
See also AITN 1; CA 1-4R; CANR 3, 48; DLB
6

Montgomery, Max
See Davenport, Guy (Mattison, Jr.)

Montherlant, Henry (Milon) de 1896-1972
CLC 8, 19; DAM DRAM
See also CA 85-88; 37-40R; DLB 72; MTCW

Monty Python
See Chapman, Graham; Cleese, John
(Marwood); Gilliam, Terry (Vance); Idle,
Eric; Jones, Terence Graham Parry; Palin,
Michael (Edward)
See also AAYA 7

Moodie, Susanna (Strickland) 1803-1885
NCLC 14
See also DLB 99

Mooney, Edward 1951- ....
See Mooney, Ted
See also CA 130

Mooney, Ted .... **CLC 25**
See also Mooney, Edward

Moorcock, Michael (John)
1939- .... **CLC 5, 27, 58**
See also CA 45-48; CAAS 5; CANR 2, 17, 38;
DLB 14; MTCW; SATA 93

Moore, Brian 1921- **CLC 1, 3, 5, 7, 8, 19, 32,**
90; DAB; DAC; DAM MST
See also CA 1-4R; CANR 1, 25, 42; MTCW

Moore, Edward
See Muir, Edwin

Moore, George Augustus 1852-1933**TCLC 7;**
SSC 19
See also CA 104; DLB 10, 18, 57, 135

Moore, Lorrie .... **CLC 39, 45, 68**
See also Moore, Marie Lorena

Moore, Marianne (Craig) 1887-1972**CLC 1, 2,**
4, 8, 10, 13, 19, 47; DA; DAB; DAC; DAM
MST, POET; PC 4; WLCS
See also CA 1-4R; 33-36R; CANR 3; CDALB
1929-1941; DLB 45; DLBD 7; MTCW;
SATA 20

Moore, Marie Lorena 1957- ....
See Moore, Lorrie
See also CA 116; CANR 39

Moore, Thomas 1779-1852 .... **NCLC 6**
See also DLB 96, 144

Morand, Paul 1888-1976 .... **CLC 41; SSC 22**
See also CA 69-72; DLB 65

Morante, Elsa 1918-1985 .... **CLC 8, 47**
See also CA 85-88; 117; CANR 35; DLB 177;
MTCW

Moravia, Alberto 1907-1990**CLC 2, 7, 11, 27,**
46; SSC 26
See also Pincherle, Alberto
See also DLB 177

More, Hannah 1745-1833 .... **NCLC 27**
See also DLB 107, 109, 116, 158

More, Henry 1614-1687 .... **LC 9**
See also DLB 126

More, Sir Thomas 1478-1535 .... **LC 10, 32**

Moreas, Jean .... **TCLC 18**
See also Papadiamantopoulos, Johannes

Morgan, Berry 1919-............................. **CLC 6**
See also CA 49-52; DLB 6

Morgan, Claire
See Highsmith, (Mary) Patricia

Morgan, Edwin (George) 1920- .... **CLC 31**
See also CA 5-8R; CANR 3, 43; DLB 27

Morgan, (George) Frederick 1922- .. **CLC 23**
See also CA 17-20R; CANR 21

Morgan, Harriet
See Mencken, H(enry) L(ouis)

Morgan, Jane
See Cooper, James Fenimore

Morgan, Janet 1945- .... **CLC 39**
See also CA 65-68

Morgan, Lady 1776(?)-1859 .... **NCLC 29**
See also DLB 116, 158

Morgan, Robin 1941- .... **CLC 2**
See also CA 69-72; CANR 29; MTCW; SATA 80

Morgan, Scott
See Kuttner, Henry

Morgan, Seth 1949(?)-1990 .... **CLC 65**
See also CA 132

Morgenstern, Christian 1871-1914 . **TCLC 8**
See also CA 105

Morgenstern, S.
See Goldman, William (W.)

Moricz, Zsigmond 1879-1942 .... **TCLC 33**

Morike, Eduard (Friedrich) 1804-1875**NCLC**
10
See also DLB 133

Mori Ogai .... **TCLC 14**
See also Mori Rintaro

Mori Rintaro 1862-1922 ....
See Mori Ogai
See also CA 110

Moritz, Karl Philipp 1756-1793 .... **LC 2**
See also DLB 94

Morland, Peter Henry
See Faust, Frederick (Schiller)

Morren, Theophil
See Hofmannsthal, Hugo von

Morris, Bill 1952- .... **CLC 76**

Morris, Julian
See West, Morris L(anglo)

Morris, Steveland Judkins 1950(?)- ....
See Wonder, Stevie
See also CA 111

Morris, William 1834-1896 .... **NCLC 4**
See also CDBLB 1832-1890; DLB 18, 35, 57,
156, 178

Morris, Wright 1910- ...... **CLC 1, 3, 7, 18, 37**
See also CA 9-12R; CANR 21; DLB 2; DLBY
81; MTCW

Morrison, Arthur 1863-1945 .... **TCLC 72**
See also CA 120; 157; DLB 70, 135

Morrison, Chloe Anthony Wofford
See Morrison, Toni

Morrison, James Douglas 1943-1971 ....
See Morrison, Jim
See also CA 73-76; CANR 40

Morrison, Jim .... **CLC 17**
See also Morrison, James Douglas

Morrison, Toni 1931-**CLC 4, 10, 22, 55, 81, 87;**
BLC; DA; DAB; DAC; DAM MST, MULT,
NOV, POP
See also AAYA 1, 22; BW 2; CA 29-32R;
CANR 27, 42; CDALB 1968-1988; DLB 6,
33, 143; DLBY 81; MTCW; SATA 57

Morrison, Van 1945- .... **CLC 21**
See also CA 116

Morrissy, Mary 1958- .... **CLC 99**

Mortimer, John (Clifford) 1923-**CLC 28, 43;**

See Koontz, Dean R(ay)

North, Captain George
See Stevenson, Robert Louis (Balfour)

North, Milou
See Erdrich, Louise

Northrup, B. A.
See Hubbard, L(afayette) Ron(ald)

North Staffs
See Hulme, T(homas) E(rnest)

Norton, Alice Mary
See Norton, Andre
See also MAICYA; SATA 1, 43

Norton, Andre 1912- .... CLC 12
See also Norton, Alice Mary
See also AAYA 14; CA 1-4R; CANR 2, 31; DLB 8, 52; JRDA; MTCW; SATA 91

Norton, Caroline 1808-1877 .... NCLC 47
See also DLB 21, 159

Norway, Nevil Shute 1899-1960 ....
See Shute, Nevil
See also CA 102; 93-96

Norwid, Cyprian Kamil 1821-1883 NCLC 17

Nosille, Nabrah
See Ellison, Harlan (Jay)

Nossack, Hans Erich 1901-1978 .... CLC 6
See also CA 93-96; 85-88; DLB 69

Nostradamus 1503-1566 .... LC 27

Nosu, Chuji
See Ozu, Yasujiro

Notenburg, Eleanora (Genrikhovna) von
See Guro, Elena

Nova, Craig 1945- .... CLC 7, 31
See also CA 45-48; CANR 2, 53

Novak, Joseph
See Kosinski, Jerzy (Nikodem)

Novalis 1772-1801 .... NCLC 13
See also DLB 90

Nowlan, Alden (Albert) 1933-1983 CLC 15; DAC; DAM MST
See also CA 9-12R; CANR 5; DLB 53

Noyes, Alfred 1880-1958 .... TCLC 7
See also CA 104; DLB 20

Nunn, Kem 19(?)- .... CLC 34

Nye, Robert 1939- .. CLC 13, 42; DAM NOV
See also CA 33-36R; CANR 29; DLB 14; MTCW; SATA 6

Nyro, Laura 1947- .... CLC 17

Oates, Joyce Carol
1938-CLC 1, 2, 3, 6, 9, 11, 15, 19, 33, 52; DA; DAB; DAC; DAM MST, NOV, POP; SSC 6; WLC
See also AAYA 15; AITN 1; BEST 89:2; CA 5-8R; CANR 25, 45; CDALB 1968-1988; DLB 2, 5, 130; DLBY 81; INT CANR-25; MTCW

O'Brien, Darcy 1939- .... CLC 11
See also CA 21-24R; CANR 8, 59

O'Brien, E. G.
See Clarke, Arthur C(harles)

O'Brien, Edna 1936- CLC 3, 5, 8, 13, 36, 65; DAM NOV; SSC 10
See also CA 1-4R; CANR 6, 41; CDBLB 1960 to Present; DLB 14; MTCW

O'Brien, Fitz-James 1828-1862 ..... NCLC 21
See also DLB 74

O'Brien, Flann .... CLC 1, 4, 5, 7, 10, 47
See also O Nuallain, Brian

O'Brien, Richard 1942- .... CLC 17
See also CA 124

O'Brien, (William) Tim(othy) 1946- . CLC 7, 19, 40; DAM POP
See also AAYA 16; CA 85-88; CANR 40, 58; DLB 152; DLBD 9; DLBY 80

Obstfelder, Sigbjoern 1866-1900 ... TCLC 23
See also CA 123

O'Casey, Sean 1880-1964CLC 1, 5, 9, 11, 15, 88; DAB; DAC; DAM DRAM, MST; WLCS
See also CA 89-92; CDBLB 1914-1945; DLB 10; MTCW

O'Cathasaigh, Sean
See O'Casey, Sean

Ochs, Phil 1940-1976 .... CLC 17
See also CA 65-68

O'Connor, Edwin (Greene) 1918-1968CLC 14
See also CA 93-96; 25-28R

O'Connor, (Mary) Flannery 1925-1964 C L C 1, 2, 3, 6, 10, 13, 15, 21, 66; DA; DAB; DAC; DAM MST, NOV; SSC 1, 23; WLC
See also AAYA 7; CA 1-4R; CANR 3, 41; CDALB 1941-1968; DLB 2, 152; DLBD 12; DLBY 80; MTCW

O'Connor, Frank .... CLC 23; SSC 5
See also O'Donovan, Michael John
See also DLB 162

O'Dell, Scott 1898-1989 .... CLC 30
See also AAYA 3; CA 61-64; 129; CANR 12, 30; CLR 1, 16; DLB 52; JRDA; MAICYA; SATA 12, 60

Odets, Clifford 1906-1963CLC 2, 28, 98; DAM DRAM; DC 6
See also CA 85-88; DLB 7, 26; MTCW

O'Doherty, Brian 1934- .... CLC 76
See also CA 105

O'Donnell, K. M.
See Malzberg, Barry N(athaniel)

O'Donnell, Lawrence
See Kuttner, Henry

O'Donovan, Michael John 1903-1966 .... CLC 14
See also O'Connor, Frank
See also CA 93-96

Oe, Kenzaburo 1935- CLC 10, 36, 86; DAM NOV; SSC 20
See also CA 97-100; CANR 36, 50; DLB 182; DLBY 94; MTCW

O'Faolain, Julia 1932- .... CLC 6, 19, 47
See also CA 81-84; CAAS 2; CANR 12; DLB 14; MTCW

O'Faolain, Sean 1900-1991 CLC 1, 7, 14, 32, 70; SSC 13
See also CA 61-64; 134; CANR 12; DLB 15, 162; MTCW

O'Flaherty, Liam 1896-1984CLC 5, 34; SSC 6
See also CA 101; 113; CANR 35; DLB 36, 162; DLBY 84; MTCW

Ogilvy, Gavin
See Barrie, J(ames) M(atthew)

O'Grady, Standish (James) 1846-1928T C L C 5
See also CA 104; 157

O'Grady, Timothy 1951- .... CLC 59
See also CA 138

O'Hara, Frank 1926-1966 . CLC 2, 5, 13, 78; DAM POET
See also CA 9-12R; 25-28R; CANR 33; DLB 5, 16; MTCW

O'Hara, John (Henry) 1905-1970CLC 1, 2, 3, 6, 11, 42; DAM NOV; SSC 15
See also CA 5-8R; 25-28R; CANR 31; CDALB 1929-1941; DLB 9, 86; DLBD 2; MTCW

O Hehir, Diana 1922- .... CLC 41
See also CA 93-96

Okigbo, Christopher (Ifenayichukwu) 1932-1967 .... CLC 25, 84; BLC; DAM MULT, POET; PC 7
See also BW 1; CA 77-80; DLB 125; MTCW

Okri, Ben 1959- .... CLC 87
See also BW 2; CA 130; 138; DLB 157; INT 138

Olds, Sharon 1942- .... CLC 32, 39, 85; DAM POET
See also CA 101; CANR 18, 41; DLB 120

Oldstyle, Jonathan
See Irving, Washington

Olesha, Yuri (Karlovich) 1899-1960 .. CLC 8
See also CA 85-88

Oliphant, Laurence 1829(?)-1888 .. NCLC 47
See also DLB 18, 166

Oliphant, Margaret (Oliphant Wilson) 1828-1897 .... NCLC 11, 61; SSC 25
See also DLB 18, 159

Oliver, Mary 1935- .... CLC 19, 34, 98
See also CA 21-24R; CANR 9, 43; DLB 5

Olivier, Laurence (Kerr) 1907-1989 . CLC 20
See also CA 111; 150; 129

Olsen, Tillie 1913-CLC 4, 13; DA; DAB; DAC; DAM MST; SSC 11
See also CA 1-4R; CANR 1, 43; DLB 28; DLBY 80; MTCW

Olson, Charles (John) 1910-1970CLC 1, 2, 5, 6, 9, 11, 29; DAM POET; PC 19
See also CA 13-16; 25-28R; CABS 2; CANR 35; CAP 1; DLB 5, 16; MTCW

Olson, Toby 1937- .... CLC 28
See also CA 65-68; CANR 9, 31

Olyesha, Yuri
See Olesha, Yuri (Karlovich)

Ondaatje, (Philip) Michael 1943-CLC 14, 29, 51, 76; DAB; DAC; DAM MST
See also CA 77-80; CANR 42; DLB 60

Oneal, Elizabeth 1934- ....
See Oneal, Zibby
See also CA 106; CANR 28; MAICYA; SATA 30, 82

Oneal, Zibby .... CLC 30
See also Oneal, Elizabeth
See also AAYA 5; CLR 13; JRDA

O'Neill, Eugene (Gladstone) 1888-1953TCLC 1, 6, 27, 49; DA; DAB; DAC; DAM DRAM, MST; WLC
See also AITN 1; CA 110; 132; CDALB 1929-1941; DLB 7; MTCW

Onetti, Juan Carlos 1909-1994 ... CLC 7, 10; DAM MULT, NOV; SSC 23
See also CA 85-88; 145; CANR 32; DLB 113; HW; MTCW

O Nuallain, Brian 1911-1966 ....
See O'Brien, Flann
See also CA 21-22; 25-28R; CAP 2

Oppen, George 1908-1984 ...... CLC 7, 13, 34
See also CA 13-16R; 113; CANR 8; DLB 5, 165

Oppenheim, E(dward) Phillips 1866-1946 TCLC 45
See also CA 111; DLB 70

Origen c. 185-c. 254 .... CMLC 19

Orlovitz, Gil 1918-1973 .... CLC 22
See also CA 77-80; 45-48; DLB 2, 5

Orris
See Ingelow, Jean

Ortega y Gasset, Jose 1883-1955 .... TCLC 9; DAM MULT; HLC
See also CA 106; 130; HW; MTCW

Ortese, Anna Maria 1914- .... CLC 89
See also DLB 177

Ortiz, Simon J(oseph) 1941- .. CLC 45; DAM MULT, POET; PC 17
See also CA 134; DLB 120, 175; NNAL

Orton, Joe .... CLC 4, 13, 43; DC 3
See also Orton, John Kingsley
See also CDBLB 1960 to Present; DLB 13

Orton, John Kingsley 1933-1967 ....
See Orton, Joe
See also CA 85-88; CANR 35; DAM DRAM; MTCW

Orwell, George . TCLC 2, 6, 15, 31, 51; DAB; WLC

See also Blair, Eric (Arthur)
See also CDBLB 1945-1960; DLB 15, 98

Osborne, David
See Silverberg, Robert

Osborne, George
See Silverberg, Robert

Osborne, John (James) 1929-1994CLC 1, 2, 5, 11, 45; DA; DAB; DAC; DAM DRAM, MST; WLC
See also CA 13-16R; 147; CANR 21, 56; CDBLB 1945-1960; DLB 13; MTCW

Osborne, Lawrence 1958- .... CLC 50

Oshima, Nagisa 1932- .... CLC 20
See also CA 116; 121

Oskison, John Milton 1874-1947 .. TCLC 35; DAM MULT
See also CA 144; DLB 175; NNAL

Ossoli, Sarah Margaret (Fuller marchesa d') 1810-1850 ....
See Fuller, Margaret
See also SATA 25

Ostrovsky, Alexander 1823-1886NCLC 30, 57

Otero, Blas de 1916-1979 .... CLC 11
See also CA 89-92; DLB 134

Otto, Whitney 1955- .... CLC 70
See also CA 140

Ouida .... TCLC 43
See also De La Ramee, (Marie) Louise
See also DLB 18, 156

Ousmane, Sembene 1923- .... CLC 66; BLC
See also BW 1; CA 117; 125; MTCW

Ovid 43B.C.-18(?)CMLC 7; DAM POET; PC 2

Owen, Hugh
See Faust, Frederick (Schiller)

Owen, Wilfred (Edward Salter) 1893-1918 TCLC 5, 27; DA; DAB; DAC; DAM MST, POET; PC 19; WLC
See also CA 104; 141; CDBLB 1914-1945; DLB 20

Owens, Rochelle 1936- .... CLC 8
See also CA 17-20R; CAAS 2; CANR 39

Oz, Amos 1939-CLC 5, 8, 11, 27, 33, 54; DAM NOV
See also CA 53-56; CANR 27, 47; MTCW

Ozick, Cynthia 1928- CLC 3, 7, 28, 62; DAM NOV, POP; SSC 15
See also BEST 90:1; CA 17-20R; CANR 23, 58; DLB 28, 152; DLBY 82; INT CANR-23; MTCW

Ozu, Yasujiro 1903-1963 .... CLC 16
See also CA 112

Pacheco, C.
See Pessoa, Fernando (Antonio Nogueira)

Pa Chin .... CLC 18
See also Li Fei-kan

Pack, Robert 1929- .... CLC 13
See also CA 1-4R; CANR 3, 44; DLB 5

Padgett, Lewis
See Kuttner, Henry

Padilla (Lorenzo), Heberto 1932- ..... CLC 38
See also AITN 1; CA 123; 131; HW

Page, Jimmy 1944- .... CLC 12

Page, Louise 1955- .... CLC 40
See also CA 140

Page, P(atricia) K(athleen) 1916- CLC 7, 18; DAC; DAM MST; PC 12
See also CA 53-56; CANR 4, 22; DLB 68; MTCW

Page, Thomas Nelson 1853-1922 .... SSC 23
See also CA 118; DLB 12, 78; DLBD 13

Paget, Violet 1856-1935 ....
See Lee, Vernon
See also CA 104

Paget-Lowe, Henry
See Lovecraft, H(oward) P(hillips)

Paglia, Camille (Anna) 1947- .... CLC 68
See also CA 140

Paige, Richard
See Koontz, Dean R(ay)

Paine, Thomas 1737-1809 .... NCLC 62
See also CDALB 1640-1865; DLB 31, 43, 73, 158

Pakenham, Antonia
See Fraser, (Lady) Antonia (Pakenham)

Palamas, Kostes 1859-1943 .... TCLC 5
See also CA 105

Palazzeschi, Aldo 1885-1974 .... CLC 11
See also CA 89-92; 53-56; DLB 114

Paley, Grace 1922-CLC 4, 6, 37; DAM POP; SSC 8
See also CA 25-28R; CANR 13, 46; DLB 28; INT CANR-13; MTCW

Palin, Michael (Edward) 1943- .... CLC 21
See also Monty Python
See also CA 107; CANR 35; SATA 67

Palliser, Charles 1947- .... CLC 65
See also CA 136

Palma, Ricardo 1833-1919 .... TCLC 29

Pancake, Breece Dexter 1952-1979 ....
See Pancake, Breece D'J
See also CA 123; 109

Pancake, Breece D'J .... CLC 29
See also Pancake, Breece Dexter
See also DLB 130

Panko, Rudy
See Gogol, Nikolai (Vasilyevich)

Papadiamantis, Alexandros 1851-1911T C L C 29

Papadiamantopoulos, Johannes 1856-1910 ..

See Moreas, Jean
See also CA 117

Papini, Giovanni 1881-1956 .... **TCLC 22**
See also CA 121

Paracelsus 1493-1541 .... **LC 14**
See also DLB 179

Parasol, Peter
See Stevens, Wallace

Pareto, Vilfredo 1848-1923 .... **TCLC 69**

Parfenie, Maria
See Codrescu, Andrei

Parini, Jay (Lee) 1948- .... **CLC 54**
See also CA 97-100; CAAS 16; CANR 32

Park, Jordan
See Kornbluth, C(yril) M.; Pohl, Frederik

Park, Robert E(zra) 1864-1944 ...... **TCLC 73**
See also CA 122

Parker, Bert
See Ellison, Harlan (Jay)

Parker, Dorothy (Rothschild) 1893-1967 **C L C 15, 68; DAM POET; SSC 2**
See also CA 19-20; 25-28R; CAP 2; DLB 11, 45, 86; MTCW

Parker, Robert B(rown) 1932- **CLC 27; DAM NOV, POP**
See also BEST 89:4; CA 49-52; CANR 1, 26, 52; INT CANR-26; MTCW

Parkin, Frank 1940- .... **CLC 43**
See also CA 147

Parkman, Francis, Jr. 1823-1893 .. **NCLC 12**
See also DLB 1, 30

Parks, Gordon (Alexander Buchanan) 1912-
CLC 1, 16; BLC; DAM MULT
See also AITN 2; BW 2; CA 41-44R; CANR 26; DLB 33; SATA 8

Parmenides c. 515B.C.-c. 450B.C. **CMLC 22**
See also DLB 176

Parnell, Thomas 1679-1718 .... **LC 3**
See also DLB 94

Parra, Nicanor 1914- ...... **CLC 2, 102; DAM MULT; HLC**
See also CA 85-88; CANR 32; HW; MTCW

Parrish, Mary Frances
See Fisher, M(ary) F(rances) K(ennedy)

Parson
See Coleridge, Samuel Taylor

Parson Lot
See Kingsley, Charles

Partridge, Anthony
See Oppenheim, E(dward) Phillips

Pascal, Blaise 1623-1662 .... **LC 35**

Pascoli, Giovanni 1855-1912 .... **TCLC 45**

Pasolini, Pier Paolo 1922-1975 **CLC 20, 37; PC 17**
See also CA 93-96; 61-64; DLB 128, 177; MTCW

Pasquini
See Silone, Ignazio

Pastan, Linda (Olenik) 1932- **CLC 27; DAM POET**
See also CA 61-64; CANR 18, 40; DLB 5

Pasternak, Boris (Leonidovich) 1890-1960
CLC 7, 10, 18, 63; DA; DAB; DAC; DAM MST, NOV, POET; PC 6; WLC
See also CA 127; 116; MTCW

Patchen, Kenneth 1911-1972 ... **CLC 1, 2, 18; DAM POET**
See also CA 1-4R; 33-36R; CANR 3, 35; DLB 16, 48; MTCW

Pater, Walter (Horatio) 1839-1894 .. **NCLC 7**
See also CDBLB 1832-1890; DLB 57, 156

Paterson, A(ndrew) B(arton) 1864-1941
TCLC 32
See also CA 155

Paterson, Katherine (Womeldorf) 1932-**C L C 12, 30**
See also AAYA 1; CA 21-24R; CANR 28, 59; CLR 7; DLB 52; JRDA; MAICYA; MTCW; SATA 13, 53, 92

Patmore, Coventry Kersey Dighton 1823-1896
NCLC 9
See also DLB 35, 98

Paton, Alan (Stewart) 1903-1988 **CLC 4, 10, 25, 55; DA; DAB; DAC; DAM MST, NOV; WLC**
See also CA 13-16; 125; CANR 22; CAP 1; MTCW; SATA 11; SATA-Obit 56

Paton Walsh, Gillian 1937- ....
See Walsh, Jill Paton
See also CANR 38; JRDA; MAICYA; SAAS 3; SATA 4, 72

Paulding, James Kirke
1778-1860 .... **NCLC 2**
See also DLB 3, 59, 74

Paulin, Thomas Neilson 1949- ....
See Paulin, Tom
See also CA 123; 128

Paulin, Tom .... **CLC 37**
See also Paulin, Thomas Neilson
See also DLB 40

Paustovsky, Konstantin (Georgievich)
1892-1968 .... **CLC 40**
See also CA 93-96; 25-28R

Pavese, Cesare 1908-1950 ... **TCLC 3; PC 13; SSC 19**
See also CA 104; DLB 128, 177

Pavic, Milorad 1929- .... **CLC 60**
See also CA 136; DLB 181

Payne, Alan
See Jakes, John (William)

Paz, Gil
See Lugones, Leopoldo

Paz, Octavio 1914-**CLC 3, 4, 6, 10, 19, 51, 65; DA; DAB; DAC; DAM MST, MULT, POET; HLC; PC 1; WLC**
See also CA 73-76; CANR 32; DLBY 90; HW; MTCW

p'Bitek, Okot 1931-1982**CLC 96; BLC; DAM MULT**
See also BW 2; CA 124; 107; DLB 125; MTCW

Peacock, Molly 1947- .... **CLC 60**
See also CA 103; CAAS 21; CANR 52; DLB 120

Peacock, Thomas Love 1785-1866 . **NCLC 22**
See also DLB 96, 116

Peake, Mervyn 1911-1968 .... **CLC 7, 54**
See also CA 5-8R; 25-28R; CANR 3; DLB 15, 160; MTCW; SATA 23

Pearce, Philippa .... **CLC 21**
See also Christie, (Ann) Philippa
See also CLR 9; DLB 161; MAICYA; SATA 1, 67

Pearl, Eric
See Elman, Richard

Pearson, T(homas) R(eid) 1956- .... **CLC 39**
See also CA 120; 130; INT 130

Peck, Dale 1967- .... **CLC 81**
See also CA 146

Peck, John 1941- .... **CLC 3**
See also CA 49-52; CANR 3

Peck, Richard (Wayne) 1934- .... **CLC 21**
See also AAYA 1; CA 85-88; CANR 19, 38; CLR 15; INT CANR-19; JRDA; MAICYA; SAAS 2; SATA 18, 55

Peck, Robert Newton 1928- ..... **CLC 17; DA; DAC; DAM MST**
See also AAYA 3; CA 81-84; CANR 31; CLR 45; JRDA; MAICYA; SAAS 1; SATA 21, 62

Peckinpah, (David) Sam(uel) 1925-1984**C L C 20**
See also CA 109; 114

Pedersen, Knut 1859-1952 ....
See Hamsun, Knut
See also CA 104; 119; MTCW

Peeslake, Gaffer
See Durrell, Lawrence (George)

Peguy, Charles Pierre 1873-1914 .. **TCLC 10**
See also CA 107

Pena, Ramon del Valle y
See Valle-Inclan, Ramon (Maria) del

Pendennis, Arthur Esquir
See Thackeray, William Makepeace

Penn, William 1644-1718 .... **LC 25**
See also DLB 24

Pepys, Samuel 1633-1703 **LC 11; DA; DAB; DAC; DAM MST; WLC**
See also CDBLB 1660-1789; DLB 101

Percy, Walker 1916-1990**CLC 2, 3, 6, 8, 14, 18, 47, 65; DAM NOV, POP**

Author Index

See also CA 1-4R; 131; CANR 1, 23; DLB 2; DLBY 80, 90; MTCW

Perec, Georges 1936-1982 .... **CLC 56**
See also CA 141; DLB 83

Pereda (y Sanchez de Porrua), Jose Maria de 1833-1906 .... **TCLC 16**
See also CA 117

Pereda y Porrua, Jose Maria de
See Pereda (y Sanchez de Porrua), Jose Maria de

Peregoy, George Weems
See Mencken, H(enry) L(ouis)

Perelman, S(idney) J(oseph) 1904-1979 **C L C 3, 5, 9, 15, 23, 44, 49; DAM DRAM**
See also AITN 1, 2; CA 73-76; 89-92; CANR 18; DLB 11, 44; MTCW

Peret, Benjamin 1899-1959 .... **TCLC 20**
See also CA 117

Peretz, Isaac Loeb 1851(?)-1915 ... **TCLC 16; SSC 26**
See also CA 109

Peretz, Yitzkhok Leibush
See Peretz, Isaac Loeb

Perez Galdos, Benito 1843-1920 .... **TCLC 27**
See also CA 125; 153; HW

Perrault, Charles 1628-1703 .... **LC 2**
See also MAICYA; SATA 25

Perry, Brighton
See Sherwood, Robert E(mmet)

Perse, St.-John .... **CLC 4, 11, 46**
See also Leger, (Marie-Rene Auguste) Alexis Saint-Leger

Perutz, Leo 1882-1957 .... **TCLC 60**
See also DLB 81

Peseenz, Tulio F.
See Lopez y Fuentes, Gregorio

Pesetsky, Bette 1932- .... **CLC 28**
See also CA 133; DLB 130

Peshkov, Alexei Maximovich 1868-1936 ....
See Gorky, Maxim
See also CA 105; 141; DA; DAC; DAM DRAM, MST, NOV

Pessoa, Fernando (Antonio Nogueira) 1888-1935 .... **TCLC 27; HLC**
See also CA 125

Peterkin, Julia Mood 1880-1961 .... **CLC 31**
See also CA 102; DLB 9

Peters, Joan K(aren) 1945- .... **CLC 39**
See also CA 158

Peters, Robert L(ouis) 1924- .... **CLC 7**
See also CA 13-16R; CAAS 8; DLB 105

Petofi, Sandor 1823-1849 .... **NCLC 21**

Petrakis, Harry Mark 1923- .... **CLC 3**
See also CA 9-12R; CANR 4, 30

Petrarch 1304-1374 **CMLC 20; DAM POET; PC 8**

Petrov, Evgeny .... **TCLC 21**
See also Kataev, Evgeny Petrovich

Petry, Ann (Lane) 1908-1997 ... **CLC 1, 7, 18**
See also BW 1; CA 5-8R; 157; CAAS 6; CANR 4, 46; CLR 12; DLB 76; JRDA; MAICYA; MTCW; SATA 5; SATA-Obit 94

Petursson, Halligrimur 1614-1674 .... **LC 8**

Philips, Katherine 1632-1664 .... **LC 30**
See also DLB 131

Philipson, Morris H. 1926- .... **CLC 53**
See also CA 1-4R; CANR 4

Phillips, Caryl 1958- .. **CLC 96; DAM MULT**
See also BW 2; CA 141; DLB 157

Phillips, David Graham 1867-1911 **TCLC 44**
See also CA 108; DLB 9, 12

Phillips, Jack
See Sandburg, Carl (August)

Phillips, Jayne Anne 1952-**CLC 15, 33; SSC 16**
See also CA 101; CANR 24, 50; DLBY 80; INT CANR-24; MTCW

Phillips, Richard
See Dick, Philip K(indred)

Phillips, Robert (Schaeffer) 1938- .... **CLC 28**
See also CA 17-20R; CAAS 13; CANR 8; DLB 105

Phillips, Ward
See Lovecraft, H(oward) P(hillips)

Piccolo, Lucio 1901-1969 .... **CLC 13**
See also CA 97-100; DLB 114

Pickthall, Marjorie L(owry) C(hristie) 1883-1922 .... **TCLC 21**
See also CA 107; DLB 92

Pico della Mirandola, Giovanni 1463-1494**LC 15**

Piercy, Marge 1936- **CLC 3, 6, 14, 18, 27, 62**
See also CA 21-24R; CAAS 1; CANR 13, 43; DLB 120; MTCW

Piers, Robert
See Anthony, Piers

Pieyre de Mandiargues, Andre 1909-1991
See Mandiargues, Andre Pieyre de
See also CA 103; 136; CANR 22

Pilnyak, Boris .... **TCLC 23**
See also Vogau, Boris Andreyevich

Pincherle, Alberto 1907-1990 ... **CLC 11, 18; DAM NOV**
See Moravia, Alberto
See also CA 25-28R; 132; CANR 33; MTCW

Pinckney, Darryl 1953- .... **CLC 76**
See also BW 2; CA 143

Pindar 518B.C.-446B.C. ..... **CMLC 12; PC 19**
See also DLB 176

Pineda, Cecile 1942- .... **CLC 39**
See also CA 118

Pinero, Arthur Wing 1855-1934 ... **TCLC 32; DAM DRAM**
See also CA 110; 153; DLB 10

Pinero, Miguel (Antonio Gomez) 1946-1988 **CLC 4, 55**
See also CA 61-64; 125; CANR 29; HW

Pinget, Robert 1919- .... **CLC 7, 13, 37**
See also CA 85-88; DLB 83

Pink Floyd
See Barrett, (Roger) Syd; Gilmour, David; Mason, Nick; Waters, Roger; Wright, Rick

Pinkney, Edward 1802-1828 .... **NCLC 31**

Pinkwater, Daniel Manus 1941- .... **CLC 35**
See also Pinkwater, Manus
See also AAYA 1; CA 29-32R; CANR 12, 38; CLR 4; JRDA; MAICYA; SAAS 3; SATA 46, 76

Pinkwater, Manus
See Pinkwater, Daniel Manus
See also SATA 8

Pinsky, Robert 1940-**CLC 9, 19, 38, 94; DAM POET**
See also CA 29-32R; CAAS 4; CANR 58; DLBY 82

Pinta, Harold
See Pinter, Harold

Pinter, Harold 1930-**CLC 1, 3, 6, 9, 11, 15, 27, 58, 73; DA; DAB; DAC; DAM DRAM, MST; WLC**
See also CA 5-8R; CANR 33; CDBLB 1960 to Present; DLB 13; MTCW

Piozzi, Hester Lynch (Thrale) 1741-1821 **NCLC 57**
See also DLB 104, 142

Pirandello, Luigi 1867-1936**TCLC 4, 29; DA; DAB; DAC; DAM DRAM, MST; DC 5; SSC 22; WLC**
See also CA 104; 153

Pirsig, Robert M(aynard) 1928-**CLC 4, 6, 73; DAM POP**
See also CA 53-56; CANR 42; MTCW; SATA 39

Pisarev, Dmitry Ivanovich 1840-1868 **NCLC 25**

Pix, Mary (Griffith) 1666-1709 .... **LC 8**
See also DLB 80

Pixerecourt, Guilbert de 1773-1844**NCLC 39**

Plaatje, Sol(omon) T(shekisho) 1876-1932 **TCLC 73**
See also BW 2; CA 141

Plaidy, Jean
See Hibbert, Eleanor Alice Burford

Planche, James Robinson 1796-1880**NCLC 42**

Plant, Robert 1948- .... **CLC 12**

Plante, David (Robert) 1940- **CLC 7, 23, 38;**
DAM NOV
See also CA 37-40R; CANR 12, 36, 58; DLBY
83; INT CANR-12; MTCW

Plath, Sylvia 1932-1963 **CLC 1, 2, 3, 5, 9, 11,**
14, 17, 50, 51, 62; DA; DAB; DAC; DAM
MST, POET; PC 1; WLC
See also AAYA 13; CA 19-20; CANR 34; CAP
2; CDALB 1941-1968; DLB 5, 6, 152;
MTCW

Plato 428(?)B.C.-348(?)B.C. ... **CMLC 8; DA;**
DAB; DAC; DAM MST; WLCS
See also DLB 176

Platonov, Andrei .... **TCLC 14**
See also Klimentov, Andrei Platonovich

Platt, Kin 1911- .... **CLC 26**
See also AAYA 11; CA 17-20R; CANR 11;
JRDA; SAAS 17; SATA 21, 86

Plautus c. 251B.C.-184B.C. .... **DC 6**

Plick et Plock
See Simenon, Georges (Jacques Christian)

Plimpton, George (Ames) 1927- .... **CLC 36**
See also AITN 1; CA 21-24R; CANR 32;
MTCW; SATA 10

Pliny the Elder c. 23-79 .... **CMLC 23**

Plomer, William Charles Franklin 1903-1973
CLC 4, 8
See also CA 21-22; CANR 34; CAP 2; DLB
20, 162; MTCW; SATA 24

Plowman, Piers
See Kavanagh, Patrick (Joseph)

Plum, J.
See Wodehouse, P(elham) G(renville)

Plumly, Stanley (Ross) 1939- .... **CLC 33**
See also CA 108; 110; DLB 5; INT 110

Plumpe, Friedrich Wilhelm 1888-1931 **TCLC**
53
See also CA 112

Poe, Edgar Allan 1809-1849 **NCLC 1, 16, 55;**
DA; DAB; DAC; DAM MST, POET; PC
1; SSC 1, 22; WLC
See also AAYA 14; CDALB 1640-1865; DLB
3, 59, 73, 74; SATA 23

Poet of Titchfield Street, The
See Pound, Ezra (Weston Loomis)

Pohl, Frederik 1919- .... **CLC 18; SSC 25**
See also CA 61-64; CAAS 1; CANR 11, 37;
DLB 8; INT CANR-11; MTCW; SATA 24

Poirier, Louis 1910- ....
See Gracq, Julien
See also CA 122; 126

Poitier, Sidney 1927- .... **CLC 26**
See also BW 1; CA 117

Polanski, Roman 1933- .... **CLC 16**
See also CA 77-80

Poliakoff, Stephen 1952- .... **CLC 38**
See also CA 106; DLB 13

Police, The
See Copeland, Stewart (Armstrong); Summers,
Andrew James; Sumner, Gordon Matthew

Polidori, John William 1795-1821 . **NCLC 51**
See also DLB 116

Pollitt, Katha 1949- .... **CLC 28**
See also CA 120; 122; MTCW

Pollock, (Mary) Sharon 1936- **CLC 50; DAC;**
DAM DRAM, MST
See also CA 141; DLB 60

Polo, Marco 1254-1324 .... **CMLC 15**

Polonsky, Abraham (Lincoln) 1910- **CLC 92**
See also CA 104; DLB 26; INT 104

Polybius c. 200B.C.-c. 118B.C. ...... **CMLC 17**
See also DLB 176

Pomerance, Bernard 1940- .... **CLC 13; DAM**
DRAM
See also CA 101; CANR 49

Ponge, Francis (Jean Gaston Alfred) 1899-1988
CLC 6, 18; DAM POET
See also CA 85-88; 126; CANR 40

Pontoppidan, Henrik 1857-1943 .... **TCLC 29**

Poole, Josephine .... **CLC 17**
See also Helyar, Jane Penelope Josephine
See also SAAS 2; SATA 5

Popa, Vasko 1922-1991 .... **CLC 19**
See also CA 112; 148; DLB 181

Pope, Alexander 1688-1744 **LC 3; DA; DAB;**
DAC; DAM MST, POET; WLC
See also CDBLB 1660-1789; DLB 95, 101

Porter, Connie (Rose) 1959(?)- .... **CLC 70**
See also BW 2; CA 142; SATA 81

Porter, Gene(va Grace) Stratton 1863(?)-1924
TCLC 21
See also CA 112

Porter, Katherine Anne 1890-1980 **CLC 1, 3, 7,**
10, 13, 15, 27, 101; DA; DAB; DAC; DAM
MST, NOV; SSC 4
See also AITN 2; CA 1-4R; 101; CANR 1; DLB
4, 9, 102; DLBD 12; DLBY 80; MTCW;
SATA 39; SATA-Obit 23

Porter, Peter (Neville Frederick) 1929- **CLC 5,**
13, 33
See also CA 85-88; DLB 40

Porter, William Sydney 1862-1910 ....
See Henry, O.
See also CA 104; 131; CDALB 1865-1917; DA;
DAB; DAC; DAM MST; DLB 12, 78, 79;
MTCW; YABC 2

Portillo (y Pacheco), Jose Lopez
See Lopez Portillo (y Pacheco), Jose

Post, Melville Davisson 1869-1930 **TCLC 39**
See also CA 110

Potok, Chaim 1929- . **CLC 2, 7, 14, 26; DAM**
NOV
See also AAYA 15; AITN 1, 2; CA 17-20R;
CANR 19, 35; DLB 28, 152; INT CANR-
19; MTCW; SATA 33

Potter, (Helen) Beatrix 1866-1943 ....
See Webb, (Martha) Beatrice (Potter)
See also MAICYA

Potter, Dennis (Christopher George) 1935-1994
CLC 58, 86
See also CA 107; 145; CANR 33; MTCW

Pound, Ezra (Weston Loomis) 1885-1972
CLC 1, 2, 3, 4, 5, 7, 10, 13, 18, 34, 48, 50;
DA; DAB; DAC; DAM MST, POET; PC
4; WLC
See also CA 5-8R; 37-40R; CANR 40; CDALB
1917-1929; DLB 4, 45, 63; DLBD 15;
MTCW

Povod, Reinaldo 1959-1994 .... **CLC 44**
See also CA 136; 146

Powell, Adam Clayton, Jr. 1908-1972 **CLC 89;**
BLC; DAM MULT
See also BW 1; CA 102; 33-36R

Powell, Anthony (Dymoke) 1905- **CLC 1, 3, 7,**
9, 10, 31
See also CA 1-4R; CANR 1, 32; CDBLB 1945-
1960; DLB 15; MTCW

Powell, Dawn 1897-1965 .... **CLC 66**
See also CA 5-8R

Powell, Padgett 1952- .... **CLC 34**
See also CA 126

Power, Susan .... **CLC 91**

Powers, J(ames) F(arl) 1917- **CLC 1, 4, 8, 57;**
SSC 4
See also CA 1-4R; CANR 2; DLB 130; MTCW

Powers, John J(ames) 1945- ....
See Powers, John R.
See also CA 69-72

Powers, John R. .... **CLC 66**
See also Powers, John J(ames)

Powers, Richard (S.) 1957- .... **CLC 93**
See also CA 148

Pownall, David 1938- .... **CLC 10**
See also CA 89-92; CAAS 18; CANR 49; DLB
14

Powys, John Cowper 1872-1963 **CLC 7, 9, 15,**
46
See also CA 85-88; DLB 15; MTCW

Powys, T(heodore) F(rancis) 1875-1953
TCLC 9
See also CA 106; DLB 36, 162

Prager, Emily 1952- .... **CLC 56**

Pratt, E(dwin) J(ohn) 1883(?)-1964 **CLC 19;**
DAC; DAM POET
See also CA 141; 93-96; DLB 92

Premchand .... **TCLC 21**
See also Srivastava, Dhanpat Rai

Preussler, Otfried 1923- .... **CLC 17**
See also CA 77-80; SATA 24

Prevert, Jacques (Henri Marie) 1900-1977

Radiguet, Raymond 1903-1923 ...... **TCLC 29**
See also DLB 65

Radnoti, Miklos 1909-1944 .... **TCLC 16**
See also CA 118

Rado, James 1939- .... **CLC 17**
See also CA 105

Radvanyi, Netty 1900-1983 ....
See Seghers, Anna
See also CA 85-88; 110

Rae, Ben
See Griffiths, Trevor

Raeburn, John (Hay) 1941- .... **CLC 34**
See also CA 57-60

Ragni, Gerome 1942-1991 .... **CLC 17**
See also CA 105; 134

Rahv, Philip 1908-1973 .... **CLC 24**
See also Greenberg, Ivan
See also DLB 137

Raine, Craig 1944- .... **CLC 32**
See also CA 108; CANR 29, 51; DLB 40

Raine, Kathleen (Jessie) 1908- ...... **CLC 7, 45**
See also CA 85-88; CANR 46; DLB 20; MTCW

Rainis, Janis 1865-1929 .... **TCLC 29**

Rakosi, Carl .... **CLC 47**
See also Rawley, Callman
See also CAAS 5

Raleigh, Richard
See Lovecraft, H(oward) P(hillips)

Raleigh, Sir Walter 1554(?)-1618 . **LC 31, 39**
See also CDBLB Before 1660; DLB 172

Rallentando, H. P.
See Sayers, Dorothy L(eigh)

Ramal, Walter
See de la Mare, Walter (John)

Ramon, Juan
See Jimenez (Mantecon), Juan Ramon

Ramos, Graciliano 1892-1953 .... **TCLC 32**

Rampersad, Arnold 1941- .... **CLC 44**
See also BW 2; CA 127; 133; DLB 111; INT 133

Rampling, Anne
See Rice, Anne

Ramsay, Allan 1684(?)-1758 .... **LC 29**
See also DLB 95

Ramuz, Charles-Ferdinand 1878-1947 **T C L C 33**

Rand, Ayn 1905-1982 **CLC 3, 30, 44, 79; DA; DAC; DAM MST, NOV, POP; WLC**
See also AAYA 10; CA 13-16R; 105; CANR 27; MTCW

Randall, Dudley (Felker) 1914- **CLC 1; BLC; DAM MULT**
See also BW 1; CA 25-28R; CANR 23; DLB 41

Randall, Robert
See Silverberg, Robert

Ranger, Ken
See Creasey, John

Ransom, John Crowe 1888-1974 **CLC 2, 4, 5, 11, 24; DAM POET**
See also CA 5-8R; 49-52; CANR 6, 34; DLB 45, 63; MTCW

Rao, Raja 1909- ...... **CLC 25, 56; DAM NOV**
See also CA 73-76; CANR 51; MTCW

Raphael, Frederic (Michael) 1931- **CLC 2, 14**
See also CA 1-4R; CANR 1; DLB 14

Ratcliffe, James P.
See Mencken, H(enry) L(ouis)

Rathbone, Julian 1935- .... **CLC 41**
See also CA 101; CANR 34

Rattigan, Terence (Mervyn) 1911-1977 **CLC 7; DAM DRAM**
See also CA 85-88; 73-76; CDBLB 1945-1960; DLB 13; MTCW

Ratushinskaya, Irina 1954- .... **CLC 54**
See also CA 129

Raven, Simon (Arthur Noel) 1927- .. **CLC 14**
See also CA 81-84

Rawley, Callman 1903- ....
See Rakosi, Carl
See also CA 21-24R; CANR 12, 32

Rawlings, Marjorie Kinnan 1896-1953 **T C L C 4**
See also AAYA 20; CA 104; 137; DLB 9, 22, 102; JRDA; MAICYA; YABC 1

Ray, Satyajit 1921-1992 .. **CLC 16, 76; DAM MULT**
See also CA 114; 137

Read, Herbert Edward 1893-1968 ..... **CLC 4**
See also CA 85-88; 25-28R; DLB 20, 149

Read, Piers Paul 1941- .... **CLC 4, 10, 25**
See also CA 21-24R; CANR 38; DLB 14; SATA 21

Reade, Charles 1814-1884 .... **NCLC 2**
See also DLB 21

Reade, Hamish
See Gray, Simon (James Holliday)

Reading, Peter 1946- .... **CLC 47**
See also CA 103; CANR 46; DLB 40

Reaney, James 1926- .. **CLC 13; DAC; DAM MST**
See also CA 41-44R; CAAS 15; CANR 42; DLB 68; SATA 43

Rebreanu, Liviu 1885-1944 .... **TCLC 28**

Rechy, John (Francisco) 1934- **CLC 1, 7, 14, 18; DAM MULT; HLC**
See also CA 5-8R; CAAS 4; CANR 6, 32; DLB 122; DLBY 82; HW; INT CANR-6

Redcam, Tom 1870-1933 .... **TCLC 25**

Reddin, Keith .... **CLC 67**

Redgrove, Peter (William) 1932- .. **CLC 6, 41**
See also CA 1-4R; CANR 3, 39; DLB 40

Redmon, Anne .... **CLC 22**
See also Nightingale, Anne Redmon
See also DLBY 86

Reed, Eliot
See Ambler, Eric

Reed, Ishmael 1938- **CLC 2, 3, 5, 6, 13, 32, 60; BLC; DAM MULT**
See also BW 2; CA 21-24R; CANR 25, 48; DLB 2, 5, 33, 169; DLBD 8; MTCW

Reed, John (Silas) 1887-1920 .... **TCLC 9**
See also CA 106

Reed, Lou ....**CLC 21**
See also Firbank, Louis

Reeve, Clara 1729-1807 .... **NCLC 19**
See also DLB 39

Reich, Wilhelm 1897-1957 .... **TCLC 57**

Reid, Christopher (John) 1949- .... **CLC 33**
See also CA 140; DLB 40

Reid, Desmond
See Moorcock, Michael (John)

Reid Banks, Lynne 1929- ....
See Banks, Lynne Reid
See also CA 1-4R; CANR 6, 22, 38; CLR 24; JRDA; MAICYA; SATA 22, 75

Reilly, William K.
See Creasey, John

Reiner, Max
See Caldwell, (Janet Miriam) Taylor (Holland)

Reis, Ricardo
See Pessoa, Fernando (Antonio Nogueira)

Remarque, Erich Maria 1898-1970 **CLC 21; DA; DAB; DAC; DAM MST, NOV**
See also CA 77-80; 29-32R; DLB 56; MTCW

Remizov, A.
See Remizov, Aleksei (Mikhailovich)

Remizov, A. M.
See Remizov, Aleksei (Mikhailovich)

Remizov, Aleksei (Mikhailovich) 1877-1957 **TCLC 27**
See also CA 125; 133

Renan, Joseph Ernest
1823-1892 .... **NCLC 26**

Renard, Jules 1864-1910 .... **TCLC 17**
See also CA 117

Renault, Mary .... **CLC 3, 11, 17**
See also Challans, Mary
See also DLBY 83

Rendell, Ruth (Barbara)
1930- .... **CLC 28, 48; DAM POP**
See also Vine, Barbara
See also CA 109; CANR 32, 52; DLB 87; INT CANR-32; MTCW

TCLC 8
See also CA 105; CLR 33; DLB 92; SATA 88;
SATA-Brief 29

Roberts, Elizabeth Madox 1886-1941 **T C L C
68**
See also CA 111; DLB 9, 54, 102; SATA 33;
SATA-Brief 27

Roberts, Kate 1891-1985 .... **CLC 15**
See also CA 107; 116

Roberts, Keith (John Kingston) 1935-**CLC 14**
See also CA 25-28R; CANR 46

Roberts, Kenneth (Lewis) 1885-1957**TCLC 23**
See also CA 109; DLB 9

Roberts, Michele (B.) 1949- .... **CLC 48**
See also CA 115; CANR 58

Robertson, Ellis
See Ellison, Harlan (Jay); Silverberg, Robert

Robertson, Thomas William 1829-1871**NCLC
35; DAM DRAM**

Robeson, Kenneth
See Dent, Lester

Robinson, Edwin Arlington 1869-1935**T C L C
5; DA; DAC; DAM MST, POET; PC 1**
See also CA 104; 133; CDALB 1865-1917;
DLB 54; MTCW

Robinson, Henry Crabb 1775-1867**NCLC 15**
See also DLB 107

Robinson, Jill 1936-............................. **CLC 10**
See also CA 102; INT 102

Robinson, Kim Stanley 1952-............ **CLC 34**
See also CA 126

Robinson, Lloyd
See Silverberg, Robert

Robinson, Marilynne 1944- .... **CLC 25**
See also CA 116

Robinson, Smokey .... CLC 21
See also Robinson, William, Jr.

Robinson, William, Jr. 1940- ....
See Robinson, Smokey
See also CA 116

Robison, Mary 1949- .... **CLC 42, 98**
See also CA 113; 116; DLB 130; INT 116

Rod, Edouard 1857-1910 .... **TCLC 52**

Roddenberry, Eugene Wesley 1921-1991 ......
See Roddenberry, Gene
See also CA 110; 135; CANR 37; SATA 45;
SATA-Obit 69

Roddenberry, Gene.............................. CLC 17
See also Roddenberry, Eugene Wesley
See also AAYA 5; SATA-Obit 69

Rodgers, Mary 1931-.......................... **CLC 12**
See also CA 49-52; CANR 8, 55; CLR 20; INT
CANR-8; JRDA; MAICYA; SATA 8

Rodgers, W(illiam) R(obert) 1909-1969**CLC 7**
See also CA 85-88; DLB 20

Rodman, Eric
See Silverberg, Robert

Rodman, Howard 1920(?)-1985 .... **CLC 65**
See also CA 118

Rodman, Maia
See Wojciechowska, Maia (Teresa)

Rodriguez, Claudio 1934- .... **CLC 10**
See also DLB 134

Roelvaag, O(le) E(dvart) 1876-1931**TCLC 17**
See also CA 117; DLB 9

Roethke, Theodore (Huebner) 1908-1963**CLC
1, 3, 8, 11, 19, 46, 101; DAM POET; PC 15**
See also CA 81-84; CABS 2; CDALB 1941-
1968; DLB 5; MTCW

Rogers, Thomas Hunton 1927- .... **CLC 57**
See also CA 89-92; INT 89-92

Rogers, Will(iam Penn Adair) 1879-1935
TCLC 8, 71; DAM MULT
See also CA 105; 144; DLB 11; NNAL

Rogin, Gilbert 1929-.......................... **CLC 18**
See also CA 65-68; CANR 15

Rohan, Koda .... TCLC 22
See also Koda Shigeyuki

Rohmer, Eric .... CLC 16
See also Scherer, Jean-Marie Maurice

Rohmer, Sax .... TCLC 28
See also Ward, Arthur Henry Sarsfield
See also DLB 70

Roiphe, Anne (Richardson) 1935- ..**CLC 3, 9**
See also CA 89-92; CANR 45; DLBY 80; INT
89-92

Rojas, Fernando de 1465-1541 ....**LC 23**

**Rolfe, Frederick (William Serafino Austin
Lewis Mary)** 1860-1913 ....
TCLC 12
See also CA 107; DLB 34, 156

Rolland, Romain 1866-1944 .... **TCLC 23**
See also CA 118; DLB 65

Rolle, Richard c. 1300-c. 1349 ...... **CMLC 21**
See also DLB 146

Rolvaag, O(le) E(dvart)
See Roelvaag, O(le) E(dvart)

Romain Arnaud, Saint
See Aragon, Louis

Romains, Jules 1885-1972 .... **CLC 7**
See also CA 85-88; CANR 34; DLB 65; MTCW

Romero, Jose Ruben 1890-1952 .... **TCLC 14**
See also CA 114; 131; HW

Ronsard, Pierre de 1524-1585 ...**LC 6; PC 11**

Rooke, Leon 1934- .. **CLC 25, 34; DAM POP**
See also CA 25-28R; CANR 23, 53

Roosevelt, Theodore
1858-1919 .... **TCLC 69**
See also CA 115; DLB 47

Roper, William 1498-1578 .... **LC 10**

Roquelaure, A. N.
See Rice, Anne

Rosa, Joao Guimaraes 1908-1967 .... **CLC 23**
See also CA 89-92; DLB 113

Rose, Wendy 1948-**CLC 85; DAM MULT; PC
13**
See also CA 53-56; CANR 5, 51; DLB 175;
NNAL; SATA 12

Rosen, Richard (Dean) 1949- .... **CLC 39**
See also CA 77-80; INT CANR-30

Rosenberg, Isaac 1890-1918 .... **TCLC 12**
See also CA 107; DLB 20

Rosenblatt, Joe .... CLC 15
See also Rosenblatt, Joseph

Rosenblatt, Joseph 1933- ....
See Rosenblatt, Joe
See also CA 89-92; INT 89-92

Rosenfeld, Samuel 1896-1963 ....
See Tzara, Tristan
See also CA 89-92

Rosenstock, Sami
See Tzara, Tristan

Rosenstock, Samuel
See Tzara, Tristan

Rosenthal, M(acha) L(ouis) 1917-1996 . **C L C
28**
See also CA 1-4R; 152; CAAS 6; CANR 4, 51;
DLB 5; SATA 59

Ross, Barnaby
See Dannay, Frederic

Ross, Bernard L.
See Follett, Ken(neth Martin)

Ross, J. H.
See Lawrence, T(homas) E(dward)

Ross, Martin
See Martin, Violet Florence
See also DLB 135

Ross, (James) Sinclair 1908- **CLC 13; DAC;
DAM MST; SSC 24**
See also CA 73-76; DLB 88

Rossetti, Christina (Georgina) 1830-1894
**NCLC 2, 50; DA; DAB; DAC; DAM MST,
POET; PC 7; WLC**
See also DLB 35, 163; MAICYA; SATA 20

Rossetti, Dante Gabriel 1828-1882 .**NCLC 4;
DA; DAB; DAC; DAM MST, POET; WLC**
See also CDBLB 1832-1890; DLB 35

Rossner, Judith (Perelman)
1935- .... **CLC 6, 9, 29**
See also AITN 2; BEST 90:3; CA 17-20R;
CANR 18, 51; DLB 6; INT CANR-18;
MTCW

Rostand, Edmond (Eugene Alexis)
1868-1918**TCLC 6, 37; DA; DAB; DAC; DAM
DRAM, MST**
See also CA 104; 126; MTCW

Roger) de 1900-1944 ....
TCLC 2, 56; DAM NOV; WLC
See also CA 108; 132; CLR 10; DLB 72;
MAICYA; MTCW; SATA 20

St. John, David
See Hunt, E(verette) Howard, (Jr.)

Saint-John Perse
See Leger, (Marie-Rene Auguste) Alexis Saint-Leger

Saintsbury, George (Edward Bateman) 1845-1933 .... **TCLC 31**
See also DLB 57, 149

Sait Faik .... **TCLC 23**
See also Abasiyanik, Sait Faik

Saki .... **TCLC 3; SSC 12**
See also Munro, H(ector) H(ugh)

Sala, George Augustus .... **NCLC 46**

Salama, Hannu 1936- .... **CLC 18**

Salamanca, J(ack) R(ichard) 1922-**CLC 4, 15**
See also CA 25-28R

Sale, J. Kirkpatrick
See Sale, Kirkpatrick

Sale, Kirkpatrick 1937- .... **CLC 68**
See also CA 13-16R; CANR 10

Salinas, Luis Omar 1937- ...... **CLC 90; DAM MULT; HLC**
See also CA 131; DLB 82; HW

Salinas (y Serrano), Pedro 1891(?)-1951
TCLC 17
See also CA 117; DLB 134

Salinger, J(erome) D(avid) 1919-**CLC 1, 3, 8, 12, 55, 56; DA; DAB; DAC; DAM MST, NOV, POP; SSC 2; WLC**
See also AAYA 2; CA 5-8R; CANR 39; CDALB 1941-1968; CLR 18; DLB 2, 102, 173; MAICYA; MTCW; SATA 67

Salisbury, John
See Caute, David

Salter, James 1925- .... **CLC 7, 52, 59**
See also CA 73-76; DLB 130

Saltus, Edgar (Everton)
1855-1921 .... **TCLC 8**
See also CA 105

Saltykov, Mikhail Evgrafovich
1826-1889 .... **NCLC 16**

Samarakis, Antonis 1919- .... **CLC 5**
See also CA 25-28R; CAAS 16; CANR 36

Sanchez, Florencio 1875-1910 .... **TCLC 37**
See also CA 153; HW

Sanchez, Luis Rafael 1936- .... **CLC 23**
See also CA 128; DLB 145; HW

Sanchez, Sonia
1934- .... **CLC 5; BLC; DAM MULT; PC 9**
See also BW 2; CA 33-36R; CANR 24, 49; CLR 18; DLB 41; DLBD 8; MAICYA; MTCW; SATA 22

Sand, George 1804-1876**NCLC 2, 42, 57; DA; DAB; DAC; DAM MST, NOV; WLC**
See also DLB 119

Sandburg, Carl (August) 1878-1967**CLC 1, 4, 10, 15, 35; DA; DAB; DAC; DAM MST, POET; PC 2; WLC**
See also CA 5-8R; 25-28R; CANR 35; CDALB 1865-1917; DLB 17, 54; MAICYA; MTCW; SATA 8

Sandburg, Charles
See Sandburg, Carl (August)

Sandburg, Charles A.
See Sandburg, Carl (August)

Sanders, (James) Ed(ward) 1939- .... **CLC 53**
See also CA 13-16R; CAAS 21; CANR 13, 44; DLB 16

Sanders, Lawrence 1920-**CLC 41; DAM POP**
See also BEST 89:4; CA 81-84; CANR 33; MTCW

Sanders, Noah
See Blount, Roy (Alton), Jr.

Sanders, Winston P.
See Anderson, Poul (William)

Sandoz, Mari(e Susette) 1896-1966 .. **CLC 28**
See also CA 1-4R; 25-28R; CANR 17; DLB 9; MTCW; SATA 5

Saner, Reg(inald Anthony) 1931- .... **CLC 9**
See also CA 65-68

Sannazaro, Jacopo 1456(?)-1530 .... **LC 8**

Sansom, William 1912-1976 **CLC 2, 6; DAM NOV; SSC 21**
See also CA 5-8R; 65-68; CANR 42; DLB 139; MTCW

Santayana, George 1863-1952 .... **TCLC 40**
See also CA 115; DLB 54, 71; DLBD 13

Santiago, Danny .... **CLC 33**
See also James, Daniel (Lewis)
See also DLB 122

Santmyer, Helen Hoover 1895-1986 . **CLC 33**
See also CA 1-4R; 118; CANR 15, 33; DLBY 84; MTCW

Santoka, Taneda 1882-1940 .... **TCLC 72**

Santos, Bienvenido N(uqui) 1911-1996 . **C L C 22; DAM MULT**
See also CA 101; 151; CANR 19, 46

Sapper .... **TCLC 44**
See also McNeile, Herman Cyril

Sapphire 1950- .... **CLC 99**

Sappho fl. 6th cent. B.C.- ...... **CMLC 3; DAM POET; PC 5**
See also DLB 176

Sarduy, Severo 1937-1993 .... **CLC 6, 97**
See also CA 89-92; 142; CANR 58; DLB 113; HW

Sargeson, Frank 1903-1982 .... **CLC 31**
See also CA 25-28R; 106; CANR 38

Sarmiento, Felix Ruben Garcia
See Dario, Ruben

Saroyan, William 1908-1981**CLC 1, 8, 10, 29, 34, 56; DA; DAB; DAC; DAM DRAM, MST, NOV; SSC 21; WLC**
See also CA 5-8R; 103; CANR 30; DLB 7, 9, 86; DLBY 81; MTCW; SATA 23; SATA-Obit 24

Sarraute, Nathalie 1900-**CLC 1, 2, 4, 8, 10, 31, 80**
See also CA 9-12R; CANR 23; DLB 83; MTCW

Sarton, (Eleanor) May 1912-1995**CLC 4, 14, 49, 91; DAM POET**
See also CA 1-4R; 149; CANR 1, 34, 55; DLB 48; DLBY 81; INT CANR-34; MTCW; SATA 36; SATA-Obit 86

Sartre, Jean-Paul 1905-1980**CLC 1, 4, 7, 9, 13, 18, 24, 44, 50, 52; DA; DAB; DAC; DAM DRAM, MST, NOV; DC 3; WLC**
See also CA 9-12R; 97-100; CANR 21; DLB 72; MTCW

Sassoon, Siegfried (Lorraine) 1886-1967**CLC 36; DAB; DAM MST, NOV, POET; PC 12**
See also CA 104; 25-28R; CANR 36; DLB 20; MTCW

Satterfield, Charles
See Pohl, Frederik

Saul, John (W. III) 1942-**CLC 46; DAM NOV, POP**
See also AAYA 10; BEST 90:4; CA 81-84; CANR 16, 40

Saunders, Caleb
See Heinlein, Robert A(nson)

Saura (Atares), Carlos 1932- .... **CLC 20**
See also CA 114; 131; HW

Sauser-Hall, Frederic 1887-1961 ...... **CLC 18**
See also Cendrars, Blaise
See also CA 102; 93-96; CANR 36; MTCW

Saussure, Ferdinand de 1857-1913 **TCLC 49**

Savage, Catharine
See Brosman, Catharine Savage

Savage, Thomas 1915- .... **CLC 40**
See also CA 126; 132; CAAS 15; INT 132

Savan, Glenn 19(?)- .... **CLC 50**

Sayers, Dorothy L(eigh) 1893-1957 **TCLC 2, 15; DAM POP**
See also CA 104; 119; CDBLB 1914-1945; DLB 10, 36, 77, 100; MTCW

Sayers, Valerie 1952- .... **CLC 50**
See also CA 134

Sayles, John (Thomas) 1950- . **CLC 7, 10, 14**
See also CA 57-60; CANR 41; DLB 44

Scammell, Michael 1935- .... **CLC 34**
See also CA 156

Scannell, Vernon
1922- .... **CLC 49**
See also CA 5-8R; CANR 8, 24, 57; DLB 27; SATA 59

36; DLBY 86; INT CANR-20; MTCW

Seger, Bob 1945- .... **CLC 35**

Seghers, Anna .... **CLC 7**
See also Radvanyi, Netty
See also DLB 69

Seidel, Frederick (Lewis) 1936- .... **CLC 18**
See also CA 13-16R; CANR 8; DLBY 84

Seifert, Jaroslav 1901-1986 .. **CLC 34, 44, 93**
See also CA 127; MTCW

Sei Shonagon c. 966-1017(?) .... **CMLC 6**

Selby, Hubert, Jr. 1928-**CLC 1, 2, 4, 8; SSC 20**
See also CA 13-16R; CANR 33; DLB 2

Selzer, Richard 1928- .... **CLC 74**
See also CA 65-68; CANR 14

Sembene, Ousmane
See Ousmane, Sembene

Senancour, Etienne Pivert de 1770-1846
NCLC 16
See also DLB 119

Sender, Ramon (Jose) 1902-1982**CLC 8; DAM MULT; HLC**
See also CA 5-8R; 105; CANR 8; HW; MTCW

Seneca, Lucius Annaeus 4B.C.-65 . **CMLC 6; DAM DRAM; DC 5**

Senghor, Leopold Sedar 1906-**CLC 54; BLC; DAM MULT, POET**
See also BW 2; CA 116; 125; CANR 47; MTCW

Serling, (Edward) Rod(man) 1924-1975**C L C 30**
See also AAYA 14; AITN 1; CA 65-68; 57-60;
DLB 26

Serna, Ramon Gomez de la
See Gomez de la Serna, Ramon

Serpieres
See Guillevic, (Eugene)

Service, Robert
See Service, Robert W(illiam)
See also DAB; DLB 92

Service, Robert W(illiam) 1874(?)-1958**TCLC 15; DA; DAC; DAM MST, POET; WLC**
See also Service, Robert
See also CA 115; 140; SATA 20

Seth, Vikram 1952-**CLC 43, 90; DAM MULT**
See also CA 121; 127; CANR 50; DLB 120;
INT 127

Seton, Cynthia Propper 1926-1982 .. **CLC 27**
See also CA 5-8R; 108; CANR 7

Seton, Ernest (Evan) Thompson 1860-1946
TCLC 31
See also CA 109; DLB 92; DLBD 13; JRDA;
SATA 18

Seton-Thompson, Ernest
See Seton, Ernest (Evan) Thompson

Settle, Mary Lee 1918- .... **CLC 19, 61**
See also CA 89-92; CAAS 1; CANR 44; DLB

6; INT 89-92

Seuphor, Michel
See Arp, Jean

Sevigne, Marie (de Rabutin-Chantal) Marquise de 1626-1696 .... **LC 11**

Sewall, Samuel 1652-1730 .... **LC 38**
See also DLB 24

Sexton, Anne (Harvey) 1928-1974**CLC 2, 4, 6, 8, 10, 15, 53; DA; DAB; DAC; DAM MST, POET; PC 2; WLC**
See also CA 1-4R; 53-56; CABS 2; CANR 3, 36; CDALB 1941-1968; DLB 5, 169;
MTCW; SATA 10

Shaara, Michael (Joseph, Jr.) 1929-1988**CLC 15; DAM POP**
See also AITN 1; CA 102; 125; CANR 52;
DLBY 83

Shackleton, C. C.
See Aldiss, Brian W(ilson)

Shacochis, Bob .... **CLC 39**
See also Shacochis, Robert G.

Shacochis, Robert G. 1951- ....
See Shacochis, Bob
See also CA 119; 124; INT 124

Shaffer, Anthony (Joshua) 1926- .... **CLC 19; DAM DRAM**
See also CA 110; 116; DLB 13

Shaffer, Peter (Levin) 1926-**CLC 5, 14, 18, 37, 60; DAB; DAM DRAM, MST; DC 7**
See also CA 25-28R; CANR 25, 47; CDBLB
1960 to Present; DLB 13; MTCW

Shakey, Bernard
See Young, Neil

Shalamov, Varlam (Tikhonovich) 1907(?)-1982
CLC 18
See also CA 129; 105

Shamlu, Ahmad 1925- .... **CLC 10**

Shammas, Anton 1951- .... **CLC 55**

Shange, Ntozake 1948-**CLC 8, 25, 38, 74; BLC; DAM DRAM, MULT; DC 3**
See also AAYA 9; BW 2; CA 85-88; CABS 3;
CANR 27, 48; DLB 38; MTCW

Shanley, John Patrick 1950- .... **CLC 75**
See also CA 128; 133

Shapcott, Thomas W(illiam) 1935-... **CLC 38**
See also CA 69-72; CANR 49

Shapiro, Jane .... **CLC 76**

Shapiro, Karl (Jay)
1913- .... **CLC 4, 8, 15, 53**
See also CA 1-4R; CAAS 6; CANR 1, 36; DLB
48; MTCW

Sharp, William 1855-1905 .... **TCLC 39**
See also DLB 156

Sharpe, Thomas Ridley 1928- ....
See Sharpe, Tom
See also CA 114; 122; INT 122

Sharpe, Tom .... **CLC 36**
See also Sharpe, Thomas Ridley
See also DLB 14

Shaw, Bernard .... **TCLC 45**
See also Shaw, George Bernard
See also BW 1

Shaw, G. Bernard
See Shaw, George Bernard

Shaw, George Bernard 1856-1950**TCLC 3, 9, 21; DA; DAB; DAC; DAM DRAM, MST; WLC**
See also Shaw, Bernard
See also CA 104; 128; CDBLB 1914-1945;
DLB 10, 57; MTCW

Shaw, Henry Wheeler 1818-1885 .. **NCLC 15**
See also DLB 11

Shaw, Irwin 1913-1984 **CLC 7, 23, 34; DAM DRAM, POP**
See also AITN 1; CA 13-16R; 112; CANR 21;
CDALB 1941-1968; DLB 6, 102; DLBY 84;
MTCW

Shaw, Robert 1927-1978 .... **CLC 5**
See also AITN 1; CA 1-4R; 81-84; CANR 4;
DLB 13, 14

Shaw, T. E.
See Lawrence, T(homas) E(dward)

Shawn, Wallace 1943- .... **CLC 41**
See also CA 112

Shea, Lisa 1953- .... **CLC 86**
See also CA 147

Sheed, Wilfrid (John Joseph) 1930-**CLC 2, 4, 10, 53**
See also CA 65-68; CANR 30; DLB 6; MTCW

Sheldon, Alice Hastings Bradley 1915(?)-1987

See Tiptree, James, Jr.
See also CA 108; 122; CANR 34; INT 108;
MTCW

Sheldon, John
See Bloch, Robert (Albert)

Shelley, Mary Wollstonecraft (Godwin) 1797-1851**NCLC 14, 59; DA; DAB; DAC; DAM MST, NOV; WLC**
See also AAYA 20; CDBLB 1789-1832; DLB
110, 116, 159, 178; SATA 29

Shelley, Percy Bysshe 1792-1822 . **NCLC 18; DA; DAB; DAC; DAM MST, POET; PC 14; WLC**
See also CDBLB 1789-1832; DLB 96, 110, 158

Shepard, Jim 1956- .... **CLC 36**
See also CA 137; CANR 59; SATA 90

Shepard, Lucius 1947- .... **CLC 34**
See also CA 128; 141

Shepard, Sam 1943-**CLC 4, 6, 17, 34, 41, 44; DAM DRAM; DC 5**
See also AAYA 1; CA 69-72; CABS 3; CANR
22; DLB 7; MTCW

Shepherd, Michael
See Ludlum, Robert

Sinclair, Iain 1943- .... **CLC 76**
See also CA 132

Sinclair, Iain MacGregor
See Sinclair, Iain

Sinclair, Irene
See Griffith, D(avid Lewelyn) W(ark)

Sinclair, Mary Amelia St. Clair 1865(?)-1946

See Sinclair, May
See also CA 104

Sinclair, May .... **TCLC 3, 11**
See also Sinclair, Mary Amelia St. Clair
See also DLB 36, 135

Sinclair, Roy
See Griffith, D(avid Lewelyn) W(ark)

Sinclair, Upton (Beall) 1878-1968 **CLC 1, 11, 15, 63; DA; DAB; DAC; DAM MST, NOV; WLC**
See also CA 5-8R; 25-28R; CANR 7; CDALB 1929-1941; DLB 9; INT CANR-7; MTCW; SATA 9

Singer, Isaac
See Singer, Isaac Bashevis

Singer, Isaac Bashevis 1904-1991 **CLC 1, 3, 6, 9, 11, 15, 23, 38, 69; DA; DAB; DAC; DAM MST, NOV; SSC 3; WLC**
See also AITN 1, 2; CA 1-4R; 134; CANR 1, 39; CDALB 1941-1968; CLR 1; DLB 6, 28, 52; DLBY 91; JRDA; MAICYA; MTCW; SATA 3, 27; SATA-Obit 68

Singer, Israel Joshua 1893-1944 .... **TCLC 33**

Singh, Khushwant 1915- .... **CLC 11**
See also CA 9-12R; CAAS 9; CANR 6

Singleton, Ann
See Benedict, Ruth (Fulton)

Sinjohn, John
See Galsworthy, John

Sinyavsky, Andrei (Donatevich) 1925- **CLC 8**
See also CA 85-88

Sirin, V.
See Nabokov, Vladimir (Vladimirovich)

Sissman, L(ouis) E(dward) 1928-1976 **CLC 9, 18**
See also CA 21-24R; 65-68; CANR 13; DLB 5

Sisson, C(harles) H(ubert) 1914- .... **CLC 8**
See also CA 1-4R; CAAS 3; CANR 3, 48; DLB 27

Sitwell, Dame Edith 1887-1964 **CLC 2, 9, 67; DAM POET; PC 3**
See also CA 9-12R; CANR 35; CDBLB 1945-1960; DLB 20; MTCW

Sjoewall, Maj 1935- .... **CLC 7**
See also CA 65-68

Sjowall, Maj
See Sjoewall, Maj

Skelton, Robin 1925- .... **CLC 13**
See also AITN 2; CA 5-8R; CAAS 5; CANR

28; DLB 27, 53

Skolimowski, Jerzy 1938- .... **CLC 20**
See also CA 128

Skram, Amalie (Bertha) 1847-1905 **TCLC 25**

Skvorecky, Josef (Vaclav) 1924- **CLC 15, 39, 69; DAC; DAM NOV**
See also CA 61-64; CAAS 1; CANR 10, 34; MTCW

Slade, Bernard .... **CLC 11, 46**
See also Newbound, Bernard Slade
See also CAAS 9; DLB 53

Slaughter, Carolyn 1946- .... **CLC 56**
See also CA 85-88

Slaughter, Frank G(ill) 1908- .... **CLC 29**
See also AITN 2; CA 5-8R; CANR 5; INT CANR-5

Slavitt, David R(ytman) 1935- ...... **CLC 5, 14**
See also CA 21-24R; CAAS 3; CANR 41; DLB 5, 6

Slesinger, Tess 1905-1945 .... **TCLC 10**
See also CA 107; DLB 102

Slessor, Kenneth 1901-1971 .... **CLC 14**
See also CA 102; 89-92

Slowacki, Juliusz 1809-1849 .... **NCLC 15**

Smart, Christopher 1722-1771 .. **LC 3; DAM POET; PC 13**
See also DLB 109

Smart, Elizabeth 1913-1986 .... **CLC 54**
See also CA 81-84; 118; DLB 88

Smiley, Jane (Graves) 1949- **CLC 53, 76; DAM POP**
See also CA 104; CANR 30, 50; INT CANR-30

Smith, A(rthur) J(ames) M(arshall) 1902-1980 **CLC 15; DAC**
See also CA 1-4R; 102; CANR 4; DLB 88

Smith, Adam 1723-1790 .... **LC 36**
See also DLB 104

Smith, Alexander 1829-1867 .... **NCLC 59**
See also DLB 32, 55

Smith, Anna Deavere 1950- .... **CLC 86**
See also CA 133

Smith, Betty (Wehner) 1896-1972 .... **CLC 19**
See also CA 5-8R; 33-36R; DLBY 82; SATA 6

Smith, Charlotte (Turner) 1749-1806 **NCLC 23**
See also DLB 39, 109

Smith, Clark Ashton 1893-1961 .... **CLC 43**
See also CA 143

Smith, Dave .... **CLC 22, 42**
See also Smith, David (Jeddie)
See also CAAS 7; DLB 5

Smith, David (Jeddie) 1942- ....
See Smith, Dave
See also CA 49-52; CANR 1, 59; DAM POET

Smith, Florence Margaret 1902-1971 ....
See Smith, Stevie
See also CA 17-18; 29-32R; CANR 35; CAP 2; DAM POET; MTCW

Smith, Iain Crichton 1928- .... **CLC 64**
See also CA 21-24R; DLB 40, 139

Smith, John 1580(?)-1631 .... **LC 9**

Smith, Johnston
See Crane, Stephen (Townley)

Smith, Joseph, Jr. 1805-1844 .... **NCLC 53**

Smith, Lee 1944- .... **CLC 25, 73**
See also CA 114; 119; CANR 46; DLB 143; DLBY 83; INT 119

Smith, Martin
See Smith, Martin Cruz

Smith, Martin Cruz 1942- ..... **CLC 25; DAM MULT, POP**
See also BEST 89:4; CA 85-88; CANR 6, 23, 43; INT CANR-23; NNAL

Smith, Mary-Ann Tirone 1944- .... **CLC 39**
See also CA 118; 136

Smith, Patti 1946- .... **CLC 12**
See also CA 93-96

Smith, Pauline (Urmson) 1882-1959 **TCLC 25**

Smith, Rosamond
See Oates, Joyce Carol

Smith, Sheila Kaye
See Kaye-Smith, Sheila

Smith, Stevie .... **CLC 3, 8, 25, 44; PC 12**
See also Smith, Florence Margaret
See also DLB 20

Smith, Wilbur (Addison) 1933- .... **CLC 33**
See also CA 13-16R; CANR 7, 46; MTCW

Smith, William Jay 1918- .... **CLC 6**
See also CA 5-8R; CANR 44; DLB 5; MAICYA; SAAS 22; SATA 2, 68

Smith, Woodrow Wilson
ttner, Henry

Smolenskin, Peretz
1842-1885 .... **NCLC 30**

Smollett, Tobias (George) 1721-1771 .... **LC 2**
See also CDBLB 1660-1789; DLB 39, 104

Snodgrass, W(illiam) D(e Witt) 1926- **CLC 2, 6, 10, 18, 68; DAM POET**
See also CA 1-4R; CANR 6, 36; DLB 5; MTCW

Snow, C(harles) P(ercy) 1905-1980 **CLC 1, 4, 6, 9, 13, 19; DAM NOV**
See also CA 5-8R; 101; CANR 28; CDBLB 1945-1960; DLB 15, 77; MTCW

Snow, Frances Compton
See Adams, Henry (Brooks)

Snyder, Gary (Sherman) 1930- **CLC 1, 2, 5, 9, 32; DAM POET**
See also CA 17-20R; CANR 30; DLB 5, 16, 165

Swinnerton, Frank Arthur 1884-1982 **CLC 31**
See also CA 108; DLB 34

Swithen, John
See King, Stephen (Edwin)

Sylvia
See Ashton-Warner, Sylvia (Constance)

Symmes, Robert Edward
See Duncan, Robert (Edward)

Symonds, John Addington 1840-1893 **N C L C 34**
See also DLB 57, 144

Symons, Arthur 1865-1945 .... **TCLC 11**
See also CA 107; DLB 19, 57, 149

Symons, Julian (Gustave) 1912-1994 **CLC 2, 14, 32**
See also CA 49-52; 147; CAAS 3; CANR 3, 33, 59; DLB 87, 155; DLBY 92; MTCW

Synge, (Edmund) J(ohn) M(illington) 1871-1909 ... **TCLC 6, 37; DAM DRAM; DC 2**
See also CA 104; 141; CDBLB 1890-1914; DLB 10, 19

Syruc, J.
See Milosz, Czeslaw

Szirtes, George 1948- .... **CLC 46**
See also CA 109; CANR 27

Szymborska, Wislawa 1923- .... **CLC 99**
See also CA 154; DLBY 96

T. O., Nik
See Annensky, Innokenty (Fyodorovich)

Tabori, George 1914- .... **CLC 19**
See also CA 49-52; CANR 4

Tagore, Rabindranath 1861-1941 **TCLC 3, 53; DAM DRAM, POET; PC 8**
See also CA 104; 120; MTCW

Taine, Hippolyte Adolphe 1828-1893 . **N C L C 15**

Talese, Gay 1932- .... **CLC 37**
See also AITN 1; CA 1-4R; CANR 9, 58; INT CANR-9; MTCW

Tallent, Elizabeth (Ann) 1954- .... **CLC 45**
See also CA 117; DLB 130

Tally, Ted 1952- .... **CLC 42**
See also CA 120; 124; INT 124

Tamayo y Baus, Manuel 1829-1898 **NCLC 1**

Tammsaare, A(nton) H(ansen) 1878-1940 .... **TCLC 27**

Tam'si, Tchicaya U
See Tchicaya, Gerald Felix

Tan, Amy (Ruth) 1952- .... **CLC 59; DAM MULT, NOV, POP**
See also AAYA 9; BEST 89:3; CA 136; CANR 54; DLB 173; SATA 75

Tandem, Felix
See Spitteler, Carl (Friedrich Georg)

Tanizaki, Jun'ichiro 1886-1965 **CLC 8, 14, 28; SSC 21**
See also CA 93-96; 25-28R; DLB 180

Tanner, William
See Amis, Kingsley (William)

Tao Lao
See Storni, Alfonsina

Tarassoff, Lev
See Troyat, Henri

Tarbell, Ida M(inerva) 1857-1944 . **TCLC 40**
See also CA 122; DLB 47

Tarkington, (Newton) Booth 1869-1946 **TCLC 9**
See also CA 110; 143; DLB 9, 102; SATA 17

Tarkovsky, Andrei (Arsenyevich) 1932-1986 **CLC 75**
See also CA 127

Tartt, Donna 1964(?)- .... **CLC 76**
See also CA 142

Tasso, Torquato 1544-1595 .... **LC 5**

Tate, (John Orley) Allen 1899-1979 **CLC 2, 4, 6, 9, 11, 14, 24**
See also CA 5-8R; 85-88; CANR 32; DLB 4, 45, 63; MTCW

Tate, Ellalice
See Hibbert, Eleanor Alice Burford

Tate, James (Vincent) 1943- ..... **CLC 2, 6, 25**
See also CA 21-24R; CANR 29, 57; DLB 5, 169

Tavel, Ronald 1940- .... **CLC 6**
See also CA 21-24R; CANR 33

Taylor, C(ecil) P(hilip) 1929-1981 .... **CLC 27**
See also CA 25-28R; 105; CANR 47

Taylor, Edward 1642(?)-1729 ..... **LC 11; DA; DAB; DAC; DAM MST, POET**
See also DLB 24

Taylor, Eleanor Ross 1920- .... **CLC 5**
See also CA 81-84

Taylor, Elizabeth 1912-1975 ..... **CLC 2, 4, 29**
See also CA 13-16R; CANR 9; DLB 139; MTCW; SATA 13

Taylor, Henry (Splawn) 1942- .... **CLC 44**
See also CA 33-36R; CAAS 7; CANR 31; DLB 5

Taylor, Kamala (Purnaiya) 1924- ....
See Markandaya, Kamala
See also CA 77-80

Taylor, Mildred D. .... **CLC 21**
See also AAYA 10; BW 1; CA 85-88; CANR 25; CLR 9; DLB 52; JRDA; MAICYA; SAAS 5; SATA 15, 70

Taylor, Peter (Hillsman) 1917-1994 **CLC 1, 4, 18, 37, 44, 50, 71; SSC 10**
See also CA 13-16R; 147; CANR 9, 50; DLBY 81, 94; INT CANR-9; MTCW

Taylor, Robert Lewis 1912- .... **CLC 14**

See also CA 1-4R; CANR 3; SATA 10

Tchekhov, Anton
See Chekhov, Anton (Pavlovich)

Tchicaya, Gerald Felix 1931-1988 .. **CLC 101**
See also CA 129; 125

Tchicaya U Tam'si
See Tchicaya, Gerald Felix

Teasdale, Sara 1884-1933 .... **TCLC 4**
See also CA 104; DLB 45; SATA 32

Tegner, Esaias 1782-1846 .... **NCLC 2**

Teilhard de Chardin, (Marie Joseph) Pierre 1881-1955 .... **TCLC 9**
See also CA 105

Temple, Ann
See Mortimer, Penelope (Ruth)

Tennant, Emma (Christina) 1937- **CLC 13, 52**
See also CA 65-68; CAAS 9; CANR 10, 38, 59; DLB 14

Tenneshaw, S. M.
See Silverberg, Robert

Tennyson, Alfred 1809-1892 . **NCLC 30; DA; DAB; DAC; DAM MST, POET; PC 6; WLC**
See also CDBLB 1832-1890; DLB 32

Teran, Lisa St. Aubin de .... **CLC 36**
See also St. Aubin de Teran, Lisa

Terence 195(?)B.C.-159B.C. **CMLC 14; DC 7**

Teresa de Jesus, St. 1515-1582 .... **LC 18**

Terkel, Louis 1912- ....
See Terkel, Studs
See also CA 57-60; CANR 18, 45; MTCW

Terkel, Studs .... **CLC 38**
See also Terkel, Louis
See also AITN 1

Terry, C. V.
See Slaughter, Frank G(ill)

Terry, Megan 1932- .... **CLC 19**
See also CA 77-80; CABS 3; CANR 43; DLB 7

Tertz, Abram
See Sinyavsky, Andrei (Donatevich)

Tesich, Steve 1943(?)-1996 .... **CLC 40, 69**
See also CA 105; 152; DLBY 83

Teternikov, Fyodor Kuzmich 1863-1927 ....
See Sologub, Fyodor
See also CA 104

Tevis, Walter 1928-1984 .... **CLC 42**
See also CA 113

Tey, Josephine .... **TCLC 14**
See also Mackintosh, Elizabeth
See also DLB 77

Thackeray, William Makepeace 1811-1863 **NCLC 5, 14, 22, 43; DA; DAB; DAC; DAM MST, NOV; WLC**
See also CDBLB 1832-1890; DLB 21, 55, 159,

163; SATA 23

Thakura, Ravindranatha
See Tagore, Rabindranath

Tharoor, Shashi 1956- .... **CLC 70**
See also CA 141

Thelwell, Michael Miles 1939- .... **CLC 22**
See also BW 2; CA 101

Theobald, Lewis, Jr.
See Lovecraft, H(oward) P(hillips)

Theodorescu, Ion N. 1880-1967 ....
See Arghezi, Tudor
See also CA 116

Theriault, Yves 1915-1983 .... **CLC 79; DAC; DAM MST**
See also CA 102; DLB 88

Theroux, Alexander (Louis) 1939- **CLC 2, 25**
See also CA 85-88; CANR 20

Theroux, Paul (Edward) 1941- **CLC 5, 8, 11, 15, 28, 46; DAM POP**
See also BEST 89:4; CA 33-36R; CANR 20, 45; DLB 2; MTCW; SATA 44

Thesen, Sharon 1946- .... **CLC 56**

Thevenin, Denis
See Duhamel, Georges

Thibault, Jacques Anatole Francois 1844-1924

See France, Anatole
See also CA 106; 127; DAM NOV; MTCW

Thiele, Colin (Milton) 1920- .... **CLC 17**
See also CA 29-32R; CANR 12, 28, 53; CLR 27; MAICYA; SAAS 2; SATA 14, 72

Thomas, Audrey (Callahan) 1935- **CLC 7, 13, 37; SSC 20**
See also AITN 2; CA 21-24R; CAAS 19; CANR 36, 58; DLB 60; MTCW

Thomas, D(onald) M(ichael) 1935- . **CLC 13, 22, 31**
See also CA 61-64; CAAS 11; CANR 17, 45; CDBLB 1960 to Present; DLB 40; INT CANR-17; MTCW

Thomas, Dylan (Marlais) 1914-1953 **TCLC 1, 8, 45; DA; DAB; DAC; DAM DRAM, MST, POET; PC 2; SSC 3; WLC**
See also CA 104; 120; CDBLB 1945-1960; DLB 13, 20, 139; MTCW; SATA 60

Thomas, (Philip) Edward 1878-1917 . **TCLC 10; DAM POET**
See also CA 106; 153; DLB 19

Thomas, Joyce Carol 1938- .... **CLC 35**
See also AAYA 12; BW 2; CA 113; 116; CANR 48; CLR 19; DLB 33; INT 116; JRDA; MAICYA; MTCW; SAAS 7; SATA 40, 78

Thomas, Lewis 1913-1993 .... **CLC 35**
See also CA 85-88; 143; CANR 38; MTCW

Thomas, Paul
See Mann, (Paul) Thomas

Thomas, Piri 1928- .... **CLC 17**

See also CA 73-76; HW

Thomas, R(onald) S(tuart) 1913- **CLC 6, 13, 48; DAB; DAM POET**
See also CA 89-92; CAAS 4; CANR 30; CDBLB 1960 to Present; DLB 27; MTCW

Thomas, Ross (Elmore) 1926-1995 ... **CLC 39**
See also CA 33-36R; 150; CANR 22

Thompson, Francis Clegg
See Mencken, H(enry) L(ouis)

Thompson, Francis Joseph 1859-1907 **TCLC 4**
See also CA 104; CDBLB 1890-1914; DLB 19

Thompson, Hunter S(tockton) 1939- . **CLC 9, 17, 40; DAM POP**
See also BEST 89:1; CA 17-20R; CANR 23, 46; MTCW

Thompson, James Myers
See Thompson, Jim (Myers)

Thompson, Jim (Myers) 1906-1977(?) **CLC 69**
See also CA 140

Thompson, Judith .... **CLC 39**

Thomson, James 1700-1748 **LC 16, 29; DAM POET**
See also DLB 95

Thomson, James 1834-1882 **NCLC 18; DAM POET**
See also DLB 35

Thoreau, Henry David 1817-1862 **NCLC 7, 21, 61; DA; DAB; DAC; DAM MST; WLC**
See also CDALB 1640-1865; DLB 1

Thornton, Hall
See Silverberg, Robert

Thucydides c. 455B.C.-399B.C. .... **CMLC 17**
See also DLB 176

Thurber, James (Grover) 1894-1961 . **CLC 5, 11, 25; DA; DAB; DAC; DAM DRAM, MST, NOV; SSC 1**
See also CA 73-76; CANR 17, 39; CDALB 1929-1941; DLB 4, 11, 22, 102; MAICYA; MTCW; SATA 13

Thurman, Wallace (Henry) 1902-1934 **TCLC 6; BLC; DAM MULT**
See also BW 1; CA 104; 124; DLB 51

Ticheburn, Cheviot
See Ainsworth, William Harrison

Tieck, (Johann) Ludwig 1773-1853 **NCLC 5, 46**
See also DLB 90

Tiger, Derry
See Ellison, Harlan (Jay)

Tilghman, Christopher 1948(?)- .... **CLC 65**

Tillinghast, Richard (Williford) 1940- **CLC 29**
See also CA 29-32R; CAAS 23; CANR 26, 51

Timrod, Henry 1828-1867 .... **NCLC 25**
See also DLB 3

Tindall, Gillian 1938- .... **CLC 7**

See also CA 21-24R; CANR 11

Tiptree, James, Jr. .... **CLC 48, 50**
See also Sheldon, Alice Hastings Bradley
See also DLB 8

Titmarsh, Michael Angelo
See Thackeray, William Makepeace

Tocqueville, Alexis (Charles Henri Maurice Clerel Comte) 1805-1859 .... **NCLC 7**

Tolkien, J(ohn) R(onald) R(euel) 1892-1973 **CLC 1, 2, 3, 8, 12, 38; DA; DAB; DAC; DAM MST, NOV, POP; WLC**
See also AAYA 10; AITN 1; CA 17-18; 45-48; CANR 36; CAP 2; CDBLB 1914-1945; DLB 15, 160; JRDA; MAICYA; MTCW; SATA 2, 32; SATA-Obit 24

Toller, Ernst 1893-1939 .... **TCLC 10**
See also CA 107; DLB 124

Tolson, M. B.
See Tolson, Melvin B(eaunorus)

Tolson, Melvin B(eaunorus) 1898(?)-1966 **CLC 36; BLC; DAM MULT, POET**
See also BW 1; CA 124; 89-92; DLB 48, 76

Tolstoi, Aleksei Nikolaevich
See Tolstoy, Alexey Nikolaevich

Tolstoy, Alexey Nikolaevich 1882-1945 **TCLC 18**
See also CA 107; 158

Tolstoy, Count Leo
See Tolstoy, Leo (Nikolaevich)

Tolstoy, Leo (Nikolaevich) 1828-1910 **TCLC 4, 11, 17, 28, 44; DA; DAB; DAC; DAM MST, NOV; SSC 9; WLC**
See also CA 104; 123; SATA 26

Tomasi di Lampedusa, Giuseppe 1896-1957 .
See Lampedusa, Giuseppe (Tomasi) di
See also CA 111

Tomlin, Lily .... **CLC 17**
See also Tomlin, Mary Jean

Tomlin, Mary Jean 1939(?)- ....
See Tomlin, Lily
See also CA 117

Tomlinson, (Alfred) Charles 1927- **CLC 2, 4, 6, 13, 45; DAM POET; PC 17**
See also CA 5-8R; CANR 33; DLB 40

Tomlinson, H(enry) M(ajor) 1873-1958 **TCLC 71**
See also CA 118; DLB 36, 100

Tonson, Jacob
See Bennett, (Enoch) Arnold

Toole, John Kennedy 1937-1969 **CLC 19, 64**
See also CA 104; DLBY 81

Toomer, Jean 1894-1967 .... **CLC 1, 4, 13, 22; BLC; DAM MULT; PC 7; SSC 1; WLCS**
See also BW 1; CA 85-88; CDALB 1917-1929; DLB 45, 51; MTCW

Torley, Luke
See Blish, James (Benjamin)

Tornimparte, Alessandra
See Ginzburg, Natalia

Torre, Raoul della
See Mencken, H(enry) L(ouis)

Torrey, E(dwin) Fuller 1937- .... **CLC 34**
See also CA 119

Torsvan, Ben Traven
See Traven, B.

Torsvan, Benno Traven
See Traven, B.

Torsvan, Berick Traven
See Traven, B.

Torsvan, Berwick Traven
See Traven, B.

Torsvan, Bruno Traven
See Traven, B.

Torsvan, Traven
See Traven, B.

Tournier, Michel (Edouard) 1924-**CLC 6, 23, 36, 95**
See also CA 49-52; CANR 3, 36; DLB 83; MTCW; SATA 23

Tournimparte, Alessandra
See Ginzburg, Natalia

Towers, Ivar
See Kornbluth, C(yril) M.

Towne, Robert (Burton) 1936(?)- ..... **CLC 87**
See also CA 108; DLB 44

Townsend, Sue 1946- .... **CLC 61; DAB; DAC**
See also CA 119; 127; INT 127; MTCW; SATA 55, 93; SATA-Brief 48

Townshend, Peter (Dennis Blandford) 1945-
CLC 17, 42
See also CA 107

Tozzi, Federigo 1883-1920 .... **TCLC 31**

Traill, Catharine Parr 1802-1899 .. **NCLC 31**
See also DLB 99

Trakl, Georg 1887-1914 .... **TCLC 5**
See also CA 104

Transtroemer, Tomas (Goesta) 1931-**CLC 52, 65; DAM POET**
See also CA 117; 129; CAAS 17

Transtromer, Tomas Gosta
See Transtroemer, Tomas (Goesta)

Traven, B. (?)-1969 .... **CLC 8, 11**
See also CA 19-20; 25-28R; CAP 2; DLB 9, 56; MTCW

Treitel, Jonathan 1959- .... **CLC 70**

Tremain, Rose
1943- .... **CLC 42**
See also CA 97-100; CANR 44; DLB 14

Tremblay, Michel 1942- **CLC 29, 102; DAC; DAM MST**
See also CA 116; 128; DLB 60; MTCW

Trevanian .... **CLC 29**
See also Whitaker, Rod(ney)

Trevor, Glen
See Hilton, James

Trevor, William 1928- . **CLC 7, 9, 14, 25, 71; SSC 21**
See also Cox, William Trevor
See also DLB 14, 139

Trifonov, Yuri (Valentinovich) 1925-1981
CLC 45
See also CA 126; 103; MTCW

Trilling, Lionel 1905-1975 ...... **CLC 9, 11, 24**
See also CA 9-12R; 61-64; CANR 10; DLB 28, 63; INT CANR-10; MTCW

Trimball, W. H.
See Mencken, H(enry) L(ouis)

Tristan
See Gomez de la Serna, Ramon

Tristram
See Housman, A(lfred) E(dward)

Trogdon, William (Lewis) 1939- ....
See Heat-Moon, William Least
See also CA 115; 119; CANR 47; INT 119

Trollope, Anthony 1815-1882**NCLC 6, 33; DA; DAB; DAC; DAM MST, NOV; WLC**
See also CDBLB 1832-1890; DLB 21, 57, 159; SATA 22

Trollope, Frances 1779-1863 .... **NCLC 30**
See also DLB 21, 166

Trotsky, Leon 1879-1940 .... **TCLC 22**
See also CA 118

Trotter (Cockburn), Catharine 1679-1749**LC 8**
See also DLB 84

Trout, Kilgore
See Farmer, Philip Jose

Trow, George W. S. 1943- .... **CLC 52**
See also CA 126

Troyat, Henri 1911- .... **CLC 23**
See also CA 45-48; CANR 2, 33; MTCW

Trudeau, G(arretson) B(eekman) 1948- ....
See Trudeau, Garry B.
See also CA 81-84; CANR 31; SATA 35

Trudeau, Garry B. .... **CLC 12**
See also Trudeau, G(arretson) B(eekman)
See also AAYA 10; AITN 2

Truffaut, Francois 1932-1984 .. **CLC 20, 101**
See also CA 81-84; 113; CANR 34

Trumbo, Dalton 1905-1976 .... **CLC 19**
See also CA 21-24R; 69-72; CANR 10; DLB 26

Trumbull, John
1750-1831 .... **NCLC 30**
See also DLB 31

Trundlett, Helen B.
See Eliot, T(homas) S(tearns)

Tryon, Thomas 1926-1991 . **CLC 3, 11; DAM POP**
See also AITN 1; CA 29-32R; 135; CANR 32; MTCW

Tryon, Tom
See Tryon, Thomas

Ts'ao Hsueh-ch'in 1715(?)-1763 .... **LC 1**

Tsushima, Shuji 1909-1948 ....
See Dazai, Osamu
See also CA 107

Tsvetaeva (Efron), Marina (Ivanovna) 1892-1941 .... **TCLC 7, 35; PC 14**
See also CA 104; 128; MTCW

Tuck, Lily 1938- .... **CLC 70**
See also CA 139

Tu Fu 712-770 .... **PC 9**
See also DAM MULT

Tunis, John R(oberts) 1889-1975 ...... **CLC 12**
See also CA 61-64; DLB 22, 171; JRDA; MAICYA; SATA 37; SATA-Brief 30

Tuohy, Frank .... **CLC 37**
See also Tuohy, John Francis
See also DLB 14, 139

Tuohy, John Francis 1925- ....
See Tuohy, Frank
See also CA 5-8R; CANR 3, 47

Turco, Lewis (Putnam) 1934- ...... **CLC 11, 63**
See also CA 13-16R; CAAS 22; CANR 24, 51; DLBY 84

Turgenev, Ivan 1818-1883 .... **NCLC 21; DA; DAB; DAC; DAM MST, NOV; DC 7; SSC 7; WLC**

Turgot, Anne-Robert-Jacques 1727-1781 **LC 26**

Turner, Frederick 1943- .... **CLC 48**
See also CA 73-76; CAAS 10; CANR 12, 30, 56; DLB 40

Tutu, Desmond M(pilo) 1931- **CLC 80; BLC; DAM MULT**
See also BW 1; CA 125

Tutuola, Amos 1920- .... **CLC 5, 14, 29; BLC; DAM MULT**
See also BW 2; CA 9-12R; CANR 27; DLB 125; MTCW

Twain, Mark **TCLC 6, 12, 19, 36, 48, 59; SSC 26; WLC**
See also Clemens, Samuel Langhorne
See also AAYA 20; DLB 11, 12, 23, 64, 74

Tyler, Anne 1941- . **CLC 7, 11, 18, 28, 44, 59; DAM NOV, POP**
See also AAYA 18; BEST 89:1; CA 9-12R; CANR 11, 33, 53; DLB 6, 143; DLBY 82; MTCW; SATA 7, 90

Tyler, Royall 1757-1826 .... **NCLC 3**
See also DLB 37

Tynan, Katharine
1861-1931 .... **TCLC 3**
See also CA 104; DLB 153

Tyutchev, Fyodor 1803-1873 .... NCLC 34

Tzara, Tristan 1896-1963 ...... CLC 47; DAM
POET
See also Rosenfeld, Samuel; Rosenstock, Sami;
Rosenstock, Samuel
See also CA 153

Uhry, Alfred 1936- ... CLC 55; DAM DRAM,
POP
See also CA 127; 133; INT 133

Ulf, Haerved
See Strindberg, (Johan) August

Ulf, Harved
See Strindberg, (Johan) August

Ulibarri, Sabine R(eyes) 1919-CLC 83; DAM
MULT
See also CA 131; DLB 82; HW

Unamuno (y Jugo), Miguel de 1864-1936
TCLC 2, 9; DAM MULT, NOV; HLC; SSC
11
See also CA 104; 131; DLB 108; HW; MTCW

Undercliffe, Errol
See Campbell, (John) Ramsey

Underwood, Miles
See Glassco, John

Undset, Sigrid 1882-1949TCLC 3; DA; DAB;
DAC; DAM MST, NOV; WLC
See also CA 104; 129; MTCW

Ungaretti, Giuseppe 1888-1970CLC 7, 11, 15
See also CA 19-20; 25-28R; CAP 2; DLB 114

Unger, Douglas 1952- .... CLC 34
See also CA 130

Unsworth, Barry (Forster) 1930- ..... CLC 76
See also CA 25-28R; CANR 30, 54

Updike, John (Hoyer) 1932-CLC 1, 2, 3, 5, 7,
9, 13, 15, 23, 34, 43, 70; DA; DAB; DAC;
DAM MST, NOV, POET, POP; SSC 13, 27;
WLC
See also CA 1-4R; CABS 1; CANR 4, 33, 51;
CDALB 1968-1988; DLB 2, 5, 143; DLBD
3; DLBY 80, 82; MTCW

Upshaw, Margaret Mitchell
See Mitchell, Margaret (Munnerlyn)

Upton, Mark
See Sanders, Lawrence

Urdang, Constance (Henriette) 1922-CLC 47
See also CA 21-24R; CANR 9, 24

Uriel, Henry
See Faust, Frederick (Schiller)

Uris, Leon (Marcus) 1924- CLC 7, 32; DAM
NOV, POP
See also AITN 1, 2; BEST 89:2; CA 1-4R;
CANR 1, 40; MTCW; SATA 49

Urmuz
See Codrescu, Andrei

Urquhart, Jane
1949- .... CLC 90; DAC
See also CA 113; CANR 32

Ustinov, Peter (Alexander) 1921- .... CLC 1
See also AITN 1; CA 13-16R; CANR 25, 51;
DLB 13

U Tam'si, Gerald Felix Tchicaya
See Tchicaya, Gerald Felix

U Tam'si, Tchicaya
See Tchicaya, Gerald Felix

Vaculik, Ludvik 1926- .... CLC 7
See also CA 53-56

Vaihinger, Hans 1852-1933 .... TCLC 71
See also CA 116

Valdez, Luis (Miguel) 1940- .. CLC 84; DAM
MULT; HLC
See also CA 101; CANR 32; DLB 122; HW

Valenzuela, Luisa 1938-CLC 31; DAM MULT;
SSC 14
See also CA 101; CANR 32; DLB 113; HW

Valera y Alcala-Galiano, Juan 1824-1905
TCLC 10
See also CA 106

Valery, (Ambroise) Paul (Toussaint Jules) 1871-
1945 ..... TCLC 4, 15; DAM POET; PC 9
See also CA 104; 122; MTCW

Valle-Inclan, Ramon (Maria) del 1866-1936
TCLC 5; DAM MULT; HLC
See also CA 106; 153; DLB 134

Vallejo, Antonio Buero
See Buero Vallejo, Antonio

Vallejo, Cesar (Abraham) 1892-1938TCLC 3,
56; DAM MULT; HLC
See also CA 105; 153; HW

Vallette, Marguerite Eymery
See Rachilde

Valle Y Pena, Ramon del
See Valle-Inclan, Ramon (Maria) del

Van Ash, Cay 1918- .... CLC 34

Vanbrugh, Sir John 1664-1726 LC 21; DAM
DRAM
See also DLB 80

Van Campen, Karl
See Campbell, John W(ood, Jr.)

Vance, Gerald
See Silverberg, Robert

Vance, Jack .... CLC 35
See also Kuttner, Henry; Vance, John Holbrook
See also DLB 8

Vance, John Holbrook 1916- ....
See Queen, Ellery; Vance, Jack
See also CA 29-32R; CANR 17; MTCW

Van Den Bogarde, Derek Jules Gaspard Ulric
Niven 1921- ....
See Bogarde, Dirk
See also CA 77-80

Vandenburgh, Jane .... CLC 59

Vanderhaeghe, Guy 1951- .... CLC 41

See also CA 113

van der Post, Laurens (Jan) 1906-1996CLC 5
See also CA 5-8R; 155; CANR 35

van de Wetering, Janwillem 1931- ... CLC 47
See also CA 49-52; CANR 4

Van Dine, S. S. .... TCLC 23
See also Wright, Willard Huntington

Van Doren, Carl (Clinton) 1885-1950 T C L C
18
See also CA 111

Van Doren, Mark 1894-1972 .... CLC 6, 10
See also CA 1-4R; 37-40R; CANR 3; DLB 45;
MTCW

Van Druten, John (William) 1901-1957TCLC
2
See also CA 104; DLB 10

Van Duyn, Mona (Jane) 1921- CLC 3, 7, 63;
DAM POET
See also CA 9-12R; CANR 7, 38; DLB 5

Van Dyne, Edith
See Baum, L(yman) Frank

van Itallie, Jean-Claude 1936- .... CLC 3
See also CA 45-48; CAAS 2; CANR 1, 48; DLB
7

van Ostaijen, Paul 1896-1928 .... TCLC 33

Van Peebles, Melvin 1932- CLC 2, 20; DAM
MULT
See also BW 2; CA 85-88; CANR 27

Vansittart, Peter 1920- .... CLC 42
See also CA 1-4R; CANR 3, 49

Van Vechten, Carl 1880-1964 .... CLC 33
See also CA 89-92; DLB 4, 9, 51

Van Vogt, A(lfred) E(lton) 1912- .... CLC 1
See also CA 21-24R; CANR 28; DLB 8; SATA
14

Varda, Agnes 1928- .... CLC 16
See also CA 116; 122

Vargas Llosa, (Jorge) Mario (Pedro) 1936-
CLC 3, 6, 9, 10, 15, 31, 42, 85; DA; DAB;
DAC; DAM MST, MULT, NOV; HLC
See also CA 73-76; CANR 18, 32, 42; DLB 145;
HW; MTCW

Vasiliu, Gheorghe 1881-1957 ....
See Bacovia, George
See also CA 123

Vassa, Gustavus
See Equiano, Olaudah

Vassilikos, Vassilis 1933- .... CLC 4, 8
See also CA 81-84

Vaughan, Henry 1621-1695 .... LC 27
See also DLB 131

Vaughn, Stephanie .... CLC 62

Vazov, Ivan (Minchov)
1850-1921 .... TCLC 25
See also CA 121; DLB 147

Veblen, Thorstein (Bunde) 1857-1929 **T C L C 31**
See also CA 115

Vega, Lope de 1562-1635 .... **LC 23**

Venison, Alfred
See Pound, Ezra (Weston Loomis)

Verdi, Marie de
See Mencken, H(enry) L(ouis)

Verdu, Matilde
See Cela, Camilo Jose

Verga, Giovanni (Carmelo) 1840-1922 T C L C 3; SSC 21
See also CA 104; 123

Vergil 70B.C.-19B.C. ... **CMLC 9; DA; DAB; DAC; DAM MST, POET; PC 12; WLCS**

Verhaeren, Emile (Adolphe Gustave) 1855-1916 **TCLC 12**
See also CA 109

Verlaine, Paul (Marie) 1844-1896 **NCLC 2, 51; DAM POET; PC 2**

Verne, Jules (Gabriel) 1828-1905 **TCLC 6, 52**
See also AAYA 16; CA 110; 131; DLB 123; JRDA; MAICYA; SATA 21

Very, Jones 1813-1880 .... **NCLC 9**
See also DLB 1

Vesaas, Tarjei 1897-1970 .... **CLC 48**
See also CA 29-32R

Vialis, Gaston
See Simenon, Georges (Jacques Christian)

Vian, Boris 1920-1959 .... **TCLC 9**
See also CA 106; DLB 72

Viaud, (Louis Marie) Julien 1850-1923 ....
See Loti, Pierre
See also CA 107

Vicar, Henry
See Felsen, Henry Gregor

Vicker, Angus
See Felsen, Henry Gregor

Vidal, Gore 1925-**CLC 2, 4, 6, 8, 10, 22, 33, 72; DAM NOV, POP**
See also AITN 1; BEST 90:2; CA 5-8R; CANR 13, 45; DLB 6, 152; INT CANR-13; MTCW

Viereck, Peter (Robert Edwin) 1916- . **CLC 4**
See also CA 1-4R; CANR 1, 47; DLB 5

Vigny, Alfred (Victor) de 1797-1863 **NCLC 7; DAM POET**
See also DLB 119

Vilakazi, Benedict Wallet 1906-1947 **TCLC 37**

Villiers de l'Isle Adam, Jean Marie Mathias Philippe Auguste Comte 1838-1889 **NCLC 3; SSC 14**
See also DLB 123

Villon, Francois 1431-1463(?) .... **PC 13**

Vinci, Leonardo da 1452-1519 .... **LC 12**

Vine, Barbara .... **CLC 50**
See also Rendell, Ruth (Barbara)
See also BEST 90:4

Vinge, Joan D(ennison) 1948-**CLC 30; SSC 24**
See also CA 93-96; SATA 36

Violis, G.
See Simenon, Georges (Jacques Christian)

Visconti, Luchino 1906-1976 .... **CLC 16**
See also CA 81-84; 65-68; CANR 39

Vittorini, Elio 1908-1966 .... **CLC 6, 9, 14**
See also CA 133; 25-28R

Vizinczey, Stephen 1933- .... **CLC 40**
See also CA 128; INT 128

Vliet, R(ussell) G(ordon) 1929-1984 **CLC 22**
See also CA 37-40R; 112; CANR 18

Vogau, Boris Andreyevich 1894-1937(?) ....
See Pilnyak, Boris
See also CA 123

Vogel, Paula A(nne) 1951- .... **CLC 76**
See also CA 108

Voight, Ellen Bryant 1943- .... **CLC 54**
See also CA 69-72; CANR 11, 29, 55; DLB 120

Voigt, Cynthia 1942-.......................... **CLC 30**
See also AAYA 3; CA 106; CANR 18, 37, 40; CLR 13; INT CANR-18; JRDA; MAICYA; SATA 48, 79; SATA-Brief 33

Voinovich, Vladimir (Nikolaevich) 1932-**C L C 10, 49**
See also CA 81-84; CAAS 12; CANR 33; MTCW

Vollmann, William T. 1959-... **CLC 89; DAM NOV, POP**
See also CA 134

Voloshinov, V. N.
See Bakhtin, Mikhail Mikhailovich

Voltaire 1694-1778 . **LC 14; DA; DAB; DAC; DAM DRAM, MST; SSC 12; WLC**

von Daeniken, Erich
1935- .... **CLC 30**
See also AITN 1; CA 37-40R; CANR 17, 44

von Daniken, Erich
See von Daeniken, Erich

von Heidenstam, (Carl Gustaf) Verner
See Heidenstam, (Carl Gustaf) Verner von

von Heyse, Paul (Johann Ludwig)
See Heyse, Paul (Johann Ludwig von)

von Hofmannsthal, Hugo
See Hofmannsthal, Hugo von

von Horvath, Odon
See Horvath, Oedoen von

von Horvath, Oedoen
See Horvath, Oedoen von

von Liliencron, (Friedrich Adolf Axel) Detlev
See Liliencron, (Friedrich Adolf Axel) Detlev von

Vonnegut, Kurt, Jr. 1922-**CLC 1, 2, 3, 4, 5, 8, 12, 22, 40, 60; DA; DAB; DAC; DAM MST, NOV, POP; SSC 8; WLC**
See also AAYA 6; AITN 1; BEST 90:4; CA 1-4R; CANR 1, 25, 49; CDALB 1968-1988; DLB 2, 8, 152; DLBD 3; DLBY 80; MTCW

Von Rachen, Kurt
See Hubbard, L(afayette) Ron(ald)

von Rezzori (d'Arezzo), Gregor
See Rezzori (d'Arezzo), Gregor von

von Sternberg, Josef
See Sternberg, Josef von

Vorster, Gordon 1924-....................... **CLC 34**
See also CA 133

Vosce, Trudie
See Ozick, Cynthia

Voznesensky, Andrei (Andreievich) 1933- **CLC 1, 15, 57; DAM POET**
See also CA 89-92; CANR 37; MTCW

Waddington, Miriam 1917- .... **CLC 28**
See also CA 21-24R; CANR 12, 30; DLB 68

Wagman, Fredrica 1937- .... **CLC 7**
See also CA 97-100; INT 97-100

Wagner, Richard 1813-1883 .... **NCLC 9**
See also DLB 129

Wagner-Martin, Linda 1936- .... **CLC 50**

Wagoner, David (Russell) 1926- **CLC 3, 5, 15**
See also CA 1-4R; CAAS 3; CANR 2; DLB 5; SATA 14

Wah, Fred(erick James) 1939- .... **CLC 44**
See also CA 107; 141; DLB 60

Wahloo, Per 1926-1975 .... **CLC 7**
See also CA 61-64

Wahloo, Peter
See Wahloo, Per

Wain, John (Barrington) 1925-1994 . **CLC 2, 11, 15, 46**
See also CA 5-8R; 145; CAAS 4; CANR 23, 54; CDBLB 1960 to Present; DLB 15, 27, 139, 155; MTCW

Wajda, Andrzej 1926- .... **CLC 16**
See also CA 102

Wakefield, Dan 1932- .... **CLC 7**
See also CA 21-24R; CAAS 7

Wakoski, Diane 1937- **CLC 2, 4, 7, 9, 11, 40; DAM POET; PC 15**
See also CA 13-16R; CAAS 1; CANR 9; DLB 5; INT CANR-9

Wakoski-Sherbell, Diane
See Wakoski, Diane

Walcott, Derek (Alton) 1930-**CLC 2, 4, 9, 14, 25, 42, 67, 76; BLC; DAB; DAC; DAM MST, MULT, POET; DC 7**
See also BW 2; CA 89-92; CANR 26, 47; DLB 117; DLBY 81; MTCW

Waldman, Anne 1945- .... **CLC 7**

See also CA 37-40R; CAAS 17; CANR 34; DLB 16

Waldo, E. Hunter
See Sturgeon, Theodore (Hamilton)

Waldo, Edward Hamilton
See Sturgeon, Theodore (Hamilton)

Walker, Alice (Malsenior) 1944- CLC 5, 6, 9, 19, 27, 46, 58; BLC; DA; DAB; DAC; DAM MST, MULT, NOV, POET, POP; SSC 5; WLCS
See also AAYA 3; BEST 89:4; BW 2; CA 37-40R; CANR 9, 27, 49; CDALB 1968-1988; DLB 6, 33, 143; INT CANR-27; MTCW; SATA 31

Walker, David Harry 1911-1992 .... CLC 14
See also CA 1-4R; 137; CANR 1; SATA 8; SATA-Obit 71

Walker, Edward Joseph 1934- ....
See Walker, Ted
See also CA 21-24R; CANR 12, 28, 53

Walker, George F. 1947- . CLC 44, 61; DAB; DAC; DAM MST
See also CA 103; CANR 21, 43, 59; DLB 60

Walker, Joseph A. 1935- .... CLC 19; DAM DRAM, MST
See also BW 1; CA 89-92; CANR 26; DLB 38

Walker, Margaret (Abigail) 1915- CLC 1, 6; BLC; DAM MULT
See also BW 2; CA 73-76; CANR 26, 54; DLB 76, 152; MTCW

Walker, Ted .... CLC 13
See also Walker, Edward Joseph
See also DLB 40

Wallace, David Foster 1962- .... CLC 50
See also CA 132; CANR 59

Wallace, Dexter
See Masters, Edgar Lee

Wallace, (Richard Horatio) Edgar 1875-1932 TCLC 57
See also CA 115; DLB 70

Wallace, Irving 1916-1990 CLC 7, 13; DAM NOV, POP
See also AITN 1; CA 1-4R; 132; CAAS 1; CANR 1, 27; INT CANR-27; MTCW

Wallant, Edward Lewis 1926-1962 CLC 5, 10
See also CA 1-4R; CANR 22; DLB 2, 28, 143; MTCW

Walley, Byron
See Card, Orson Scott

Walpole, Horace 1717-1797 .... LC 2
See also DLB 39, 104

Walpole, Hugh (Seymour) 1884-1941 TCLC 5
See also CA 104; DLB 34

Walser, Martin 1927- .... CLC 27
See also CA 57-60; CANR 8, 46; DLB 75, 124

Walser, Robert
1878-1956 .... TCLC 18; SSC 20
See also CA 118; DLB 66

Walsh, Jill Paton .... CLC 35
See also Paton Walsh, Gillian
See also AAYA 11; CLR 2; DLB 161; SAAS 3

Walter, Villiam Christian
See Andersen, Hans Christian

Wambaugh, Joseph (Aloysius, Jr.) 1937-CLC 3, 18; DAM NOV, POP
See also AITN 1; BEST 89:3; CA 33-36R; CANR 42; DLB 6; DLBY 83; MTCW

Wang Wei
699(?)-761(?) .... PC 18

Ward, Arthur Henry Sarsfield 1883-1959 ....
See Rohmer, Sax
See also CA 108

Ward, Douglas Turner 1930- .... CLC 19
See also BW 1; CA 81-84; CANR 27; DLB 7, 38

Ward, Mary Augusta
See Ward, Mrs. Humphry

Ward, Mrs. Humphry 1851-1920 .. TCLC 55
See also DLB 18

Ward, Peter
See Faust, Frederick (Schiller)

Warhol, Andy 1928(?)-1987 .... CLC 20
See also AAYA 12; BEST 89:4; CA 89-92; 121; CANR 34

Warner, Francis (Robert le Plastrier) 1937-CLC 14
See also CA 53-56; CANR 11

Warner, Marina 1946- .... CLC 59
See also CA 65-68; CANR 21, 55

Warner, Rex (Ernest) 1905-1986 ...... CLC 45
See also CA 89-92; 119; DLB 15

Warner, Susan (Bogert) 1819-1885 NCLC 31
See also DLB 3, 42

Warner, Sylvia (Constance) Ashton
See Ashton-Warner, Sylvia (Constance)

Warner, Sylvia Townsend 1893-1978 CLC 7, 19; SSC 23
See also CA 61-64; 77-80; CANR 16; DLB 34, 139; MTCW

Warren, Mercy Otis 1728-1814 ..... NCLC 13
See also DLB 31

Warren, Robert Penn 1905-1989 CLC 1, 4, 6, 8, 10, 13, 18, 39, 53, 59; DA; DAB; DAC; DAM MST, NOV, POET; SSC 4; WLC
See also AITN 1; CA 13-16R; 129; CANR 10, 47; CDALB 1968-1988; DLB 2, 48, 152; DLBY 80, 89; INT CANR-10; MTCW; SATA 46; SATA-Obit 63

Warshofsky, Isaac
See Singer, Isaac Bashevis

Warton, Thomas 1728-1790 ..... LC 15; DAM POET
See also DLB 104, 109

Waruk, Kona
See Harris, (Theodore) Wilson

Warung, Price 1855-1911 .... TCLC 45

Warwick, Jarvis
See Garner, Hugh

Washington, Alex
See Harris, Mark

Washington, Booker T(aliaferro) 1856-1915 TCLC 10; BLC; DAM MULT
See also BW 1; CA 114; 125; SATA 28

Washington, George 1732-1799 .... LC 25
See also DLB 31

Wassermann, (Karl) Jakob 1873-1934 TCLC 6
See also CA 104; DLB 66

Wasserstein, Wendy 1950- ... CLC 32, 59, 90; DAM DRAM; DC 4
See also CA 121; 129; CABS 3; CANR 53; INT 129; SATA 94

Waterhouse, Keith (Spencer) 1929- . CLC 47
See also CA 5-8R; CANR 38; DLB 13, 15; MTCW

Waters, Frank (Joseph) 1902-1995 .. CLC 88
See also CA 5-8R; 149; CAAS 13; CANR 3, 18; DLBY 86

Waters, Roger 1944- .... CLC 35

Watkins, Frances Ellen
See Harper, Frances Ellen Watkins

Watkins, Gerrold
See Malzberg, Barry N(athaniel)

Watkins, Gloria 1955(?)- ....
See hooks, bell
See also BW 2; CA 143

Watkins, Paul 1964- .... CLC 55
See also CA 132

Watkins, Vernon Phillips 1906-1967 CLC 43
See also CA 9-10; 25-28R; CAP 1; DLB 20

Watson, Irving S.
See Mencken, H(enry) L(ouis)

Watson, John H.
See Farmer, Philip Jose

Watson, Richard F.
See Silverberg, Robert

Waugh, Auberon (Alexander) 1939- .. CLC 7
See also CA 45-48; CANR 6, 22; DLB 14

Waugh, Evelyn (Arthur St. John) 1903-1966 CLC 1, 3, 8, 13, 19, 27, 44; DA; DAB; DAC; DAM MST, NOV, POP; WLC
See also CA 85-88; 25-28R; CANR 22; CDBLB 1914-1945; DLB 15, 162; MTCW

Waugh, Harriet
1944- .... CLC 6
See also CA 85-88; CANR 22

Ways, C. R.
See Blount, Roy (Alton), Jr.

Waystaff, Simon
See Swift, Jonathan

See Douglas, Ellen
See also CA 17-20R; 114; CANR 39

Williamson, Jack .... CLC 29
See also Williamson, John Stewart
See also CAAS 8; DLB 8

Williamson, John Stewart 1908- ....
See Williamson, Jack
See also CA 17-20R; CANR 23

Willie, Frederick
See Lovecraft, H(oward) P(hillips)

Willingham, Calder (Baynard, Jr.)
1922-1995 .... CLC 5, 51
See also CA 5-8R; 147; CANR 3; DLB 2, 44;
MTCW

Willis, Charles
See Clarke, Arthur C(harles)

Willy
See Colette, (Sidonie-Gabrielle)

Willy, Colette
See Colette, (Sidonie-Gabrielle)

Wilson, A(ndrew) N(orman) 1950- ... CLC 33
See also CA 112; 122; DLB 14, 155

Wilson, Angus (Frank Johnstone) 1913-1991
CLC 2, 3, 5, 25, 34; SSC 21
See also CA 5-8R; 134; CANR 21; DLB 15,
139, 155; MTCW

Wilson, August 1945- CLC 39, 50, 63; BLC;
DA; DAB; DAC; DAM DRAM, MST,
MULT; DC 2; WLCS
See also AAYA 16; BW 2; CA 115; 122; CANR
42, 54; MTCW

Wilson, Brian 1942- .... CLC 12

Wilson, Colin 1931- .... CLC 3, 14
See also CA 1-4R; CAAS 5; CANR 1, 22, 33;
DLB 14; MTCW

Wilson, Dirk
See Pohl, Frederik

Wilson, Edmund
1895-1972 .... CLC 1, 2, 3, 8, 24
See also CA 1-4R; 37-40R; CANR 1, 46; DLB
63; MTCW

Wilson, Ethel Davis (Bryant) 1888(?)-1980
CLC 13; DAC; DAM POET
See also CA 102; DLB 68; MTCW

Wilson, John 1785-1854 .... NCLC 5

Wilson, John (Anthony) Burgess 1917-1993 .
See Burgess, Anthony
See also CA 1-4R; 143; CANR 2, 46; DAC;
DAM NOV; MTCW

Wilson, Lanford 1937- CLC 7, 14, 36; DAM
DRAM
See also CA 17-20R; CABS 3; CANR 45; DLB
7

Wilson, Robert M. 1944- .... CLC 7, 9
See also CA 49-52; CANR 2, 41; MTCW

Wilson, Robert McLiam 1964- .... CLC 59
See also CA 132

Wilson, Sloan
1920- .... CLC 32
See also CA 1-4R; CANR 1, 44

Wilson, Snoo 1948- .... CLC 33
See also CA 69-72

Wilson, William S(mith) 1932- .... CLC 49
See also CA 81-84

Winchilsea, Anne (Kingsmill) Finch Counte
1661-1720 .... LC 3

Windham, Basil
See Wodehouse, P(elham) G(renville)

Wingrove, David (John) 1954- .... CLC 68
See also CA 133

Wintergreen, Jane
See Duncan, Sara Jeannette

Winters, Janet Lewis .... CLC 41
See also Lewis, Janet
See also DLBY 87

Winters, (Arthur) Yvor 1900-1968 CLC 4, 8,
32
See also CA 11-12; 25-28R; CAP 1; DLB 48;
MTCW

Winterson, Jeanette 1959-CLC 64; DAM POP
See also CA 136; CANR 58

Winthrop, John 1588-1649 .... LC 31
See also DLB 24, 30

Wiseman, Frederick 1930- .... CLC 20

Wister, Owen 1860-1938 .... TCLC 21
See also CA 108; DLB 9, 78; SATA 62

Witkacy
See Witkiewicz, Stanislaw Ignacy

Witkiewicz, Stanislaw Ignacy 1885-1939
TCLC 8
See also CA 105

Wittgenstein, Ludwig (Josef Johann) 1889-1951
TCLC 59
See also CA 113

Wittig, Monique 1935(?)- .... CLC 22
See also CA 116; 135; DLB 83

Wittlin, Jozef 1896-1976 .... CLC 25
See also CA 49-52; 65-68; CANR 3

Wodehouse, P(elham) G(renville) 1881-1975
CLC 1, 2, 5, 10, 22; DAB; DAC; DAM
NOV; SSC 2
See also AITN 2; CA 45-48; 57-60; CANR 3,
33; CDBLB 1914-1945; DLB 34, 162;
MTCW; SATA 22

Woiwode, L.
See Woiwode, Larry (Alfred)

Woiwode, Larry (Alfred) 1941- .... CLC 6, 10
See also CA 73-76; CANR 16; DLB 6; INT
CANR-16

Wojciechowska, Maia (Teresa) 1927-CLC 26
See also AAYA 8; CA 9-12R; CANR 4, 41; CLR
1; JRDA; MAICYA; SAAS 1; SATA 1, 28,
83

Wolf, Christa 1929- .... CLC 14, 29, 58
See also CA 85-88; CANR 45; DLB 75; MTCW

Wolfe, Gene (Rodman) 1931- CLC 25; DAM
POP
See also CA 57-60; CAAS 9; CANR 6, 32; DLB
8

Wolfe, George C. 1954- .... CLC 49
See also CA 149

Wolfe, Thomas (Clayton) 1900-1938TCLC 4,
13, 29, 61; DA; DAB; DAC; DAM MST,
NOV; WLC
See also CA 104; 132; CDALB 1929-1941;
DLB 9, 102; DLBD 2; DLBY 85; MTCW

Wolfe, Thomas Kennerly, Jr. 1931- ....
See Wolfe, Tom
See also CA 13-16R; CANR 9, 33; DAM POP;
INT CANR-9; MTCW

Wolfe, Tom .... CLC 1, 2, 9, 15, 35, 51
See also Wolfe, Thomas Kennerly, Jr.
See also AAYA 8; AITN 2; BEST 89:1; DLB
152

Wolff, Geoffrey (Ansell) 1937- .... CLC 41
See also CA 29-32R; CANR 29, 43

Wolff, Sonia
See Levitin, Sonia (Wolff)

Wolff, Tobias (Jonathan Ansell) 1945- . C L C
39, 64
See also AAYA 16; BEST 90:2; CA 114; 117;
CAAS 22; CANR 54; DLB 130; INT 117

Wolfram von Eschenbach c. 1170-c. 1220
CMLC 5
See also DLB 138

Wolitzer, Hilma 1930- .... CLC 17
See also CA 65-68; CANR 18, 40; INT CANR-
18; SATA 31

Wollstonecraft, Mary 1759-1797 .... LC 5
See also CDBLB 1789-1832; DLB 39, 104, 158

Wonder, Stevie .... CLC 12
See also Morris, Steveland Judkins

Wong, Jade Snow 1922- .... CLC 17
See also CA 109

Woodcott, Keith
See Brunner, John (Kilian Houston)

<indexbody>**Woodruff, Robert W.**
See Mencken, H(enry) L(ouis)

Woolf, (Adeline) Virginia 1882-1941TCLC 1,
5, 20, 43, 56; DA; DAB; DAC; DAM MST,
NOV; SSC 7; WLC
See also CA 104; 130; CDBLB 1914-1945;
DLB 36, 100, 162; DLBD 10; MTCW

Woollcott, Alexander (Humphreys) 1887-1943
TCLC 5
See also CA 105; DLB 29

Woolrich, Cornell 1903-1968 .... CLC 77
See also Hopley-Woolrich, Cornell George

Wordsworth, Dorothy
1771-1855 .... NCLC 25
See also DLB 107

Wordsworth, William 1770-1850.. **NCLC 12, 38; DA; DAB; DAC; DAM MST, POET; PC 4; WLC**
See also CDBLB 1789-1832; DLB 93, 107

Wouk, Herman 1915-**CLC 1, 9, 38; DAM NOV, POP**
See also CA 5-8R; CANR 6, 33; DLBY 82; INT CANR-6; MTCW

Wright, Charles (Penzel, Jr.) 1935-**CLC 6, 13, 28**
See also CA 29-32R; CAAS 7; CANR 23, 36; DLB 165; DLBY 82; MTCW

Wright, Charles Stevenson 1932- ... **CLC 49; BLC 3; DAM MULT, POET**
See also BW 1; CA 9-12R; CANR 26; DLB 33

Wright, Jack R.
See Harris, Mark

Wright, James (Arlington) 1927-1980**CLC 3, 5, 10, 28; DAM POET**
See also AITN 2; CA 49-52; 97-100; CANR 4, 34; DLB 5, 169; MTCW

Wright, Judith (Arandell) 1915- **CLC 11, 53; PC 14**
See also CA 13-16R; CANR 31; MTCW; SATA 14

Wright, L(aurali) R. 1939- .... **CLC 44**
See also CA 138

Wright, Richard (Nathaniel) 1908-1960 **C L C 1, 3, 4, 9, 14, 21, 48, 74; BLC; DA; DAB; DAC; DAM MST, MULT, NOV; SSC 2; WLC**
See also AAYA 5; BW 1; CA 108; CDALB 1929-1941; DLB 76, 102; DLBD 2; MTCW

Wright, Richard B(ruce) 1937- .... **CLC 6**
See also CA 85-88; DLB 53

Wright, Rick 1945- .... **CLC 35**

Wright, Rowland
See Wells, Carolyn

Wright, Stephen Caldwell 1946- .... **CLC 33**
See also BW 2

Wright, Willard Huntington 1888-1939 ....
See Van Dine, S. S.
See also CA 115

Wright, William 1930- .... **CLC 44**
See also CA 53-56; CANR 7, 23

Wroth, LadyMary 1587-1653(?) .... **LC 30**
See also DLB 121

Wu Ch'eng-en 1500(?)-1582(?) .... **LC 7**

Wu Ching-tzu 1701-1754 .... **LC 2**

Wurlitzer, Rudolph 1938(?)- .... **CLC 2, 4, 15**
See also CA 85-88; DLB 173

Wycherley, William 1641-1715**LC 8, 21; DAM DRAM**
See also CDBLB 1660-1789; DLB 80

Wylie, Elinor (Morton Hoyt) 1885-1928 **TCLC 8**
See also CA 105; DLB 9, 45

Wylie, Philip (Gordon) 1902-1971 ... **CLC 43**
See also CA 21-22; 33-36R; CAP 2; DLB 9

Wyndham, John .... **CLC 19**
See also Harris, John (Wyndham Parkes Lucas) Beynon

Wyss, Johann David Von 1743-1818**NCLC 10**
See also JRDA; MAICYA; SATA 29; SATA-Brief 27

Xenophon c. 430B.C.-c. 354B.C. ... **CMLC 17**
See also DLB 176

Yakumo Koizumi
See Hearn, (Patricio) Lafcadio (Tessima Carlos)

Yanez, Jose Donoso
See Donoso (Yanez), Jose

Yanovsky, Basile S.
See Yanovsky, V(assily) S(emenovich)

Yanovsky, V(assily) S(emenovich) 1906-1989 **CLC 2, 18**
See also CA 97-100; 129

Yates, Richard 1926-1992 .... **CLC 7, 8, 23**
See also CA 5-8R; 139; CANR 10, 43; DLB 2; DLBY 81, 92; INT CANR-10

Yeats, W. B.
See Yeats, William Butler

Yeats, William Butler 1865-1939**TCLC 1, 11, 18, 31; DA; DAB; DAC; DAM DRAM, MST, POET; WLC**
See also CA 104; 127; CANR 45; CDBLB 1890-1914; DLB 10, 19, 98, 156; MTCW

Yehoshua, A(braham) B. 1936-.. **CLC 13, 31**
See also CA 33-36R; CANR 43

Yep, Laurence Michael 1948-............ **CLC 35**
See also AAYA 5; CA 49-52; CANR 1, 46; CLR 3, 17; DLB 52; JRDA; MAICYA; SATA 7, 69

Yerby, Frank G(arvin) 1916-1991 .**CLC 1, 7, 22; BLC; DAM MULT**
See also BW 1; CA 9-12R; 136; CANR 16, 52; DLB 76; INT CANR-16; MTCW

Yesenin, Sergei Alexandrovich
See Esenin, Sergei (Alexandrovich)

Yevtushenko, Yevgeny (Alexandrovich) 1933- **CLC 1, 3, 13, 26, 51; DAM POET**
See also CA 81-84; CANR 33, 54; MTCW

Yezierska, Anzia 1885(?)-1970 .... **CLC 46**
See also CA 126; 89-92; DLB 28; MTCW

Yglesias, Helen 1915- .... **CLC 7, 22**
See also CA 37-40R; CAAS 20; CANR 15; INT CANR-15; MTCW

Yokomitsu Riichi 1898-1947 .... **TCLC 47**

Yonge, Charlotte (Mary) 1823-1901**TCLC 48**
See also CA 109; DLB 18, 163; SATA 17

York, Jeremy
See Creasey, John

York, Simon
See Heinlein, Robert A(nson)

Yorke, Henry Vincent 1905-1974...... **CLC 13**
See also Green, Henry
See also CA 85-88; 49-52

Yosano Akiko 1878-1942 .... **TCLC 59; PC 11**

Yoshimoto, Banana .... **CLC 84**
See also Yoshimoto, Mahoko

Yoshimoto, Mahoko 1964- ....
See Yoshimoto, Banana
See also CA 144

Young, Al(bert James) 1939-.**CLC 19; BLC; DAM MULT**
See also BW 2; CA 29-32R; CANR 26; DLB 33

Young, Andrew (John) 1885-1971 ...... **CLC 5**
See also CA 5-8R; CANR 7, 29

Young, Collier
See Bloch, Robert (Albert)

Young, Edward 1683-1765 .... **LC 3**
See also DLB 95

Young, Marguerite (Vivian) 1909-1995 **C L C 82**
See also CA 13-16; 150; CAP 1

Young, Neil 1945- .... **CLC 17**
See also CA 110

Young Bear, Ray A. 1950-...... **CLC 94; DAM MULT**
See also CA 146; DLB 175; NNAL

Yourcenar, Marguerite 1903-1987**CLC 19, 38, 50, 87; DAM NOV**
See also CA 69-72; CANR 23; DLB 72; DLBY 88; MTCW

Yurick, Sol 1925-................................. **CLC 6**
See also CA 13-16R; CANR 25

Zabolotskii, Nikolai Alekseevich 1903-1958 **TCLC 52**
See also CA 116

Zamiatin, Yevgenii
See Zamyatin, Evgeny Ivanovich

Zamora, Bernice (B. Ortiz) 1938- .. **CLC 89; DAM MULT; HLC**
See also CA 151; DLB 82; HW

Zamyatin, Evgeny Ivanovich 1884-1937 **TCLC 8, 37**
See also CA 105

Zangwill, Israel 1864-1926 .... **TCLC 16**
See also CA 109; DLB 10, 135

Zappa, Francis Vincent, Jr. 1940-1993 ....
See Zappa, Frank
See also CA 108; 143; CANR 57

Zappa, Frank .... **CLC 17**
See also Zappa, Francis Vincent, Jr.

Zaturenska, Marya 1902-1982 ...... **CLC 6, 11**
See also CA 13-16R; 105; CANR 22

Zeami 1363-1443 .... **DC 7**

Zelazny, Roger (Joseph) 1937-1995 . **CLC 21**

See also AAYA 7; CA 21-24R; 148; CANR 26;
DLB 8; MTCW; SATA 57; SATA-Brief 39

Zhdanov, Andrei A(lexandrovich) 1896-1948
TCLC 18
See also CA 117

Zhukovsky, Vasily 1783-1852 .... **NCLC 35**

Ziegenhagen, Eric .... **CLC 55**

Zimmer, Jill Schary
See Robinson, Jill

Zimmerman, Robert
See Dylan, Bob

Zindel, Paul 1936-**CLC 6, 26; DA; DAB; DAC;
DAM DRAM, MST, NOV; DC 5**
See also AAYA 2; CA 73-76; CANR 31; CLR
3, 45; DLB 7, 52; JRDA; MAICYA; MTCW;
SATA 16, 58

Zinov'Ev, A. A.
See Zinoviev, Alexander (Aleksandrovich)

Zinoviev, Alexander (Aleksandrovich) 1922-
CLC 19
See also CA 116; 133; CAAS 10

Zoilus
See Lovecraft, H(oward) P(hillips)

Zola, Emile (Edouard Charles Antoine) 1840-
1902**TCLC 1, 6, 21, 41; DA; DAB; DAC;
DAM MST, NOV; WLC**
See also CA 104; 138; DLB 123

Zoline, Pamela 1941- .... **CLC 62**

Zorrilla y Moral, Jose 1817-1893 .... **NCLC 6**

Zoshchenko, Mikhail (Mikhailovich) 1895-1958
TCLC 15; SSC 15
See also CA 115

Zuckmayer, Carl 1896-1977 .... **CLC 18**
See also CA 69-72; DLB 56, 124

Zuk, Georges
See Skelton, Robin

Zukofsky, Louis 1904-1978**CLC 1, 2, 4, 7, 11,
18; DAM POET; PC 11**
See also CA 9-12R; 77-80; CANR 39; DLB 5,
165; MTCW

Zweig, Paul 1935-1984 .... **CLC 34, 42**
See also CA 85-88; 113

Zweig, Stefan 1881-1942 .... **TCLC 17**
See also CA 112; DLB 81, 118

Zwingli, Huldreich 1484-1531 .... **LC 37**
See also DLB 179

Literary Criticism Series
Cumulative Topic Index

This index lists all topic entries in Gale's *Classical and Medieval Literature Criticism, Contemporary Literary Criticism, Literature Criticism from 1400 to 1800, Nineteenth-Century Literature Criticism,* and *Twentieth-Century Literary Criticism.*

Topic Index

Topic Index

Topic Index

Topic Index

Twentieth-Century Literary Criticism
Cumulative Nationality Index

Nationality Index